Atomic Masses of the Elements

Name	Symbol	Atomic Number	Atomic Mass[a]	Name	Symbol	At	
Actinium	Ac	89	(227)[b]	Mendelevium	Md		
Aluminum	Al	13	26.98	Mercury	Hg	80	
Americium	Am	95	(243)	Molybdenum	Mo	42	95.94
Antimony	Sb	51	121.8	Neodymium	Nd	60	144.2
Argon	Ar	18	39.95	Neon	Ne	10	20.18
Arsenic	As	33	74.92	Neptunium	Np	93	(237)
Astatine	At	85	(210)	Nickel	Ni	28	58.69
Barium	Ba	56	137.3	Niobium	Nb	41	92.91
Berkelium	Bk	97	(247)	Nitrogen	N	7	14.01
Beryllium	Be	4	9.012	Nobelium	No	102	(259)
Bismuth	Bi	83	209.0	Osmium	Os	76	190.2
Bohrium	Bh	107	(264)	Oxygen	O	8	16.00
Boron	B	5	10.81	Palladium	Pd	46	106.4
Bromine	Br	35	79.90	Phosphorus	P	15	30.97
Cadmium	Cd	48	112.4	Platinum	Pt	78	195.1
Calcium	Ca	20	40.08	Plutonium	Pu	94	(244)
Californium	Cf	98	(251)	Polonium	Po	84	(209)
Carbon	C	6	12.01	Potassium	K	19	39.10
Cerium	Ce	58	140.1	Praseodymium	Pr	59	140.9
Cesium	Cs	55	132.9	Promethium	Pm	61	(145)
Chlorine	Cl	17	35.45	Protactinium	Pa	91	231.0
Chromium	Cr	24	52.00	Radium	Ra	88	(226)
Cobalt	Co	27	58.93	Radon	Rn	86	(222)
Copernicium	Cn	112	(285)	Rhenium	Re	75	186.2
Copper	Cu	29	63.55	Rhodium	Rh	45	102.9
Curium	Cm	96	(247)	Roentgenium	Rg	111	(272)
Darmstadtium	Ds	110	(271)	Rubidium	Rb	37	85.47
Dubnium	Db	105	(262)	Ruthenium	Ru	44	101.1
Dysprosium	Dy	66	162.5	Rutherfordium	Rf	104	(261)
Einsteinium	Es	99	(252)	Samarium	Sm	62	150.4
Erbium	Er	68	167.3	Scandium	Sc	21	44.96
Europium	Eu	63	152.0	Seaborgium	Sg	106	(266)
Fermium	Fm	100	(257)	Selenium	Se	34	78.96
Flerovium	Fl	114	(289)	Silicon	Si	14	28.09
Fluorine	F	9	19.00	Silver	Ag	47	107.9
Francium	Fr	87	(223)	Sodium	Na	11	22.99
Gadolinium	Gd	64	157.3	Strontium	Sr	38	87.62
Gallium	Ga	31	69.72	Sulfur	S	16	32.07
Germanium	Ge	32	72.64	Tantalum	Ta	73	180.9
Gold	Au	79	197.0	Technetium	Tc	43	(99)
Hafnium	Hf	72	178.5	Tellurium	Te	52	127.6
Hassium	Hs	108	(265)	Terbium	Tb	65	158.9
Helium	He	2	4.003	Thallium	Tl	81	204.4
Holmium	Ho	67	164.9	Thorium	Th	90	232.0
Hydrogen	H	1	1.008	Thulium	Tm	69	168.9
Indium	In	49	114.8	Tin	Sn	50	118.7
Iodine	I	53	126.9	Titanium	Ti	22	47.87
Iridium	Ir	77	192.2	Tungsten	W	74	183.8
Iron	Fe	26	55.85	Uranium	U	92	238.0
Krypton	Kr	36	83.80	Vanadium	V	23	50.94
Lanthanum	La	57	138.9	Xenon	Xe	54	131.3
Lawrencium	Lr	103	(262)	Ytterbium	Yb	70	173.0
Lead	Pb	82	207.2	Yttrium	Y	39	88.91
Lithium	Li	3	6.941	Zinc	Zn	30	65.41
Livermorium	Lv	116	(293)	Zirconium	Zr	40	91.22
Lutetium	Lu	71	175.0	—	—	113	(284)
Magnesium	Mg	12	24.31	—	—	115	(288)
Manganese	Mn	25	54.94	—	—	117	(293)
Meitnerium	Mt	109	(268)	—	—	118	(294)

[a]Values for atomic masses are given to four significant figures.
[b]Values in parentheses are the mass number of an important radioactive isotope.

Karen C. Timberlake

General, Organic, and Biological Chemistry
Structures of Life

CHEM 2A

Second Custom Edition for Pasadena City College

Taken from:
General, Organic, and Biological Chemistry: Structures of Life, Fifth Edition
by Karen C. Timberlake

Cover Art: Courtesy of Pearson Learning Solutions.

Taken from:

General, Organic, and Biological Chemistry: Structures of Life, Fifth Edition
by Karen C. Timberlake
Copyright © 2015, 2013, 2010, 2007 Pearson Education, Inc.
New York, New York 10013

This special edition published in cooperation with Pearson Learning Solutions.

Pearson Learning Solutions, 330 Hudson Street, New York, New York 10013
A Pearson Education Company
www.pearsoned.com

Printed in the United States of America

4 5 6 7 8 9 10 V092 16 15

000200010271970824

EEB

ISBN 10: 1-323-11047-X
ISBN 13: 978-1-323-11047-8

Brief Contents

Contents

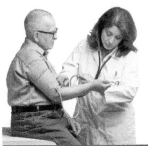

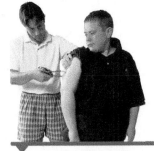

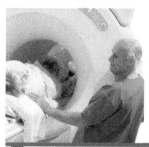

6
Ionic and Molecular Compounds   183

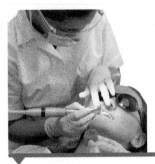

7
Chemical Reactions and Quantities   235

9
Solutions   324

8
Gases   288

10
Reaction Rates and Chemical Equilibrium 370

11
Acids and Bases 399

12
Introduction to Organic Chemistry: Hydrocarbons 443

About the Author

Karen at the Natural History Museum where she is a supporter of children's environmental programs.

KAREN TIMBERLAKE is Professor Emerita of chemistry at Los Angeles Valley College, where **she taught chemistry for allied health and preparatory chemistry for 36 years.** She received her bachelor's degree in chemistry from the University of Washington and her master's degree in biochemistry from the University of California at Los Angeles.

Professor Timberlake has been writing chemistry textbooks for 40 years. During that time, her name **has become associated with the strategic use of pedagogical tools that promote student success in chemistry and the application of chemistry to real-life situations.** More than one million students have learned chemistry using texts, laboratory manuals, and study guides written by Karen Timberlake. In addition to *General, Organic, and Biological Chemistry: Structures of Life,* fifth edition, she is also the author of *Chemistry: An Introduction to General, Organic, and Biological Chemistry,* twelfth edition, with the accompanying *Study Guide and Selected Solutions Manual,* and *Basic Chemistry,* fourth edition, with the accompanying *Study Guide and Selected Solutions Manual, Laboratory Manual,* and *Essentials Laboratory Manual.*

Professor Timberlake belongs to numerous scientific and educational organizations including the American Chemical Society (ACS) and the National Science Teachers Association (NSTA). She has been the Western Regional Winner of Excellence in College Chemistry Teaching Award given by the Chemical Manufacturers Association. She received the McGuffey Award in Physical Sciences from the Textbook Authors Association for her textbook *Chemistry: An Introduction to General, Organic, and Biological Chemistry,* eighth edition, which has demonstrated her excellence over time. She received the "Texty" Textbook Excellence Award from the Textbook Authors Association for the first edition of *Basic Chemistry.* She has participated in education grants for science teaching including the Los Angeles Collaborative for Teaching Excellence (LACTE) and a Title III grant at her college. She speaks at conferences and educational meetings on the use of student-centered teaching methods in chemistry to promote the learning success of students.

When Professor Timberlake is not writing textbooks, she and her husband relax by playing tennis, ballroom dancing, traveling, trying new restaurants, cooking, and taking care of their grandchildren, Daniel and Emily.

DEDICATION

I dedicate this book to

- My husband, Bill, for his patience, loving support, and preparation of late meals

- My son, John, daughter-in-law, Cindy, grandson, Daniel, and granddaughter, Emily, for the precious things in life

- The wonderful students over many years whose hard work and commitment always motivated me and put purpose in my writing

FAVORITE QUOTES

The whole art of teaching is only the art of awakening the natural curiosity of young minds.

—Anatole France

One must learn by doing the thing; though you think you know it, you have no certainty until you try.

—Sophocles

Discovery consists of seeing what everybody has seen and thinking what nobody has thought.

—Albert Szent-Györgyi

I never teach my pupils; I only attempt to provide the conditions in which they can learn.

—Albert Einstein

Preface

Welcome to the fifth edition of *General, Organic, and Biological Chemistry: Structures of Life*. This chemistry text was written and designed to help you prepare for a career in a health-related profession, such as nursing, dietetics, respiratory therapy, and environmental and agricultural science. This text assumes no prior knowledge of chemistry. My main objective in writing this text is to make the study of chemistry an engaging and a positive experience for you by relating the structure and behavior of matter to its role in health and the environment.

It is my goal to help you become a critical thinker by understanding scientific concepts that will form a basis for making important decisions about issues concerning health and the environment. Thus, I have utilized materials that

- help you to learn and enjoy chemistry
- relate chemistry to clinical stories and careers that interest you
- develop problem-solving skills that lead to your success in chemistry
- promote learning and success in chemistry

New for the Fifth Edition

This new edition introduces chemistry in a clinical environment beginning with the stories of patients in the Chapter Openers and Clinical Updates that follow the diagnosis and treatment for the patients. New problem-solving strategies include Key Math Skills; Core Chemistry Skills; new Analyze the Problem features; more Guides to Problem Solving; and new Clinical Applications throughout each chapter that add clinical relevance to the chemistry content.

- **NEW AND UPDATED! Chapter Openers** now provide engaging clinical stories in which a metabolic or genetic condition introduces the content of each chapter.
- **NEW! Clinical Careers** include lipidology nurse, exercise physiologist, hepatology nurse. and public health nurse.
- **NEW! Clinical Updates** give a follow up of the diagnosis and treatment for each patient in the Chapter Openers.
- **NEW! Clinical Applications** are added to Questions and Problems sets that show the relevance between the chemistry content and the clinical story.
- **NEW! Biochemistry Chapters 19 to 24** contain new and expanded material on recent topics in biochemistry including **CH 19** Alzheimer's and beta-amyloid proteins that form plaques in the brain, **CH 20** lactose intolerance and breath hydrogen test, **CH 21** transcription factors, the estrogen receptor, and the impact of altered genes BRAC1 and BRAC2 in breast cancer, **CH 22** enzyme deficiencies in glycogen storage diseases, and **CH 23** malate-aspartate

pathway added, ATP energy values updated to 2.5 ATP for NADH and 1.5 ATP for $FADH_2$, and **CH 24** updated beta-oxidation and synthesis of fatty acids.

- **NEW! Ribbon Models** of proteins have been added including lactase with amino acids in the active site, transaminase, trypsin, chymotrypsin, carboxypeptidase, alanine amino transferase, estrogen receptor, cytochrome c, and aspartate transaminase.
- **NEW AND UPDATED! Diagrams** are updated using current models for allosteric enzymes, covalent modification including phosphorylation, 2- and 3-dimensional models of tRNA, DNA transcription, transcription factors in the promoter region, the sites in electron transport blocked by toxins, and urea cycle showing transport between the mitochondrial matrix and the cytosol.
- **NEW AND UPDATED! New biochemistry problems** include action of viruses, transcription and the estrogen receptor, energy diagram for the hydrolysis of ATP, defective enzymes that block the degradation of glycogen, and current values for ATP energy from NADH and $FADH_2$.
- **NEW! Interactive Videos** give students the experience of step-by-step problem solving for problems from the text.
- **NEW! Chapter Readiness** sections at the beginning of each chapter list the Key Math Skills and Core Chemistry Skills from the previous chapters, which provide the foundation for learning new chemistry principles in the current chapter.
- **NEW! Key Math Skills** review basic math relevant to the chemistry you are learning throughout the text. A **Key Math Skill Review** at the end of each chapter summarizes and gives additional examples.
- **NEW! Core Chemistry Skills** identify the key chemical principles in each chapter that are required for successfully learning chemistry. A **Core Chemistry Skill Review** at the end of each chapter helps reinforce the material and gives additional examples.
- **UPDATED! Analyze the Problem** features included in the solutions of the Sample Problems strengthen critical-thinking skills and illustrate the breakdown of a word problem into the components required to solve it.
- **UPDATED! Questions and Problems, Sample Problems, and art** are directly related to nursing and health applications to better demonstrate the connection between the chemistry being discussed and how these skills will be needed in professional experience.
- **UPDATED! Combining Ideas** features offer sets of integrated problems that test students' understanding by integrating topics from two or more previous chapters.

Chapter Organization of the Fifth Edition

In each textbook I write, I consider it essential to relate every chemical concept to real-life issues of health and environment. Because a chemistry course may be taught in different time frames, it may be difficult to cover all the chapters in this text. However, each chapter is a complete package, which allows some chapters to be skipped or the order of presentation to be changed.

Chapter 1, Chemistry in our Lives, now discusses the Scientific Method in everyday terms, guides students in developing a study plan for learning chemistry, and now has a new section of Key Math Skills that review the basic math including scientific notation needed in chemistry calculations.

- A new chapter opener tells the story of a murder and features the work and career of a forensic scientist.
- A new Clinical Update feature follows up with forensic scientists that help solve the murder and includes Clinical Applications related to the story.
- A new section, "Scientific Method: Thinking Like a Scientist," has been added, which discusses the scientific method in everyday terms.
- A new section, "Key Math Skills," reviews basic math required in chemistry, such as Identifying Place Values (1.4A), Using Positive and Negative Numbers in Calculations (1.4B) including a new feature Calculator Operations, Calculating Percentages (1.4C), Solving Equations (1.4D), Interpreting Graphs (1.4E), and Writing Numbers in Scientific Notation (1.4 F).
- New sample problems with nursing applications are added. New Sample Problem 1.5 requires the interpretation of a graph to determine the decrease in a child's temperature when given Tylenol.
- New art includes a photo of a plastic strip thermometer placed on a baby's forehead to determine body temperature.

Chapter 2, Chemistry and Measurements, looks at measurement and emphasizes the need to understand numerical relationships of the metric system. Significant numbers are discussed in the determination of final answers. Prefixes from the metric system are used to write equalities and conversion factors for problem-solving strategies. Density is discussed and used as a conversion factor.

- A new chapter opener tells the story of a patient with high blood pressure and features the work and career of a registered nurse.
- A new Clinical Update describes the patient's follow-up visit with his doctor.
- New material is added that illustrates how to count significant figures in equalities and in conversion factors used in a problem setup.
- New abbreviation mcg for microgram is introduced as used in health and medicine.

- New Core Chemistry Skills are added: Counting Significant Figures (2.2), Using Significant Figures in Calculations (2.3), Using Prefixes (2.4), Writing Conversion Factors from Equalities (2.5), Using Conversion Factors (2.6), and Using Density as a Conversion Factor (2.7).
- New photos, including an endoscope, a urine dipstick, a pint of blood, Keflex capsules, and salmon for omega-3 fatty acids, are added to improve visual introduction to clinical applications of chemistry.
- Updated Guides to Problem Solving (GPS) use color blocks as visual guides through the solution pathway.
- Updated Sample Problems relate questions and problem solving to health-related topics such as the measurements that a nurse would make, blood volume, omega-3 fatty acids, radiological imaging, and medication orders.
- New Clinical Applications feature questions about health-related settings including measurements made by a nurse, daily values for minerals and vitamins, equalities and conversion factors for medications, and health questions related to the Clinical Update story.

Chapter 3, Matter and Energy, classifies matter and states of matter, describes temperature measurement, and discusses energy, specific heat, and energy in nutrition. Physical and chemical changes and physical and chemical properties are now discussed in more depth.

- A new chapter opener describes diet and exercise for an overweight child with type 2 diabetes and features the work and career of a dietitian. A new Clinical Update describes the new diet for weight loss.
- Chapter 3 has a new order of topics: 3.1 Classification of Matter, 3.2 States and Properties of Matter, 3.3 Temperature, 3.4 Energy, 3.5 Energy and Nutrition, 3.6 Specific Heat, and 3.7 Changes of State. Section 3.7 Changes of State now includes heat of fusion and vaporization, and combinations of energy calculations.
- New Core Chemistry Skills are added: Classifying Matter (3.1), Identifying Physical and Chemical Changes (3.2), Converting between Temperature Scales (3.3), Using Energy Units (3.4), and Using the Heat Equation (3.6).
- New Questions and Problems and Sample Problems now have more clinical applications to nursing and health, including Sample Problem 3.4, high temperatures used in cancer treatment; Sample Problem 3.5, the energy produced by a high-energy shock output of a defibrillator; Sample Problem 3.7, body temperature lowering using a cooling cap; and Sample Problem 3.8, ice bag therapy for muscle injury.
- The interchapter problem set, Combining Ideas from Chapters 1 to 3, completes the chapter.

Chapter 4, Atoms, introduces elements and atoms and the periodic table. The names and symbols of element 114, Flerovium, Fl, and 116, Livermorium, Lv, have been added to update the periodic table. Atomic numbers and mass number are determined for isotopes. Atomic mass is calculated using the masses of the naturally occurring isotopes and their abundances. Electron arrangements are written using orbital diagrams, electron configurations, and abbreviated electron configurations. Trends in the properties of elements are discussed, including atomic size, Lewis symbols, ionization energy, and metallic character.

- A new chapter opener features chemistry in agriculture and the career of a farmer.
- A new Clinical Update describes the improvement in crop production by the farmer.
- New Core Chemistry Skills are added: Counting Protons and Neutrons (4.4), Writing Atomic Symbols for Isotopes (4.5), Writing Electron Configurations (4.7), Using the Periodic Table to Write Electron Configurations (4.7), Identifying Trends in Periodic Properties (4.8), and Drawing Lewis Symbols (4.8).
- A new weighted average analogy uses 8-lb and 14-lb bowling balls and the percent abundance of each to calculate weighted average of a bowling ball.
- New nursing and clinical applications are added to Sample Problems/Questions and Problems.
- Updated Chemistry Link to Health, "Biological Reactions to UV Light," adds information on using light for neonatal jaundice.
- Updated photos and diagrams including a new diagram for the electromagnetic spectrum are added.

Chapter 5, Nuclear Chemistry, looks at the types of radiation emitted from the nuclei of radioactive atoms. Nuclear equations are written and balanced for both naturally occurring radioactivity and artificially produced radioactivity. The half-lives of radioisotopes are discussed, and the amount of time for a sample to decay is calculated. Radioisotopes important in the field of nuclear medicine are described.

- A new chapter opener about the work and career of a nuclear medicine technologist is added.
- A new Clinical Update discusses cardiac imaging using the radioisotope Tl-201.
- New Core Chemistry Skills are added: Writing Nuclear Equations (5.2) and Using Half-Lives (5.4).
- New Sample Problems and Questions and Problems use nursing and clinical examples, including Sample Problem 5.3 that describe the radioisotope yttrium-90 use in cancer and arthritis treatments. Sample Problem 5.6 that uses phosphorus-32 for the treatment of leukemia and Sample Problem 5.9 that uses titanium seeds containing a radioactive isotope implanted in the body to treat cancer.
- Clinical applications include radioisotopes in nuclear medicine, activity, half-lives, and dosage of radioisotopes.

Chapter 6, Ionic and Molecular Compounds, describes the formation of ionic and covalent bonds. Chemical formulas are written, and ionic compounds—including those with polyatomic ions—and molecular compounds are named. Section 6.2 is titled "Writing Formulas for Ionic Compounds," 6.5 is titled "Molecular Compounds: Sharing Electrons," and 6.6 is titled "Lewis Structure for Molecules and Polyatomic Ions."

- The chapter opener describes aspirin as a molecular compound and features the work and career of a pharmacy technician.
- A new Clinical Update describes several types of compounds at a pharmacy and includes Clinical Applications.
- "Ions: Transfer of Electrons" has been rewritten to emphasize the stability of the electron configuration of a noble gas.
- New Core Chemistry Skills are added: Writing Positive and Negative Ions (6.1), Writing Ionic Formulas (6.2), Naming Ionic Compounds (6.3), Writing the Names and Formulas for Molecular Compounds (6.5), Drawing Lewis Structures (6.6), Using Electronegativity (6.7), Predicting Shape (6.8), Identifying Polarity of Molecules (6.8), and Identifying Attractive Forces (6.9).
- A new art comparing the particles and bonding of ionic compounds and molecular compounds has been added.
- Bismuth was added to Table 6.5, Some Metals That Form More Than One Positive Ion.
- Analyze the Problem feature was updated for Sample Problems 6.4, 6.5, 6.6, 6.9, 6.10.
- The interchapter problem set, Combining Ideas from Chapters 4 to 6, completes the chapter.

Chapter 7, Chemical Reactions and Quantities, introduces moles and molar masses of compounds, which are used in calculations to determine the mass or number of particles in a given quantity. Students learn to balance chemical equations and to recognize the types of chemical reactions: combination, decomposition, single replacement, double replacement, and combustion reactions. Section 7.3 discusses Oxidation–Reduction Reactions using real-life examples, including biological reactions. Section 7.6, Mole Relationships in Chemical Equations, and Section 7.7, Mass Calculations for Reactions, prepare students for the quantitative relationships of reactants and products in reactions. Section 7.8, Limiting Reactants and Percent Yield, identifies limiting reactants and calculates percent yield, and Section 7.9, Energy in Chemical Reactions, calculates the energy in exothermic and endothermic chemical reactions.

- A chapter opener describes the chemical reaction that is used to whiten teeth and features the work and career of a dental hygienist.
- Sample Problems and problem sets include Clinical Applications for nursing.
- New Core Chemistry Skills are added: Balancing a Chemical Equation (7.1), Classifying Types of Chemical Reactions (7.2), Identifying Oxidized and Reduced Substances (7.3), Converting Particles to Moles (7.4), Calculating Molar Mass (7.5), Using Molar Mass as a Conversion Factor (7.5), Using Mole–Mole Factors (7.6), Converting Grams to Grams (7.7), Calculating Quantity of Product from a Limiting Reactant (7.8), Calculating Percent Yield (7.8), and Using the Heat of Reaction (7.9).

Chapter 8, Gases, discusses the properties of gases and calculates changes in gases using the gas laws: Boyle's, Charles's, Gay-Lussac's, Avogadro's, Dalton's, and the Ideal Gas Law. Problem-solving strategies enhance the discussion and calculations with gas laws including chemical reactions using the ideal gas law.

- The chapter opener describes a child with asthma and her treatment with oxygen and features the work and career of a respiratory therapist is added. A new Clinical Update describes exercises to prevent exercise-induced asthma. Clinical Applications are related to lung volume and gas laws.
- New Sample Problems and Challenge Problems use nursing and medical examples, including Sample Problem 8.3, calculating the volume of oxygen gas delivered through a face mask during oxygen therapy; and Sample Problem 8.12, preparing a heliox breathing mixture for a scuba diver.
- New Core Chemistry Skills are added: Using the Gas Laws (8.2, 8.3, 8.4, 8.5, 8.6), Using the Ideal Gas Law (8.7), Calculating Mass or Volume of a Gas in a Chemical Reaction (8.7), and Calculating Partial Pressure (8.8).
- Clinical applications includes calculations of mass or pressure of oxygen in uses of hyperbaric chambers.
- The interchapter problem set, Combining Ideas from Chapters 7 and 8, completes the chapter.

Chapter 9, Solutions, describes solutions, electrolytes, saturation and solubility, insoluble salts, concentrations, and osmosis. New problem-solving strategies clarify the use of concentrations to determine volume or mass of solute. The volumes and concentrations of solutions are used in calculations of dilutions, reactions, and titrations. Properties of solutions, osmosis in the body, and dialysis are discussed.

- The chapter opener describes a patient with kidney failure and dialysis treatment and features the work and career of a dialysis nurse.
- New Core Chemistry Skills are added: Using Solubility Rules (9.3), Calculating Concentration (9.4), Using Concentration as a Conversion Factor (9.4), Calculating the Quantity of a Reactant or Product (9.4), and Calculating the Boiling Point/Freezing Point of a Solution (9.6).
- Table 9.6 Electrolytes in Blood Plasma and Selected Intravenous Solutions is updated. Table 9.7 Solubility Rules for Ionic Solids in Water is updated.
- Molality is removed.
- New clinical applications include saline solutions, mass of solution in a mannitol, a lactated Ringer's solution, and a Pedialyte solution, solutions of medications, electrolytes in dialysis, and reactions of antacids.

Chapter 10, Reaction Rates and Chemical Equilibrium, looks at the rates of reactions and the equilibrium condition when forward and reverse rates for a reaction become equal. Equilibrium expressions for reactions are written and equilibrium constants are calculated. Le Châtelier's principle is used to evaluate the impact on concentrations when stress is placed on the system.

- A new chapter opener describes the symptoms of *infant respiratory distress syndrome* (IRDS) and discusses the career of a neonatal nurse.
- The Clinical Update describes a child with anemia, hemoglobin-oxygen equilibrium, and a diet that is high in iron-containing foods.
- New Core Chemistry Skills are added: Writing the Equilibrium Constant (10.3), Calculating an Equilibrium Constant (10.3), Calculating Equilibrium Concentrations (10.4), and Using Le Châtelier's Principle (10.5).
- New problems that visually represent equilibrium situations are added.
- Clinical applications include hemoglobin equilibrium and anemia.
- A new diagram represents the transport of O_2 by hemoglobin from the lungs to the tissues and muscles.
- Updates of Analyze the Problem include Sample Problems 10.4 and 10.5.

Chapter 11, Acids and Bases, discusses acids and bases and their strengths, conjugate acid–base pairs. The dissociation of strong and weak acids and bases is related to their strengths as acids or bases. The dissociation of water leads to the water dissociation constant expression, K_w, the pH scale, and the calculation of pH. Chemical equations for acids in reactions are balanced and titration of an acid is illustrated. Buffers are discussed along with their role in the blood. The pH of a buffer is calculated.

- A new chapter opener describes a blood sample for an emergency room patient sent to the clinical laboratory for analysis of blood pH and CO_2 gas and features the work and career of a clinical laboratory technician.
- Section 11.2 is now a discussion of Brønsted–Lowry Acids and Bases.
- A new Clinical Update discusses the symptoms and treatment of acid reflux disease.
- Analyze the Problem was updated in Sample Problems 11.3, 11.6, 11.8, 11.10, 11.12, and 11.13.
- Key Math Skills are added: Calculating pH from $[H_3O^+]$ (11.6) and Calculating $[H_3O^+]$ from pH (11.6).
- New Core Chemistry Skills are added: Identifying Conjugate Acid–Base Pairs (11.2), Calculating $[H_3O^+]$ and $[OH^-]$ in Solutions (11.5), Writing Equations for Reactions of Acids and Bases (11.7), Calculating Molarity or Volume of an Acid or Base in a Titration (11.8), and Calculating the pH of a Buffer (11.9).
- A new Guide to Writing Conjugate Acid–Base Pairs has been added. Guide to Calculating pH of an Aqueous Solutions, Calculating $[H_3O^+]$ from pH, Calculations for an Acid-Base Titration, and Calculating pH of a Buffer were updated.
- Clinical applications include calculating $[OH^-]$ or $[H_3O^+]$ of body fluids, foods, blood plasma, pH of body fluids, grams of antacids to neutralize stomach acid, and buffers for stomach acid.
- New visuals include the ionization of the weak acid hydrofluoric acid, a new photo of calcium hydroxide and information about its use in the food industry and

dentistry, as well as a new photo of sodium bicarbonate reacting with acetic acid.

- The interchapter problem set, Combining Ideas from Chapters 9 to 11, completes the chapter.

Chapter 12, Introduction to Organic Chemistry: Hydrocarbons, combines Chapters 11 and 12 of GOB, fourth edition. This new chapter compares inorganic and organic compounds, and describes the structures and naming of alkanes, alkenes including cis–trans isomers, alkynes, and aromatic compounds.

- A new chapter opener describes a fire victim and the search for traces of accelerants and fuel at the arson scene and features the work and career of a firefighter/emergency medical technician.
- A Clinical Update describes treatment for a burn patient and the identification of the fuels at the arson scene.
- Chapter 12 has a new order of topics: 12.1 Organic Compounds, 12.2 Alkanes, 12.3 Alkanes with Substituents, 12.4 Properties of Alkanes, 12.5 Alkenes and Alkynes, 12.6 Cis–Trans Isomers, 12.7 Addition Reactions, and 12.8 Aromatic Compounds.

- The wedge-dash models of methane and ethane have been added.
- New Core Chemistry Skills are added: Naming and Drawing Alkanes (12.2) and Writing Equations for Hydrogenation, Hydration, and Polymerization Hydration, and Polymerization of Alkenes (12.7).
- Line-angle structural formulas were added to Table 12.2.
- Guides to Drawing Structural Formulas for Alkanes, and Naming Alkanes with Substituents have been added.
- The Chemistry Link to Industry *Crude Oil* has been removed.
- Polymerization was added to Table 12.8, Summary of Addition Reactions.
- The Analyze the Problem features were updated in Sample Problem 12.7, 12.9, and 12.10.

Acknowledgments

The preparation of a new text is a continuous effort of many people. I am thankful for the support, encouragement, and dedication of many people who put in hours of tireless effort to produce a high-quality book that provides an outstanding learning package. I am extremely grateful to Dr. Laura Frost, who provided new and expanded material on current topics in the Biochemistry Chapters 19–24. The editorial team at Pearson has done an exceptional job. I want to thank Jeanne Zalesky, Editor-in-Chief, and Terry Haugen, Senior Acquisitions Editor who supported our vision of this fifth edition.

I appreciate all the wonderful work of Lisa Pierce, project manager, who skillfully brought together reviews, art, web site materials, and all the things it takes to prepare a book for production. I appreciate the work of Meeta Pendharkar and Jenna Vittorioso, project managers, and of Lumina Datamatics, Inc., who brilliantly coordinated all phases of the manuscript to the final pages of a beautiful book. Thanks to Mark Quirie, manuscript and accuracy reviewer, and Lumina Datamatics copy editor and proofreaders, who precisely analyzed and edited the initial and final manuscripts and pages to make sure the words and problems were correct to help students learn chemistry. Their keen eyes and thoughtful comments were extremely helpful in the development of this text.

I am especially proud of the art program in this text, which lends beauty and understanding to chemistry. I would like to thank Wynne Au Yeung, art specialist; Derek Bacchus, Design Manager, and Jerilyn Bockorick, interior and cover designers, whose creative ideas provided the outstanding design for the cover and pages of the book. Stephen Merland and Jen Simmons, photo researchers, were outstanding in researching and selecting vivid photos for the text so that students can see the beauty of chemistry, and to William Opaluch, text permissions manager for clearing third party content. Thanks also to *Bio-Rad Laboratories* for their courtesy and use of *KnowItAll ChemWindows*, drawing software that helped us produce chemical structures for the manuscript. The macro-to-micro illustrations designed by Imagineering give students visual impressions of the atomic and molecular organization of everyday things and are a fantastic learning tool. I also appreciate the hard work of Will Moore, Product Marketing Manager, and Chris Barker, Field Marketing Manager for their dedication in conveying the ideas of this revision through their marketing expertise.

I am extremely grateful to an incredible group of peers for their careful assessment of all the new ideas for the text; for their suggested additions, corrections, changes, and deletions; and for providing an incredible amount of feedback about improvements for the book. I admire and appreciate every one of you.

If you would like to share your experience with chemistry, or have questions and comments about this text, I would appreciate hearing from you.

Karen Timberlake
Email: khemist@aol.com

Feature	Description	Benefit	Page
Chapter Opener 	**Chapter Openers** begin with **Clinical Conditions** and discuss careers in fields such as nursing, agriculture, exercise physiology, and anesthesia.	Connects a clinical situation with the chemistry in the chapter and show you how health professionals use chemistry every day.	183
Chemistry Link to Health Chemistry Link to **Health** Losing and Gaining Weight The number of kilocalories or kilojoules needed in the daily diet of an adult depends on gender, age, and level of physical activity. Some typical levels of energy needs are given in Table 3.9. A person gains weight when food intake exceeds energy output.	**Chemistry Links to Health** apply chemical concepts to health and medicine such as weight loss and weight gain, trans fats, anabolic steroids, alcohol abuse, blood buffers, kidney dialysis, and cancer.	Provide you with connections that illustrate the importance of understanding chemistry in real-life health and medical situations.	78
Clinical Update Clinical Update A Diet and Exercise Program for Charles It has been two weeks since Charles met with Daniel, a dietitian, who provided Charles with a menu for weight loss. Charles and his mother are going back to see Daniel again with a chart of the food Charles has eaten. The following is what Charles ate in one day:	**Clinical Updates** give a follow-up to the medical condition and treatment discussed in the chapter opener and include Clinical Application questions.	Continue a clinical theme through the entire chapter utilizing the chemistry content of the chapter.	90
Macro-to-Micro Art 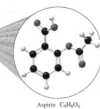 Aspirin $C_9H_8O_4$	**Macro-to-Micro Art** utilizes photographs and drawings to illustrate the atomic structure of chemical phenomena.	Helps you connect the world of atoms and molecules to the macroscopic world.	253
Chemistry Link to the **Environment** Carbon Dioxide and Climate Change The Earth's climate is a product of interactions between sunlight, the atmosphere, and the oceans. The Sun provides us with energy in the form of solar radiation. Some of this radiation is reflected back into space. The rest is absorbed by the clouds, atmospheric gases including carbon dioxide, and the Earth's surface. For millions of	**Chemistry Links to the Environment** relate chemistry to environmental topics such as climate change, radon in our homes, and pheromones.	Helps you extend your understanding of the impact of chemistry on the environment	75

Feature	Description	Benefit	Page
LEARNING GOAL Account for the ATP produced by the complete oxidation of glucose.	**Learning Goals** at the beginning and end of each section identify the key concepts for that section and provide a roadmap for your study.	Help you focus your studying by emphasizing what is most important in each section.	851
15.1 Carbohydrates Carbohydrates such as table sugar, lactose, and cellulose and oxygen. Simple sugars, which have formulas of C hydrates of carbon, thus the name *carbohydrate*. In a ser sis, energy from the Sun is used to combine the carbon	Timberlake's accessible **Writing Style** is based on careful development of chemical concepts suited to the skills and backgrounds of students in chemistry.	Helps you understand new terms and chemical concepts.	551
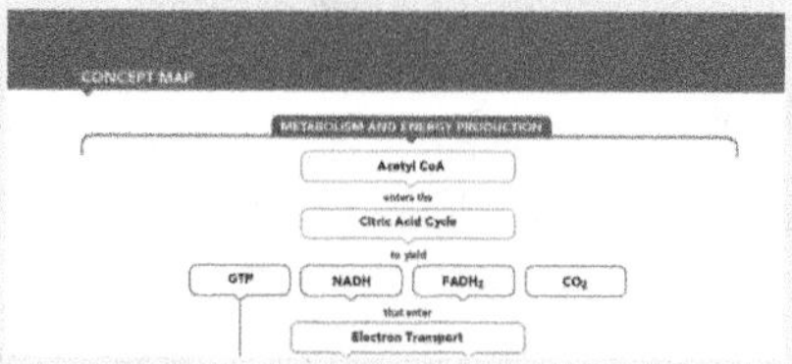 CONCEPT MAP METABOLISM AND ENERGY PRODUCTION Acetyl CoA enters the Citric Acid Cycle to yield GTP / NADH / FADH₂ / CO₂ that enter Electron Transport	**Concept Maps** at the end of each chapter show how all the key concepts fit together.	Encourage learning by providing a visual guide to the interrelationship among all the concepts in each chapter.	859
KEY MATH SKILL Interpreting Graphs	**Key Math Skills** review the basic math required needed for chemistry. Instructors can also assign these through MasteringChemistry.	Help you master the basic quantitative skills to succeed in chemistry.	14
CORE CHEMISTRY SKILL Describing the Reactions in the Citric Acid Cycle	**Core Chemistry Skills** identify content crucial to problem-solving strategies related to chemistry. Instructors can also assign these through MasteringChemistry.	Help you master the basic problem-solving skills needed to succeed in chemistry.	837
 FIGURE 15.3 ▶ Lactose, a disaccharid found in milk and milk products, contair galactose and glucose.	The **Art and Photo Program** is beautifully rendered, pedagogically effective, and includes questions with all the figures.	Helps you think critically using photos and illustrations.	565
CHAPTER REVIEW 19.1 Proteins and Amino Acids **LEARNING GOAL** Classify proteins by their functions. Give the name and abbreviations for an amino acid, and draw its zwitterion. • Some proteins are enzymes or hormones, whereas others are important in structure, transport, protection, storage, and muscle contraction. 	The **Chapter Reviews** include Learning Goals and visual thumbnails to summarize the key points in each section.	Help you determine your mastery of the chapter concepts and study for your tests.	715
Explore Your World Sugar and Sweeteners	**Explore Your World** features are hands-on activities that use everyday materials to encourage you to explore selected chemistry topics.	Helps you interact with chemistry, learn scientific method, and support critical thinking.	580

Tools to engage students in chemistry and show them how to solve problems

Feature	Description	Benefit	Page
Clinical Applications 3.19 **a.** A patient with hyperthermia has a temperature of 106 °F. What does this read on a Celsius thermometer? **b.** Because high fevers can cause convulsions in children, the doctor needs to be called if the child's temperature goes over 40.0 °C. Should the doctor be called if a child has a temperature of 103 °F?	Clinical Applications connect the chemistry in each section with health and clinical problems.	Shows you how the chemistry you are learning is related to health and medicine.	73
Guide to Problem Solving Using Conversion Factors STEP 1 State the given and needed quantities. STEP 2 Write a plan to convert the	**Guides to Problem Solving** (GPS) illustrate the steps needed to solve problems.	Visually guide you step-by-step through each problem-solving strategy.	44
ANALYZE THE PROBLEM — Given: 7.5 qt of blood, density of blood (1.06 g/mL); Need: grams of blood	**Analyze the Problems** included in Sample Problem Solutions convert information in a word problem into components for problem solving.	Help you identify and utilize the components within a word problem to set up a solution strategy.	51
QUESTIONS AND PROBLEMS **15.1 Carbohydrates** **LEARNING GOAL** Classify a monosaccharide as an aldose or a ketose, and indicate the number of carbon atoms. 15.1 What reactants are needed for photosynthesis and respiration? 15.2 What is the relationship between photosynthesis and respiration?	**Questions and Problems** are placed at the end of each section. Problems are paired and the **Answers** to the odd-numbered problems are given at the end of each chapter.	Encourage you to become involved immediately in the process of problem solving.	554
SAMPLE PROBLEM 2.9 Problem Solving Using Conversion Factors Greg's doctor has ordered a PET scan of his heart. In radiological imaging such as PET or CT scans, dosages of pharmaceuticals are based on body mass. If Greg weighs 144 lb, what is his body mass in kilograms? SOLUTION STEP 1 State the given and needed quantities. ANALYZE THE PROBLEM — Given: 144 lb; Need: kilograms STEP 2 Write a plan to convert the given unit to the needed unit. The conversion factor relates the given unit in the U.S. system of measurement and the needed unit in the metric system.	**Sample Problems** illustrate worked-out solutions with step-by-step explanations and required calculations. Study Checks associated with each Sample Problem allow you to check your problem solving strategies with the **Answer.**	Provide the intermediate steps to guide you successfully through each type of problem.	44
UNDERSTANDING THE CONCEPTS The chapter sections to review are shown in parentheses at the end of each question.	**Understanding the Concepts** are questions with visual representations placed at the end of each chapter.	Build an understanding of newly learned chemical concepts.	22
ADDITIONAL QUESTIONS AND PROBLEMS	**Additional Questions and Problems** at the end of each chapter provide further study and application of the topics from the entire chapter. Problems are paired and the Answers to the odd-numbered problems are given at the end of each chapter.	Promote critical thinking.	22
CHALLENGE QUESTIONS	**Challenge Questions** at the end of each chapter provide complex questions.	Promote critical thinking, group work, and cooperative learning environments.	23
COMBINING IDEAS FROM Chapters 7 and 8	**Combining Ideas** are sets of integrated problems placed after every 2 to 4 chapters that are useful as Practice exams.	Test your understanding of the concepts from previous chapters by integrating topics.	322

Resources

General, Organic, and Biological Chemistry: Structures of Life, fifth edition, provides an integrated teaching and learning package of support material for both students and professors.

Name of Supplement	Available in Print	Available Online	Instructor or Student Supplement	Description
Study Guide and Selected Solutions Manual (ISBN 0133891917)	✓		Resource for Students	The *Study Guide and Selected Solutions Manual*, by Karen Timberlake and Mark Quirie, promotes active learning through a variety of exercises with answers as well as practice tests that are connected directly to the learning goals of the textbook. Complete solutions to odd-numbered problems are included.
MasteringChemistry® (www.masteringchemistry.com) (ISBN 0133858375)		✓	Resource for Students and Instructors	MasteringChemistry® from Pearson is the leading online teaching and learning system designed to improve results by engaging students before, during, and after class with powerful content. Ensure that students arrive ready to learn by assigning educationally effective content before class, and encourage critical thinking and retention with in-class resources such as Learning Catalytics. Students can further master concepts after class through traditional homework assignments that provide hints and answer-specific feedback. The Mastering gradebook records scores for all automatically graded assignments while diagnostic tools give instructors access to rich data to assess student understanding and misconceptions.
MasteringChemistry with Pearson eText (ISBN 0133899306)		✓	Resource for Students	The fifth edition of *General, Organic, and Biological Chemistry: Structures of Life* features a Pearson eText enhanced with media within Mastering. In conjunction with Mastering assessment capabilities, Interactive Videos and 3D animations will improve student engagement and knowledge retention. Each chapter will contain a balance of interactive animations, videos, sample calculations, and self-assessments/quizzes embedded directly in the eText. Additionally, the Pearson eText offers students the power to create notes, highlight text in different colors, create bookmarks, zoom, and view single or multiple pages.
Instructor's Solutions Manual–Download Only (ISBN 0133891909)		✓	Resource for Instructors	Prepared by Mark Quirie, the solutions manual highlights chapter topics, and includes answers and solutions for all questions and problems in the text.
Instructor Resource Materials–Download Only (ISBN 0133891887)		✓	Resource for Instructors	Includes all the art, photos, and tables from the book in JPEG format for use in classroom projection or when creating study materials and tests. In addition, the instructors can access modifiable PowerPoint™ lecture outlines. Also available are downloadable files of the Instructor's Solutions Manual and a set of "clicker questions" designed for use with classroom-response systems. Also visit the Pearson Education catalog page for Timberlake's *General, Organic, and Biological Chemistry: Structures of Life* fifth Edition, at www.pearsonhighered.com to download available instructor supplements.
TestGen Test Bank–Download Only (ISBN 0133891895)		✓	Resource for Instructors	Prepared by William Timberlake, this resource includes more than 2000 questions in multiple-choice, matching, true/false, and short-answer format.
Laboratory Manual by Karen Timberlake (ISBN 0321811852)	✓		Resource for Students	This best-selling lab manual coordinates 35 experiments with the topics in *General, Organic, and Biological Chemistry: Structures of Life* fifth edition, uses laboratory investigations to explore chemical concepts, develop skills of manipulating equipment, reporting data, solving problems, making calculations, and drawing conclusions.
Online Instructor Manual for Laboratory Manual (ISBN 0321812859)		✓	Resource for Instructors	This manual contains answers to report sheet pages for the *Laboratory Manual* and a list of the materials needed for each experiment with amounts given for 20 students working in pairs, available for download at www.pearsonhighered.com.

Highlighting Relevancy and Clinical Applications

Designed to prepare students for health-related careers, *General, Organic, and Biological Chemistry: Structures of Life* breaks chemical concepts and problem solving into clear, manageable pieces, ensuring students follow along and stay motivated throughout their first, and often only, chemistry course. Timberlake's friendly writing style, student focus, strong problems, and engaging health-related applications continue to help students make connections between chemistry and their future careers as they develop problem-solving skills they'll need beyond the classroom.

Clinical Conditions, Applications, and Updates

Clinical features throughout the chapter connect chemistry to real life. Each chapter begins with an image and details of a Clinical Condition being addressed in the field by professionals from nursing, agriculture, exercise physiology, and anesthesia. **Clinical Updates** throughout the chapter follow the medical condition and treatment discussed in the chapter opener. **Clinical Applications** within the chapter and end-of-chapter show students how the chemistry they are learning applies specifically to health and medicine.

1

Chemistry in Our Lives

A CALL CAME IN TO 911 FROM A MAN WHO FOUND

his wife lying on the floor of their home. When the police arrived at the home, they determined that the woman was dead. The husband said he had worked late, and just arrived at their home. The victim's body was lying on the floor of the living room. There was no blood at the scene, but the police did find a glass on the side table that contained a small amount of liquid. In an adjacent laundry room/garage, the police found a half-empty bottle of antifreeze. The bottle, glass, and liquid were bagged and sent to the forensic laboratory.

In another 911 call, a man was found lying on the grass outside his home. Blood was present on his body, and some bullet casings were found on the grass. Inside the victim's home, a weapon was recovered. The bullet casings and the weapon were bagged and sent to the forensic laboratory.

Sarah and Mark, forensic scientists, use scientific procedures and chemical tests to examine the evidence from law enforcement agencies. Sarah proceeds to analyze blood, stomach contents, and the unknown liquid from the first victim's home. She will look for the presence of drugs, poisons, and alcohol. Her lab partner Mark will analyze the fingerprints on the glass. He will also match the characteristics of the weapon that was found at the second crime scene.

Evidence from a crime scene is sent to the forensic laboratory.

CAREER Forensic Scientist

Most forensic scientists work in crime laboratories that are part of city or county legal systems where they analyze bodily fluids and tissue samples collected by crime scene investigators. In analyzing these samples, forensic scientists identify the presence or absence of specific chemicals within the body to help solve the criminal case. Some of the chemicals they look for include alcohol, illegal or prescription drugs, poisons, arson debris, metals, and various gases such as carbon monoxide. In order to identify these substances, a variety of chemical instruments and highly specific methodologies are used. Forensic scientists also analyze samples from criminal suspects, athletes, and potential employees. They also work on cases involving environmental contamination and animal samples for wildlife crimes. Forensic scientists usually have a bachelor's degree that includes courses in math, chemistry, and biology.

1

℞ Clinical Update
Forensic Evidence Solves the Murder

Using a variety of laboratory tests, Sarah finds ethylene glycol in the victim's blood. The quantitative tests indicate that the victim had ingested 125 g of ethylene glycol. Sarah determines that the liquid in the glass found at the crime scene was ethylene glycol that had been added to an alcoholic beverage. Ethylene glycol is a clear, sweet-tasting, thick liquid that is odorless and mixes with water. It is easy to obtain since it is used as antifreeze in automobiles and in brake fluid. Because the initial symptoms of ethylene glycol poisoning are similar to being intoxicated, the victim is often unaware of its presence.

If ingestion of ethylene glycol occurs, it can cause depression of the central nervous system, cardiovascular damage, and kidney failure. If discovered quickly, hemodialysis may be used to remove ethylene glycol from the blood. A toxic amount of ethylene glycol is 1.5 g of ethylene glycol/kg of body mass. Thus, 75 g could be fatal for a 50-kg (110 lb) person.

Mark determines that a fingerprint on the glass found in the victim's home is match to the victim's husband. This evidence along with the container of antifreeze found in the home led to the arrest and conviction of the husband for poisoning his wife.

🔬 Clinical Applications

1.29 A container was found in the home of the victim that contained 120 g of ethylene glycol in 450 g of liquid. What was the percentage of ethylene glycol? Express your answer to the ones place.

1.30 How many drinks, each containing 100 g of the liquid in problem 1.29, would a 50-kg victim need to consume to reach a toxic level of ethylene glycol?

Interactive Videos

Interactive videos and demonstrations help students through some of the more challenging topics by showing how chemistry works in real life and introducing a bit of humor into chemical problem solving and demonstrations. Topics include Using Conversion Factors, Balancing Nuclear Equations, Chemical v. Physical Change, and Dehydration of Sucrose.

Sample Calculations walk students through the most challenging chemistry problems and provide a fresh perspective on how to approach individual problems and reach their solutions. Topics include Using Conversion Factors, Mass Calculations for Reactions, and Concentration of Solutions.

Green play button icons appear in the margins throughout the text. In the eText, the icons link to new interactive videos that the student can use to clarify and reinforce important concepts. All Interactive Videos are available in web and mobile-friendly formats through the eText, and are assignable activities in MasteringChemistry.

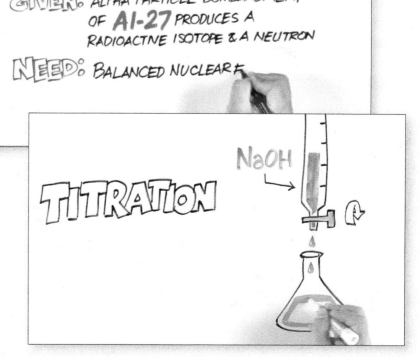

ANALYZE THE PROBLEM

GIVEN: ALPHA PARTICLE BOMBARDMENT OF **Al-27** PRODUCES A RADIOACTIVE ISOTOPE & A NEUTRON

NEED: BALANCED NUCLEAR E.

TITRATION   NaOH

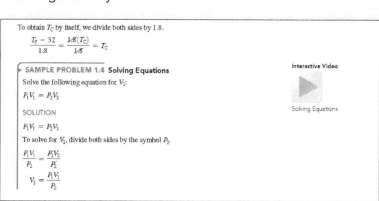

To obtain T_C by itself, we divide both sides by 1.8.

$$\frac{T_F - 32}{1.8} = \frac{1.8(T_C)}{1.8} = T_C$$

SAMPLE PROBLEM 1.4 Solving Equations

Solve the following equation for V_2:

$$P_1V_1 = P_2V_2$$

SOLUTION

$$P_1V_1 = P_2V_2$$

To solve for V_2, divide both sides by the symbol P_2.

$$\frac{P_1V_1}{P_2} = \frac{P_2V_2}{P_2}$$

$$V_2 = \frac{P_1V_1}{P_2}$$

Interactive Video

Solving Equations

MasteringChemistry®

MasteringChemistry® from Pearson is the leading online teaching and learning system designed to improve results by engaging students before, during, and after class with powerful content. Ensure that students arrive ready to learn by assigning educationally effective content before class, and encourage critical thinking and retention with in-class resources such as Learning Catalytics. Students can further master concepts after class through traditional homework assignments that provide hints and answer-specific feedback. The Mastering gradebook records scores for all automatically graded assignments while diagnostic tools give instructors access to rich data to assess student understanding and misconceptions.

Mastering brings learning full circle by continuously adapting to each student and making learning more personal than ever—before, during, and after class.

Before Class

Dynamic Study Modules

Help students quickly learn chemistry!

Now assignable, Dynamic Study Modules (DSMs) enable your students to study on their own and be better prepared with the basic math and chemistry skills needed to succeed in the GOB course. The mobile app is available for iOS and Android devices for study on the go and results can be tracked in the MasteringChemistry gradebook.

Reading Quizzes

Reading Quizzes give instructors the opportunity to assign reading and test students on their comprehension of chapter content.

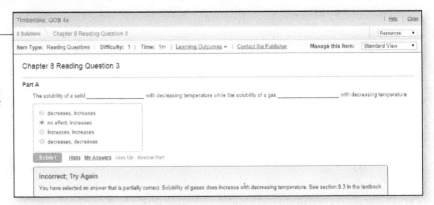

During Class

▶ Learning Catalytics

Learning Catalytics is a "bring your own device" student engagement, assessment, and classroom intelligence system. With Learning Catalytics you can:

- Assess students in real time, using open-ended tasks to probe student understanding.
- Understand immediately where students are and adjust your lecture accordingly.
- Manage student interactions with intelligent grouping and timing.

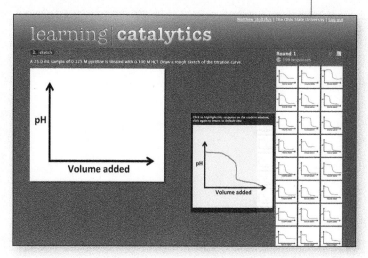

After Class

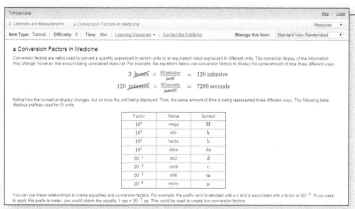

Tutorials and Coaching

Students learn chemistry by practicing chemistry.

Tutorials, featuring specific wrong-answer feedback, hints, and a wide variety of educationally effective content, guide your students through the toughest topics in General, Organic, and Biological chemistry.

▶ Adaptive Follow-Ups

Mastering continuously adapts to each student, making learning more personal than ever.

Adaptive Follow-Ups are personalized assignments that pair Mastering's powerful content with Knewton's adaptive learning engine to provide personalized help to students before misconceptions take hold. These assignments are based on each student's performance on homework assignments and on all work in the course to date, including core prerequisite topics.

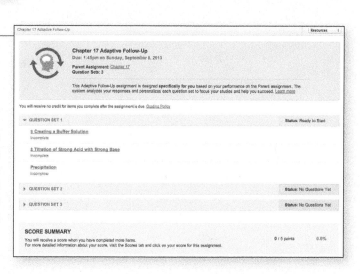

1

Chemistry in Our Lives

A CALL CAME IN TO 911 FROM A MAN WHO FOUND

his wife lying on the floor of their home. When the police arrived at the home, they determined that the woman was dead. The husband said he had worked late, and just arrived at their home. The victim's body was lying on the floor of the living room. There was no blood at the scene, but the police did find a glass on the side table that contained a small amount of liquid. In an adjacent laundry room/garage, the police found a half-empty bottle of antifreeze. The bottle, glass, and liquid were bagged and sent to the forensic laboratory.

In another 911 call, a man was found lying on the grass outside his home. Blood was present on his body, and some bullet casings were found on the grass. Inside the victim's home, a weapon was recovered. The bullet casings and the weapon were bagged and sent to the forensic laboratory.

Sarah and Mark, forensic scientists, use scientific procedures and chemical tests to examine the evidence from law enforcement agencies. Sarah proceeds to analyze blood, stomach contents, and the unknown liquid from the first victim's home. She will look for the presence of drugs, poisons, and alcohol. Her lab partner Mark will analyze the fingerprints on the glass. He will also match the characteristics of the bullet casings to the weapon that was found at the second crime scene.

Evidence from a crime scene is sent to the forensic laboratory.

CAREER Forensic Scientist

Most forensic scientists work in crime laboratories that are part of city or county legal systems where they analyze bodily fluids and tissue samples collected by crime scene investigators. In analyzing these samples, forensic scientists identify the presence or absence of specific chemicals within the body to help solve the criminal case. Some of the chemicals they look for include alcohol, illegal or prescription drugs, poisons, arson debris, metals, and various gases such as carbon monoxide. In order to identify these substances, a variety of chemical instruments and highly specific methodologies are used. Forensic scientists also analyze samples from criminal suspects, athletes, and potential employees. They also work on cases involving environmental contamination and animal samples for wildlife crimes. Forensic scientists usually have a bachelor's degree that includes courses in math, chemistry, and biology.

Chemists working in research laboratories test new products and develop new pharmaceuticals.

LEARNING GOAL

Define the term chemistry and identify substances as chemicals.

N ow that you are in a chemistry class, you may be wondering what you will be learning. What questions in science have you been curious about? Perhaps you are interested in what hemoglobin does in the body or how aspirin relieves a headache. Just like you, chemists are curious about the world we live in.

▶ What does hemoglobin do in the body? Hemoglobin consists of four polypeptide chains, each containing a heme group with an iron atom that binds to oxygen (O_2) in the lungs. From the lungs, hemoglobin transports oxygen to the tissues of the body where it is used to provide energy. Once the oxygen is released, hemoglobin binds to carbon dioxide (CO_2) for transport to the lungs where it is released.

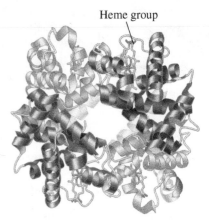

Heme group

Hemoglobin transports oxygen to the tissues and carbon dioxide to the lungs.

▶ Why does aspirin relieve a headache? When a part of the body is injured, substances called prostaglandins are produced, which cause inflammation and pain. Aspirin acts to block the production of prostaglandins, thereby reducing inflammation, pain, and fever.

Chemists in the medical field develop new treatments for diabetes, genetic defects, cancer, AIDS, and other diseases. Researchers in the environmental field study the ways in which human development impacts the environment and develop processes that help reduce environmental degradation. For the chemist in the forensic laboratory, the nurse in the dialysis unit, the dietitian, or the agricultural scientist, chemistry plays a central role in understanding problems, assessing possible solutions, and making important decisions.

1.1 Chemistry and Chemicals

Chemistry is the study of the composition, structure, properties, and reactions of matter. *Matter* is another word for all the substances that make up our world. Perhaps you imagine that chemistry takes place only in a laboratory where a chemist is working in a white coat and goggles. Actually, chemistry happens all around you every day and has an impact on everything you use and do. You are doing chemistry when you cook food, add bleach to your laundry, or start your car. A chemical reaction has taken place when silver tarnishes or an antacid tablet fizzes when dropped into water. Plants grow because chemical reactions convert carbon dioxide, water, and energy to carbohydrates. Chemical reactions take place when you digest food and break it down into substances that you need for energy and health.

Antacid tablets undergo a chemical reaction when dropped into water.

Chemicals

A **chemical** is a substance that always has the same composition and properties wherever it is found. All the things you see around you are composed of one or more chemicals. Chemical processes take place in chemistry laboratories, manufacturing plants, and pharmaceutical labs as well as every day in nature and in our bodies. Often the terms *chemical* and *substance* are used interchangeably to describe a specific type of matter.

Every day, you use products containing substances that were developed and prepared by chemists. Soaps and shampoos contain chemicals that remove oils on your skin and scalp. When you brush your teeth, the substances in toothpaste clean your teeth, prevent plaque formation, and stop tooth decay. Some of the chemicals used to make toothpaste are listed in Table 1.1.

In cosmetics and lotions, chemicals are used to moisturize, prevent deterioration of the product, fight bacteria, and thicken the product. Your clothes may be made of natural materials such as cotton or synthetic substances such as nylon or polyester. Perhaps you wear a ring or watch made of gold, silver, or platinum. Your breakfast cereal is probably fortified with iron, calcium, and phosphorus, whereas the milk you drink is enriched with vitamins A and D. Antioxidants are chemicals added to food to prevent it from spoiling. Some of the chemicals you may encounter when you cook in the kitchen are shown in Figure 1.1.

Toothpaste is a combination of many chemicals.

TABLE 1.1 Chemicals Commonly Used in Toothpaste

Chemical	Function
Calcium carbonate	Used as an abrasive to remove plaque
Sorbitol	Prevents loss of water and hardening of toothpaste
Sodium lauryl sulfate	Used to loosen plaque
Titanium dioxide	Makes toothpaste white and opaque
Triclosan	Inhibits bacteria that cause plaque and gum disease
Sodium fluorophosphate	Prevents formation of cavities by strengthening tooth enamel with fluoride
Methyl salicylate	Gives toothpaste a pleasant wintergreen flavor

FIGURE 1.1 ▶ Many of the items found in a kitchen are chemicals or products of chemical reactions.

What are some other chemicals found in a kitchen?

QUESTIONS AND PROBLEMS

1.1 Chemistry and Chemicals

LEARNING GOAL Define the term chemistry and identify substances as chemicals.

In every chapter, odd-numbered exercises in the *Questions and Problems* are paired with even-numbered exercises. The answers for the magenta, odd-numbered *Questions and Problems* are given at the end of each chapter. The complete solutions to the odd-numbered *Questions and Problems* are in the *Student Solutions Manual*.

1.1 Write a one-sentence definition for each of the following:
a. chemistry
b. chemical

1.2 Ask two of your friends (not in this class) to define the terms in problem 1.1. Do their answers agree with the definitions you provided?

1.3 Obtain a bottle of multivitamins and read the list of ingredients. What are four chemicals from the list?

1.4 Obtain a box of breakfast cereal and read the list of ingredients. What are four chemicals from the list?

℞ Clinical Applications

1.5 Read the labels on some items found in your medicine cabinet. What are the names of some chemicals contained in those items?

1.6 Read the labels on products used to wash your dishes. What are the names of some chemicals contained in those products?

LEARNING GOAL

Describe the activities that are part of the scientific method.

Linus Pauling won the Nobel Prize in Chemistry in 1954.

Explore Your World

Nobel Prize Winners in Chemistry

Use the Internet to find information about each of the following:
1. Who won the latest Nobel Prize in Chemistry?
2. What was the area of research for question **1**?

1.2 Scientific Method: Thinking Like a Scientist

When you were very young, you explored the things around you by touching and tasting. As you grew, you asked questions about the world in which you live. What is lightning? Where does a rainbow come from? Why is water blue? As an adult, you may have wondered how antibiotics work or why vitamins are important to your health. Every day, you ask questions and seek answers to organize and make sense of the world around you.

When the late Nobel Laureate Linus Pauling described his student life in Oregon, he recalled that he read many books on chemistry, mineralogy, and physics. "I mulled over the properties of materials: why are some substances colored and others not, why are some minerals or inorganic compounds hard and others soft?" He said, "I was building up this tremendous background of empirical knowledge and at the same time asking a great number of questions." Linus Pauling won two Nobel Prizes: the first, in 1954, was in chemistry for his work on the nature of chemical bonds and the determination of the structures of complex substances; the second, in 1962, was the Peace Prize.

Scientific Method

Although the process of trying to understand nature is unique to each scientist, a set of general principles, called the **scientific method**, helps to describe how a scientist thinks.

1. **Observations** The first step in the scientific method is to make *observations* about nature and ask questions about what you observe.
2. **Hypothesis** Propose a *hypothesis*, which states a possible explanation of the observations. The hypothesis must be stated in such a way that it can be tested by experiments.
3. **Experiments** Several *experiments* may be done to test the hypothesis.
4. **Conclusion** When the results of the experiments are analyzed, a *conclusion* is made as to whether the hypothesis is *true* or *false*. When experiments give consistent results, the hypothesis may be confirmed. Even then, a hypothesis continues to be tested and, based on new experimental results, may need to be modified or replaced.

Chemistry Link to Health
Early Chemist: Paracelsus

Paracelsus (1493–1541) was a physician and an alchemist who thought that alchemy should be about preparing new medicines. Using observation and experimentation, he proposed that a healthy body was regulated by a series of chemical processes that could be unbalanced by certain chemical compounds and rebalanced by using minerals and medicines. For example, he determined that inhaled dust, not underground spirits, caused lung disease in miners. He also thought that goiter was a problem caused by contaminated water, and he treated syphilis with compounds of mercury. His opinion of medicines was that the right dose makes the difference between a poison and a cure. Paracelsus changed alchemy in ways that helped to establish modern medicine and chemistry.

Swiss physician and alchemist Paracelsus (1493–1541) believed that chemicals and minerals could be used as medicines.

Using the Scientific Method in Everyday Life

You may be surprised to realize that you use the scientific method in your everyday life. Suppose you visit a friend in her home. Soon after you arrive, your eyes start to itch and you begin to sneeze. Then you observe that your friend has a new cat. Perhaps you ask yourself why you are sneezing and you form the hypothesis that you are allergic to cats. To test your hypothesis, you leave your friend's home. If the sneezing stops, perhaps your hypothesis is correct. You test your hypothesis further by visiting another friend who also has a cat. If you start to sneeze again, your experimental results support your hypothesis and you come to the conclusion that you are allergic to cats. However, if you continue sneezing after you leave your friend's home, your hypothesis is not supported. Now you need to form a new hypothesis, which could be that you have a cold.

Scientific Method

Observations

↓

Hypothesis   The hypothesis is modified if the results of the experiments do not support it.

↓

Experiments

↓

Conclusion

The scientific method develops conclusions using observations, hypotheses, and experiments.

Through observation you may determine that you are allergic to cat hair and dander.

QUESTIONS AND PROBLEMS

1.2 Scientific Method: Thinking Like a Scientist

LEARNING GOAL Describe the activities that are part of the scientific method.

1.7 Identify each activity, **a** to **f**, as an observation (O), a hypothesis (H), an experiment (E), or a conclusion (C).
At a popular restaurant, where Chang is the head chef, the following occurred:
a. Chang determined that sales of the house salad had dropped.
b. Chang decided that the house salad needed a new dressing.
c. In a taste test, Chang prepared four bowls of lettuce, each with a new dressing: sesame seed, olive oil and balsamic vinegar, creamy Italian, and blue cheese.
d. The tasters rated the sesame seed salad dressing as the favorite.
e. After two weeks, Chang noted that the orders for the house salad with the new sesame seed dressing had doubled.
f. Chang decided that the sesame seed dressing improved the sales of the house salad because the sesame seed dressing enhanced the taste.

1.8 Identify each activity, **a** to **f**, as an observation (O), a hypothesis (H), an experiment (E), or a conclusion (C).
Lucia wants to develop a process for dyeing shirts so that the color will not fade when the shirt is washed. She proceeds with the following activities:

Customers rated the sesame seed dressing as the best.

a. Lucia notices that the dye in a design fades when the shirt is washed.
b. Lucia decides that the dye needs something to help it combine with the fabric.

c. She places a spot of dye on each of four shirts and then places each one separately in water, salt water, vinegar, and baking soda and water.
d. After one hour, all the shirts are removed and washed with a detergent.
e. Lucia notices that the dye has faded on the shirts in water, salt water, and baking soda, whereas the dye did not fade on the shirt soaked in vinegar.
f. Lucia thinks that the vinegar binds with the dye so it does not fade when the shirt is washed.

℞ Clinical Applications

1.9 Identify each of the following as an observation (O), a hypothesis (H), an experiment (E), or a conclusion (C):
a. One hour after drinking a glass of regular milk, Jim experienced stomach cramps.
b. Jim thinks he may be lactose intolerant.
c. Jim drinks a glass of lactose-free milk and does not have any stomach cramps.
d. Jim drinks a glass of regular milk to which he has added lactase, an enzyme that breaks down lactose, and has no stomach cramps.

1.10 Identify each of the following as an observation (O), a hypothesis (H), an experiment (E), or a conclusion (C):
a. Sally thinks she may be allergic to shrimp.
b. Yesterday, one hour after Sally ate a shrimp salad, she broke out in hives.
c. Today, Sally had some soup that contained shrimp, but she did not break out in hives.
d. Sally realizes that she does not have an allergy to shrimp.

LEARNING GOAL

Develop a study plan for learning chemistry.

📱 **KEY MATH SKILL**

⚛ **CORE CHEMISTRY SKILL**

1.3 Learning Chemistry: A Study Plan

Here you are taking chemistry, perhaps for the first time. Whatever your reasons for choosing to study chemistry, you can look forward to learning many new and exciting ideas.

Features in This Text Help You Study Chemistry

This text has been designed with study features to complement your individual learning style. On the inside of the front cover is a periodic table of the elements. On the inside of the back cover are tables that summarize useful information needed throughout your study of chemistry. Each chapter begins with *Looking Ahead*, which outlines the topics in the chapter. At the end of the text, there is a comprehensive *Glossary and Index*, which lists and defines key terms used in the text. *Key Math Skills* and *Core Chemistry Skills* that are critical to learning chemistry are indicated by icons in the margin, and summarized at the end of each chapter. In the *Chapter Readiness* list at the beginning of every chapter, the *Key Math Skills* and *Core Chemistry Skills* from previous chapters related to the current chapter concepts are highlighted for your review.

Before you begin reading, obtain an overview of a chapter by reviewing the topics in *Looking Ahead*. As you prepare to read a section of the chapter, look at the section title and turn it into a question. For example, for section 1.1, "Chemistry and Chemicals," you could ask, "What is chemistry?" or "What are chemicals?" When you come to a *Sample Problem*, take the time to work it through and compare your solution to the one provided. Then try the associated *Study Check*. Many *Sample Problem*s are accompanied by a *Guide to Problem Solving*, which gives the steps needed to work the problem. In some *Sample Problem*s, an *Analyze the Problem* feature shows how to organize the data in the word problem to obtain a solution. At the end of each chapter section, you will find a set of *Questions and Problems* that allows you to apply problem solving immediately to the new concepts.

ANALYZE THE PROBLEM	Given	Need
	165 lb	kilograms

Throughout each chapter, boxes titled "Chemistry Link to Health" and "Chemistry Link to the Environment" help you connect the chemical concepts you are learning to real-life situations. Many of the figures and diagrams use macro-to-micro illustrations to depict the atomic level of organization of ordinary objects. These visual models illustrate the concepts described in the text and allow you to "see" the world in a microscopic way. The *Explore Your World* features investigate concepts with materials found at home.

At the end of each chapter, you will find several study aids that complete the chapter. *Chapter Reviews* provide a summary in easy-to-read bullet points and *Concept Maps* visually show the connections between important topics. The *Key Terms*, which are in boldface type within the chapter, are listed with their definitions. *Understanding the Concepts*, a set of questions that use art and models, helps you visualize concepts. *Additional Questions and Problems* and *Challenge Problems* provide additional exercises to test your understanding of the topics in the chapter. The problems are paired, which means that each of the odd-numbered problems is matched to the following even-numbered problem. *Clinical Applications* are groups of problems that apply section content to health-related topics. The answers to all the *Study Checks* are included with the Sample Problems and the answers to all the odd-numbered problems are provided at the end of the chapter. If the answers provided match your answers, you most likely understand the topic; if not, you need to study the section again.

After some chapters, problem sets called *Combining Ideas* test your ability to solve problems containing material from more than one chapter.

Using Active Learning

A student who is an active learner continually interacts with the chemical ideas while reading the text, working problems, and attending lectures. Let's see how this is done.

As you read and practice problem solving, you remain actively involved in studying, which enhances the learning process. In this way, you learn small bits of information at a time and establish the necessary foundation for understanding the next section. You may also note questions you have about the reading to discuss with your professor or laboratory instructor. Table 1.2 summarizes these steps for active learning. The time you spend in a lecture is also a useful learning time. By keeping track of the class schedule and reading the assigned material before a lecture, you become aware of the new terms and concepts you need to learn. Some questions that occur during your reading may be answered during the lecture. If not, you can ask your professor for further clarification.

Many students find that studying with a group can be beneficial to learning. In a group, students motivate each other to study, fill in gaps, and correct misunderstandings by teaching and learning together. Studying alone does not allow the process of peer correction. In a group, you can cover the ideas more thoroughly as you discuss the reading and problem solve with other students. You may find that it is easier to retain new material and new ideas if you study in short sessions throughout the week rather than all at once. Waiting to study until the night before an exam does not give you time to understand concepts and practice problem solving.

Studying in a group can be beneficial to learning.

TABLE 1.2 Steps in Active Learning

1. Read each *Learning Goal* for an overview of the material.

2. Form a question from the title of the section you are going to read.

3. Read the section, looking for answers to your question.

4. Self-test by working *Sample Problems* and *Study Checks*.

5. Complete the *Questions and Problems* that follow that section, and check the answers for the magenta odd-numbered problems.

6. Proceed to the next section and repeat the steps.

Making a Study Plan

As you embark on your journey into the world of chemistry, think about your approach to studying and learning chemistry. You might consider some of the ideas in the following list. Check those ideas that will help you successfully learn chemistry. Commit to them now. *Your* success depends on *you*.

My study plan for learning chemistry will include the following:

_____ reading the chapter before lecture

_____ going to lecture

_____ reviewing the *Learning Goals*

_____ keeping a problem notebook

_____ reading the text as an active learner

_____ working the *Questions and Problems* following each section and checking answers at the end of the chapter

_____ being an active learner in lecture

_____ organizing a study group

_____ seeing the professor during office hours

_____ reviewing *Key Math Skills* and *Core Chemistry Skills*

_____ attending review sessions

_____ organizing my own review sessions

_____ studying as often as I can

Students discuss a chemistry problem with their professor during office hours.

▶ **SAMPLE PROBLEM 1.1** A Study Plan for Learning Chemistry

Which of the following activities would you include in your study plan for learning chemistry successfully?

a. skipping lecture
b. going to the professor's office hours
c. keeping a problem notebook
d. waiting to study until the night before the exam
e. becoming an active learner

SOLUTION

Your success in chemistry can be improved by

b. going to the professor's office hours
c. keeping a problem notebook
e. becoming an active learner

STUDY CHECK 1.1

Which of the following will help you learn chemistry?

a. skipping review sessions
b. working assigned problems
c. staying up all night before an exam
d. reading the assignment before a lecture

ANSWER

b and **d**

QUESTIONS AND PROBLEMS

1.3 Learning Chemistry: A Study Plan

LEARNING GOAL Develop a study plan for learning chemistry.

1.11 What are four things you can do to help yourself to succeed in chemistry?

1.12 What are four things that would make it difficult for you to learn chemistry?

1.13 A student in your class asks you for advice on learning chemistry. Which of the following might you suggest?
 a. forming a study group
 b. skipping a lecture

 c. visiting the professor during office hours
 d. waiting until the night before an exam to study
 e. being an active learner

1.14 A student in your class asks you for advice on learning chemistry. Which of the following might you suggest?
 a. doing the assigned problems
 b. not reading the text; it's never on the test
 c. attending review sessions
 d. reading the assignment before a lecture
 e. keeping a problem notebook

1.4 Key Math Skills for Chemistry

During your study of chemistry, you will work many problems that involve numbers. You will need various math skills and operations. We will review some of the key math skills that are particularly important for chemistry. As we move through the chapters, we will also reference the key math skills as they apply.

A. Identifying Place Values

For any number, we can identify the *place value* for each of the digits in that number. These place values have names such as the ones place (first place to the left of the decimal point) or the tens place (second place to the left of the decimal point). A premature baby has a mass of 2518 g. We can indicate the place values for the number 2518 as follows:

Digit	Place Value
2	thousands
5	hundreds
1	tens
8	ones

We also identify place values such as the tenths place (first place to the right of the decimal point) and the hundredths place (second place to the right of the decimal place). A silver coin has a mass of 6.407 g. We can indicate the place values for the number 6.407 as follows:

Digit	Place Value
6	ones
4	ten**ths**
0	hundred**ths**
7	thousand**ths**

Note that place values ending with the suffix *ths* refer to the decimal places to the right of the decimal point.

LEARNING GOAL

Review math concepts used in chemistry: place values, positive and negative numbers, percentages, solving equations, interpreting graphs, and writing numbers in scientific notation.

 **KEY MATH SKILL**

Identifying Place Values

▶ SAMPLE PROBLEM 1.2 **Identifying Place Values**

A bullet found at a crime scene has a mass of 15.24 g. What are the place values for the digits in the mass of the bullet?

SOLUTION

Digit	Place Value
1	tens
5	ones
2	tenths
4	hundredths

STUDY CHECK 1.2

A bullet found at a crime scene contains 0.925 g of lead. What are the place values for the digits in the mass of the lead?

ANSWER

Digit	Place Value
9	tenths
2	hundredths
5	thousandths

📟 KEY MATH SKILL

Using Positive and Negative Numbers in Calculations

B. Using Positive and Negative Numbers in Calculations

A *positive number* is any number that is greater than zero and has a positive sign ($+$). Often the positive sign is understood and not written in front of the number. For example, the number $+8$ can also be written as 8. A *negative number* is any number that is less than zero and is written with a negative sign ($-$). For example, a negative eight is written as -8.

Multiplication and Division of Positive and Negative Numbers

When two positive numbers or two negative numbers are multiplied, the answer is positive ($+$).

$$2 \times 3 = +6$$
$$(-2) \times (-3) = +6$$

When a positive number and a negative number are multiplied, the answer is negative ($-$).

$$2 \times (-3) = -6$$
$$(-2) \times 3 = -6$$

The rules for the division of positive and negative numbers are the same as the rules for multiplication. When two positive numbers or two negative numbers are divided, the answer is positive ($+$).

$$\frac{6}{3} = 2 \qquad \frac{-6}{-3} = 2$$

When a positive number and a negative number are divided, the answer is negative ($-$).

$$\frac{-6}{3} = -2 \qquad \frac{6}{-3} = -2$$

Addition of Positive and Negative Numbers

When positive numbers are added, the sign of the answer is positive.

$3 + 4 = 7$ The $+$ sign $(+7)$ is understood.

When negative numbers are added, the sign of the answer is negative.

$(-3) + (-4) = -7$

When a positive number and a negative number are added, the smaller number is subtracted from the larger number, and the result has the same sign as the larger number.

$12 + (-15) = -3$

Subtraction of Positive and Negative Numbers

When two numbers are subtracted, change the sign of the number to be subtracted and follow the rules for addition shown above.

$$12 - (+5) = 12 - 5 = 7$$
$$12 - (-5) = 12 + 5 = 17$$
$$-12 - (-5) = -12 + 5 = -7$$
$$-12 - (+5) = -12 - 5 = -17$$

Calculator Operations

On your calculator, there are four keys that are used for basic mathematical operations. The change sign $\boxed{+/-}$ key is used to change the sign of a number.

To practice these basic calculations on the calculator, work through the problem going from the left to the right doing the operations in the order they occur. If your calculator has a change sign $\boxed{+/-}$ key, a negative number is entered by pressing the number and then pressing the change sign $\boxed{+/-}$ key. At the end, press the equals $\boxed{=}$ key or ANS or ENTER.

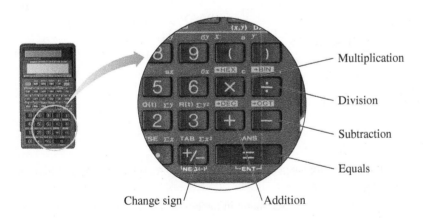

Multiplication

Division

Subtraction

Equals

Change sign   Addition

Addition and Subtraction

Example 1: $15 - 8 + 2 =$

Solution: $15 \boxed{-} 8 \boxed{+} 2 \boxed{=} 9$

Example 2: $4 + (-10) - 5 =$

Solution: $4 \boxed{+} 10 \boxed{+/-} \boxed{-} 5 \boxed{=} -11$

Multiplication and Division

Example 3: $2 \times (-3) =$

Solution: $2 \boxed{\times} 3 \boxed{+/-} \boxed{=} -6$

Example 4: $\dfrac{8 \times 3}{4} =$

Solution: $8 \boxed{\times} 3 \boxed{\div} 4 \boxed{=} 6$

C. Calculating Percentages

To determine a percentage, divide the parts by the total (whole) and multiply by 100%. For example, if an aspirin tablet contains 325 mg of aspirin (active ingredient) and the tablet has a mass of 545 mg, what is the percentage of aspirin in the tablet?

$$\frac{325 \text{ mg aspirin}}{545 \text{ mg tablet}} \times 100\% = 59.6\% \text{ aspirin}$$

When a value is described as a percentage (%), it represents the number of parts of an item in 100 of those items. If the percentage of red balls is 5, it means there are 5 red balls in every 100 balls. If the percentage of green balls is 50, there are 50 green balls in every 100 balls.

$$5\% \text{ red balls} = \frac{5 \text{ red balls}}{100 \text{ balls}} \qquad 50\% \text{ green balls} = \frac{50 \text{ green balls}}{100 \text{ balls}}$$

A bullet casing at a crime scene is marked as evidence.

> ▶ **SAMPLE PROBLEM 1.3** Calculating a Percentage
>
> In the forensic laboratory, a bullet found at a crime scene may be used as evidence in a trial if the percentage of three metals, usually lead, tin, and antimony, is a match to the composition of metals in a bullet from the suspect's ammunition. If a bullet found at the crime scene contains 13.9 g of lead, 0.3 g of tin, and 0.9 g of antimony, what is the percentage of each metal in the bullet? Express your answers to the ones place.
>
> **SOLUTION**
>
> Total mass = 13.9 g + 0.3 g + 0.9 g = 15.1 g
>
> Percentage of lead
>
> $$\frac{13.9 \text{ g}}{15.1 \text{ g}} \times 100\% = 92\% \text{ lead}$$
>
> Percentage of tin
>
> $$\frac{0.3 \text{ g}}{15.1 \text{ g}} \times 100\% = 2\% \text{ tin}$$
>
> Percentage of antimony
>
> $$\frac{0.9 \text{ g}}{15.1 \text{ g}} \times 100\% = 6\% \text{ antimony}$$
>
> **STUDY CHECK 1.3**
>
> A bullet seized from the suspect's ammunition has a composition of lead 11.6 g, tin 0.5 g, and antimony 0.4 g.
>
> **a.** What is the percentage of each metal in the bullet? Express your answers to the ones place.
> **b.** Could the bullet removed from the suspect's ammunition be considered as evidence that the suspect was at the crime scene?
>
> **ANSWER**
>
> **a.** The bullet from the suspect's ammunition is lead 93%, tin 4%, and antimony 3%.
> **b.** The bullet in part **a** does not match the bullet from the crime scene and cannot be used as evidence.

D. Solving Equations

In chemistry, we use equations that express the relationship between certain variables. Let's look at how we would solve for x in the following equation:

$$2x + 8 = 14$$

Our overall goal is to rearrange the items in the equation to obtain x on one side.

1. *Place all like terms on one side.* The numbers 8 and 14 are like terms. To remove the 8 from the left side of the equation, we subtract 8. To keep a balance, we need to subtract 8 from the 14 on the other side.

$$2x + 8 - 8 = 14 - 8$$
$$2x = 6$$

2. *Isolate the variable you need to solve for.* In this problem, we obtain x by dividing both sides of the equation by 2. The value of x is the result when 6 is divided by 2.

$$\frac{2x}{2} = \frac{6}{2}$$
$$x = 3$$

3. *Check your answer.* Check your answer by substituting your value for x back into the original equation.

$$2(3) + 8 = 14$$
$$6 + 8 = 14$$
$$14 = 14 \quad \text{Your answer } x = 3 \text{ is correct.}$$

Summary: To solve an equation for a particular variable, be sure you perform the same mathematical operations on *both* sides of the equation.

If you eliminate a symbol or number by subtracting, you need to subtract that same symbol or number on the opposite side.

If you eliminate a symbol or number by adding, you need to add that same symbol or number on the opposite side.

If you cancel a symbol or number by dividing, you need to divide both sides by that same symbol or number.

If you cancel a symbol or number by multiplying, you need to multiply both sides by that same symbol or number.

When we work with temperature, we may need to convert between degrees Celsius and degrees Fahrenheit using the following equation:

$$T_F = 1.8(T_C) + 32$$

To obtain the equation for converting degrees Fahrenheit to degrees Celsius, we subtract 32 from both sides.

$$T_F = 1.8(T_C) + 32$$
$$T_F - 32 = 1.8(T_C) + 32 - 32$$
$$T_F - 32 = 1.8(T_C)$$

To obtain T_C by itself, we divide both sides by 1.8.

$$\frac{T_F - 32}{1.8} = \frac{1.8(T_C)}{1.8} = T_C$$

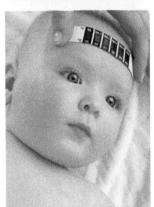

A plastic strip thermometer changes color to indicate body temperature.

SAMPLE PROBLEM 1.4 Solving Equations

Solve the following equation for V_2:

$$P_1V_1 = P_2V_2$$

SOLUTION

$$P_1V_1 = P_2V_2$$

To solve for V_2, divide both sides by the symbol P_2.

$$\frac{P_1V_1}{P_2} = \frac{P_2V_2}{P_2}$$
$$V_2 = \frac{P_1V_1}{P_2}$$

Interactive Video

Solving Equations

STUDY CHECK 1.4

Solve the following equation for m:

$$\text{heat} = m \times \Delta T \times SH$$

ANSWER

$$m = \frac{\text{heat}}{\Delta T \times SH}$$

KEY MATH SKILL

Interpreting Graphs

E. Interpreting Graphs

A graph represents the relationship between two variables. These quantities are plotted along two perpendicular axes, which are the x axis (horizontal) and y axis (vertical).

Example

In the following graph, the volume of a gas in a balloon is plotted against its temperature.

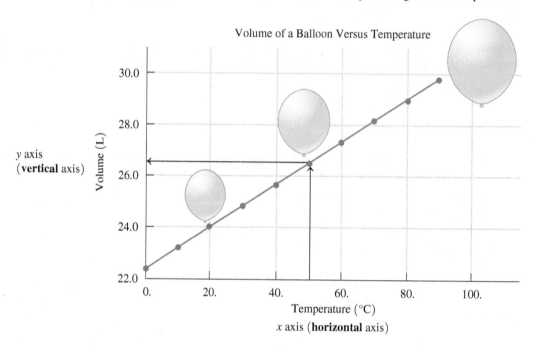

Volume of a Balloon Versus Temperature

y axis (**vertical** axis)

Volume (L)

Temperature (°C)

x axis (**horizontal** axis)

Title

Look at the title. What does it tell us about the graph? The title indicates that the volume of a balloon was measured at different temperatures.

Vertical Axis

Look at the label and the numbers on the vertical (y) axis. The label indicates that the volume of the balloon was measured in liters (L). The numbers, which are chosen to include the low and high measurements of the volume of the gas, are evenly spaced from 22.0 L to 30.0 L.

Horizontal Axis

The label on the horizontal (x) axis indicates that the temperature of the balloon was measured in degrees Celsius (°C). The numbers are measurements of the Celsius temperature, which are evenly spaced from 0. °C to 100. °C.

Points on the Graph

Each point on the graph represents a volume in liters that was measured at a specific temperature. When these points are connected, a straight line is obtained.

Interpreting the Graph

From the graph, we see that the volume of the gas increases as the temperature of the gas increases. This is called a *direct relationship*. Now we use the graph to determine the volume at various temperatures. For example, suppose we want to know the volume of the gas at 50. °C. We would start by finding 50. °C on the *x* axis and then drawing a line up to the plotted line. From there, we would draw a horizontal line that intersects the *y* axis and read the volume value where the line crosses the *y* axis.

▶ SAMPLE PROBLEM 1.5 Interpreting a Graph

A nurse administers Tylenol to lower a child's fever. The graph shows the body temperature of the child plotted against time.

a. What is measured on the vertical axis?
b. What is the range of values on the vertical axis?
c. What is measured on the horizontal axis?
d. What is the range of values on the horizontal axis?

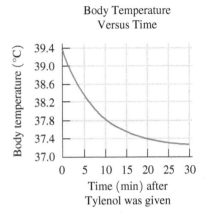

Body Temperature
Versus Time

SOLUTION

a. temperature in degrees Celsius
b. 37.0 °C to 39.4 °C
c. time, in minutes, after Tylenol was given
d. 0 min to 30 min

STUDY CHECK 1.5

a. Using the graph in Sample Problem 1.5, what was the child's temperature 15 min after Tylenol was given?
b. How many minutes elapsed before the temperature decreased to 38.0 °C?

ANSWER

a. 37.6 °C   b. 8 min

F. Writing Numbers in Scientific Notation

In chemistry, we use numbers that are very large and very small. We might measure something as tiny as the width of a human hair, which is about 0.000 008 m. Or perhaps we want to count the number of hairs on the average human scalp, which is about 100 000 hairs. In this text, we add spaces between sets of three digits when it helps make the places easier to count. However, we will see that it is more convenient to write large and small numbers in *scientific notation*.

📱 **KEY MATH SKILL**

Writing Numbers in Scientific Notation

1×10^5 hairs

8×10^{-6} m

Humans have an average of 1×10^5 hairs on their scalps. Each hair is about 8×10^{-6} m wide.

Standard Number	Scientific Notation
0.000 008 m	8×10^{-6} m
100 000 hairs	1×10^5 hairs

A number written in **scientific notation** has two parts: a coefficient and a power of 10. For example, the number 2400 is written in scientific notation as 2.4×10^3. The coefficient, 2.4, is obtained by moving the decimal point to the left to give a number that is at least 1 but less than 10. Because we moved the decimal point three places to the left, the power of 10 is a positive 3, which is written as 10^3. When a number greater than 1 is converted to scientific notation, the power of 10 is positive.

$$2400. \quad = \quad 2.4 \quad \times \quad 10^3$$
$$\longleftarrow \text{3 places} \qquad \text{Coefficient} \qquad \text{Power of 10}$$

In another example, a number smaller than 1, 0.000 86, is written in scientific notation as 8.6×10^{-4}. The coefficient, 8.6, is obtained by moving the decimal point to the right. Because the decimal point is moved four places to the right, the power of 10 is a negative 4, written as 10^{-4}. When a number less than 1 is written in scientific notation, the power of 10 is negative.

$$0.00086 \quad = \quad 8.6 \quad \times \quad 10^{-4}$$
$$\text{4 places} \longrightarrow \qquad \text{Coefficient} \qquad \text{Power of 10}$$

Table 1.3 gives some examples of numbers written as positive and negative powers of 10. The powers of 10 are a way of keeping track of the decimal point in the number. Table 1.4 gives several examples of writing measurements in scientific notation.

TABLE 1.3 Some Powers of 10

Number	Multiples of 10	Scientific Notation	
10 000	$10 \times 10 \times 10 \times 10$	1×10^4	
1 000	$10 \times 10 \times 10$	1×10^3	
100	10×10	1×10^2	Some positive powers of 10
10	10	1×10^1	
1	0	1×10^0	
0.1	$\dfrac{1}{10}$	1×10^{-1}	
0.01	$\dfrac{1}{10} \times \dfrac{1}{10} = \dfrac{1}{100}$	1×10^{-2}	
0.001	$\dfrac{1}{10} \times \dfrac{1}{10} \times \dfrac{1}{10} = \dfrac{1}{1\,000}$	1×10^{-3}	Some negative powers of 10
0.0001	$\dfrac{1}{10} \times \dfrac{1}{10} \times \dfrac{1}{10} \times \dfrac{1}{10} = \dfrac{1}{10\,000}$	1×10^{-4}	

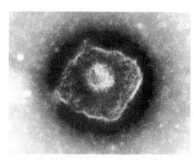

A chickenpox virus has a diameter of 3×10^{-7} m.

TABLE 1.4 Some Measurements Written in Scientific Notation

Measured Quantity	Standard Number	Scientific Notation
Volume of gasoline used in the United States each year	550 000 000 000 L	5.5×10^{11} L
Diameter of the Earth	12 800 000 m	1.28×10^7 m
Average volume of blood pumped in 1 day	8500 L	8.5×10^3 L
Time for light to travel from the Sun to the Earth	500 s	5×10^2 s
Mass of a typical human	68 kg	6.8×10^1 kg
Mass of stirrup bone in ear	0.003 g	3×10^{-3} g
Diameter of a chickenpox (*Varicella zoster*) virus	0.000 000 3 m	3×10^{-7} m
Mass of bacterium (mycoplasma)	0.000 000 000 000 000 000 1 kg	1×10^{-19} kg

Scientific Notation and Calculators

You can enter a number in scientific notation on many calculators using the $\boxed{\text{EE or EXP}}$ key. After you enter the coefficient, press the $\boxed{\text{EE or EXP}}$ key and enter only the power of 10, because the $\boxed{\text{EE or EXP}}$ key already includes the $\times$ 10 value. To enter a negative power of 10, press the $\boxed{+/-}$ key or the $\boxed{-}$ key, depending on your calculator.

Number to Enter	Procedure	Calculator Display		
4×10^6	4 $\boxed{\text{EE or EXP}}$ 6	$4\ 06$ or 4^{06} or $4E06$		
2.5×10^{-4}	2.5 $\boxed{\text{EE or EXP}}$ $\boxed{+/-}$ 4	$2.5-04$ or 2.5^{-04} or $2.5E-04$		

When a calculator display appears in scientific notation, it is shown as a number between 1 and 10 followed by a space and the power of 10. To express this display in scientific notation, write the coefficient value, write $\times$ 10, and use the power of 10 as an exponent.

Calculator Display	Expressed in Scientific Notation
$7.52\ 04$ or 7.52^{04} or $7.52E04$	7.52×10^4
$5.8-02$ or 5.8^{-02} or $5.8E-02$	5.8×10^{-2}

On many scientific calculators, a number is converted into scientific notation using the appropriate keys. For example, the number 0.000 52 is entered, followed by pressing the 2nd or 3rd function key and the SCI key. The scientific notation appears in the calculator display as a coefficient and the power of 10.

0.000 52 $\boxed{2^{\text{nd}} \text{ or } 3^{\text{rd}} \text{ function key}}$ $\boxed{\text{SCI}}$ $=$ $5.2-04$ or 5.2^{-04} or $5.2E-04$ $=$ 5.2×10^{-4}

Calculator display

▶ **SAMPLE PROBLEM 1.6 Scientific Notation**

Write each of the following in scientific notation:

a. 3500   **b.** 0.000 016

SOLUTION

a. 3500

STEP **1** Move the decimal point to obtain a coefficient that is at least 1 but less than 10. For a number greater than 1, the decimal point is moved to the left three places to give a coefficient of 3.5.

STEP **2** Express the number of places moved as a power of 10. Moving the decimal point three places to the left gives a power of 3, written as 10^3.

STEP **3** Write the product of the coefficient multiplied by the power of 10. 3.5×10^3

b. 0.000 016

STEP **1** Move the decimal point to obtain a coefficient that is at least 1 but less than 10. For a number less than one, the decimal point is moved to the right five places to give a coefficient of 1.6.

STEP **2** Express the number of places moved as a power of 10. Moving the decimal point five places to the right gives a power of negative 5, written as 10^{-5}.

STEP **3** Write the product of the coefficient multiplied by the power of 10. 1.6×10^{-5}

Guide to Writing a Number in Scientific Notation

STEP **1**
Move the decimal point to obtain a coefficient that is at least 1 but less than 10.

STEP **2**
Express the number of places moved as a power of 10.

STEP **3**
Write the product of the coefficient multiplied by the power of 10.

STUDY CHECK 1.6

Write each of the following in scientific notation:

a. 425 000   **b.** 0.000 000 86

ANSWER

a. 4.25×10^5 **b.** 8.6×10^{-7}

QUESTIONS AND PROBLEMS

1.4 Key Math Skills in Chemistry

LEARNING GOAL Review math concepts used in chemistry: place values, positive and negative numbers, percentages, solving equations, interpreting graphs, and writing numbers in scientific notation.

1.15 What is the place value for the bold digit?
    a. 7.32**8**8
    b. 16.1**2**34
    c. 4675.9**9**

1.16 What is the place value for the bold digit?
    a. 97.5**6**89
    b. **3**75.88
    c. 46.1**0**00

1.17 Evaluate each of the following:
    a. $15 - (-8) =$ _____
    b. $-8 + (-22) =$ _____
    c. $4 \times (-2) + 6 =$ _____

1.18 Evaluate each of the following:
    a. $-11 - (-9) =$ _____
    b. $34 + (-55) =$ _____
    c. $\dfrac{-56}{8} =$ _____

1.19 a. A clinic had 25 patients on Friday morning. If 21 patients were given flu shots, what percentage of the patients received flu shots? Express your answer to the ones place.
    b. An alloy contains 56 g of pure silver and 22 g of pure copper. What is the percentage of silver in the alloy? Express your answer to the ones place.
    c. A collection of coins contains 11 nickels, 5 quarters, and 7 dimes. What is the percentage of dimes in the collection? Express your answer to the ones place.

1.20 a. At a local hospital, 35 babies were born. If 22 were boys, what percentage of the newborns were boys? Express your answer to the ones place.
    b. An alloy contains 67 g of pure gold and 35 g of pure zinc. What is the percentage of zinc in the alloy? Express your answer to the ones place.
    c. A collection of coins contains 15 pennies, 14 dimes, and 6 quarters. What is the percentage of pennies in the collection? Express your answer to the ones place.

1.21 Solve each of the following for a:
    a. $4a + 4 = 40$ **b.** $\dfrac{a}{6} = 7$

1.22 Solve each of the following for b:
    a. $2b + 7 = b + 10$ **b.** $3b - 4 = 24 - b$

Use the following graph for questions 1.23 and 1.24:

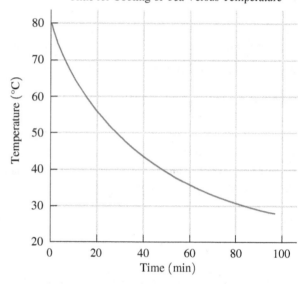

Time for Cooling of Tea Versus Temperature

1.23 a. What does the title indicate about the graph?
    b. What is measured on the vertical axis?
    c. What is the range of values on the vertical axis?
    d. Does the temperature increase or decrease with an increase in time?

1.24 a. What is measured on the horizontal axis?
    b. What is the range of values on the horizontal axis?
    c. What is the temperature of the tea after 20 min?
    d. How many minutes were needed to reach a temperature of 45 °C?

1.25 Write each of the following in scientific notation:
    a. 55 000   **b.** 480
    c. 0.000 005   **d.** 0.000 14
    e. 0.0072   **f.** 670 000

1.26 Write each of the following in scientific notation:
    a. 180 000 000   **b.** 0.000 06
    c. 750   **d.** 0.15
    e. 0.024   **f.** 1500

1.27 Which number in each of the following pairs is larger?
    a. 7.2×10^3 or 8.2×10^2 **b.** 4.5×10^{-4} or 3.2×10^{-2}
    c. 1×10^4 or 1×10^{-4} **d.** 0.000 52 or 6.8×10^{-2}

1.28 Which number in each of the following pairs is smaller?
    a. 4.9×10^{-3} or 5.5×10^{-9} **b.** 1250 or 3.4×10^2
    c. 0.000 000 4 or 5.0×10^2 **d.** 2.50×10^2 or 4×10^5

Clinical Update
Forensic Evidence Solves the Murder

Using a variety of laboratory tests, Sarah finds ethylene glycol in the victim's blood. The quantitative tests indicate that the victim had ingested 125 g of ethylene glycol. Sarah determines that the liquid in the glass found at the crime scene was ethylene glycol that had been added to an alcoholic beverage. Ethylene glycol is a clear, sweet-tasting, thick liquid that is odorless and mixes with water. It is easy to obtain since it is used as antifreeze in automobiles and in brake fluid. Because the initial symptoms of ethylene glycol poisoning are similar to being intoxicated, the victim is often unaware of its presence.

If ingestion of ethylene glycol occurs, it can cause depression of the central nervous system, cardiovascular damage, and kidney failure. If discovered quickly, hemodialysis may be used to remove ethylene glycol from the blood. A toxic amount of ethylene glycol is 1.5 g of ethylene glycol/kg of body mass. Thus, 75 g could be fatal for a 50-kg (110 lb) person.

Mark determines that a fingerprint on the glass found in the victim's home is match to the victim's husband. This evidence along with the container of antifreeze found in the home led to the arrest and conviction of the husband for poisoning his wife.

Clinical Applications

1.29 A container was found in the home of the victim that contained 120 g of ethylene glycol in 450 g of liquid. What was the percentage of ethylene glycol? Express your answer to the ones place.

1.30 If the toxic quantity is 1.5 g per 1000 g of body mass, what percentage of ethylene glycol is fatal?

CONCEPT MAP

CHEMISTRY IN OUR LIVES

deals with
Substances
called
Chemicals

uses the
Scientific Method
starting with
Observations
that lead to
Hypothesis
Experiments
Conclusion

is learned by
Reading the Text
Practicing Problem Solving
Self-Testing
Working with a Group

uses key math skills
Identifying Place Values
Using Positive and Negative Numbers
Calculating Percentages
Solving Equations
Interpreting Graphs
Writing Numbers in Scientific Notation

CHAPTER REVIEW

1.1 Chemistry and Chemicals
LEARNING GOAL Define the term chemistry and identify substances as chemicals.
- Chemistry is the study of the composition, structure, properties, and reactions of matter.
- A chemical is any substance that always has the same composition and properties wherever it is found.

1.2 Scientific Method: Thinking Like a Scientist
LEARNING GOAL Describe the activities that are part of the scientific method.
- The scientific method is a process of explaining natural phenomena beginning with making observations, forming a hypothesis, and performing experiments.
- After repeated experiments, a conclusion may be reached as to whether the hypothesis is true or not.

1.3 Learning Chemistry: A Study Plan
LEARNING GOAL Develop a study plan for learning chemistry.
- A study plan for learning chemistry utilizes the features in the text and develops an active learning approach to study.
- By using the *Learning Goals* in the chapter and working the *Sample Problems*, *Study Checks*, and the *Questions and Problems* at the end of each section, you can successfully learn the concepts of chemistry.

1.4 Key Math Skills for Chemistry
LEARNING GOAL Review math concepts used in chemistry: place values, positive and negative numbers, percentages, solving equations, interpreting graphs, and writing numbers in scientific notation.

1×10^5 hairs 8×10^{-6} m

- Solving chemistry problems involves a number of math skills: identifying place values, using positive and negative numbers, calculating percentages, solving equations, interpreting graphs, and writing numbers in scientific notation.

KEY TERMS

chemical A substance that has the same composition and properties wherever it is found.

chemistry The study of the composition, structure, properties, and reactions of matter.

conclusion An explanation of an observation that has been validated by repeated experiments that support a hypothesis.

experiment A procedure that tests the validity of a hypothesis.

hypothesis An unverified explanation of a natural phenomenon.

observation Information determined by noting and recording a natural phenomenon.

scientific method The process of making observations, proposing a hypothesis, testing the hypothesis, and making a conclusion as to the validity of the hypothesis.

scientific notation A form of writing large and small numbers using a coefficient that is at least 1 but less than 10, followed by a power of 10.

KEY MATH SKILLS

The chapter section containing each Key Math Skill is shown in parentheses at the end of each heading.

Identifying Place Values (1.4A)
- The place value identifies the numerical value of each digit in a number.

Example: Identify the place value for each of the digits in the number 456.78.

Answer:

Digit	Place Value
4	hundreds
5	tens
6	ones
7	tenths
8	hundredths

Using Positive and Negative Numbers in Calculations (1.4B)

- A *positive number* is any number that is greater than zero and has a positive sign $(+)$. A *negative number* is any number that is less than zero and is written with a negative sign $(-)$.
- When two positive numbers are added, multiplied, or divided, the answer is positive.
- When two negative numbers are multiplied or divided, the answer is positive. When two negative numbers are added, the answer is negative.
- When a positive and a negative number are multiplied or divided, the answer is negative.
- When a positive and a negative number are added, the smaller number is subtracted from the larger number and the result has the same sign as the larger number.
- When two numbers are subtracted, change the sign of the number to be subtracted then follow the rules for addition.

Example: Evaluate each of the following:
  a. $-8 - 14 = $ _____
  b. $6 \times (-3) = $ _____
Answer: **a.** $-8 - 14 = -22$
  b. $6 \times (-3) = -18$

Calculating Percentages (1.4C)

- A percentage is the part divided by the total (whole) multiplied by 100%.

Example: A drawer contains 6 white socks and 18 black socks. What is the percentage of white socks?

Answer: $\dfrac{6 \text{ white socks}}{24 \text{ total socks}} \times 100\% = 25\%$ white socks

Solving Equations (1.4D)

An equation in chemistry often contains an unknown. To rearrange an equation to obtain the unknown factor by itself, you keep it balanced by performing matching mathematical operations on both sides of the equation.

- If you eliminate a number or symbol by subtracting, subtract that same number or symbol on the opposite side.
- If you eliminate a number or symbol by adding, add that same number or symbol on the opposite side.
- If you cancel a number or symbol by dividing, divide both sides by that same number or symbol.
- If you cancel a number or symbol by multiplying, multiply both sides by that same number or symbol.

Example: Solve the equation for a: $3a - 8 = 28$
Answer: *Add 8 to both sides* $3a - \cancel{8} + \cancel{8} = 28 + 8$
  $3a = 36$

  Divide both sides by 3 $\dfrac{3a}{3} = \dfrac{36}{3}$

  $a = 12$

Check: $3(12) - 8 = 28$
  $36 - 8 = 28$
  $28 = 28$

Your answer $a = 12$ is correct.

Interpreting Graphs (1.4E)

A graph represents the relationship between two variables. These quantities are plotted along two perpendicular axes, which are the x axis (horizontal) and y axis (vertical). The title indicates the components of the x and y axes. Numbers on the x and y axes show the range of values of the variables. The graph shows the relationship between the component on the y axis and that on the x axis.

Example:

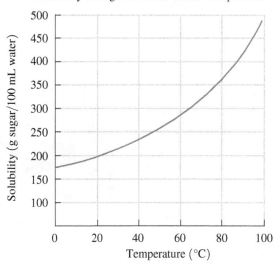

Solubility of Sugar in Water Versus Temperature

a. Does the amount of sugar that dissolves in 100 mL of water increase or decrease when the temperature increases?
b. How many grams of sugar dissolve in 100 mL of water at 70 °C?
c. At what temperature (°C) will 275 g of sugar dissolve in 100 mL of water?

Answer: **a.** increase
  b. 320 g
  c. 55 °C

Writing Numbers in Scientific Notation (1.4F)

A number is written in scientific notation by:

- Moving the decimal point to obtain a coefficient that is at least 1 but less than 10.
- Expressing the number of places moved as a power of 10. The power of 10 is positive if the decimal point is moved to the left, negative if the decimal point is moved to the right.
- A number written in scientific notation consists of a coefficient and a power of 10.

Example: Write the number 28 000 in scientific notation.
Answer: Moving the decimal point four places to the left gives a coefficient of 2.8 and a positive power of 10, 10^4. The number 28 000 written in scientific notation is 2.8×10^4.
Example: Write the number 0.000 056 in scientific notation.
Answer: Moving the decimal point five places to the right gives a coefficient of 5.6 and a negative power of 10, 10^{-5}. The number 0.000 056 written in scientific notation is 5.6×10^{-5}.

UNDERSTANDING THE CONCEPTS

The chapter sections to review are shown in parentheses at the end of each question.

1.31 A "chemical-free" shampoo includes the following ingredients: water, cocomide, glycerin, and citric acid. Is the shampoo truly "chemical-free"? (1.1)

1.32 A "chemical-free" sunscreen includes the following ingredients: titanium dioxide, vitamin E, and vitamin C. Is the sunscreen truly "chemical-free"? (1.1)

1.33 According to Sherlock Holmes, "One must follow the rules of scientific inquiry, gathering, observing, and testing data, then formulating, modifying, and rejecting hypotheses, until only one remains." Did Holmes use the scientific method? Why or why not? (1.2)

Sherlock Holmes is a fictional detective in novels written by Arthur Conan Doyle.

1.34 In *A Scandal in Bohemia*, Sherlock Holmes receives a mysterious note. He states, "I have no data yet. It is a capital mistake to theorize before one has data. Insensibly one begins to twist facts to suit theories, instead of theories to suit facts." What do you think Holmes meant? (1.2)

1.35 Classify each of the following statements as an observation (O) or a hypothesis (H): (1.2)
 a. A patient breaks out in hives after receiving penicillin.
 b. Dinosaurs became extinct when a large meteorite struck the Earth and caused a huge dust cloud that severely decreased the amount of light reaching the Earth.
 c. The 100-yd dash was run in 9.8 s.

1.36 Classify each of the following statements as an observation (O) or a hypothesis (H): (1.2)
 a. Analysis of 10 ceramic dishes showed that four dishes contained lead levels that exceeded federal safety standards.
 b. Marble statues undergo corrosion in acid rain.
 c. A child with a high fever and a rash may have chicken pox.

1.37 For each of the following, indicate if the answer has a positive or negative sign: (1.4)
 a. Two negative numbers are added.
 b. A positive and negative number are multiplied.

1.38 For each of the following, indicate if the answer has a positive or negative sign: (1.4)
 a. A negative number is subtracted from a positive number.
 b. Two negative numbers are divided.

ADDITIONAL QUESTIONS AND PROBLEMS

1.39 Identify each of the following as an observation (O), a hypothesis (H), an experiment (E), or a conclusion (C): (1.2)
 a. During an assessment in the emergency room, a nurse writes that the patient has a resting pulse of 30 beats/min.
 b. A nurse thinks that an incision from a recent surgery that is red and swollen is infected.
 c. Repeated studies show that lowering sodium in the diet leads to a decrease in blood pressure.

Nurses make observations in the hospital.

1.40 Identify each of the following as an observation (O), a hypothesis (H), an experiment (E), or a conclusion (C): (1.2)
 a. Drinking coffee at night keeps me awake.
 b. If I stop drinking coffee in the afternoon, I will be able to sleep at night.
 c. I will try drinking coffee only in the morning.

1.41 Select the correct phrase(s) to complete the following statement: If experimental results do not support your hypothesis, you should (1.2)
 a. pretend that the experimental results support your hypothesis
 b. modify your hypothesis
 c. do more experiments

1.42 Select the correct phrase(s) to complete the following statement: A conclusion confirms a hypothesis when (1.2)
 a. one experiment proves the hypothesis
 b. many experiments validate the hypothesis
 c. you think your hypothesis is correct

1.43 Which of the following will help you develop a successful study plan? (1.3)
 a. skipping lecture and just reading the text
 b. working the *Sample Problems* as you go through a chapter
 c. going to your professor's office hours
 d. reading through the chapter, but working the problems later

1.44 Which of the following will help you develop a successful study plan? (1.3)
 a. studying all night before the exam
 b. forming a study group and discussing the problems together
 c. working problems in a notebook for easy reference
 d. copying the homework answers from a friend

1.45 Evaluate each of the following: (1.4)
    a. $4 \times (-8) =$ _____
    b. $-12 - 48 =$ _____
    c. $\dfrac{-168}{-4} =$ _____

1.46 Evaluate each of the following: (1.4)
    a. $-95 - (-11) =$ _____
    b. $\dfrac{152}{-19} =$ _____
    c. $4 - 56 =$ _____

1.47 A bag of gumdrops contains 16 orange gumdrops, 8 yellow gumdrops, and 16 black gumdrops. (1.4)
    a. What is the percentage of yellow gumdrops? Express your answer to the ones place.
    b. What is the percentage of black gumdrops? Express your answer to the ones place.

1.48 On the first chemistry test, 12 students got As, 18 students got Bs, and 20 students got Cs. (1.4)
    a. What is the percentage of students who received Bs? Express your answer to the ones place.
    b. What is the percentage of students who received Cs? Express your answer to the ones place.

1.49 Express each of the following numbers in scientific notation: (1.4)
    a. 120 000
    b. 0.000 000 34
    c. 0.066
    d. 2700

1.50 Express each of the following numbers in scientific notation: (1.4)
    a. 0.0042
    b. 310
    c. 890 000 000
    d. 0.000 000 056

CHALLENGE QUESTIONS

The following groups of questions are related to the topics in this chapter. However, they do not all follow the chapter order, and they require you to combine concepts and skills from several sections. These questions will help you increase your critical thinking skills and prepare for your next exam.

1.51 Classify each of the following as an observation (O), a hypothesis (H), or an experiment (E): (1.2)
    a. The bicycle tire is flat.
    b. If I add air to the bicycle tire, it will expand to the proper size.
    c. When I added air to the bicycle tire, it was still flat.
    d. The bicycle tire must have a leak in it.

1.52 Classify each of the following as an observation (O), a hypothesis (H), or an experiment (E): (1.2)
    a. A big log in the fire does not burn well.
    b. If I chop the log into smaller wood pieces, it will burn better.
    c. The small wood pieces burn brighter and make a hotter fire.
    d. The small wood pieces are used up faster than burning the big log.

1.53 Solve each of the following for x: (1.4)
    a. $2x + 5 = 41$ **b.** $\dfrac{5x}{3} = 40$

1.54 Solve each of the following for z: (1.4)
    a. $3z - (-6) = 12$ **b.** $\dfrac{4z}{-12} = -8$

Use the following graph for problems 1.55 and 1.56:

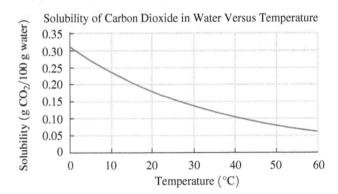

1.55 **a.** What does the title indicate about the graph? (1.4)
    b. What is measured on the vertical axis?
    c. What is the range of values on the vertical axis?
    d. Does the solubility of carbon dioxide increase or decrease with an increase in temperature?

1.56 **a.** What is measured on the horizontal axis? (1.4)
    b. What is the range of values on the horizontal axis?
    c. What is the solubility of carbon dioxide in water at 25 °C?
    d. At what temperature does carbon dioxide have a solubility of 0.20 g/100 g water?

ANSWERS

Answers to Selected Questions and Problems

1.1 a. Chemistry is the study of the composition, structure, properties, and reactions of matter.
   b. A chemical is a substance that has the same composition and properties wherever it is found.

1.3 Many chemicals are listed on a vitamin bottle such as vitamin A, vitamin B_3, vitamin B_{12}, vitamin C, and folic acid.

1.5 Typical items found in a medicine cabinet and some of the chemicals they contain are as follows:

Antacid tablets: calcium carbonate, cellulose, starch, stearic acid, silicon dioxide

Mouthwash: water, alcohol, thymol, glycerol, sodium benzoate, benzoic acid

Cough suppressant: menthol, beta-carotene, sucrose, glucose

1.7 a. observation (O)   **b.** hypothesis (H)
   c. experiment (E)   **d.** observation (O)
   e. observation (O)   **f.** conclusion (C)

1.9 a. observation (O)   **b.** hypothesis (H)
   c. experiment (E)   **d.** experiment (E)

1.11 There are several things you can do that will help you successfully learn chemistry: forming a study group, going to lecture, working *Sample Problems* and *Study Checks*, working *Questions and Problems* and checking answers, reading the assignment ahead of class, and keeping a problem notebook.

1.13 a, c, and **e**

1.15 a. thousandths   **b.** ones   **c.** hundreds

1.17 a. 23   **b.** −30   **c.** −2

1.19 a. 84%   **b.** 72%   **c.** 30%

1.21 a. 9   **b.** 42

1.23 a. The graph shows the relationship between the temperature of a cup of tea and time.
   b. temperature, in °C
   c. 20 °C to 80 °C
   d. decrease

1.25 a. 5.5×10^4 **b.** 4.8×10^2
   c. 5×10^{-6} **d.** 1.4×10^{-4}
   e. 7.2×10^{-3} **f.** 6.7×10^5

1.27 a. 7.2×10^3 **b.** 3.2×10^{-2}
   c. 1×10^4 **d.** 6.8×10^{-2}

1.29 27% ethylene glycol

1.31 No. All of the ingredients are chemicals.

1.33 Yes. Sherlock's investigation includes making observations (gathering data), formulating a hypothesis, testing the hypothesis, and modifying it until one of the hypotheses is validated.

1.35 a. observation (O)   **b.** hypothesis (H)
   c. observation (O)

1.37 a. negative   **b.** negative

1.39 a. observation (O)   **b.** hypothesis (H)
   c. conclusion (C)

1.41 b

1.43 b and **c**

1.45 a. −32   **b.** −60   **c.** 42

1.47 a. 20%   **b.** 40%

1.49 a. 1.2×10^5 **b.** 3.4×10^{-7}
   c. 6.6×10^{-2} **d.** 2.7×10^3

1.51 a. observation (O)   **b.** hypothesis (H)
   c. experiment (E)   **d.** hypothesis (H)

1.53 a. 18   **b.** 24

1.55 a. The graph shows the relationship between the solubility of carbon dioxide in water and temperature.
   b. solubility of carbon dioxide (g CO_2/100 g water)
   c. 0 to 0.35 g of CO_2/100 g of water
   d. decrease

2

Chemistry and Measurements

DURING THE PAST FEW MONTHS, GREG HAS BEEN experiencing an increased number of headaches, and frequently feels dizzy and nauseous. He goes to his doctor's office where, Sandra, the registered nurse completes the initial part of the exam by recording several measurements: weight 65.5 kg, height 171 cm, temperature 37.2 °C, and blood pressure 155/95. Normal blood pressure is 120/80 or below.

When Greg sees his doctor, he is diagnosed as having high blood pressure (hypertension). The doctor prescribes 80. mg of Inderal (propranolol). Inderal is a beta blocker, which relaxes the muscles of the heart. It is used to treat hypertension, angina (chest pain), arrhythmia, and migraine headaches.

Two weeks later, Greg visits his doctor again, who determines that Greg's blood pressure is now 152/90. The doctor increases the dosage of Inderal to 160 mg. The registered nurse, Sandra, informs Greg that he needs to increase his daily dosage from two tablets to four tablets.

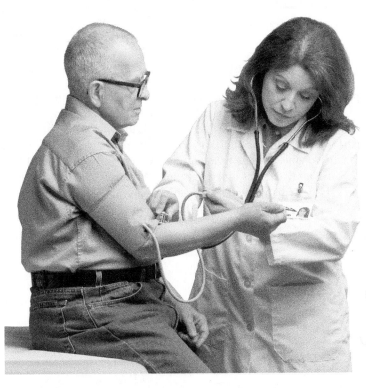

CAREER Registered Nurse

In addition to assisting physicians, registered nurses work to promote patient health, and prevent and treat disease. They provide patient care and help patients cope with illness. They take measurements such as a patient's weight, height, temperature, and blood pressure; make conversions; and calculate drug dosage rates. Registered nurses also maintain detailed medical records of patient symptoms and prescribed medications.

C hemistry and measurements are an important part of our everyday lives. Levels of toxic materials in the air, soil, and water are discussed in our newspapers. We read about radon gas in our homes, holes in the ozone layer, trans fatty acids, and climate change. Understanding chemistry and measurement helps us make proper choices about our world.

Think about your day. You probably took some measurements. Perhaps you checked your weight by stepping on a bathroom scale. If you made some rice for dinner, you added two cups of water to one cup of rice. If you did not feel well, you may have taken your temperature. Whenever you take a measurement, you use a measuring device such as a balance, a measuring cup, or a thermometer. Over the years, you have learned to read the markings on each device to take a correct measurement.

Your weight on a bathroom scale is a measurement.

Measurement is an essential part of health careers such as nursing, dental hygiene, respiratory therapy, nutrition, and veterinary technology. The temperature, height, and weight of a patient are measured and recorded. Samples of blood and urine are collected and sent to a laboratory where glucose, pH, urea, and protein are measured by the clinical technicians. By learning about measurement, you develop skills for solving problems and working with numbers.

CHAPTER READINESS*

🖩 KEY MATH SKILLS

- Identifying Place Values (1.4A)
- Using Positive and Negative Numbers in Calculations (1.4B)

- Calculating Percentages (1.4C)
- Writing Numbers in Scientific Notation (1.4F)

*These Key Math Skills from the previous chapter are listed here for your review as you proceed to the new material in this chapter.

LEARNING GOAL

Write the names and abbreviations for the metric or SI units used in measurements of length, volume, mass, temperature, and time.

2.1 Units of Measurement

Scientists and health professionals throughout the world use the **metric system** of measurement. It is also the common measuring system in all but a few countries in the world. The **International System of Units (SI)**, or Système International, is the official system of measurement throughout the world except for the United States. In chemistry, we use metric units and SI units for length, volume, mass, temperature, and time, as listed in Table 2.1.

Suppose you walked 1.3 mi to campus today, carrying a backpack that weighs 26 lb. The temperature was 72 °F. Perhaps you weigh 128 lb and your height is 65 in. These measurements and units may seem familiar to you because they are stated in the U.S.

TABLE 2.1 Units of Measurement and Their Abbreviations

Measurement	Metric	SI
Length	meter (m)	meter (m)
Volume	liter (L)	cubic meter (m^3)
Mass	gram (g)	kilogram (kg)
Temperature	degree Celsius (°C)	kelvin (K)
Time	second (s)	second (s)

system of measurement. However, in chemistry, we use the *metric system* in making our measurements. Using the metric system, you walked 2.1 km to campus, carrying a back-pack that has a mass of 12 kg, when the temperature was 22 °C. You have a mass of 58.2 kg and a height of 1.65 m.

8:30 A.M.

1.65 m (65 in.)

22 °C (72 °F)

58.2 kg (128 lb)

12 kg (26 lb)

2.1 km (1.3 mi)

There are many measurements in everyday life.

Length

The metric and SI unit of length is the **meter (m)**. A meter is 39.4 inches (in.), which makes it slightly longer than a yard (yd). The **centimeter (cm)**, a smaller unit of length, is com-monly used in chemistry and is about equal to the width of your little finger. For comparison, there are 2.54 cm in 1 in. (see Figure 2.1). Some relationships between units for length are

$$1 \text{ m} = 100 \text{ cm}$$
$$1 \text{ m} = 39.4 \text{ in.}$$
$$1 \text{ m} = 1.09 \text{ yd}$$
$$2.54 \text{ cm} = 1 \text{ in.}$$

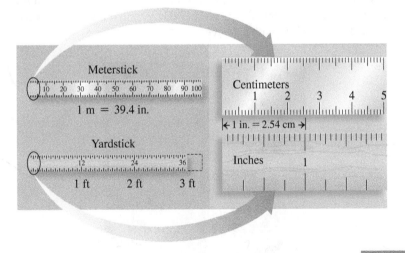

Meterstick

10 20 30 40 50 60 70 80 90 100

1 m = 39.4 in.

Yardstick

12   24   36

1 ft   2 ft   3 ft

Centimeters

1   2   3   4   5

← 1 in. = 2.54 cm →

Inches   1

FIGURE 2.1 ▶ Length in the metric (SI) system is based on the meter, which is slightly longer than a yard.

Ⓠ How many centimeters are in a length of 1 inch?

Volume

Volume is the amount of space a substance occupies. A **liter (L)** is slightly larger than a quart (qt), (1 L = 1.06 qt). In a laboratory or a hospital, chemists work with metric units of volume that are smaller and more convenient, such as the **milliliter (mL)**. There are 1000 mL in 1 L. A comparison of metric and U.S. units for volume appears in Figure 2.2. Some relationships between units for volume are

$$1 \text{ L} = 1000 \text{ mL}$$
$$1 \text{ L} = 1.06 \text{ qt}$$
$$946 \text{ mL} = 1 \text{ qt}$$

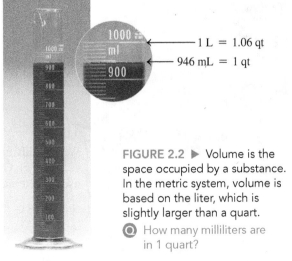

1 L = 1.06 qt

946 mL = 1 qt

FIGURE 2.2 ▶ Volume is the space occupied by a substance. In the metric system, volume is based on the liter, which is slightly larger than a quart.

Ⓠ How many milliliters are in 1 quart?

The standard kilogram for the United States is stored at the National Institute of Standards and Technology (NIST).

Mass

The **mass** of an object is a measure of the quantity of material it contains. The SI unit of mass, the **kilogram (kg)**, is used for larger masses such as body mass. In the metric system, the unit for mass is the **gram (g)**, which is used for smaller masses. There are 1000 g in 1 kg. It takes 2.20 lb to make 1 kg, and 454 g is equal to 1 lb. Some relationships between units for mass are

$$1 \text{ kg} = 1000 \text{ g}$$
$$1 \text{ kg} = 2.20 \text{ lb}$$
$$454 \text{ g} = 1 \text{ lb}$$

You may be more familiar with the term *weight* than with mass. *Weight* is a measure of the gravitational pull on an object. On the Earth, an astronaut with a mass of 75.0 kg has a weight of 165 lb. On the Moon where the gravitational pull is one-sixth that of the Earth, the astronaut has a weight of 27.5 lb. However, the mass of the astronaut is the same as on Earth, 75.0 kg. Scientists measure mass rather than weight because mass does not depend on gravity.

In a chemistry laboratory, an electronic balance is used to measure the mass in grams of a substance (see Figure 2.3).

FIGURE 2.3 ▶ On an electronic balance, the digital readout gives the mass of a nickel, which is 5.01 g.

Ⓠ What is the mass of 10 nickels?

Temperature

Temperature tells us how hot something is, how cold it is outside, or helps us determine if we have a fever (see Figure 2.4). In the metric system, temperature is measured using Celsius temperature. On the **Celsius (°C) temperature scale**, water freezes at 0 °C and boils at 100 °C, whereas on the Fahrenheit (°F) scale, water freezes at 32 °F and boils at 212 °F. In the SI system, temperature is measured using the **Kelvin (K) temperature scale** on which the lowest possible temperature is 0 K. A unit on the Kelvin scale is called a kelvin (K) and is not written with a degree sign.

FIGURE 2.4 ▶ A thermometer is used to determine temperature.

Ⓠ What kinds of temperature readings have you made today?

Time

We typically measure time in units such as years (yr), days, hours (h), minutes (min), or seconds (s). Of these, the SI and metric unit of time is the **second (s)**. The standard now used to determine a second is an atomic clock.

A stopwatch is used to measure the time of a race.

> **SAMPLE PROBLEM 2.1 Units of Measurement**
>
> On a typical day, a nurse encounters several situations involving measurement. State the name and type of measurement indicated by the units in each of the following:
>
> **a.** A patient has a temperature of 38.5 °C.
> **b.** A physician orders 1.5 g of Cefuroxime for injection.
> **c.** A physician orders 1 L of a sodium chloride solution to be given intravenously.
> **d.** A medication is to be given to a patient every 4 h.
>
> **SOLUTION**
>
> **a.** Degrees Celsius is a unit of temperature.
> **b.** A gram is a unit of mass.
> **c.** A liter is a unit of volume.
> **d.** An hour is a unit of time.
>
> **STUDY CHECK 2.1**
>
> State the name and type of measurement indicated by an infant that is 32.5 cm long.
>
> **ANSWER**
>
> A centimeter is a unit of length.

Explore Your World

Units Listed on Labels

Read the labels on a variety of products such as sugar, salt, soft drinks, vitamins, and dental floss.

Questions

1. What metric or SI units of measurement are listed?
2. What type of measurement (mass, volume, etc.) does each indicate?
3. Write each quantity as a number and a metric or SI unit.

QUESTIONS AND PROBLEMS

2.1 Units of Measurement

LEARNING GOAL Write the names and abbreviations for the metric or SI units used in measurements of length, volume, mass, temperature, and time.

2.1 State the type of measurement in each of the following statements:
    a. I put 12 L of gasoline in my gas tank.
    b. My friend is 170 cm tall.
    c. We are 385 000 km away from the Moon.
    d. The horse won the race by 1.2 s.

2.2 State the type of measurement in each of the following statements:
    a. I rode my bicycle 15 km today.
    b. My dog weighs 12 kg.
    c. It is hot today. It is 30 °C.
    d. I added 2 L of water to my fish tank.

2.3 State the name of the unit and the type of measurement indicated for each of the following quantities:
    a. 4.8 m   **b.** 325 g   **c.** 1.5 mL
    d. 4.8×10^2 s   **e.** 28 °C

2.4 State the name of the unit and the type of measurement indicated for each of the following quantities:
    a. 0.8 L   **b.** 3.6 cm   **c.** 4 kg
    d. 3.5 h   **e.** 373 K

℞ Clinical Applications

2.5 On a typical day, a nurse encounters several situations involving measurement. State the name and type of measurement indicated by the units in each of the following:
    a. The prothrombin time (clotting time) for a blood sample is 12 s.
    b. A premature baby weighs 2.0 kg.
    c. An antacid tablet contains 1.0 g of calcium carbonate.
    d. An infant has a temperature 39.2 °C.

2.6 On a typical day, a nurse encounters several situations involving measurement. State the name and type of measurement indicated by the units in each of the following:
    a. During open-heart surgery, the temperature of a patient is lowered to 29 °C.
    b. The circulation time of a red blood cell through the body is 20 s.
    c. A patient with a persistent cough is given 10. mL of cough syrup.
    d. The amount of iron in the red blood cells of the body is 2.5 g.

A volume of 10. mL of cough syrup is measured for a patient.

LEARNING GOAL

Identify a number as measured or exact; determine the number of significant figures in a measured number.

(a)

(b)

(c)

FIGURE 2.5 ▶ The lengths of the rectangular objects are measured as **(a)** 4.5 cm and **(b)** 4.55 cm.
❓ What is the length of the object in **(c)**?

⚙ **CORE CHEMISTRY SKILL**

Counting Significant Figures

2.2 Measured Numbers and Significant Figures

When you make a measurement, you use some type of measuring device. For example, you may use a meterstick to measure your height, a scale to check your weight, or a thermometer to take your temperature.

Measured Numbers

Measured numbers are the numbers you obtain when you measure a quantity such as your height, weight, or temperature. Suppose you are going to measure the lengths of the objects in Figure 2.5. The metric ruler that you use may have lines marked in 1-cm divisions or perhaps in divisions of 0.1 cm. To report the length of the object, you observe the numerical values of the marked lines at the end of the object. Then you can *estimate* by visually dividing the space between the marked lines. This estimated value is the final digit in a measured number.

For example, in Figure 2.5a, the end of the object is between the marks of 4 cm and 5 cm, which means that the length is more than 4 cm but less than 5 cm. This is written as 4 cm plus an estimated digit. If you estimate that the end of the object is halfway between 4 cm and 5 cm, you would report its length as 4.5 cm. The last digit in a measured number may differ because people do not always estimate in the same way. Thus, someone else might report the length of the same object as 4.4 cm.

The metric ruler shown in Figure 2.5b is marked at every 0.1 cm. With this ruler, you can estimate to the hundredths place (0.01 cm). Now you can determine that the end of the object is between 4.5 cm and 4.6 cm. Perhaps you report its length as 4.55 cm, whereas another student reports its length as 4.56 cm. Both results are acceptable.

In Figure 2.5c, the end of the object appears to line up with the 3-cm mark. Because the divisions are marked in units of 1 cm, the length of the object is between 3 cm and 4 cm. Because the end of the object is on the 3-cm mark, the estimated digit is 0, which means the measurement is reported as 3.0 cm.

Significant Figures

In a measured number, the **significant figures (SFs)** are all the digits including the estimated digit. Nonzero numbers are always counted as significant figures. However, a zero may or may not be a significant figure depending on its position in a number. Table 2.2 gives the rules and examples of counting significant figures.

TABLE 2.2 Significant Figures in Measured Numbers

Rule	Measured Number	Number of Significant Figures
1. A number is a *significant figure* if it is		
a. not a zero	4.5 g	2
	122.35 m	5
b. a zero between nonzero digits	205 m	3
	5.008 kg	4
c. a zero at the end of a decimal number	50. L	2
	25.0 °C	3
	16.00 g	4
d. in the coefficient of a number written in scientific notation	4.8×10^5 m	2
	5.70×10^{-3} g	3
2. A zero is *not significant* if it is		
a. at the beginning of a decimal number	0.0004 s	1
	0.075 cm	2
b. used as a placeholder in a large number without a decimal point	850 000 m	2
	1 250 000 g	3

Significant Zeros and Scientific Notation

When one or more zeros in a large number are significant, they are shown clearly by writing the number in scientific notation. For example, if the first zero in the measurement 300 m is significant, but the second zero is not, the measurement is written as 3.0×10^2 m. *In this text, we will place a decimal point after a significant zero at the end of a number.* For example, if a measurement is written as 500. g, the decimal point after the second zero indicates that *both zeros* are significant. To show this more clearly, we can write it as 5.00×10^2 g. We will assume that zeros at the end of large standard numbers without a decimal point are not significant. Therefore, we write 400 000 g as 4×10^5 g, which has only one significant figure.

▶ **SAMPLE PROBLEM 2.2 Significant Zeros**

Identify the significant zeros in each of the following measured numbers:

a. 0.000 250 m   **b.** 70.040 g   **c.** 1 020 000 L

SOLUTION

a. The zero in the last decimal place following the 5 is significant. The zeros preceding the 2 are not significant.
b. Zeros between nonzero digits or at the end of decimal numbers are significant. All the zeros in 70.040 g are significant.
c. Zeros between nonzero digits are significant. Zeros at the end of a large number with no decimal point are placeholders but not significant. The zero between 1 and 2 is significant, but the four zeros following the 2 are not significant.

STUDY CHECK 2.2

Identify the significant zeros in each of the following measured numbers:

a. 0.04008 m   **b.** 6.00×10^3 g

ANSWER

a. The zeros between 4 and 8 are significant. The zeros preceding the first nonzero digit 4 are not significant.
b. All zeros in the coefficient of a number written in scientific notation are significant.

Exact Numbers

Exact numbers *are those numbers obtained by counting items or using a definition that compares two units in the same measuring system.* Suppose a friend asks you how many classes you are taking. You would answer by counting the number of classes in your schedule. It would not use any measuring tool. Suppose you are asked to state the number of seconds in one minute. Without using any measuring device, you would give the definition: There are 60 s in 1 min. *Exact numbers are not measured, do not have a limited number of significant figures, and do not affect the number of significant figures in a calculated answer.* For more examples of exact numbers, see Table 2.3.

TABLE 2.3 Examples of Some Exact Numbers

Counted Numbers	Defined Equalities	
Items	Metric System	U.S. System
8 doughnuts	1 L = 1000 mL	1 ft = 12 in.
2 baseballs	1 m = 100 cm	1 qt = 4 cups
5 capsules	1 kg = 1000 g	1 lb = 16 oz

For example, a mass of 42.2 g and a length of 5.0×10^{-3} cm are measured numbers because they are obtained using measuring tools. There are three SFs in 42.2 g because all nonzero digits are always significant. There are two SFs in 5.0×10^{-3} cm because all the digits in the coefficient of a number written in scientific notation are significant. However, a quantity of three eggs is an exact number that is obtained by counting the eggs. In the equality 1 kg = 1000 g, the masses of 1 kg and 1000 g are both exact numbers because this equality is a definition in the metric system of measurement.

The number of baseballs is counted, which means 2 is an exact number.

QUESTIONS AND PROBLEMS

2.2 Measured Numbers and Significant Figures

LEARNING GOAL Identify a number as measured or exact; determine the number of significant figures in a measured number.

2.7 Identify the numbers in each of the following statements as measured or exact:
  a. A patient has a mass of 67.5 kg.
  b. A patient is given 2 tablets of medication.
  c. In the metric system, 1 L is equal to 1000 mL.
  d. The distance from Denver, Colorado, to Houston, Texas, is 1720 km.

2.8 Identify the numbers in each of the following statements as measured or exact:
  a. There are 31 students in the laboratory.
  b. The oldest known flower lived 1.20×10^8 yr ago.
  c. The largest gem ever found, an aquamarine, has a mass of 104 kg.
  d. A laboratory test shows a blood cholesterol level of 184 mg/dL.

2.9 Identify the measured number(s), if any, in each of the following pairs of numbers:
  a. 3 hamburgers and 6 oz of hamburger
  b. 1 table and 4 chairs
  c. 0.75 lb of grapes and 350 g of butter
  d. 60 s = 1 min

2.10 Identify the exact number(s), if any, in each of the following pairs of numbers:
  a. 5 pizzas and 50.0 g of cheese
  b. 6 nickels and 16 g of nickel
  c. 3 onions and 3 lb of onions
  d. 5 miles and 5 cars

2.11 Indicate if the zeros are significant in each of the following measurements:
  a. 0.0038 m   **b.** 5.04 cm
  c. 800. L   **d.** 3.0×10^{-3} kg
  e. 85 000 g

2.12 Indicate if the zeros are significant in each of the following measurements:
  a. 20.05 °C   **b.** 5.00 m
  c. 0.000 02 g   **d.** 120 000 yr
  e. 8.05×10^2 L

2.13 How many significant figures are in each of the following?
  a. 11.005 g
  b. 0.000 32 m
  c. 36 000 000 km
  d. 1.80×10^4 kg
  e. 0.8250 L
  f. 30.0 °C

2.14 How many significant figures are in each of the following?
  a. 20.60 mL
  b. 1036.48 kg
  c. 4.00 m
  d. 20.8 °C
  e. 60 800 000 g
  f. 5.0×10^{-3} L

2.15 In which of the following pairs do both numbers contain the same number of significant figures?
  a. 11.0 m and 11.00 m
  b. 0.0250 m and 0.205 m
  c. 0.000 12 s and 12 000 s
  d. 250.0 L and 2.5×10^{-2} L

2.16 In which of the following pairs do both numbers contain the same number of significant figures?
  a. 0.005 75 g and 5.75×10^{-3} g
  b. 405 K and 405.0 K
  c. 150 000 s and 1.50×10^4 s
  d. 3.8×10^{-2} L and 3.0×10^5 L

Ⓡ Clinical Applications

2.17 Identify the number of significant figures in each of the following:
  a. The mass of a neonate is 1.607 kg.
  b. The Daily Value (DV) for iodine for an infant is 130 mcg.
  c. There are 4.02×10^6 red blood cells in a blood sample.

2.18 Identify the number of significant figures in each of the following:
  a. An adult with the flu has a temperature of 103.5 °F.
  b. A brain contains 1.20×10^{10} neurons.
  c. The time for a nerve impulse to travel from the feet to the brain is 0.46 s.

LEARNING GOAL

Adjust calculated answers to give the correct number of significant figures.

2.3 Significant Figures in Calculations

In the sciences, we measure many things: the length of a bacterium, the volume of a gas sample, the temperature of a reaction mixture, or the mass of iron in a sample. The numbers obtained from these types of measurements are often used in calculations. The number of significant figures in the measured numbers determines the number of significant figures in the calculated answer.

Using a calculator will help you perform calculations faster. However, calculators cannot think for you. It is up to you to enter the numbers correctly, press the correct function keys, and give an answer with the correct number of significant figures.

Rounding Off

Suppose you decide to buy carpeting for a room that measures 5.52 m by 3.58 m. Each of these measurements has three significant figures because the measuring tape limits your estimated place to 0.01 m. To determine how much carpeting you need, you would calculate the area of the room by multiplying 5.52 times 3.58 on your calculator. The calculator shows the number 19.7616 in its display. However, this is not the correct final answer because there are too many digits, which is the result of the multiplication process. Because each of the original measurements has only three significant figures, the displayed number (19.7616) must be *rounded off* to three significant figures, 19.8. Therefore, you can order carpeting that will cover an area of 19.8 m^2.

Each time you use a calculator, it is important to look at the original measurements and determine the number of significant figures that can be used for the answer. You can use the following rules to round off the numbers shown in a calculator display.

Rules for Rounding Off

1. If the first digit to be dropped is *4 or less*, then it and all following digits are simply dropped from the number.
2. If the first digit to be dropped is *5 or greater*, then the last retained digit of the number is increased by 1.

Number to Round Off	Three Significant Figures	Two Significant Figures
8.4234	8.42 (drop 34)	8.4 (drop 234)
14.780	14.8 (drop 80, increase the last retained digit by 1)	15 (drop 780, increase the last retained digit by 1)
3256	3260* (drop 6, increase the last retained digit by 1, add 0) (3.26×10^3)	3300* (drop 56, increase the last retained digit by 1, add 00) (3.3×10^3)

*The value of a large number is retained by using placeholder zeros to replace dropped digits.

A technician uses a calculator in the laboratory.

▶ **SAMPLE PROBLEM 2.3 Rounding Off**

Round off each of the following numbers to three significant figures:

a. 35.7823 m
b. 0.002 621 7 L
c. 3.8268×10^3 g

SOLUTION

a. To round off 35.7823 m to three significant figures, drop 823 and increase the last retained digit by 1 to give 35.8 m.
b. To round off 0.002 621 7 L to three significant figures, drop 17 to give 0.002 62 L.
c. To round off 3.8268×10^3 g to three significant figures, drop 68 and increase the last retained digit by 1 to give 3.83×10^3 g.

STUDY CHECK 2.3

Round off each of the numbers in Sample Problem 2.3 to two significant figures.

ANSWER

a. 36 m
b. 0.0026 L
c. 3.8×10^3 g

Using Significant Figures in
Calculations

A calculator is helpful in working
problems and doing calculations
faster.

Multiplication and Division with Measured Numbers

*In multiplication or division, the final answer is written so that it has the same number of
significant figures (SFs) as the measurement with the fewest SFs.* An example of rounding
off a calculator display follows:

Perform the following operations with measured numbers:

$$\frac{2.8 \times 67.40}{34.8} =$$

When the problem has multiple steps, the numbers in the numerator are multiplied and
then divided by each of the numbers in the denominator.

2.8	×	67.40	÷	34.8	=	5.4229885D6	=	5.4
Two SFs		Four SFs		Three SFs		Calculator display		Answer, rounded off to two SFs

Because the calculator display has more digits than the significant figures in the measured
numbers allow, we need to round off. Using the measured number that has the fewest number
(two) of significant figures, 2.8, we round off the calculator display to the answer with two SFs.

Adding Significant Zeros

Sometimes, a calculator display gives a small whole number. Then we add one or more significant zeros to the calculator display to obtain the correct number of significant figures. For
example, suppose the calculator display is 4, but you used measurements that have three
significant numbers. Then two significant zeros are *added* to give 4.00 as the correct answer.

$$\frac{\overset{\text{Three SFs}}{8.00}}{\underset{\text{Three SFs}}{2.00}} = \qquad \underset{\text{Calculator display}}{4.} \qquad = \qquad \underset{\substack{\text{Final answer, two zeros}\\\text{added to give three SFs}}}{4.00}$$

▶ **SAMPLE PROBLEM 2.4** **Significant Figures in Multiplication and Division**

Perform the following calculations of measured numbers. Round off the calculator display or add zeros to give each answer with the correct number of significant figures.

a. 56.8×0.37 **b.** $\dfrac{(2.075)(0.585)}{(8.42)(0.0045)}$ **c.** $\dfrac{25.0}{5.00}$

SOLUTION
a. 21 **b.** 32 **c.** 5.00 (add two significant zeros)

STUDY CHECK 2.4

Perform the following calculations of measured numbers and give the answers with the
correct number of significant figures:

a. $45.26 \times 0.010\,88$ **b.** $2.6 \div 324$ **c.** $\dfrac{4.0 \times 8.00}{16}$

ANSWER
a. 0.4924 **b.** 0.0080 or 8.0×10^{-3} **c.** 2.0

Addition and Subtraction with Measured Numbers

*In addition or subtraction, the final answer is written so that it has the same number of
decimal places as the measurement having the fewest decimal places.*

2.045	Thousandths place
+ 34.1	Tenths place
36.145	Calculator display
36.1	Answer, rounded off to the tenths place

When numbers are added or subtracted to give an answer ending in zero, the zero does not appear after the decimal point in the calculator display. For example, 14.5 g − 2.5 g = 12.0 g. However, if you do the subtraction on your calculator, the display shows 12. To write the correct answer, a significant zero is written after the decimal point.

▶ **SAMPLE PROBLEM 2.5 Significant Figures in Addition and Subtraction**

Perform the following calculations and round off the calculator display or add zeros to give each answer with the correct number of decimal places:

a. 104.45 mL + 0.838 mL + 46 mL   **b.** 153.247 g − 14.82 g

SOLUTION

a.   104.45 mL   Hundredths place
           0.838 mL   Thousandths place
       ☐+ 46 mL   Ones place
           151 mL   Answer, rounded off to the ones place

b.   153.247 g   Thousandths place
       ☐− 14.82 g   Hundredths place
           138.43 g   Answer, rounded off to the hundredths place

STUDY CHECK 2.5

Perform the following calculations and give the answers with the correct number of decimal places:

a. 82.45 mg + 1.245 mg + 0.000 56 mg   **b.** 4.259 L − 3.8 L

ANSWER

a. 83.70 mg   **b.** 0.5 L

QUESTIONS AND PROBLEMS

2.3 Significant Figures in Calculations

LEARNING GOAL Adjust calculated answers to give the correct number of significant figures.

2.19 Why do we usually need to round off calculations that use measured numbers?

2.20 Why do we sometimes add a zero to a number in a calculator display?

2.21 Round off each of the following measurements to three significant figures:
  a. 1.854 kg   **b.** 88.2038 L
  c. 0.004 738 265 cm   **d.** 8807 m
  e. 1.832×10^5 s

2.22 Round off each of the measurements in problem 2.21 to two significant figures.

2.23 Round off to three significant figures and express in scientific notation.
  a. 5080 L   **b.** 37 400 g
  c. 104 720 m   **d.** 0.000 250 82 s

2.24 Round off to three significant figures and express in scientific notation.
  a. 5 100 000 L   **b.** 26 711 s
  c. 0.003 378 m   **d.** 56.982 g

2.25 Perform each of the following calculations, and give an answer with the correct number of significant figures:
  a. 45.7×0.034 **b.** $0.002\ 78 \times 5$
  c. $\dfrac{34.56}{1.25}$ **d.** $\dfrac{(0.2465)(25)}{1.78}$

2.26 Perform each of the following calculations, and give an answer with the correct number of significant figures:
  a. 400×185 **b.** $\dfrac{2.40}{(4)(125)}$
  c. $0.825 \times 3.6 \times 5.1$ **d.** $\dfrac{3.5 \times 0.261}{8.24 \times 20.0}$

2.27 Perform each of the following calculations, and give an answer with the correct number of decimal places:
  a. 45.48 cm + 8.057 cm
  b. 23.45 g + 104.1 g + 0.025 g
  c. 145.675 mL − 24.2 mL
  d. 1.08 L − 0.585 L

2.28 Perform each of the following calculations, and give an answer with the correct number of decimal places:
  a. 5.08 g + 25.1 g
  b. 85.66 cm + 104.10 cm + 0.025 cm
  c. 24.568 mL − 14.25 mL
  d. 0.2654 L − 0.2585 L

Use the numerical values of prefixes to write a metric equality.

TABLE 2.5 Daily Values for Selected Nutrients

Nutrient	Amount Recommended
Protein	50 g
Vitamin C	60 mg
Vitamin B_{12}	6 μg (6 mcg)
Calcium	1000 mg
Copper	2 mg
Iodine	150 μg (150 mcg)
Iron	18 mg
Magnesium	400 mg
Niacin	20 mg
Potassium	3500 mg
Selenium	70 μg (70 mcg)
Sodium	2400 mg
Zinc	15 mg

⚛ CORE CHEMISTRY SKILL

Using Prefixes

2.4 Prefixes and Equalities

The special feature of the SI as well as the metric system is that a **prefix** can be placed in front of any unit to increase or decrease its size by some factor of 10. For example, the prefixes *milli* and *micro* are used to make the smaller units, milligram (mg) and microgram (μg). Table 2.4 lists some of the metric prefixes, their symbols, and their numerical values.

The prefix *centi* is like cents in a dollar. One cent would be a "centidollar" or 0.01 of a dollar. That also means that one dollar is the same as 100 cents. The prefix *deci* is like dimes in a dollar. One dime would be a "decidollar" or 0.1 of a dollar. That also means that one dollar is the same as 10 dimes.

The U.S. Food and Drug Administration has determined the Daily Values (DV) for nutrients for adults and children aged 4 or older. Examples of these recommended Daily Values, some of which use prefixes, are listed in Table 2.5.

The relationship of a prefix to a unit can be expressed by replacing the prefix with its numerical value. For example, when the prefix *kilo* in kilometer is replaced with its value of 1000, we find that a kilometer is equal to 1000 m. Other examples follow:

1 **kilo**meter (1 km) = **1000** meters (1000 m = 10^3 m)
1 **kilo**liter (1 kL) = **1000** liters (1000 L = 10^3 L)
1 **kilo**gram (1 kg) = **1000** grams (1000 g = 10^3 g)

TABLE 2.4 Metric and SI Prefixes

Prefix	Symbol	Numerical Value	Scientific Notation	Equality
Prefixes That Increase the Size of the Unit				
peta	P	1 000 000 000 000 000	10^{15}	1 Pg = 1 × 10^{15} g 1 g = 1 × 10^{-15} Pg
tera	T	1 000 000 000 000	10^{12}	1 Ts = 1 × 10^{12} s 1 s = 1 × 10^{-12} Ts
giga	G	1 000 000 000	10^9	1 Gm = 1 × 10^9 m 1 m = 1 × 10^{-9} Gm
mega	M	1 000 000	10^6	1 Mg = 1 × 10^6 g 1 g = 1 × 10^{-6} Mg
kilo	k	1 000	10^3	1 km = 1 × 10^3 m 1 m = 1 × 10^{-3} km
Prefixes That Decrease the Size of the Unit				
deci	d	0.1	10^{-1}	1 dL = 1 × 10^{-1} L 1 L = 10 dL
centi	c	0.01	10^{-2}	1 cm = 1 × 10^{-2} m 1 m = 100 cm
milli	m	0.001	10^{-3}	1 ms = 1 × 10^{-3} s 1 s = 1 × 10^3 ms
micro	μ*	0.000 001	10^{-6}	1 μg = 1 × 10^{-6} g 1 g = 1 × 10^6 μg
nano	n	0.000 000 001	10^{-9}	1 nm = 1 × 10^{-9} m 1 m = 1 × 10^9 nm
pico	p	0.000 000 000 001	10^{-12}	1 ps = 1 × 10^{-12} s 1 s = 1 × 10^{12} ps
femto	f	0.000 000 000 000 001	10^{-15}	1 fs = 1 × 10^{-15} s 1 s = 1 × 10^{15} fs

*In medicine and nursing, the abbreviation mc for the prefix micro is used because the symbol μ may be misread, which could result in a medication error. Thus, 1 μg would be written as 1 mcg.

▶**SAMPLE PROBLEM 2.6 Prefixes and Equalities**

An endoscopic camera has a width of 1 mm. Complete each of the following equalities involving millimeters:

a. 1 m = _____ mm   **b.** 1 cm = _____ mm

SOLUTION

a. 1 m = 1000 mm   **b.** 1 cm = 10 mm

STUDY CHECK 2.6

What is the relationship between millimeters and micrometers?

ANSWER

1 mm = 1000 μm (mcm)

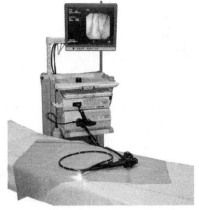

An endoscope, used to see inside the body, has a tiny video camera with a width of 1 mm attached to the end of a long, thin cable.

Measuring Length

An ophthalmologist may measure the diameter of the retina of an eye in centimeters (cm), whereas a surgeon may need to know the length of a nerve in millimeters (mm). When the prefix *centi* is used with the unit meter, it becomes *centimeter*, a length that is one-hundredth of a meter (0.01 m). When the prefix *milli* is used with the unit meter, it becomes *millimeter*, a length that is one-thousandth of a meter (0.001 m). There are 100 cm and 1000 mm in a meter.

If we compare the lengths of a millimeter and a centimeter, we find that 1 mm is 0.1 cm; there are 10 mm in 1 cm. These comparisons are examples of **equalities**, which show the relationship between two units that measure the same quantity. In every equality, each quantity has both a number and a unit. Examples of equalities between different metric units of length follow:

$$1 \text{ m} = 100 \text{ cm} = 1 \times 10^2 \text{ cm}$$
$$1 \text{ m} = 1000 \text{ mm} = 1 \times 10^3 \text{ mm}$$
$$1 \text{ cm} = 10 \text{ mm} = 1 \times 10^1 \text{ mm}$$

Some metric units for length are compared in Figure 2.6.

Using a retinal camera, an ophthalmologist photographs the retina of an eye.

First quantity		Second quantity	
1	m	100	cm
↑	↑	↑	↑
Number + unit		Number + unit	

This example of an equality shows the relationship between meters and centimeters.

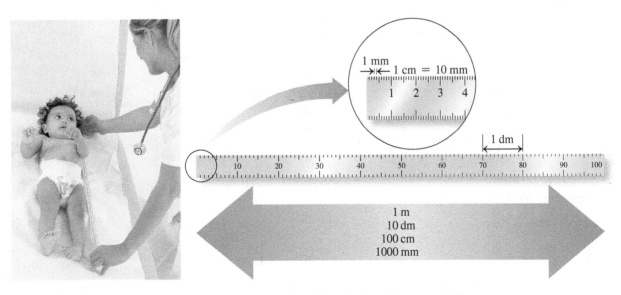

FIGURE 2.6 ▶ The metric length of 1 m is the same length as 10 dm, 100 cm, or 1000 mm.
How many millimeters (mm) are in 1 centimeter (cm)?

FIGURE 2.7 ▶ A plastic intravenous fluid container contains 1000 mL.

Q How many liters of solution are in the intravenous fluid container?

Measuring Volume

Volumes of 1 L or smaller are common in the health sciences. When a liter is divided into 10 equal portions, each portion is a deciliter (dL). There are 10 dL in 1 L. Laboratory results for blood work are often reported in mass per deciliter. Table 2.6 lists typical laboratory test values for some substances in the blood.

TABLE 2.6 Some Typical Laboratory Test Values

Substance in Blood	Typical Range
Albumin	3.5–5.0 g/dL
Ammonia	20–150 mcg/dL
Calcium	8.5–10.5 mg/dL
Cholesterol	105–250 mg/dL
Iron (male)	80–160 mcg/dL
Protein (total)	6.0–8.0 g/dL

When a liter is divided into a thousand parts, each of the smaller volumes is called a milliliter (mL). In a 1-L container of physiological saline, there are 1000 mL of solution (see Figure 2.7). Examples of equalities between different metric units of volume follow:

$$1 \text{ L} = 10 \text{ dL} = 1 \times 10^1 \text{ dL}$$
$$1 \text{ L} = 1000 \text{ mL} = 1 \times 10^3 \text{ mL}$$
$$1 \text{ dL} = 100 \text{ mL} = 1 \times 10^2 \text{ mL}$$

The **cubic centimeter** (abbreviated as **cm³** or **cc**) is the volume of a cube whose dimensions are 1 cm on each side. A cubic centimeter has the same volume as a milliliter, and the units are often used interchangeably.

$$1 \text{ cm}^3 = 1 \text{ cc} = 1 \text{ mL}$$

When you see *1 cm*, you are reading about length; when you see *1 cm³* or *1 cc* or *1 mL*, you are reading about volume. A comparison of units of volume is illustrated in Figure 2.8.

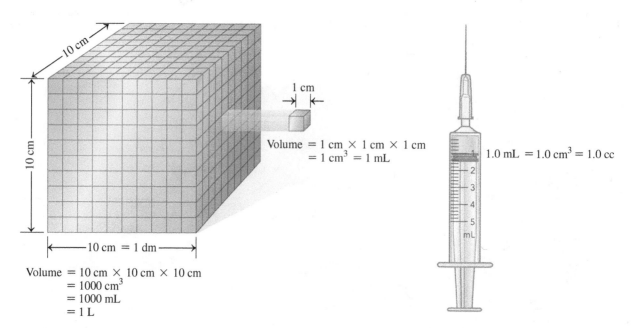

FIGURE 2.8 ▶ A cube measuring 10 cm on each side has a volume of 1000 cm³, or 1 L; a cube measuring 1 cm on each side has a volume of 1 cm³ (cc) or 1 mL.

Q What is the relationship between a milliliter (mL) and a cubic centimeter (cm³)?

Measuring Mass

When you go to the doctor for a physical examination, your mass is recorded in kilograms, whereas the results of your laboratory tests are reported in grams, milligrams (mg), or micrograms (μg or mcg). A kilogram is equal to 1000 g. One gram represents the same mass as 1000 mg, and one mg equals 1000 μg (or 1000 mcg). Examples of equalities between different metric units of mass follow:

$$1 \text{ kg} = 1000 \text{ g} \qquad\qquad = 1 \times 10^3 \text{ g}$$
$$1 \text{ g} = 1000 \text{ mg} \qquad\qquad = 1 \times 10^3 \text{ mg}$$
$$1 \text{ mg} = 1000\,\mu\text{g (or 1000 mcg)} = 1 \times 10^3\,\mu\text{g (or } 1 \times 10^3 \text{ mcg)}$$

QUESTIONS AND PROBLEMS

2.4 Prefixes and Equalities

LEARNING GOAL Use the numerical values of prefixes to write a metric equality.

2.29 The speedometer is marked in both km/h and mi/h, or mph. What is the meaning of each abbreviation?

2.30 In a French car, the odometer reads 22269. What units would this be? What units would it be if this were an odometer in a car made for the United States?

2.31 Write the abbreviation for each of the following units:
a. milligram
b. deciliter
c. kilometer
d. femtogram

2.32 Write the abbreviation for each of the following units:
a. gigagram
b. megameter
c. microliter
d. nanosecond

2.33 Write the complete name for each of the following units:
a. cL
b. kg
c. ms
d. Gm

2.34 Write the complete name for each of the following units:
a. dL
b. Ts
c. mcg
d. pm

2.35 Write the numerical value for each of the following prefixes:
a. centi
b. tera
c. milli
d. deci

2.36 Write the numerical value for each of the following prefixes:
a. giga
b. micro
c. mega
d. nano

2.37 Use a prefix to write the name for each of the following:
a. 0.1 g
b. 10^{-6} g
c. 1000 g
d. 0.01 g

2.38 Use a prefix to write the name for each of the following:
a. 10^9 m
b. 10^6 m
c. 0.001 m
d. 10^{-15} m

2.39 Complete each of the following metric relationships:
a. 1 m = _____ cm
b. 1 m = _____ nm
c. 1 mm = _____ m
d. 1 L = _____ mL

2.40 Complete each of the following metric relationships:
a. 1 Mg = _____ g
b. 1 mL = _____ μL
c. 1 g = _____ kg
d. 1 g = _____ mg

2.41 For each of the following pairs, which is the larger unit?
a. milligram or kilogram
b. milliliter or microliter
c. m or km
d. kL or dL
e. nanometer or picometer

2.42 For each of the following pairs, which is the smaller unit?
a. mg or g
b. centimeter or nanometer
c. millimeter or micrometer
d. mL or dL
e. centigram or megagram

2.5 Writing Conversion Factors

LEARNING GOAL

Write a conversion factor for two units that describe the same quantity.

Many problems in chemistry and the health sciences require you to change from one unit to another unit. You make changes in units every day. For example, suppose you worked 2.0 hours (h) on your homework, and someone asked you how many minutes that was. You would answer 120 minutes (min). You must have multiplied 2.0 h × 60 min/h because you knew the equality (1 h = 60 min) that related the two units. When you expressed 2.0 h as 120 min, you did not change the amount of time you spent studying. You changed only the unit of measurement used to express the time. *Any equality can be written as fractions called* **conversion factors** *with one of the quantities in the numerator and the other quantity in the denominator.* Be sure to include the units when you write the conversion factors. Two conversion factors are always possible from any equality.

Explore Your World

SI and Metric Equalities on Product Labels

Read the labels on some food products on your kitchen shelves and in your refrigerator, or refer to the labels in Figure 2.9. List the amount of product given in different units. Write a relationship for two of the amounts for the same product and container. Look for measurements of grams and pounds or quarts and milliliters.

Questions

1. Use the stated measurement to derive a metric–U.S. conversion factor.
2. How do your results compare with the conversion factors we have described in this text?

CORE CHEMISTRY SKILL

Writing Conversion Factors from Equalities

TABLE 2.7 Some Common Equalities

Quantity	Metric (SI)	U.S.	Metric–U.S.
Length	1 km = 1000 m	1 ft = 12 in.	2.54 cm = 1 in. (exact)
	1 m = 1000 mm	1 yd = 3 ft	1 m = 39.4 in.
	1 cm = 10 mm	1 mi = 5280 ft	1 km = 0.621 mi
Volume	1 L = 1000 mL	1 qt = 4 cups	946 mL = 1 qt
	1 dL = 100 mL	1 qt = 2 pt	1 L = 1.06 qt
	1 mL = 1 cm³	1 gal = 4 qt	473 mL = 1 pt
	1 mL = 1 cc*		1 mL = 15 drops*
			5 mL = 1 tsp*
			15 mL = 1 T (tbsp)*
Mass	1 kg = 1000 g	1 lb = 16 oz	1 kg = 2.20 lb
	1 g = 1000 mg		454 g = 1 lb
	1 mg = 1000 mcg*		
Time	1 h = 60 min	1 h = 60 min	
	1 min = 60 s	1 min = 60 s	

*Used in nursing and medicine.

Two Conversion Factors for the Equality: 60 min = 1 h

$$\text{Numerator} \longrightarrow \frac{60 \text{ min}}{1 \text{ h}} \quad \text{and} \quad \frac{1 \text{ h}}{60 \text{ min}} \longleftarrow \text{Denominator}$$

These factors are read as "60 minutes per 1 hour" and "1 hour per 60 minutes." The term *per* means "divide." Some common relationships are given in Table 2.7. It is important that the equality you select to form a conversion factor is a *true* relationship.

The numbers in any equality between two metric units or between two U.S. system units are obtained by definition. Because numbers in a definition are exact, they are not used to determine significant figures. For example, the equality of 1 g = 1000 mg is defined, which means that both the numbers 1 and 1000 are exact. *However, when an equality consists of a metric unit and a U.S. unit, one of the numbers in the equality is obtained by measurement and counts toward the significant figures in the answer.* For example, the equality of 1 lb = 454 g is obtained by measuring the grams in exactly 1 lb. In this equality, the measured quantity 454 g has three significant figures, whereas the 1 is exact. An exception is the relationship of 1 in. = 2.54 cm where 2.54 has been defined as exact.

Metric Conversion Factors

We can write metric conversion factors for any of the metric relationships. For example, from the equality for meters and centimeters, we can write the following factors:

Metric Equality	Conversion Factors	
1 m = 100 cm	$\dfrac{100 \text{ cm}}{1 \text{ m}}$ and	$\dfrac{1 \text{ m}}{100 \text{ cm}}$

Both are proper conversion factors for the relationship; one is just the inverse of the other. *The usefulness of conversion factors is enhanced by the fact that we can turn a conversion factor over and use its inverse.* The number 100 and 1 in this equality and its conversion factors are both *exact* numbers.

Metric–U.S. System Conversion Factors

Suppose you need to convert from pounds, a unit in the U.S. system, to kilograms in the metric (or SI) system. A relationship you could use is

1 kg = 2.20 lb

The corresponding conversion factors would be

$$\frac{2.20 \text{ lb}}{1 \text{ kg}} \quad \text{and} \quad \frac{1 \text{ kg}}{2.20 \text{ lb}}$$

Figure 2.9 illustrates the contents of some packaged foods in both U.S. and metric units.

> **SAMPLE PROBLEM 2.7** **Writing Conversion Factors**
>
> Identify the correct conversion factor(s) for the equality: 1 pt of blood contains 473 mL of blood.
>
> **a.** $\dfrac{473 \text{ pt}}{1 \text{ mL}}$ **b.** $\dfrac{1 \text{ pt}}{473 \text{ mL}}$
>
> **c.** $\dfrac{473 \text{ mL}}{1 \text{ pt}}$ **d.** $\dfrac{1 \text{ mL}}{473 \text{ pt}}$
>
> **SOLUTION**
>
> The equality for pints and milliliters is 1 pt = 473 mL. Answers **b** and **c** are correctly written conversion factors for the equality.
>
> **STUDY CHECK 2.7**
>
> What are the two correctly written conversion factors for the equality: 1000 mm = 1 m?
>
> **ANSWER**
>
> $\dfrac{1000 \text{ mm}}{1 \text{ m}} \quad \text{and} \quad \dfrac{1 \text{ m}}{1000 \text{ mm}}$

FIGURE 2.9 ▶ In the United States, the contents of many packaged foods are listed in both U.S. and metric units.

◉ What are some advantages of using the metric system?

Equalities and Conversion Factors Stated Within a Problem

An equality may also be stated within a problem that applies only to that problem. For example, the speed of a car in kilometers per hour or the milligrams of vitamin C in a tablet would be specific relationships for that problem only. However, it is possible to identify these relationships within a problem and to write corresponding conversion factors.

From each of the following statements, we can write an equality, and its conversion factors, and identify each number as exact or give its significant figures.

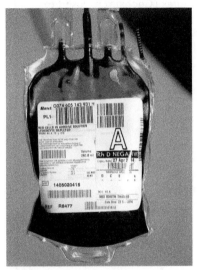

1 pt of blood contains 473 mL.

The car was traveling at a speed of 85 km/h.

Equality	Conversion Factors	Significant Figures or Exact
85 km = 1 h	$\dfrac{85 \text{ km}}{1 \text{ h}}$ and $\dfrac{1 \text{ h}}{85 \text{ km}}$	The 85 km is measured: It has two significant figures. The 1 h is exact.

One tablet contains 500 mg of vitamin C.

Equality	Conversion Factors	Significant Figures or Exact
1 tablet = 500 mg of vitamin C	$\dfrac{500 \text{ mg vitamin C}}{1 \text{ tablet}}$ and $\dfrac{1 \text{ tablet}}{500 \text{ mg vitamin C}}$	The 500 mg is measured: It has one significant figure. The 1 tablet is exact.

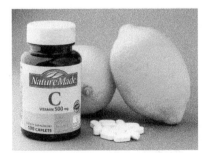

Vitamin C, an antioxidant needed by the body, is found in fruits such as lemons.

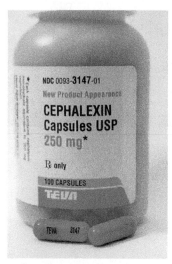

Keflex (Cephalexin), used to treat respiratory infections, is available in 250-mg capsules.

The thickness of the skin fold at the abdomen is used to determine the percentage of body fat.

Conversion Factors from Dosage Problems

Equalities stated within dosage problems for medications can also be written as conversion factors. For example, Keflex (Cephalexin), an antibiotic used for respiratory and ear infections, is available in 250-mg capsules. The quantity of Keflex in a capsule can be written as an equality from which two conversion factors are possible.

Equality	Conversion Factors	Significant Figures or Exact
1 capsule = 250 mg of Keflex	$\dfrac{250 \text{ mg Keflex}}{1 \text{ capsule}}$ and $\dfrac{1 \text{ capsule}}{250 \text{ mg Keflex}}$	The 250 mg is measured: It has two significant figures. The 1 capsule is exact.

Conversion Factors from a Percentage, ppm, and ppb

A percentage (%) is written as a conversion factor by choosing a unit and expressing the numerical relationship of the parts of this unit to 100 parts of the whole. For example, a person might have 18% body fat by mass. The percentage quantity can be written as 18 mass units of body fat in every 100 mass units of body mass. Different mass units such as grams (g), kilograms (kg), or pounds (lb) can be used, but both units in the factor must be the same.

Equality	Conversion Factors	Significant Figures or Exact
18 kg of body fat = 100 kg of body mass	$\dfrac{18 \text{ kg body fat}}{100 \text{ kg body mass}}$ and $\dfrac{100 \text{ kg body mass}}{18 \text{ kg body fat}}$	The 18 kg is measured: It has two significant figures. The 100 kg is exact.

When scientists want to indicate very small ratios, they use numerical relationships called *parts per million* (ppm) or *parts per billion* (ppb). The ratio of parts per million is the same as the milligrams of a substance per kilogram (mg/kg). The ratio of parts per billion equals the micrograms per kilogram (μg/kg, mcg/kg).

Ratio	Units
parts per million (ppm)	milligrams per kilogram (mg/kg)
parts per billion (ppb)	micrograms per kilogram (μg/kg, mcg/kg)

For example, the maximum amount of lead that is allowed by the Food and Drug Administration (FDA) in glazed pottery bowls is 2 ppm, which is 2 mg/kg.

Equality	Conversion Factors	Significant Figures or Exact
2 mg of lead = 1 kg of glaze	$\dfrac{2 \text{ mg lead}}{1 \text{ kg glaze}}$ and $\dfrac{1 \text{ kg glaze}}{2 \text{ mg lead}}$	The 2 mg is measured: It has one significant figure. The 1 kg is exact.

> **SAMPLE PROBLEM 2.8 Equalities and Conversion Factors Stated in a Problem**
>
> Write the equality and conversion factors, and identify each number as exact or give the number of significant figures for each of the following:
>
> **a.** The medication that Greg takes for his high blood pressure contains 40. mg of propranolol in 1 tablet.
> **b.** Cold water fish such as salmon contains 1.9% omega-3 fatty acids by mass.
> **c.** The U.S. Environmental Protection Agency (EPA) has set the maximum level for mercury in tuna at 0.5 ppm.

SOLUTION

a. There are 40. mg of propranolol in 1 tablet.

Equality	Conversion Factors	Significant Figures or Exact
1 tablet = 40. mg of propranolol	$\dfrac{40.\ \text{mg propranolol}}{1\ \text{tablet}}$ and $\dfrac{1\ \text{tablet}}{40.\ \text{mg propranolol}}$	The 40. mg is measured: It has two significant figures. The 1 tablet is exact.

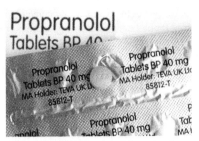

Propranolol is used to lower high blood pressure.

b. Cold water fish such as salmon contains 1.9% omega-3 fatty acids by mass.

Equality	Conversion Factors	Significant Figures or Exact
1.9 g of omega-3 fatty acids = 100 g of salmon	$\dfrac{1.9\ \text{g omega-3 fatty acids}}{100\ \text{g salmon}}$ and $\dfrac{100\ \text{g salmon}}{1.9\ \text{g omega-3 fatty acids}}$	The 1.9 g is measured: It has two significant figures. The 100 g is exact.

Salmon contains high levels of omega-3 fatty acids.

c. The EPA has set the maximum level for mercury in tuna at 0.5 ppm.

Equality	Conversion Factors	Significant Figures or Exact
0.5 mg of mercury = 1 kg of tuna	$\dfrac{0.5\ \text{mg mercury}}{1\ \text{kg tuna}}$ and $\dfrac{1\ \text{kg tuna}}{0.5\ \text{mg mercury}}$	The 0.5 mg is measured: It has one significant figure. The 1 kg is exact.

STUDY CHECK 2.8

Levsin (hyoscyamine), used to treat stomach and bladder problems, is available as drops with 0.125 mg Levsin per 1 mL of solution. Write the equality and its corresponding conversion factors, and identify each number as exact or give the number of significant figures.

The maximum amount of mercury allowed in tuna is 0.5 ppm.

ANSWER

0.125 mg of Levsin = 1 mL of solution

$$\frac{0.125\ \text{mg Levsin}}{1\ \text{mL solution}} \quad \text{and} \quad \frac{1\ \text{mL solution}}{0.125\ \text{mg Levsin}}$$

The 0.125 mg is measured: It has three SFs. The 1 mL is exact.

QUESTIONS AND PROBLEMS

2.5 Writing Conversion Factors

LEARNING GOAL Write a conversion factor for two units that describe the same quantity.

2.43 Write the equality and conversion factors for each of the following pairs of units:
- **a.** centimeters and meters
- **b.** milligrams and grams
- **c.** liters and milliliters
- **d.** deciliters and milliliters

2.44 Write the equality and conversion factors for each of the following pairs of units:
- **a.** centimeters and inches
- **b.** pounds and kilograms
- **c.** pounds and grams
- **d.** quarts and liters

2.45 Write the equality and conversion factors, and identify the numbers as exact or give the number of significant figures for each of the following:
- **a.** One yard is 3 ft.
- **b.** One kilogram is 2.20 lb.
- **c.** One minute is 60 s.
- **d.** A car goes 27 mi on 1 gal of gas.
- **e.** Sterling silver is 93% silver by mass.

2.46 Write the equality and conversion factors, and identify the numbers as exact or give the number of significant figures for each of the following:
   a. One liter is 1.06 qt.
   b. At the store, oranges are $1.29 per lb.
   c. There are 7 days in 1 week.
   d. One deciliter contains 100 mL.
   e. An 18-carat gold ring contains 75% gold by mass.

2.47 Write the equality and conversion factors, and identify the numbers as exact or give the number of significant figures for each of the following:
   a. A bee flies at an average speed of 3.5 m per second.
   b. The Daily Value (DV) for potassium is 4700 mg.
   c. An automobile traveled 46.0 km on 1 gal of gasoline.
   d. The pesticide level in plums was 29 ppb.

2.48 Write the equality and conversion factors, and identify the numbers as exact or give the number of significant figures for each of the following:
   a. The Daily Value (DV) for iodine is 150 mcg.
   b. The nitrate level in well water was 32 ppm.
   c. Gold jewelry contains 58% gold by mass.
   d. The price of a liter of milk is $1.65.

R Clinical Applications

2.49 Write the equality and conversion factors, and identify the numbers as exact or give the number of significant figures for each of the following:
   a. A calcium supplement contains 630 mg of calcium per tablet.
   b. The Daily Value (DV) for vitamin C is 60 mg.

   c. The label on a bottle reads 50 mg of atenolol per tablet.
   d. A low-dose aspirin contains 81 mg of aspirin per tablet.

2.50 Write the equality and conversion factors, and identify the numbers as exact or give the number of significant figures for each of the following:
   a. The label on a bottle reads 10 mg of furosemide per 1 mL.
   b. The Daily Value (DV) for selenium is 70. mcg.
   c. An IV of normal saline solution has a flow rate of 85 mL per hour.
   d. One capsule of fish oil contains 360 mg of omega-3 fatty acids.

2.51 Write an equality and two conversion factors for each of the following medications in stock:
   a. 10 mg of Atarax per 5 mL of Atarax syrup
   b. 0.25 g of Lanoxin per 1 tablet of Lanoxin
   c. 300 mg of Motrin per 1 tablet of Motrin

2.52 Write an equality and two conversion factors for each of the following medications in stock:
   a. 2.5 mg of Coumadin per 1 tablet of Coumadin
   b. 100 mg of Clozapine per 1 tablet of Clozapine
   c. 1.5 g of Cefuroxime per 1 mL of Cefuroxime

Use conversion factors to change from one unit to another.

2.6 Problem Solving Using Unit Conversion

The process of problem solving in chemistry often requires one or more conversion factors to change a given unit to the needed unit. For the problem, the unit of the given quantity and the unit of the needed quantity are identified. From there, the problem is set up with one or more conversion factors used to convert the given unit to the needed unit as seen in the following Sample Problem.

Given unit × one or more conversion factors = needed unit

Guide to Problem Solving Using Conversion Factors

STEP **1**
State the given and needed quantities.

STEP **2**
Write a plan to convert the given unit to the needed unit.

STEP **3**
State the equalities and conversion factors.

STEP **4**
Set up the problem to cancel units and calculate the answer.

▶ **SAMPLE PROBLEM 2.9** **Problem Solving Using Conversion Factors**

Greg's doctor has ordered a PET scan of his heart. In radiological imaging such as PET or CT scans, dosages of pharmaceuticals are based on body mass. If Greg weighs 144 lb, what is his body mass in kilograms?

SOLUTION

STEP **1** State the given and needed quantities.

ANALYZE THE PROBLEM	Given	Need
	144 lb	kilograms

STEP **2** Write a plan to convert the given unit to the needed unit. The conversion factor relates the given unit in the U.S. system of measurement and the needed unit in the metric system.

pounds $\dfrac{\text{U.S.–Metric}}{\text{factor}}$ kilograms

STEP **3** State the equalities and conversion factors.

$$1 \text{ kg} = 2.20 \text{ lb}$$

$$\frac{2.20 \text{ lb}}{1 \text{ kg}} \quad \text{and} \quad \frac{1 \text{ kg}}{2.20 \text{ lb}}$$

STEP **4** Set up the problem to cancel units and calculate the answer. Write the given, 144 lb, and multiply by the conversion factor that has the unit lb in the denominator (bottom number) to cancel out the given unit (lb) in the numerator.

Unit for answer goes here
↓

$$144 \text{ l\!b} \quad \times \quad \frac{1 \text{ kg}}{2.20 \text{ l\!b}} \quad = \quad 65.5 \text{ kg}$$

Given   Conversion factor   Answer

Look at how the units cancel. The given unit lb cancels out and the needed unit kg is in the numerator. *The unit you want in the final answer is the one that remains after all the other units have canceled out.* This is a helpful way to check that you set up a problem properly.

$$\text{l\!b} \times \frac{\text{kg}}{\text{l\!b}} = \text{kg} \quad \text{Unit needed for answer}$$

The calculator display gives the numerical answer, which is adjusted to give a final answer with the proper number of significant figures (SFs).

Exact

$$144 \quad \times \quad \frac{1}{2.20} \quad = \quad 144 \div 2.20 \quad = \quad \boxed{65.45454545} \quad = \quad 65.5$$

Three SFs   Three SFs   Calculator   Three SFs
                                          display   (rounded off)

The value of 65.5 combined with the unit, kg, gives the final answer of 65.5 kg. With few exceptions, answers to numerical problems contain a number and a unit.

STUDY CHECK 2.9

A total of 2500 mL of a boric acid antiseptic solution is prepared from boric acid concentrate. How many quarts of boric acid has been prepared?

ANSWER

2.6 qt

Interactive Video

Conversion Factors

Using Two or More Conversion Factors

In problem solving, two or more conversion factors are often needed to complete the change of units. In setting up these problems, one factor follows the other. Each factor is arranged to cancel the preceding unit until the needed unit is obtained. Once the problem is set up to cancel units properly, the calculations can be done without writing intermediate results. The process is worth practicing until you understand unit cancelation, the steps on the calculator, and rounding off to give a final answer. In this text, when two or more conversion factors are required, the final answer will be based on obtaining a final calculator display and rounding off (or adding zeros) to give the correct number of significant figures.

⚛ CORE CHEMISTRY SKILL

Using Conversion Factors

▶ **SAMPLE PROBLEM 2.10** Using Two or More Conversion Factors

A doctor's order for 0.50 g of Keflex is available as 250-mg tablets. How many tablets of Keflex are needed? In the following setup, fill in the missing parts of the conversion factors, show the canceled units, and give the correct answer:

$$0.50 \text{ g Keflex} \times \frac{\underline{\hspace{1em}} \text{ mg Keflex}}{1 \text{ g Keflex}} \times \frac{1 \text{ tablet}}{\underline{\hspace{1em}} \text{ mg Keflex}} =$$

SOLUTION

$$0.50 \text{ g } \cancel{\text{Keflex}} \times \frac{1000 \text{ mg } \cancel{\text{Keflex}}}{1 \text{ g } \cancel{\text{Keflex}}} \times \frac{1 \text{ tablet}}{250 \text{ mg } \cancel{\text{Keflex}}} = 2 \text{ tablets}$$

STUDY CHECK 2.10

A newborn has a length of 450 mm. In the following setup that calculates the baby's length in inches, fill in the missing parts of the conversion factors, show the canceled units, and give the correct answer:

$$450 \text{ mm} \times \frac{1 \text{ cm}}{\underline{\hspace{1em}} \text{ mm}} \times \frac{1 \text{ in.}}{\underline{\hspace{1em}} \text{ cm}} =$$

ANSWER

$$450 \cancel{\text{mm}} \times \frac{1 \cancel{\text{cm}}}{10 \cancel{\text{mm}}} \times \frac{1 \text{ in.}}{2.54 \cancel{\text{cm}}} = 18 \text{ in.}$$

▶ **SAMPLE PROBLEM 2.11** Problem Solving Using Two Conversion Factors

Synthroid is used as a replacement or supplemental therapy for diminished thyroid function. A doctor's order prescribes a dosage of 0.150 mg of Synthroid. If tablets in stock contain 75 mcg of Synthroid, how many tablets are required to provide the prescribed medication?

SOLUTION

STEP **1** State the given and needed quantities.

ANALYZE THE PROBLEM	Given	Need
	0.150 mg of Synthroid	number of tablets

STEP **2** Write a plan to convert the given unit to the needed unit.

milligrams → Metric factor → micrograms → Clinical factor → number of tablets

STEP **3** State the equalities and conversion factors.

1 mg = 1000 mcg	1 tablet = 75 mcg of Synthroid
$\dfrac{1 \text{ mg}}{1000 \text{ mcg}}$ and $\dfrac{1000 \text{ mcg}}{1 \text{ mg}}$	$\dfrac{1 \text{ tablet}}{75 \text{ mcg Synthroid}}$ and $\dfrac{75 \text{ mcg Synthroid}}{1 \text{ tablet}}$

STEP **4** Set up the problem to cancel units and calculate the answer. The problem can be set up using the metric factor to cancel milligrams, and then the clinical factor to obtain the number of tablets as the final unit.

$$\underset{\text{Three SFs}}{0.150 \cancel{\text{ mg Synthroid}}} \times \underset{\text{Exact}}{\frac{\overset{\text{Exact}}{1000 \cancel{\text{ mcg}}}}{1 \cancel{\text{ mg}}}} \times \underset{\text{Two SFs}}{\frac{\overset{\text{Exact}}{1 \text{ tablet}}}{75 \cancel{\text{ mcg Synthroid}}}} = 2 \text{ tablets}$$

STUDY CHECK 2.11

A bottle contains 120 mL of cough syrup. If one teaspoon (5 mL) is given four times a day, how many days will elapse before a refill is needed?

ANSWER

6 days

▶ **SAMPLE PROBLEM 2.12 Using a Percentage as a Conversion Factor**

A person who exercises regularly has 16% body fat by mass. If this person weighs 155 lb, what is the mass, in kilograms, of body fat?

SOLUTION

STEP **1** State the given and needed quantities.

ANALYZE THE PROBLEM	Given	Need
	155 lb body weight, 16% body fat	kilograms of body fat

Exercising regularly helps reduce body fat.

STEP **2** Write a plan to convert the given unit to the needed unit.

pounds of body weight	U.S.–Metric factor	kilograms of body mass	Percentage factor	kilograms of body fat

STEP **3** State the equalities and conversion factors.

1 kg of body mass = 2.20 lb of body weight   16 kg of body fat = 100 kg of body mass

$$\frac{2.20 \text{ lb body weight}}{1 \text{ kg body mass}} \text{ and } \frac{1 \text{ kg body mass}}{2.20 \text{ lb body weight}} \qquad \frac{16 \text{ kg body fat}}{100 \text{ kg body mass}} \text{ and } \frac{100 \text{ kg body mass}}{16 \text{ kg body fat}}$$

STEP **4** Set up the problem to cancel units and calculate the answer. We set up the problem using conversion factors to cancel each unit, starting with lb of body weight, until we obtain the final unit, kg of body fat, in the numerator.

$$255 \text{ lb body weight} \times \underset{\text{Three SFs}}{\frac{1 \text{ kg body mass}}{2.20 \text{ lb body weight}}} \times \underset{\text{Exact}}{\frac{16 \text{ kg body fat}}{100 \text{ kg body mass}}} = \underset{\text{Two SFs}}{11 \text{ kg of body fat}}$$

STUDY CHECK 2.12

Uncooked lean ground beef can contain up to 22% fat by mass. How many grams of fat would be contained in 0.25 lb of the ground beef?

ANSWER

25 g of fat

Chemistry Link to **Health**
Toxicology and Risk–Benefit Assessment

Each day, we make choices about what we do or what we eat, often without thinking about the risks associated with these choices. We are aware of the risks of cancer from smoking or the risks of lead poisoning, and we know there is a greater risk of having an accident if we cross a street where there is no light or crosswalk.

A basic concept of toxicology is the statement of Paracelsus that the dose is the difference between a poison and a cure. To evaluate the level of danger from various substances, natural or synthetic, a risk assessment is made by exposing laboratory animals to the substances and monitoring the health effects. Often, doses very much greater than humans might ordinarily encounter are given to the test animals.

Many hazardous chemicals or substances have been identified by these tests. One measure of toxicity is the LD_{50}, or lethal dose, which is the concentration of the substance that causes death in 50% of the test animals. A dosage is typically measured in milligrams per kilogram (mg/kg) of body mass or micrograms per kilogram (mcg/kg) of body mass.

Other evaluations need to be made, but it is easy to compare LD_{50} values. Parathion, a pesticide, with an LD_{50} of 3 mg/kg, would be highly toxic. This means that 3 mg of parathion per kg of body mass would be fatal to half the test animals. Table salt (sodium chloride) with an LD_{50} of 3000 mg/kg would have a much lower toxicity. You would need to ingest a huge amount of salt before any toxic effect would be observed. Although the risk to animals can be evaluated in the laboratory, it is more difficult to determine the impact in the environment since there is also a difference between continued exposure and a single, large dose of the substance.

Table 2.8 lists some LD_{50} values and compares substances in order of increasing toxicity.

The LD_{50} of caffeine is 192 mg/kg.

TABLE 2.8 Some LD_{50} Values for Substances Tested in Rats

Substance	LD_{50} (mg/kg)
Table sugar	29 700
Boric acid	5140
Baking soda	4220
Table salt	3300
Ethanol	2080
Aspirin	1100
Codeine	800
Oxycodone	480
Caffeine	192
DDT	113
Cocaine (injected)	95
Dichlorvos (pesticide strips)	56
Ricin	30
Sodium cyanide	6
Parathion	3

QUESTIONS AND PROBLEMS

2.6 Problem Solving Using Unit Conversion

LEARNING GOAL Use conversion factors to change from one unit to another.

2.53 Use metric conversion factors to solve each of the following problems:
   a. The height of a student is 175 cm. How tall is the student in meters?
   b. A cooler has a volume of 5500 mL. What is the capacity of the cooler in liters?
   c. A Bee Hummingbird has a mass of 0.0018 kg. What is the mass of the hummingbird in grams?

2.54 Use metric conversion factors to solve each of the following problems:
   a. The Daily Value (DV) for phosphorus is 800 mg. How many grams of phosphorus are recommended?
   b. A glass of orange juice contains 0.85 dL of juice. How many milliliters of orange juice is that?
   c. A package of chocolate instant pudding contains 2840 mg of sodium. How many grams of sodium is that?

2.55 Solve each of the following problems using one or more conversion factors:
   a. A container holds 0.500 qt of liquid. How many milliliters of lemonade will it hold?
   b. What is the mass, in kilograms, of a person who weighs 175 lb?
   c. An athlete has 15% body fat by mass. What is the weight of fat, in pounds, of a 74-kg athlete?
   d. A plant fertilizer contains 15% nitrogen (N) by mass. In a container of soluble plant food, there are 10.0 oz of fertilizer. How many grams of nitrogen are in the container?

Agricultural fertilizers applied to a field provide nitrogen for plant growth.

2.56 Solve each of the following problems using one or more conversion factors:
   a. Wine is 12% alcohol by volume. How many milliliters of alcohol are in a 0.750-L bottle of wine?
   b. Blueberry high-fiber muffins contain 51% dietary fiber by mass. If a package with a net weight of 12 oz contains six muffins, how many grams of fiber are in each muffin?
   c. A jar of crunchy peanut butter contains 1.43 kg of peanut butter. If you use 8.0% of the peanut butter for a sandwich, how many ounces of peanut butter did you take out of the container?
   d. In a candy factory, the nutty chocolate bars contain 22.0% pecans by mass. If 5.0 kg of pecans were used for candy last Tuesday, how many pounds of nutty chocolate bars were made?

℞ Clinical Applications

2.57 Using conversion factors, solve each of the following clinical problems:
   a. You have used 250 L of distilled water for a dialysis patient. How many gallons of water is that?
   b. A patient needs 0.024 g of a sulfa drug. There are 8-mg tablets in stock. How many tablets should be given?

c. The daily dose of ampicillin for the treatment of an ear infection is 115 mg/kg of body weight. What is the daily dose for a 34-lb child?

d. You need 4.0 oz of a steroid ointment. If there are 16 oz in 1 lb, how many grams of ointment does the pharmacist need to prepare?

2.58 Using conversion factors, solve each of the following clinical problems:

a. The physician has ordered 1.0 g of tetracycline to be given every six hours to a patient. If your stock on hand is 500-mg tablets, how many will you need for one day's treatment?

b. An intramuscular medication is given at 5.00 mg/kg of body weight. What is the dose for a 180-lb patient?

c. A physician has ordered 0.50 mg of atropine, intramuscularly. If atropine were available as 0.10 mg/mL of solution, how many milliliters would you need to give?

d. During surgery, a patient receives 5.0 pt of plasma. How many milliliters of plasma were given?

2.59 Using conversion factors, solve each of the following clinical problems:

a. A nurse practitioner prepares 500. mL of an IV of normal saline solution to be delivered at a rate of 80. mL/h. What is the infusion time, in hours, to deliver 500. mL?

b. A nurse practitioner orders Medrol to be given 1.5 mg/kg of body weight. Medrol is an anti-inflammatory administered as an intramuscular injection. If a child weighs 72.6 lb and the available stock of Medrol is 20. mg/mL, how many milliliters does the nurse administer to the child?

2.60 Using conversion factors, solve each of the following clinical problems:

a. A nurse practitioner prepares an injection of promethazine, an antihistamine used to treat allergic rhinitis. If the stock bottle is labeled 25 mg/mL and the order is a dose of 12.5 mg, how many milliliters will the nurse draw up in the syringe?

b. You are to give ampicillin 25 mg/kg to a child with a mass of 28 kg. If stock on hand is 250 mg/capsule, how many capsules should be given?

2.61 Using Table 2.8, calculate the number of grams that would provide the LD_{50} for a 175-lb person for each of the following:
a. table salt   **b.** sodium cyanide   **c.** aspirin

2.62 Using Table 2.8, calculate the number of grams that would provide the LD_{50} for a 148-lb person for each of the following:
a. ethanol   **b.** ricin   **c.** baking soda

2.7 Density

LEARNING GOAL

Calculate the density of a substance; use the density to calculate the mass or volume of a substance.

The mass and volume of any object can be measured. If we compare the mass of the object to its volume, we obtain a relationship called **density**.

$$\text{Density} = \frac{\text{mass of substance}}{\text{volume of substance}}$$

Every substance has a unique density, which distinguishes it from other substances. For example, lead has a density of 11.3 g/mL, whereas cork has a density of 0.26 g/mL. From these densities, we can predict if these substances will sink or float in water. *If an object is less dense than a liquid, the object floats when placed in the liquid.* If a substance, such as cork, is less dense than water, it will float. However, a lead object sinks because its density is greater than that of water (see Figure 2.10).

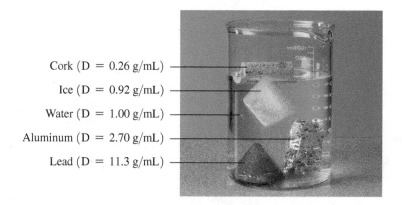

Cork (D = 0.26 g/mL)
Ice (D = 0.92 g/mL)
Water (D = 1.00 g/mL)
Aluminum (D = 2.70 g/mL)
Lead (D = 11.3 g/mL)

FIGURE 2.10 ▶ Objects that sink in water are more dense than water; objects that float are less dense.

Q Why does an ice cube float and a piece of aluminum sink?

Metals such as gold and lead tend to have higher densities, whereas gases have low densities. In the metric system, the densities of solids and liquids are usually expressed as grams per cubic centimeter (g/cm^3) or grams per milliliter (g/mL). The densities of gases are usually stated as grams per liter (g/L). Table 2.9 gives the densities of some common substances.

TABLE 2.9 Densities of Some Common Substances

Solids (at 25 °C)	Density (g/mL)	Liquids (at 25 °C)	Density (g/mL)	Gases (at 0 °C)	Density (g/L)
Cork	0.26	Gasoline	0.74	Hydrogen	0.090
Body fat	0.909	Ethanol	0.79	Helium	0.179
Ice (at 0 °C)	0.92	Olive oil	0.92	Methane	0.714
Muscle	1.06	Water (at 4 °C)	1.00	Neon	0.902
Sugar	1.59	Urine	1.012–1.030	Nitrogen	1.25
Bone	1.80	Plasma (blood)	1.03	Air (dry)	1.29
Salt (NaCl)	2.16	Milk	1.04	Oxygen	1.43
Aluminum	2.70	Blood	1.06	Carbon dioxide	1.96
Iron	7.86	Mercury	13.6		
Copper	8.92				
Silver	10.5				
Lead	11.3				
Gold	19.3				

Calculating Density

We can calculate the density of a substance from its mass and volume. High-density lipoprotein (HDL) is a type of cholesterol, sometimes called "good cholesterol," that is measured in a routine blood test. If we have a 0.258-g sample of HDL with a volume of 0.22 mL, we can calculate the density of the HDL as follows:

$$\text{Density} = \frac{\text{mass of HDL sample}}{\text{volume of HDL sample}} = \frac{\overset{\text{Three SFs}}{0.258 \text{ g}}}{\underset{\text{Two SFs}}{0.22 \text{ mL}}} = \underset{\text{Two SFs}}{1.2 \text{ g/mL}}$$

Density of Solids

The volume of a solid can be determined by volume displacement. When a solid is completely submerged in water, it displaces a volume that is equal to the volume of the solid. In Figure 2.11, the water level rises from 35.5 mL to 45.0 mL after the zinc object is added. This means that 9.5 mL of water is displaced and that the volume of the object is 9.5 mL. The density of the zinc is calculated using volume displacement as follows:

$$\text{Density} = \frac{\overset{\text{Four SFs}}{68.60 \text{ g zinc}}}{\underset{\text{Two SFs}}{9.5 \text{ mL}}} = \underset{\text{Two SFs}}{7.2 \text{ g/mL}}$$

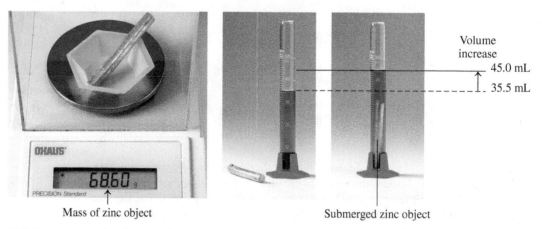

Mass of zinc object

Submerged zinc object

Volume increase
45.0 mL
35.5 mL

FIGURE 2.11 ▶ The density of a solid can be determined by volume displacement because a submerged object displaces a volume of water equal to its own volume.

❓ How is the volume of the zinc object determined?

Chemistry Link to Health

Bone Density

The density of our bones determines their health and strength. Our bones are constantly gaining and losing minerals such as calcium, magnesium, and phosphate. In childhood, bones form at a faster rate than they break down. As we age, the breakdown of bone occurs more rapidly than new bone forms. As the loss of bone minerals increases, bones begin to thin, causing a decrease in mass and density. Thinner bones lack strength, which increases the risk of fracture. Hormonal changes, disease, and certain medications can also contribute to the thinning of bone. Eventually, a condition of severe thinning of bone known as *osteoporosis* may occur. *Scanning electron micrographs* (SEMs) show (a) normal bone and (b) bone with osteoporosis due to loss of bone minerals.

Bone density is often determined by passing low-dose X-rays through the narrow part at the top of the femur (hip) and the spine (c). These locations are where fractures are more likely to occur, especially as we age. Bones with high density will block more of the X-rays compared to bones that are less dense. The results of a bone density test are compared to a healthy young adult as well as to other people of the same age.

Recommendations to improve bone strength include supplements of calcium and vitamin D. Weight-bearing exercise such as walking and lifting weights can also improve muscle strength, which in turn increases bone strength.

(a) Normal bone

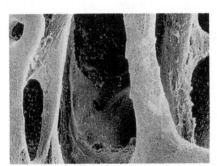

(b) Bone with osteoporosis

(c) Viewing a low-dose X-ray of the spine

Problem Solving Using Density

Density can be used as a conversion factor. For example, if the volume and the density of a sample are known, the mass in grams of the sample can be calculated as shown in the following Sample Problem.

⚛ CORE CHEMISTRY SKILL

Using Density as a Conversion Factor

▶ **SAMPLE PROBLEM 2.13 Problem Solving with Density**

Ken, a 195-lb male patient, has a blood volume of 7.5 qt. If the density of blood is 1.06 g/mL, what is the mass, in grams, of Ken's blood?

SOLUTION

STEP 1 State the given and needed quantities.

ANALYZE THE PROBLEM	Given	Need
	7.5 qt of blood, density of blood (1.06 g/mL)	grams of blood

STEP 2 Write a plan to calculate the needed quantity.

quarts → U.S.–Metric factor → milliliters → Density factor → grams

Guide to Using Density

STEP 1
State the given and needed quantities.

STEP 2
Write a plan to calculate the needed quantity.

STEP 3
Write the equalities and their conversion factors including density.

STEP 4
Set up the problem to calculate the needed quantity.

STEP **3** Write the equalities and their conversion factors including density.

$$1 \text{ qt} = 946 \text{ mL}$$

$$\frac{946 \text{ mL}}{1 \text{ qt}} \quad \text{and} \quad \frac{1 \text{ qt}}{946 \text{ mL}}$$

$$1 \text{ mL of blood} = 1.06 \text{ g of blood}$$

$$\frac{1 \text{ mL}}{1.06 \text{ g blood}} \quad \text{and} \quad \frac{1.06 \text{ g blood}}{1 \text{ mL}}$$

STEP **4** Set up the problem to calculate the needed quantity.

$$7.5 \text{ qt blood} \times \underset{\text{Three SFs}}{\frac{946 \text{ mL}}{1 \text{ qt}}} \times \underset{\text{Three SFs}}{\frac{1.06 \text{ g blood}}{1 \text{ mL}}} = 7500 \text{ g of blood}$$

Two SFs   Exact   Exact   Two SFs

STUDY CHECK 2.13

During surgery, a patient receives 3.0 pt of blood. How many kilograms of blood (density = 1.06 g/mL) were needed for the transfusion?

ANSWER

1.5 kg of blood

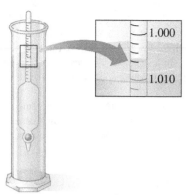

FIGURE 2.12 ▶ A hydrometer is used to measure the specific gravity of urine, which, for adults, is 1.012 to 1.030.

❓ If the hydrometer reading is 1.006, what is the density of the urine?

A dipstick is used to measure the specific gravity of a urine sample.

Specific Gravity

Specific gravity (sp gr) is a relationship between the density of a substance and the density of water. Specific gravity is calculated by dividing the density of a sample by the density of water, which is 1.00 g/mL at 4 °C. A substance with a specific gravity of 1.00 has the same density as water (1.00 g/mL).

$$\text{Specific gravity} = \frac{\text{density of sample}}{\text{density of water}}$$

Specific gravity is one of the few unitless values you will encounter in chemistry. An instrument called a hydrometer is often used to measure the specific gravity of fluids such as wine or a sample of urine. The specific gravity of the urine helps to evaluate the water balance in the body and the substances in the urine. In Figure 2.12, a hydrometer is used to measure the specific gravity of urine. The normal range of specific gravity for urine is 1.012 to 1.030. The specific gravity can decrease with *type 2 diabetes* and kidney disease. Increased specific gravity may occur with dehydration, kidney infection, and liver disease. In a clinic or hospital, a dipstick containing chemical pads is used to evaluate specific gravity.

QUESTIONS AND PROBLEMS

2.7 Density

LEARNING GOAL Calculate the density of a substance; use the density to calculate the mass or volume of a substance.

2.63 What is the density (g/mL) of each of the following samples?

Lightweight heads on golf clubs are made of titanium.

a. A solid object with a mass of 1.65 lb and a volume of 170 mL.
b. A gem has a mass of 4.50 g. When the gem is placed in a graduated cylinder containing 20.00 mL of water, the water level rises to 21.45 mL.
c. A lightweight head on the driver of a golf club is made of titanium. The volume of a sample of titanium is 114 cm^3 and the mass is 514.1 g.

2.64 What is the density (g/mL) of each of the following samples?
   a. A medication, if 3.00 mL has a mass of 3.85 g.
   b. The fluid in a car battery, if it has a volume of 125 mL and a mass of 155 g.
   c. A syrup is added to an empty container with a mass of 115.25 g. When 0.100 pt of syrup is added, the total mass of the container and syrup is 182.48 g.

115.25 g   **182.48 g**

2.65 Solve the following problems:
   a. What is the mass, in grams, of 150 mL of a liquid with a density of 1.4 g/mL?
   b. What is the mass of a glucose solution that fills a 0.500-L intravenous bottle if the density of the glucose solution is 1.15 g/mL?
   c. A sculptor has prepared a mold for casting a bronze figure. The figure has a volume of 225 mL. If bronze has a density of 7.8 g/mL, how many ounces of bronze are needed in the preparation of the bronze figure?

2.66 Use Table 2.9 to solve the following problems:
   a. A graduated cylinder contains 18.0 mL of water. What is the new water level after 35.6 g of silver metal with a density of 10.5 g/mL is submerged in the water?
   b. A thermometer containing 8.3 g of mercury has broken. If mercury has a density of 13.6 g/mL, what volume spilled?

   c. A fish tank holds 35 gal of water. Using the density of 1.00 g/mL for water, determine the number of pounds of water in the fish tank.

Clinical Applications

2.67 Solve each of the following problems:
   a. A urine sample has a density of 1.030 g/mL. What is the specific gravity of the sample?
   b. A 20.0-mL sample of a glucose IV solution that has a mass of 20.6 g. What is the density of the glucose solution?
   c. The specific gravity of a vegetable oil is 0.85. What is its density?
   d. A 0.200-mL sample of high-density lipoprotein (HDL) has a mass of 0.230 g. What is the density of the HDL?

2.68 Solve each of the following problems:
   a. A glucose solution has a density of 1.02 g/mL. What is its specific gravity?
   b. A bottle containing 325 g of cleaning solution is used to clean hospital equipment. If the cleaning solution has a specific gravity of 0.850, what volume, in milliliters, of solution was used?
   c. Butter has a specific gravity of 0.86. What is the mass, in grams, of 2.15 L of butter?
   d. A 5.000-mL urine sample has a mass of 5.025 g. If the normal range for the specific gravity of urine is 1.012 to 1.030, would the specific gravity of this urine sample indicate that the patient could have type 2 diabetes?

 # Clinical Update
Greg's Follow-Up Visit with His Doctor

On Greg's last visit to his doctor, he complained of feeling tired. His doctor orders a blood test for iron. Sandra, the registered nurse, does a venipuncture and withdraws 8.0 mL of blood. About 70% of the iron in the body is used to form hemoglobin, which is a protein in the red blood cells that carries oxygen to the cells of the body. About 30% is stored in ferritin, bone marrow, and the liver. When the iron level is low, a person may have fatigue and decreased immunity.

The normal range for serum iron in men is 80 to 160 mcg/dL. Greg's iron test showed a blood serum iron level of 42 mcg/dL, which indicates that Greg has iron deficiency anemia. His doctor orders an iron supplement to be taken twice daily (b.i.d.). One tablet of the iron supplement contains 65 mg of iron.

Clinical Applications

2.69 **a.** Write an equality and two conversion factors for Greg's serum iron level.
   b. How many micrograms of iron were in the 8.0 mL sample of Greg's blood?

2.70 **a.** Write an equality and two conversion factors for one tablet of the iron supplement.
   b. How many grams of iron will Greg consume in one week?

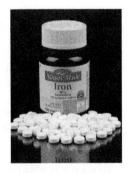

Each tablet contains 65 mg of iron, which is given for iron supplementation.

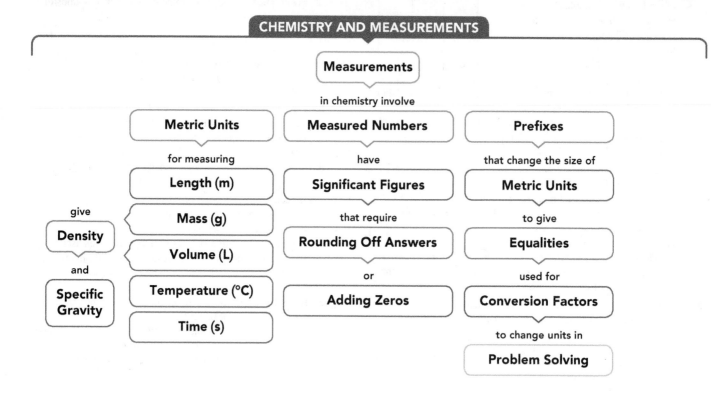

CHEMISTRY AND MEASUREMENTS

Measurements

in chemistry involve

Metric Units	Measured Numbers	Prefixes
for measuring	have	that change the size of
Length (m)	Significant Figures	Metric Units
Mass (g)	that require	to give
Volume (L)	Rounding Off Answers	Equalities
Temperature (°C)	or	used for
Time (s)	Adding Zeros	Conversion Factors

give

Density

and

Specific Gravity

to change units in

Problem Solving

CHAPTER REVIEW

2.1 Units of Measurement
LEARNING GOAL Write the names and abbreviations for the metric or SI units used in measurements of length, volume, mass, temperature, and time.

—1 L = 1.06 qt
—946 mL = 1 qt

- In science, physical quantities are described in units of the metric or International System of Units (SI).
- Some important units are meter (m) for length, liter (L) for volume, gram (g) and kilogram (kg) for mass, degree Celsius (°C) and Kelvin (K) for temperature, and second (s) for time.

2.2 Measured Numbers and Significant Figures
LEARNING GOAL Identify a number as measured or exact; determine the number of significant figures in a measured number.

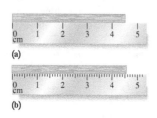

- A measured number is any number obtained by using a measuring device.
- An exact number is obtained by counting items or from a definition; no measuring device is needed.
- Significant figures are the numbers reported in a measurement including the estimated digit.
- Zeros in front of a decimal number or at the end of a nondecimal number are not significant.

2.3 Significant Figures in Calculations
LEARNING GOAL Adjust calculated answers to give the correct number of significant figures.

- In multiplication and division, the final answer is written so that it has the same number of significant figures as the measurement with the fewest significant figures.
- In addition and subtraction, the final answer is written so that it has the same number of decimal places as the measurement with the fewest decimal places.

2.4 Prefixes and Equalities

LEARNING GOAL Use the numerical values of prefixes to write a metric equality.

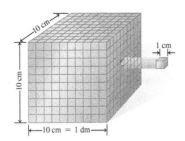

- A prefix placed in front of a metric or SI unit changes the size of the unit by factors of 10.
- Prefixes such as *centi*, *milli*, and *micro* provide smaller units; prefixes such as *kilo*, *mega*, and *tera* provide larger units.
- An equality shows the relationship between two units that measure the same quantity of length, volume, mass, or time.
- Examples of metric equalities are 1 m = 100 cm, 1 L = 1000 mL, 1 kg = 1000 g, and 1 min = 60 s.

2.5 Writing Conversion Factors

LEARNING GOAL Write a conversion factor for two units that describe the same quantity.

- Conversion factors are used to express a relationship in the form of a fraction.
- Two conversion factors can be written for any relationship in the metric or U.S. system.
- A percentage is written as a conversion factor by expressing matching units as the parts in 100 parts of the whole.

2.6 Problem Solving Using Unit Conversion

LEARNING GOAL Use conversion factors to change from one unit to another.

- Conversion factors are useful when changing a quantity expressed in one unit to a quantity expressed in another unit.
- In the problem-solving process, a given unit is multiplied by one or more conversion factors that cancel units until the needed answer is obtained.

2.7 Density

LEARNING GOAL Calculate the density of a substance; use the density to calculate the mass or volume of a substance.

- The density of a substance is a ratio of its mass to its volume, usually g/mL or g/cm³.
- The units of density can be used to write conversion factors that convert between the mass and volume of a substance.
- Specific gravity (sp gr) compares the density of a substance to the density of water, 1.00 g/mL.

KEY TERMS

Celsius (°C) temperature scale A temperature scale on which water has a freezing point of 0 °C and a boiling point of 100 °C.

centimeter (cm) A unit of length in the metric system; there are 2.54 cm in 1 in.

conversion factor A ratio in which the numerator and denominator are quantities from an equality or given relationship. For example, the conversion factors for the relationship 1 kg = 2.20 lb are written as

$$\frac{2.20 \text{ lb}}{1 \text{ kg}} \quad \text{and} \quad \frac{1 \text{ kg}}{2.20 \text{ lb}}$$

cubic centimeter (cm³, cc) The volume of a cube that has 1-cm sides; 1 cm³ is equal to 1 mL.

density The relationship of the mass of an object to its volume expressed as grams per cubic centimeter (g/cm³), grams per milliliter (g/mL), or grams per liter (g/L).

equality A relationship between two units that measure the same quantity.

exact number A number obtained by counting or by definition.

gram (g) The metric unit used in measurements of mass.

International System of Units (SI) An international system of units that modifies the metric system.

Kelvin (K) temperature scale A temperature scale on which the lowest possible temperature is 0 K.

kilogram (kg) A metric mass of 1000 g, equal to 2.20 lb. The kilogram is the SI standard unit of mass.

liter (L) The metric unit for volume that is slightly larger than a quart.

mass A measure of the quantity of material in an object.

measured number A number obtained when a quantity is determined by using a measuring device.

meter (m) The metric unit for length that is slightly longer than a yard. The meter is the SI standard unit of length.

metric system A system of measurement used by scientists and in most countries of the world.

milliliter (mL) A metric unit of volume equal to one-thousandth of a liter (0.001 L).

prefix The part of the name of a metric unit that precedes the base unit and specifies the size of the measurement. All prefixes are related on a decimal scale.

second (s) A unit of time used in both the SI and metric systems.

significant figures (SFs) The numbers recorded in a measurement.

specific gravity (sp gr) A relationship between the density of a substance and the density of water:

$$\text{sp gr} = \frac{\text{density of sample}}{\text{density of water}}$$

temperature An indicator of the hotness or coldness of an object.

volume The amount of space occupied by a substance.

📠 KEY MATH SKILL

The chapter section containing each Key Math Skill is shown in parentheses at the end of each heading.

Rounding Off (2.3)

Calculator displays are rounded off to give the correct number of significant figures.

- If the first digit to be dropped is *4 or less*, then it and all following digits are simply dropped from the number.
- If the first digit to be dropped is *5 or greater*, then the last retained digit of the number is increased by 1.

One or more significant zeros are added when the calculator display has fewer digits than the needed number of significant figures.

Example: Round off each of the following to three significant figures:

3.608 92 L	**Answer:** 3.61 L
0.003 870 298 m	0.003 87 m
6 g	6.00 g

⚛ CORE CHEMISTRY SKILLS

The chapter section containing each Core Chemistry Skill is shown in parentheses at the end of each heading.

Counting Significant Figures (2.2)

The significant figures are all the *measured* numbers including the last, estimated digit:

- All nonzero digits
- Zeros between nonzero digits
- Zeros within a decimal number
- All digits in a coefficient of a number written in scientific notation

An *exact* number is obtained from counting or a definition and has no effect on the number of significant figures in the final answer.

Example: State the number of significant figures in each of the following:

0.003 045 mm	**Answer:**	four SFs
15 000 m		two SFs
45.067 kg		five SFs
5.30×10^3 g		three SFs
2 cans of soda		exact

Using Significant Figures in Calculations (2.3)

- In multiplication or division, the final answer is written so that it has the same number of significant figures as the measurement with the fewest significant figures (SFs).
- In addition or subtraction, the final answer is written so that it has the same number of decimal places as the measurement having the fewest decimal places.

Perform the following calculations using measured numbers and give answers with the correct number of SFs:

Example: 4.05 m × 0.6078 m

Answer: 2.461 59 rounded off to 2.46 m² (three SFs)

Example: $\dfrac{4.50\ g}{3.27\ mL}$

Answer: 1.376 146 789 rounded off to 1.38 g/mL (three SFs)

Example: 0.758 g + 3.10 g

Answer: 3.858 rounded off to 3.86 g (hundredths place)

Example: 13.538 km − 8.6 km

Answer: 4.938 rounded off to 4.9 km (tenths place)

Using Prefixes (2.4)

- In the metric and SI systems of units, a prefix attached to any unit increases or decreases its size by some factor of 10.
- When the prefix *centi* is used with the unit meter, it becomes centimeter, a length that is one-hundredth of a meter (0.01 m).
- When the prefix *milli* is used with the unit meter, it becomes millimeter, a length that is one-thousandth of a meter (0.001 m).

Example: Complete the following statements with the correct prefix symbol:

a. 1000 m = 1 ____ m   **b.** 0.01 g = 1 ____ g

Answer: **a.** 1000 m = 1 km   **b.** 0.01 g = 1 cg

Writing Conversion Factors from Equalities (2.5)

- A conversion factor allows you to change from one unit to another.
- Two conversion factors can be written for any equality in the metric, U.S., or metric–U.S. systems of measurement.
- Two conversion factors can be written for a relationship stated within a problem.

Example: Write two conversion factors for the equality:
1 L = 1000 mL.

Answer: $\dfrac{1000\ mL}{1\ L}$ and $\dfrac{1\ L}{1000\ mL}$

Using Conversion Factors (2.6)

In problem solving, conversion factors are used to cancel the given unit and to provide the needed unit for the answer.

- State the given and needed quantities.
- Write a plan to convert the given unit to the needed unit.
- State the equalities and conversion factors.
- Set up the problem to cancel units and calculate the answer.

Example: A computer chip has a width of 0.75 in. What is that distance in millimeters?

Answer:

Equalities: 1 in. = 2.54 cm; 1 cm = 10 mm

Conversion Factors: $\dfrac{2.54 \text{ cm}}{1 \text{ in.}}$ and $\dfrac{1 \text{ in.}}{2.54 \text{ cm}}$; $\dfrac{10 \text{ mm}}{1 \text{ cm}}$ and $\dfrac{1 \text{ cm}}{10 \text{ mm}}$

Problem Setup: $0.75 \text{ in.} \times \dfrac{2.54 \text{ cm}}{1 \text{ in.}} \times \dfrac{10 \text{ mm}}{1 \text{ cm}} = 19 \text{ mm}$

Using Density as a Conversion Factor (2.7)

Density is an equality of mass and volume for a substance, which is written as the *density expression*.

$$\text{Density} = \frac{\text{mass of substance}}{\text{volume of substance}}$$

Density is useful as a conversion factor to convert between mass and volume.

Example: The element tungsten used in light bulb filaments has a density of 19.3 g/cm³. What is the volume, in cubic centimeters, of 250 g of tungsten?

Answer: *Equality:* $1 \text{ cm}^3 = 19.3 \text{ g}$

Conversion Factors: $\dfrac{19.3 \text{ g}}{1 \text{ cm}^3}$ and $\dfrac{1 \text{ cm}^3}{19.3 \text{ g}}$

Problem Setup: $250 \text{ g} \times \dfrac{1 \text{ cm}^3}{19.3 \text{ g}} = 13 \text{ cm}^3$

UNDERSTANDING THE CONCEPTS

The chapter sections to review are shown in parentheses at the end of each question.

2.71 In which of the following pairs do both numbers contain the same number of significant figures? (2.2)
  a. 2.0500 m and 0.0205 m
  b. 600.0 K and 60 K
  c. 0.000 75 s and 75 000 s
  d. 6.240 L and 6.240×10^{-2} L

2.72 In which of the following pairs do both numbers contain the same number of significant figures? (2.2)
  a. 3.44×10^{-3} g and 0.0344 g
  b. 0.0098 s and 9.8×10^4 s
  c. 6.8×10^3 m and 68 000 m
  d. 258.000 g and 2.58×10^{-2} g

2.73 Indicate if each of the following is answered with an exact number or a measured number: (2.2)

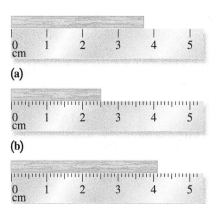

  a. number of legs
  b. height of table
  c. number of chairs at the table
  d. area of tabletop

2.74 Measure the length of each of the objects in diagrams **(a)**, **(b)**, and **(c)** using the metric ruler in the figure. Indicate the number of significant figures for each and the estimated digit for each. (2.2)

(a)

(b)

(c)

2.75 The length of this rug is 38.4 in. and the width is 24.2 in. (2.3)

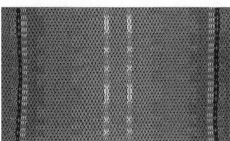

  a. What is the length of this rug measured in centimeters?
  b. What is the width of this rug measured in centimeters?
  c. How many significant figures are in the length measurement?
  d. Calculate the area of the rug, in cm², to the correct number of significant figures.

2.76 Each of the following diagrams represents a container of water and a cube. Some cubes float while others sink. Match diagrams **1**, **2**, **3**, or **4** with one of the following descriptions and explain your choices: (2.7)

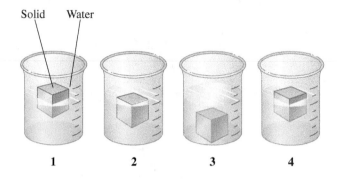

Solid   Water

1	**2**	**3**	**4**

a. The cube has a greater density than water.
b. The cube has a density that is 0.80 g/mL.
c. The cube has a density that is one-half the density of water.
d. The cube has the same density as water.

2.77 What is the density of the solid object that is weighed and submerged in water? (2.7)

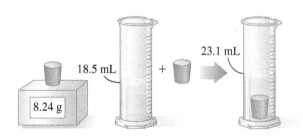

23.1 mL

18.5 mL   +

8.24 g

2.78 Consider the following solids. The solids **A**, **B**, and **C** represent aluminum, gold, and silver. If each has a mass of 10.0 g, what is the identity of each solid? (2.7)

Density of aluminum = 2.70 g/mL
Density of gold = 19.3 g/mL
Density of silver = 10.5 g/mL

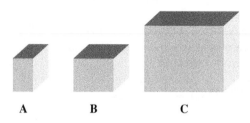

A   **B**   **C**

2.79 A graduated cylinder contains three liquids **A**, **B**, and **C**, which have different densities and do not mix: mercury (D = 13.6 g/mL), vegetable oil (D = 0.92 g/mL), and water (D = 1.00 g/mL). Identify the liquids **A**, **B**, and **C** in the cylinder. (2.7)

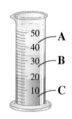

50 — A
40
30 — B
20
10 — C

2.80 Suppose you have two 100-mL graduated cylinders. In each cylinder, there is 40.0 mL of water. You also have two cubes: One is lead, and the other is aluminum. Each cube measures 2.0 cm on each side. After you carefully lower each cube into the water of its own cylinder, what will the new water level be in each of the cylinders? (2.7)

ADDITIONAL QUESTIONS AND PROBLEMS

2.81 Round off or add zeros to the following calculated answers to give a final answer with three significant figures: (2.2)
a. 0.000 012 58 L
b. 3.528×10^2 kg
c. 125 111 m

2.82 Round off or add zeros to the following calculated answers to give a final answer with three significant figures: (2.2)
a. 58.703 g
b. 3×10^{-3} s
c. 0.010 826 g

2.83 A dessert contains 137.25 g of vanilla ice cream, 84 g of fudge sauce, and 43.7 g of nuts. (2.3, 2.6)
a. What is the total mass, in grams, of the dessert?
b. What is the total weight, in pounds, of the dessert?

2.84 A fish company delivers 22 kg of salmon, 5.5 kg of crab, and 3.48 kg of oysters to your seafood restaurant. (2.3, 2.6)
a. What is the total mass, in kilograms, of the seafood?
b. What is the total number of pounds?

2.85 In France, grapes are 1.75 Euros per kilogram. What is the cost of grapes, in dollars per pound, if the exchange rate is 1.36 dollars/Euro? (2.6)

2.86 In Mexico, avocados are 48 pesos per kilogram. What is the cost, in cents, of an avocado that weighs 0.45 lb if the exchange rate is 13 pesos to the dollar? (2.6)

2.87 Bill's recipe for onion soup calls for 4.0 lb of thinly sliced onions. If an onion has an average mass of 115 g, how many onions does Bill need? (2.6)

2.88 The price of 1 lb of potatoes is $1.75. If all the potatoes sold today at the store bring in $1420, how many kilograms of potatoes did grocery shoppers buy? (2.6)

2.89 The density of lead is 11.3 g/mL. The water level in a graduated cylinder initially at 215 mL rises to 285 mL after a piece of lead is submerged. What is the mass, in grams, of the lead? (2.7)

2.90 A graduated cylinder contains 155 mL of water. A 15.0-g piece of iron (density = 7.86 g/mL) and a 20.0-g piece of lead (density = 11.3 g/mL) are added. What is the new water level, in milliliters, in the cylinder? (2.7)

2.91 How many cubic centimeters (cm^3) of olive oil have the same mass as 1.50 L of gasoline (see Table 2.9)? (2.7)

2.92 Ethanol has a density of 0.79 g/mL. What is the volume, in quarts, of 1.50 kg of alcohol? (2.7)

℞ Clinical Applications

2.93 The following nutrition information is listed on a box of crackers: (2.6)

Serving size 0.50 oz (6 crackers)
Fat 4 g per serving; Sodium 140 mg per serving

a. If the box has a net weight (contents only) of 8.0 oz, about how many crackers are in the box?

b. If you ate 10 crackers, how many ounces of fat are you consuming?

c. How many servings of crackers in part **a** would it take to obtain the Daily Value (DV) for sodium, which is 2300 mg?

2.94 A dialysis unit requires 75 000 mL of distilled water. How many gallons of water are needed? (1 gal = 4 qt) (2.6)

2.95 To prevent bacterial infection, a doctor orders 4 tablets of amoxicillin per day for 10 days. If each tablet contains 250 mg of amoxicillin, how many ounces of the medication are given in 10 days? (2.6)

2.96 Celeste's diet restricts her intake of protein to 24 g per day. If she eats 1.2 oz of protein, has she exceeded her protein limit for the day? (2.6)

2.97 A doctor orders 5.0 mL of phenobarbital elixir. If the phenobarbital elixir is available as 30. mg per 7.5 mL, how many milligrams is given to the patient? (2.6)

2.98 A doctor orders 2.0 mg of morphine. The vial of morphine on hand is 10. mg per 1.0 mL. How many milliliters of morphine should you administer to the patient? (2.6)

CHALLENGE QUESTIONS

The following groups of questions are related to the topics in this chapter. However, they do not all follow the chapter order, and they require you to combine concepts and skills from several sections. These questions will help you increase your critical thinking skills and prepare for your next exam.

2.99 A balance measures mass to 0.001 g. If you determine the mass of an object that weighs about 30 g, would you record the mass as 30 g, 31 g, 31.2 g, 31.16 g, or 31.075 g? Explain your choice by writing two to three complete sentences that describe your thinking. (2.3)

2.100 When three students use the same meterstick to measure the length of a paper clip, they obtain results of 5.8 cm, 5.75 cm, and 5.76 cm. If the meterstick has millimeter markings, what are some reasons for the different values? (2.3)

2.101 A car travels at 55 mi/h and gets 11 km/L of gasoline. How many gallons of gasoline are needed for a 3.0-h trip? (2.6)

2.102 A 50.0-g silver object and a 50.0-g gold object are both added to 75.5 mL of water contained in a graduated cylinder. What is the new water level, in milliliters, in the cylinder? (2.7)

2.103 In the manufacturing of computer chips, cylinders of silicon are cut into thin wafers that are 3.00 in. in diameter and have a mass of 1.50 g of silicon. How thick, in millimeters, is each wafer if silicon has a density of 2.33 g/cm^3? (The volume of a cylinder is $V = \pi r^2 h$.) (2.6)

2.104 A sunscreen preparation contains 2.50% benzyl salicylate by mass. If a tube contains 4.0 oz of sunscreen, how many kilograms of benzyl salicylate are needed to manufacture 325 tubes of sunscreen? (2.6)

℞ Clinical Applications

2.105 For a 180-lb person, calculate the quantity of each of the following that must be ingested to provide the LD$_{50}$ for caffeine given in Table 2.8: (2.6)

a. cups of coffee if one cup is 12 fl oz and there is 100. mg of caffeine per 6 fl oz of drip-brewed coffee

b. cans of cola if one can contains 50. mg of caffeine

c. tablets of No-Doz if one tablet contains 100. mg of caffeine

2.106 A dietary supplement contains the following components. If a person uses the dietary supplement once a day, how many milligrams of each component would that person consume in one week? (2.6)

a. calcium 0.20 g
b. iron 0.50 mg
c. iodine 53 mcg
d. chromium 45 mcg
e. threonine 0.285 g

2.107 a. Some athletes have as little as 3.0% body fat. If such a person has a body mass of 65 kg, how many pounds of body fat does that person have? (2.6)

b. In liposuction, a doctor removes fat deposits from a person's body. If body fat has a density of 0.94 g/mL and 3.0 L of fat is removed, how many pounds of fat were removed from the patient?

2.108 A mouthwash is 21.6% ethanol by mass. If each bottle contains 0.358 pt of mouthwash with a density of 0.876 g/mL, how many kilograms of ethanol are in 180 bottles of the mouthwash? (2.6, 2.7)

A mouthwash may contain over 20% ethanol.

ANSWERS

Answers to Selected Questions and Problems

2.1 a. volume **b.** length
c. length **d.** time

2.3 a. meter, length **b.** gram, mass
c. milliliter, volume **d.** second, time
e. degree Celsius, temperature

2.5 a. second, time **b.** kilogram, mass
c. gram, mass **d.** degrees Celsius, temperature

2.7 a. measured **b.** exact
c. exact **d.** measured

2.9 a. 6 oz **b.** none
c. 0.75 lb, 350 g **d.** none (definitions are exact)

2.11 a. not significant **b.** significant
c. significant **d.** significant
e. not significant

2.13 a. 5 SFs **b.** 2 SFs **c.** 2 SFs
d. 3 SFs **e.** 4 SFs **f.** 3 SFs

2.15 b and c

2.17 a. 4 **b.** 2 **c.** 3

2.19 A calculator often gives more digits than the number of significant figures allowed in the answer.

2.21 a. 1.85 kg **b.** 88.2 L
c. 0.004 74 cm **d.** 8810 m
e. 1.83×10^5 s

2.23 a. 5.08×10^3 L **b.** 3.74×10^4 g
c. 1.05×10^5 m **d.** 2.51×10^{-4} s

2.25 a. 1.6 **b.** 0.01
c. 27.6 **d.** 3.5

2.27 a. 53.54 cm **b.** 127.6 g
c. 121.5 mL **d.** 0.50 L

2.29 km/h is kilometers per hour; mi/h is miles per hour.

2.31 a. mg **b.** dL
c. km **d.** fg

2.33 a. centiliter **b.** kilogram
c. millisecond **d.** gigameter

2.35 a. 0.01 **b.** 10^{12}
c. 0.001 **d.** 0.1

2.37 a. decigram **b.** microgram
c. kilogram **d.** centigram

2.39 a. 100 cm **b.** 1×10^9 nm
c. 0.001 m **d.** 1000 mL

2.41 a. kilogram **b.** milliliter
c. km **d.** kL
e. nanometer

2.43 a. 1 m = 100 cm; $\dfrac{100 \text{ cm}}{1 \text{ m}}$ and $\dfrac{1 \text{ m}}{100 \text{ cm}}$

b. 1 g = 1000 mg; $\dfrac{1000 \text{ mg}}{1 \text{ g}}$ and $\dfrac{1 \text{ g}}{1000 \text{ mg}}$

c. 1 L = 1000 mL; $\dfrac{1000 \text{ mL}}{1 \text{ L}}$ and $\dfrac{1 \text{ L}}{1000 \text{ mL}}$

d. 1 dL = 100 mL; $\dfrac{100 \text{ mL}}{1 \text{ dL}}$ and $\dfrac{1 \text{ dL}}{100 \text{ mL}}$

2.45 a. 1 yd = 3 ft; $\dfrac{3 \text{ ft}}{1 \text{ yd}}$ and $\dfrac{1 \text{ yd}}{3 \text{ ft}}$
The 1 yd and 3 ft are both exact.

b. 1 kg = 2.20 lb; $\dfrac{2.20 \text{ lb}}{1 \text{ kg}}$ and $\dfrac{1 \text{ kg}}{2.20 \text{ lb}}$
The 2.20 lb is measured: It has three SFs. The 1 kg is exact.

c. 1 min = 60 s; $\dfrac{60 \text{ s}}{1 \text{ min}}$ and $\dfrac{1 \text{ min}}{60 \text{ s}}$
The 1 min and 60 s are both exact.

d. 1 gal = 27 mi; $\dfrac{1 \text{ gal}}{27 \text{ mi}}$ and $\dfrac{27 \text{ mi}}{1 \text{ gal}}$
The 27 mi is measured: It has two SFs. The 1 gal is exact.

e. 93 g of silver = 100 g of sterling;
$\dfrac{93 \text{ g silver}}{100 \text{ g sterling}}$ and $\dfrac{100 \text{ g sterling}}{93 \text{ g silver}}$
The 93 g is measured: It has two SFs. The 100 g is exact.

2.47 a. 3.5 m = 1 s; $\dfrac{3.5 \text{ m}}{1 \text{ s}}$ and $\dfrac{1 \text{ s}}{3.5 \text{ m}}$
The 3.5 m is measured: It has two SFs. The 1 s is exact.

b. 4700 mg of potassium = 1 day;
$\dfrac{4700 \text{ mg potassium}}{1 \text{ day}}$ and $\dfrac{1 \text{ day}}{4700 \text{ mg potassium}}$
The 4700 mg is measured: It has two SFs. The 1 day is exact.

c. 46.0 km = 1 gal; $\dfrac{46.0 \text{ km}}{1 \text{ gal}}$ and $\dfrac{1 \text{ gal}}{46.0 \text{ km}}$
The 46.0 km is measured: It has three SFs. The 1 gal is exact.

d. 29 mcg of pesticide = 1 kg of plums;
$\dfrac{29 \text{ mcg pesticide}}{1 \text{ kg plums}}$ and $\dfrac{1 \text{ kg plums}}{29 \text{ mcg pesticide}}$
The 29 mcg is measured: It has two SFs. The 1 kg is exact.

2.49 a. 1 tablet = 630 mg of calcium;
$\dfrac{630 \text{ mg calcium}}{1 \text{ tablet}}$ and $\dfrac{1 \text{ tablet}}{630 \text{ mg calcium}}$
The 630 mg is measured: It has two SFs. The 1 tablet is exact.

b. 60 mg of vitamin C = 1 day;
$\dfrac{60 \text{ mg vitamin C}}{1 \text{ day}}$ and $\dfrac{1 \text{ day}}{60 \text{ mg vitamin C}}$
The 60 mg is measured: It has one SF. The 1 day is exact.

c. 1 tablet = 50 mg of atenolol;
$\dfrac{50 \text{ mg atenolol}}{1 \text{ tablet}}$ and $\dfrac{1 \text{ tablet}}{50 \text{ mg atenolol}}$
The 50 mg is measured: It has one SF. The 1 tablet is exact.

d. 1 tablet = 81 mg of aspirin;
$\dfrac{81 \text{ mg aspirin}}{1 \text{ tablet}}$ and $\dfrac{1 \text{ tablet}}{81 \text{ mg aspirin}}$
The 81 mg is measured: It has two SFs. The 1 tablet is exact.

2.51 a. 10 mg of Atarax = 5 mL of syrup;
$\dfrac{10 \text{ mg Atarax}}{5 \text{ mL syrup}}$ and $\dfrac{5 \text{ mL syrup}}{10 \text{ mg Atarax}}$

b. 1 tablet = 0.25 g of Lanoxin;
$\dfrac{0.25 \text{ g Lanoxin}}{1 \text{ tablet}}$ and $\dfrac{1 \text{ tablet}}{0.25 \text{ g Lanoxin}}$

c. 1 tablet = 300 mg of Motrin;
$\dfrac{300 \text{ mg Motrin}}{1 \text{ tablet}}$ and $\dfrac{1 \text{ tablet}}{300 \text{ mg Motrin}}$

2.53 a. 1.75 m   **b.** 5.5 L   **c.** 1.8 g

2.55 a. 473 mL   **b.** 79.5 kg
c. 24 lb   **d.** 43 g

2.57 a. 66 gal   **b.** 3 tablets
c. 1800 mg   **d.** 110 g

2.59 a. 6.3 h   **b.** 2.5 mL

2.61 a. 260 g   **b.** 0.5 g   **c.** 88 g

2.63 a. 4.4 g/mL   **b.** 3.10 g/mL
c. 4.51 g/mL

2.65 a. 210 g   **b.** 575 g   **c.** 62 oz

2.67 a. 1.03   **b.** 1.03 g/mL
c. 0.85 g/mL   **d.** 1.15 g/mL

2.69 a. 42 mcg of iron = 1 dL of blood;

$$\frac{42 \text{ mcg iron}}{1 \text{ dL blood}} \quad \text{and} \quad \frac{1 \text{ dL blood}}{42 \text{ mcg iron}}$$

b. 3.4 mcg of iron

2.71 c and **d**

2.73 a. exact   **b.** measured
c. exact   **d.** measured

2.75 a. length = 97.5 cm   **b.** width = 61.5 cm
c. 3 SFs   **d.** 6.00×10^3 cm^2

2.77 1.8 g/mL

2.79 A is vegetable oil, **B** is water, and **C** is mercury.

2.81 a. 0.000 012 6 L
b. 3.53×10^2 kg
c. 125 000 m

2.83 a. 265 g   **b.** 0.584 lb

2.85 $1.08 per lb

2.87 16 onions

2.89 790 g

2.91 1200 cm^3

2.93 a. 96 crackers
b. 0.2 oz of fat
c. 16 servings

2.95 0.35 oz

2.97 20. mg

2.99 You would record the mass as 31.075 g. Since the balance will weigh to the nearest 0.001 g, the mass value would be reported to 0.001 g.

2.101 6.4 gal

2.103 0.141 mm

2.105 a. 79 cups
b. 310 cans
c. 160 tablets

2.107 a. 4.3 lb of body fat
b. 6.2 lb

3

Matter and Energy

CHARLES IS 13 YEARS OLD AND OVERWEIGHT.

His doctor is worried that Charles is at risk for type 2 diabetes and advises his mother to make an appointment with a dietitian. Daniel, a dietitian, explains to them that choosing the appropriate foods is important to living a healthy lifestyle, losing weight, and preventing or managing diabetes.

Daniel also explains that food contains potential or stored energy, and different foods contain different amounts of potential energy. For instance, carbohydrates contain 4 kcal/g (17 kJ/g) whereas fats contain 9 kcal/g (38 kJ/g). He then explains that diets high in fat require more exercise to burn the fats, as they contain more potential energy. When Daniel looks at Charles' typical daily diet, he calculates that Charles is obtaining 3800 kcal for one day. The American Heart Association recommends 1800 kcal for boys 9 to 13 years of age. Daniel encourages Charles and his mother to include whole grains, fruits, and vegetables in their diet instead of foods high in fat. They also discuss food labels and the fact that smaller serving sizes of healthy foods are necessary to lose weight. Daniel also recommends that Charles participate in at least 60 min of exercise every day. Before leaving, Charles and his mother are given a menu for the following two weeks, as well as a diary to keep track of what, and how much, they actually consume.

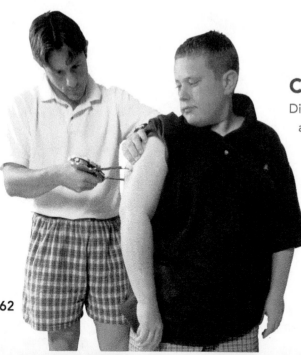

CAREER Dietitian

Dietitians specialize in helping individuals learn about good nutrition and the need for a balanced diet. This requires them to understand biochemical processes, the importance of vitamins, and food labels, as well as the differences between carbohydrates, fats, and proteins in terms of their energy value and how they are metabolized. Dietitians work in a variety of environments including hospitals, nursing homes, school cafeterias, and public health clinics. In these environments, they create specialized diets for individuals diagnosed with a specific disease or create meal plans for those in a nursing home.

E very day, we see a variety of materials with many different shapes and forms. To a scientist, all of this material is *matter*. Matter is everywhere around us: the orange juice we had for breakfast, the water we put in the coffee maker, the plastic bag we put our sandwich in, our toothbrush and toothpaste, the oxygen we inhale, and the carbon dioxide we exhale.

When we look around, we see that matter takes the physical form of a solid, a liquid, or a gas. Water is a familiar example that we routinely observe in all three states. In the solid state, water can be an ice cube or a snowflake. It is a liquid when it comes out of a faucet or fills a pool. Water forms a gas, or vapor, when it evaporates from wet clothes or boils in a pan. In these examples, water changes its state by gaining or losing energy. For example, energy is added to melt ice cubes and to boil water in a teakettle. Conversely, energy is removed to freeze liquid water in an ice cube tray and to condense water vapor to liquid droplets.

Almost everything we do involves energy. We use energy when we heat water, cook food, turn on lights, walk, study, use a washing machine, or drive our cars. Of course, that energy has to come from something. In our bodies, the food we eat provides us with energy. Energy from burning fossil fuels or the Sun is used to heat a home or water for a pool.

CHAPTER READINESS*

🖩 KEY MATH SKILLS

- Using Positive and Negative Numbers in Calculations (1.4B)
- Solving Equations (1.4D)
- Interpreting Graphs (1.4E)
- Writing Numbers in Scientific Notation (1.4F)
- Rounding Off (2.3)

⚛ CORE CHEMISTRY SKILLS

- Counting Significant Figures (2.2)
- Using Significant Figures in Calculations (2.3)
- Writing Conversion Factors from Equalities (2.5)
- Using Conversion Factors (2.6)

*These Key Math Skills and Core Chemistry Skills from previous chapters are listed here for your review as you proceed to the new material in this chapter.

3.1 Classification of Matter

Matter is anything that has mass and occupies space. Matter makes up all the things we use such as water, wood, plates, plastic bags, clothes, and shoes. The different types of matter are classified by their composition.

Pure Substances: Elements and Compounds

A **pure substance** is matter that has a fixed or definite composition. There are two kinds of pure substances: elements and compounds. An **element**, the simplest type of a pure substance, is composed of only one type of material such as silver, iron, or aluminum. Every element is composed of *atoms*, which are extremely tiny particles that make up each type of matter. Silver is composed of silver atoms, iron of iron atoms, and aluminum of aluminum atoms. A full list of the elements is found on the inside front cover of this text.

LEARNING GOAL

Classify examples of matter as pure substances or mixtures.

⚛ CORE CHEMISTRY SKILL

Classifying Matter

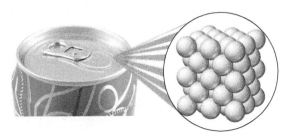

An aluminum can consists of many atoms of aluminum.

A molecule of water, H_2O, consists of two atoms of hydrogen (white) for one atom of oxygen (red).

A **compound** is also a pure substance, but it consists of atoms of two or more elements always chemically combined in the same proportion. In compounds, the atoms are held together by attractions called *bonds*, which form small groups of atoms called *molecules*. For example, a molecule of the compound water has two hydrogen atoms for every one oxygen atom and is represented by the formula H_2O. This means that water found anywhere always has the same composition of H_2O. Another compound that consists of a chemical combination of hydrogen and oxygen is hydrogen peroxide. It has two hydrogen atoms for every two oxygen atoms, and is represented by the formula H_2O_2. Thus, water (H_2O) and hydrogen peroxide (H_2O_2) are different compounds that have different properties.

Pure substances that are compounds can be broken down by chemical processes into their elements. They cannot be broken down through physical methods such as boiling or sifting. For example, ordinary table salt consists of the compound NaCl, which can be separated by chemical processes into sodium metal and chlorine gas, as seen in Figure 3.1. Elements cannot be broken down further.

A molecule of hydrogen peroxide, H_2O_2, consists of two atoms of hydrogen (white) for every two atoms of oxygen (red).

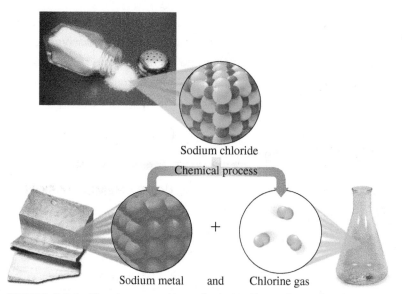

Sodium chloride

Chemical process

Sodium metal   and   Chlorine gas

FIGURE 3.1 ▶ The decomposition of salt, NaCl, produces the elements sodium and chlorine.

Ⓠ How do elements and compounds differ?

Mixtures

In a **mixture**, two or more different substances are physically mixed, but not chemically combined. Much of the matter in our everyday lives consists of mixtures. The air we breathe is a mixture of mostly oxygen and nitrogen gases. The steel in buildings and railroad tracks is a mixture of iron, nickel, carbon, and chromium. The brass in doorknobs and fixtures is a mixture of zinc and copper (see Figure 3.2). Tea, coffee, and ocean water are mixtures too. Unlike compounds, the proportions of the substances in a mixture are not consistent but can vary. For example, two sugar–water mixtures may look the same, but the one with the higher ratio of sugar to water would taste sweeter.

Physical processes can be used to separate mixtures because there are no chemical interactions between the components. For example, different coins, such as nickels, dimes, and

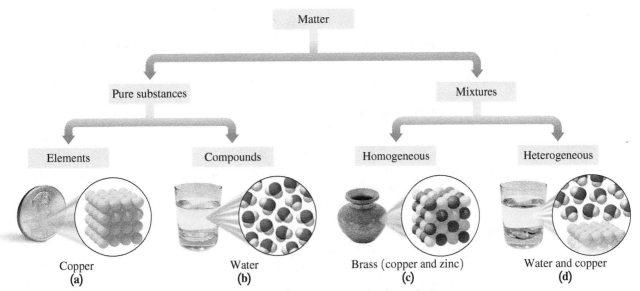

FIGURE 3.2 ▶ Matter is organized by its components: elements, compounds, and mixtures. **(a)** The element copper consists of copper atoms. **(b)** The compound water consists of H_2O molecules. **(c)** Brass is a homogeneous mixture of copper and zinc atoms. **(d)** Copper metal in water is a heterogeneous mixture of copper atoms and H_2O molecules.

◉ Why are copper and water pure substances, but brass is a mixture?

quarters, can be separated by size; iron particles mixed with sand can be picked up with a magnet; and water is separated from cooked spaghetti by using a strainer (see Figure 3.3).

Types of Mixtures

Mixtures are classified further as homogeneous or heterogeneous. In a *homogeneous mixture*, also called a *solution*, the composition is uniform throughout the sample. Familiar examples of homogeneous mixtures are air, which contains oxygen and nitrogen gases, and seawater, a solution of salt and water.

In a *heterogeneous mixture*, the components do not have a uniform composition throughout the sample. For example, a mixture of oil and water is heterogeneous because the oil floats on the surface of the water. Other examples of heterogeneous mixtures are a cookie with raisins and pulp in orange juice.

In the chemistry laboratory, mixtures are separated by various methods. Solids are separated from liquids by *filtration*, which involves pouring a mixture through a filter paper set in a funnel. In *chromatography*, different components of a liquid mixture separate as they move at different rates up the surface of a piece of chromatography paper.

FIGURE 3.3 ▶ A mixture of spaghetti and water is separated using a strainer, a physical method of separation.

◉ Why can physical methods be used to separate mixtures but not compounds?

(a) A mixture of a liquid and a solid is separated by filtration. **(b)** Different substances are separated as they travel at different rates up the surface of chromatography paper.

(a)　　　　(b)

▸ **SAMPLE PROBLEM 3.1 Classifying Mixtures**

Classify each of the following as a pure substance (element or compound) or a mixture (homogeneous or heterogeneous):

a. copper in copper wire
b. a chocolate-chip cookie
c. nitrox, a combination of oxygen and nitrogen used to fill scuba tanks

SOLUTION

a. Copper is an element, which is a pure substance.
b. A chocolate-chip cookie does not have a uniform composition, which makes it a heterogeneous mixture.
c. The gases oxygen and nitrogen have a uniform composition in nitrox, which makes it a homogeneous mixture.

STUDY CHECK 3.1

A salad dressing is prepared with oil, vinegar, and chunks of blue cheese. Is this a homogeneous or heterogeneous mixture?

ANSWER

heterogeneous

Chemistry Link to Health
Breathing Mixtures

The air we breathe is composed mostly of the gases oxygen (21%) and nitrogen (79%). The homogeneous breathing mixtures used by scuba divers differ from the air we breathe depending on the depth of the dive. Nitrox is a mixture of oxygen and nitrogen, but with more oxygen gas (up to 32%) and less nitrogen gas (68%) than air. A breathing mixture with less nitrogen gas decreases the risk of *nitrogen narcosis* associated with breathing regular air while diving. Heliox contains oxygen and helium, which is typically used for diving to more than 200 ft. By replacing nitrogen with helium, nitrogen narcosis does not occur. However, at dive depths over 300 ft, helium is associated with severe shaking and body temperature drop.

A breathing mixture used for dives over 400 ft is trimix, which contains oxygen, helium, and some nitrogen. The addition of some nitrogen lessens the problem of shaking that comes with breathing high levels of helium. Heliox and trimix are used only by professional, military, or other highly trained divers.

In hospitals, heliox may be used as a treatment for respiratory disorders and lung constriction in adults and premature infants. Heliox is less dense than air, which reduces the effort of breathing, and helps distribute the oxygen gas to the tissues.

A nitrox mixture is used to fill scuba tanks.

QUESTIONS AND PROBLEMS

3.1 Classification of Matter

LEARNING GOAL Classify examples of matter as pure substances or mixtures.

3.1 Classify each of the following as a pure substance or a mixture:
  a. baking soda ($NaHCO_3$)   **b.** a blueberry muffin
  c. ice (H_2O)   **d.** zinc (Zn)
  e. trimix (oxygen, nitrogen, and helium) in a scuba tank

3.2 Classify each of the following as a pure substance or a mixture:
  a. a soft drink   **b.** propane (C_3H_8)
  c. a cheese sandwich   **d.** an iron (Fe) nail
  e. salt substitute (KCl)

3.3 Classify each of the following pure substances as an element or a compound:
  a. a silicon (Si) chip   **b.** hydrogen peroxide (H_2O_2)
  c. oxygen (O_2)   **d.** rust (Fe_2O_3)
  e. methane (CH_4) in natural gas

3.4 Classify each of the following pure substances as an element or a compound:
  a. helium gas (He)   **b.** mercury (Hg) in a thermometer
  c. sugar ($C_{12}H_{22}O_{11}$)   **d.** sulfur (S)
  e. lye (NaOH)

3.5 Classify each of the following mixtures as homogeneous or heterogeneous:
  a. vegetable soup   **b.** seawater
  c. tea   **d.** tea with ice and lemon slices
  e. fruit salad

3.6 Classify each of the following mixtures as homogeneous or heterogeneous:
  a. nonfat milk   **b.** chocolate-chip ice cream
  c. gasoline   **d.** peanut butter sandwich
  e. cranberry juice

3.2 States and Properties of Matter

On Earth, matter exists in one of three *physical forms* called the **states of matter**: solids, liquids, and gases. A **solid**, such as a pebble or a baseball, has a definite shape and volume. You can probably recognize several solids within your reach right now such as books, pencils, or a computer mouse. In a solid, strong attractive forces hold the particles such as atoms or molecules close together. The particles in a solid are arranged in such a rigid pattern, their only movement is to vibrate slowly in fixed positions. For many solids, this rigid structure produces a crystal such as that seen in amethyst.

A **liquid** has a definite volume, but not a definite shape. In a liquid, the particles move in random directions but are sufficiently attracted to each other to maintain a definite volume, although not a rigid structure. Thus, when water, oil, or vinegar is poured from one container to another, the liquid maintains its own volume but takes the shape of the new container.

A **gas** does not have a definite shape or volume. In a gas, the particles are far apart, have little attraction to each other, and move at high speeds, taking the shape and volume of their container. When you inflate a bicycle tire, the air, which is a gas, fills the entire volume of the tire. The propane gas in a tank fills the entire volume of the tank. Table 3.1 compares the three states of matter.

Identify the states and the physical and chemical properties of matter.

Amethyst, a solid, is a purple form of quartz (SiO_2).

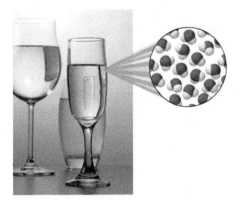

Water as a liquid takes the shape of its container.

A gas takes the shape and volume of its container.

TABLE 3.1 A Comparison of Solids, Liquids, and Gases

Characteristic	Solid	Liquid	Gas
Shape	Has a definite shape	Takes the shape of the container	Takes the shape of the container
Volume	Has a definite volume	Has a definite volume	Fills the volume of the container
Arrangement of Particles	Fixed, very close	Random, close	Random, far apart
Interaction between Particles	Very strong	Strong	Essentially none
Movement of Particles	Very slow	Moderate	Very fast
Examples	Ice, salt, iron	Water, oil, vinegar	Water vapor, helium, air

Physical Properties and Physical Changes

One way to describe matter is to observe its properties. For example, if you were asked to describe yourself, you might list your characteristics such as the color of your eyes and skin or the length, color, and texture of your hair.

Physical properties are those characteristics that can be observed or measured without affecting the identity of a substance. In chemistry, typical physical properties include the shape, color, melting point, boiling point, and physical state of a substance. For example, a penny has the physical properties of a round shape, an orange-red color, solid state, and a shiny luster. Table 3.2 gives more examples of physical properties of copper found in pennies, electrical wiring, and copper pans.

Water is a substance that is commonly found in all three states: solid, liquid, and gas. When matter undergoes a **physical change**, its state, size, or its appearance will change, but its composition remains the same. The solid state of water, snow or ice, has a different appearance than its liquid or gaseous state, but all three states are water.

TABLE 3.2 Some Physical Properties of Copper

State at 25 °C	Solid
Color	Orange-red
Odor	Odorless
Melting Point	1083 °C
Boiling Point	2567 °C
Luster	Shiny
Conduction of Electricity	Excellent
Conduction of Heat	Excellent

The evaporation of water from seawater gives white, solid crystals of salt (sodium chloride).

Copper, used in cookware, is a good conductor of heat.

The physical appearance of a substance can change in other ways too. Suppose that you dissolve some salt in water. The appearance of the salt changes, but you could re-form the salt crystals by evaporating the water. Thus in a physical change of state, no new substances are produced. Table 3.3 gives more examples of physical changes.

Chemical Properties and Chemical Changes

Chemical properties are those that describe the ability of a substance to change into a new substance. When a **chemical change** takes place, the original substance is converted into one or more new substances, which have different physical and chemical properties. For example, the rusting or corrosion of a metal such as iron is a chemical property. In the rain, an iron (Fe) nail undergoes a chemical change when it reacts with oxygen (O_2) to form rust (Fe_2O_3). A chemical change has taken place: Rust is a new substance with new physical and chemical properties. Table 3.4 gives examples of some chemical changes.

Flan has a topping of caramelized sugar.

TABLE 3.3 Examples of Some Physical Changes

Water boils to form water vapor.

Sugar dissolves in water to form a solution.

Copper is drawn into thin copper wires.

Paper is cut into tiny pieces of confetti.

Pepper is ground into flakes.

TABLE 3.4 Examples of Some Chemical Changes

Shiny, silver metal reacts in air to give a black, grainy coating.

A piece of wood burns with a bright flame and produces heat, ashes, carbon dioxide, and water vapor.

Heating white, granular sugar forms a smooth, caramel-colored substance.

Iron, which is gray and shiny, combines with oxygen to form orange-red rust.

A gold ingot is hammered to form gold leaf.

Interactive Video

Chemical vs. Physical Changes

▶ **SAMPLE PROBLEM 3.2 Physical and Chemical Changes**

Classify each of the following as a physical or chemical change:

a. A gold ingot is hammered to form gold leaf.
b. Gasoline burns in air.
c. Garlic is chopped into small pieces.

SOLUTION

a. A physical change occurs when the gold ingot changes shape.
b. A chemical change occurs when gasoline burns and forms different substances with new properties.
c. A physical change occurs when the size of the garlic pieces changes.

STUDY CHECK 3.2

Classify each of the following as a physical or chemical change:

a. Water freezes on a pond.
b. Gas bubbles form when baking powder is placed in vinegar.
c. A log is cut for firewood.

ANSWER

a. physical change   **b.** chemical change   **c.** physical change

QUESTIONS AND PROBLEMS

3.2 States and Properties of Matter

LEARNING GOAL Identify the states and the physical and chemical properties of matter.

3.7 Indicate whether each of the following describes a gas, a liquid, or a solid:
   a. The gaseous breathing mixture in a scuba tank has no definite volume or shape.
   b. The neon atoms in a lighting display do not interact with each other.
   c. The particles in an ice cube are held in a rigid structure.

3.8 Indicate whether each of the following describes a gas, a liquid, or a solid:
   a. Lemonade has a definite volume but takes the shape of its container.
   b. The particles in a tank of oxygen are very far apart.
   c. Helium occupies the entire volume of a balloon.

3.9 Describe each of the following as a physical or chemical property:
   a. Chromium is a steel-gray solid.
   b. Hydrogen reacts readily with oxygen.
   c. A patient has a temperature of 40.2 °C.
   d. Milk will sour when left in a warm room.
   e. Butane gas in an igniter burns in oxygen.

3.10 Describe each of the following as a physical or chemical property:
   a. Neon is a colorless gas at room temperature.
   b. Apple slices turn brown when they are exposed to air.
   c. Phosphorus will ignite when exposed to air.
   d. At room temperature, mercury is a liquid.
   e. Propane gas is compressed to a liquid for placement in a small cylinder.

3.11 What type of change, physical or chemical, takes place in each of the following?
   a. Water vapor condenses to form rain.
   b. Cesium metal reacts explosively with water.
   c. Gold melts at 1064 °C.
   d. A puzzle is cut into 1000 pieces.
   e. Cheese is grated.

3.12 What type of change, physical or chemical, takes place in each of the following?
   a. Pie dough is rolled into thin pieces for a crust.
   b. A silver pin tarnishes in the air.
   c. A tree is cut into boards at a saw mill.
   d. Food is digested.
   e. A chocolate bar melts.

3.13 Describe each property of the element fluorine as physical or chemical.
   a. is highly reactive
   b. is a gas at room temperature
   c. has a pale, yellow color
   d. will explode in the presence of hydrogen
   e. has a melting point of −220 °C

3.14 Describe each property of the element zirconium as physical or chemical.
   a. melts at 1852 °C
   b. is resistant to corrosion
   c. has a grayish white color
   d. ignites spontaneously in air when finely divided
   e. is a shiny metal

3.3 Temperature

LEARNING GOAL
Given a temperature, calculate a corresponding temperature on another scale.

CORE CHEMISTRY SKILL
Converting between Temperature Scales

Temperatures in science are measured and reported in *Celsius* (°C) units. On the Celsius scale, the reference points are the freezing point of water, defined as 0 °C, and the boiling point, 100 °C. In the United States, everyday temperatures are commonly reported in *Fahrenheit* (°F) units. On the Fahrenheit scale, water freezes at exactly 32 °F and boils at 212 °F. A typical room temperature of 22 °C would be the same as 72 °F. Normal human body temperature is 37.0 °C, which is the same temperature as 98.6 °C.

On the Celsius and Fahrenheit temperature scales, the temperature difference between freezing and boiling is divided into smaller units called *degrees*. On the Celsius scale, there are 100 degrees Celsius between the freezing and boiling points of water, whereas the Fahrenheit scale has 180 degrees Fahrenheit between the freezing and boiling points of water. That makes a degree Celsius almost twice the size of a degree Fahrenheit: 1 °C = 1.8 °F (see Figure 3.4).

$$180 \text{ degrees Fahrenheit} = 100 \text{ degrees Celsius}$$

$$\frac{180 \text{ degrees Fahrenheit}}{100 \text{ degrees Celsius}} = \frac{1.8 \text{ °F}}{1 \text{ °C}}$$

We can write a temperature equation that relates a Fahrenheit temperature and its corresponding Celsius temperature.

$$T_F = 1.8(T_C) + 32$$

Changes °C to °F / Adjusts freezing point

Temperature equation to obtain degrees Fahrenheit

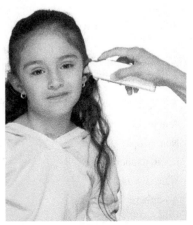
A digital ear thermometer is used to measure body temperature.

FIGURE 3.4 ▶ A comparison of the Fahrenheit, Celsius, and Kelvin temperature scales between the freezing and boiling points of water.

Q What is the difference in the freezing points of water on the Celsius and Fahrenheit temperature scales?

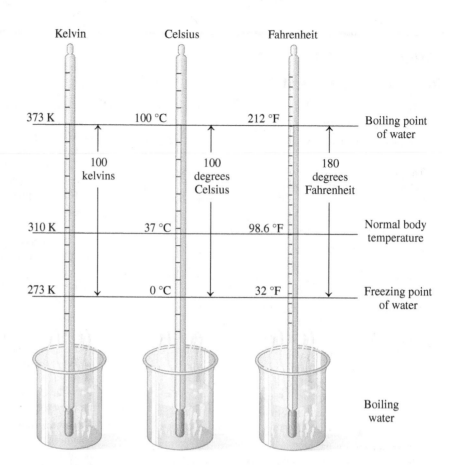

In this equation, the Celsius temperature is multiplied by 1.8 to change °C to °F; then 32 is added to adjust the freezing point from 0 °C to the Fahrenheit freezing point, 32 °F. The values, 1.8 and 32, used in the temperature equation are exact numbers and are not used to determine significant figures in the answer.

To convert from degrees Fahrenheit to degrees Celsius, the temperature equation is rearranged to solve for T_C. First, we subtract 32 from both sides since we must apply the same operation to both sides of the equation.

$$T_F - 32 = 1.8(T_C) + \cancel{32} - \cancel{32}$$
$$T_F - 32 = 1.8(T_C)$$

Second, we solve the equation for T_C by dividing both sides by 1.8.

$$\frac{T_F - 32}{1.8} = \frac{\cancel{1.8}(T_C)}{\cancel{1.8}}$$

$$\frac{T_F - 32}{1.8} = T_C \quad \text{Temperature equation to obtain degrees Celsius}$$

Scientists have learned that the coldest temperature possible is −273 °C (more precisely, −273.15 °C). On the *Kelvin* scale, this temperature, called *absolute zero*, has the value of 0 K. Units on the Kelvin scale are called kelvins (K); *no degree symbol is used*. Because there are no lower temperatures, the Kelvin scale has no negative temperature values. Between the freezing point of water, 273 K, and the boiling point, 373 K, there are 100 kelvins, which makes a kelvin equal in size to a degree Celsius.

$$1 \text{ K} = 1 \text{ °C}$$

We can write an equation that relates a Celsius temperature to its corresponding Kelvin temperature by adding 273 to the Celsius temperature. Table 3.5 gives a comparison of some temperatures on the three scales.

TABLE 3.5 A Comparison of Temperatures

Example	Fahrenheit (°F)	Celsius (°C)	Kelvin (K)
Sun	9937	5503	5776
A hot oven	450	232	505
A desert	120	49	322
A high fever	104	40	313
Normal body temperature	98.6	37.0	310
Room temperature	70	21	294
Water freezes	32	0	273
A northern winter	−66	−54	219
Nitrogen liquefies	−346	−210	63
Helium boils	−452	−269	4
Absolute zero	−459	−273	0

$T_K = T_C + 273$ Temperature equation to obtain kelvins

Suppose that a dermatologist uses liquid nitrogen at $-196\,°C$ to remove skin lesions and some skin cancer. We can calculate the temperature of the liquid nitrogen in kelvins by adding 273 to the temperature in degrees Celsius.

$T_K = -196 + 273 = 77\ K$

▶ **SAMPLE PROBLEM 3.3 Converting from Degrees Celsius to Degrees Fahrenheit**

The typical temperature in a hospital room is set at 21 °C. What is that temperature in degrees Fahrenheit?

SOLUTION

STEP **1** State the given and needed quantities.

ANALYZE THE PROBLEM	Given	Need
	21 °C	T in degrees Fahrenheit

STEP **2** Write a temperature equation.

$$T_F = 1.8(T_C) + 32$$

STEP **3** Substitute in the known values and calculate the new temperature.

$T_F = 1.8(21) + 32$ 1.8 is exact; 32 is exact
    Two SFs

$T_F = 38 + 32$
$\quad\ = 70.\,°F$ Answer to the ones place

In the equation, *the values of 1.8 and 32 are exact numbers*, which do not affect the number of SFs used in the answer.

STUDY CHECK 3.3

In the process of making ice cream, rock salt is added to crushed ice to chill the ice cream mixture. If the temperature drops to $-11\,°C$, what is it in degrees Fahrenheit?

ANSWER
12 °F

Guide to Calculating Temperature

STEP **1**
State the given and needed quantities.

STEP **2**
Write a temperature equation.

STEP **3**
Substitute in the known values and calculate the new temperature.

▶ **SAMPLE PROBLEM 3.4 Converting from Degrees Fahrenheit to Degrees Celsius**

In a type of cancer treatment called *thermotherapy*, temperatures as high as 113 °F are used to destroy cancer cells or make them more sensitive to radiation. What is that temperature in degrees Celsius?

SOLUTION

STEP **1** State the given and needed quantities.

ANALYZE THE PROBLEM	Given	Need
	113 °F	T in degrees Celsius

STEP **2** Write a temperature equation.

$$T_C = \frac{T_F - 32}{1.8}$$

STEP **3** Substitute in the known values and calculate the new temperature.

$$T_C = \frac{(113 - 32)}{1.8} \quad \text{32 is exact; 1.8 is exact}$$

$$= \frac{81}{1.8} = 45\,°C \quad \text{Answer to the ones place}$$

STUDY CHECK 3.4

A child has a temperature of 103.6 °F. What is this temperature on a Celsius thermometer?

ANSWER

39.8 °C

Chemistry Link to Health

Variation in Body Temperature

Normal body temperature is considered to be 37.0 °C, although it varies throughout the day and from person to person. Oral temperatures of 36.1 °C are common in the morning and climb to a high of 37.2 °C between 6 P.M. and 10 P.M. Temperatures above 37.2 °C for a person at rest are usually an indication of illness. Individuals who are involved in prolonged exercise may also experience elevated temperatures. Body temperatures of marathon runners can range from 39 °C to 41 °C as heat production during exercise exceeds the body's ability to lose heat.

Changes of more than 3.5 °C from the normal body temperature begin to interfere with bodily functions. Body temperatures above 41 °C, *hyperthermia*, can lead to convulsions, particularly in children, which may cause permanent brain damage. Heatstroke occurs above 41.1 °C. Sweat production stops, and the skin becomes hot and dry. The pulse rate is elevated, and respiration becomes weak and rapid. The person can become lethargic and lapse into a coma. Damage to internal organs is a major concern, and treatment, which must be immediate, may include immersing the person in an ice-water bath.

At the low temperature extreme of *hypothermia*, body temperature can drop as low as 28.5 °C. The person may appear cold and pale and have an irregular heartbeat. Unconsciousness can occur if the body temperature drops below 26.7 °C. Respiration becomes slow and shallow, and oxygenation of the tissues decreases. Treatment involves providing oxygen and increasing blood volume with glucose and saline fluids. Injecting warm fluids (37.0 °C) into the peritoneal cavity may restore the internal temperature.

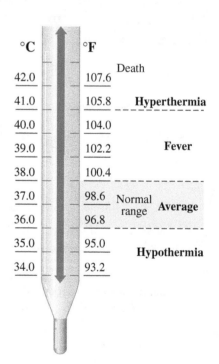

QUESTIONS AND PROBLEMS

3.3 Temperature

LEARNING GOAL Given a temperature, calculate a corresponding temperature on another scale.

3.15 Your friend who is visiting from Canada just took her temperature. When she reads 99.8 °F, she becomes concerned that she is quite ill. How would you explain this temperature to your friend?

3.16 You have a friend who is using a recipe for flan from a Mexican cookbook. You notice that he set your oven temperature at 175 °F. What would you advise him to do?

3.17 Calculate the unknown temperature in each of the following:
a. 37.0 °C = _____ °F
b. 65.3 °F = _____ °C
c. −27 °C = _____ K
d. 62 °C = _____ K
e. 114 °F = _____ °C

3.18 Calculate the unknown temperature in each of the following:
a. 25 °C = _____ °F
b. 155 °C = _____ °F
c. −25 °F = _____ °C
d. 224 K = _____ °C
e. 145 °C = _____ K

3.19 **a.** A patient with hyperthermia has a temperature of 106 °F. What does this read on a Celsius thermometer?

    b. Because high fevers can cause convulsions in children, the doctor needs to be called if the child's temperature goes over 40.0 °C. Should the doctor be called if a child has a temperature of 103 °F?

3.20 **a.** Hot compresses for a patient are prepared with water heated to 145 °F. What is the temperature of the hot water in degrees Celsius?

    b. During extreme hypothermia, a boy's temperature dropped to 20.6 °C. What was his temperature in degrees Fahrenheit?

3.4 Energy

When you are running, walking, dancing, or thinking, you are using energy to do *work*, any activity that requires energy. In fact, **energy** is defined as the ability to do work. Suppose you are climbing a steep hill and you become too tired to go on. At that moment, you do not have the energy to do any more work. Now suppose you sit down and have lunch. In a while, you will have obtained some energy from the food, and you will be able to do more work and complete the climb.

LEARNING GOAL

Identify energy as potential or kinetic; convert between units of energy.

Kinetic and Potential Energy

Energy can be classified as kinetic energy or potential energy. **Kinetic energy** is the energy of motion. Any object that is moving has kinetic energy. **Potential energy** is determined by the position of an object or by the chemical composition of a substance. A boulder resting on top of a mountain has potential energy because of its location. If the boulder rolls down the mountain, the potential energy becomes kinetic energy. Water stored in a reservoir has potential energy. When the water goes over the dam and falls to the stream below, its potential energy is converted to kinetic energy. Foods and fossil fuels have potential energy in their molecules. When you digest food or burn gasoline in your car, potential energy is converted to kinetic energy to do work.

Water at the top of the dam stores potential energy. When the water flows over the dam, potential energy is converted to kinetic energy.

Heat and Energy

Heat is the energy associated with the motion of particles. An ice cube feels cold because heat flows from your hand into the ice cube. The faster the particles move, the greater the heat or thermal energy of the substance. In the ice cube, the particles are moving very slowly. As heat is added, the motion of the particles in the ice cube increases. Eventually, the particles have enough energy to make the ice cube melt as it changes from a solid to a liquid.

Units of Energy

The SI unit of energy and work is the **joule (J)** (pronounced "jewel"). The joule is a small amount of energy, so scientists often use the kilojoule (kJ), 1000 joules. To heat water for one cup of tea, you need about 75 000 J or 75 kJ of heat. Table 3.6 shows a comparison of energy in joules for several energy sources.

You may be more familiar with the unit **calorie (cal)**, from the Latin *caloric*, meaning "heat." The calorie was originally defined as the amount of energy (heat) needed to raise the temperature of 1 g of water by 1 °C. Now one calorie is defined as exactly 4.184 J. This equality can be written as two conversion factors:

$$1 \text{ cal} = 4.184 \text{ J (exact)} \qquad \frac{4.184 \text{ J}}{1 \text{ cal}} \quad \text{and} \quad \frac{1 \text{ cal}}{4.184 \text{ J}}$$

One *kilocalorie* (kcal) is equal to 1000 calories, and one *kilojoule* (kJ) is equal to 1000 joules. The equalities and conversion factors follow:

$$1 \text{ kcal} = 1000 \text{ cal} \qquad \frac{1000 \text{ cal}}{1 \text{ kcal}} \quad \text{and} \quad \frac{1 \text{ kcal}}{1000 \text{ cal}}$$

$$1 \text{ kJ} = 1000 \text{ J} \qquad \frac{1000 \text{ J}}{1 \text{ kJ}} \quad \text{and} \quad \frac{1 \text{ kJ}}{1000 \text{ J}}$$

⚙ **CORE CHEMISTRY SKILL**

Using Energy Units

TABLE 3.6 A Comparison of Energy for Various Resources

Energy in Joules

- 10^{27}
- 10^{24} — Energy radiated by the Sun in 1 s (10^{26})
- 10^{21} — World reserves of fossil fuel (10^{23})
- 10^{18} — Energy consumption for 1 yr in the United States (10^{20})
- 10^{15} — Solar energy reaching the Earth in 1 s (10^{17})
- 10^{12} — Energy use per person in 1 yr in the United States (10^{11})
- 10^{9} — Energy from 1 gal of gasoline (10^{8})
- 10^{6} — Energy from one serving of pasta, a doughnut, or needed to bicycle for 1 h (10^{6})
- 10^{3} — Energy used to sleep for 1 h (10^{5})
- 10^{0}

A defibrillator provides electrical energy to heart muscle to re-establish normal rhythm.

▶ **SAMPLE PROBLEM 3.5 Energy Units**

A defibrillator gives a high-energy-shock output of 360 J. What is this quantity of energy in calories?

SOLUTION

STEP 1 State the given and needed quantities.

ANALYZE THE PROBLEM	Given	Need
	360 J	calories

STEP 2 Write a plan to convert the given unit to the needed unit.

joules → Energy factor → calories

STEP 3 State the equalities and conversion factors.

$$1 \text{ cal} = 4.184 \text{ J}$$

$$\frac{4.184 \text{ J}}{1 \text{ cal}} \quad \text{and} \quad \frac{1 \text{ cal}}{4.184 \text{ J}}$$

STEP 4 Set up the problem to calculate the needed quantity.

$$360 \text{ J} \times \frac{1 \text{ cal (Exact)}}{4.184 \text{ J}} = 86 \text{ cal}$$

Two SFs   Exact   Two SFs

STUDY CHECK 3.5

When 1.0 g of glucose is metabolized in the body, it produces 3.8 kcal. How many kilojoules are produced?

ANSWER

16 kJ

QUESTIONS AND PROBLEMS

3.4 Energy

LEARNING GOAL Identify energy as potential or kinetic; convert between units of energy.

3.21 Discuss the changes in the potential and kinetic energy of a roller-coaster ride as the roller-coaster car climbs to the top and goes down the other side.

3.22 Discuss the changes in the potential and kinetic energy of a ski jumper taking the elevator to the top of the jump and going down the ramp.

3.23 Indicate whether each of the following statements describes potential or kinetic energy:
  a. water at the top of a waterfall
  b. kicking a ball
  c. the energy in a lump of coal
  d. a skier at the top of a hill

3.24 Indicate whether each of the following statements describes potential or kinetic energy:
  a. the energy in your food
  b. a tightly wound spring
  c. an earthquake
  d. a car speeding down the freeway

3.25 The energy needed to keep a 75-watt light bulb burning for 1.0 h is 270 kJ. Calculate the energy required to keep the light bulb burning for 3.0 h in each of the following energy units:
  a. joules
  b. kilocalories

3.26 A person uses 750 kcal on a long walk. Calculate the energy used for the walk in each of the following energy units:
  a. joules
  b. kilojoules

Chemistry Link to the Environment

Carbon Dioxide and Climate Change

The Earth's climate is a product of interactions between sunlight, the atmosphere, and the oceans. The Sun provides us with energy in the form of solar radiation. Some of this radiation is reflected back into space. The rest is absorbed by the clouds, atmospheric gases including carbon dioxide, and the Earth's surface. For millions of years, concentrations of carbon dioxide (CO_2) have fluctuated. However in the last 100 years, the amount of carbon dioxide (CO_2) gas in our atmosphere has increased significantly. From the years 1000 to 1800, the atmospheric carbon dioxide averaged 280 ppm. The concentration of ppm indicates the parts per million by volume, which for gases is the same as mL of CO_2 per kL of air. But since the beginning of the Industrial Revolution in 1800 up until 2005, the level of atmospheric carbon dioxide has risen from about 280 ppm to about 394 ppm in 2013, a 40% increase.

As the atmospheric CO_2 level increases, more solar radiation is trapped by the atmospheric gases, which raises the temperature at the surface of the Earth. Some scientists have estimated that if the carbon dioxide level doubles from its level before the Industrial Revolution, the average global temperature could increase by 2.0 to 4.4 °C. Although this seems to be a small temperature change, it could have dramatic impact worldwide. Even now, glaciers and snow cover in much of the world have diminished. Ice sheets in Antarctica and Greenland are melting faster and breaking apart. Although no one knows for sure how rapidly the ice in the polar regions is melting, this accelerating change will contribute to a rise in sea level. In the twenti-

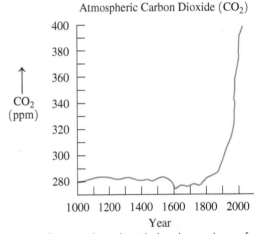

Atmospheric Carbon Dioxide (CO_2)

Atmospheric carbon dioxide levels are shown for the years from 1000 C.E. to 2010 C.E.

eth century, the sea level rose by 15 to 23 cm. Some scientists predict the sea level will rise by 1 m in this century. Such an increase will have a major impact on coastal areas.

Until recently, the carbon dioxide level was maintained as algae in the oceans and the trees in the forests utilized the carbon dioxide. However, the ability of these and other forms of plant life to absorb carbon dioxide is not keeping up with the increase in carbon dioxide. Most scientists agree that the primary source of the increase of carbon dioxide is the burning of fossil fuels such as gasoline, coal, and natural gas. The cutting and burning of trees in the rainforests (deforestation) also reduces the amount of carbon dioxide removed from the atmosphere.

Worldwide efforts are being made to reduce the carbon dioxide produced by burning fossil fuels that heat our homes, run our cars, and provide energy for industries. Scientists are exploring ways to provide alternative energy sources and to reduce the effects of deforestation. Meanwhile, we can reduce energy use in our homes by using appliances that are more energy efficient such as replacing incandescent light bulbs with fluorescent lights. Such an effort worldwide will reduce the possible impact of climate change and at the same time save our fuel resources.

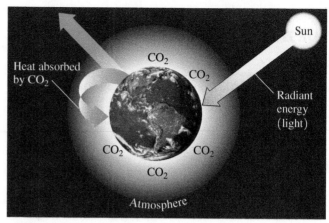

Heat from the Sun is trapped by the CO_2 layer in the atmosphere.

LEARNING GOAL

Use the energy values to calculate the kilocalories (kcal) or kilojoules (kJ) for a food.

3.5 Energy and Nutrition

The food we eat provides energy to do work in the body, which includes the growth and repair of cells. Carbohydrates are the primary fuel for the body, but if the carbohydrate reserves are exhausted, fats and then proteins are used for energy.

For many years in the field of nutrition, the energy from food was measured as Calories or kilocalories. The nutritional unit *Calorie, Cal* (with an uppercase C), is the same as 1000 cal, or 1 kcal. The international unit, kilojoule (kJ), is becoming more prevalent. For example, a baked potato has an energy value of 100 Calories, which is 100 kcal or 440 kJ. A typical diet that provides 2100 Cal (kcal) is the same as an 8800 kJ diet.

$$1 \text{ Cal} = 1 \text{ kcal} = 1000 \text{ cal}$$
$$1 \text{ Cal} = 4.184 \text{ kJ} = 4184 \text{ J}$$

In the nutrition laboratory, foods are burned in a *calorimeter* to determine their *energy value* (kcal/g or kJ/g) (see Figure 3.5). A sample of food is placed in a steel container called a calorimeter filled with oxygen. A measured amount of water is added to fill the area surrounding the combustion chamber. The food sample is ignited, releasing heat that increases the temperature of the water. From the known mass of the food and water as well as the measured temperature increase, the energy value for the food is calculated. We will assume that the energy absorbed by the calorimeter is negligible.

FIGURE 3.5 ▶ Heat released from burning a food sample in a calorimeter is used to determine the energy value for the food.

Q What happens to the temperature of water in a calorimeter during the combustion of a food sample?

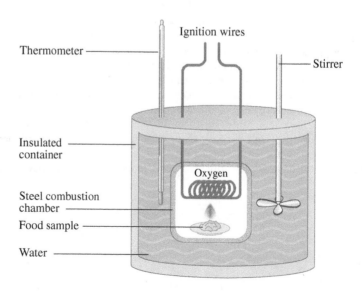

Energy Values for Foods

The **energy values** for food are the kilocalories or kilojoules obtained from burning 1 g of carbohydrate, fat, or protein, which are listed in Table 3.7.

Using these energy values, we can calculate the total energy for a food if the mass of each food type is known.

$$\text{kilocalories} = \not{g} \times \frac{\text{kcal}}{\not{g}} \qquad\qquad \text{kilojoules} = \not{g} \times \frac{\text{kJ}}{\not{g}}$$

On packaged food, the energy content is listed on the Nutrition Facts label, usually in terms of the number of Calories or kilojoules for one serving. The general composition and energy content for some foods are given in Table 3.8. The total energy, in kilocalories, for each food type was calculated using energy values in kilocalories. Total energy, in kilojoules, was calculated using energy values in kilojoules. The energy for each food type was rounded off to the tens place.

TABLE 3.7 Typical Energy Values for the Three Food Types

Food Type	kcal/g	kJ/g
Carbohydrate	4	17
Fat	9	38
Protein	4	17

TABLE 3.8 General Composition and Energy Content for Some Foods

Food	Carbohydrate (g)	Fat (g)	Protein (g)	Energy
Apple, 1 medium	15	0	0	60 kcal (260 kJ)
Banana, 1 medium	26	0	1	110 kcal (460 kJ)
Beef, ground, 3 oz	0	14	22	220 kcal (900 kJ)
Broccoli, 3 oz	4	0	3	30 kcal (120 kJ)
Carrots, 1 cup	11	0	2	50 kcal (220 kJ)
Chicken, no skin, 3 oz	0	3	20	110 kcal (450 kJ)
Egg, 1 large	0	6	6	70 kcal (330 kJ)
Milk, nonfat, 1 cup	12	0	9	90 kcal (350 kJ)
Potato, baked	23	0	3	100 kcal (440 kJ)
Salmon, 3 oz	0	5	16	110 kcal (460 kJ)
Steak, 3 oz	0	27	19	320 kcal (1350 kJ)

▶ **SAMPLE PROBLEM 3.6 Energy Content for a Food Using Nutrition Facts**

The Nutrition Facts label for crackers states that 1 serving contains 19 g of carbohydrate, 4 g of fat, and 2 g of protein. What is the energy from each food type and the total energy, in kilocalories, for one serving of crackers? Round off the kilocalories for each food type to the tens place.

SOLUTION

STEP 1 State the given and needed quantities.

	Given	**Need**
ANALYZE THE PROBLEM	carbohydrate, 19 g fat, 4 g protein, 2 g	kilocalories for each food type, total number of kilocalories

The Nutrition Facts include the total Calories and kilojoules, and the grams of carbohydrate, fat, and protein per serving.

Guide to Calculating the Energy from a Food

STEP 1
State the given and needed quantities.

STEP 2
Use the energy value for each food type and calculate the kcal or kJ rounded off to the tens place.

STEP 3
Add the energy for each food type to give the total energy from the food.

STEP 2 Use the energy value for each food type and calculate the kcal rounded off to the tens place. Using the energy values for carbohydrate, fat, and protein (see Table 3.7), we can calculate the energy for each type of food.

Food Type	Mass		Energy Value		Energy
Carbohydrate	19 g	×	$\dfrac{4 \text{ kcal}}{1 \text{ g}}$	=	80 kcal
Fat	4 g	×	$\dfrac{9 \text{ kcal}}{1 \text{ g}}$	=	40 kcal
Protein	2 g	×	$\dfrac{4 \text{ kcal}}{1 \text{ g}}$	=	10 kcal

STEP 3 Add the energy for each food type to give the total energy from the food.

Total energy = 80 kcal + 40 kcal + 10 kcal = 130 kcal

STUDY CHECK 3.6

a. Using the nutrition values for one serving of crackers in Sample Problem 3.6, calculate the energy, in kilojoules, for each food type. Round off the kilojoules for each food type to the tens place.
b. What is the total energy, in kilojoules, for one serving of crackers?

ANSWER

a. carbohydrate, 320 kJ; fat, 150 kJ; protein, 30 kJ
b. 500 kJ

Explore Your World

Counting Calories

Obtain a food item that has a Nutrition Facts label. From the information on the label, determine the number of grams of carbohydrate, fat, and protein in one serving. Using the energy values for each food type, calculate the total Calories (kilocalories) for one serving. (For most products, the kilocalories for each food type are rounded off to the tens place.)

Question

How does your total for the Calories (kilocalories) in one serving compare to the Calories (kilocalories) stated on the label for a single serving?

Chemistry Link to Health

Losing and Gaining Weight

The number of kilocalories or kilojoules needed in the daily diet of an adult depends on gender, age, and level of physical activity. Some typical levels of energy needs are given in Table 3.9.

A person gains weight when food intake exceeds energy output. The amount of food a person eats is regulated by the hunger center in the hypothalamus, which is located in the brain. Food intake is normally proportional to the nutrient stores in the body. If these nutrient stores are low, you feel hungry; if they are high, you do not feel like eating.

TABLE 3.9 Typical Energy Requirements for Adults

Gender	Age	Moderately Active kcal (kJ)	Highly Active kcal (kJ)
Female	19–30	2100 (8800)	2400 (10 000)
	31–50	2000 (8400)	2200 (9200)
Male	19–30	2700 (11 300)	3000 (12 600)
	31–50	2500 (10 500)	2900 (12 100)

A person loses weight when food intake is less than energy output. Many diet products contain cellulose, which has no nutritive value but provides bulk and makes you feel full. Some diet drugs depress the hunger center and must be used with caution, because they excite the nervous system and can elevate blood pressure. Because muscular exercise is an important way to expend energy, an increase in daily exercise aids weight loss. Table 3.10 lists some activities and the amount of energy they require.

One hour of swimming uses 2100 kJ of energy.

TABLE 3.10 Energy Expended by a 70.0-kg (154-lb) Adult

Activity	Energy (kcal/h)	Energy (kJ/h)
Sleeping	60	250
Sitting	100	420
Walking	200	840
Swimming	500	2100
Running	750	3100

QUESTIONS AND PROBLEMS

3.5 Energy and Nutrition

LEARNING GOAL Use the energy values to calculate the kilocalories (kcal) or kilojoules (kJ) for a food.

3.27 Calculate the kilocalories for each of the following:
  a. one stalk of celery that produces 125 kJ when burned in a calorimeter
  b. a waffle that produces 870. kJ when burned in a calorimeter

3.28 Calculate the kilocalories for each of the following:
  a. one cup of popcorn that produces 131 kJ when burned in a calorimeter
  b. a sample of butter that produces 23.4 kJ when burned in a calorimeter

3.29 Using the energy values for foods (see Table 3.7), determine each of the following (round off the answers in kilocalories or kilojoules to the tens place):
  a. the total kilojoules for one cup of orange juice that contains 26 g of carbohydrate, no fat, and 2 g of protein
  b. the grams of carbohydrate in one apple if the apple has no fat and no protein and provides 72 kcal of energy
  c. the kilocalories in one tablespoon of vegetable oil, which contains 14 g of fat and no carbohydrate or protein
  d. the grams of fat in one avocado that has 405 kcal, 13 g of carbohydrate, and 5 g of protein

3.30 Using the energy values for foods (see Table 3.7), determine each of the following (round off the answers in kilocalories or kilojoules to the tens place):
  a. the total kilojoules in two tablespoons of crunchy peanut butter that contains 6 g of carbohydrate, 16 g of fat, and 7 g of protein

  b. the grams of protein in one cup of soup that has 110 kcal with 9 g of carbohydrate and 6 g of fat
  c. the kilocalories in one can of cola if it has 40. g of carbohydrate and no fat or protein
  d. the total kilocalories for a diet that consists of 68 g of carbohydrate, 9 g of fat, and 150 g of protein

3.31 One cup of clam chowder contains 16 g of carbohydrate, 12 g of fat, and 9 g of protein. How much energy, in kilocalories and kilojoules, is in the clam chowder? (Round off the kilocalories and kilojoules to the tens place.)

3.32 A high-protein diet contains 70.0 g of carbohydrate, 5.0 g of fat, and 150 g of protein. How much energy, in kilocalories and kilojoules, does this diet provide? (Round off the kilocalories and kilojoules to the tens place.)

Rx **Clinical Applications**

3.33 A patient receives 3.2 L of glucose solution intravenously (IV). If 100. mL of the solution contains 5.0 g of glucose (carbohydrate), how many kilocalories did the patient obtain from the glucose solution?

3.34 For lunch, a patient consumed 3 oz of skinless chicken, 3 oz of broccoli, 1 medium apple, and 1 cup of nonfat milk (see Table 3.8). How many kilocalories did the patient obtain from the lunch?

3.6 Specific Heat

Every substance has its own characteristic ability to absorb heat. When you bake a potato, you place it in a hot oven. If you are cooking pasta, you add the pasta to boiling water. You already know that adding heat to water increases its temperature until it boils. Certain substances must absorb more heat than others to reach a certain temperature.

The energy requirements for different substances are described in terms of a physical property called *specific heat*. The **specific heat (SH)** for a substance is defined as the amount of heat needed to raise the temperature of exactly 1 g of a substance by exactly 1 °C. This temperature change is written as ΔT (*delta T*), where the delta symbol means "change in."

TABLE 3.11 Specific Heats for Some Substances

Substance	cal/g °C	J/g °C
Elements		
Aluminum, Al(s)	0.214	0.897
Copper, Cu(s)	0.0920	0.385
Gold, Au(s)	0.0308	0.129
Iron, Fe(s)	0.108	0.452
Silver, Ag(s)	0.0562	0.235
Titanium, Ti(s)	0.125	0.523
Compounds		
Ammonia, NH$_3$(g)	0.488	2.04
Ethanol, C$_2$H$_5$OH(l)	0.588	2.46
Sodium chloride, NaCl(s)	0.207	0.864
Water, H$_2$O(l)	1.00	4.184
Water, H$_2$O(s)	0.485	2.03

$$\text{Specific heat } (SH) = \frac{\text{heat}}{\text{grams} \times \Delta T} = \frac{\text{cal (or J)}}{\text{g °C}}$$

The specific heat for water is written using our definition of the calorie and joule.

$$SH \text{ for H}_2\text{O}(l) = \frac{1.00 \text{ cal}}{\text{g °C}} = \frac{4.184 \text{ J}}{\text{g °C}}$$

If we look at Table 3.11, we see that 1 g of water requires 1.00 cal or 4.184 J to increase its temperature by 1 °C. Water has a large specific heat that is about five times the specific heat of aluminum. Aluminum has a specific heat that is about twice that of copper. However, adding the same amount of heat (1.00 cal or 4.184 J) will raise the temperature of 1 g of aluminum by about 5 °C and 1 g of copper by about 10 °C. The low specific heats of aluminum and copper mean they transfer heat efficiently, which makes them useful in cookware.

The high specific heat of water has a major impact on the temperatures in a coastal city compared to an inland city. A large mass of water near a coastal city can absorb or release five times the energy absorbed or released by the same mass of rock near an inland city. This means that in the summer a body of water absorbs large quantities of heat, which cools a coastal city, and then in the winter that same body of water releases large quantities of heat, which provides warmer temperatures. A similar effect happens with our bodies, which contain 70% water by mass. Water in the body absorbs or releases large quantities of heat to maintain an almost constant body temperature.

The high specific heat of water keeps temperatures more moderate in summer and winter.

Calculations Using Specific Heat

When we know the specific heat of a substance, we can calculate the heat lost or gained by measuring the mass of the substance and the initial and final temperature. We can substitute these measurements into the specific heat expression that is rearranged to solve for heat, which we call the *heat equation*.

$$
\begin{array}{ccccc}
\text{Heat} = & \text{mass} & \times & \text{temperature change} & \times & \text{specific heat} \\
\text{Heat} = & m & \times & \Delta T & \times & SH \\
\text{cal} = & \cancel{g} & \times & \cancel{°C} & \times & \dfrac{\text{cal}}{\cancel{g}\ \cancel{°C}} \\
\text{J} = & \cancel{g} & \times & \cancel{°C} & \times & \dfrac{\text{J}}{\cancel{g}\ \cancel{°C}}
\end{array}
$$

A cooling cap lowers the body temperature to reduce the oxygen required by the tissues.

▶ **SAMPLE PROBLEM 3.7 Calculating Heat Loss**

During surgery or when a patient has suffered a cardiac arrest or stroke, lowering the body temperature will reduce the amount of oxygen needed by the body. Some methods used to lower body temperature include cooled saline solution, cool water blankets, or cooling caps worn on the head. How many kilojoules are lost when the body temperature of a surgery patient with a blood volume of 5500 mL is cooled from 38.5 °C to 33.2 °C? (Assume that the specific heat and density of blood is the same as for water.)

SOLUTION

STEP **1** State the given and needed quantities.

	Given	Need
ANALYZE THE PROBLEM	5500 mL of blood = 5500 g of blood, cooled from 38.5 °C to 33.2 °C	kilojoules removed

STEP **2** Calculate the temperature change (ΔT).

$\Delta T = 38.5\,°C - 33.2\,°C = 5.3\,°C$

STEP **3** Write the heat equation and needed conversion factors.

$\text{Heat} = m \times \Delta T \times SH$

$$SH_{water} = \frac{4.184\ \text{J}}{\text{g\ °C}} \qquad 1\ \text{kJ} = 1000\ \text{J}$$

$$\frac{4.184\ \text{J}}{\text{g\ °C}} \ \text{and} \ \frac{\text{g\ °C}}{4.184\ \text{J}} \qquad \frac{1000\ \text{J}}{1\ \text{kJ}} \ \text{and} \ \frac{1\ \text{kJ}}{1000\ \text{J}}$$

STEP **4** Substitute in the given values and calculate the heat, making sure units cancel.

$$\text{Heat} = 5500\ \text{g} \times 5.3\ °C \times \overset{\text{Exact}}{\frac{4.184\ \text{J}}{\text{g\ °C}}} \times \overset{\text{Exact}}{\frac{1\ \text{kJ}}{1000\ \text{J}}} = 120\ \text{kJ}$$

Two SFs Two SFs Exact Two SFs

STUDY CHECK 3.7

How many kilocalories are lost when 560 g of water cools from 67 °C to 22 °C?

ANSWER

25 kcal

Guide to Calculations Using Specific Heat

STEP **1**
State the given and needed quantities.

STEP **2**
Calculate the temperature change (ΔT).

STEP **3**
Write the heat equation and needed conversion factors.

STEP **4**
Substitute in the given values and calculate the heat, making sure units cancel.

QUESTIONS AND PROBLEMS

3.6 Specific Heat

LEARNING GOAL Use specific heat to calculate heat loss or gain.

3.35 If the same amount of heat is supplied to samples of 10.0 g each of aluminum, iron, and copper all at 15.0 °C, which sample would reach the highest temperature (see Table 3.11)?

3.36 Substances **A** and **B** are the same mass and at the same initial temperature. When they are heated, the final temperature of **A** is 55 °C higher than the temperature of **B**. What does this tell you about the specific heats of **A** and **B**?

3.37 Use the heat equation to calculate the energy for each of the following (see Table 3.11):
a. calories to heat 8.5 g of water from 15 °C to 36 °C
b. 2600 joules lost when 25 g of water cools from 86 °C to 61 °C
c. 9.3 kilocalories to heat 150 g of water from 15 °C to 77 °C
d. kilojoules to heat 175 g of copper from 28 °C to 188 °C

3.38 Use the heat equation to calculate the energy for each of the following (see Table 3.11):

a. calories lost when 85 g of water cools from 45 °C to 25 °C
b. joules to heat 75 g of water from 22 °C to 66 °C
c. kilocalories to heat 5.0 kg of water from 22 °C to 28 °C
d. kilojoules to heat 224 g of gold from 18 °C to 185 °C

3.39 Use the heat equation to calculate the energy, in joules and calories, for each of the following (see Table 3.11):
a. to heat 25.0 g of water from 12.5 °C to 25.7 °C
b. to heat 38.0 g of copper from 122 °C to 246 °C
c. lost when 15.0 g of ethanol, C_2H_5OH, cools from 60.5 °C to −42.0 °C
d. lost when 125 g of iron cools from 118 °C to 55 °C

3.40 Use the heat equation to calculate the energy, in joules and calories, for each of the following (see Table 3.11):
a. to heat 5.25 g of water from 5.5 °C to 64.8 °C
b. lost when 75.0 g of water cools from 86.4 °C to 2.1 °C
c. to heat 10.0 g of silver from 112 °C to 275 °C
d. lost when 18.0 g of gold cools from 224 °C to 118 °C

3.7 Changes of State

Matter undergoes a **change of state** when it is converted from one state to another state (see Figure 3.6).

LEARNING GOAL

Describe the changes of state between solids, liquids, and gases; calculate the energy involved.

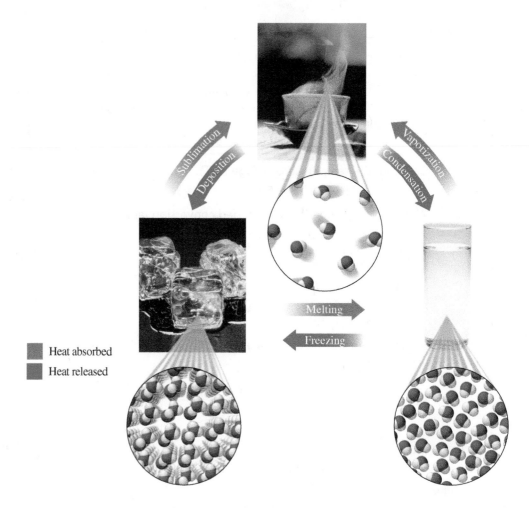

Heat absorbed

Heat released

FIGURE 3.6 ▶ Changes of state include melting and freezing, vaporization and condensation, sublimation and deposition.

Q Is heat added or released when liquid water freezes?

Solid   + Heat   Liquid
Melting
Freezing
− Heat

Melting and freezing are reversible processes.

Melting and Freezing

When heat is added to a solid, the particles move faster. At a temperature called the **melting point (mp)**, the particles of a solid gain sufficient energy to overcome the attractive forces that hold them together. The particles in the solid separate and move about in random patterns. The substance is **melting**, changing from a solid to a liquid.

If the temperature of a liquid is lowered, the reverse process takes place. Kinetic energy is lost, the particles slow down, and attractive forces pull the particles close together. The substance is **freezing**. A liquid changes to a solid at the **freezing point (fp)**, which is the same temperature as its melting point. Every substance has its own freezing (melting) point: Solid water (ice) melts at 0 °C when heat is added, and freezes at 0 °C when heat is removed. Gold melts at 1064 °C when heat is added, and freezes at 1064 °C when heat is removed.

During a change of state, the temperature of a substance remains constant. Suppose we have a glass containing ice and water. The ice melts when heat is added at 0 °C, forming more liquid. When heat is removed at 0 °C, the liquid water freezes, forming more solid. The process of melting requires heat; the process of freezing releases heat. Melting and freezing are reversible at 0 °C.

Heat of Fusion

During melting, the **heat of fusion** is the energy that must be added to convert exactly 1 g of solid to liquid at the melting point. For example, 80. cal (334 J) of heat is needed to melt exactly 1 g of ice at its melting point (0 °C).

$$H_2O(s) + 80.\ \text{cal/g (or 334 J/g)} \longrightarrow H_2O(l)$$

Heat of Fusion for Water

$$\frac{80.\ \text{cal}}{1\ \text{g}\ H_2O} \quad \text{and} \quad \frac{1\ \text{g}\ H_2O}{80.\ \text{cal}} \qquad \frac{334\ \text{J}}{1\ \text{g}\ H_2O} \quad \text{and} \quad \frac{1\ \text{g}\ H_2O}{334\ \text{J}}$$

The heat of fusion (80. cal/g or 334 J/g) is also the quantity of heat that must be removed to freeze exactly 1 g of water at its freezing point (0 °C).

Water is sometimes sprayed in fruit orchards during subfreezing weather. If the air temperature drops to 0 °C, the water begins to freeze. Because heat is released as the water molecules form solid ice, the air warms above 0 °C and protects the fruit.

$$H_2O(l) \longrightarrow H_2O(s) + 80.\,cal/g\ (or\ 334\,J/g)$$

The heat of fusion can be used as a conversion factor in calculations. For example, to determine the heat needed to melt a sample of ice, the mass of ice, in grams, is multiplied by the heat of fusion. Because the temperature remains constant as long as the ice is melting, there is no temperature change given in the calculation, as shown in Sample Problem 3.8.

Calculating Heat to Melt (or Freeze) Water

Heat = mass × heat of fusion

$$cal = g \times \frac{80.\,cal}{g} \qquad J = g \times \frac{334\,J}{g}$$

SAMPLE PROBLEM 3.8 **Heat of Fusion**

Ice bag therapy is used by sports trainers to treat muscle injuries. If 260. g of ice are placed in an ice bag, how much heat, in joules, will be absorbed to melt all the ice at 0 °C?

An ice bag is used to treat a sports injury.

SOLUTION

STEP 1 State the given and needed quantities.

ANALYZE THE PROBLEM	Given	Need
	260. g of ice at 0 °C, heat of fusion = 334 J/g	joules to melt ice at 0 °C

STEP 2 Write a plan to convert the given quantity to the needed quantity.

grams of ice → Heat of fusion → joules

STEP 3 Write the heat conversion factor and any metric factor.

$$1\,g\ of\ H_2O(s \rightarrow l) = 334\,J$$

$$\frac{334\,J}{1\,g\,H_2O} \quad and \quad \frac{1\,g\,H_2O}{334\,J}$$

STEP 4 Set up the problem and calculate the needed quantity.

Three SFs

$$260.\ g\,H_2O \times \frac{334\,J}{1\,g\,H_2O} = 86\,800\,J\ (8.68 \times 10^4\,J)$$

Three SFs   Exact   Three SFs

STUDY CHECK 3.8

In a freezer, 150 g of water at 0 °C is placed in an ice cube tray. How much heat, in kilocalories, must be removed to form ice cubes at 0 °C?

ANSWER

12 kcal

Guide to Using a Heat Conversion Factor

STEP 1 State the given and needed quantities.

STEP 2 Write a plan to convert the given quantity to the needed quantity.

STEP 3 Write the heat conversion factor and any metric factor.

STEP 4 Set up the problem and calculate the needed quantity.

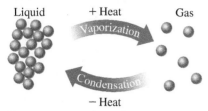

Liquid   + Heat   Gas

Vaporization

Condensation

− Heat

Vaporization and condensation are reversible processes.

Evaporation, Boiling, and Condensation

Water in a mud puddle disappears, unwrapped food dries out, and clothes hung on a line dry. **Evaporation** is taking place as water molecules with sufficient energy escape from the liquid surface and enter the gas phase (see Figure 3.7a). The loss of the "hot" water molecules removes heat, which cools the remaining liquid water. As heat is added, more and more water molecules gain sufficient energy to evaporate. At the **boiling point (bp)**, the molecules within a liquid have enough energy to overcome their attractive forces and become a gas. We observe the **boiling** of a liquid such as water as gas bubbles form throughout the liquid, rise to the surface, and escape (see Figure 3.7b).

When heat is removed, a reverse process takes place. In **condensation**, water vapor is converted back to liquid as the water molecules lose kinetic energy and slow down. Condensation occurs at the same temperature as boiling but differs because heat is removed. You may have noticed that condensation occurs when you take a hot shower and the water vapor forms water droplets on a mirror. Because a substance loses heat as it condenses, its surroundings become warmer. That is why, when a rainstorm is approaching, you may notice a warming of the air as gaseous water molecules condense to rain.

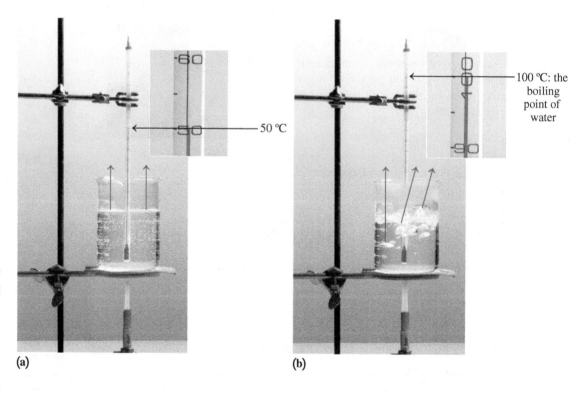

FIGURE 3.7 ▶ **(a)** Evaporation occurs at the surface of a liquid. **(b)** Boiling occurs as bubbles of gas form throughout the liquid.

❓ Why does water evaporate faster at 85 °C than at 15 °C?

50 °C

100 °C: the boiling point of water

(a)   **(b)**

Dry ice sublimes at −78 °C.

Sublimation

In a process called **sublimation**, the particles on the surface of a solid change directly to a gas with no temperature change and without going through the liquid state. In the reverse process called **deposition**, gas particles change directly to a solid. For example, dry ice, which is solid carbon dioxide, sublimes at −78 °C. It is called "dry" because it does not form a liquid as it warms. In extremely cold areas, snow does not melt but sublimes directly to water vapor.

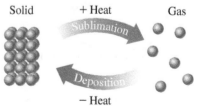

Solid   + Heat   Gas

Sublimation

Deposition

− Heat

Sublimation and deposition are reversible processes.

When frozen foods are left in the freezer for a long time, so much water sublimes that foods, especially meats, become dry and shrunken, a condition called *freezer burn*. Deposition occurs in a freezer when water vapor forms ice crystals on the surface of freezer bags and frozen food.

Freeze-dried foods prepared by sublimation are convenient for long-term storage and for camping and hiking. A food that has been frozen is placed in a vacuum chamber where it dries as the ice sublimes. The dried food retains all of its nutritional value and needs only water to be edible. A food that is freeze-dried does not need refrigeration because bacteria cannot grow without moisture.

Water vapor will change to solid on contact with a cold surface.

Heat of Vaporization

The **heat of vaporization** is the energy that must be added to convert exactly 1 g of liquid to gas at its boiling point. For water, 540 cal (2260 J) is needed to convert 1 g of water to vapor at 100 °C.

$$H_2O(l) + 540 \text{ cal/g (or 2260 J/g)} \longrightarrow H_2O(g)$$

This same amount of heat is released when 1 g of water vapor (gas) changes to liquid at 100 °C.

$$H_2O(g) \longrightarrow H_2O(l) + 540 \text{ cal/g (or 2260 J/g)}$$

Therefore, 2260 J/g or 540 cal/g is also the *heat of condensation* of water.

Freeze-dried foods have a long shelf life because they contain no water.

Heat of Vaporization for Water

$$\frac{540 \text{ cal}}{1 \text{ g H}_2\text{O}} \quad \text{and} \quad \frac{1 \text{ g H}_2\text{O}}{540 \text{ cal}} \qquad \frac{2260 \text{ J}}{1 \text{ g H}_2\text{O}} \quad \text{and} \quad \frac{1 \text{ g H}_2\text{O}}{2260 \text{ J}}$$

To determine the heat needed to boil a sample of water, the mass, in grams, is multiplied by the heat of vaporization. Because the temperature remains constant as long as the water is boiling, there is no temperature change given in the calculation, as shown in Sample Problem 3.9.

Calculating Heat to Vaporize (or Condense) Water

Heat = mass × heat of vaporization

$$\text{cal} = \cancel{g} \times \frac{540 \text{ cal}}{\cancel{g}} \qquad\qquad J = \cancel{g} \times \frac{2260 \text{ J}}{\cancel{g}}$$

▶ **SAMPLE PROBLEM 3.9 Using Heat of Vaporization**

In a sauna, 122 g of water is converted to steam at 100 °C. How many kilojoules of heat are needed?

SOLUTION

STEP **1** State the given and needed quantities.

ANALYZE THE PROBLEM	Given	Need
	122 g of water at 100 °C, heat of vaporization = 2260 J/g	kilojoules to convert to steam at 100 °C

STEP **2** Write a plan to convert the given quantity to the needed quantity.

grams of water → Heat of vaporization → joules → Metric factor → kilojoules

STEP **3** Write the heat conversion factor and any metric factor.

$$1 \text{ g of H}_2\text{O}(l \rightarrow g) = 2260 \text{ J} \qquad\qquad 1 \text{ kJ} = 1000 \text{ J}$$

$$\frac{2260 \text{ J}}{1 \text{ g H}_2\text{O}} \quad \text{and} \quad \frac{1 \text{ g H}_2\text{O}}{2260 \text{ J}} \qquad\qquad \frac{1000 \text{ J}}{1 \text{ kJ}} \quad \text{and} \quad \frac{1 \text{ kJ}}{1000 \text{ J}}$$

STEP **4**   Set up the problem and calculate the needed quantity.

$$122 \text{ g H}_2\text{O} \times \frac{2260 \text{ J}}{1 \text{ g H}_2\text{O}} \times \frac{1 \text{ kJ}}{1000 \text{ J}} = 276 \text{ kJ}$$

Three SFs ··· Three SFs ··· Exact ··· Exact ··· Three SFs

STUDY CHECK 3.9

When steam from a pan of boiling water reaches a cool window, it condenses. How much heat, in kilojoules, is released when 25.0 g of steam condenses at 100 °C?

ANSWER

56.5 kJ released

Chemistry Link to Health

Steam Burns

Hot water at 100 °C will cause burns and damage to the skin. However, getting steam on the skin is even more dangerous. If 25 g of hot water at 100 °C falls on a person's skin, the temperature of the water will drop to body temperature, 37 °C. The heat released during cooling can cause severe burns. The amount of heat can be calculated from the mass, the temperature change, 100 °C − 37 °C = 63 °C, and the specific heat of water, 4.184 J/g °C.

$$25 \text{ g} \times 63 \text{ °C} \times \frac{4.184 \text{ J}}{\text{g °C}} = 6600 \text{ J of heat released when water cools}$$

However, getting steam on the skin is even more damaging. The condensation of the same quantity of steam to liquid at 100 °C releases much more heat—almost ten times as much. This amount of heat can be calculated using the heat of vaporization, which is 2260 J/g for water at 100 °C.

$$25 \text{ g} \times \frac{2260 \text{ J}}{1 \text{ g}} = 57\,000 \text{ J released when water (gas) condenses to water (liquid) at 100 °C}$$

The total heat released is calculated by combining the heat from the condensation at 100 °C and the heat from cooling of the steam from 100 °C to 37 °C (body temperature). We can see that most of the heat is from the condensation of steam. This large amount of heat released on the skin is what causes damage from steam burns.

Condensation (100 °C)	= 57 000 J
Cooling (100 °C to 37 °C) =	6 600 J
Heat released	= 64 000 J (rounded off)

The amount of heat released from steam is almost ten times greater than the heat from the same amount of hot water.

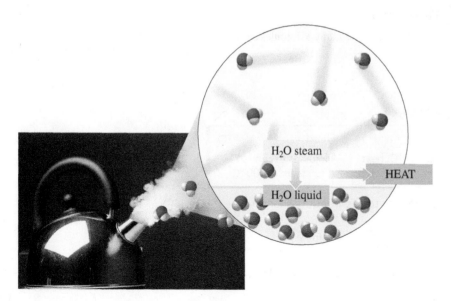

When 1 g of steam condenses, 2260 J is released.

Heating and Cooling Curves

All the changes of state during the heating or cooling of a substance can be illustrated visually. On a **heating curve** or **cooling curve**, the temperature is shown on the vertical axis and the loss or gain of heat is shown on the horizontal axis.

Steps on a Heating Curve

The first diagonal line indicates a warming of a solid as heat is added. When the melting temperature is reached, a horizontal line, or plateau, indicates that the solid is melting. As melting takes place, the solid is changing to liquid without any change in temperature (see Figure 3.8).

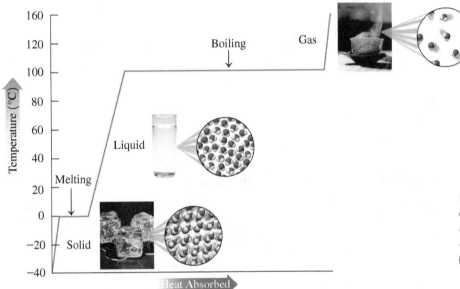

FIGURE 3.8 ▶ A heating curve diagrams the temperature increases and changes of state as heat is added.

ⓠ What does the plateau at 100 °C represent on the heating curve for water?

Once all the particles are in the liquid state, heat that is added will increase the temperature of the liquid. This increase is drawn as a diagonal line from the melting point temperature to the boiling point temperature. Once the liquid reaches its boiling point, a horizontal line indicates that the temperature is constant as liquid changes to gas. Because the heat of vaporization is greater than the heat of fusion, the horizontal line at the boiling point is longer than the line at the melting point. Once all the liquid becomes gas, adding more heat increases the temperature of the gas.

Steps on a Cooling Curve

A cooling curve is a diagram of the cooling process in which the temperature decreases as heat is removed. Initially, a diagonal line to the boiling (condensation) point is drawn to show that heat is removed from a gas until it begins to condense. At the boiling (condensation) point, a horizontal line is drawn that indicates a change of state as gas condenses to form a liquid. After all the gas has changed into liquid, further cooling lowers the temperature. The decrease in temperature is shown as a diagonal line from the condensation temperature to the freezing temperature. At the freezing point, another horizontal line indicates that liquid is changing to solid at the freezing point temperature. Once all the substance is frozen, the removal of more heat decreases the temperature of the solid below its freezing point, which is shown as a diagonal line below its freezing point.

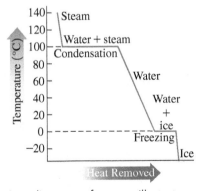

A cooling curve for water illustrates the change in temperature and changes of state as heat is removed.

▶ **SAMPLE PROBLEM 3.10 Using a Cooling Curve**

Using the cooling curve for water, identify the state or change of state for water as solid, liquid, gas, condensation, or freezing.

a. at 120 °C   **b.** at 100 °C   **c.** at 40 °C

SOLUTION

a. A temperature of 120 °C occurs on the diagonal line above the boiling (condensation) point, which indicates that water is a gas.

b. A temperature of 100 °C, shown as a horizontal line, indicates that the water vapor is changing to liquid water, or condensing.

c. A temperature of 40 °C occurs on the diagonal line below the boiling point but above the freezing point, which indicates that the water is in the liquid state.

STUDY CHECK 3.10

Using the cooling curve for water, identify the state or change of state for water as solid, liquid, gas, condensation, or freezing.

a. at 0 °C   **b.** at −20 °C

ANSWER

a. freezing   **b.** solid

Combining Energy Calculations

Up to now, we have calculated one step in a heating or cooling curve. However, many problems require a combination of steps that include a temperature change as well as a change of state. The heat is calculated for each step separately and then added together to find the total energy, as seen in Sample Problem 3.11.

▶ **SAMPLE PROBLEM 3.11 Combining Heat Calculations**

Charles has increased his activity by doing more exercise. After a session of using small weights, he has a sore arm. An ice bag is filled with 125 g of ice at 0.0 °C. The heat of fusion for ice is 334 J/g. How much heat, in kilojoules, is absorbed to melt the ice, and to raise the temperature of the water to body temperature, 37.0 °C?

SOLUTION

STEP 1 State the given and needed quantities.

	Given	Need
ANALYZE THE PROBLEM	125 g of ice at 0.0 °C, heat of fusion of ice = 334 J/g	total kilojoules to melt ice at 0.0 °C and to raise temperature of water to 37.0 °C

STEP 2 Write a plan to convert the given quantity to the needed quantity.

Total heat = kilojoules needed to melt the ice and heat the water from 0.0 °C (freezing point) to 37.0 °C

STEP 3 Write the heat conversion factor and any metric factor.

$$1 \text{ g of } H_2O(s \rightarrow l) = 334 \text{ J} \qquad SH_{water} = \frac{4.184 \text{ J}}{\text{g °C}} \qquad 1 \text{ kJ} = 1000 \text{ J}$$

$$\frac{334 \text{ J}}{1 \text{ g } H_2O} \text{ and } \frac{1 \text{ g } H_2O}{334 \text{ J}} \qquad \frac{4.184 \text{ J}}{\text{g °C}} \text{ and } \frac{\text{g °C}}{4.184 \text{ J}} \qquad \frac{1000 \text{ J}}{1 \text{ kJ}} \text{ and } \frac{1 \text{ kJ}}{1000 \text{ J}}$$

STEP **4** Set up the problem and calculate the needed quantity.
$$\Delta T = 37.0\,^{\circ}\text{C} - 0.0\,^{\circ}\text{C} = 37.0\,^{\circ}\text{C}$$

Heat needed to change ice (solid) to water (liquid) at 0.0 °C:

Three SFs   Exact

$$125\text{ g ice} \times \frac{334\text{ J}}{1\text{ g ice}} \times \frac{1\text{ kJ}}{1000\text{ J}} = 41.8\text{ kJ}$$

Three SFs   Exact   Exact   Three SFs

Heat needed to warm water (liquid) from 0.0 °C to water (liquid) at 37.0 °C:

Exact   Exact

$$125\text{ g} \times 37.0\,^{\circ}\text{C} \times \frac{4.184\text{ J}}{\text{g}\,^{\circ}\text{C}} \times \frac{1\text{ kJ}}{1000\text{ J}} = 19.4\text{ kJ}$$

Three SFs   Three SFs   Exact   Three SFs

Calculate the total heat:

Melting ice at 0.0 °C	41.8 kJ
Heating water (0.0 °C to 37.0 °C)	19.4 kJ
Total heat needed	61.2 kJ

STUDY CHECK 3.11

How many kilojoules are released when 75.0 g of steam at 100 °C condenses, cools to 0 °C, and freezes at 0 °C? (*Hint*: The solution will require three energy calculations.)

ANSWER

226 kJ

QUESTIONS AND PROBLEMS

3.7 Changes of State

LEARNING GOAL Describe the changes of state between solids, liquids, and gases; calculate the energy involved.

3.41 Identify each of the following changes of state as melting, freezing, sublimation, or deposition:
 a. The solid structure of a substance breaks down as liquid forms.
 b. Coffee is freeze-dried.
 c. Water on the street turns to ice during a cold wintry night.
 d. Ice crystals form on a package of frozen corn.

3.42 Identify each of the following changes of state as melting, freezing, sublimation, or deposition:
 a. Dry ice in an ice-cream cart disappears.
 b. Snow on the ground turns to liquid water.
 c. Heat is removed from 125 g of liquid water at 0 °C.
 d. Frost (ice) forms on the walls of a freezer unit of a refrigerator.

3.43 Calculate the heat change at 0 °C for each of the following, and indicate whether heat was absorbed or released:
 a. calories to melt 65 g of ice
 b. joules to melt 17.0 g of ice
 c. kilocalories to freeze 225 g of water
 d. kilojoules to freeze 50.0 g of water

3.44 Calculate the heat change at 0 °C for each of the following, and indicate whether heat was absorbed or released:
 a. calories to freeze 35 g of water
 b. joules to freeze 275 g of water
 c. kilocalories to melt 140 g of ice
 d. kilojoules to melt 5.00 g of ice

3.45 Identify each of the following changes of state as evaporation, boiling, or condensation:
 a. The water vapor in the clouds changes to rain.
 b. Wet clothes dry on a clothesline.
 c. Lava flows into the ocean and steam forms.
 d. After a hot shower, your bathroom mirror is covered with water.

3.46 Identify each of the following changes of state as evaporation, boiling, or condensation:
 a. At 100 °C, the water in a pan changes to steam.
 b. On a cool morning, the windows in your car fog up.
 c. A shallow pond dries up in the summer.
 d. Your teakettle whistles when the water is ready for tea.

3.47 Calculate the heat change at 100 °C for each of the following, and indicate whether heat was absorbed or released:
 a. calories to vaporize 10.0 g of water
 b. joules to vaporize 5.00 g of water
 c. kilocalories to condense 8.0 kg of steam
 d. kilojoules to condense 175 g of steam

3.48 Calculate the heat change at 100 °C for each of the following, and indicate whether heat was absorbed or released:
 a. calories to condense 10.0 g of steam
 b. joules to condense 7.60 g of steam
 c. kilocalories to vaporize 44 g of water
 d. kilojoules to vaporize 5.00 kg of water

3.49 Draw a heating curve for a sample of ice that is heated from −20 °C to 150 °C. Indicate the segment of the graph that corresponds to each of the following:
a. solid
b. melting
c. liquid
d. boiling
e. gas

3.50 Draw a cooling curve for a sample of steam that cools from 110 °C to −10 °C. Indicate the segment of the graph that corresponds to each of the following:
a. solid
b. freezing
c. liquid
d. condensation
e. gas

3.51 Using the values for the heat of fusion, specific heat of water, and/or heat of vaporization, calculate the amount of heat energy in each of the following:
a. joules needed to melt 50.0 g of ice at 0 °C and to warm the liquid to 65.0 °C
b. kilocalories released when 15.0 g of steam condenses at 100 °C and the liquid cools to 0 °C
c. kilojoules needed to melt 24.0 g of ice at 0 °C, warm the liquid to 100 °C, and change it to steam at 100 °C

3.52 Using the values for the heat of fusion, specific heat of water, and/or heat of vaporization, calculate the amount of heat energy in each of the following:
a. joules released when 125 g of steam at 100 °C condenses and cools to liquid at 15.0 °C
b. kilocalories needed to melt a 525-g ice sculpture at 0 °C and to warm the liquid to 15.0 °C
c. kilojoules released when 85.0 g of steam condenses at 100 °C, cools, and freezes at 0 °C

Rx Clinical Applications

3.53 A patient arrives in the emergency room with a burn caused by steam. Calculate the heat, in kilocalories, that is released when 18.0 g of steam at 100. °C hits the skin, condenses, and cools to body temperature of 37.0 °C.

3.54 A sports trainer applies an ice bag to the back of an injured athlete. Calculate the heat, in kilocalories, that is absorbed if 145 g of ice at 0.0 °C is placed in an ice bag, melts, and rises to body temperature of 37.0 °C.

Clinical Update
A Diet and Exercise Program for Charles

It has been two weeks since Charles met with Daniel, a dietitian, who provided Charles with a menu for weight loss. Charles and his mother are going back to see Daniel again with a chart of the food Charles has eaten. The following is what Charles ate in one day:

Breakfast
1 banana, 1 cup of nonfat milk, 1 egg

Lunch
1 cup of carrots, 3 oz of ground beef, 1 apple, 1 cup of nonfat milk

Dinner
6 oz of skinless chicken, 1 baked potato, 3 oz of broccoli, 1 cup of nonfat milk

Rx Clinical Applications

3.55 Using energy values from Table 3.8, determine each of the following:
a. the total kilocalories for each meal
b. the total kilocalories for one day
c. If Charles consumes 1800 kcal per day, he will maintain his weight. Would he lose weight on his new diet?
d. If the loss of 3500 kcal is equal to a loss of 1.0 lb, how many days will it take Charles to lose 5.0 lb?

3.56 a. During one week, Charles swam for a total of 2.5 h and walked for a total of 8.0 h. If Charles expends 340 kcal/h swimming and 160 kcal/h walking, how many total kilocalories did he expend for one week?
b. For the amount of exercise that Charles did for one week in part a, how much weight, in pounds, did he lose?
c. How many hours would Charles have to walk to lose 1.0 lb?
d. How many hours would Charles have to swim to lose 1.0 lb?

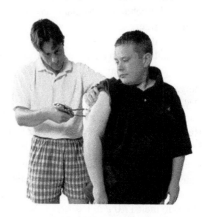

MATTER AND ENERGY

Matter		Energy

Matter — has states of —
Energy — affects —

Solid	Liquid	Gas	Particle Motion

can be (Solid/Liquid) — *undergo* (Gas) — *as* (Particle Motion)

Pure Substances	Mixtures	Changes of State	Heat

that are — *that are* — *gain/loss of heat during* — *measured in*

Elements	Homogeneous	Melting or Freezing	Calories or Joules

or — *or* — — *using*

Compounds	Heterogeneous	Boiling or Condensation	Temperature Change

require — Specific Heat

		Heat of Fusion	Mass

		Heat of Vaporization	

are drawn as a

Heating or Cooling Curve

CHAPTER REVIEW

3.1 Classification of Matter
LEARNING GOAL Classify examples of matter as pure substances or mixtures.

- Matter is anything that has mass and occupies space.
- Matter is classified as pure substances or mixtures.
- Pure substances, which are elements or compounds, have fixed compositions, and mixtures have variable compositions.
- The substances in mixtures can be separated using physical methods.

3.2 States and Properties of Matter
LEARNING GOAL Identify the states and the physical and chemical properties of matter.

- The three states of matter are solid, liquid, and gas.
- A physical property is a characteristic of a substance in that it can be observed or measured without affecting the identity of the substance.
- A physical change occurs when physical properties change, but not the composition of the substance.
- A chemical property indicates the ability of a substance to change into another substance.
- A chemical change occurs when one or more substances react to form a substance with new physical and chemical properties.

3.3 Temperature

LEARNING GOAL Given a temperature, calculate a corresponding temperature on another scale.

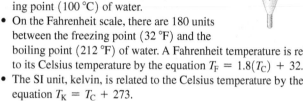

- In science, temperature is measured in degrees Celsius (°C) or kelvins (**K**).
- On the Celsius scale, there are 100 units between the freezing point (0 °C) and the boiling point (100 °C) of water.
- On the Fahrenheit scale, there are 180 units between the freezing point (32 °F) and the boiling point (212 °F) of water. A Fahrenheit temperature is related to its Celsius temperature by the equation $T_F = 1.8(T_C) + 32$.
- The SI unit, kelvin, is related to the Celsius temperature by the equation $T_K = T_C + 273$.

3.4 Energy

LEARNING GOAL Identify energy as potential or kinetic; convert between units of energy.

- Energy is the ability to do work.
- Potential energy is stored energy; kinetic energy is the energy of motion.
- Common units of energy are the calorie (cal), kilocalorie (kcal), joule (J), and kilojoule (kJ).
- One calorie is equal to 4.184 J.

3.5 Energy and Nutrition

LEARNING GOAL Use the energy values to calculate the kilocalories (kcal) or kilojoules (kJ) for a food.

- The nutritional Calorie is the same amount of energy as 1 kcal or 1000 calories.
- The energy of a food is the sum of kilocalories or kilojoules from carbohydrate, fat, and protein.

3.6 Specific Heat

LEARNING GOAL Use specific heat to calculate heat loss or gain.

- Specific heat is the amount of energy required to raise the temperature of exactly 1 g of a substance by exactly 1 °C.
- The heat lost or gained by a substance is determined by multiplying its mass, the temperature change, and its specific heat.

3.7 Changes of State

LEARNING GOAL Describe the changes of state between solids, liquids, and gases; calculate the energy involved.

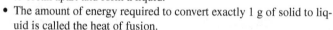

- Melting occurs when the particles in a solid absorb enough energy to break apart and form a liquid.
- The amount of energy required to convert exactly 1 g of solid to liquid is called the heat of fusion.
- For water, 80. cal (334 J) is needed to melt 1 g of ice or must be removed to freeze 1 g of water.
- Evaporation occurs when particles in a liquid state absorb enough energy to break apart and form gaseous particles.
- Boiling is the vaporization of liquid at its boiling point. The heat of vaporization is the amount of heat needed to convert exactly 1 g of liquid to vapor.
- For water, 540 cal (2260 J) is needed to vaporize 1 g of water or must be removed to condense 1 g of steam.
- A heating or cooling curve illustrates the changes in temperature and state as heat is added to or removed from a substance. Plateaus on the graph indicate changes of state.
- The total heat absorbed or removed from a substance undergoing temperature changes and changes of state is the sum of energy calculations for change(s) of state and change(s) in temperature.
- Sublimation is a process whereby a solid changes directly to a gas.

KEY TERMS

boiling The formation of bubbles of gas throughout a liquid.

boiling point (bp) The temperature at which a liquid changes to gas (boils) and gas changes to liquid (condenses).

calorie (cal) The amount of heat energy that raises the temperature of exactly 1 g of water by exactly 1 °C.

change of state The transformation of one state of matter to another; for example, solid to liquid, liquid to solid, liquid to gas.

chemical change A change during which the original substance is converted into a new substance that has a different composition and new physical and chemical properties.

chemical properties The properties that indicate the ability of a substance to change into a new substance.

compound A pure substance consisting of two or more elements, with a definite composition, that can be broken down into simpler substances only by chemical methods.

condensation The change of state from a gas to a liquid.

cooling curve A diagram that illustrates temperature changes and changes of state for a substance as heat is removed.

deposition The change of a gas directly into a solid; the reverse of sublimation.

element A pure substance containing only one type of matter, which cannot be broken down by chemical methods.

energy The ability to do work.

energy value The kilocalories (or kilojoules) obtained per gram of the food types: carbohydrate, fat, and protein.

evaporation The formation of a gas (vapor) by the escape of high-energy molecules from the surface of a liquid.

freezing The change of state from liquid to solid.

freezing point (fp) The temperature at which a liquid changes to a solid (freezes), a solid changes to a liquid (melts).

gas A state of matter that does not have a definite shape or volume.

heat The energy associated with the motion of particles in a substance.

heat of fusion The energy required to melt exactly 1 g of a substance at its melting point. For water, 80. cal (334 J) is needed to melt 1 g of ice; 80. cal (334 J) is released when 1 g of water freezes.

heat of vaporization The energy required to vaporize exactly 1 g of a substance at its boiling point. For water, 540 cal (2260 J) is needed to vaporize 1 g of liquid; 1 g of steam gives off 540 cal (2260 J) when it condenses.

heating curve A diagram that illustrates the temperature changes and changes of state of a substance as it is heated.

joule (J) The SI unit of heat energy; 4.184 J = 1 cal.

kinetic energy The energy of moving particles.

liquid A state of matter that takes the shape of its container but has a definite volume.

matter The material that makes up a substance and has mass and occupies space.

melting The change of state from a solid to a liquid.

melting point (mp) The temperature at which a solid becomes a liquid (melts). It is the same temperature as the freezing point.

mixture The physical combination of two or more substances that does not change the identities of the mixed substances.

physical change A change in which the physical properties of a substance change but its identity stays the same.

physical properties The properties that can be observed or measured without affecting the identity of a substance.

potential energy A type of energy related to position or composition of a substance.

pure substance A type of matter that has a definite composition.

solid A state of matter that has its own shape and volume.

specific heat (*SH*) A quantity of heat that changes the temperature of exactly 1 g of a substance by exactly 1 °C.

states of matter Three forms of matter: solid, liquid, and gas.

sublimation The change of state in which a solid is transformed directly to a gas without forming a liquid first.

⚛ CORE CHEMISTRY SKILLS

The chapter section containing each Core Chemistry Skill is shown in parentheses at the end of each heading.

Classifying Matter (3.1)

- A pure substance is matter that has a fixed or constant composition.
- An element, the simplest type of a pure substance, is composed of only one type of matter, such as silver, iron, or aluminum.
- A compound is also a pure substance, but it consists of two or more elements chemically combined in the same proportion.
- In a *homogeneous mixture*, also called a *solution*, the composition of the substances in the mixture is uniform.
- In a *heterogeneous mixture*, the components are visible and do not have a uniform composition throughout the sample.

Example: Classify each of the following as a pure substance (element or compound) or a mixture (homogeneous or heterogeneous):
   a. iron in a nail
   b. black coffee
   c. carbon dioxide, a greenhouse gas

Answer: **a.** Iron is a pure substance, which is an element.
   b. Black coffee contains different substances with uniform composition, which makes it a homogeneous mixture.
   c. The gas carbon dioxide, which is a pure substance that contains two elements chemically combined, is a compound.

Identifying Physical and Chemical Changes (3.2)

- When matter undergoes a physical change, its state or its appearance changes, but its composition remains the same.
- When a chemical change takes place, the original substance is converted into a new substance, which has different physical and chemical properties.

Example: Classify each of the following as a physical or chemical property:
   a. Helium in a balloon is a gas.
   b. Methane, in natural gas, burns.
   c. Hydrogen sulfide smells like rotten eggs.

Answer: **a.** A gas is a state of matter, which makes it a physical property.
   b. When methane burns, it changes to different substances with new properties, which is a chemical property.
   c. The odor of hydrogen sulfide is a physical property.

Converting between Temperature Scales (3.3)

- The temperature equation $T_F = 1.8(T_C) + 32$ is used to convert from Celsius to Fahrenheit and can be rearranged to convert from Fahrenheit to Celsius.
- The temperature equation $T_K = T_C + 273$ is used to convert from Celsius to Kelvin and can be rearranged to convert from Kelvin to Celsius.

Example: Convert 75.0 °C to degrees Fahrenheit.

Answer: $T_F = 1.8(T_C) + 32$
   $T_F = 1.8(75.0) + 32 = 135 + 32$
   $= 167 °F$

Example: Convert 355 K to degrees Celsius.

Answer: $T_K = T_C + 273$
   To solve the equation for T_C, subtract 273 from both sides.
   $T_K - 273 = T_C + 273 - 273$
   $T_C = T_K - 273$
   $T_C = 355 - 273$
   $= 82 °C$

Using Energy Units (3.4)

- Equalities for energy units include 1 cal = 4.184 J, 1 kcal = 1000 cal, and 1 kJ = 1000 J.
- Each equality for energy units can be written as two conversion factors:

$$\frac{4.184 \text{ J}}{1 \text{ cal}} \text{ and } \frac{1 \text{ cal}}{4.184 \text{ J}} \quad \frac{1000 \text{ cal}}{1 \text{ kcal}} \text{ and } \frac{1 \text{ kcal}}{1000 \text{ cal}} \quad \frac{1000 \text{ J}}{1 \text{ kJ}} \text{ and } \frac{1 \text{ kJ}}{1000 \text{ J}}$$

- The energy unit conversion factors are used to cancel given units of energy and to obtain the needed unit of energy.

Example: Convert 45 000 J to kilocalories.

Answer: Using the conversion factors above, we start with the given 45 000 J and convert it to kilocalories.

$$45\,000 \text{ J} \times \frac{1 \text{ cal}}{4.184 \text{ J}} \times \frac{1 \text{ kcal}}{1000 \text{ cal}} = 11 \text{ kcal}$$

Using the Heat Equation (3.6)

- The quantity of heat absorbed or lost by a substance is calculated using the heat equation.

    Heat $= m \times \Delta T \times SH$

- Heat, in joules, is obtained when the specific heat of a substance in J/g °C is used.
- To cancel, the unit grams is used for mass, and the unit °C is used for temperature change.

Example: How many joules are required to heat 5.25 g of titanium from 85.5 °C to 132.5 °C?

Answer: $m = 5.25$ g, $\Delta T = 132.5\,°C - 85.5\,°C = 47.0\,°C$
SH for titanium $= 0.523$ J/g °C

The known values are substituted into the heat equation making sure units cancel.

$$\text{Heat} = m \times \Delta T \times SH = 5.25\ \cancel{g} \times 47.0\ \cancel{°C} \times \frac{0.523\ \text{J}}{\cancel{g}\ \cancel{°C}}$$

$$= 129\ \text{J}$$

UNDERSTANDING THE CONCEPTS

The chapter sections to review are shown in parentheses at the end of each question.

3.57 Identify each of the following as an element, a compound, or a mixture. Explain your choice. (3.1)

a. b.

c.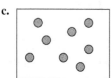

3.58 Identify each of the following as a homogeneous or heterogeneous mixture. Explain your choice. (3.1)

a. 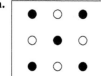 b.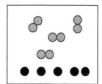

c.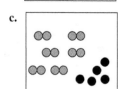

3.59 Classify each of the following as a homogeneous or heterogeneous mixture: (3.1)
 a. lemon-flavored water
 b. stuffed mushrooms
 c. eye drops

3.60 Classify each of the following as a homogeneous or heterogeneous mixture: (3.1)
 a. ketchup b. hard-boiled egg c. tortilla soup

3.61 State the temperature on the Celsius thermometer and convert to Fahrenheit. (3.3)

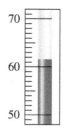

3.62 State the temperature on the Celsius thermometer and convert to Fahrenheit. (3.3)

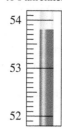

3.63 Compost can be made at home from grass clippings, some kitchen scraps, and dry leaves. As microbes break down organic matter, heat is generated and the compost can reach a temperature of 155 °F, which kills most pathogens. What is this temperature in degrees Celsius? In kelvins? (3.3)

Compost produced from decayed plant material is used to enrich the soil.

3.64 After a week, biochemical reactions in compost slow, and the temperature drops to 45 °C. The dark brown organic-rich mixture is ready for use in the garden. What is this temperature in degrees Fahrenheit? In kelvins? (3.3)

3.65 Calculate the energy to heat two cubes (gold and aluminum) each with a volume of 10.0 cm³ from 15 °C to 25 °C. Refer to Tables 2.9 and 3.11. (3.6)

3.66 Calculate the energy to heat two cubes (silver and copper), each with a volume of 10.0 cm³ from 15 °C to 25 °C. Refer to Tables 2.9 and 3.11. (3.6)

Clinical Applications

3.67 A 70.0-kg person had a quarter-pound cheeseburger, french fries, and a chocolate shake. (3.5)

Item	Carbohydrate (g)	Fat (g)	Protein (g)
Cheeseburger	46	40.	47
French fries	47	16	4
Chocolate shake	76	10.	10.

a. Using Table 3.7, calculate the total kilocalories for each food type in this meal (round off the kilocalories to the tens place).
b. Determine the total kilocalories for the meal (round off to the tens place).
c. Using Table 3.10, determine the number of hours of sleep needed to burn off the kilocalories in this meal.
d. Using Table 3.10, determine the number of hours of running needed to burn off the kilocalories in this meal.

3.68 Your friend, who has a mass of 70.0 kg, has a slice of pizza, a cola soft drink, and ice cream. (3.5)

Item	Carbohydrate (g)	Fat (g)	Protein (g)
Pizza	29	10.	13
Cola	51	0	0
Ice cream	44	28	8

a. Using Table 3.7, calculate the total kilocalories for each food type in this meal (round off the kilocalories to the tens place).
b. Determine the total kilocalories for the meal (round off to the tens place).
c. Using Table 3.10, determine the number of hours of sitting needed to burn off the kilocalories in this meal.
d. Using Table 3.10, determine the number of hours of swimming needed to burn off the kilocalories in this meal.

ADDITIONAL QUESTIONS AND PROBLEMS

3.69 Classify each of the following as an element, a compound, or a mixture: (3.1)
a. carbon in pencils
b. carbon monoxide (CO) in automobile exhaust
c. orange juice

3.70 Classify each of the following as an element, a compound, or a mixture: (3.1)
a. neon gas in lights
b. a salad dressing of oil and vinegar
c. sodium hypochlorite (NaOCl) in bleach

3.71 Classify each of the following mixtures as homogeneous or heterogeneous: (3.1)
a. hot fudge sundae   **b.** herbal tea   **c.** vegetable oil

3.72 Classify each of the following mixtures as homogeneous or heterogeneous: (3.1)
a. water and sand   **b.** mustard   **c.** blue ink

3.73 Identify each of the following as solid, liquid, or gas: (3.2)
a. vitamin tablets in a bottle   **b.** helium in a balloon
c. milk in a bottle   **d.** the air you breathe
e. charcoal briquettes on a barbecue

3.74 Identify each of the following as solid, liquid, or gas: (3.2)
a. popcorn in a bag   **b.** water in a garden hose
c. a computer mouse   **d.** air in a tire
e. hot tea in a teacup

3.75 Identify each of the following as a physical or chemical property: (3.2)
a. Gold is shiny.
b. Gold melts at 1064 °C.
c. Gold is a good conductor of electricity.
d. When gold reacts with yellow sulfur, a black sulfide compound forms.

3.76 Identify each of the following as a physical or chemical property: (3.2)
a. A candle is 10 in. high and 2 in. in diameter.
b. A candle burns.
c. The wax of a candle softens on a hot day.
d. A candle is blue.

3.77 Identify each of the following as a physical or chemical change: (3.2)
a. A plant grows a new leaf.
b. Chocolate is melted for a dessert.
c. Wood is chopped for the fireplace.
d. Wood burns in a woodstove.

3.78 Identify each of the following as a physical or chemical change: (3.2)
a. Aspirin tablets are broken in half.
b. Carrots are grated for use in a salad.
c. Malt undergoes fermentation to make beer.
d. A copper pipe reacts with air and turns green.

3.79 Calculate each of the following temperatures in degrees Celsius and kelvins: (3.3)
  a. The highest recorded temperature in the continental United States was 134 °F in Death Valley, California, on July 10, 1913.
  b. The lowest recorded temperature in the continental United States was −69.7 °F in Rodgers Pass, Montana, on January 20, 1954.

3.80 Calculate each of the following temperatures in kelvins and degrees Fahrenheit: (3.3)
  a. The highest recorded temperature in the world was 58.0 °C in El Azizia, Libya, on September 13, 1922.
  b. The lowest recorded temperature in the world was −89.2 °C in Vostok, Antarctica, on July 21, 1983.

3.81 What is −15 °F in degrees Celsius and in kelvins? (3.3)

3.82 On a hot sunny day, you get out of the swimming pool and sit in a metal chair, which is very hot. Would you predict that the specific heat of the metal is higher or lower than that of water? Explain. (3.6)

3.83 On a hot day, the beach sand gets hot but the water stays cool. Would you predict that the specific heat of sand is higher or lower than that of water? Explain. (3.6)

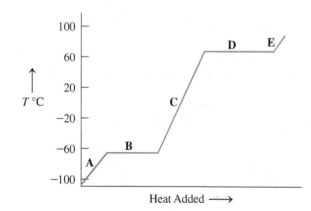

On a sunny day, the sand gets hot but the water stays cool.

3.84 A large bottle containing 883 g of water at 4 °C is removed from the refrigerator. How many kilojoules are absorbed to warm the water to room temperature of 22 °C? (3.6)

3.85 A 0.50-g sample of vegetable oil is placed in a calorimeter. When the sample is burned, 18.9 kJ is given off. What is the energy value (kcal/g) for the oil? (3.5)

3.86 A 1.3-g sample of rice is placed in a calorimeter. When the sample is burned, 22 kJ is given off. What is the energy value (kcal/g) for the rice? (3.5)

3.87 The following graph is a heating curve for chloroform, a solvent for fats, oils, and waxes: (3.7)

  a. What is the approximate melting point of chloroform?
  b. What is the approximate boiling point of chloroform?

  c. On the heating curve, identify the segments **A**, **B**, **C**, **D**, and **E** as solid, liquid, gas, melting, or boiling.
  d. At the following temperatures, is chloroform a solid, liquid, or gas?
        −80 °C; −40 °C; 25 °C; 80 °C

3.88 Associate the contents of the beakers (**1** to **5**) with segments (**A** to **E**) on the following heating curve for water: (3.7)

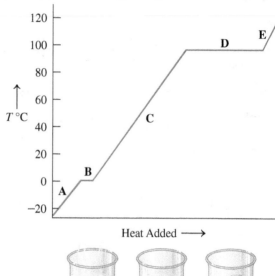

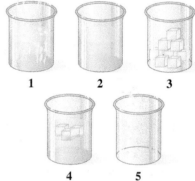

3.89 The melting point of dibromomethane is −53 °C and its boiling point is 97 °C. Sketch a heating curve for dibromomethane from −100 °C to 120 °C. (3.7)
  a. What is the state of dibromomethane at −75 °C?
  b. What happens on the curve at −53 °C?
  c. What is the state of dibromomethane at −18 °C?
  d. What is the state of dibromomethane at 110 °C?
  e. At what temperature will both solid and liquid be present?

3.90 The melting point of benzene is 5.5 °C and its boiling point is 80.1 °C. Sketch a heating curve for benzene from 0 °C to 100 °C. (3.7)
  a. What is the state of benzene at 15 °C?
  b. What happens on the curve at 5.5 °C?
  c. What is the state of benzene at 63 °C?
  d. What is the state of benzene at 98 °C?
  e. At what temperature will both liquid and gas be present?

℞ **Clinical Applications**

3.91 If you want to lose 1 lb of "body fat," which is 15% water, how many kilocalories do you need to expend? (3.5)

3.92 The highest recorded body temperature that a person has survived is 46.5 °C. Calculate that temperature in degrees Fahrenheit and in kelvins. (3.3)

3.93 A hot-water bottle for a patient contains 725 g of water at 65 °C. If the water cools to body temperature (37 °C), how many kilojoules of heat could be transferred to sore muscles? (3.6)

3.94 A young patient drinks whole milk as part of her diet. Calculate the total kilocalories if the glass of milk contains 12 g of carbohydrate, 9 g of fat, and 9 g of protein. (Round off answers for each food type to the tens place.) (3.5)

CHALLENGE QUESTIONS

The following groups of questions are related to the topics in this chapter. However, they do not all follow the chapter order, and they require you to combine concepts and skills from several sections. These questions will help you increase your critical thinking skills and prepare for your next exam.

3.95 When a 0.66-g sample of olive oil is burned in a calorimeter, the heat released increases the temperature of 370 g of water from 22.7 °C to 38.8 °C. What is the energy value for the olive oil in kcal/g? (3.5, 3.6)

3.96 A 45-g piece of ice at 0.0 °C is added to a sample of water at 8.0 °C. All of the ice melts and the temperature of the water decreases to 0.0 °C. How many grams of water were in the sample? (3.6, 3.7)

3.97 In a large building, oil is used in a steam boiler heating system. The combustion of 1.0 lb of oil provides 2.4×10^7 J. (3.4, 3.6)
   a. How many kilograms of oil are needed to heat 150 kg of water from 22 °C to 100 °C?
   b. How many kilograms of oil are needed to change 150 kg of water to steam at 100 °C?

3.98 When 1.0 g of gasoline burns, it releases 11 kcal of heat. The density of gasoline is 0.74 g/mL. (3.4, 3.6)
   a. How many megajoules are released when 1.0 gal of gasoline burns?
   b. If a television requires 150 kJ/h to run, how many hours can the television run on the energy provided by 1.0 gal of gasoline?

3.99 An ice bag containing 275 g of ice at 0 °C was used to treat sore muscles. When the bag was removed, the ice had melted and the liquid water had a temperature of 24.0 °C. How many kilojoules of heat were absorbed? (3.6, 3.7)

3.100 A 115-g sample of steam at 100 °C is emitted from a volcano. It condenses, cools, and falls as snow at 0 °C. How many kilojoules of heat were released? (3.6, 3.7)

3.101 A 70.0-g piece of copper metal at 54.0 °C is placed in 50.0 g of water at 26.0 °C. If the final temperature of the water and metal is 29.2 °C, what is the specific heat (J/g °C) of copper? (3.6)

3.102 A 125-g piece of metal is heated to 288 °C and dropped into 85.0 g of water at 12.0 °C. The metal and water come to the same temperature of 24.0 °C. What is the specific heat, in J/g °C, of the metal? (3.6)

3.103 A metal is thought to be titanium or aluminum. When 4.7 g of the metal absorbs 11 J, its temperature rises by 4.5 °C. (3.6)
   a. What is the specific heat (J/g °C) of the metal?
   b. Would you identify the metal as titanium or aluminum (see Table 3.11)?

3.104 A metal is thought to be copper or gold. When 18 g of the metal absorbs 58 cal, its temperature rises by 35 °C. (3.6)
   a. What is the specific heat, in cal/g °C, of the metal?
   b. Would you identify the metal as copper or gold (see Table 3.11)?

ANSWERS

Answers to Selected Questions and Problems

3.1 a. pure substance   **b.** mixture
   c. pure substance   **d.** pure substance
   e. mixture

3.3 a. element   **b.** compound
   c. element   **d.** compound
   e. compound

3.5 a. heterogeneous   **b.** homogeneous
   c. homogeneous   **d.** heterogeneous
   e. heterogeneous

3.7 a. gas   **b.** gas
   c. solid

3.9 a. physical   **b.** chemical
   c. physical   **d.** chemical
   e. chemical

3.11 a. physical   **b.** chemical
   c. physical   **d.** physical
   e. physical

3.13 a. chemical   **b.** physical
   c. physical   **d.** chemical
   e. physical

3.15 In the United States, we still use the Fahrenheit temperature scale. In °F, normal body temperature is 98.6. On the Celsius scale, her temperature would be 37.7 °C, a mild fever.

3.17 a. 98.6 °F   **b.** 18.5 °C
   c. 246 K   **d.** 335 K
   e. 46 °C

3.19 a. 41 °C
   b. No. The temperature is equivalent to 39 °C.

3.21 When the roller-coaster car is at the top of the ramp, it has its maximum potential energy. As it descends, potential energy changes to kinetic energy. At the bottom, all the energy is kinetic.

3.23 a. potential   **b.** kinetic
   c. potential   **d.** potential

3.25 a. 8.1×10^5 J   **b.** 190 kcal

3.27 a. 29.9 kcal   **b.** 208 kcal

3.29 a. 470 kJ   **b.** 18 g
      c. 130 kcal   **d.** 37 g

3.31 210 kcal, 880 kJ

3.33 640 kcal

3.35 Copper has the lowest specific heat of the samples and will reach the highest temperature.

3.37 a. 180 cal   **b.** 14 000 J
      c. 2600 J   **d.** 10.8 kJ

3.39 a. 1380 J, 330. cal   **b.** 1810 J, 434 cal
      c. 3780 J, 904 cal   **d.** 3600 J, 850 cal

3.41 a. melting   **b.** sublimation
      c. freezing   **d.** deposition

3.43 a. 5200 cal absorbed   **b.** 5680 J absorbed
      c. 18 kcal released   **d.** 16.7 kJ released

3.45 a. condensation   **b.** evaporation
      c. boiling   **d.** condensation

3.47 a. 5400 cal absorbed   **b.** 11 300 J absorbed
      c. 4300 kcal released   **d.** 396 kJ released

3.49

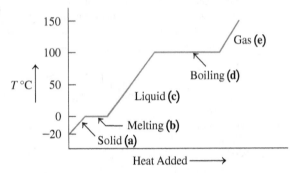

3.51 a. 30 300 J   **b.** 9.6 kcal
      c. 72.2 kJ

3.53 11 kcal

3.55 a. Breakfast 270 kcal; Lunch 420 kcal; Dinner 440 kcal
      b. 1130 kcal total
      c. Yes. Charles should be losing weight.
      d. 26 days

3.57 a. compound, the molecules have a definite 2:1 ratio of atoms
      b. mixture, has two different kinds of atoms and molecules
      c. element, has a single kind of atom

3.59 a. homogeneous   **b.** heterogeneous
      c. homogeneous

3.61 61.4 °C, 143 °F

3.63 68.3 °C, 341 K

3.65 gold, 250 J or 60.0 cal; aluminum, 240 J or 58 cal

3.67 a. carbohydrate, 680 kcal; fat, 590 kcal; protein, 240 kcal
      b. 1510 kcal
      c. 25 h
      d. 2.0 h

3.69 a. element   **b.** compound
      c. mixture

3.71 a. heterogeneous   **b.** homogeneous
      c. homogeneous

3.73 a. solid   **b.** gas
      c. liquid   **d.** gas
      e. solid

3.75 a. physical   **b.** physical
      c. physical   **d.** chemical

3.77 a. chemical   **b.** physical
      c. physical   **d.** chemical

3.79 a. 56.7 °C, 330. K   **b.** −56.5 °C, 217 K

3.81 −26 °C, 247 K

3.83 The same amount of heat causes a greater temperature change in the sand than in the water; thus the sand must have a lower specific heat than that of water.

3.85 9.0 kcal/g

3.87 a. about −60 °C
      b. about 60 °C
      c. The diagonal line A represents the solid state as temperature increases. The horizontal line B represents the change from solid to liquid or melting of the substance. The diagonal line C represents the liquid state as temperature increases. The horizontal line D represents the change from liquid to gas or boiling of the liquid. The diagonal line E represents the gas state as temperature increases.
      d. At −80 °C, solid; at −40 °C, liquid; at 25 °C, liquid; at 80 °C, gas

3.89

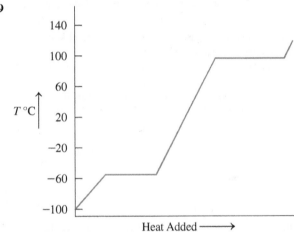

      a. solid   **b.** solid dibromomethane melts
      c. liquid   **d.** gas
      e. −53 °C

3.91 3500 kcal

3.93 85 kJ

3.95 9.0 kcal/g

3.97 a. 0.93 kg   **b.** 6.4 kg

3.99 119.5 kJ

3.101 Specific heat = 0.385 J/g °C

3.103 a. 0.52 J/g °C   **b.** titanium

CI.1 Gold, one of the most sought-after metals in the world, has a density of 19.3 g/cm^3, a melting point of 1064 °C, a specific heat of 0.129 J/g °C, and a heat of fusion of 63.6 J/g. A gold nugget found in Alaska in 1998 weighs 20.17 lb. (2.4, 2.6, 2.7, 3.3, 3.6, 3.7)

Gold nuggets, also called native gold, can be found in streams and mines.

a. How many significant figures are in the measurement of the weight of the nugget?

b. Which is the mass of the nugget in kilograms?

c. If the nugget were pure gold, what would its volume be in cm^3?

d. What is the melting point of gold in degrees Fahrenheit and kelvins?

e. How many kilocalories are required to raise the temperature of the nugget from 500. °C to 1064 °C and melt all the gold to liquid at 1064 °C?

f. If the price of gold is $45.98 per gram, what is the nugget worth, in dollars?

CI.2 The mileage for a motorcycle with a fuel-tank capacity of 22 L is 35 mi/gal. (2.5, 2.6, 2.7, 3.4)

a. How long a trip, in kilometers, can be made on one full tank of gasoline?

b. If the price of gasoline is $3.82 per gallon, what would be the cost of fuel for the trip?

c. If the average speed during the trip is 44 mi/h, how many hours will it take to reach the destination?

When 1.00 g of gasoline burns, 47 kJ of energy are released.

d. If the density of gasoline is 0.74 g/mL, what is the mass, in grams, of the fuel in the tank?

e. When 1.00 g of gasoline burns, 47 kJ of energy is released. How many kilojoules are produced when the fuel in one full tank is burned?

CI.3 Answer the following questions for the water samples **A** and **B** shown in the diagrams: (3.1, 3.2, 3.6)

A   B

a. In which sample (**A** or **B**) does the water have its own shape?

b. Which diagram (**1** or **2** or **3**) represents the arrangement of particles in water sample **A**?

c. Which diagram (**1** or **2** or **3**) represents the arrangement of particles in water sample **B**?

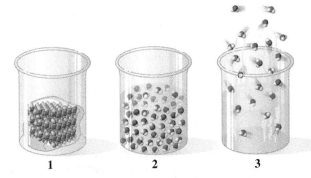

1   2   3

Answer the following for diagrams **1**, **2**, and **3**: (3.2, 3.3)

d. The state of matter indicated in diagram **1** is a _____; in diagram **2**, it is a _____; and in diagram **3**, it is a _____.

e. The motion of the particles is slowest in diagram _____.

f. The arrangement of particles is farthest apart in diagram _____.

g. The particles fill the volume of the container in diagram _____.

h. If the water in diagram **2** has a mass of 19 g and a temperature of 45 °C, how much heat, in kilojoules, is removed to cool the liquid to 0 °C?

CI.4 The label of a black cherry almond energy bar with a mass of 68 g lists the nutrition facts as 39 g of carbohydrate, 5 g of fat, and 10. g of protein. (2.5, 2.6, 3.4, 3.5)

a. Using the energy values for carbohydrates, fats, and proteins (see Table 3.7), what are the total kilocalories (Calories) listed for a black cherry almond bar? (Round off answers for each food type to the tens place.)

b. What are the kilojoules for the black cherry almond bar? (Round off answers for each food type to the tens place.)

An energy bar contains carbohydrate, fat, and protein.

c. If you obtain 160 kJ, how many grams of the black cherry almond bar did you eat?

d. If you are walking and using energy at a rate of 840 kJ/h, how many minutes will you need to walk to expend the energy from two black cherry almond bars?

CI.5 In one box of nails, there are 75 iron nails weighing 0.250 lb. The density of iron is 7.86 g/cm³. The specific heat of iron is 0.452 J/g °C. The melting point of iron is 1535 °C. The heat of fusion for iron is 272 J/g.(2.5, 2.6, 2.7, 3.4, 3.6, 3.7)

Nails made of iron have a density of 7.86 g/cm³.

a. What is the volume, in cm³, of the iron nails in the box?
b. If 30 nails are added to a graduated cylinder containing 17.6 mL of water, what is the new level of water, in milliliters, in the cylinder?
c. How much heat, in joules, must be added to the nails in the box to raise their temperature from 16 °C to 125 °C?
d. How much heat, in joules, is required to heat one nail from 25 °C to its melting point and change it to liquid iron?

CI.6 A hot tub is filled with 450 gal of water. (2.5, 2.6, 2.7, 3.3, 3.4, 3.6)

A hot tub filled with water is heated to 105 °F.

a. What is the volume of water, in liters, in the tub?
b. What is the mass, in kilograms, of water in the tub?
c. How many kilocalories are needed to heat the water from 62 °F to 105 °F?
d. If the hot-tub heater provides 5900 kJ/min, how long, in minutes, will it take to heat the water in the hot tub from 62 °F to 105 °F?

ANSWERS

CI.1 a. 4 significant figures
 b. 9.17 kg
 c. 475 cm³
 d. 1947 °F; 1337 K
 e. 298 kcal
 f. $422 000

CI.3 a. B
 b. A is represented by diagram **2**.
 c. B is represented by diagram **1**.
 d. solid; liquid; gas

 e. diagram **1**
 f. diagram **3**
 g. diagram **3**
 h. 3.6 kJ

CI.5 a. 14.4 cm³
 b. 23.4 mL
 c. 5590 J
 d. 1440 J

4

Atoms

JOHN IS PREPARING FOR THE NEXT GROWING

season as he decides how much of each crop should be planted and their location on his farm. Part of this decision is determined by the quality of the soil including the pH, the amount of moisture, and the nutrient content in the soil. He begins by sampling the soil and performing a few chemical tests on the soil. John determines that several of his fields need additional fertilizer before the crops can be planted. John considers several different types of fertilizers as each supplies different nutrients to the soil to help increase crop production. Plants need three basic elements for growth. These elements are potassium, nitrogen, and phosphorus. Potassium (K on the periodic table) is a metal, whereas nitrogen (N) and phosphorus (P) are nonmetals. Fertilizers may also contain several other elements including calcium (Ca), magnesium (Mg), and sulfur (S). John applies a fertilizer containing a mixture of all of these elements to his soil and plans to re-check the soil nutrient content in a few days.

CAREER Farmer

Farming involves much more than growing crops and raising animals. Farmers must understand how to perform chemical tests and how to apply fertilizer to soil and pesticides or herbicides to crops. Pesticides are chemicals used to kill insects that could destroy the crop, whereas herbicides are chemicals used to kill weeds that would compete for the crop's water and nutrient supply. This requires knowledge of how these chemicals work, their safety, effectiveness, and their storage. In using this information, farmers are able to grow crops that produce a higher yield, greater nutritional value, and better taste.

LEARNING GOAL

Given the name of an element, write its correct symbol; from the symbol, write the correct name.

All matter is composed of *elements*, of which there are 118 different kinds. Of these, 88 elements occur naturally and make up all the substances in our world. Many elements are already familiar to you. Perhaps you use aluminum in the form of foil or drink soft drinks from aluminum cans. You may have a ring or necklace made of gold, silver, or perhaps platinum. If you play tennis or golf, then you may have noticed that your racket or clubs may be made from the elements titanium or carbon. In our bodies, calcium and phosphorus form the structure of bones and teeth, iron and copper are needed in the formation of red blood cells, and iodine is required for the proper functioning of the thyroid.

The correct amounts of certain elements are crucial to the proper growth and function of the body. Low levels of iron can lead to anemia, whereas lack of iodine can cause hypothyroidism and goiter. Some elements known as microminerals, such as chromium, cobalt, and selenium, are needed in our bodies in very small amounts. Laboratory tests are used to confirm that these elements are within normal ranges in our bodies.

CHAPTER READINESS*

📱 KEY MATH SKILLS
- Using Positive and Negative Numbers in Calculations (1.4B)
- Calculating Percentages (1.4C)
- Rounding Off (2.3)

⚛ CORE CHEMISTRY SKILLS
- Counting Significant Figures (2.2)
- Using Significant Figures in Calculations (2.3)

*These Key Math Skills and Core Chemistry Skills from previous chapters are listed here for your review as you proceed to the new material in this chapter.

4.1 Elements and Symbols

Elements are pure substances from which all other things are built. Elements cannot be broken down into simpler substances. Over the centuries, elements have been named for planets, mythological figures, colors, minerals, geographic locations, and famous people. Some sources of names of elements are listed in Table 4.1. A complete list of all the elements and their symbols are found on the inside front cover of this text.

Chemical Symbols

Chemical symbols are one- or two-letter abbreviations for the names of the elements. Only the first letter of an element's symbol is capitalized. If the symbol has a second letter, it is lowercase so that we know when a different element is indicated. If two letters are

TABLE 4.1 Some Elements, Symbols, and Source of Names

Element	Symbol	Source of Name
Uranium	U	The planet Uranus
Titanium	Ti	Titans (mythology)
Chlorine	Cl	*Chloros*: "greenish yellow" (Greek)
Iodine	I	*Ioeides*: "violet" (Greek)
Magnesium	Mg	Magnesia, a mineral
Californium	Cf	California
Curium	Cm	Marie and Pierre Curie
Copernicium	Cn	Nicolaus Copernicus

capitalized, they represent the symbols of two different elements. For example, the element cobalt has the symbol Co. However, the two capital letters CO specify two elements, carbon (C) and oxygen (O).

Although most of the symbols use letters from the current names, some are derived from their ancient names. For example, Na, the symbol for sodium, comes from the Latin word *natrium*. The symbol for iron, Fe, is derived from the Latin name *ferrum*. Table 4.2 lists the names and symbols of some common elements. Learning their names and symbols will greatly help your learning of chemistry.

One-Letter Symbols		Two-Letter Symbols	
C	Carbon	Co	Cobalt
S	Sulfur	Si	Silicon
N	Nitrogen	Ne	Neon
I	Iodine	Ni	Nickel

TABLE 4.2 Names and Symbols of Some Common Elements

Name*	Symbol	Name*	Symbol	Name*	Symbol
Aluminum	Al	Gallium	Ga	Oxygen	O
Argon	Ar	Gold (*aurum*)	Au	Phosphorus	P
Arsenic	As	Helium	He	Platinum	Pt
Barium	Ba	Hydrogen	H	Potassium (*kalium*)	K
Boron	B	Iodine	I	Radium	Ra
Bromine	Br	Iron (*ferrum*)	Fe	Silicon	Si
Cadmium	Cd	Lead (*plumbum*)	Pb	Silver (*argentum*)	Ag
Calcium	Ca	Lithium	Li	Sodium (*natrium*)	Na
Carbon	C	Magnesium	Mg	Strontium	Sr
Chlorine	Cl	Manganese	Mn	Sulfur	S
Chromium	Cr	Mercury (*hydrargyrum*)	Hg	Tin (*stannum*)	Sn
Cobalt	Co	Neon	Ne	Titanium	Ti
Copper (*cuprum*)	Cu	Nickel	Ni	Uranium	U
Fluorine	F	Nitrogen	N	Zinc	Zn

*Names given in parentheses are ancient Latin or Greek words from which the symbols are derived.

▶ **SAMPLE PROBLEM 4.1 Names and Symbols of Chemical Elements**

Complete the following table with the correct symbol or name of each element:

Name	Symbol
nickel	____
nitrogen	____
____	Zn
____	K
iron	____

SOLUTION

Name	Symbol
nickel	<u>Ni</u>
nitrogen	<u>N</u>
<u>zinc</u>	Zn
<u>potassium</u>	K
iron	<u>Fe</u>

STUDY CHECK 4.1

Write the chemical symbols for the elements silicon, sulfur, and silver.

ANSWER

Si, S, and Ag

Aluminum

Carbon

Gold

Silver

Sulfur

Chemistry Link to **Health**
Latin Names for Elements in Clinical Usage

In medicine, the Latin name *natrium* is often used for sodium, an important electrolyte in body fluids and cells. An increase in serum sodium, a condition called *hypernatremia*, may occur when water is lost because of profuse sweating, severe diarrhea, or vomiting, or when there is inadequate water intake. A decrease in sodium, a condition called *hyponatremia*, may occur when a person takes in a large amount of water or fluid-replacement solutions. Conditions that occur in cardiac failure, liver failure, and malnutrition can also cause hyponatremia.

The Latin name *kalium* is often used for potassium, the most common electrolyte inside the cells. Potassium regulates osmotic pressure,

acid–base balance, nerve and muscle excitability, and the function of cellular enzymes. Serum potassium measures potassium outside the cells, which amounts to only 2% of total body potassium. An increase in serum potassium (*hyperkalemia* or *hyperpotassemia*) may occur when cells are severely injured, in renal failure when potassium is not properly excreted, and in Addison's disease. A severe loss of potassium (*hypokalemia* or *hypopotassemia*) may occur during excessive vomiting, diarrhea, renal tubular defects, and glucose or insulin therapy.

Chemistry Link to **Health**
Toxicity of Mercury

Mercury is a silvery, shiny element that is a liquid at room temperature. Mercury can enter the body through inhaled mercury vapor, contact with the skin, or ingestion of foods or water contaminated with mercury. In the body, mercury destroys proteins and disrupts cell function. Long-term exposure to mercury can damage the brain and kidneys, cause mental retardation, and decrease physical development. Blood, urine, and hair samples are used to test for mercury.

In both freshwater and seawater, bacteria convert mercury into toxic methylmercury, which attacks the central nervous system. Because fish absorb methylmercury, we are exposed to mercury by consuming mercury-contaminated fish. As levels of mercury ingested from fish became a concern, the Food and Drug Administration set a maximum level of one part mercury per million parts seafood (1 ppm), which is the same as 1 mg of mercury in every kilogram of seafood. Fish higher in the food chain, such as swordfish and shark, can have such high levels of mercury that the Environmental Protection Agency recommends they be consumed no more than once a week.

One of the worst incidents of mercury poisoning occurred in Minamata and Niigata, Japan, in 1950. At that time, the ocean was polluted with high levels of mercury from industrial wastes. Because fish were a major food in the diet, more than 2000 people were affected with mercury poisoning and died or developed neural damage. In the United States between 1988 and 1997, the use of mercury decreased by 75%

when the use of mercury was banned in paint and pesticides, and regulated in batteries and other products. Certain batteries and compact fluorescent light bulbs (CFL) contain mercury, and instructions for their safe disposal should be followed.

The element mercury is a silvery, shiny liquid at room temperature.

QUESTIONS AND PROBLEMS

4.1 Elements and Symbols

LEARNING GOAL Given the name of an element, write its correct symbol; from the symbol, write the correct name.

4.1 Write the symbols for the following elements:
   a. copper   **b.** platinum   **c.** calcium   **d.** manganese
   e. iron   **f.** barium   **g.** lead   **h.** strontium

4.2 Write the symbols for the following elements:
   a. oxygen   **b.** lithium   **c.** uranium   **d.** titanium
   e. hydrogen   **f.** chromium   **g.** tin   **h.** gold

℞ Clinical Applications

4.3 Write the name for the symbol of each of the following elements essential in the body:
   a. C   **b.** Cl   **c.** I   **d.** Se
   e. N   **f.** S   **g.** Zn   **h.** Co

4.4 Write the name for the symbol of each of the following elements essential in the body:
   a. V   **b.** P   **c.** Na   **d.** As
   e. Ca   **f.** Mo   **g.** Mg   **h.** Si

4.5 Write the names for the elements in each of the following formulas of compounds used in health and medicine:
  a. table salt, NaCl
  b. plaster casts, $CaSO_4$
  c. Demerol, $C_{15}H_{22}ClNO_2$
  d. treatment of bipolar disorder, Li_2CO_3

4.6 Write the names for the elements in each of the following formulas of compounds used in health and medicine:
  a. salt substitute, KCl
  b. dental cement, $Zn_3(PO_4)_2$
  c. antacid, $Mg(OH)_2$
  d. contrast agent for X-ray, $BaSO_4$

4.2 The Periodic Table

As more elements were discovered, it became necessary to organize them into some type of classification system. By the late 1800s, scientists recognized that certain elements looked alike and behaved much the same way. In 1872, a Russian chemist, Dmitri Mendeleev, arranged the 60 elements known at that time into groups with similar properties and placed them in order of increasing atomic masses. Today, this arrangement of 118 elements is known as the **periodic table** (see Figure 4.1).

LEARNING GOAL

Use the periodic table to identify the group and the period of an element; identify the element as a metal, a nonmetal, or a metalloid.

Periodic Table of Elements

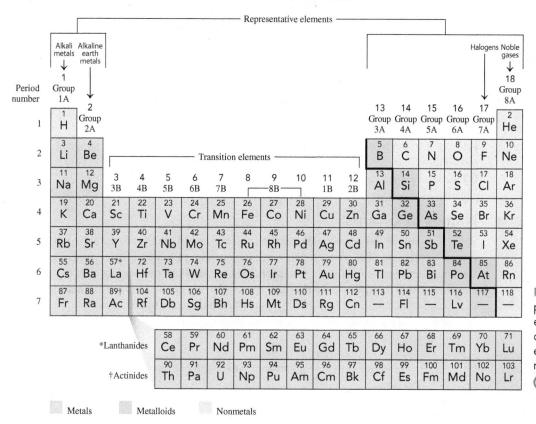

FIGURE 4.1 ▶ On the periodic table, groups are the elements arranged as vertical columns, and periods are the elements in each horizontal row.

◉ What is the symbol of the alkali metal in Period 3?

Periods and Groups

Each horizontal row in the periodic table is a **period** (see Figure 4.2). The periods are counted from the top of the table as Periods 1 to 7. The first period contains two elements: hydrogen (H) and helium (He). The second period contains eight elements: lithium (Li), beryllium (Be), boron (B), carbon (C), nitrogen (N), oxygen (O), fluorine (F), and neon (Ne). The third period also contains eight elements beginning with sodium (Na) and ending with argon (Ar). The fourth period, which begins with potassium (K), and the fifth period, which begins with rubidium (Rb), have 18 elements each. The sixth period, which begins with cesium (Cs), has 32 elements. The seventh period, as of today, contains 32 elements, for a total of 118 elements.

Each vertical column on the periodic table contains a **group** (or family) of elements that have similar properties. A **group number** is written at the top of each vertical column (group) in the periodic table. For many years, the **representative elements** have had group numbers 1A to 8A. In the center of the periodic table is a block of elements known as the **transition**

elements, which have had group numbers followed by the letter "B." A newer system assigns numbers of 1 to 18 to all of the groups going left to right across the periodic table. Because both systems are currently in use, they are both shown on the periodic table in this text and are included in our discussions of elements and group numbers. The two rows of 14 elements called the *lanthanides* and *actinides* (or the inner transition elements), which are part of Periods 6 and 7, are placed at the bottom of the periodic table to allow it to fit on a page.

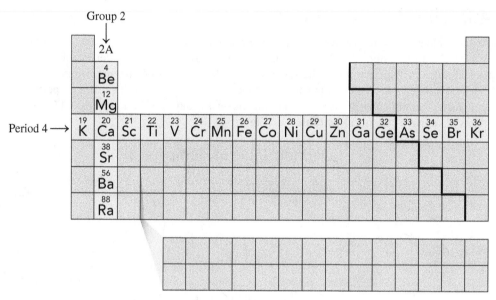

FIGURE 4.2 ▶ On the periodic table, each vertical column represents a group of elements and each horizontal row of elements represents a period.

◉ Are the elements Si, P, and S part of a group or a period?

Names of Groups

Several groups in the periodic table have special names (see Figure 4.3). Group 1A (1) elements—lithium (Li), sodium (Na), potassium (K), rubidium (Rb), cesium (Cs), and francium (Fr)—are a family of elements known as the **alkali metals** (see Figure 4.4). The elements within this group are soft, shiny metals that are good conductors of heat and electricity and have relatively low melting points. Alkali metals react vigorously with water and form white products when they combine with oxygen.

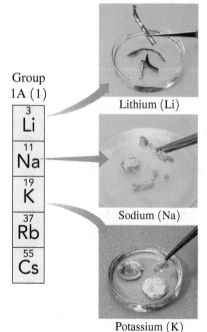

FIGURE 4.4 ▶ Lithium (Li), sodium (Na), and potassium (K) are some alkali metals from Group 1A (1).

◉ What physical properties do these alkali metals have in common?

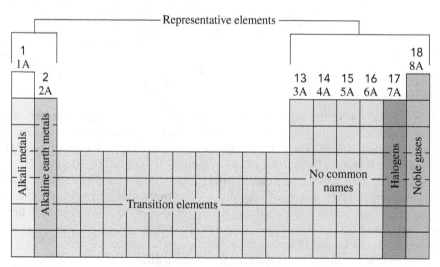

FIGURE 4.3 ▶ Certain groups on the periodic table have common names.

◉ What is the common name for the group of elements that includes helium and argon?

Although hydrogen (H) is at the top of Group 1A (1), it is not an alkali metal and has very different properties than the rest of the elements in this group. Thus hydrogen is not included in the alkali metals.

The **alkaline earth metals** are found in Group 2A (2). They include the elements beryllium (Be), magnesium (Mg), calcium (Ca), strontium (Sr), barium (Ba), and radium (Ra). The alkaline earth metals are shiny metals like those in Group 1A (1), but they are not as reactive.

The **halogens** are found on the right side of the periodic table in Group 7A (17). They include the elements fluorine (F), chlorine (Cl), bromine (Br), iodine (I), and astatine (At) (see Figure 4.5). The halogens, especially fluorine and chlorine, are highly reactive and form compounds with most of the elements.

The **noble gases** are found in Group 8A (18). They include helium (He), neon (Ne), argon (Ar), krypton (Kr), xenon (Xe), and radon (Rn). They are quite unreactive and are seldom found in combination with other elements.

Metals, Nonmetals, and Metalloids

Another feature of the periodic table is the heavy zigzag line that separates the elements into the *metals* and the *nonmetals*. *Except for hydrogen*, the metals are to the left of the line with the nonmetals to the right (see Figure 4.6).

In general, most **metals** are shiny solids, such as copper (Cu), gold (Au), and silver (Ag). Metals can be shaped into wires (ductile) or hammered into a flat sheet (malleable). Metals are good conductors of heat and electricity. They usually melt at higher temperatures than nonmetals. All the metals are solids at room temperature, except for mercury (Hg), which is a liquid.

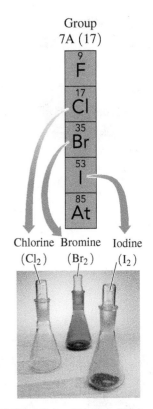

Group 7A (17)

FIGURE 4.5 ▶ Chlorine (Cl_2), bromine (Br_2), and iodine (I_2) are examples of halogens from Group 7A (17).

What elements are in the halogen group?

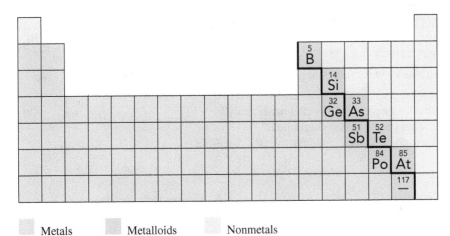

Metals Metalloids Nonmetals

FIGURE 4.6 ▶ Along the heavy zigzag line on the periodic table that separates the metals and nonmetals are metalloids, which exhibit characteristics of both metals and nonmetals.

On which side of the heavy zigzag line are the nonmetals located?

Nonmetals are not especially shiny, ductile, or malleable, and they are often poor conductors of heat and electricity. They typically have low melting points and low densities. Some examples of nonmetals are hydrogen (H), carbon (C), nitrogen (N), oxygen (O), chlorine (Cl), and sulfur (S).

Except for aluminum, the elements located along the heavy line are **metalloids**: B, Si, Ge, As, Sb, Te, Po, and At. Metalloids are elements that exhibit some properties that are typical of the metals and other properties that are characteristic of the nonmetals. For example, they are better conductors of heat and electricity than the nonmetals, but not as good as the metals. The metalloids are *semiconductors* because they can be modified to function as conductors or insulators. Table 4.3 compares some characteristics of silver, a metal, with those of antimony, a metalloid, and sulfur, a nonmetal.

A silver cup is shiny, antimony is a blue-gray solid, and sulfur is a dull, yellow color.

TABLE 4.3 Some Characteristics of a Metal, a Metalloid, and a Nonmetal

Silver (Ag)	Antimony (Sb)	Sulfur (S)
Metal	Metalloid	Nonmetal
Shiny	Blue-gray, shiny	Dull, yellow
Extremely ductile	Brittle	Brittle
Can be hammered into sheets (malleable)	Shatters when hammered	Shatters when hammered
Good conductor of heat and electricity	Poor conductor of heat and electricity	Poor conductor of heat and electricity, good insulator
Used in coins, jewelry, tableware	Used to harden lead, color glass and plastics	Used in gunpowder, rubber, fungicides
Density 10.5 g/mL	Density 6.7 g/mL	Density 2.1 g/mL
Melting point 962 °C	Melting point 630 °C	Melting point 113 °C

▶SAMPLE PROBLEM 4.2 **Metals, Nonmetals, and Metalloids**

Use the periodic table to classify each of the following elements by its group and period, group name (if any), and as a metal, a nonmetal, or a metalloid:

a. Na, important in nerve impulses, regulates blood pressure
b. I, needed to produce thyroid hormones
c. Si, needed for tendons and ligaments

SOLUTION

a. Na (sodium), Group 1A (1), Period 3, is an alkali metal.
b. I (iodine), Group 7A (17), Period 5, halogen, is a nonmetal.
c. Si (silicon), Group 4A (14), Period 3, is a metalloid.

STUDY CHECK 4.2

Strontium is an element that gives a brilliant red color to fireworks.

a. In what group is strontium found?
b. What is the name of this chemical family?
c. In what period is strontium found?
d. Is strontium a metal, a nonmetal, or a metalloid?

ANSWER

a. Group 2A (2)
b. alkaline earth metals
c. Period 5
d. metal

Strontium provides the red color in fireworks.

 # Chemistry Link to Health
Elements Essential to Health

Of all the elements, only about 20 are essential for the well-being and survival of the human body. Of those, four elements—oxygen, carbon, hydrogen, and nitrogen—which are representative elements in Period 1 and Period 2 on the periodic table, make up 96% of our body mass. Most of the food in our daily diet provides these elements to maintain a healthy body. These elements are found in carbohydrates, fats, and proteins. Most of the hydrogen and oxygen is found in water, which makes up 55 to 60% of our body mass.

The *macrominerals*—Ca, P, K, Cl, S, Na, and Mg—are representative elements located in Period 3 and Period 4 of the periodic table. They are involved in the formation of bones and teeth, maintenance of heart and blood vessels, muscle contraction, nerve impulses, acid–base balance of body fluids, and regulation of cellular metabolism.

The macrominerals are present in lower amounts than the major elements, so that smaller amounts are required in our daily diets.

The other essential elements, called *microminerals* or *trace elements*, are mostly transition elements in Period 4 along with Si in Period 3 and Mo and I in Period 5. They are present in the human body in very small amounts, some less than 100 mg. In recent years, the detection of such small amounts has improved so that researchers can more easily identify the roles of trace elements. Some trace elements such as arsenic, chromium, and selenium are toxic at high levels in the body but are still required by the body. Other elements, such as tin and nickel, are thought to be essential, but their metabolic role has not yet been determined. Some examples and the amounts present in a 60.-kg person are listed in Table 4.4.

	1 Group 1A	2 Group 2A												13 Group 3A	14 Group 4A	15 Group 5A	16 Group 6A	17 Group 7A	18 Group 8A
1	1 H																		2 He
2	3 Li	4 Be												5 B	6 C	7 N	8 O	9 F	10 Ne
3	11 Na	12 Mg	3 3B	4 4B	5 5B	6 6B	7 7B	8	9 8B	10	11 1B	12 2B	13 Al	14 Si	15 P	16 S	17 Cl	18 Ar
4	19 K	20 Ca	21 Sc	22 Ti	23 V	24 Cr	25 Mn	26 Fe	27 Co	28 Ni	29 Cu	30 Zn	31 Ga	32 Ge	33 As	34 Se	35 Br	36 Kr
5	37 Rb	38 Sr	39 Y	40 Zr	41 Nb	42 Mo	43 Tc	44 Ru	45 Rh	46 Pd	47 Ag	48 Cd	49 In	50 Sn	51 Sb	52 Te	53 I	54 Xe
6	55 Cs	56 Ba	57* La	72 Hf	73 Ta	74 W	75 Re	76 Os	77 Ir	78 Pt	79 Au	80 Hg	81 Tl	82 Pb	83 Bi	84 Po	85 At	86 Rn
7	87 Fr	88 Ra	89† Ac	104 Rf	105 Db	106 Sg	107 Bh	108 Hs	109 Mt	110 Ds	111 Rg	112 Cn	113 —	114 Fl	115 —	116 Lv	117 —	118 —

☐ Major elements in the human body   ☐ Macrominerals   ☐ Microminerals (trace elements)

TABLE 4.4 Typical Amounts of Essential Elements in a 60.-kg Adult

Element	Quantity	Function
Major Elements		
Oxygen (O)	39 kg	Building block of biomolecules and water (H_2O)
Carbon (C)	11 kg	Building block of organic and biomolecules
Hydrogen (H)	6 kg	Component of biomolecules, water (H_2O), and pH of body fluids, stomach acid (HCl)
Nitrogen (N)	1.5 kg	Component of proteins and nucleic acids
Macrominerals		
Calcium (Ca)	1000 g	Needed for bones and teeth, muscle contraction, nerve impulses
Phosphorus (P)	600 g	Needed for bones and teeth, nucleic acids
Potassium (K)	120 g	Most prevalent positive ion (K^+) in cells, muscle contraction, nerve impulses
Chlorine (Cl)	100 g	Most prevalent negative ion (Cl^-) in fluids outside cells, stomach acid (HCl)
Sulfur (S)	86 g	Component of proteins, liver, vitamin B_1, insulin
Sodium (Na)	60 g	Most prevalent positive ion (Na^+) in fluids outside cells, water balance, muscle contraction, nerve impulses
Magnesium (Mg)	36 g	Component of bones, required for metabolic reactions
Microminerals (trace elements)		
Iron (Fe)	3600 mg	Component of oxygen carrier hemoglobin
Silicon (Si)	3000 mg	Needed for growth and maintenance of bones and teeth, tendons and ligaments, hair and skin
Zinc (Zn)	2000 mg	Used in metabolic reactions in cells, DNA synthesis, growth of bones, teeth, connective tissue, immune system
Copper (Cu)	240 mg	Needed for blood vessels, blood pressure, immune system
Manganese (Mn)	60 mg	Needed for growth of bones, blood clotting, necessary for metabolic reactions
Iodine (I)	20 mg	Needed for proper thyroid function
Molybdenum (Mo)	12 mg	Needed to process Fe and N from food
Arsenic (As)	3 mg	Needed for growth and reproduction
Chromium (Cr)	3 mg	Needed for maintenance of blood sugar levels, synthesis of biomolecules
Cobalt (Co)	3 mg	Component of vitamin B_{12}, red blood cells
Selenium (Se)	2 mg	Used in the immune system, health of heart and pancreas
Vanadium (V)	2 mg	Needed in the formation of bones and teeth, energy from food

QUESTIONS AND PROBLEMS

4.2 The Periodic Table

LEARNING GOAL Use the periodic table to identify the group and the period of an element; identify the element as a metal, a nonmetal, or a metalloid.

4.7 Identify the group or period number described by each of the following:
   a. contains the elements C, N, and O
   b. begins with helium
   c. contains the alkali metals
   d. ends with neon

4.8 Identify the group or period number described by each of the following:
   a. contains Na, K, and Rb
   b. begins with Li
   c. contains the noble gases
   d. contains F, Cl, Br, and I

4.9 Give the symbol of the element described by each of the following:
   a. Group 4A (14), Period 2
   b. a noble gas in Period 1
   c. an alkali metal in Period 3
   d. Group 2A (2), Period 4
   e. Group 3A (13), Period 3

4.10 Give the symbol of the element described by each of the following:
   a. an alkaline earth metal in Period 2
   b. Group 5A (15), Period 3
   c. a noble gas in Period 4
   d. a halogen in Period 5
   e. Group 4A (14), Period 4

4.11 Identify each of the following elements as a metal, a nonmetal, or a metalloid:
   a. calcium
   b. sulfur
   c. a shiny element
   d. an element that is a gas at room temperature
   e. located in Group 8A (18)
   f. bromine
   g. boron
   h. silver

4.12 Identify each of the following elements as a metal, a nonmetal, or a metalloid:
   a. located in Group 2A (2)
   b. a good conductor of electricity
   c. chlorine
   d. arsenic
   e. an element that is not shiny
   f. oxygen
   g. nitrogen
   h. tin

℞ Clinical Applications

4.13 Using Table 4.4, identify the function of each of the following in the body and classify each as an alkali metal, an alkaline earth metal, a transition element, or a halogen:
   a. Ca   b. Fe   c. K   d. Cl

4.14 Using Table 4.4, identify the function of each of the following in the body and classify each as an alkali metal, an alkaline earth metal, a transition element, or a halogen:
   a. Mg   b. Cu   c. I   d. Na

4.15 Using the Chemistry Link to Health: Elements Essential to Health, answer each of the following:
   a. What is a macromineral?
   b. What is the role of sulfur in the human body?
   c. How many grams of sulfur would be a typical amount in a 60.-kg adult?

4.16 Using the Chemistry Link to Health: Elements Essential to Health, answer each of the following:
   a. What is a micromineral?
   b. What is the role of iodine in the human body?
   c. How many milligrams of iodine would be a typical amount in a 60.-kg adult?

LEARNING GOAL

Describe the electrical charge and location in an atom for a proton, a neutron, and an electron.

4.3 The Atom

All the elements listed on the periodic table are made up of atoms. An **atom** is the smallest particle of an element that retains the characteristics of that element. Imagine that you are tearing a piece of aluminum foil into smaller and smaller pieces. Now imagine that you have a microscopic piece so small that it cannot be divided any further. Then you would have a single atom of aluminum.

The concept of the atom is relatively recent. Although the Greek philosophers in 500 B.C.E. reasoned that everything must contain minute particles they called *atomos*, the idea of atoms did not become a scientific theory until 1808. Then John Dalton (1766–1844) developed an atomic theory that proposed that atoms were responsible for the combinations of elements found in compounds.

Dalton's Atomic Theory

1. All matter is made up of tiny particles called atoms.
2. All atoms of a given element are similar to one another and different from atoms of other elements.
3. Atoms of two or more different elements combine to form compounds. A particular compound is always made up of the same kinds of atoms and always has the same number of each kind of atom.
4. A chemical reaction involves the rearrangement, separation, or combination of atoms. Atoms are neither created nor destroyed during a chemical reaction.

Dalton's atomic theory formed the basis of current atomic theory, although we have modified some of Dalton's statements. We now know that atoms of the same element are not completely identical to each other and consist of even smaller particles. However, an atom is still the smallest particle that retains the properties of an element.

Although atoms are the building blocks of everything we see around us, we cannot see an atom or even a billion atoms with the naked eye. However, when billions and billions of atoms are packed together, the characteristics of each atom are added to those of the next until we can see the characteristics we associate with the element. For example, a small piece of the shiny element nickel consists of many, many nickel atoms. A special kind of microscope called a *scanning tunneling microscope* (STM) produces images of individual atoms (see Figure 4.7).

Electrical Charges in an Atom

By the end of the 1800s, experiments with electricity showed that atoms were not solid spheres but were composed of even smaller bits of matter called **subatomic particles**, three of which are the *proton*, *neutron*, and *electron*. Two of these subatomic particles were discovered because they have electrical charges.

An electrical charge can be positive or negative. Experiments show that like charges repel or push away from each other. When you brush your hair on a dry day, electrical charges that are alike build up on the brush and in your hair. As a result, your hair flies away from the brush. However, opposite or unlike charges attract. The crackle of clothes taken from the clothes dryer indicates the presence of electrical charges. The clinginess of the clothing results from the attraction of opposite, unlike charges (see Figure 4.8).

Structure of the Atom

In 1897, J. J. Thomson, an English physicist, applied electricity to a glass tube, which produced streams of small particles called *cathode rays*. Because these rays were attracted to a positively charged electrode, Thomson realized that the particles in the rays must be negatively charged. In further experiments, these particles called **electrons** were found to be much smaller than the atom and to have extremely small masses. Because atoms are neutral, scientists soon discovered that atoms contained positively charged particles called **protons** that were much heavier than the electrons.

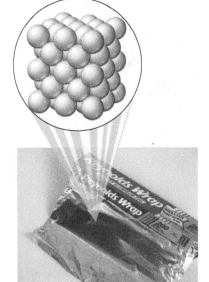

Aluminum foil consists of atoms of aluminum.

FIGURE 4.7 ▶ Images of nickel atoms are produced when nickel is magnified millions of times by a scanning tunneling microscope (STM).

🅠 Why is a microscope with extremely high magnification needed to see these atoms?

Positive charges repel

Negative charges repel

Unlike charges attract

FIGURE 4.8 ▶ Like charges repel and unlike charges attract.

🅠 Why are the electrons attracted to the protons in the nucleus of an atom?

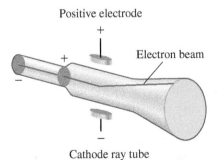

Positive electrode

Electron beam

Cathode ray tube

Negatively charged cathode rays (electrons) are attracted to the positive electrode.

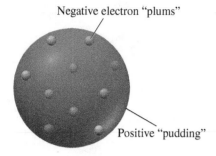

Negative electron "plums"

Positive "pudding"

Thomson's "plum-pudding" model had protons and electrons scattered throughout the atom.

Thomson proposed a "plum-pudding" model for the atom in which the electrons and protons were randomly distributed in a positively charged cloud like "plums in a pudding" or "chocolate chips in a cookie." In 1911, Ernest Rutherford worked with Thomson to test this model. In Rutherford's experiment, positively charged particles were aimed at a thin sheet of gold foil (see Figure 4.9). If the Thomson model were correct, the particles would travel in straight paths through the gold foil. Rutherford was greatly surprised to find that some of the particles were deflected as they passed through the gold foil, and a few particles were deflected so much that they went back in the opposite direction. According to Rutherford, it was as though he had shot a cannonball at a piece of tissue paper, and it bounced back at him.

From his gold-foil experiments, Rutherford realized that the protons must be contained in a small, positively charged region at the center of the atom, which he called the **nucleus**. He proposed that the electrons in the atom occupy the space surrounding the nucleus through which most of the particles traveled undisturbed. Only the particles that came near this dense, positive center were deflected. If an atom were the size of a football stadium, the nucleus would be about the size of a golf ball placed in the center of the field.

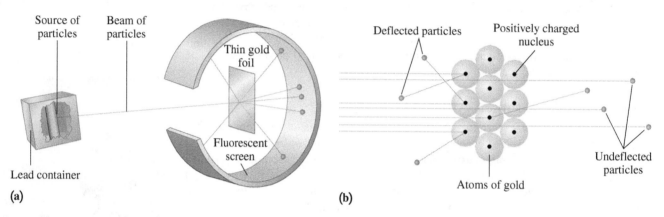

FIGURE 4.9 ▶ **(a)** Positive particles are aimed at a piece of gold foil. **(b)** Particles that come close to the atomic nuclei are deflected from their straight path.

Why are some particles deflected whereas most pass through the gold foil undeflected?

Interactive Video

Rutherford Gold-Foil Experiment

Scientists knew that the nucleus was heavier than the mass of the protons, so they looked for another subatomic particle. Eventually, they discovered that the nucleus also contained a particle that is neutral, which they called a **neutron**. Thus, the masses of the protons and neutrons in the nucleus determine the mass of an atom (see Figure 4.10).

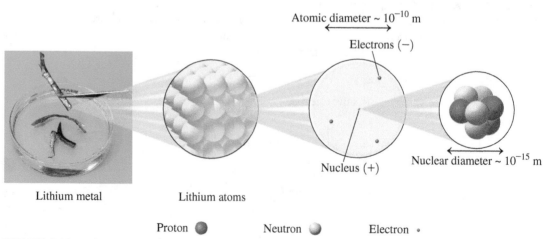

FIGURE 4.10 ▶ In an atom, the protons and neutrons that make up almost all the mass are packed into the tiny volume of the nucleus. The rapidly moving electrons (negative charge) surround the nucleus and account for the large volume of the atom.

Why can we say that the atom is mostly empty space?

Mass of the Atom

All the subatomic particles are extremely small compared with the things you see around you. One proton has a mass of 1.67×10^{-24} g, and the neutron is about the same. However, the electron has a mass 9.11×10^{-28} g, which is much less than the mass of either a proton or neutron. Because the masses of subatomic particles are so small, chemists use a very small unit of mass called an **atomic mass unit (amu)**. An amu is defined as one-twelfth of the mass of a carbon atom, which has a nucleus containing six protons and six neutrons. In biology, the atomic mass unit is called a *Dalton* (Da) in honor of John Dalton. On the amu scale, the proton and neutron each have a mass of about 1 amu. Because the electron mass is so small, it is usually ignored in atomic mass calculations. Table 4.5 summarizes some information about the subatomic particles in an atom.

TABLE 4.5 Subatomic Particles in the Atom

Particle	Symbol	Charge	Mass (amu)	Location in Atom
Proton	p or p^+	1+	1.007	Nucleus
Neutron	n or n^0	0	1.008	Nucleus
Electron	e^-	1-	0.000 55	Outside nucleus

▶**SAMPLE PROBLEM 4.3** **Subatomic Particles**

Indicate whether each of the following is *true* or *false*:

a. A proton is heavier than an electron.
b. An electron is attracted to a neutron.
c. The nucleus contains all the protons and neutrons of an atom.

SOLUTION

a. True
b. False; an electron is attracted to a proton.
c. True

STUDY CHECK 4.3

Is the following statement *true* or *false*?
The nucleus occupies a large volume in an atom.

ANSWER

False, most of the volume of the atom is outside the nucleus.

 Explore Your World
Repulsion and Attraction

Tear a small piece of paper into bits. Brush your hair several times, and place the brush just above the bits of paper. Use your knowledge of electrical charges to give an explanation for your observations. Try the same experiment with a comb.

Questions

1. What happens when objects with like charges are placed close together?
2. What happens when objects with unlike charges are placed close together?

QUESTIONS AND PROBLEMS

4.3 The Atom

LEARNING GOAL Describe the electrical charge and location in an atom for a proton, a neutron, and an electron.

4.17 Identify each of the following as describing either a proton, a neutron, or an electron:
a. has the smallest mass
b. has a 1+ charge
c. is found outside the nucleus
d. is electrically neutral

4.18 Identify each of the following as describing either a proton, a neutron, or an electron:
a. has a mass about the same as a proton
b. is found in the nucleus
c. is attracted to the protons
d. has a 1- charge

4.19 What did Rutherford determine about the structure of the atom from his gold-foil experiment?

4.20 How did Thomson determine that the electrons have a negative charge?

4.21 Is each of the following statements *true* or *false*?
a. A proton and an electron have opposite charges.
b. The nucleus contains most of the mass of an atom.
c. Electrons repel each other.
d. A proton is attracted to a neutron.

4.22 Is each of the following statements *true* or *false*?
a. A proton is attracted to an electron.
b. A neutron has twice the mass of a proton.
c. Neutrons repel each other.
d. Electrons and neutrons have opposite charges.

4.23 On a dry day, your hair flies apart when you brush it. How would you explain this?

4.24 Sometimes clothes cling together when removed from a dryer. What kinds of charges are on the clothes?

4.4 Atomic Number and Mass Number

All the atoms of the same element always have the same number of protons. This feature distinguishes atoms of one element from atoms of all the other elements.

Atomic Number

The **atomic number** of an element is equal to the number of protons in every atom of that element. The atomic number is the whole number that appears above the symbol of each element on the periodic table.

Atomic number = number of protons in an atom

The periodic table on the inside front cover of this text shows the elements in order of atomic number from 1 to 118. We can use an atomic number to identify the number of protons in an atom of any element. For example, a lithium atom, with atomic number 3, has 3 protons. Every lithium atom has 3 and only 3 protons. Any atom with 3 protons is always a lithium atom. In the same way, we determine that a carbon atom, with atomic number 6, has 6 protons. Every carbon atom has 6 protons, and any atom with 6 protons is carbon; every copper atom, with atomic number 29, has 29 protons and any atom with 29 protons is copper.

An atom is electrically neutral. That means that the number of protons in an atom is equal to the number of electrons, which gives every atom an overall charge of zero. Thus, for every atom, the atomic number also gives the number of electrons.

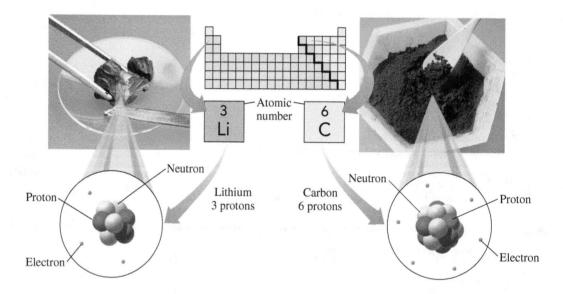

All atoms of lithium (left) contain three protons, and all atoms of carbon (right) contain six protons.

Mass Number

We now know that the protons and neutrons determine the mass of the nucleus. Thus, for a single atom, we assign a **mass number**, which is the total number of protons and neutrons in its nucleus. However, the mass number does not appear on the periodic table because it applies to single atoms only.

Mass number = number of protons + number of neutrons

For example, the nucleus of a single oxygen atom that contains 8 protons and 8 neutrons has a mass number of 16. An atom of iron that contains 26 protons and 32 neutrons has a mass number of 58.

If we are given the mass number of an atom and its atomic number, we can calculate the number of neutrons in its nucleus.

Number of neutrons in a nucleus = mass number − number of protons

For example, if we are given a mass number of 37 for an atom of chlorine (atomic number 17), we can calculate the number of neutrons in its nucleus.

Number of neutrons = 37 (mass number) − 17 (protons) = 20 neutrons

Table 4.6 illustrates these relationships between atomic number, mass number, and the number of protons, neutrons, and electrons in examples of single atoms for different elements.

TABLE 4.6 Composition of Some Atoms of Different Elements

Element	Symbol	Atomic Number	Mass Number	Number of Protons	Number of Neutrons	Number of Electrons
Hydrogen	H	1	1	1	0	1
Nitrogen	N	7	14	7	7	7
Oxygen	O	8	16	8	8	8
Chlorine	Cl	17	37	17	20	17
Potassium	K	19	39	19	20	19
Iron	Fe	26	58	26	32	26
Gold	Au	79	197	79	118	79

▶ SAMPLE PROBLEM 4.4 **Calculating Numbers of Protons, Neutrons, and Electrons**

Zinc, a micromineral, is needed for metabolic reactions in cells, DNA synthesis, the growth of bones, teeth, and connective tissue, and the proper functioning of the immune system. For an atom of zinc that has a mass number of 68, determine the following:

a. the number of protons   **b.** the number of neutrons   **c.** the number of electrons

SOLUTION

	Given	Need
ANALYZE THE PROBLEM	zinc (Zn), mass number 68	number of protons, number of neutrons, number of electrons

a. Zinc (Zn), with an atomic number of 30, has 30 protons.
b. The number of neutrons in this atom is found by subtracting number of protons (atomic number) from the mass number.

Mass number − atomic number = number of neutrons
    68   −   30   =   38

c. Because the zinc atom is neutral, the number of electrons is equal to the number of protons. A zinc atom has 30 electrons.

STUDY CHECK 4.4

How many neutrons are in the nucleus of a bromine atom that has a mass number of 80?

ANSWER
45

Chemistry Link to the Environment

Many Forms of Carbon

Carbon has the symbol C. However, its atoms can be arranged in different ways to give several different substances. Two forms of carbon—diamond and graphite—have been known since prehistoric times. In diamond, carbon atoms are arranged in a rigid structure. A diamond is transparent and harder than any other substance, whereas graphite is black and soft. In graphite, carbon atoms are arranged in sheets that slide over each other. Graphite is used as pencil lead, as lubricants, and as carbon fibers for the manufacture of lightweight golf clubs and tennis rackets.

Two other forms of carbon have been discovered more recently. In the form called *Buckminsterfullerene* or *buckyball* (named after

R. Buckminster Fuller, who popularized the geodesic dome), 60 carbon atoms are arranged as rings of five and six atoms to give a spherical, cage-like structure. When a fullerene structure is stretched out, it produces a cylinder with a diameter of only a few nanometers called a *nanotube*. Practical uses for buckyballs and nanotubes are not yet developed, but they are expected to find use in lightweight structural materials, heat conductors, computer parts, and medicine. Recent research has shown that carbon nanotubes (CNTs) can carry many drug molecules that can be released once the CNTs enter the targeted cells.

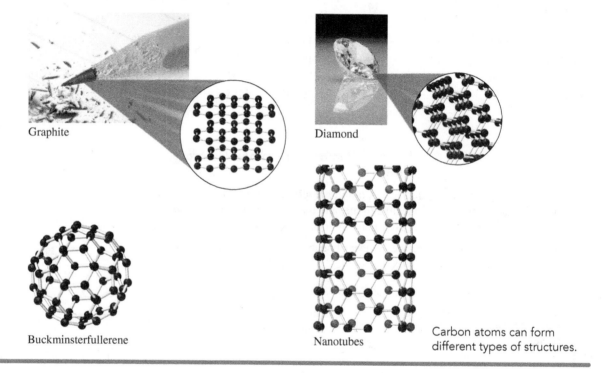

Graphite

Diamond

Buckminsterfullerene

Nanotubes

Carbon atoms can form different types of structures.

QUESTIONS AND PROBLEMS

4.4 Atomic Number and Mass Number

LEARNING GOAL Given the atomic number and the mass number of an atom, state the number of protons, neutrons, and electrons.

4.25 Would you use the atomic number, mass number, or both to determine each of the following?
- **a.** number of protons in an atom
- **b.** number of neutrons in an atom
- **c.** number of particles in the nucleus
- **d.** number of electrons in a neutral atom

4.26 Identify the type of subatomic particles described by each of the following:
- **a.** atomic number
- **b.** mass number
- **c.** mass number − atomic number
- **d.** mass number + atomic number

4.27 Write the names and symbols for the elements with the following atomic numbers:
- **a.** 3
- **b.** 9
- **c.** 20
- **d.** 30
- **e.** 10
- **f.** 14
- **g.** 53
- **h.** 8

4.28 Write the names and symbols for the elements with the following atomic numbers:
- **a.** 1
- **b.** 11
- **c.** 19
- **d.** 82
- **e.** 35
- **f.** 47
- **g.** 15
- **h.** 2

4.29 How many protons and electrons are there in a neutral atom of each of the following elements?
- **a.** argon
- **b.** manganese
- **c.** iodine
- **d.** cadmium

4.30 How many protons and electrons are there in a neutral atom of each of the following elements?
- **a.** carbon
- **b.** fluorine
- **c.** tin
- **d.** nickel

® **Clinical Applications**

4.31 Complete the following table for atoms of essential elements in the body:

Name of the Element	Symbol	Atomic Number	Mass Number	Number of Protons	Number of Neutrons	Number of Electrons
	Zn		66			
		12			12	
Potassium					20	
				16	15	
			56			26

4.32 Complete the following table for atoms of essential elements in the body:

Name of the Element	Symbol	Atomic Number	Mass Number	Number of Protons	Number of Neutrons	Number of Electrons
	N		15			
Calcium			42			
				53	72	
		14			16	
		29	65			

4.5 Isotopes and Atomic Mass

We have seen that all atoms of the same element have the same number of protons and electrons. However, the atoms of any one element are not entirely identical because the atoms of most elements have different numbers of neutrons. When a sample of an element consists of two or more atoms with differing numbers of neutrons, those atoms are called *isotopes*.

Atoms and Isotopes

Isotopes are atoms of the same element that have the same atomic number but different numbers of neutrons. For example, all atoms of the element magnesium (Mg) have an atomic number of 12. Thus every magnesium atom always has 12 protons. However, some naturally occurring magnesium atoms have 12 neutrons, others have 13 neutrons, and still others have 14 neutrons. The different numbers of neutrons give the magnesium atoms different mass numbers but do not change their chemical behavior. The three isotopes of magnesium have the same atomic number but different mass numbers.

To distinguish between the different isotopes of an element, we write an **atomic symbol** for a particular isotope that indicates the mass number in the upper left corner and the atomic number in the lower left corner.

An isotope may be referred to by its name or symbol, followed by its mass number, such as magnesium-24 or Mg-24. Magnesium has three naturally occurring isotopes, as

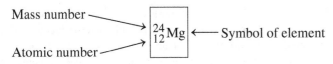

Atomic symbol for an isotope of magnesium, Mg-24.

shown in Table 4.7. In a large sample of naturally occurring magnesium atoms, each type of isotope can be present as a low percentage or a high percentage. For example, the Mg-24 isotope makes up almost 80% of the total sample, whereas Mg-25 and Mg-26 each make up only about 10% of the total number of magnesium atoms.

TABLE 4.7 Isotopes of Magnesium

Atomic Symbol	$^{24}_{12}$Mg	$^{25}_{12}$Mg	$^{26}_{12}$Mg
Name	Mg-24	Mg-25	Mg-26
Number of Protons	12	12	12
Number of Electrons	12	12	12
Mass Number	24	25	26
Number of Neutrons	12	13	14
Mass of Isotope (amu)	23.99	24.99	25.98
Percent Abundance	78.70	10.13	11.17

LEARNING GOAL

Determine the number of protons, neutrons, and electrons in one or more of the isotopes of an element; calculate the atomic mass of an element using the percent abundance and mass of its naturally occurring isotopes.

⊗ **CORE CHEMISTRY SKILL**

Writing Atomic Symbols for Isotopes

Atoms of Mg

Isotopes of Mg

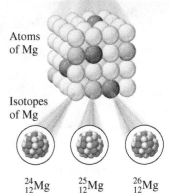

$^{24}_{12}$Mg $^{25}_{12}$Mg $^{26}_{12}$Mg

The nuclei of three naturally occurring magnesium isotopes have the same number of protons but different numbers of neutrons.

SAMPLE PROBLEM 4.5 Identifying Protons and Neutrons in Isotopes

Chromium, a micromineral needed for maintenance of blood sugar levels, has four naturally occurring isotopes:

a. $^{50}_{24}Cr$ **b.** $^{52}_{24}Cr$ **c.** $^{53}_{24}Cr$ **d.** $^{54}_{24}Cr$

Determine the number of protons and number of neutrons in each of these isotopes.

SOLUTION

ANALYZE THE PROBLEM	Given	Need
	atomic symbols for Cr isotopes	number of protons, number of neutrons

In the atomic symbol, the mass number is shown in the upper left corner of the symbol, and the atomic number is shown in the lower left corner of the symbol. Thus, each isotope of Cr, atomic number 24, has 24 protons. The number of neutrons is found by subtracting the number of protons (24) from the mass number of each isotope.

Atomic Symbol	Atomic Number	Mass Number	Number of Protons	Number of Neutrons
a. $^{50}_{24}Cr$	24	50	24	26 (50 − 24)
b. $^{52}_{24}Cr$	24	52	24	28 (52 − 24)
c. $^{53}_{24}Cr$	24	53	24	29 (53 − 24)
d. $^{54}_{24}Cr$	24	53	24	30 (54 − 24)

STUDY CHECK 4.5

Vanadium is a micromineral needed in the formation of bones and teeth. Write the atomic symbol for the single naturally occurring isotope of vanadium, which has 27 neutrons.

ANSWER

$^{50}_{23}V$

Vanadium along with calcium is important in forming strong bones and preventing osteoporosis.

Atomic Mass

In laboratory work, a chemist generally uses samples with many atoms that contain all the different atoms or isotopes of an element. Because each isotope has a different mass, chemists have calculated an **atomic mass** for an "average atom," which is a *weighted average* of the masses of all the naturally occurring isotopes of that element. On the periodic table, the atomic mass is the number including decimal places that is given below the symbol of each element. Most elements consist of two or more isotopes, which is one reason that the atomic masses on the periodic table are seldom whole numbers.

Weighted Average Analogy

To understand how the atomic mass as a weighted average for a group of isotopes is calculated, we will use an analogy of bowling balls with different weights. Suppose that a bowling alley has ordered 5 bowling balls that weigh 8 lb each and 20 bowling balls that weigh 14 lb each. In this group of bowling balls, there are more 14-lb balls than 8-lb balls. The abundance of the 14-lb balls is 80.% (20/25), and the abundance of the 8-lb balls is 20.% (5/25). Now we can calculate a weighted average for the "average" bowling ball using the weight and percent abundance of the two types of bowling balls.

The weighted average of 8-lb and 14-lb bowling balls is calculated using their percent abundance.

	Weight		Percent Abundance		Weight from Each Type
14-lb bowling balls	14 lb	×	$\dfrac{80.}{100}$	=	11.2 lb
8-lb bowling balls	8 lb	×	$\dfrac{20.}{100}$	=	1.6 lb
	Weighted average of a bowling ball			=	12.8 lb
	"Atomic mass" of a bowling ball			=	12.8 lb

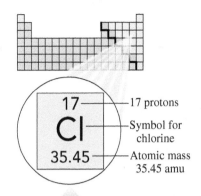

17 — 17 protons

Cl — Symbol for chlorine

35.45 — Atomic mass 35.45 amu

Calculating Atomic Mass

To calculate the atomic mass of an element, we need to know the percentage abundance and the mass of each isotope, which must be determined experimentally. For example, a large sample of naturally occurring chlorine atoms consists of 75.76% of $^{35}_{17}Cl$ atoms and 24.24% of $^{37}_{17}Cl$ atoms. The $^{35}_{17}Cl$ isotope has a mass of 34.97 amu and the $^{37}_{17}Cl$ isotope has a mass of 36.97 amu.

$$\text{Atomic mass of Cl} = \text{mass of } ^{35}_{17}Cl \times \frac{^{35}_{17}Cl\%}{100\%} + \text{mass of } ^{37}_{17}Cl \times \frac{^{37}_{17}Cl\%}{100\%}$$

$$\underbrace{\qquad\qquad}_{\text{amu from } ^{35}_{17}Cl} \qquad\qquad \underbrace{\qquad\qquad}_{\text{amu from } ^{37}_{17}Cl}$$

Atomic Symbol	Mass (amu)	×	Abundance (%)	=	Contribution to Average Cl Atom
$^{35}_{17}Cl$	34.97	×	$\dfrac{75.76}{100}$	=	26.49 amu
$^{37}_{17}Cl$	36.97	×	$\dfrac{24.24}{100}$	=	8.962 amu
			Atomic mass of Cl	=	35.45 amu (weighted average mass)

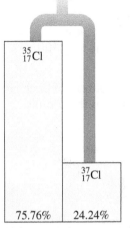

Chlorine, with two naturally occurring isotopes, has an atomic mass of 35.45 amu.

The atomic mass of 35.45 amu is the weighted average mass of a sample of Cl atoms, although no individual Cl atom actually has this mass. An atomic mass of 35.45, which is closer to the mass number of Cl-35, also indicates there is a higher percentage of $^{35}_{17}Cl$ atoms in the chlorine sample. In fact, there are about three atoms of $^{35}_{17}Cl$ for every one atom of $^{37}_{17}Cl$ in a sample of chlorine atoms.

Table 4.8 lists the naturally occurring isotopes of some selected elements and their atomic masses along with their most prevalent isotopes.

TABLE 4.8 The Atomic Mass of Some Elements

Element	Atomic Symbols	Atomic Mass (weighted average)	Most Prevalent Isotope
Lithium	$^{6}_{3}Li, ^{7}_{3}Li$	6.941 amu	$^{7}_{3}Li$
Carbon	$^{12}_{6}C, ^{13}_{6}C, ^{14}_{6}C$	12.01 amu	$^{12}_{6}C$
Oxygen	$^{16}_{8}O, ^{17}_{8}O, ^{18}_{8}O$	16.00 amu	$^{16}_{8}O$
Fluorine	$^{19}_{9}F$	19.00 amu	$^{19}_{9}F$
Sulfur	$^{32}_{16}S, ^{33}_{16}S, ^{34}_{16}S, ^{36}_{16}S$	32.07 amu	$^{32}_{16}S$
Potassium	$^{39}_{19}K, ^{40}_{19}K, ^{41}_{19}K$	39.10 amu	$^{39}_{19}K$
Copper	$^{63}_{29}Cu, ^{65}_{29}Cu$	63.55 amu	$^{63}_{29}Cu$

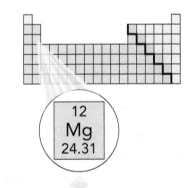

12 Mg 24.31

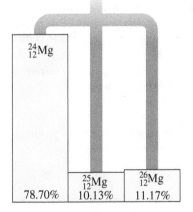

Magnesium, with three naturally occurring isotopes, has an atomic mass of 24.31 amu.

> SAMPLE PROBLEM 4.6 **Calculating Atomic Mass**

Magnesium is a macromineral needed in the contraction of muscles and metabolic reactions. Using Table 4.7, calculate the atomic mass for magnesium using the weighted average mass method.

SOLUTION

STEP **1** Multiply the mass of each isotope by its percent abundance divided by 100.

Atomic Symbol	Mass (amu)		Abundance (%)		Contribution to the Atomic Mass
$^{24}_{12}Mg$	23.99	×	$\dfrac{78.70}{100}$	=	18.88 amu
$^{25}_{12}Mg$	24.99	×	$\dfrac{10.13}{100}$	=	2.531 amu
$^{26}_{12}Mg$	25.98	×	$\dfrac{11.17}{100}$	=	2.902 amu

STEP **2** Add the contribution of each isotope to obtain the atomic mass. Add the contribution of each isotope to give the weighted average mass, which is the atomic mass.

$$\text{Atomic mass of Mg} = 18.88 \text{ amu} + 2.531 \text{ amu} + 2.902 \text{ amu}$$
$$= 24.31 \text{ amu (weighted average mass)}$$

STUDY CHECK 4.6

There are two naturally occurring isotopes of boron. The isotope $^{10}_{5}B$ has a mass of 10.01 amu with an abundance of 19.80%, and the isotope $^{11}_{5}B$ has a mass of 11.01 amu with an abundance of 80.20%. Calculate the atomic mass for boron using the weighted average mass method.

ANSWER

10.81 amu

Guide to Calculating Atomic Mass

STEP 1
Multiply the mass of each isotope by its percent abundance divided by 100.

STEP 2
Add the contribution of each isotope to obtain the atomic mass.

QUESTIONS AND PROBLEMS

4.5 Isotopes and Atomic Mass

LEARNING GOAL Determine the number of protons, neutrons, and electrons in one or more of the isotopes of an element; calculate the atomic mass of an element using the percent abundance and mass of its naturally occurring isotopes.

4.33 What are the number of protons, neutrons, and electrons in the following isotopes?
  a. $^{89}_{38}Sr$ b. $^{52}_{24}Cr$
  c. $^{34}_{16}S$ d. $^{81}_{35}Br$

4.34 What are the number of protons, neutrons, and electrons in the following isotopes?
  a. $^{2}_{1}H$ b. $^{14}_{7}N$
  c. $^{26}_{14}Si$ d. $^{70}_{30}Zn$

4.35 Write the atomic symbol for the isotope with each of the following characteristics:
  a. 15 protons and 16 neutrons
  b. 35 protons and 45 neutrons
  c. 50 electrons and 72 neutrons
  d. a chlorine atom with 18 neutrons
  e. a mercury atom with 122 neutrons

4.36 Write the atomic symbol for the isotope with each of the following characteristics:
  a. an oxygen atom with 10 neutrons
  b. 4 protons and 5 neutrons
  c. 25 electrons and 28 neutrons
  d. a mass number of 24 and 13 neutrons
  e. a nickel atom with 32 neutrons

4.37 Argon has three naturally occurring isotopes, with mass numbers 36, 38, and 40.
  a. Write the atomic symbol for each of these atoms.
  b. How are these isotopes alike?
  c. How are they different?
  d. Why is the atomic mass of argon listed on the periodic table not a whole number?
  e. Which isotope is the most prevalent in a sample of argon?

4.38 Strontium has four naturally occurring isotopes, with mass numbers 84, 86, 87, and 88.
  a. Write the atomic symbol for each of these atoms.
  b. How are these isotopes alike?
  c. How are they different?
  d. Why is the atomic mass of strontium listed on the periodic table not a whole number?
  e. Which isotope is the most prevalent in a sample of strontium?

4.39 Two isotopes of gallium are naturally occurring, with $^{69}_{31}\text{Ga}$ at 60.11% (68.93 amu) and $^{71}_{31}\text{Ga}$ at 39.89% (70.92 amu). Calculate the atomic mass for gallium using the weighted average mass method.

4.40 Two isotopes of rubidium occur naturally, with $^{85}_{37}\text{Rb}$ at 72.17% (84.91 amu) and $^{87}_{37}\text{Rb}$ at 27.83% (86.91 amu). Calculate the atomic mass for rubidium using the weighted average mass method.

4.6 Electron Energy Levels

When we listen to a radio, use a microwave oven, turn on a light, see the colors of a rainbow, or have an X-ray taken, we are experiencing various forms of *electromagnetic radiation*. Light and other electromagnetic radiation consist of energy particles that move as waves of energy. In a wave, just like the waves in an ocean, the distance between the peaks is called the *wavelength*. All forms of electromagnetic radiation travel in space at the speed of light, 3.0×10^8 m/s, but differ in energy and wavelength. High-energy radiation has short wavelengths compared to low-energy radiation, which has longer wavelengths. The *electromagnetic spectrum* shows the arrangement of different types of electromagnetic radiation in order of increasing energy (see Figure 4.11).

When the light from the Sun passes through a prism, the light separates into a continuous color spectrum, which consists of the colors we see in a rainbow. In contrast, when light from a heated element passes through a prism, it separates into distinct lines of color separated by dark areas called an *atomic spectrum*. Each element has its own unique atomic spectrum.

LEARNING GOAL

Describe the energy levels, sublevels, and orbitals for the electrons in an atom.

A rainbow forms when light passes through water droplets.

Light passes through a slit   Prism   Film

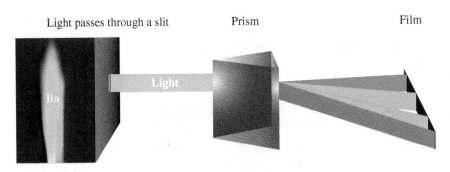

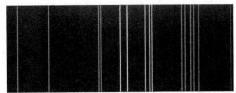

Barium light spectrum

In an atomic spectrum, light from a heated element separates into distinct lines.

Electron Energy Levels

Scientists have now determined that the lines in the atomic spectra of elements are associated with changes in the energies of the electrons. In an atom, each electron has a specific energy known as its **energy level**, which is assigned values called *principal quantum numbers* (n), ($n = 1, n = 2, \dots$). Generally, electrons in the lower energy levels are closer to the nucleus, whereas electrons in the higher energy levels are farther away. The energy of an electron is *quantized*, which means that the energy of an electron can only have specific energy values, but cannot have values between them.

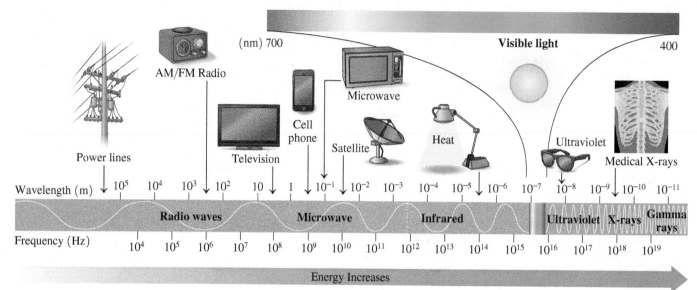

FIGURE 4.11 ▶ The electromagnetic spectrum shows the arrangement of wavelengths of electromagnetic radiation. The visible portion consists of wavelengths from 700 nm to 400 nm.

How does the wavelength of ultraviolet light compare to that of a microwave?

Order of Increasing Energy of Levels

$$1 < 2 < 3 < 4 < 5 < 6 < 7$$

Lowest energy ⟶ Highest energy

All the electrons with the same energy are grouped in the same energy level. As an analogy, we can think of the energy levels of an atom as similar to the shelves in a bookcase. The first shelf is the lowest energy level; the second shelf is the second energy level,

 # Chemistry Link to Health
Biological Reactions to UV Light

Our everyday life depends on sunlight, but exposure to sunlight can have damaging effects on living cells, and too much exposure can even cause their death. The light energy, especially ultraviolet (UV), excites electrons and may lead to unwanted chemical reactions. The list of damaging effects of sunlight includes sunburn; wrinkling; premature aging of the skin; changes in the DNA of the cells, which can lead to skin cancers; inflammation of the eyes; and perhaps cataracts. Some drugs, like the acne medications Accutane and Retin-A, as well as antibiotics, diuretics, sulfonamides, and estrogen, make the skin extremely sensitive to light.

However, medicine does take advantage of the beneficial effect of sunlight. *Phototherapy* can be used to treat certain skin conditions, including psoriasis, eczema, and dermatitis. In the treatment of psoriasis, for example, oral drugs are given to make the skin more photosensitive; exposure to UV follows. Low-energy light is used to break down bilirubin in neonatal jaundice. Sunlight is also a factor in stimulating the immune system.

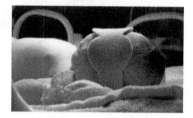

Babies with neonatal jaundice are treated with UV light.

In a disorder called *seasonal affective disorder* or SAD, people experience mood swings and depression during the winter. Some research suggests that SAD is the result of a decrease of serotonin, or an increase in melatonin, when there are fewer hours of sunlight. One treatment for SAD is therapy using bright light provided by a lamp called a light box. A daily exposure to intense light for 30 to 60 min seems to reduce symptoms of SAD.

and so on. If we are arranging books on the shelves, it would take less energy to fill the bottom shelf first, and then the second shelf, and so on. However, we could never get any book to stay in the space between any of the shelves. Similarly, the energy of an electron must be at specific energy levels, and not between.

Unlike standard bookcases, however, there is a large difference between the energy of the first and second levels, but then the higher energy levels are closer together. Another difference is that the lower electron energy levels hold fewer electrons than the higher energy levels.

Changes in Electron Energy Level

An electron can change from one energy level to a higher level only if it absorbs the energy equal to the difference in energy levels. When an electron changes to a lower energy level, it emits energy equal to the difference between the two levels (see Figure 4.12). If the energy emitted is in the visible range, we see one of the colors of visible light. The yellow color of sodium streetlights and the red color of neon lights are examples of electrons emitting energy in the visible color range.

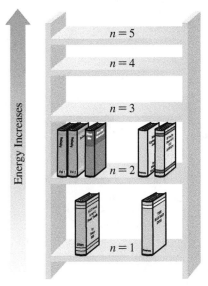

Nucleus

An electron can have only the energy of one of the energy levels in an atom.

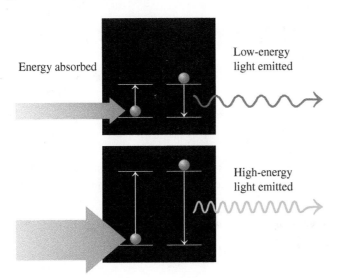

Energy absorbed

Low-energy light emitted

High-energy light emitted

FIGURE 4.12 ▶ Electrons absorb a specific amount of energy to move to a higher energy level. When electrons lose energy, a specific quantity of energy is emitted.

❓ What causes electrons to move to higher energy levels?

 # Chemistry Link to the Environment

Energy-Saving Fluorescent Bulbs

Compact fluorescent lights (CFL) are replacing the standard light bulb we use in our homes and workplaces. Compared to a standard light bulb, the CFL has a longer life and uses less electricity. Within about 20 days of use, the CFL saves enough money in electricity costs to pay for its higher initial cost.

A standard incandescent light bulb has a thin tungsten filament inside a sealed glass bulb. When the light is switched on, electricity flows through this filament, and electrical energy is converted to heat energy. When the filament reaches a temperature around 2300 °C, we see white light.

A fluorescent bulb produces light in a different way. When the switch is turned on, electrons move between two electrodes and collide with mercury atoms in a mixture of mercury and argon gas inside the light. When the electrons in the mercury atoms absorb energy from the collisions, they are raised to higher energy levels. As electrons fall to lower energy levels emitting ultraviolet radiation, they strike the phosphor coating inside the tube, and fluorescence occurs as visible light is emitted.

The production of light in a fluorescent bulb is more efficient than in an incandescent light bulb. A 75-watt incandescent bulb can be replaced by a 20-watt CFL that gives the same amount of light, providing a 70% reduction in electricity costs. A typical incandescent light bulb lasts for one to two months, whereas a CFL lasts from 1 to 2 yr. One drawback of the CFL is that each contains about 4 mg of mercury. As long as the bulb stays intact, no mercury is released. However, used CFL bulbs should not be disposed of in household trash but rather should be taken to a recycling center.

A compact fluorescent light (CFL) uses up to 70% less energy.

Sublevels

We have seen that the protons and neutrons are contained in the small, dense nucleus of an atom. However, it is the electrons within the atoms that determine the physical and chemical properties of the elements. Therefore, we will look at the arrangement of electrons within the large volume of space surrounding the nucleus.

Each of the energy levels consists of one or more **sublevels**, in which electrons with identical energy are found. The sublevels are identified by the letters s, p, d, and f. The number of sublevels within an energy level is equal to the principal quantum number, n. For example, the first energy level ($n = 1$) has only one sublevel, $1s$. The second energy level ($n = 2$) has two sublevels, $2s$ and $2p$. The third energy level ($n = 3$) has three sublevels, $3s$, $3p$, and $3d$. The fourth energy level ($n = 4$) has four sublevels, $4s$, $4p$, $4d$, and $4f$. Energy levels $n = 5$, $n = 6$, and $n = 7$ also have as many sublevels as the value of n, but only s, p, d, and f sublevels are needed to hold the electrons in atoms of the 118 known elements (see Figure 4.13).

FIGURE 4.13 ▶ The number of sublevels in an energy level is the same as the principal quantum number, n.

Q How many sublevels are in the $n = 5$ energy level?

Energy Level	Number of Sublevels	Types of Sublevels
$n = 4$	4	s p d f
$n = 3$	3	
$n = 2$	2	
$n = 1$	1	

Within each energy level, the s sublevel has the lowest energy. If there are additional sublevels, the p sublevel has the next lowest energy, then the d sublevel, and finally the f sublevel.

Order of Increasing Energy of Sublevels in an Energy Level

$$s < p < d < f$$

Lowest energy $\longrightarrow$ Highest energy

Orbitals

There is no way to know the exact location of an electron in an atom. Instead, scientists describe the location of an electron in terms of probability. The **orbital** is the three-dimensional volume in which electrons have the highest probability of being found.

As an analogy, imagine that you could draw a circle with a 100-m radius around your chemistry classroom. There is a high probability of finding you within that circle when your chemistry class is in session. But once in a while, you may be outside that circle because you were sick or your car did not start.

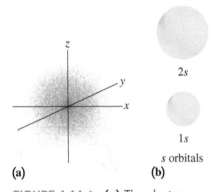

3s

2s

1s

s orbitals

(a)   (b)

FIGURE 4.14 ▶ **(a)** The electron cloud of an s orbital represents the highest probability of finding an s electron. **(b)** The s orbitals are shown as spheres. The sizes of the s orbitals increase because they contain electrons at higher energy levels.

Q Is the probability high or low of finding an s electron outside an s orbital?

Shapes of Orbitals

Each type of orbital has a unique three-dimensional shape. Electrons in an s orbital are most likely found in a region with a spherical shape. Imagine that you take a picture of the location of an electron in an s orbital every second for an hour. When all these pictures are overlaid, the result, called a *probability density*, would look like the electron cloud shown in Figure 4.14a. For convenience, we draw this electron cloud as a sphere called an s orbital. There is one s orbital for every energy level starting with $n = 1$. For example, in the first, second, and third energy levels there are s orbitals designated as $1s$, $2s$, and $3s$. As the principal quantum number increases, there is an increase in the size of the s orbitals, although the shape is the same (see Figure 4.14b).

The orbitals occupied by p, d, and f electrons have three-dimensional shapes different from those of the s electrons. There are three p orbitals, starting with $n = 2$. Each p orbital has two lobes like a balloon tied in the middle. The three p orbitals are arranged in three perpendicular directions, along the x, y, and z axes around the nucleus (see Figure 4.15). As with s orbitals, the shape of p orbitals is the same, but the volume increases at higher energy levels.

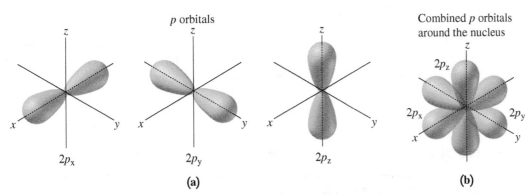

FIGURE 4.15 ▶ A p orbital has two regions of high probability, which gives a "dumbbell" shape. **(a)** Each p orbital is aligned along a different axis from the other p orbitals. **(b)** All three p orbitals are shown around the nucleus.

Ⓠ What are some similarities and differences of the p orbitals in the $n = 3$ energy level?

In summary, the $n = 2$ energy level, which has $2s$ and $2p$ sublevels, consists of one s orbital and three p orbitals.

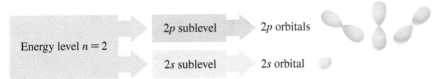

Energy level $n = 2$ consists of one $2s$ orbital and three $2p$ orbitals.

Energy level $n = 3$ consists of three sublevels s, p, and d. The d sublevels contain five d orbitals (see Figure 4.16).

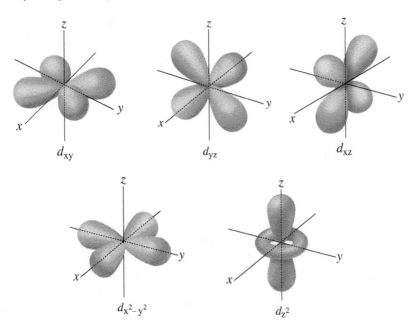

FIGURE 4.16 ▶ Four of the five d orbitals consist of four lobes that are aligned along or between different axes. One d orbital consists of two lobes and a doughnut-shaped ring around its center.

Ⓠ How many orbitals are there in the $5d$ sublevel?

Energy level $n = 4$ consists of four sublevels s, p, d, and f. In the f sublevel, there are seven f orbitals. The shapes of f orbitals are complex and so we have not included them in this text.

Orbital Capacity and Electron Spin

The *Pauli exclusion principle* states that each orbital can hold a maximum of two electrons. According to a useful model for electron behavior, an electron is seen as spinning on its axis, which generates a magnetic field. When two electrons are in the same orbital, they will repel each other unless their magnetic fields cancel. This happens only when the two electrons spin in opposite directions. We can represent the spins of the electrons in the same orbital with one arrow pointing up and the other pointing down.

Electron spinning counterclockwise   Electron spinning clockwise

Opposite spins of electrons in an orbital

An orbital can hold up to two electrons with opposite spins.

Number of Electrons in Sublevels

There is a maximum number of electrons that can occupy each sublevel. An s sublevel holds one or two electrons. Because each p orbital can hold up to two electrons, the three p orbitals in a p sublevel can accommodate six electrons. A d sublevel with five d orbitals can hold a maximum of 10 electrons. With seven f orbitals, an f sublevel can hold up to 14 electrons.

As mentioned earlier, higher energy levels such as $n = 5$, 6, and 7 would have 5, 6, and 7 sublevels, but those beyond sublevel f are not utilized by the atoms of the elements known today. The total number of electrons in all the sublevels adds up to give the electrons allowed in an energy level. The number of sublevels, the number of orbitals, and the maximum number of electrons for energy levels 1 to 4 are shown in Table 4.9.

TABLE 4.9 Electron Capacity in Sublevels for Energy Levels 1 to 4

Energy Level (n)	Number of Sublevels	Type of Sublevel	Number of Orbitals	Maximum Number of Electrons	Total Electrons
4	4	$4f$	7	14	
		$4d$	5	10	
		$4p$	3	6	32
		$4s$	1	2	
3	3	$3d$	5	10	
		$3p$	3	6	18
		$3s$	1	2	
2	2	$2p$	3	6	
		$2s$	1	2	8
1	1	$1s$	1	2	2

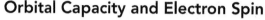

QUESTIONS AND PROBLEMS

4.6 Electron Energy Levels

LEARNING GOAL Describe the energy levels, sublevels, and orbitals for the electrons in an atom.

4.41 Describe the shape of each of the following orbitals:
   a. $1s$ **b.** $2p$ **c.** $5s$

4.42 Describe the shape of each of the following orbitals:
   a. $3p$ **b.** $6s$ **c.** $4p$

4.43 Match statements **1** to **3** with **a** to **d**:
   1. They have the same shape.
   2. The maximum number of electrons is the same.
   3. They are in the same energy level.

   a. $1s$ and $2s$ orbitals   **b.** $3s$ and $3p$ sublevels
   c. $3p$ and $4p$ sublevels   **d.** three $3p$ orbitals

4.44 Match statements **1** to **3** with **a** to **d**:
1. They have the same shape.
2. The maximum number of electrons is the same.
3. They are in the same energy level.

a. 5s and 6s orbitals   b. 3p and 4p orbitals
c. 3s and 4s sublevels   d. 2s and 2p orbitals

4.45 Indicate the number of each in the following:
a. orbitals in the 3d sublevel
b. sublevels in the $n = 1$ energy level
c. orbitals in the 6s sublevel
d. orbitals in the $n = 3$ energy level

4.46 Indicate the number of each in the following:
a. orbitals in the $n = 2$ energy level
b. sublevels in the $n = 4$ energy level
c. orbitals in the 5f sublevel
d. orbitals in the 6p sublevel

4.47 Indicate the maximum number of electrons in the following:
a. 2p orbital   b. 3p sublevel
c. $n = 4$ energy level   d. 5d sublevel

4.48 Indicate the maximum number of electrons in the following:
a. 3s sublevel   b. 4p orbital
c. $n = 3$ energy level   d. 4f sublevel

4.7 Electron Configurations

LEARNING GOAL

Draw the orbital diagram and write the electron configuration for an element.

We can now look at how electrons are arranged in the orbitals within an atom. An **orbital diagram** shows the placement of the electrons in the orbitals in order of increasing energy (Figure 4.17). In this energy diagram, we see that the electrons in the 1s orbital have the lowest energy level. The energy level is higher for the 2s orbital and is even higher for the 2p orbitals.

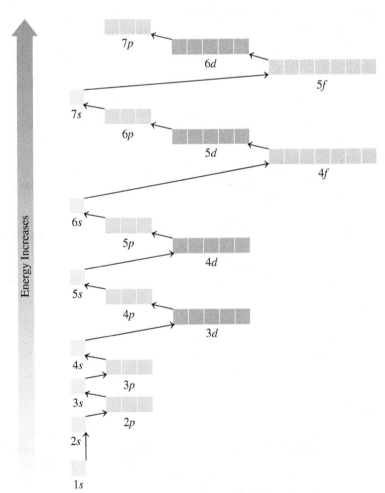

FIGURE 4.17 ▶ The orbitals in an atom fill in order of increasing energy beginning with 1s.

🔘 Why do 3d orbitals fill after the 4s orbital?

We begin our discussion of electron configuration by using orbital diagrams in which boxes represent the orbitals. Any orbital can have a maximum of two electrons.

To draw an orbital diagram, the lowest energy orbitals are filled first. For example, we can draw the orbital diagram for carbon. The atomic number of carbon is 6, which means that a carbon atom has six electrons. The first two electrons go into the $1s$ orbital; the next two electrons go into the $2s$ orbital. In the orbital diagram, the two electrons in the $1s$ and $2s$ orbitals are shown with opposite spins; the first arrow is up and the second is down. The last two electrons in carbon begin to fill the $2p$ sublevel, which has the next lowest energy. However, there are three $2p$ orbitals of equal energy. Because the negatively charged electrons repel each other, they are placed in separate $2p$ orbitals. With few exceptions (which will be noted later in this chapter) lower energy sublevels are filled first, and then the "building" of electrons continues to the next lowest energy sublevel that is available until all the electrons are placed.

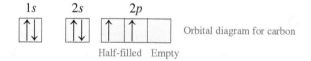

Orbital diagram for carbon

<table>
</table>

CORE CHEMISTRY SKILL

Writing Electron Configurations

Electron Configurations

Chemists use a notation called the **electron configuration** to indicate the placement of the electrons of an atom in order of increasing energy. The electron configuration is written with the lowest energy sublevel first, followed by the next lowest energy sublevel. The number of electrons in each sublevel is shown as a superscript.

Electron Configuration for Carbon

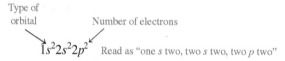

$1s^2 2s^2 2p^2$ Read as "one s two, two s two, two p two"

Period 1: Hydrogen and Helium

We will draw orbital diagrams and write electron configurations for the elements H and He in Period 1. The $1s$ orbital (which is the $1s$ sublevel) is written first because it has the lowest energy. Hydrogen has one electron in the $1s$ sublevel; helium has two. In the orbital diagram, the electrons for helium are shown as arrows pointing in opposite directions.

Element	Atomic Number	Orbital Diagram	Electron Configuration
H	1	↑	$1s^1$
He	2	↑↓	$1s^2$

Period 2: Lithium to Neon

Period 2 begins with lithium, which has three electrons. The first two electrons fill the $1s$ orbital, whereas the third electron goes into the $2s$ orbital, the sublevel with the next lowest energy. In beryllium, another electron is added to complete the $2s$ orbital. The next six electrons are used to fill the $2p$ orbitals. The electrons are added one at a time from boron to nitrogen, which gives three half-filled $2p$ orbitals.

From oxygen to neon, the remaining three electrons are paired up using opposite spins to complete the $2p$ sublevel. In writing the electron configurations for the elements in Period 2, begin with the $1s$ orbital followed by the $2s$ and then the $2p$ orbitals.

An electron configuration can also be written in an *abbreviated configuration*. The electron configuration of the preceding noble gas is replaced by writing its element symbol inside square brackets. For example, the electron configuration for lithium, $1s^22s^1$, can be abbreviated as $[\text{He}]2s^1$ where $[\text{He}]$ replaces $1s^2$.

Element	Atomic Number	Orbital Diagram	Electron Configuration	Abbreviated Electron Configuration
Li	3	1s 2s ↑↓ ↑	$1s^22s^1$	$[\text{He}]2s^1$
Be	4	↑↓ ↑↓	$1s^22s^2$	$[\text{He}]2s^2$
B	5	2p ↑↓ ↑↓ ↑	$1s^22s^22p^1$	$[\text{He}]2s^22p^1$
C	6	↑↓ ↑↓ ↑ ↑	$1s^22s^22p^2$	$[\text{He}]2s^22p^2$
N	7	↑↓ ↑↓ ↑ ↑ ↑	$1s^22s^22p^3$	$[\text{He}]2s^22p^3$
O	8	↑↓ ↑↓ ↑↓ ↑ ↑	$1s^22s^22p^4$	$[\text{He}]2s^22p^4$
F	9	↑↓ ↑↓ ↑↓ ↑↓ ↑	$1s^22s^22p^5$	$[\text{He}]2s^22p^5$
Ne	10	↑↓ ↑↓ ↑↓ ↑↓ ↑↓	$1s^22s^22p^6$	$[\text{He}]2s^22p^6$

(Unpaired electrons)

▶ **SAMPLE PROBLEM 4.7 Drawing Orbital Diagrams**

Nitrogen is an element that is used in the formation of amino acids, proteins, and nucleic acids. Draw the orbital diagram for nitrogen.

SOLUTION

STEP 1 Draw boxes to represent the occupied orbitals. Nitrogen has atomic number 7, which means it has seven electrons. For the orbital diagram, we draw boxes to represent the $1s$, $2s$, and $2p$ orbitals.

1s 2s 2p
☐ ☐ ☐☐☐

STEP 2 Place a pair of electrons with opposite spins in each filled orbital. First, we place a pair of electrons with opposite spins in both the $1s$ and $2s$ orbitals.

1s 2s 2p
↑↓ ↑↓ ☐☐☐

STEP 3 Place the remaining electrons in the last occupied sublevel in separate orbitals. Then we place the three remaining electrons in three separate $2p$ orbitals with arrows drawn in the same direction.

1s 2s 2p
↑↓ ↑↓ ↑ ↑ ↑
Orbital diagram for nitrogen (N)

> **Guide to Drawing Orbital Diagrams**
>
> **STEP 1**
> Draw boxes to represent the occupied orbitals.
>
> **STEP 2**
> Place a pair of electrons with opposite spins in each filled orbital.
>
> **STEP 3**
> Place the remaining electrons in the last occupied sublevel in separate orbitals.

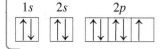

Period 3: Sodium to Argon

In Period 3, electrons enter the orbitals of the $3s$ and $3p$ sublevels, but not the $3d$ sublevel. We notice that the elements sodium to argon, which are directly below the elements lithium to neon in Period 2, have a similar pattern of filling their s and p orbitals. In sodium and magnesium, one and two electrons go into the $3s$ orbital. The electrons for aluminum, silicon, and phosphorus go into separate $3p$ orbitals. The remaining electrons in sulfur, chlorine, and argon are paired up (opposite spins) with the electrons already in the $3p$ orbitals. For the abbreviated electron configurations of Period 3, the symbol $[Ne]$ replaces $1s^2 2s^2 2p^6$.

Element	Atomic Number	Orbital Diagram (3s and 3p orbitals only)	Electron Configuration	Abbreviated Electron Configuration
Na	11	$[Ne]$ ↑ ☐ ☐ ☐	$1s^2 2s^2 2p^6 3s^1$	$[Ne]3s^1$
Mg	12	$[Ne]$ ↑↓ ☐ ☐ ☐	$1s^2 2s^2 2p^6 3s^2$	$[Ne]3s^2$
Al	13	$[Ne]$ ↑↓ ↑ ☐ ☐	$1s^2 2s^2 2p^6 3s^2 3p^1$	$[Ne]3s^2 3p^1$
Si	14	$[Ne]$ ↑↓ ↑ ↑ ☐	$1s^2 2s^2 2p^6 3s^2 3p^2$	$[Ne]3s^2 3p^2$
P	15	$[Ne]$ ↑↓ ↑ ↑ ↑	$1s^2 2s^2 2p^6 3s^2 3p^3$	$[Ne]3s^2 3p^3$
S	16	$[Ne]$ ↑↓ ↑↓ ↑ ↑	$1s^2 2s^2 2p^6 3s^2 3p^4$	$[Ne]3s^2 3p^4$
Cl	17	$[Ne]$ ↑↓ ↑↓ ↑↓ ↑	$1s^2 2s^2 2p^6 3s^2 3p^5$	$[Ne]3s^2 3p^5$
Ar	18	$[Ne]$ ↑↓ ↑↓ ↑↓ ↑↓	$1s^2 2s^2 2p^6 3s^2 3p^6$	$[Ne]3s^2 3p^6$

▶ **SAMPLE PROBLEM 4.8** Orbital Diagrams and Electron Configurations

Silicon is a micromineral needed for the growth of bones, tendons, and ligaments. Draw or write each of the following for silicon:

a. orbital diagram
b. abbreviated orbital diagram
c. electron configuration
d. abbreviated electron configuration

SOLUTION

	Given	Need
ANALYZE THE PROBLEM	silicon (Si)	orbital diagram, abbreviated orbital diagram, electron configuration, abbreviated electron configuration

a. Place two electrons in each orbital, and single electrons in the highest energy level.

Complete orbital diagram for Si

b. Write the symbol for the preceding noble gas followed by the orbitals for the remaining electrons.

[Ne]

Abbreviated orbital diagram for Si

c. List the sublevels in order of filling and add the number of electrons.

$1s^2 2s^2 2p^6 3s^2 3p^2$ Electron configuration for Si

d. Write the symbol for the preceding noble gas followed by the configuration for the remaining electrons.

$[Ne]3s^2 3p^2$ Abbreviated electron configuration for Si

STUDY CHECK 4.8

Write the complete and abbreviated electron configurations for sulfur, which is a macromineral in proteins, vitamin B_1, and insulin.

ANSWER

$1s^2 2s^2 2p^6 3s^2 3p^4$, $[Ne]3s^2 3p^4$

Electron Configurations and the Periodic Table

The electron configurations of the elements are also related to their position on the periodic table. Different sections or blocks within the periodic table correspond to the s, p, d, and f sublevels (see Figure 4.18).

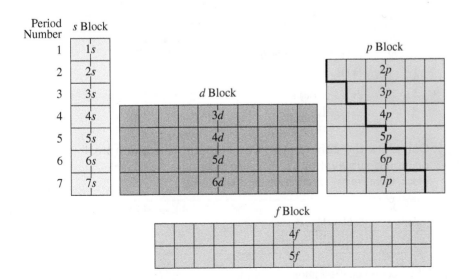

FIGURE 4.18 ▶ Electron configurations follow the order of occupied sublevels on the periodic table.

Q If neon is in Group 8A (18), Period 2, how many electrons are in the 1s, 2s, and 2p sublevels of neon?

Blocks on the Periodic Table

1. The *s* **block** includes hydrogen and helium as well as the elements in Group 1A (1) and Group 2A (2). This means that the final one or two electrons in the elements of the *s* block are located in an *s* orbital. The period number indicates the particular *s* orbital that is filling: 1*s*, 2*s*, and so on.

2. The *p* **block** consists of the elements in Group 3A (13) to Group 8A (18). There are six *p* block elements in each period because three *p* orbitals can hold up to six electrons. The period number indicates the particular *p* sublevel that is filling: 2*p*, 3*p*, and so on.

3. The *d* **block**, containing the transition elements, first appears after calcium (atomic number 20). There are 10 elements in each period of the *d* block because five *d* orbitals can hold up to 10 electrons. The particular *d* sublevel is one less $(n - 1)$ than the period number. For example, in Period 4, the *d* block is the 3*d* sublevel. In Period 5, the *d* block is the 4*d* sublevel.

4. The *f* **block**, the inner transition elements, are the two rows at the bottom of the periodic table. There are 14 elements in each *f* block because seven *f* orbitals can hold up to 14 electrons. Elements that have atomic numbers higher than 57 (La) have electrons in the 4*f* block. The particular *f* sublevel is two less $(n - 2)$ than the period number. For example, in Period 6, the *f* block is the 4*f* sublevel. In Period 7, the *f* block is the 5*f* sublevel.

Writing Electron Configurations Using Sublevel Blocks

Now we can write electron configurations using the sublevel blocks on the periodic table. As before, each configuration begins at H. But now we move across the table from left to right, writing down each sublevel block we come to until we reach the element for which we are writing an electron configuration. We show how to write the electron configuration for chlorine (atomic number 17) using the sublevel blocks on the periodic table in Sample Problem 4.9.

SAMPLE PROBLEM 4.9 Using Sublevel Blocks to Write Electron Configurations

Chlorine is a macromineral that is prevalent in extracellular fluids and stomach acid. Use the sublevel blocks on the periodic table to write the electron configuration for chlorine.

SOLUTION

STEP 1 Locate the element on the periodic table. Chlorine (atomic number 17) is in Group 7A (17) and Period 3.

STEP 2 Write the filled sublevels in order, going across each period.

Period	Sublevel Block Filling	Sublevel Block Notation (filled)
1	1*s* (H → He)	$1s^2$
2	2*s* (Li → Be) and 2*p* (B → Ne)	$2s^2 2p^6$
3	3*s* (Na → Mg)	$3s^2$

STEP 3 Complete the configuration by counting the electrons in the last occupied sublevel block. Because chlorine is the fifth element in the 3*p* block, there are five electrons in the 3*p* sublevel.

Period	Sublevel Block Filling	Sublevel Block Notation
3	3*p* (Al → Cl)	$3p^5$

The electron configuration for chlorine (Cl) is: $1s^2 2s^2 2p^6 3s^2 3p^5$.

STUDY CHECK 4.9

Use the sublevel blocks on the periodic table to write the electron configuration for magnesium, a macromineral needed to form bones and required for metabolic reactions.

ANSWER

$1s^2 2s^2 2p^6 3s^2$

Electron Configurations for Period 4 and Above

Up to Period 4, the filling of the sublevels has progressed in order. However, if we look at the sublevel blocks in Period 4, we see that the $4s$ sublevel fills before the $3d$ sublevel. This occurs because the electrons in the $4s$ sublevel have slightly lower energy than the electrons in the $3d$ sublevel. This order occurs again in Period 5 when the $5s$ sublevel fills before the $4d$ sublevel and again in Period 6 when the $6s$ fills before the $5d$.

At the beginning of Period 4, the electrons in potassium (19) and calcium (20) go into the $4s$ sublevel. In scandium, the next electron added goes into the $3d$ block, which continues to fill until it is complete with 10 electrons at zinc (30). Once the $3d$ block is complete, the next six electrons, gallium to krypton, go into the $4p$ block.

Element	Atomic Number	Electron Configuration	Abbreviated Electron Configuration	
4s Block				
K	19	$1s^2 2s^2 2p^6 3s^2 3p^6 4s^1$	$[Ar]4s^1$	
Ca	20	$1s^2 2s^2 2p^6 3s^2 3p^6 4s^2$	$[Ar]4s^2$	
3d Block				
Sc	21	$1s^2 2s^2 2p^6 3s^2 3p^6 4s^2 3d^1$	$[Ar]4s^2 3d^1$	
Ti	22	$1s^2 2s^2 2p^6 3s^2 3p^6 4s^2 3d^2$	$[Ar]4s^2 3d^2$	
V	23	$1s^2 2s^2 2p^6 3s^2 3p^6 4s^2 3d^3$	$[Ar]4s^2 3d^3$	
Cr*	24	$1s^2 2s^2 2p^6 3s^2 3p^6 4s^1 3d^5$	$[Ar]4s^1 3d^5$	(half-filled d sublevel is stable)
Mn	25	$1s^2 2s^2 2p^6 3s^2 3p^6 4s^2 3d^5$	$[Ar]4s^2 3d^5$	
Fe	26	$1s^2 2s^2 2p^6 3s^2 3p^6 4s^2 3d^6$	$[Ar]4s^2 3d^6$	
Co	27	$1s^2 2s^2 2p^6 3s^2 3p^6 4s^2 3d^7$	$[Ar]4s^2 3d^7$	
Ni	28	$1s^2 2s^2 2p^6 3s^2 3p^6 4s^2 3d^8$	$[Ar]4s^2 3d^8$	
Cu*	29	$1s^2 2s^2 2p^6 3s^2 3p^6 4s^1 3d^{10}$	$[Ar]4s^1 3d^{10}$	(filled d sublevel is stable)
Zn	30	$1s^2 2s^2 2p^6 3s^2 3p^6 4s^2 3d^{10}$	$[Ar]4s^2 3d^{10}$	
4p Block				
Ga	31	$1s^2 2s^2 2p^6 3s^2 3p^6 4s^2 3d^{10} 4p^1$	$[Ar]4s^2 3d^{10} 4p^1$	
Ge	32	$1s^2 2s^2 2p^6 3s^2 3p^6 4s^2 3d^{10} 4p^2$	$[Ar]4s^2 3d^{10} 4p^2$	
As	33	$1s^2 2s^2 2p^6 3s^2 3p^6 4s^2 3d^{10} 4p^3$	$[Ar]4s^2 3d^{10} 4p^3$	
Se	34	$1s^2 2s^2 2p^6 3s^2 3p^6 4s^2 3d^{10} 4p^4$	$[Ar]4s^2 3d^{10} 4p^4$	
Br	35	$1s^2 2s^2 2p^6 3s^2 3p^6 4s^2 3d^{10} 4p^5$	$[Ar]4s^2 3d^{10} 4p^5$	
Kr	36	$1s^2 2s^2 2p^6 3s^2 3p^6 4s^2 3d^{10} 4p^6$	$[Ar]4s^2 3d^{10} 4p^6$	

*Exceptions to the order of filling

▶ SAMPLE PROBLEM 4.10 Using Sublevel Blocks to Write Electron Configurations

Selenium is a micromineral used in the immune system and cardiac health. Use the sublevel blocks on the periodic table to write the electron configuration for selenium.

SOLUTION

STEP 1 Locate the element on the periodic table. Selenium is in Period 4 and Group 6A (16).

STEP 2 Write the filled sublevels in order, going across each period.

Period	Sublevel Block Filling	Sublevel Block Notation (filled)
1	$1s$ (H → He)	$1s^2$
2	$2s$ (Li → Be) and $2p$ (B → Ne)	$2s^2 2p^6$
3	$3s$ (Na → Mg) and $3p$ (Al → Ar)	$3s^2 3p^6$
4	$4s$ (K → Ca) and $3d$ (Sc → Zn)	$4s^2 3d^{10}$

STEP 3 Complete the configuration by counting the electrons in the last occupied sublevel block. Because selenium is the fourth element in the $4p$ block, there are four electrons to place in the $4p$ sublevel.

Period	Sublevel Block Filling	Sublevel Block Notation
4	$4p$ (Ga → Se)	$4p^4$

The electron configuration for selenium (Se) is: $1s^2 2s^2 2p^6 3s^2 3p^6 4s^2 3d^{10} 4p^4$.

STUDY CHECK 4.10

Use the sublevel blocks on the periodic table to write the electron configuration for iodine, a micromineral needed for thyroid function.

ANSWER

$1s^2 2s^2 2p^6 3s^2 3p^6 4s^2 3d^{10} 4p^6 5s^2 4d^{10} 5p^5$

Some Exceptions in Sublevel Block Order

Within the filling of the $3d$ sublevel, exceptions occur for chromium and copper. In Cr and Cu, the $3d$ sublevel is close to being a half-filled or filled sublevel, which is particularly stable. Thus, the electron configuration for chromium has only one electron in the $4s$ and five electrons in the $3d$ sublevel to give the added stability of a half-filled d sublevel. This is shown in the abbreviated orbital diagram for chromium:

Abbreviated orbital diagram for chromium

A similar exception occurs when copper achieves a stable, filled $3d$ sublevel with 10 electrons and only one electron in the $4s$ orbital. This is shown in the abbreviated orbital diagram for copper:

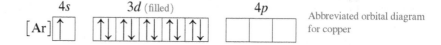

Abbreviated orbital diagram for copper

After the 4s and 3d sublevels are completed, the 4p sublevel fills as expected from gallium to krypton, the noble gas that completes Period 4. There are also exceptions in filling for the higher d and f electron sublevels, some caused by the added stability of half-filled shells and others where the cause is not known.

QUESTIONS AND PROBLEMS

4.7 Electron Configurations

LEARNING GOAL Draw the orbital diagram and write the electron configuration for an element.

4.49 Compare the terms *electron configuration* and *abbreviated electron configuration*.

4.50 Compare the terms *orbital diagram* and *electron configuration*.

4.51 Draw the orbital diagram for each of the following:
   a. boron   **b.** aluminum
   c. phosphorus   **d.** argon

4.52 Draw the orbital diagram for each of the following:
   a. fluorine   **b.** sulfur
   c. magnesium   **d.** beryllium

4.53 Write a complete electron configuration for each of the following:
   a. boron   **b.** sodium
   c. lithium   **d.** magnesium

4.54 Write a complete electron configuration for each of the following:
   a. nitrogen   **b.** chlorine
   c. oxygen   **d.** neon

4.55 Write an abbreviated electron configuration for each of the following:
   a. carbon   **b.** silicon
   c. phosphorus   **d.** fluorine

4.56 Write an abbreviated electron configuration for each of the following:
   a. magnesium   **b.** oxygen
   c. sulfur   **d.** nitrogen

4.57 Give the symbol of the element with each of the following electron or abbreviated electron configurations:
   a. $1s^2 2s^1$ **b.** $1s^2 2s^2 2p^6 3s^2 3p^4$
   c. $[Ne]3s^2 3p^2$ **d.** $[He]2s^2 2p^5$

4.58 Give the symbol of the element with each of the following electron or abbreviated electron configurations:
   a. $1s^2 2s^2 2p^4$ **b.** $[Ne]3s^2$
   c. $1s^2 2s^2 2p^6 3s^2 3p^6$ **d.** $[Ne]3s^2 3p^1$

4.59 Give the symbol of the element that meets the following conditions:
   a. has three electrons in the $n = 3$ energy level
   b. has two 2p electrons

   c. completes the 3p sublevel
   d. completes the 2s sublevel

4.60 Give the symbol of the element that meets the following conditions:
   a. has five electrons in the 3p sublevel
   b. has four 2p electrons
   c. completes the 3s sublevel
   d. has one electron in the 3s sublevel

4.61 Use the sublevel blocks on the periodic table to write a complete electron configuration and abbreviated electron configuration for an atom of each of the following:
   a. arsenic   **b.** iron
   c. indium   **d.** iodine
   e. titanium

4.62 Use the sublevel blocks on the periodic table to write a complete electron configuration and abbreviated electron configuration for an atom of each of the following:
   a. calcium   **b.** cobalt
   c. gallium   **d.** cadmium
   e. tin

4.63 Use the periodic table to give the symbol of the element that meets the following conditions:
   a. has three electrons in the $n = 4$ energy level
   b. has three 2p electrons
   c. completes the 5p sublevel
   d. has two electrons in the 4d sublevel

4.64 Use the periodic table to give the symbol of the element that meets the following conditions:
   a. has five electrons in the $n = 3$ energy level
   b. has one electron in the 6p sublevel
   c. completes the 7s sublevel
   d. has four 5p electrons

4.65 Use the periodic table to give the number of electrons in the indicated sublevels for the following:
   a. 3d in zinc   **b.** 2p in sodium
   c. 4p in arsenic   **d.** 5s in rubidium

4.66 Use the periodic table to give the number of electrons in the indicated sublevels for the following:
   a. 3d in manganese   **b.** 5p in antimony
   c. 6p in lead   **d.** 3s in magnesium

4.8 Trends in Periodic Properties

LEARNING GOAL

Use the electron configurations of elements to explain the trends in periodic properties.

The electron configurations of atoms are an important factor in the physical and chemical properties of the elements and in the properties of the compounds that they form. In this section, we will look at the *valence electrons* in atoms, the trends in *atomic size*, *ionization energy*, and *metallic character*. Going across a period, there is a pattern of regular change in these properties from one group to the next. Known as *periodic properties*, each property increases or decreases across a period, and then the trend is repeated in each successive period. We can use the seasonal changes in temperatures as an analogy for periodic properties. In the winter, temperatures are cold and become warmer in the spring. By summer, the outdoor temperatures are hot but begin to cool in the fall. By winter, we expect cold temperatures again as the pattern of decreasing and increasing temperatures repeats for another year.

Group Number and Valence Electrons

The chemical properties of representative elements are mostly due to the **valence electrons**, which are the electrons in the outermost energy level. These valence electrons occupy the s and p sublevels with the highest principal quantum number n. The group numbers indicate the number of valence (outer) electrons for the elements in each vertical column. For example, the elements in Group 1A (1), such as lithium, sodium, and potassium, all have one electron in an s orbital. Looking at the sublevel block, we can represent the valence electron in the alkali metals of Group 1A (1) as ns^1. All the elements in Group 2A (2), the alkaline earth metals, have two valence electrons, ns^2. The halogens in Group 7A (17) have seven valence electrons, ns^2np^5.

We can see the repetition of the outermost s and p electrons for the representative elements for Periods 1 to 4 in Table 4.10. Helium is included in Group 8A (18) because it is a noble gas, but it has only two electrons in its complete energy level.

TABLE 4.10 Valence Electron Configuration for Representative Elements in Periods 1 to 4

1A (1)	2A (2)	3A (13)	4A (14)	5A (15)	6A (16)	7A (17)	8A (18)
1 H $1s^1$							2 He $1s^2$
3 Li $2s^1$	4 Be $2s^2$	5 B $2s^22p^1$	6 C $2s^22p^2$	7 N $2s^22p^3$	8 O $2s^22p^4$	9 F $2s^22p^5$	10 Ne $2s^22p^6$
11 Na $3s^1$	12 Mg $3s^2$	13 Al $3s^23p^1$	14 Si $3s^23p^2$	15 P $3s^23p^3$	16 S $3s^23p^4$	17 Cl $3s^23p^5$	18 Ar $3s^23p^6$
19 K $4s^1$	20 Ca $4s^2$	31 Ga $4s^24p^1$	32 Ge $4s^24p^2$	33 As $4s^24p^3$	34 Se $4s^24p^4$	35 Br $4s^24p^5$	36 Kr $4s^24p^6$

▶ **SAMPLE PROBLEM 4.11 Using Group Numbers**

Using the periodic table, write the group number, the period, and the valence electron configuration for the following:

a. calcium   **b.** iodine   **c.** lead

SOLUTION

The valence electrons are the outermost s and p electrons. Although there may be electrons in the d or f sublevels, they are not valence electrons.

a. Calcium is in Group 2A (2), Period 4. It has a valence electron configuration of $4s^2$.
b. Iodine is in Group 7A (17), Period 5. It has a valence electron configuration of $5s^25p^5$.
c. Lead is in Group 4A (14), Period 6. It has a valence electron configuration of $6s^26p^2$.

STUDY CHECK 4.11

What are the group numbers, the periods, and the valence electron configurations for sulfur and strontium?

ANSWER

Sulfur is in Group 6A (16), Period 3, and has a $3s^23p^4$ valence electron configuration. Strontium is in Group 2A (2), Period 5, and has a $5s^2$ valence electron configuration.

Lewis Symbols

A **Lewis symbol** is a convenient way to represent the valence electrons, which are shown as dots placed on the sides, top, or bottom of the symbol for the element. One to four valence electrons are arranged as single dots. When there are five to eight electrons, one or more electrons are paired. Any of the following would be an acceptable Lewis symbol for magnesium, which has two valence electrons:

⊛ **CORE CHEMISTRY SKILL**

Drawing Lewis Symbols

Lewis Symbols for Magnesium

$$\text{Mg·} \quad \text{Mg} \quad \text{·Mg} \quad \text{·Mg·} \quad \text{Mg·} \quad \text{·Mg}$$

Lewis symbols for selected elements are given in Table 4.11.

Number of Valence Electrons Increases →

TABLE 4.11 Lewis Symbols for Selected Elements in Periods 1 to 4

	Group Number							
	IA (1)	2A (2)	3A (13)	4A (14)	5A (15)	6A (16)	7A (17)	8A (18)
Number of Valence Electrons	1	2	3	4	5	6	7	8*
Lewis Symbol	H·							He:*
	Li·	Be·	·B·	·C·	·N·	·O:	·F:	:Ne:
	Na·	Mg·	·Al·	·Si·	·P·	·S:	·Cl:	:Ar:
	K·	Ca·	·Ga·	·Ge·	·As·	·Se:	·Br:	:Kr:

*Helium (He) is stable with two valence electrons.

SAMPLE PROBLEM 4.12 Drawing Lewis Symbols

Draw the Lewis symbol for each of the following:

a. bromine
b. aluminum

SOLUTION

a. The Lewis symbol for bromine, which is in Group 7A (17), has seven valence electrons. Thus, three pairs of dots and one single dot are drawn on the sides of the Br symbol.

·Br:

b. The Lewis symbol for aluminum, which is in Group 3A (13), has three valence electrons drawn as single dots on the sides of the Al symbol.

·Al·

STUDY CHECK 4.12

Draw the Lewis symbol for phosphorus, a macromineral needed for bones and teeth.

ANSWER

·P·

Atomic Size

The **atomic size** of an atom is determined by the distance of the valence electrons from the nucleus. For each group of representative elements, the atomic size *increases* going from the top to the bottom because the outermost electrons in each energy level are farther from the nucleus. For example, in Group 1A (1), Li has a valence electron in energy level 2; Na has a valence electron in energy level 3; and K has a valence electron in energy level 4. This means that the K atom is larger than the Na atom, and the Na atom is larger than the Li atom (see Figure 4.19).

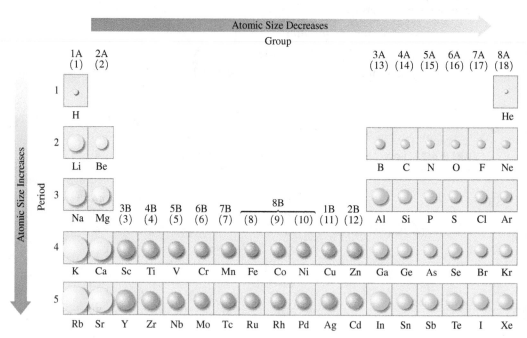

FIGURE 4.19 ▶ The atomic size increases going down a group but decreases going from left to right across a period.

Why does the atomic size increase going down a group?

The atomic size of representative elements is affected by the attractive forces of the protons in the nucleus on the electrons in the outermost level. For the elements going across a period, the increase in the number of protons in the nucleus increases the positive charge of the nucleus. As a result, the electrons are pulled closer to the nucleus, which means that the atomic size of representative elements decreases going from left to right across a period.

The size of atoms of transition elements within the same period changes only slightly because electrons are filling *d* orbitals rather than the outermost energy level. Because the increase in nuclear charge is canceled by an increase in *d* electrons, the attraction of the valence electrons by the nucleus remains about the same. Because there is little change in the nuclear attraction for the valence electrons, the atomic size remains relatively constant for the transition elements.

▶ SAMPLE PROBLEM 4.13 **Size of Atoms**

Identify the smaller atom in each of the following pairs:

a. N or F   **b.** K or Kr   **c.** Ca and Sr

SOLUTION

a. The F atom has a greater positive charge on the nucleus, which pulls electrons closer, and makes the F atom smaller than the N atom. Atomic size decreases going from left to right across a period.

b. The Kr atom has a greater positive charge on the nucleus, which pulls electrons closer, and makes the Kr atom smaller than the K atom. Atomic size decreases going from left to right across a period.

c. The outer electrons in the Ca atom are closer to the nucleus than in the Sr atom, which makes the Ca atom smaller than the Sr atom. Atomic size increases going down a group.

STUDY CHECK 4.13

Which atom has the largest atomic size, P, As, or Se?

ANSWER

As

Ionization Energy

In an atom, negatively charged electrons are attracted to the positive charge of the protons in the nucleus. Therefore, energy is required to remove an electron from an atom. The **ionization energy** is the energy needed to remove one electron from an atom in the gaseous (g) state. When an electron is removed from a neutral atom, a cation with a $1+$ charge is formed.

$$Na(g) + energy\ (ionization) \longrightarrow Na^+(g) + e^-$$

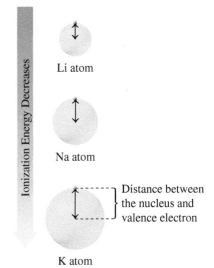

The attraction of a nucleus for the outermost electrons decreases as those electrons are farther from the nucleus. Thus the ionization energy decreases going down a group (see Figure 4.20). However, going across a period from left to right, the positive charge of the nucleus increases because there is an increase in the number of protons. Thus the ionization energy increases going from left to right across the periodic table.

In summary, the ionization energy is low for the metals and high for the nonmetals. The high ionization energies of the noble gases indicate that their electron configurations are especially stable.

FIGURE 4.20 ▶ As the distance from the nucleus to the valence electron in Li, Na, and K atoms increases in Group 1A (1), the ionization energy decreases and less energy is required to remove the valence electron.

Why would Cs have a lower ionization energy than K?

▶ SAMPLE PROBLEM 4.14 **Ionization Energy**

Indicate the element in each group that has the higher ionization energy and explain your choice.

a. K or Na   **b.** Mg or Cl   **c.** F, N, or C

SOLUTION

a. Na. In Na, an electron is removed from an energy level closer to the nucleus, which requires a higher ionization energy for Na compared to K.
b. Cl. The increased nuclear charge of Cl increases the attraction for the valence electrons, which requires a higher ionization energy for Cl compared to Mg.
c. F. The increased nuclear charge of F increases the attraction for the valence electrons, which requires a higher ionization energy for F compared to C or N.

STUDY CHECK 4.14

Arrange Sn, Sr, and I in order of increasing ionization energy.

ANSWER

Ionization energy increases going from left to right across a period: Sr, Sn, I.

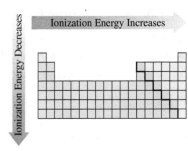

Ionization energy decreases going down a group and increases going from left to right across a period.

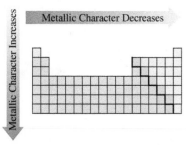

Metallic character increases going down a group and decreases going from left to right across a period.

Metallic Character

An element that has **metallic character** is an element that loses valence electrons easily. Metallic character is more prevalent in the elements (metals) on the left side of the periodic table and decreases going from left to right across a period. The elements (nonmetals) on the right side of the periodic table do not easily lose electrons, which means they are less metallic. Most of the metalloids between the metals and nonmetals tend to lose electrons, but not as easily as the metals. Thus, in Period 3, sodium, which loses electrons most easily, would be the most metallic. Going across from left to right in Period 3, metallic character decreases to argon, which has the least metallic character.

For elements in the same group of representative elements, metallic character increases going from top to bottom. Atoms at the bottom of any group have more electron levels, which makes it easier to lose electrons. Thus, the elements at the bottom of a group on the periodic table have lower ionization energy and are more metallic compared to the elements at the top.

A summary of the trends in periodic properties we have discussed is given in Table 4.12.

TABLE 4.12 Summary of Trends in Periodic Properties of Representative Elements

Periodic Property	Top to Bottom within a Group	Left to Right across a Period
Valence Electrons	Remains the same	Increases
Atomic Size	Increases because of the increase in the number of energy levels	Decreases as the number of protons increases, which strengthens the attraction of the nucleus for the valence electrons, and pulls them closer to the nucleus
Ionization Energy	Decreases because the valence electrons are easier to remove when they are farther from the nucleus	Increases as the increase in the number of protons strengthens the attraction of the nucleus for the valence electrons, and more energy is required to remove an electron
Metallic Character	Increases because the valence electrons are easier to remove when they are farther from the nucleus	Decreases as the number of protons increases, which strengthens the attraction of the nucleus for the valence electrons, and makes it more difficult to remove a valence electron

QUESTIONS AND PROBLEMS

4.8 Trends in Periodic Properties

LEARNING GOAL Use the electron configurations of elements to explain the trends in periodic properties.

4.67 Indicate the number of valence electrons in each of the following:
   a. aluminum
   b. Group 5A
   c. barium
   d. F, Cl, Br, and I

4.68 Indicate the number of valence electrons in each of the following:
   a. Li, Na, K, Rb, and Cs
   b. Se
   c. C, Si, Ge, Sn, and Pb
   d. Group 8A

4.69 Write the group number and Lewis symbol for each of the following elements:
   a. sulfur
   b. nitrogen
   c. calcium
   d. sodium
   e. gallium

4.70 Write the group number and Lewis symbol for each of the following elements:
   a. carbon
   b. oxygen
   c. argon
   d. lithium
   e. chlorine

4.71 Select the larger atom in each pair.
   a. Na or Cl
   b. Na or Rb
   c. Na or Mg
   d. Rb or I

4.72 Select the larger atom in each pair.
   a. S or Ar
   b. S or O
   c. S or K
   d. S or Mg

4.73 Arrange each set of elements in order of decreasing atomic size.
   a. Al, Si, Mg
   b. Cl, I, Br
   c. Sb, Sr, I
   d. P, Si, Na

4.74 Arrange each set of elements in order of decreasing atomic size.
  a. Cl, S, P
  b. Ge, Si, C
  c. Ba, Ca, Sr
  d. S, O, Se

4.75 Select the element in each pair with the higher ionization energy.
  a. Br or I
  b. Mg or Sr
  c. Si or P
  d. I or Xe

4.76 Select the element in each pair with the higher ionization energy.
  a. O or Ne
  b. K or Br
  c. Ca or Ba
  d. N or Ne

4.77 Arrange each set of elements in order of increasing ionization energy.
  a. F, Cl, Br
  b. Na, Cl, Al
  c. Na, K, Cs
  d. As, Ca, Br

4.78 Arrange each set of elements in order of increasing ionization energy.
  a. O, N, C
  b. S, P, Cl
  c. P, As, N
  d. Al, Si, P

4.79 Arrange the following in order of decreasing metallic character:
  Br, Ge, Ca, Ga

4.80 Arrange the following in order of increasing metallic character:
  Na, P, Al, Ar

4.81 Fill in each of the following blanks using *higher* or *lower*, *more* or *less*: Sr has a _____ ionization energy and _____ metallic character than Sb.

4.82 Fill in each of the following blanks using *higher* or *lower*, *more* or *less*: N has a _____ ionization energy and _____ metallic character than As.

4.83 Complete each of the following statements **a** to **d** using **1**, **2**, or **3**:
  1. decreases   **2.** increases   **3.** remains the same

  Going down Group 6A (16),
  a. the ionization energy _____
  b. the atomic size _____
  c. the metallic character _____
  d. the number of valence electrons _____

4.84 Complete each of the following statements **a** to **d** using **1**, **2**, or **3**:
  1. decreases   **2.** increases   **3.** remains the same

  Going from left to right across Period 3,
  a. the ionization energy _____
  b. the atomic size _____
  c. the metallic character _____
  d. the number of valence electrons _____

4.85 Which statements completed with **a** to **e** will be *true* and which will be *false*?

  An atom of N compared to an atom of Li has a larger (greater)
  a. atomic size
  b. ionization energy
  c. number of protons
  d. metallic character
  e. number of valence electrons

4.86 Which statements completed with **a** to **e** will be *true* and which will be *false*?

  An atom of C compared to an atom of Sn has a larger (greater)
  a. atomic size
  b. ionization energy
  c. number of protons
  d. metallic character
  e. number of valence electrons

Clinical Update
Improving Crop Production

In plants, potassium is needed for metabolic processes including the regulation of plant growth. Potassium (K) is required by plants for protein synthesis, photosynthesis, enzymes, and ionic balance. Potassium-deficient potato plants may show purple or brown spots and plant, root, and seed growth is reduced. John has noticed that the leaves of his recent crop of potatoes had brown spots, the potatoes were undersized, and the crop yield was low.

Tests on soil samples indicated that the potassium levels were below 100 ppm, which indicated that supplemental potassium was needed. John applied a fertilizer containing potassium chloride (KCl). To apply the correct amount of potassium, John needs to apply 170 kg of fertilizer per hectare.

℞ Clinical Applications

4.87 **a.** What is the group number and name of the group that contains potassium?
  b. Is potassium a metal, a nonmetal, or a metalloid?
  c. How many protons are in an atom of potassium?
  d. What is the most prevalent isotope of potassium (see Table 4.8)?
  e. Potassium has three naturally occurring isotopes. They are K-39 (93.26%, 38.964 amu), K-40 (0.0117%, 39.964 amu),

and K-41 (6.73%, 40.962 amu). Calculate the atomic mass of potassium from the naturally occurring isotopes and their abundance using the weighted average mass method.

4.88 **a.** How many neutrons are in K-41?
  b. Write the electron configuration for potassium.
  c. Which is the larger atom, K or Cs?
  d. Which is the smallest atom, K, As, or Br?
  e. If John's potato farm has an area of 34.5 hectares, how many pounds of fertilizer does John need to use?

A mineral deficiency of potassium causes brown spots on potato leaves.

CONCEPT MAP

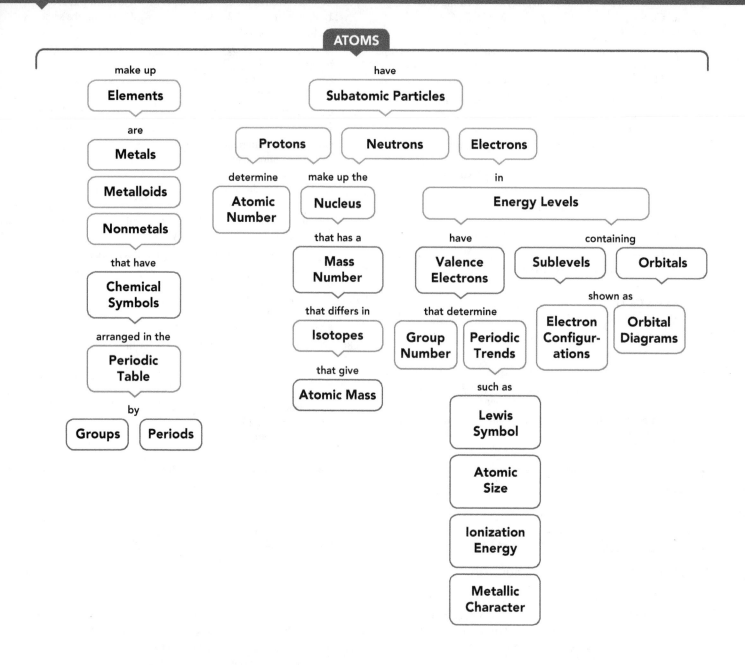

ATOMS

make up → **Elements**
are → **Metals** / **Metalloids** / **Nonmetals**
that have → **Chemical Symbols**
arranged in the → **Periodic Table**
by → **Groups** / **Periods**

have → **Subatomic Particles**
→ **Protons** / **Neutrons** / **Electrons**

determine → **Atomic Number**

make up the → **Nucleus**
that has a → **Mass Number**
that differs in → **Isotopes**
that give → **Atomic Mass**

in → **Energy Levels**
have → **Valence Electrons**
that determine → **Group Number** / **Periodic Trends**
such as → **Lewis Symbol** / **Atomic Size** / **Ionization Energy** / **Metallic Character**

containing → **Sublevels** / **Orbitals**
shown as → **Electron Configurations** / **Orbital Diagrams**

CHAPTER REVIEW

4.1 Elements and Symbols
LEARNING GOAL Given the name of an element, write its correct symbol; from the symbol, write the correct name.
- Elements are the primary substances of matter.
- Chemical symbols are one- or two-letter abbreviations of the names of the elements.

4.2 The Periodic Table
LEARNING GOAL Use the periodic table to identify the group and the period of an element; identify the element as a metal, a nonmetal, or a metalloid.
- The periodic table is an arrangement of the elements by increasing atomic number.

- A horizontal row is called a *period*.
A vertical column on the periodic table containing elements with similar properties is called a *group*.
- Elements in Group 1A (1) are called the *alkali metals*; Group 2A (2), the *alkaline earth metals*; Group 7A (17), the *halogens*; and Group 8A (18), the *noble gases*.
- On the periodic table, *metals* are located on the left of the heavy zigzag line, and *nonmetals* are to the right of the heavy zigzag line.
- Except for aluminum, elements located along the heavy zigzag line are called *metalloids*.

4.3 The Atom
LEARNING GOAL Describe the electrical charge and location in an atom for a proton, a neutron, and an electron.

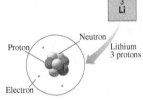

- An atom is the smallest particle that retains the characteristics of an element.
- Atoms are composed of three types of subatomic particles.
- Protons have a positive charge ($+$), electrons carry a negative charge ($-$), and neutrons are electrically neutral.
- The protons and neutrons are found in the tiny, dense nucleus; electrons are located outside the nucleus.

4.4 Atomic Number and Mass Number
LEARNING GOAL Given the atomic number and the mass number of an atom, state the number of protons, neutrons, and electrons.

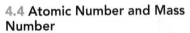

- The atomic number gives the number of protons in all the atoms of the same element.
- In a neutral atom, the number of protons and electrons is equal.
- The mass number is the total number of protons and neutrons in an atom.

4.5 Isotopes and Atomic Mass
LEARNING GOAL Determine the number of protons, neutrons, and electrons in one or more of the isotopes of an element; calculate the atomic mass of an element using the percent abundance and mass of its naturally occurring isotopes.

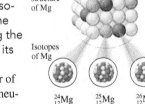

- Atoms that have the same number of protons but different numbers of neutrons are called *isotopes*.
- The atomic mass of an element is the weighted average mass of all the isotopes in a naturally occurring sample of that element.

4.6 Electron Energy Levels
LEARNING GOAL Describe the energy levels, sublevels, and orbitals for the electrons in an atom.

- Electromagnetic radiation such as radio waves and visible light is energy that travels at the speed of light.
- Each particular type of radiation has a specific wavelength and frequency.
- Long-wavelength radiation has low frequencies, whereas short-wavelength radiation has high frequencies.

- Radiation with a high frequency has high energy.
- The atomic spectra of elements are related to the specific energy levels occupied by electrons.
- When an electron absorbs energy, it attains a higher energy level. When an electron drops to a lower energy level, energy is emitted.
- An orbital is a region around the nucleus where an electron with a specific energy is most likely to be found.
- Each orbital holds a maximum of two electrons, which must have opposite spins.
- In each energy level (n), electrons occupy orbitals of identical energy within sublevels.
- An *s* sublevel contains one *s* orbital, a *p* sublevel contains three *p* orbitals, a *d* sublevel contains five *d* orbitals, and an *f* sublevel contains seven *f* orbitals.

4.7 Electron Configurations
LEARNING GOAL Draw the orbital diagram and write the electron configuration for an element.

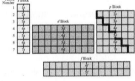

- Within a sublevel, electrons enter orbitals in the same energy level one at a time until all the orbitals are half-filled.
- Additional electrons enter with opposite spins until the orbitals in that sublevel are filled with two electrons each.
- The orbital diagram for an element such as silicon shows the orbitals that are occupied by paired and unpaired electrons:

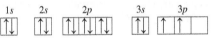

- The electron configuration for an element such as silicon shows the number of electrons in each sublevel: $1s^22s^22p^63s^23p^2$.
- An abbreviated electron configuration for an element such as silicon places the symbol of a noble gas in brackets to represent the filled sublevels: $[\text{Ne}]3s^23p^2$.
- The periodic table consists of *s*, *p*, *d*, and *f* sublevel blocks.
- An electron configuration can be written following the order of the sublevel blocks on the periodic table.
- Beginning with $1s$, an electron configuration is obtained by writing the sublevel blocks in order going across each period on the periodic table until the element is reached.

4.8 Trends in Periodic Properties
LEARNING GOAL Use the electron configurations of elements to explain the trends in periodic properties.

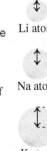

- The properties of elements are related to the valence electrons of the atoms.
- With only a few exceptions, each group of elements has the same arrangement of valence electrons differing only in the energy level.
- Valence electrons are represented as dots around the symbol of the element.
- The size of an atom increases going down a group and decreases going from left to right across a period.
- The energy required to remove a valence electron is the ionization energy, which decreases going down a group, and generally increases going from left to right across a period.
- The metallic character of an element increases going down a group and decreases going from left to right across a period.

KEY TERMS

alkali metal An element in Group 1A (1), except hydrogen, that is a soft, shiny metal with one electron in its outermost energy level.

alkaline earth metal An element in Group 2A (2) that has two electrons in its outermost energy level.

atom The smallest particle of an element that retains the characteristics of the element.

atomic mass The weighted average mass of all the naturally occurring isotopes of an element.

atomic mass unit (amu) A small mass unit used to describe the mass of extremely small particles such as atoms and subatomic particles; 1 amu is equal to one-twelfth the mass of a $^{12}_{6}C$ atom.

atomic number A number that is equal to the number of protons in an atom.

atomic size The distance between the outermost electrons and the nucleus.

atomic symbol An abbreviation used to indicate the mass number and atomic number of an isotope.

chemical symbol An abbreviation that represents the name of an element.

***d* block** The block of ten elements from Groups 3B (3) to 2B (12) in which electrons fill the five *d* orbitals in the *d* sublevels.

electron A negatively charged subatomic particle having a minute mass that is usually ignored in mass calculations; its symbol is e^-.

electron configuration A list of the number of electrons in each sublevel within an atom, arranged by increasing energy.

energy level A group of electrons with similar energy.

***f* block** The block of 14 elements in the rows at the bottom of the periodic table in which electrons fill the seven *f* orbitals in the 4*f* and 5*f* sublevels.

group A vertical column in the periodic table that contains elements having similar physical and chemical properties.

group number A number that appears at the top of each vertical column (group) in the periodic table and indicates the number of electrons in the outermost energy level.

halogen An element in Group 7A (17)—fluorine, chlorine, bromine, iodine, and astatine—that has seven electrons in its outermost energy level.

ionization energy The energy needed to remove the least tightly bound electron from the outermost energy level of an atom.

isotope An atom that differs only in mass number from another atom of the same element. Isotopes have the same atomic number (number of protons), but different numbers of neutrons.

Lewis symbol The representation of an atom that shows valence electrons as dots around the symbol of the element.

mass number The total number of protons and neutrons in the nucleus of an atom.

metal An element that is shiny, malleable, ductile, and a good conductor of heat and electricity. The metals are located to the left of the heavy zigzag line on the periodic table.

metallic character A measure of how easily an element loses a valence electron.

metalloid Elements with properties of both metals and nonmetals located along the heavy zigzag line on the periodic table.

neutron A neutral subatomic particle having a mass of about 1 amu and found in the nucleus of an atom; its symbol is n or n^0.

noble gas An element in Group 8A (18) of the periodic table, generally unreactive and seldom found in combination with other elements, that has eight electrons (helium has two electrons) in its outermost energy level.

nonmetal An element with little or no luster that is a poor conductor of heat and electricity. The nonmetals are located to the right of the heavy zigzag line on the periodic table.

nucleus The compact, extremely dense center of an atom, containing the protons and neutrons of the atom.

orbital The region around the nucleus where electrons of a certain energy are more likely to be found. The *s* orbitals are spherical; the *p* orbitals have two lobes.

orbital diagram A diagram that shows the distribution of electrons in the orbitals of the energy levels.

***p* block** The elements in Groups 3A (13) to 8A (18) in which electrons fill the *p* orbitals in the *p* sublevels.

period A horizontal row of elements in the periodic table.

periodic table An arrangement of elements by increasing atomic number such that elements having similar chemical behavior are grouped in vertical columns.

proton A positively charged subatomic particle having a mass of about 1 amu and found in the nucleus of an atom; its symbol is p or p^+.

representative element An element in the first two columns on the left of the periodic table and the last six columns on the right that has a group number of 1A through 8A or 1, 2, and 13 through 18.

***s* block** The elements in Groups 1A (1) and 2A (2) in which electrons fill the *s* orbitals.

subatomic particle A particle within an atom; protons, neutrons, and electrons are subatomic particles.

sublevel A group of orbitals of equal energy within an energy level. The number of sublevels in each energy level is the same as the principal quantum number (n).

transition element An element in the center of the periodic table that is designated with the letter "B" or the group number of 3 through 12.

valence electrons Electrons in the highest energy level of an atom.

⚛ CORE CHEMISTRY SKILLS

The chapter section containing each Core Chemistry Skill is shown in parentheses at the end of each heading.

Counting Protons and Neutrons (4.4)

- The atomic number of an element is equal to the number of protons in every atom of that element. The atomic number is the whole number that appears above the symbol of each element on the periodic table.

  Atomic number = number of protons in an atom

- Because atoms are neutral, the number of electrons is equal to the number of protons. Thus, the atomic number gives the number of electrons.
- The mass number is the total number of protons and neutrons in the nucleus of an atom.

  Mass number = number of protons + number of neutrons

- The number of neutrons is calculated from the mass number and atomic number.

  Number of neutrons = mass number − number of protons

Example: Calculate the number of protons, neutrons, and electrons in a krypton atom with a mass number of 80.

Answer:

Element	Atomic Number	Mass Number	Number of Protons	Number of Neutrons	Number of Electrons
Kr	36	80	equal to atomic number (36)	equal to mass number − number of protons 80 − 36 = 44	equal to number of protons (36)

Writing Atomic Symbols for Isotopes (4.5)

- Isotopes are atoms of the same element that have the same atomic number but different numbers of neutrons.
- An atomic symbol is written for a particular isotope, with its mass number (protons and neutrons) shown in the upper left corner and its atomic number (protons) shown in the lower left corner.

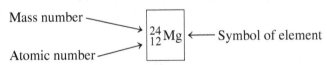

Mass number ⟶ $^{24}_{12}$Mg ⟵ Symbol of element
Atomic number ⟶

Example: Calculate the number of protons and neutrons in the cadmium isotope $^{112}_{48}$Cd.

Answer:

Atomic Symbol	Atomic Number	Mass Number	Number of Protons	Number of Neutrons
$^{112}_{48}$Cd	number (48) in lower left corner	number (112) in upper left corner	equal to atomic number (48)	equal to mass number − number of protons 112 − 48 = 64

Writing Electron Configurations (4.7)

- The electron configuration for an atom specifies the energy levels and sublevels occupied by the electrons of an atom.

- An electron configuration is written starting with the lowest energy sublevel, followed by the next lowest energy sublevel.
- The number of electrons in each sublevel is shown as a superscript.

Example: Write the electron configuration for palladium.

Answer: Palladium has atomic number 46, which means it has 46 protons and 46 electrons.

$$1s^2 2s^2 2p^6 3s^2 3p^6 4s^2 3d^{10} 4p^6 5s^2 4d^8$$

Using the Periodic Table to Write Electron Configurations (4.7)

- An electron configuration corresponds to the location of an element on the periodic table, where different blocks within the periodic table are identified as the *s*, *p*, *d*, and *f* sublevels.

Example: Use the periodic table to write the electron configuration for sulfur.

Answer: Sulfur (atomic number 16) is in Group 6A (16) and Period 3.

Period	Sublevel Block Filling	Sublevel Block Notation (filled)
1	$1s$ (H → He)	$1s^2$
2	$2s$ (Li → Be) and $2p$ (B → Ne)	$2s^2 2p^6$
3	$3s$ (Na → Mg)	$3s^2$
	$3p$ (Al → S)	$3p^4$

The electron configuration for sulfur (S) is: $1s^2 2s^2 2p^6 3s^2 3p^4$.

Identifying Trends in Periodic Properties (4.8)

- The size of an atom increases going down a group and decreases going from left to right across a period.
- The ionization energy decreases going down a group and increases going from left to right across a period.
- The metallic character of an element increases going down a group and decreases going from left to right across a period.

Example: For Mg, P, and Cl, identify which has the

  a. largest atomic size
  b. highest ionization energy
  c. most metallic character

Answer: **a.** Mg   **b.** Cl   **c.** Mg

Drawing Lewis Symbols (4.8)

- The valence electrons are the electrons in the outermost energy level.
- The number of valence electrons is the same as the group number for the representative elements.
- A Lewis symbol represents the number of valence electrons shown as dots placed around the symbol for the element.

Example: Give the group number and number of valence electrons, and draw the Lewis symbol for each of the following:

  a. Rb   **b.** Se   **c.** Xe

Answer: **a.** Group 1A (1), one valence electron, Rb·

  b. Group 6A (16), six valence electrons, ·S̈e:

  c. Group 8A (18), eight valence electrons, :Ẍe:

UNDERSTANDING THE CONCEPTS

The chapter sections to review are shown in parentheses at the end of each question.

4.89 According to Dalton's atomic theory, which of the following are *true* or *false*? If false, correct the statement to make it true. (4.3)

   a. Atoms of an element are identical to atoms of other elements.

   b. Every element is made of atoms.

   c. Atoms of different elements combine to form compounds.

   d. In a chemical reaction, some atoms disappear and new atoms appear.

4.90 Use Rutherford's gold-foil experiment to answer each of the following: (4.3)

   a. What did Rutherford expect to happen when he aimed particles at the gold foil?

   b. How did the results differ from what he expected?

   c. How did he use the results to propose a model of the atom?

4.91 Match the subatomic particles (**1** to **3**) to each of the descriptions below: (4.4)

   1. protons   **2.** neutrons   **3.** electrons

   a. atomic mass

   b. atomic number

   c. positive charge

   d. negative charge

   e. mass number – atomic number

4.92 Match the subatomic particles (**1** to **3**) to each of the descriptions below: (4.4)

   1. protons   **2.** neutrons   **3.** electrons

   a. mass number

   b. surround the nucleus

   c. in the nucleus

   d. charge of 0

   e. equal to number of electrons

4.93 Consider the following atoms in which X represents the chemical symbol of the element: (4.4, 4.5)

$$^{16}_{8}X \quad ^{16}_{9}X \quad ^{18}_{10}X \quad ^{17}_{8}X \quad ^{18}_{8}X$$

   a. What atoms have the same number of protons?

   b. Which atoms are isotopes? Of what element?

   c. Which atoms have the same mass number?

4.94 Consider the following atoms in which X represents the chemical symbol of the element: (4.4, 4.5)

$$^{124}_{47}X \quad ^{116}_{49}X \quad ^{116}_{50}X \quad ^{124}_{50}X \quad ^{116}_{48}X$$

   a. What atoms have the same number of protons?

   b. Which atoms are isotopes? Of what element?

   c. Which atoms have the same mass number?

4.95 Complete the following table for three of the naturally occurring isotopes of germanium, which is a metalloid used in semiconductors: (4.4, 4.5)

	Atomic Symbol		
	$^{70}_{32}$Ge	$^{73}_{32}$Ge	$^{76}_{32}$Ge
Atomic Number			
Mass Number			
Number of Protons			
Number of Neutrons			
Number of Electrons			

4.96 Complete the following table for the three naturally occurring isotopes of silicon, the major component in computer chips: (4.4, 4.5)

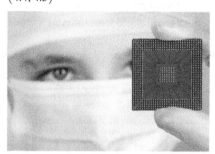

Computer chips consist primarily of the element silicon.

	Atomic Symbol		
	$^{28}_{14}$Si	$^{29}_{14}$Si	$^{30}_{14}$Si
Atomic Number			
Mass Number			
Number of Protons			
Number of Neutrons			
Number of Electrons			

4.97 For each representation of a nucleus **A** through **E**, write the atomic symbol, and identify which are isotopes. (4.4, 4.5)

Proton ⬤

Neutron 🔵

  A   **B**   **C**   **D**   **E**

4.98 Identify the element represented by each nucleus **A** through **E** in problem 4.97 as a metal, a nonmetal, or a metalloid. (4.3)

4.99 Indicate whether or not the following orbital diagrams are possible and explain. When possible, indicate the element it represents. (4.7)

a.
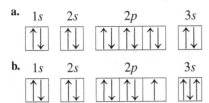

b.
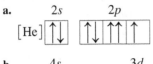

4.100 Indicate whether or not the following abbreviated orbital diagrams are possible and explain. When possible, indicate the element it represents. (4.7)

a.

b.

4s   3d

[Ar]⬆ ⬆ ⬆ ⬆ ⬆ ⬆

4.101 Match the spheres **A** through **D** with atoms of Li, Na, K, and Rb. (4.8)

A   B   C   D

4.102 Match the spheres **A** through **D** with atoms of K, Ge, Ca, and Kr. (4.8)

A   B   C   D

4.103 Of the elements Na, Mg, Si, S, Cl, and Ar, identify one that fits each of the following: (4.2, 4.6, 4.7, 4.8)
a. largest atomic size
b. a halogen
c. electron configuration $1s^2 2s^2 2p^6 3s^2 3p^2$
d. highest ionization energy
e. in Group 6A (16)
f. most metallic character
g. two valence electrons

4.104 Of the elements Sn, Xe, Te, Sr, I, and Rb, identify one that fits each of the following: (4.2, 4.6, 4.7, 4.8)
a. smallest atomic size
b. an alkaline earth metal
c. a metalloid
d. lowest ionization energy
e. in Group 4A (14)
f. least metallic character
g. seven valence electrons

ADDITIONAL QUESTIONS AND PROBLEMS

4.105 Give the group and period number for each of the following elements: (4.2)
a. bromine   **b.** argon
c. lithium   **d.** radium

4.106 Give the group and period number for each of the following elements: (4.2)
a. radon   **b.** tin
c. carbon   **d.** magnesium

4.107 The following trace elements have been found to be crucial to the functions of the body. Indicate each as a metal, a nonmetal, or a metalloid. (4.2)
a. zinc   **b.** cobalt
c. manganese   **d.** iodine

4.108 The following trace elements have been found to be crucial to the functions of the body. Indicate each as a metal, a nonmetal, or a metalloid. (4.2)
a. copper   **b.** selenium
c. arsenic   **d.** chromium

4.109 Indicate if each of the following statements is *true* or *false*: (4.3)
a. The proton is a negatively charged particle.
b. The neutron is 2000 times as heavy as a proton.
c. The atomic mass unit is based on a carbon atom with 6 protons and 6 neutrons.

d. The nucleus is the largest part of the atom.
e. The electrons are located outside the nucleus.

4.110 Indicate if each of the following statements is *true* or *false*: (4.3)
a. The neutron is electrically neutral.
b. Most of the mass of an atom is because of the protons and neutrons.
c. The charge of an electron is equal, but opposite, to the charge of a neutron.
d. The proton and the electron have about the same mass.
e. The mass number is the number of protons.

4.111 For the following atoms, give the number of protons, neutrons, and electrons: (4.3)
a. $^{114}_{48}Cd$ **b.** $^{98}_{43}Tc$ **c.** $^{199}_{79}Au$
d. $^{222}_{86}Rn$ **e.** $^{136}_{54}Xe$

4.112 For the following atoms, give the number of protons, neutrons, and electrons: (4.3)
a. $^{202}_{80}Hg$ **b.** $^{127}_{53}I$ **c.** $^{75}_{35}Br$
d. $^{133}_{55}Cs$ **e.** $^{195}_{78}Pt$

4.113 Complete the following table: (4.3)

Name of the Element	Atomic Symbol	Number of Protons	Number of Neutrons	Number of Electrons
	$^{80}_{34}$Se			
		28	34	
Magnesium			14	
	$^{228}_{88}$Ra			

4.114 Complete the following table: (4.3)

Name of the Element	Atomic Symbol	Number of Protons	Number of Neutrons	Number of Electrons
Potassium			22	
	$^{51}_{23}$V			
		48	64	
Barium			82	

4.115 a. What electron sublevel starts to fill after completion of the 3s sublevel? (4.7)
  b. What electron sublevel starts to fill after completion of the 4p sublevel?
  c. What electron sublevel starts to fill after completion of the 3d sublevel?
  d. What electron sublevel starts to fill after completion of the 3p sublevel?

4.116 a. What electron sublevel starts to fill after completion of the 5s sublevel? (4.7)
  b. What electron sublevel starts to fill after completion of the 4d sublevel?
  c. What electron sublevel starts to fill after completion of the 4f sublevel?
  d. What electron sublevel starts to fill after completion of the 5p sublevel?

4.117 a. How many 3d electrons are in Fe? (4.7)
  b. How many 5p electrons are in Ba?
  c. How many 4d electrons are in I?
  d. How many 7s electrons are in Ra?

4.118 a. How many 4d electrons are in Cd? (4.7)
  b. How many 4p electrons are in Br?
  c. How many 6p electrons are in Bi?
  d. How many 5s electrons are in Zn?

4.119 Name the element that corresponds to each of the following: (4.7, 4.8)
  a. $1s^22s^22p^63s^23p^3$
  b. alkali metal with the smallest atomic size
  c. $[Kr]5s^24d^{10}$
  d. Group 5A (15) element with the highest ionization energy
  e. Period 3 element with the largest atomic size

4.120 Name the element that corresponds to each of the following: (4.7, 4.8)
  a. $1s^22s^22p^63s^23p^64s^13d^5$
  b. $[Xe]6s^24f^{14}5d^{10}6p^5$
  c. halogen with the highest ionization energy
  d. Group 2A (2) element with the smallest ionization energy
  e. Period 4 element with the smallest atomic size

4.121 Of the elements Na, P, Cl, and F, which (4.2, 4.7, 4.8)
  a. is a metal?
  b. is in Group 5A (15)?
  c. has the highest ionization energy?
  d. loses an electron most easily?
  e. is found in Group 7A (17), Period 3?

4.122 Of the elements K, Ca, Br, and Kr, which (4.2, 4.7, 4.8)
  a. is a halogen?
  b. has the smallest atomic size?
  c. has the lowest ionization energy?
  d. requires the most energy to remove an electron?
  e. is found in Group 2A (2), Period 4?

CHALLENGE QUESTIONS

The following groups of questions are related to the topics in this chapter. However, they do not all follow the chapter order, and they require you to combine concepts and skills from several sections. These questions will help you increase your critical thinking skills and prepare for you next exam.

4.123 The most abundant isotope of lead is $^{208}_{82}$Pb. (4.4)
  a. How many protons, neutrons, and electrons are in $^{208}_{82}$Pb?
  b. What is the atomic symbol of another isotope of lead with 132 neutrons?
  c. What is the name and symbol of an atom with the same mass number as in part **b** and 131 neutrons?

4.124 The most abundant isotope of silver is $^{107}_{47}$Ag. (4.4)
  a. How many protons, neutrons, and electrons are in $^{107}_{47}$Ag?
  b. What is the symbol of another isotope of silver with 62 neutrons?
  c. What is the name and symbol of an atom with the same mass number as in part **b** and 61 neutrons?

4.125 Give the symbol of the element that has the (4.8)
  a. smallest atomic size in Group 6A (16)
  b. smallest atomic size in Period 3
  c. highest ionization energy in Group 4A (14)
  d. lowest ionization energy in Period 3
  e. most metallic character in Group 2A (2)

4.126 Give the symbol of the element that has the (4.8)
  a. largest atomic size in Group 1A (1)
  b. largest atomic size in Period 4
  c. highest ionization energy in Group 2A (2)
  d. lowest ionization energy in Group 7A (17)
  e. least metallic character in Group 4A (14)

4.127 Silicon has three naturally occurring isotopes: Si-28 that has a percent abundance of 92.23% and a mass of 27.977 amu, Si-29 that has a 4.68% abundance and a mass of 28.976 amu, and Si-30 that has a percent abundance of 3.09% and a mass of 29.974 amu. Calculate the atomic mass for silicon using the weighted average mass method. (4.5)

4.128 Antimony (Sb) has two naturally occurring isotopes: Sb-121 that has a percent abundance of 57.21% and a mass of 120.90 amu, and Sb-123 that has a percent abundance of 42.79% and a mass of 122.90 amu. Calculate the atomic mass for antimony using the weighted average mass method. (4.5)

4.129 Consider three elements with the following abbreviated electron configurations: (4.2, 4.7, 4.8)

$$X = [Ar]4s^2 \qquad Y = [Ne]3s^23p^4$$
$$Z = [Ar]4s^23d^{10}4p^4$$

   a. Identify each element as a metal, a nonmetal, or a metalloid.
   b. Which element has the largest atomic size?
   c. Which elements have similar properties?
   d. Which element has the highest ionization energy?
   e. Which element has the smallest atomic size?

4.130 Consider three elements with the following abbreviated electron configurations: (4.2, 4.7, 4.8)

$$X = [Ar]4s^23d^5 \qquad Y = [Ar]4s^23d^{10}4p^1$$
$$Z = [Ar]4s^23d^{10}4p^6$$

   a. Identify each element as a metal, a nonmetal, or a metalloid.
   b. Which element has the smallest atomic size?
   c. Which elements have similar properties?
   d. Which element has the highest ionization energy?
   e. Which element has a half-filled sublevel?

ANSWERS

Answers to Selected Questions and Problems

4.1 a. Cu   **b.** Pt   **c.** Ca   **d.** Mn
   e. Fe   **f.** Ba   **g.** Pb   **h.** Sr

4.3 a. carbon   **b.** chlorine   **c.** iodine   **d.** selenium
   e. nitrogen   **f.** sulfur   **g.** zinc   **h.** cobalt

4.5 a. sodium, chlorine
   b. calcium, sulfur, oxygen
   c. carbon, hydrogen, chlorine, nitrogen, oxygen
   d. lithium, carbon, oxygen

4.7 a. Period 2   **b.** Group 8A (18)
   c. Group 1A (1)   **d.** Period 2

4.9 a. C   **b.** He   **c.** Na
   d. Ca   **e.** Al

4.11 a. metal   **b.** nonmetal   **c.** metal   **d.** nonmetal
   e. nonmetal   **f.** nonmetal   **g.** metalloid   **h.** metal

4.13 a. needed for bones and teeth, muscle contraction, nerve impulses; alkaline earth metal
   b. component of hemoglobin; transition element
   c. muscle contraction, nerve impulses; alkali metal
   d. found in fluids outside cells; halogen

4.15 a. A macromineral is an element essential to health, which is present in the body in amounts from 5 to 1000 g.
   b. Sulfur is a component of proteins, liver, vitamin B_1, and insulin.
   c. 86 g

4.17 a. electron   **b.** proton
   c. electron   **d.** neutron

4.19 Rutherford determined that an atom contains a small, compact nucleus that is positively charged.

4.21 a. True   **b.** True
   c. True   **d.** False; a proton is attracted to an electron

4.23 In the process of brushing hair, strands of hair become charged with like charges that repel each other.

4.25 a. atomic number   **b.** both
   c. mass number   **d.** atomic number

4.27 a. lithium, Li   **b.** fluorine, F
   c. calcium, Ca   **d.** zinc, Zn
   e. neon, Ne   **f.** silicon, Si
   g. iodine, I   **h.** oxygen, O

4.29 a. 18 protons and 18 electrons
   b. 25 protons and 25 electrons
   c. 53 protons and 53 electrons
   d. 48 protons and 48 electrons

4.31

Name of the Element	Symbol	Atomic Number	Mass Number	Number of Protons	Number of Neutrons	Number of Electrons
Zinc	Zn	30	66	30	36	30
Magnesium	Mg	12	24	12	12	12
Potassium	K	19	39	19	20	19
Sulfur	S	16	31	16	15	16
Iron	Fe	26	56	26	30	26

4.33 a. 38 protons, 51 neutrons, 38 electrons
   b. 24 protons, 28 neutrons, 24 electrons
   c. 16 protons, 18 neutrons, 16 electrons
   d. 35 protons, 46 neutrons, 35 electrons

4.35 a. $^{31}_{15}P$ **b.** $^{80}_{35}Br$ **c.** $^{122}_{50}Sn$
   d. $^{35}_{17}Cl$ **e.** $^{202}_{80}Hg$

4.37 a. $^{36}_{18}Ar$ $^{38}_{18}Ar$ $^{40}_{18}Ar$
   b. They all have the same number of protons and electrons.
   c. They have different numbers of neutrons, which gives them different mass numbers.
   d. The atomic mass of Ar listed on the periodic table is the weighted average atomic mass of all the naturally occurring isotopes.
   e. The isotope Ar-40 is most prevalent because its mass is closest to the atomic mass of Ar on the periodic table.

4.39 69.72 amu

4.41 a. spherical   **b.** two lobes   **c.** spherical

4.43 a. 1 and 2   **b.** 3
   c. 1 and 2   **d.** 1, 2, and 3

4.45 a. There are five orbitals in the $3d$ sublevel.
   b. There is one sublevel in the $n = 1$ energy level.
   c. There is one orbital in the $6s$ sublevel.
   d. There are nine orbitals in the $n = 3$ energy level.

4.47 a. There is a maximum of two electrons in a $2p$ orbital.
   b. There is a maximum of six electrons in the $3p$ sublevel.
   c. There is a maximum of 32 electrons in the $n = 4$ energy level.
   d. There is a maximum of 10 electrons in the $5d$ sublevel.

4.49 The electron configuration shows the number of electrons in each sublevel of an atom. The abbreviated electron configuration uses the symbol of the preceding noble gas to show completed sublevels.

4.51 a.

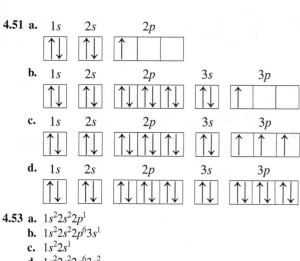

4.53 a. $1s^22s^22p^1$
b. $1s^22s^22p^63s^1$
c. $1s^22s^1$
d. $1s^22s^22p^63s^2$

4.55 a. $[He]2s^22p^2$ **b.** $[Ne]3s^23p^2$
c. $[Ne]3s^23p^3$ **d.** $[He]2s^22p^5$

4.57 a. Li   **b.** S   **c.** Si   **d.** F

4.59 a. Al   **b.** C   **c.** Ar   **d.** Be

4.61 a. $1s^22s^22p^63s^23p^64s^23d^{10}4p^3$, $[Ar]4s^23d^{10}4p^3$
b. $1s^22s^22p^63s^23p^64s^23d^6$, $[Ar]4s^23d^6$
c. $1s^22s^22p^63s^23p^64s^23d^{10}4p^65s^24d^{10}5p^1$, $[Kr]5s^24d^{10}5p^1$
d. $1s^22s^22p^63s^23p^64s^23d^{10}4p^65s^24d^{10}5p^5$, $[Kr]5s^24d^{10}5p^5$
e. $1s^22s^22p^63s^23p^64s^23d^2$, $[Ar]4s^23d^2$

4.63 a. Ga   **b.** N   **c.** Xe   **d.** Zr

4.65 a. 10   **b.** 6   **c.** 3   **d.** 1

4.67 a. 3   **b.** 5   **c.** 2   **d.** 7

4.69 a. Sulfur is in Group 6A (16); ⋅S̈⋅
b. Nitrogen is in Group 5A (15); ⋅N̈⋅
c. Calcium is in Group 2A (2); Ca⋅
d. Sodium is in Group 1A (1); Na⋅
e. Gallium is in Group 3A (13); ⋅Ga⋅

4.71 a. Na   **b.** Rb   **c.** Na   **d.** Rb

4.73 a. Mg, Al, Si   **b.** I, Br, Cl
c. Sr, Sb, I   **d.** Na, Si, P

4.75 a. Br   **b.** Mg   **c.** P   **d.** Xe

4.77 a. Br, Cl, F   **b.** Na, Al, Cl
c. Cs, K, Na   **d.** Ca, As, Br

4.79 Ca, Ga, Ge, Br

4.81 lower, more

4.83 a. 1. decreases   **b. 2.** increases
c. 2. increases   **d. 3.** remains the same

4.85 a. false   **b.** true   **c.** true   **d.** false   **e.** true

4.87 a. Group 1A (1), alkali metals   **b.** metal
c. 19 protons   **d.** K-39
e. 39.10 amu

4.89 a. False; All atoms of a given element are different from atoms of other elements.
b. True
c. True
d. False; In a chemical reaction, atoms are neither created nor destroyed.

4.91 a. 1 + 2   **b.** 1   **c.** 1
d. 3   **e.** 2

4.93 a. $^{16}_8X$, $^{17}_8X$, $^{18}_8X$ all have eight protons.
b. $^{16}_8X$, $^{17}_8X$, $^{18}_8X$ are all isotopes of oxygen.

c. $^{16}_8X$ and $^{16}_9X$ have mass numbers of 16, and $^{18}_{10}X$ and $^{18}_8X$ have mass numbers of 18.

4.95

	Atomic Symbol		
	$^{70}_{32}Ge$	$^{73}_{32}Ge$	$^{76}_{32}Ge$
Atomic Number	32	32	32
Mass Number	70	73	76
Number of Protons	32	32	32
Number of Neutrons	38	41	44
Number of Electrons	32	32	32

4.97 a. ^9_4Be **b.** $^{11}_5B$ **c.** $^{13}_6C$ **d.** $^{10}_5B$ **e.** $^{12}_6C$
Representations **B** and **D** are isotopes of boron; **C** and **E** are isotopes of carbon.

4.99 a. This is possible. This element is magnesium.
b. Not possible. The $2p$ sublevel would fill before the $3s$, and only two electrons are allowed in an s orbital.

4.101 Li is **D**, Na is **A**, K is **C**, and Rb is **B**.

4.103 a. Na   **b.** Cl   **c.** Si   **d.** Ar
e. S   **f.** Na   **g.** Mg

4.105 a. Group 7A (17), Period 4
b. Group 8A (18), Period 3
c. Group 1A (1), Period 2
d. Group 2A (2), Period 7

4.107 a. metal   **b.** metal
c. metal   **d.** nonmetal

4.109 a. false   **b.** false   **c.** true
d. false   **e.** true

4.111 a. 48 protons, 66 neutrons, 48 electrons
b. 43 protons, 55 neutrons, 43 electrons
c. 79 protons, 120 neutrons, 79 electrons
d. 86 protons, 136 neutrons, 86 electrons
e. 54 protons, 82 neutrons, 54 electrons

4.113

Name of the Element	Atomic Symbol	Number of Protons	Number of Neutrons	Number of Electrons
Selenium	$^{80}_{34}Se$	34	46	34
Nickel	$^{62}_{28}Ni$	28	34	28
Magnesium	$^{26}_{12}Mg$	12	14	12
Radium	$^{228}_{88}Ra$	88	140	88

4.115 a. $3p$ **b.** $5s$ **c.** $4p$ **d.** $4s$

4.117 a. 6   **b.** 6   **c.** 10   **d.** 2

4.119 a. phosphorus   **b.** lithium (H is a nonmetal.)
c. cadmium   **d.** nitrogen
e. sodium

4.121 a. Na   **b.** P   **c.** F   **d.** Na   **e.** Cl

4.123 a. 82 protons, 126 neutrons, 82 electrons
b. $^{214}_{82}Pb$
c. $^{214}_{83}Bi$

4.125 a. O   **b.** Ar   **c.** C   **d.** Na   **e.** Ra

4.127 28.09 amu

4.129 a. X is a metal; Y and Z are nonmetals.
b. X has the largest atomic size.
c. Y and Z have six valence electrons and are in Group 6A (16).
d. Y has the highest ionization energy.
e. Y has the smallest atomic size.

5

Nuclear Chemistry

SIMONE'S DOCTOR IS CONCERNED ABOUT HER

elevated cholesterol, which could lead to coronary heart disease and a heart attack. He sends her to a nuclear medicine center to undergo a cardiac stress test. Paul, the nuclear medicine technician, explains to Simone that a nuclear stress test measures the blood flow to her heart muscle at rest and then during stress. The test is performed in a similar way as a routine exercise stress test, but images are produced that show areas of low blood flow through the heart and areas of damaged heart muscle. It involves taking two sets of images of her heart, one when the heart is at rest, and one when she is exercising on a treadmill.

Paul tells Simone that he will inject thallium-201 into her bloodstream. He explains that Tl-201 is a radioactive isotope that has a half-life of 3.0 days. Simone is curious about the term "half-life." Paul explains that a half-life is the amount of time it takes for one-half of a radio-active sample to break down. He assures her that after four half-lives, the radiation emitted will be almost zero. Paul tells Simone that Tl-201 decays to Hg-201 and emits energy similar to X-rays and gamma rays. When the Tl-201 reaches any areas within her heart with restricted blood supply, small amounts of the radioisotope will accumulate.

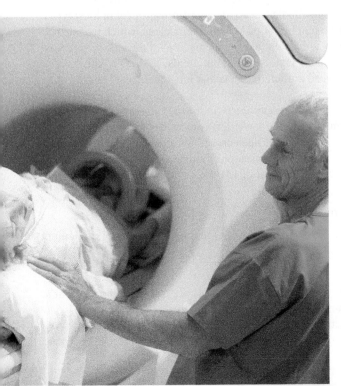

CAREER Nuclear Medicine Technologist

A nuclear medicine technologist works in a hospital or imaging center where nuclear medicine is used to diagnose and treat a variety of medical conditions. Typically, a nuclear medicine technologist prepares radioisotopes, which are given to patients for diagnostic or therapeutic procedures. In a diagnostic test, the nuclear medicine technologist uses a scanner, which converts radiation from various parts of the body into images. The images are evaluated to determine any abnormalities in the body. A nuclear medicine technologist operates the instrumentation and computers associated with nuclear medicine such as Computed Tomography (CT), Magnetic Resonance Imaging (MRI), and Positron Emission Tomography (PET). A nuclear medicine technologist must know how to handle radioisotopes safely, use the necessary type of shielding, and give radioactive isotopes to patients. In addition, they must physically and mentally prepare patients for imaging by explaining the procedure to them.

With the production of artificial radioactive substances in 1934, the field of nuclear medicine was established. In 1937, the first radioactive isotope was used to treat a person with leukemia at the University of California at Berkeley. Major strides in the use of radioactivity in medicine occurred in 1946, when a radioactive iodine isotope was successfully used to diagnose thyroid function and to treat hyperthyroidism and thyroid cancer. Radioactive substances are now used to produce images of organs, such as liver, spleen, thyroid gland, kidneys, and the brain, and to detect heart disease. Today, procedures in nuclear medicine provide information about the function and structure of every organ in the body, which allows the nuclear physician to diagnose and treat diseases early.

CHAPTER READINESS*

🖩 KEY MATH SKILLS
- Using Positive and Negative Numbers in Calculations (1.4B)
- Solving Equations (1.4D)
- Interpreting a Graph (1.4E)

⚛ CORE CHEMISTRY SKILLS
- Using Conversion Factors (2.6)
- Counting Protons and Neutrons (4.4)
- Writing Atomic Symbols for Isotopes (4.5)

*These Key Math Skills and Core Chemistry Skills from previous chapters are listed here for your review as you proceed to the new material in this chapter.

LEARNING GOAL

Describe alpha, beta, positron, and gamma radiation.

5.1 Natural Radioactivity

Most naturally occurring isotopes of elements up to atomic number 19 have stable nuclei. Elements with atomic numbers 20 and higher usually have one or more isotopes that have unstable nuclei in which the nuclear forces cannot offset the repulsions between the protons. An unstable nucleus is *radioactive*, which means that it spontaneously emits small particles of energy called **radiation** to become more stable. Radiation may take the form of alpha (α) and beta (β) particles, positrons (β^+), or pure energy such as gamma (γ) rays. An isotope of an element that emits radiation is called a **radioisotope**. For most types of radiation, there is a change in the number of protons in the nucleus, which means that an atom is converted into an atom of a different element. This kind of nuclear change was not evident to Dalton when he made his predictions about atoms. Elements with atomic numbers of 93 and higher are produced artificially in nuclear laboratories and consist only of radioactive isotopes.

The atomic symbols for the different isotopes are written with the mass number in the upper left corner and the atomic number in the lower left corner. The mass number is the sum of the number of protons and neutrons in the nucleus, and the atomic number is equal to the number of protons. For example, a radioactive isotope of iodine used in the diagnosis and treatment of thyroid conditions has a mass number of 131 and an atomic number of 53.

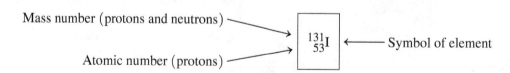

Mass number (protons and neutrons) ⟶ $^{131}_{53}\text{I}$ ⟵ Symbol of element
Atomic number (protons) ⟶

Radioactive isotopes are identified by writing the mass number after the element's name or symbol. Thus, in this example, the isotope is called iodine-131 or I-131. Table 5.1 compares some stable, nonradioactive isotopes with some radioactive isotopes.

TABLE 5.1 Stable and Radioactive Isotopes of Some Elements

Magnesium	Iodine	Uranium
Stable Isotopes		
$^{24}_{12}Mg$	$^{127}_{53}I$	None
Magnesium-24	Iodine-127	
Radioactive Isotopes		
$^{23}_{12}Mg$	$^{125}_{53}I$	$^{235}_{92}U$
Magnesium-23	Iodine-125	Uranium-235
$^{27}_{12}Mg$	$^{131}_{53}I$	$^{238}_{92}U$
Magnesium-27	Iodine-131	Uranium-238

Types of Radiation

By emitting radiation, an unstable nucleus forms a more stable, lower energy nucleus. One type of radiation consists of *alpha particles*. An **alpha particle** is identical to a helium (He) nucleus, which has two protons and two neutrons. An alpha particle has a mass number of 4, an atomic number of 2, and a charge of 2+. The symbol for an alpha particle is the Greek letter alpha (α) or the symbol of a helium nucleus except that the 2+ charge is omitted.

Another type of radiation occurs when a radioisotope emits a *beta particle*. A **beta particle**, which is a high-energy electron, has a charge of 1−, and because its mass is so much less than the mass of a proton, it has a mass number of 0. It is represented by the Greek letter beta (β) or by the symbol for the electron including the mass number and the charge ($^{0}_{-1}e$). A beta particle is formed when a neutron in an unstable nucleus changes into a proton.

A **positron**, similar to a beta particle, has a positive (1+) charge with a mass number of 0. It is represented by the Greek letter beta with a 1+ charge, β^{+}, or by the symbol of an electron, which includes the mass number and the charge ($^{0}_{+1}e$). A positron is produced by an unstable nucleus when a proton is transformed into a neutron and a positron.

A positron is an example of *antimatter*, a term physicists use to describe a particle that is the opposite of another particle, in this case, an electron. When an electron and a positron collide, their minute masses are completely converted to energy in the form of *gamma rays*.

$$^{0}_{-1}e + ^{0}_{+1}e \longrightarrow 2\,^{0}_{0}\gamma$$

Gamma rays are high-energy radiation, released when an unstable nucleus undergoes a rearrangement of its particles to give a more stable, lower energy nucleus. Gamma rays are often emitted along with other types of radiation. A gamma ray is written as the Greek letter gamma ($^{0}_{0}\gamma$). Because gamma rays are energy only, zeros are used to show that a gamma ray has no mass or charge.

Table 5.2 summarizes the types of radiation we will use in nuclear equations.

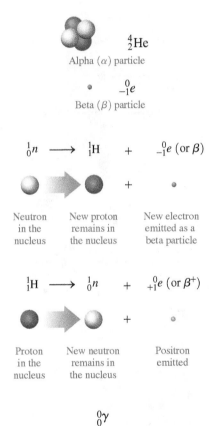

$^{4}_{2}He$
Alpha (α) particle

$^{0}_{-1}e$
Beta (β) particle

$^{1}_{0}n \longrightarrow \ ^{1}_{1}H \ + \ ^{0}_{-1}e$ (or β)

| Neutron in the nucleus | New proton remains in the nucleus | New electron emitted as a beta particle |

$^{1}_{1}H \longrightarrow \ ^{1}_{0}n \ + \ ^{0}_{+1}e$ (or β^{+})

| Proton in the nucleus | New neutron remains in the nucleus | Positron emitted |

$^{0}_{0}\gamma$
Gamma (γ) ray

TABLE 5.2 Some Forms of Radiation

Type of Radiation	Symbol		Change in Nucleus	Mass Number	Charge
Alpha Particle	α	$^{4}_{2}He$	Two protons and two neutrons are emitted as an alpha particle.	4	2+
Beta Particle	β	$^{0}_{-1}e$	A neutron changes to a proton and an electron is emitted.	0	1−
Positron	β^{+}	$^{0}_{+1}e$	A proton changes to a neutron and a positron is emitted.	0	1+
Gamma Ray	γ	$^{0}_{0}\gamma$	Energy is lost to stabilize the nucleus.	0	0
Proton	p	$^{1}_{1}H$	A proton is emitted.	1	1+
Neutron	n	$^{1}_{0}n$	A neutron is emitted.	1	0

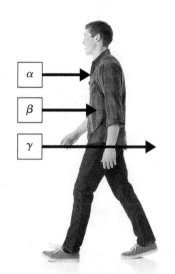

Different types of radiation penetrate the body to different depths.

> **SAMPLE PROBLEM 5.1 Radiation Particles**
>
> Identify and write the symbol for each of the following types of radiation:
>
> **a.** contains two protons and two neutrons
> **b.** has a mass number of 0 and a 1− charge
>
> SOLUTION
>
> **a.** An alpha (α) particle, $_2^4\text{He}$, has two protons and two neutrons.
> **b.** A beta (β) particle, $_{-1}^0 e$, is like an electron with a mass number of 0 and a 1− charge.
>
> **STUDY CHECK 5.1**
>
> Identify and write the symbol for the type of radiation that has a mass number of zero and a 1+ charge.
>
> ANSWER
>
> A positron, $_{+1}^0 e$, has a mass number of 0 and a 1+ charge.

Biological Effects of Radiation

When radiation strikes molecules in its path, electrons may be knocked away, forming unstable ions. If this *ionizing radiation* passes through the human body, it may interact with water molecules, removing electrons and producing H_2O^+, which can cause undesirable chemical reactions.

The cells most sensitive to radiation are the ones undergoing rapid division—those of the bone marrow, skin, reproductive organs, and intestinal lining, as well as all cells of growing children. Damaged cells may lose their ability to produce necessary materials. For example, if radiation damages cells of the bone marrow, red blood cells may no longer be produced. If sperm cells, ova, or the cells of a fetus are damaged, birth defects may result. In contrast, cells of the nerves, muscles, liver, and adult bones are much less sensitive to radiation because they undergo little or no cellular division.

Cancer cells are another example of rapidly dividing cells. Because cancer cells are highly sensitive to radiation, large doses of radiation are used to destroy them. The normal tissue that surrounds cancer cells divides at a slower rate and suffers less damage from radiation. However, radiation may cause malignant tumors, leukemia, anemia, and genetic mutations.

Radiation Protection

Nuclear medicine technologists, chemists, doctors, and nurses who work with radioactive isotopes must use proper radiation protection. Proper *shielding* is necessary to prevent exposure. Alpha particles, which have the largest mass and charge of the radiation particles, travel only a few centimeters in the air before they collide with air molecules, acquire electrons, and become helium atoms. A piece of paper, clothing, and our skin are protection against alpha particles. Lab coats and gloves will also provide sufficient shielding. However, if alpha emitters are ingested or inhaled, the alpha particles they give off can cause serious internal damage.

Beta particles have a very small mass and move much faster and farther than alpha particles, traveling as much as several meters through air. They can pass through paper and penetrate as far as 4 to 5 mm into body tissue. External exposure to beta particles can burn the surface of the skin, but they do not travel far enough to reach the internal organs. Heavy clothing such as lab coats and gloves are needed to protect the skin from beta particles.

Gamma rays travel great distances through the air and pass through many materials, including body tissues. Because gamma rays penetrate so deeply, exposure to gamma rays can be extremely hazardous. Only very dense shielding, such as lead or concrete, will stop them. Syringes used for injections of radioactive materials use shielding made of lead or heavy-weight materials such as tungsten and plastic composites.

When working with radioactive materials, medical personnel wear protective clothing and gloves and stand behind a shield (see Figure 5.1). Long tongs may be used to pick up vials of radioactive material, keeping them away from the hands and body. Table 5.3 summarizes the shielding materials required for the various types of radiation.

TABLE 5.3 Properties of Radiation and Shielding Required

Property	Alpha (α) Particle	Beta (β) Particle	Gamma (γ) Ray
Travel Distance in Air	2 to 4 cm	200 to 300 cm	500 m
Tissue Depth	0.05 mm	4 to 5 mm	50 cm or more
Shielding	Paper, clothing	Heavy clothing, lab coats, gloves	Lead, thick concrete
Typical Source	Radium-226	Carbon-14	Technetium-99m

If you work in an environment where radioactive materials are present, such as a nuclear medicine facility, try to keep the time you spend in a radioactive area to a minimum. Remaining in a radioactive area twice as long exposes you to twice as much radiation.

Keep your distance! The greater the distance from the radioactive source, the lower the intensity of radiation received. By doubling your distance from the radiation source, the intensity of radiation drops to $\left(\frac{1}{2}\right)^2$, or one-fourth of its previous value.

QUESTIONS AND PROBLEMS

5.1 Natural Radioactivity

LEARNING GOAL Describe alpha, beta, positron, and gamma radiation.

5.1 Identify the type of particle or radiation for each of the following:
  a. ^4_2He **b.** $^0_{+1}e$ **c.** $^0_0\gamma$

5.2 Identify the type of particle or radiation for each of the following:
  a. $^0_{-1}e$ **b.** ^1_1H **c.** ^1_0n

5.3 Naturally occurring potassium consists of three isotopes: potassium-39, potassium-40, and potassium-41.
  a. Write the atomic symbol for each isotope.
  b. In what ways are the isotopes similar, and in what ways do they differ?

5.4 Naturally occurring iodine is iodine-127. Medically, radioactive isotopes of iodine-125 and iodine-131 are used.
  a. Write the atomic symbol for each isotope.
  b. In what ways are the isotopes similar, and in what ways do they differ?

5.5 Identify each of the following:
  a. $^0_{-1}X$ **b.** ^4_2X **c.** ^1_0X
  d. $^{38}_{18}X$ **e.** $^{14}_6X$

5.6 Identify each of the following:
  a. ^1_1X **b.** $^{81}_{35}X$ **c.** ^0_0X
  d. $^{59}_{26}X$ **e.** $^0_{+1}X$

℞ Clinical Applications

5.7 Write the symbol for each of the following isotopes used in nuclear medicine:
  a. copper-64   **b.** selenium-75
  c. sodium-24   **d.** nitrogen-15

5.8 Write the symbol for each of the following isotopes used in nuclear medicine:
  a. indium-111   **b.** palladium-103
  c. barium-131   **d.** rubidium-82

5.9 Supply the missing information in the following table:

Medical Use	Atomic Symbol	Mass Number	Number of Protons	Number of Neutrons
Heart imaging	$^{201}_{81}Tl$			
Radiation therapy		60	27	
Abdominal scan			31	36
Hyperthyroidism	$^{131}_{53}I$			
Leukemia treatment		32		17

5.10 Supply the missing information in the following table:

Medical Use	Atomic Symbol	Mass Number	Number of Protons	Number of Neutrons
Cancer treatment	$^{131}_{55}Cs$			
Brain scan			43	56
Blood flow		141	58	
Bone scan		85		47
Lung function	$^{133}_{54}Xe$			

5.11 Match the type of radiation (**1** to **3**) with each of the following statements:
  1. alpha particle
  2. beta particle
  3. gamma radiation

  a. does not penetrate skin
  b. shielding protection includes lead or thick concrete
  c. can be very harmful if ingested

5.12 Match the type of radiation (**1** to **3**) with each of the following statements:
  1. alpha particle
  2. beta particle
  3. gamma radiation

  a. penetrates farthest into skin and body tissues
  b. shielding protection includes lab coats and gloves
  c. travels only a short distance in air

Write a balanced nuclear equation showing mass numbers and atomic numbers for radioactive decay.

⚛ **CORE CHEMISTRY SKILL**

Writing Nuclear Equations

5.2 Nuclear Reactions

In a process called **radioactive decay**, a nucleus spontaneously breaks down by emitting radiation. This process is shown by writing a *nuclear equation* with the atomic symbols of the original radioactive nucleus on the left, an arrow, and the new nucleus and the type of radiation emitted on the right.

$$\text{Radioactive nucleus} \longrightarrow \text{new nucleus} + \text{radiation } (\alpha, \beta, \beta^+, \gamma)$$

In a nuclear equation, the sum of the mass numbers and the sum of the atomic numbers on one side of the arrow must equal the sum of the mass numbers and the sum of the atomic numbers on the other side.

Alpha Decay

An unstable nucleus may emit an alpha particle, which consists of two protons and two neutrons. Thus, the mass number of the radioactive nucleus decreases by 4, and its atomic number decreases by 2. For example, when uranium-238 emits an alpha particle, the new nucleus that forms has a mass number of 234. Compared to uranium with 92 protons, the new nucleus has 90 protons, which is thorium.

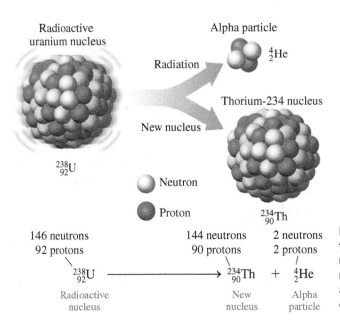

Radioactive uranium nucleus

Alpha particle

^4_2He

Radiation

Thorium-234 nucleus

New nucleus

$^{238}_{92}\text{U}$

◯ Neutron

⬤ Proton

$^{234}_{90}\text{Th}$

146 neutrons
92 protons

144 neutrons
90 protons

2 neutrons
2 protons

$$^{238}_{92}\text{U} \longrightarrow {}^{234}_{90}\text{Th} + {}^4_2\text{He}$$

Radioactive nucleus

New nucleus

Alpha particle

In the nuclear equation for alpha decay, the mass number of the new nucleus decreases by 4 and its atomic number decreases by 2.

We can look at writing a balanced nuclear equation for americium-241, which undergoes alpha decay as shown in Sample Problem 5.2.

▶ **SAMPLE PROBLEM 5.2 Writing an Equation for Alpha Decay**

Smoke detectors that are used in homes and apartments contain americium-241, which undergoes alpha decay. When alpha particles collide with air molecules, charged particles are produced that generate an electrical current. If smoke particles enter the detector, they interfere with the formation of charged particles in the air, and the electrical current is interrupted. This causes the alarm to sound and warns the occupants of the danger of fire. Write the balanced nuclear equation for the decay of americium-241.

SOLUTION

ANALYZE THE PROBLEM	Given	Need
	Am-241, alpha decay	balanced nuclear equation

A smoke detector sounds an alarm when smoke enters its ionization chamber.

STEP 1 Write the incomplete nuclear equation.

$$^{241}_{95}\text{Am} \longrightarrow ? + ^{4}_{2}\text{He}$$

STEP 2 Determine the missing mass number. In the equation, the mass number of the americium, 241, is equal to the sum of the mass numbers of the new nucleus and the alpha particle.

241   = ? + 4
241 − 4 = ?
241 − 4 = 237 (mass number of new nucleus)

STEP 3 Determine the missing atomic number. The atomic number of americium, 95, must equal the sum of the atomic numbers of the new nucleus and the alpha particle.

95   = ? + 2
95 − 2 = ?
95 − 2 = 93 (atomic number of new nucleus)

STEP 4 Determine the symbol of the new nucleus. On the periodic table, the element that has atomic number 93 is neptunium, Np. The nucleus of this isotope of Np is written as $^{237}_{93}\text{Np}$.

STEP 5 Complete the nuclear equation.

$$^{241}_{95}\text{Am} \longrightarrow ^{237}_{93}\text{Np} + ^{4}_{2}\text{He}$$

STUDY CHECK 5.2

Write the balanced nuclear equation for the alpha decay of Po-214.

ANSWER

$$^{214}_{84}\text{Po} \longrightarrow ^{210}_{82}\text{Pb} + ^{4}_{2}\text{He}$$

> **Guide to Completing a Nuclear Equation**
>
> **STEP 1**
> Write the incomplete nuclear equation.
>
> **STEP 2**
> Determine the missing mass number.
>
> **STEP 3**
> Determine the missing atomic number.
>
> **STEP 4**
> Determine the symbol of the new nucleus.
>
> **STEP 5**
> Complete the nuclear equation.

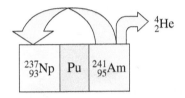

$^{4}_{2}\text{He}$

| $^{237}_{93}\text{Np}$ | Pu | $^{241}_{95}\text{Am}$ |

Chemistry Link to Health
Radon in Our Homes

The presence of radon gas has become a much publicized environmental and health issue because of the radiation danger it poses. Radioactive isotopes such as radium-226 are naturally present in many types of rocks and soils. Radium-226 emits an alpha particle and is converted into radon gas, which diffuses out of the rocks and soil.

$$^{226}_{88}\text{Ra} \longrightarrow ^{222}_{86}\text{Rn} + ^{4}_{2}\text{He}$$

Outdoors, radon gas poses little danger because it disperses in the air. However, if the radioactive source is under a house or building, the radon gas can enter the house through cracks in the foundation or other openings. Those who live or work there may inhale the radon. Inside the lungs, radon-222 emits alpha particles to form polonium-218, which is known to cause lung cancer.

$$^{222}_{86}\text{Rn} \longrightarrow ^{218}_{84}\text{Po} + ^{4}_{2}\text{He}$$

The Environmental Protection Agency (EPA) recommends that the maximum level of radon not exceed 4 picocuries (pCi) per liter of air in a home. One picocurie (pCi) is equal to 10^{-12} curies (Ci); curies are described in section 5.3. In California, 1% of all the houses surveyed exceeded the EPA's recommended maximum radon level.

A radon gas detector is used to determine radon levels in buildings.

Beta Decay

The formation of a beta particle is the result of the breakdown of a neutron into a proton and an electron (beta particle). Because the proton remains in the nucleus, the number of protons increases by one, whereas the number of neutrons decreases by one. Thus, in a nuclear equation for beta decay, the mass number of the radioactive nucleus and the mass number of the new nucleus are the same. However, the atomic number of the new nucleus increases by one, which makes it a nucleus of a different element (*transmutation*). For example, the beta decay of a carbon-14 nucleus produces a nitrogen-14 nucleus.

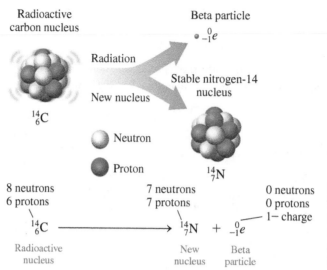

Radioactive carbon nucleus

Beta particle
$_{-1}^{0}e$

Radiation

Stable nitrogen-14 nucleus

New nucleus

$_{6}^{14}C$

○ Neutron

● Proton

$_{7}^{14}N$

8 neutrons
6 protons

7 neutrons
7 protons

0 neutrons
0 protons
1− charge

$_{6}^{14}C \longrightarrow _{7}^{14}N + _{-1}^{0}e$

Radioactive nucleus

New nucleus

Beta particle

In the nuclear equation for beta decay, the mass number of the new nucleus remains the same and its atomic number increases by 1.

A radioisotope is injected into joint of the hand to relieve the pain caused by arthritis.

▶ **SAMPLE PROBLEM 5.3** **Writing a Nuclear Equation for Beta Decay**

The radioactive isotope yttrium-90, a beta emitter, is used in cancer treatment and as a colloidal injection into large joints to relieve the pain caused by arthritis. Write the balanced nuclear equation for the beta decay of yttrium-90.

SOLUTION

ANALYZE THE PROBLEM	Given	Need
	Y-90, beta decay	balanced nuclear equation

STEP 1 Write the incomplete nuclear equation.

$$_{39}^{90}Y \longrightarrow \; ? \; + _{-1}^{0}e$$

STEP 2 Determine the missing mass number. In the equation, the mass number of the yttrium, 90, is equal to the sum of the mass numbers of the new nucleus and the beta particle.

90 $\;= ? + 0$
90 − 0 $= ?$
90 − 0 $= 90$ (mass number of new nucleus)

STEP 3 Determine the missing atomic number. The atomic number of yttrium, 39, must equal the sum of the atomic numbers of the new nucleus and the beta particle.

39 $\;= ? − 1$
39 + 1 $= ?$
39 + 1 $= 40$ (atomic number of new nucleus)

STEP 4 Determine the symbol of the new nucleus. On the periodic table, the element that has atomic number 40 is zirconium, Zr. The nucleus of this isotope of Zr is written as $_{40}^{90}Zr$.

STEP 5 Complete the nuclear equation.

$$_{39}^{90}Y \longrightarrow _{40}^{90}Zr + _{-1}^{0}e$$

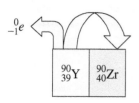

$_{-1}^{0}e$

| $_{39}^{90}Y$ | $_{40}^{90}Zr$ |

STUDY CHECK 5.3

Write the balanced nuclear equation for the beta decay of chromium-51.

ANSWER

$$^{51}_{24}\text{Cr} \longrightarrow {}^{51}_{25}\text{Mn} + {}^{0}_{-1}e$$

Positron Emission

In positron emission, a proton in an unstable nucleus is converted to a neutron and a positron. The neutron remains in the nucleus, but the positron is emitted from the nucleus. In a nuclear equation for positron emission, the mass number of the radioactive nucleus and the mass number of the new nucleus are the same. However, the atomic number of the new nucleus decreases by one, indicating a change of one element into another. For example, an aluminum-24 nucleus undergoes positron emission to produce a magnesium-24 nucleus. The atomic number of magnesium (12) and the charge of the positron (1+) give the atomic number of aluminum (13).

$$^{24}_{13}\text{Al} \longrightarrow {}^{24}_{12}\text{Mg} + {}^{0}_{+1}e$$

▶ **SAMPLE PROBLEM 5.4 Writing a Nuclear Equation for Positron Emission**

Write the balanced nuclear equation for manganese-49, which decays by emitting a positron.

SOLUTION

ANALYZE THE PROBLEM	Given	Need
	Mn-49, positron emission	balanced nuclear equation

STEP 1 Write the incomplete nuclear equation.

$$^{49}_{25}\text{Mn} \longrightarrow ? + {}^{0}_{+1}e$$

STEP 2 Determine the missing mass number. In the equation, the mass number of the manganese, 49, is equal to the sum of the mass numbers of the new nucleus and the positron.

$$49 = ? + 0$$
$$49 - 0 = ?$$
$$49 - 0 = 49 \text{ (mass number of new nucleus)}$$

STEP 3 Determine the missing atomic number. The atomic number of manganese, 25, must equal the sum of the atomic numbers of the new nucleus and the positron.

$$25 = ? + 1$$
$$25 - 1 = ?$$
$$25 - 1 = 24 \text{ (atomic number of new nucleus)}$$

STEP 4 Determine the symbol of the new nucleus. On the periodic table, the element that has atomic number 24 is chromium (Cr). The nucleus of this isotope of Cr is written as $^{49}_{24}\text{Cr}$.

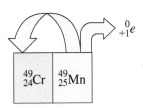

STEP 5 Complete the nuclear equation.

$$^{49}_{25}\text{Mn} \longrightarrow {}^{49}_{24}\text{Cr} + {}^{0}_{+1}e$$

STUDY CHECK 5.4

Write the balanced nuclear equation for xenon-118, which undergoes positron emission.

ANSWER

$$^{118}_{54}\text{Xe} \longrightarrow {}^{118}_{53}\text{I} + {}^{0}_{+1}e$$

Radiation Source	Radiation	New Nucleus
Alpha emitter	$_2^4\text{He}$ +	New element
		Mass number -4 Atomic number -2
Beta emitter	$_{-1}^0 e$ +	New element
		Mass number same Atomic number $+1$
Positron emitter	$_{+1}^0 e$ +	New element
		Mass number same Atomic number -1
Gamma emitter	$_0^0\gamma$ +	Stable nucleus of the same element
		Mass number same Atomic number same

Gamma Emission

Pure gamma emitters are rare, although gamma radiation accompanies most alpha and beta radiation. In radiology, one of the most commonly used gamma emitters is technetium (Tc). The unstable isotope of technetium is written as the *metastable* (symbol m) isotope technetium-99m, Tc-99m, or $_{43}^{99m}\text{Tc}$. By emitting energy in the form of gamma rays, the nucleus becomes more stable.

$$_{43}^{99m}\text{Tc} \longrightarrow _{43}^{99}\text{Tc} + _0^0\gamma$$

Figure 5.2 summarizes the changes in the nucleus for alpha, beta, positron, and gamma radiation.

Producing Radioactive Isotopes

Today, many radioisotopes are produced in small amounts by bombarding stable, nonradioactive isotopes with high-speed particles such as alpha particles, protons, neutrons, and small nuclei. When one of these particles is absorbed, the stable nucleus is converted to a radioactive isotope and usually some type of radiation particle.

FIGURE 5.2 ▶ When the nuclei of alpha, beta, positron, and gamma emitters emit radiation, new, more stable nuclei are produced.

◉ What changes occur in the number of protons and neutrons when an alpha emitter gives off radiation?

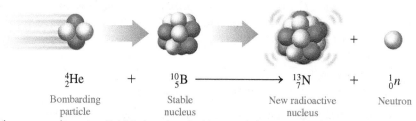

$$_2^4\text{He} \quad + \quad _5^{10}\text{B} \longrightarrow _7^{13}\text{N} \quad + \quad _0^1 n$$

Bombarding particle · · · · Stable nucleus · · · · New radioactive nucleus · · · · Neutron

When nonradioactive B-10 is bombarded by an alpha particle, the products are radioactive N-13 and a neutron.

All elements that have an atomic number greater than 92 have been produced by bombardment. Most have been produced in only small amounts and exist for only a short time, making it difficult to study their properties. For example, when californium-249 is bombarded with nitrogen-15, the radioactive element dubnium-260 and four neutrons are produced.

$$_7^{15}\text{N} + _{98}^{249}\text{Cf} \longrightarrow _{105}^{260}\text{Db} + 4_0^1 n$$

Technetium-99m is a radioisotope used in nuclear medicine for several diagnostic procedures, including the detection of brain tumors and examinations of the liver and spleen. The source of technetium-99m is molybdenum-99, which is produced in a nuclear reactor by neutron bombardment of molybdenum-98.

$$_0^1 n + _{42}^{98}\text{Mo} \longrightarrow _{42}^{99}\text{Mo}$$

Many radiology laboratories have small generators containing molybdenum-99, which decays to the technetium-99m radioisotope.

$$^{99}_{42}\text{Mo} \longrightarrow ^{99m}_{43}\text{Tc} + ^{0}_{-1}e$$

The technetium-99m radioisotope decays by emitting gamma rays. Gamma emission is desirable for diagnostic work because the gamma rays pass through the body to the detection equipment.

$$^{99m}_{43}\text{Tc} \longrightarrow ^{99}_{43}\text{Tc} + ^{0}_{0}\gamma$$

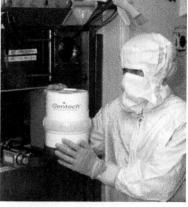

A generator is used to prepare technetium-99m.

▶ **SAMPLE PROBLEM 5.5** **Writing an Equation for an Isotope Produced by Bombardment**

Write the balanced nuclear equation for the bombardment of nickel-58 by a proton, $^{1}_{1}\text{H}$, which produces a radioactive isotope and an alpha particle.

SOLUTION

ANALYZE THE PROBLEM	**Given**	**Need**
	proton bombardment of Ni-58	balanced nuclear equation

STEP 1 Write the incomplete nuclear equation.

$$^{1}_{1}\text{H} + ^{58}_{28}\text{Ni} \longrightarrow ? + ^{4}_{2}\text{He}$$

STEP 2 Determine the missing mass number. In the equation, the sum of the mass numbers of the proton, 1, and the nickel, 58, must equal the sum of the mass numbers of the new nucleus and the alpha particle.

$1 + 58 = ? + 4$
$59 - 4 = ?$
$59 - 4 = 55$ (mass number of new nucleus)

STEP 3 Determine the missing atomic number. The sum of the atomic numbers of the proton, 1, and nickel, 28, must equal the sum of the atomic numbers of the new nucleus and the alpha particle.

$1 + 28 = ? + 2$
$29 - 2 = ?$
$29 - 2 = 27$ (atomic number of new nucleus)

STEP 4 Determine the symbol of the new nucleus. On the periodic table, the element that has atomic number 27 is cobalt, Co. The nucleus of this isotope of Co is written as $^{55}_{27}\text{Co}$.

STEP 5 Complete the nuclear equation.

$$^{1}_{1}\text{H} + ^{58}_{28}\text{Ni} \longrightarrow ^{55}_{27}\text{Co} + ^{4}_{2}\text{He}$$

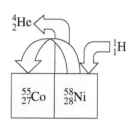

STUDY CHECK 5.5

The first radioactive isotope was produced in 1934 by the bombardment of aluminum-27 by an alpha particle to produce a radioactive isotope and one neutron. Write the balanced nuclear equation for this bombardment.

Interactive Video

Writing Equations for an Isotope Produced by Bombardment

ANSWER

$$^{4}_{2}\text{He} + ^{27}_{13}\text{Al} \longrightarrow ^{30}_{15}\text{P} + ^{1}_{0}n$$

QUESTIONS AND PROBLEMS

5.2 Nuclear Reactions

LEARNING GOAL Write a balanced nuclear equation showing mass numbers and atomic numbers for radioactive decay.

5.13 Write a balanced nuclear equation for the alpha decay of each of the following radioactive isotopes:
 a. $^{208}_{84}Po$ 　　　　 b. $^{232}_{90}Th$
 c. $^{251}_{102}No$ 　　　　 d. radon-220

5.14 Write a balanced nuclear equation for the alpha decay of each of the following radioactive isotopes:
 a. curium-243 　　　　 b. $^{252}_{99}Es$
 c. $^{251}_{98}Cf$ 　　　　 d. $^{261}_{107}Bh$

5.15 Write a balanced nuclear equation for the beta decay of each of the following radioactive isotopes:
 a. $^{25}_{11}Na$ 　　　　 b. $^{20}_{8}O$
 c. strontium-92 　　　　 d. iron-60

5.16 Write a balanced nuclear equation for the beta decay of each of the following radioactive isotopes:
 a. $^{44}_{19}K$ 　　　　 b. iron-59
 c. potassium-42 　　　　 d. $^{141}_{56}Ba$

5.17 Write a balanced nuclear equation for the positron emission of each of the following radioactive isotopes:
 a. silicon-26 　　　　 b. cobalt-54
 c. $^{77}_{37}Rb$ 　　　　 d. $^{93}_{45}Rh$

5.18 Write a balanced nuclear equation for the positron emission of each of the following radioactive isotopes:
 a. boron-8 　　　　 b. $^{15}_{8}O$
 c. $^{40}_{19}K$ 　　　　 d. nitrogen-13

5.19 Complete each of the following nuclear equations and describe the type of radiation:
 a. $^{28}_{13}Al \longrightarrow ? + ^{0}_{-1}e$ 　　 b. $^{180m}_{73}Ta \longrightarrow ^{180}_{73}Ta + ?$
 c. $^{66}_{29}Cu \longrightarrow ^{66}_{30}Zn + ?$ 　　 d. $? \longrightarrow ^{234}_{90}Th + ^{4}_{2}He$
 e. $^{188}_{80}Hg \longrightarrow ? + ^{0}_{+1}e$

5.20 Complete each of the following nuclear equations and describe the type of radiation:
 a. $^{11}_{6}C \longrightarrow ^{11}_{5}B + ?$ 　　 b. $^{35}_{16}S \longrightarrow ? + ^{0}_{-1}e$
 c. $? \longrightarrow ^{90}_{39}Y + ^{0}_{-1}e$ 　　 d. $^{210}_{83}Bi \longrightarrow ? + ^{4}_{2}He$
 e. $? \longrightarrow ^{89}_{39}Y + ^{0}_{+1}e$

5.21 Complete each of the following bombardment reactions:
 a. $^{1}_{0}n + ^{9}_{4}Be \longrightarrow ?$
 b. $^{1}_{0}n + ^{131}_{52}Te \longrightarrow ? + ^{0}_{-1}e$
 c. $^{1}_{0}n + ? \longrightarrow ^{24}_{11}Na + ^{4}_{2}He$
 d. $^{4}_{2}He + ^{14}_{7}N \longrightarrow ? + ^{1}_{1}H$

5.22 Complete each of the following bombardment reactions:
 a. $? + ^{40}_{18}Ar \longrightarrow ^{43}_{19}K + ^{1}_{1}H$
 b. $^{1}_{0}n + ^{238}_{92}U \longrightarrow ?$
 c. $^{1}_{0}n + ? \longrightarrow ^{14}_{6}C + ^{1}_{1}H$
 d. $? + ^{64}_{28}Ni \longrightarrow ^{272}_{111}Rg + ^{1}_{0}n$

LEARNING GOAL

Describe the detection and measurement of radiation.

5.3 Radiation Measurement

One of the most common instruments for detecting beta and gamma radiation is the Geiger counter. It consists of a metal tube filled with a gas such as argon. When radiation enters a window on the end of the tube, it forms charged particles in the gas, which produce an electrical current. Each burst of current is amplified to give a click and a reading on a meter.

$$Ar + radiation \longrightarrow Ar^{+} + e^{-}$$

Measuring Radiation

Radiation is measured in several different ways. When a radiology laboratory obtains a radioisotope, the *activity* of the sample is measured in terms of the number of nuclear disintegrations per second. The **curie (Ci)**, the original unit of activity, was defined as the

A radiation counter is used to determine radiation levels in workers at the Fukushima Daiichi nuclear power plant.

number of disintegrations that occur in 1 s for 1 g of radium, which is equal to 3.7×10^{10} disintegrations/s. The unit was named for the Polish scientist Marie Curie, who along with her husband, Pierre, discovered the radioactive elements radium and polonium. The SI unit of radiation activity is the **becquerel (Bq)**, which is 1 disintegration/s.

The **rad (radiation absorbed dose)** is a unit that measures the amount of radiation absorbed by a gram of material such as body tissue. The SI unit for absorbed dose is the **gray (Gy)**, which is defined as the joules of energy absorbed by 1 kg of body tissue. The gray is equal to 100 rad.

The **rem (radiation equivalent in humans)** is a unit that measures the biological effects of different kinds of radiation. Although alpha particles do not penetrate the skin, if they should enter the body by some other route, they can cause extensive damage within a short distance in tissue. High-energy radiation, such as beta particles, high-energy protons, and neutrons that travel into tissue, causes more damage. Gamma rays are damaging because they travel a long way through body tissue.

To determine the **equivalent dose** or rem dose, the absorbed dose (rad) is multiplied by a factor that adjusts for biological damage caused by a particular form of radiation. For beta and gamma radiation the factor is 1, so the biological damage in rems is the same as the absorbed radiation (rad). For high-energy protons and neutrons, the factor is about 10, and for alpha particles it is 20.

$$\text{Biological damage (rem)} = \text{Absorbed dose (rad)} \times \text{Factor}$$

Often, the measurement for an equivalent dose will be in units of millirems (mrem). One rem is equal to 1000 mrem. The SI unit is the **sievert (Sv)**. One sievert is equal to 100 rem. Table 5.4 summarizes the units used to measure radiation.

 # Chemistry Link to Health
Radiation and Food

Foodborne illnesses caused by pathogenic bacteria such as *Salmonella*, *Listeria*, and *Escherichia coli* have become a major health concern in the United States. The Centers for Disease Control and Prevention estimates that each year, *E. coli* in contaminated foods infects 20 000 people in the United States and that 500 people die. *E. coli* has been responsible for outbreaks of illness from contaminated ground beef, fruit juices, lettuce, and alfalfa sprouts.

The U.S. Food and Drug Administration (FDA) has approved the use of 0.3 kGy to 1 kGy of radiation produced by cobalt-60 or cesium-137 for the treatment of foods. The irradiation technology is much like that used to sterilize medical supplies. Cobalt pellets are placed in stainless steel tubes, which are arranged in racks. When food moves through the series of racks, the gamma rays pass through the food and kill the bacteria.

It is important for consumers to understand that when food is irradiated, it never comes in contact with the radioactive source. The gamma rays pass through the food to kill bacteria, but that does not make the food radioactive. The radiation kills bacteria because it stops their ability to divide and grow. We cook or heat food thoroughly for the same purpose. Radiation, as well as heat, has little effect on the food itself because its cells are no longer dividing or growing. Thus irradiated food is not harmed, although a small amount of vitamin B_1 and C may be lost.

Currently, tomatoes, blueberries, strawberries, and mushrooms are being irradiated to allow them to be harvested when completely ripe and extend their shelf life (see Figure 5.3). The FDA has also approved the irradiation of pork, poultry, and beef to decrease potential infections and to extend shelf life. Currently, irradiated vegetable and meat products are available in retail markets in more than 40 countries. In the United States, irradiated foods such as tropical fruits,

spinach, and ground meats are found in some stores. *Apollo 17* astronauts ate irradiated foods on the Moon, and some U.S. hospitals and nursing homes now use irradiated poultry to reduce the possibility of salmonella infections among residents. The extended shelf life of irradiated food also makes it useful for campers and military personnel. Soon, consumers concerned about food safety will have a choice of irradiated meats, fruits, and vegetables at the market.

(a)

(b)

FIGURE 5.3 ▶ **(a)** The FDA requires this symbol to appear on irradiated retail foods. **(b)** After two weeks, the irradiated strawberries on the right show no spoilage. Mold is growing on the nonirradiated ones on the left.

Why are irradiated foods used on spaceships and in nursing homes?

A dosimeter measures radiation exposure.

TABLE 5.5 Average Annual Radiation Received by a Person in the United States

Source	Dose (mrem)
Natural	
Ground	20
Air, water, food	30
Cosmic rays	40
Wood, concrete, brick	50
Medical	
Chest X-ray	20
Dental X-ray	20
Mammogram	40
Hip X-ray	60
Lumbar spine X-ray	70
Upper gastrointestinal tract X-ray	200
Other	
Nuclear power plants	0.1
Television	20
Air travel	10
Radon	200*

*Varies widely.

TABLE 5.6 Lethal Doses of Radiation for Some Life Forms

Life Form	LD$_{50}$ (rem)
Insect	100 000
Bacterium	50 000
Rat	800
Human	500
Dog	300

TABLE 5.4 Units of Radiation Measurement

Measurement	Common Unit	SI Unit	Relationship
Activity	curie (Ci) 1 Ci = 3.7×10^{10} disintegrations/s	becquerel (Bq) 1 Bq = 1 disintegration/s	1 Ci = 3.7×10^{10} Bq
Absorbed Dose	rad	gray (Gy) 1 Gy = 1 J/kg of tissue	1 Gy = 100 rad
Biological Damage	rem	sievert (Sv)	1 Sv = 100 rem

People who work in radiology laboratories wear dosimeters attached to their clothing to determine any exposure to radiation such as X-rays, gamma rays, or beta particles. A dosimeter can be thermoluminescent (TLD), optically stimulated luminescence (OSL), or electronic personal (EPD). Dosimeters provide real time radiation levels measured by monitors in the work area.

▶ **SAMPLE PROBLEM 5.6 Radiation Measurement**

One treatment for bone pain involves intravenous administration of the radioisotope phosphorus-32, which is incorporated into bone. A typical dose of 7 mCi can produce up to 450 rad in the bone. What is the difference between the units of mCi and rad?

SOLUTION

The millicuries (mCi) indicate the activity of the P-32 in terms of nuclei that break down in 1 s. The radiation absorbed dose (rad) is a measure of amount of radiation absorbed by the bone.

STUDY CHECK 5.6

For Sample Problem 5.6, what is the absorbed dose of radiation in grays (Gy)?

ANSWER

4.5 Gy

Exposure to Radiation

Every day, we are exposed to low levels of radiation from naturally occurring radioactive isotopes in the buildings where we live and work, in our food and water, and in the air we breathe. For example, potassium-40, a naturally occurring radioactive isotope, is present in any potassium-containing food. Other naturally occurring radioisotopes in air and food are carbon-14, radon-222, strontium-90, and iodine-131. The average person in the United States is exposed to about 360 mrem of radiation annually. Medical sources of radiation, including dental, hip, spine, and chest X-rays and mammograms, add to our radiation exposure. Table 5.5 lists some common sources of radiation.

Another source of background radiation is cosmic radiation produced in space by the Sun. People who live at high altitudes or travel by airplane receive a greater amount of cosmic radiation because there are fewer molecules in the atmosphere to absorb the radiation. For example, a person living in Denver receives about twice the cosmic radiation as a person living in Los Angeles. A person living close to a nuclear power plant normally does not receive much additional radiation, perhaps 0.1 mrem in 1 yr. (One rem equals 1000 mrem.) However, in the accident at the Chernobyl nuclear power plant in 1986 in Ukraine, it is estimated that people in a nearby town received as much as 1 rem/h.

Radiation Sickness

The larger the dose of radiation received at one time, the greater the effect on the body. Exposure to radiation of less than 25 rem usually cannot be detected. Whole-body exposure of 100 rem produces a temporary decrease in the number of white blood cells. If the exposure to radiation is greater than 100 rem, a person may suffer the symptoms of radiation sickness: nausea, vomiting, fatigue, and a reduction in white-cell count. A whole-body dosage greater than

300 rem can decrease the white-cell count to zero. The person suffers diarrhea, hair loss, and infection. Exposure to radiation of 500 rem is expected to cause death in 50% of the people receiving that dose. This amount of radiation to the whole body is called the *lethal dose for one-half the population*, or the LD_{50}. The LD_{50} varies for different life forms, as Table 5.6 shows. Whole-body radiation of 600 rem or greater would be fatal to all humans within a few weeks.

QUESTIONS AND PROBLEMS

5.3 Radiation Measurement

LEARNING GOAL Describe the detection and measurement of radiation.

5.23 Match each property (**1** to **3**) with its unit of measurement.
   1. activity
   2. absorbed dose
   3. biological damage

   a. rad   **b.** mrem
   c. mCi   **d.** Gy

5.24 Match each property (**1** to **3**) with its unit of measurement.
   1. activity
   2. absorbed dose
   3. biological damage

   a. mrad   **b.** gray
   c. becquerel   **d.** Sv

℞ Clinical Applications

5.25 Two technicians in a nuclear laboratory were accidentally exposed to radiation. If one was exposed to 8 mGy and the other to 5 rad, which technician received more radiation?

5.26 Two samples of a radioisotope were spilled in a nuclear laboratory. The activity of one sample was 8 kBq and the other 15 mCi. Which sample produced the higher amount of radiation?

5.27 **a.** The recommended dosage of iodine-131 is 4.20 μCi/kg of body mass. How many microcuries of iodine-131 are needed for a 70.0-kg person with hyperthyroidism?
   b. A person receives 50 rad of gamma radiation. What is that amount in grays?

5.28 **a.** The dosage of technetium-99m for a lung scan is 20. μCi/kg of body mass. How many millicuries of technetium-99m should be given to a 50.0-kg person (1 mCi = 1000 μCi)?
   b. Suppose a person absorbed 50 mrad of alpha radiation. What would be the equivalent dose in millirems?

5.4 Half-Life of a Radioisotope

LEARNING GOAL

Given the half-life of a radioisotope, calculate the amount of radioisotope remaining after one or more half-lives.

The **half-life** of a radioisotope is the amount of time it takes for one-half of a sample to decay. For example, $^{131}_{53}$I has a half-life of 8.0 days. As $^{131}_{53}$I decays, it produces the nonradioactive isotope $^{131}_{54}$Xe and a beta particle.

$$^{131}_{53}\text{I} \longrightarrow {}^{131}_{54}\text{Xe} + {}^{0}_{-1}e$$

Suppose we have a sample that initially contains 20. mg of $^{131}_{53}$I. In 8.0 days, one-half (10. mg) of all the I-131 nuclei in the sample will decay, which leaves 10. mg of I-131. After 16 days (two half-lives), 5.0 mg of the remaining I-131 decays, which leaves 5.0 mg of I-131. After 24 days (three half-lives), 2.5 mg of the remaining I-131 decays, which leaves 2.5 mg of I-131 nuclei still capable of producing radiation.

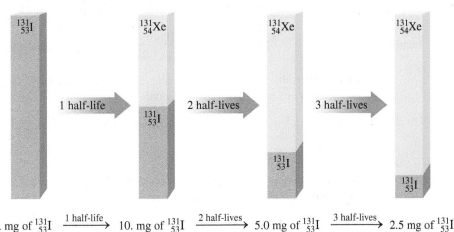

A **decay curve** is a diagram of the decay of a radioactive isotope. Figure 5.4 shows such a curve for the $^{131}_{53}$I we have discussed.

FIGURE 5.4 ▶ The decay curve for iodine-131 shows that one-half of the radioactive sample decays and one-half remains radioactive after each half-life of 8.0 days.

Q How many milligrams of the 20.-mg sample remain radioactive after two half-lives?

⚛ **CORE CHEMISTRY SKILL**

Using Half-Lives

Guide to Using Half-Lives

STEP 1
State the given and needed quantities.

STEP 2
Write a plan to calculate the unknown quantity.

STEP 3
Write the half-life equality and conversion factors.

STEP 4
Set up the problem to calculate the needed quantity.

▶ **SAMPLE PROBLEM 5.7 Using Half-Lives of a Radioisotope**

Phosphorus-32, a radioisotope used in the treatment of leukemia, has a half-life of 14.3 days. If a sample contains 8.0 mg of phosphorus-32, how many milligrams of phosphorus-32 remain after 42.9 days?

SOLUTION

STEP 1 State the given and needed quantities.

ANALYZE THE PROBLEM	Given	Need
	8.0 mg of P-32, 42.9 days elapsed, half-life = 14.3 days	milligrams of P-32 remaining

STEP 2 Write a plan to calculate the unknown quantity.

days → $\boxed{\text{Half-life}}$ → number of half-lives

milligrams of $^{32}_{15}P$ → $\boxed{\text{Number of half-lives}}$ → milligrams of $^{32}_{15}P$ remaining

STEP 3 Write the half-life equality and conversion factors.

$$1 \text{ half-life} = 14.3 \text{ days}$$

$$\frac{14.3 \text{ days}}{1 \text{ half-life}} \quad \text{and} \quad \frac{1 \text{ half-life}}{14.3 \text{ days}}$$

STEP 4 Set up the problem to calculate the needed quantity. First, we determine the number of half-lives in the amount of time that has elapsed.

$$\text{number of half-lives} = 42.9 \text{ days} \times \frac{1 \text{ half-life}}{14.3 \text{ days}} = 3.00 \text{ half-lives}$$

Now we can determine how much of the sample decays in three half-lives and how many grams of the phosphorus remain.

8.0 mg of $^{32}_{15}P$ $\xrightarrow{\text{1 half-life}}$ 4.0 mg of $^{32}_{15}P$ $\xrightarrow{\text{2 half-lives}}$ 2.0 mg of $^{32}_{15}P$ $\xrightarrow{\text{3 half-lives}}$ 1.0 mg of $^{32}_{15}P$

Interactive Video

▶

Half-Lives

STUDY CHECK 5.7

Iron-59 has a half-life of 44 days. If a nuclear laboratory receives a sample of 8.0 μg of iron-59, how many micrograms of iron-59 are still active after 176 days?

ANSWER

0.50 μg of iron-59

TABLE 5.7 Half-Lives of Some Radioisotopes

Element	Radioisotope	Half-Life	Type of Radiation
Naturally Occurring Radioisotopes			
Carbon-14	$^{14}_{6}C$	5730 yr	Beta
Potassium-40	$^{40}_{19}K$	1.3×10^9 yr	Beta, gamma
Radium-226	$^{226}_{88}Ra$	1600 yr	Alpha
Strontium-90	$^{90}_{38}Sr$	38.1 yr	Alpha
Uranium-238	$^{238}_{92}U$	4.5×10^9 yr	Alpha
Some Medical Radioisotopes			
Carbon-11	$^{11}_{6}C$	20 min	Positron
Chromium-51	$^{51}_{24}Cr$	28 days	Gamma
Iodine-131	$^{131}_{53}I$	8.0 days	Gamma
Oxygen-15	$^{15}_{8}O$	2.0 min	Positron
Iron-59	$^{59}_{26}Fe$	44 days	Beta, gamma
Radon-222	$^{222}_{86}Rn$	3.8 days	Alpha
Technetium-99m	$^{99m}_{43}Tc$	6.0 h	Beta, gamma

Naturally occurring isotopes of the elements usually have long half-lives, as shown in Table 5.7. They disintegrate slowly and produce radiation over a long period of time, even hundreds or millions of years. In contrast, the radioisotopes used in nuclear medicine have much shorter half-lives. They disintegrate rapidly and produce almost all their radiation in a short period of time. For example, technetium-99m emits half of its radiation in the first 6 h. This means that a small amount of the radioisotope given to a patient is essentially gone within two days. The decay products of technetium-99m are totally eliminated by the body.

Chemistry Link to the Environment

Dating Ancient Objects

Radiological dating is a technique used by geologists, archaeologists, and historians to determine the age of ancient objects. The age of an object derived from plants or animals (such as wood, fiber, natural pigments, bone, and cotton or woolen clothing) is determined by measuring the amount of carbon-14, a naturally occurring radioactive form of carbon. In 1960, Willard Libby received the Nobel Prize for the work he did developing carbon-14 dating techniques during the 1940s. Carbon-14 is produced in the upper atmosphere by the bombardment of $^{14}_{7}N$ by high-energy neutrons from cosmic rays.

$$^{1}_{0}n + ^{14}_{7}N \longrightarrow ^{14}_{6}C + ^{1}_{1}H$$

Neutron from cosmic rays   Nitrogen in atmosphere   Radioactive carbon-14   Proton

The carbon-14 reacts with oxygen to form radioactive carbon dioxide, $^{14}_{6}CO_2$. Living plants continuously absorb carbon dioxide, which incorporates carbon-14 into the plant material. The uptake of carbon-14 stops when the plant dies.

$$^{14}_{6}C \longrightarrow ^{14}_{7}N + ^{0}_{-1}e$$

As the carbon-14 decays, the amount of radioactive carbon-14 in the plant material steadily decreases. In a process called *carbon dating*, scientists use the half-life of carbon-14 (5730 yr) to calculate the length of time since the plant died. For example, a wooden beam found in an ancient dwelling might have one-half of the carbon-14 found in living plants today. Because one half-life of carbon-14 is 5730 yr, the dwelling was constructed about 5730 yr ago. Carbon-14 dating was used to determine that the Dead Sea Scrolls are about 2000 yr old.

The age of the Dead Sea Scrolls was determined using carbon-14.

A radiological dating method used for determining the age of much older items is based on the radioisotope uranium-238, which decays through a series of reactions to lead-206. The uranium-238 isotope has an incredibly long half-life, about 4×10^9 (4 billion) yr. Measurements of the amounts of uranium-238 and lead-206 enable geologists to determine the age of rock samples. The older rocks will have a higher percentage of lead-206 because more of the uranium-238 has decayed. The age of rocks brought back from the Moon by the *Apollo* missions, for example, was determined using uranium-238. They were found to be about 4×10^9 yr old, approximately the same age calculated for the Earth.

The age of a bone sample from a skeleton can be determined by carbon dating.

SAMPLE PROBLEM 5.8 Dating Using Half-Lives

Carbon material in the bones of humans and animals assimilates carbon until death. Using radiocarbon dating, the number of half-lives of carbon-14 from a bone sample determines the age of the bone. Suppose a sample is obtained from a prehistoric animal and used for radiocarbon dating. We can calculate the age of the bone or the years elapsed since the animal died by using the half-life of carbon-14, which is 5730 yr. If the sample shows that four half-lives have passed, how much time has elapsed since the animal died?

SOLUTION

STEP 1 State the given and needed quantities.

ANALYZE THE PROBLEM	Given	Need
	1 half-life of C-14 = 5730 yr, 4 half-lives elapsed	years elapsed

STEP 2 Write a plan to calculate the unknown quantity.

4 half-lives   Half-life   years elapsed

STEP 3 Write the half-life equality and conversion factors.

$$1 \text{ half-life} = 5730 \text{ yr}$$

$$\frac{5730 \text{ yr}}{1 \text{ half-life}} \quad \text{and} \quad \frac{1 \text{ half-life}}{5730 \text{ yr}}$$

STEP 4 Set up the problem to calculate the needed quantity.

$$\text{Years elapsed} = 4.0 \text{ half-lives} \times \frac{5730 \text{ yr}}{1 \text{ half-life}} = 23\,000 \text{ yr}$$

We would estimate that the animal lived 23 000 yr ago.

STUDY CHECK 5.8

Suppose that a piece of wood found in a tomb had one-eighth of its original carbon-14 activity. About how many years ago was the wood part of a living tree?

ANSWER

17 200 yr

QUESTIONS AND PROBLEMS

5.4 Half-Life of a Radioisotope

LEARNING GOAL Given the half-life of a radioisotope, calculate the amount of radioisotope remaining after one or more half-lives.

5.29 For each of the following, indicate if the number of half-lives elapsed is:
1. one half-life
2. two half-lives
3. three half-lives

a. a sample of Pd-103 with a half-life of 17 days after 34 days
b. a sample of C-11 with a half-life of 20 min after 20 min
c. a sample of At-211 with a half-life of 7 h after 21 h

5.30 For each of the following, indicate if the number of half-lives elapsed is:
1. one half-life
2. two half-lives
3. three half-lives

a. a sample of Ce-141 with a half-life of 32.5 days after 32.5 days
b. a sample of F-18 with a half-life of 110 min after 330 min
c. a sample of Au-198 with a half-life of 2.7 days after 5.4 days

℞ **Clinical Applications**

5.31 Technetium-99m is an ideal radioisotope for scanning organs because it has a half-life of 6.0 h and is a pure gamma emitter. Suppose that 80.0 mg were prepared in the technetium generator this morning. How many milligrams of technetium-99m would remain after each of the following intervals?
 a. one half-life   **b.** two half-lives
 c. 18 h   **d.** 24 h

5.32 A sample of sodium-24 with an activity of 12 mCi is used to study the rate of blood flow in the circulatory system. If sodium-24 has a half-life of 15 h, what is the activity after each of the following intervals?
 a. one half-life   **b.** 30 h
 c. three half-lives   **d.** 2.5 days

5.33 Strontium-85, used for bone scans, has a half-life of 65 days.
 a. How long will it take for the radiation level of strontium-85 to drop to one-fourth of its original level?
 b. How long will it take for the radiation level of strontium-85 to drop to one-eighth of its original level?

5.34 Fluorine-18, which has a half-life of 110 min, is used in PET scans.
 a. If 100. mg of fluorine-18 is shipped at 8:00 A.M., how many milligrams of the radioisotope are still active after 110 min?
 b. If 100. mg of fluorine-18 is shipped at 8:00 A.M., how many milligrams of the radioisotope are still active when the sample arrives at the radiology laboratory at 1:30 P.M.?

5.5 Medical Applications Using Radioactivity

To determine the condition of an organ in the body, a nuclear medicine technologist may use a radioisotope that concentrates in that organ. The cells in the body do not differentiate between a nonradioactive atom and a radioactive one, so these radioisotopes are easily incorporated. Then the radioactive atoms are detected because they emit radiation. Some radioisotopes used in nuclear medicine are listed in Table 5.8.

LEARNING GOAL

Describe the use of radioisotopes in medicine.

TABLE 5.8 Medical Applications of Radioisotopes

Isotope	Half-Life	Radiation	Medical Application
Au-198	2.7 days	Beta	Liver imaging; treatment of abdominal carcinoma
Ce-141	32.5 days	Beta	Gastrointestinal tract diagnosis; measuring blood flow to the heart
Cs-131	9.7 days	Gamma	Prostate brachytherapy
F-18	110 min	Positron	Positron emission tomography (PET)
Ga-67	78 h	Gamma	Abdominal imaging; tumor detection
Ga-68	68 min	Gamma	Detection of pancreatic cancer
I-123	13.2 h	Gamma	Treatment of thyroid, brain, and prostate cancer
I-131	8.0 days	Beta	Treatment of Graves' disease, goiter, hyperthyroidism, thyroid and prostate cancer
Ir-192	74 days	Gamma	Treatment of breast and prostate cancer
P-32	14.3 days	Beta	Treatment of leukemia, excess red blood cells, and pancreatic cancer
Pd-103	17 days	Gamma	Prostate brachytherapy
Sr-85	65 days	Gamma	Detection of bone lesions; brain scans
Tc-99m	6.0 h	Gamma	Imaging of skeleton and heart muscle, brain, liver, heart, lungs, bone, spleen, kidney, and thyroid; most widely used radioisotope in nuclear medicine
Y-90	2.7 days	Beta	Treatment of liver cancer

▶**SAMPLE PROBLEM 5.9** **Medical Applications of Radioactivity**

In the treatment of abdominal carcinoma, a person is treated with "seeds" of gold-198, which is a beta emitter. Write the balanced nuclear equation for the beta decay of gold-198.

SOLUTION

ANALYZE THE PROBLEM	Given	Need
	gold-198, beta decay	balanced nuclear equation

Titanium "seeds" filled with a radioactive isotope are implanted in the body to treat cancer.

We can write the incomplete nuclear equation starting with gold-198.

$$^{198}_{79}\text{Au} \longrightarrow ? + ^{0}_{-1}e$$

In beta decay, the mass number, 198, does not change, but the atomic number of the new nucleus increases by one. The new atomic number is 80, which is mercury, Hg.

$$^{198}_{79}\text{Au} \longrightarrow ^{198}_{80}\text{Hg} + ^{0}_{-1}e$$

STUDY CHECK 5.9

In an experimental treatment, a person is given boron-10, which is taken up by malignant tumors. When bombarded with neutrons, boron-10 decays by emitting alpha particles that destroy the surrounding tumor cells. Write the balanced nuclear equation for the reaction for this experimental procedure.

ANSWER

$$^{1}_{0}n + ^{10}_{5}\text{B} \longrightarrow ^{7}_{3}\text{Li} + ^{4}_{2}\text{He}$$

Scans with Radioisotopes

After a person receives a radioisotope, the radiologist determines the level and location of radioactivity emitted by the radioisotope. An apparatus called a *scanner* is used to produce an image of the organ. The scanner moves slowly across the body above the region where the organ containing the radioisotope is located. The gamma rays emitted from the radioisotope in the organ can be used to expose a photographic plate, producing a *scan* of the organ. On a scan, an area of decreased or increased radiation can indicate conditions such as a disease of the organ, a tumor, a blood clot, or edema.

A common method of determining thyroid function is the use of *radioactive iodine uptake*. Taken orally, the radioisotope iodine-131 mixes with the iodine already present in the thyroid. Twenty-four hours later, the amount of iodine taken up by the thyroid is determined. A detection tube held up to the area of the thyroid gland detects the radiation coming from the iodine-131 that has located there (see Figure 5.5).

A person with a hyperactive thyroid will have a higher than normal level of radioactive iodine, whereas a person with a hypoactive thyroid will have lower values. If a person has hyperthyroidism, treatment is begun to lower the activity of the thyroid. One treatment involves giving a therapeutic dosage of radioactive iodine, which has a higher radiation level than the diagnostic dose. The radioactive iodine goes to the thyroid where its radiation destroys some of the thyroid cells. The thyroid produces less thyroid hormone, bringing the hyperthyroid condition under control.

Positron Emission Tomography

Positron emitters with short half-lives such as carbon-11, oxygen-15, nitrogen-13, and fluorine-18 are used in an imaging method called *positron emission tomography* (PET). A positron-emitting isotope such as fluorine-18 combined with substances in the body such as glucose is used to study brain function, metabolism, and blood flow.

$$^{18}_{9}\text{F} \longrightarrow ^{18}_{8}\text{O} + ^{0}_{+1}e$$

As positrons are emitted, they combine with electrons to produce gamma rays that are detected by computerized equipment to create a three-dimensional image of the organ (see Figure 5.6).

(a)

(b)

FIGURE 5.5 ▶ **(a)** A scanner detects radiation from a radioisotope in an organ. **(b)** A scan shows radioactive iodine-131 in the thyroid.

Q What type of radiation would move through body tissues to create a scan?

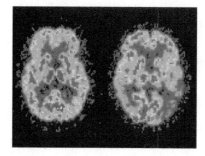

FIGURE 5.6 ▶ These PET scans of the brain show a normal brain on the left and a brain affected by Alzheimer's disease on the right.

Q When positrons collide with electrons, what type of radiation is produced that gives an image of an organ?

Computed Tomography

Another imaging method used to scan organs such as the brain, lungs, and heart is *computed tomography* (CT). A computer monitors the absorption of 30 000 X-ray beams directed at successive layers of the target organ. Based on the densities of the tissues and fluids in the organ, the differences in absorption of the X-rays provide a series of images of the organ. This technique is successful in the identification of hemorrhages, tumors, and atrophy.

Magnetic Resonance Imaging

Magnetic resonance imaging (MRI) is a powerful imaging technique that does not involve X-ray radiation. It is the least invasive imaging method available. MRI is based on the absorption of energy when the protons in hydrogen atoms are excited by a strong magnetic field. Hydrogen atoms make up 63% of all the atoms in the body. In the hydrogen nuclei, the protons act like tiny bar magnets. With no external field, the protons have random orientations. However, when placed within a strong magnetic field, the protons align with the field. A proton aligned with the field has a lower energy than one that is aligned against the field. As the MRI scan proceeds, radiofrequency pulses of energy are applied and the hydrogen nuclei resonate at a certain frequency. Then the radio waves are quickly turned off, and the protons slowly return to their natural alignment within the magnetic field and resonate at a different frequency. They release the energy absorbed from the radio wave pulses. The difference in energy between the two states is released, which produces the electromagnetic signal that the scanner detects. These signals are sent to a computer system, where a color image of the body is generated. Because hydrogen atoms in the body are in different chemical environments, different energies are absorbed. MRI is particularly useful in obtaining images of soft tissues, which contain large amounts of hydrogen atoms in the form of water.

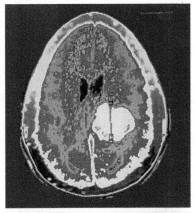

A CT scan shows a tumor (yellow) in the brain.

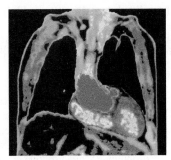

An MRI scan provides images of the heart and lungs.

 Chemistry Link to Health

Brachytherapy

The process called *brachytherapy*, or seed implantation, is an internal form of radiation therapy. The prefix *brachy* is from the Greek word for short distance. With internal radiation, a high dose of radiation is delivered to a cancerous area, whereas normal tissue sustains minimal damage. Because higher doses are used, fewer treatments of shorter duration are needed. Conventional external treatment delivers a lower dose per treatment, but requires six to eight weeks of treatment.

Permanent Brachytherapy

One of the most common forms of cancer in males is prostate cancer. In addition to surgery and chemotherapy, one treatment option is to place 40 or more titanium capsules, or "seeds," in the malignant area. Each seed, which is the size of a grain of rice, contains radioactive iodine-125, palladium-103, or cesium-131, which decay by gamma emission. The radiation from the seeds destroys the cancer by interfering with the reproduction of cancer cells with minimal damage to adjacent normal tissues. Ninety percent (90%) of the radioisotopes decay within a few months because they have short half-lives.

Isotope	I-125	Pd-103	Cs-131
Radiation	Gamma	Gamma	Gamma
Half-Life	60 days	17 days	10 days
Time Required to Deliver 90% of Radiation	7 months	2 months	1 month

Almost no radiation passes out of the patient's body. The amount of radiation received by a family member is no greater than that received on a long plane flight. Because the radioisotopes decay to products that are not radioactive, the inert titanium capsules can be left in the body.

Temporary Brachytherapy

In another type of treatment for prostate cancer, long needles containing iridium-192 are placed in the tumor. However, the needles are removed after 5 to 10 min, depending on the activity of the iridium isotope. Compared to permanent brachytherapy, temporary brachytherapy can deliver a higher dose of radiation over a shorter time. The procedure may be repeated in a few days.

Brachytherapy is also used following breast cancer lumpectomy. An iridium-192 isotope is inserted into the catheter implanted in the space left by the removal of the tumor. The isotope is removed after 5 to 10 min, depending on the activity of the iridium source. Radiation is delivered primarily to the tissue surrounding the cavity that contained the tumor and where the cancer is most likely to recur. The procedure is repeated twice a day for five days to give an absorbed dose of 34 Gy (3400 rad). The catheter is removed, and no radioactive material remains in the body.

In conventional external beam therapy for breast cancer, a patient is given 2 Gy once a day for six to seven weeks, which gives a total absorbed dose of about 80 Gy or 8000 rad. The external beam therapy irradiates the entire breast, including the tumor cavity.

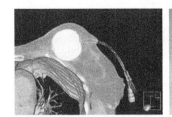 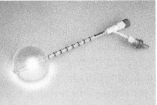

A catheter placed temporarily in the breast for radiation from Ir-192.

QUESTIONS AND PROBLEMS

5.5 Medical Applications Using Radioactivity

LEARNING GOAL Describe the use of radioisotopes in medicine.

℞ **Clinical Applications**

5.35 Bone and bony structures contain calcium and phosphorus.
   a. Why would the radioisotopes calcium-47 and phosphorus-32 be used in the diagnosis and treatment of bone diseases?
   b. During nuclear tests, scientists were concerned that strontium-85, a radioactive product, would be harmful to the growth of bone in children. Explain.

5.36 **a.** Technetium-99m emits only gamma radiation. Why would this type of radiation be used in diagnostic imaging rather than an isotope that also emits beta or alpha radiation?

b. A person with *polycythemia vera* (excess production of red blood cells) receives radioactive phosphorus-32. Why would this treatment reduce the production of red blood cells in the bone marrow of the patient?

5.37 In a diagnostic test for leukemia, a person receives 4.0 mL of a solution containing selenium-75. If the activity of the selenium-75 is 45 μCi/mL, what dose, in microcuries, does the patient receive?

5.38 A vial contains radioactive iodine-131 with an activity of 2.0 mCi/mL. If a thyroid test requires 3.0 mCi in an "atomic cocktail," how many milliliters are used to prepare the iodine-131 solution?

LEARNING GOAL

Describe the processes of nuclear fission and fusion.

5.6 Nuclear Fission and Fusion

During the 1930s, scientists bombarding uranium-235 with neutrons discovered that the U-235 nucleus splits into two smaller nuclei and produces a great amount of energy. This was the discovery of nuclear **fission**. The energy generated by splitting the atom was called *atomic energy*. A typical equation for nuclear fission is:

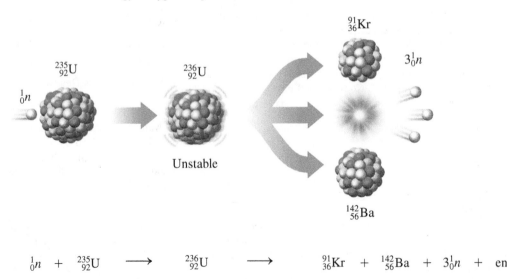

$${}^{1}_{0}n + {}^{235}_{92}U \longrightarrow {}^{236}_{92}U \longrightarrow {}^{91}_{36}Kr + {}^{142}_{56}Ba + 3{}^{1}_{0}n + \text{energy}$$

If we could determine the mass of the products krypton, barium, and three neutrons, with great accuracy, we would find that their total mass is slightly less than the mass of the starting materials. The missing mass has been converted into an enormous amount of energy, consistent with the famous equation derived by Albert Einstein.

$$E = mc^2$$

where E is the energy released, m is the mass lost, and c is the speed of light, 3×10^8 m/s. Even though the mass loss is very small, when it is multiplied by the speed of light squared, the result is a large value for the energy released. The fission of 1 g of uranium-235 produces about as much energy as the burning of 3 tons of coal.

Chain Reaction

Fission begins when a neutron collides with the nucleus of a uranium atom. The resulting nucleus is unstable and splits into smaller nuclei. This fission process also releases several neutrons and large amounts of gamma radiation and energy. The neutrons emitted have high energies and bombard other uranium-235 nuclei. In a **chain reaction**, there is a rapid increase in the number of high-energy neutrons available to react with more uranium. To sustain a nuclear chain reaction, sufficient quantities of uranium-235 must be brought together to provide a *critical mass* in which almost all the neutrons immediately collide with more uranium-235 nuclei. So much heat and energy build up that an atomic explosion can occur (see Figure 5.7).

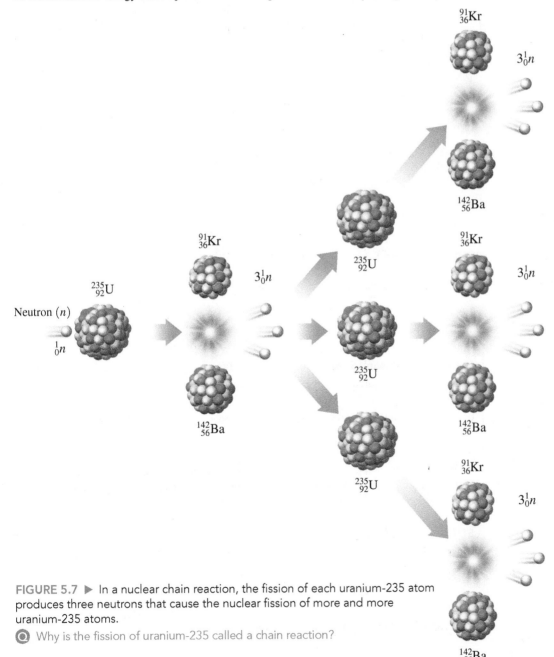

FIGURE 5.7 ▶ In a nuclear chain reaction, the fission of each uranium-235 atom produces three neutrons that cause the nuclear fission of more and more uranium-235 atoms.

🔘 Why is the fission of uranium-235 called a chain reaction?

Nuclear Fusion

In **fusion**, two small nuclei combine to form a larger nucleus. Mass is lost, and a tremendous amount of energy is released, even more than the energy released from nuclear fission. However, a fusion reaction requires a temperature of 100 000 000 °C to overcome the repulsion of the hydrogen nuclei and cause them to undergo fusion. Fusion reactions occur continuously in the Sun and other stars, providing us with heat and light. The huge amounts of energy produced by our sun come from the fusion of 6×10^{11} kg of hydrogen every second. In a fusion reaction, isotopes of hydrogen combine to form helium and large amounts of energy.

Scientists expect less radioactive waste with shorter half-lives from fusion reactors. However, fusion is still in the experimental stage because the extremely high temperatures needed have been difficult to reach and even more difficult to maintain. Research groups around the world are attempting to develop the technology needed to make the harnessing of the fusion reaction for energy a reality in our lifetime.

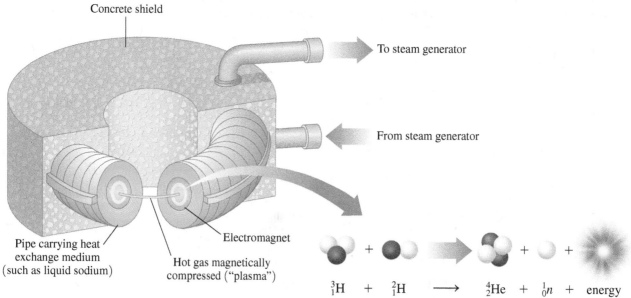

Concrete shield

To steam generator

From steam generator

Pipe carrying heat exchange medium (such as liquid sodium)

Electromagnet

Hot gas magnetically compressed ("plasma")

$${}^{3}_{1}H \ + \ {}^{2}_{1}H \ \longrightarrow \ {}^{4}_{2}He \ + \ {}^{1}_{0}n \ + \ \text{energy}$$

In a fusion reactor, high temperatures are needed to combine hydrogen atoms.

▶ **SAMPLE PROBLEM 5.10 Identifying Fission and Fusion**

Classify the following as pertaining to fission, fusion, or both:

a. A large nucleus breaks apart to produce smaller nuclei.
b. Large amounts of energy are released.
c. Extremely high temperatures are needed for reaction.

SOLUTION

a. When a large nucleus breaks apart to produce smaller nuclei, the process is fission.
b. Large amounts of energy are generated in both the fusion and fission processes.
c. An extremely high temperature is required for fusion.

STUDY CHECK 5.10

Classify the following nuclear equation as pertaining to fission, fusion, or both:

$${}^{3}_{1}H + {}^{2}_{1}H \longrightarrow {}^{4}_{2}He + {}^{1}_{0}n + \text{energy}$$

ANSWER

When small nuclei combine to release energy, the process is fusion.

QUESTIONS AND PROBLEMS

5.6 Nuclear Fission and Fusion

LEARNING GOAL Describe the processes of nuclear fission and fusion.

5.39 What is nuclear fission?

5.40 How does a chain reaction occur in nuclear fission?

5.41 Complete the following fission reaction:

$$_0^1 n + _{92}^{235}U \longrightarrow _{50}^{131}Sn + ? + 2_0^1 n + \text{energy}$$

5.42 In another fission reaction, uranium-235 bombarded with a neutron produces strontium-94, another small nucleus, and three neutrons. Write the balanced nuclear equation for the fission reaction.

5.43 Indicate whether each of the following is characteristic of the fission or fusion process, or both:
a. Neutrons bombard a nucleus.
b. The nuclear process occurs in the Sun.
c. A large nucleus splits into smaller nuclei.
d. Small nuclei combine to form larger nuclei.

5.44 Indicate whether each of the following is characteristic of the fission or fusion process, or both:
a. Very high temperatures are required to initiate the reaction.
b. Less radioactive waste is produced.
c. Hydrogen nuclei are the reactants.
d. Large amounts of energy are released when the nuclear reaction occurs.

Chemistry Link to the Environment
Nuclear Power Plants

In a nuclear power plant, the quantity of uranium-235 is held below a critical mass, so it cannot sustain a chain reaction. The fission reactions are slowed by placing control rods, which absorb some of the fast-moving neutrons, among the uranium samples. In this way, less fission occurs, and there is a slower, controlled production of energy. The heat from the controlled fission is used to produce steam. The steam drives a generator, which produces electricity. Approximately 10% of the electrical energy produced in the United States is generated in nuclear power plants.

Although nuclear power plants help meet some of our energy needs, there are some problems associated with nuclear power. One of the most serious problems is the production of radioactive byproducts that have very long half-lives, such as plutonium-239 with a half-life of 24 000 yr. It is essential that these waste products be stored safely in a place where they do not contaminate the environment. Several countries are now in the process of selecting areas where nuclear waste can be placed in caverns 1000 m below the surface of the Earth. In the United States, a current proposed repository site for nuclear waste is Yucca Mountain, Nevada.

Nuclear power plants supply about 10% of electricity in the United States.

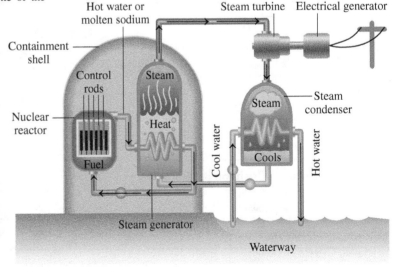

Heat from nuclear fission is used to generate electricity.

Clinical Update
Cardiac Imaging Using a Radioisotope

As part of her nuclear stress test, Simone starts to walk on the treadmill. When she reaches the maximum level, Paul injects a radioactive dye with Tl-201 with an activity of 74 MBq. The radiation emitted from areas of heart is detected by a scanner and produces images of her heart muscle. After Simone rests for 3 h, Paul injects more dye with Tl-201 and she is placed under the scanner again. A second set of images of her heart muscle at rest are taken. When Simone's doctor reviews her scans, he assures her that she had normal blood flow to her heart muscle, both at rest and under stress.

Clinical Applications

5.45 What is the activity of the radioactive dye injection for Simone
    a. in curies?
    b. in millicuries?

5.46 If the half-life of Tl-201 is 3.0 days, what is its activity, in megabecquerels
    a. after 3.0 days?
    b. after 6.0 days?

5.47 How many days will it take until the activity of the Tl-201 in Simone's body is one-eighth of the initial activity?

5.48 Radiation from Tl-201 to Simone's kidneys can be 24 mGy. What is this amount of radiation in rads?

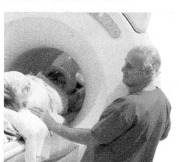

CONCEPT MAP

NUCLEAR CHEMISTRY

Radioisotopes

emit → **Radiation and Energy**

are measured by their → **Activity**

measured in → **Becquerel**

decay by one-half in one → **Half-Life**

from the nucleus as → **Alpha** **Beta** **Positron** **Gamma**

or → **Biological Effect**

Curie

and are used in → **Nuclear Medicine**

as shown in → **Nuclear Equations**

as absorbed → **Rad** **Gray**

as exposure → **Rem** **Sievert**

and in → **Fission** **Fusion**

CHAPTER REVIEW

5.1 Natural Radioactivity

LEARNING GOAL Describe alpha, beta, positron, and gamma radiation.

$^4_2$He
Alpha (α) particle

- Radioactive isotopes have unstable nuclei that break down (decay), spontaneously emitting alpha (α), beta (β), positron (β^+), and gamma (γ) radiation.
- Because radiation can damage the cells in the body, proper protection must be used: shielding, limiting the time of exposure, and distance.

5.2 Nuclear Reactions

LEARNING GOAL Write a balanced nuclear equation showing mass numbers and atomic numbers for radioactive decay.

Radioactive carbon nucleus
Beta particle
$_{-1}^0 e$
Radiation
Stable nitrogen-14 nucleus
New nucleus
$^{14}_6$C
$^{14}_7$N

- A balanced nuclear equation is used to represent the changes that take place in the nuclei of the reactants and products.
- The new isotopes and the type of radiation emitted can be determined from the symbols that show the mass numbers and atomic numbers of the isotopes in the nuclear equation.
- A radioisotope is produced artificially when a nonradioactive isotope is bombarded by a small particle.

5.3 Radiation Measurement

LEARNING GOAL Describe the detection and measurement of radiation.

- In a Geiger counter, radiation produces charged particles in the gas contained in a tube, which generates an electrical current.
- The curie (Ci) and the becquerel (Bq) measure the activity, which is the number of nuclear transformations per second.
- The amount of radiation absorbed by a substance is measured in rads or the gray (Gy).
- The rem and the sievert (Sv) are units used to determine the biological damage from the different types of radiation.

5.4 Half-Life of a Radioisotope

LEARNING GOAL Given the half-life of a radioisotope, calculate the amount of radioisotope remaining after one or more half-lives.

- Every radioisotope has its own rate of emitting radiation.
- The time it takes for one-half of a radioactive sample to decay is called its half-life.
- For many medical radioisotopes, such as Tc-99m and I-131, half-lives are short.
- For other isotopes, usually naturally occurring ones such as C-14, Ra-226, and U-238, half-lives are extremely long.

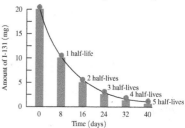

5.5 Medical Applications Using Radioactivity

LEARNING GOAL Describe the use of radioisotopes in medicine.

- In nuclear medicine, radioisotopes that go to specific sites in the body are given to the patient.
- By detecting the radiation they emit, an evaluation can be made about the location and extent of an injury, disease, tumor, or the level of function of a particular organ.
- Higher levels of radiation are used to treat or destroy tumors.

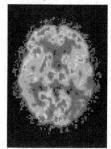

5.6 Nuclear Fission and Fusion

LEARNING GOAL Describe the processes of nuclear fission and fusion.

- In fission, the bombardment of a large nucleus breaks it apart into smaller nuclei, releasing one or more types of radiation and a great amount of energy.
- In fusion, small nuclei combine to form larger nuclei while great amounts of energy are released.

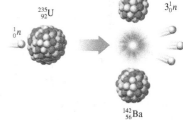
$^{91}_{36}$Kr
$3^1_0 n$
$^{235}_{92}$U
$^1_0 n$
$^{142}_{56}$Ba

KEY TERMS

alpha particle A nuclear particle identical to a helium nucleus, symbol α or $^4_2$He.

becquerel (Bq) A unit of activity of a radioactive sample equal to one disintegration per second.

beta particle A particle identical to an electron, symbol $_{-1}^0 e$ or β, that forms in the nucleus when a neutron changes to a proton and an electron.

chain reaction A fission reaction that will continue once it has been initiated by a high-energy neutron bombarding a heavy nucleus such as uranium-235.

curie (Ci) A unit of activity of a radioactive sample equal to 3.7×10^{10} disintegrations/s.

decay curve A diagram of the decay of a radioactive element.

equivalent dose The measure of biological damage from an absorbed dose that has been adjusted for the type of radiation.

fission A process in which large nuclei are split into smaller pieces, releasing large amounts of energy.

fusion A reaction in which large amounts of energy are released when small nuclei combine to form larger nuclei.

gamma ray High-energy radiation, symbol $^0_0 \gamma$, emitted by an unstable nucleus.

gray (Gy) A unit of absorbed dose equal to 100 rad.

half-life The length of time it takes for one-half of a radioactive sample to decay.

positron A particle of radiation with no mass and a positive charge, symbol β^+ or $_{+1}^{0}e$, produced when a proton is transformed into a neutron and a positron.

rad (radiation absorbed dose) A measure of an amount of radiation absorbed by the body.

radiation Energy or particles released by radioactive atoms.

radioactive decay The process by which an unstable nucleus breaks down with the release of high-energy radiation.

radioisotope A radioactive atom of an element.

rem (radiation equivalent in humans) A measure of the biological damage caused by the various kinds of radiation (rad $\times$ radiation biological factor).

sievert (Sv) A unit of biological damage (equivalent dose) equal to 100 rem.

⚛ CORE CHEMISTRY SKILLS

The chapter section containing each Core Chemistry Skill is shown in parentheses at the end of each heading.

Writing Nuclear Equations (5.2)

- A nuclear equation is written with the atomic symbols of the original radioactive nucleus on the left, an arrow, and the new nucleus and the type of radiation emitted on the right.
- The sum of the mass numbers and the sum of the atomic numbers on one side of the arrow must equal the sum of the mass numbers and the sum of the atomic numbers on the other side.
- When an alpha particle is emitted, the mass number of the new nucleus decreases by 4, and its atomic number decreases by 2.
- When a beta particle is emitted, there is no change in the mass number of the new nucleus, but its atomic number increases by one.
- When a positron is emitted, there is no change in the mass number of the new nucleus, but its atomic number decreases by one.
- In gamma emission, there is no change in the mass number or the atomic number of the new nucleus.

Example: a. Write a balanced nuclear equation for the alpha decay of Po-210.

      b. Write a balanced nuclear equation for the beta decay of Co-60.

Answer: a. When an alpha particle is emitted, we calculate the decrease of 4 in the mass number (210) of the polonium, and a decrease of 2 in its atomic number.

$$_{84}^{210}\text{Po} \longrightarrow \,_{82}^{206}? + \,_{2}^{4}\text{He}$$

Because lead has atomic number 82, the new nucleus must be an isotope of lead.

$$_{84}^{210}\text{Po} \longrightarrow \,_{82}^{206}\text{Pb} + \,_{2}^{4}\text{He}$$

b. When a beta particle is emitted, there is no change in the mass number (60) of the cobalt, but there is an increase of 1 in its atomic number.

$$_{27}^{60}\text{Co} \longrightarrow \,_{28}^{60}? + \,_{-1}^{0}e$$

Because nickel has atomic number 28, the new nucleus must be an isotope of nickel.

$$_{27}^{60}\text{Co} \longrightarrow \,_{28}^{60}\text{Ni} + \,_{-1}^{0}e$$

Using Half-Lives (5.4)

- The half-life of a radioisotope is the amount of time it takes for one-half of a sample to decay.
- The remaining amount of a radioisotope is calculated by dividing its quantity or activity by one-half for each half-life that has elapsed.

Example: Co-60 has a half-life of 5.3 yr. If the initial sample of Co-60 has an activity of 1200 Ci, what is its activity after 15.9 yr?

Answer:

Years	Number of Half-Lives	Co-60 (Activity)
0	0	1200 Ci
5.3	1	600 Ci
10.6	2	300 Ci
15.9	3	150 Ci

In 15.9 yr, three half-lives have passed. Thus, the activity was reduced from 1200 Ci to 150 Ci.

$$1200 \text{ Ci} \xrightarrow{\text{1 half-life}} 600 \text{ Ci} \xrightarrow{\text{2 half-lives}} 300 \text{ Ci} \xrightarrow{\text{3 half-lives}} 150 \text{ Ci}$$

UNDERSTANDING THE CONCEPTS

The chapter sections to review are shown in parentheses at the end of each question.

In problems 5.49 to 5.52, a nucleus is shown with protons and neutrons.

proton
neutron

5.49 Draw the new nucleus when this isotope emits a positron to complete the following figure: (5.2)

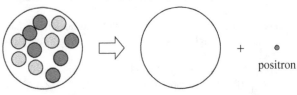
positron

5.50 Draw the nucleus that emits a beta particle to complete the following figure: (5.2)

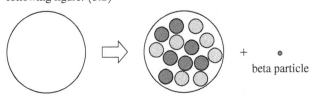

5.51 Draw the nucleus of the isotope that is bombarded in the following figure: (5.2)

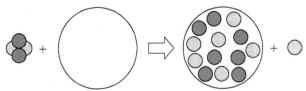

5.52 Complete the following bombardment reaction by drawing the nucleus of the new isotope that is produced in the following figure: (5.2)

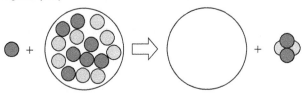

5.53 Carbon dating of small bits of charcoal used in cave paintings has determined that some of the paintings are from 10 000 to 30 000 yr old. Carbon-14 has a half-life of 5730 yr. In a 1 μg-sample of carbon from a live tree, the activity of carbon-14 is 6.4 μCi. If researchers determine that 1 μg of charcoal from a prehistoric cave painting in France has an activity of 0.80 μCi, what is the age of the painting? (5.4)

The technique of carbon dating is used to determine the age of ancient cave paintings.

5.54 Use the following decay curve for iodine-131 to answer questions **a** to **c**: (5.4)
  a. Complete the values for the mass of radioactive iodine-131 on the vertical axis.
  b. Complete the number of days on the horizontal axis.
  c. What is the half-life, in days, of iodine-131?

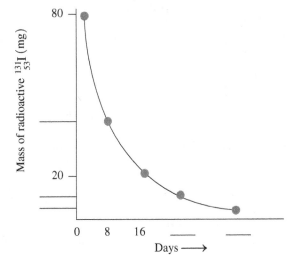

ADDITIONAL QUESTIONS AND PROBLEMS

5.55 Determine the number of protons and number of neutrons in the nucleus of each of the following: (5.1)
  a. sodium-25
  b. nickel-61
  c. rubidium-84
  d. silver-110

5.56 Determine the number of protons and number of neutrons in the nucleus of each of the following: (5.1)
  a. boron-10
  b. zinc-72
  c. iron-59
  d. gold-198

5.57 Identify each of the following as alpha decay, beta decay, positron emission, or gamma emission: (5.1, 5.2)
  a. $^{27m}_{13}\text{Al} \longrightarrow ^{27}_{13}\text{Al} + ^{0}_{0}\gamma$
  b. $^{8}_{5}\text{B} \longrightarrow ^{8}_{4}\text{Be} + ^{0}_{+1}e$
  c. $^{220}_{86}\text{Rn} \longrightarrow ^{216}_{84}\text{Po} + ^{4}_{2}\text{He}$

5.58 Identify each of the following as alpha decay, beta decay, positron emission, or gamma emission: (5.1, 5.2)
  a. $^{127}_{55}\text{Cs} \longrightarrow ^{127}_{54}\text{Xe} + ^{0}_{+1}e$
  b. $^{90}_{38}\text{Sr} \longrightarrow ^{90}_{39}\text{Y} + ^{0}_{-1}e$
  c. $^{218}_{85}\text{At} \longrightarrow ^{214}_{83}\text{Bi} + ^{4}_{2}\text{He}$

5.59 Write the balanced nuclear equation for each of the following: (5.1, 5.2)
  a. Th-225 (α decay)
  b. Bi-210 (α decay)
  c. cesium-137 (β decay)
  d. tin-126 (β decay)
  e. F-18 (β^+ emission)

5.60 Write the balanced nuclear equation for each of the following: (5.1, 5.2)
  a. potassium-40 (β decay)
  b. sulfur-35 (β decay)
  c. platinum-190 (α decay)
  d. Ra-210 (α decay)
  e. In-113m (γ emission)

5.61 Complete each of the following nuclear equations: (5.2)

a. $^{4}_{2}He + ^{14}_{7}N \longrightarrow ? + ^{1}_{1}H$

b. $^{4}_{2}He + ^{27}_{13}Al \longrightarrow ^{30}_{14}Si + ?$

c. $^{1}_{0}n + ^{235}_{92}U \longrightarrow ^{90}_{38}Sr + 3^{1}_{0}n + ?$

d. $^{23m}_{12}Mg \longrightarrow ? + ^{0}_{0}\gamma$

5.62 Complete each of the following nuclear equations: (5.2)

a. $? + ^{59}_{27}Co \longrightarrow ^{56}_{25}Mn + ^{4}_{2}He$

b. $? \longrightarrow ^{14}_{7}N + ^{0}_{-1}e$

c. $^{0}_{-1}e + ^{76}_{36}Kr \longrightarrow ?$

d. $^{4}_{2}He + ^{241}_{95}Am \longrightarrow ? + 2^{1}_{0}n$

5.63 Write the balanced nuclear equation for each of the following: (5.2)

a. When two oxygen-16 atoms collide, one of the products is an alpha particle.

b. When californium-249 is bombarded by oxygen-18, a new element, seaborgium-263, and four neutrons are produced.

c. Radon-222 undergoes alpha decay.

d. An atom of strontium-80 emits a positron.

5.64 Write the balanced nuclear equation for each of the following: (5.2)

a. Polonium-210 decays to give lead-206.

b. Bismuth-211 emits an alpha particle.

c. A radioisotope emits a positron to form titanium-48.

d. An atom of germanium-69 emits a positron.

5.65 A 120-mg sample of technetium-99m is used for a diagnostic test. If technetium-99m has a half-life of 6.0 h, how many milligrams of the technetium-99m sample remains active 24 h after the test? (5.4)

5.66 The half-life of oxygen-15 is 124 s. If a sample of oxygen-15 has an activity of 4000 Bq, how many minutes will elapse before it has an activity of 500 Bq? (5.4)

5.67 What is the difference between fission and fusion? (5.6)

5.68 a. What are the products in the fission of uranium-235 that make possible a nuclear chain reaction? (5.6)

b. What is the purpose of placing control rods among uranium samples in a nuclear reactor?

5.69 Where does fusion occur naturally? (5.6)

5.70 Why are scientists continuing to try to build a fusion reactor even though the very high temperatures it requires have been difficult to reach and maintain? (5.6)

℞ Clinical Applications

5.71 The activity of K-40 in a 70.-kg human body is estimated to be 120 nCi. What is this activity in becquerels? (5.3)

5.72 The activity of C-14 in a 70.-kg human body is estimated to be 3.7 kBq. What is this activity in microcuries? (5.3)

5.73 If the amount of radioactive phosphorus-32, used to treat leukemia, in a sample decreases from 1.2 mg to 0.30 mg in 28.6 days, what is the half-life of phosphorus-32? (5.4)

5.74 If the amount of radioactive iodine-123, used to treat thyroid cancer, in a sample decreases from 0.4 mg to 0.1 mg in 26.4 h, what is the half-life of iodine-123? (5.4)

5.75 Calcium-47, used to evaluate bone metabolism, has a half-life of 4.5 days. (5.2, 5.4)

a. Write the balanced nuclear equation for the beta decay of calcium-47.

b. How many milligrams of a 16-mg sample of calcium-47 remain after 18 days?

c. How many days have passed if 4.8 mg of calcium-47 decayed to 1.2 mg of calcium-47?

5.76 Cesium-137, used in cancer treatment, has a half-life of 30 yr. (5.2, 5.4)

a. Write the balanced nuclear equation for the beta decay of cesium-137.

b. How many milligrams of a 16-mg sample of cesium-137 remain after 90 yr?

c. How many years are required for 28 mg of cesium-137 to decay to 3.5 mg of cesium-137?

CHALLENGE QUESTIONS

The following groups of questions are related to the topics in this chapter. However, they do not all follow the chapter order, and they require you to combine concepts and skills from several sections. These questions will help you increase your critical thinking skills and prepare for your next exam.

5.77 Write the balanced nuclear equation for each of the following radioactive emissions: (5.2)

a. an alpha particle from Hg-180

b. a beta particle from Au-198

c. a positron from Rb-82

5.78 Write the balanced nuclear equation for each of the following radioactive emissions: (5.2)

a. an alpha particle from Gd-148

b. a beta particle from Sr-90

c. a positron from Al-25

5.79 All the elements beyond uranium, the transuranium elements, have been prepared by bombardment and are not naturally occurring elements. The first transuranium element neptunium, Np, was prepared by bombarding U-238 with neutrons to form a neptunium atom and a beta particle. Complete the following equation: (5.2)

$$^{1}_{0}n + ^{238}_{92}U \longrightarrow ? + ?$$

5.80 One of the most recent transuranium elements ununoctium-294 (Uuo-294), atomic number 118, was prepared by bombarding californium-249 with another isotope. Complete the following equation for the preparation of this new element: (5.2)

$$? + ^{249}_{98}Cf \longrightarrow ^{294}_{118}Uuo + 3^{1}_{0}n$$

5.81 A 64-μCi sample of Tl-201 decays to 4.0 μCi in 12 days. What is the half-life, in days, of Tl-201? (5.3, 5.4)

5.82 A wooden object from the site of an ancient temple has a carbon-14 activity of 10 counts/min compared with a reference piece of wood cut today that has an activity of 40 counts/min. If the half-life for carbon-14 is 5730 yr, what is the age of the ancient wood object? (5.3, 5.4)

5.83 The half-life for the radioactive decay of calcium-47 is 4.5 days. If a sample has an activity of 1.0 μCi after 27 days, what was the initial activity, in microcuries, of the sample? (5.3, 5.4)

5.84 The half-life for the radioactive decay of Ce-141 is 32.5 days. If a sample has an activity of 4.0 μCi after 130 days have elapsed, what was the initial activity, in microcuries, of the sample? (5.3, 5.4)

5.85 Element 114 was recently named flerovium, symbol Fl. The reaction for its synthesis involves bombarding Pu-244 with Ca-48. Write the balanced nuclear equation for the synthesis of flerovium. (5.2)

5.86 Element 116 was recently named livermorium, symbol Lv. The reaction for its synthesis involves bombarding Cm-248 with Ca-48. Write the balanced nuclear equation for the synthesis of livermorium. (5.2)

Rx **Clinical Applications**

5.87 A nuclear technician was accidentally exposed to potassium-42 while doing brain scans for possible tumors. The error was not discovered until 36 h later when the activity of the potassium-42 sample was 2.0 μCi. If potassium-42 has a half-life of 12 h, what was the activity of the sample at the time the technician was exposed? (5.3, 5.4)

5.88 The radioisotope sodium-24 is used to determine the levels of electrolytes in the body. A 16-μg sample of sodium-24 decays to 2.0 μg in 45 h. What is the half-life, in hours, of sodium-24? (5.4)

ANSWERS

Answers to Selected Questions and Problems

5.1 a. alpha particle
b. positron
c. gamma radiation

5.3 a. $^{39}_{19}K$, $^{40}_{19}K$, $^{41}_{19}K$
b. They all have 19 protons and 19 electrons, but they differ in the number of neutrons.

5.5 a. β or $^{0}_{-1}e$
b. α or $^{4}_{2}He$
c. n or $^{1}_{0}n$
d. $^{38}_{18}Ar$
e. $^{14}_{6}C$

5.7 a. $^{64}_{29}Cu$
b. $^{75}_{34}Se$
c. $^{24}_{11}Na$
d. $^{15}_{7}N$

5.9

Medical Use	Atomic Symbol	Mass Number	Number of Protons	Number of Neutrons
Heart imaging	$^{201}_{81}Tl$	201	81	120
Radiation therapy	$^{60}_{27}Co$	60	27	33
Abdominal scan	$^{67}_{31}Ga$	67	31	36
Hyperthyroidism	$^{131}_{53}I$	131	53	78
Leukemia treatment	$^{32}_{15}P$	32	15	17

5.11 a. 1. alpha particle
b. 3. gamma radiation
c. 1. alpha particle

5.13 a. $^{208}_{84}Po \longrightarrow ^{204}_{82}Pb + ^{4}_{2}He$
b. $^{232}_{90}Th \longrightarrow ^{228}_{88}Ra + ^{4}_{2}He$
c. $^{251}_{102}No \longrightarrow ^{247}_{100}Fm + ^{4}_{2}He$
d. $^{220}_{86}Rn \longrightarrow ^{216}_{84}Po + ^{4}_{2}He$

5.15 a. $^{25}_{11}Na \longrightarrow ^{25}_{12}Mg + ^{0}_{-1}e$
b. $^{20}_{8}O \longrightarrow ^{20}_{9}F + ^{0}_{-1}e$
c. $^{92}_{38}Sr \longrightarrow ^{92}_{39}Y + ^{0}_{-1}e$
d. $^{60}_{26}Fe \longrightarrow ^{60}_{27}Co + ^{0}_{-1}e$

5.17 a. $^{26}_{14}Si \longrightarrow ^{26}_{13}Al + ^{0}_{+1}e$
b. $^{54}_{27}Co \longrightarrow ^{54}_{26}Fe + ^{0}_{+1}e$
c. $^{77}_{37}Rb \longrightarrow ^{77}_{36}Kr + ^{0}_{+1}e$
d. $^{93}_{45}Rh \longrightarrow ^{93}_{44}Ru + ^{0}_{+1}e$

5.19 a. $^{28}_{14}Si$, beta decay
b. $^{0}_{0}\gamma$, gamma emission
c. $^{0}_{-1}e$, beta decay
d. $^{238}_{92}U$, alpha decay
e. $^{188}_{79}Au$, positron emission

5.21 a. $^{10}_{4}Be$
b. $^{132}_{53}I$
c. $^{27}_{13}Al$
d. $^{17}_{8}O$

5.23 a. 2. absorbed dose
b. 3. biological damage
c. 1. activity
d. 2. absorbed dose

5.25 The technician exposed to 5 rad received the higher amount of radiation.

5.27 a. 294 μCi
b. 0.5 Gy

5.29 a. two half-lives
b. one half-life
c. three half-lives

5.31 a. 40.0 mg
b. 20.0 mg
c. 10.0 mg
d. 5.00 mg

5.33 a. 130 days
b. 195 days

5.35 a. Because the elements Ca and P are part of the bone, the radioactive isotopes of Ca and P will become part of the bony structures of the body, where their radiation can be used to diagnose or treat bone diseases.
b. Strontium (Sr) acts much like calcium (Ca) because both are Group 2A (2) elements. The body will accumulate radioactive strontium in bones in the same way that it incorporates calcium. Radioactive strontium is harmful to children because the radiation it produces causes more damage in cells that are dividing rapidly.

5.37 180 μCi

5.39 Nuclear fission is the splitting of a large atom into smaller fragments with the release of large amounts of energy.

5.41 $^{103}_{42}Mo$

5.43 a. fission
    c. fission
    b. fusion
    d. fusion

5.45 a. 2.0×10^{-3} Ci
    b. 2.0 mCi

5.47 9.0 days

5.49

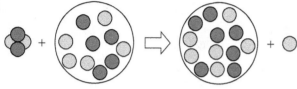

5.51

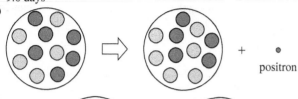

5.53 17 200 yr old

5.55 a. 11 protons and 14 neutrons
    b. 28 protons and 33 neutrons
    c. 37 protons and 47 neutrons
    d. 47 protons and 63 neutrons

5.57 a. gamma emission
    b. positron emission
    c. alpha decay

5.59 a. $^{225}_{90}Th \longrightarrow {}^{221}_{88}Ra + {}^{4}_{2}He$
    b. $^{210}_{83}Bi \longrightarrow {}^{206}_{81}Tl + {}^{4}_{2}He$
    c. $^{137}_{55}Cs \longrightarrow {}^{137}_{56}Ba + {}^{0}_{-1}e$
    d. $^{126}_{50}Sn \longrightarrow {}^{126}_{51}Sb + {}^{0}_{-1}e$
    e. $^{18}_{9}F \longrightarrow {}^{18}_{8}O + {}^{0}_{+1}e$

5.61 a. $^{17}_{8}O$
    b. $^{1}_{1}H$
    c. $^{143}_{54}Xe$
    d. $^{23}_{12}Mg$

5.63 a. $^{16}_{8}O + {}^{16}_{8}O \longrightarrow {}^{28}_{14}Si + {}^{4}_{2}He$
    b. $^{18}_{8}O + {}^{249}_{98}Cf \longrightarrow {}^{263}_{106}Sg + 4{}^{1}_{0}n$
    c. $^{222}_{86}Rn \longrightarrow {}^{218}_{84}Po + {}^{4}_{2}He$
    d. $^{80}_{38}Sr \longrightarrow {}^{80}_{37}Rb + {}^{0}_{+1}e$

5.65 7.5 mg of Tc-99m

5.67 In the fission process, an atom splits into smaller nuclei. In fusion, small nuclei combine (fuse) to form a larger nucleus.

5.69 Fusion occurs naturally in the Sun and other stars.

5.71 4.4×10^{3} Bq

5.73 14.3 days

5.75 a. $^{47}_{20}Ca \longrightarrow {}^{47}_{21}Sc + {}^{0}_{-1}e$
    b. 1.0 mg of Ca-47
    c. 9.0 days

5.77 a. $^{180}_{80}Hg \longrightarrow {}^{176}_{78}Pt + {}^{4}_{2}He$
    b. $^{198}_{79}Au \longrightarrow {}^{198}_{80}Hg + {}^{0}_{-1}e$
    c. $^{82}_{37}Rb \longrightarrow {}^{82}_{36}Kr + {}^{0}_{+1}e$

5.79 $^{1}_{0}n + {}^{238}_{92}U \longrightarrow {}^{239}_{93}Np + {}^{0}_{-1}e$

5.81 3.0 days

5.83 64 μCi

5.85 $^{48}_{20}Ca + {}^{244}_{94}Pu \longrightarrow {}^{292}_{114}Fl$

5.87 16 μCi

6

Ionic and Molecular Compounds

RICHARD'S DOCTOR HAS RECOMMENDED THAT

he take a low-dose aspirin (81 mg) every day to prevent a heart attack or stroke. Richard is concerned about taking aspirin and asks Sarah, a pharmacy technician working at a local pharmacy, about the effects of aspirin. Sarah explains to Richard that aspirin is acetylsalicylic acid, and has the chemical formula $C_9H_8O_4$. Aspirin is a molecular compound, often referred to as an organic molecule because it contains the nonmetals carbon (C), hydrogen (H), and oxygen (O). Sarah explains to Richard that aspirin is used to relieve minor pains, to reduce inflammation and fever, and to slow blood clotting. Aspirin is one of several nonsteroidal anti-inflammatory drugs (NSAIDs) that reduce pain and fever by blocking the formation of prostaglandins, which are chemical messengers that transmit pain signals to the brain and cause fever. Some potential side effects of aspirin may include heartburn, upset stomach, nausea, and an increased risk of a stomach ulcer.

CAREER Pharmacy Technician

Pharmacy technicians work under the supervision of a pharmacist, and their main responsibility is to fill prescriptions by preparing pharmaceutical medications. They obtain the proper medication, calculate, measure, and label the patient's medication, which is then approved by the pharmacist. After the prescription is filled, the technician prices and files the prescription. Pharmacy technicians also provide customer service by receiving prescription requests, interacting with customers, and answering any questions they may have about the drugs and their health condition. Pharmacy technicians also prepare insurance claims, and create and maintain patient profiles.

The ionic formulas of gemstones contain metallic ions that produce their different colors.

n nature, atoms of almost all the elements on the periodic table are found in combination with other atoms. Only the atoms of the noble gases—He, Ne, Ar, Kr, Xe, and Rn—do not combine in nature with other atoms. A *compound* is composed of two or more elements, with a definite composition.

Compounds may be ionic or molecular. In an *ionic compound*, one or more electrons are transferred from metals to nonmetals, which form positive and negative ions. The attraction between these ions is called an *ionic bond*.

We utilize ionic compounds every day, including salt, NaCl, and baking soda, $NaHCO_3$. Milk of magnesia, $Mg(OH)_2$, or calcium carbonate, $CaCO_3$, may be taken to settle an upset stomach. In a mineral supplement, iron may be present as iron(II) sulfate, $FeSO_4$, iodine as potassium iodide, KI, and manganese as manganese(II) sulfate, $MnSO_4$. Some sunscreens contain zinc oxide, ZnO, and tin(II) fluoride, SnF_2, in toothpaste provides fluoride to help prevent tooth decay. Precious and semiprecious gemstones are examples of ionic compounds called minerals that are cut and polished to make jewelry. For example, sapphires and rubies are made of aluminum oxide, Al_2O_3. Impurities of chromium ions make rubies red, and iron and titanium ions make sapphires blue.

A *molecular compound* consists of two or more nonmetals that share one or more valence electrons. The resulting molecules are held together by *covalent bonds*. There are many more molecular compounds than there are ionic ones. For example, water (H_2O) and carbon dioxide (CO_2) are both molecular compounds. Molecular compounds consist of molecules, which are discrete groups of atoms in a definite proportion. A molecule of water (H_2O) consists of two atoms of hydrogen and one atom of oxygen. When you have iced tea, perhaps you add molecules of sugar ($C_{12}H_{22}O_{11}$), which is a molecular compound. Other molecular compounds include propane (C_3H_8), alcohol (C_2H_6O), the antibiotic amoxicillin ($C_{16}H_{19}N_3O_5S$), and the antidepressant Prozac ($C_{17}H_{18}F_3NO$).

CHAPTER READINESS*

🖩 KEY MATH SKILLS
- Using Positive and Negative Numbers in Calculations (1.4B)
- Solving Equations (1.4D)

⚛ CORE CHEMISTRY SKILLS
- Writing Electron Configurations (4.7)
- Drawing Lewis Symbols (4.8)

*These Key Math Skills and Core Chemistry Skills from previous chapters are listed here for your review as you proceed to the new material in this chapter.

LEARNING GOAL

Write the symbols for the simple ions of the representative elements.

6.1 Ions: Transfer of Electrons

Most of the elements, except the noble gases, are found in nature combined as compounds. The noble gases are so stable that they form compounds only under extreme conditions. One explanation for the stability of noble gases is that they have a filled valence electron energy level.

Compounds form when electrons are transferred or shared to give stable electron configuration to the atoms. In the formation of either an *ionic bond* or a *covalent bond*, atoms lose, gain, or share valence electrons to acquire an **octet** of eight valence electrons. This tendency of atoms to attain a stable electron configuration is known as the **octet rule** and provides a key to our understanding of the ways in which atoms bond and form compounds.

A few elements achieve the stability of helium with two valence electrons. However, we do not use the octet rule with transition elements.

Ionic bonds occur when the valence electrons of atoms of a metal are transferred to atoms of nonmetals. For example, sodium atoms lose electrons and chlorine atoms gain electrons to form the ionic compound NaCl. *Covalent bonds* form when atoms of nonmetals share valence electrons. In the molecular compounds H_2O and C_3H_8, atoms share electrons.

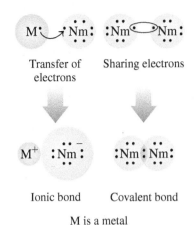

Transfer of electrons

Sharing electrons

Ionic bond

Covalent bond

M is a metal
Nm is a nonmetal

Type	Ionic Compounds	Molecular Compounds	
Particles	Ions	Molecules	
Bonding	Ionic bonds	Covalent bonds	
Examples	$Na^+ Cl^-$ ions	H_2O molecules	C_3H_8 molecules

Positive Ions: Loss of Electrons

In ionic bonding, **ions**, which have electrical charges, form when atoms lose or gain electrons to form a stable electron configuration. Because the ionization energies of metals of Groups 1A (1), 2A (2), and 3A (13) are low, metal atoms readily lose their valence electrons. In doing so, they form ions with positive charges. A metal atom obtains the same electron configuration as its nearest noble gas (usually eight valence electrons). For example, when a sodium atom loses its single valence electron, the remaining electrons have a stable electron configuration. By losing an electron, sodium has 10 negatively charged electrons instead of 11. Because there are still 11 positively charged protons in its nucleus, the atom is no longer neutral. It is now a sodium ion with a positive electrical charge, called an **ionic charge**, of 1+. In the Lewis symbol for the sodium ion, the ionic charge of 1+ is written in the upper right-hand corner, Na^+, where the 1 is understood. The sodium ion is smaller than the sodium atom because the ion has lost its outermost electron from the third energy level. The positively charged ions of metals are called **cations** (pronounced *cat-eye-uns*) and use the name of the element.

$$\text{Ionic charge} = \text{Charge of protons} + \text{Charge of electrons}$$
$$1+ = (11+) \qquad + (10-)$$

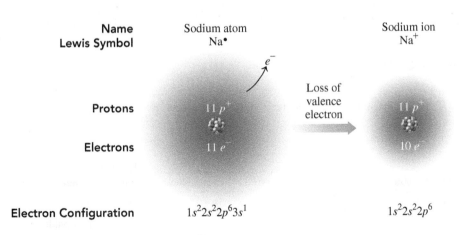

Name Lewis Symbol	Sodium atom Na•		Sodium ion Na^+
		Loss of valence electron	
Protons	$11\,p^+$		$11\,p^+$
Electrons	$11\,e^-$		$10\,e^-$
Electron Configuration	$1s^2 2s^2 2p^6 3s^1$		$1s^2 2s^2 2p^6$

Magnesium, a metal in Group 2A (2), obtains a stable electron configuration by losing two valence electrons to form a magnesium ion with a 2+ ionic charge, Mg^{2+}. A metal ion is named by its element name. Thus, Mg^{2+} is named the *magnesium ion*. The magnesium ion is smaller than the magnesium atom because the outermost electrons in the third energy level were removed. The octet in the magnesium ion is made up of electrons that fill its second energy level.

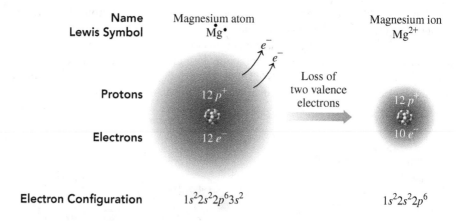

Negative Ions: Gain of Electrons

The ionization energy of a nonmetal atom in Groups 5A (15), 6A (16), or 7A (17) is high. In an ionic compound, a nonmetal atom gains one or more valence electrons to obtain a stable electron configuration. By gaining electrons, a nonmetal atom forms a negatively charged ion. For example, an atom of chlorine with seven valence electrons gains one electron to form an octet. Because it now has 18 electrons and 17 protons in its nucleus, the chlorine atom is no longer neutral. It is a *chloride ion* with an ionic charge of 1−, which is written as Cl^-, with the 1 understood. A negatively charged ion, called an **anion** (pronounced *an-eye-un*), is named by using the first syllable of its element name followed by *ide*. The chloride ion is larger than the chlorine atom because the ion has an additional electron, which completes its outermost energy level.

$$\text{Ionic charge} = \text{Charge of protons} + \text{Charge of electrons}$$
$$1- = (17+) + (18-)$$

	Name	Chlorine atom		Chloride ion
	Lewis Symbol	$:\overset{..}{\underset{.}{Cl}}\cdot$	e^- Gain of one valence electron	$:\overset{..}{\underset{..}{Cl}}:$
	Protons	17 p		17 p
	Electrons	17 e		18 e
	Electron Configuration	$1s^2 2s^2 2p^6 3s^2 3p^5$		$1s^2 2s^2 2p^6 3s^2 3p^6$

Table 6.1 lists the names of some important metal and nonmetal ions.

TABLE 6.1 Formulas and Names of Some Common Ions

Metals			Nonmetals		
Group Number	Cation	Name of Cation	Group Number	Anion	Name of Anion
1A (1)	Li^+	Lithium	5A (15)	N^{3-}	Nitride
	Na^+	Sodium		P^{3-}	Phosphide
	K^+	Potassium	6A (16)	O^{2-}	Oxide
2A (2)	Mg^{2+}	Magnesium		S^{2-}	Sulfide
	Ca^{2+}	Calcium	7A (17)	F^-	Fluoride
	Ba^{2+}	Barium		Cl^-	Chloride
3A (13)	Al^{3+}	Aluminum		Br^-	Bromide
				I^-	Iodide

> **SAMPLE PROBLEM 6.1 Ions**

a. Write the symbol and name for the ion that has 7 protons and 10 electrons.
b. Write the symbol and name for the ion that has 20 protons and 18 electrons.

SOLUTION

a. The element with seven protons is nitrogen. In an ion of nitrogen with 10 electrons, the ionic charge would be $3-$, $[(7+) + (10-) = 3-]$. The ion, written as N^{3-}, is the *nitride* ion.
b. The element with 20 protons is calcium. In an ion of calcium with 18 electrons, the ionic charge would be $2+$, $[(20+) + (18-) = 2+]$. The ion, written as Ca^{2+}, is the *calcium* ion.

STUDY CHECK 6.1

How many protons and electrons are in each of the following ions?

a. S^{2-} **b.** Al^{3+}

ANSWER

a. 16 protons, 18 electrons   **b.** 13 protons, 10 electrons

Ionic Charges from Group Numbers

In ionic compounds, representative elements usually lose or gain electrons to give eight valence electrons like their nearest noble gas (or two for helium). We can use the group numbers in the periodic table to determine the charges for the ions of the representative elements. The elements in Group 1A (1) lose one electron to form ions with a 1+ charge. The elements in Group 2A (2) lose two electrons to form ions with a 2+ charge. The elements in Group 3A (13) lose three electrons to form ions with a 3+ charge. In this text, we do not use the group numbers of the transition elements to determine their ionic charges.

In ionic compounds, the elements in Group 7A (17) gain one electron to form ions with a 1− charge. The elements in Group 6A (16) gain two electrons to form ions with a 2− charge. The elements in Group 5A (15) gain three electrons to form ions with a 3− charge.

The nonmetals of Group 4A (14) do not typically form ions. However, the metals Sn and Pb in Group 4A (14) lose electrons to form positive ions. Table 6.2 lists the ionic charges for some common monatomic ions of representative elements.

TABLE 6.2 Examples of Monatomic Ions and Their Nearest Noble Gases

Noble Gases		Metals Lose Valence Electrons 1A (1)	2A (2)	3A (13)	Nonmetals Gain Valence Electrons 5A (15)	6A (16)	7A (17)		Noble Gases
He	⇐	Li^+							
Ne	⇐	Na^+	Mg^{2+}	Al^{3+}	N^{3-}	O^{2-}	F^-	⇒	Ne
Ar	⇐	K^+	Ca^{2+}		P^{3-}	S^{2-}	Cl^-	⇒	Ar
Kr	⇐	Rb^+	Sr^{2+}				Br^-	⇒	Kr
Xe	⇐	Cs^+	Ba^{2+}				I^-	⇒	Xe

> ▶ **SAMPLE PROBLEM 6.2 Writing Symbols for Ions**
>
> Consider the elements aluminum and oxygen.
>
> **a.** Identify each as a metal or a nonmetal.
> **b.** State the number of valence electrons for each.
> **c.** State the number of electrons that must be lost or gained for each to achieve an octet.
> **d.** Write the symbol, including its ionic charge, and name for each resulting ion.
>
> **SOLUTION**
>
> | Aluminum | Oxygen |
> |---|---|
> | **a.** metal | nonmetal |
> | **b.** three valence electrons | six valence electrons |
> | **c.** loses 3 e^- | gains 2 e^- |
> | **d.** Al^{3+}, $[(13+) + (10-) = 3+]$, aluminum ion | O^{2-}, $[(8+) + (10-) = 2-]$, oxide ion |
>
> **STUDY CHECK 6.2**
>
> Write the symbols for the ions formed by potassium and sulfur.
>
> **ANSWER**
> K^+ and S^{2-}

Chemistry Link to Health

Some Important Ions in the Body

Several ions in body fluids have important physiological and metabolic functions. Some are listed in Table 6.3.

Foods such as bananas, milk, cheese, and potatoes provide the body with ions that are important in regulating body functions.

Milk, cheese, bananas, cereal, and potatoes provide ions for the body.

TABLE 6.3 Ions in the Body

Ion	Occurrence	Function	Source	Result of Too Little	Result of Too Much
Na^+	Principal cation outside the cell	Regulation and control of body fluids	Salt, cheese, pickles	Hyponatremia, anxiety, diarrhea, circulatory failure, decrease in body fluid	Hypernatremia, little urine, thirst, edema
K^+	Principal cation inside the cell	Regulation of body fluids and cellular functions	Bananas, orange juice, milk, prunes, potatoes	Hypokalemia (hypopotassemia), lethargy, muscle weakness, failure of neurological impulses	Hyperkalemia (hyperpotassemia), irritability, nausea, little urine, cardiac arrest
Ca^{2+}	Cation outside the cell; 90% of calcium in the body in bones as $Ca_3(PO_4)_2$ or $CaCO_3$	Major cation of bones; needed for muscle contraction	Milk, yogurt, cheese, greens, spinach	Hypocalcemia, tingling fingertips, muscle cramps, osteoporosis	Hypercalcemia, relaxed muscles, kidney stones, deep bone pain
Mg^{2+}	Cation outside the cell; 50% of magnesium in the body in bone structure	Essential for certain enzymes, muscles, nerve control	Widely distributed (part of chlorophyll of all green plants), nuts, whole grains	Disorientation, hypertension, tremors, slow pulse	Drowsiness
Cl^-	Principal anion outside the cell	Gastric juice, regulation of body fluids	Salt	Same as for Na^+	Same as for Na^+

QUESTIONS AND PROBLEMS

6.1 Ions: Transfer of Electrons

LEARNING GOAL Write the symbols for the simple ions of the representative elements.

6.1 State the number of electrons that must be lost by atoms of each of the following to achieve a stable electron configuration:
a. Li   **b.** Ca   **c.** Ga   **d.** Cs   **e.** Ba

6.2 State the number of electrons that must be gained by atoms of each of the following to achieve a stable electron configuration:
a. Cl   **b.** Se   **c.** N   **d.** I   **e.** S

6.3 State the number of electrons lost or gained when the following elements form ions:
a. Sr   **b.** P   **c.** Group 7A (17)
d. Na   **e.** Br

6.4 State the number of electrons lost or gained when the following elements form ions:
a. O   **b.** Group 2A (2)   **c.** F
d. K   **e.** Rb

6.5 Write the symbols for the ions with the following number of protons and electrons:
a. 3 protons, 2 electrons   **b.** 9 protons, 10 electrons
c. 12 protons, 10 electrons   **d.** 26 protons, 23 electrons

6.6 Write the symbols for the ions with the following number of protons and electrons:
a. 8 protons, 10 electrons   **b.** 19 protons, 18 electrons
c. 35 protons, 36 electrons   **d.** 50 protons, 46 electrons

6.7 Write the symbol for the ion of each of the following:
a. chlorine   **b.** cesium
c. nitrogen   **d.** radium

6.8 Write the symbol for the ion of each of the following:
a. fluorine   **b.** calcium
c. sodium   **d.** iodine

℞ Clinical Applications

6.9 State the number of protons and electrons in each of the following ions:
a. O^{2-}, used to build biomolecules and water
b. K^+, most prevalent positive ion in cells, needed for muscle contraction, nerve impulses
c. I^-, needed for thyroid function
d. Na^+, most prevalent positive ion in extracellular fluid

6.10 State the number of protons and electrons in each of the following ions:
a. P^{3-}, needed for bones and teeth
b. F^-, used to strengthen tooth enamel
c. Mg^{2+}, needed for bones and teeth
d. Ca^{2+}, needed for bones and teeth

6.2 Writing Formulas for Ionic Compounds

LEARNING GOAL

Using charge balance, write the correct formula for an ionic compound.

Ionic compounds consist of positive and negative ions. The ions are held together by strong electrical attractions between the oppositely charged ions, called *ionic bonds*. The positive ions are formed by *metals* losing electrons, and the negative ions are formed when *nonmetals* gain electrons. Even though noble gases are nonmetals, they already have stable electron configurations and do not form compounds.

Properties of Ionic Compounds

The physical and chemical properties of an ionic compound such as NaCl are very different from those of the original elements. For example, the original elements of NaCl were sodium, which is a soft, shiny metal, and chlorine, which is a yellow-green poisonous gas. However, when they react and form positive and negative ions, they produce NaCl, which is ordinary table salt, a hard, white, crystalline substance that is important in our diet.

In a crystal of NaCl, the larger Cl^- ions are arranged in a three-dimensional structure in which the smaller Na^+ ions occupy the spaces between the Cl^- ions (see Figure 6.1). In this crystal, every Na^+ ion is surrounded by six Cl^- ions, and every Cl^- ion is surrounded by six Na^+ ions. Thus, there are many strong attractions between the positive and negative ions, which account for the high melting points of ionic compounds. For example, the melting point of NaCl is 801 °C. At room temperature, ionic compounds are solids.

Chemical Formulas of Ionic Compounds

The **chemical formula** of a compound represents the symbols and subscripts in the lowest whole-number ratio of the atoms or ions. In the formula of an ionic compound, the sum of the ionic charges in the formula is always zero. *Thus, the total amount of positive charge is equal to the total amount of negative charge.* For example, to achieve a stable electron configuration, one Na atom (metal) loses its one valence electron to form Na^+, and one Cl

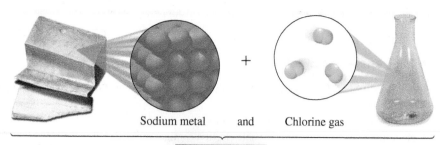

FIGURE 6.1 ▶ The elements sodium and chlorine react to form the ionic compound sodium chloride, the compound that makes up table salt. The magnification of NaCl crystals shows the arrangement of Na⁺ and Cl⁻ ions.

Ⓠ What is the type of bonding between Na⁺ and Cl⁻ ions in NaCl?

atom (nonmetal) gains one electron to form a Cl⁻ ion. The formula NaCl indicates that the compound has charge balance because there is one sodium ion, Na⁺, for every chloride ion, Cl⁻. Although the ions are positively or negatively charged, they are not shown in the formula of the compound.

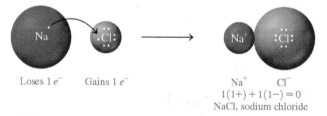

Subscripts in Formulas

Consider a compound of magnesium and chlorine. To achieve a stable electron configuration, one Mg atom (metal) loses its two valence electrons to form Mg^{2+}. Two Cl atoms (nonmetals) each gain one electron to form two Cl⁻ ions. The two Cl⁻ ions are needed to balance the positive charge of Mg^{2+}. This gives the formula $MgCl_2$, magnesium chloride, in which the subscript 2 shows that two Cl⁻ ions are needed for charge balance.

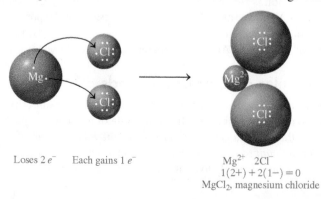

Writing Ionic Formulas from Ionic Charges

The subscripts in the formula of an ionic compound represent the number of positive and negative ions that give an overall charge of zero. Thus, we can now write a formula directly from the ionic charges of the positive and negative ions. Suppose we wish to write the formula for the ionic compound containing Na^+ and S^{2-} ions. To balance the ionic charge of the S^{2-} ion, we will need to place two Na^+ ions in the formula. This gives the formula Na_2S, which has an overall charge of zero. In the formula of an ionic compound, the cation is written first followed by the anion. Appropriate subscripts are used to show the number of each of the ions. This formula, which is the lowest ratio of the ions in an ionic compound, is called a *formula unit*.

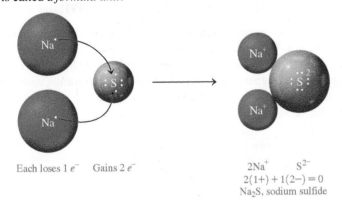

Each loses 1 e^- Gains 2 e^-

$2Na^+$ S^{2-}
$2(1+) + 1(2-) = 0$
Na_2S, sodium sulfide

▶ **SAMPLE PROBLEM 6.3** **Writing Formulas from Ionic Charges**

Write the symbols for the ions, and the correct formula for the ionic compound formed when lithium and nitrogen react.

SOLUTION

Lithium, which is a metal in Group 1A (1), forms Li^+; nitrogen, which is a nonmetal in Group 5A (15), forms N^{3-}. The charge of 3− is balanced by three Li^+ ions.

$$3(1+) + 1(3-) = 0$$

Writing the cation (positive ion) first and the anion (negative ion) second gives the formula Li_3N.

STUDY CHECK 6.3

Write the symbols for the ions, and the correct formula for the ionic compound that would form when calcium and oxygen react.

ANSWER

Ca^{2+}, O^{2-}, CaO

QUESTIONS AND PROBLEMS

6.2 Writing Formulas for Ionic Compounds

LEARNING GOAL Using charge balance, write the correct formula for an ionic compound.

6.11 Which of the following pairs of elements are likely to form an ionic compound?
    a. lithium and chlorine   **b.** oxygen and bromine
    c. potassium and oxygen   **d.** sodium and neon
    e. cesium and magnesium   **f.** nitrogen and fluorine

6.12 Which of the following pairs of elements are likely to form an ionic compound?
    a. helium and oxygen   **b.** magnesium and chlorine
    c. chlorine and bromine   **d.** potassium and sulfur
    e. sodium and potassium   **f.** nitrogen and iodine

6.13 Write the correct ionic formula for the compound formed between each of the following pairs of ions:
    a. Na^+ and O^{2-} **b.** Al^{3+} and Br^- **c.** Ba^{2+} and N^{3-}
    d. Mg^{2+} and F^- **e.** Al^{3+} and S^{2-}

6.14 Write the correct ionic formula for the compound formed between each of the following pairs of ions:
  a. Al^{3+} and Cl^- **b.** Ca^{2+} and S^{2-} **c.** Li^+ and S^{2-}
  d. Rb^+ and P^{3-} **e.** Cs^+ and I^-

6.15 Write the symbols for the ions, and the correct formula for the ionic compound formed by each of the following:
  a. potassium and sulfur   **b.** sodium and nitrogen
  c. aluminum and iodine   **d.** gallium and oxygen

6.16 Write the symbols for the ions, and the correct formula for the ionic compound formed by each of the following:
  a. calcium and chlorine   **b.** rubidium and bromine
  c. sodium and phosphorus   **d.** magnesium and oxygen

LEARNING GOAL

Given the formula of an ionic compound, write the correct name; given the name of an ionic compound, write the correct formula.

⚛ CORE CHEMISTRY SKILL

Naming Ionic Compounds

Iodized salt contains KI to prevent iodine deficiency.

Guide to Naming Ionic Compounds with Metals That Form a Single Ion

STEP **1**
Identify the cation and anion.

STEP **2**
Name the cation by its element name.

STEP **3**
Name the anion by using the first syllable of its element name followed by *ide*.

STEP **4**
Write the name for the cation first and the name for the anion second.

6.3 Naming and Writing Ionic Formulas

In the name of an ionic compound made up of two elements, the name of the metal ion, which is written first, is the same as its element name. The name of the nonmetal ion is obtained by using the first syllable of its element name followed by *ide*. In the name of any ionic compound, a space separates the name of the cation from the name of the anion. Subscripts are not used; they are understood because of the charge balance of the ions in the compound (see Table 6.4).

TABLE 6.4 Names of Some Ionic Compounds

Compound	Metal Ion	Nonmetal Ion	Name
KI	K^+ Potassium	I^- Iodide	Potassium iodide
$MgBr_2$	Mg^{2+} Magnesium	Br^- Bromide	Magnesium bromide
Al_2O_3	Al^{3+} Aluminum	O^{2-} Oxide	Aluminum oxide

▷ **SAMPLE PROBLEM 6.4 Naming Ionic Compounds**

Write the name for the ionic compound Mg_3N_2.

SOLUTION

ANALYZE THE PROBLEM	Given	Ions	Need
	Mg_3N_2	cation, Mg^{2+} anion, N^{3-}	name of compound

STEP **1** Identify the cation and anion. The cation, Mg^{2+}, is from Group 2A (2), and the anion, N^{3-}, is from Group 5A (15).

STEP **2** Name the cation by its element name. The cation Mg^{2+} is magnesium.

STEP **3** Name the anion by using the first syllable of its element name followed by *ide*. The anion N^{3-} is nitride.

STEP **4** Write the name for the cation first and the name for the anion second. Mg_3N_2 magnesium nitride

STUDY CHECK 6.4

Name the compound Ga_2S_3.

ANSWER

gallium sulfide

Metals with Variable Charges

We have seen that the charge of an ion of a representative element can be obtained from its group number. However, we cannot determine the charge of a transition element because it typically forms two or more positive ions. The transition elements lose electrons, but they are lost from the highest energy level and sometimes from a lower energy level as well. This is also true for metals of representative elements in Groups 4A (14) and 5A (15), such as Pb, Sn, and Bi.

In some ionic compounds, iron is in the Fe^{2+} form, but in other compounds, it has the Fe^{3+} form. Copper also forms two different ions, Cu^+ and Cu^{2+}. When a metal can form two or more types of ions, it has *variable charge*. Then we cannot predict the ionic charge from the group number.

For metals that form two or more ions, a naming system is used to identify the particular cation. To do this, a Roman numeral that is equal to the ionic charge is placed in parentheses immediately after the name of the metal. For example, Fe^{2+} is iron(II), and Fe^{3+} is iron(III). Table 6.5 lists the ions of some metals that produce more than one ion.

Figure 6.2 shows some ions and their location on the periodic table. The transition elements form more than one positive ion except for zinc (Zn^{2+}), cadmium (Cd^{2+}), and silver (Ag^+), which form only one ion. Thus, no Roman numerals are used with zinc, cadmium, and silver when naming their cations in ionic compounds. Metals in Groups 4A (14) and 5A (15) also form more than one type of positive ion. For example, lead and tin in Group 4A (14) form cations with charges of 2+ and 4+, and bismuth in Group 5A (15) forms cations with charges of 3+ and 5+.

Determination of Variable Charge

When you name an ionic compound, you need to determine if the metal is a representative element or a transition element. If it is a transition element, except for zinc, cadmium, or silver, you will need to use its ionic charge as a Roman numeral as part of its name. The calculation of ionic charge depends on the negative charge of the anions in the formula. For example, we use charge balance to determine the charge of a copper cation in the ionic compound $CuCl_2$. Because there are two chloride ions, each with a $1-$ charge, the total negative charge is $2-$. To balance this $2-$ charge, the copper ion must have a charge of $2+$, or Cu^{2+}:

$CuCl_2$

$$\text{Cu charge} + 2\,Cl^- \text{ charge} = 0$$
$$? \qquad + 2(1-) \qquad = 0$$
$$2+ \qquad + 2- \qquad = 0$$

To indicate the $2+$ charge for the copper ion Cu^{2+}, we place the Roman numeral (II) immediately after copper when naming this compound: copper(II) chloride.

TABLE 6.5 Some Metals That Form More Than One Positive Ion

Element	Possible Ions	Name of Ion
Bismuth	Bi^{3+}	Bismuth(III)
	Bi^{5+}	Bismuth(V)
Chromium	Cr^{2+}	Chromium(II)
	Cr^{3+}	Chromium(III)
Cobalt	Co^{2+}	Cobalt(II)
	Co^{3+}	Cobalt(III)
Copper	Cu^+	Copper(I)
	Cu^{2+}	Copper(II)
Gold	Au^+	Gold(I)
	Au^{3+}	Gold(III)
Iron	Fe^{2+}	Iron(II)
	Fe^{3+}	Iron(III)
Lead	Pb^{2+}	Lead(II)
	Pb^{4+}	Lead(IV)
Manganese	Mn^{2+}	Manganese(II)
	Mn^{3+}	Manganese(III)
Mercury	Hg_2^{2+}	Mercury(I)*
	Hg^{2+}	Mercury(II)
Nickel	Ni^{2+}	Nickel(II)
	Ni^{3+}	Nickel(III)
Tin	Sn^{2+}	Tin(II)
	Sn^{4+}	Tin(IV)

*Mercury(I) ions form an ion pair with a 2+ charge.

FIGURE 6.2 ▶ In ionic compounds, metals form positive ions, and nonmetals form negative ions.

What are the typical ions of calcium, copper, and oxygen in ionic compounds?

The growth of barnacles is prevented by using a paint with Cu_2O on the bottom of a boat.

Guide to Naming Ionic Compounds with Variable Charge Metals

STEP 1
Determine the charge of the cation from the anion.

STEP 2
Name the cation by its element name and use a Roman numeral in parentheses for the charge.

STEP 3
Name the anion by using the first syllable of its element name followed by *ide*.

STEP 4
Write the name for the cation first and the name for the anion second.

TABLE 6.6 Some Ionic Compounds of Metals That Form Two Kinds of Positive Ions

Compound	Systematic Name
$FeCl_2$	Iron(II) chloride
Fe_2O_3	Iron(III) oxide
Cu_3P	Copper(I) phosphide
$CrBr_2$	Chromium(II) bromide
$SnCl_2$	Tin(II) chloride
PbS_2	Lead(IV) sulfide
BiF_3	Bismuth(III) fluoride

▶ **SAMPLE PROBLEM 6.5** Naming Ionic Compounds with Variable Charge Metal Ions

Antifouling paint contains Cu_2O, which prevents the growth of barnacles and algae on the bottoms of boats. What is the name of Cu_2O?

SOLUTION

ANALYZE THE PROBLEM	Given	Need
	Cu_2O	name

STEP 1 Determine the charge of the cation from the anion.

	Metal	Nonmetal
Elements	copper (Cu)	oxygen (O)
Groups	transition element	6A (16)
Ions	Cu?	O^{2-}
Charge Balance	$2Cu?$ +	$2- = 0$
	$\dfrac{2Cu?}{2} = \dfrac{2+}{2} = 1+$	
Ions	Cu^+	O^{2-}

STEP 2 Name the cation by its element name and use a Roman numeral in parentheses for the charge. copper(I)

STEP 3 Name the anion by using the first syllable of its element name followed by *ide*. oxide

STEP 4 Write the name for the cation first and the name for the anion second. copper(I) oxide

STUDY CHECK 6.5

Write the name for the compound with the formula Mn_2S_3.

ANSWER

manganese(III) sulfide

Table 6.6 lists the names of some ionic compounds in which the transition elements and metals from Groups 4A (14) and 5A (15) have more than one positive ion.

Writing Formulas from the Name of an Ionic Compound

The formula for an ionic compound is written from the first part of the name that describes the metal ion, including its charge, and the second part of the name that specifies the nonmetal ion. Subscripts are added, as needed, to balance the charge. The steps for writing a formula from the name of an ionic compound are shown in Sample Problem 6.6.

▶ **SAMPLE PROBLEM 6.6** Writing Formulas for Ionic Compounds

Write the correct formula for iron(III) chloride.

SOLUTION

ANALYZE THE PROBLEM	Given	Need
	iron(III) chloride	ionic formula

STEP 1 Identify the cation and anion. Iron(III) chloride consists of a metal and a nonmetal, which means that it is an ionic compound.

Type of Ion	Cation	Anion
Name	iron(III)	chloride
Group	transition element	7A (17)
Symbol of Ion	Fe^{3+}	Cl^-

STEP **2** Balance the charges.

Fe^{3+} Cl^-

           Cl^-

           Cl^-
_____

$\mathbf{1}(3+) + \mathbf{3}(1-) = 0$

↑

Becomes a subscript in the formula

STEP **3** Write the formula, cation first, using subscripts from the charge balance. $FeCl_3$

STUDY CHECK 6.6

Write the correct formula for chromium(III) oxide.

ANSWER

Cr_2O_3

Guide to Writing Formulas from the Name of an Ionic Compound

STEP **1**
Identify the cation and anion.

STEP **2**
Balance the charges.

STEP **3**
Write the formula, cation first, using subscripts from the charge balance.

The pigment chrome oxide green contains chromium(III) oxide.

QUESTIONS AND PROBLEMS

6.3 Naming and Writing Ionic Formulas

LEARNING GOAL Given the formula of an ionic compound, write the correct name; given the name of an ionic compound, write the correct formula.

6.17 Write the name for each of the following ionic compounds:
  a. Al_2O_3 **b.** $CaCl_2$ **c.** Na_2O
  d. Mg_3P_2 **e.** KI   **f.** BaF_2

6.18 Write the name for each of the following ionic compounds:
  a. $MgCl_2$ **b.** K_3P **c.** Li_2S
  d. CsF   **e.** MgO   **f.** $SrBr_2$

6.19 Write the name for each of the following ions (include the Roman numeral when necessary):
  a. Fe^{2+} **b.** Cu^{2+} **c.** Zn^{2+}
  d. Pb^{4+} **e.** Cr^{3+} **f.** Mn^{2+}

6.20 Write the name for each of the following ions (include the Roman numeral when necessary):
  a. Ag^+ **b.** Cu^+ **c.** Bi^{3+}
  d. Sn^{2+} **e.** Au^{3+} **f.** Ni^{2+}

6.21 Write the name for each of the following ionic compounds:
  a. $SnCl_2$ **b.** FeO   **c.** Cu_2S
  d. CuS   **e.** $CdBr_2$ **f.** $HgCl_2$

6.22 Write the name for each of the following ionic compounds:
  a. Ag_3P **b.** PbS   **c.** SnO_2
  d. $MnCl_3$ **e.** Bi_2O_3 **f.** $CoCl_2$

6.23 Write the symbol for the cation in each of the following ionic compounds:
  a. $AuCl_3$ **b.** Fe_2O_3 **c.** PbI_4 **d.** $SnCl_2$

6.24 Write the symbol for the cation in each of the following ionic compounds:
  a. $FeCl_2$ **b.** CrO   **c.** Ni_2S_3 **d.** AlP

6.25 Write the formula for each of the following ionic compounds:
  a. magnesium chloride   **b.** sodium sulfide
  c. copper(I) oxide   **d.** zinc phosphide
  e. gold(III) nitride   **f.** cobalt(III) fluoride

6.26 Write the formula for each of the following ionic compounds:
  a. nickel(III) oxide   **b.** barium fluoride
  c. tin(IV) chloride   **d.** silver sulfide
  e. bismuth(V) chloride   **f.** potassium nitride

6.27 Write the formula for each of the following ionic compounds:
  a. cobalt(III) chloride   **b.** lead(IV) oxide
  c. silver iodide   **d.** calcium nitride
  e. copper(I) phosphide   **f.** chromium(II) chloride

6.28 Write the formula for each of the following ionic compounds:
  a. zinc bromide   **b.** iron(III) sulfide
  c. manganese(IV) oxide   **d.** chromium(III) iodide
  e. lithium nitride   **f.** gold(I) oxide

℞ Clinical Applications

6.29 The following compounds contain ions that are required in small amounts by the body. Write the formula for each:
   a. potassium phosphide   **b.** copper(II) chloride
   c. iron(III) bromide   **d.** magnesium oxide

6.30 The following compounds contain ions that are required in small amounts by the body. Write the formula for each:
   a. calcium chloride   **b.** nickel(II) iodide
   c. manganese(II) oxide   **d.** zinc nitride

Vitamins and minerals are substances required in small amounts by the body for growth and activity.

LEARNING GOAL

Write the name and formula for an ionic compound containing a polyatomic ion.

6.4 Polyatomic Ions

An ionic compound may also contain a *polyatomic ion* as one of its cations or anions. A **polyatomic ion** is a group of covalently bonded atoms that has an overall ionic charge. Most polyatomic ions consist of a nonmetal such as phosphorus, sulfur, carbon, or nitrogen covalently bonded to oxygen atoms.

Almost all the polyatomic ions are anions with charges $1-$, $2-$, or $3-$. Only one common polyatomic ion, NH_4^+, has a positive charge. Some models of common polyatomic ions are shown in Figure 6.3.

Plaster cast
$CaSO_4$

Fertilizer
NH_4NO_3

Ca^{2+} SO_4^{2-} NH_4^+ NO_3^-
                 Sulfate ion   Ammonium ion   Nitrate ion

FIGURE 6.3 ▶ Many products contain polyatomic ions, which are groups of atoms that have an ionic charge.

ⓠ What is the charge of a sulfate ion?

Names of Polyatomic Ions

The names of the most common polyatomic ions end in *ate*, such as nitrate and sulfate. When a related ion has one less oxygen atom, the *ite* ending is used for its name such as nitrite and sulfite. Recognizing these endings will help you identify polyatomic ions in the name of a compound. The hydroxide ion (OH^-) and cyanide ion (CN^-) are exceptions to this naming pattern.

By learning the formulas, charges, and names of the polyatomic ions shown in bold type in Table 6.7, you can derive the related ions. Note that both the *ate* ion and *ite* ion of a particular nonmetal have the same ionic charge. For example, the sulfate ion is SO_4^{2-}, and the sulfite ion, which has one less oxygen atom, is SO_3^{2-}. Phosphate and phosphite ions

TABLE 6.7 Names and Formulas of Some Common Polyatomic Ions

Nonmetal	Formula of Ion*	Name of Ion
Hydrogen	OH^-	Hydroxide
Nitrogen	NH_4^+	Ammonium
	NO_3^-	**Nitrate**
	NO_2^-	Nitrite
Chlorine	ClO_4^-	Perchlorate
	ClO_3^-	**Chlorate**
	ClO_2^-	Chlorite
	ClO^-	Hypochlorite
Carbon	**CO_3^{2-}**	**Carbonate**
	HCO_3^-	Hydrogen carbonate (or bicarbonate)
	CN^-	Cyanide
	$C_2H_3O_2^-$	Acetate
Sulfur	**SO_4^{2-}**	**Sulfate**
	HSO_4^-	Hydrogen sulfate (or bisulfate)
	SO_3^{2-}	Sulfite
	HSO_3^-	Hydrogen sulfite (or bisulfite)
Phosphorus	**PO_4^{3-}**	**Phosphate**
	HPO_4^{2-}	Hydrogen phosphate
	$H_2PO_4^-$	Dihydrogen phosphate
	PO_3^{3-}	Phosphite

*Formulas and names in bold type indicate the most common polyatomic ion for that element.

each have a 3− charge; nitrate and nitrite each have a 1− charge; and perchlorate, chlorate, chlorite, and hypochlorite all have a 1− charge. The halogens form four different polyatomic ions with oxygen.

The formula of hydrogen carbonate, or *bicarbonate*, is written by placing a hydrogen in front of the polyatomic ion formula for carbonate (CO_3^{2-}), and the charge is decreased from 2− to 1− to give HCO_3^-.

$$H^+ + CO_3^{2-} = HCO_3^-$$

Writing Formulas for Compounds Containing Polyatomic Ions

No polyatomic ion exists by itself. Like any ion, a polyatomic ion must be associated with ions of opposite charge. The bonding between polyatomic ions and other ions is one of electrical attraction. For example, the compound sodium chlorite consists of sodium ions (Na^+) and chlorite ions (ClO_2^-) held together by ionic bonds.

To write correct formulas for compounds containing polyatomic ions, we follow the same rules of charge balance that we used for writing the formulas for simple ionic compounds. The total negative and positive charges must equal zero. For example, consider the formula for a compound containing sodium ions and chlorite ions. The ions are written as

$$Na^+ \qquad ClO_2^-$$

Sodium ion   Chlorite ion

Ionic charge: $(1+) + (1-) = 0$

Because one ion of each balances the charge, the formula is written as

$$NaClO_2$$

Sodium chlorite

When more than one polyatomic ion is needed for charge balance, parentheses are used to enclose the formula of the ion. A subscript is written outside the right parenthesis

Sodium chlorite is used in the processing and bleaching of pulp from wood fibers and recycled cardboard.

of the polyatomic ion to indicate the number needed for charge balance. Consider the formula for magnesium nitrate. The ions in this compound are the magnesium ion and the nitrate ion, a polyatomic ion.

$$Mg^{2+} \qquad NO_3^-$$

Magnesium ion   Nitrate ion

To balance the positive charge of 2+ on the magnesium ion, two nitrate ions are needed. In the formula of the compound, parentheses are placed around the nitrate ion, and the subscript 2 is written outside the right parenthesis.

$$NO_3^-$$

$$Mg^{2+}$$

$$NO_3^-$$

$$(2+) + 2(1-) = 0$$

Magnesium nitrate

$$Mg(NO_3)_2$$

Parentheses enclose the formula of the nitrate ion

Subscript outside the parenthesis indicates the use of two nitrate ions

---

> **SAMPLE PROBLEM 6.7** Writing Formulas Containing Polyatomic Ions

An antacid called Amphojel contains aluminum hydroxide, which treats acid indigestion and heartburn. Write the formula for aluminum hydroxide.

SOLUTION

STEP **1** Identify the cation and polyatomic ion (anion).

Cation	Polyatomic Ion (anion)
aluminum	hydroxide
Al^{3+}	OH^-

STEP **2** Balance the charges.

$$Al^{3+} \qquad OH^-$$
$$OH^-$$
$$OH^-$$
$$\overline{1(3+) \; + \; 3(1-) = 0}$$
$$\uparrow$$

Becomes a subscript in the formula

STEP **3** Write the formula, cation first, using the subscripts from charge balance. The formula for the compound is written by enclosing the formula of the hydroxide ion, OH^-, in parentheses and writing the subscript 3 outside the right parenthesis.

$$Al(OH)_3$$

STUDY CHECK 6.7

Write the formula for a compound containing ammonium ions and phosphate ions.

ANSWER

$(NH_4)_3PO_4$

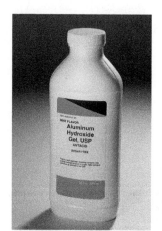

Aluminum hydroxide is an antacid used to treat acid indigestion.

Guide to Writing Formulas with Polyatomic Ions

STEP **1**
Identify the cation and polyatomic ion (anion).

STEP **2**
Balance the charges.

STEP **3**
Write the formula, cation first, using the subscripts from charge balance.

Naming Ionic Compounds Containing Polyatomic Ions

When naming ionic compounds containing polyatomic ions, we first write the positive ion, usually a metal, and then we write the name for the polyatomic ion. It is important that you learn to recognize the polyatomic ion in the formula and name it correctly. As with other ionic compounds, no prefixes are used.

Na_2SO_4 $FePO_4$ $Al_2(CO_3)_3$

Na_2 $\boxed{SO_4}$ Fe $\boxed{PO_4}$ $Al_2(\boxed{CO_3})_3$

Sodium sulfate   Iron(III) phosphate   Aluminum carbonate

Table 6.8 lists the formulas and names of some ionic compounds that include polyatomic ions and also gives their uses in medicine and industry.

TABLE 6.8 Some Ionic Compounds That Contain Polyatomic Ions

Formula	Name	Medical Use
$BaSO_4$	Barium sulfate	Contrast medium for X-rays
$CaCO_3$	Calcium carbonate	Antacid, calcium supplement
$Ca_3(PO_4)_2$	Calcium phosphate	Calcium dietary supplement
$CaSO_4$	Calcium sulfate	Plaster casts
$AgNO_3$	Silver nitrate	Topical anti-infective
$NaHCO_3$	Sodium bicarbonate or sodium hydrogen carbonate	Antacid
$Zn_3(PO_4)_2$	Zinc phosphate	Dental cement
K_2CO_3	Potassium carbonate	Alkalizer, diuretic
$Al_2(SO_4)_3$	Aluminum sulfate	Antiperspirant, anti-infective
$AlPO_4$	Aluminum phosphate	Antacid
$MgSO_4$	Magnesium sulfate	Cathartic, Epsom salts

A solution of Epsom salts, magnesium sulfate, $MgSO_4$, may be used to soothe sore muscles.

▶ **SAMPLE PROBLEM 6.8** Naming Compounds Containing Polyatomic Ions

Name the following ionic compounds:

a. $Cu(NO_2)_2$ **b.** $KClO_3$

SOLUTION

	STEP 1		STEP 2	STEP 3	STEP 4
Formula	Cation	Anion	Name of Cation	Name of Anion	Name of Compound
a. $Cu(NO_2)_2$	Cu^{2+}	NO_2^-	Copper(II) ion	Nitrite ion	Copper(II) nitrite
b. $KClO_3$	K^+	ClO_3^-	Potassium ion	Chlorate ion	Potassium chlorate

STUDY CHECK 6.8

What is the name of $Co_3(PO_4)_2$?

ANSWER

cobalt(II) phosphate

Guide to Naming Ionic Compounds with Polyatomic Ions

STEP **1**
Identify the cation and polyatomic ion (anion).

STEP **2**
Name the cation using a Roman numeral, if needed.

STEP **3**
Name the polyatomic ion.

STEP **4**
Write the name for the compound, cation first and the polyatomic ion second.

QUESTIONS AND PROBLEMS

6.4 Polyatomic Ions

LEARNING GOAL Write the name and formula for an ionic compound containing a polyatomic ion.

6.31 Write the formula including the charge for each of the following polyatomic ions:
  a. hydrogen carbonate (bicarbonate) **b.** ammonium
  c. phosphite **d.** chlorate

6.32 Write the formula including the charge for each of the following polyatomic ions:
  a. nitrite **b.** sulfite
  c. hydroxide **d.** acetate

6.33 Name the following polyatomic ions:
  a. SO_4^{2-} **b.** CO_3^{2-} **c.** HSO_3^- **d.** NO_3^-

6.34 Name the following polyatomic ions:
  a. OH^- **b.** PO_4^{3-} **c.** CN^- **d.** NO_2^-

6.35 Complete the following table with the formula and name of the compound that forms between each pair of ions:

	NO_2^-	CO_3^{2-}	HSO_4^-	PO_4^{3-}
Li^+				
Cu^{2+}				
Ba^{2+}				

6.36 Complete the following table with the formula and name of the compound that forms between each pair of ions:

	NO_3^-	HCO_3^-	SO_3^{2-}	HPO_4^{2-}
NH_4^+				
Al^{3+}				
Pb^{4+}				

6.37 Write the correct formula for the following ionic compounds:
  a. barium hydroxide **b.** sodium hydrogen sulfate
  c. iron(II) nitrite **d.** zinc phosphate
  e. iron(III) carbonate

6.38 Write the correct formula for the following ionic compounds:
  a. aluminum chlorate **b.** ammonium oxide
  c. magnesium bicarbonate **d.** sodium nitrite
  e. copper(I) sulfate

6.39 Write the formula for the polyatomic ion and name each of the following compounds:
  a. Na_2CO_3 **b.** $(NH_4)_2S$
  c. $Ba_3(PO_4)_2$ **d.** $Sn(NO_2)_2$

6.40 Write the formula for the polyatomic ion and name each of the following compounds:
  a. $MnCO_3$ **b.** Au_2SO_4
  c. $Mg_3(PO_4)_2$ **d.** $Fe(HCO_3)_3$

Clinical Applications

6.41 Name each of the following ionic compounds:
  a. $Zn(C_2H_3O_2)_2$, cold remedy
  b. $Mg_3(PO_4)_2$, antacid
  c. NH_4Cl, expectorant
  d. $NaHCO_3$, corrects pH imbalance

6.42 Name each of the following ionic compounds:
  a. Li_2CO_3, antidepressant
  b. $MgSO_4$, Epsom salts
  c. $NaClO$, disinfectant
  d. Na_3PO_4, laxative

LEARNING GOAL

Given the formula of a molecular compound, write its correct name; given the name of a molecular compound, write its formula.

CORE CHEMISTRY SKILL

Writing the Names and Formulas for Molecular Compounds

6.5 Molecular Compounds: Sharing Electrons

A **molecular compound** contains two or more nonmetals that form *covalent bonds*. Because nonmetals have high ionization energies, valence electrons are shared by nonmetal atoms to achieve stability. When atoms share electrons, the bond is a **covalent bond**. When two or more atoms share electrons, they form a **molecule**.

Names and Formulas of Molecular Compounds

When naming a molecular compound, the first nonmetal in the formula is named by its element name; the second nonmetal is named using the first syllable of its element name, followed by *ide*. When a subscript indicates two or more atoms of an element, a prefix is shown in front of its name. Table 6.9 lists prefixes used in naming molecular compounds.

The names of molecular compounds need prefixes because several different compounds can be formed from the same two nonmetals. For example, carbon and oxygen can form two different compounds, carbon monoxide, CO, and carbon dioxide, CO_2, in which the number of atoms of oxygen in each compound is indicated by the prefixes *mono* or *di* in their names.

When the vowels *o* and *o* or *a* and *o* appear together, the first vowel is omitted, as in carbon monoxide. In the name of a molecular compound, the prefix *mono* is usually omitted, as in NO, nitrogen oxide. Traditionally, however, CO is named carbon monoxide. Table 6.10 lists the formulas, names, and commercial uses of some molecular compounds.

TABLE 6.9 Prefixes Used in Naming Molecular Compounds

1 mono	6 hexa
2 di	7 hepta
3 tri	8 octa
4 tetra	9 nona
5 penta	10 deca

TABLE 6.10 Some Common Molecular Compounds

Formula	Name	Commercial Uses
CS_2	Carbon disulfide	Manufacture of rayon
CO_2	Carbon dioxide	Fire extinguishers, dry ice, propellant in aerosols, carbonation of beverages
NO	Nitrogen oxide	Stabilizer, biochemical messenger in cells
N_2O	Dinitrogen oxide	Inhalation anesthetic, "laughing gas"
SO_2	Sulfur dioxide	Preserving fruits, vegetables; disinfectant in breweries; bleaching textiles
SO_3	Sulfur trioxide	Manufacture of explosives
SF_6	Sulfur hexafluoride	Electrical circuits

▶ **SAMPLE PROBLEM 6.9** **Naming Molecular Compounds**

Name the molecular compound NCl_3.

SOLUTION

ANALYZE THE PROBLEM	Given	Need
	NCl_3	name

STEP 1 Name the first nonmetal by its element name. In NCl_3, the first nonmetal (N) is nitrogen.

Symbol of Element	N	Cl
Name	nitrogen	chloride
Subscript	1	3
Prefix	none	tri

STEP 2 Name the second nonmetal by using the first syllable of its element name followed by *ide*. The second nonmetal (Cl) is named chloride.

STEP 3 Add prefixes to indicate the number of atoms (subscripts). Because there is one nitrogen atom, no prefix is needed. The subscript 3 for the Cl atoms is shown as the prefix *tri*. The name of NCl_3 is nitrogen trichloride.

STUDY CHECK 6.9

Write the name for each of the following molecular compounds:

a. $SiBr_4$

b. Br_2O

ANSWER

a. silicon tetrabromide

b. dibromine oxide

> **Guide to Naming Molecular Compounds**
>
> **STEP 1**
> Name the first nonmetal by its element name.
>
> **STEP 2**
> Name the second nonmetal by using the first syllable of its element name followed by *ide*.
>
> **STEP 3**
> Add prefixes to indicate the number of atoms (subscripts).

Writing Formulas from the Names of Molecular Compounds

In the name of a molecular compound, the names of two nonmetals are given along with prefixes for the number of atoms of each. To write the formula from the name, we use the symbol for each element and a subscript if a prefix indicates two or more atoms.

> **SAMPLE PROBLEM 6.10** Writing Formulas for Molecular Compounds

Write the formula for the molecular compound diboron trioxide.

SOLUTION

ANALYZE THE PROBLEM	Given	Need
	diboron trioxide	formula

Guide to Writing Formulas for Molecular Compounds

STEP 1
Write the symbols in the order of the elements in the name.

STEP 2
Write any prefixes as subscripts.

STEP 1 Write the symbols in the order of the elements in the name.

Name of Element	boron	oxygen
Symbol of Element	B	O
Subscript	2 (di)	3 (tri)

STEP 2 Write any prefixes as subscripts. The prefix *di* in *di*boron indicates that there are two atoms of boron, shown as a subscript 2 in the formula. The prefix *tri* in *tri*oxide indicates that there are three atoms of oxygen, shown as a subscript 3 in the formula.

$$B_2O_3$$

STUDY CHECK 6.10

Write the formula for the molecular compound iodine pentafluoride.

ANSWER

IF_5

Summary of Naming Ionic and Molecular Compounds

We have now examined strategies for naming ionic and molecular compounds. In general, compounds having two elements are named by stating the first element name followed by the name of the second element with an *ide* ending. If the first element is a metal, the compound is usually ionic; if the first element is a nonmetal, the compound is usually molecular. For ionic compounds, it is necessary to determine whether the metal can form more than one type of positive ion; if so, a Roman numeral following the name of the metal indicates the particular ionic charge. One exception is the ammonium ion, NH_4^+, which is also written first as a positively charged polyatomic ion. Ionic compounds having three or more elements include some type of polyatomic ion. They are named by ionic rules but have an *ate* or *ite* ending when the polyatomic ion has a negative charge.

In naming molecular compounds having two elements, prefixes are necessary to indicate two or more atoms of each nonmetal as shown in that particular formula (see Figure 6.4).

> **SAMPLE PROBLEM 6.11** Naming Ionic and Molecular Compounds

Identify each of the following compounds as ionic or molecular and give its name:

a. K_3P **b.** $NiSO_4$ **c.** SO_3

SOLUTION

a. K_3P, consisting of a metal and a nonmetal, is an ionic compound. As a representative element in Group 1A (1), K forms the potassium ion, K^+. Phosphorus, as a representative element in Group 5A (15), forms a phosphide ion, P^{3-}. Writing the name of the cation followed by the name of the anion gives the name potassium phosphide.

b. NiSO$_4$, consisting of a cation of a transition element and a polyatomic ion SO$_4^{2-}$, is an ionic compound. As a transition element, Ni forms more than one type of ion. In this formula, the 2− charge of SO$_4^{2-}$ is balanced by one nickel ion, Ni^{2+}. In the name, a Roman numeral written after the metal name, nickel(II), specifies the 2+ charge. The anion SO$_4^{2-}$ is a polyatomic ion named sulfate. The compound is named nickel(II) sulfate.

c. SO$_3$ consists of two nonmetals, which indicates that it is a molecular compound. The first element S is sulfur (no prefix is needed). The second element O, oxide, has subscript 3, which requires a prefix *tri* in the name. The compound is named sulfur trioxide.

STUDY CHECK 6.11

What is the name of Fe(NO$_3$)$_3$?

ANSWER

iron(III) nitrate

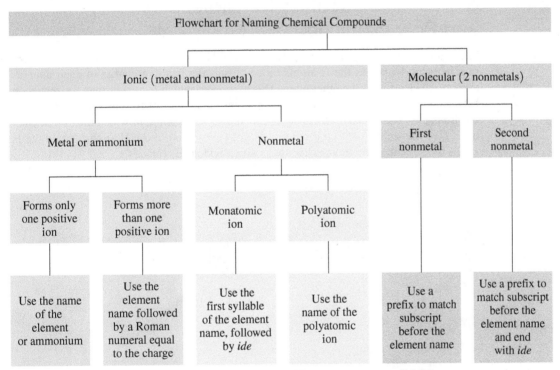

Flowchart for Naming Chemical Compounds

- **Ionic (metal and nonmetal)**
  - **Metal or ammonium**
    - Forms only one positive ion → Use the name of the element or ammonium
    - Forms more than one positive ion → Use the element name followed by a Roman numeral equal to the charge
  - **Nonmetal**
    - Monatomic ion → Use the first syllable of the element name, followed by *ide*
    - Polyatomic ion → Use the name of the polyatomic ion
- **Molecular (2 nonmetals)**
  - First nonmetal → Use a prefix to match subscript before the element name
  - Second nonmetal → Use a prefix to match subscript before the element name and end with *ide*

FIGURE 6.4 ▶ A flowchart illustrates naming for ionic and molecular compounds.

○ Why are the names of some metal ions followed by a Roman numeral in the name of a compound?

QUESTIONS AND PROBLEMS

6.5 Molecular Compounds: Sharing Electrons

LEARNING GOAL Given the formula of a molecular compound, write its correct name; given the name of a molecular compound, write its formula.

6.43 Name each of the following molecular compounds:
    a. PBr$_3$ **b.** Cl$_2$O   **c.** CBr$_4$ **d.** HF   **e.** NF$_3$

6.44 Name each of the following molecular compounds:
    a. CS$_2$ **b.** P$_2$O$_5$ **c.** SiO$_2$ **d.** PCl$_3$ **e.** CO

6.45 Name each of the following molecular compounds:
    a. N$_2$O$_3$ **b.** Si$_2$Br$_6$ **c.** P$_4$S$_3$ **d.** PCl$_5$ **e.** SeF$_6$

6.46 Name each of the following molecular compounds:
    a. SiF$_4$ **b.** IBr$_3$ **c.** CO$_2$ **d.** N$_2$F$_2$ **e.** N$_2$S$_3$

6.47 Write the formula for each of the following molecular compounds:
    a. carbon tetrachloride   **b.** carbon monoxide
    c. phosphorus trichloride   **d.** dinitrogen tetroxide

6.48 Write the formula for each of the following molecular compounds:
    a. sulfur dioxide
    b. silicon tetrachloride
    c. iodine trifluoride
    d. dinitrogen oxide

6.49 Write the formula for each of the following molecular compounds:
    a. oxygen difluoride
    b. boron trichloride
    c. dinitrogen trioxide
    d. sulfur hexafluoride

6.50 Write the formula for each of the following molecular compounds:
    a. sulfur dibromide
    b. carbon disulfide
    c. tetraphosphorus hexoxide
    d. dinitrogen pentoxide

℞ Clinical Applications

6.51 Name each of the following ionic or molecular compounds:
    a. $Al_2(SO_4)_3$, antiperspirant
    b. $CaCO_3$, antacid
    c. N_2O, "laughing gas," inhaled anesthetic
    d. $Mg(OH)_2$, laxative

6.52 Name each of the following ionic or molecular compounds:
    a. $Al(OH)_3$, antacid
    b. $FeSO_4$, iron supplement in vitamins
    c. NO, vasodilator
    d. $Cu(OH)_2$, fungicide

LEARNING GOAL

Draw the Lewis structures for molecular compounds or polyatomic ions.

6.6 Lewis Structures for Molecules and Polyatomic Ions

The simplest molecule is hydrogen, H_2. When two H atoms are far apart, there is no attraction between them. As the H atoms move closer, the positive charge of each nucleus attracts the electron of the other atom. This attraction, which is greater than the repulsion between the valence electrons, pulls the H atoms closer until they share a pair of valence electrons (see Figure 6.5). The result is called a *covalent bond*, in which the shared electrons give the stable electron configuration of He to *each* of the H atoms. When the H atoms form H_2, they are more stable than two individual H atoms.

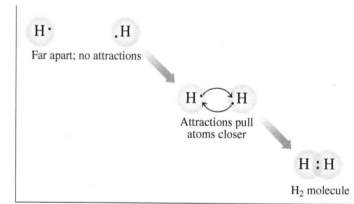

FIGURE 6.5 ▶ A covalent bond forms as H atoms move close together to share electrons.

Q What determines the attraction between two H atoms?

The elements hydrogen, nitrogen, oxygen, fluorine, chlorine, bromine, and iodine exist as diatomic molecules.

Lewis Structures for Molecular Compounds

A molecule is represented by a **Lewis structure** in which the valence electrons of all the atoms are arranged to give octets except two electrons for hydrogen. The shared electrons, or *bonding pairs*, are shown as two dots or a single line between atoms. The nonbonding pairs of electrons, or *lone pairs*, are placed on the outside. For example, a fluorine molecule, F_2, consists of two fluorine atoms, which are in Group 7A (17), each with seven valence electrons. In the Lewis structure of the F_2 molecule, each F atom achieves an octet by sharing its unpaired valence electron.

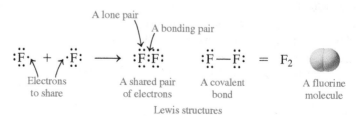

Hydrogen (H_2) and fluorine (F_2) are examples of nonmetal elements whose natural state is diatomic; that is, they contain two like atoms. The elements that exist as diatomic molecules are listed in Table 6.11.

Sharing Electrons Between Atoms of Different Elements

The number of electrons that a nonmetal atom shares and the number of covalent bonds it forms are usually equal to the number of electrons it needs to achieve a stable electron configuration. Table 6.12 gives the most typical bonding patterns for some nonmetals.

TABLE 6.11 Elements That Exist as Diatomic Molecules

Diatomic Molecule	Name
H_2	Hydrogen
N_2	Nitrogen
O_2	Oxygen
F_2	Fluorine
Cl_2	Chlorine
Br_2	Bromine
I_2	Iodine

TABLE 6.12 Typical Bonding Patterns of Some Nonmetals

1A (1)	3A (13)	4A (14)	5A (15)	6A (16)	7A (17)
*H 1 bond					
	*B 3 bonds	C 4 bonds	N 3 bonds	O 2 bonds	F 1 bond
		Si 4 bonds	P 3 bonds	S 2 bonds	Cl, Br, I 1 bond

*H and B do not form octets. H atoms share one electron pair; B atoms share three electron pairs for a set of six electrons.

Drawing Lewis Structures

To draw the Lewis structure for CH_4, we first draw the Lewis symbols for carbon and hydrogen.

$$\cdot \overset{\displaystyle \cdot}{\underset{\displaystyle \cdot}{C}} \cdot \qquad \cdot H$$

Then we can determine the number of valence electrons needed for carbon and hydrogen. When a carbon atom shares its four electrons with four hydrogen atoms, carbon obtains an octet and each hydrogen atom is complete with two shared electrons. The Lewis structure is drawn with the carbon atom as the central atom, with the hydrogen atoms on each of the sides. The bonding pairs of electrons, which are single covalent bonds, may also be shown as single lines between the carbon atom and each of the hydrogen atoms.

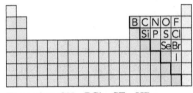

Examples: CH_4, PCl_3, SF_2, HBr

The number of covalent bonds that a nonmetal atom forms is usually equal to the number of electrons it needs to achieve a stable electron configuration.

⚛ **CORE CHEMISTRY SKILL**

Drawing Lewis Structures

TABLE 6.13 Lewis Structures for Some Molecular Compounds

CH_4	NH_3	H_2O
Lewis Structures		
H H:C:H H	H:N:H H	:O:H H
Formulas Using Bonds and Electron Dots		
H H—C—H H	H—N—H H	:O—H H
Molecular Models		

Methane molecule | Ammonia molecule | Water molecule

H

H:C:H

H

        H
        |
H — C — H
        |
        H

Table 6.13 gives the formulas and three-dimensional models of some molecules.

When we draw a Lewis structure for a molecule or polyatomic ion, we show the sequence of atoms, the bonding pairs of electrons shared between atoms, and the nonbonding or *lone pairs* of electrons. From the formula, we identify the central atom, which is the element that has the fewer atoms. Then, the central atom is bonded to the other atoms, as shown in Sample Problem 6.12.

▶ **SAMPLE PROBLEM 6.12** Drawing Lewis Structures

Draw the Lewis structure for PCl_3, phosphorus trichloride, used commercially to prepare insecticides and flame retardants.

SOLUTION

STEP **1** Determine the arrangement of atoms. In PCl_3, the central atom is P because there is only one P atom.

$$Cl \quad P \quad Cl$$
$$Cl$$

STEP **2** Determine the total number of valence electrons. We use the group number to determine the number of valence electrons for each of the atoms in the molecule.

Element	Group	Atoms		Valence Electrons	=	Total
P	5A (15)	1 P	×	$5\,e^-$	=	$5\,e^-$
Cl	7A (17)	3 Cl	×	$7\,e^-$	=	$21\,e^-$
		Total valence electrons for PCl_3			=	$26\,e^-$

STEP **3** Attach each bonded atom to the central atom with a pair of electrons. Each bonding pair can also be represented by a bond line.

$$Cl\!:\!P\!:\!Cl \quad \text{or} \quad Cl-P-Cl$$
$$Cl \quad\quad\quad\quad\quad Cl$$

STEP **4** Place the remaining electrons using single or multiple bonds to complete the octets. Six electrons ($3 \times 2\,e^-$) are used to bond the central P atom to three Cl atoms. Twenty valence electrons are left.

$$26 \text{ valence } e^- - 6 \text{ bonding } e^- = 20\,e^- \text{ remaining}$$

We use the remaining 20 electrons as lone pairs, which are placed around the outer Cl atoms and on the P atom, such that all the atoms have octets.

$$:\!\ddot{C}l\!:\!P\!:\!\ddot{C}l\!: \quad \text{or} \quad :\!\ddot{C}l\!-\!\ddot{P}\!-\!\ddot{C}l\!:$$
$$:\!\ddot{C}l\!: \quad\quad\quad\quad\quad :\!\ddot{C}l\!:$$

STUDY CHECK 6.12

Draw the Lewis structure for Cl_2O.

ANSWER

$$:\!\ddot{C}l\!:\!\ddot{O}\!:\!\ddot{C}l\!: \quad \text{or} \quad :\!\ddot{C}l\!-\!\ddot{O}\!-\!\ddot{C}l\!:$$

Guide to Drawing Lewis Structures

STEP 1
Determine the arrangement of atoms.

STEP 2
Determine the total number of valence electrons.

STEP 3
Attach each bonded atom to the central atom with a pair of electrons.

STEP 4
Place the remaining electrons using single or multiple bonds to complete octets (two for H).

The ball-and-stick model of PCl_3 consists of P and Cl atoms connected by single bonds.

▶ SAMPLE PROBLEM 6.13 **Drawing Lewis Structures for Polyatomic Ions**

Sodium chlorite, $NaClO_2$, is a component of mouthwashes, toothpastes, and contact lens cleaning solutions. Draw the Lewis structure for the chlorite ion, ClO_2^-.

SOLUTION

STEP **1** Determine the arrangement of atoms. For the polyatomic ion ClO_2^-, the central atom is Cl because there is only one Cl atom. For a polyatomic ion, the atoms and electrons are placed in brackets, and the charge is written outside to the upper right.

$$\left[O \quad Cl \quad O \right]^-$$

STEP **2** Determine the total number of valence electrons. We use the group numbers to determine the number of valence electrons for each of the atoms in the ion. Because the ion has a negative charge, one more electron is added to the valence electrons.

Element	Group	Atoms	Valence Electrons	=	Total
O	6A (16)	2 O	× 6 e^-	=	12 e^-
Cl	7A (17)	1 Cl	× 7 e^-	=	7 e^-
Ionic charge (negative) add			1 e^-	=	1 e^-
	Total valence electrons for ClO_2^-			=	20 e^-

STEP **3** Attach each bonded atom to the central atom with a pair of electrons. Each bonding pair can also be represented by a line, which indicates a single bond.

$$\left[O:Cl:O \right]^- \quad \text{or} \quad \left[O - Cl - O \right]^-$$

STEP **4** Place the remaining electrons using single or multiple bonds to complete the octets. Four electrons are used to bond the O atoms to the central Cl atom, which leaves 16 valence electrons. Of these, 12 electrons are drawn as lone pairs to complete the octets of the O atoms.

$$\left[:\ddot{O}:Cl:\ddot{O}: \right]^- \quad \text{or} \quad \left[:\ddot{O} - Cl - \ddot{O}: \right]^-$$

The remaining four electrons are placed as two lone pairs on the central Cl atom.

$$\left[:\ddot{O}:\ddot{Cl}:\ddot{O}: \right]^- \quad \text{or} \quad \left[:\ddot{O} - \ddot{Cl} - \ddot{O}: \right]^-$$

In ClO_2^-, the central Cl atom is bonded to two O atoms.

STUDY CHECK 6.13

Draw the Lewis structure for the polyatomic ion NH_2^-.

ANSWER

$$\left[H:\ddot{N}:H \right]^- \quad \text{or} \quad \left[H - \ddot{N} - H \right]^-$$

Double and Triple Bonds

Up to now, we have looked at bonding in molecules having only single bonds. In many molecular compounds, atoms share two or three pairs of electrons to complete their octets.

Double and triple bonds form when the number of valence electrons is not enough to complete the octets of all the atoms in the molecule. Then one or more lone pairs of electrons from the atoms attached to the central atom are shared with the central atom. A **double bond** occurs when two pairs of electrons are shared; in a **triple bond**, three pairs of electrons are shared. Atoms of carbon, oxygen, nitrogen, and sulfur are most likely to form multiple bonds.

Atoms of hydrogen and the halogens do not form double or triple bonds. The process of drawing a Lewis structure with multiple bonds is shown in Sample Problem 6.14.

▶**SAMPLE PROBLEM 6.14** Drawing Lewis Structures with Multiple Bonds

Draw the Lewis structure for carbon dioxide, CO_2, in which the central atom is C.

SOLUTION

STEP **1** Determine the arrangement of atoms. O C O

STEP **2** Determine the total number of valence electrons. Using the group number to determine valence electrons, the carbon atom has four valence electrons, and each oxygen atom has six valence electrons, which gives a total of 16 valence electrons.

Element	Group	Atoms	Valence Electrons	=	Total
C	4A (14)	1 C	× 4 e^-	=	4 e^-
O	6A (16)	2 O	× 6 e^-	=	12 e^-
		Total valence electrons for CO_2		=	16 e^-

STEP **3** Attach each bonded atom to the central atom with a pair of electrons.

$$\text{O:C:O} \quad \text{or} \quad \text{O—C—O}$$

STEP **4** Place the remaining electrons to complete octets. Because we used four valence electrons to attach the C atom to two O atoms, there are 12 valence electrons remaining.

$$16 \text{ valence } e^- - 4 \text{ bonding } e^- = 12 \text{ } e^- \text{ remaining}$$

The 12 remaining electrons are placed as six lone pairs of electrons on the outside O atoms. However, this does not complete the octet of the C atom.

$$\text{:Ö:C:Ö:} \quad \text{or} \quad \text{:Ö—C—Ö:}$$

To obtain an octet, the C atom must share lone pairs of electrons from each of the O atoms. When two bonding pairs occur between atoms, it is known as a double bond.

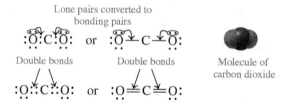

Lone pairs converted to bonding pairs

:Ö:C:Ö: or   :Ö⤴C⤴Ö:

Double bonds   Double bonds

:O::C::O: or   :O=C=O:

Molecule of carbon dioxide

STUDY CHECK 6.14

Draw the Lewis structure for HCN, which has a triple bond.

ANSWER

H:C⋮⋮N: or   H—C≡N:

Exceptions to the Octet Rule

Although the octet rule is useful for bonding in many compounds, there are exceptions. We have already seen that a hydrogen (H_2) molecule requires just two electrons or a single bond. Usually the nonmetals form octets. However, in BCl_3, the B atom has only three valence electrons to share. Boron compounds typically have six valence electrons on the central B atoms and form just three bonds. Although we will generally see compounds of P, S, Cl, Br, and I with octets, they can form molecules in which they share more of their valence electrons. This expands their valence electrons to 10, 12, or even 14 electrons. For example, we have seen that the P atom in PCl_3 has an octet, but in PCl_5, the P atom has five bonds with 10 valence electrons. In H_2S, the S atom has an octet, but in SF_6, there are six bonds to sulfur with 12 valence electrons.

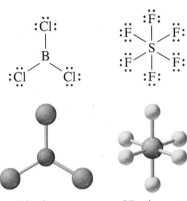

In BCl_3, the central B atom is bonded to three Cl atoms.

In SF_6, the central S atom is bonded to six F atoms.

QUESTIONS AND PROBLEMS

6.6 Lewis Structures for Molecules and Polyatomic Ions

LEARNING GOAL Draw the Lewis structures for molecular compounds or polyatomic ions.

6.53 Determine the total number of valence electrons for each of the following:
  a. H_2S **b.** I_2 **c.** CCl_4 **d.** OH^-

6.54 Determine the total number of valence electrons for each of the following:
  a. SBr_2 **b.** NBr_3 **c.** CH_3OH **d.** NH_4^+

6.55 Draw the Lewis structure for each of the following molecules or ions:
  a. HF   **b.** SF_2 **c.** NBr_3 **d.** BH_4^-

6.56 Draw the Lewis structure for each of the following molecules or ions:
  a. H_2O **b.** CCl_4 **c.** H_3O^+ **d.** SiF_4

6.57 When is it necessary to draw a multiple bond in a Lewis structure?

6.58 If the available number of valence electrons for a molecule or polyatomic ion does not complete all of the octets in a Lewis structure, what should you do?

6.59 Draw the Lewis structure for each of the following molecules or ions:
  a. CO
  b. NO_3^- (N is the central atom)
  c. H_2CO (C is the central atom)

6.60 Draw the Lewis structure for each of the following molecules or ions:
  a. HCCH (ethyne)
  b. CS_2
  c. NO^+

6.7 Electronegativity and Bond Polarity

We can learn more about the chemistry of compounds by looking at how bonding electrons are shared between atoms. The bonding electrons are shared equally in a bond between identical nonmetal atoms. However, when a bond is between atoms of different elements, the electron pairs are usually shared unequally. Then the shared pairs of electrons are attracted to one atom in the bond more than the other.

The **electronegativity** of an atom is its ability to attract the shared electrons in a chemical bond. Nonmetals have higher electronegativities than do metals, because nonmetals have a greater attraction for electrons than metals. On the electronegativity scale, fluorine was assigned a value of 4.0, and the electronegativities for all other elements were determined relative to the attraction of fluorine for shared electrons. The nonmetal fluorine, which has the highest electronegativity (4.0), is located in the upper right corner of the periodic table. The metal cesium, which has the lowest electronegativity (0.7), is located in the lower left corner of the periodic table. The electronegativities for the representative elements are shown in Figure 6.6. Note that there are no electronegativity values for the noble gases because they do not typically form bonds. The electronegativity values for transition elements are also low, but we have not included them in our discussion.

LEARNING GOAL

Use electronegativity to determine the polarity of a bond.

⚛ CORE CHEMISTRY SKILL

Using Electronegativity

FIGURE 6.6 ▶ The electro-
negativity values of representative
elements in Group 1A (1) to Group
7A (17), which indicate the ability
of atoms to attract shared
electrons, increase going across a
period from left to right and
decrease going down a group.

🔍 What element on the periodic table has the strongest
attraction for shared
electrons?

Electronegativity Increases

H 2.1

18
Group
8A

Electronegativity Decreases

1 Group 1A	2 Group 2A		13 Group 3A	14 Group 4A	15 Group 5A	16 Group 6A	17 Group 7A
Li 1.0	Be 1.5		B 2.0	C 2.5	N 3.0	O 3.5	F 4.0
Na 0.9	Mg 1.2		Al 1.5	Si 1.8	P 2.1	S 2.5	Cl 3.0
K 0.8	Ca 1.0		Ga 1.6	Ge 1.8	As 2.0	Se 2.4	Br 2.8
Rb 0.8	Sr 1.0		In 1.7	Sn 1.8	Sb 1.9	Te 2.1	I 2.5
Cs 0.7	Ba 0.9		Tl 1.8	Pb 1.9	Bi 1.9	Po 2.0	At 2.1

Polarity of Bonds

The difference in the electronegativity values of two atoms can be used to predict the type
of chemical bond, ionic or covalent, that forms. For the H—H bond, the electronegativity
difference is zero ($2.1 - 2.1 = 0$), which means the bonding electrons are shared equally.
A bond between atoms with identical or very similar electronegativity values is a **nonpolar covalent bond**. However, when bonds are between atoms with different electronegativity values, the electrons are shared unequally; the bond is a **polar covalent bond**. For
the H—Cl bond, there is an electronegativity difference of $3.0\,(Cl) - 2.1(H) = 0.9$,
which means that the H—Cl bond is polar covalent (see Figure 6.7).

FIGURE 6.7 ▶ In the nonpolar
covalent bond of H_2, electrons are
shared equally. In the polar
covalent bond of HCl, electrons are
shared unequally.

🔍 H_2 has a nonpolar covalent
bond, but HCl has a polar
covalent bond. Explain.

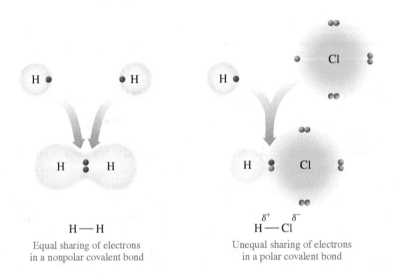

H—H
Equal sharing of electrons
in a nonpolar covalent bond

$\overset{\delta^+}{H}$—$\overset{\delta^-}{Cl}$
Unequal sharing of electrons
in a polar covalent bond

Dipoles and Bond Polarity

The **polarity** of a bond depends on the difference in the electronegativity values of its
atoms. In a polar covalent bond, the shared electrons are attracted to the more electronegative atom, which makes it partially negative, because of the negatively charged electrons

around that atom. At the other end of the bond, the atom with the lower electronegativity becomes partially positive because of the lack of electrons at that atom.

A bond becomes more *polar* as the electronegativity difference increases. A polar covalent bond that has a separation of charges is called a **dipole**. The positive and negative ends of the dipole are indicated by the lowercase Greek letter delta with a positive or negative sign, δ^+ and δ^-. Sometimes we use an arrow that points from the positive charge to the negative charge $\longmapsto$ to indicate the dipole.

Examples of Dipoles in Polar Covalent Bonds

$$\overset{\delta^+}{C}\!-\!\overset{\delta^-}{O} \qquad \overset{\delta^+}{N}\!-\!\overset{\delta^-}{O} \qquad \overset{\delta^+}{Cl}\!-\!\overset{\delta^-}{F}$$

$$\longmapsto \qquad \longmapsto \qquad \longmapsto$$

Variations in Bonding

The variations in bonding are continuous; there is no definite point at which one type of bond stops and the next starts. When the electronegativity difference is between 0.0 and 0.4, the electrons are considered to be shared equally in a *nonpolar covalent bond*. For example, the C—C bond $(2.5 - 2.5 = 0.0)$ and the C—H bond $(2.5 - 2.1 = 0.4)$ are classified as nonpolar covalent bonds. As the electronegativity difference increases, the shared electrons are attracted more strongly to the more electronegative atom, which increases the polarity of the bond. When the electronegativity difference is from 0.5 to 1.8, the bond is a *polar covalent bond*. For example, the O—H bond $(3.5 - 2.1 = 1.4)$ is classified as a polar covalent bond (see Table 6.14).

TABLE 6.14 Electronegativity Differences and Types of Bonds

Electronegativity Difference	0	0.4	1.8	3.3
Bond Type	Nonpolar covalent	Polar covalent	Ionic	
Electron Bonding	Electrons shared equally	Electrons shared unequally	Electrons transferred	

When the electronegativity difference is greater than 1.8, electrons are transferred from one atom to another, which results in an *ionic bond*. For example, the electronegativity difference for the ionic compound NaCl is $3.0 - 0.9 = 2.1$. Thus, for large differences in electronegativity, we would predict an ionic bond (see Table 6.15).

TABLE 6.15 Predicting Bond Type from Electronegativity Differences

Molecule	Bond	Type of Electron Sharing	Electronegativity Difference*	Type of Bond	Reason
H_2	H—H	Shared equally	$2.1 - 2.1 = 0.0$	Nonpolar covalent	Between 0.0 and 0.4
BrCl	Br—Cl	Shared about equally	$3.0 - 2.8 = 0.2$	Nonpolar covalent	Between 0.0 and 0.4
HBr	$\overset{\delta^+}{H}\!-\!\overset{\delta^-}{Br}$	Shared unequally	$2.8 - 2.1 = 0.7$	Polar covalent	Greater than 0.4, but less than 1.8
HCl	$\overset{\delta^+}{H}\!-\!\overset{\delta^-}{Cl}$	Shared unequally	$3.0 - 2.1 = 0.9$	Polar covalent	Greater than 0.4, but less than 1.8
NaCl	Na^+Cl^-	Electron transfer	$3.0 - 0.9 = 2.1$	Ionic	Greater than 1.8
MgO	$Mg^{2+}O^{2-}$	Electron transfer	$3.5 - 1.2 = 2.3$	Ionic	Greater than 1.8

*Values are taken from Figure 6.6.

> ▶ **SAMPLE PROBLEM 6.15 Bond Polarity**
>
> Using electronegativity values, classify each of the following bonds as nonpolar covalent, polar covalent, or ionic:
>
> O—K, Cl—As, N—N, P—Br
>
> **SOLUTION**
>
> For each bond, we obtain the electronegativity values and calculate the difference in electronegativity.
>
> | Bond | Electronegativity Difference | Type of Bond |
> |------|------------------------------|--------------|
> | O—K | $3.5 - 0.8 = 2.7$ | Ionic |
> | Cl—As | $3.0 - 2.0 = 1.0$ | Polar covalent |
> | N—N | $3.0 - 3.0 = 0.0$ | Nonpolar covalent |
> | P—Br | $2.8 - 2.1 = 0.7$ | Polar covalent |
>
> **STUDY CHECK 6.15**
>
> Using electronegativity values, classify each of the following bonds as nonpolar covalent, polar covalent, or ionic:
>
> **a.** P—Cl **b.** Br—Br **c.** Na—O
>
> **ANSWER**
>
> **a.** polar covalent (0.9) **b.** nonpolar covalent (0.0) **c.** ionic (2.6)

QUESTIONS AND PROBLEMS

6.7 Electronegativity and Bond Polarity

LEARNING GOAL Use electronegativity to determine the polarity of a bond.

6.61 Describe the trend in electronegativity as *increases* or *decreases* for each of the following:
  a. from B to F **b.** from Mg to Ba **c.** from F to I

6.62 Describe the trend in electronegativity as *increases* or *decreases* for each of the following:
  a. from Al to Cl **b.** from Br to K **c.** from Li to Cs

6.63 Using the periodic table, arrange the atoms in each of the following sets in order of increasing electronegativity:
  a. Li, Na, K **b.** Na, Cl, P **c.** Se, Ca, O

6.64 Using the periodic table, arrange the atoms in each of the following sets in order of increasing electronegativity:
  a. Cl, F, Br **b.** B, O, N **c.** Mg, F, S

6.65 Predict whether each of the following bonds is nonpolar covalent, polar covalent, or ionic:
  a. Si—Br **b.** Li—F **c.** Br—F
  d. I—I **e.** N—P **f.** C—P

6.66 Predict whether each of the following bonds is nonpolar covalent, polar covalent, or ionic:
  a. Si—O **b.** K—Cl **c.** S—F
  d. P—Br **e.** Li—O **f.** N—S

6.67 For each of the following bonds, indicate the positive end with δ^+ and the negative end with δ^-. Draw an arrow to show the dipole for each.
  a. N—F **b.** Si—Br **c.** C—O
  d. P—Br **e.** N—P

6.68 For each of the following bonds, indicate the positive end with δ^+ and the negative end with δ^-. Draw an arrow to show the dipole for each.
  a. P—Cl **b.** Se—F **c.** Br—F
  d. N—H **e.** B—Cl

LEARNING GOAL

Predict the three-dimensional structure of a molecule, and classify it as polar or nonpolar.

6.8 Shapes and Polarity of Molecules

Using the Lewis structures, we can predict the three-dimensional shapes of many molecules. The shape is important in our understanding of how molecules interact with enzymes or certain antibiotics or produce our sense of taste and smell.

The three-dimensional shape of a molecule is determined by drawing its Lewis structure and identifying the number of electron groups (one or more electron pairs) around the central atom. We count lone pairs of electrons, single, double, or triple bonds as *one* electron group. In the **valence shell electron-pair repulsion (VSEPR) theory,** the electron groups are arranged as far apart as possible around the central atom to minimize the repulsion between their negative charges. Once we have counted the number of electron groups surrounding the central atom, we can determine its specific shape from the number of atoms bonded to the central atom.

Central Atoms with Two Electron Groups

In the Lewis structure for CO_2, there are two electron groups (two double bonds) attached to the central atom. According to VSEPR theory, minimal repulsion occurs when two electron groups are on opposite sides of the central C atom. This gives the CO_2 molecule a *linear* electron-group geometry and a *linear shape* with a bond angle of 180°.

180°

:Ö=C=Ö:

Linear
electron-group
geometry

Linear shape

Central Atoms with Three Electron Groups

In the Lewis structure for formaldehyde, H_2CO, the central atom C is attached to two H atoms by single bonds and to the O atom by a double bond. Minimal repulsion occurs when three electron groups are as far apart as possible around the central C atom, which gives 120° bond angles. This type of electron-group geometry is *trigonal planar* and gives a shape for H_2CO called *trigonal planar*.

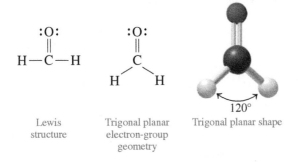

:O:
‖
H—C—H

Lewis
structure

:O:
‖
C
H   H

Trigonal planar
electron-group
geometry

120°

Trigonal planar shape

In the Lewis structure for SO_2, there are also three electron groups around the central S atom: a single bond to an O atom, a double bond to another O atom, and a lone pair of electrons. As in H_2CO, three electron groups have minimal repulsion when they form trigonal planar electron-group geometry. However, in SO_2 one of the electron groups is a lone pair of electrons. Therefore, the shape of the SO_2 molecule is determined by the two O atoms bonded to the central S atom, which gives the SO_2 molecule a *bent shape* with a bond angle of 120°. When there are one or more lone pairs on the central atom, the shape has a different name than that of the electron-group geometry.

:Ö—S̈=O:

Lewis
structure

S̈
:O: O:

Trigonal planar
electron-group
geometry

120°

Bent shape

Central Atom with Four Electron Groups

In a molecule of methane, CH_4, the central C atom is bonded to four H atoms. From the Lewis structure, you may think that CH_4 is planar with 90° bond angles. However, the best geometry for minimal repulsion is *tetrahedral*, giving bond angles of 109°. When there are four atoms attached to four electron groups, the shape of the molecule is *tetrahedral*.

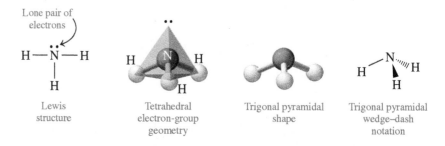

| Lewis structure | Tetrahedral electron-group geometry | Tetrahedral shape | Tetrahedral wedge–dash notation |

A way to represent the three-dimensional structure of methane is to use the wedge–dash notation. In this representation, the two bonds connecting carbon to hydrogen by solid lines are in the plane of the paper. The wedge represents a carbon-to-hydrogen bond coming out of the page toward us, whereas the dash represents a carbon-to-hydrogen bond going into the page away from us.

Now we can look at molecules that have four electron groups, of which one or more are lone pairs of electrons. Then the central atom is attached to only two or three atoms. For example, in the Lewis structure for ammonia, NH_3, four electron groups have a tetrahedral electron-group geometry. However, in NH_3 one of the electron groups is a lone pair of electrons. Therefore, the shape of NH_3 is determined by the three H atoms bonded to the central N atom. Therefore, the shape of the NH_3 molecule is *trigonal pyramidal*, with a bond angle of 109°. The wedge–dash notation can also represent this three-dimensional structure of ammonia with one N—H bond in the plane, one N—H bond coming toward us, and one N—H bond going away from us.

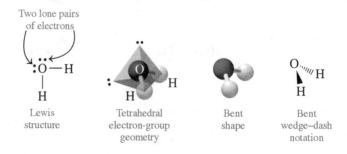

Lone pair of electrons

| Lewis structure | Tetrahedral electron-group geometry | Trigonal pyramidal shape | Trigonal pyramidal wedge–dash notation |

In the Lewis structure for water, H_2O, there are also four electron groups, which have minimal repulsion when the electron-group geometry is tetrahedral. However, in H_2O, two of the electron groups are lone pairs of electrons. Because the shape of H_2O is determined by the two H atoms bonded to the central O atom, the H_2O molecule has a *bent shape* with a bond angle of 109°. Table 6.16 gives the shapes of molecules with two, three, or four bonded atoms.

Two lone pairs of electrons

| Lewis structure | Tetrahedral electron-group geometry | Bent shape | Bent wedge–dash notation |

TABLE 6.16 Molecular Shapes for a Central Atom with Two, Three, and Four Bonded Atoms

Electron Groups	Electron-Group Geometry	Bonded Atoms	Lone Pairs	Bond Angle*	Molecular Shape	Example	Three-Dimensional Model
2	Linear	2	0	180°	Linear	CO_2	
3	Trigonal planar	3	0	120°	Trigonal planar	H_2CO	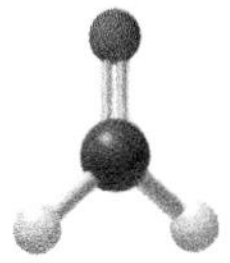
3	Trigonal planar	2	1	120°	Bent	SO_2	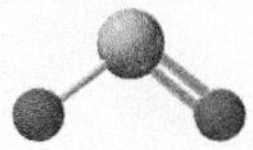
4	Tetrahedral	4	0	109°	Tetrahedral	CH_4	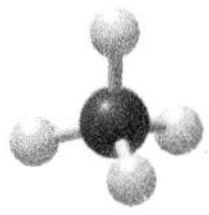
4	Tetrahedral	3	1	109°	Trigonal pyramidal	NH_3	
4	Tetrahedral	2	2	109°	Bent	H_2O	

*The bond angles in actual molecules may vary slightly.

▶ **SAMPLE PROBLEM 6.16 Shapes of Molecules**

Predict the shape of a molecule of $SiCl_4$.

SOLUTION

ANALYZE THE PROBLEM	Given	Need
	$SiCl_4$	shape

STEP 1 Draw the Lewis structure. Using $32\ e^-$, we draw the bonds and lone pairs for the Lewis structure of $SiCl_4$.

Name of Element	Silicon	Chlorine
Symbol of Element	Si	Cl
Atoms of Element	1	4
Valence Electrons	$4\ e^-$	$7\ e^-$
Total Electrons	$1(4\ e^-)$ +	$4(7\ e^-) = 32\ e^-$

$$
\begin{array}{c}
:\ddot{Cl}: \\
:\ddot{Cl}:\ddot{Si}:\ddot{Cl}: \\
:\ddot{Cl}:
\end{array}
$$

STEP 2 Arrange the electron groups around the central atom to minimize repulsion. To minimize repulsion, the electron-group geometry would be tetrahedral.

STEP 3 Use the atoms bonded to the central atom to determine the shape. Because the central Si atom has four bonded pairs and no lone pairs of electrons, the $SiCl_4$ molecule has a tetrahedral shape.

Guide to Predicting Shape (VSEPR Theory)

STEP 1
Draw the Lewis structure.

STEP 2
Arrange the electron groups around the central atom to minimize repulsion.

STEP 3
Use the atoms bonded to the central atom to determine the shape.

STUDY CHECK 6.16

Predict the shape of SCl_2.

ANSWER

The central atom S has four electron groups: two bonded atoms and two lone pairs of electrons. The shape of SCl_2 is bent, 109°.

> **SAMPLE PROBLEM 6.17 Predicting Shape of an Ion**
>
> Use VSEPR theory to predict the shape of the polyatomic ion NO_3^-.
>
> SOLUTION
>
> STEP **1** Draw the Lewis structure. The polyatomic ion, NO_3^-, contains three electron groups (two single bonds between the central N atom and O atoms, and one double bond between N and O). Note that the double bond can be drawn to any of the O atoms.
>
> $$\left[\ddot{\underset{..}{O}} - N = \ddot{O} : \atop | \atop :\underset{..}{O}: \right]^{-}$$
>
> STEP **2** Arrange the electron groups around the central atom to minimize repulsion. To minimize repulsion, three electron groups would have a trigonal planar geometry.
>
> STEP **3** Use the atoms bonded to the central atom to determine the shape. Because NO_3^- has three bonded atoms, it has a trigonal planar shape.
>
> **STUDY CHECK 6.17**
>
> Use VSEPR theory to predict the shape of ClO_2^-.
>
> ANSWER
>
> With two bonded atoms and two lone pairs of electrons, the shape of ClO_2^- is bent with a bond angle of 109°.

⊗ **CORE CHEMISTRY SKILL**

Identifying Polarity of Molecules

Polarity of Molecules

We have seen that covalent bonds in molecules can be polar or nonpolar. Now we will look at how the bonds in a molecule and its shape determine whether that molecule is classified as polar or nonpolar.

Nonpolar Molecules

In a **nonpolar molecule**, all the bonds are nonpolar or the polar bonds cancel each other out. Molecules such as H_2, Cl_2, and CH_4 are nonpolar because they contain only nonpolar covalent bonds.

$$H-H \qquad Cl-Cl \qquad H-\underset{\displaystyle |}{\overset{\displaystyle |}{C}}-H$$

Nonpolar molecules

A *nonpolar molecule* also occurs when polar bonds (dipoles) cancel each other because they are in a symmetrical arrangement. For example, CO_2, a linear molecule, contains two equal polar covalent bonds whose dipoles point in opposite directions. As a result, the dipoles cancel out, which makes a CO_2 molecule nonpolar.

O=C=O

Dipoles cancel

CO_2 is a nonpolar molecule.

Another example of a nonpolar molecule is the CCl_4 molecule, which has four polar bonds symmetrically arranged around the central C atom. Each of the C—Cl bonds has the same polarity, but because they have a tetrahedral arrangement, their opposing dipoles cancel out. As a result, a molecule of CCl_4 is nonpolar.

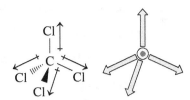

The four C—Cl dipoles cancel out.

Polar Molecules

In a **polar molecule**, one end of the molecule is more negatively charged than the other end. Polarity in a molecule occurs when the dipoles from the individual polar bonds do not cancel each other. For example, HCl is a polar molecule because it has one covalent bond that is polar.

In molecules with two or more electron groups, the shape, such as bent or trigonal pyramidal, determines whether the dipoles cancel. For example, we have seen that H_2O has a bent shape. Thus, a water molecule is polar because the individual dipoles do not cancel.

A single dipole does not cancel.

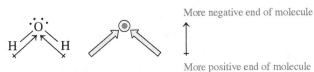

H_2O is a polar molecule because its dipoles do not cancel.

The NH_3 molecule has a tetrahedral electron-group geometry with three bonded atoms, which gives it a trigonal pyramidal shape. Thus, the NH_3 molecule is polar because the individual N—H dipoles do not cancel.

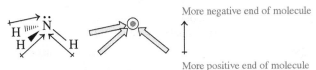

NH_3 is a polar molecule because its dipoles do not cancel.

In the molecule CH_3F, the C—F bond is polar covalent, but the three C—H bonds are nonpolar covalent. Because there is only one dipole in CH_3F, which does not cancel, CH_3F is a polar molecule.

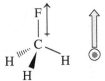

CH_3F is a polar molecule.

▶ **SAMPLE PROBLEM 6.18** **Polarity of Molecules**

Determine whether a molecule of OF_2 is polar or nonpolar.

SOLUTION

STEP 1 Determine if the bonds are polar covalent or nonpolar covalent. From Figure 6.6, F and O have an electronegativity difference of 0.5 ($4.0 - 3.5 = 0.5$), which makes each of the O—F bonds polar covalent.

STEP 2 If the bonds are polar covalent, draw the Lewis structure and determine if the dipoles cancel. The Lewis structure for OF_2 has four electron groups and two bonded atoms. The molecule has a bent shape in which the dipoles of the O—F bonds do not cancel. The OF_2 molecule would be polar.

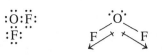

OF_2 is a polar molecule.

STUDY CHECK 6.18

Would a PCl_3 molecule be polar or nonpolar?

ANSWER

polar

Guide to Determining the Polarity of a Molecule

STEP 1
Determine if the bonds are polar covalent or nonpolar covalent.

STEP 2
If the bonds are polar covalent, draw the Lewis structure and determine if the dipoles cancel.

QUESTIONS AND PROBLEMS

6.8 Shapes and Polarity of Molecules

LEARNING GOAL Predict the three-dimensional structure of a molecule, and classify it as polar or nonpolar.

6.69 Choose the shape (**1** to **6**) that matches each of the following descriptions (**a** to **c**):

    1. linear   **2.** bent (109°)   **3.** trigonal planar
    4. bent (120°)   **5.** trigonal pyramidal   **6.** tetrahedral

    a. a molecule with a central atom that has four electron groups and four bonded atoms

    b. a molecule with a central atom that has four electron groups and three bonded atoms

    c. a molecule with a central atom that has three electron groups and three bonded atoms

6.70 Choose the shape (**1** to **6**) that matches each of the following descriptions (**a** to **c**):

    1. linear   **2.** bent (109°)   **3.** trigonal planar
    4. bent (120°)   **5.** trigonal pyramidal   **6.** tetrahedral

    a. a molecule with a central atom that has four electron groups and two bonded atoms

    b. a molecule with a central atom that has two electron groups and two bonded atoms

    c. a molecule with a central atom that has three electron groups and two bonded atoms

6.71 Complete each of the following statements for a molecule of SeO_3:

    a. There are _____ electron groups around the central Se atom.

    b. The electron-group geometry is _____.

    c. The number of atoms attached to the central Se atom is

    _____.

    d. The shape of the molecule is _____.

6.72 Complete each of the following statements for a molecule of H_2S:

    a. There are _____ electron groups around the central S atom.

    b. The electron-group geometry is _____.

    c. The number of atoms attached to the central S atom is

    _____.

    d. The shape of the molecule is _____.

6.73 Compare the Lewis structures of PH_3 and NH_3. Why do these molecules have the same shape?

6.74 Compare the Lewis structures of CH_4 and H_2O. Why do these molecules have approximately the same bond angles but different molecular shapes?

6.75 Use VSEPR theory to predict the shape of each of the following:

    a. $SeBr_2$ **b.** CCl_4 **c.** OBr_2

6.76 Use VSEPR theory to predict the shape of each of the following:

    a. NCl_3 **b.** SeO_2 **c.** SiF_2Cl_2

6.77 The molecule Cl_2 is nonpolar, but HCl is polar. Explain.

6.78 The molecules CH_4 and CH_3Cl both contain four bonds. Why is CH_4 nonpolar whereas CH_3Cl is polar?

6.79 Identify each of the following molecules as polar or nonpolar:

    a. HBr   **b.** NF_3 **c.** CHF_3

6.80 Identify each of the following molecules as polar or nonpolar:

    a. SeF_2 **b.** PBr_3 **c.** $SiCl_4$

LEARNING GOAL

Describe the attractive forces between ions, polar covalent molecules, and nonpolar covalent molecules.

⚛ CORE CHEMISTRY SKILL

Identifying Attractive Forces

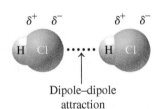

Dipole–dipole
attraction

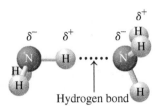

Hydrogen bond

6.9 Attractive Forces in Compounds

In gases, the interactions between particles are minimal, which allows gas molecules to move far apart from each other. In solids and liquids, there are sufficient interactions between the particles to hold them close together, although some solids have low melting points whereas others have very high melting points. Such differences in properties are explained by looking at the various kinds of attractive forces between particles including *dipole–dipole attractions, hydrogen bonding, dispersion forces*, as well as *ionic bonds*.

    Ionic compounds have high melting points. For example, solid NaCl melts at 801 °C. Large amounts of energy are needed to overcome the strong attractive forces between positive and negative ions. In solids containing molecules with covalent bonds, there are attractive forces too, but they are weaker than those of an ionic compound.

Dipole–Dipole Attractions

For polar molecules, attractive forces called **dipole–dipole attractions** occur between the positive end of one molecule and the negative end of another. For a polar molecule with a dipole such as HCl, the partially positive H atom of one HCl molecule attracts the partially negative Cl atom in another HCl molecule.

Hydrogen Bonds

Polar molecules containing hydrogen atoms bonded to highly electronegative atoms of nitrogen, oxygen, or fluorine form especially strong dipole–dipole attractions. This type of attraction, called a **hydrogen bond**, occurs between the partially positive hydrogen atom in one molecule and the partially negative fluorine, oxygen, or nitrogen atom in another molecule. Hydrogen bonds are the strongest type of attractive forces between polar covalent molecules. They are a major factor in the formation and structure of biological molecules such as proteins and DNA.

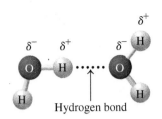

Hydrogen bond

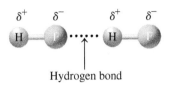

Hydrogen bond

Dispersion Forces

Nonpolar compounds do form solids, but at low temperatures. Very weak attractions called **dispersion forces** occur between nonpolar molecules. Usually, the electrons in a nonpolar covalent molecule are distributed symmetrically. However, electrons may accumulate more in one part of the molecule than another, which forms a *temporary dipole*. Although dispersion forces are very weak, they make it possible for nonpolar molecules to form liquids and solids.

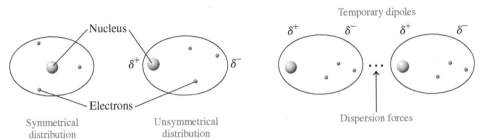

Nonpolar covalent molecules have weak attractions when they form temporary dipoles.

The melting points of substances are related to the strength of the attractive forces. Compounds with weak attractive forces, such as dispersion forces, have low melting points because only a small amount of energy is needed to separate the molecules and form a liquid. Compounds with hydrogen bonds and dipole–dipole attractions require more energy to break the attractive forces between the molecules. The highest melting points are seen with ionic compounds that have very strong attractions between ions. Table 6.17 compares the melting points of some substances with various kinds of attractive forces. The various types of attractions between particles in solids and liquids are summarized in Table 6.18.

TABLE 6.17 Melting Points of Selected Substances

Substance	Melting Point (°C)
Ionic Bonds	
MgF_2	1248
NaCl	801
Hydrogen Bonds	
H_2O	0
NH_3	−78
Dipole–Dipole Attractions	
HBr	−89
HCl	−115
Dispersion Forces	
Cl_2	−101
F_2	−220

TABLE 6.18 Comparison of Bonding and Attractive Forces

Type of Force	Particle Arrangement	Example	Strength
Between Atoms or Ions			Strong
Ionic bond		Na^+Cl^-	
Covalent bond (X = nonmetal)	X : X	Cl—Cl	
Between Molecules			
Hydrogen bond (X = F, O, or N)	$\overset{\delta^+}{H} \overset{\delta^-}{X} \cdots \overset{\delta^+}{H} \overset{\delta^-}{X}$	$H^{\delta^+}—F^{\delta^-} \cdots H^{\delta^+}—F^{\delta^-}$	
Dipole–dipole attractions (X and Y = nonmetals)	$\overset{\delta^+}{Y} \overset{\delta^-}{X} \cdots \overset{\delta^+}{Y} \overset{\delta^-}{X}$	$Br^{\delta^+}—Cl^{\delta^-} \cdots Br^{\delta^+}—Cl^{\delta^-}$	
Dispersion forces (temporary shift of electrons in nonpolar bonds)	$\overset{\delta^+}{X} : \overset{\delta^-}{X} \cdots \overset{\delta^+}{X} : \overset{\delta^-}{X}$ (temporary dipoles)	$F^{\delta^+}—F^{\delta^-} \cdots F^{\delta^+}—F^{\delta^-}$	Weak

SAMPLE PROBLEM 6.19 **Attractive Forces Between Particles**

Indicate the major type of molecular interaction—dipole–dipole attractions, hydrogen bonding, or dispersion forces—expected of each of the following:

a. HF
b. Br_2
c. PCl_3

SOLUTION

a. HF is a polar molecule that interacts with other HF molecules by hydrogen bonding.
b. Br_2 is nonpolar; only dispersion forces provide attractive forces.
c. The polarity of the PCl_3 molecules provides dipole–dipole attractions.

STUDY CHECK 6.19

Why is the melting point of H_2S lower than that of H_2O?

ANSWER

The attractive forces between H_2S molecules are dipole–dipole attractions, whereas the attractive forces between H_2O molecules are hydrogen bonds, which are stronger and require more energy to break.

Chemistry Link to Health

Attractive Forces in Biological Compounds

The proteins in our bodies are biological molecules that have many different functions. They are needed for structural components such as cartilage, muscles, hair, and nails, and for the formation of enzymes that regulate biological reactions. Other proteins, such as hemoglobin and myoglobin, transport oxygen in the blood and muscle.

Proteins are composed of building blocks called *amino acids*. Every amino acid has a central carbon atom bonded to $-NH_3^+$ from an amine, a $-COO^-$ from a carboxylic acid, an H atom, and a side chain called an R group, which is unique for each amino acid. For example, the R group for the amino acid alanine is a methyl group ($-CH_3$).

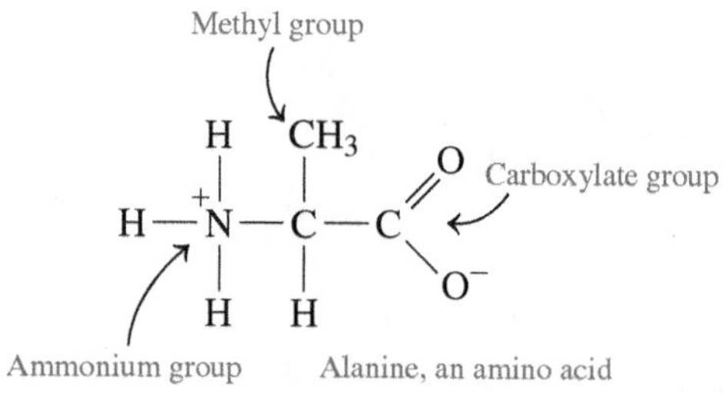

Methyl group

Alanine, an amino acid

Ammonium group   Carboxylate group

The ionized form of alanine contains $-NH_3^+$, $-COO^-$, H, and a $-CH_3$ group.

Several of the amino acids have side chains that contain groups such as hydroxyl $-OH$, amide $-CONH_2$, amine $-NH_2$, which is ionized as ammonium $-NH_3^+$, and carboxyl $-COOH$, which is ionized as carboxylate $-COO^-$.

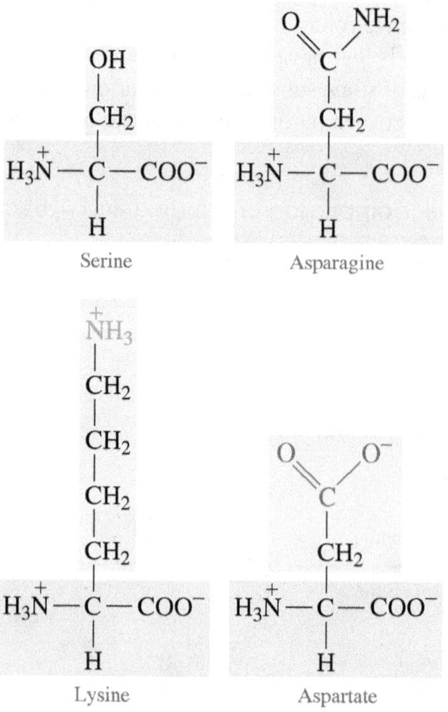

Serine

Asparagine

Lysine

Aspartate

In the primary structure of proteins, amino acids are linked together by peptide bonds, which are amide bonds that form between the —COO$^-$ group of one amino acid and the —NH$_3^+$ group of the next amino acid. When there are more than 50 amino acids in a chain, it is called a protein. Every protein in our body has a unique sequence of amino acids in a primary structure that determines its biological function. In addition, proteins have higher levels of structure. In an *alpha helix*, hydrogen bonds form between the hydrogen atom of the N—H groups and the oxygen atom of a C=O group in the next turn. Because many hydrogen bonds form, the backbone of a protein takes a helical shape similar to a corkscrew or a spiral staircase.

Shapes of Biologically Active Proteins

Many proteins have compact, spherical shapes because sections of the chain fold over on top of other sections of the chain. This shape is stabilized by attractive forces between functional groups of side chains (R groups), causing the protein to twist and bend into a specific three-dimensional shape.

Hydrogen bonds form between the side chains within the protein. For example, a hydrogen bond can occur between the —OH groups on two serines or between the —OH of a serine and the —NH$_2$ of asparagine. Hydrogen bonding also occurs between the polar side chains of the amino acids on the outer surface of the protein and —OH or —H of polar water molecules in the external aqueous environment.

Ionic bonds can form between the positively and negatively charged R groups of acidic and basic amino acids. For example, an ionic bond can form between the —NH$_3^+$ in the R group of lysine and the —COO$^-$ of aspartate.

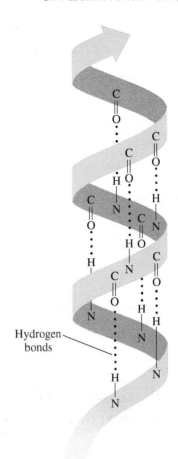

The shape of an alpha helix is stabilized by hydrogen bonds.

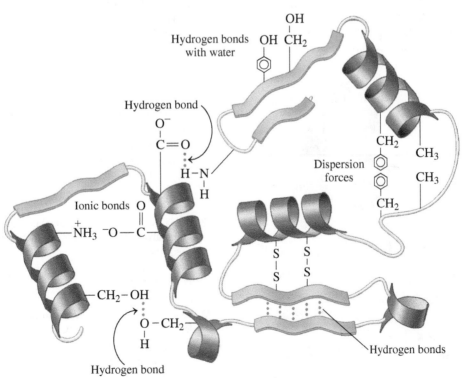

Attractive forces hold the protein in a specific shape.

QUESTIONS AND PROBLEMS

6.9 Attractive Forces in Compounds

LEARNING GOAL Describe the attractive forces between ions, polar covalent molecules, and nonpolar covalent molecules.

6.81 Identify the major type of attractive force between the particles of each of the following:
    a. BrF   **b.** KCl   **c.** NF_3 **d.** Cl_2

6.82 Identify the major type of attractive force between the particles of each of the following:
    a. HCl   **b.** MgF_2 **c.** PBr_3 **d.** NH_3

6.83 Identify the strongest attractive forces between the particles of each of the following:
    a. CH_3OH **b.** CO
    c. CF_4 **d.** $CH_3{-}CH_3$

6.84 Identify the strongest attractive forces between the particles of each of the following:
    a. O_2 **b.** SiH_4
    c. CH_3Cl **d.** H_2O_2

6.85 Identify the substance in each of the following pairs that would have the higher boiling point and explain your choice:
    a. HF or HBr   **b.** HF or NaF
    c. $MgBr_2$ or PBr_3 **d.** CH_4 or CH_3OH

6.86 Identify the substance in each of the following pairs that would have the higher boiling point and explain your choice:
    a. NaCl or HCl   **b.** H_2O or H_2Se
    c. NH_3 or PH_3 **d.** F_2 or HF

Clinical Update
Compounds at the Pharmacy

A few days ago, Richard went back to the pharmacy to pick up aspirin, $C_9H_8O_4$, and acetaminophen, $C_8H_9NO_2$. He also wanted to talk to Sarah about a way to treat his sore toe. Sarah recommended soaking his foot in a solution of Epsom salts, which is magnesium sulfate. Richard also asked Sarah to recommend an antacid for his upset stomach and an iron supplement. Sarah suggested an antacid that contains calcium carbonate, aluminum hydroxide, and iron(II) sulfate as an iron supplement. Richard also picked up toothpaste containing tin(II) fluoride, and carbonated water, which contains carbon dioxide.

℞ Clinical Applications

6.87 Write the chemical formula for each of the following:
    a. magnesium sulfate
    b. calcium carbonate
    c. aluminum hydroxide

6.88 Write the chemical formula for each of the following:
    a. tin(II) fluoride
    b. carbon dioxide
    c. iron(II) sulfate

6.89 Identify each of the compounds in problem 6.87 as ionic or molecular.

6.90 Identify each of the compounds in problem 6.88 as ionic or molecular.

6.91 Using the electronegativity values in Figure 6.6, calculate the electronegativity difference for the following bonds present in aspirin:
    a. C$-$C
    b. C$-$H
    c. C$-$O

6.92 Using the electronegativity values in Figure 6.6, calculate the electronegativity difference for the following bonds present in acetaminophen:
    a. C$-$N
    b. N$-$H
    c. H$-$O

6.93 Classify each of the bonds in problem 6.91 as nonpolar covalent, polar covalent, or ionic.

6.94 Classify each of the bonds in problem 6.92 as nonpolar covalent, polar covalent, or ionic.

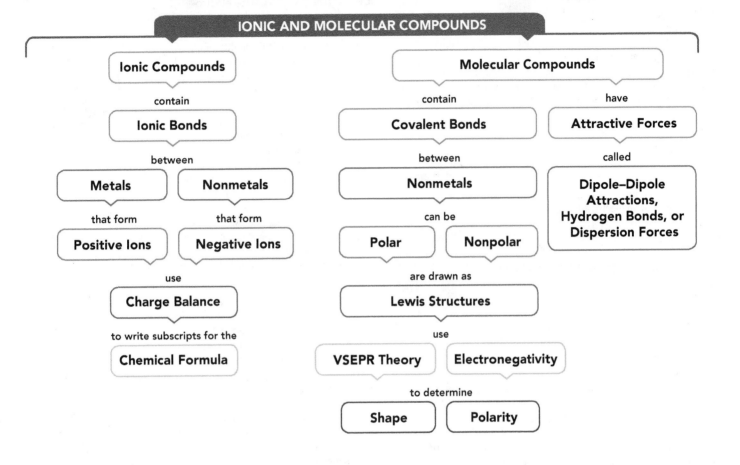

IONIC AND MOLECULAR COMPOUNDS

Ionic Compounds

contain

Ionic Bonds

between

Metals   Nonmetals

that form   that form

Positive Ions   Negative Ions

use

Charge Balance

to write subscripts for the

Chemical Formula

Molecular Compounds

contain   have

Covalent Bonds   Attractive Forces

between   called

Nonmetals   Dipole–Dipole Attractions, Hydrogen Bonds, or Dispersion Forces

can be

Polar   Nonpolar

are drawn as

Lewis Structures

use

VSEPR Theory   Electronegativity

to determine

Shape   Polarity

CHAPTER REVIEW

6.1 Ions: Transfer of Electrons

LEARNING GOAL Write the symbols for the simple ions of the representative elements.

Transfer of electrons

Ionic bond

- The stability of the noble gases is associated with a stable electron configuration in the outermost energy level.
- With the exception of helium, which has two electrons, noble gases have eight valence electrons, which is an octet.
- Atoms of elements in Groups 1A–7A (1, 2, 13–17) achieve stability by losing, gaining, or sharing their valence electrons in the formation of compounds.
- Metals of the representative elements lose valence electrons to form positively charged ions (cations): Group 1A (1), 1+, Group 2A (2), 2+, and Group 3A (13), 3+.
- When reacting with metals, nonmetals gain electrons to form octets and form negatively charged ions (anions): Groups 5A (15), 3−, 6A (16), 2−, and 7A (17), 1−.

6.2 Writing Formulas for Ionic Compounds

LEARNING GOAL Using charge balance, write the correct formula for an ionic compound.

- The total positive and negative ionic charge is balanced in the formula of an ionic compound.
- Charge balance in a formula is achieved by using subscripts after each symbol so that the overall charge is zero.

Sodium chloride

6.3 Naming and Writing Ionic Formulas

LEARNING GOAL Given the formula of an ionic compound, write the correct name; given the name of an ionic compound, write the correct formula.

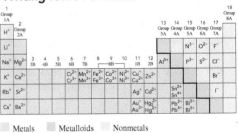

Metals   Metalloids   Nonmetals

- In naming ionic compounds, the positive ion is given first followed by the name of the negative ion.
- The names of ionic compounds containing two elements end with *ide*.
- Except for Ag, Cd, and Zn, transition elements form cations with two or more ionic charges.
- The charge of the cation is determined from the total negative charge in the formula and included as a Roman numeral immediately following the name of the metal that has a variable charge.

6.4 Polyatomic Ions

LEARNING GOAL Write the name and formula for an ionic compound containing a polyatomic ion.

Plaster cast $CaSO_4$

Ca^{2+} SO_4^{2-}
Sulfate ion

- A polyatomic ion is a covalently bonded group of atoms with an electrical charge; for example, the carbonate ion has the formula CO_3^{2-}.
- Most polyatomic ions have names that end with *ate* or *ite*.
- Most polyatomic ions contain a nonmetal and one or more oxygen atoms.
- The ammonium ion, NH_4^+, is a positive polyatomic ion.
- When more than one polyatomic ion is used for charge balance, parentheses enclose the formula of the polyatomic ion.

6.5 Molecular Compounds: Sharing Electrons

LEARNING GOAL Given the formula of a molecular compound, write its correct name; given the name of a molecular compound, write its formula.

1	mono
2	di
3	tri
4	tetra
5	penta

- In a covalent bond, atoms of nonmetals share valence electrons such that each atom has a stable electron configuration.
- The first nonmetal in a molecular compound uses its element name; the second nonmetal uses the first syllable of its element name followed by *ide*.
- The name of a molecular compound with two different atoms uses prefixes to indicate the subscripts in the formula.

6.6 Lewis Structures for Molecules and Polyatomic Ions

LEARNING GOAL Draw the Lewis structures for molecular compounds or polyatomic ions.

- The total number of valence electrons is determined for all the atoms in the molecule or polyatomic ion.
- Any negative charge is added to the total valence electrons, whereas any positive charge is subtracted.
- In the Lewis structure, a bonding pair of electrons is placed between the central atom and each of the attached atoms.
- Any remaining valence electrons are used as lone pairs to complete the octets of the surrounding atoms and then the central atom.
- If octets are not completed, one or more lone pairs of electrons are placed as bonding pairs forming double or triple bonds.

6.7 Electronegativity and Bond Polarity

LEARNING GOAL Use electronegativity to determine the polarity of a bond.

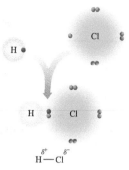

Unequal sharing of electrons in a polar covalent bond

- Electronegativity is the ability of an atom to attract the electrons it shares with another atom. In general, the electronegativities of metals are low, whereas nonmetals have high electronegativities.
- In a nonpolar covalent bond, atoms share electrons equally.
- In a polar covalent bond, the electrons are unequally shared because they are attracted to the more electronegative atom.
- The atom in a polar bond with the lower electronegativity is partially positive (δ^+), and the atom with the higher electronegativity is partially negative (δ^-).
- Atoms that form ionic bonds have large differences in electronegativities.

6.8 Shapes and Polarity of Molecules

LEARNING GOAL Predict the three-dimensional structure of a molecule, and classify it as polar or nonpolar.

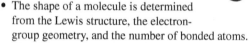
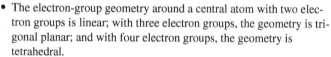

- The shape of a molecule is determined from the Lewis structure, the electron-group geometry, and the number of bonded atoms.
- The electron-group geometry around a central atom with two electron groups is linear; with three electron groups, the geometry is trigonal planar; and with four electron groups, the geometry is tetrahedral.
- When all the electron groups are bonded to atoms, the shape has the same name as the electron arrangement.
- A central atom with three electron groups and two bonded atoms has a bent shape, 120°.
- A central atom with four electron groups and three bonded atoms has a trigonal pyramidal shape.
- A central atom with four electron groups and two bonded atoms has a bent shape, 109°.
- Nonpolar molecules contain nonpolar covalent bonds or have an arrangement of bonded atoms that causes the dipoles to cancel out.
- In polar molecules, the dipoles do not cancel.

6.9 Attractive Forces in Compounds

LEARNING GOAL Describe the attractive forces between ions, polar covalent molecules, and nonpolar covalent molecules.

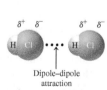

Dipole–dipole attraction

- In ionic solids, oppositely charged ions are held in a rigid structure by ionic bonds.
- Attractive forces called dipole–dipole attractions and hydrogen bonds hold the solid and liquid states of polar molecular compounds together.
- Nonpolar compounds form solids and liquids by weak attractions between temporary dipoles called dispersion forces.

KEY TERMS

anion A negatively charged ion such as Cl^-, O^{2-}, or SO_4^{2-}.

cation A positively charged ion such as Na^+, Mg^{2+}, Al^{3+}, or NH_4^+.

chemical formula The group of symbols and subscripts that represents the atoms or ions in a compound.

covalent bond A sharing of valence electrons by atoms.

dipole The separation of positive and negative charges in a polar bond indicated by an arrow that is drawn from the more positive atom to the more negative atom.

dipole–dipole attractions Attractive forces between oppositely charged ends of polar molecules.

dispersion forces Weak dipole bonding that results from a momentary polarization of nonpolar molecules.

double bond A sharing of two pairs of electrons by two atoms.

electronegativity The relative ability of an element to attract electrons in a bond.

hydrogen bond The attraction between a partially positive H atom and a strongly electronegative atom of F, O, or N.

ion An atom or group of atoms having an electrical charge because of a loss or gain of electrons.

ionic charge The difference between the number of protons (positive) and the number of electrons (negative) written in the upper right corner of the symbol for the element or polyatomic ion.

ionic compound A compound of positive and negative ions held together by ionic bonds.

Lewis structure A representation of a molecule or ion that shows the valence electrons.

molecular compound A combination of atoms in which stable electron configurations are attained by sharing electrons.

molecule The smallest unit of two or more atoms held together by covalent bonds.

nonpolar covalent bond A covalent bond in which the electrons are shared equally between atoms.

nonpolar molecule A molecule that has only nonpolar bonds or in which the bond dipoles cancel.

octet A set of eight valence electrons.

octet rule Elements in Groups 1A–7A (1, 2, 13–17) react with other elements by forming ionic or covalent bonds to produce a stable electron configuration, usually eight electrons in the outer shell.

polar covalent bond A covalent bond in which the electrons are shared unequally between atoms.

polar molecule A molecule containing bond dipoles that do not cancel.

polarity A measure of the unequal sharing of electrons indicated by the difference in electronegativities.

polyatomic ion A group of covalently bonded nonmetal atoms that has an overall electrical charge.

triple bond A sharing of three pairs of electrons by two atoms.

valence shell electron-pair repulsion (VSEPR) theory A theory that predicts the shape of a molecule by placing the electron pairs on a central atom as far apart as possible to minimize the mutual repulsion of the electrons.

⚛ CORE CHEMISTRY SKILLS

The chapter section containing each Core Chemistry Skill is shown in parentheses at the end of each heading.

Writing Positive and Negative Ions (6.1)

• In the formation of an ionic bond, atoms of a metal lose and atoms of a nonmetal gain valence electrons to acquire a stable electron configuration, usually eight valence electrons.

• This tendency of atoms to attain a stable electron configuration is known as the octet rule.

Example: State the number of electrons lost or gained by atoms and the ion formed for each of the following to obtain a stable electron configuration:

    a. Br   **b.** Ca   **c.** S

Answer: **a.** Br atoms gain one electron to achieve a stable electron configuration, Br^-.

    b. Ca atoms lose two electrons to achieve a stable electron configuration, Ca^{2+}.

    c. S atoms gain two electrons to achieve a stable electron configuration, S^{2-}.

Writing Ionic Formulas (6.2)

• The chemical formula of a compound represents the lowest whole-number ratio of the atoms or ions.

• In the chemical formula of an ionic compound, the sum of the positive and negative charges is always zero.

• Thus, in a chemical formula of an ionic compound, the total positive charge is equal to the total negative charge.

Example: Write the formula for magnesium phosphate.

Answer: Magnesium phosphate is an ionic compound that contains the ions Mg^{2+} and PO_4^{3-}.

Using charge balance, we determine the number(s) of each type of ion.

$$3(2+) + 2(3-) = 0$$

$3Mg^{2+}$ and $2PO_4^{3-}$ give the formula $Mg_3(PO_4)_2$.

Naming Ionic Compounds (6.3)

• In the name of an ionic compound made up of two elements, the name of the metal ion, which is written first, is the same as its element name.

• For metals that form two or more different ions, a Roman numeral that is equal to the ionic charge is placed in parentheses immediately after the name of the metal.

• The name of a nonmetal ion is obtained by using the first syllable of its element name followed by *ide*.

• The name of a polyatomic ion usually ends in *ate* or *ite*.

Example: What is the name of $PbSO_4$?

Answer: This compound contains the polyatomic ion SO_4^{2-}, which is sulfate with a 2− charge.

For charge balance, the positive ion must have a charge of 2+.

$$Pb? + (2-) = 0; \quad Pb = 2+$$

Because lead can form two different positive ions, a Roman numeral (II) is used in the name of the compound: lead(II) sulfate.

Writing the Names and Formulas for Molecular Compounds (6.5)

- When naming a molecular compound, the first nonmetal in the formula is named by its element name; the second nonmetal is named using the first syllable of its element name followed by *ide*.

Example: Name the molecular compound BrF_5.

Answer: Two nonmetals share electrons and form a molecular compound. Br (first nonmetal) is bromine; F (second nonmetal) is fluoride. In the name for a molecular compound, prefixes indicate the subscripts in the formulas. The subscript 1 is understood for Br. The subscript 5 for fluoride is written with the prefix *penta*. The name is bromine pentafluoride.

Drawing Lewis Structures (6.6)

- The Lewis structure for a molecule shows the sequence of atoms, the bonding pairs of electrons shared between atoms, and the nonbonding or *lone pairs* of electrons.
- Double or triple bonds result when a second or third electron pair is shared between the same atoms to complete octets.

Example: Draw the Lewis structure for CS_2.

Answer: The central atom in the atom arrangement is C.

S   C   S

Determine the total number of valence electrons.

$$1\,C \times 4\,e^- = 4\,e^-$$
$$\underline{2\,S \times 6\,e^- = 12\,e^-}$$
$$\text{Total} = 16\,e^-$$

Attach each bonded atom to the central atom using a pair of electrons. Two bonding pairs use four electrons.

S:C:S

Place the 12 remaining electrons as lone pairs around the S atoms.

:S̈:C:S̈:

To complete the octet for C, a lone pair of electrons from each of the S atoms is shared with C, which forms two double bonds.

:S̈::C::S̈:   or   :S̈=C=S̈:

Using Electronegativity (6.7)

- The electronegativity values indicate the ability of atoms to attract shared electrons.
- Electronegativity values increase going across a period from left to right, and decrease going down a group.
- A nonpolar covalent bond occurs between atoms with identical or very similar electronegativity values such that the electronegativity difference is 0.0 to 0.4.
- A polar covalent bond occurs when electrons are shared unequally between atoms with electronegativity differences from 0.5 to 1.8.
- An ionic bond typically occurs when the difference in electronegativity for two atoms is greater than 1.8.

Example: Use electronegativity values to classify each of the following bonds as nonpolar covalent, polar covalent, or ionic:

   a. Sr—Cl   **b.** C—S   **c.** O—Br

Answer: **a.** An electronegativity difference of 2.0 (Cl 3.0 − Sr 1.0) makes this an ionic bond.
   b. An electronegativity difference of 0.0 (C 2.5 − S 2.5) makes this a nonpolar covalent bond.
   c. An electronegativity difference of 0.7 (O 3.5 − Br 2.8) makes this a polar covalent bond.

Predicting Shape (6.8)

- The three-dimensional shape of a molecule or polyatomic ion is determined by drawing a Lewis structure and identifying the number of electron groups (one or more electron pairs) around the central atom and the number of bonded atoms.
- In the valence shell electron-pair repulsion (VSEPR) theory, the electron groups are arranged as far apart as possible around a central atom to minimize the repulsion.
- A central atom with two electron groups bonded to two atoms is linear. A central atom with three electron groups bonded to three atoms is trigonal planar, and to two atoms is bent (120°). A central atom with four electron groups bonded to four atoms is tetrahedral, to three atoms is trigonal pyramidal, and to two atoms is bent (109°).

Identifying Polarity of Molecules (6.8)

- A molecule is nonpolar if all of its bonds are nonpolar or it has polar bonds that cancel out. CCl_4 is a nonpolar molecule that consists of four polar bonds that cancel out.

- A molecule is polar if it contains polar bonds that do not cancel out. H_2O is a polar molecule that consists of polar bonds that do not cancel out.

Example: Predict whether $AsCl_3$ is polar or nonpolar.

Answer: From its Lewis structure, we see that $AsCl_3$ has four electron groups with three bonded atoms.

:C̈l:Äs:C̈l:
   :C̈l:

The shape of a molecule of $AsCl_3$ would be trigonal pyramidal with three polar bonds (As—Cl = 3.0 − 2.0 = 1.0) that do not cancel. Thus, it is a polar molecule.

Identifying Attractive Forces (6.9)

- Dipole–dipole attractions occur between the dipoles in polar compounds because the positively charged end of one molecule is attracted to the negatively charged end of another molecule.

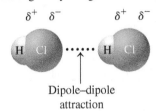

$$\delta^+ \quad \delta^- \qquad \delta^+ \quad \delta^-$$

H Cl ••••• H Cl

Dipole–dipole
attraction

- Strong dipole–dipole attractions called hydrogen bonds occur in compounds in which H is bonded to F, O, or N. The partially positive H atom in one molecule has a strong attraction to the partially negative F, O, or N in another molecule.
- Dispersion forces are very weak attractive forces between nonpolar molecules that occur when *temporary dipoles* form as electrons are unequally distributed.

Example: Identify the strongest type of attractive forces in each of the following:

   a. HF   **b.** F_2 **c.** NF_3

Answer: **a.** HF molecules, which are polar with H bonded to F, have hydrogen bonding.
   b. Nonpolar F_2 molecules have only dispersion forces.
   c. NF_3 molecules, which are polar, have dipole–dipole attractions.

UNDERSTANDING THE CONCEPTS

The chapter sections to review are shown in parentheses at the end of each question.

6.95 **a.** How does the octet rule explain the formation of a magnesium ion? (6.1)
   b. What noble gas has the same electron configuration as the magnesium ion?
   c. Why are Group 1A (1) and Group 2A (2) elements found in many compounds, but not Group 8A (18) elements?

6.96 **a.** How does the octet rule explain the formation of a chloride ion? (6.1)
   b. What noble gas has the same electron configuration as the chloride ion?
   c. Why are Group 7A (17) elements found in many compounds, but not Group 8A (18) elements?

6.97 Identify each of the following atoms or ions: (6.1)

18 e^-	8 e^-	28 e^-	23 e^-
15 p^+	8 p^+	30 p^+	26 p^+
16 n	8 n	35 n	28 n
A	**B**	**C**	**D**

6.98 Identify each of the following atoms or ions: (6.1)

2 e^-	0 e^-	3 e^-	10 e^-
3 p^+	1 p^+	3 p^+	7 p^+
4 n		4 n	8 n
A	**B**	**C**	**D**

6.99 Consider the following Lewis symbols for elements X and Y: (6.1, 6.2, 6.5)

$$\dot{X}\cdot \qquad \cdot\ddot{Y}\cdot$$

   a. What are the group numbers of X and Y?
   b. Will a compound of X and Y be ionic or molecular?
   c. What ions would be formed by X and Y?
   d. What would be the formula of a compound of X and Y?
   e. What would be the formula of a compound of X and sulfur?
   f. What would be the formula of a compound of Y and chlorine?
   g. Is the compound in part **f** ionic or molecular?

6.100 Consider the following Lewis symbols for elements X and Y: (6.1, 6.5)

$$\dot{X}\cdot \qquad \cdot\ddot{Y}\cdot$$

   a. What are the group numbers of X and Y?
   b. Will a compound of X and Y be ionic or molecular?
   c. What ions would be formed by X and Y?
   d. What would be the formula of a compound of X and Y?
   e. What would be the formula of a compound of X and sulfur?
   f. What would be the formula of a compound of Y and chlorine?
   g. Is the compound in part **f** ionic or molecular?

6.101 Match each of the Lewis structures (**a** to **c**) with the correct diagram (**1** to **3**) of its shape, and name the shape; indicate if each molecule is polar or nonpolar. (Assume X and Y are nonmetals and all bonds are polar covalent.) (6.8)

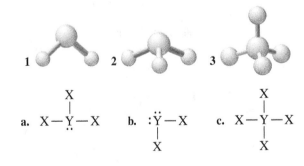

1   2   3

   a. X—Ẏ—X (with X above and X below the central Y)
   b. :Ÿ—X
   c. X—Y—X (with X above and X below the central Y)

6.102 Match each of the formulas (**a** to **c**) with the correct diagram (**1** to **3**) of its shape, and name the shape; indicate if each molecule is polar or nonpolar. (6.8)

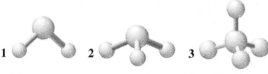

1   **2**   **3**

a. PBr_3 b. $SiCl_4$ c. OF_2

6.103 Using each of the following electron configurations, give the formulas of the cation and anion that form, the formula for the compound they form, and its name. (6.2, 6.3)

Electron Configurations		Cation	Anion	Formula of Compound	Name of Compound
$1s^2 2s^2 2p^6 3s^2$	$1s^2 2s^2 2p^3$				
$1s^2 2s^2 2p^6 3s^2 3p^6 4s^1$	$1s^2 2s^2 2p^4$				
$1s^2 2s^2 2p^6 3s^2 3p^1$	$1s^2 2s^2 2p^6 3s^2 3p^5$				

6.104 Using each of the following electron configurations, give the formulas of the cation and anion that form, the formula of the compound they form, and its name. (6.2, 6.3)

Electron Configurations		Cation	Anion	Formula of Compound	Name of Compound
$1s^2 2s^2 2p^6 3s^1$	$1s^2 2s^2 2p^5$				
$1s^2 2s^2 2p^6 3s^2 3p^6 4s^2$	$1s^2 2s^2 2p^6 3s^2 3p^4$				
$1s^2 2s^2 2p^6 3s^2 3p^1$	$1s^2 2s^2 2p^6 3s^2 3p^3$				

6.105 State the number of valence electrons, bonding pairs, and lone pairs in each of the following Lewis structures: (6.5)

a. H:H   b. H:$\ddot{\text{Br}}$:   c. :$\ddot{\text{Br}}$:$\ddot{\text{Br}}$:

6.106 State the number of valence electrons, bonding pairs, and lone pairs in each of the following Lewis structures: (6.5)

a. H:$\ddot{\text{O}}$:   b. H:$\ddot{\text{N}}$:H (with H below)   c. :$\ddot{\text{Br}}$:$\ddot{\text{O}}$:$\ddot{\text{Br}}$:

ADDITIONAL QUESTIONS AND PROBLEMS

6.107 Write the electron configuration for the following: (6.1)
a. N^{3-} b. Mg^{2+} c. P^{3-} d. Al^{3+} e. Li^+

6.108 Write the electron configuration for the following: (6.1)
a. K^+ b. Na^+ c. S^{2-} d. Cl^- e. Ca^{2+}

6.109 Consider an ion with the symbol X^{2+} formed from a representative element. (6.1, 6.2, 6.3)
a. What is the group number of the element?
b. What is the Lewis symbol of the element?
c. If X is in Period 3, what is the element?
d. What is the formula of the compound formed from X and the nitride ion?

6.110 Consider an ion with the symbol Y^{3-} formed from a representative element. (6.1, 6.2, 6.3)
a. What is the group number of the element?
b. What is the Lewis symbol of the element?
c. If Y is in Period 3, what is the element?
d. What is the formula of the compound formed from the barium ion and Y?

6.111 One of the ions of tin is tin(IV). (6.1, 6.2, 6.3, 6.4)
a. What is the symbol for this ion?
b. How many protons and electrons are in the ion?
c. What is the formula of tin(IV) oxide?
d. What is the formula of tin(IV) phosphate?

6.112 One of the ions of gold is gold(III). (6.1, 6.2, 6.3, 6.4)
a. What is the symbol for this ion?
b. How many protons and electrons are in the ion?
c. What is the formula of gold(III) sulfate?
d. What is the formula of gold(III) nitrate?

6.113 Write the formula for each of the following ionic compounds: (6.2, 6.3)
a. tin(II) sulfide   b. lead(IV) oxide
c. silver chloride   d. calcium nitride
e. copper(I) phosphide   f. chromium(II) bromide

6.114 Write the formula for each of the following ionic compounds: (6.2, 6.3)
a. nickel(III) oxide   b. iron(III) sulfide
c. lead(II) sulfate   d. chromium(III) iodide
e. lithium nitride   f. gold(I) oxide

6.115 Name each of the following molecular compounds: (6.5)
a. NCl_3 b. N_2S_3 c. N_2O
d. IF   e. BF_3 f. P_2O_5

6.116 Name each of the following molecular compounds: (6.5)
a. CBr_4 b. SF_6 c. BrCl
d. N_2O_4 e. SO_2 f. CS_2

6.117 Write the formula for each of the following molecular compounds: (6.5)
a. carbon sulfide   b. diphosphorus pentoxide
c. dihydrogen sulfide   d. sulfur dichloride

6.118 Write the formula for each of the following molecular compounds: (6.5)
a. silicon dioxide   b. carbon tetrabromide
c. diphosphorus tetraiodide   d. dinitrogen trioxide

6.119 Classify each of the following as ionic or molecular, and give its name: (6.3, 6.5)
a. $FeCl_3$ b. Na_2SO_4 c. NO_2
d. N_2 e. PF_5 f. CF_4

6.120 Classify each of the following as ionic or molecular, and give its name: (6.3, 6.5)
a. $Al_2(CO_3)_3$ b. ClF_5 c. H_2
d. Mg_3N_2 e. ClO_2 f. $CrPO_4$

6.121 Write the formula for each of the following: (6.3, 6.4, 6.5)
a. tin(II) carbonate   b. lithium phosphide
c. silicon tetrachloride   d. manganese(III) oxide
e. bromine   f. calcium bromide

6.122 Write the formula for each of the following: (6.3, 6.4, 6.5)
  a. sodium carbonate **b.** nitrogen dioxide
  c. aluminum nitrate **d.** copper(I) nitride
  e. potassium phosphate **f.** cobalt(III) sulfate

6.123 Draw the Lewis structure for each of the following: (6.6)
  a. BF_4^- **b.** Cl_2O
  c. H_2NOH (N is the central atom)
  d. H_2CCCl_2

6.124 Draw the Lewis structure for each of the following: (6.6)
  a. H_3COCH_3 (the atoms are in the order C O C)
  b. HNO_2 (the atoms are in the order HONO)
  c. ClO_2^- **d.** BrO^-

6.125 Draw the Lewis structure for each of the following: (6.6)
  a. N_3^- **b.** NO_2^+ **c.** CNS^-

6.126 Draw the Lewis structure for each of the following: (6.6)
  a. NO_3^- **b.** CO_3^{2-} **c.** SCN^-

6.127 Select the more polar bond in each of the following pairs: (6.7)
  a. C—N or C—O **b.** N—F or N—Br
  c. Br—Cl or S—Cl **d.** Br—Cl or Br—I
  e. N—F or N—O

6.128 Select the more polar bond in each of the following pairs: (6.7)
  a. C—C or C—O **b.** P—Cl or P—Br
  c. Si—S or Si—Cl **d.** F—Cl or F—Br
  e. P—O or P—S

6.129 Calculate the electronegativity difference and classify each of the following bonds as nonpolar covalent, polar covalent, or ionic: (6.7)
  a. Si—Cl **b.** C—C
  c. Na—Cl **d.** C—H
  e. F—F

6.130 Calculate the electronegativity difference and classify each of the following bonds as nonpolar covalent, polar covalent, or ionic: (6.7)
  a. C—N **b.** Cl—Cl
  c. K—Br **d.** H—H
  e. N—F

6.131 Predict the shape and polarity of each of the following molecules: (6.8)
  a. A central atom with three identical bonded atoms and one lone pair.
  b. A central atom with two bonded atoms and two lone pairs.

6.132 Predict the shape and polarity of each of the following molecules: (6.8)
  a. A central atom with four identical bonded atoms and no lone pairs.
  b. A central atom with four bonded atoms that are not identical and no lone pairs.

6.133 Classify the following molecules as polar or nonpolar: (6.8)
  a. NH_3 **b.** CH_3Cl **c.** SiF_4

6.134 Classify the following molecules as polar or nonpolar: (6.8)
  a. GeH_4 **b.** SeO_2 **c.** SCl_2

6.135 Predict the shape and polarity of each of the following molecules: (6.8)
  a. SI_2 **b.** PF_3

6.136 Predict the shape and polarity of each of the following molecules: (6.8)
  a. H_2O **b.** CF_4

6.137 Indicate the major type of attractive force—(1) ionic bonds, (2) dipole–dipole attractions, (3) hydrogen bonds, (4) dispersion forces—that occurs between particles of the following substances: (6.9)
  a. NH_3 **b.** HI **c.** I_2 **d.** Cs_2O

6.138 Indicate the major type of attractive force—(1) ionic bonds, (2) dipole–dipole attractions, (3) hydrogen bonds, (4) dispersion forces—that occurs between particles of the following substances: (6.9)
  a. CHF_3 **b.** H_2O **c.** LiCl **d.** N_2

CHALLENGE QUESTIONS

The following groups of questions are related to the topics in this chapter. However, they do not all follow the chapter order, and they require you to combine concepts and skills from several sections. These questions will help you increase your critical thinking skills and prepare for your next exam.

6.139 Complete the following table for atoms or ions: (6.1)

Atom or Ion	Number of Protons	Number of Electrons	Electrons Lost/ Gained
K^+			
	$12\ p^+$	$10\ e^-$	
	$8\ p^+$		$2\ e^-$ gained
		$10\ e^-$	$3\ e^-$ lost

6.140 Complete the following table for atoms or ions: (6.1)

Atom or Ion	Number of Protons	Number of Electrons	Electrons Lost/ Gained
	$30\ p^+$		$2\ e^-$ lost
	$36\ p^+$	$36\ e^-$	
	$16\ p^+$		$2\ e^-$ gained
		$46\ e^-$	$4\ e^-$ lost

6.141 Identify the group number in the periodic table of X, a representative element, in each of the following ionic compounds: (6.2)
  a. XCl_3 **b.** Al_2X_3 **c.** XCO_3

6.142 Identify the group number in the periodic table of X, a representative element, in each of the following ionic compounds: (6.2)
  a. X_2O_3 **b.** X_2SO_3 **c.** Na_3X

6.143 Classify each of the following as ionic or molecular, and name each: (6.2, 6.3, 6.4, 6.5)
a. Li_2HPO_4 b. $Cr(NO_2)_2$ c. $Mg(ClO_2)_2$
d. NF_3 e. $Ca(HSO_4)_2$ f. $KClO_4$
g. $Au_2(SO_3)_3$ h. I_2

6.144 Classify each of the following as ionic or molecular, and name each: (6.2, 6.3, 6.4, 6.5)
a. $FePO_3$ b. Cl_2O_7 c. Br_2
d. $Ca_3(PO_4)_2$ e. PCl_3 f. $Al(ClO_2)_3$
g. $Pb(C_2H_3O_2)_2$ h. $MgCO_3$

ANSWERS

Answers to Selected Questions and Problems

6.1 a. 1   **b.** 2   **c.** 3   **d.** 1   **e.** 2

6.3 a. $2\,e^-$ lost   **b.** $3\,e^-$ gained   **c.** $1\,e^-$ gained
d. $1\,e^-$ lost   **e.** $1\,e^-$ gained

6.5 a. Li^+ **b.** F^- **c.** Mg^{2+} **d.** Fe^{3+}

6.7 a. Cl^- **b.** Cs^+ **c.** N^{3-} **d.** Ra^{2+}

6.9 a. 8 protons, 10 electrons   **b.** 19 protons, 18 electrons
c. 53 protons, 54 electrons   **d.** 11 protons, 10 electrons

6.11 a and c

6.13 a. Na_2O **b.** $AlBr_3$ **c.** Ba_3N_2
d. MgF_2 **e.** Al_2S_3

6.15 a. K^+ and S^{2-}, K_2S **b.** Na^+ and N^{3-}, Na_3N
c. Al^{3+} and I^-, AlI_3 **d.** Ga^{3+} and O^{2-}, Ga_2O_3

6.17 a. aluminum oxide   **b.** calcium chloride
c. sodium oxide   **d.** magnesium phosphide
e. potassium iodide   **f.** barium fluoride

6.19 a. iron(II)   **b.** copper(II)
c. zinc   **d.** lead(IV)
e. chromium(III)   **f.** manganese(II)

6.21 a. tin(II) chloride   **b.** iron(II) oxide
c. copper(I) sulfide   **d.** copper(II) sulfide
e. cadmium bromide   **f.** mercury(II) chloride

6.23 a. Au^{3+} **b.** Fe^{3+} **c.** Pb^{4+} **d.** Sn^{2+}

6.25 a. $MgCl_2$ **b.** Na_2S **c.** Cu_2O **d.** Zn_3P_2
e. AuN **f.** CoF_3

6.27 a. $CoCl_3$ **b.** PbO_2 **c.** AgI **d.** Ca_3N_2
e. Cu_3P **f.** $CrCl_2$

6.29 a. K_3P **b.** $CuCl_2$ **c.** $FeBr_3$ **d.** MgO

6.31 a. HCO_3^- **b.** NH_4^+ **c.** PO_3^{3-} **d.** ClO_3^-

6.33 a. sulfate   **b.** carbonate
c. hydrogen sulfite (bisulfite)   **d.** nitrate

6.35

	NO_2^-	CO_3^{2-}	HSO_4^-	PO_4^{3-}
Li^+	$LiNO_2$ Lithium nitrite	Li_2CO_3 Lithium carbonate	$LiHSO_4$ Lithium hydrogen sulfate	Li_3PO_4 Lithium phosphate
Cu^{2+}	$Cu(NO_2)_2$ Copper(II) nitrite	$CuCO_3$ Copper(II) carbonate	$Cu(HSO_4)_2$ Copper(II) hydrogen sulfate	$Cu_3(PO_4)_2$ Copper(II) phosphate
Ba^{2+}	$Ba(NO_2)_2$ Barium nitrite	$BaCO_3$ Barium carbonate	$Ba(HSO_4)_2$ Barium hydrogen sulfate	$Ba_3(PO_4)_2$ Barium phosphate

6.37 a. $Ba(OH)_2$ **b.** $NaHSO_4$ **c.** $Fe(NO_2)_2$
d. $Zn_3(PO_4)_2$ **e.** $Fe_2(CO_3)_3$

6.39 a. CO_3^{2-}, sodium carbonate   **b.** NH_4^+, ammonium sulfide
c. PO_4^{3-}, barium phosphate   **d.** NO_2^-, tin(II) nitrite

6.41 a. zinc acetate   **b.** magnesium phosphate
c. ammonium chloride
d. sodium bicarbonate or sodium hydrogen bicarbonate

6.43 a. phosphorus tribromide   **b.** dichlorine oxide
c. carbon tetrabromide   **d.** hydrogen fluoride
e. nitrogen trifluoride

6.45 a. dinitrogen trioxide   **b.** disilicon hexabromide
c. tetraphosphorus trisulfide   **d.** phosphorus pentachloride
e. selenium hexafluoride

6.47 a. CCl_4 **b.** CO **c.** PCl_3 **d.** N_2O_4

6.49 a. OF_2 **b.** BCl_3 **c.** N_2O_3 **d.** SF_6

6.51 a. aluminum sulfate   **b.** calcium carbonate
c. dinitrogen oxide   **d.** magnesium hydroxide

6.53 a. 8 valence electrons   **b.** 14 valence electrons
c. 32 valence electrons   **d.** 8 valence electrons

6.55 a. HF $(8\,e^-)$ H:F̈: or H—F̈:

b. SF_2 $(20\,e^-)$:F̈:S̈:F̈: or :F̈—S̈—F̈:

c. NBr_3 $(26\,e^-)$:Br̈:N̈:Br̈: or :Br̈—N̈—Br̈: (with :Br̈: above)

d. BH_4^- $(8\,e^-)$ [H:B̈:H]⁻ or [H—B—H]⁻ (with H above and below)

6.57 If complete octets cannot be formed by using all the valence electrons, it is necessary to draw multiple bonds.

6.59 a. CO $(10\,e^-)$:C::O: or :C≡O:

b. NO_3^- $(24\,e^-)$ [:Ö:N:Ö:]⁻ or [:Ö—N—Ö:]⁻ (with :O: above)

c. H_2CO $(12\,e^-)$ H:C̈:H or H—C—H (with :O: above)

6.61 a. increases   **b.** decreases   **c.** decreases

6.63 a. K, Na, Li   **b.** Na, P, Cl   **c.** Ca, Se, O

6.65 a. polar covalent   **b.** ionic
c. polar covalent   **d.** nonpolar covalent
e. polar covalent   **f.** nonpolar covalent

6.67 a. N $\overset{\delta^+ \quad \delta^-}{—}$ F
$\xrightarrow{\quad}$

b. Si $\overset{\delta^+ \quad \delta^-}{—}$ Br
$\xrightarrow{\quad}$

c. C $\overset{\delta^+ \quad \delta^-}{—}$ O
$\xrightarrow{\quad}$

d. P $\overset{\delta^+ \quad \delta^-}{—}$ Br
$\xrightarrow{\quad}$

e. N $\overset{\delta^- \quad \delta^+}{—}$ P
$\xleftarrow{\quad}$

6.69 a. 6. tetrahedral   **b. 5.** trigonal pyramidal
c. 3. trigonal planar

6.71 a. three   **b.** trigonal planar
c. three   **d.** trigonal planar

6.73 In both PH_3 and NH_3, there are three bonded atoms and one lone pair of electrons on the central atoms. The shapes of both are trigonal pyramidal.

6.75 a. bent, 109°   **b.** tetrahedral   **c.** bent, 109°

6.77 Cl_2 is a nonpolar molecule because there is a nonpolar covalent bond between Cl atoms, which have identical electronegativity values. In HCl, the bond is a polar bond, which makes HCl a polar molecule.

6.79 a. polar   **b.** polar   **c.** polar

6.81 a. dipole–dipole attractions   **b.** ionic bonds
c. dipole–dipole attractions   **d.** dispersion forces

6.83 a. hydrogen bonds   **b.** dipole–dipole attractions
c. dispersion forces   **d.** dispersion forces

6.85 a. HF; hydrogen bonds are stronger than the dipole–dipole attractions in HBr.
b. NaF; ionic bonds are stronger than the hydrogen bonds in HF.
c. $MgBr_2$; ionic bonds are stronger than the dipole–dipole attractions in PBr_3.
d. CH_3OH; hydrogen bonds are stronger than the dispersion forces in CH_4.

6.87 a. $MgSO_4$ **b.** $CaCO_3$ **c.** $Al(OH)_3$

6.89 a. ionic   **b.** ionic   **c.** ionic

6.91 a. 0.0   **b.** 0.4   **c.** 1.0

6.93 a. nonpolar covalent   **b.** nonpolar covalent
c. polar covalent

6.95 a. By losing two valence electrons from the third energy level, magnesium achieves an octet in the second energy level.
b. The magnesium ion Mg^{2+} has the same electron configuration as Ne $(1s^2 2s^2 2p^6)$.
c. Group 1A (1) and 2A (2) elements achieve octets by losing electrons to form compounds. Group 8A (18) elements are stable with octets (or two electrons for helium).

6.97 a. P^{3-} ion   **b.** O atom
c. Zn^{2+} ion   **d.** Fe^{3+} ion

6.99 a. X = Group 1A (1), Y = Group 6A (16)
b. ionic   **c.** X^+ and Y^{2-} **d.** X_2Y
e. X_2S **f.** YCl_2 **g.** molecular

6.101 a. 2. trigonal pyramidal, polar
b. 1. bent, 109°, polar
c. 3. tetrahedral, nonpolar

6.103

Electron Configurations		Cation	Anion	Formula of Compound	Name of Compound
$1s^2 2s^2 2p^6 3s^2$	$1s^2 2s^2 2p^3$	Mg^{2+}	N^{3-}	Mg_3N_2	Magnesium nitride
$1s^2 2s^2 2p^6 3s^2 3p^6 4s^1$	$1s^2 2s^2 2p^4$	K^+	O^{2-}	K_2O	Potassium oxide
$1s^2 2s^2 2p^6 3s^2 3p^1$	$1s^2 2s^2 2p^6 3s^2 3p^5$	Al^{3+}	Cl^-	$AlCl_3$	Aluminum chloride

6.105 a. two valence electrons, one bonding pair, no lone pairs
b. eight valence electrons, one bonding pair, three lone pairs
c. 14 valence electrons, one bonding pair, six lone pairs

6.107 a. $1s^2 2s^2 2p^6$ **b.** $1s^2 2s^2 2p^6$ **c.** $1s^2 2s^2 2p^6 3s^2 3p^6$
d. $1s^2 2s^2 2p^6$ **e.** $1s^2$

6.109 a. 2A (2)   **b.** $\dot{X}\cdot$ **c.** Mg   **d.** X_3N_2

6.111 a. Sn^{4+}
b. 50 protons and 46 electrons
c. SnO_2
d. $Sn_3(PO_4)_4$

6.113 a. SnS   **b.** PbO_2 **c.** AgCl
d. Ca_3N_2 **e.** Cu_3P **f.** $CrBr_2$

6.115 a. nitrogen trichloride   **b.** dinitrogen trisulfide
c. dinitrogen oxide   **d.** iodine fluoride
e. boron trifluoride   **f.** diphosphorus pentoxide

6.117 a. CS   **b.** P_2O_5 **c.** H_2S **d.** SCl_2

6.119 a. ionic, iron(III) chloride
b. ionic, sodium sulfate
c. molecular, nitrogen dioxide
d. molecular, nitrogen
e. molecular, phosphorus pentafluoride
f. molecular, carbon tetrafluoride

6.121 a. $SnCO_3$ **b.** Li_3P **c.** $SiCl_4$
d. Mn_2O_3 **e.** Br_2 **f.** $CaBr_2$

6.123 a. BF_4^- $(32\ e^-)$
$$\left[:\overset{..}{\underset{..}{F}}:\overset{..}{\underset{..}{B}}:\overset{..}{\underset{..}{F}}: \right]^- \text{ or } \left[:\overset{..}{F}—\overset{..}{\underset{..}{B}}—\overset{..}{F}: \right]^-$$

b. Cl_2O $(20\ e^-)$ $:\overset{..}{\underset{..}{Cl}}:\overset{..}{\underset{..}{O}}:\overset{..}{\underset{..}{Cl}}:$ or $:\overset{..}{\underset{..}{Cl}}—\overset{..}{\underset{..}{O}}—\overset{..}{\underset{..}{Cl}}:$

c. H_2NOH $(14\ e^-)$ $H:\overset{H}{\underset{}{N}}:\overset{..}{\underset{..}{O}}:H$ or $H—\overset{H}{\underset{}{N}}—\overset{..}{\underset{..}{O}}—H$

d. H_2CCCl_2 $(24\ e^-)$ $H:\overset{H}{\underset{}{C}}::C:\overset{:\overset{..}{Cl}:}{\underset{..}{Cl}}:$ or

$$H—\overset{H}{\underset{}{C}}=\overset{:\overset{..}{Cl}:}{\underset{}{C}}—\overset{..}{\underset{..}{Cl}}:$$

6.125

a. 16 valence electrons $\left[:\overset{..}{N}::N::\overset{..}{N}: \right]^-$ or $\left[:\overset{..}{N}=N=\overset{..}{N}: \right]^-$

b. 16 valence electrons $\left[:\overset{..}{O}::N::\overset{..}{O}: \right]^+$ or $\left[:\overset{..}{O}=N=\overset{..}{O}: \right]^+$

c. 16 valence electrons $\left[:C::N:\overset{..}{\underset{.}{S}}: \right]^-$ or $\left[:C\equiv N—\overset{..}{\underset{..}{S}}: \right]^-$

6.127 a. C—O   **b.** N—F   **c.** S—Cl
d. Br—I   **e.** N—F

6.129 a. polar covalent (Cl 3.0 − Si 1.8 = 1.2)
b. nonpolar covalent (C 2.5 − C 2.5 = 0.0)
c. ionic (Cl 3.0 − Na 0.9 = 2.1)
d. nonpolar covalent (C 2.5 − H 2.1 = 0.4)
e. nonpolar covalent (F 4.0 − F 4.0 = 0.0)

6.131 a. trigonal pyramidal, polar
b. bent 109°, polar

6.133 a. polar   **b.** polar   **c.** nonpolar

6.135 a. bent 109°, nonpolar
b. trigonal pyramidal, polar

6.137 a. (3) hydrogen bonds   **b.** (2) dipole–dipole attractions
c. (4) dispersion forces   **d.** (1) ionic bonds

6.139

Atom or Ion	Number of Protons	Number of Electrons	Electrons Lost/ Gained
K^+	$19\ p^+$	$18\ e^-$	$1\ e^-$ lost
Mg^{2+}	$12\ p^+$	$10\ e^-$	$2\ e^-$ lost
O^{2-}	$8\ p^+$	$10\ e^-$	$2\ e^-$ gained
Al^{3+}	$13\ p^+$	$10\ e^-$	$3\ e^-$ lost

6.141 a. Group 3A (13)   **b.** Group 6A (16)   **c.** Group 2A (2)

6.143 a. ionic, lithium hydrogen phosphate
b. ionic, chromium(II) nitrite
c. ionic, magnesium chlorite
d. molecular, nitrogen trifluoride
e. ionic, calcium bisulfate or calcium hydrogen sulfate
f. ionic, potassium perchlorate
g. ionic, gold(III) sulfite
h. molecular, iodine

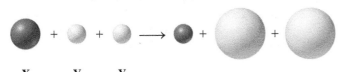

CI.7 For parts **a** to **f**, consider the loss of electrons by atoms of the element X, and a gain of electrons by atoms of the element Y, if X is in Group 2A (2), Period 3, and Y is in Group 7A (17), Period 3. (4.6, 6.1, 6.2, 6.3, 6.7)

X   Y   Y

a. Which reactant has the higher electronegativity?
b. What are the ionic charges of **X** and **Y** in the product?
c. Write the electron configurations for the atoms **X** and **Y**.
d. Write the electron configurations for the ions of **X** and **Y**.
e. Give the names for the noble gases with the same electron configurations as each of these ions.
f. Write the formula and name for the ionic compound formed by the ions of **X** and **Y**.

CI.8 A sterling silver bracelet, which is 92.5% silver by mass, has a volume of 25.6 cm^3 and a density of 10.2 g/cm^3. (2.7, 4.5, 5.2, 5.4)

Sterling silver is 92.5% silver by mass.

a. What is the mass, in kilograms, of the bracelet?
b. Determine the number of protons and neutrons in each of the two stable isotopes of silver:

$^{107}_{47}Ag$ $^{109}_{47}Ag$

c. Silver (Ag) has two naturally occurring isotopes: Ag-107 (106.905 amu) with an abundance of 51.84% and Ag-109 (108.905 amu) with an abundance of 48.16%. Calculate the atomic mass for silver using the weighted average mass method.
d. Ag-112 decays by beta emission. Write the balanced nuclear equation for the decay of Ag-112.
e. A 64.0-μCi sample of Ag-112 decays to 8.00 μCi in 9.3 h. What is the half-life of Ag-112?

CI.9 Some of the isotopes of silicon are listed in the following table: (4.5, 4.6, 5.2, 5.4, 6.7, 6.8)

Isotope	% Natural Abundance	Atomic Mass	Half-Life (radioactive)	Radiation
$^{27}_{14}Si$		26.987	4.9 s	Positron
$^{28}_{14}Si$	92.23	27.977	Stable	None
$^{29}_{14}Si$	4.683	28.976	Stable	None
$^{30}_{14}Si$	3.087	29.974	Stable	None
$^{31}_{14}Si$		30.975	2.6 h	Beta

a. In the following table, indicate the number of protons, neutrons, and electrons for each isotope listed:

Isotope	Number of Protons	Number of Neutrons	Number of Electrons
$^{27}_{14}Si$			
$^{28}_{14}Si$			
$^{29}_{14}Si$			
$^{30}_{14}Si$			
$^{31}_{14}Si$			

b. What is the electron configuration of silicon?
c. Calculate the atomic mass for silicon using the weighted average mass method.
d. Write the balanced nuclear equations for the positron emission of Si-27 and the beta decay of Si-31.
e. Draw the Lewis structure and predict the shape of $SiCl_4$.
f. How many hours are needed for a sample of Si-31 with an activity of 16 μCi to decay to 2.0 μCi?

CI.10 The iceman known as Ötzi was discovered in a high mountain pass on the Austrian–Italian border. Samples of his hair and bones had carbon-14 activity that was 50% of that present in new hair or bone. Carbon-14 undergoes beta decay and has a half-life of 5730 yr. (5.2, 5.4)

The mummified remains of Ötzi were discovered in 1991.

a. How long ago did Ötzi live?
b. Write a balanced nuclear equation for the decay of carbon-14.

CI.11 K$^+$ is an electrolyte required by the human body and is found in many foods as well as salt substitutes. One of the isotopes of potassium is potassium-40, which has a natural abundance of 0.012% and a half-life of 1.30×10^9 yr. The isotope potassium-40 decays to calcium-40 or to argon-40. A typical activity for potassium-40 is 7.0 μCi per gram. (5.2, 5.3, 5.4)

Potassium chloride is used as a salt substitute.

a. Write a balanced nuclear equation for each type of decay and identify the particle emitted.
b. A shaker of salt substitute contains 1.6 oz of K. What is the activity, in millicuries and becquerels, of the potassium in the shaker?

CI.12 Of much concern to environmentalists is radon-222, which is a radioactive noble gas that can seep from the ground into basements of homes and buildings. Radon-222 is a product of the decay of radium-226 that occurs naturally in rocks and soil in much of the United States. Radon-222, which has a half-life of 3.8 days, decays by emitting an alpha particle. Radon-222, which is a gas, can be inhaled into the lungs where it is can cause lung cancer. Radon levels in a home can be measured with a home radon-detection kit. Environmental agencies have set the maximum level of radon-222 in a home at 4 picocuries per liter (pCi/L) of air. (5.2, 5.3, 5.4)

A home detection kit is used to measure the level of radon-222.

a. Write the balanced nuclear equation for the decay of Ra-226.
b. Write the balanced nuclear equation for the decay of Rn-222.
c. If a room contains 24 000 atoms of radon-222, how many atoms of radon-222 remain after 15.2 days?
d. Suppose a room has a volume of 72 000 L (7.2×10^4 L). If the radon level is the maximum allowed (4 pCi/L), how many alpha particles are emitted from Rn-222 in 1 day? (1 Ci = 3.7×10^{10} disintegrations/s)

ANSWERS

CI.7 **a.** Y has the higher electronegativity.
b. X^{2+}, Y^-
c. X = $1s^2 2s^2 2p^6 3s^2$ Y = $1s^2 2s^2 2p^6 3s^2 3p^5$
d. X^{2+} = $1s^2 2s^2 2p^6$ Y^- = $1s^2 2s^2 2p^6 3s^2 3p^6$
e. X^{2+} has the same electron configuration as Ne. Y^- has the same electron configuration as Ar.
f. $MgCl_2$, magnesium chloride

CI.9 **a.**

Isotope	Number of Protons	Number of Neutrons	Number of Electrons
$^{27}_{14}Si$	14	13	14
$^{28}_{14}Si$	14	14	14
$^{29}_{14}Si$	14	15	14
$^{30}_{14}Si$	14	16	14
$^{31}_{14}Si$	14	17	14

b. $1s^2 2s^2 2p^6 3s^2 3p^2$
c. 28.09 amu
d. $^{27}_{14}Si \longrightarrow {}^{27}_{13}Al + {}^{0}_{+1}e$
$^{31}_{14}Si \longrightarrow {}^{31}_{15}P + {}^{0}_{-1}e$

e.

$$:\ddot{C}l-Si-\ddot{C}l:$$

Tetrahedral

$:\ddot{C}l:$

f. 7.8 h

CI.11 **a.** $^{40}_{19}K \longrightarrow {}^{40}_{20}Ca + {}^{0}_{-1}e$ Beta particle
$^{40}_{19}K \longrightarrow {}^{40}_{18}Ar + {}^{0}_{+1}e$ Positron
b. 3.8×10^{-5} mCi; 1.4×10^3 Bq

7

Chemical Reactions and Quantities

JANE'S TEETH HAVE BECOME BADLY STAINED

because of drinking excessive amounts of coffee. Dark colored compounds in coffee, tea, fruit juices, wine, and smoke cause discoloration of the teeth when they penetrate the hydroxyapatite, which is a porous compound in the enamel layer. Jane makes an appointment with Kimberly, her dental hygienist, to have her teeth whitened. After Kimberly cleans Jane's teeth, she begins the process of whitening by placing a gel composed of 15 to 35% hydrogen peroxide (H_2O_2) on the surface of Jane's teeth. The hydrogen peroxide penetrates the enamel of Jane's teeth where it causes a chemical reaction occurs that produces oxygen (O_2). As the O_2 reacts with the discoloration in the enamel, the teeth are whitened.

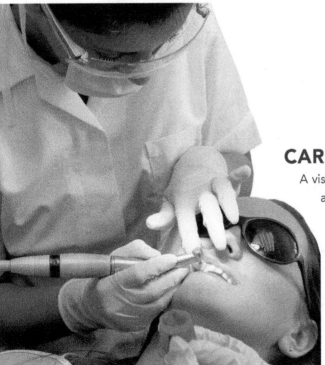

CAREER Dental Hygienist

A visit to the dentist frequently begins with a dental hygienist who cleans and polishes the patient's teeth by removing tartar, stains, and plaque. This requires the hygienist to use a variety of tools, including hand and rotary instruments, as well as ultrasonic equipment. The hygienist also discusses the proper technique for brushing and flossing with each patient. The dental hygienist may also take X-rays of a patient's teeth to detect any abnormalities. A dental hygienist must be knowledgeable about the proper safety procedures for taking X-rays and how to protect themselves from disease transmission by wearing the proper safety attire like safety glasses, surgical masks, and gloves.

C hemical reactions occur everywhere. The fuel in our cars burns with oxygen to make the car move and run the air conditioner. When we cook our food or bleach our hair, chemical reactions take place. In our bodies, chemical reactions convert food into molecules that build muscles and move them. In the leaves of trees and plants, carbon dioxide and water are converted into carbohydrates.

Some chemical reactions are simple, whereas others are quite complex. However, they can all be written with chemical equations that chemists use to describe chemical reactions. In every chemical reaction, the atoms in the reacting substances, called *reactants*, are rearranged to give new substances called *products*.

In chemistry, you calculate and measure the amounts of substances to use in lab. Actually, measuring the amount of a substance is something you do every day. When you cook, you measure out the proper amounts of ingredients so you don't have too much of one or too little of another. At the gas station, you pump a certain amount of fuel into your gas tank. If you paint the walls of a room, you measure the area and purchase the amount of paint that will cover the walls. In the lab, the chemical formula of a substance tells you the number and kinds of atoms it has, which you then use to determine the mass of the substance to use in an experiment.

You do the same thing at home when you use a recipe to make cookies. At the automotive repair shop, a mechanic goes through a similar process when adjusting the fuel system of an engine to allow for the correct amounts of fuel and oxygen. In the body, a certain amount of O_2 must reach the tissues for efficient metabolic reactions. If the oxygenation of the blood is low, the respiratory therapist will oxygenate the patient and recheck the blood levels.

CHAPTER READINESS*

KEY MATH SKILLS
- Calculating Percentages (1.4C)
- Solving Equations (1.4D)
- Writing Numbers in Scientific Notation (1.4F)

CORE CHEMISTRY SKILLS
- Counting Significant Figures (2.2)
- Using Significant Figures in Calculations (2.3)

- Writing Conversion Factors from Equalities (2.5)
- Using Conversion Factors (2.6)
- Using Energy Units (3.4)
- Writing Ionic Formulas (6.2)
- Naming Ionic Compounds (6.3)
- Writing the Names and Formulas for Molecular Compounds (6.5)

*These Key Math Skills and Core Chemistry Skills from previous chapters are listed here for your review as you proceed to the new material in this chapter.

LEARNING GOAL

Write a balanced chemical equation from the formulas of the reactants and products for a reaction; determine the number of atoms in the reactants and products.

7.1 Equations for Chemical Reactions

A *chemical change* occurs when a substance is converted into one or more new substances that have different formulas and different properties. For example, when silver tarnishes, the shiny silver metal (Ag) reacts with sulfur (S) to become the dull, black substance we call tarnish (Ag_2S) (see Figure 7.1).

A chemical change:
the tarnishing of silver

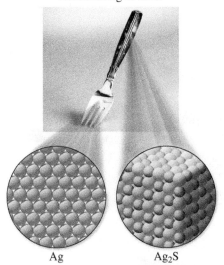

Ag   Ag$_2$S

FIGURE 7.1 ▶ A chemical change produces new substances with new properties.

🅀 Why is the formation of tarnish a chemical change?

Fe   Fe$_2$O$_3$

FIGURE 7.2 ▶ Chemical reactions involve chemical changes. When iron (Fe) reacts with oxygen (O$_2$), the product is rust (Fe$_2$O$_3$).

🅀 What is the evidence for chemical change in this chemical reaction?

A *chemical reaction* always involves chemical change because atoms of the reacting substances form new combinations with new properties. For example, a chemical reaction takes place when a piece of iron (Fe) combines with oxygen (O$_2$) in the air to produce a new substance, rust (Fe$_2$O$_3$), which has a reddish-brown color (see Figure 7.2). During a chemical change, new properties become visible, which are an indication that a chemical reaction has taken place (see Table 7.1).

When you build a model airplane, prepare a new recipe, or mix a medication, you follow a set of directions. These directions tell you what materials to use and the products you will obtain. In chemistry, a *chemical equation* tells us the materials we need and the products that will form.

TABLE 7.1 Types of Visible Evidence of a Chemical Reaction

1. Change in color
2. Formation of a gas (bubbles)
3. Formation of a solid (precipitate)
4. Heat (or a flame) produced or heat absorbed

Writing a Chemical Equation

Suppose you work in a bicycle shop, assembling wheels and frames into bicycles. You could represent this process by a simple equation:

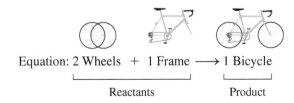

Equation: 2 Wheels + 1 Frame ⟶ 1 Bicycle

Reactants   Product

When you burn charcoal in a grill, the carbon in the charcoal combines with oxygen to form carbon dioxide. We can represent this reaction by a chemical equation.

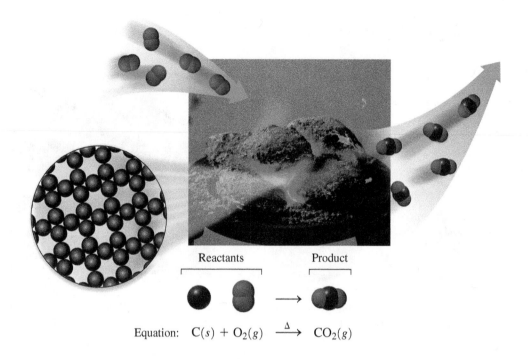

Equation: $C(s) + O_2(g) \xrightarrow{\Delta} CO_2(g)$

Symbol	Meaning
+	Separates two or more formulas
$\longrightarrow$	Reacts to form products
$\xrightarrow{\Delta}$	Reactants are heated
(s)	Solid
(l)	Liquid
(g)	Gas
(aq)	Aqueous

In a **chemical equation**, the formulas of the **reactants** are written on the left of the arrow and the formulas of the **products** on the right. When there are two or more formulas on the same side, they are separated by plus (+) signs. The delta sign (Δ) indicates that heat was used to start the reaction.

Generally, each formula in an equation is followed by an abbreviation, in parentheses, that gives the physical state of the substance: solid (s), liquid (l), or gas (g). If a substance is dissolved in water, it is an aqueous (aq) solution. Table 7.2 summarizes some of the symbols used in equations.

Identifying a Balanced Chemical Equation

When a chemical reaction takes place, the bonds between the atoms of the reactants are broken and new bonds are formed to give the products. All atoms are conserved, which means that atoms cannot be gained, lost, or changed into other types of atoms during a chemical reaction. Every chemical reaction must be written as a **balanced equation**, which shows the same number of atoms for each element in the reactants as well as in the products. For example, the chemical equation we wrote previously for burning carbon is balanced because there is one carbon atom and two oxygen atoms in both the reactants and the products:

$$C(s) + O_2(g) \xrightarrow{\Delta} CO_2(g)$$

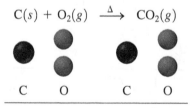

C	O	C	O

Reactant atoms   =   Product atoms

Now consider the reaction in which hydrogen reacts with oxygen to form water written as follows:

$$H_2(g) + O_2(g) \longrightarrow H_2O(g) \qquad \text{Unbalanced}$$

In the *balanced* equation, there are whole numbers called **coefficients** in front of the formulas. On the reactant side, the coefficient of 2 in front of the H_2 formula represents two molecules of hydrogen, which is 4 atoms of H. A coefficient of 1 is understood for O_2,

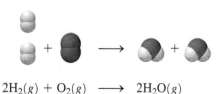

$$2H_2(g) + O_2(g) \longrightarrow 2H_2O(g)$$

Balanced

which gives 2 atoms of O. On the product side, the coefficient of 2 in front of the H_2O formula represents 2 molecules of water. Because the coefficient of 2 multiplies all the atoms in H_2O, there are 4 hydrogen atoms and 2 oxygen atoms in the products. Because there are the same number of hydrogen atoms and oxygen atoms in the reactants as in the products, we know that the equation is *balanced*. This illustrates the *Law of Conservation of Matter*, which states that matter cannot be created or destroyed during a chemical reaction.

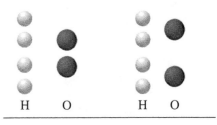

Reactant atoms   =   Product atoms

▶ SAMPLE PROBLEM 7.1 Number of Atoms in Balanced Chemical Equations

Indicate the number of each type of atom in the following balanced chemical equation:

$$Fe_2S_3(s) + 6HCl(aq) \longrightarrow 2FeCl_3(aq) + 3H_2S(g)$$

	Reactants	Products
Fe		
S		
H		
Cl		

SOLUTION

The total number of atoms in each formula is obtained by multiplying the coefficient by each subscript in a chemical formula.

	Reactants	Products
Fe	2 (1 × 2)	2 (2 × 1)
S	3 (1 × 3)	3 (3 × 1)
H	6 (6 × 1)	6 (3 × 2)
Cl	6 (6 × 1)	6 (2 × 3)

STUDY CHECK 7.1

When ethane, C_2H_6, burns in oxygen, the products are carbon dioxide and water. The balanced chemical equation is written as

$$2C_2H_6(g) + 7O_2(g) \xrightarrow{\Delta} 4CO_2(g) + 6H_2O(g)$$

Calculate the number of each type of atom in the reactants and in the products.

ANSWER

In both the reactants and products, there are 4 C atoms, 12 H atoms, and 14 O atoms.

Balancing a Chemical Equation

The chemical reaction that occurs in the flame of a gas burner you use in the laboratory or a gas cooktop is the reaction of methane gas, CH_4, and oxygen to produce carbon dioxide and water. We now show the process of balancing a chemical equation in Sample Problem 7.2.

⚛ **CORE CHEMISTRY SKILL**

Balancing a Chemical Equation

▶ SAMPLE PROBLEM 7.2 Balancing a Chemical Equation

The chemical reaction of methane, CH_4, and oxygen gas, O_2, produces carbon dioxide (CO_2) and water (H_2O). Write a balanced chemical equation for this reaction.

Guide to Balancing a Chemical Equation

STEP 1
Write an equation using the correct formulas for the reactants and products.

STEP 2
Count the atoms of each element in the reactants and products.

STEP 3
Use coefficients to balance each element.

STEP 4
Check the final equation to confirm it is balanced.

SOLUTION

STEP 1 Write an equation using the correct formulas for the reactants and products.

$$CH_4(g) + O_2(g) \xrightarrow{\Delta} CO_2(g) + H_2O(g)$$

CH$_4$ O$_2$ CO$_2$ H$_2$O

STEP 2 Count the atoms of each element in the reactants and products. When we compare the atoms on the reactant side and the atoms on the product side, we see that there are more H atoms in the reactants and more O atoms in the products.

$$CH_4(g) + O_2(g) \xrightarrow{\Delta} CO_2(g) + H_2O(g)$$

Reactants	Products	
1 C atom	1 C atom	Balanced
4 H atoms	2 H atoms	Not balanced
2 O atoms	3 O atoms	Not balanced

STEP 3 Use coefficients to balance each element. We will start by balancing the H atoms in CH$_4$ because it has the most atoms. By placing a coefficient of 2 in front of the formula for H$_2$O, a total of 4 H atoms in the products is obtained. *Only use coefficients to balance an equation. Do not change any of the subscripts: This would alter the chemical formula of a reactant or product.*

$$CH_4(g) + O_2(g) \xrightarrow{\Delta} CO_2(g) + 2H_2O(g)$$

Reactants	Products	
1 C atom	1 C atom	Balanced
4 H atoms	4 H atoms	Balanced
2 O atoms	4 O atoms	Not balanced

We can balance the O atoms on the reactant side by placing a coefficient of 2 in front of the formula O$_2$. There are now 4 O atoms in both the reactants and products.

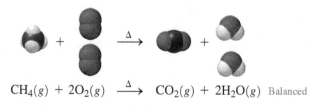

$$CH_4(g) + 2O_2(g) \xrightarrow{\Delta} CO_2(g) + 2H_2O(g) \quad \text{Balanced}$$

STEP 4 Check the final equation to confirm it is balanced. In the final equation, the numbers of atoms of C, H, and O are the same in both the reactants and the products. The equation is balanced.

$$CH_4(g) + 2O_2(g) \xrightarrow{\Delta} CO_2(g) + 2H_2O(g)$$

Reactants	Products	
1 C atom	1 C atom	Balanced
4 H atoms	4 H atoms	Balanced
4 O atoms	4 O atoms	Balanced

In a balanced chemical equation, the coefficients must be the *lowest possible whole numbers*. Suppose you had obtained the following for the balanced equation:

$$2CH_4(g) + 4O_2(g) \xrightarrow{\Delta} 2CO_2(g) + 4H_2O(g) \quad \text{Incorrect}$$

Although there are equal numbers of atoms on both sides of the equation, this is not written correctly. To obtain coefficients that are the lowest whole numbers, we divide all the coefficients by 2.

STUDY CHECK 7.2

Balance the following chemical equation:

$$Al(s) + Cl_2(g) \longrightarrow AlCl_3(s)$$

ANSWER

$$2Al(s) + 3Cl_2(g) \longrightarrow 2AlCl_3(s)$$

▶ **SAMPLE PROBLEM 7.3 Balancing Chemical Equations with Polyatomic Ions**

Balance the following chemical equation:

$$Na_3PO_4(aq) + MgCl_2(aq) \longrightarrow Mg_3(PO_4)_2(s) + NaCl(aq)$$

SOLUTION

STEP **1** Write an equation using the correct formulas for the reactants and products.

$$Na_3PO_4(aq) + MgCl_2(aq) \longrightarrow Mg_3(PO_4)_2(s) + NaCl(aq) \quad \text{Unbalanced}$$

STEP **2** Count the atoms of each element in the reactants and products. When we compare the number of ions in the reactants and products, we find that the equation is not balanced. In this equation, we can balance the phosphate ion as a group of atoms because it appears on both sides of the equation.

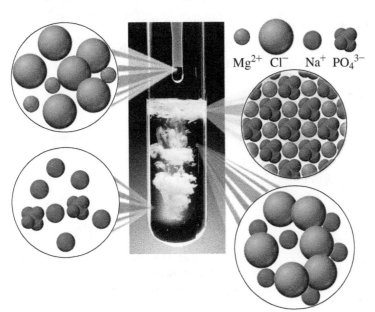

Mg^{2+} Cl^- Na^+ $PO_4{}^{3-}$

$$Na_3PO_4(aq) + MgCl_2(aq) \longrightarrow Mg_3(PO_4)_2(s) + NaCl(aq)$$

Reactants	Products	
3 Na^+	1 Na^+	Not balanced
1 PO_4^{3-}	2 PO_4^{3-}	Not balanced
1 Mg^{2+}	3 Mg^{2+}	Not balanced
2 Cl^-	1 Cl^-	Not balanced

STEP 3   Use coefficients to balance each element. We begin with the formula that has the highest subscript values, which in this equation is $Mg_3(PO_4)_2$. The subscript 3 in $Mg_3(PO_4)_2$ is used as a coefficient for $MgCl_2$ to balance magnesium. The subscript 2 in $Mg_3(PO_4)_2$ is used as a coefficient for Na_3PO_4 to balance the phosphate ion.

$$2Na_3PO_4(aq) + 3MgCl_2(aq) \longrightarrow Mg_3(PO_4)_2(s) + NaCl(aq)$$

Reactants	Products	
6 Na^+	1 Na^+	Not balanced
2 PO_4^{3-}	2 PO_4^{3-}	Balanced
3 Mg^{2+}	3 Mg^{2+}	Balanced
6 Cl^-	1 Cl^-	Not balanced

In the reactants and products, we see that the sodium and chloride ions are not yet balanced. A coefficient of 6 is placed in front of the NaCl to balance the equation.

$$2Na_3PO_4(aq) + 3MgCl_2(aq) \longrightarrow Mg_3(PO_4)_2(s) + 6NaCl(aq)$$

STEP 4   Check the final equation to confirm it is balanced. A check of the total number of ions confirms the equation is balanced. A coefficient of 1 is understood and not usually written.

$$2Na_3PO_4(aq) + 3MgCl_2(aq) \longrightarrow Mg_3(PO_4)_2(s) + 6NaCl(aq) \quad \text{Balanced}$$

Reactants	Products	
6 Na^+	6 Na^+	Balanced
2 PO_4^{3-}	2 PO_4^{3-}	Balanced
3 Mg^{2+}	3 Mg^{2+}	Balanced
6 Cl^-	6 Cl^-	Balanced

STUDY CHECK 7.3

Balance the following chemical equation:

$$Pb(NO_3)_2(aq) + AlBr_3(aq) \longrightarrow PbBr_2(s) + Al(NO_3)_3(aq)$$

ANSWER

$$3Pb(NO_3)_2(aq) + 2AlBr_3(aq) \longrightarrow 3PbBr_2(s) + 2Al(NO_3)_3(aq)$$

QUESTIONS AND PROBLEMS

7.1 Equations for Chemical Reactions

LEARNING GOAL Write a balanced chemical equation from the formulas of the reactants and products for a reaction; determine the number of atoms in the reactants and products.

7.1   Balance each of the following chemical equations:
   a. $N_2(g) + O_2(g) \longrightarrow NO(g)$
   b. $HgO(s) \longrightarrow Hg(l) + O_2(g)$
   c. $Fe(s) + O_2(g) \longrightarrow Fe_2O_3(s)$
   d. $Na(s) + Cl_2(g) \longrightarrow NaCl(s)$
   e. $Cu_2O(s) + O_2(g) \longrightarrow CuO(s)$

7.2   Balance each of the following chemical equations:
   a. $Ca(s) + Br_2(l) \longrightarrow CaBr_2(s)$
   b. $P_4(s) + O_2(g) \longrightarrow P_4O_{10}(s)$

  c. $C_4H_8(g) + O_2(g) \xrightarrow{\Delta} CO_2(g) + H_2O(g)$
  d. $Ca(OH)_2(aq) + HNO_3(aq) \longrightarrow$
  $\qquad\qquad\qquad\qquad Ca(NO_3)_2(aq) + H_2O(l)$
  e. $Fe_2O_3(s) + C(s) \longrightarrow Fe(s) + CO(g)$

7.3 Balance each of the following chemical equations:
  a. $Mg(s) + AgNO_3(aq) \longrightarrow Mg(NO_3)_2(aq) + Ag(s)$
  b. $CuCO_3(s) \longrightarrow CuO(s) + CO_2(g)$
  c. $Al(s) + CuSO_4(aq) \longrightarrow Cu(s) + Al_2(SO_4)_3(aq)$
  d. $Pb(NO_3)_2(aq) + NaCl(aq) \longrightarrow PbCl_2(s) + NaNO_3(aq)$
  e. $Al(s) + HCl(aq) \longrightarrow AlCl_3(aq) + H_2(g)$

7.4 Balance each of the following chemical equations:
  a. $Zn(s) + HNO_3(aq) \longrightarrow Zn(NO_3)_2(aq) + H_2(g)$
  b. $Al(s) + H_2SO_4(aq) \longrightarrow Al_2(SO_4)_3(aq) + H_2(g)$
  c. $K_2SO_4(aq) + BaCl_2(aq) \longrightarrow BaSO_4(s) + KCl(aq)$
  d. $CaCO_3(s) \longrightarrow CaO(s) + CO_2(g)$
  e. $AlCl_3(aq) + KOH(aq) \longrightarrow Al(OH)_3(s) + KCl(aq)$

7.5 Balance each of the following chemical equations:
  a. $Fe_2O_3(s) + CO(g) \longrightarrow Fe(s) + CO_2(g)$
  b. $Li_3N(s) \longrightarrow Li(s) + N_2(g)$
  c. $Al(s) + HBr(aq) \longrightarrow AlBr_3(aq) + H_2(g)$
  d. $Ba(OH)_2(aq) + Na_3PO_4(aq) \longrightarrow$
  $\qquad\qquad\qquad\qquad Ba_3(PO_4)_2(s) + NaOH(aq)$
  e. $As_4S_6(s) + O_2(g) \longrightarrow As_4O_6(s) + SO_2(g)$

7.6 Balance each of the following chemical equations:
  a. $K(s) + H_2O(l) \longrightarrow KOH(aq) + H_2(g)$
  b. $Cr(s) + S_8(s) \longrightarrow Cr_2S_3(s)$
  c. $BCl_3(s) + H_2O(l) \longrightarrow H_3BO_3(aq) + HCl(aq)$
  d. $Fe(OH)_3(s) + H_2SO_4(aq) \longrightarrow Fe_2(SO_4)_3(aq) + H_2O(l)$
  e. $BaCl_2(aq) + Na_3PO_4(aq) \longrightarrow$
  $\qquad\qquad\qquad\qquad Ba_3(PO_4)_2(s) + NaCl(aq)$

7.7 Write a balanced equation using the correct formulas and include conditions (s, l, g, or aq) for each of the following chemical reactions:
  a. Lithium metal reacts with liquid water to form hydrogen gas and aqueous lithium hydroxide.
  b. Solid phosphorus reacts with chlorine gas to form solid phosphorus pentachloride.

  c. Solid iron(II) oxide reacts with carbon monoxide gas to form solid iron and carbon dioxide gas.
  d. Liquid pentene (C_5H_{10}) burns in oxygen gas to form carbon dioxide gas and water vapor.
  e. Hydrogen sulfide gas and solid iron(III) chloride react to form solid iron(III) sulfide and hydrogen chloride gas.

7.8 Write a balanced equation using the correct formulas and include conditions (s, l, g, or aq) for each of the following chemical reactions:
  a. Solid sodium carbonate decomposes to produce solid sodium oxide and carbon dioxide gas.
  b. Nitrogen oxide gas reacts with carbon monoxide gas to produce nitrogen gas and carbon dioxide gas.
  c. Iron metal reacts with solid sulfur to produce solid iron(III) sulfide.
  d. Solid calcium reacts with nitrogen gas to produce solid calcium nitride.
  e. In the *Apollo* lunar module, hydrazine gas, N_2H_4, reacts with dinitrogen tetroxide gas to produce gaseous nitrogen and water vapor.

Clinical Applications

7.9 Dinitrogen oxide, also known as laughing gas, is a sweet-tasting gas used in dentistry. When solid ammonium nitrate is heated, the products are gaseous water and gaseous dinitrogen oxide. Write the balanced chemical equation for the reaction.

7.10 When ethanol $C_2H_6O(aq)$ is consumed, it reacts with O_2 gas in the body to produce gaseous carbon dioxide and liquid water. Write the balanced chemical equation for the reaction.

7.11 In the body, the amino acid alanine $C_3H_7NO_2(aq)$ reacts with O_2 gas to produce gaseous carbon dioxide, liquid water, and urea, $CH_4N_2O(aq)$. Write the balanced chemical equation for the reaction.

7.12 In the body, the amino acid asparagine $C_4H_8N_2O_3(aq)$ reacts with O_2 gas in the body to produce gaseous carbon dioxide, liquid water, and urea, $CH_4N_2O(aq)$. Write the balanced chemical equation for the reaction.

7.2 Types of Reactions

A great number of reactions occur in nature, in biological systems, and in the laboratory. However, there are some general patterns among all reactions that help us classify reactions. Some reactions may fit into more than one reaction type.

Combination Reactions

In a **combination reaction**, two or more elements or compounds bond to form one product. For example, sulfur and oxygen combine to form the product sulfur dioxide.

$$S(s) + O_2(g) \longrightarrow SO_2(g)$$

In Figure 7.3, the elements magnesium and oxygen combine to form a single product, which is the ionic compound magnesium oxide formed from Mg^{2+} and O^{2-} ions.

$$2Mg(s) + O_2(g) \longrightarrow 2MgO(s)$$

LEARNING GOAL

Identify a reaction as a combination, decomposition, single replacement, double replacement, or combustion.

Combination

Two or more reactants	combine to yield	a single product
+	$\longrightarrow$	

CORE CHEMISTRY SKILL

Classifying Types of Chemical Reactions

In other examples of combination reactions, elements or compounds combine to form a single product.

$$N_2(g) + 3H_2(g) \longrightarrow 2NH_3(g)$$
Ammonia

$$Cu(s) + S(s) \longrightarrow CuS(s)$$

$$MgO(s) + CO_2(g) \longrightarrow MgCO_3(s)$$

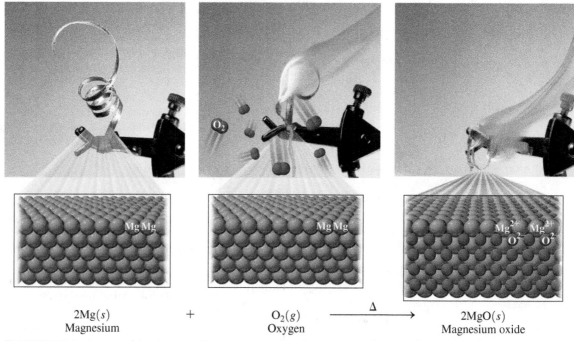

$$\begin{array}{ccccc} 2Mg(s) & + & O_2(g) & \xrightarrow{\Delta} & 2MgO(s) \\ \text{Magnesium} & & \text{Oxygen} & & \text{Magnesium oxide} \end{array}$$

FIGURE 7.3 ▶ In a combination reaction, two or more substances combine to form one substance as product.

Q What happens to the atoms in the reactants in a combination reaction?

Decomposition Reactions

Decomposition

A   splits   two or more
reactant into   products
 $\longrightarrow$ +

In a **decomposition reaction**, a reactant splits into two or more simpler products. For example, when mercury(II) oxide is heated, the compound breaks apart into mercury atoms and oxygen (see Figure 7.4).

$$2HgO(s) \xrightarrow{\Delta} 2Hg(l) + O_2(g)$$

In another example of a decomposition reaction, calcium carbonate breaks apart into simpler compounds of calcium oxide and carbon dioxide.

$$CaCO_3(s) \xrightarrow{\Delta} CaO(s) + CO_2(g)$$

Replacement Reactions

In a replacement reaction, elements in a compound are replaced by other elements. In a **single replacement reaction**, a reacting element switches place with an element in the other reacting compound.

Single replacement

One element   replaces   another element
A + B C $\longrightarrow$ A C + B

In the single replacement reaction shown in Figure 7.5, zinc replaces hydrogen in hydrochloric acid, HCl(aq).

$$Zn(s) + 2HCl(aq) \longrightarrow H_2(g) + ZnCl_2(aq)$$

In another single replacement reaction, chlorine replaces bromine in the compound potassium bromide.

$$Cl_2(g) + 2KBr(s) \longrightarrow 2KCl(s) + Br_2(l)$$

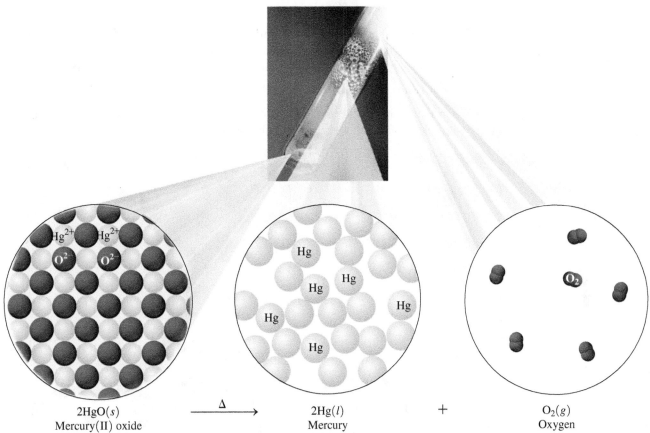

$$2HgO(s) \xrightarrow{\Delta} 2Hg(l) + O_2(g)$$

Mercury(II) oxide   Mercury   Oxygen

FIGURE 7.4 ▶ In a decomposition reaction, one reactant breaks down into two or more products.

Q How do the differences in the reactant and products classify this as a decomposition reaction?

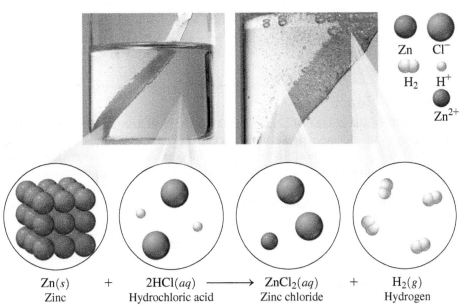

$$Zn(s) + 2HCl(aq) \longrightarrow ZnCl_2(aq) + H_2(g)$$

Zinc   Hydrochloric acid   Zinc chloride   Hydrogen

FIGURE 7.5 ▶ In a single replacement reaction, an atom or ion replaces an atom or ion in a compound.

Q What changes in the formulas of the reactants identify this equation as a single replacement?

In a **double replacement reaction**, the positive ions in the reacting compounds switch places.

Double replacement

Two elements   replace   each other

$$\boxed{A} \boxed{B} + \boxed{C} \boxed{D} \longrightarrow \boxed{A} \boxed{D} + \boxed{C} \boxed{B}$$

In the reaction shown in Figure 7.6, barium ions change places with sodium ions in the reactants to form sodium chloride and a white solid precipitate of barium sulfate. The formulas of the products depend on the charges of the ions.

$$BaCl_2(aq) + Na_2SO_4(aq) \longrightarrow BaSO_4(s) + 2NaCl(aq)$$

When sodium hydroxide and hydrochloric acid (HCl) react, sodium and hydrogen ions switch places, forming water and sodium chloride.

$$NaOH(aq) + HCl(aq) \longrightarrow H_2O(l) + NaCl(aq)$$

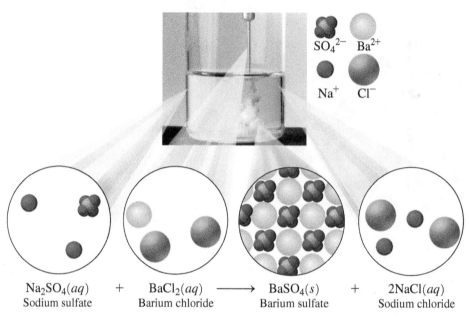

SO_4^{2-} Ba^{2+}

Na^+ Cl^-

$$\underset{\substack{\text{Sodium sulfate}}}{Na_2SO_4(aq)} + \underset{\substack{\text{Barium chloride}}}{BaCl_2(aq)} \longrightarrow \underset{\substack{\text{Barium sulfate}}}{BaSO_4(s)} + \underset{\substack{\text{Sodium chloride}}}{2NaCl(aq)}$$

FIGURE 7.6 ▶ In a double replacement reaction, the positive ions in the reactants replace each other.

Q How do the changes in the formulas of the reactants identify this equation as a double replacement reaction?

Combustion Reactions

The burning of a candle and the burning of fuel in the engine of a car are examples of combustion reactions. In a **combustion reaction**, a carbon-containing compound, usually a fuel, burns in oxygen from the air to produce carbon dioxide (CO_2), water (H_2O), and energy in the form of heat or a flame. For example, methane gas (CH_4) undergoes combustion when used to cook our food on a gas cooktop and to heat our homes. In the equation for the combustion of methane, each element in the fuel (CH_4) forms a compound with oxygen.

$$CH_4(g) + 2O_2(g) \xrightarrow{\Delta} CO_2(g) + 2H_2O(g) + energy$$
Methane

The balanced equation for the combustion of propane (C_3H_8) is

$$C_3H_8(g) + 5O_2(g) \xrightarrow{\Delta} 3CO_2(g) + 4H_2O(g) + energy$$

In a combustion reaction, a candle burns using the oxygen in the air.

Propane is the fuel used in portable heaters and gas barbecues. Gasoline, a mixture of liquid hydrocarbons, is the fuel that powers our cars, lawn mowers, and snow blowers.

Table 7.3 summarizes the reaction types and gives examples.

TABLE 7.3 Summary of Reaction Types

Reaction Type	Example
Combination	
$A + B \longrightarrow AB$	$Ca(s) + Cl_2(g) \longrightarrow CaCl_2(s)$
Decomposition	
$AB \longrightarrow A + B$	$Fe_2S_3(s) \longrightarrow 2Fe(s) + 3S(s)$
Single Replacement	
$A + BC \longrightarrow AC + B$	$Cu(s) + 2AgNO_3(aq) \longrightarrow Cu(NO_3)_2(aq) + 2Ag(s)$
Double Replacement	
$AB + CD \longrightarrow AD + CB$	$BaCl_2(aq) + K_2SO_4(aq) \longrightarrow BaSO_4(s) + 2KCl(aq)$
Combustion	
$C_XH_Y + ZO_2(g) \xrightarrow{\Delta} XCO_2(g) + \frac{Y}{2}H_2O(g) + \text{energy}$	$CH_4(g) + 2O_2(g) \xrightarrow{\Delta} CO_2(g) + 2H_2O(g) + \text{energy}$

▶ **SAMPLE PROBLEM 7.4 Identifying Reactions and Predicting Products**

Classify each of the following as a combination, decomposition, single replacement, double replacement, or combustion reaction:

a. $2Fe_2O_3(s) + 3C(s) \longrightarrow 3CO_2(g) + 4Fe(s)$
b. $2KClO_3(s) \xrightarrow{\Delta} 2KCl(s) + 3O_2(g)$
c. $C_2H_4(g) + 3O_2(g) \xrightarrow{\Delta} 2CO_2(g) + 2H_2O(g) + \text{energy}$

SOLUTION

a. In this single replacement reaction, a C atom replaces Fe in Fe_2O_3 to form the compound CO_2 and Fe atoms.
b. When one reactant breaks down to produce two products, the reaction is decomposition.
c. The reaction of a carbon compound with oxygen to produce carbon dioxide, water, and energy makes this a combustion reaction.

STUDY CHECK 7.4

Nitrogen gas (N_2) and oxygen gas (O_2) react to form nitrogen dioxide gas. Write the balanced chemical equation using the correct chemical formulas of the reactants and product, and identify the reaction type.

ANSWER

$N_2(g) + 2O_2(g) \longrightarrow 2NO_2(g)$ combination

Chemistry Link to Health

Incomplete Combustion: Toxicity of Carbon Monoxide

When a propane heater, fireplace, or woodstove is used in a closed room, there must be adequate ventilation. If the supply of oxygen is limited, incomplete combustion from burning gas, oil, or wood produces carbon monoxide. The incomplete combustion of methane in natural gas is written

$$2CH_4(g) + 3O_2(g) \xrightarrow{\Delta} 2CO(g) + 4H_2O(g) + \text{heat}$$
Limited oxygen supply   Carbon monoxide

Carbon monoxide (CO) is a colorless, odorless, poisonous gas. When inhaled, CO passes into the bloodstream, where it attaches to hemoglobin, which reduces the amount of oxygen (O_2) reaching the cells.

As a result, a person can experience a reduction in exercise capability, visual perception, and manual dexterity.

Hemoglobin is the protein that transports O_2 in the blood. When the amount of hemoglobin bound to CO (COHb) is about 10%, a person may experience shortness of breath, mild headache, and drowsiness. Heavy smokers can have levels of COHb in their blood as high as 9%. When as much as 30% of the hemoglobin is bound to CO, a person may experience more severe symptoms, including dizziness, mental confusion, severe headache, and nausea. If 50% or more of the hemoglobin is bound to CO, a person could become unconscious and die if not treated immediately with oxygen.

QUESTIONS AND PROBLEMS

7.2 Types of Reactions

LEARNING GOAL Identify a reaction as a combination, decomposition, single replacement, double replacement, or combustion.

7.13 Classify each of the following as a combination, decomposition, single replacement, double replacement, or combustion reaction:
 a. $2Al_2O_3(s) \xrightarrow{\Delta} 4Al(s) + 3O_2(g)$
 b. $Br_2(g) + BaI_2(s) \longrightarrow BaBr_2(s) + I_2(g)$
 c. $2C_2H_2(g) + 5O_2(g) \xrightarrow{\Delta} 4CO_2(g) + 2H_2O(g)$
 d. $BaCl_2(aq) + K_2CO_3(aq) \longrightarrow BaCO_3(s) + 2KCl(aq)$
 e. $Pb(s) + O_2(g) \longrightarrow PbO_2(s)$

7.14 Classify each of the following as a combination, decomposition, single replacement, double replacement, or combustion reaction:
 a. $H_2(g) + Br_2(g) \longrightarrow 2HBr(g)$
 b. $AgNO_3(aq) + NaCl(aq) \longrightarrow AgCl(s) + NaNO_3(aq)$
 c. $2H_2O_2(aq) \longrightarrow 2H_2O(l) + O_2(g)$
 d. $Zn(s) + CuCl_2(aq) \longrightarrow Cu(s) + ZnCl_2(aq)$
 e. $C_5H_8(g) + 7O_2(g) \xrightarrow{\Delta} 5CO_2(g) + 4H_2O(g)$

7.15 Classify each of the following as a combination, decomposition, single replacement, double replacement, or combustion reaction:
 a. $4Fe(s) + 3O_2(g) \longrightarrow 2Fe_2O_3(s)$
 b. $Mg(s) + 2AgNO_3(aq) \longrightarrow Mg(NO_3)_2(aq) + 2Ag(s)$
 c. $CuCO_3(s) \xrightarrow{\Delta} CuO(s) + CO_2(g)$

 d. $Al_2(SO_4)_3(aq) + 6KOH(aq) \longrightarrow$
   $2Al(OH)_3(s) + 3K_2SO_4(aq)$
 e. $C_4H_8(g) + 6O_2(g) \xrightarrow{\Delta} 4CO_2(g) + 4H_2O(g)$

7.16 Classify each of the following as a combination, decomposition, single replacement, double replacement, or combustion reaction:
 a. $CuO(s) + 2HCl(aq) \longrightarrow CuCl_2(aq) + H_2O(l)$
 b. $2Al(s) + 3Br_2(g) \longrightarrow 2AlBr_3(s)$
 c. $2C_2H_2(g) + 5O_2(g) \xrightarrow{\Delta} 4CO_2(g) + 2H_2O(g)$
 d. $Fe_2O_3(s) + 3C(s) \longrightarrow 2Fe(s) + 3CO(g)$
 e. $C_6H_{12}O_6(aq) \longrightarrow 2C_2H_6O(aq) + 2CO_2(g)$

7.17 Using Table 7.3, predict the products that would result from each of the following reactions and balance:
 a. combination: $Mg(s) + Cl_2(g) \longrightarrow$
 b. decomposition: $HBr(g) \longrightarrow$
 c. single replacement: $Mg(s) + Zn(NO_3)_2(aq) \longrightarrow$
 d. double replacement: $K_2S(aq) + Pb(NO_3)_2(aq) \longrightarrow$
 e. combustion: $C_2H_6(g) + O_2(g) \xrightarrow{\Delta}$

7.18 Using Table 7.3, predict the products that would result from each of the following reactions and balance:
 a. combination: $Ca(s) + O_2(g) \longrightarrow$
 b. combustion: $C_6H_6(g) + O_2(g) \xrightarrow{\Delta}$
 c. decomposition: $PbO_2(s) \xrightarrow{\Delta}$
 d. single replacement: $KI(s) + Cl_2(g) \longrightarrow$
 e. double replacement: $CuCl_2(aq) + Na_2S(aq) \longrightarrow$

Define the terms oxidation and reduction; identify the reactants oxidized and reduced.

Rust forms when the oxygen in the air reacts with iron.

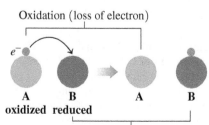

Oxidation (loss of electron)

e^-

A **B** **A** **B**
oxidized reduced

Reduction (gain of electron)

7.3 Oxidation–Reduction Reactions

Perhaps you have never heard of an oxidation and reduction reaction. However, this type of reaction has many important applications in your everyday life. When you see a rusty nail, tarnish on a silver spoon, or corrosion on metal, you are observing oxidation.

$$4Fe(s) + 3O_2(g) \longrightarrow 2Fe_2O_3(s) \quad \text{Fe is oxidized}$$
Rust

When we turn the lights on in our automobiles, an oxidation–reduction reaction within the car battery provides the electricity. On a cold, wintry day, we might build a fire. As the wood burns, oxygen combines with carbon and hydrogen to produce carbon dioxide, water, and heat. In the previous section, we called this a combustion reaction, but it is also an *oxidation–reduction reaction*. When we eat foods with starches in them, the starches break down to give glucose, which is oxidized in our cells to give us energy along with carbon dioxide and water. Every breath we take provides oxygen to carry out oxidation in our cells.

$$C_6H_{12}O_6(aq) + 6O_2(g) \longrightarrow 6CO_2(g) + 6H_2O(l) + \text{energy}$$
Glucose

Oxidation–Reduction Reactions

In an **oxidation–reduction reaction** (*redox*), electrons are transferred from one substance to another. If one substance loses electrons, another substance must gain electrons. **Oxidation** is defined as the *loss* of electrons; **reduction** is the *gain* of electrons.

One way to remember these definitions is to use the following acronym:

OIL RIG

Oxidation **I**s **L**oss of electrons
Reduction **I**s **G**ain of electrons

Oxidation–Reduction

In general, atoms of metals lose electrons to form positive ions, whereas nonmetals gain electrons to form negative ions. Now we can say that metals are oxidized and nonmetals are reduced.

The green color that appears on copper surfaces from weathering, known as *patina*, is a mixture of $CuCO_3$ and CuO. We can now look at the oxidation and reduction reactions that take place when copper metal reacts with oxygen in the air to produce copper(II) oxide.

$$2Cu(s) + O_2(g) \longrightarrow 2CuO(s)$$

The element Cu in the reactants has a charge of 0, but in the CuO product, it is present as Cu^{2+}, which has a 2+ charge. Because the Cu atom lost two electrons, the charge is more positive. This means that Cu was oxidized in the reaction.

$$Cu^0(s) \longrightarrow Cu^{2+}(s) + 2\,e^- \quad \text{Oxidation: loss of electrons by Cu}$$

At the same time, the element O in the reactants has a charge of 0, but in the CuO product, it is present as O^{2-}, which has a 2− charge. Because the O atom has gained two electrons, the charge is more negative. This means that O was reduced in the reaction.

$$O_2^0(g) + 4\,e^- \longrightarrow 2O^{2-}(s) \quad \text{Reduction: gain of electrons by O}$$

Thus, the overall equation for the formation of CuO involves an oxidation and a reduction that occur simultaneously. In every oxidation and reduction, the number of electrons lost must be equal to the number of electrons gained. Therefore, we multiply the oxidation reaction of Cu by 2. Canceling the $4\,e^-$ on each side, we obtain the overall oxidation–reduction equation for the formation of CuO.

$$
\begin{array}{ll}
2Cu(s) \longrightarrow 2Cu^{2+}(s) + \cancel{4e^-} & \text{Oxidation} \\
O_2(g) + \cancel{4e^-} \longrightarrow 2O^{2-}(s) & \text{Reduction} \\
\hline
2Cu(s) + O_2(g) \longrightarrow 2CuO(s) & \text{Oxidation–reduction equation}
\end{array}
$$

As we see in the next reaction between zinc and copper(II) sulfate, there is always an oxidation with every reduction (see Figure 7.7).

$$Zn(s) + CuSO_4(aq) \longrightarrow ZnSO_4(aq) + Cu(s)$$

We rewrite the equation to show the atoms and ions.

$$\mathbf{Zn}(s) + \mathbf{Cu^{2+}}(aq) + SO_4{}^{2-}(aq) \longrightarrow \mathbf{Zn^{2+}}(aq) + SO_4{}^{2-}(aq) + \mathbf{Cu}(s)$$

The green patina on copper is due to oxidation.

Reduced		Oxidized
Na	Oxidation: Lose e^- →	$Na^+ + e^-$
Ca		$Ca^{2+} + 2\,e^-$
$2Br^-$	← Reduction: Gain e	$Br_2 + 2\,e^-$
Fe^{2+}		$Fe^{3+} + e^-$

Oxidation is a loss of electrons; reduction is a gain of electrons.

⚛ **CORE CHEMISTRY SKILL**

Identifying Oxidized and Reduced Substances

FIGURE 7.7 ▶ In this single replacement reaction, Zn(s) is oxidized to $Zn^{2+}(aq)$ when it provides two electrons to reduce $Cu^{2+}(aq)$ to Cu(s):

$$Zn(s) + Cu^{2+}(aq) \longrightarrow Cu(s) + Zn^{2+}(aq)$$

❓ In the oxidation, does Zn(s) lose or gain electrons?

Explore Your World

Oxidation of Fruits and Vegetables

Freshly cut surfaces of fruits and vegetables discolor when exposed to oxygen in the air. Cut three slices of a fruit or vegetable such as apple, potato, avocado, or banana. Leave one piece on the kitchen counter (uncovered). Wrap one piece in plastic wrap and leave it on the kitchen counter. Dip one piece in lemon juice and leave it uncovered.

Questions

1. What changes take place in each sample after 1 to 2 h?
2. Why would wrapping fruits and vegetables slow the rate of discoloration?
3. If lemon juice contains vitamin C (an antioxidant), why would dipping a fruit or vegetable in lemon juice affect the oxidation reaction on the surface of the fruit or vegetable?
4. Other kinds of antioxidants are vitamin E, citric acid, and BHT. Look for these antioxidants on the labels of cereals, potato chips, and other foods in your kitchen. Why are antioxidants added to food products that will be stored on our kitchen shelves?

In this reaction, Zn atoms lose two electrons to form Zn^{2+}. The increase in positive charge indicates that Zn is oxidized. At the same time, Cu^{2+} gains two electrons. The decrease in charge indicates that Cu is reduced. The SO_4^{2-} ions are *spectator ions*, which are present in both the reactants and products and do not change.

$$Zn(s) \longrightarrow Zn^{2+}(aq) + 2\,e^- \quad \text{Oxidation of Zn}$$
$$Cu^{2+}(aq) + 2\,e^- \longrightarrow Cu(s) \quad \text{Reduction of } Cu^{2+}$$

In this single replacement reaction, zinc was oxidized and copper(II) ion was reduced.

Oxidation and Reduction in Biological Systems

Oxidation may also involve the addition of oxygen or the loss of hydrogen, and reduction may involve the loss of oxygen or the gain of hydrogen. In the cells of the body, oxidation of organic (carbon) compounds involves the transfer of hydrogen atoms (H), which are composed of electrons and protons. For example, the oxidation of a typical biochemical molecule can involve the transfer of two hydrogen atoms (or $2H^+$ and $2\,e^-$) to a hydrogen ion acceptor such as the coenzyme FAD (flavin adenine dinucleotide). The coenzyme is reduced to $FADH_2$.

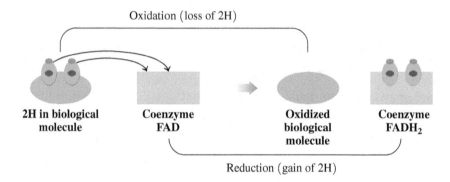

In many biochemical oxidation–reduction reactions, the transfer of hydrogen atoms is necessary for the production of energy in the cells. For example, methyl alcohol (CH_3OH), a poisonous substance, is metabolized in the body by the following reactions:

$$CH_3OH \longrightarrow H_2CO + 2H \quad \text{Oxidation: loss of H atoms}$$
Methyl alcohol   Formaldehyde

The formaldehyde can be oxidized further, this time by the addition of oxygen, to produce formic acid.

$$2H_2CO + O_2 \longrightarrow 2H_2CO_2 \quad \text{Oxidation: addition of O atoms}$$
Formaldehyde   Formic acid

Finally, formic acid is oxidized to carbon dioxide and water.

$$2H_2CO_2 + O_2 \longrightarrow 2CO_2 + 2H_2O \quad \text{Oxidation: addition of O atoms}$$
Formic acid

The intermediate products of the oxidation of methyl alcohol are quite toxic, causing blindness and possibly death as they interfere with key reactions in the cells of the body.

In summary, we find that the particular definition of oxidation and reduction we use depends on the process that occurs in the reaction. All these definitions are summarized in Table 7.4. Oxidation always involves a loss of electrons, but it may also be seen as an addition of oxygen or the loss of hydrogen atoms. A reduction always involves a gain of electrons and may also be seen as the loss of oxygen or the gain of hydrogen.

TABLE 7.4 Characteristics of Oxidation and Reduction

Always Involves	May Involve
Oxidation	
Loss of electrons	Addition of oxygen
	Loss of hydrogen
Reduction	
Gain of electrons	Loss of oxygen
	Gain of hydrogen

QUESTIONS AND PROBLEMS

7.3 Oxidation–Reduction Reactions

LEARNING GOAL Define the terms oxidation and reduction; identify the reactants oxidized and reduced.

7.19 Identify each of the following as an oxidation or a reduction:
 a. $Na^+(aq) + e^- \longrightarrow Na(s)$
 b. $Ni(s) \longrightarrow Ni^{2+}(aq) + 2\,e^-$
 c. $Cr^{3+}(aq) + 3\,e^- \longrightarrow Cr(s)$
 d. $2H^+(aq) + 2\,e^- \longrightarrow H_2(g)$

7.20 Identify each of the following as an oxidation or a reduction:
 a. $O_2(g) + 4\,e^- \longrightarrow 2O^{2-}(aq)$
 b. $Ag(s) \longrightarrow Ag^+(aq) + e^-$
 c. $Fe^{3+}(aq) + e^- \longrightarrow Fe^{2+}(aq)$
 d. $2Br^-(aq) \longrightarrow Br_2(l) + 2\,e^-$

7.21 In each of the following reactions, identify the reactant that is oxidized and the reactant that is reduced:
 a. $Zn(s) + Cl_2(g) \longrightarrow ZnCl_2(s)$
 b. $Cl_2(g) + 2NaBr(aq) \longrightarrow 2NaCl(aq) + Br_2(l)$
 c. $2PbO(s) \longrightarrow 2Pb(s) + O_2(g)$
 d. $2Fe^{3+}(aq) + Sn^{2+}(aq) \longrightarrow 2Fe^{2+}(aq) + Sn^{4+}(aq)$

7.22 In each of the following reactions, identify the reactant that is oxidized and the reactant that is reduced:
 a. $2Li(s) + F_2(g) \longrightarrow 2LiF(s)$
 b. $Cl_2(g) + 2KI(aq) \longrightarrow 2KCl(aq) + I_2(s)$
 c. $2Al(s) + 3Sn^{2+}(aq) \longrightarrow 2Al^{3+}(aq) + 3Sn(s)$
 d. $Fe(s) + CuSO_4(aq) \longrightarrow FeSO_4(aq) + Cu(s)$

Rx Clinical Applications

7.23 In the mitochondria of human cells, energy is provided by the oxidation and reduction reactions of the iron ions in the cytochromes in electron transport. Identify each of the following reactions as an oxidation or reduction:
 a. $Fe^{3+} + e^- \longrightarrow Fe^{2+}$ **b.** $Fe^{2+} \longrightarrow Fe^{3+} + e^-$

7.24 Chlorine (Cl_2) is a strong germicide used to disinfect drinking water and to kill microbes in swimming pools. If the product is Cl^-, was the elemental chlorine oxidized or reduced?

7.25 When linoleic acid, an unsaturated fatty acid, reacts with hydrogen, it forms a saturated fatty acid. Is linoleic acid oxidized or reduced in the hydrogenation reaction?

$$C_{18}H_{32}O_2 + 2H_2 \longrightarrow C_{18}H_{36}O_2$$
Linoleic acid

7.26 In one of the reactions in the citric acid cycle, which provides energy, succinic acid is converted to fumaric acid.

$$C_4H_6O_4 \longrightarrow C_4H_4O_4 + 2H$$
Succinic acid   Fumaric acid

The reaction is accompanied by a coenzyme, flavin adenine dinucleotide (FAD).

$$FAD + 2H \longrightarrow FADH_2$$

 a. Is succinic acid oxidized or reduced?
 b. Is FAD oxidized or reduced?
 c. Why would the two reactions occur together?

7.4 The Mole

At the grocery store, you buy eggs by the dozen or soda by the case. In an office-supply store, pencils are ordered by the gross and paper by the ream. The terms *dozen*, *case*, *gross*, and *ream* are used to count the number of items present. For example, when you buy a dozen eggs, you know that there will be 12 eggs in the carton.

LEARNING GOAL

Use Avogadro's number to determine the number of particles in a given number of moles.

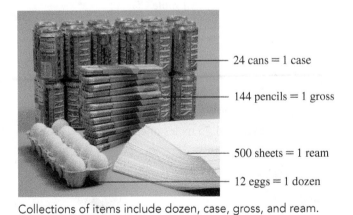

24 cans = 1 case

144 pencils = 1 gross

500 sheets = 1 ream

12 eggs = 1 dozen

Collections of items include dozen, case, gross, and ream.

Avogadro's Number

In chemistry, particles such as atoms, molecules, and ions are counted by the **mole**, which contains 6.02×10^{23} items. This value, known as **Avogadro's number**, is a very big number because atoms are so small that it takes an extremely large number of atoms to provide a sufficient amount to weigh and use in chemical reactions. Avogadro's number is named for Amedeo Avogadro (1776–1856), an Italian physicist.

CORE CHEMISTRY SKILL

Converting Particles to Moles

One mole of sulfur contains 6.02×10^{23} sulfur atoms.

Avogadro's number

$$602\ 000\ 000\ 000\ 000\ 000\ 000\ 000 = 6.02 \times 10^{23}$$

One mole of any element always contains Avogadro's number of atoms. For example, 1 mole of carbon contains 6.02×10^{23} carbon atoms; 1 mole of aluminum contains 6.02×10^{23} aluminum atoms; 1 mole of sulfur contains 6.02×10^{23} sulfur atoms.

$$1 \text{ mole of an element} = 6.02 \times 10^{23} \text{ atoms of that element}$$

Avogadro's number tells us that one mole of a compound contains 6.02×10^{23} of the particular type of particles that make up that compound. One mole of a molecular compound contains Avogadro's number of molecules. For example, 1 mole of CO_2 contains 6.02×10^{23} molecules of CO_2. One mole of an ionic compound contains Avogadro's number of **formula units**, which are the groups of ions represented by the formula of an ionic compound. One mole of NaCl contains 6.02×10^{23} formula units of NaCl (Na^+, Cl^-). Table 7.5 gives examples of the number of particles in some 1-mole quantities.

TABLE 7.5 Number of Particles in 1-Mole Samples

Substance	Number and Type of Particles
1 mole of Al	6.02×10^{23} atoms of Al
1 mole of S	6.02×10^{23} atoms of S
1 mole of water (H_2O)	6.02×10^{23} molecules of H_2O
1 mole of vitamin C ($C_6H_8O_6$)	6.02×10^{23} molecules of vitamin C
1 mole of NaCl	6.02×10^{23} formula units of NaCl

We use Avogadro's number as a conversion factor to convert between the moles of a substance and the number of particles it contains.

$$\frac{6.02 \times 10^{23} \text{ particles}}{1 \text{ mole}} \quad \text{and} \quad \frac{1 \text{ mole}}{6.02 \times 10^{23} \text{ particles}}$$

For example, we use Avogadro's number to convert 4.00 moles of sulfur to atoms of sulfur.

$$4.00 \text{ moles S} \times \frac{6.02 \times 10^{23} \text{ atoms S}}{1 \text{ mole S}} = 2.41 \times 10^{24} \text{ atoms of S}$$

Avogadro's number as a conversion factor

We also use Avogadro's number to convert 3.01×10^{24} molecules of CO_2 to moles of CO_2.

$$3.01 \times 10^{24} \text{ molecules CO}_2 \times \frac{1 \text{ mole CO}_2}{6.02 \times 10^{23} \text{ molecules CO}_2} = 5.00 \text{ moles of CO}_2$$

Avogadro's number as a conversion factor

In calculations that convert between moles and particles, the number of moles will be a small number compared to the number of atoms or molecules, which will be large.

▶ **SAMPLE PROBLEM 7.5 Calculating the Number of Molecules**

How many molecules are present in 1.75 moles of carbon dioxide, CO_2?

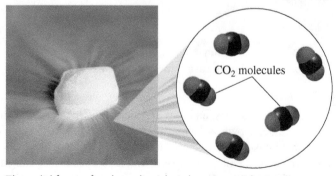

CO_2 molecules

The solid form of carbon dioxide is known as "dry ice."

SOLUTION

STEP 1 State the given and needed quantities.

ANALYZE THE PROBLEM	Given	Need
	1.75 moles of CO_2	molecules of CO_2

STEP 2 Write a plan to convert moles to atoms or molecules.

moles of CO_2 Avogadro's number   molecules of CO_2

STEP 3 Use Avogadro's number to write conversion factors.

$$1 \text{ mole of } CO_2 = 6.02 \times 10^{23} \text{ molecules of } CO_2$$

$$\frac{6.02 \times 10^{23} \text{ molecules } CO_2}{1 \text{ mole } CO_2} \quad \text{and} \quad \frac{1 \text{ mole } CO_2}{6.02 \times 10^{23} \text{ molecules } CO_2}$$

STEP 4 Set up the problem to calculate the number of particles.

$$1.75 \text{ moles } CO_2 \times \frac{6.02 \times 10^{23} \text{ molecules } CO_2}{1 \text{ mole } CO_2} = 1.05 \times 10^{24} \text{ molecules of } CO_2$$

STUDY CHECK 7.5

How many moles of water, H_2O, contain 2.60×10^{23} molecules of water?

ANSWER

0.432 mole of H_2O

> **Guide to Calculating the Atoms or Molecules of a Substance**
>
> **STEP 1**
> State the given and needed quantities.
>
> **STEP 2**
> Write a plan to convert moles to atoms or molecules.
>
> **STEP 3**
> Use Avogadro's number to write conversion factors.
>
> **STEP 4**
> Set up the problem to calculate the number of particles.

Moles of Elements in a Chemical Formula

We have seen that the subscripts in the chemical formula of a compound indicate the number of atoms of each type of element in the compound. For example, aspirin, $C_9H_8O_4$, is a drug used to reduce pain and inflammation in the body. Using the subscripts in the chemical formula of aspirin shows that there are 9 carbon atoms, 8 hydrogen atoms, and 4 oxygen atoms in each molecule of aspirin. The subscripts also tell us the number of moles of each element in 1 mole of aspirin: 9 moles of C atoms, 8 moles of H atoms, and 4 moles of O atoms.

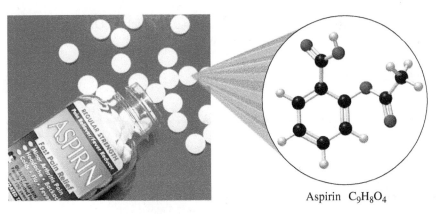

Number of atoms in 1 molecule
Carbon (C)   Hydrogen (H)   Oxygen (O)

Aspirin $C_9H_8O_4$

The chemical formula subscripts specify the	$C_9H_8O_4$		
	Carbon	**Hydrogen**	**Oxygen**
Atoms in 1 molecule	9 atoms of C	8 atoms of H	4 atoms of O
Moles of each element in 1 mole	9 moles of C	8 moles of H	4 moles of O

Using the subscripts from the formula, $C_9H_8O_4$, we can write the conversion factors for each of the elements in 1 mole of aspirin.

$$\frac{9 \text{ moles C}}{1 \text{ mole } C_9H_8O_4} \qquad \frac{8 \text{ moles H}}{1 \text{ mole } C_9H_8O_4} \qquad \frac{4 \text{ moles O}}{1 \text{ mole } C_9H_8O_4}$$

$$\frac{1 \text{ mole } C_9H_8O_4}{9 \text{ moles C}} \qquad \frac{1 \text{ mole } C_9H_8O_4}{8 \text{ moles H}} \qquad \frac{1 \text{ mole } C_9H_8O_4}{4 \text{ moles O}}$$

Guide to Calculating the Moles of an Element in a Compound

STEP 1
State the given and needed quantities.

STEP 2
Write a plan to convert moles of compound to moles of an element.

STEP 3
Write equalities and conversion factors using subscripts.

STEP 4
Set up the problem to calculate the moles of an element.

The compound propyl acetate provides the odor and taste of pears.

▶ **SAMPLE PROBLEM 7.6   Calculating the Moles of an Element in a Compound**

Propyl acetate, $C_5H_{10}O_2$, gives the odor and taste to pears. How many moles of C are present in 1.50 moles of propyl acetate?

SOLUTION

STEP 1   State the given and needed quantities.

ANALYZE THE PROBLEM	Given	Need
	1.50 moles of propyl acetate, chemical formula $C_5H_{10}O_2$	moles of C

STEP 2   Write a plan to convert moles of compound to moles of an element.

moles of $C_5H_{10}O_2$ [Subscript]   moles of C atoms

STEP 3   Write equalities and conversion factors using subscripts.

1 mole of $C_5H_{10}O_2$ = 5 moles of C

$$\frac{5 \text{ moles C}}{1 \text{ mole } C_5H_{10}O_2} \quad \text{and} \quad \frac{1 \text{ mole } C_5H_{10}O_2}{5 \text{ moles C}}$$

STEP 4   Set up the problem to calculate the moles of an element.

$$1.50 \text{ moles } \cancel{C_5H_{10}O_2} \times \frac{5 \text{ moles C}}{1 \text{ mole } \cancel{C_5H_{10}O_2}} = 7.50 \text{ moles of C}$$

STUDY CHECK 7.6

How many moles of propyl acetate, $C_5H_{10}O_2$, contain 0.480 mole of O?

ANSWER

0.240 mole of propyl acetate

QUESTIONS AND PROBLEMS

7.4 The Mole

LEARNING GOAL Use Avogadro's number to determine the number of particles in a given number of moles.

7.27   What is a mole?

7.28   What is Avogadro's number?

7.29   Calculate each of the following:
   a. number of C atoms in 0.500 mole of C
   b. number of SO_2 molecules in 1.28 moles of SO_2
   c. moles of Fe in 5.22×10^{22} atoms of Fe
   d. moles of C_2H_6O in 8.50×10^{24} molecules of C_2H_6O

7.30   Calculate each of the following:
   a. number of Li atoms in 4.5 moles of Li
   b. number of CO_2 molecules in 0.0180 mole of CO_2
   c. moles of Cu in 7.8×10^{21} atoms of Cu
   d. moles of C_2H_6 in 3.75×10^{23} molecules of C_2H_6

7.31   Calculate each of the following quantities in 2.00 moles of H_3PO_4:
   a. moles of H   **b.** moles of O
   c. atoms of P   **d.** atoms of O

7.32 Calculate each of the following quantities in 0.185 mole of $C_6H_{14}O$:
   a. moles of C   **b.** moles of O
   c. atoms of H   **d.** atoms of C

Ⓡ Clinical Applications

7.33 Quinine, $C_{20}H_{24}N_2O_2$, is a component of tonic water and bitter lemon.
   a. How many moles of H are in 1.0 mole of quinine?
   b. How many moles of C are in 5.0 moles of quinine?
   c. How many moles of N are in 0.020 mole of quinine?

7.34 Aluminum sulfate, $Al_2(SO_4)_3$, is used in some antiperspirants.
   a. How many moles of S are present in 3.0 moles of $Al_2(SO_4)_3$?
   b. How many moles of aluminum ions (Al^{3+}) are present in 0.40 mole of $Al_2(SO_4)_3$?
   c. How many moles of sulfate ions (SO_4^{2-}) are present in 1.5 moles of $Al_2(SO_4)_3$?

7.35 Naproxen is used to treat the pain and inflammation caused by arthritis. Naproxen has a formula of $C_{14}H_{14}O_3$.
   a. How many moles of C are present in 2.30 moles of naproxen?
   b. How many moles of H are present in 0.444 mole of naproxen?

   c. How many moles of O are present in 0.0765 mole of naproxen?

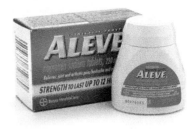

Naproxen is used to treat pain and inflammation caused by arthritis.

7.36 Benadryl is an over-the-counter drug used to treat allergy symptoms. The formula of benadryl is $C_{17}H_{21}NO$.
   a. How many moles of C are present in 0.733 mole of benadryl?
   b. How many moles of H are present in 2.20 moles of benadryl?
   c. How many moles of N are present in 1.54 moles of benadryl?

7.5 Molar Mass and Calculations

A single atom or molecule is much too small to weigh, even on the most accurate balance. In fact, it takes a huge number of atoms or molecules to make enough of a substance for you to see. An amount of water that contains Avogadro's number of water molecules is only a few sips. In the laboratory, we can use a balance to weigh out Avogadro's number of particles or 1 mole of a substance.

For any element, the quantity called **molar mass** is the quantity in grams that equals the atomic mass of that element. We are counting 6.02×10^{23} atoms of an element when we weigh out the number of grams equal to its molar mass. For example, carbon has an atomic mass of 12.01 on the periodic table. This means 1 mole of carbon atoms has a mass of 12.01 g. Then to obtain 1 mole of carbon atoms, we would weigh out 12.01 g of carbon. The molar mass of carbon is found by looking at its atomic mass on the periodic table.

LEARNING GOAL

Calculate the molar mass for a substance given its chemical formula; use molar mass to convert between grams and moles.

6.02×10^{23} atoms of C

⇕

1 mole of C atoms

⇕

12.01 g of C atoms

47	6	16
Ag	**C**	**S**
107.9	12.01	32.07
1 mole of silver atoms has a mass of 107.9 g	1 mole of carbon atoms has a mass of 12.01 g	1 mole of sulfur atoms has a mass of 32.07 g

Calculating Molar Mass

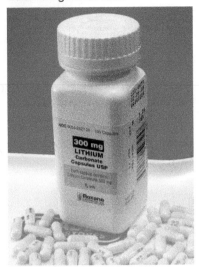

Lithium carbonate is used to treat bipolar disorder.

Guide to Calculating Molar Mass

STEP 1
Obtain the molar mass of each element.

STEP 2
Multiply each molar mass by the number of moles (subscript) in the formula.

STEP 3
Calculate the molar mass by adding the masses of the elements.

 Explore Your World

Calculating Moles in the Kitchen

The labels on food products list the components in grams and milligrams. It is possible to convert those values to moles, which is also interesting. Read the labels of some products in the kitchen and convert the amounts given in grams or milligrams to moles using molar mass. Here are some examples.

Questions

1. How many moles of NaCl are in a box of salt?
2. How many moles of sugar are contained in a 5-lb bag of sugar if sugar has the formula $C_{12}H_{22}O_{11}$?
3. A serving of cereal contains 90 mg of potassium. If there are 11 servings of cereal in the box, how many moles of K^+ are present in the cereal in the box?

The molar mass of an element is useful to convert moles of an element to grams, or grams to moles. For example, 1 mole of sulfur has a mass of 32.07 g. We can express the molar mass of sulfur as an equality

$$1 \text{ mole of S} = 32.07 \text{ g of S}$$

From this equality, two conversion factors can be written as

$$\frac{32.07 \text{ g S}}{1 \text{ mole S}} \quad \text{and} \quad \frac{1 \text{ mole S}}{32.07 \text{ g S}}$$

Molar Mass of a Compound

To calculate the molar mass for a compound, we multiply the molar mass of each element by its subscript in the formula, and add the results as shown in Sample Problem 7.7.

▶ **SAMPLE PROBLEM 7.7   Calculating the Molar Mass for a Compound**

Calculate the molar mass for lithium carbonate, Li_2CO_3, used to treat bipolar disorder.

SOLUTION

ANALYZE THE PROBLEM	**Given**	**Need**
	formula Li_2CO_3	molar mass of Li_2CO_3

STEP 1 Obtain the molar mass of each element.

$$\frac{6.941 \text{ g Li}}{1 \text{ mole Li}} \qquad \frac{12.01 \text{ g C}}{1 \text{ mole C}} \qquad \frac{16.00 \text{ g O}}{1 \text{ mole O}}$$

STEP 2 Multiply each molar mass by the number of moles (subscript) in the formula.

Grams from 2 moles of Li:

$$2 \text{ moles Li} \times \frac{6.941 \text{ g Li}}{1 \text{ mole Li}} = 13.88 \text{ g of Li}$$

Grams from 1 mole of C:

$$1 \text{ mole C} \times \frac{12.01 \text{ g C}}{1 \text{ mole C}} = 12.01 \text{ g of C}$$

Grams from 3 moles of O:

$$3 \text{ moles O} \times \frac{16.00 \text{ g O}}{1 \text{ mole O}} = 48.00 \text{ g of O}$$

STEP 3 Calculate the molar mass by adding the masses of the elements.

2 moles of Li	=	13.88 g of Li
1 mole of C	=	12.01 g of C
3 moles of O	=	+48.00 g of O
Molar mass of Li_2CO_3	=	73.89 g

STUDY CHECK 7.7

Calculate the molar mass for salicylic acid, $C_7H_6O_3$, used to treat skin conditions such as acne, psoriasis, and dandruff.

ANSWER

138.12 g

Figure 7.8 shows some 1-mole quantities of substances. Table 7.6 lists the molar mass for several 1-mole samples.

1-Mole Quantities

| S | Fe | NaCl | K₂Cr₂O₇ | C₁₂H₂₂O₁₁ |

FIGURE 7.8 ▶ 1-mole samples: sulfur, S (32.07 g); iron, Fe (55.85 g); salt, NaCl (58.44 g); potassium dichromate, $K_2Cr_2O_7$ (294.2 g); and sucrose, $C_{12}H_{22}O_{11}$ (342.3 g).

Q How is the molar mass for $K_2Cr_2O_7$ obtained?

Calculations Using Molar Mass

We can now change from moles to grams, or grams to moles, using the conversion factors derived from the molar mass as shown in Sample Problem 7.8. (Remember, you must determine the molar mass of the substance first.)

▶**SAMPLE PROBLEM 7.8 Converting Moles of an Element to Grams**

Silver metal is used in the manufacture of tableware, mirrors, jewelry, and dental alloys. If the design for a piece of jewelry requires 0.750 mole of silver, how many grams of silver are needed?

SOLUTION

STEP **1** State the given and needed quantities.

ANALYZE THE PROBLEM	Given	Need
	0.750 mole of Ag	grams of Ag

STEP **2** Write a plan to convert moles to grams.

moles of Ag   Molar mass factor   grams of Ag

STEP **3** Determine the molar mass and write conversion factors.

$$1 \text{ mole of Ag} = 107.9 \text{ g of Ag}$$

$$\frac{107.9 \text{ g Ag}}{1 \text{ mole Ag}} \quad \text{and} \quad \frac{1 \text{ mole Ag}}{107.9 \text{ g Ag}}$$

TABLE 7.6 The Molar Mass of Selected Elements and Compounds

Substance	Molar Mass
1 mole of C	12.01 g
1 mole of Na	22.99 g
1 mole of Fe	55.85 g
1 mole of NaF	41.99 g
1 mole of $C_6H_{12}O_6$ (glucose)	180.16 g
1 mole of $C_8H_{10}N_4O_2$ (caffeine)	194.20 g

⚛ **CORE CHEMISTRY SKILL**

Using Molar Mass as a Conversion Factor

Silver metal is used to make jewelry.

Guide to Calculating the Moles (or Grams) of a Substance from Grams (or Moles)

STEP 1
State the given and needed quantities.

STEP 2
Write a plan to convert moles to grams (or grams to moles).

STEP 3
Determine the molar mass and write conversion factors.

STEP 4
Set up the problem to convert moles to grams (or grams to moles).

Table salt is sodium chloride, NaCl.

STEP 4 **Set up the problem to convert moles to grams.** Calculate the grams of silver using the molar mass factor that cancels mole Ag.

$$0.750 \; \cancel{\text{mole Ag}} \times \frac{107.9 \text{ g Ag}}{1 \; \cancel{\text{mole Ag}}} = 80.9 \text{ g of Ag}$$

STUDY CHECK 7.8

A dentist orders gold to prepare dental crowns and fillings. Calculate the number of grams of gold (Au) present in 0.124 mole of gold.

ANSWER

24.4 g of Au

The conversion factors for a compound are also written from the molar mass. For example, the molar mass of the compound H_2O is written

$$1 \text{ mole of } H_2O = 18.02 \text{ g of } H_2O$$

From this equality, conversion factors for the molar mass of H_2O are written as

$$\frac{18.02 \text{ g } H_2O}{1 \text{ mole } H_2O} \quad \text{and} \quad \frac{1 \text{ mole } H_2O}{18.02 \text{ g } H_2O}$$

▶ SAMPLE PROBLEM 7.9 Converting the Mass of a Compound to Moles

A box of salt contains 737 g of NaCl. How many moles of NaCl are present?

SOLUTION

STEP 1 State the given and needed quantities.

ANALYZE THE PROBLEM	Given	Need
	737 g of NaCl	moles of NaCl

STEP 2 Write a plan to convert grams to moles.

grams of NaCl   Molar mass factor   moles of NaCl

STEP 3 Determine the molar mass and write conversion factors.
$$(1 \times 22.99) + (1 \times 35.45) = 58.44 \text{ g/mole}$$

$$1 \text{ mole of NaCl} = 58.44 \text{ g of NaCl}$$
$$\frac{58.44 \text{ g NaCl}}{1 \text{ mole NaCl}} \quad \text{and} \quad \frac{1 \text{ mole NaCl}}{58.44 \text{ g NaCl}}$$

STEP 4 Set up the problem to convert grams to moles.

$$737 \; \cancel{\text{g NaCl}} \times \frac{1 \text{ mole NaCl}}{58.44 \; \cancel{\text{g NaCl}}} = 12.6 \text{ moles of NaCl}$$

STUDY CHECK 7.9

One tablet of an antacid contains 680. mg of $CaCO_3$. How many moles of $CaCO_3$ are present?

ANSWER

0.00679 mole of $CaCO_3$

We can summarize the calculations to show the connections between the moles of a compound, its mass in grams, number of molecules (or formula units if ionic), and the moles and atoms of each element in that compound in the following flowchart:

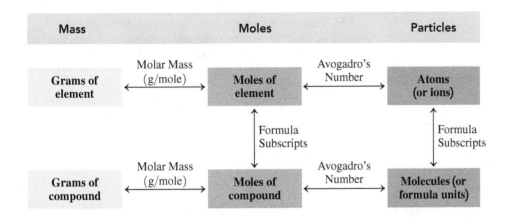

QUESTIONS AND PROBLEMS

7.5 Molar Mass and Calculations

LEARNING GOAL Calculate the molar mass for a substance given its chemical formula; use molar mass to convert between grams and moles.

7.37 Calculate the molar mass for each of the following:
    a. $KC_4H_5O_6$ (cream of tartar)
    b. Fe_2O_3 (rust)
    c. $Al_2(SO_4)_3$ (antiperspirant)
    d. $Mg(OH)_2$ (antacid)

7.38 Calculate the molar mass for each of the following:
    a. $FeSO_4$ (iron supplement)
    b. Al_2O_3 (absorbent and abrasive)
    c. $C_7H_5NO_3S$ (saccharin)
    d. $(NH_4)_2CO_3$ (baking powder)

7.39 Calculate the molar mass for each of the following:
    a. Cl_2 **b.** $C_3H_6O_3$
    c. $Mg_3(PO_4)_2$ **d.** AlF_3

7.40 Calculate the molar mass for each of the following:
    a. O_2 **b.** KH_2PO_4
    c. $Fe(ClO_4)_3$ **d.** $C_4H_8O_4$

7.41 Calculate the mass, in grams, for each of the following:
    a. 2.00 moles of Na   **b.** 2.80 moles of Ca
    c. 0.125 mole of Sn   **d.** 1.76 moles of Cu

7.42 Calculate the mass, in grams, for each of the following:
    a. 1.50 moles of K   **b.** 2.5 moles of C
    c. 0.25 mole of P   **d.** 12.5 moles of He

7.43 Calculate the number of grams in each of the following:
    a. 0.500 mole of NaCl   **b.** 1.75 moles of Na_2O
    c. 0.225 mole of H_2O **d.** 4.42 moles of CO_2

7.44 Calculate the number of grams in each of the following:
    a. 2.0 moles of $MgCl_2$ **b.** 3.5 moles of C_6H_6
    c. 5.00 moles of C_2H_6O **d.** 0.488 mole of $C_3H_6O_3$

7.45 How many moles are contained in each of the following?
    a. 50.0 g of Ag   **b.** 0.200 g of C
    c. 15.0 g of NH_3 **d.** 75.0 g of SO_2

7.46 How many moles are contained in each of the following?
    a. 25.0 g of Ca   **b.** 5.00 g of S
    c. 40.0 g of H_2O **d.** 100.0 g of O_2

7.47 Calculate the number of moles in 25.0 g of each of the following:
    a. Ne   **b.** O_2
    c. $Al(OH)_3$ **d.** Ga_2S_3

7.48 Calculate the number of moles in 4.00 g of each of the following:
    a. He   **b.** SnO_2
    c. $Cr(OH)_3$ **d.** Ca_3N_2

7.49 How many moles of S are in each of the following quantities?
    a. 25 g of S   **b.** 125 g of SO_2 **c.** 2.0 moles of Al_2S_3

7.50 How many moles of C are in each of the following quantities?
    a. 75 g of C   **b.** 0.25 mole of C_2H_6 **c.** 88 g of CO_2

℞ Clinical Applications

7.51 **a.** The compound $MgSO_4$, Epsom salts, is used to soothe sore feet and muscles. How many grams will you need to prepare a bath containing 5.00 moles of Epsom salts?
    b. Potassium iodide, KI, is used as an expectorant. How many grams of KI are in 0.450 mole of KI?

7.52 **a.** Cyclopropane, C_3H_6, is an anesthetic given by inhalation. How many grams are in 0.25 mole of cyclopropane?
    b. The sedative Demerol hydrochloride has the formula $C_{15}H_{22}ClNO_2$. How many grams are in 0.025 mole of Demerol hydrochloride?

7.53 Dinitrogen oxide (or nitrous oxide), N_2O, also known as laughing gas, is widely used as an anesthetic in dentistry.
    a. How many grams of the compound are in 1.50 moles of N_2O?
    b. How many moles of the compound are in 34.0 g of N_2O?
    c. How many grams of N are in 34.0 g of N_2O?

7.54 Allyl sulfide, $C_6H_{10}S$, is the substance that gives garlic, onions, and leeks their characteristic odor. Some studies indicate that garlic may be beneficial for the heart and in lowering cholesterol.

a. How many moles of H are in 0.75 mole of $C_6H_{10}S$?

b. How many moles of S are in 23.2 g of $C_6H_{10}S$?

c. How many grams of C are in 44.0 g of $C_6H_{10}S$?

The characteristic odor of garlic is a sulfur-containing compound.

7.55 Calculate the molar mass for each of the following:

a. Paxil, an antidepressant, $C_{19}H_{20}FNO_3$

b. calcium citrate, a calcium supplement, $Ca_3C_{12}H_{10}O_{14}$

c. rubbing alcohol, C_3H_8O

d. Cipro, used to treat a range of bacterial infections, $C_{17}H_{18}FN_3O_3$

7.56 Calculate the molar mass for each of the following:

a. Propofol, used to induce anesthesia during surgery, $C_{12}H_{18}O$

b. Carboplatin, used in chemotherapy, $C_6H_{12}N_2O_4Pt$

c. calcium sulfate, used to make casts to protect broken bones, $CaSO_4$

d. Amoxicillin, an antibiotic, $C_{16}H_{19}N_3O_5S$

Given a quantity in moles of reactant or product, use a mole–mole factor from the balanced chemical equation to calculate the number of moles of another substance in the reaction.

7.6 Mole Relationships in Chemical Equations

In any chemical reaction, the total amount of matter in the reactants is equal to the total amount of matter in the products. Thus, the total mass of all the reactants must be equal to the total mass of all the products. This is known as the *law of conservation of mass*, which states that there is no change in the total mass of the substances reacting in a chemical reaction. Thus, no material is lost or gained as original substances are changed to new substances.

For example, tarnish (Ag_2S) forms when silver reacts with sulfur to form silver sulfide.

$$2Ag(s) + S(s) \longrightarrow Ag_2S(s)$$

In the chemical reaction of Ag and S, the mass of the reactants is the same as the mass of the product, Ag_2S.

In this reaction, the number of silver atoms that reacts is twice the number of sulfur atoms. When 200 silver atoms react, 100 sulfur atoms are required. However, in the actual chemical reaction, many more atoms of both silver and sulfur would react. If we are dealing with moles of silver and sulfur, then the coefficients in the equation can be interpreted in terms of moles. Thus, 2 moles of silver react with 1 mole of sulfur to form 1 mole of Ag_2S. Because the molar mass of each can be determined, the moles of Ag, S, and Ag_2S can also be stated in terms of mass in grams of each. Thus, 215.8 g of Ag and 32.1 g of S react to form 247.9 g of Ag_2S. The total mass of the reactants (247.9 g) is equal to the mass of product (247.9 g). The various ways in which a chemical equation can be interpreted are seen in Table 7.7.

TABLE 7.7 Information Available from a Balanced Equation

	Reactants		Products
Equation	$2Ag(s)$	$+ S(s)$	$\longrightarrow Ag_2S(s)$
Atoms	2 Ag atoms	+ 1 S atom	$\longrightarrow$ 1 Ag_2S formula unit
	200 Ag atoms	+ 100 S atoms	$\longrightarrow$ 100 Ag_2S formula units
Avogadro's Number of Atoms	$2(6.02 \times 10^{23})$ Ag atoms	$+ 1(6.02 \times 10^{23})$ S atoms	$\longrightarrow 1(6.02 \times 10^{23})\ Ag_2S$ formula units
Moles	2 moles of Ag	+ 1 mole of S	$\longrightarrow$ 1 mole of Ag_2S
Mass (g)	$2(107.9\ g)$ of Ag	$+ 1(32.07\ g)$ of S	$\longrightarrow 1(247.9\ g)$ of Ag_2S
Total Mass (g)	247.9 g		$\longrightarrow$ 247.9 g

Mole–Mole Factors from an Equation

When iron reacts with sulfur, the product is iron(III) sulfide.

$$2Fe(s) + 3S(s) \longrightarrow Fe_2S_3(s)$$

Iron (Fe)   Sulfur (S)   Iron(III) sulfide (Fe_2S_3)
$2Fe(s)$ $+$ $3S(s)$ $\longrightarrow$ $Fe_2S_3(s)$

In the chemical reaction of Fe and S, the mass of the reactants is the same as the mass of the product, Fe_2S_3.

From the balanced chemical equation, we see that 2 moles of iron reacts with 3 moles of sulfur to form 1 mole of iron(III) sulfide. Actually, any amount of iron or sulfur may be used, but the *ratio* of iron reacting with sulfur will always be the same. From the coefficients, we can write **mole–mole factors** between reactants and between reactants and products. The coefficients used in the mole–mole factors are *exact* numbers; they do not limit the number of significant figures.

Fe and S:	$\dfrac{2 \text{ moles Fe}}{3 \text{ moles S}}$	and	$\dfrac{3 \text{ moles S}}{2 \text{ moles Fe}}$
Fe and Fe_2S_3:	$\dfrac{2 \text{ moles Fe}}{1 \text{ mole } Fe_2S_3}$	and	$\dfrac{1 \text{ mole } Fe_2S_3}{2 \text{ moles Fe}}$
S and Fe_2S_3:	$\dfrac{3 \text{ moles S}}{1 \text{ mole } Fe_2S_3}$	and	$\dfrac{1 \text{ mole } Fe_2S_3}{3 \text{ moles S}}$

Using Mole–Mole Factors in Calculations

Whenever you prepare a recipe, adjust an engine for the proper mixture of fuel and air, or prepare medicines in a pharmaceutical laboratory, you need to know the proper amounts of reactants to use and how much of the product will form. Now that we have written all the possible conversion factors for the balanced equation $2Fe(s) + 3S(s) \longrightarrow Fe_2S_3(s)$, we will use those mole–mole factors in a chemical calculation in Sample Problem 7.10.

 **CORE CHEMISTRY SKILL**

Using Mole–Mole Factors

▶ **SAMPLE PROBLEM 7.10 Calculating Moles of a Reactant**

In the chemical reaction of iron and sulfur, how many moles of sulfur are needed to react with 1.42 moles of iron?

$$2Fe(s) + 3S(s) \longrightarrow Fe_2S_3(s)$$

SOLUTION

Guide to Calculating the Quantities of Reactants and Products in a Chemical Reaction

STEP 1
State the given and needed quantities (moles or grams).

STEP 2
Write a plan to convert the given to the needed quantity (moles or grams).

STEP 3
Use coefficients to write mole–mole factors; write molar mass factors if needed.

STEP 4
Set up the problem to give the needed quantity (moles or grams).

STEP 1 State the given and needed quantities (moles).

ANALYZE THE PROBLEM	Given	Need
	1.42 moles of Fe	moles of S
	Equation	
	$2Fe(s) + 3S(s) \longrightarrow Fe_2S_3(s)$	

STEP 2 Write a plan to convert the given to the needed quantity (moles).

moles of Fe   ⟶ Mole–mole factor ⟶   moles of S

STEP 3 Use coefficients to write mole–mole factors.

$$2 \text{ moles of Fe} = 3 \text{ moles of S}$$

$$\frac{2 \text{ moles Fe}}{3 \text{ moles S}} \quad \text{and} \quad \frac{3 \text{ moles S}}{2 \text{ moles Fe}}$$

STEP 4 Set up the problem to give the needed quantity (moles).

Exact

$$1.42 \text{ moles Fe} \times \frac{3 \text{ moles S}}{2 \text{ moles Fe}} = 2.13 \text{ moles of S}$$

Three SFs   Exact   Three SFs

STUDY CHECK 7.10

Using the equation in Sample Problem 7.10, calculate the number of moles of iron needed to react with 2.75 moles of sulfur.

ANSWER

1.83 moles of iron

QUESTIONS AND PROBLEMS

7.6 Mole Relationships in Chemical Equations

LEARNING GOAL Given a quantity in moles of reactant or product, use a mole–mole factor from the balanced chemical equation to calculate the number of moles of another substance in the reaction.

7.57 Write all the mole–mole factors for each of the following chemical equations:
   a. $2SO_2(g) + O_2(g) \longrightarrow 2SO_3(g)$
   b. $4P(s) + 5O_2(g) \longrightarrow 2P_2O_5(s)$

7.58 Write all the mole–mole factors for each of the following chemical equations:
   a. $2Al(s) + 3Cl_2(g) \longrightarrow 2AlCl_3(s)$
   b. $4HCl(g) + O_2(g) \longrightarrow 2Cl_2(g) + 2H_2O(g)$

7.59 The chemical reaction of hydrogen with oxygen produces water.
   $$2H_2(g) + O_2(g) \longrightarrow 2H_2O(g)$$
   a. How many moles of O_2 are required to react with 2.0 moles of H_2?
   b. How many moles of H_2 are needed to react with 5.0 moles of O_2?
   c. How many moles of H_2O form when 2.5 moles of O_2 reacts?

7.60 Ammonia is produced by the chemical reaction of nitrogen and hydrogen.

$$N_2(g) + 3H_2(g) \longrightarrow 2NH_3(g)$$
Ammonia

a. How many moles of H_2 are needed to react with 1.0 mole of N_2?
b. How many moles of N_2 reacted if 0.60 mole of NH_3 is produced?
c. How many moles of NH_3 are produced when 1.4 moles of H_2 reacts?

7.61 Carbon disulfide and carbon monoxide are produced when carbon is heated with sulfur dioxide.

$$5C(s) + 2SO_2(g) \xrightarrow{\Delta} CS_2(l) + 4CO(g)$$

a. How many moles of C are needed to react with 0.500 mole of SO_2?
b. How many moles of CO are produced when 1.2 moles of C reacts?

c. How many moles of SO_2 are needed to produce 0.50 mole of CS_2?
d. How many moles of CS_2 are produced when 2.5 moles of C reacts?

7.62 In the acetylene torch, acetylene gas (C_2H_2) burns in oxygen to produce carbon dioxide and water.

$$2C_2H_2(g) + 5O_2(g) \xrightarrow{\Delta} 4CO_2(g) + 2H_2O(g)$$

a. How many moles of O_2 are needed to react with 2.00 moles of C_2H_2?
b. How many moles of CO_2 are produced when 3.5 moles of C_2H_2 reacts?
c. How many moles of C_2H_2 are needed to produce 0.50 mole of H_2O?
d. How many moles of CO_2 are produced from 0.100 mole of O_2?

7.7 Mass Calculations for Reactions

When we have the balanced chemical equation for a reaction, we can use the mass of one of the substances (A) in the reaction to calculate the mass of another substance (B) in the reaction. However, the calculations require us to convert the mass of A to moles of A using the molar mass factor for A. Then we use the mole–mole factor that links substance A to substance B, which we obtain from the coefficients in the balanced equation. This mole–mole factor (B/A) will convert the moles of A to moles of B. Then the molar mass factor of B is used to calculate the grams of substance B.

LEARNING GOAL

Given the mass in grams of a substance in a reaction, calculate the mass in grams of another substance in the reaction.

⚛ **CORE CHEMISTRY SKILL**

Converting Grams to Grams

Substance A   **Substance B**

grams of A	Molar mass factor A	moles of A	Mole–mole factor B/A	moles of B	Molar mass factor B	grams of B

> ▶ **SAMPLE PROBLEM 7.11 Mass of Product**
>
> When acetylene, C_2H_2, burns in oxygen, high temperatures are produced that are used for welding metals.
>
> $$2C_2H_2(g) + 5O_2(g) \xrightarrow{\Delta} 4CO_2(g) + 2H_2O(g)$$
>
> How many grams of CO_2 are produced when 54.6 g of C_2H_2 is burned?
>
> **SOLUTION**
> **STEP 1** State the given and needed quantities (grams).

	Given	Need
ANALYZE THE PROBLEM	54.6 g of C_2H_2	grams of CO_2
	Equation	
	$2C_2H_2(g) + 5O_2(g) \xrightarrow{\Delta} 4CO_2(g) + 2H_2O(g)$ + energy	

STEP 2 Write a plan to convert the given to the needed quantity (grams).

grams of C_2H_2	Molar mass	moles of C_2H_2	Mole–mole factor	moles of CO_2	Molar mass	grams of CO_2

A mixture of acetylene and oxygen undergoes combustion during the welding of metals.

STEP 3　Use coefficients to write mole–mole factors; write molar mass factors if needed.

$$1 \text{ mole of } C_2H_2 = 26.04 \text{ g of } C_2H_2$$

$$\frac{26.04 \text{ g } C_2H_2}{1 \text{ mole } C_2H_2} \quad \text{and} \quad \frac{1 \text{ mole } C_2H_2}{26.04 \text{ g } C_2H_2}$$

$$2 \text{ moles of } C_2H_2 = 4 \text{ moles of } CO_2 \qquad\qquad 1 \text{ mole of } CO_2 = 44.01 \text{ g of } CO_2$$

$$\frac{2 \text{ moles } C_2H_2}{4 \text{ moles } CO_2} \quad \text{and} \quad \frac{4 \text{ moles } CO_2}{2 \text{ moles } C_2H_2} \qquad \frac{44.01 \text{ g } CO_2}{1 \text{ mole } CO_2} \quad \text{and} \quad \frac{1 \text{ mole } CO_2}{44.01 \text{ g } CO_2}$$

STEP 4　Set up the problem to give the needed quantity (grams).

Exact　　　　　　　　Exact　　　　　　　　Four SFs

$$54.6 \text{ g } C_2H_2 \times \frac{1 \text{ mole } C_2H_2}{26.04 \text{ g } C_2H_2} \times \frac{4 \text{ moles } CO_2}{2 \text{ moles } C_2H_2} \times \frac{44.01 \text{ g } CO_2}{1 \text{ mole } CO_2} = 185 \text{ g of } CO_2$$

Three SFs　　　　　Four SFs　　　　　Exact　　　　　Exact　　　　　Three SFs

STUDY CHECK 7.11

Using the equation in Sample Problem 7.11, calculate the grams of CO_2 that can be produced when 25.0 g of O_2 reacts.

ANSWER

27.5 g of CO_2

QUESTIONS AND PROBLEMS

7.7 Mass Calculations for Reactions

LEARNING GOAL Given the mass in grams of a substance in a reaction, calculate the mass in grams of another substance in the reaction.

7.63　Sodium reacts with oxygen to produce sodium oxide.

$$4Na(s) + O_2(g) \longrightarrow 2Na_2O(s)$$

　a. How many grams of Na_2O are produced when 57.5 g of Na reacts?
　b. If you have 18.0 g of Na, how many grams of O_2 are needed for the reaction?
　c. How many grams of O_2 are needed in a reaction that produces 75.0 g of Na_2O?

7.64　Nitrogen gas reacts with hydrogen gas to produce ammonia.

$$N_2(g) + 3H_2(g) \longrightarrow 2NH_3(g)$$

　a. If you have 3.64 g of H_2, how many grams of NH_3 can be produced?
　b. How many grams of H_2 are needed to react with 2.80 g of N_2?
　c. How many grams of NH_3 can be produced from 12.0 g of H_2?

7.65　Ammonia and oxygen react to form nitrogen and water.

$$4NH_3(g) + 3O_2(g) \longrightarrow 2N_2(g) + 6H_2O(g)$$

　a. How many grams of O_2 are needed to react with 13.6 g of NH_3?
　b. How many grams of N_2 can be produced when 6.50 g of O_2 reacts?
　c. How many grams of H_2O are formed from the reaction of 34.0 g of NH_3?

7.66　Iron(III) oxide reacts with carbon to give iron and carbon monoxide.

$$Fe_2O_3(s) + 3C(s) \longrightarrow 2Fe(s) + 3CO(g)$$

　a. How many grams of C are required to react with 16.5 g of Fe_2O_3?
　b. How many grams of CO are produced when 36.0 g of C reacts?
　c. How many grams of Fe can be produced when 6.00 g of Fe_2O_3 reacts?

7.67　Nitrogen dioxide and water react to produce nitric acid, HNO_3, and nitrogen oxide.

$$3NO_2(g) + H_2O(l) \longrightarrow 2HNO_3(aq) + NO(g)$$

　a. How many grams of H_2O are needed to react with 28.0 g of NO_2?
　b. How many grams of NO are produced from 15.8 g of NO_2?
　c. How many grams of HNO_3 are produced from 8.25 g of NO_2?

7.68　Calcium cyanamide reacts with water to form calcium carbonate and ammonia.

$$CaCN_2(s) + 3H_2O(l) \longrightarrow CaCO_3(s) + 2NH_3(g)$$

　a. How many grams of H_2O are needed to react with 75.0 g of $CaCN_2$?
　b. How many grams of NH_3 are produced from 5.24 g of $CaCN_2$?
　c. How many grams of $CaCO_3$ form if 155 g of H_2O reacts?

7.69 When solid lead(II) sulfide ore burns in oxygen gas, the products are solid lead(II) oxide and sulfur dioxide gas.

Interactive Video

Stoichiometry

a. Write the balanced chemical equation for the reaction.
b. How many grams of oxygen are required to react with 30.0 g of lead(II) sulfide?
c. How many grams of sulfur dioxide can be produced when 65.0 g of lead(II) sulfide reacts?
d. How many grams of lead(II) sulfide are used to produce 128 g of lead(II) oxide?

7.70 When the gases dihydrogen sulfide and oxygen react, they form the gases sulfur dioxide and water vapor.
a. Write the balanced chemical equation for the reaction.
b. How many grams of oxygen are needed to react with 2.50 g of dihydrogen sulfide?
c. How many grams of sulfur dioxide can be produced when 38.5 g of oxygen reacts?
d. How many grams of oxygen are needed to produce 55.8 g of water vapor?

℞ **Clinical Applications**

7.71 In the body, the amino acid glycine, $C_2H_5NO_2$, reacts according to the following equation:

$$2C_2H_5NO_2(aq) + 3O_2(g) \longrightarrow$$
$$\text{Glycine} \qquad 3CO_2(g) + 3H_2O(l) + CH_4N_2O(aq)$$
$$\text{Urea}$$

a. How many grams of O_2 are needed to react with 15.0 g of glycine?
b. How many grams of urea are produced from 15.0 g of glycine?
c. How many grams of CO_2 are produced from 15.0 g of glycine?

7.72 In the body, ethanol, C_2H_6O, reacts according to the following equation:

$$C_2H_6O(aq) + 3O_2(g) \longrightarrow 2CO_2(g) + 3H_2O(l)$$
$$\text{Ethanol}$$

a. How many grams of O_2 are needed to react with 8.40 g of ethanol?
b. How many grams of H_2O are produced from 8.40 g of ethanol?
c. How many grams of CO_2 are produced from 8.40 g of ethanol?

7.8 Limiting Reactants and Percent Yield

LEARNING GOAL

Identify a limiting reactant and calculate the amount of product formed from the limiting reactant. Given the actual quantity of product, determine the percent yield for a reaction.

When you make peanut butter sandwiches for lunch, you need 2 slices of bread and 1 tablespoon of peanut butter for each sandwich. As an equation, we could write:

2 slices of bread + 1 tablespoon of peanut butter $\longrightarrow$ 1 peanut butter sandwich

If you have 8 slices of bread and a full jar of peanut butter, you will run out of bread after you make 4 peanut butter sandwiches. You cannot make any more sandwiches once the bread is used up, even though there is a lot of peanut butter left in the jar. The number of slices of bread has limited the number of sandwiches you can make.

On a different day, you might have 8 slices of bread but only a tablespoon of peanut butter left in the peanut butter jar. You will run out of peanut butter after you make just 1 peanut butter sandwich and have 6 slices of bread left over. The small amount of peanut butter available has limited the number of sandwiches you can make.

8 slices of bread + 1 jar of peanut butter → make → 4 peanut butter sandwiches + peanut butter left over

8 slices of bread + 1 tablespoon of peanut butter → make → 1 peanut butter sandwich + 6 slices of bread left over

The reactant that is completely used up is the **limiting reactant**. The reactant that does not completely react and is left over is called the *excess reactant*.

Bread	Peanut Butter	Sandwiches	Limiting Reactant	Excess Reactant
1 loaf (20 slices)	1 tablespoon	1	Peanut butter	Bread
4 slices	1 full jar	2	Bread	Peanut butter
8 slices	1 full jar	4	Bread	Peanut butter

CORE CHEMISTRY SKILL

Calculating Quantity of Product from a Limiting Reactant

Calculating Moles of Product from a Limiting Reactant

In a similar way, the reactants in a chemical reaction do not always combine in quantities that allow each to be used up at exactly the same time. In many reactions, there is a limiting reactant that determines the amount of product that can be formed. When we know the quantities of the reactants of a chemical reaction, we calculate the amount of product that is possible from each reactant if it were completely consumed. We are looking for the *limiting reactant*, which is the one that runs out first, producing the smaller amount of product.

▶ **SAMPLE PROBLEM 7.12 Moles of Product from Limiting Reactant**

The chemical reaction of carbon monoxide and hydrogen is used to produce methanol, CH_3OH.

$$CO(g) + 2H_2(g) \longrightarrow CH_3OH(g)$$

If 3.00 moles of CO and 5.00 moles of H_2 are the initial reactants, what is the limiting reactant and how many moles of methanol can be produced?

SOLUTION

STEP 1 State the given and needed moles.

ANALYZE THE PROBLEM	Given	Need
	3.00 moles of CO, 5.00 moles of H_2	moles of CH_3OH produced, limiting reactant
	Equation	
	$CO(g) + 2H_2(g) \longrightarrow CH_3OH(g)$	

Guide to Calculating the Moles of Product from a Limiting Reactant

STEP 1
State the given and needed moles.

STEP 2
Write a plan to convert the moles of each reactant to moles of product.

STEP 3
Write the mole–mole factors from the equation.

STEP 4
Calculate the number of moles of product from each reactant and select the smaller number of moles as the amount of product from the limiting reactant.

STEP 2 Write a plan to convert the moles of each reactant to moles of product.

moles of CO → Mole–mole factor → moles of CH_3OH

moles of H_2 → Mole–mole factor → moles of CH_3OH

STEP 3 Write the mole–mole factors from the equation.

1 mole of CO = 1 mole of CH_3OH

$$\frac{1 \text{ mole CO}}{1 \text{ mole } CH_3OH} \quad \text{and} \quad \frac{1 \text{ mole } CH_3OH}{1 \text{ mole CO}}$$

2 moles of H_2 = 1 mole of CH_3OH

$$\frac{2 \text{ moles } H_2}{1 \text{ mole } CH_3OH} \quad \text{and} \quad \frac{1 \text{ mole } CH_3OH}{2 \text{ moles } H_2}$$

STEP **4** Calculate the number of moles of product from each reactant and select the smaller number of moles as the amount of product from the limiting reactant.

Moles of CH₃OH (product) from CO:

Exact

$$3.00 \text{ moles CO} \times \frac{1 \text{ mole CH}_3\text{OH}}{1 \text{ mole CO}} = 3.00 \text{ moles of CH}_3\text{OH}$$

Three SFs · Exact · Three SFs

Moles of CH₃OH (product) from H₂:

Three SFs · Exact

$$5.00 \text{ moles H}_2 \times \frac{1 \text{ mole CH}_3\text{OH}}{2 \text{ moles H}_2} = 2.50 \text{ moles of CH}_3\text{OH}$$ Smaller amount of product

Limiting reactant · Exact · Three SFs

The smaller amount, 2.50 moles of CH₃OH, is the maximum amount of methanol that can be produced from the limiting reactant, H₂, when it is completely consumed.

STUDY CHECK 7.12

If the initial mixture of reactants for Sample Problem 7.12 contains 4.00 moles of CO and 4.00 moles of H_2, what is the limiting reactant and how many moles of methanol can be produced?

ANSWER

H_2 is the limiting reactant; 2.00 moles of methanol can be produced.

Calculating Mass of Product from a Limiting Reactant

The quantities of the reactants can also be given in grams. The calculations to identify the limiting reactant are the same as before, but the grams of each reactant must first be converted to moles, then to moles of product, and finally to grams of product. Then select the smaller mass of product, which is from complete use of the limiting reactant. This calculation is shown in Sample Problem 7.13.

A ceramic brake disc in a sports car withstands temperatures of 1400 °C.

▶ SAMPLE PROBLEM 7.13 Mass of Product from a Limiting Reactant

When silicon dioxide (sand) and carbon are heated, the products are silicon carbide, SiC, and carbon monoxide. Silicon carbide is a ceramic material that tolerates extreme temperatures and is used as an abrasive and in the brake discs of sports cars. How many grams of CO are formed from 70.0 g of SiO_2 and 50.0 g of C?

$$SiO_2(s) + 3C(s) \xrightarrow{\text{Heat}} SiC(s) + 2CO(g)$$

SOLUTION

STEP **1** State the given and needed grams.

	Given	Need
ANALYZE THE PROBLEM	70.0 g of SiO₂, 50.0 g of C	grams of CO from limiting reactant
	Equation	
	$SiO_2(s) + 3C(s) \xrightarrow{\text{Heat}} SiC(s) + 2CO(g)$	

Guide to Calculating the Grams of Product from a Limiting Reactant

STEP **1**
State the given and needed grams.

STEP **2**
Write a plan to convert the grams of each reactant to grams of product.

STEP **3**
Write the molar mass factors and the mole–mole factors from the equation.

STEP **4**
Calculate the number of grams of product from each reactant and select the smaller number of grams as the amount of product from the limiting reactant.

STEP 2 Write a plan to convert the grams of each reactant to grams of product.

grams of SiO$_2$ $\xrightarrow{\text{Molar mass}}$ moles of SiO$_2$ $\xrightarrow{\text{Mole–mole factor}}$ moles of CO $\xrightarrow{\text{Molar mass}}$ grams of CO

grams of C $\xrightarrow{\text{Molar mass}}$ moles of C $\xrightarrow{\text{Mole–mole factor}}$ moles of CO $\xrightarrow{\text{Molar mass}}$ grams of CO

STEP 3 Write the molar mass factors and mole–mole factors from the equation.

Molar mass factors:

1 mole of SiO$_2$ = 60.09 g of SiO$_2$
$$\frac{1 \text{ mole SiO}_2}{60.09 \text{ g SiO}_2} \quad \text{and} \quad \frac{60.09 \text{ g SiO}_2}{1 \text{ mole SiO}_2}$$

1 mole of C = 12.01 g of C
$$\frac{1 \text{ mole C}}{12.01 \text{ g C}} \quad \text{and} \quad \frac{12.01 \text{ g C}}{1 \text{ mole C}}$$

1 mole of CO = 28.01 g of CO
$$\frac{1 \text{ mole CO}}{28.01 \text{ g CO}} \quad \text{and} \quad \frac{28.01 \text{ g CO}}{1 \text{ mole CO}}$$

Mole–mole factors:

2 moles of CO = 1 mole of SiO$_2$
$$\frac{2 \text{ moles CO}}{1 \text{ mole SiO}_2} \quad \text{and} \quad \frac{1 \text{ mole SiO}_2}{2 \text{ moles CO}}$$

2 moles of CO = 3 moles of C
$$\frac{2 \text{ moles CO}}{3 \text{ moles C}} \quad \text{and} \quad \frac{3 \text{ moles C}}{2 \text{ moles CO}}$$

STEP 4 Calculate the number of grams of product from each reactant and select the smaller number of grams as the amount of product from the limiting reactant.

Grams of CO (product) from SiO$_2$:

$$\underset{\text{Limiting reactant}}{\overset{\text{Three SFs}}{70.0 \text{ g SiO}_2}} \times \underset{\text{Four SFs}}{\overset{\text{Exact}}{\frac{1 \text{ mole SiO}_2}{60.09 \text{ g SiO}_2}}} \times \underset{\text{Exact}}{\overset{\text{Exact}}{\frac{2 \text{ moles CO}}{1 \text{ mole SiO}_2}}} \times \underset{\text{Exact}}{\overset{\text{Four SFs}}{\frac{28.01 \text{ g CO}}{1 \text{ mole CO}}}} = \underset{\substack{\text{Smaller amount} \\ \text{of product}}}{\overset{\text{Three SFs}}{65.3 \text{ g of CO}}}$$

Grams of CO (product) from C:

$$\overset{\text{Three SFs}}{50.0 \text{ g C}} \times \underset{\text{Four SFs}}{\overset{\text{Exact}}{\frac{1 \text{ mole C}}{12.01 \text{ g C}}}} \times \underset{\text{Exact}}{\overset{\text{Exact}}{\frac{2 \text{ moles CO}}{3 \text{ moles C}}}} \times \underset{\text{Exact}}{\overset{\text{Four SFs}}{\frac{28.01 \text{ g CO}}{1 \text{ mole CO}}}} = \overset{\text{Three SFs}}{77.7 \text{ g of CO}}$$

The smaller amount, 65.3 g of CO, is the most CO that can be produced.

STUDY CHECK 7.13

Hydrogen sulfide burns with oxygen to give sulfur dioxide and water. How many grams of sulfur dioxide are formed from the reaction of 8.52 g of H$_2$S and 9.60 g of O$_2$?

$$2H_2S(g) + 3O_2(g) \xrightarrow{\Delta} 2SO_2(g) + 2H_2O(g)$$

ANSWER

12.8 g of SO$_2$

Percent Yield

In our problems up to now, we assumed that all of the reactants changed completely to product. Thus, we have calculated the amount of product as the maximum quantity possible, or 100%. While this would be an ideal situation, it does not usually happen. As we carry out a reaction and transfer products from one container to another, some product is usually lost. In the lab as well as commercially, the starting materials may not be completely pure, and side reactions may use some of the reactants to give unwanted products. Thus, 100% of the desired product is not actually obtained.

When we do a chemical reaction in the laboratory, we measure out specific quantities of the reactants. We calculate the **theoretical yield** for the reaction, which is the amount of product (100%) we would expect if all the reactants were converted to the desired product. When the reaction ends, we collect and measure the mass of the product, which is the **actual yield** for the product. Because some product is usually lost, the actual yield is less than the theoretical yield. Using the actual yield and the theoretical yield for a product, we can calculate the **percent yield**.

$$\text{Percent yield (\%)} = \frac{\text{actual yield}}{\text{theoretical yield}} \times 100\%$$

⚛ **CORE CHEMISTRY SKILL**

Calculating Percent Yield

▶ **SAMPLE PROBLEM 7.14 Calculating Percent Yield**

On a space shuttle, LiOH is used to absorb exhaled CO_2 from breathing air to form $LiHCO_3$.

$$LiOH(s) + CO_2(g) \longrightarrow LiHCO_3(s)$$

What is the percent yield of $LiHCO_3$ for the reaction if 50.0 g of LiOH gives 72.8 g of $LiHCO_3$?

SOLUTION

STEP 1 State the given and needed quantities.

ANALYZE THE PROBLEM	Given	Need
	50.0 g of LiOH (reactant), 72.8 g of $LiHCO_3$ (actual product)	theoretical yield of $LiHCO_3$, percent yield of $LiHCO_3$
	Equation	
	$LiOH(s) + CO_2(g) \longrightarrow LiHCO_3(s)$	

STEP 2 Write a plan to calculate the theoretical yield and the percent yield.

Calculation of theoretical yield:

grams of LiOH → Molar mass → moles of LiOH → Mole–mole factor → moles of $LiHCO_3$ → Molar mass → grams of $LiHCO_3$ Theoretical yield

Calculation of percent yield:

$$\text{Percent yield (\%)} = \frac{\text{actual yield of } LiHCO_3}{\text{theoretical yield of } LiHCO_3} \times 100\%$$

STEP 3 Write the molar mass factors and the mole–mole factor from the balanced equation.

Molar mass factors:

1 mole of LiOH = 23.95 g of LiOH

$$\frac{1 \text{ mole LiOH}}{23.95 \text{ g LiOH}} \text{ and } \frac{23.95 \text{ g LiOH}}{1 \text{ mole LiOH}}$$

1 mole of $LiHCO_3$ = 67.96 g of $LiHCO_3$

$$\frac{1 \text{ mole } LiHCO_3}{67.96 \text{ g } LiHCO_3} \text{ and } \frac{67.96 \text{ g } LiHCO_3}{1 \text{ mole } LiHCO_3}$$

Mole–mole factors:

1 mole of $LiHCO_3$ = 1 mole of LiOH

$$\frac{1 \text{ mole } LiHCO_3}{1 \text{ mole LiOH}} \text{ and } \frac{1 \text{ mole LiOH}}{1 \text{ mole } LiHCO_3}$$

Guide to Calculations for Percent Yield

STEP 1
State the given and needed quantities.

STEP 2
Write a plan to calculate the theoretical yield and the percent yield.

STEP 3
Write the molar mass factors and the mole–mole factors from the balanced equation.

STEP 4
Calculate the percent yield by dividing the actual yield (given) by the theoretical yield and multiplying the result by 100%.

On a space shuttle, the LiOH in the canisters removes CO_2 from the air.

STEP 4 Calculate the percent yield by dividing the actual yield (given) by the theoretical yield and multiplying the result by 100%.

Calculation of theoretical yield:

$$50.0 \text{ g LiOH} \times \underset{\text{Three SFs}}{\overset{\text{Exact}}{\frac{1 \text{ mole LiOH}}{23.95 \text{ g LiOH}}}} \times \underset{\text{Four SFs}}{\frac{1 \text{ mole LiHCO}_3}{1 \text{ mole LiOH}}} \times \underset{\text{Exact}}{\overset{\text{Four SFs}}{\frac{67.96 \text{ g LiHCO}_3}{1 \text{ mole LiHCO}_3}}}$$

$$= \underset{\text{Three SFs}}{142 \text{ g of LiHCO}_3}$$

Calculation of percent yield:

$$\frac{\text{actual yield (given)}}{\text{theoretical yield (calculated)}} \times 100\% = \underset{\text{Three SFs}}{\frac{72.8 \text{ g LiHCO}_3}{142 \text{ g LiHCO}_3}} \times 100\% = \underset{\text{Three SFs}}{51.3\%}$$

A percent yield of 51.3% means that 72.8 g of the theoretical amount of 142 g of LiHCO$_3$ was actually produced by the reaction.

STUDY CHECK 7.14

For the reaction in Sample Problem 7.14, what is the percent yield of LiHCO$_3$ if 8.00 g of CO$_2$ produces 10.5 g of LiHCO$_3$?

ANSWER

84.7%

QUESTIONS AND PROBLEMS

7.8 Limiting Reactants and Percent Yield

LEARNING GOAL Identify a limiting reactant and calculate the amount of product formed from the limiting reactant. Given the actual quantity of product, determine the percent yield for a reaction.

7.73 A taxi company has 10 taxis.
   a. On a certain day, only eight taxi drivers show up for work. How many taxis can be used to pick up passengers?
   b. On another day, 10 taxi drivers show up for work but three taxis are in the repair shop. How many taxis can be driven?

7.74 A clock maker has 15 clock faces. Each clock requires one face and two hands.
   a. If the clock maker has 42 hands, how many clocks can be produced?
   b. If the clock maker has only eight hands, how many clocks can be produced?

7.75 Nitrogen and hydrogen react to form ammonia.

$$N_2(g) + 3H_2(g) \longrightarrow 2NH_3(g)$$

Determine the limiting reactant in each of the following mixtures of reactants:
   a. 3.0 moles of N$_2$ and 5.0 moles of H$_2$
   b. 8.0 moles of N$_2$ and 4.0 moles of H$_2$
   c. 3.0 moles of N$_2$ and 12.0 moles of H$_2$

7.76 Iron and oxygen react to form iron(III) oxide.

$$4Fe(s) + 3O_2(g) \longrightarrow 2Fe_2O_3(s)$$

Determine the limiting reactant in each of the following mixtures of reactants:
   a. 2.0 moles of Fe and 6.0 moles of O$_2$

   b. 5.0 moles of Fe and 4.0 moles of O$_2$
   c. 16.0 moles of Fe and 20.0 moles of O$_2$

7.77 For each of the following reactions, 20.0 g of each reactant is present initially. Determine the limiting reactant, and calculate the grams of product in parentheses that would be produced.
   a. $2Al(s) + 3Cl_2(g) \longrightarrow 2AlCl_3(s)$ (AlCl$_3$)
   b. $4NH_3(g) + 5O_2(g) \longrightarrow 4NO(g) + 6H_2O(g)$ (H$_2$O)
   c. $CS_2(g) + 3O_2(g) \overset{\Delta}{\longrightarrow} CO_2(g) + 2SO_2(g)$ (SO$_2$)

7.78 For each of the following reactions, 20.0 g of each reactant is present initially. Determine the limiting reactant, and calculate the grams of product in parentheses that would be produced.
   a. $4Al(s) + 3O_2(g) \longrightarrow 2Al_2O_3(s)$ (Al$_2$O$_3$)
   b. $3NO_2(g) + H_2O(l) \longrightarrow 2HNO_3(aq) + NO(g)$ (HNO$_3$)
   c. $C_2H_5OH(l) + 3O_2(g) \overset{\Delta}{\longrightarrow} 2CO_2(g) + 3H_2O(g)$ (H$_2$O)

7.79 For each of the following reactions, calculate the grams of indicated product when 25.0 g of the first reactant and 40.0 g of the second reactant is used:
   a. $2SO_2(g) + O_2(g) \longrightarrow 2SO_3(g)$ (SO$_3$)
   b. $3Fe(s) + 4H_2O(l) \longrightarrow Fe_3O_4(s) + 4H_2(g)$ (Fe$_3$O$_4$)
   c. $C_7H_{16}(g) + 11O_2(g) \overset{\Delta}{\longrightarrow} 7CO_2(g) + 8H_2O(g)$ (CO$_2$)

7.80 For each of the following reactions, calculate the grams of indicated product when 15.0 g of the first reactant and 10.0 g of the second reactant is used:
   a. $4Li(s) + O_2(g) \longrightarrow 2Li_2O(s)$ (Li$_2$O)
   b. $Fe_2O_3(s) + 3H_2(g) \longrightarrow 2Fe(s) + 3H_2O(l)$ (Fe)
   c. $Al_2S_3(s) + 6H_2O(l) \longrightarrow$
$$2Al(OH)_3(aq) + 3H_2S(g)   (H_2S)$$

7.81 Carbon disulfide is produced by the reaction of carbon and sulfur dioxide.

$$5C(s) + 2SO_2(g) \longrightarrow CS_2(g) + 4CO(g)$$

a. What is the percent yield of carbon disulfide if the reaction of 40.0 g of carbon produces 36.0 g of carbon disulfide?

b. What is the percent yield of carbon disulfide if the reaction of 32.0 g of sulfur dioxide produces 12.0 g of carbon disulfide?

7.82 Iron(III) oxide reacts with carbon monoxide to produce iron and carbon dioxide.

$$Fe_2O_3(s) + 3CO(g) \longrightarrow 2Fe(s) + 3CO_2(g)$$

a. What is the percent yield of iron if the reaction of 65.0 g of iron(III) oxide produces 15.0 g of iron?

b. What is the percent yield of carbon dioxide if the reaction of 75.0 g of carbon monoxide produces 85.0 g of carbon dioxide?

7.83 Aluminum reacts with oxygen to produce aluminum oxide.

$$4Al(s) + 3O_2(g) \longrightarrow 2Al_2O_3(s)$$

Calculate the mass of Al_2O_3 that can be produced if the reaction of 50.0 g of aluminum and sufficient oxygen has a 75.0% yield.

7.84 Propane (C_3H_8) burns in oxygen to produce carbon dioxide and water.

$$C_3H_8(g) + 5O_2(g) \xrightarrow{\Delta} 3CO_2(g) + 4H_2O(g)$$

Calculate the mass of CO_2 that can be produced if the reaction of 45.0 g of propane and sufficient oxygen has a 60.0% yield.

7.85 When 30.0 g of carbon is heated with silicon dioxide, 28.2 g of carbon monoxide is produced. What is the percent yield of carbon monoxide for this reaction?

$$SiO_2(s) + 3C(s) \longrightarrow SiC(s) + 2CO(g)$$

7.86 When 56.6 g of calcium is reacted with nitrogen gas, 32.4 g of calcium nitride is produced. What is the percent yield of calcium nitride for this reaction?

$$3Ca(s) + N_2(g) \longrightarrow Ca_3N_2(s)$$

7.9 Energy in Chemical Reactions

LEARNING GOAL

Given the heat of reaction, calculate the loss or gain of heat for an exothermic or endothermic reaction.

Almost every chemical reaction involves a loss or gain of energy. To discuss energy change for a reaction, we look at the energy of the reactants before the reaction and the energy of the products after the reaction.

Energy Units for Chemical Reactions

The SI unit for energy is the *joule* (J). Often, the unit of *kilojoules* (kJ) is used to show the energy change in a reaction.

1 kilojoule (kJ) = 1000 joules (J)

Heat of Reaction

The **heat of reaction** is the amount of heat absorbed or released during a reaction that takes place at constant pressure. A change of energy occurs as reactants interact, bonds break apart, and products form. We determine a heat of reaction or *enthalpy change*, symbol ΔH, as the difference in the energy of the products and the reactants.

$$\Delta H = H_{products} - H_{reactants}$$

Exothermic Reactions

In an **exothermic reaction** (*exo* means "out"), the energy of the products is lower than that of the reactants. This means that heat is released along with the products that form. Let us look at the equation for the exothermic reaction in which 185 kJ of heat is released when 1 mole of hydrogen and 1 mole of chlorine react to form 2 moles of hydrogen chloride. For an exothermic reaction, the heat of reaction can be written as one of the products. It can also be written as a ΔH value with a negative sign ($-$).

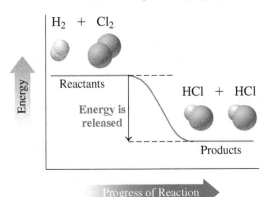

Exothermic, Heat Released	Heat Is a Product
$H_2(g) + Cl_2(g) \longrightarrow 2HCl(g) + 185\,kJ$	$\Delta H = -185\,kJ$ Negative sign

Endothermic Reactions

In an **endothermic reaction** (*endo* means "within"), the energy of the products is higher than that of the reactants. Heat is required to convert the reactants to products. Let us look at the equation for the endothermic reaction in which 180 kJ of heat is needed to convert 1 mole of nitrogen and 1 mole of oxygen to 2 moles of nitrogen oxide. For an endothermic reaction, the heat of reaction can be written as one of the reactants. It can also be written as a ΔH value with a positive sign ($+$).

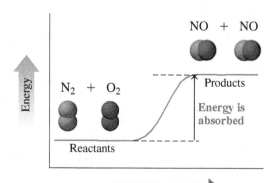

Endothermic, Heat Absorbed	Heat Is a Reactant
$N_2(g) + O_2(g) + 180\,kJ \longrightarrow 2NO(g)$	$\Delta H = +180\,kJ$ Positive sign

Reaction	Energy Change	Heat in the Equation	Sign of ΔH
Endothermic	Heat absorbed	Reactant side	Positive sign ($+$)
Exothermic	Heat released	Product side	Negative sign ($-$)

Calculations of Heat in Reactions

The value of ΔH refers to the heat change for each substance in the balanced equation. Consider the following decomposition reaction:

$$2H_2O(l) \longrightarrow 2H_2(g) + O_2(g) \quad \Delta H = +572\,kJ$$
$$2H_2O(l) + 572\,kJ \longrightarrow 2H_2(g) + O_2(g)$$

For this reaction, 572 kJ are absorbed by 2 moles of H_2O to produce 2 moles of H_2 and 1 mole of O_2. We can write heat conversion factors for each substance in this reaction as follows:

$$\frac{+572\,kJ}{2\ moles\ H_2O} \qquad \frac{+572\,kJ}{2\ moles\ H_2} \qquad \frac{+572\,kJ}{1\ mole\ O_2}$$

Suppose in this reaction that 9.00 g of H_2O undergoes reaction. We can calculate the amount of heat absorbed as

$$9.00\ \text{g}\ H_2O \times \frac{1\ \text{mole}\ H_2O}{18.02\ \text{g}\ H_2O} \times \frac{+572\,kJ}{2\ \text{moles}\ H_2O} = +143\,kJ$$

▶ **SAMPLE PROBLEM 7.15** Calculating Heat in a Reaction

How much heat, in kilojoules, is released when nitrogen and hydrogen react to form 50.0 g of ammonia?

$$N_2(g) + 3H_2(g) \longrightarrow 2NH_3(g) \qquad \Delta H = -92.2 \text{ kJ}$$

⊗ **CORE CHEMISTRY SKILL**

Using the Heat of Reaction

SOLUTION

STEP 1 State the given and needed quantities.

ANALYZE THE PROBLEM	Given	Need
	50.0 g of NH_3, $\Delta H = -92.2$ kJ	heat released, in kilojoules
	Equation	
	$N_2(g) + 3H_2(g) \longrightarrow 2NH_3(g)$	

STEP 2 Write a plan using the heat of reaction and any molar mass needed.

grams of NH_3 → Molar mass → moles of NH_3 → Heat of reaction → kilojoules

STEP 3 Write the conversion factors including heat of reaction.

1 mole of NH_3 = 17.03 g of NH_3 2 moles of NH_3 = −92.2 kJ

$$\frac{17.03 \text{ g } NH_3}{1 \text{ mole } NH_3} \quad \text{and} \quad \frac{1 \text{ mole } NH_3}{17.03 \text{ g } NH_3} \qquad \frac{-92.2 \text{ kJ}}{2 \text{ moles } NH_3} \quad \text{and} \quad \frac{2 \text{ moles } NH_3}{-92.2 \text{ kJ}}$$

STEP 4 Set up the problem to calculate the heat.

$$50.0 \text{ g } NH_3 \times \frac{1 \text{ mole } NH_3}{17.03 \text{ g } NH_3} \times \frac{-92.2 \text{ kJ}}{2 \text{ moles } NH_3} = -135 \text{ kJ}$$

Three SFs   Four SFs   Exact   Three SFs

(Exact — 1 mole NH₃; Three SFs — −92.2 kJ)

Guide to Calculations Using the Heat of Reaction

STEP 1
State the given and needed quantities.

STEP 2
Write a plan using the heat of reaction and any molar mass needed.

STEP 3
Write the conversion factors including heat of reaction.

STEP 4
Set up the problem to calculate the heat.

STUDY CHECK 7.15

Mercury(II) oxide decomposes to mercury and oxygen.

$$2HgO(s) \longrightarrow 2Hg(l) + O_2(g) \qquad \Delta H = +182 \text{ kJ}$$

a. Is the reaction exothermic or endothermic?
b. How many kilojoules are needed to react 25.0 g of mercury(II) oxide?

ANSWER

a. endothermic   **b.** 20.5 kJ

❤ Chemistry Link to Health

Cold Packs and Hot Packs

In a hospital, at a first-aid station, or at an athletic event, an instant *cold pack* may be used to reduce swelling from an injury, remove heat from inflammation, or decrease capillary size to lessen the effect of hemorrhaging. Inside the plastic container of a cold pack, there is a compartment containing solid ammonium nitrate

(NH_4NO_3) that is separated from a compartment containing water. The pack is activated when it is hit or squeezed hard enough to break the walls between the compartments and cause the ammonium nitrate to mix with the water (shown as H_2O over the reaction arrow). In an endothermic process, 1 mole of NH_4NO_3 that dissolves absorbs

26 kJ of heat. The temperature drops to about 4 to 5 °C to give a cold pack that is ready to use.

Endothermic Reaction in a Cold Pack

$$NH_4NO_3(s) + 26\,kJ \xrightarrow{H_2O} NH_4NO_3(aq)$$

Hot packs are used to relax muscles, lessen aches and cramps, and increase circulation by expanding capillary size. Constructed in the same way as cold packs, a hot pack contains a salt such as $CaCl_2$. When 1 mole of $CaCl_2$ dissolves in water, 82 kJ are released as heat. The temperature increases as much as 66 °C to give a hot pack that is ready to use.

Exothermic Reaction in a Hot Pack

$$CaCl_2(s) \xrightarrow{H_2O} CaCl_2(aq) + 82\,kJ$$

Cold packs use an endothermic reaction.

QUESTIONS AND PROBLEMS

7.9 Energy in Chemical Reactions

LEARNING GOAL Given the heat of reaction, calculate the loss or gain of heat for an exothermic or endothermic reaction.

7.87 In an exothermic reaction, is the energy of the products higher or lower than that of the reactants?

7.88 In an endothermic reaction, is the energy of the products higher or lower than that of the reactants?

7.89 Classify each of the following as exothermic or endothermic:
a. A reaction releases 550 kJ.
b. The energy level of the products is higher than that of the reactants.
c. The metabolism of glucose in the body provides energy.

7.90 Classify each of the following as exothermic or endothermic:
a. The energy level of the products is lower than that of the reactants.
b. In the body, the synthesis of proteins requires energy.
c. A reaction absorbs 125 kJ.

7.91 Classify each of the following as exothermic or endothermic and give the ΔH for each:
a. $CH_4(g) + 2O_2(g) \xrightarrow{\Delta} CO_2(g) + 2H_2O(g) + 802\,kJ$
b. $Ca(OH)_2(s) + 65.3\,kJ \longrightarrow CaO(s) + H_2O(l)$
c. $2Al(s) + Fe_2O_3(s) \longrightarrow Al_2O_3(s) + 2Fe(l) + 850\,kJ$

The thermite reaction of aluminum and iron(III) oxide produces very high temperatures used to cut or weld railroad tracks.

7.92 Classify each of the following as exothermic or endothermic and give the ΔH for each:
a. $C_3H_8(g) + 5O_2(g) \xrightarrow{\Delta} 3CO_2(g) + 4H_2O(g) + 2220\,kJ$
b. $2Na(s) + Cl_2(g) \longrightarrow 2NaCl(s) + 819\,kJ$
c. $PCl_5(g) + 67\,kJ \longrightarrow PCl_3(g) + Cl_2(g)$

7.93 a. How many kilojoules are released when 125 g of Cl_2 reacts with silicon?

$$Si(s) + 2Cl_2(g) \longrightarrow SiCl_4(g) \quad \Delta H = -657\,kJ$$

b. How many kilojoules are absorbed when 278 g of PCl_5 reacts?

$$PCl_5(g) \longrightarrow PCl_3(g) + Cl_2(g) \quad \Delta H = +67\,kJ$$

7.94 a. How many kilojoules are released when 75.0 g of methanol reacts?

$$2CH_3OH(l) + 3O_2(g) \xrightarrow{\Delta} 2CO_2(g) + 4H_2O(l)$$
$$\Delta H = -726\,kJ$$

b. How many kilojoules are absorbed when 315 g of $Ca(OH)_2$ reacts?

$$Ca(OH)_2(s) \longrightarrow CaO(s) + H_2O(l) \quad \Delta H = +65.3\,kJ$$

Rx Clinical Applications

7.95 In photosynthesis, glucose, $C_6H_{12}O_6$, and O_2 are produced from CO_2 and H_2O. Glucose from starches is the major fuel for the body.

$$6CO_2(g) + 6H_2O(l) + 680\,kcal \longrightarrow C_6H_{12}O_6(aq) + 6O_2(g)$$
Glucose

a. Is the reaction endothermic or exothermic?
b. How many grams of glucose are produced from 18.0 g of CO_2?
c. How much heat, in kilojoules, is needed to produce 25.0 g of $C_6H_{12}O_6$?

7.96 Ethanol, C_2H_6O, reacts in the body using the following equation:

$$C_2H_6O(aq) + 3O_2(g) \longrightarrow 2CO_2(g) + 3H_2O(l) + 327\,kcal$$
Ethanol

a. Is the reaction endothermic or exothermic?
b. How much heat, in kilocalories, is produced when 5.00 g of ethanol reacts with O_2 gas?
c. How many grams of ethanol react if 1250 kJ are produced?

Clinical Update
Whitening of Tooth Enamel

The reaction of hydrogen peroxide, $H_2O_2(aq)$, placed on Jane's teeth produces water, $H_2O(l)$, and oxygen gas. After Jane had her teeth cleaned and whitened, Kimberly recommended that she use a toothpaste with tin(II) fluoride when she brushes her teeth. Most toothpastes and mouthwashes contain fluoride ions. Tooth enamel, which is composed of hydroxyapatite, $Ca_5(PO_4)_3OH$, is strengthened when it reacts with fluoride ions to form fluoroapatite, $Ca_5(PO_4)_3F$.

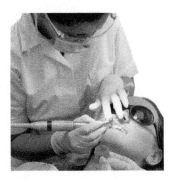

Clinical Applications

7.97 The hydroxyapatite that makes up the enamel of teeth has the formula $Ca_5(PO_4)_3OH$.
   a. How many moles of phosphorus (P) are in 0.0500 mole of hydroxyapatite?
   b. How many calcium ions (Ca^{2+}) are in 0.250 mole of hydroxyapatite?
   c. How many moles of hydroxyapatite contain 8.5×10^{23} atoms of hydrogen (H)?
   d. What is the molar mass of hydroxyapatite?

7.98 The fluoroapatite that makes up the enamel of teeth has the formula $Ca_5(PO_4)_3F$.
   a. How many moles of oxygen (O) are in 0.0500 mole of fluoroapatite?
   b. How many calcium ions (Ca^{2+}) are in 0.460 mole of fluoroapatite?

   c. How many moles of fluoroapatite contain 7.2×10^{23} fluoride (F^-) ions?
   d. What is the molar mass of fluoroapatite?

7.99 a. Write the balanced chemical equation for the reaction when aqueous hydrogen peroxide, H_2O_2, reacts to form liquid water and O_2 gas.
   b. Classify the reaction in part **a** as a combination, decomposition, single replacement, double replacement, or combustion reaction.
   Use your balanced chemical equation in part **a** to make the following calculations:
   c. the moles of O_2 that can be produced from 1.65 moles of H_2O_2
   d. the grams of H_2O_2 that react to produce 4.28 g of O_2
   e. If 3.0 g of a gel, which is 25% H_2O_2 by mass, is applied to Jane's teeth, how many grams of O_2 are produced?
   f. What is the percent yield for the reaction if 8.00 g of H_2O_2 gives 2.33 g of O_2?

7.100 a. Write the balanced chemical equation for the reaction of solid tin(II) oxide with aqueous hydrogen fluoride to produce aqueous tin(II) fluoride and water.
   b. Classify the reaction in part **a** as a combination, decomposition, single replacement, double replacement, or combustion reaction.
   Use your balanced chemical equation in part **a** to make the following calculations:
   c. the moles of HF needed to react with 0.725 mole of SnO
   d. the grams of HF that need to react to produce 4.28 g of SnF_2
   e. If 5.00 g of HF completely reacts, what is the theoretical yield of SnF_2?
   f. What is the percent yield for the reaction in part **e** if 16.2 g of SnF_2 are produced?

CHEMICAL REACTIONS AND QUANTITIES

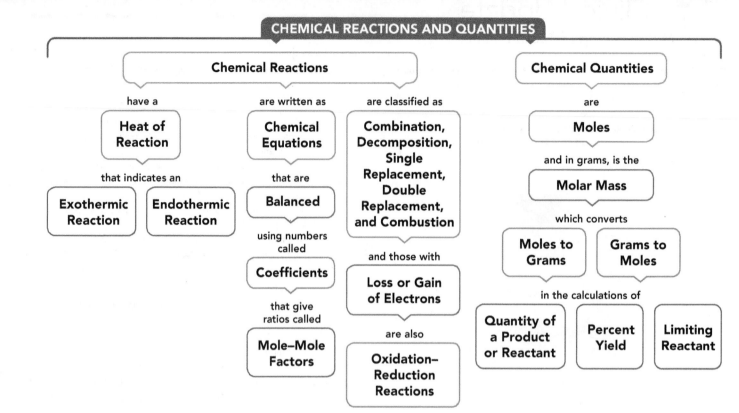

Chemical Reactions

have a → **Heat of Reaction** → that indicates an → **Exothermic Reaction** / **Endothermic Reaction**

are written as → **Chemical Equations** → that are → **Balanced** → using numbers called → **Coefficients** → that give ratios called → **Mole–Mole Factors**

are classified as → **Combination, Decomposition, Single Replacement, Double Replacement, and Combustion**

and those with → **Loss or Gain of Electrons** → are also → **Oxidation–Reduction Reactions**

Chemical Quantities

are → **Moles** → and in grams, is the → **Molar Mass** → which converts → **Moles to Grams** / **Grams to Moles** → in the calculations of → **Quantity of a Product or Reactant** / **Percent Yield** / **Limiting Reactant**

CHAPTER REVIEW

7.1 Equations for Chemical Reactions

LEARNING GOAL Write a balanced chemical equation from the formulas of the reactants and products for a reaction; determine the number of atoms in the reactants and products.

$2H_2(g) + O_2(g) \longrightarrow 2H_2O(g)$
Balanced

- A chemical change occurs when the atoms of the initial substances rearrange to form new substances.
- A chemical equation shows the formulas of the substances that react on the left side of a reaction arrow and the products that form on the right side of the reaction arrow.
- A chemical equation is balanced by writing coefficients, small whole numbers, in front of formulas to equalize the atoms of each of the elements in the reactants and the products.

7.2 Types of Reactions

LEARNING GOAL

Identify a reaction as a combination, decomposition, single replacement, double replacement, or combustion.

Single replacement

One element   replaces   another element

A + B C ⟶ A C + B

- Many chemical reactions can be organized by reaction type: combination, decomposition, single replacement, double replacement, or combustion.

7.3 Oxidation–Reduction Reactions

LEARNING GOAL Define the terms oxidation and reduction; identify the reactants oxidized and reduced.

Oxidation (loss of electron)

e^-

A   B   A   B
oxidized reduced

Reduction (gain of electron)

- When electrons are transferred in a reaction, it is an oxidation–reduction reaction.
- One reactant loses electrons, and another reactant gains electrons.
- Overall, the number of electrons lost and gained is equal.

7.4 The Mole

LEARNING GOAL Use Avogadro's number to determine the number of particles in a given number of moles.

- One mole of an element contains 6.02×10^{23} atoms.
- One mole of a compound contains 6.02×10^{23} molecules or formula units.

7.5 Molar Mass and Calculations

LEARNING GOAL Calculate the molar mass for a substance given its chemical formula; use molar mass to convert between grams and moles.

- The molar mass (g/mole) of any substance is the mass in grams equal numerically to its atomic mass, or the sum of the atomic masses, which have been multiplied by their subscripts in a formula.
- The molar mass is used as a conversion factor to change a quantity in grams to moles or to change a given number of moles to grams.

7.6 Mole Relationships in Chemical Equations

LEARNING GOAL Given a quantity in moles of reactant or product, use a mole–mole factor from the balanced chemical equation to calculate the number of moles of another substance in the reaction.

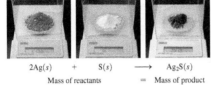

$2Ag(s)$ + $S(s)$ $\longrightarrow$ $Ag_2S(s)$

Mass of reactants = Mass of product

- In a balanced equation, the total mass of the reactants is equal to the total mass of the products.
- The coefficients in an equation describing the relationship between the moles of any two components are used to write mole–mole factors.
- When the number of moles for one substance is known, a mole–mole factor is used to find the moles of a different substance in the reaction.

7.7 Mass Calculations for Reactions

LEARNING GOAL Given the mass in grams of a substance in a reaction, calculate the mass in grams of another substance in the reaction.

- In calculations using equations, the molar masses of the substances and their mole–mole factors are used to change the number of grams of one substance to the corresponding grams of a different substance.

7.8 Limiting Reactants and Percent Yield

LEARNING GOAL Identify a limiting reactant and calculate the amount of product formed from the limiting reactant. Given the actual quantity of product, determine the percent yield for a reaction.

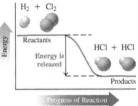

- A limiting reactant is the reactant that produces the smaller amount of product while the other reactant is left over.
- When the masses of two reactants are given, the mass of a product is calculated from the limiting reactant.
- The percent yield for a reaction indicates the percent of product actually produced during a reaction.
- The percent yield is calculated by dividing the actual yield in grams of a product by the theoretical yield in grams and multiplying by 100%.

7.9 Energy in Chemical Reactions

LEARNING GOAL Given the heat of reaction, calculate the loss or gain of heat for an exothermic or endothermic reaction.

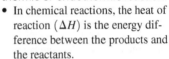

- In chemical reactions, the heat of reaction (ΔH) is the energy difference between the products and the reactants.
- In an exothermic reaction, the energy of the products is lower than that of the reactants. Heat is released, and ΔH is negative.
- In an endothermic reaction, the energy of the products is higher than that of the reactants; heat is absorbed, and ΔH is positive.

KEY TERMS

actual yield The actual amount of product produced by a reaction.

Avogadro's number The number of items in a mole, equal to 6.02×10^{23}.

balanced equation The final form of a chemical equation that shows the same number of atoms of each element in the reactants and products.

chemical equation A shorthand way to represent a chemical reaction using chemical formulas to indicate the reactants and products and coefficients to show reacting ratios.

coefficients Whole numbers placed in front of the formulas to balance the number of atoms or moles of atoms of each element on both sides of an equation.

combination reaction A chemical reaction in which reactants combine to form a single product.

combustion reaction A chemical reaction in which a fuel containing carbon and hydrogen reacts with oxygen to produce CO_2, H_2O, and energy.

decomposition reaction A reaction in which a single reactant splits into two or more simpler substances.

double replacement reaction A reaction in which parts of two different reactants exchange places.

endothermic reaction A reaction that requires heat; the energy of the products is higher than the energy of the reactants.

exothermic reaction A reaction that releases heat; the energy of the products is lower than the energy of the reactants.

formula unit The group of ions represented by the formula of an ionic compound.

heat of reaction The heat (symbol ΔH) absorbed or released when a reaction takes place at constant pressure.

limiting reactant The reactant used up during a chemical reaction, which limits the amount of product that can form.

molar mass The mass in grams of 1 mole of an element equal numerically to its atomic mass. The molar mass of a compound is equal to the sum of the masses of the elements multiplied by their subscripts in the formula.

mole A group of atoms, molecules, or formula units that contains 6.02×10^{23} of these items.

mole–mole factor A conversion factor that relates the number of moles of two compounds derived from the coefficients in an equation.

oxidation The loss of electrons by a substance. Biological oxidation may involve the addition of oxygen or the loss of hydrogen.

oxidation–reduction reaction A reaction in which the oxidation of one reactant is always accompanied by the reduction of another reactant.

percent yield The ratio of the actual yield for a reaction to the theoretical yield possible for the reaction.

products The substances formed as a result of a chemical reaction.

reactants The initial substances that undergo change in a chemical reaction.

reduction The gain of electrons by a substance. Biological reduction may involve the loss of oxygen or the gain of hydrogen.

single replacement reaction A reaction in which an element replaces a different element in a compound.

theoretical yield The maximum amount of product that a reaction can produce from a given amount of reactant.

⚛ CORE CHEMISTRY SKILLS

The chapter section containing each Core Chemistry Skill is shown in parentheses at the end of each heading.

Balancing a Chemical Equation (7.1)

- In a *balanced* equation, whole numbers called coefficients multiply each of the atoms in the chemical formulas so that the number of each type of atom in the reactants is equal to the number of the same type of atom in the products.

Example: Balance the following chemical equation:

$$SnCl_4(s) + H_2O(l) \longrightarrow Sn(OH)_4(s) + HCl(aq) \quad \text{Unbalanced}$$

Answer: When we compare the atoms on the reactant side and the product side, we see that there are more Cl atoms in the reactants and more O and H atoms in the products.

To balance the equation, we need to use coefficients in front of the formulas containing the Cl atoms, H atoms, and O atoms.

- Place a 4 in front of the formula HCl to give 8 H atoms and 4 Cl atoms in the products.

$$SnCl_4(s) + H_2O(l) \longrightarrow Sn(OH)_4(s) + 4HCl(aq)$$

- Place a 4 in front of the formula H_2O to give 8 H atoms and 4 O atoms in the reactants.

$$SnCl_4(s) + 4H_2O(l) \longrightarrow Sn(OH)_4(s) + 4HCl(aq)$$

- The total number of Sn (1), Cl (4), H (8), and O (4) atoms is now equal on both sides of the equation.

$$SnCl_4(s) + 4H_2O(l) \longrightarrow Sn(OH)_4(s) + 4HCl(aq) \quad \text{Balanced}$$

Classifying Types of Chemical Reactions (7.2)

- Chemical reactions are classified by identifying general patterns in their equations.
- In a combination reaction, two or more elements or compounds bond to form one product.
- In a decomposition reaction, a single reactant splits into two or more products.
- In a single replacement reaction, an uncombined element takes the place of an element in a compound.
- In a double replacement reaction, the positive ions in the reacting compounds switch places.

- In combustion reaction, a carbon-containing compound that is the fuel burns in oxygen from the air to produce carbon dioxide (CO_2), water (H_2O), and energy.

Example: Classify the type of the following reaction:

$$2Al(s) + Fe_2O_3(s) \xrightarrow{\Delta} Al_2O_3(s) + 2Fe(l)$$

Answer: The iron in iron(III) oxide is replaced by aluminum, which makes this a single replacement reaction.

Identifying Oxidized and Reduced Substances (7.3)

- In an oxidation–reduction reaction (abbreviated *redox*), one reactant is oxidized when it loses electrons, and another reactant is reduced when it gains electrons.
- Oxidation is the *loss* of electrons; reduction is the *gain* of electrons.

Example: For the following redox reaction, identify the reactant that is oxidized, and the reactant that is reduced:

$$Fe(s) + Cu^{2+}(aq) \longrightarrow Fe^{2+}(aq) + Cu(s)$$

Answer: $Fe^0(s) \longrightarrow Fe^{2+}(aq) + 2\,e^-$

Fe loses electrons; it is oxidized.

$$Cu^{2+}(aq) + 2\,e^- \longrightarrow Cu^0(s)$$

Cu^{2+} gains electrons; it is reduced.

Converting Particles to Moles (7.4)

- In chemistry, atoms, molecules, and ions are counted by the mole, a unit that contains 6.02×10^{23} items, which is Avogadro's number.
- For example, 1 mole of carbon contains 6.02×10^{23} atoms of carbon and 1 mole of H_2O contains 6.02×10^{23} molecules of H_2O.
- Avogadro's number is used to convert between particles and moles.

Example: How many moles of nickel contain 2.45×10^{24} Ni atoms?

Answer: 2.45×10^{24} ~~Ni atoms~~ $\times \dfrac{\overset{\text{Exact}}{1 \text{ mole Ni}}}{\underset{\text{Three SFs}}{6.02 \times 10^{23} \text{ ~~Ni atoms~~}}}$

Three SFs

$= 4.07$ moles of Ni

Three SFs

Calculating Molar Mass (7.5)

- The molar mass of a compound is the sum of the molar mass of each element in its chemical formula multiplied by its subscript in the formula.

Pinene is a component of pine sap.

Example: Pinene, $C_{10}H_{16}$, which is found in pine tree sap and essential oils, has anti-inflammatory properties. Calculate the molar mass for pinene.

Answer:
$$10 \text{ moles C} \times \frac{12.01 \text{ g C}}{1 \text{ mole C}} = 120.1 \text{ g of C}$$

$$16 \text{ moles H} \times \frac{1.008 \text{ g H}}{1 \text{ mole H}} = 16.13 \text{ g of H}$$

$$\text{Molar mass of } C_{10}H_{16} = 136.2 \text{ g}$$

Using Molar Mass as a Conversion Factor (7.5)

- The molar mass of an element is its mass in grams equal numerically to its atomic mass.
- The molar mass of a compound is its mass in grams equal numerically to the sum of the masses of its elements.
- Molar mass is used as a conversion factor to convert between the moles and grams of a substance.

Some bicycles have aluminum frames.

Equality: 1 mole of Al = 26.98 g of Al

Conversion Factors: $\dfrac{26.98 \text{ g Al}}{1 \text{ mole Al}}$ and $\dfrac{1 \text{ mole Al}}{26.98 \text{ g Al}}$

Example: The frame of a bicycle contains 6500 g of aluminum. How many moles of aluminum are in the bicycle frame?

Answer:
$$6500 \text{ g Al} \times \underset{\text{Four SFs}}{\frac{1 \text{ mole Al}}{26.98 \text{ g Al}}} = \underset{\text{Two SFs}}{240 \text{ moles of Al}}$$

Two SFs

Using Mole–Mole Factors (7.6)

Consider the balanced chemical equation

$$4Na(s) + O_2(g) \longrightarrow 2Na_2O(s)$$

- The coefficients in a balanced chemical equation represent the moles of reactants and the moles of products. Thus, 4 moles of Na react with 1 mole of O_2 to form 2 moles of Na_2O.
- From the coefficients, mole–mole factors can be written for any two substances as follows:

Na and O_2	$\dfrac{4 \text{ moles Na}}{1 \text{ mole } O_2}$	and	$\dfrac{1 \text{ mole } O_2}{4 \text{ moles Na}}$
Na and Na_2O	$\dfrac{4 \text{ moles Na}}{2 \text{ moles } Na_2O}$	and	$\dfrac{2 \text{ moles } Na_2O}{4 \text{ moles Na}}$
O_2 and Na_2O	$\dfrac{1 \text{ mole } O_2}{2 \text{ moles } Na_2O}$	and	$\dfrac{2 \text{ moles } Na_2O}{1 \text{ mole } O_2}$

- A mole–mole factor is used to convert the number of moles of one substance in the reaction to the number of moles of another substance in the reaction.

Example: How many moles of sodium are needed to produce 3.5 moles of sodium oxide?

Answer: **Given:** 3.5 moles of Na_2O **Need:** moles of Na

$$3.5 \text{ moles } Na_2O \times \underset{\text{Exact}}{\frac{4 \text{ moles Na}}{2 \text{ moles } Na_2O}} = 7.0 \text{ moles of Na}$$

Two SFs   Exact   Two SFs

Converting Grams to Grams (7.7)

- When we have the balanced chemical equation for a reaction, we can use the mass of substance A and then calculate the mass of substance B.

$$A \longrightarrow B$$

- The process is as follows:

(1) Use the molar mass factor of A to convert the mass, in grams, of A to moles of A.
(2) Use the mole–mole factor that converts moles of A to moles of B.
(3) Use the molar mass factor of B to calculate the mass, in grams, of B.

$$\text{grams of A} \xrightarrow{\underset{\text{mass A}}{\text{molar}}} \text{moles of A} \xrightarrow{\underset{\text{factor}}{\text{mole–mole}}} \text{moles of B} \xrightarrow{\underset{\text{mass B}}{\text{molar}}} \text{grams of B}$$

Example: How many grams of O_2 are needed to completely react with 14.6 g of Na?

$$4Na(s) + O_2(g) \longrightarrow 2Na_2O(s)$$

Answer:

$$14.6 \text{ g Na} \times \underset{\text{Four SFs}}{\frac{1 \text{ mole Na}}{22.99 \text{ g Na}}} \times \underset{\text{Exact}}{\frac{1 \text{ mole } O_2}{4 \text{ moles Na}}} \times \underset{\text{Exact}}{\frac{32.00 \text{ g } O_2}{1 \text{ mole } O_2}} = 5.08 \text{ g of } O_2$$

Three SFs   Four SFs   Exact   Exact   Three SFs

Calculating Quantity of Product from a Limiting Reactant (7.8)

Often in reactions, the reactants are not consumed at exactly the same time. Then one of the reactants, called the *limiting reactant*, determines the maximum amount of product that can form.

- To determine the limiting reactant, we calculate the amount of product that is possible from each reactant.
- The limiting reactant is the one that produces the smaller amount of product.

Example: If 12.5 g of S reacts with 17.2 g of O_2, what is the limiting reactant and the mass, in grams, of SO_3 produced?

$$2S(s) + 3O_2(g) \longrightarrow 2SO_3(g)$$

Answer:

Mass of SO_3 from S:

$$12.5 \text{ g S} \times \underset{\text{Four SFs}}{\frac{1 \text{ mole S}}{32.07 \text{ g S}}} \times \underset{\text{Exact}}{\frac{2 \text{ moles } SO_3}{2 \text{ moles S}}} \times \underset{\text{Four SFs}}{\frac{80.07 \text{ g } SO_3}{1 \text{ mole } SO_3}} = 31.2 \text{ g of } SO_3$$

Three SFs   Four SFs   Exact   Exact   Three SFs

Mass of SO_3 from O_2:

$$17.2 \text{ g } O_2 \times \underset{\text{Four SFs}}{\frac{1 \text{ mole } O_2}{32.00 \text{ g } O_2}} \times \underset{\text{Exact}}{\frac{2 \text{ moles } SO_3}{3 \text{ moles } O_2}} \times \underset{\text{Exact}}{\frac{80.07 \text{ g } SO_3}{1 \text{ mole } SO_3}}$$

Three SFs   Four SFs   Exact   Exact

Limiting reactant   = 28.7 g of SO_3 Smaller amount of SO_3

Three SFs

Calculating Percent Yield (7.8)

- The *theoretical yield* for a reaction is the amount of product (100%) formed if all the reactants were converted to desired product.
- The *actual yield* for the reaction is the mass, in grams, of the product obtained at the end of the experiment. Because some product is usually lost, the actual yield is less than the theoretical yield.
- The *percent yield* is calculated from the actual yield divided by the theoretical yield and multiplied by 100%.

$$\text{Percent yield (\%)} = \frac{\text{actual yield}}{\text{theoretical yield}} \times 100\%$$

Example: If 22.6 g of Al reacts completely with O_2, and 37.8 g of Al_2O_3 is obtained, what is the percent yield of Al_2O_3 for the reaction?

$$4Al(s) + 3O_2(g) \longrightarrow 2Al_2O_3(s)$$

Answer:

Calculation of theoretical yield:

Three SFs — Exact — Exact — Five SFs

$$22.6 \ \cancel{g \ Al} \times \frac{1 \ \text{mole } \cancel{Al}}{26.98 \ \cancel{g \ Al}} \times \frac{2 \ \text{moles } Al_2O_3}{4 \ \text{moles } \cancel{Al}} \times \frac{101.96 \ g \ Al_2O_3}{1 \ \text{mole } \cancel{Al_2O_3}}$$

Four SFs — Exact — Exact

$$= 42.7 \ g \ \text{of} \ Al_2O_3 \quad \text{Theoretical yield}$$

Three SFs

Calculation of percent yield:

$$\frac{\text{actual yield (given)}}{\text{theoretical yield (calculated)}} \times 100\% = \frac{\overset{\text{Three SFs}}{37.8 \ \cancel{g \ Al_2O_3}}}{42.7 \ \cancel{g \ Al_2O_3}} \times 100\%$$

Three SFs

$$= 88.5\%$$

Three SFs

Using the Heat of Reaction (7.9)

- The heat of reaction is the amount of heat, in kJ or kcal, that is absorbed or released during a reaction.
- The heat of reaction, symbol ΔH, is the difference in the energy of the products and the reactants.

$$\Delta H = H_{\text{products}} - H_{\text{reactants}}$$

- In an exothermic reaction (*exo* means "out"), the energy of the products is lower than that of the reactants. This means that heat is released along with the products that form. Then the sign for the heat of reaction, ΔH, is negative.
- In an endothermic reaction (*endo* means "within"), the energy of the products is higher than that of the reactants. The heat is required to convert the reactants to products. Then the sign for the heat of reaction, ΔH, is positive.

Example: How many kilojoules are released when 3.50 g of CH_4 undergoes combustion?

$$CH_4(g) + 2O_2(g) \overset{\Delta}{\longrightarrow} CO_2(g) + 2H_2O(g) \quad \Delta H = -802 \ kJ$$

Exact — Three SFs

Answer: $3.50 \ \cancel{g \ CH_4} \times \dfrac{1 \ \text{mole } \cancel{CH_4}}{16.04 \ \cancel{g \ CH_4}} \times \dfrac{-802 \ kJ}{1 \ \text{mole } \cancel{CH_4}} = -175 \ kJ$

Three SFs — Four SFs — Exact — Three SFs

UNDERSTANDING THE CONCEPTS

The chapter sections to review are shown in parentheses at the end of each question.

7.101 Balance each of the following by adding coefficients, and identify the type of reaction for each: (7.1, 7.2)

a.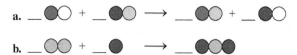

b.

7.102 Balance each of the following by adding coefficients, and identify the type of reaction for each: (7.1, 7.2)

a.

b.

7.103 If red spheres represent oxygen atoms, blue spheres represent nitrogen atoms, and all the molecules are gases, (7.1, 7.2)

Reactants   Products

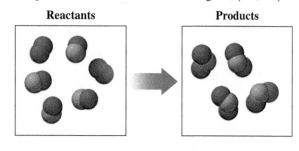

a. write the formula for each of the reactants and products.
b. write a balanced equation for the reaction.
c. indicate the type of reaction as combination, decomposition, single replacement, double replacement, or combustion.

7.104 If purple spheres represent iodine atoms, white spheres represent hydrogen atoms, and all the molecules are gases, (7.1, 7.2)

Reactants   **Products**

a. write the formula for each of the reactants and products.
b. write a balanced equation for the reaction.
c. indicate the type of reaction as combination, decomposition, single replacement, double replacement, or combustion.

7.105 If blue spheres represent nitrogen atoms, purple spheres represent iodine atoms, the reacting molecules are solid, and the products are gases, (7.1, 7.2)

Reactants **Products**

a. write the formula for each of the reactants and products.
b. write a balanced equation for the reaction.
c. indicate the type of reaction as combination, decomposition, single replacement, double replacement, or combustion.

7.106 If green spheres represent chlorine atoms, yellow-green spheres represent fluorine atoms, white spheres represent hydrogen atoms, and all the molecules are gases, (7.1, 7.2)

Reactants **Products**

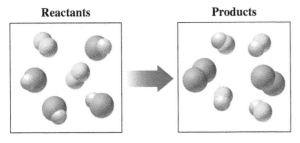

a. write the formula for each of the reactants and products.
b. write a balanced equation for the reaction.
c. indicate the type of reaction as combination, decomposition, single replacement, double replacement, or combustion.

7.107 If green spheres represent chlorine atoms, red spheres represent oxygen atoms, and all the molecules are gases, (7.1, 7.2)

Reactants **Products**

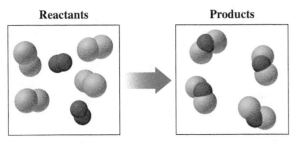

a. write the formula for each of the reactants and products.
b. write a balanced equation for the reaction.
c. indicate the type of reaction as combination, decomposition, single replacement, double replacement, or combustion.

7.108 If blue spheres represent nitrogen atoms, purple spheres represent iodine atoms, the reacting molecules are gases, and the products are solid, (7.1, 7.2)

Reactants **Products**

a. write the formula for each of the reactants and products.
b. write a balanced equation for the reaction.

c. indicate the type of reaction as combination, decomposition, single replacement, double replacement, or combustion.

7.109 Using the models of the molecules (black = C, white = H, yellow = S, green = Cl), determine each of the following for models of compounds **1** and **2**: (7.4, 7.5)

1. **2.**

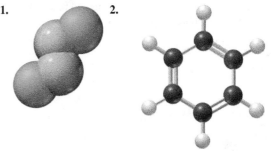

a. molecular formula
b. molar mass
c. number of moles in 10.0 g

7.110 Using the models of the molecules (black = C, white = H, yellow = S, red = O), determine each of the following for models of compounds **1** and **2**: (7.4, 7.5)

1. **2.**

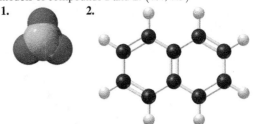

a. molecular formula
b. molar mass
c. number of moles in 10.0 g

7.111 A dandruff shampoo contains dipyrithione, $C_{10}H_8N_2O_2S_2$, which acts as an antibacterial and antifungal agent. (7.4, 7.5)
a. What is the molar mass of dipyrithione?
b. How many moles of dipyrithione are in 25.0 g?
c. How many moles of C are in 25.0 g of dipyrithione?
d. How many moles of dipyrithione contain 8.2×10^{24} atoms of N?

Dandruff shampoo contains dipyrithione.

7.112 Ibuprofen, an anti-inflammatory, has the formula $C_{13}H_{18}O_2$. (7.4, 7.5)

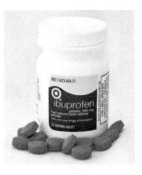

Ibuprofen is an anti-inflammatory.

a. What is the molar mass of ibuprofen?
b. How many grams of ibuprofen are in 0.525 mole?
c. How many moles of C are in 12.0 g of ibuprofen?
d. How many moles of ibuprofen contain 1.22×10^{23} atoms of C?

7.113 If red spheres represent oxygen atoms and blue spheres represent nitrogen atoms, (7.1, 7.8)

Reactants   **Products**

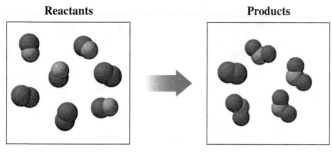

a. write a balanced equation for the reaction.
b. identify the limiting reactant.

7.114 If green spheres represent chlorine atoms, yellow-green spheres represent fluorine atoms, and white spheres represent hydrogen atoms, (7.1, 7.8)

Reactants   **Products**

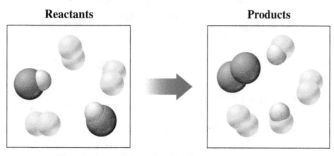

a. write a balanced equation for the reaction.
b. identify the limiting reactant.

7.115 If blue spheres represent nitrogen atoms and white spheres represent hydrogen atoms, (7.1, 7.8)

Reactants

Products
A   B

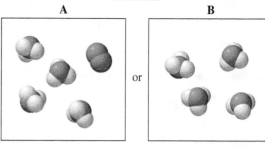

or

a. write a balanced equation for the reaction.
b. identify the diagram that shows the products.

7.116 If purple spheres represent iodine atoms and white spheres represent hydrogen atoms, (7.1, 7.8)
a. write a balanced equation for the reaction.
b. identify the diagram that shows the products.

Reactants

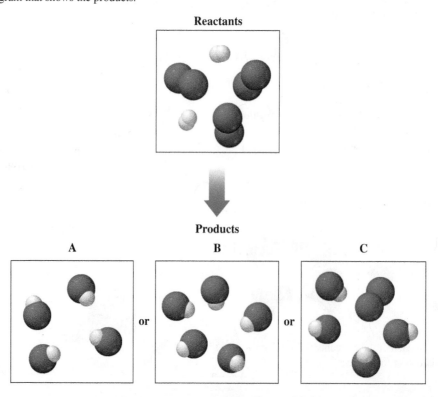

Products
A   B   C

or   or

7.117 If blue spheres represent nitrogen atoms and purple spheres represent iodine atoms, (7.1, 7.8)

Reactants   **Actual products**

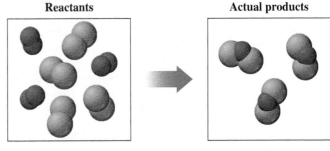

a. write a balanced equation for the reaction.
b. from the diagram of the actual products that result, calculate the percent yield for the reaction.

7.118 If green spheres represent chlorine atoms and red spheres represent oxygen atoms, (7.1, 7.8)

Reactants   **Actual products**

a. write a balanced equation for the reaction.
b. identify the limiting reactant.
c. from the diagram of the actual products that result, calculate the percent yield for the reaction.

ADDITIONAL QUESTIONS AND PROBLEMS

7.119 Identify the type of reaction for each of the following as combination, decomposition, single replacement, double replacement, or combustion: (7.2)
   a. A metal and a nonmetal form an ionic compound.
   b. A compound of hydrogen and carbon reacts with oxygen to produce carbon dioxide and water.
   c. Heating calcium carbonate produces calcium oxide and carbon dioxide.
   d. Zinc replaces copper in $Cu(NO_3)_2$.

7.120 Identify the type of reaction for each of the following as combination, decomposition, single replacement, double replacement, or combustion: (7.2)
   a. A compound breaks apart into its elements.
   b. Copper and bromine form copper(II) bromide.
   c. Iron(II) sulfite breaks down to iron(II) oxide and sulfur dioxide.
   d. Silver ion from $AgNO_3(aq)$ forms a solid with bromide ion from $KBr(aq)$.

7.121 Balance each of the following chemical equations, and identify the type of reaction: (7.1, 7.2)
   a. $NH_3(g) + HCl(g) \longrightarrow NH_4Cl(s)$
   b. $C_4H_8(g) + O_2(g) \xrightarrow{\Delta} CO_2(g) + H_2O(g)$
   c. $Sb(s) + Cl_2(g) \longrightarrow SbCl_3(s)$
   d. $NI_3(s) \longrightarrow N_2(g) + I_2(g)$
   e. $KBr(aq) + Cl_2(aq) \longrightarrow KCl(aq) + Br_2(l)$
   f. $Fe(s) + H_2SO_4(aq) \longrightarrow Fe_2(SO_4)_3(aq) + H_2(g)$
   g. $Al_2(SO_4)_3(aq) + NaOH(aq) \longrightarrow$
      $Na_2SO_4(aq) + Al(OH)_3(s)$

7.122 Balance each of the following chemical equations, and identify the type of reaction: (7.1, 7.2)
   a. $Si_3N_4(s) \longrightarrow Si(s) + N_2(g)$
   b. $Mg(s) + N_2(g) \longrightarrow Mg_3N_2(s)$
   c. $Al(s) + H_3PO_4(aq) \longrightarrow AlPO_4(aq) + H_2(g)$
   d. $C_3H_4(g) + O_2(g) \xrightarrow{\Delta} CO_2(g) + H_2O(g)$
   e. $Cr_2O_3(s) + H_2(g) \longrightarrow Cr(s) + H_2O(g)$
   f. $Al(s) + Cl_2(g) \longrightarrow AlCl_3(s)$
   g. $MgCl_2(aq) + AgNO_3(aq) \longrightarrow$
      $Mg(NO_3)_2(aq) + AgCl(s)$

7.123 Predict the products and write a balanced equation for each of the following: (7.1, 7.2)
   a. single replacement:
      $Zn(s) + HCl(aq) \longrightarrow \underline{\hspace{1cm}} + \underline{\hspace{1cm}}$
   b. decomposition: $BaCO_3(s) \xrightarrow{\Delta} \underline{\hspace{1cm}} + \underline{\hspace{1cm}}$
   c. double replacement:
      $NaOH(aq) + HCl(aq) \longrightarrow \underline{\hspace{1cm}} + \underline{\hspace{1cm}}$
   d. combination: $Al(s) + F_2(g) \longrightarrow \underline{\hspace{1cm}}$

7.124 Predict the products and write a balanced equation for each of the following: (7.1, 7.2)
   a. decomposition: $NaCl(s) \xrightarrow{Electricity} \underline{\hspace{1cm}} + \underline{\hspace{1cm}}$
   b. combination: $Ca(s) + Br_2(g) \longrightarrow \underline{\hspace{1cm}}$
   c. combustion:
      $C_2H_4(g) + O_2(g) \xrightarrow{\Delta} \underline{\hspace{1cm}} + \underline{\hspace{1cm}}$
   d. double replacement:
      $NiCl_2(aq) + NaOH(aq) \longrightarrow \underline{\hspace{1cm}} + \underline{\hspace{1cm}}$

7.125 Calculate the molar mass for each of the following: (7.5)
   a. $ZnSO_4$, zinc sulfate, zinc supplement
   b. $Ca(IO_3)_2$, calcium iodate, iodine source in table salt
   c. $C_5H_8NNaO_4$, monosodium glutamate, flavor enhancer
   d. $C_6H_{12}O_2$, isoamyl formate, used to make artificial fruit syrups

7.126 Calculate the molar mass for each of the following: (7.5)
   a. $MgCO_3$, magnesium carbonate, used in antacids
   b. $Au(OH)_3$, gold(III) hydroxide, used in gold plating
   c. $C_{18}H_{34}O_2$, oleic acid, from olive oil
   d. $C_{21}H_{26}O_5$, prednisone, anti-inflammatory

7.127 How many grams are in 0.150 mole of each of the following? (7.5)
   a. K   **b.** Cl_2 **c.** Na_2CO_3

7.128 How many grams are in 2.25 moles of each of the following? (7.5)
   a. N_2 **b.** NaBr   **c.** C_6H_{14}

7.129 How many moles are in 25.0 g of each of the following compounds? (7.5)
   a. CO_2 **b.** Al_2O_3 **c.** $MgCl_2$

7.130 How many moles are in 4.00 g of each of the following compounds? (7.5)
   a. NH_3
   b. $Ca(NO_3)_2$
   c. SO_3

7.131 When ammonia (NH_3) reacts with fluorine, the products are dinitrogen tetrafluoride (N_2F_4) and hydrogen fluoride (HF). (7.1, 7.5, 7.6, 7.7)
   a. Write the balanced chemical equation.
   b. How many moles of each reactant are needed to produce 4.00 moles of HF?
   c. How many grams of F_2 are needed to react with 25.5 g of NH_3?
   d. How many grams of N_2F_4 can be produced when 3.40 g of NH_3 reacts?

7.132 When nitrogen dioxide (NO_2) from car exhaust combines with water in the air, it forms nitric acid (HNO_3), which causes acid rain, and nitrogen oxide. (7.1, 7.5, 7.6, 7.7)
   a. Write the balanced chemical equation.
   b. How many moles of each product are produced from 0.250 mole of H_2O?
   c. How many grams of HNO_3 are produced when 60.0 g of NO_2 completely reacts?
   d. How many grams of NO_2 are needed to form 75.0 g of HNO_3?

7.133 When hydrogen peroxide (H_2O_2) is used in rocket fuels, it produces water and oxygen (O_2). (7.5, 7.6, 7.7)
$$2H_2O_2(l) \longrightarrow 2H_2O(l) + O_2(g)$$
   a. How many moles of H_2O_2 are needed to produce 3.00 moles of H_2O?
   b. How many grams of H_2O_2 are required to produce 36.5 g of O_2?
   c. How many grams of H_2O can be produced when 12.2 g of H_2O_2 reacts?

7.134 Propane gas (C_3H_8) reacts with oxygen to produce carbon dioxide and water. (7.5, 7.6, 7.7)
$$C_3H_8(g) + 5O_2(g) \xrightarrow{\Delta} 3CO_2(g) + 4H_2O(l)$$
   a. How many moles of H_2O form when 5.00 moles of C_3H_8 completely reacts?
   b. How many grams of CO_2 are produced from 18.5 g of oxygen gas?
   c. How many grams of H_2O can be produced when 46.3 g of C_3H_8 reacts?

7.135 When 12.8 g of Na and 10.2 g of Cl_2 react, what is the mass, in grams, of NaCl that is produced? (7.5, 7.6, 7.7)
$$2Na(s) + Cl_2(g) \longrightarrow 2NaCl(s)$$

7.136 If 35.8 g of CH_4 and 75.5 g of S react, how many grams of H_2S are produced? (7.5, 7.6, 7.7)
$$CH_4(g) + 4S(g) \longrightarrow CS_2(g) + 2H_2S(g)$$

7.137 Pentane gas (C_5H_{12}) reacts with oxygen to produce carbon dioxide and water. (7.5, 7.6, 7.7)
$$C_5H_{12}(g) + 8O_2(g) \xrightarrow{\Delta} 5CO_2(g) + 6H_2O(g)$$
   a. How many moles of C_5H_{12} must react to produce 4.00 moles of water?
   b. How many grams of CO_2 are produced from 32.0 g of O_2?
   c. How many grams of CO_2 are formed if 44.5 g of C_5H_{12} is mixed with 108 g of O_2?

7.138 Gasohol is a fuel that contains ethanol (C_2H_6O) that burns in oxygen (O_2) to give carbon dioxide and water. (7.5, 7.6, 7.7, 7.8)
$$C_2H_6O(g) + 3O_2(g) \xrightarrow{\Delta} 2CO_2(g) + 3H_2O(g)$$
   a. How many moles of O_2 are needed to completely react with 4.0 moles of C_2H_6O?
   b. If a car produces 88 g of CO_2, how many grams of O_2 are used up in the reaction?
   c. How many grams of CO_2 are produced if 50.0 g of C_2H_6O are mixed with 75.0 g of O_2?

7.139 The gaseous hydrocarbon acetylene (C_2H_2) used in welders' torches, burns according to the following equation: (7.5, 7.6, 7.7, 7.8)
$$2C_2H_2(g) + 5O_2(g) \xrightarrow{\Delta} 4CO_2(g) + 2H_2O(g)$$
   a. What is the theoretical yield, in grams, of CO_2, if 22.0 g of C_2H_2 completely reacts?
   b. If the actual yield in part **a** is 64.0 g of CO_2, what is the percent yield of CO_2 for the reaction?

7.140 The equation for the decomposition of potassium chlorate is written as (7.5, 7.6, 7.7, 7.8)
$$2KClO_3(s) \xrightarrow{\Delta} 2KCl(s) + 3O_2(g)$$
   a. When 46.0 g of $KClO_3$ is completely decomposed, what is the theoretical yield, in grams, of O_2?
   b. If 12.1 g of O_2 is produced, what is the percent yield of O_2?

7.141 When 28.0 g of acetylene reacts with hydrogen, 24.5 g of ethane is produced. What is the percent yield of C_2H_6 for the reaction? (7.5, 7.6, 7.7, 7.8)
$$C_2H_2(g) + 2H_2(g) \xrightarrow{Pt} C_2H_6(g)$$

7.142 When 50.0 g of iron(III) oxide reacts with carbon monoxide, 32.8 g of iron is produced. What is the percent yield of Fe for the reaction? (7.5, 7.6, 7.7, 7.8)
$$Fe_2O_3(s) + 3CO(g) \longrightarrow 2Fe(s) + 3CO_2(g)$$

7.143 The equation for the reaction of nitrogen and oxygen to form nitrogen oxide is written as (7.5, 7.6, 7.7, 7.9)
$$N_2(g) + O_2(g) \longrightarrow 2NO(g) \qquad \Delta H = +90.2 \text{ kJ}$$
   a. How many kilojoules are required to form 3.00 g of NO?
   b. What is the complete equation (including heat) for the decomposition of NO?
   c. How many kilojoules are released when 5.00 g of NO decomposes to N_2 and O_2?

7.144 The equation for the reaction of iron and oxygen gas to form rust (Fe_2O_3) is written as (7.5, 7.6, 7.7, 7.9)
$$4Fe(s) + 3O_2(g) \longrightarrow 2Fe_2O_3(s) \qquad \Delta H = -1.7 \times 10^3 \text{ kJ}$$
   a. How many kilojoules are released when 2.00 g of Fe reacts?
   b. How many grams of rust form when 150 kJ are released?

Rx Clinical Applications

7.145 Each of the following is a reaction that occurs in the cells of the body. Identify which is exothermic and endothermic. (7.9)
   a. Succinyl CoA + $H_2O \longrightarrow$ succinate + CoA + 8.9 kcal
   b. GDP + P_i + 34 kJ $\longrightarrow$ GTP + H_2O

7.146 Each of the following is a reaction that is needed by the cells of the body. Identify which is exothermic and endothermic. (7.9)
   a. Phosphocreatine + $H_2O \longrightarrow$ creatine + P_i + 10.2 kcal
   b. Fructose-6-phosphate + P_i + 16 kJ $\longrightarrow$
       fructose-1,6-bisphosphate

CHALLENGE QUESTIONS

The following groups of questions are related to the topics in this chapter. However, they do not all follow the chapter order, and they require you to combine concepts and skills from several sections. These questions will help you increase your critical thinking skills and prepare for your next exam.

7.147 At a winery, glucose ($C_6H_{12}O_6$) in grapes undergoes fermentation to produce ethanol (C_2H_6O) and carbon dioxide. (7.6, 7.7)

$$C_6H_{12}O_6 \longrightarrow 2C_2H_6O + 2CO_2$$
Glucose   Ethanol

Glucose in grapes ferments to produce ethanol.

  a. How many grams of glucose are required to form 124 g of ethanol?
  b. How many grams of ethanol would be formed from the reaction of 0.240 kg of glucose?

7.148 Gasohol is a fuel containing ethanol (C_2H_6O) that burns in oxygen (O_2) to give carbon dioxide and water. (7.1, 7.6, 7.7)
  a. Write the balanced chemical equation.
  b. How many moles of O_2 are needed to completely react with 8.0 moles of C_2H_6O?
  c. If a car produces 4.4 g of CO_2, how many grams of O_2 are used up in the reaction?
  d. If you burn 125 g of C_2H_6O, how many grams of CO_2 and H_2O can be produced?

7.149 Consider the following *unbalanced* equation: (7.1, 7.2, 7.6, 7.7)

$$Al(s) + O_2(g) \longrightarrow Al_2O_3(s)$$

  a. Write the balanced chemical equation.
  b. Identify the type of reaction.
  c. How many moles of O_2 are needed to react with 4.50 moles of Al?
  d. How many grams of Al_2O_3 are produced when 50.2 g of Al reacts?
  e. When Al is reacted in a closed container with 8.00 g of O_2, how many grams of Al_2O_3 can form?

7.150 A toothpaste contains 0.240% by mass sodium fluoride used to prevent dental caries and 0.30% by mass triclosan $C_{12}H_7Cl_3O_2$, an antigingivitis agent. One tube contains 119 g of toothpaste. (7.4, 7.5)

Components in toothpaste include triclosan and NaF.

  a. How many moles of NaF are in the tube of toothpaste?
  b. How many fluoride ions, F^-, are in the tube of toothpaste?
  c. How many grams of sodium ion, Na^+, are in 1.50 g of toothpaste?
  d. How many molecules of triclosan are in the tube of toothpaste?

7.151 Chromium and oxygen combine to form chromium(III) oxide. (7.6, 7.7, 7.8)

$$4Cr(s) + 3O_2(g) \longrightarrow 2Cr_2O_3(s)$$

  a. How many moles of O_2 react with 4.50 moles of Cr?
  b. How many grams of Cr_2O_3 are produced when 24.8 g of Cr reacts?
  c. When 26.0 g of Cr reacts with 8.00 g of O_2, how many grams of Cr_2O_3 can form?
  d. If 74.0 g of Cr and 62.0 g of O_2 are mixed, and 87.3 g of Cr_2O_3 is actually obtained, what is the percent yield of Cr_2O_3 for the reaction?

7.152 Aluminum and chlorine combine to form aluminum chloride. (7.6, 7.7, 7.8)

$$2Al(s) + 3Cl_2(g) \longrightarrow 2AlCl_3(s)$$

  a. How many moles of Cl_2 are needed to react with 2.50 moles of Al?
  b. How many grams of $AlCl_3$ are produced when 37.7 g of Al reacts?
  c. When 13.5 g of Al reacts with 8.00 g of Cl_2, how many grams of $AlCl_3$ can form?
  d. If 45.0 g of Al and 62.0 g of Cl_2 are mixed, and 66.5 g of $AlCl_3$ is actually obtained, what is the percent yield of $AlCl_3$ for the reaction?

7.153 The combustion of propyne (C_3H_4) releases heat when it burns according to the following equation: (7.6, 7.7, 7.8)

$$C_3H_4(g) + 4O_2(g) \xrightarrow{\Delta} 3CO_2(g) + 2H_2O(g)$$

  a. How many moles of O_2 are needed to react completely with 0.225 mole of C_3H_4?
  b. How many grams of water are produced from the complete reaction of 64.0 g of O_2?
  c. How many grams of CO_2 are produced from the complete reaction of 78.0 g of C_3H_4?
  d. If the reaction in part **c** produces 186 g of CO_2, what is the percent yield of CO_2 for the reaction?

7.154 The gaseous hydrocarbon butane (C_4H_{10}) burns according to the following equation: (7.6, 7.7, 7.8)

$$2C_4H_{10}(g) + 13O_2(g) \xrightarrow{\Delta} 8CO_2(g) + 10H_2O(g)$$

  a. How many moles of H_2O are produced from the complete reaction of 2.50 moles of C_4H_{10}?
  b. How many grams of O_2 are needed to react completely with 22.5 g of C_4H_{10}?
  c. How many grams of CO_2 are produced from the complete reaction of 55.0 g of C_4H_{10}?
  d. If the reaction in part **c** produces 145 g of CO_2, what is the percent yield of CO_2 for the reaction?

7.155 Sulfur trioxide decomposes to sulfur and oxygen. (7.6, 7.7, 7.9)

$$2SO_3(g) \longrightarrow 2S(s) + 3O_2(g) \quad \Delta H = +790 \text{ kJ}$$

a. Is the reaction endothermic or exothermic?
b. How many kilojoules are required when 1.5 moles of SO_3 reacts?
c. How many kilojoules are required when 150 g of O_2 is formed?

7.156 When hydrogen peroxide (H_2O_2) is used in rocket fuels, it produces water, oxygen, and heat. (7.6, 7.7, 7.9)

$$2H_2O_2(l) \longrightarrow 2H_2O(l) + O_2(g) \quad \Delta H = -196 \text{ kJ}$$

a. Is the reaction endothermic or exothermic?
b. How many kilojoules are released when 2.50 moles of H_2O_2 reacts?
c. How many kilojoules are released when 275 g of O_2 is produced?

ANSWERS

Answers to Selected Questions and Problems

7.1 a. $N_2(g) + O_2(g) \longrightarrow 2NO(g)$
  b. $2HgO(s) \longrightarrow 2Hg(l) + O_2(g)$
  c. $4Fe(s) + 3O_2(g) \longrightarrow 2Fe_2O_3(s)$
  d. $2Na(s) + Cl_2(g) \longrightarrow 2NaCl(s)$
  e. $2Cu_2O(s) + O_2(g) \longrightarrow 4CuO(s)$

7.3 a. $Mg(s) + 2AgNO_3(aq) \longrightarrow Mg(NO_3)_2(aq) + 2Ag(s)$
  b. $CuCO_3(s) \longrightarrow CuO(s) + CO_2(g)$
  c. $2Al(s) + 3CuSO_4(aq) \longrightarrow 3Cu(s) + Al_2(SO_4)_3(aq)$
  d. $Pb(NO_3)_2(aq) + 2NaCl(aq) \longrightarrow$
      $PbCl_2(s) + 2NaNO_3(aq)$
  e. $2Al(s) + 6HCl(aq) \longrightarrow 2AlCl_3(aq) + 3H_2(g)$

7.5 a. $Fe_2O_3(s) + 3CO(g) \longrightarrow 2Fe(s) + 3CO_2(g)$
  b. $2Li_3N(s) \longrightarrow 6Li(s) + N_2(g)$
  c. $2Al(s) + 6HBr(aq) \longrightarrow 2AlBr_3(aq) + 3H_2(g)$
  d. $3Ba(OH)_2(aq) + 2Na_3PO_4(aq) \longrightarrow$
      $Ba_3(PO_4)_2(s) + 6NaOH(aq)$
  e. $As_4S_6(s) + 9O_2(g) \longrightarrow As_4O_6(s) + 6SO_2(g)$

7.7 a. $2Li(s) + 2H_2O(l) \longrightarrow H_2(g) + 2LiOH(aq)$
  b. $2P(s) + 5Cl_2(g) \longrightarrow 2PCl_5(s)$
  c. $FeO(s) + CO(g) \longrightarrow Fe(s) + CO_2(g)$
  d. $2C_5H_{10}(l) + 15O_2(g) \xrightarrow{\Delta} 10CO_2(g) + 10H_2O(g)$
  e. $3H_2S(g) + 2FeCl_3(s) \longrightarrow Fe_2S_3(s) + 6HCl(g)$

7.9 $NH_4NO_3(s) \xrightarrow{\Delta} 2H_2O(g) + N_2O(g)$

7.11 $2C_3H_7NO_2(aq) + 6O_2(g) \longrightarrow$
      $5CO_2(g) + 5H_2O(l) + CH_4N_2O(aq)$

7.13 a. decomposition   **b.** single replacement
  c. combustion   **d.** double replacement
  e. combination

7.15 a. combination   **b.** single replacement
  c. decomposition   **d.** double replacement
  e. combustion

7.17 a. $Mg(s) + Cl_2(g) \longrightarrow MgCl_2(s)$
  b. $2HBr(g) \longrightarrow H_2(g) + Br_2(g)$
  c. $Mg(s) + Zn(NO_3)_2(aq) \longrightarrow Zn(s) + Mg(NO_3)_2(aq)$
  d. $K_2S(aq) + Pb(NO_3)_2(aq) \longrightarrow 2KNO_3(aq) + PbS(s)$
  e. $2C_2H_6(g) + 7O_2(g) \xrightarrow{\Delta} 4CO_2(g) + 6H_2O(g)$

7.19 a. reduction   **b.** oxidation
  c. reduction   **d.** reduction

7.21 a. Zn is oxidized, Cl_2 is reduced.
  b. The Br^- in NaBr is oxidized, Cl_2 is reduced.
  c. The O^{2-} in PbO is oxidized, the Pb^{2+} in PbO is reduced.
  d. Sn^{2+} is oxidized, Fe^{3+} is reduced.

7.23 a. reduction   **b.** oxidation

7.25 Linoleic acid gains hydrogen atoms and is reduced.

7.27 One mole contains 6.02×10^{23} atoms of an element, molecules of a molecular substance, or formula units of an ionic substance.

7.29 a. 3.01×10^{23} atoms of C
  b. 7.71×10^{23} molecules of SO_2
  c. 0.0867 mole of Fe
  d. 14.1 moles of C_2H_6O

7.31 a. 6.00 moles of H
  b. 8.00 moles of O
  c. 1.20×10^{24} atoms of P
  d. 4.82×10^{24} atoms of O

7.33 a. 24 moles of H   **b.** 1.0×10^2 moles of C
  c. 0.040 mole of N

7.35 a. 32.2 moles of C   **b.** 6.22 moles of H
  c. 0.230 mole of O

7.37 a. 188.18 g   **b.** 159.7 g
  c. 342.2 g   **d.** 58.33 g

7.39 a. 70.90 g   **b.** 90.08 g   **c.** 262.9 g   **d.** 83.98 g

7.41 a. 46.0 g   **b.** 112 g   **c.** 14.8 g   **d.** 112 g

7.43 a. 29.2 g   **b.** 108 g   **c.** 4.05 g   **d.** 195 g

7.45 a. 0.463 mole of Ag   **b.** 0.0167 mole of C
  c. 0.881 mole of NH_3 **d.** 1.17 moles of SO_2

7.47 a. 1.24 moles of Ne   **b.** 0.781 mole of O_2
  c. 0.321 mole of $Al(OH)_3$ **d.** 0.106 mole of Ga_2S_3

7.49 a. 0.78 mole of S   **b.** 1.95 moles of S
  c. 6.0 moles of S

7.51 a. 602 g   **b.** 74.7 g

7.53 a. 66.0 g of N_2O **b.** 0.772 mole of N_2O
  c. 21.6 g of N

7.55 a. 329.4 g   **b.** 498.4 g
  c. 60.09 g   **d.** 331.4 g

7.57 a. $\dfrac{2 \text{ moles } SO_2}{1 \text{ mole } O_2}$ and $\dfrac{1 \text{ mole } O_2}{2 \text{ moles } SO_2}$

  $\dfrac{2 \text{ moles } SO_2}{2 \text{ moles } SO_3}$ and $\dfrac{2 \text{ moles } SO_3}{2 \text{ moles } SO_2}$

  $\dfrac{2 \text{ moles } SO_3}{1 \text{ mole } O_2}$ and $\dfrac{1 \text{ mole } O_2}{2 \text{ moles } SO_3}$

  b. $\dfrac{4 \text{ moles } P}{5 \text{ moles } O_2}$ and $\dfrac{5 \text{ moles } O_2}{4 \text{ moles } P}$

  $\dfrac{4 \text{ moles } P}{2 \text{ moles } P_2O_5}$ and $\dfrac{2 \text{ moles } P_2O_5}{4 \text{ moles } P}$

  $\dfrac{5 \text{ moles } O_2}{2 \text{ moles } P_2O_5}$ and $\dfrac{2 \text{ moles } P_2O_5}{5 \text{ moles } O_2}$

7.59 a. 1.0 mole of O_2 **b.** 10. moles of H_2
     c. 5.0 moles of H_2O

7.61 a. 1.25 moles of C   **b.** 0.96 mole of CO
     c. 1.0 mole of SO_2 **d.** 0.50 mole of CS_2

7.63 a. 77.5 g of Na_2O **b.** 6.26 g of O_2
     c. 19.4 g of O_2

7.65 a. 19.2 g of O_2 **b.** 3.79 g of N_2
     c. 54.0 g of H_2O

7.67 a. 3.66 g of H_2O **b.** 3.44 g of NO
     c. 7.53 g of HNO_3

7.69 a. $2PbS(s) + 3O_2(g) \longrightarrow 2PbO(s) + 2SO_2(g)$
     b. 6.02 g of O_2
     c. 17.4 g of SO_2
     d. 137 g of PbS

7.71 a. 9.59 g of O_2 **b.** 6.00 g of urea
     c. 13.2 g of CO_2

7.73 a. Eight taxis can be used to pick up passengers.
     b. Seven taxis can be driven.

7.75 a. 5.0 moles of H_2 **b.** 4.0 moles of H_2
     c. 3.0 moles of N_2

7.77 a. 25.1 g of $AlCl_3$ **b.** 13.5 g of H_2O
     c. 26.7 g of SO_2

7.79 a. 31.2 g of SO_3 **b.** 34.6 g of Fe_3O_4
     c. 35.0 g of CO_2

7.81 a. 71.0%   **b.** 63.2%

7.83 70.9 g of Al_2O_3

7.85 60.5%

7.87 In exothermic reactions, the energy of the products is lower than that of the reactants.

7.89 a. exothermic   **b.** endothermic
     c. exothermic

7.91 a. Heat is released, exothermic, $\Delta H = -802$ kJ
     b. Heat is absorbed, endothermic, $\Delta H = +65.3$ kJ
     c. Heat is released, exothermic, $\Delta H = -850$ kJ

7.93 a. 579 kJ   **b.** 89 kJ

7.95 a. endothermic   **b.** 12.3 g of glucose
     c. 390 kJ

7.97 a. 0.150 mole of P   **b.** 7.53×10^{23} Ca^{2+} ions
     c. 1.41 moles of hydroxyapatite   **d.** 502.3 g/mole

7.99 a. $2H_2O_2(aq) \longrightarrow 2H_2O(l) + O_2(g)$
     b. decomposition   **c.** 0.825 mole of O_2
     d. 9.10 g of H_2O_2 **e.** 0.35 g of O_2
     f. 62.0% yield

7.101 a. 1,1,2 combination   **b.** 2,2,1 decomposition

7.103 a. reactants NO and O_2; product NO_2
     b. $2NO(g) + O_2(g) \longrightarrow 2NO_2(g)$
     c. combination

7.105 a. reactant NI_3; product N_2 and I_2
     b. $2NI_3(s) \longrightarrow N_2(g) + 3I_2(g)$
     c. decomposition

7.107 a. reactants Cl_2 and O_2; product OCl_2
     b. $2Cl_2(g) + O_2(g) \longrightarrow 2OCl_2(g)$
     c. combination

7.109 1. a. S_2Cl_2 **b.** 135.04 g/mole
     c. 0.0741 mole

     2. a. C_6H_6 **b.** 78.11 g/mole
     c. 0.128 mole

7.111 a. 252.3 g/mole
     b. 0.0991 mole of dipyrithione
     c. 0.991 mole of C
     d. 6.8 moles of dipyrithione

7.113 a. $2NO + O_2 \longrightarrow 2NO_2$
     b. NO is the limiting reactant.

7.115 a. $N_2 + 3H_2 \longrightarrow 2NH_3$ **b.** A

7.117 a. $2NI_3 \longrightarrow N_2 + 3I_2$ **b.** 67%

7.119 a. combination   **b.** combustion
     c. decomposition   **d.** single replacement

7.121 a. $NH_3(g) + HCl(g) \longrightarrow NH_4Cl(s)$ combination
     b. $C_4H_8(g) + 6O_2(g) \xrightarrow{\Delta}$
         $4CO_2(g) + 4H_2O(g)$ combustion
     c. $2Sb(s) + 3Cl_2(g) \longrightarrow 2SbCl_3(s)$ combination
     d. $2NI_3(s) \longrightarrow N_2(g) + 3I_2(g)$ decomposition
     e. $2KBr(aq) + Cl_2(aq) \longrightarrow$
         $2KCl(aq) + Br_2(l)$ single replacement
     f. $2Fe(s) + 3H_2SO_4(aq) \longrightarrow$
         $Fe_2(SO_4)_3(aq) + 3H_2(g)$ single replacement
     g. $Al_2(SO_4)_3(aq) + 6NaOH(aq) \longrightarrow$
         $3Na_2SO_4(aq) + 2Al(OH)_3(s)$ double replacement

7.123 a. $Zn(s) + 2HCl(aq) \longrightarrow ZnCl_2(aq) + H_2(g)$
     b. $BaCO_3(s) \xrightarrow{\Delta} BaO(s) + CO_2(g)$
     c. $NaOH(aq) + HCl(aq) \longrightarrow NaCl(aq) + H_2O(l)$
     d. $2Al(s) + 3F_2(g) \longrightarrow 2AlF_3(s)$

7.125 a. 161.48 g/mole   **b.** 389.9 g/mole
     c. 169.11 g/mole   **d.** 116.16 g/mole

7.127 a. 5.87 g   **b.** 10.6 g   **c.** 15.9 g

7.129 a. 0.568 mole   **b.** 0.245 mole   **c.** 0.263 mole

7.131 a. $2NH_3(g) + 5F_2(g) \longrightarrow N_2F_4(g) + 6HF(g)$
     b. 1.33 moles of NH_3 and 3.33 moles of F_2
     c. 142 g of F_2
     d. 10.4 g of N_2F_4

7.133 a. 3.00 moles of H_2O_2 **b.** 77.6 g of H_2O_2
     c. 6.46 g of H_2O

7.135 16.8 g of NaCl

7.137 a. 0.667 mole of C_5H_{12} **b.** 27.5 g of CO_2
     c. 92.8 g of CO_2

7.139 a. 74.4 g of CO_2 **b.** 86.0%

7.141 75.9%

7.143 a. 4.51 kJ
     b. $2NO(g) \longrightarrow N_2(g) + O_2(g) + 90.2$ kJ
     c. 7.51 kJ

7.145 a. exothermic   **b.** endothermic

7.147 a. 242 g of glucose   **b.** 123 g of ethanol

7.149 a. $4Al(s) + 3O_2(g) \longrightarrow 2Al_2O_3(s)$
     b. combination   **c.** 3.38 moles of oxygen
     d. 94.9 g of Al_2O_3 **e.** 17.0 g of Al_2O_3

7.151 a. 3.38 moles of oxygen
     b. 36.2 g of chromium(III) oxide
     c. 25.3 g of chromium(III) oxide
     d. 80.8%

7.153 a. 0.900 mole of oxygen
     b. 18.0 g of water
     c. 257 g of carbon dioxide
     d. 72.4%

7.155 a. endothermic   **b.** 590 kJ
     c. 1200 kJ

8

Gases

AFTER SOCCER PRACTICE, WHITNEY COMPLAINED

that she was having difficulty breathing. Her father took her to the emergency room where she was seen by Sam, a respiratory therapist, who listened to Whitney's chest and then tested her breathing capacity. Based on her limited breathing capacity and the wheezing noise in her chest, Whitney was diagnosed as having asthma.

Sam gave Whitney a nebulizer containing a bronchodilator that opens the airways and allows more air to go into the lungs. During the breathing treatment, he measured the amount of oxygen (O_2) in her blood and explained to Whitney and her father that air is a mixture of gases containing 78% nitrogen (N_2) gas and 21% oxygen (O_2) gas. Because Whitney had difficulty obtaining sufficient oxygen breathing air, Sam gave her supplemental oxygen through an oxygen mask. Within a short period of time, Whitney's breathing returned to normal. The therapist then explained that the lungs work according to Boyle's law: The volume of the lungs increases upon inhalation, and the pressure decreases to make air flow in. However, during an asthma attack, the airways become restricted, and it becomes more difficult to expand the volume of the lungs.

CAREER Respiratory Therapist

Respiratory therapists assess and treat a range of patients, including premature infants whose lungs have not developed and asthmatics or patients with emphysema or cystic fibrosis. In assessing patients, they perform a variety of diagnostic tests including breathing capacity, concentrations of oxygen and carbon dioxide in a patient's blood, as well as blood pH.

In order to treat patients, therapists provide oxygen or aerosol medications to the patient, as well as chest physiotherapy to remove mucus from their lungs. Respiratory therapists also educate patients on how to correctly use their inhalers.

We all live at the bottom of a sea of gases called the atmosphere. The most important of these gases is oxygen, which constitutes about 21% of the atmosphere. Without oxygen, life on this planet would be impossible: Oxygen is vital to all life processes of plants and animals. Ozone (O_3), formed in the upper atmosphere by the interaction of oxygen with ultraviolet light, absorbs some of the harmful radiation before it can strike the Earth's surface. The other gases in the atmosphere include nitrogen (78% of the atmosphere), argon, carbon dioxide (CO_2), and water vapor. Carbon dioxide gas, a product of combustion and metabolism, is used by plants in photosynthesis, a process that produces the oxygen that is essential for humans and animals.

The atmosphere has become a dumping ground for other gases, such as methane, chlorofluorocarbons, and nitrogen oxides as well as volatile organic compounds (VOCs), which are gases from paints, paint thinners, and cleaning supplies. The chemical reactions of these gases with sunlight and oxygen in the air are contributing to air pollution, ozone depletion, climate change, and acid rain. Such chemical changes can seriously affect our health and our lifestyle. An understanding of gases and some of the laws that govern gas behavior can help us understand the nature of matter and allow us to make decisions concerning important environmental and health issues.

CHAPTER READINESS*

🖩 KEY MATH SKILL
- Solving Equations (1.4D)

⚛ CORE CHEMISTRY SKILLS
- Using Significant Figures in Calculations (2.3)
- Writing Conversion Factors from Equalities (2.5)
- Using Conversion Factors (2.6)
- Using Molar Mass as a Conversion Factor (7.5)
- Using Mole–Mole Factors (7.6)

*These Key Math Skills and Core Chemistry Skills from previous chapters are listed here for your review as you proceed to the new material in this chapter.

8.1 Properties of Gases

We are surrounded by gases, but are not often aware of their presence. Of the elements on the periodic table, only a handful exist as gases at room temperature: H_2, N_2, O_2, F_2, Cl_2, and the noble gases. Another group of gases includes the oxides of the nonmetals on the upper right corner of the periodic table, such as CO, CO_2, NO, NO_2, SO_2, and SO_3. Generally molecules that are gases at room temperature have fewer than five atoms from the first or second period.

The behavior of gases is quite different from that of liquids and solids. Gas particles are far apart, whereas particles of both liquids and solids are held close together. A gas has no definite shape or volume and will completely fill any container. Because there are great distances between gas particles, a gas is less dense than a solid or liquid, and easy to compress. A model for the behavior of a gas, called the **kinetic molecular theory of gases**, helps us understand gas behavior.

LEARNING GOAL

Describe the kinetic molecular theory of gases and the units of measurement used for gases.

Interactive Video

Kinetic Molecular Theory

Kinetic Molecular Theory of Gases

1. **A gas consists of small particles (atoms or molecules) that move randomly with high velocities.** Gas molecules moving in random directions at high speeds cause a gas to fill the entire volume of a container.

2. **The attractive forces between the particles of a gas are usually very small.** Gas particles are far apart and fill a container of any size and shape.

3. **The actual volume occupied by gas molecules is extremely small compared with the volume that the gas occupies.** The volume of the gas is considered equal to the volume of the container. Most of the volume of a gas is empty space, which allows gases to be easily compressed.

4. **Gas particles are in constant motion, moving rapidly in straight paths.** When gas particles collide, they rebound and travel in new directions. Every time they hit the walls of the container, they exert pressure. An increase in the number or force of collisions against the walls of the container causes an increase in the pressure of the gas.

5. **The average kinetic energy of gas molecules is proportional to the Kelvin temperature.** Gas particles move faster as the temperature increases. At higher temperatures, gas particles hit the walls of the container more often and with more force, producing higher pressures.

The kinetic molecular theory helps explain some of the characteristics of gases. For example, we can quickly smell perfume when a bottle is opened on the other side of a room, because its particles move rapidly in all directions. At room temperature, the molecules in the air are moving at about 450 m/s, which is 1000 mi/h. They move faster at higher temperatures and more slowly at lower temperatures. Sometimes tires or gas-filled containers explode when temperatures are too high. From the kinetic molecular theory, we know that gas particles move faster when heated, hit the walls of a container with more force, and cause a buildup of pressure inside a container.

When we talk about a gas, we describe it in terms of four properties: pressure, volume, temperature, and the amount of gas.

Pressure (P)

Gas particles are extremely small and move rapidly. When they hit the walls of a container, they exert **pressure** (see Figure 8.1). If we heat the container, the molecules move faster and smash into the walls more often and with increased force, thus increasing the pressure. The gas particles in the air, mostly oxygen and nitrogen, exert a pressure on us called **atmospheric pressure** (see Figure 8.2). As you go to higher altitudes, the atmospheric pressure is less because there are fewer particles in the air. The most common units used for gas pressure measurement are the *atmosphere* (atm) and *millimeters of mercury* (mmHg). On the TV weather report, you may hear or see the atmospheric pressure given in inches of mercury, or kilopascals in countries other than the United States. In a hospital, the unit torr or psi (pounds per square inch) may be used.

Volume (V)

The volume of gas equals the size of the container in which the gas is placed. When you inflate a tire or a basketball, you are adding more gas particles. The increase in the number of particles hitting the walls of the tire or basketball increases the volume. Sometimes, on a cold morning, a tire looks flat. The volume of the tire has decreased because a lower temperature decreases the speed of the molecules, which in turn reduces the force of their impacts on the walls of the tire. The most common units for volume measurement are liters (L) and milliliters (mL).

Temperature (T)

The temperature of a gas is related to the kinetic energy of its particles. For example, if we have a gas at 200 K in a rigid container and heat it to a temperature of 400 K, the gas particles will have twice the kinetic energy that they did at 200 K. This also means that the gas at 400 K exerts twice the pressure of the gas at 200 K. Although you measure gas

FIGURE 8.1 ▶ Gas particles which move in straight lines within a container, exert pressure when they collide with the walls of the container.

Q Why does heating the container increase the pressure of the gas within it?

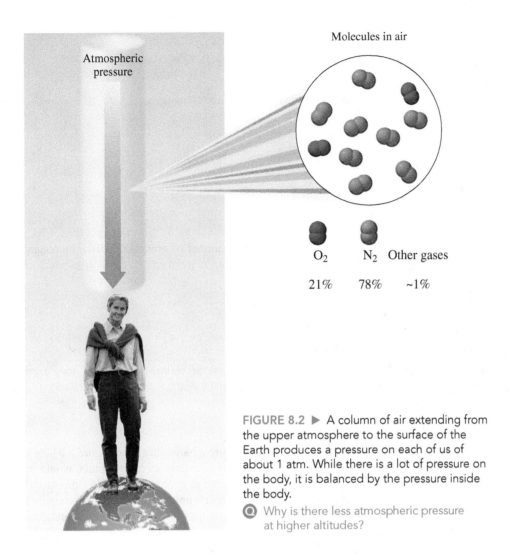

FIGURE 8.2 ▶ A column of air extending from the upper atmosphere to the surface of the Earth produces a pressure on each of us of about 1 atm. While there is a lot of pressure on the body, it is balanced by the pressure inside the body.

Why is there less atmospheric pressure at higher altitudes?

temperature using a Celsius thermometer, all comparisons of gas behavior and all calculations related to temperature must use the Kelvin temperature scale. No one has quite created the conditions for absolute zero (0 K), but we predict that the particles will have zero kinetic energy and the gas will exert zero pressure at absolute zero.

Amount of Gas (*n*)

When you add air to a bicycle tire, you increase the amount of gas, which results in a higher pressure in the tire. Usually we measure the amount of gas by its mass in grams. In gas law calculations, we need to change the grams of gas to moles.

A summary of the four properties of a gas are given in Table 8.1.

TABLE 8.1 Properties That Describe a Gas

Property	Description	Units of Measurement
Pressure (*P*)	The force exerted by a gas against the walls of the container	atmosphere (atm); millimeters of mercury (mmHg); torr (Torr); pascal (Pa)
Volume (*V*)	The space occupied by a gas	liter (L); milliliter (mL)
Temperature (*T*)	The determining factor of the kinetic energy and rate of motion of gas particles	degree Celsius (°C); Kelvin (K) *is required in calculations*
Amount (*n*)	The quantity of gas present in a container	grams (g); moles (*n*) *is required in calculations*

Explore Your World
Forming a Gas

Obtain baking soda and a jar or a plastic bottle. You will also need an elastic glove that fits over the mouth of the jar or a balloon that fits snugly over the top of the plastic bottle. Place a cup of vinegar in the jar or bottle. Sprinkle some baking soda into the fingertips of the glove or into the balloon. Carefully fit the glove or balloon over the top of the jar or bottle. Slowly lift the fingers of the glove or the balloon so that the baking soda falls into the vinegar. Watch what happens. Squeeze the glove or balloon.

Questions

1. Describe the properties of gas that you observe as the reaction takes place between vinegar and baking soda.
2. How do you know that a gas was formed?

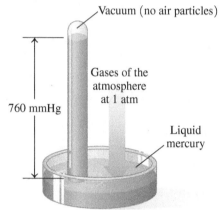

FIGURE 8.3 ► **A barometer:** The pressure exerted by the gases in the atmosphere is equal to the downward pressure of a mercury column in a closed glass tube. The height of the mercury column measured in mmHg is called atmospheric pressure.

🔘 Why does the height of the mercury column change from day to day?

Vacuum (no air particles)

Gases of the atmosphere at 1 atm

760 mmHg

Liquid mercury

▶ **SAMPLE PROBLEM 8.1** **Properties of Gases**

Identify the property of a gas that is described by each of the following:

a. increases the kinetic energy of gas particles
b. the force of the gas particles hitting the walls of the container
c. the space that is occupied by a gas

SOLUTION

a. temperature
b. pressure
c. volume

STUDY CHECK 8.1

As more helium gas is added to a balloon, the number of grams of helium increases. What property of a gas is described?

ANSWER

The mass, in grams, gives the amount of gas.

Measurement of Gas Pressure

When billions and billions of gas particles hit against the walls of a container, they exert *pressure*, which is defined as a force acting on a certain area.

$$\text{Pressure } (P) = \frac{\text{force}}{\text{area}}$$

The atmospheric pressure can be measured using a barometer (see Figure 8.3). At a pressure of exactly 1 atmosphere (atm), a mercury column in an inverted tube would be *exactly* 760 mm high. One **atmosphere (atm)** is defined as *exactly* 760 mmHg (millimeters of mercury). One atmosphere is also 760 Torr, a pressure unit named to honor Evangelista Torricelli, the inventor of the barometer. Because the units of torr and mmHg are equal, they are used interchangeably. One atmosphere is also equivalent to 29.9 in. of mercury (inHg).

1 atm = 760 mmHg = 760 Torr (exact)

1 atm = 29.9 inHg

1 mmHg = 1 Torr (exact)

In SI units, pressure is measured in pascals (Pa); 1 atm is equal to 101 325 Pa. Because a pascal is a very small unit, pressures are usually reported in kilopascals.

1 atm = 1.01325×10^5 Pa = 101.325 kPa

The U.S. equivalent of 1 atm is 14.7 lb/in.² (psi). When you use a pressure gauge to check the air pressure in the tires of a car, it may read 30 to 35 psi. This measurement is actually 30 to 35 psi above the pressure that the atmosphere exerts on the outside of the tire.

1 atm = 14.7 lb/in.²

Table 8.2 summarizes the various units and their symbols used in the measurement of pressure.

TABLE 8.2 Units for Measuring Pressure

Unit	Abbreviation	Unit Equivalent to 1 atm
atmosphere	atm	1 atm (exact)
millimeters of Hg	mmHg	760 mmHg (exact)
torr	Torr	760 Torr (exact)
inches of Hg	inHg	29.9 inHg
pounds per square inch	lb/in.² (psi)	14.7 lb/in.²
pascal	Pa	101 325 Pa
kilopascal	kPa	101.325 kPa

Atmospheric pressure changes with variations in weather and altitude. On a hot, sunny day, a column of air has more particles, which increases the pressure on the mercury surface. The mercury column rises, indicating a higher atmospheric pressure. On a rainy day, the atmosphere exerts less pressure, which causes the mercury column to fall. In the weather report, this type of weather is called a *low-pressure system*. Above sea level, the density of the gases in the air decreases, which causes lower atmospheric pressures; the atmospheric pressure is greater than 760 mmHg at the Dead Sea because it is below sea level (see Table 8.3).

$P = 0.70$ atm (530 mmHg) $P = 1.0$ atm (760 mmHg)

Sea level

The atmospheric pressure decreases as the altitude increases.

TABLE 8.3 Altitude and Atmospheric Pressure

Location	Altitude (km)	Atmospheric Pressure (mmHg)
Dead Sea	−0.40	800
Sea level	0.00	760
Los Angeles	0.09	752
Las Vegas	0.70	700
Denver	1.60	630
Mount Whitney	4.50	440
Mount Everest	8.90	253

Divers must be concerned about increasing pressures on their ears and lungs when they dive below the surface of the ocean. Because water is more dense than air, the pressure on a diver increases rapidly as the diver descends. At a depth of 33 ft below the surface of the ocean, an additional 1 atm of pressure is exerted by the water on a diver, for a total of 2 atm. At 100 ft, there is a total pressure of 4 atm on a diver. The regulator that a diver uses continuously adjusts the pressure of the breathing mixture to match the increase in pressure.

A patient with severe COPD obtains oxygen from an oxygen tank.

▶ **SAMPLE PROBLEM 8.2 Units of Pressure**

The oxygen in a tank in the hospital respiratory unit has a pressure of 4820 mmHg. Calculate the pressure, in atmospheres, of the oxygen gas (see Table 8.2).

SOLUTION

The equality 1 atm = 760 mmHg can be written as two conversion factors:

$$\frac{760 \text{ mmHg}}{1 \text{ atm}} \quad \text{and} \quad \frac{1 \text{ atm}}{760 \text{ mmHg}}$$

Using the conversion factor that cancels mmHg and gives atm, we can set up the problem as

$$4820 \text{ mmHg} \times \frac{\overset{\text{Exact}}{1 \text{ atm}}}{760 \text{ mmHg}} = 6.34 \text{ atm}$$

Three SFs   Exact   Three SFs

STUDY CHECK 8.2

A tank of nitrous oxide (N_2O) used as an anesthetic has a pressure of 48 psi. What is that pressure in atmospheres (see Table 8.2)?

ANSWER

3.3 atm

The anesthetic N_2O gas is used for pain relief.

Chemistry Link to Health
Measuring Blood Pressure

Your blood pressure is one of the vital signs a doctor or nurse checks during a physical examination. It actually consists of two separate measurements. Acting like a pump, the heart contracts to create the pressure that pushes blood through the circulatory system. During contraction, the blood pressure is at its highest; this is your *systolic* pressure. When the heart muscles relax, the blood pressure falls; this is your *diastolic* pressure. The normal range for systolic pressure is 100 to 120 mmHg. For diastolic pressure, it is 60 to 80 mmHg. These two measurements are usually expressed as a ratio such as 100/80. These values are somewhat higher in older people. When blood pressures are elevated, such as 140/90, there is a greater risk of stroke, heart attack, or kidney damage. Low blood pressure prevents the brain from receiving adequate oxygen, causing dizziness and fainting.

The blood pressures are measured by a sphygmomanometer, an instrument consisting of a stethoscope and an inflatable cuff connected to a tube of mercury called a manometer. After the cuff is wrapped around the upper arm, it is pumped up with air until it cuts off the flow of blood through the arm. With the stethoscope over the artery, the air is slowly released from the cuff, decreasing the pressure on the artery. When the blood flow first starts again in the artery, a noise can be heard through the stethoscope signifying the systolic blood pressure as the pressure shown on the manometer. As air continues to be released, the cuff deflates until no sound is heard in the artery. A second pressure reading is taken at the moment of silence and denotes the diastolic pressure, the pressure when the heart is not contracting.

The use of digital blood pressure monitors is becoming more common. However, they have not been validated for use in all situations and can sometimes give inaccurate readings.

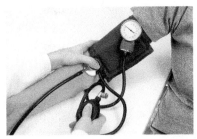

The measurement of blood pressure is part of a routine physical exam.

QUESTIONS AND PROBLEMS

8.1 Properties of Gases

LEARNING GOAL Describe the kinetic molecular theory of gases and the units of measurement used for gases.

8.1 Use the kinetic molecular theory of gases to explain each of the following:
   a. Gases move faster at higher temperatures.
   b. Gases can be compressed much more than liquids or solids.
   c. Gases have low densities.

8.2 Use the kinetic molecular theory of gases to explain each of the following:
   a. A container of nonstick cooking spray explodes when thrown into a fire.
   b. The air in a hot-air balloon is heated to make the balloon rise.
   c. You can smell the odor of cooking onions from far away.

8.3 Identify the property of a gas that is measured in each of the following:
   a. 350 K
   b. 125 mL
   c. 2.00 g of O_2
   d. 755 mmHg

8.4 Identify the property of a gas that is measured in each of the following:
   a. 425 K
   b. 1.0 atm
   c. 10.0 L
   d. 0.50 mole of He

8.5 Which of the following statement(s) describes the pressure of a gas?
   a. the force of the gas particles on the walls of the container
   b. the number of gas particles in a container
   c. 4.5 L of helium gas
   d. 750 Torr
   e. 28.8 lb/in.^{2}

8.6 Which of the following statement(s) describes the pressure of a gas?
   a. the temperature of the gas
   b. the volume of the container
   c. 3.00 atm
   d. 0.25 mole of O_2
   e. 101 kPa

Clinical Applications

8.7 A tank contains oxygen (O_2) at a pressure of 2.00 atm. What is the pressure in the tank in terms of the following units?
   a. torr
   b. mmHg

8.8 On a climb up Mt. Whitney, the atmospheric pressure drops to 467 mmHg. What is the pressure in terms of the following units?
   a. atm
   b. torr

8.2 Pressure and Volume (Boyle's Law)

Imagine that you can see air particles hitting the walls inside a bicycle tire pump. What happens to the pressure inside the pump as you push down on the handle? As the volume decreases, there is a decrease in the surface area of the container. The air particles are crowded together, more collisions occur, and the pressure increases within the container.

When a change in one property (in this case, volume) causes a change in another property (in this case, pressure), the properties are related. If the changes occur in opposite directions, the properties have an *inverse relationship*. The inverse relationship between the pressure and volume of a gas is known as **Boyle's law**. The law states that the volume (V) of a sample of gas changes inversely with the pressure (P) of the gas as long as there is no change in the temperature (T) or amount of gas (n) (see Figure 8.4).

If the volume or pressure of a gas sample changes without any change in the temperature or in the amount of the gas, then the final volume will give the same PV product as the initial pressure and volume. Then we can set the initial and final PV products equal to each other.

Boyle's Law

$$P_1 V_1 = P_2 V_2 \quad \text{No change in number of moles and temperature}$$

▶ **SAMPLE PROBLEM 8.3** Calculating Volume When Pressure Changes

When Whitney had her asthma attack, oxygen was delivered through a face mask. The gauge on a 12-L tank of compressed oxygen reads 3800 mmHg. How many liters would this same gas occupy at a pressure of 0.75 atm when temperature and amount of gas do not change?

SOLUTION

STEP **1** Organize the data in a table of initial and final conditions. To match the units for the initial and final pressures, we can convert either atm to mmHg or mmHg to atm.

$$0.75 \ \text{atm} \times \frac{760 \ \text{mmHg}}{1 \ \text{atm}} = 570 \ \text{mmHg}$$

or

$$3800 \ \text{mmHg} \times \frac{1 \ \text{atm}}{760 \ \text{mmHg}} = 5.0 \ \text{atm}$$

We place the gas data using units of mmHg for pressure and liters for volume in a table. (We could have both pressures in units of atm as well.) The properties that do not change, which are temperature and amount of gas, are shown below the table. We know that pressure decreases, and can predict that the volume increases.

	Conditions 1	Conditions 2	Know	Predict
ANALYZE THE PROBLEM	P_1 = 3800 mmHg (5.0 atm)	P_2 = 570 mmHg (0.75 atm)	P decreases	
	V_1 = 12 L	V_2 = ? L		V increases

Factors that remain constant: T and n

STEP **2** Rearrange the gas law equation to solve for the unknown quantity. For a PV relationship, we use Boyle's law and solve for V_2 by dividing both sides by P_2. According to Boyle's law, a decrease in the pressure will cause an increase in the volume when T and n remain constant.

$$P_1 V_1 = P_2 V_2$$

$$\frac{P_1 V_1}{P_2} = \frac{P_2 V_2}{P_2}$$

$$V_2 = V_1 \times \frac{P_1}{P_2}$$

LEARNING GOAL

Use the pressure–volume relationship (Boyle's law) to determine the final pressure or volume when the temperature and amount of gas are constant.

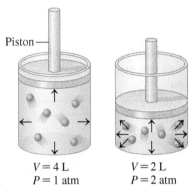

Piston

$V = 4 \ \text{L}$
$P = 1 \ \text{atm}$

$V = 2 \ \text{L}$
$P = 2 \ \text{atm}$

FIGURE 8.4 ▶ **Boyle's law:** As volume decreases, gas molecules become more crowded, which causes the pressure to increase. Pressure and volume are inversely related.

Q If the volume of a gas increases, what will happen to its pressure?

Oxygen therapy increases the oxygen available to the tissues of the body.

⊛ CORE CHEMISTRY SKILL

Using the Gas Laws

Guide to Using the Gas Laws

STEP 1
Organize the data in a table of initial and final conditions.

STEP 2
Rearrange the gas law equation to solve for the unknown quantity.

STEP 3
Substitute values into the gas law equation and calculate.

STEP 3 Substitute values into the gas law equation and calculate. When we substitute in the values with pressures in units of mmHg or atm, the ratio of pressures (pressure factor) is greater than 1, which increases the volume as predicted in Step 1.

$$V_2 = 12\text{ L} \times \frac{3800\text{ mmHg}}{570\text{ mmHg}} = 80.\text{ L}$$

Pressure factor
increases volume

or

$$V_2 = 12\text{ L} \times \frac{5.0\text{ atm}}{0.75\text{ atm}} = 80.\text{ L}$$

Pressure factor
increases volume

STUDY CHECK 8.3

In an underground natural gas reserve, a bubble of methane gas, CH_4, has a volume of 45.0 mL at 1.60 atm. What volume, in milliliters, will the gas bubble occupy when it reaches the surface where the atmospheric pressure is 744 mmHg, if there is no change in the temperature or amount of gas?

ANSWER

73.5 mL

Chemistry Link to Health

Pressure–Volume Relationship in Breathing

The importance of Boyle's law becomes more apparent when you consider the mechanics of breathing. Our lungs are elastic, balloon-like structures contained within an airtight chamber called the thoracic cavity. The diaphragm, a muscle, forms the flexible floor of the cavity.

Inspiration

The process of taking a breath of air begins when the diaphragm contracts and the rib cage expands, causing an increase in the volume of the thoracic cavity. The elasticity of the lungs allows them to expand when the thoracic cavity expands. According to Boyle's law, the pressure inside the lungs decreases when their volume increases, causing the pressure inside the lungs to fall below the pressure of the atmosphere. This difference in pressures produces a *pressure gradient* between the lungs and the atmosphere. In a pressure gradient, molecules flow from an area of higher pressure to an area of lower pressure. During the inhalation phase of breathing, air flows into the lungs (*inspiration*), until the pressure within the lungs becomes equal to the pressure of the atmosphere.

Expiration

Expiration, or the exhalation phase of breathing, occurs when the diaphragm relaxes and moves back up into the thoracic cavity to its

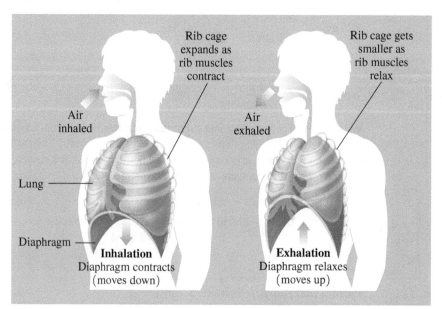

resting position. The volume of the thoracic cavity decreases, which squeezes the lungs and decreases their volume. Now the pressure in the lungs is higher than the pressure of the atmosphere, so air flows out of the lungs. Thus, breathing is a process in which pressure gradients are continuously created between the lungs and the environment because of the changes in the volume and pressure.

QUESTIONS AND PROBLEMS

8.2 Pressure and Volume (Boyle's Law)

LEARNING GOAL Use the pressure–volume relationship (Boyle's law) to determine the final pressure or volume when the temperature and amount of gas are constant.

8.9 Why do scuba divers need to exhale air when they ascend to the surface of the water?

8.10 Why does a sealed bag of chips expand when you take it to a higher altitude?

8.11 The air in a cylinder with a piston has a volume of 220 mL and a pressure of 650 mmHg.

    a. To obtain a higher pressure inside the cylinder at constant temperature and amount of gas, would the cylinder change as shown in **A** or **B**? Explain your choice.

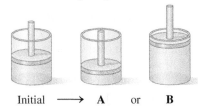

Initial ⟶ **A** or **B**

    b. If the pressure inside the cylinder increases to 1.2 atm, what is the final volume, in milliliters, of the cylinder? Complete the following data table:

Property	Conditions 1	Conditions 2	Know	Predict
Pressure (P)				
Volume (V)				

8.12 A balloon is filled with helium gas. When each of the following changes are made at constant temperature, which of the following diagrams (**A**, **B**, or **C**) shows the final volume of the balloon?

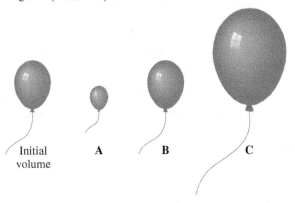

Initial
volume   **A**   **B**   **C**

    a. The balloon floats to a higher altitude where the outside pressure is lower.
    b. The balloon is taken inside the house, but the atmospheric pressure does not change.
    c. The balloon is put in a hyperbaric chamber in which the pressure is increased.

8.13 A gas with a volume of 4.0 L is in a closed container. Indicate the changes (*increases, decreases, does not change*) in pressure when the volume undergoes the following changes at constant temperature and amount of gas:
    a. The volume is compressed to 2.0 L.
    b. The volume expands to 12 L.
    c. The volume is compressed to 0.40 L.

8.14 A gas at a pressure of 2.0 atm is in a closed container. Indicate the changes (*increases, decreases, does not change*) in its volume when the pressure undergoes the following changes at constant temperature and amount of gas:
    a. The pressure increases to 6.0 atm.
    b. The pressure remains at 2.0 atm.
    c. The pressure drops to 0.40 atm.

8.15 A 10.0-L balloon contains helium gas at a pressure of 655 mmHg. What is the final pressure, in millimeters of mercury, of the helium gas at each of the following volumes, if there is no change in temperature and amount of gas?
    a. 20.0 L   **b.** 2.50 L
    c. 13 800 mL   **d.** 1250 mL

8.16 The air in a 5.00-L tank has a pressure of 1.20 atm. What is the final pressure, in atmospheres, when the air is placed in tanks that have the following volumes, if there is no change in temperature and amount of gas?
    a. 1.00 L   **b.** 2500. mL
    c. 750. mL   **d.** 8.00 L

8.17 A sample of nitrogen (N_2) has a volume of 50.0 L at a pressure of 760. mmHg. What is the final volume, in liters, of the gas at each of the following pressures, if there is no change in temperature and amount of gas?
    a. 725 mmHg   **b.** 2.0 atm
    c. 0.500 atm   **d.** 850 Torr

8.18 A sample of methane (CH_4) has a volume of 25 mL at a pressure of 0.80 atm. What is the final volume, in milliliters, of the gas at each of the following pressures, if there is no change in temperature and amount of gas?
    a. 0.40 atm   **b.** 2.00 atm
    c. 2500 mmHg   **d.** 80.0 Torr

℞ Clinical Applications

8.19 Cyclopropane, C_3H_6, is a general anesthetic. A 5.0-L sample has a pressure of 5.0 atm. What is the volume, in liters, of the anesthetic given to a patient at a pressure of 1.0 atm with no change in temperature and amount of gas?

8.20 The volume of air in a person's lungs is 615 mL at a pressure of 760. mmHg. Inhalation occurs as the pressure in the lungs drops to 752 mmHg with no change in temperature and amount of gas. To what volume, in milliliters, did the lungs expand?

8.21 Use the word *inspiration* or *expiration* to describe the part of the breathing cycle that occurs as a result of each of the following:
    a. The diaphragm contracts (flattens out).
    b. The volume of the lungs decreases.
    c. The pressure within the lungs is less than that of the atmosphere.

8.22 Use the word *inspiration* or *expiration* to describe the part of the breathing cycle that occurs as a result of each of the following:
    a. The diaphragm relaxes, moving up into the thoracic cavity.
    b. The volume of the lungs expands.
    c. The pressure within the lungs is greater than that of the atmosphere.

Use the temperature–volume relationship (Charles's law) to determine the final temperature or volume when the pressure and amount of gas are constant.

As the gas in a hot-air balloon is heated, it expands.

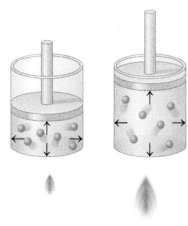

$T = 200$ K $T = 400$ K
$V = 1$ L $V = 2$ L

FIGURE 8.5 ▶ **Charles's law:** The Kelvin temperature of a gas is directly related to the volume of the gas when there is no change in the pressure and amount. When the temperature increases, making the molecules move faster, the volume must increase to maintain constant pressure.

◉ If the temperature of a gas decreases at constant pressure and amount of gas, how will the volume change?

8.3 Temperature and Volume (Charles's Law)

Suppose that you are going to take a ride in a hot-air balloon. The captain turns on a propane burner to heat the air inside the balloon. As the air is heated, it expands and becomes less dense than the air outside, causing the balloon and its passengers to lift off. In 1787, Jacques Charles, a balloonist as well as a physicist, proposed that the volume of a gas is related to the temperature. This became **Charles's law**, which states that the volume (V) of a gas is directly related to the temperature (T) when there is no change in the pressure (P) or amount (n) of gas. A *direct relationship* is one in which the related properties increase or decrease together. For two conditions, initial and final, we can write Charles's law as follows:

Charles's Law

$$\frac{V_1}{T_1} = \frac{V_2}{T_2} \quad \text{No change in number of moles and pressure}$$

All temperatures used in gas law calculations must be converted to their corresponding Kelvin (K) temperatures.

To determine the effect of changing temperature on the volume of a gas, the pressure and the amount of gas are kept constant. If we increase the temperature of a gas sample, we know from the kinetic molecular theory that the motion (kinetic energy) of the gas particles will also increase. To keep the pressure constant, the volume of the container must increase (see Figure 8.5). If the temperature of the gas decreases, the volume of the container must decrease to maintain the same pressure when the amount of gas is constant.

▶ **SAMPLE PROBLEM 8.4** Calculating Volume When Temperature Changes

Helium gas is used to inflate the abdomen during laparoscopic surgery. A sample of helium gas has a volume of 5.40 L and a temperature of 15 °C. What is the final volume, in liters, of the gas if the temperature has been increased to 42 °C at constant pressure and amount of gas?

SOLUTION

STEP **1** Organize the data in a table of initial and final conditions. The properties that change, which are the temperature and volume, are listed in the following table. The properties that do not change, which are pressure and amount of gas, are shown below the table. When the temperature is given in degrees Celsius, it must be changed to kelvins. Because we know the initial and final temperatures of the gas, we know that the temperature increases. Thus, we can predict that the volume increases.

$T_1 = 15\,°C + 273 = 288$ K
$T_2 = 42\,°C + 273 = 315$ K

ANALYZE THE PROBLEM	Conditions 1	Conditions 2	Know	Predict
	$T_1 = 288$ K	$T_2 = 315$ K	T increases	
	$V_1 = 5.40$ L	$V_2 = ?$ L		V increases

Factors that remain constant: P and n

STEP **2** Rearrange the gas law equation to solve for the unknown quantity. In this problem, we want to know the final volume (V_2) when the temperature increases. Using Charles's law, we solve for V_2 by multiplying both sides by T_2.

$$\frac{V_1}{T_1} = \frac{V_2}{T_2}$$

$$\frac{V_1}{T_1} \times T_2 = \frac{V_2}{\cancel{T_2}} \times \cancel{T_2}$$

$$V_2 = V_1 \times \frac{T_2}{T_1}$$

STEP **3** Substitute values into the gas law equation and calculate. From the table, we see that the temperature has increased. Because temperature is directly related to volume, the volume must increase. When we substitute in the values, we see that the ratio of the temperatures (temperature factor) is greater than 1, which increases the volume as predicted in Step 1.

$$V_2 = 5.40\,\text{L} \times \frac{315\,\text{K}}{288\,\text{K}} = 5.91\,\text{L}$$

Temperature factor
increases volume

STUDY CHECK 8.4

A mountain climber with a body temperature of 37 °C inhales 486 mL of air at a temperature of −8 °C. What volume, in milliliters, will the air occupy in the lungs, if the pressure and amount of gas do not change?

ANSWER

569 mL

QUESTIONS AND PROBLEMS

8.3 Temperature and Volume (Charles's Law)

LEARNING GOAL Use the temperature–volume relationship (Charles's law) to determine the final temperature or volume when the pressure and amount of gas are constant.

8.23 Select the diagram that shows the final volume of a balloon when the following changes are made at constant pressure and amount of gas:

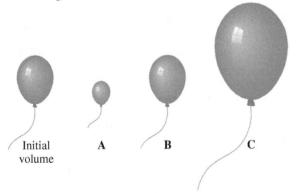

Initial   **A**   **B**   **C**
volume

a. The temperature changes from 100 K to 300 K.
b. The balloon is placed in a freezer.
c. The balloon is first warmed and then returned to its starting temperature.

8.24 Indicate whether the final volume of gas in each of the following is the *same*, *larger*, or *smaller* than the initial volume, if pressure and amount of gas do not change:
   a. A volume of 505 mL of air on a cold winter day at −15 °C is breathed into the lungs, where body temperature is 37 °C.
   b. The heater used to heat the air in a hot-air balloon is turned off.
   c. A balloon filled with helium at the amusement park is left in a car on a hot day.

8.25 A sample of neon initially has a volume of 2.50 L at 15 °C. What final temperature, in degrees Celsius, is needed to change the volume of the gas to each of the following, if *n* and *P* do not change?
   a. 5.00 L   b. 1250 mL
   c. 7.50 L   d. 3550 mL

8.26 A gas has a volume of 4.00 L at 0 °C. What final temperature, in degrees Celsius, is needed to change the volume of the gas to each of the following, if *n* and *P* do not change?
   a. 1.50 L   b. 1200 mL
   c. 10.0 L   d. 50.0 mL

8.27 A balloon contains 2500 mL of helium gas at 75 °C. What is the final volume, in milliliters, of the gas when the temperature changes to each of the following, if n and P do not change?
a. 55 °C
b. 680. K
c. −25 °C
d. 240. K

8.28 An air bubble has a volume of 0.500 L at 18 °C. What is the final volume, in liters, of the gas when the temperature changes to each of the following, if n and P do not change?
a. 0 °C
b. 425 K
c. −12 °C
d. 575 K

$T = 200$ K $T = 400$ K
$P = 1$ atm $P = 2$ atm

FIGURE 8.6 ▶ **Gay-Lussac's law:** When the Kelvin temperature of a gas doubles at constant volume and amount of gas, the pressure also doubles.

Q How does a decrease in the temperature of a gas affect its pressure at constant volume and amount of gas?

8.4 Temperature and Pressure (Gay-Lussac's Law)

If we could observe the molecules of a gas as the temperature rises, we would notice that they move faster and hit the sides of the container more often and with greater force. If we maintain a constant volume and amount of gas, the pressure will increase. In the temperature–pressure relationship known as **Gay-Lussac's law**, the pressure of a gas is directly related to its Kelvin temperature. This means that an increase in temperature increases the pressure of a gas and a decrease in temperature decreases the pressure of the gas, as long as the volume and amount of gas do not change (see Figure 8.6).

Gay-Lussac's Law

$$\frac{P_1}{T_1} = \frac{P_2}{T_2} \qquad \text{No change in number of moles and volume}$$

All temperatures used in gas law calculations must be converted to their corresponding Kelvin (K) temperatures.

▶ **SAMPLE PROBLEM 8.5 Calculating Pressure When Temperature Changes**

Home oxygen tanks, which provide an oxygen-rich environment, can be dangerous if they are heated, because they can explode. Suppose an oxygen tank has a pressure of 120 atm at a room temperature of 25 °C. If a fire in the room causes the temperature of the gas inside the oxygen tank to reach 402 °C, what will be its pressure in atmospheres? The oxygen tank may rupture if the pressure inside exceeds 180 atm. Would you expect it to rupture?

SOLUTION

STEP **1** Organize the data in a table of initial and final conditions. We list the properties that change, which are the pressure and temperature, in a table. The properties that do not change, which are volume and amount of gas, are shown below the table. The temperatures given in degrees Celsius must be changed to kelvins. Because we know the initial and final temperatures of the gas, we know that the temperature increases. Thus, we can predict that the pressure increases.

$$T_1 = 25\,°C + 273 = 298\ K$$
$$T_2 = 402\,°C + 273 = 675\ K$$

ANALYZE THE PROBLEM	Conditions 1	Conditions 2	Know	Predict
	$P_1 = 120$ atm	$P_2 = ?$ atm		P increases
	$T_1 = 298$ K	$T_2 = 675$ K	T increases	

Factors that remain constant: V and n

STEP **2** Rearrange the gas law equation to solve for the unknown quantity.
Using Gay-Lussac's law, we can solve for P_2 by multiplying both sides by T_2.

$$\frac{P_1}{T_1} = \frac{P_2}{T_2}$$

$$\frac{P_1}{T_1} \times T_2 = \frac{P_2}{\cancel{T_2}} \times \cancel{T_2}$$

$$P_2 = P_1 \times \frac{T_2}{T_1}$$

STEP **3** Substitute values into the gas law equation and calculate. When we substitute in the values, we see that the ratio of the temperatures (temperature factor), is greater than 1, which increases pressure as predicted in Step 1.

$$P_2 = 120 \text{ atm} \times \underbrace{\frac{675 \text{ K}}{298 \text{ K}}}_{\substack{\text{Temperature factor} \\ \text{increases pressure}}} = 270 \text{ atm}$$

Because the calculated pressure of 270 atm of the gas exceeds the limit of 180 atm, we would expect the oxygen tank to rupture.

STUDY CHECK 8.5

In a storage area of a hospital where the temperature has reached 55 °C, the pressure of oxygen gas in a 15.0-L steel cylinder is 965 Torr. To what temperature, in degrees Celsius, would the gas have to be cooled to reduce the pressure to 850. Torr when the volume and amount of the gas do not change?

ANSWER

16 °C

Vapor Pressure and Boiling Point

When liquid molecules with sufficient kinetic energy break away from the surface, they become gas particles or vapor. In an open container, all the liquid will eventually evaporate. In a closed container, the vapor accumulates and creates pressure called **vapor pressure**. Each liquid exerts its own vapor pressure at a given temperature. As temperature increases, more vapor forms, and vapor pressure increases. Table 8.4 lists the vapor pressure of water at various temperatures.

A liquid reaches its boiling point when its vapor pressure becomes equal to the external pressure. As boiling occurs, bubbles of the gas form within the liquid and quickly rise to the surface. For example, at an atmospheric pressure of 760 mmHg, water will boil at 100 °C, the temperature at which its vapor pressure reaches 760 mmHg (see Table 8.4).

At high altitudes, where atmospheric pressures are lower than 760 mmHg, the boiling point of water is lower than 100 °C. For example, a typical atmospheric pressure in Denver is 630 mmHg. This means that water in Denver boils when the vapor pressure is 630 mmHg. From Table 8.5, we see that water has a vapor pressure of 630 mmHg at 95 °C, which means that water boils at 95 °C in Denver.

In a closed container such as a pressure cooker, a pressure greater than 1 atm can be obtained, which means that water boils at a temperature higher than 100 °C. Laboratories and hospitals use closed containers called *autoclaves* to sterilize laboratory and surgical equipment. Table 8.5 shows how the boiling point of water increases as pressure increases.

TABLE 8.4 Vapor Pressure of Water

Temperature (°C)	Vapor Pressure (mmHg)
0	5
10	9
20	18
30	32
37*	47
40	55
50	93
60	149
70	234
80	355
90	528
100	760

*At body temperature

TABLE 8.5 Pressure and the Boiling Point of Water

Pressure (mmHg)	Boiling Point (°C)
270	70
467	87
630	95
752	99
760	100
800	100.4
1075	110
1520 (2 atm)	120
3800 (5 atm)	160
7600 (10 atm)	180

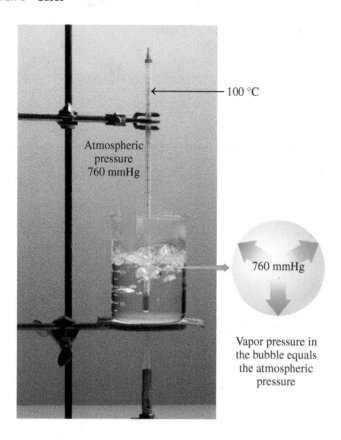

100 °C

Atmospheric
pressure
760 mmHg

760 mmHg

Vapor pressure in
the bubble equals
the atmospheric
pressure

An autoclave used to sterilize equipment attains
a temperature higher than 100 °C.

QUESTIONS AND PROBLEMS

8.4 Temperature and Pressure (Gay-Lussac's Law)

LEARNING GOAL Use the temperature–pressure relationship (Gay-Lussac's law) to determine the final temperature or pressure when the volume and amount of gas are constant.

8.29 Calculate the final pressure, in millimeters of mercury, for each of the following, if n and V do not change:
  a. A gas with an initial pressure of 1200 Torr at 155 °C is cooled to 0 °C.
  b. A gas in an aerosol can at an initial pressure of 1.40 atm at 12 °C is heated to 35 °C.

8.30 Calculate the final pressure, in atmospheres, for each of the following, if n and V do not change:
  a. A gas with an initial pressure of 1.20 atm at 75 °C is cooled to −32 °C.
  b. A sample of N_2 with an initial pressure of 780. mmHg at −75 °C is heated to 28 °C.

8.31 Calculate the final temperature, in degrees Celsius for each of the following, if n and V do not change:
  a. A sample of xenon gas at 25 °C and 740. mmHg is cooled to give a pressure of 620. mmHg.
  b. A tank of argon gas with a pressure of 0.950 atm at −18 °C is heated to give a pressure of 1250 Torr.

8.32 Calculate the final temperature, in degrees Celsius, for each of the following, if n and V do not change:
  a. A sample of helium gas with a pressure of 250 Torr at 0 °C is heated to give a pressure of 1500 Torr.
  b. A sample of air at 40 °C and 740. mmHg is cooled to give a pressure of 680. mmHg.

Clinical Applications

8.33 A tank contains isoflurane, an inhaled anesthetic, at a pressure of 1.8 atm and 5 °C. What is the pressure, in atmospheres, if the gas is warmed to a temperature of 22 °C, if n and V do not change?

8.34 Bacteria and viruses are inactivated by temperatures above 135 °C in an autoclave. An autoclave contains steam at 1.00 atm and 100 °C. At what pressure, in atmospheres, will the temperature of the steam in the autoclave reach 135 °C, if n and V do not change?

8.5 The Combined Gas Law

All of the pressure–volume–temperature relationships for gases that we have studied may be combined into a single relationship called the **combined gas law**. This expression is useful for studying the effect of changes in two of these variables on the third as long as the amount of gas (number of moles) remains constant.

Combined Gas Law

$$\frac{P_1 V_1}{T_1} = \frac{P_2 V_2}{T_2} \qquad \text{No change in number of moles of gas}$$

By using the combined gas law, we can derive any of the gas laws by omitting those properties that do not change as seen in Table 8.6.

TABLE 8.6 Summary of Gas Laws

Combined Gas Law	Properties Held Constant	Relationship	Name of Gas Law
$\dfrac{P_1 V_1}{\cancel{T_1}} = \dfrac{P_2 V_2}{\cancel{T_2}}$	T, n	$P_1 V_1 = P_2 V_2$	Boyle's law
$\dfrac{\cancel{P_1} V_1}{T_1} = \dfrac{\cancel{P_2} V_2}{T_2}$	P, n	$\dfrac{V_1}{T_1} = \dfrac{V_2}{T_2}$	Charles's law
$\dfrac{P_1 \cancel{V_1}}{T_1} = \dfrac{P_2 \cancel{V_2}}{T_2}$	V, n	$\dfrac{P_1}{T_1} = \dfrac{P_2}{T_2}$	Gay-Lussac's law

> **SAMPLE PROBLEM 8.6 Using the Combined Gas Law**
>
> A 25.0-mL bubble is released from a diver's air tank at a pressure of 4.00 atm and a temperature of 11 °C. What is the volume, in milliliters, of the bubble when it reaches the ocean surface, where the pressure is 1.00 atm and the temperature is 18 °C? (Assume the amount of gas in the bubble does not change.)

SOLUTION

STEP **1** Organize the data in a table of initial and final conditions. We list the properties that change, which are the pressure, volume, and temperature, in a table. The property that remains constant, which is the amount of gas, is shown below the table. The temperatures in degrees Celsius must be changed to kelvins.

$T_1 = 11\,°C + 273 = 284\ K$

$T_2 = 18\,°C + 273 = 291\ K$

ANALYZE THE PROBLEM	Conditions 1	Conditions 2
	$P_1 = 4.00\ atm$	$P_2 = 1.00\ atm$
	$V_1 = 25.0\ mL$	$V_2 = ?\ mL$
	$T_1 = 284\ K$	$T_2 = 291\ K$

Factor that remains constant: n

STEP **2** Rearrange the gas law equation to solve for the unknown quantity.

$$\frac{P_1 V_1}{T_1} = \frac{P_2 V_2}{T_2}$$

$$\frac{P_1 V_1}{T_1} \times \frac{T_2}{P_2} = \frac{\cancel{P_2} V_2}{\cancel{T_2}} \times \frac{\cancel{T_2}}{\cancel{P_2}}$$

$$V_2 = V_1 \times \frac{P_1}{P_2} \times \frac{T_2}{T_1}$$

Under water, the pressure on a diver is greater than the atmospheric pressure.

STEP 3 Substitute values into the gas law equation and calculate. From the data table, we determine that both the pressure decrease and the temperature increase will increase the volume.

$$V_2 = 25.0 \text{ mL} \times \frac{4.00 \text{ atm}}{1.00 \text{ atm}} \times \frac{291 \text{ K}}{284 \text{ K}} = 102 \text{ mL}$$

Pressure factor
increases volume

Temperature factor
increases volume

However, when the unknown value is decreased by one change but increased by the second change, it is difficult to predict the overall change for the unknown.

STUDY CHECK 8.6

A weather balloon is filled with 15.0 L of helium at a temperature of 25 °C and a pressure of 685 mmHg. What is the pressure, in millimeters of mercury, of the helium in the balloon in the upper atmosphere when the temperature is −35 °C and the final volume becomes 34.0 L, if the amount of He does not change?

ANSWER
241 mmHg

QUESTIONS AND PROBLEMS

8.5 The Combined Gas Law

LEARNING GOAL Use the combined gas law to calculate the final pressure, volume, or temperature of a gas when changes in two of these properties are given and the amount of gas is constant.

8.35 A sample of helium gas has a volume of 6.50 L at a pressure of 845 mmHg and a temperature of 25 °C. What is the final pressure of the gas, in atmospheres, when the volume and temperature of the gas sample are changed to the following, if the amount of gas does not change?
 a. 1850 mL and 325 K
 b. 2.25 L and 12 °C
 c. 12.8 L and 47 °C

8.36 A sample of argon gas has a volume of 735 mL at a pressure of 1.20 atm and a temperature of 112 °C. What is the final volume of the gas, in milliliters, when the pressure and temperature of

the gas sample are changed to the following, if the amount of gas does not change?
 a. 658 mmHg and 281 K
 b. 0.55 atm and 75 °C
 c. 15.4 atm and −15 °C

8.37 A 124-mL bubble of hot gases at 212 °C and 1.80 atm is emitted from an active volcano. What is the final temperature, in degrees Celsius, of the gas in the bubble outside the volcano if the final volume of the bubble is 138 mL and the pressure is 0.800 atm, if the amount of gas does not change?

8.38 A scuba diver 60 ft below the ocean surface inhales 50.0 mL of compressed air from a scuba tank at a pressure of 3.00 atm and a temperature of 8 °C. What is the final pressure of air, in atmospheres, in the lungs when the gas expands to 150.0 mL at a body temperature of 37 °C, if the amount of gas does not change?

LEARNING GOAL

Use Avogadro's law to calculate the amount or volume of a gas when the pressure and temperature are constant.

8.6 Volume and Moles (Avogadro's Law)

In our study of the gas laws, we have looked at changes in properties for a specified amount (n) of gas. Now we will consider how the properties of a gas change when there is a change in the number of moles or grams of the gas.

When you blow up a balloon, its volume increases because you add more air molecules. If the balloon has a hole in it, air leaks out, causing its volume to decrease. In 1811, Amedeo Avogadro formulated **Avogadro's law**, which states that the volume of a gas is directly related to the number of moles of a gas when temperature and pressure do not change. For example, if the number of moles of a gas is doubled, then the volume will also double as long as we do not change the pressure or the temperature (see Figure 8.7). At constant pressure and temperature, we can write Avogadro's law:

Avogadro's Law

$$\frac{V_1}{n_1} = \frac{V_2}{n_2}$$ No change in pressure and temperature

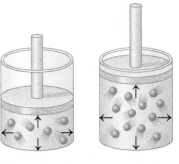

$n = 1$ mole $n = 2$ moles
$V = 1$ L $V = 2$ L

FIGURE 8.7 ▶ **Avogadro's law:** The volume of a gas is directly related to the number of moles of the gas. If the number of moles is doubled, the volume must double at constant temperature and pressure.

Q If a balloon has a leak, what happens to its volume?

▶ **SAMPLE PROBLEM 8.7** **Calculating Volume for a Change in Moles**

A weather balloon with a volume of 44 L is filled with 2.0 moles of helium. What is the final volume, in liters, if 3.0 moles of helium gas are added, to give a total of 5.0 moles of helium gas, if the pressure and temperature do not change?

SOLUTION

STEP 1 Organize the data in a table of initial and final conditions. We list those properties that change, which are volume and amount (moles) of gas, in a table. The properties that do not change, which are pressure and temperature, are shown below the table. Because there is an increase in the number of moles of gas, we can predict that the volume increases.

	Conditions 1	Conditions 2	Know	Predict
ANALYZE THE PROBLEM	$V_1 = 44$ L	$V_2 = ?$ L		V increases
	$n_1 = 2.0$ moles	$n_2 = 5.0$ moles	n increases	

Factors that remain constant: P and T

STEP 2 Rearrange the gas law equation to solve for the unknown quantity. Using Avogadro's law, we can solve for V_2 by multiplying both sides by n_2.

$$\frac{V_1}{n_1} = \frac{V_2}{n_2}$$

$$\frac{V_1}{n_1} \times n_2 = \frac{V_2}{n_2} \times n_2$$

$$V_2 = V_1 \times \frac{n_2}{n_1}$$

STEP 3 Substitute values into the gas law equation and calculate. When we substitute in the values, we see that the ratio of the moles (mole factor) is greater than 1, which increases the volume as predicted in Step 1.

$$V_2 = 44 \text{ L} \times \frac{5.0 \text{ moles}}{2.0 \text{ moles}} = 110 \text{ L}$$

Mole factor
increases volume

STUDY CHECK 8.7

A sample containing 8.00 g of oxygen gas has a volume of 5.00 L. What is the final volume, in liters, after 4.00 g of oxygen gas is added to the 8.00 g of oxygen in the balloon, if the temperature and pressure do not change?

ANSWER

7.50 L

STP and Molar Volume

Using Avogadro's law, we can say that any two gases will have equal volumes if they contain the same number of moles of gas at the same temperature and pressure. To help us make comparisons between different gases, arbitrary conditions called *standard temperature* (273 K) and *standard pressure* (1 atm) together abbreviated **STP**, were selected by scientists:

The molar volume of a gas at STP is about the same as the volume of three basketballs.

STP Conditions

Standard temperature is *exactly* 0 °C (273 K).

Standard pressure is *exactly* 1 atm (760 mmHg).

At STP, one mole of any gas occupies a volume of 22.4 L, which is about the same as the volume of three basketballs. This volume, 22.4 L, of any gas at STP is called its **molar volume** (see Figure 8.8).

When a gas is at STP conditions (0 °C and 1 atm), its molar volume can be used to write conversion factors between the number of moles of gas and its volume, in liters.

Molar Volume Conversion Factors

$$1 \text{ mole of gas} = 22.4 \text{ L of gas (STP)}$$

$$\frac{1 \text{ mole gas}}{22.4 \text{ L gas (STP)}} \quad \text{and} \quad \frac{22.4 \text{ L gas (STP)}}{1 \text{ mole gas}}$$

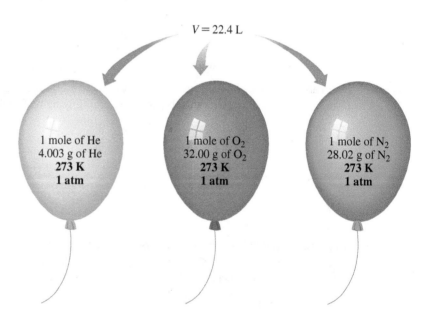

FIGURE 8.8 ▶ Avogadro's law indicates that 1 mole of any gas at STP has a volume of 22.4 L.

ⓠ What volume of gas, in liters, is occupied by 16.0 g of methane gas, CH_4, at STP?

▶ **SAMPLE PROBLEM 8.8** Using Molar Volume to Find Volume at STP

What is the volume, in liters, of 64.0 g of O_2 gas at STP?

SOLUTION

STEP **1** State the given and needed quantities.

ANALYZE THE PROBLEM	Given	Need
	64.0 g of $O_2(g)$ at STP	liters of O_2 gas at STP

STEP **2** Write a plan to calculate the needed quantity. The grams of O_2 are converted to moles using molar mass. Then a molar volume conversion factor is used to convert the number of moles to volume (L).

grams of O_2 Molar mass   moles of O_2 Molar volume   liters of O_2

STEP **3** Write the equalities and conversion factors including 22.4 L/mole at STP.

1 mole of O_2 = 32.00 g of O_2

$$\frac{32.00 \text{ g } O_2}{1 \text{ mole } O_2} \quad and \quad \frac{1 \text{ mole } O_2}{32.00 \text{ g } O_2}$$

1 mole of O_2 = 22.4 L of O_2 (STP)

$$\frac{22.4 \text{ L } O_2 \text{ (STP)}}{1 \text{ mole } O_2} \quad and \quad \frac{1 \text{ mole } O_2}{22.4 \text{ L } O_2 \text{ (STP)}}$$

STEP **4** Set up the problem with factors to cancel units.

$$64.0 \text{ g } O_2 \quad \times \quad \frac{1 \text{ mole } O_2}{32.00 \text{ g } O_2} \quad \times \quad \frac{22.4 \text{ L } O_2 \text{ (STP)}}{1 \text{ mole } O_2} = 44.8 \text{ L of } O_2 \text{ (STP)}$$

> ### Guide to Using Molar Volume
> **STEP 1**
> State the given and needed quantities.
>
> **STEP 2**
> Write a plan to calculate the needed quantity.
>
> **STEP 3**
> Write the equalities and conversion factors including 22.4 L/mole at STP.
>
> **STEP 4**
> Set up the problem with factors to cancel units.

STUDY CHECK 8.8

How many grams of $N_2(g)$ are in 5.6 L of $N_2(g)$ at STP?

ANSWER

7.0 g of N_2

QUESTIONS AND PROBLEMS

8.6 Volume and Moles (Avogadro's Law)

LEARNING GOAL Use Avogadro's law to calculate the amount or volume of a gas when the pressure and temperature are constant.

8.39 What happens to the volume of a bicycle tire or a basketball when you use an air pump to add air?

8.40 Sometimes when you blow up a balloon and release it, it flies around the room. What is happening to the air that was in the balloon and its volume?

8.41 A sample containing 1.50 moles of Ne gas has an initial volume of 8.00 L. What is the final volume of the gas, in liters, when each of the following changes occurs in the quantity of the gas at constant pressure and temperature?
a. A leak allows one-half of the Ne atoms to escape.
b. A sample of 3.50 moles of Ne is added to the 1.50 moles of Ne gas in the container.
c. A sample of 25.0 g of Ne is added to the 1.50 moles of Ne gas in the container.

8.42 A sample containing 4.80 g of O_2 gas has an initial volume of 15.0 L. What is the final volume, in liters, when each of the

following changes occurs in the quantity of the gas at constant pressure and temperature?
a. A sample of 0.500 mole of O_2 is added to the 4.80 g of O_2 in the container.
b. A sample of 2.00 g of O_2 is removed.
c. A sample of 4.00 g of O_2 is added to the 4.80 g of O_2 gas in the container.

8.43 Use molar volume to calculate each of the following at STP:
a. the number of moles of O_2 in 44.8 L of O_2 gas
b. the volume, in liters, occupied by 0.420 mole of He gas

8.44 Use molar volume to calculate each of the following at STP:
a. the volume, in liters, occupied by 2.50 moles of N_2 gas
b. the number of moles of CO_2 in 4.00 L of CO_2 gas

8.45 Use molar volume to calculate each of the following at STP:
a. the volume, in liters, occupied by 6.40 g of O_2 gas
b. the number of grams of H_2 in 1620 mL of H_2 gas

8.46 Use molar volume to calculate each of the following at STP:
a. the number of grams of Ne in 11.2 L of Ne gas
b. the volume, in liters, occupied by 50.0 g of Ar gas

8.7 The Ideal Gas Law

The **ideal gas law** is the combination of the four properties used in the measurement of a gas—pressure (*P*), volume (*V*), temperature (*T*), and amount of a gas (*n*)—to give a single expression, which is written as

Ideal Gas Law

$$PV = nRT$$

Rearranging the ideal gas law equation shows that the four gas properties equal the gas law constant, *R*.

$$\frac{PV}{nT} = R$$

To calculate the value of *R*, we substitute the STP conditions for molar volume into the expression: 1.00 mole of any gas occupies 22.4 L at STP (273 K and 1.00 atm).

$$R = \frac{(1.00\ \text{atm})(22.4\ \text{L})}{(1.00\ \text{mole})(273\ \text{K})} = \frac{0.0821\ \text{L} \cdot \text{atm}}{\text{mole} \cdot \text{K}}$$

The value for the **ideal gas constant, *R*,** is 0.0821 L • atm per mole • K. If we use 760. mmHg for the pressure, we obtain another useful value for *R* of 62.4 L • mmHg per mole • K.

$$R = \frac{(760.\ \text{mmHg})(22.4\ \text{L})}{(1.00\ \text{mole})(273\ \text{K})} = \frac{62.4\ \text{L} \cdot \text{mmHg}}{\text{mole} \cdot \text{K}}$$

The ideal gas law is a useful expression when you are given the quantities for any three of the four properties of a gas. Although real gases show some deviations in behavior, the ideal gas law closely approximates the behavior of real gases at typical conditions. In working problems using the ideal gas law, the units of each variable must match the units in the *R* you select.

	$\dfrac{0.0821\ \text{L} \cdot \text{atm}}{\text{mole} \cdot \text{K}}$	$\dfrac{62.4\ \text{L} \cdot \text{mmHg}}{\text{mole} \cdot \text{K}}$
Ideal Gas Constant (*R*)		
Pressure (*P*)	atm	mmHg
Volume (*V*)	L	L
Amount (*n*)	mole	mole
Temperature (*T*)	K	K

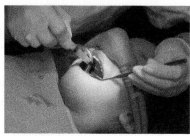

Dinitrogen oxide is used as an anesthetic in dentistry.

▶ **SAMPLE PROBLEM 8.9** Using the Ideal Gas Law

Dinitrogen oxide, N_2O, which is used in dentistry, is an anesthetic also called laughing gas. What is the pressure, in atmospheres, of 0.350 mole of N_2O at 22 °C in a 5.00-L container?

SOLUTION

STEP **1** State the given and needed quantities. When three of the four quantities (*P, V, n,* and *T*) are known, we use the ideal gas law equation to solve for the unknown quantity. It is helpful to organize the data in a table. The temperature is converted from degrees Celsius to kelvins so that the units of *V, n,* and *T* match the unit of the gas constant *R*.

		P	**V**	**n**	**R**	**T**
ANALYZE THE PROBLEM	**Given**		5.00 L	0.350 mole	$\dfrac{0.0821\ \text{L} \cdot \text{atm}}{\text{mole} \cdot \text{K}}$	22 °C + 273 = 295 K
	Need	atm				

STEP **2** Rearrange the ideal gas law equation to solve for the needed quantity. By dividing both sides of the ideal gas law equation by V, we solve for pressure, P.

$$PV = nRT \quad \text{Ideal gas law equation}$$

$$\frac{P\cancel{V}}{\cancel{V}} = \frac{nRT}{V}$$

$$P = \frac{nRT}{V}$$

STEP **3** Substitute the gas data into the equation and calculate the needed quantity.

$$P = \frac{0.350 \, \cancel{\text{mole}} \times \dfrac{0.0821 \, \cancel{L} \cdot \text{atm}}{\cancel{\text{mole}} \cdot \cancel{K}} \times 295 \, \cancel{K}}{5.00 \, \cancel{L}} = 1.70 \, \text{atm}$$

> ### Guide to Using the Ideal Gas Law
>
> **STEP 1**
> State the given and needed quantities.
>
> **STEP 2**
> Rearrange the ideal gas law equation to solve for the needed quantity.
>
> **STEP 3**
> Substitute the gas data into the equation and calculate the needed quantity.

STUDY CHECK 8.9

Chlorine gas, Cl_2, is used to purify water. How many moles of chlorine gas are in a 7.00-L tank if the gas has a pressure of 865 mmHg and a temperature of 24 °C?

ANSWER

0.327 mole of Cl_2

Many times we need to know the amount of gas, in grams, involved in a reaction. Then the ideal gas law equation can be rearranged to solve for the amount (n) of gas, which is converted to mass in grams using its molar mass as shown in Sample Problem 8.10.

▶ **SAMPLE PROBLEM 8.10 Calculating Mass Using the Ideal Gas Law**

Butane, C_4H_{10}, is used as a fuel for camping stoves. If you have 108 mL of butane gas at 715 mmHg and 25 °C, what is the mass, in grams, of butane?

SOLUTION

STEP **1** State the given and needed quantities. When three of the quantities (P, V, and T) are known, we use the ideal gas law equation to solve for the unknown quantity, moles (n). Because the pressure is given in mmHg, we will use R in mmHg. The volume given in milliliters (mL) is converted to a volume in liters (L). The temperature is converted from degrees Celsius to kelvins.

When camping, butane is used as a fuel for a portable stove.

		P	V	n	R	T
ANALYZE THE PROBLEM	**Given**	715 mmHg	108 mL (0.108 L)		$\dfrac{62.4 \, L \cdot mmHg}{mole \cdot K}$	25 °C + 273 = 298 K
	Need			g of C_4H_{10} (mole of C_4H_{10})		

STEP **2** Rearrange the ideal gas law equation to solve for the needed quantity. By dividing both sides of the ideal gas law equation by RT, we solve for moles, n.

$$PV = nRT \quad \text{Ideal gas law equation}$$

$$\frac{PV}{RT} = \frac{n\cancel{RT}}{\cancel{RT}}$$

$$n = \frac{PV}{RT}$$

STEP **3** Substitute the gas data into the equation and calculate the needed quantity.

$$n = \frac{715 \text{ mmHg} \times 0.108 \text{ L}}{\dfrac{62.4 \text{ L} \cdot \text{mmHg}}{\text{mole} \cdot \text{K}} \times 298 \text{ K}} = 0.00415 \text{ mole } (4.15 \times 10^{-3} \text{ mole})$$

Now we can convert the moles of butane to grams using its molar mass of 58.12 g/mole:

$$0.00415 \text{ mole C}_4\text{H}_{10} \times \frac{58.12 \text{ g C}_4\text{H}_{10}}{1 \text{ mole C}_4\text{H}_{10}} = 0.241 \text{ g of C}_4\text{H}_{10}$$

STUDY CHECK 8.10

What is the volume, in liters, of 1.20 g of carbon monoxide at 8 °C if it has a pressure of 724 mmHg?

ANSWER

1.04 L

Chemistry Link to Health

Hyperbaric Chambers

A burn patient may undergo treatment for burns and infections in a hyperbaric chamber, a device in which pressures can be obtained that are two to three times greater than atmospheric pressure. A greater oxygen pressure increases the level of dissolved oxygen in the blood and tissues, where it fights bacterial infections. High levels of oxygen are toxic to many strains of bacteria. The hyperbaric chamber may also be used during surgery, to help counteract carbon monoxide (CO) poisoning, and to treat some cancers.

The blood is normally capable of dissolving up to 95% of the oxygen. Thus, if the partial pressure of the oxygen in the hyperbaric chamber is 2280 mmHg (3 atm), about 2170 mmHg of oxygen can dissolve in the blood where it saturates the tissues. In the treatment for carbon monoxide poisoning, oxygen at high pressure is used to displace the CO from the hemoglobin faster than breathing pure oxygen at 1 atm.

A patient undergoing treatment in a hyperbaric chamber must also undergo decompression (reduction of pressure) at a rate that slowly reduces the concentration of dissolved oxygen in the blood. If decompression is too rapid, the oxygen dissolved in the blood may form gas bubbles in the circulatory system.

Similarly, if a scuba diver does not decompress slowly, a condition called the "bends" may occur. While below the surface of the ocean, a

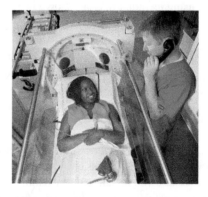

A hyperbaric chamber is used in the treatment of certain diseases.

diver uses a breathing mixture with a higher pressure. If there is nitrogen in the mixture, higher quantities of nitrogen gas will dissolve in the blood. If the diver ascends to the surface too quickly, the dissolved nitrogen forms gas bubbles that can block a blood vessel and cut off the flow of blood in the joints and tissues of the body and be quite painful. A diver suffering from the bends is placed immediately into a hyperbaric chamber where pressure is first increased and then slowly decreased. The dissolved nitrogen can then diffuse through the lungs until atmospheric pressure is reached.

CORE CHEMISTRY SKILL

Calculating Mass or Volume of a Gas in a Chemical Reaction

Gas Laws and Chemical Reactions

Gases are involved as reactants and products in many chemical reactions. Typically, the information given for a gas in a reaction is its pressure (P), volume (V), and temperature (T). Then we can use the ideal gas law equation to determine the moles of a gas in a reaction. If we know the number of moles for one of the gases in a reaction, we can use mole–mole factors to determine the moles of any other substance.

▶SAMPLE PROBLEM 8.11 **Gases in Chemical Reactions**

Calcium carbonate, $CaCO_3$, in antacids reacts with HCl in the stomach to reduce acid reflux.

$$CaCO_3(s) + 2HCl(aq) \longrightarrow CO_2(g) + H_2O(l) + CaCl_2(aq)$$

How many liters of CO_2 are produced at 752 mmHg and 24 °C from a 25.0-g sample of calcium carbonate?

SOLUTION

STEP 1 State the given and needed quantities.

ANALYZE THE PROBLEM	Given	Need
	reactant: 25.0 g of $CaCO_3$	liters of $CO_2(g)$
	product: $CO_2(g)$ at 752 mmHg, 24 °C (24 °C + 273 = 297 K)	
	Equation	
	$CaCO_3(s) + 2HCl(aq) \longrightarrow CO_2(g) + H_2O(l) + CaCl_2(aq)$	

STEP 2 Write a plan to convert the given quantity to the needed moles.

grams of $CaCO_3$ ⟶ Molar mass ⟶ moles of $CaCO_3$ ⟶ Mole–mole factor ⟶ moles of CO_2

STEP 3 Write the equalities and conversion factors for molar mass and mole–mole factors.

$$1 \text{ mole of } CaCO_3 = 100.09 \text{ g of } CaCO_3$$
$$\frac{100.09 \text{ g } CaCO_3}{1 \text{ mole } CaCO_3} \quad \text{and} \quad \frac{1 \text{ mole } CaCO_3}{100.09 \text{ g } CaCO_3}$$

$$1 \text{ mole of } CaCO_3 = 1 \text{ mole of } CO_2$$
$$\frac{1 \text{ mole } CaCO_3}{1 \text{ mole } CO_2} \quad \text{and} \quad \frac{1 \text{ mole } CO_2}{1 \text{ mole } CaCO_3}$$

STEP 4 Set up the problem to calculate moles of needed quantity.

$$25.0 \text{ g } CaCO_3 \times \frac{1 \text{ mole } CaCO_3}{100.09 \text{ g } CaCO_3} \times \frac{1 \text{ mole } CO_2}{1 \text{ mole } CaCO_3} = 0.250 \text{ mole of } CO_2$$

STEP 5 Convert the moles of needed quantity to mass or volume using the molar mass or the ideal gas law equation.

$$V = \frac{nRT}{P}$$

$$V = \frac{0.250 \text{ mole} \times \dfrac{62.4 \text{ L} \cdot \text{mmHg}}{\text{mole} \cdot \text{K}} \times 297 \text{ K}}{752 \text{ mmHg}} = 6.16 \text{ L of } CO_2$$

STUDY CHECK 8.11

If 12.8 g of aluminum reacts with HCl, how many liters of H_2 would be formed at 715 mmHg and 19 °C?

$$2Al(s) + 6HCl(aq) \longrightarrow 3H_2(g) + 2AlCl_3(aq)$$

ANSWER

18.1 L of H_2

Guide to Using the Ideal Gas Law for Reactions

STEP 1
State the given and needed quantities.

STEP 2
Write a plan to convert the given quantity to the needed moles.

STEP 3
Write the equalities and conversion factors for molar mass and mole–mole factors.

STEP 4
Set up the problem to calculate moles of needed quantity.

STEP 5
Convert the moles of needed quantity to mass or volume using the molar mass or the ideal gas law equation.

When aluminum reacts with HCl, bubbles of H_2 gas form.

QUESTIONS AND PROBLEMS

8.7 The Ideal Gas Law

LEARNING GOAL Use the ideal gas law equation to solve for P, V, T, or n of a gas when given three of the four values in the ideal gas law equation. Calculate mass or volume of a gas in a chemical reaction.

8.47 Calculate the pressure, in atmospheres, of 2.00 moles of helium gas in a 10.0-L container at 27 °C.

8.48 What is the volume, in liters, of 4.00 moles of methane gas, CH_4, at 18 °C and 1.40 atm?

8.49 An oxygen gas container has a volume of 20.0 L. How many grams of oxygen are in the container if the gas has a pressure of 845 mmHg at 22 °C?

8.50 A 10.0-g sample of krypton has a temperature of 25 °C at 575 mmHg. What is the volume, in milliliters, of the krypton gas?

8.51 A 25.0-g sample of nitrogen, N_2, has a volume of 50.0 L and a pressure of 630. mmHg. What is the temperature, in kelvins and degrees Celsius, of the gas?

8.52 A 0.226-g sample of carbon dioxide, CO_2, has a volume of 525 mL and a pressure of 455 mmHg. What is the temperature, in kelvins and degrees Celsius, of the gas?

8.53 Mg metal reacts with HCl to produce hydrogen gas.

$$Mg(s) + 2HCl(aq) \longrightarrow H_2(g) + MgCl_2(aq)$$

a. What volume, in liters, of hydrogen at 0 °C and 1.00 atm (STP) is released when 8.25 g of Mg reacts?

b. How many grams of magnesium are needed to prepare 5.00 L of H_2 at 735 mmHg and 18 °C?

8.54 When heated to 350 °C at 0.950 atm, ammonium nitrate decomposes to produce nitrogen, water, and oxygen gases.

$$2NH_4NO_3(s) \xrightarrow{\Delta} 2N_2(g) + 4H_2O(g) + O_2(g)$$

a. How many liters of water vapor are produced when 25.8 g of NH_4NO_3 decomposes?

b. How many grams of NH_4NO_3 are needed to produce 10.0 L of oxygen?

8.55 Butane undergoes combustion when it reacts with oxygen to produce carbon dioxide and water. What volume, in liters, of oxygen is needed to react with 55.2 g of butane at 0.850 atm and 25 °C?

$$2C_4H_{10}(g) + 13O_2(g) \xrightarrow{\Delta} 8CO_2(g) + 10H_2O(g)$$

8.56 Potassium nitrate decomposes to potassium nitrite and oxygen. What volume, in liters, of O_2 can be produced from the decomposition of 50.0 g of KNO_3 at 35 °C and 1.19 atm?

$$2KNO_3(s) \longrightarrow 2KNO_2(s) + O_2(g)$$

8.57 Aluminum and oxygen react to form aluminum oxide. How many liters of oxygen at 0 °C and 760 mmHg (STP) are required to completely react with 5.4 g of aluminum?

$$4Al(s) + 3O_2(g) \longrightarrow 2Al_2O_3(s)$$

8.58 Nitrogen dioxide reacts with water to produce oxygen and ammonia. How many grams of NH_3 can be produced when 4.00 L of NO_2 reacts at 415 °C and 725 mmHg?

$$4NO_2(g) + 6H_2O(g) \longrightarrow 7O_2(g) + 4NH_3(g)$$

℞ Clinical Applications

8.59 A single-patient hyperbaric chamber has a volume of 640 L. At a temperature of 24 °C, how many grams of oxygen are needed to give a pressure of 1.6 atm?

8.60 A multipatient hyperbaric chamber has a volume of 3400 L. At a temperature of 22 °C, how many grams of oxygen are needed to give a pressure of 2.4 atm?

LEARNING GOAL

Use Dalton's law of partial pressures to calculate the total pressure of a mixture of gases.

8.8 Partial Pressures (Dalton's Law)

Many gas samples are a mixture of gases. For example, the air you breathe is a mixture of mostly oxygen and nitrogen gases. In gas mixtures, scientists observed that all gas particles behave in the same way. Therefore, the total pressure of the gases in a mixture is a result of the collisions of the gas particles regardless of what type of gas they are.

In a gas mixture, each gas exerts its **partial pressure**, which is the pressure it would exert if it were the only gas in the container. **Dalton's law** states that the total pressure of a gas mixture is the sum of the partial pressures of the gases in the mixture.

Dalton's Law

$$P_{total} = P_1 + P_2 + P_3 + \cdots$$

Total pressure = Sum of the partial pressures
of a gas mixture   of the gases in the mixture

⚛ CORE CHEMISTRY SKILL

Calculating Partial Pressure

Suppose we have two separate tanks, one filled with helium at 2.0 atm and the other filled with argon at 4.0 atm. When the gases are combined in a single tank at the same volume and temperature, the number of gas molecules, not the type of gas, determines the pressure in a container. Then the pressure of the gases in the gas mixture would be 6.0 atm, which is the sum of their individual or partial pressures.

$$P_{total} = P_{He} + P_{Ar}$$
$$= 2.0 \text{ atm} + 4.0 \text{ atm}$$
$$= 6.0 \text{ atm}$$

$P_{He} = 2.0 \text{ atm}$ $P_{Ar} = 4.0 \text{ atm}$

The total pressure of two gases is the sum of their partial pressures.

SAMPLE PROBLEM 8.12 Partial Pressure of a Gas in a Mixture

A heliox breathing mixture of oxygen and helium is prepared for a patient with COPD (chronic obstructive pulmonary disease). The gas mixture has a total pressure of 7.00 atm. If the partial pressure of the oxygen in the tank is 1140 mmHg, what is the partial pressure, in atmospheres, of the helium in the breathing mixture?

SOLUTION

STEP 1 Write the equation for the sum of the partial pressures.

$$P_{total} = P_{O_2} + P_{He}$$

STEP 2 Rearrange the equation to solve for the unknown pressure. To solve for the partial pressure of helium (P_{He}), we rearrange the equation to give the following:

$$P_{He} = P_{total} - P_{O_2}$$

Convert units to match.

$$P_{O_2} = 1140 \text{ mmHg} \times \frac{1 \text{ atm}}{760 \text{ mmHg}} = 1.50 \text{ atm}$$

STEP 3 Substitute known pressures into the equation and calculate the unknown partial pressure.

$$P_{He} = P_{total} - P_{O_2}$$
$$P_{He} = 7.00 \text{ atm} - 1.50 \text{ atm} = 5.50 \text{ atm}$$

STUDY CHECK 8.12

An anesthetic consists of a mixture of cyclopropane gas, C_3H_6, and oxygen gas, O_2. If the mixture has a total pressure of 1.09 atm, and the partial pressure of the cyclopropane is 73 mmHg, what is the partial pressure, in millimeters of mercury, of the oxygen in the anesthetic?

ANSWER
755 mmHg

> **Guide to Calculating Partial Pressure**
>
> **STEP 1**
> Write the equation for the sum of the partial pressures.
>
> **STEP 2**
> Rearrange the equation to solve for the unknown pressure.
>
> **STEP 3**
> Substitute known pressures into the equation and calculate the unknown partial pressure.

Chemistry Link to Health

Blood Gases

Our cells continuously use oxygen and produce carbon dioxide. Both gases move in and out of the lungs through the membranes of the alveoli, the tiny air sacs at the ends of the airways in the lungs. An exchange of gases occurs in which oxygen from the air diffuses into the lungs and into the blood, while carbon dioxide produced in the cells is carried to the lungs to be exhaled. In Table 8.7, partial pressures are given for the gases in air that we inhale (inspired air), air in the alveoli, and air that we exhale (expired air).

At sea level, oxygen normally has a partial pressure of 100 mmHg in the alveoli of the lungs. Because the partial pressure of oxygen in venous blood is 40 mmHg, oxygen diffuses from the alveoli into the

bloodstream. The oxygen combines with hemoglobin, which carries it to the tissues of the body where the partial pressure of oxygen can be very low, less than 30 mmHg. Oxygen diffuses from the blood, where the partial pressure of O_2 is high, into the tissues where O_2 pressure is low.

As oxygen is used in the cells of the body during metabolic processes, carbon dioxide is produced, so the partial pressure of CO_2 may be as high as 50 mmHg or more. Carbon dioxide diffuses from the tissues into the bloodstream and is carried to the lungs. There it diffuses out of the blood, where CO_2 has a partial pressure of 46 mmHg, into the alveoli, where the CO_2 is at 40 mmHg and is exhaled. Table 8.8 gives the partial pressures of blood gases in the tissues and in oxygenated and deoxygenated blood.

TABLE 8.7 Partial Pressures of Gases During Breathing

Gas	Partial Pressure (mmHg)		
	Inspired Air	Alveolar Air	Expired Air
Nitrogen, N_2	594	573	569
Oxygen, O_2	160.	100.	116
Carbon dioxide, CO_2	0.3	40.	28
Water vapor, H_2O	5.7	47	47
Total	760.	760.	760.

TABLE 8.8 Partial Pressures of Oxygen and Carbon Dioxide in Blood and Tissues

Gas	Partial Pressure (mmHg)		
	Oxygenated Blood	Deoxygenated Blood	Tissues
O_2	100	40	30 or less
CO_2	40	46	50 or greater

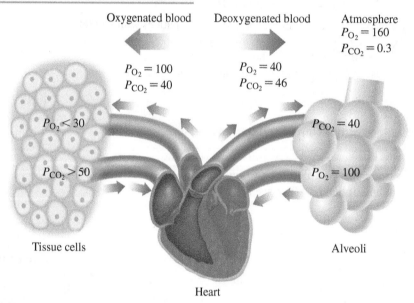

QUESTIONS AND PROBLEMS

8.8 Partial Pressures (Dalton's Law)

LEARNING GOAL Use Dalton's law of partial pressures to calculate the total pressure of a mixture of gases.

8.61 In a gas mixture, the partial pressures are nitrogen 425 Torr, oxygen 115 Torr, and helium 225 Torr. What is the total pressure, in torr, exerted by the gas mixture?

8.62 In a gas mixture, the partial pressures are argon 415 mmHg, neon 75 mmHg, and nitrogen 125 mmHg. What is the total pressure, in millimeters of mercury, exerted by the gas mixture?

8.63 A gas mixture containing oxygen, nitrogen, and helium exerts a total pressure of 925 Torr. If the partial pressures are oxygen

425 Torr and helium 75 Torr, what is the partial pressure, in torr, of the nitrogen in the mixture?

8.64 A gas mixture containing oxygen, nitrogen, and neon exerts a total pressure of 1.20 atm. If helium added to the mixture increases the pressure to 1.50 atm, what is the partial pressure, in atmospheres, of the helium?

℞ Clinical Applications

8.65 In certain lung ailments such as emphysema, there is a decrease in the ability of oxygen to diffuse into the blood.

a. How would the partial pressure of oxygen in the blood change?

b. Why does a person with severe emphysema sometimes use a portable oxygen tank?

8.66 An accident to the head can affect the ability of a person to ventilate (breathe in and out).

a. What would happen to the partial pressures of oxygen and carbon dioxide in the blood if a person cannot properly ventilate?

b. When a person who cannot breathe properly is placed on a ventilator, an air mixture is delivered at pressures that are alternately above the air pressure in the person's lung, and then below. How will this move oxygen gas into the lungs, and carbon dioxide out?

8.67 An air sample in the lungs contains oxygen at 93 mmHg, nitrogen at 565 mmHg, carbon dioxide at 38 mmHg, and water vapor at 47 mmHg. What is the total pressure, in atmospheres, exerted by the gas mixture?

8.68 A nitrox II gas mixture for scuba diving contains oxygen gas at 53 atm and nitrogen gas at 94 atm. What is the total pressure, in torr, of the scuba gas mixture?

Clinical Update
Exercise-Induced Asthma

Vigorous exercise with high levels of physical activity can induce asthma particularly in children. When Whitney had her asthma attack, her breathing became more rapid, the temperature within her airways increased, and the muscles around the bronchi contracted causing a narrowing of the airways. Whitney's symptoms, which may occur  within 5 to 20 min after the start of vigorous exercise, include shortness of breath, wheezing, and coughing.

Whitney now does several things to prevent exercise-induced asthma. She uses a pre-exercise inhaled medication before she starts her activity. The medication relaxes the muscles that surround the airways and opens up the airways. Then she does a warm-up set of exercises. If pollen counts are high, she avoids exercising outdoors.

℞ Clinical Applications

8.69 Whitney's lung capacity was measured as 3.2 L at a body temperature of 37 °C and a pressure of 745 mmHg. How many moles of oxygen is in her lungs if air contains 21% oxygen?

8.70 Whitney's tidal volume, which is the volume of air that she inhales and exhales, was 0.54 L. Her tidal volume was measured at a body temperature of 37 °C and a pressure of 745 mmHg. How many moles of nitrogen does she inhale in one breath if air contains 78% nitrogen?

CONCEPT MAP

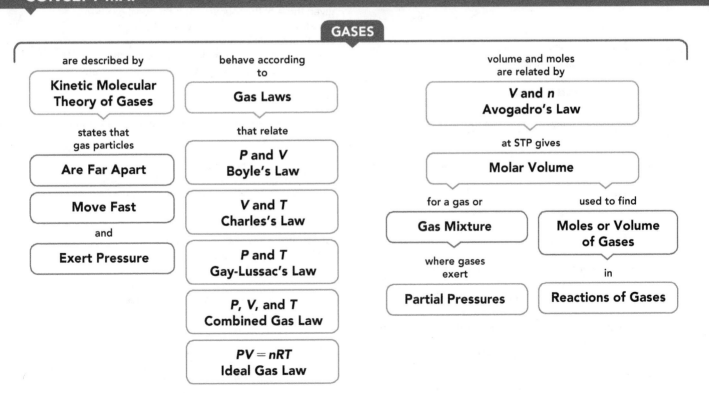

GASES

are described by
Kinetic Molecular Theory of Gases

behave according to
Gas Laws

volume and moles are related by
V and n
Avogadro's Law

states that gas particles
Are Far Apart

Move Fast

and

Exert Pressure

that relate
P and V
Boyle's Law

V and T
Charles's Law

P and T
Gay-Lussac's Law

P, V, and T
Combined Gas Law

PV = nRT
Ideal Gas Law

at STP gives
Molar Volume

for a gas or
Gas Mixture

where gases exert
Partial Pressures

used to find
Moles or Volume of Gases

in
Reactions of Gases

CHAPTER REVIEW

8.1 Properties of Gases

LEARNING GOAL Describe the kinetic molecular theory of gases and the units of measurement used for gases.

- In a gas, particles are so far apart and moving so fast that their attractions are negligible.
- A gas is described by the physical properties of pressure (P), volume (V), temperature (T) in kelvins (K), and the amount in moles (n).
- A gas exerts pressure, the force of the gas particles striking the walls of a container.
- Gas pressure is measured in units such as torr, mmHg, atm, and Pa.

8.2 Pressure and Volume (Boyle's Law)

LEARNING GOAL Use the pressure–volume relationship (Boyle's law) to determine the final pressure or volume when the temperature and amount of gas are constant.

Piston

$V = 4$ L $V = 2$ L
$P = 1$ atm $P = 2$ atm

- The volume (V) of a gas changes inversely with the pressure (P) of the gas if there is no change in the temperature and the amount of gas.

$$P_1V_1 = P_2V_2$$

- The pressure increases if volume decreases; pressure decreases if volume increases.

8.3 Temperature and Volume (Charles's Law)

LEARNING GOAL Use the temperature–volume relationship (Charles's law) to determine the final temperature or volume when the pressure and amount of gas are constant.

- The volume (V) of a gas is directly related to its Kelvin temperature (T) when there is no change in the pressure and amount of the gas.

$$\frac{V_1}{T_1} = \frac{V_2}{T_2}$$

$T = 200$ K $T = 400$ K
$V = 1$ L $V = 2$ L

- As temperature of a gas increases, its volume increases; if its temperature decreases, volume decreases.

8.4 Temperature and Pressure (Gay-Lussac's Law)

LEARNING GOAL Use the temperature–pressure relationship (Gay-Lussac's law) to determine the final temperature or pressure when the volume and amount of gas are constant.

- The pressure (P) of a gas is directly related to its Kelvin temperature (T) when there is no change in the volume and amount of the gas.

$T = 200$ K $T = 400$ K
$P = 1$ atm $P = 2$ atm

$$\frac{P_1}{T_1} = \frac{P_2}{T_2}$$

- As temperature of a gas increases, its pressure increases; if its temperature decreases, pressure decreases.
- Vapor pressure is the pressure of the gas that forms when a liquid evaporates.
- At the boiling point of a liquid, the vapor pressure equals the external pressure.

8.5 The Combined Gas Law

LEARNING GOAL Use the combined gas law to calculate the final pressure, volume, or temperature of a gas when changes in two of these properties are given and the amount of gas is constant.

- The combined gas law is the relationship of pressure (P), volume (V), and temperature (T) for a constant amount (n) of gas.

$$\frac{P_1V_1}{T_1} = \frac{P_2V_2}{T_2}$$

- The combined gas law is used to determine the effect of changes in two of the variables on the third.

8.6 Volume and Moles (Avogadro's Law)

LEARNING GOAL Use Avogadro's law to calculate the amount or volume of a gas when the pressure and temperature are constant.

$V = 22.4$ L

1 mole of O_2
32.00 g of O_2
273 K
1 atm

- The volume (V) of a gas is directly related to the number of moles (n) of the gas when the pressure and temperature of the gas do not change.

$$\frac{V_1}{n_1} = \frac{V_2}{n_2}$$

- If the moles of gas are increased, the volume must increase; if the moles of gas are decreased, the volume must decrease.
- At standard temperature (273 K) and standard pressure (1 atm), abbreviated STP, one mole of any gas has a volume of 22.4 L.

8.7 The Ideal Gas Law

LEARNING GOAL Use the ideal gas law equation to solve for P, V, T, or n of a gas when given three of the four values in the ideal gas law equation. Calculate mass or volume of a gas in a chemical reaction.

- The ideal gas law gives the relationship of the quantities P, V, n, and T that describe and measure a gas.

$$PV = nRT$$

- Any of the four variables can be calculated if the values of the other three are known.
- The ideal gas law equation is used to convert the quantities (P, V, and T) of gases to moles in a chemical reaction.
- The moles of gases can be used to determine the number of moles or grams of other substances in the reaction.

8.8 Partial Pressures (Dalton's Law)

LEARNING GOAL Use Dalton's law of partial pressures to calculate the total pressure of a mixture of gases.

$P_{total} = P_{He} + P_{Ar}$
$= 2.0$ atm $+ 4.0$ atm
$= 6.0$ atm

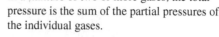
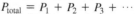

- In a mixture of two or more gases, the total pressure is the sum of the partial pressures of the individual gases.

$$P_{total} = P_1 + P_2 + P_3 + \cdots$$

- The partial pressure of a gas in a mixture is the pressure it would exert if it were the only gas in the container.

KEY TERMS

atmosphere (atm) A unit equal to pressure exerted by a column of mercury 760 mm high.

atmospheric pressure The pressure exerted by the atmosphere.

Avogadro's law A gas law stating that the volume of a gas is directly related to the number of moles of gas when pressure and temperature do not change.

Boyle's law A gas law stating that the pressure of a gas is inversely related to the volume when temperature and moles of the gas do not change.

Charles's law A gas law stating that the volume of a gas changes directly with a change in Kelvin temperature when pressure and moles of the gas do not change.

combined gas law A relationship that combines several gas laws relating pressure, volume, and temperature when the amount of gas does not change.

$$\frac{P_1 V_1}{T_1} = \frac{P_2 V_2}{T_2}$$

Dalton's law A gas law stating that the total pressure exerted by a mixture of gases in a container is the sum of the partial pressures that each gas would exert alone.

Gay-Lussac's law A gas law stating that the pressure of a gas changes directly with a change in the Kelvin temperature when the number of moles of a gas and its volume do not change.

ideal gas constant, *R* A numerical value that relates the quantities *P*, *V*, *n*, and *T* in the ideal gas law, $PV = nRT$.

ideal gas law A law that combines the four measured properties of a gas.

$$PV = nRT$$

kinetic molecular theory of gases A model used to explain the behavior of gases.

molar volume A volume of 22.4 L occupied by 1 mole of a gas at STP conditions of 0 °C (273 K) and 1 atm.

partial pressure The pressure exerted by a single gas in a gas mixture.

pressure The force exerted by gas particles that hit the walls of a container.

STP Standard conditions of exactly 0 °C (273 K) temperature and 1 atm pressure used for the comparison of gases.

vapor pressure The pressure exerted by the particles of vapor above a liquid.

⚛ CORE CHEMISTRY SKILLS

The chapter section containing each Core Chemistry Skill is shown in parentheses at the end of each heading.

Using the Gas Laws (8.2, 8.3, 8.4, 8.5, 8.6)

- Boyle's, Charles's, Gay-Lussac's, and Avogadro's laws show the relationships between two properties of a gas.

$$P_1 V_1 = P_2 V_2 \quad \text{Boyle's law}$$
$$\frac{V_1}{T_1} = \frac{V_2}{T_2} \quad \text{Charles's law}$$
$$\frac{P_1}{T_1} = \frac{P_2}{T_2} \quad \text{Gay-Lussac's law}$$
$$\frac{V_1}{n_1} = \frac{V_2}{n_2} \quad \text{Avogadro's law}$$

- The combined gas law shows the relationship between *P*, *V*, and *T* for a gas.

$$\frac{P_1 V_1}{T_1} = \frac{P_2 V_2}{T_2}$$

- When two properties of a gas vary and the other two are constant, we list the initial and final conditions of each property in a table.

Example: A sample of helium gas (He) has a volume of 6.8 L and a pressure of 2.5 atm. What is the final volume, in liters, if it has a final pressure of 1.2 atm with no change in temperature and amount of gas?

Answer:

ANALYZE THE PROBLEM	Conditions 1	Conditions 2	Know	Predict
	$P_1 = 2.5$ atm	$P_2 = 1.2$ atm	*P* decreases	
	$V_1 = 6.8$ L	$V_2 = ?$ L		*V* increases

Factors that remain constant: *T* and *n*

Using Boyle's law, we can write the relationship for V_2, which we predict will increase.

$$V_2 = V_1 \times \frac{P_1}{P_2}$$
$$V_2 = 6.8 \text{ L} \times \frac{2.5 \text{ atm}}{1.2 \text{ atm}} = 14 \text{ L}$$

Using the Ideal Gas Law (8.7)

- The ideal gas law equation combines the relationships of the four properties of a gas into one equation.

$$PV = nRT$$

- When three of the four properties are given, we rearrange the ideal gas law equation for the needed quantity.

Example: What is the volume, in liters, of 0.750 mole of CO_2 at a pressure of 1340 mmHg and a temperature of 295 K?

Answer: $V = \dfrac{nRT}{P}$

$$= \frac{0.750 \text{ mole} \times \dfrac{62.4 \text{ L} \cdot \text{mmHg}}{\text{mole} \cdot \text{K}} \times 295 \text{ K}}{1340 \text{ mmHg}} = 10.3 \text{ L}$$

Calculating Mass or Volume of a Gas in a Chemical Reaction (8.7)

- The ideal gas law equation is used to calculate the pressure, volume, moles (or grams) of a gas in a chemical reaction.

Example: What is the volume, in liters, of N_2 required to react with 18.5 g of magnesium at a pressure of 1.20 atm and a temperature of 303 K?

$$3Mg(s) + N_2(g) \longrightarrow Mg_3N_2(s)$$

Answer: Initially, we convert the grams of Mg to moles and use a mole–mole factor from the balanced equation to calculate the moles of N_2 gas.

$$18.5 \text{ g Mg} \times \frac{1 \text{ mole Mg}}{24.31 \text{ g Mg}} \times \frac{1 \text{ mole } N_2}{3 \text{ moles Mg}} = 0.254 \text{ mole of } N_2$$

Now, we use the moles of N_2 in the ideal gas law equation and solve for liters, the needed quantity.

$$V = \frac{nRT}{P} = \frac{0.254 \text{ mole } N_2 \times \dfrac{0.0821 \text{ L} \cdot \text{atm}}{\text{mole} \cdot \text{K}} \times 303 \text{ K}}{1.20 \text{ atm}} = 5.27 \text{ L}$$

Calculating Partial Pressure (8.8)

- In a gas mixture, each gas exerts its partial pressure, which is the pressure it would exert if it were the only gas in the container.
- Dalton's law states that the total pressure of a gas mixture is the sum of the partial pressures of the gases in the mixture.

$$P_{total} = P_1 + P_2 + P_3 + \cdots$$

Example: A gas mixture with a total pressure of 1.18 atm contains helium gas at a partial pressure of 465 mmHg and nitrogen gas. What is the partial pressure, in atmospheres, of the nitrogen gas?

Answer: Initially, we convert the partial pressure of helium gas from mmHg to atm.

$$465 \text{ mmHg} \times \frac{1 \text{ atm}}{760 \text{ mmHg}} = 0.612 \text{ atm of He gas}$$

Using Dalton's law, we solve for the needed quantity, P_{N_2} in atm.

$$P_{total} = P_{N_2} + P_{He}$$
$$P_{N_2} = P_{total} - P_{He}$$
$$P_{N_2} = 1.18 \text{ atm} - 0.612 \text{ atm} = 0.57 \text{ atm}$$

UNDERSTANDING THE CONCEPTS

The chapter sections to review are shown in parentheses at the end of each question.

8.71 Two flasks of equal volume and at the same temperature contain different gases. One flask contains 10.0 g of Ne, and the other flask contains 10.0 g of He. Is each of the following statements *true* or *false*? Explain. (8.1)

    a. The flask that contains He has a higher pressure than the flask that contains Ne.

    b. The densities of the gases are the same.

8.72 Two flasks of equal volume and at the same temperature contain different gases. One flask contains 5.0 g of O_2, and the other flask contains 5.0 g of H_2. Is each of the following statements *true* or *false*? Explain. (8.1)

    a. Both flasks contain the same number of molecules.

    b. The pressures in the flasks are the same.

8.73 At 100 °C, which of the following diagrams (**1, 2,** or **3**) represents a gas sample that exerts the (8.1)

    a. lowest pressure?   **b.** highest pressure?

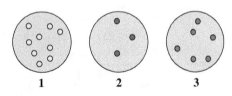

        1   **2**   **3**

8.74 Indicate which diagram (**1, 2,** or **3**) represents the volume of the gas sample in a flexible container when each of the following changes (**a** to **e**) takes place: (8.2, 8.3, 8.4)

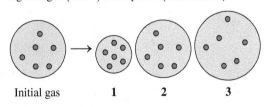

    Initial gas   **1**   **2**   **3**

    a. Temperature increases at constant pressure.

    b. Temperature decreases at constant pressure.

    c. Atmospheric pressure increases at constant temperature.

    d. Atmospheric pressure decreases at constant temperature.

    e. Doubling the atmospheric pressure and doubling the Kelvin temperature.

8.75 A balloon is filled with helium gas with a partial pressure of 1.00 atm and neon gas with a partial pressure of 0.50 atm. For each of the following changes of the initial balloon, select the diagram (**A, B,** or **C**) that shows the final volume of the balloon: (8.2, 8.3, 8.4, 8.6)

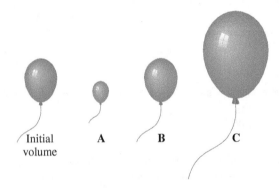

    Initial   **A**   **B**   **C**
    volume

    a. The balloon is put in a cold storage unit (*P* and *n* constant).

    b. The balloon floats to a higher altitude where the pressure is less (*n* and *T* constant).

    c. All of the neon gas is removed (*T* and *P* constant).

    d. The Kelvin temperature doubles and half of the gas atoms leak out (*P* constant).

    e. 2.0 moles of O_2 gas is added (*T* and *P* constant).

8.76 Indicate if pressure *increases*, *decreases*, or *stays the same* in each of the following: (8.2, 8.4, 8.6)

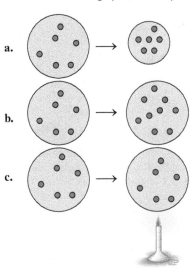

a.

b.

c.

8.77 At a restaurant, a customer chokes on a piece of food. You put your arms around the person's waist and use your fists to push up on the person's abdomen, an action called the Heimlich maneuver. (8.2)

a. How would this action change the volume of the chest and lungs?

b. Why does it cause the person to expel the food item from the airway?

8.78 An airplane is pressurized with air to 650. mmHg. (8.8)

a. If air is 21% oxygen, what is the partial pressure of oxygen on the plane?

b. If the partial pressure of oxygen drops below 100. mmHg, passengers become drowsy. If this happens, oxygen masks are released. What is the total cabin pressure at which oxygen masks are dropped?

ADDITIONAL QUESTIONS AND PROBLEMS

8.79 A sample of hydrogen (H_2) gas at 127 °C has a pressure of 2.00 atm. At what final temperature, in degrees Celsius, will the pressure of the H_2 decrease to 0.25 atm, if V and n are constant? (8.4)

8.80 A fire extinguisher has a pressure of 10. atm at 25 °C. What is the final pressure, in atmospheres, when the fire extinguisher is used at a temperature of 75 °C, if V and n are constant? (8.4)

8.81 In 1783, Jacques Charles launched his first balloon filled with hydrogen gas (H_2), which he chose because it was lighter than air. The balloon had a volume of 31 000 L at a pressure of 755 mmHg and a temperature of 22 °C. When the balloon reached an altitude of 1000 m, the pressure was 658 mmHg and the temperature was −8 °C. What was the volume, in liters, of the balloon at these conditions, if the amount of hydrogen remains the same? (8.5)

Jacques Charles used hydrogen to launch his balloon in 1783.

8.82 During laparoscopic surgery, carbon dioxide gas is used to expand the abdomen to help create a larger working space. If 4.80 L of CO_2 gas at 18 °C at 785 mmHg is used, what is the final volume, in liters, of the gas at 37 °C and a pressure of 745 mmHg, if the amount of CO_2 remains the same? (8.5)

8.83 A 2.00-L container is filled with methane gas, CH_4, at a pressure of 2500. mmHg and a temperature of 18 °C. How many grams of methane are in the container? (8.7)

8.84 A steel cylinder with a volume of 15.0 L is filled with 50.0 g of nitrogen gas at 25 °C. What is the pressure, in atmospheres, of the N_2 gas in the cylinder? (8.7)

8.85 How many grams of CO_2 are in 35.0 L of $CO_2(g)$ at 1.20 atm and 5 °C? (8.7)

8.86 A container is filled with 0.644 g of O_2 at 5 °C and 845 mmHg. What is the volume, in milliliters, of the container? (8.7)

8.87 How many liters of H_2 gas can be produced at 0 °C and 1.00 atm (STP) from 25.0 g of Zn? (8.7)

$$Zn(s) + 2HCl(aq) \longrightarrow H_2(g) + ZnCl_2(aq)$$

8.88 In the formation of smog, nitrogen and oxygen gas react to form nitrogen dioxide. How many grams of NO_2 will be produced when 2.0 L of nitrogen at 840 mmHg and 24 °C are completely reacted? (8.7)

$$N_2(g) + 2O_2(g) \longrightarrow 2NO_2(g)$$

8.89 Nitrogen dioxide reacts with water to produce oxygen and ammonia. A 5.00-L sample of $H_2O(g)$ reacts at a temperature of 375 °C and a pressure of 725 mmHg. How many grams of NH_3 can be produced? (8.7)

$$4NO_2(g) + 6H_2O(g) \longrightarrow 7O_2(g) + 4NH_3(g)$$

8.90 Hydrogen gas can be produced in the laboratory through the reaction of magnesium metal with hydrochloric acid. When 12.0 g of Mg reacts, what volume, in liters, of H_2 gas is produced at 24 °C and 835 mmHg? (8.7)

$$Mg(s) + 2HCl(aq) \longrightarrow H_2(g) + MgCl_2(aq)$$

8.91 A gas mixture contains oxygen and argon at partial pressures of 0.60 atm and 425 mmHg. If nitrogen gas added to the sample increases the total pressure to 1250 Torr, what is the partial pressure, in torr, of the nitrogen added? (8.8)

8.92 What is the total pressure, in millimeters of mercury, of a gas mixture containing argon gas at 0.25 atm, helium gas at 350 mmHg, and nitrogen gas at 360 Torr? (8.8)

CHALLENGE QUESTIONS

The following groups of questions are related to the topics in this chapter. However, they do not all follow the chapter order, and they require you to combine concepts and skills from several sections. These questions will help you increase your critical thinking skills and prepare for your next exam.

8.93   Your spaceship has docked at a space station above Mars. The temperature inside the space station is a carefully controlled 24 °C at a pressure of 745 mmHg. A balloon with a volume of 425 mL drifts into the airlock where the temperature is −95 °C and the pressure is 0.115 atm. What is the final volume, in milliliters, of the balloon if *n* remains constant and the balloon is very elastic? (8.5)

8.94   You are doing research on planet X. The temperature inside the space station is a carefully controlled 24 °C and the pressure is 755 mmHg. Suppose that a balloon, which has a volume of 850. mL inside the space station, is placed into the airlock, and floats out to planet X. If planet X has an atmospheric pressure of 0.150 atm and the volume of the balloon changes to 3.22 L, what is the temperature, in degrees Celsius, on planet X (*n* does not change)? (8.5)

8.95   A gas sample has a volume of 4250 mL at 15 °C and 745 mmHg. What is the final temperature, in degrees Celsius, after the sample is transferred to a different container with a volume of 2.50 L and a pressure of 1.20 atm when *n* is constant? (8.5)

8.96   In the fermentation of glucose (wine making), 780 mL of CO_2 gas was produced at 37 °C and 1.00 atm. What is the final volume, in liters, of the gas when measured at 22 °C and 675 mmHg, when *n* is constant? (8.5)

8.97   The propane, C_3H_8, in a fuel cylinder, undergoes combustion with oxygen in the air. How many liters of CO_2 are produced at STP if the cylinder contains 881 g of propane? (8.7)

$$C_3H_8(g) + 5O_2(g) \xrightarrow{\Delta} 3CO_2(g) + 4H_2O(g)$$

8.98   When sensors in a car detect a collision, they cause the reaction of sodium azide, NaN_3, which generates nitrogen gas to fill the airbags within 0.03 s. How many liters of N_2 are produced at STP if the airbag contains 132 g of NaN_3? (8.7)

$$2NaN_3(s) \longrightarrow 2Na(s) + 3N_2(g)$$

8.99   Glucose, $C_6H_{12}O_6$, is metabolized in living systems. How many grams of water can be produced from the reaction of 18.0 g of glucose and 7.50 L of O_2 at 1.00 atm and 37 °C? (8.7)

$$C_6H_{12}O_6(s) + 6O_2(g) \longrightarrow 6CO_2(g) + 6H_2O(l)$$

8.100   2.00 L of N_2, at 25 °C and 1.08 atm, is mixed with 4.00 L of O_2, at 25 °C and 0.118 atm, and the mixture is allowed to react. How much NO, in grams, is produced? (8.7)

$$N_2(g) + O_2(g) \longrightarrow 2NO(g)$$

℞ Clinical Applications

8.101   Hyperbaric therapy uses 100% oxygen at pressure to help heal wounds and infections, and to treat carbon monoxide poisoning. If the pressure inside a hyperbaric chamber is 3.0 atm, what is the volume, in liters, of the chamber containing 2400 g of O_2 at 28 °C? (8.7)

8.102   A hyperbaric chamber has a volume of 1510 L. How many kilograms of O_2 gas are needed to give an oxygen pressure of 2.04 atm at 25 °C? (8.7)

8.103   Laparoscopic surgery involves inflating the abdomen with carbon dioxide gas to separate the internal organs and the abdominal wall. If the CO_2 injected into the abdomen produces a pressure of 20. mmHg and a volume of 4.00 L at 32 °C, how many grams of CO_2 were used? (8.7)

8.104   In another laparoscopic surgery, helium is used to inflate the abdomen to separate the internal organs and the abdominal wall. If the He injected into the abdomen produces a pressure of 15 mmHg and a volume of 3.1 L at 28 °C, how many grams of He were used? (8.7)

ANSWERS

Answers to Selected Questions and Problems

8.1   a.   At a higher temperature, gas particles have greater kinetic energy, which makes them move faster.
   b.   Because there are great distances between the particles of a gas, they can be pushed closer together and still remain a gas.
   c.   Gas particles are very far apart, which means that the mass of a gas in a certain volume is very small, resulting in a low density.

8.3   a.   temperature   **b.**   volume
   c.   amount   **d.**   pressure

8.5   a, d, and **e** describe the pressure of a gas.

8.7   a.   1520 Torr   **b.**   1520 mmHg

8.9   As a diver ascends to the surface, external pressure decreases. If the air in the lungs were not exhaled, its volume would expand and severely damage the lungs. The pressure in the lungs must adjust to changes in the external pressure.

8.11   a.   The pressure is greater in cylinder **A**. According to Boyle's law, a decrease in volume pushes the gas particles closer together, which will cause an increase in the pressure.
   b.

Property	Conditions 1	Conditions 2	Know	Predict
Pressure (P)	650 mmHg	1.2 atm (910 mmHg)	P increases	
Volume (V)	220 mL	160 mL		V decreases

8.13   a.   increases   **b.**   decreases   **c.**   increases
8.15   a.   328 mmHg   **b.**   2620 mmHg
   c.   475 mmHg   **d.**   5240 mmHg
8.17   a.   52.4 L   **b.**   25 L
   c.   100. L   **d.**   45 L

8.19 25 L of cyclopropane

8.21 **a.** inspiration   **b.** expiration   **c.** inspiration

8.23 **a.** C   **b.** A   **c.** B

8.25 **a.** 303 °C   **b.** −129 °C
     c. 591 °C   **d.** 136 °C

8.27 **a.** 2400 mL   **b.** 4900 mL
     c. 1800 mL   **d.** 1700 mL

8.29 **a.** 770 mmHg   **b.** 1150 mmHg

8.31 **a.** −23 °C   **b.** 168 °C

8.33 1.9 atm

8.35 **a.** 4.26 atm   **b.** 3.07 atm   **c.** 0.606 atm

8.37 −33 °C

8.39 The volume increases because the number of gas particles is increased.

8.41 **a.** 4.00 L   **b.** 26.7 L   **c.** 14.6 L

8.43 **a.** 2.00 moles of O_2 **b.** 9.41 L of He

8.45 **a.** 4.48 L of O_2 **b.** 0.146 g of H_2

8.47 4.93 atm

8.49 29.4 g of O_2

8.51 566 K (293 °C)

8.53 **a.** 7.60 L of H_2 **b.** 4.92 g of Mg

8.55 178 L of O_2

8.57 3.4 L of O_2

8.59 1300 g of O_2

8.61 765 Torr

8.63 425 Torr

8.65 **a.** The partial pressure of oxygen will be lower than normal.
     b. Breathing a higher concentration of oxygen will help to increase the supply of oxygen in the lungs and blood and raise the partial pressure of oxygen in the blood.

8.67 0.978 atm

8.69 0.025 mole of O_2

8.71 **a.** True. The flask containing helium has more moles of helium and thus more helium atoms.
     b. True. The mass and volume of each are the same, which means the mass/volume ratio or density is the same in both flasks.

8.73 **a.** 2   **b.** 1

8.75 **a.** A   **b.** C
     c. A   **d.** B
     e. C

8.77 **a.** The volume of the chest and lungs is decreased.
     b. The decrease in volume increases the pressure, which can dislodge the food in the trachea.

8.79 −223 °C

8.81 32 000 L

8.83 4.41 g of CH_4

8.85 81.0 g of CO_2

8.87 8.56 L of H_2

8.89 1.02 g of NH_3

8.91 370 Torr

8.93 2170 mL

8.95 −66 °C

8.97 1340 L of CO_2

8.99 5.31 g of water

8.101 620 L

8.103 0.18 g of CO_2

CI.13 In the following diagram, blue spheres represent the element **A** and yellow spheres represent the element **B**: (6.5, 7.1, 7.2)

Reactants   **Products**

a. Write the formulas for each of the reactants and products.
b. Write a balanced chemical equation for the reaction.
c. Indicate the type of reaction as combination, decomposition, single replacement, double replacement, or combustion.

CI.14 The active ingredient in Tums is calcium carbonate. One Tums tablet contains 500. mg of calcium carbonate. (6.3, 6.4, 7.4, 7.5)

The active ingredient in Tums neutralizes excess stomach acid.

a. What is the formula of calcium carbonate?
b. What is the molar mass of calcium carbonate?
c. How many moles of calcium carbonate are in one roll of Tums that contains 12 tablets?
d. If a person takes two Tums tablets, how many grams of calcium are obtained?
e. If the daily recommended quantity of Ca^{2+} to maintain bone strength in older women is 1500 mg, how many Tums tablets are needed each day to supply the needed calcium?

CI.15 Tamiflu (Oseltamivir), $C_{16}H_{28}N_2O_4$, is an antiviral drug used to treat influenza. The preparation of Tamiflu begins with the extraction of shikimic acid from the seedpods of star anise. From 2.6 g of star anise, 0.13 g of shikimic acid can be obtained and used to produce one capsule containing 75 mg of Tamiflu. The usual adult dosage for treatment of influenza is two capsules of Tamiflu daily for 5 days. (7.4, 7.5)

Shikimic acid is the basis for the antiviral drug in Tamiflu.

The spice called star anise is a plant source of shikimic acid.

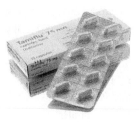

Each capsule contains 75 mg of Tamiflu.

a. If black spheres are carbon atoms, white spheres are hydrogen atoms, and red spheres are oxygen atoms, what is the formula of shikimic acid?
b. What is the molar mass of shikimic acid?
c. How many moles of shikimic acid are contained in 130 g of shikimic acid?
d. How many capsules containing 75 mg of Tamiflu could be produced from 155 g of star anise?
e. What is the molar mass of Tamiflu?
f. How many kilograms of Tamiflu would be needed to treat all the people in a city with a population of 500 000 if each person consumes two Tamiflu capsules a day for 5 days?

CI.16 The compound butyric acid gives rancid butter its characteristic odor. (6.7, 7.4, 7.5)

Butyric acid produces the characteristic odor of rancid butter.

a. If black spheres are carbon atoms, white spheres are hydrogen atoms, and red spheres are oxygen atoms, what is the molecular formula of butyric acid?
b. What is the molar mass of butyric acid?
c. How many grams of butyric acid contain 3.28×10^{23} atoms of oxygen?
d. How many grams of carbon are in 5.28 g of butyric acid?
e. Butyric acid has a density of 0.959 g/mL at 20 °C. How many moles of butyric acid are contained in 1.56 mL of butyric acid?
f. Identify the bonds C—C, C—H, and C—O in a molecule of butyric acid as polar covalent or nonpolar covalent.

CI.17 Methane is a major component of purified natural gas used for heating and cooking. When 1.0 mole of methane gas burns with oxygen to produce carbon dioxide and water, 883 kJ is produced. Methane gas has a density of 0.715 g/L at STP. For transport, the natural gas is cooled to −163 °C to form liquefied natural gas (LNG) with a density of 0.45 g/mL. A tank on a ship can hold 7.0 million gallons of LNG. (2.7, 6.6, 7.1, 7.5, 7.7, 7.9, 8.6)

An LNG carrier transports liquefied natural gas.

a. Draw the Lewis structure formula for methane, which has the formula CH_4.
b. What is the mass, in kilograms, of LNG (assume that LNG is all methane) transported in one tank on a ship?
c. What is the volume, in liters, of LNG (methane) from one tank when the LNG is converted to gas at STP?
d. Write a balanced chemical equation for the combustion of methane in a gas burner, including the heat of reaction.

Methane is the fuel burned in a gas cooktop.

e. How many kilograms of oxygen are needed to react with all of the methane provided by one tank of LNG?
f. How much heat, in kilojoules, is released from burning all of the methane in one tank of LNG?

CI.18 Automobile exhaust is a major cause of air pollution. One pollutant is nitrogen oxide, which forms from nitrogen and oxygen gases in the air at the high temperatures in an automobile engine. Once emitted into the air, nitrogen oxide reacts with oxygen to produce nitrogen dioxide, a reddish brown gas with a sharp, pungent odor that makes up smog. One component of gasoline is heptane, C_7H_{16}, which has a density of 0.684 g/mL. In one year, a typical automobile uses 550 gal of gasoline and produces 41 lb of nitrogen oxide. (7.1, 7.5, 7.7, 8.6)

Two gases found in automobile exhaust are carbon dioxide and nitrogen oxide.

a. Write a balanced chemical equations for the production of nitrogen oxide and nitrogen dioxide.
b. If all the nitrogen oxide emitted by one automobile is converted to nitrogen dioxide in the atmosphere, how many kilograms of nitrogen dioxide are produced in one year by a single automobile?
c. Write a balanced chemical equation for the combustion of heptane.
d. How many moles of CO_2 are produced from the gasoline used by the typical automobile in one year, assuming the gasoline is all heptane?
e. How many liters of carbon dioxide at STP are produced in one year from the gasoline used by the typical automobile?

ANSWERS

CI.13 a. Reactants: A and B_2; Products: AB_3
    b. $2A + 3B_2 \longrightarrow 2AB_3$
    c. combination

CI.15 a. $C_7H_{10}O_5$ **b.** 174.15 g/mole
    c. 0.75 mole   **d.** 59 capsules
    e. 312.4 g/mole   **f.** 400 kg

CI.17 a.

$$H:\overset{\displaystyle H}{\underset{\displaystyle H}{\ddot{C}}}:H \quad \text{or} \quad H-\overset{\displaystyle H}{\underset{\displaystyle H}{\overset{|}{\underset{|}{C}}}}-H$$

    b. 1.2×10^7 kg of LNG (methane)
    c. 1.7×10^{10} L of LNG (methane) at STP
    d. $CH_4(g) + 2O_2(g) \xrightarrow{\Delta} CO_2(g) + 2H_2O(g) + 883$ kJ
    e. 4.8×10^7 kg of O_2
    f. 6.6×10^{11} kJ

9

Solutions

OUR KIDNEYS PRODUCE URINE, WHICH CARRIES WASTE
products and excess fluid from the body. They also reabsorb electrolytes such as potassium and produce hormones that regulate blood pressure and calcium blood levels. Diseases such as diabetes and high blood pressure can cause a decrease in kidney function. Symptoms of kidney malfunction include protein in the urine, an abnormal level of urea nitrogen in the blood, frequent urination, and swollen feet. If kidney failure occurs, it may be treated with dialysis or transplantation.

Michelle has been suffering from kidney disease because of severe strep throat as a child. When her kidneys stopped functioning, Michelle was placed on dialysis three times a week. As she enters the dialysis unit, her dialysis nurse, Amanda, asks Michelle how she is feeling. Michelle indicates that she feels tired today and has considerable swelling around her ankles. The dialysis nurse informs her that these side effects occur because of her body's inability to regulate the amount of water in her cells. Amanda explains that the amount of water is regulated by the concentration of electrolytes in her body fluids and the rate at which waste products are removed from her body. Amanda explains that although water is essential for the many chemical reactions that occur in the body, the amount of water can become too high or too low because of various diseases and conditions. Because Michelle's kidneys no longer perform dialysis, she cannot regulate the amount of electrolytes or waste in her body fluids. As a result, she has an electrolyte imbalance and a buildup of waste products, so her body is retaining water. Amanda then explains that the dialysis machine does the work of her kidneys to reduce the high levels of electrolytes and waste products.

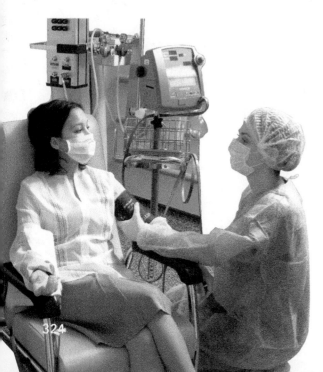

CAREER Dialysis Nurse

A dialysis nurse specializes in assisting patients with kidney disease undergoing dialysis. This requires monitoring the patient before, during, and after dialysis for any complications such as a drop in blood pressure or cramping. The dialysis nurse connects the patient to the dialysis unit via a dialysis catheter that is inserted into the neck or chest, which must be kept clean to prevent infection. A dialysis nurse must have considerable knowledge about how the dialysis machine functions to ensure that it is operating correctly at all times.

Solutions are everywhere around us. Most of the gases, liquids, and solids we see are mixtures of at least one substance dissolved in another. There are different types of solutions. The air we breathe is a solution that is primarily oxygen and nitrogen gases. Carbon dioxide gas dissolved in water makes carbonated drinks. When we make solutions of coffee or tea, we use hot water to dissolve substances from coffee beans or tea leaves. The ocean is also a solution, consisting of many ionic compounds such as sodium chloride dissolved in water. In your medicine cabinet, the antiseptic tincture of iodine is a solution of iodine dissolved in ethanol.

Our body fluids contain water and dissolved substances such as glucose and urea and electrolytes such as K^+, Na^+, Cl^-, Mg^{2+}, HCO_3^-, and HPO_4^{2-}. Proper amounts of each of these dissolved substances and water must be maintained in the body fluids. Small changes in electrolyte levels can seriously disrupt cellular processes and endanger our health. Solutions can be described by their concentration, which is the amount of solute in a specific amount of that solution. These relationships, which include mass % (m/m), volume % (v/v), mass /volume % (m/v), and molarity (M), can be used to convert between the amount of a solute and the quantity of its solution. Solutions are also diluted by adding a specific amount of solvent to a solution.

In the processes of osmosis and dialysis, water, essential nutrients, and waste products enter and leave the cells of the body. The kidneys utilize osmosis and dialysis to regulate the amount of water and electrolytes that are excreted.

CHAPTER READINESS*

🖩 KEY MATH SKILLS
- Calculating a Percentage (1.4C)
- Solving Equations (1.4D)
- Interpreting a Graph (1.4E)

⚛ CORE CHEMISTRY SKILLS
- Writing Conversion Factors from Equalities (2.5)
- Using Conversion Factors (2.6)
- Identifying Attractive Forces (6.9)
- Using Mole–Mole Factors (7.6)

*These Key Math Skills and Core Chemistry Skills from previous chapters are listed here for your review as you proceed to the new material in this chapter.

9.1 Solutions

A **solution** is a homogeneous mixture in which one substance, called the **solute**, is uniformly dispersed in another substance called the **solvent**. Because the solute and the solvent do not react with each other, they can be mixed in varying proportions. A solution of a little salt dissolved in water tastes slightly salty. When a large amount of salt is dissolved in water, the solution tastes very salty. Usually, the solute (in this case, salt) is the substance present in the lesser amount, whereas the solvent (in this case, water) is present in the greater amount. For example, in a solution composed of 5.0 g of salt and 50. g of water, salt is the solute and water is the solvent. In a solution, the particles of the solute are evenly dispersed among the molecules within the solvent (see Figure 9.1).

A solution has at least one solute dispersed in a solvent.

LEARNING GOAL

Identify the solute and solvent in a solution; describe the formation of a solution.

Solute: The substance present in lesser amount

Salt

Water

Solvent: The substance present in greater amount

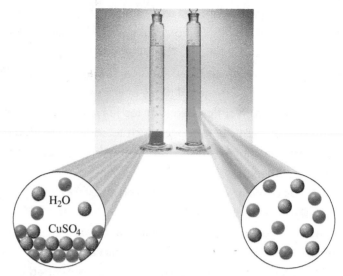

FIGURE 9.1 ▶ A solution of copper(II) sulfate ($CuSO_4$) forms as particles of solute dissolve, move away from the crystal, and become evenly dispersed among the solvent (water) molecules.

Q What does the uniform blue color in the graduated cylinder on the right indicate?

Types of Solutes and Solvents

Solutes and solvents may be solids, liquids, or gases. The solution that forms has the same physical state as the solvent. When sugar crystals are dissolved in water, the resulting sugar solution is liquid. Sugar is the solute, and water is the solvent. Soda water and soft drinks are prepared by dissolving carbon dioxide gas in water. The carbon dioxide gas is the solute, and water is the solvent. Table 9.1 lists some solutes and solvents and their solutions.

TABLE 9.1 Some Examples of Solutions

Type	Example	Primary Solute	Solvent
Gas Solutions			
Gas in a gas	Air	$O_2(g)$	$N_2(g)$
Liquid Solutions			
Gas in a liquid	Soda water	$CO_2(g)$	$H_2O(l)$
	Household ammonia	$NH_3(g)$	$H_2O(l)$
Liquid in a liquid	Vinegar	$HC_2H_3O_2(l)$	$H_2O(l)$
Solid in a liquid	Seawater	$NaCl(s)$	$H_2O(l)$
	Tincture of iodine	$I_2(s)$	$C_2H_5OH(l)$
Solid Solutions			
Solid in a solid	Brass	$Zn(s)$	$Cu(s)$
	Steel	$C(s)$	$Fe(s)$

Water as a Solvent

Water is one of the most common solvents in nature. In the H_2O molecule, an oxygen atom shares electrons with two hydrogen atoms. Because oxygen is much more electronegative than hydrogen, the O—H bonds are polar. In each polar bond, the oxygen atom has a partial negative (δ^-) charge and the hydrogen atom has a partial positive (δ^+) charge. Because the shape of a water molecule is bent, not linear, its dipoles do not cancel out. Thus, water is polar, and is a *polar solvent*.

Attractive forces known as *hydrogen bonds* occur between molecules where partially positive hydrogen atoms are attracted to the partially negative atoms F, O, or N. As seen in the diagram, the hydrogen bonds are shown as a series of dots. Although hydrogen bonds are much weaker than covalent or ionic bonds, there are many of them linking water molecules together. Hydrogen bonds are important in the properties of biological compounds such as proteins, carbohydrates, and DNA.

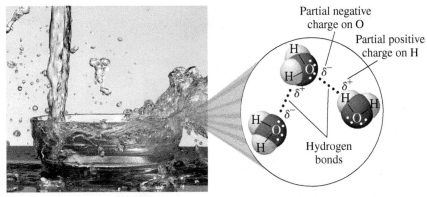

In water, hydrogen bonds form between an oxygen atom in one water molecule and the hydrogen atom in another.

 # Chemistry Link to Health
Water in the Body

The average adult is about 60% water by mass, and the average infant about 75%. About 60% of the body's water is contained within the cells as intracellular fluids; the other 40% makes up extracellular fluids, which include the interstitial fluid in tissue and the plasma in the blood. These external fluids carry nutrients and waste materials between the cells and the circulatory system.

Typical water gain and loss during 24 hours

Water Gain	
Liquid	1000 mL
Food	1200 mL
Metabolism	300 mL
Total	2500 mL

Water Loss	
Urine	1500 mL
Perspiration	300 mL
Breath	600 mL
Feces	100 mL
Total	2500 mL

The water lost from the body is replaced by the intake of fluids.

Every day you lose between 1500 and 3000 mL of water from the kidneys as urine, from the skin as perspiration, from the lungs as you exhale, and from the gastrointestinal tract. Serious dehydration can occur in an adult if there is a 10% net loss in total body fluid; a 20% loss of fluid can be fatal. An infant suffers severe dehydration with only a 5 to 10% loss in body fluid.

Water loss is continually replaced by the liquids and foods in the diet and from metabolic processes that produce water in the cells of the body. Table 9.2 lists the percentage by mass of water contained in some foods.

TABLE 9.2 Percentage of Water in Some Foods

Food	Water (% by mass)	Food	Water (% by mass)
Vegetables		**Meats/Fish**	
Carrot	88	Chicken, cooked	71
Celery	94	Hamburger, broiled	60
Cucumber	96	Salmon	71
Tomato	94		
Fruits		**Milk Products**	
Apple	85	Cottage cheese	78
Cantaloupe	91	Milk, whole	87
Orange	86	Yogurt	88
Strawberry	90		
Watermelon	93		

Formation of Solutions

The interactions between solute and solvent will determine whether a solution will form. Initially, energy is needed to separate the particles in the solute and the solvent particles. Then energy is released as solute particles move between the solvent particles to form a solution. However, there must be attractions between the solute and the solvent particles to provide the energy for the initial separation. These attractions occur when the solute and the solvent have similar polarities. The expression "like dissolves like" is a way of saying that the polarities of a solute and a solvent must be similar in order for a solution to form (see Figure 9.2). In the absence of attractions between a solute and a solvent, there is insufficient energy to form a solution (see Table 9.3).

Explore Your World

Like Dissolves Like

Obtain small samples of vegetable oil, water, vinegar, salt, and sugar. Then combine and mix the substances as listed in **a** through **e**.

a. oil and water
b. water and vinegar
c. salt and water
d. sugar and water
e. salt and oil

Questions

1. Which of the mixtures formed a solution?
2. Which of the mixtures did not form a solution?
3. Why do some mixtures form solutions, but others do not?

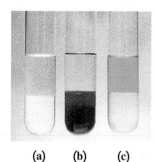

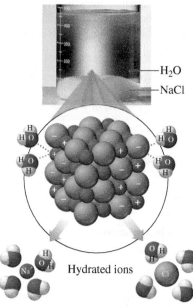

FIGURE 9.3 ▶ Ions on the surface of a crystal of NaCl dissolve in water as they are attracted to the polar water molecules that pull the ions into solution and surround them.

Q What helps keep Na^+ and Cl^- ions in solution?

FIGURE 9.2 ▶ Like dissolves like. In each test tube, the lower layer is CH_2Cl_2 (more dense), and the upper layer is water (less dense).
(a) CH_2Cl_2 is nonpolar and water is polar; the two layers do not mix. **(b)** The nonpolar solute I_2 (purple) is soluble in the nonpolar solvent CH_2Cl_2. **(c)** The ionic solute $Ni(NO_3)_2$ (green) is soluble in the polar solvent water.

Q In which layer would polar molecules of sucrose ($C_{12}H_{22}O_{11}$) be soluble?

(a)   (b)   (c)

TABLE 9.3 Possible Combinations of Solutes and Solvents

Solutions Will Form		Solutions Will Not Form	
Solute	Solvent	Solute	Solvent
Polar	Polar	Polar	Nonpolar
Nonpolar	Nonpolar	Nonpolar	Polar

Solutions with Ionic and Polar Solutes

In ionic solutes such as sodium chloride, NaCl, there are strong ionic bonds between positively charged Na^+ ions and negatively charged Cl^- ions. In water, a polar solvent, the hydrogen bonds provide strong solvent–solvent attractions. When NaCl crystals are placed in water, partially negative oxygen atoms in water molecules attract positive Na^+ ions, and the partially positive hydrogen atoms in other water molecules attract negative Cl^- ions (see Figure 9.3). As soon as the Na^+ ions and the Cl^- ions form a solution, they undergo **hydration** as water molecules surround each ion. Hydration of the ions diminishes their attraction to other ions and keeps them in solution.

In the equation for the formation of the NaCl solution, the solid and aqueous NaCl are shown with the formula H_2O over the arrow, which indicates that water is needed for the dissociation process but is not a reactant.

$$NaCl(s) \xrightarrow[\text{Dissociation}]{H_2O} Na^+(aq) + Cl^-(aq)$$

In another example, we find that a polar molecular compound such as methanol, CH_3-OH, is soluble in water because methanol has a polar $-OH$ group that forms hydrogen bonds with water (see Figure 9.4). Polar solutes require polar solvents for a solution to form.

Solutions with Nonpolar Solutes

Compounds containing nonpolar molecules, such as iodine (I_2), oil, or grease, do not dissolve in water because there are essentially no attractions between the particles of a nonpolar solute and the polar solvent. Nonpolar solutes require nonpolar solvents for a solution to form.

Methanol (CH_3-OH) solute

Water solvent

Methanol–water solution with hydrogen bonding

FIGURE 9.4 ▶ Molecules of methanol, CH_3-OH, form hydrogen bonds with polar water molecules to form a methanol–water solution.

Q Why are there attractions between the solute methanol and the solvent water?

QUESTIONS AND PROBLEMS

9.1 Solutions

LEARNING GOAL Identify the solute and solvent in a solution; describe the formation of a solution.

9.1 Identify the solute and the solvent in each solution composed of the following:
   a. 10.0 g of NaCl and 100.0 g of H_2O
   b. 50.0 mL of ethanol, C_2H_5OH, and 10.0 mL of H_2O
   c. 0.20 L of O_2 and 0.80 L of N_2

9.2 Identify the solute and the solvent in each solution composed of the following:
   a. 10.0 mL of acetic acid and 200. mL of water
   b. 100.0 mL of water and 5.0 g of sugar
   c. 1.0 g of Br_2 and 50.0 mL of methylene chloride(l)

9.3 Describe the formation of an aqueous KI solution, when solid KI dissolves in water.

9.4 Describe the formation of an aqueous LiBr solution, when solid LiBr dissolves in water.

℞ Clinical Applications

9.5 Water is a polar solvent and carbon tetrachloride (CCl_4) is a nonpolar solvent. In which solvent is each of the following, which is found or used in the body, more likely to be soluble?
   a. $CaCO_3$ (calcium supplement), ionic
   b. retinol (vitamin A), nonpolar
   c. sucrose (table sugar), polar
   d. cholesterol (lipid), nonpolar

9.6 Water is a polar solvent and hexane is a nonpolar solvent. In which solvent is each of the following, which is found or used in the body, more likely to be soluble?
   a. vegetable oil, nonpolar
   b. oleic acid (lipid), nonpolar
   c. niacin (vitamin B_3), polar
   d. $FeSO_4$ (iron supplement), ionic

9.2 Electrolytes and Nonelectrolytes

Solutes can be classified by their ability to conduct an electrical current. When **electrolytes** dissolve in water, the process of *dissociation* separates them into ions forming solutions that conduct electricity. When **nonelectrolytes** dissolve in water, they do not separate into ions and their solutions do not conduct electricity.

To test solutions for the presence of ions, we can use an apparatus that consists of a battery and a pair of electrodes connected by wires to a light bulb. The light bulb glows when electricity can flow, which can only happen when electrolytes provide ions that move between the electrodes to complete the circuit.

Types of Electrolytes

Electrolytes can be further classified as *strong electrolytes* or *weak electrolytes*. For a **strong electrolyte**, such as sodium chloride (NaCl), there is 100% dissociation of the solute into ions. When the electrodes from the light bulb apparatus are placed in the NaCl solution, the light bulb glows very brightly.

In an equation for dissociation of a compound in water, the charges must balance. For example, magnesium nitrate dissociates to give one magnesium ion for every two nitrate ions. However, only the ionic bonds between Mg^{2+} and NO_3^- are broken, not the covalent bonds within the polyatomic ion. The equation for the dissociation of $Mg(NO_3)_2$ is written as follows:

$$Mg(NO_3)_2(s) \xrightarrow[\text{Dissociation}]{H_2O} Mg^{2+}(aq) + 2NO_3^-(aq)$$

A **weak electrolyte** is a compound that dissolves in water mostly as molecules. Only a few of the dissolved solute molecules undergo *dissociation*, producing a small number of ions in solution. Thus solutions of weak electrolytes do not conduct electrical current as well as solutions of strong electrolytes. When the electrodes are placed in a solution of a weak electrolyte, the glow of the light bulb is very dim. In an aqueous solution of the weak electrolyte HF, a few HF molecules dissociate to produce H^+ and F^- ions. As more H^+ and F^- ions form, some recombine to give HF molecules. These forward and reverse reactions of molecules to ions and back again are indicated by two arrows between reactant and products that point in opposite directions:

$$HF(aq) \underset{\text{Recombination}}{\overset{\text{Dissociation}}{\rightleftharpoons}} H^+(aq) + F^-(aq)$$

LEARNING GOAL

Identify solutes as electrolytes or nonelectrolytes.

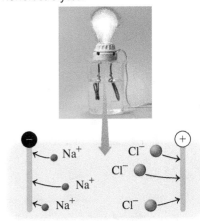

(a) Strong electrolyte

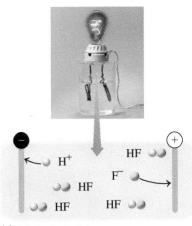

(b) Weak electrolyte

TABLE 9.4 Classification of Solutes in Aqueous Solutions

Type of Solute	In Solution	Type(s) of Particles in Solution	Conducts Electricity?	Examples
Strong electrolyte	Dissociates completely	Ions only	Yes	Ionic compounds such as NaCl, KBr, $MgCl_2$, $NaNO_3$; bases such as NaOH, KOH; acids such as HCl, HBr, HI, HNO_3, $HClO_4$, H_2SO_4
Weak electrolyte	Ionizes partially	Mostly molecules and a few ions	Weakly	HF, H_2O, NH_3, $HC_2H_3O_2$ (acetic acid)
Nonelectrolyte	No ionization	Molecules only	No	Carbon compounds such as CH_3OH (methanol), C_2H_5OH (ethanol), $C_{12}H_{22}O_{11}$ (sucrose), CH_4N_2O (urea)

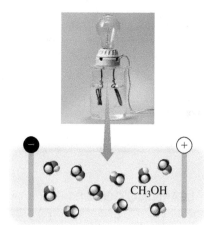

(c) Nonelectrolyte

A nonelectrolyte such as methanol (CH_3OH) dissolves in water only as molecules, which do not ionize. When electrodes of the light bulb apparatus are placed in a solution of a nonelectrolyte, the light bulb does not glow, because the solution does not contain ions and cannot conduct electricity.

$$CH_3OH(l) \xrightarrow{H_2O} CH_3OH(aq)$$

Table 9.4 summarizes the classification of solutes in aqueous solutions.

▶ **SAMPLE PROBLEM 9.1 Solutions of Electrolytes and Nonelectrolytes**

Indicate whether solutions of each of the following contain only ions, only molecules, or mostly molecules and a few ions. Write the equation for the formation of a solution for each of the following:

a. $Na_2SO_4(s)$, a strong electrolyte
b. sucrose, $C_{12}H_{22}O_{11}(s)$, a nonelectrolyte
c. acetic acid, $HC_2H_3O_2(l)$, a weak electrolyte

SOLUTION

a. An aqueous solution of $Na_2SO_4(s)$ contains only the ions Na^+ and SO_4^{2-}.

$$Na_2SO_4(s) \xrightarrow{H_2O} 2Na^+(aq) + SO_4^{2-}(aq)$$

b. A nonelectrolyte such as sucrose, $C_{12}H_{22}O_{11}(s)$, produces only molecules when it dissolves in water.

$$C_{12}H_{22}O_{11}(s) \xrightarrow{H_2O} C_{12}H_{22}O_{11}(aq)$$

c. A weak electrolyte such as $HC_2H_3O_2(l)$ produces mostly molecules and a few ions when it dissolves in water.

$$HC_2H_3O_2(l) \underset{}{\overset{H_2O}{\rightleftarrows}} H^+(aq) + C_2H_3O_2^-(aq)$$

STUDY CHECK 9.1

Boric acid, $H_3BO_3(s)$, is a weak electrolyte. Would you expect a boric acid solution to contain only ions, only molecules, or mostly molecules and a few ions?

ANSWER

A solution of a weak electrolyte would contain mostly molecules and a few ions.

Equivalents

Body fluids and intravenous (IV) solutions contain a mixture of electrolytes, such as Na^+, Cl^-, K^+, and Ca^{2+}. We measure each individual ion in terms of an **equivalent (Eq)**, which is the amount of that ion equal to 1 mole of positive or negative electrical charge. For example, 1 mole of Na^+ ions and 1 mole of Cl^- ions are each 1 equivalent because they each contain 1 mole of charge. For an ion with a charge of 2+ or 2-, there are 2 equivalents for each mole. Some examples of ions and equivalents are shown in Table 9.5.

TABLE 9.5 Equivalents of Electrolytes in Clinical Intravenous (IV) Solutions

Ion	Ionic Charge	Number of Equivalents in 1 Mole
Na^+, K^+, Li^+, NH_4^+	1+	1 Eq
Ca^{2+}, Mg^{2+}	2+	2 Eq
Fe^{3+}	3+	3 Eq
Cl^-, $C_2H_3O_2^-$ (acetate), $H_2PO_4^-$, $C_3H_5O_3^-$ (lactate)	1−	1 Eq
CO_3^{2-}, HPO_4^{2-}	2−	2 Eq
PO_4^{3-}, $C_6H_5O_7^{3-}$ (citrate)	3−	3 Eq

In any solution, the charge of the positive ions is always balanced by the charge of the negative ions. The concentrations of electrolytes in intravenous fluids are expressed in milliequivalents per liter (mEq/L); 1 Eq = 1000 mEq. For example, a solution containing 25 mEq/L of Na^+ and 4 mEq/L of K^+ has a total positive charge of 29 mEq/L. If Cl^- is the only anion, its concentration must be 29 mEq/L.

► **SAMPLE PROBLEM 9.2 Electrolyte Concentration**

The laboratory tests for a patient indicate a blood calcium level of 8.8 mEq/L.

a. How many moles of calcium ion are in 0.50 L of blood?
b. If chloride ion is the only other ion present, what is its concentration in mEq/L?

SOLUTION

a. Using the volume and the electrolyte concentration in mEq/L, we can find the number of equivalents in 0.50 L of blood.

$$0.50 \, \cancel{L} \times \frac{8.8 \, \cancel{mEq \, Ca^{2+}}}{1 \, \cancel{L}} \times \frac{1 \, Eq \, Ca^{2+}}{1000 \, \cancel{mEq \, Ca^{2+}}} = 0.0044 \, Eq \, of \, Ca^{2+}$$

We can then convert equivalents to moles (for Ca^{2+} there are 2 Eq per mole).

$$0.0044 \, \cancel{Eq \, Ca^{2+}} \times \frac{1 \, mole \, Ca^{2+}}{2 \, \cancel{Eq \, Ca^{2+}}} = 0.0022 \, mole \, of \, Ca^{2+}$$

b. If the concentration of Ca^{2+} is 8.8 mEq/L, then the concentration of Cl^- must be 8.8 mEq/L to balance the charge.

STUDY CHECK 9.2

A lactated Ringer's solution for intravenous fluid replacement contains 109 mEq of Cl^- per liter of solution. If a patient received 1250 mL of Ringer's solution, how many moles of chloride ion were given?

ANSWER

0.136 mole of Cl^-

Chemistry Link to Health
Electrolytes in Body Fluids

Electrolytes in the body play an important role in maintaining the proper function of the cells and organs in the body. Typically, the electrolytes sodium, potassium, chloride, and bicarbonate are measured in a blood test. Sodium ions regulate the water content in the body and are important in carrying electrical impulses through the nervous system. Potassium ions are also involved in the transmission of electrical impulses and play a role in the maintenance of a regular heartbeat. Chloride ions balance the charges of the positive ions and also control the balance of fluids in the body. Bicarbonate is important in maintaining the proper pH of the blood. Sometimes when vomiting, diarrhea, or sweating is excessive, the concentrations of certain electrolytes may decrease. Then fluids such as Pedialyte may be given to return electrolyte levels to normal.

An intravenous solution is used to replace electrolytes in the body.

The concentrations of electrolytes present in body fluids and in intravenous fluids given to a patient are often expressed in milliequivalents per liter (mEq/L) of solution. For example, one liter of Pedialyte contains the following electrolytes: Na^+ 45 mEq, Cl^- 35 mEq, K^+ 20 mEq, and citrate^{3-} 30 mEq.

Table 9.6 gives the concentrations of some typical electrolytes in blood plasma and various types of solutions. There is a charge balance because the total number of positive charges is equal to the total number of negative charges. The use of a specific intravenous solution depends on the nutritional, electrolyte, and fluid needs of the individual patient.

TABLE 9.6 Electrolytes in Blood Plasma and Selected Intravenous Solutions

		Normal Concentrations of Ions (mEq/L)			
	Blood Plasma	Normal Saline 0.9% NaCl	Lactated Ringer's Solution	Maintenance Solution	Replacement Solution (extracellular)
Purpose		Replaces fluid loss	Hydration	Maintains electrolytes and fluids	Replaces electrolytes
Cations					
Na^+	135–145	154	130	40	140
K^+	3.5–5.5		4	35	10
Ca^{2+}	4.5–5.5		3		5
Mg^{2+}	1.5–3.0				3
Total		154	137	75	158
Anions					
Acetate$^-$					47
Cl^-	95–105	154	109	40	103
HCO_3^-	22–28				
Lactate$^-$			28	20	
HPO_4^{2-}	1.8–2.3			15	
Citrate^{3-}					8
Total		154	137	75	158

QUESTIONS AND PROBLEMS

9.2 Electrolytes and Nonelectrolytes

LEARNING GOAL Identify solutes as electrolytes or nonelectrolytes.

9.7   KF is a strong electrolyte, and HF is a weak electrolyte. How is the solution of KF different from that of HF?

9.8   NaOH is a strong electrolyte, and CH_3OH is a nonelectrolyte. How is the solution of NaOH different from that of CH_3OH?

9.9   Write a balanced equation for the dissociation of each of the following strong electrolytes in water:
a. KCl   b. $CaCl_2$
c. K_3PO_4 d. $Fe(NO_3)_3$

9.10   Write a balanced equation for the dissociation of each of the following strong electrolytes in water:
a. LiBr   b. $NaNO_3$
c. $CuCl_2$ d. K_2CO_3

9.11   Indicate whether aqueous solutions of each of the following solutes contain only ions, only molecules, or mostly molecules and a few ions:
a. acetic acid, $HC_2H_3O_2$, a weak electrolyte
b. NaBr, a strong electrolyte
c. fructose, $C_6H_{12}O_6$, a nonelectrolyte

9.12   Indicate whether aqueous solutions of each of the following solutes contain only ions, only molecules, or mostly molecules and a few ions:
a. NH_4Cl, a strong electrolyte
b. ethanol, C_2H_5OH, a nonelectrolyte
c. HCN, hydrocyanic acid, a weak electrolyte

9.13 Classify the solute represented in each of the following equations as a strong, weak, or nonelectrolyte:

a. $K_2SO_4(s) \xrightarrow{H_2O} 2K^+(aq) + SO_4^{2-}(aq)$

b. $NH_3(g) + H_2O(l) \rightleftharpoons NH_4^+(aq) + OH^-(aq)$

c. $C_6H_{12}O_6(s) \xrightarrow{H_2O} C_6H_{12}O_6(aq)$

9.14 Classify the solute represented in each of the following equations as a strong, weak, or nonelectrolyte:

a. $CH_3OH(l) \xrightarrow{H_2O} CH_3OH(aq)$

b. $MgCl_2(s) \xrightarrow{H_2O} Mg^{2+}(aq) + 2Cl^-(aq)$

c. $HClO(aq) \rightleftharpoons H^+(aq) + ClO^-(aq)$

9.15 Calculate the number of equivalents in each of the following:
a. 1 mole of K^+　　b. 2 moles of OH^-
c. 1 mole of Ca^{2+}　　d. 3 moles of CO_3^{2-}

9.16 Calculate the number of equivalents in each of the following:
a. 1 mole of Mg^{2+}　　b. 0.5 mole of H^+
c. 4 moles of Cl^-　　d. 2 moles of Fe^{3+}

Clinical Applications

9.17 An intravenous saline solution contains 154 mEq/L each of Na^+ and Cl^-. How many moles each of Na^+ and Cl^- are in 1.00 L of the saline solution?

9.18 An intravenous solution to replace potassium loss contains 40. mEq/L each of K^+ and Cl^-. How many moles each of K^+ and Cl^- are in 1.5 L of the solution?

9.19 An intravenous solution contains 40. mEq/L of Cl^- and 15 mEq/L of HPO_4^{2-}. If Na^+ is the only cation in the solution, what is the Na^+ concentration, in milliequivalents per liter?

9.20 A Ringer's solution contains the following concentrations (mEq/L) of cations: Na^+ 147, K^+ 4, and Ca^{2+} 4. If Cl^- is the only anion in the solution, what is the Cl^- concentration, in milliequivalents per liter?

9.21 When Amanda's blood was tested, the chloride level was 0.45 g/dL.
a. What is this value in milliequivalents per liter?
b. According to Table 9.6, is this value above, below, or within the normal range?

9.22 After dialysis, the level of magnesium in Amanda's blood was 0.0026 g/dL.
a. What is this value in milliequivalents per liter?
b. According to Table 9.6, is this value above, below, or within the normal range?

9.3 Solubility

The term *solubility* is used to describe the amount of a solute that can dissolve in a given amount of solvent. Many factors, such as the type of solute, the type of solvent, and the temperature, affect the solubility of a solute. **Solubility**, usually expressed in grams of solute in 100 g of solvent, is the maximum amount of solute that can be dissolved at a certain temperature. If a solute readily dissolves when added to the solvent, the solution does not contain the maximum amount of solute. We call this solution an **unsaturated solution**.

A solution that contains all the solute that can dissolve is a **saturated solution**. When a solution is saturated, the rate at which the solute dissolves becomes equal to the rate at which solid forms, a process known as *recrystallization*. Then there is no further change in the amount of dissolved solute in solution.

LEARNING GOAL

Define solubility; distinguish between an unsaturated and a saturated solution. Identify an ionic compound as soluble or insoluble.

$$\text{Solute + solvent} \underset{\text{Solute recrystallizes}}{\overset{\text{Solute dissolves}}{\rightleftharpoons}} \text{saturated solution}$$

We can prepare a saturated solution by adding an amount of solute greater than that needed to reach solubility. Stirring the solution will dissolve the maximum amount of solute and leave the excess on the bottom of the container. Once we have a saturated solution, the addition of more solute will only increase the amount of undissolved solute.

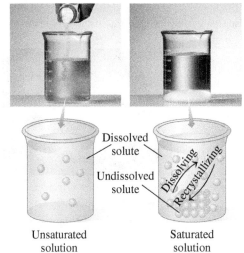

Dissolved solute

Undissolved solute

Unsaturated solution

Saturated solution

Additional solute can dissolve in an unsaturated solution, but not in a saturated solution.

▶SAMPLE PROBLEM 9.3 **Saturated Solutions**

At 20 °C, the solubility of KCl is 34 g/100 g of H_2O. In the laboratory, a student mixes 75 g of KCl with 200. g of H_2O at a temperature of 20 °C.

a. How much of the KCl will dissolve?
b. Is the solution saturated or unsaturated?
c. What is the mass, in grams, of any solid KCl left undissolved on the bottom of the container?

SOLUTION

a. At 20 °C, KCl has a solubility of 34 g of KCl in 100 g of water. Using the solubility as a conversion factor, we can calculate the maximum amount of KCl that can dissolve in 200. g of water as follows:

$$200. \text{ g } H_2O \times \frac{34 \text{ g KCl}}{100 \text{ g } H_2O} = 68 \text{ g of KCl}$$

b. Because 75 g of KCl exceeds the maximum amount (68 g) that can dissolve in 200. g of water, the KCl solution is saturated.

c. If we add 75 g of KCl to 200. g of water and only 68 g of KCl can dissolve, there is 7 g (75 g − 68 g) of solid (undissolved) KCl on the bottom of the container.

STUDY CHECK 9.3

At 40 °C, the solubility of KNO_3 is 65 g/100 g of H_2O. How many grams of KNO_3 will dissolve in 120 g of H_2O at 40 °C?

ANSWER

78 g of KNO_3

Chemistry Link to Health

Gout and Kidney Stones: A Problem of Saturation in Body Fluids

The conditions of gout and kidney stones involve compounds in the body that exceed their solubility levels and form solid products. Gout affects adults, primarily men, over the age of 40. Attacks of gout may occur when the concentration of uric acid in blood plasma exceeds its solubility, which is 7 mg/100 mL of plasma at 37 °C. Insoluble deposits of needle-like crystals of uric acid can form in the cartilage, tendons, and soft tissues where they cause painful gout attacks. They may also form in the tissues of the kidneys, where they can cause renal damage. High levels of uric acid in the body can be caused by an increase in uric acid production, failure of the kidneys to remove uric acid, or a diet with an overabundance of foods containing purines, which are metabolized to uric acid in the body. Foods in the diet that contribute to high levels of uric acid include certain meats, sardines, mushrooms, asparagus, and beans. Drinking alcoholic beverages may also significantly increase uric acid levels and bring about gout attacks.

Treatment for gout involves diet changes and drugs. Medications, such as probenecid, which helps the kidneys eliminate uric acid, or allopurinol, which blocks the production of uric acid by the body may be useful.

Kidney stones are solid materials that form in the urinary tract. Most kidney stones are composed of calcium phosphate and calcium oxalate, although they can be solid uric acid. Insufficient water intake and high levels of calcium, oxalate, and phosphate in the urine can lead to the formation of kidney stones. When a kidney stone passes through the urinary tract, it causes considerable pain and discomfort, necessitating the use of painkillers and surgery. Sometimes ultrasound is used to break up kidney stones. Persons prone to kidney stones are advised to drink six to eight glasses of water every day to prevent saturation levels of minerals in the urine.

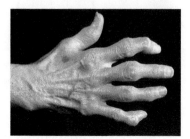

Gout occurs when uric acid exceeds its solubility.

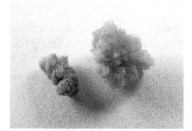

Kidney stones form when calcium phosphate exceeds its solubility.

Effect of Temperature on Solubility

The solubility of most solids is greater as temperature increases, which means that solutions usually contain more dissolved solute at higher temperature. A few substances show little change in solubility at higher temperatures, and a few are less soluble (see Figure 9.5). For example, when you add sugar to iced tea, some undissolved sugar may form on the bottom of the glass. But if you add sugar to hot tea, many teaspoons of sugar are needed before solid sugar appears. Hot tea dissolves more sugar than does cold tea because the solubility of sugar is much greater at a higher temperature.

When a saturated solution is carefully cooled, it becomes a *supersaturated solution* because it contains more solute than the solubility allows. Such a solution is unstable, and if the solution is agitated or if a solute crystal is added, the excess solute will recrystallize to give a saturated solution again.

Conversely, the solubility of a gas in water decreases as the temperature increases. At higher temperatures, more gas molecules have the energy to escape from the solution. Perhaps you have observed the bubbles escaping from a cold carbonated soft drink as it warms. At high temperatures, bottles containing carbonated solutions may burst as more gas molecules leave the solution and increase the gas pressure inside the bottle. Biologists have found that increased temperatures in rivers and lakes cause the amount of dissolved oxygen to decrease until the warm water can no longer support a biological community. Electricity-generating plants are required to have their own ponds to use with their cooling towers to lessen the threat of thermal pollution in surrounding waterways.

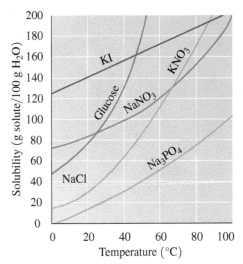

FIGURE 9.5 ▶ In water, most common solids are more soluble as the temperature increases.

Compare the solubility of $NaNO_3$ at 20 °C and 60 °C.

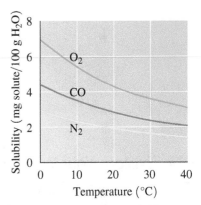

In water, gases are less soluble as the temperature increases.

Explore Your World

Preparing Rock Candy

Need: one cup of water, three cups of granulated sugar, clean narrow glass or jar, wooden stick (skewer) or thick string that is the height of the glass, pencil, and food coloring (optional)

Process:
1. Place the water and two cups of sugar in a pan and begin heating and stirring. The sugar should all dissolve. Continue heating, but not boiling, adding small amounts of the remaining sugar and

stirring thoroughly each time, until some of the sugar no longer dissolves. There may be some sugar crystals on the bottom of the pan. Carefully pour the sugar solution into the glass or jar. Add two to three drops of food coloring, if desired.
2. Wet the wooden stick and roll it in granulated sugar to provide crystals for the sugar solution to attach to. Place the stick in the sugar solution. If using string, tape the string to a pencil so it will hang slightly above the bottom of the glass. Wet the lower half of the string, roll it in the granulated sugar, and place the pencil across the top of the glass with the string in the sugar solution. Place the glass and wooden stick or string in a place where it will not be disturbed. You should see sugar crystals grow over the next several days.

Rock candy can be made from a saturated solution of sugar (sucrose).

Questions
1. Why did more sugar dissolve as the solution was heated?
2. How did you know when you obtained a saturated solution?
3. Why did you see crystals forming on the stick or string over time?

Henry's Law

Henry's law states that the solubility of gas in a liquid is directly related to the pressure of that gas above the liquid. At higher pressures, there are more gas molecules available to enter and dissolve in the liquid. A can of soda is carbonated by using CO_2 gas at high pressure to increase the solubility of the CO_2 in the beverage. When you open the can at atmospheric pressure, the pressure on the CO_2 drops, which decreases the solubility of CO_2. As a result, bubbles of CO_2 rapidly escape from the solution. The burst of bubbles is even more noticeable when you open a warm can of soda.

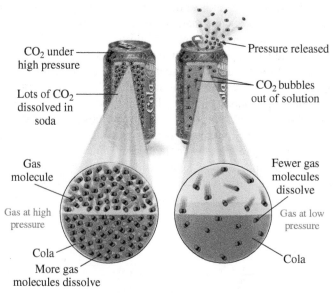

CO_2 under high pressure

Pressure released

Lots of CO_2 dissolved in soda

CO_2 bubbles out of solution

Gas molecule

Fewer gas molecules dissolve

Gas at high pressure

Gas at low pressure

Cola

Cola

More gas molecules dissolve

When the pressure of a gas above a solution decreases, the solubility of that gas in the solution also decreases.

Soluble and Insoluble Ionic Compounds

In our discussion up to now, we have considered ionic compounds that dissolve in water. However, some ionic compounds do not dissociate into ions and remain as solids even in contact with water. The **solubility rules** give some guidelines about the solubility of ionic compounds in water.

Ionic compounds that are soluble in water typically contain at least one of the ions in Table 9.7. *Only an ionic compound containing a soluble cation or anion will dissolve in water.* Most ionic compounds containing Cl^- are soluble, but $AgCl$, $PbCl_2$, and Hg_2Cl_2 are insoluble. Similarly, most ionic compounds containing SO_4^{2-} are soluble, but a few are insoluble. Most other ionic compounds are insoluble (see Figure 9.6). In an insoluble ionic compound, the ionic bonds between its positive and negative ions are too strong for the polar water molecules to break. We can use the solubility rules to predict whether a solid ionic compound would be soluble or not. Table 9.8 illustrates the use of these rules.

TABLE 9.7 Solubility Rules for Ionic Compounds in Water

An ionic compound is soluble in water if it contains one of the following:
Positive Ions: Li^+, Na^+, K^+, Rb^+, Cs^+, NH_4^+
Negative Ions: NO_3^-, $C_2H_3O_2^-$
Cl^-, Br^-, I^- except when combined with Ag^+, Pb^{2+}, or Hg_2^{2+}
SO_4^{2-} except when combined with Ba^{2+}, Pb^{2+}, Ca^{2+}, Sr^{2+}, or Hg_2^{2+}
Ionic compounds that do not contain at least one of these ions are usually insoluble.

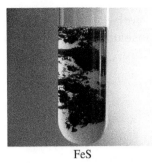

| CdS | FeS | PbI$_2$ | Ni(OH)$_2$ |

FIGURE 9.6 ▶ If an ionic compound contains a combination of a cation and an anion that are not soluble, that ionic compound is insoluble. For example, combinations of cadmium and sulfide, iron and sulfide, lead and iodide, and nickel and hydroxide do not contain any soluble ions. Thus, they form insoluble ionic compounds.

◎ Why are each of these ionic compounds insoluble in water?

TABLE 9.8 Using Solubility Rules

Ionic Compound	Solubility in Water	Reasoning
K$_2$S	Soluble	Contains K$^+$
Ca(NO$_3$)$_2$	Soluble	Contains NO$_3^-$
PbCl$_2$	Insoluble	Is an insoluble chloride
NaOH	Soluble	Contains Na$^+$
AlPO$_4$	Insoluble	Contains no soluble ions

⚛ CORE CHEMISTRY SKILL

Using Solubility Rules

In medicine, insoluble BaSO$_4$ is used as an opaque substance to enhance X-rays of the gastrointestinal tract. BaSO$_4$ is so insoluble that it does not dissolve in gastric fluids (see Figure 9.7). Other ionic barium compounds cannot be used because they would dissolve in water, releasing Ba^{2+} which is poisonous.

▶**SAMPLE PROBLEM 9.4 Soluble and Insoluble Ionic Compounds**

Predict whether each of the following ionic compounds is soluble in water and explain why:

a. Na$_3$PO$_4$ **b.** CaCO$_3$

SOLUTION

a. The ionic compound Na$_3$PO$_4$ is soluble in water because any compound that contains Na$^+$ is soluble.
b. The ionic compound CaCO$_3$ is not soluble. The compound does not contain a soluble positive ion, which means that ionic compound containing Ca^{2+} and CO$_3^{2-}$ is not soluble.

STUDY CHECK 9.4

In some electrolyte drinks, MgCl$_2$ is added to provide magnesium. Why would you expect MgCl$_2$ to be soluble in water?

ANSWER

MgCl$_2$ is soluble in water because ionic compounds that contain chloride are soluble unless they contain Ag$^+$, Pb^{2+}, or Hg$_2^{2+}$.

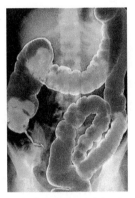

FIGURE 9.7 ▶ A barium sulfate-enhanced X-ray of the abdomen shows the lower gastrointestinal (GI) tract.

◎ Is BaSO$_4$ a soluble or an insoluble substance?

Formation of a Solid

We can use solubility rules to predict whether a solid, called a *precipitate*, forms when two solutions containing soluble reactants are mixed as shown in Sample Problem 9.5.

> SAMPLE PROBLEM 9.5 Writing Equations for the Formation of an
> Insoluble Ionic Compound

When solutions of NaCl and $AgNO_3$ are mixed, a white solid forms. Write the ionic and net ionic equations for the reaction.

SOLUTION

STEP **1** Write the ions of the reactants.

Reactants
(initial combinations)

$$Ag^+(aq) + NO_3^-(aq)$$

$$Na^+(aq) + Cl^-(aq)$$

STEP **2** Write the combinations of ions and determine if any are insoluble. When we look at the ions of each solution, we see that the combination of Ag^+ and Cl^- forms an insoluble ionic compound.

Mixture (new combinations)	Product	Soluble
$Ag^+(aq) + Cl^-(aq)$	AgCl	No
$Na^+(aq) + NO_3^-(aq)$	$NaNO_3$	Yes

STEP **3** Write the ionic equation including any solid. In the *ionic equation*, we show all the ions of the reactants. The products include the solid AgCl that forms along with the remaining ions Na^+ and NO_3^-.

$$Ag^+(aq) + NO_3^-(aq) + Na^+(aq) + Cl^-(aq) \longrightarrow AgCl(s) + Na^+(aq) + NO_3^-(aq)$$

STEP **4** Write the net ionic equation. To write a *net ionic equation*, we remove the Na^+ and NO_3^- ions, known as *spectator ions*, which are unchanged. This leaves only the ions and solid of the chemical reaction.

$$Ag^+(aq) + \underbrace{NO_3^-(aq) + Na^+(aq)}_{\text{Spectator ions}} + Cl^-(aq) \longrightarrow AgCl(s) + \underbrace{Na^+(aq) + NO_3^-(aq)}_{\text{Spectator ions}}$$

$$Ag^+(aq) + Cl^-(aq) \longrightarrow AgCl(s) \quad \text{Net ionic equation}$$

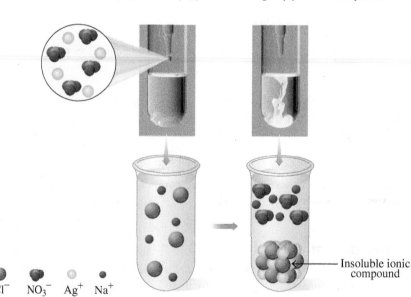

Cl⁻   NO₃⁻   Ag⁺   Na⁺

Insoluble ionic compound

Guide to Writing an Equation
for the Formation of an
Insoluble Ionic Compound

STEP **1**
Write the ions of the reactants.

STEP **2**
Write the combinations of ions
and determine if any are
insoluble.

STEP **3**
Write the ionic equation
including any solid.

STEP **4**
Write the net ionic equation.

Type of Equation				
Chemical	$AgNO_3(aq)$	$+ NaCl(aq)$	$\longrightarrow$	$AgCl(s) + NaNO_3(aq)$
Ionic	$Ag^+(aq) + NO_3^-(aq)$	$+ Na^+(aq) + Cl^-(aq)$	$\rightarrow$	$AgCl(s) + Na^+(aq) + NO_3^-(aq)$
Net Ionic	$Ag^+(aq)$	$+ Cl^-(aq)$	$\longrightarrow$	$AgCl(s)$

STUDY CHECK 9.5

Predict whether a solid might form in each of the following mixtures of solutions. If so, write the net ionic equation for the reaction.

a. $NH_4Cl(aq) + Ca(NO_3)_2(aq)$

b. $Pb(NO_3)_2(aq) + KCl(aq)$

ANSWER

a. No solid forms because the products, $NH_4NO_3(aq)$ and $CaCl_2(aq)$, are soluble.

b. $Pb^{2+}(aq) + 2Cl^-(aq) \longrightarrow PbCl_2(s)$

QUESTIONS AND PROBLEMS

9.3 Solubility

LEARNING GOAL Define solubility; distinguish between an unsaturated and a saturated solution. Identify an ionic compound as soluble or insoluble.

Use the following table for problems 9.23 to 9.26:

	Solubility (g/100 g H_2O)	
Substance	20 °C	50 °C
KCl	34	43
NaNO_3	88	110
$C_{12}H_{22}O_{11}$ (sugar)	204	260

9.23 Determine whether each of the following solutions will be saturated or unsaturated at 20 °C:
a. adding 25 g of KCl to 100. g of H_2O
b. adding 11 g of $NaNO_3$ to 25 g of H_2O
c. adding 400. g of sugar to 125 g of H_2O

9.24 Determine whether each of the following solutions will be saturated or unsaturated at 50 °C:
a. adding 25 g of KCl to 50. g of H_2O
b. adding 150. g of $NaNO_3$ to 75 g of H_2O
c. adding 80. g of sugar to 25 g of H_2O

9.25 A solution containing 80. g of KCl in 200. g of H_2O at 50 °C is cooled to 20 °C.
a. How many grams of KCl remain in solution at 20 °C?
b. How many grams of solid KCl crystallized after cooling?

9.26 A solution containing 80. g of $NaNO_3$ in 75 g of H_2O at 50 °C is cooled to 20 °C.
a. How many grams of $NaNO_3$ remain in solution at 20 °C?
b. How many grams of solid $NaNO_3$ crystallized after cooling?

9.27 Explain the following observations:
a. More sugar dissolves in hot tea than in iced tea.
b. Champagne in a warm room goes flat.
c. A warm can of soda has more spray when opened than a cold one.

9.28 Explain the following observations:
a. An open can of soda loses its "fizz" faster at room temperature than in the refrigerator.
b. Chlorine gas in tap water escapes as the sample warms to room temperature.
c. Less sugar dissolves in iced coffee than in hot coffee.

9.29 Predict whether each of the following ionic compounds is soluble in water:
a. LiCl **b.** AgCl **c.** $BaCO_3$ **d.** K_2O **e.** $Fe(NO_3)_3$

9.30 Predict whether each of the following ionic compounds is soluble in water:
a. PbS **b.** KI **c.** Na_2S **d.** Ag_2O **e.** $CaSO_4$

9.31 Determine whether a solid forms when solutions containing the following ionic compounds are mixed. If so, write the ionic equation and the net ionic equation.
a. $KCl(aq)$ and $Na_2S(aq)$ **b.** $AgNO_3(aq)$ and $K_2S(aq)$
c. $CaCl_2(aq)$ and $Na_2SO_4(aq)$ **d.** $CuCl_2(aq)$ and $Li_3PO_4(aq)$

9.32 Determine whether a solid forms when solutions containing the following ionic compounds are mixed. If so, write the ionic equation and the net ionic equation.
a. $Na_3PO_4(aq)$ and $AgNO_3(aq)$
b. $K_2SO_4(aq)$ and $Na_2CO_3(aq)$
c. $Pb(NO_3)_2(aq)$ and $Na_2CO_3(aq)$
d. $BaCl_2(aq)$ and $KOH(aq)$

9.4 Solution Concentrations and Reactions

The amount of solute dissolved in a certain amount of solution is called the **concentration** of the solution. We will look at ways to express a concentration as a ratio of a certain amount of solute in a given amount of solution. The amount of a solute may be expressed in units of grams, milliliters, or moles. The amount of a solution may be expressed in units of grams, milliliters, or liters.

$$\text{Concentration of a solution} = \frac{\text{amount of solute}}{\text{amount of solution}}$$

LEARNING GOAL

Calculate the concentration of a solute in a solution; use concentration units to calculate the amount of solute or solution. Given the volume and concentration of a solution, calculate the amount of another reactant or product in a reaction.

Add 8.00 g of KCl

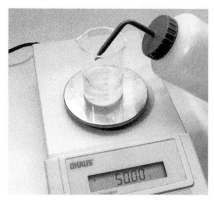

Add water until the
solution has a mass of 50.00 g

When water is added to 8.00 g of
KCl to form 50.00 g of a KCl
solution, the mass percent
concentration is 16.0% (m/m).

**Guide to Calculating
Solution Concentration**

STEP 1
State the given and needed
quantities.

STEP 2
Write the concentration
expression.

STEP 3
Substitute solute and solution
quantities into the expression
and calculate.

Mass Percent (m/m) Concentration

Mass percent (m/m) describes the mass of the solute in grams for exactly 100 g of solution. In the calculation of mass percent (m/m), the units of mass of the solute and solution must be the same. If the mass of the solute is given as grams, then the mass of the solution must also be grams. The mass of the solution is the sum of the mass of the solute and the mass of the solvent.

$$\text{Mass percent (m/m)} = \frac{\text{mass of solute (g)}}{\text{mass of solute (g)} + \text{mass of solvent (g)}} \times 100\%$$

$$= \frac{\text{mass of solute (g)}}{\text{mass of solution (g)}} \times 100\%$$

Suppose we prepared a solution by mixing 8.00 g of KCl (solute) with 42.00 g of water (solvent). Together, the mass of the solute and mass of solvent give the mass of the solution (8.00 g + 42.00 g = 50.00 g). Mass percent is calculated by substituting the mass of the solute and the mass of the solution into the mass percent expression.

$$\underbrace{\frac{8.00 \text{ g KCl}}{50.00 \text{ g solution}}}_{\underset{\text{Solute}\quad+\quad\text{Solvent}}{8.00 \text{ g KCl} + 42.00 \text{ g H}_2\text{O}}} \times 100\% = 16.0\% \text{ (m/m) KCl solution}$$

> **SAMPLE PROBLEM 9.6** Calculating Mass Percent (m/m) Concentration

What is the mass percent of NaOH in a solution prepared by dissolving 30.0 g of NaOH in 120.0 g of H_2O?

SOLUTION

STEP 1 State the given and needed quantities.

	Given	Need
ANALYZE THE PROBLEM	30.0 g of NaOH solute, 30.0 g NaOH + 120.0 g H_2O = 150.0 g of NaOH solution	mass percent (m/m)

STEP 2 Write the concentration expression.

$$\text{Mass percent (m/m)} = \frac{\text{grams of solute}}{\text{grams of solution}} \times 100\%$$

STEP 3 Substitute solute and solution quantities into the expression and calculate.

$$\text{Mass percent (m/m)} = \frac{30.0 \text{ g NaOH}}{150.0 \text{ g solution}} \times 100\%$$

$$= 20.0\% \text{ (m/m) NaOH solution}$$

STUDY CHECK 9.6

What is the mass percent (m/m) of NaCl in a solution made by dissolving 2.0 g of NaCl in 56.0 g of H_2O?

ANSWER

3.4% (m/m) NaCl solution

Volume Percent (v/v) Concentration

Because the volumes of liquids or gases are easily measured, the concentrations of their solutions are often expressed as **volume percent (v/v)**. The units of volume used in the ratio must be the same, for example, both in milliliters or both in liters.

$$\text{Volume percent (v/v)} = \frac{\text{volume of solute}}{\text{volume of solution}} \times 100\%$$

We interpret a volume percent as the volume of solute in exactly 100 mL of solution. On a bottle of extract of vanilla, a label that reads alcohol 35% (v/v) means 35 mL of ethanol solute in exactly 100 mL of vanilla solution.

The label indicates that vanilla extract contains 35% (v/v) alcohol.

▶ **SAMPLE PROBLEM 9.7** **Calculating Volume Percent (v/v) Concentration**

A bottle contains 59 mL of lemon extract solution. If the extract contains 49 mL of alcohol, what is the volume percent (v/v) of the alcohol in the solution?

SOLUTION

STEP 1 State the given and needed quantities.

ANALYZE THE PROBLEM	Given	Need
	49 mL of alcohol, 59 mL of solution	volume percent (v/v)

STEP 2 Write the concentration expression.

$$\text{Volume percent (v/v)} = \frac{\text{volume of solute}}{\text{volume of solution}} \times 100\%$$

STEP 3 Substitute solute and solution quantities into the expression and calculate.

$$\text{Volume percent (v/v)} = \frac{49 \text{ mL alcohol}}{59 \text{ mL solution}} \times 100\%$$
$$= 83\% \text{ (v/v) alcohol solution}$$

Lemon extract is a solution of lemon flavor and alcohol.

STUDY CHECK 9.7

What is the volume percent (v/v) of Br_2 in a solution prepared by dissolving 12 mL of liquid bromine (Br_2) in the solvent carbon tetrachloride (CCl_4) to make 250 mL of solution?

ANSWER

4.8% (v/v) Br_2 in CCl_4

⊛ **CORE CHEMISTRY SKILL**

Calculating Concentration

Mass/Volume Percent (m/v) Concentration

Mass/volume percent (m/v) describes the mass of the solute in grams for exactly 100 mL of solution. In the calculation of mass/volume percent, the unit of mass of the solute is grams and the unit of the solution volume is milliliters.

$$\text{Mass/volume percent (m/v)} = \frac{\text{grams of solute}}{\text{milliliters of solution}} \times 100\%$$

The mass/volume percent is widely used in hospitals and pharmacies for the preparation of intravenous solutions and medicines. For example, a 5% (m/v) glucose solution contains 5 g of glucose in 100 mL of solution. The volume of solution represents the combined volumes of the glucose and H_2O.

▶ **SAMPLE PROBLEM 9.8** **Calculating Mass/Volume Percent (m/v) Concentration**

A potassium iodide solution may be used in a diet that is low in iodine. A KI solution is prepared by dissolving 5.0 g of KI in enough water to give a final volume of 250 mL. What is the mass/volume percent (m/v) of the KI solution?

Water added to make a solution

250 mL

5.0 g of KI   250 mL of KI solution

SOLUTION

STEP 1 State the given and needed quantities.

ANALYZE THE PROBLEM	Given	Need
	5.0 g of KI solute,	mass/volume percent
	250 mL of KI solution	(m/v)

STEP 2 Write the concentration expression.

$$\text{Mass/volume percent (m/v)} = \frac{\text{mass of solute}}{\text{volume of solution}} \times 100\%$$

STEP 3 Substitute solute and solution quantities into the expression and calculate.

$$\text{Mass/volume percent (m/v)} = \frac{5.0 \text{ g KI}}{250 \text{ mL solution}} \times 100\%$$
$$= 2.0\% \text{ (m/v) KI solution}$$

STUDY CHECK 9.8

What is the mass/volume percent (m/v) of NaOH in a solution prepared by dissolving 12 g of NaOH in enough water to make 220 mL of solution?

ANSWER

5.5% (m/v) NaOH solution

Molarity (M) Concentration

When chemists work with solutions, they often use **molarity (M)**, a concentration that states the number of moles of solute in exactly 1 L of solution.

$$\text{Molarity (M)} = \frac{\text{moles of solute}}{\text{liters of solution}}$$

The molarity of a solution can be calculated knowing the moles of solute and the volume of solution in liters. For example, if 1.0 mole of NaCl were dissolved in enough water to prepare 1.0 L of solution, the resulting NaCl solution has a molarity of 1.0 M. The abbreviation M indicates the units of mole per liter (mole/L).

$$M = \frac{\text{moles of solute}}{\text{liters of solution}} = \frac{1.0 \text{ mole NaCl}}{1 \text{ L solution}} = 1.0 \text{ M NaCl solution}$$

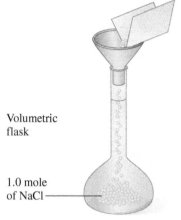

Volumetric flask

1.0 mole of NaCl

Add water until 1-liter mark is reached.

Mix

A 1.0 molar (M) NaCl solution

SAMPLE PROBLEM 9.9 Calculating Molarity

What is the molarity (M) of 60.0 g of NaOH in 0.250 L of NaOH solution?

SOLUTION

STEP 1 State the given and needed quantities.

ANALYZE THE PROBLEM	Given	Need
	60.0 g of NaOH,	molarity (mole/L)
	0.250 L of NaOH solution	

To calculate the moles of NaOH, we need to write the equality and conversion factors for the molar mass of NaOH. Then the moles in 60.0 g of NaOH can be determined.

$$1 \text{ mole of NaOH} = 40.00 \text{ g of NaOH}$$

$$\frac{1 \text{ mole NaOH}}{40.00 \text{ g NaOH}} \quad \text{and} \quad \frac{40.00 \text{ g NaOH}}{1 \text{ mole NaOH}}$$

$$\text{moles of NaOH} = 60.0 \text{ g NaOH} \times \frac{1 \text{ mole NaOH}}{40.00 \text{ g NaOH}}$$

$$= 1.50 \text{ moles of NaOH}$$

$$\text{volume of solution} = 0.250 \text{ L of NaOH solution}$$

STEP 2 Write the concentration expression.

$$\text{Molarity (M)} = \frac{\text{moles of solute}}{\text{liters of solution}}$$

STEP 3 Substitute solute and solution quantities into the expression and calculate.

$$M = \frac{1.50 \text{ moles NaOH}}{0.250 \text{ L solution}} = \frac{6.00 \text{ moles NaOH}}{1 \text{ L solution}} = 6.00 \text{ M NaOH solution}$$

STUDY CHECK 9.9

What is the molarity of a solution that contains 75.0 g of KNO_3 dissolved in 0.350 L of solution?

ANSWER

2.12 M KNO_3 solution

Table 9.9 summarizes the types of units used in the various types of concentration expressions for solutions.

TABLE 9.9 Summary of Types of Concentration Expressions and Their Units

Concentration Units	Mass Percent (m/m)	Volume Percent (v/v)	Mass/Volume Percent (m/v)	Molarity (M)
Solute	g	mL	g	mole
Solution	g	mL	mL	L

Using Concentration as a Conversion Factor

In the preparation of solutions, we often need to calculate the amount of solute or solution. Then the concentration is useful as a conversion factor. Some examples of percent concentrations and molarity, their meanings, and conversion factors are given in Table 9.10. Some examples of using percent concentration or molarity as conversion factors are given in Sample Problems 9.10 and 9.11.

⚛ **CORE CHEMISTRY SKILL**

Using Concentration as a Conversion Factor

TABLE 9.10 Conversion Factors from Concentrations

Percent Concentration	Meaning	Conversion Factors		
10% (m/m) KCl solution	10 g of KCl in 100 g of KCl solution	$\dfrac{10 \text{ g KCl}}{100 \text{ g solution}}$	and	$\dfrac{100 \text{ g solution}}{10 \text{ g KCl}}$
12% (v/v) ethanol solution	12 mL of ethanol in 100 mL of ethanol solution	$\dfrac{12 \text{ mL ethanol}}{100 \text{ mL solution}}$	and	$\dfrac{100 \text{ mL solution}}{12 \text{ mL ethanol}}$
5% (m/v) glucose solution	5 g of glucose in 100 mL of glucose solution	$\dfrac{5 \text{ g glucose}}{100 \text{ mL solution}}$	and	$\dfrac{100 \text{ mL solution}}{5 \text{ g glucose}}$
Molarity				
6.0 M HCl solution	6.0 moles of HCl in 1 liter of HCl solution	$\dfrac{6.0 \text{ moles HCl}}{1 \text{ L solution}}$	and	$\dfrac{1 \text{ L solution}}{6.0 \text{ moles HCl}}$

Guide to Using Concentration to Calculate Mass or Volume

STEP 1
State the given and needed quantities.

STEP 2
Write a plan to calculate the mass or volume.

STEP 3
Write equalities and conversion factors.

STEP 4
Set up the problem to calculate the mass or volume.

▶ **SAMPLE PROBLEM 9.10** **Using Mass/Volume Percent to Find Mass of Solute**

A topical antibiotic is 1.0% (m/v) clindamycin. How many grams of clindamycin are in 60. mL of the 1.0% (m/v) solution?

SOLUTION

STEP 1 State the given and needed quantities.

ANALYZE THE PROBLEM	Given	Need
	60. mL of 1.0% (m/v) clindamycin solution	grams of clindamycin

STEP 2 Write a plan to calculate the mass.

milliliters of solution   % (m/v) factor   grams of clindamycin

STEP 3 Write equalities and conversion factors. The percent (m/v) indicates the grams of a solute in every 100 mL of a solution. The 1.0% (m/v) can be written as two conversion factors.

$$100 \text{ mL of solution } = 1.0 \text{ g of clindamycin}$$

$$\frac{1.0 \text{ g clindamycin}}{100 \text{ mL solution}} \quad \text{and} \quad \frac{100 \text{ mL solution}}{1.0 \text{ g clindamycin}}$$

STEP 4 Set up the problem to calculate the mass. The volume of the solution is converted to mass of solute using the conversion factor that cancels mL.

$$60. \text{ mL solution} \times \frac{1.0 \text{ g clindamycin}}{100 \text{ mL solution}} = 0.60 \text{ g of clindamycin}$$

STUDY CHECK 9.10

In 2010, the FDA approved a 2.0% (m/v) morphine oral solution to treat severe or chronic pain. How many grams of morphine does a patient receive if 0.60 mL of 2.0% (m/v) morphine solution was ordered?

ANSWER

0.012 g of morphine

▶ **SAMPLE PROBLEM 9.11** **Using Molarity to Calculate Volume of Solution**

How many liters of a 2.00 M NaCl solution are needed to provide 67.3 g of NaCl?

SOLUTION

STEP 1 State the given and needed quantities.

ANALYZE THE PROBLEM	Given	Need
	67.3 g of NaCl, 2.00 M NaCl solution	liters of NaCl solution

STEP 2 Write a plan to calculate the volume.

grams of NaCl   Molar mass   moles of NaCl   Molarity   liters of NaCl solution

STEP 3   Write equalities and conversion factors.

1 mole of NaCl = 58.44 g of NaCl

$$\frac{1 \text{ mole NaCl}}{58.44 \text{ g NaCl}} \quad \text{and} \quad \frac{58.44 \text{ g NaCl}}{1 \text{ mole NaCl}}$$

1 L of NaCl solution = 2.00 moles of NaCl

$$\frac{1 \text{ L NaCl solution}}{2.00 \text{ moles NaCl}} \quad \text{and} \quad \frac{2.00 \text{ moles NaCl}}{1 \text{ L NaCl solution}}$$

STEP 4   Set up the problem to calculate the volume.

$$\text{liters of NaCl solution} = 67.3 \cancel{\text{ g NaCl}} \times \frac{1 \cancel{\text{ mole NaCl}}}{58.44 \cancel{\text{ g NaCl}}} \times \frac{1 \text{ L NaCl solution}}{2.00 \cancel{\text{ moles NaCl}}}$$

$$= 0.576 \text{ L of NaCl solution}$$

STUDY CHECK 9.11

How many milliliters of a 6.0 M HCl solution will provide 164 g of HCl?

ANSWER

750 mL of HCl solution

Chemical Reactions in Solution

When chemical reactions involve aqueous solutions, we use the balanced chemical equation, the molarity, and the volume to determine the moles or grams of the reactants or products. For example, we can determine the volume of a solution from the molarity and the grams of reactant as seen in Sample Problem 9.12.

▶ **SAMPLE PROBLEM 9.12   Volume of a Solution in a Reaction**

Zinc reacts with HCl to produce hydrogen gas, H_2, and $ZnCl_2$.

$$Zn(s) + 2HCl(aq) \longrightarrow H_2(g) + ZnCl_2(aq)$$

How many liters of a 1.50 M HCl solution completely react with 5.32 g of zinc?

SOLUTION

STEP 1   State the given and needed quantities.

ANALYZE THE PROBLEM	Given	Need
	5.32 g of Zn, 1.50 M HCl solution	liters of HCl solution
	Equation	
	$Zn(s) + 2HCl(aq) \longrightarrow H_2(g) + ZnCl_2(aq)$	

STEP 2   Write a plan to calculate the needed quantity.

grams of Zn | Molar mass | moles of Zn | Mole–mole factor | moles of HCl | Molarity | liters of HCl solution

STEP 3   Write equalities and conversion factors including mole–mole and concentration factors.

1 mole of Zn = 65.41 g of Zn

$$\frac{1 \text{ mole Zn}}{65.41 \text{ g Zn}} \quad \text{and} \quad \frac{65.41 \text{ g Zn}}{1 \text{ mole Zn}}$$

1 mole of Zn = 2 moles of HCl

$$\frac{1 \text{ mole Zn}}{2 \text{ moles HCl}} \quad \text{and} \quad \frac{2 \text{ moles HCl}}{1 \text{ mole Zn}}$$

1 L of solution = 1.50 moles of HCl

$$\frac{1 \text{ L solution}}{1.50 \text{ moles HCl}} \quad \text{and} \quad \frac{1.50 \text{ moles HCl}}{1 \text{ L solution}}$$

⚛ **CORE CHEMISTRY SKILL**

Calculating the Quantity of a Reactant or Product for a Chemical Reaction in Solution

Guide to Calculations Involving Solutions in Chemical Reactions

STEP 1
State the given and needed quantities.

STEP 2
Write a plan to calculate the needed quantity or concentration.

STEP 3
Write equalities and conversion factors including mole–mole and concentration factors.

STEP 4
Set up the problem to calculate the needed quantity or concentration.

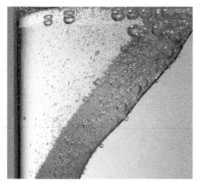

Zinc reacts when placed in a solution of HCl.

STEP **4** Set up the problem to calculate the needed quantity.

$$5.32 \text{ g Zn} \times \frac{1 \text{ mole Zn}}{65.41 \text{ g Zn}} \times \frac{2 \text{ moles HCl}}{1 \text{ mole Zn}} \times \frac{1 \text{ L solution}}{1.50 \text{ moles HCl}} = 0.108 \text{ L of HCl solution}$$

STUDY CHECK 9.12

Using the reaction in Sample Problem 9.12, how many grams of zinc can react with 225 mL of a 0.200 M HCl solution?

ANSWER

1.47 g of Zn

▶ **SAMPLE PROBLEM 9.13** Volume of a Reactant in a Solution

How many milliliters of a 0.250 M $BaCl_2$ solution are needed to react with 0.0325 L of a 0.160 M Na_2SO_4 solution?

$$Na_2SO_4(aq) + BaCl_2(aq) \longrightarrow BaSO_4(s) + 2NaCl(aq)$$

SOLUTION

STEP **1** State the given and needed quantities.

When a $BaCl_2$ solution is added to a Na_2SO_4 solution, $BaSO_4$, a white solid, forms.

	Given	Need
ANALYZE THE PROBLEM	0.0325 L of 0.160 M Na_2SO_4 solution 0.250 M $BaCl_2$ solution	milliliters of $BaCl_2$ solution
	Equation	
	$Na_2SO_4(aq) + BaCl_2(aq) \longrightarrow BaSO_4(s) + 2NaCl(aq)$	

STEP **2** Write a plan to calculate the needed quantity.

liters of Na_2SO_4 solution   Molarity   moles of Na_2SO_4 Mole–mole factor   moles of $BaCl_2$

Molarity   liters of $BaCl_2$ solution   Metric factor   milliliters of $BaCl_2$ solution

STEP **3** Write equalities and conversion factors including mole–mole and concentration factors.

1 L of solution = 0.160 mole of Na_2SO_4

$$\frac{1 \text{ L solution}}{0.160 \text{ mole } Na_2SO_4} \quad \text{and} \quad \frac{0.160 \text{ mole } Na_2SO_4}{1 \text{ L solution}}$$

1 mole of Na_2SO_4 = 1 mole of $BaCl_2$

$$\frac{1 \text{ mole } Na_2SO_4}{1 \text{ mole } BaCl_2} \quad \text{and} \quad \frac{1 \text{ mole } BaCl_2}{1 \text{ mole } Na_2SO_4}$$

1 L of solution = 0.250 mole of $BaCl_2$

$$\frac{1 \text{ L solution}}{0.250 \text{ mole } BaCl_2} \quad \text{and} \quad \frac{0.250 \text{ mole } BaCl_2}{1 \text{ L solution}}$$

1 L = 1000 mL

$$\frac{1 \text{ L}}{1000 \text{ mL}} \quad \text{and} \quad \frac{1000 \text{ mL}}{1 \text{ L}}$$

STEP **4** Set up the problem to calculate the needed quantity.

$$0.0325 \text{ L solution} \times \frac{0.160 \text{ mole } Na_2SO_4}{1 \text{ L solution}} \times \frac{1 \text{ mole } BaCl_2}{1 \text{ mole } Na_2SO_4} \times \frac{1 \text{ L solution}}{0.250 \text{ mole } BaCl_2} \times \frac{1000 \text{ mL } BaCl_2 \text{ solution}}{1 \text{ L solution}}$$

= 20.8 mL of $BaCl_2$ solution

STUDY CHECK 9.13

For the reaction in Sample Problem 9.13, how many milliliters of a 0.330 M Na_2SO_4 solution are needed to react with 26.8 mL of a 0.216 M $BaCl_2$ solution?

ANSWER

17.5 mL of Na_2SO_4 solution

Figure 9.8 gives a summary of the pathways and conversion factors needed for substances including solutions involved in chemical reactions.

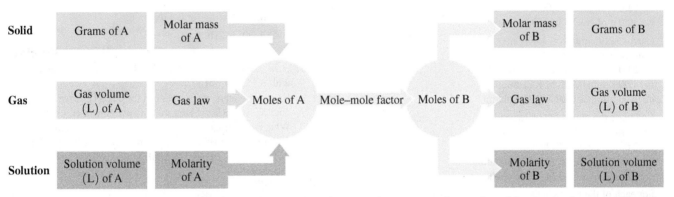

FIGURE 9.8 ▶ In calculations involving chemical reactions, substance A is converted to moles of A using molar mass (if solid), gas laws (if gas), or molarity (if solution). Then moles of A are converted to moles of substance B, which are converted to grams of solid, liters of gas, or liters of solution, as needed.

Q What sequence of conversion factors would you use to calculate the number of grams of $CaCO_3$ needed to react with 1.50 L of a 2.00 M HCl solution in the reaction $CaCO_3(s) + 2HCl(aq) \longrightarrow CO_2(g) + H_2O(l) + CaCl_2(aq)$?

QUESTIONS AND PROBLEMS

9.4 Solution Concentrations and Reactions

LEARNING GOAL Calculate the concentration of a solute in a solution; use concentration units to calculate the amount of solute or solution. Given the volume and concentration of a solution, calculate the amount of another reactant or product in a reaction.

Interactive Video

Solutions

9.33 Calculate the mass percent (m/m) for the solute in each of the following:
   a. 25 g of KCl and 125 g of H_2O
   b. 12 g of sucrose in 225 g of tea solution
   c. 8.0 g of $CaCl_2$ in 80.0 g of $CaCl_2$ solution

9.34 Calculate the mass percent (m/m) for the solute in each of the following:
   a. 75 g of NaOH in 325 g of NaOH solution
   b. 2.0 g of KOH and 20.0 g of H_2O
   c. 48.5 g of Na_2CO_3 in 250.0 g of Na_2CO_3 solution

9.35 Calculate the mass/volume percent (m/v) for the solute in each of the following:
   a. 75 g of Na_2SO_4 in 250 mL of Na_2SO_4 solution
   b. 39 g of sucrose in 355 mL of a carbonated drink

9.36 Calculate the mass/volume percent (m/v) for the solute in each of the following:
   a. 2.50 g of LiCl in 40.0 mL of LiCl solution
   b. 7.5 g of casein in 120 mL of low-fat milk

9.37 Calculate the grams or milliliters of solute needed to prepare the following:
   a. 50. g of a 5.0% (m/m) KCl solution
   b. 1250 mL of a 4.0% (m/v) NH_4Cl solution
   c. 250. mL of a 10.0% (v/v) acetic acid solution

9.38 Calculate the grams or milliliters of solute needed to prepare the following:
   a. 150. g of a 40.0% (m/m) $LiNO_3$ solution
   b. 450 mL of a 2.0% (m/v) KOH solution
   c. 225 mL of a 15% (v/v) isopropyl alcohol solution

9.39 A mouthwash contains 22.5% (v/v) alcohol. If the bottle of mouthwash contains 355 mL, what is the volume, in milliliters, of alcohol?

9.40 A bottle of champagne is 11% (v/v) alcohol. If there are 750 mL of champagne in the bottle, what is the volume, in milliliters, of alcohol?

9.41 For each of the following solutions, calculate the:
   a. grams of 25% (m/m) $LiNO_3$ solution that contains 5.0 g of $LiNO_3$
   b. milliliters of 10.0% (m/v) KOH solution that contains 40.0 g of KOH
   c. milliliters of 10.0% (v/v) formic acid solution that contains 2.0 mL of formic acid

9.42 For each of the following solutions, calculate the:
    a. grams of 2.0% (m/m) NaCl solution that contains 7.50 g of NaCl
    b. milliliters of 25% (m/v) NaF solution that contains 4.0 g of NaF
    c. milliliters of 8.0% (v/v) ethanol solution that contains 20.0 mL of ethanol

9.43 Calculate the molarity of each of the following:
    a. 2.00 moles of glucose in 4.00 L of a glucose solution
    b. 4.00 g of KOH in 2.00 L of a KOH solution
    c. 5.85 g of NaCl in 400. mL of a NaCl solution

9.44 Calculate the molarity of each of the following:
    a. 0.500 mole of glucose in 0.200 L of a glucose solution
    b. 73.0 g of HCl in 2.00 L of a HCl solution
    c. 30.0 g of NaOH in 350. mL of a NaOH solution

9.45 Calculate the grams of solute needed to prepare each of the following:
    a. 2.00 L of a 1.50 M NaOH solution
    b. 4.00 L of a 0.200 M KCl solution
    c. 25.0 mL of a 6.00 M HCl solution

9.46 Calculate the grams of solute needed to prepare each of the following:
    a. 2.00 L of a 6.00 M NaOH solution
    b. 5.00 L of a 0.100 M $CaCl_2$ solution
    c. 175 mL of a 3.00 M $NaNO_3$ solution

9.47 For each of the following solutions, calculate the:
    a. liters of a 2.00 M KBr solution to obtain 3.00 moles of KBr
    b. liters of a 1.50 M NaCl solution to obtain 15.0 moles of NaCl
    c. milliliters of a 0.800 M $Ca(NO_3)_2$ solution to obtain 0.0500 mole of $Ca(NO_3)_2$

9.48 For each of the following solutions, calculate the:
    a. liters of a 4.00 M KCl solution to obtain 0.100 mole of KCl
    b. liters of a 6.00 M HCl solution to obtain 5.00 moles of HCl
    c. milliliters of a 2.50 M K_2SO_4 solution to obtain 1.20 moles of K_2SO_4

9.49 Answer the following for the reaction:
$$Pb(NO_3)_2(aq) + 2KCl(aq) \longrightarrow$$
$$PbCl_2(s) + 2KNO_3(aq)$$
    a. How many grams of $PbCl_2$ will be formed from 50.0 mL of a 1.50 M KCl solution?
    b. How many milliliters of a 2.00 M $Pb(NO_3)_2$ solution will react with 50.0 mL of a 1.50 M KCl solution?
    c. What is the molarity of 20.0 mL of a KCl solution that reacts completely with 30.0 mL of a 0.400 M $Pb(NO_3)_2$ solution?

9.50 Answer the following for the reaction:
$$NiCl_2(aq) + 2NaOH(aq) \longrightarrow$$
$$Ni(OH)_2(s) + 2NaCl(aq)$$
    a. How many milliliters of a 0.200 M NaOH solution are needed to react with 18.0 mL of a 0.500 M $NiCl_2$ solution?
    b. How many grams of $Ni(OH)_2$ are produced from the reaction of 35.0 mL of a 1.75 M NaOH solution and excess $NiCl_2$?

    c. What is the molarity of 30.0 mL of a $NiCl_2$ solution that reacts completely with 10.0 mL of a 0.250 M NaOH solution?

9.51 Answer the following for the reaction:
$$Mg(s) + 2HCl(aq) \longrightarrow H_2(g) + MgCl_2(aq)$$
    a. How many milliliters of a 6.00 M HCl solution are required to react with 15.0 g of magnesium?
    b. How many liters of hydrogen gas can form at STP when 0.500 L of a 2.00 M HCl solution reacts with excess magnesium?
    c. What is the molarity of a HCl solution if the reaction of 45.2 mL of the HCl solution with excess magnesium produces 5.20 L of H_2 gas at 735 mmHg and 25 °C?

9.52 Answer the following for the reaction:
$$CaCO_3(s) + 2HCl(aq) \longrightarrow$$
$$CO_2(g) + H_2O(l) + CaCl_2(aq)$$
    a. How many milliliters of a 0.200 M HCl solution can react with 8.25 g of $CaCO_3$?
    b. How many liters of CO_2 gas can form at STP when 15.5 mL of a 3.00 M HCl solution reacts with excess $CaCO_3$?
    c. What is the molarity of a HCl solution if the reaction of 200. mL of the HCl solution with excess $CaCO_3$ produces 12.0 L of CO_2 gas at 725 mmHg and 18 °C?

℞ Clinical Applications

9.53 A patient receives 100. mL of 20.% (m/v) mannitol solution every hour.
    a. How many grams of mannitol are given in 1 h?
    b. How many grams of mannitol does the patient receive in 12 h?

9.54 A patient receives 250 mL of a 4.0% (m/v) amino acid solution twice a day.
    a. How many grams of amino acids are in 250 mL of solution?
    b. How many grams of amino acids does the patient receive in 1 day?

9.55 A patient needs 100. g of glucose in the next 12 h. How many liters of a 5% (m/v) glucose solution must be given?

9.56 A patient received 2.0 g of NaCl in 8 h. How many milliliters of a 0.90% (m/v) NaCl (saline) solution were delivered?

9.57 A doctor orders 0.075 g of chlorpromazine, which is used to treat schizophrenia. If the stock solution is 2.5% (m/v), how many milliliters are administered to the patient?

9.58 A doctor orders 5 mg of compazine, which is used to treat nausea, vertigo, and migraine headaches. If the stock solution is 2.5% (m/v), how many milliliters are administered to the patient?

9.59 A $CaCl_2$ solution is given to increase blood levels of calcium. If a patient receives 5.0 mL of a 10.% (m/v) $CaCl_2$ solution, how many grams of $CaCl_2$ were given?

9.60 An intravenous solution of mannitol is used as a diuretic to increase the loss of sodium and chloride by a patient. If a patient receives 30.0 mL of a 25% (m/v) mannitol solution, how many grams of mannitol were given?

9.5 Dilution of Solutions

LEARNING GOAL

Describe the dilution of a solution; calculate the unknown concentration or volume when a solution is diluted.

In chemistry and biology, we often prepare diluted solutions from more concentrated solutions. In a process called **dilution**, a solvent, usually water, is added to a solution, which increases the volume. As a result, the concentration of the solution decreases. In an everyday example, you are making a dilution when you add three cans of water to a can of concentrated orange juice.

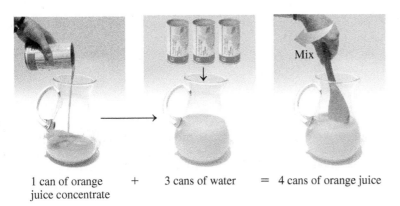

1 can of orange   +   3 cans of water   =   4 cans of orange juice
juice concentrate

Although the addition of solvent increases the volume, the amount of solute does not change; it is the same in the concentrated solution and the diluted solution (see Figure 9.9).

Grams or moles of solute = grams or moles of solute

    Concentrated solution   Diluted solution

We can write this equality in terms of the concentration, C, and the volume, V. The concentration, C, may be percent concentration or molarity.

$$C_1V_1 \quad = \quad C_2V_2$$

Concentrated   Diluted
solution   solution

If we are given any three of the four variables (C_1, C_2, V_1, or V_2), we can rearrange the dilution expression to solve for the unknown quantity as seen in Sample Problem 9.14.

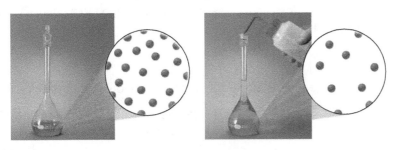

FIGURE 9.9 ▶ When water is added to a concentrated solution, there is no change in the number of particles. However, the solute particles spread out as the volume of the diluted solution increases.

Q What is the concentration of the diluted solution after an equal volume of water is added to a sample of a 6 M HCl solution?

▶ **SAMPLE PROBLEM 9.14 Dilution of a Solution**

A doctor orders 1000. mL of a 35.0% (m/v) dextrose solution. If you have a 50.0% (m/v) dextrose solution, how many milliliters would you use to prepare 1000. mL of 35.0% (m/v) dextrose solution?

SOLUTION

STEP 1 Prepare a table of the concentrations and volumes of the solutions. For our problem analysis, we organize the solution data in a table, making sure that the units of concentration and volume are the same.

Guide to Calculating
Dilution Quantities

STEP **1**
Prepare a table of the
concentrations and
volumes of the solutions.

STEP **2**
Rearrange the dilution
expression to solve for the
unknown quantity.

STEP **3**
Substitute the known
quantities into the dilution
expression and calculate.

	Concentrated Solution	Diluted Solution	Know	Predict
ANALYZE THE PROBLEM	C_1 = 50.0% (m/v) dextrose	C_2 = 35.0% (m/v) dextrose	C_1 increases	
	V_1 = ? mL	V_2 = 1000. mL		V_1 decreases

STEP **2** Rearrange the dilution expression to solve for the unknown quantity.

$$C_1 V_1 = C_2 V_2$$

$$\frac{C_1 V_1}{C_1} = \frac{C_2 V_2}{C_1} \quad \text{Divide both sides by } C_1$$

$$V_1 = V_2 \times \frac{C_2}{C_1}$$

STEP **3** Substitute the known quantities into the dilution expression and calculate.

$$V_1 = 1000. \text{ mL} \times \frac{35.0\%}{50.0\%} = 700. \text{ mL of dextrose solution}$$

Concentration factor
decreases volume

When the final volume (V_2) is multiplied by a ratio of the percent concentrations (concentration factor) that is less than 1, the initial volume (V_1) is less than the final volume (V_2) as predicted in Step 1.

STUDY CHECK 9.14

What initial volume of a 15% (m/v) mannose solution is needed to prepare 125 mL of a 3.0% (m/v) mannose solution?

ANSWER

25 mL of a 15% (m/v) mannose solution

SAMPLE PROBLEM 9.15 Molarity of a Diluted Solution

What is the molarity of a solution when 75.0 mL of a 4.00 M KCl solution is diluted to a volume of 500. mL?

SOLUTION

STEP **1** Prepare a table of the concentrations and volumes of the solutions.

	Concentrated Solution	Diluted Solution	Know	Predict
ANALYZE THE PROBLEM	C_1 = 4.00 M KCl	C_2 = ? M KCl		C (molarity) decreases
	V_1 = 75.0 mL = 0.0750 L	V_2 = 500. mL = 0.500 L	V increases	

STEP **2** Rearrange the dilution expression to solve for the unknown quantity.

$$C_1 V_1 = C_2 V_2$$

$$\frac{C_1 V_1}{V_2} = \frac{C_2 V_2}{V_2} \quad \text{Divide both sides by } V_2$$

$$C_2 = C_1 \times \frac{V_1}{V_2}$$

STEP **3** Substitute the known quantities into the dilution expression and calculate.

$$C_2 = 4.00 \text{ M} \times \frac{75.0 \text{ mL}}{500. \text{ mL}} = 0.600 \text{ M (diluted KCl solution)}$$

Volume factor
decreases concentration

When the initial molarity (C_1) is multiplied by a ratio of the volumes (volume factor) that is less than 1, the molarity of the diluted solution decreases as predicted in Step 1.

STUDY CHECK 9.15

What is the molarity of a solution when 50.0 mL of a 4.00 M KOH solution is diluted to 200. mL?

ANSWER

1.00 M KOH solution

QUESTIONS AND PROBLEMS

9.5 Dilution of Solutions

LEARNING GOAL Describe the dilution of a solution; calculate the unknown concentration or volume when a solution is diluted.

9.61 To make tomato soup, you add one can of water to the condensed soup. Why is this a dilution?

9.62 A can of frozen lemonade calls for the addition of three cans of water to make a pitcher of the beverage. Why is this a dilution?

9.63 Calculate the final concentration of each of the following:
 a. 2.0 L of a 6.0 M HCl solution is added to water so that the final volume is 6.0 L.
 b. Water is added to 0.50 L of a 12 M NaOH solution to make 3.0 L of a diluted NaOH solution.
 c. A 10.0-mL sample of a 25% (m/v) KOH solution is diluted with water so that the final volume is 100.0 mL.
 d. A 50.0-mL sample of a 15% (m/v) H_2SO_4 solution is added to water to give a final volume of 250 mL.

9.64 Calculate the final concentration of each of the following:
 a. 1.0 L of a 4.0 M HNO_3 solution is added to water so that the final volume is 8.0 L.
 b. Water is added to 0.25 L of a 6.0 M NaF solution to make 2.0 L of a diluted NaF solution.
 c. A 50.0-mL sample of an 8.0% (m/v) KBr solution is diluted with water so that the final volume is 200.0 mL.
 d. A 5.0-mL sample of a 50.0% (m/v) acetic acid ($HC_2H_3O_2$) solution is added to water to give a final volume of 25 mL.

9.65 Determine the final volume, in milliliters, of each of the following:
 a. a 1.5 M HCl solution prepared from 20.0 mL of a 6.0 M HCl solution
 b. a 2.0% (m/v) LiCl solution prepared from 50.0 mL of a 10.0% (m/v) LiCl solution
 c. a 0.500 M H_3PO_4 solution prepared from 50.0 mL of a 6.00 M H_3PO_4 solution
 d. a 5.0% (m/v) glucose solution prepared from 75 mL of a 12% (m/v) glucose solution

9.66 Determine the final volume, in milliliters, of each of the following:
 a. a 1.00% (m/v) H_2SO_4 solution prepared from 10.0 mL of a 20.0% H_2SO_4 solution
 b. a 0.10 M HCl solution prepared from 25 mL of a 6.0 M HCl solution
 c. a 1.0 M NaOH solution prepared from 50.0 mL of a 12 M NaOH solution
 d. a 1.0% (m/v) $CaCl_2$ solution prepared from 18 mL of a 4.0% (m/v) $CaCl_2$ solution

9.67 Determine the initial volume, in milliliters, required to prepare each of the following:
 a. 255 mL of a 0.200 M HNO_3 solution using a 4.00 M HNO_3 solution
 b. 715 mL of a 0.100 M $MgCl_2$ solution using a 6.00 M $MgCl_2$ solution
 c. 0.100 L of a 0.150 M KCl solution using an 8.00 M KCl solution

9.68 Determine the initial volume, in milliliters, required to prepare each of the following:
 a. 20.0 mL of a 0.250 M KNO_3 solution using a 6.00 M KNO_3 solution
 b. 25.0 mL of a 2.50 M H_2SO_4 solution using a 12.0 M H_2SO_4 solution
 c. 0.500 L of a 1.50 M NH_4Cl solution using a 10.0 M NH_4Cl solution

Rx Clinical Applications

9.69 You need 500. mL of a 5.0% (m/v) glucose solution. If you have a 25% (m/v) glucose solution on hand, how many milliliters do you need?

9.70 A doctor orders 100. mL of 2.0% (m/v) ibuprofen. If you have 8.0% (m/v) ibuprofen on hand, how many milliliters do you need?

9.6 Properties of Solutions

The size and number of solute particles in different types of mixtures play an important role in determining the properties of that mixture.

Solutions

In the solutions discussed up to now, the solute was dissolved as small particles that are uniformly dispersed throughout the solvent to give a homogeneous solution. When you observe a solution, such as salt water, you cannot visually distinguish the solute from the solvent. The solution appears transparent, although it may have a color. The particles are so small that they go through filters and through *semipermeable membranes*. A semipermeable membrane allows solvent molecules such as water and very small solute particles to pass through, but does allow the passage of large solute molecules.

Colloids

The particles in a **colloid** are much larger than solute particles in a solution. Colloidal particles are large molecules, such as proteins, or groups of molecules or ions. Colloids, similar to solutions, are homogeneous mixtures that do not separate or settle out. Colloidal particles are small enough to pass through filters, but too large to pass through semipermeable membranes. Table 9.11 lists several examples of colloids.

TABLE 9.11 Examples of Colloids

Colloid	Substance Dispersed	Dispersing Medium
Fog, clouds, hair sprays	Liquid	Gas
Dust, smoke	Solid	Gas
Shaving cream, whipped cream, soapsuds	Gas	Liquid
Styrofoam, marshmallows	Gas	Solid
Mayonnaise, homogenized milk	Liquid	Liquid
Cheese, butter	Liquid	Solid
Blood plasma, paints (latex), gelatin	Solid	Liquid

Suspensions

Suspensions are heterogeneous, nonuniform mixtures that are very different from solutions or colloids. The particles of a suspension are so large that they can often be seen with the naked eye. They are trapped by filters and semipermeable membranes.

The weight of the suspended solute particles causes them to settle out soon after mixing. If you stir muddy water, it mixes but then quickly separates as the suspended particles settle to the bottom and leave clear liquid at the top. You can find suspensions among the medications in a hospital or in your medicine cabinet. These include Kaopectate, calamine lotion, antacid mixtures, and liquid penicillin. It is important to follow the instructions on the label that states "shake well before using" so that the particles form a suspension.

Water-treatment plants make use of the properties of suspensions to purify water. When chemicals such as aluminum sulfate or iron(III) sulfate are added to untreated water, they react with impurities to form large suspended particles called *floc*. In the water-treatment plant, a system of filters traps the suspended particles, but clean water passes through.

Table 9.12 compares the different types of mixtures and Figure 9.10 illustrates some properties of solutions, colloids, and suspensions.

TABLE 9.12 Comparison of Solutions, Colloids, and Suspensions

Type of Mixture	Type of Particle	Settling	Separation
Solution	Small particles such as atoms, ions, or small molecules	Particles do not settle	Particles cannot be separated by filters or semipermeable membranes
Colloid	Larger molecules or groups of molecules or ions	Particles do not settle	Particles can be separated by semipermeable membranes but not by filters
Suspension	Very large particles that may be visible	Particles settle rapidly	Particles can be separated by filters

Chemistry Link to Health
Colloids and Solutions in the Body

In the body, colloids are retained by semipermeable membranes. For example, the intestinal lining allows solution particles to pass into the blood and lymph circulatory systems. However, the colloids from foods are too large to pass through the membrane, and they remain in the intestinal tract. Digestion breaks down large colloidal particles, such as starch and protein, into smaller particles, such as glucose and amino acids that can pass through the intestinal membrane and enter the circulatory system. Certain foods, such as bran, a fiber, cannot be broken down by human digestive processes, and they move through the intestine intact.

Because large proteins, such as enzymes, are colloids, they remain inside cells. However, many of the substances that must be obtained by cells, such as oxygen, amino acids, electrolytes, glucose, and minerals, can pass through cellular membranes. Waste products, such as urea and carbon dioxide, pass out of the cell to be excreted.

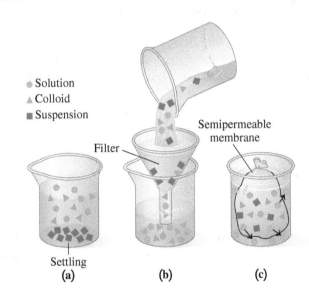

Solution
Colloid
Suspension

Semipermeable membrane

Filter

Settling
(a)   (b)   (c)

FIGURE 9.10 ▶ Properties of different types of mixtures: **(a)** suspensions settle out; **(b)** suspensions are separated by a filter; **(c)** solution particles go through a semipermeable membrane, but colloids and suspensions do not.

A filter can be used to separate suspension particles from a solution, but a semipermeable membrane is needed to separate colloids from a solution. Explain.

Boiling Point Elevation and Freezing Point Lowering

When we add a solute to water, it changes the vapor pressure, boiling point, and freezing point of pure water. Therefore, an aqueous solution will have a higher boiling point and a lower freezing point than that of pure water. These types of changes in physical properties, known as *colligative properties*, depend only on the concentration of solute particles in the solution.

We can illustrate how these changes in physical properties occur by comparing the number of evaporating solvent molecules in pure solvent with those in a solution with a nonvolatile solute in the solvent. In the solution, there are fewer solvent molecules at the surface because the solute that has been added takes up some of the space at the surface. As a result, fewer solvent molecules can evaporate compared to the pure solvent. Vapor pressure is lowered for the solution. If we add more solute molecules, the vapor pressure will be lowered even more.

Vapor pressure

Pure solvent

Lower vapor pressure

Solute and solvent

Ethylene glycol is added to a radiator to form an aqueous solution that has a lower freezing point than water.

The boiling point of a solvent is raised when a nonvolatile solute is added. The vapor pressure of a solvent must reach atmospheric pressure before it begins boiling. However, because the solute lowers the vapor pressure of the solvent, a temperature higher than the normal boiling point of the pure solvent is needed to cause the solution to boil.

The freezing point of a solvent is lowered when a nonvolatile solute is added. In this case, the solute particles prevent the organization of solvent molecules needed to form the solid state. Thus, a lower temperature is required before the molecules of the solvent can become organized enough to freeze.

Thus, when you spread salt on an icy sidewalk when temperatures drop below freezing, the particles from the salt combine with water to lower the freezing point, which causes the ice to melt. Another example is the addition of antifreeze, such as ethylene glycol $HO—CH_2—CH_2—OH$, to the water in a car radiator. Ethylene glycol forms many hydrogen bonds, which makes it very soluble in water. If an ethylene glycol and water mixture is about 50–50% by mass, it does not freeze until the temperature drops to about $-30\,°F$, and does not boil unless the temperature reaches about $225\,°F$. The solution in the radiator prevents the water in the radiator from forming ice in cold weather or boiling over on a hot desert highway.

Insects and fish in climates with subfreezing temperatures control ice formation by producing biological antifreezes made of glycerol, proteins, and sugars, such as glucose, within their bodies. Some insects can survive temperatures below $-60\,°C$. These forms of biological antifreezes may one day be applied to the long-term preservation of human organs.

The Alaska Upis beetle produces biological antifreeze to survive subfreezing temperatures.

Particles in Solution

A solute that is a nonelectrolyte dissolves as molecules, whereas a solute that is a strong electrolyte dissolves entirely as ions. The solute in antifreeze, ethylene glycol, $C_2H_6O_2$—a nonelectrolyte—dissolves as molecules.

Nonelectrolyte: 1 mole of $C_2H_6O_2(l)$ = 1 mole of $C_2H_6O_2(aq)$

However, when 1 mole of a strong electrolyte, such as NaCl or $CaCl_2$, dissolves in water, the NaCl solution will contain 2 moles of particles and the $CaCl_2$ solution will contain 3 moles of particles.

Strong electrolytes:

$$1 \text{ mole of NaCl}(s) = \underbrace{1 \text{ mole of Na}^+(aq) + 1 \text{ mole of Cl}^-(aq)}_{2 \text{ moles of particles }(aq)}$$

$$1 \text{ mole of CaCl}_2(s) = \underbrace{1 \text{ mole of Ca}^{2+}(aq) + 2 \text{ moles of Cl}^-(aq)}_{3 \text{ moles of particles }(aq)}$$

⚛️ **CORE CHEMISTRY SKILL**

Calculating the Boiling Point/ Freezing Point of a Solution

Change in Boiling Point and Freezing Point

The change in boiling point or freezing point depends on the number of particles in the solution. One mole of an electrolyte such as glucose raises the boiling point of one kilogram of pure water ($100.00\,°C$) by $0.51\,°C$, which gives a boiling point of $100.51\,°C$. If the solute is a strong electrolyte such as NaCl, one mole produces two moles of particles (ions). Then the boiling point of one kilogram of water is raised by 1.02 °C (2 × 0.51 °C), to give a boiling point of 101.02 °C.

The presence of solute particles also changes the freezing point. One mole of a non-electrolyte such as glucose lowers the freezing point (0.00 °C) of one kilogram of pure water by 1.86 °C, to give a freezing point of −1.86 °C. For NaCl, one mole dissociates to form two moles of particles (ions). Then the freezing point of one kilogram of water is lowered by 3.72 °C (2 × 1.86 °C), which gives a freezing point of −3.72 °C.

The effect of some solutes on freezing and boiling point is summarized in Table 9.13.

A truck spreads calcium chloride on the road to melt ice and snow.

TABLE 9.13 Effect of Solute Concentration on Freezing and Boiling Points of 1 kg of Water

Substance in One Kilogram of Water	Type of Solute	Moles of Solute Particles in One Kilogram of Water	Freezing Point	Boiling Point
Pure water	None	0	0.00 °C	100.00 °C
1 mole of $C_2H_6O_2$	Nonelectrolyte	1	−1.86 °C	100.51 °C
1 mole of NaCl	Strong electrolyte	2	−3.72 °C	101.02 °C
1 mole of $CaCl_2$	Strong electrolyte	3	−5.58 °C	101.53 °C

▶ **SAMPLE PROBLEM 9.16 Calculating the Freezing Point of a Solution**

In the northern United States during freezing temperatures, $CaCl_2$ is spread on icy highways to melt the ice. Calculate the freezing point of a solution containing 0.50 mole of $CaCl_2$ in 1 kg of water.

SOLUTION

STEP 1 State the given and needed quantities.

ANALYZE THE PROBLEM	Given	Need
	0.50 mole of $CaCl_2$, 1 kg of water	freezing point of solution

STEP 2 Determine the number of moles of solute particles.
$$CaCl_2(s) \longrightarrow Ca^{2+}(aq) + 2Cl^-(aq) = 3 \text{ moles of solute particles}$$

1 mole of $CaCl_2$ = 3 moles of solute particles

$$\frac{1 \text{ mole } CaCl_2}{3 \text{ moles solute particles}} \quad \text{and} \quad \frac{3 \text{ moles solute particles}}{1 \text{ mole } CaCl_2}$$

STEP 3 Determine the temperature change using the moles of solute particles and the degrees Celsius change per mole of particles.

1 mole of solute particles = 1.86 °C

$$\frac{1.86 \,°C}{1 \text{ mole solute particles}} \quad \text{and} \quad \frac{1 \text{ mole solute particles}}{1.86 \,°C}$$

$$\text{Temperature change} = 0.50 \text{ mole } CaCl_2 \times \frac{3 \text{ moles solute particles}}{1 \text{ mole } CaCl_2} \times \frac{1.86 \,°C}{1 \text{ mole solute particles}}$$

$$= 2.8 \,°C$$

STEP 4 Subtract the temperature change from the freezing point. Finally, the freezing point lowering, ΔT_f, is subtracted from 0.0 °C to obtain the new freezing point of the $CaCl_2$ solution.

$$T_{\text{solution}} = T_{\text{water}} - \Delta T_f$$
$$= 0.0 \,°C - 2.8 \,°C$$
$$= -2.8 \,°C$$

Calculating Freezing Point Lowering/Boiling Point Elevation

STEP 1
State the given and needed quantities.

STEP 2
Determine the number of moles of solute particles.

STEP 3
Determine the temperature change using the moles of solute particles and the degrees Celsius change per mole of particles.

STEP 4
Subtract the temperature change from the freezing point or add the temperature change to the boiling point.

Osmosis and Osmotic Pressure

The movement of water into and out of the cells of plants as well as the cells of our bodies is an important biological process that also depends on the solute concentration. In a process called **osmosis**, water molecules move through a semipermeable membrane from the solution with the lower concentration of solute into a solution with the higher solute concentration. In an osmosis apparatus, water is placed on one side of a semipermeable membrane and a sucrose (sugar) solution on the other side. The semipermeable membrane allows water molecules to flow back and forth but blocks the sucrose molecules because they cannot pass through the membrane. Because the sucrose solution has a higher solute concentration, more water molecules flow into the sucrose solution than out of the sucrose solution. The volume level of the sucrose solution rises as the volume level on the water side falls. The increase of water dilutes the sucrose solution to equalize (or attempt to equalize) the concentrations on both sides of the membrane.

Eventually the height of the sucrose solution creates sufficient pressure to equalize the flow of water between the two compartments. This pressure, called **osmotic pressure**, prevents the flow of additional water into the more concentrated solution. Then there is no further change in the volumes of the two solutions. The osmotic pressure depends on the concentration of solute particles in the solution. The greater the number of particles dissolved, the higher its osmotic pressure. In this example, the sucrose solution has a higher osmotic pressure than pure water, which has an osmotic pressure of zero.

Explore Your World
Everyday Osmosis

1. Place a few pieces of dried fruit such as raisins, prunes, or banana chips in water. Observe them after 1 hour or more. Look at them again the next day.
2. Place some grapes in a concentrated salt-water solution. Observe them after 1 hour or more. Look at them again the next day.
3. Place one potato slice in water and another slice in a concentrated salt-water solution. After 1 to 2 hours, observe the shapes and size of the slices. Look at them again the next day.

Questions

1. How did the shape of the dried fruit change after being in water? Explain.
2. How did the appearance of the grapes change after being in a concentrated salt solution? Explain.
3. How does the appearance of the potato slice that was placed in water compare to the appearance of the potato slice placed in salt water? Explain.
4. At the grocery store, why are sprinklers used to spray water on fresh produce such as lettuce, carrots, and cucumbers?

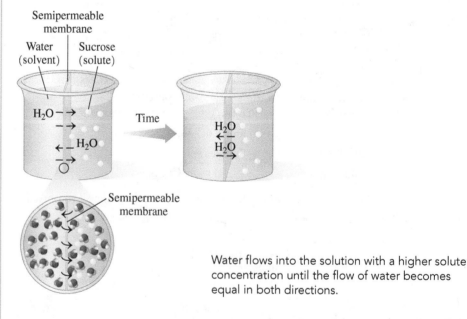

Water flows into the solution with a higher solute concentration until the flow of water becomes equal in both directions.

In a process called *reverse osmosis*, a pressure greater than the osmotic pressure is applied to a solution so that it is forced through a purification membrane. The flow of water is reversed because water flows from an area of lower water concentration to an area of higher water concentration. The molecules and ions in solution stay behind, trapped by the membrane, while water passes through the membrane. This process of reverse osmosis is used in a few desalination plants to obtain pure water from sea (salt) water. However, the pressure that must be applied requires so much energy that reverse osmosis is not yet an economical method for obtaining pure water in most parts of the world.

Osmolarity

Every molecule and every ion that dissolves in a solution contributes to its osmotic pressure. A solution with a higher concentration of dissolved particles has a higher osmotic pressure than a solution with fewer dissolved particles. Because the osmotic pressure depends on the number of particles in solution, which is equal to the number of osmoles. We use a concentration term *osmolarity* to indicate the number of osmoles dissolved in each liter of solution.

$$\text{Osmolarity (Osm)} = \frac{\text{number of osmoles}}{1\text{ L of solution}}$$

When one mole of NaCl dissolves in one liter of solution, it produces one mole of Na^+ ions and one mole of Cl^- ions, or two osmoles. This would be a 1 M NaCl or a 2 Osm solution.

$$NaCl(s) \xrightarrow{\text{H}_2\text{O}} Na^+(aq) + Cl^-(aq)$$
1 mole   1 mole   1 mole   = 2 osmoles

When one mole of K_2SO_4 dissolves, two moles of K^+ ions and one mole of SO_4^{2-} ions or three osmoles are produced from each one mole of $K_2SO_4(s)$.

$$K_2SO_4(s) \xrightarrow{\text{H}_2\text{O}} 2K^+(aq) + SO_4^{2-}(aq)$$
1 mole   2 moles   1 mole   = 3 osmoles

Using the number of moles of ions as a conversion factor, we can convert the molarity of the solution to the osmolarity. For example, a 0.10 M K_2SO_4 solution would be a 0.30 Osm K_2SO_4 solution.

$$\frac{0.10\text{ mole } K_2SO_4}{1\text{ L solution}} \times \frac{3\text{ osmoles}}{1\text{ mole } K_2SO_4} = 0.30\text{ Osm } K_2SO_4 \text{ solution}$$

The physiological solutions 0.9% (m/v) NaCl and 5% (m/v) glucose are isotonic solutions because they have the same concentration of particles and the same osmolarities as body fluids.

▶ **SAMPLE PROBLEM 9.17 Calculating the Osmolarity of a Solution**

The osmolarity of normal blood serum is 0.30 Osm. Show that the osmolarity of 0.90% (m/v) NaCl solution is the same as that of normal serum.

SOLUTION

STEP 1 State the given and needed quantities.

ANALYZE THE PROBLEM	Given	Need
	0.90% (m/v) NaCl	osmolarity (Osm) of NaCl solution

STEP 2 Determine the number of osmoles in one mole of solute.

1 mole NaCl(s) $\longrightarrow$ 1 mole $Na^+(aq)$ + 1 mole $Cl^-(aq)$ =
                                             2 moles of particles = 2 osmoles

STEP 3 Calculate the osmolarity (Osm).

$$\frac{0.90\text{ g NaCl}}{100\text{ mL solution}} \times \frac{1\text{ mole NaCl}}{58.44\text{ g NaCl}} \times \frac{2\text{ osmoles}}{1\text{ mole NaCl}} \times \frac{1000\text{ mL}}{1\text{ L}} = 0.30\text{ Osm NaCl solution}$$

The osmolarity of 0.90% (m/v) NaCl solution is 0.30 Osm, which is the same as that of normal blood serum.

STUDY CHECK 9.17

Calculate the osmolarity of 5% (m/v) glucose solution. (The molar mass of the nonelectrolyte glucose is 180 g/mole.)

ANSWER

0.3 Osm

Guide to Calculating Osmolarity

STEP 1
State the given and needed quantities.

STEP 2
Determine the number of osmoles in one mole of solute.

STEP 3
Calculate the osmolarity (Osm).

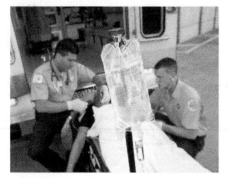

A 0.9% NaCl solution is isotonic with the solute concentration of the blood cells of the body.

Isotonic Solutions

Because the cell membranes in biological systems are semipermeable, osmosis is an ongoing process. The solutes in body solutions such as blood, tissue fluids, lymph, and plasma all exert osmotic pressure. Most intravenous (IV) solutions used in a hospital are **isotonic solutions**, which exert the same osmotic pressure as body fluids such as blood. The percent concentration typically used in IV solutions is mass/volume percent (m/v), which is a type of percent concentration we have already discussed. The most typical isotonic solutions are 0.9% (m/v) NaCl solution, or 0.9 g of NaCl/100 mL of solution, and 5% (m/v) glucose, or 5 g of glucose/100 mL of solution. Although they do not contain the same kinds of particles, a 0.9% (m/v) NaCl solution as well as a 5% (m/v) glucose solution both have the same osmolarity, 0.3 Osm. A red blood cell placed in an isotonic solution retains its volume because there is an equal flow of water into and out of the cell (see Figure 9.11a).

Hypotonic and Hypertonic Solutions

If a red blood cell is placed in a solution that is not isotonic, the differences in osmotic pressure inside and outside the cell can drastically alter the volume of the cell. When a red blood cell is placed in a **hypotonic solution**, which has a lower solute concentration (*hypo* means "lower than"), water flows into the cell by osmosis. The increase in fluid causes the cell to swell, and possibly burst—a process called **hemolysis** (see Figure 9.11b). A similar process occurs when you place dehydrated food, such as raisins or dried fruit, in water. The water enters the cells, and the food becomes plump and smooth.

If a red blood cell is placed in a **hypertonic solution**, which has a higher solute concentration (*hyper* means "greater than"), water flows out of the cell into the hypertonic solution by osmosis. Suppose a red blood cell is placed in a 10% (m/v) NaCl solution. Because the osmotic pressure in the red blood cell is the same as a 0.9% (m/v) NaCl solution, the 10% (m/v) NaCl solution has a much greater osmotic pressure. As water leaves the cell, it shrinks, a process called **crenation** (see Figure 9.11c). A similar process occurs when making pickles, which uses a hypertonic salt solution that causes the cucumbers to shrivel as they lose water.

FIGURE 9.11 ▶ **(a)** In an isotonic solution, a red blood cell retains its normal volume. **(b)** Hemolysis: In a hypotonic solution, water flows into a red blood cell, causing it to swell and burst. **(c)** Crenation: In a hypertonic solution, water leaves the red blood cell, causing it to shrink.

Q What happens to a red blood cell placed in a 4% NaCl solution?

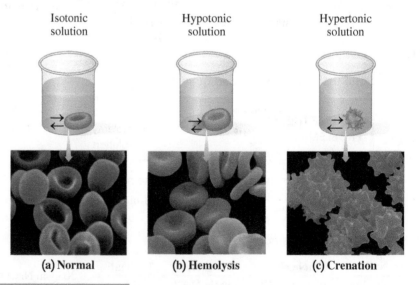

(a) Normal   (b) Hemolysis   (c) Crenation

SAMPLE PROBLEM 9.18 Isotonic, Hypotonic, and Hypertonic Solutions

Describe each of the following solutions as isotonic, hypotonic, or hypertonic. Indicate whether a red blood cell placed in each solution will undergo hemolysis, crenation, or no change.

a. a 5% (m/v) glucose solution
b. a 0.2% (m/v) NaCl solution

SOLUTION

a. A 5% (m/v) glucose solution is isotonic. A red blood cell will not undergo any change.
b. A 0.2% (m/v) NaCl solution is hypotonic. A red blood cell will undergo hemolysis.

STUDY CHECK 9.18

What will happen to a red blood cell placed in a 10% (m/v) glucose solution?

ANSWER

The red blood cell will shrink (crenate).

Dialysis

Dialysis is a process that is similar to osmosis. In dialysis, a semipermeable membrane, called a dialyzing membrane, permits small solute molecules and ions as well as solvent water molecules to pass through, but it retains large particles, such as colloids. Dialysis is a way to separate solution particles from colloids.

Suppose we fill a cellophane bag with a solution containing NaCl, glucose, starch, and protein and place it in pure water. Cellophane is a dialyzing membrane, and the sodium ions, chloride ions, and glucose molecules will pass through it into the surrounding water. However, large colloidal particles, like starch and protein, remain inside. Water molecules will flow into the cellophane bag. Eventually the concentrations of sodium ions, chloride ions, and glucose molecules inside and outside the dialysis bag become equal. To remove more NaCl or glucose, the cellophane bag must be placed in a fresh sample of pure water.

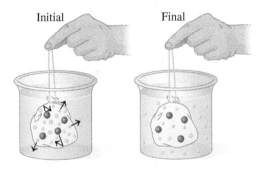

Initial   Final

○ Solution particles such as Na$^+$, Cl$^-$, glucose
● Colloidal particles such as protein, starch

Solution particles pass through a dialyzing membrane, but colloidal particles are retained.

 Chemistry Link to Health

Dialysis by the Kidneys and the Artificial Kidney

The fluids of the body undergo dialysis by the membranes of the kidneys, which remove waste materials, excess salts, and water. In an adult, each kidney contains about 2 million nephrons. At the top of each nephron, there is a network of arterial capillaries called the *glomerulus.*

As blood flows into the glomerulus, small particles, such as amino acids, glucose, urea, water, and certain ions, will move through the capillary membranes into the nephron. As this solution moves through the nephron, substances still of value to the body (such as amino acids, glucose, certain ions, and 99% of the water) are reabsorbed. The major waste product, urea, is excreted in the urine.

Hemodialysis

If the kidneys fail to dialyze waste products, increased levels of urea can become life-threatening in a relatively short time. A person with kidney failure must use an artificial kidney, which cleanses the blood by **hemodialysis**.

A typical artificial kidney machine contains a large tank filled with water containing selected electrolytes. In the center of this dialyzing bath (dialysate), there is a dialyzing coil or membrane made of cellulose tubing. As the patient's blood flows through the dialyzing coil, the highly concentrated waste products dialyze out of the blood. No blood is lost because the membrane is not permeable to large particles such as red blood cells.

Dialysis patients do not produce much urine. As a result, they retain large amounts of water between dialysis treatments, which produces a strain on the heart. The intake of fluids for a dialysis patient may be restricted to as little as a few teaspoons of water a day. In the dialysis procedure, the pressure of the blood is increased as it circulates through the dialyzing coil so water can be squeezed out of the blood. For some dialysis patients, 2 to 10 L of water may be removed during one treatment. Dialysis patients have from two to three treatments a week, each treatment requiring about 5 to 7 h. Some of the newer treatments require less time. For many patients, dialysis is done at home with a home dialysis unit.

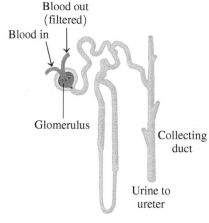

In the kidneys, each nephron contains a glomerulus where urea and waste products are removed to form urine.

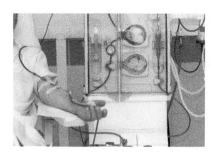

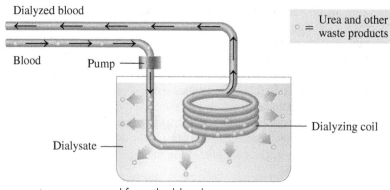

During dialysis, waste products and excess water are removed from the blood.

QUESTIONS AND PROBLEMS

9.6 Properties of Solutions

LEARNING GOAL Identify a mixture as a solution, a colloid, or a suspension. Describe how the number of particles in a solution affects the freezing point, the boiling point, and the osmotic pressure of a solution.

9.71 Identify the following as characteristic of a solution, a colloid, or a suspension:
  a. a mixture that cannot be separated by a semipermeable membrane
  b. a mixture that settles out upon standing

9.72 Identify the following as characteristic of a solution, a colloid, or a suspension:
  a. Particles of this mixture remain inside a semipermeable membrane but pass through filters.
  b. The particles of solute in this solution are very large and visible.

9.73 In each pair, identify the solution that will have a lower freezing point. Explain.
  a. 1.0 mole of glycerol (nonelectrolyte) and 2.0 moles of ethylene glycol (nonelectrolyte) each in 1.0 kg of water
  b. 0.50 mole of KCl (strong electrolyte) and 0.50 mole of $MgCl_2$ (strong electrolyte) each in 1.0 kg of water

9.74 In each pair, identify the solution that will have a higher boiling point. Explain.
  a. 1.50 moles of LiOH (strong electrolyte) and 3.00 moles of KOH (strong electrolyte) each in 1.0 kg of water

  b. 0.40 mole of $Al(NO_3)_3$ (strong electrolyte) and 0.40 mole of CsCl (strong electrolyte) each in 1.0 kg of water

9.75 Calculate the freezing point of each of the following solutions:
  a. 1.36 moles of methanol, CH_3OH, a nonelectrolyte, added to 1.00 kg of water
  b. 640. g of the antifreeze propylene glycol, $C_3H_8O_2$, a nonelectrolyte, dissolved in 1.00 kg of water
  c. 111 g of KCl, a strong electrolyte, dissolved in 1.00 kg of water

9.76 Calculate the boiling point of each of the following solutions:
  a. 2.12 moles of glucose, $C_6H_{12}O_6$, a nonelectrolyte, added to 1.00 kg of water
  b. 110. g of sucrose, $C_{12}H_{22}O_{11}$, a nonelectrolyte, dissolved in 1.00 kg of water
  c. 146 g of $NaNO_3$, a strong electrolyte, dissolved in 1.00 kg of water

9.77 A 10% (m/v) starch solution is separated from a 1% (m/v) starch solution by a semipermeable membrane. (Starch is a colloid.)
  a. Which compartment has the higher osmotic pressure?
  b. In which direction will water flow initially?
  c. In which compartment will the volume level rise?

9.78 A 0.1% (m/v) albumin solution is separated from a 2% (m/v) albumin solution by a semipermeable membrane. (Albumin is a colloid.)

a. Which compartment has the higher osmotic pressure?
b. In which direction will water flow initially?
c. In which compartment will the volume level rise?

9.79 Indicate the compartment (**A** or **B**) that will increase in volume for each of the following pairs of solutions separated by a semi-permeable membrane:

A	B
a. 5% (m/v) sucrose	10% (m/v) sucrose
b. 8% (m/v) albumin	4% (m/v) albumin
c. 0.1% (m/v) starch	10% (m/v) starch

9.80 Indicate the compartment (**A** or **B**) that will increase in volume for each of the following pairs of solutions separated by a semi-permeable membrane:

A	B
a. 20% (m/v) starch	10% (m/v) starch
b. 10% (m/v) albumin	2% (m/v) albumin
c. 0.5% (m/v) sucrose	5% (m/v) sucrose

℞ Clinical Applications

9.81 What is the osmolarity of each of the following solutions?
   a. hypertonic saline, NaCl, 3.0% (m/v) (strong electrolyte)
   b. 50.% (m/v) dextrose ($C_6H_{12}O_6$), used to treat severe hypoglycemia

9.82 What is the osmolarity of each of the following solutions?
   a. 3% (m/v) NaCl (strong electrolyte), used to treat hyponatremia
   b. 2.5% (m/v) dextrose ($C_6H_{12}O_6$), used to hydrate cells

9.83 Are the following solutions isotonic, hypotonic, or hypertonic compared with a red blood cell?
   a. distilled H_2O **b.** 1% (m/v) glucose
   c. 0.9% (m/v) NaCl   **d.** 15% (m/v) glucose

9.84 Will a red blood cell undergo crenation, hemolysis, or no change in each of the following solutions?
   a. 1% (m/v) glucose   **b.** 2% (m/v) NaCl
   c. 5% (m/v) glucose   **d.** 0.1% (m/v) NaCl

9.85 Each of the following mixtures is placed in a dialyzing bag and immersed in distilled water. Which substances will be found outside the bag in the distilled water?
   a. NaCl solution
   b. starch solution (colloid) and alanine (an amino acid) solution
   c. NaCl solution and starch solution (colloid)
   d. urea solution

9.86 Each of the following mixtures is placed in a dialyzing bag and immersed in distilled water. Which substances will be found outside the bag in the distilled water?
   a. KCl solution and glucose solution
   b. albumin solution (colloid)
   c. an albumin solution (colloid), KCl solution, and glucose solution
   d. urea solution and NaCl solution

Clinical Update

Using Dialysis for Renal Failure

As a dialysis patient, Michelle has a 4-h dialysis treatment three times a week. When she arrives at the dialysis clinic, her weight, temperature, and blood pressure are taken and blood tests are done to determine the level of electrolytes and urea in her blood. In the dialysis center, tubes to the dialyzer are connected to the catheter she has had implanted. Blood is then pumped out of her body, through the dialyzer where it is filtered, and returned to her body. As Michelle's blood flows through the dialyzer, electrolytes from the dialysate move into her blood, and waste products in her blood move into the dialysate, which is continually renewed. To achieve normal serum electrolyte levels, dialysate fluid contains sodium, chloride, and magnesium levels that are equal to serum concentrations. These electrolytes are removed from the blood only if their concentrations are higher than normal. Typically, in dialysis patients, the potassium ion level is higher than normal. Therefore, initial dialysis may start with a low concentration of potassium ion in the dialysate. During dialysis excess fluid is removed by osmosis. A 4-h dialysis session requires at least 120 L of dialysis fluid. During dialysis, the electrolytes in the dialysate are adjusted until the electrolytes have the same levels as normal serum. Initially the dialysate solution prepared for Michelle's pre-dialysis blood tests shows that the electrolyte levels in her blood are HCO_3^- 24 mEq/L, K^+ 6.0 mEq/L, Na^+ 148 mEq/L, Ca^{2+} 3.0 mEq/L, Mg^{2+} 1.0 mEq/L, Cl^- 111.0 mEq/L.

A dialysis solution is prepared for Michelle that contains the following: HCO_3^- 35.0 mEq/L, K^+ 2.0 mEq/L, Na^+ 130 mEq/L, Ca^{2+} 5.0 mEq/L, Mg^{2+} 3.0 mEq/L, Cl^- 105.0 mEq/L, glucose 5.0% (m/v).

℞ Clinical Applications

9.87 **a.** Which electrolyte concentrations are higher than normal serum values in Michelle's pre-dialysis blood test (see Table 9.6)?
   b. Which electrolyte concentrations are lower than normal serum values in Michelle's pre-dialysis blood test (see Table 9.6)?
   c. Which electrolytes need to be increased by dialysis for Michelle's blood serum?
   d. Which electrolytes are decreased by dialysis for Michelle's blood serum?

9.88 **a.** What is the total positive charge, in milliequivalents/L, of the electrolytes in the dialysate fluid?
   b. What is the total negative charge, in milliequivalents/L, of the electrolytes in the dialysate fluid?
   c. What is the net total charge, in milliequivalents/L, of the electrolytes in the dialysate fluid?
   d. What is the osmolarity of the dialysate fluid?

CONCEPT MAP

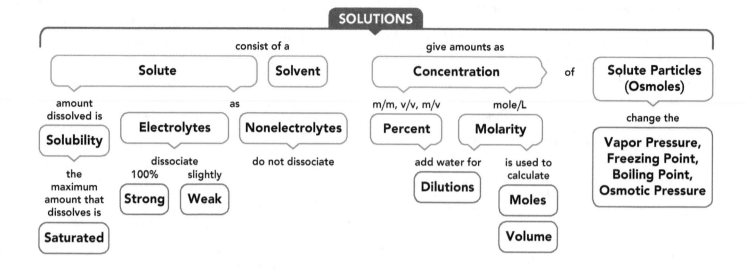

SOLUTIONS

consist of a

Solute   **Solvent**

give amounts as

Concentration of **Solute Particles (Osmoles)**

amount dissolved is

Solubility

as

Electrolytes   **Nonelectrolytes**

do not dissociate

the maximum amount that dissolves is

Saturated

dissociate
100%   slightly

Strong   **Weak**

m/m, v/v, m/v   mole/L

Percent   **Molarity**

add water for   is used to calculate

Dilutions   **Moles**

Volume

change the

Vapor Pressure, Freezing Point, Boiling Point, Osmotic Pressure

CHAPTER REVIEW

9.1 Solutions

LEARNING GOAL Identify the solute and solvent in a solution; describe the formation of a solution.

- A solution forms when a solute dissolves in a solvent.
- In a solution, the particles of solute are evenly dispersed in the solvent.
- The solute and solvent may be solid, liquid, or gas.
- The polar O—H bond leads to hydrogen bonding between water molecules.
- An ionic solute dissolves in water, a polar solvent, because the polar water molecules attract and pull the ions into solution, where they become hydrated.
- The expression *like dissolves like* means that a polar or an ionic solute dissolves in a polar solvent while a nonpolar solute dissolves in a nonpolar solvent.

9.2 Electrolytes and Nonelectrolytes

LEARNING GOAL Identify solutes as electrolytes or nonelectrolytes.

- Substances that produce ions in water are called electrolytes because their solutions will conduct an electrical current.
- Strong electrolytes are completely dissociated, whereas weak electrolytes are only partially ionized.
- Nonelectrolytes are substances that dissolve in water to produce only molecules and cannot conduct electrical currents.
- An equivalent (Eq) is the amount of an electrolyte that carries one mole of positive or negative charge.
- One mole of Na^+ is 1 Eq. One mole of Ca^{2+} has 2 Eq.

Strong electrolyte

9.3 Solubility

LEARNING GOAL Define solubility; distinguish between an unsaturated and a saturated solution. Identify an ionic compound as soluble or insoluble.

- The solubility of a solute is the maximum amount of a solute that can dissolve in 100 g of solvent.
- A solution that contains the maximum amount of dissolved solute is a saturated solution.
- A solution containing less than the maximum amount of dissolved solute is unsaturated.
- An increase in temperature increases the solubility of most solids in water, but decreases the solubility of gases in water.
- Ionic compounds that are soluble in water usually contain Li^+, Na^+, K^+, NH_4^+, NO_3^-, or acetate, $C_2H_3O_2^-$.

Dissolved solute

Undissolved solute

Saturated solution

9.4 Solution Concentrations and Reactions

LEARNING GOAL Calculate the concentration of a solute in a solution; use concentration units to calculate the amount of solute or solution. Given the volume and concentration of a solution, calculate the amount of another reactant or product in a reaction.

- Mass percent expresses the mass/mass (m/m) ratio of the mass of solute to the mass of solution multiplied by 100%.
- Percent concentration can also be expressed as volume/volume (v/v) and mass/volume (m/v) ratios.
- Molarity is the moles of solute per liter of solution.
- In calculations of grams or milliliters of solute or solution, the concentration is used as a conversion factor.
- Molarity (mole/L) is written as conversion factors to solve for moles of solute or volume of solution.

Water added to make a solution   250 mL

5.0 g of KI   250 mL of KI solution

- When solutions are involved in chemical reactions, the moles of a substance in solution can be determined from the volume and molarity of the solution.
- When mass, volume, and molarities of substances in a reaction are given, the balanced equation is used to determine the quantities or concentrations of other substances in the reaction.

9.5 Dilution of Solutions
LEARNING GOAL Describe the dilution of a solution; calculate the unknown concentration or volume when a solution is diluted.

- In dilution, a solvent such as water is added to a solution, which increases its volume and decreases its concentration.

9.6 Properties of Solutions
LEARNING GOAL Identify a mixture as a solution, a colloid, or a suspension. Describe how the number of particles in a solution affects the freezing point, the boiling point, and the osmotic pressure of a solution.

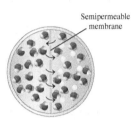

Semipermeable membrane

- Colloids contain particles that pass through most filters but do not settle out or pass through permeable membranes.
- Suspensions have very large particles that settle out of solution.
- The particles in a solution lower the vapor pressure, raise the boiling point, lower the freezing point, and increase the osmotic pressure.
- In osmosis, solvent (water) passes through a semipermeable membrane from a solution with a lower osmotic pressure (lower solute concentration) to a solution with a higher osmotic pressure (higher solute concentration).
- Isotonic solutions have osmotic pressures equal to that of body fluids.
- In osmosis, solvent (water) passes through a selectively permeable membrane from a solution with a lower solute concentration to a solution with a higher concentration.
- Isotonic solutions have osmotic pressures equal to that of body fluids.
- A red blood cell maintains its volume in an isotonic solution but swells in a hypotonic solution, and shrinks in a hypertonic solution.
- In dialysis, water and small solute particles pass through a dialyzing membrane, while larger particles are retained.

KEY TERMS

colloid A mixture having particles that are moderately large. Colloids pass through filters but cannot pass through semipermeable membranes.

concentration A measure of the amount of solute that is dissolved in a specified amount of solution.

crenation The shriveling of a cell because water leaves the cell when the cell is placed in a hypertonic solution.

dialysis A process in which water and small solute particles pass through a semipermeable membrane.

dilution A process by which water (solvent) is added to a solution to increase the volume and decrease (dilute) the concentration of the solute.

electrolyte A substance that produces ions when dissolved in water; its solution conducts electricity.

equivalent (Eq) The amount of a positive or negative ion that supplies 1 mole of electrical charge.

hemodialysis A mechanical cleansing of the blood by an artificial kidney using the principle of dialysis.

hemolysis A swelling and bursting of red blood cells in a hypotonic solution because of an increase in fluid volume.

Henry's law The solubility of a gas in a liquid is directly related to the pressure of that gas above the liquid.

hydration The process of surrounding dissolved ions by water molecules.

hypertonic solution A solution that has a higher particle concentration and higher osmotic pressure than the cells of the body.

hypotonic solution A solution that has a lower particle concentration and lower osmotic pressure than the cells of the body.

isotonic solution A solution that has the same particle concentration and osmotic pressure as that of the cells of the body.

mass percent (m/m) The grams of solute in exactly 100 g of solution.

mass/volume percent (m/v) The grams of solute in exactly 100 mL of solution.

molarity (M) The number of moles of solute in exactly 1 L of solution.

nonelectrolyte A substance that dissolves in water as molecules; its solution does not conduct an electrical current.

osmosis The flow of a solvent, usually water, through a semipermeable membrane into a solution of higher solute concentration.

osmotic pressure The pressure that prevents the flow of water into the more concentrated solution.

saturated solution A solution containing the maximum amount of solute that can dissolve at a given temperature. Any additional solute will remain undissolved in the container.

solubility The maximum amount of solute that can dissolve in exactly 100 g of solvent, usually water, at a given temperature.

solubility rules A set of guidelines that states whether an ionic compound is soluble or insoluble in water.

solute The component in a solution that is present in the lesser amount.

solution A homogeneous mixture in which the solute is made up of small particles (ions or molecules) that can pass through filters and semipermeable membranes.

solvent The substance in which the solute dissolves; usually the component present in greater amount.

strong electrolyte A compound that ionizes completely when it dissolves in water. Its solution is a good conductor of electricity.

suspension A mixture in which the solute particles are large enough and heavy enough to settle out and be retained by both filters and semipermeable membranes.

unsaturated solution A solution that contains less solute than can be dissolved.

volume percent (v/v) A percent concentration that relates the volume of the solute in exactly 100 mL of solution.

weak electrolyte A substance that produces only a few ions along with many molecules when it dissolves in water. Its solution is a weak conductor of electricity.

⚛ CORE CHEMISTRY SKILLS

The chapter section containing each Core Chemistry Skill is shown in parentheses at the end of each heading.

Using Solubility Rules (9.3)

- Soluble ionic compounds contain Li^+, Na^+, K^+, NH_4^+, NO_3^-, or $C_2H_3O_2^-$ (acetate).
- Ionic compounds containing Cl^-, Br^-, or I^- are soluble, but if they are combined with Ag^+, Pb^{2+}, or Hg_2^{2+}, the ionic compounds are insoluble.
- Most ionic compounds containing SO_4^{2-} are soluble, but if SO_4^{2-} is combined with Ba^{2+}, Pb^{2+}, Ca^{2+}, Sr^{2+}, or Hg_2^{2+}, the ionic compounds are insoluble.
- Ionic compounds that do not contain at least one of these ions are usually insoluble.

Example: Is K_2SO_4 soluble or insoluble in water?
Answer: K_2SO_4 is soluble in water because it contains K^+.

Calculating Concentration (9.4)

The amount of solute dissolved in a certain amount of solution is called the concentration of the solution.

- Mass percent $(m/m) = \dfrac{\text{mass of solute}}{\text{mass of solution}} \times 100\%$

- Volume percent $(v/v) = \dfrac{\text{volume of solute}}{\text{volume of solution}} \times 100\%$

- Mass/volume percent $(m/v) = \dfrac{\text{grams of solute}}{\text{milliliters of solution}} \times 100\%$

- Molarity $(M) = \dfrac{\text{moles of solute}}{\text{liters of solution}}$

Example: What is the mass/volume percent (m/v) and the molarity (M) of 225 mL (0.225 L) of a LiCl solution that contains 17.1 g of LiCl?

Answer:

$$\text{Mass/volume percent } (m/v) = \dfrac{\text{grams of solute}}{\text{milliliters of solution}} \times 100\%$$

$$= \dfrac{17.1 \text{ g LiCl}}{225 \text{ mL solution}} \times 100\%$$

$$= 7.60\% \ (m/v) \text{ LiCl solution}$$

$$\text{moles of LiCl} = 17.1 \text{ g LiCl} \times \dfrac{1 \text{ mole LiCl}}{42.39 \text{ g LiCl}}$$

$$= 0.403 \text{ mole of LiCl}$$

$$\text{Molarity } (M) = \dfrac{\text{moles of solute}}{\text{liters of solution}} = \dfrac{0.403 \text{ mole LiCl}}{0.225 \text{ L solution}}$$

$$= 1.79 \text{ M LiCl solution}$$

Using Concentration as a Conversion Factor (9.4)

- When we need to calculate the amount of solute or solution, we use the mass/volume percent (m/v) or the molarity (M) as a conversion factor.
- For example, the concentration of a 4.50 M HCl solution means there are 4.50 moles of HCl in 1 L of HCl solution, which gives two conversion factors written as

$$\dfrac{4.50 \text{ moles HCl}}{1 \text{ L solution}} \quad \text{and} \quad \dfrac{1 \text{ L solution}}{4.50 \text{ moles HCl}}$$

Example: How many milliliters of a 4.50 M HCl solution will provide 1.13 moles of HCl?

Answer:

$$1.13 \text{ moles HCl} \times \dfrac{1 \text{ L solution}}{4.50 \text{ moles HCl}} \times \dfrac{1000 \text{ mL solution}}{1 \text{ L solution}}$$

$$= 251 \text{ mL of HCl solution}$$

Calculating the Quantity of a Reactant or Product for a Chemical Reaction in Solution (9.4)

- When chemical reactions involve aqueous solutions of reactants or products, we use the balanced chemical equation, the molarity, and the volume to determine the moles or grams of the reactants or products.

Example: How many grams of zinc metal will react with 0.315 L of a 1.20 M HCl solution?

$$Zn(s) + 2HCl(aq) \longrightarrow H_2(g) + ZnCl_2(aq)$$

Answer:

$$0.315 \text{ L solution} \times \dfrac{1.20 \text{ moles HCl}}{1 \text{ L solution}} \times \dfrac{1 \text{ mole Zn}}{2 \text{ moles HCl}} \times \dfrac{65.41 \text{ g Zn}}{1 \text{ mole Zn}}$$

$$= 12.4 \text{ g of Zn}$$

Calculating the Boiling Point/Freezing Point of a Solution (9.6)

- The particles in a solution raise the boiling point, lower the freezing point, and increase the osmotic pressure.
- The boiling point elevation is determined from the moles of particles in one kilogram of water.
- The freezing point lowering is determined from the moles of particles in one kilogram of water.

Example: What is the boiling point of a solution that contains 1.5 moles of the strong electrolyte KCl in 1.0 kg of water?

Answer: A solution of 1.5 moles of KCl in 1.0 kg of water contains 3.0 moles of particles (1.5 moles of K^+ and 1.5 moles of Cl^-) in 1.0 kg of water and has a boiling point change of

$$3.0 \text{ moles particles} \times \dfrac{0.51 \ ^\circ C}{1 \text{ mole particles}} = 1.53 \ ^\circ C$$

The boiling point would be $100.00 \ ^\circ C + 1.53 \ ^\circ C = 101.53 \ ^\circ C$.

UNDERSTANDING THE CONCEPTS

The chapter sections to review are shown in parentheses at the end of each question.

9.89 Match the diagrams with the following: (9.1)
a. a polar solute and a polar solvent
b. a nonpolar solute and a polar solvent
c. a nonpolar solute and a nonpolar solvent

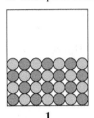 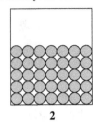

      1   **2**

9.90 If all the solute is dissolved in diagram **1**, how would heating or cooling the solution cause each of the following changes? (9.3)
a. **2** to **3**   b. **2** to **1**

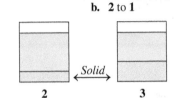

   1   **2**   ←*Solid*→   **3**

9.91 Select the diagram that represents the solution formed by a solute 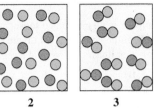 that is a (9.2)
a. nonelectrolyte
b. weak electrolyte
c. strong electrolyte

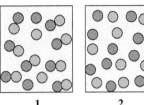

     1   **2**   **3**

9.92 Select the container that represents the dilution of a 4% (m/v) KCl solution to give each of the following: (9.5)
a. a 2% (m/v) KCl solution
b. a 1% (m/v) KCl solution

4% (m/v) KCl   **1**   **2**   **3**

Use the following illustration of beakers and solutions for problems 9.93 and 9.94:

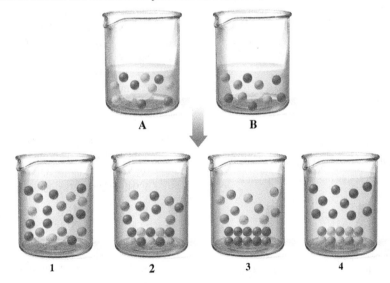

       A   **B**

    1   **2**   **3**   **4**

9.93 Use the following types of ions: (9.3)

Na^+ Cl^- Ag^+ ● NO_3^- ●

a. Select the beaker (**1**, **2**, **3**, or **4**) that contains the products after the solutions in beakers **A** and **B** are mixed.
b. If an insoluble ionic compound forms, write the ionic equation.
c. If a reaction occurs, write the net ionic equation.

9.94 Use the following types of ions: (9.3)

K^+ ● NO_3^- ● NH_4^+ ● Br^- ●

a. Select the beaker (**1**, **2**, **3**, or **4**) that contains the products after the solutions in beakers **A** and **B** are mixed.

b. If an insoluble ionic compound forms, write the ionic equation.
c. If a reaction occurs, write the net ionic equation.

9.95 A pickle is made by soaking a cucumber in brine, a salt-water solution. What makes the smooth cucumber become wrinkled like a prune? (9.6)

9.96 Why do lettuce leaves in a salad wilt after a vinaigrette dressing containing salt is added? (9.6)

9.97 A semipermeable membrane separates two compartments, **A** and **B**. If the levels in **A** and **B** are equal initially, select the diagram that illustrates the final levels in **a** to **d**: (9.6)

A B	A B	A B
1	**2**	**3**

Solution in A	Solution in B
a. 2% (m/v) starch	8% (m/v) starch
b. 1% (m/v) starch	1% (m/v) starch
c. 5% (m/v) sucrose	1% (m/v) sucrose
d. 0.1% (m/v) sucrose	1% (m/v) sucrose

9.98 Select the diagram that represents the shape of a red blood cell when placed in each of the following **a** to **e**: (9.6)

1   **2**   **3**

Normal red blood cell

a. 0.9% (m/v) NaCl solution
b. 10% (m/v) glucose solution
c. 0.01% (m/v) NaCl solution
d. 5% (m/v) glucose solution
e. 1% (m/v) glucose solution

ADDITIONAL QUESTIONS AND PROBLEMS

9.99 Why does iodine dissolve in hexane, but not in water? (9.1)

9.100 How do temperature and pressure affect the solubility of solids and gases in water? (9.3)

9.101 Potassium nitrate has a solubility of 32 g of KNO_3 in 100 g of H_2O at 20 °C. Determine if each of the following forms an unsaturated or saturated solution at 20 °C: (9.3)
a. adding 32 g of KNO_3 to 200. g of H_2O
b. adding 19 g of KNO_3 to 50. g of H_2O
c. adding 68 g of KNO_3 to 150. g of H_2O

9.102 Potassium chloride has a solubility of 43 g of KCl in 100 g of H_2O at 50 °C. Determine if each of the following forms an unsaturated or saturated solution at 50 °C: (9.3)
a. adding 25 g of KCl to 100. g of H_2O
b. adding 15 g of KCl to 25 g of H_2O
c. adding 86 g of KCl to 150. g of H_2O

9.103 Indicate whether each of the following ionic compounds is soluble or insoluble in water: (9.3)
a. KCl   **b.** $MgSO_4$ **c.** CuS
d. $AgNO_3$ **e.** $Ca(OH)_2$

9.104 Indicate whether each of the following ionic compounds is soluble or insoluble in water: (9.3)
a. $CuCO_3$ **b.** FeO   **c.** $Mg_3(PO_4)_2$
d. $(NH_4)_2SO_4$ **e.** $NaHCO_3$

9.105 Write the net ionic equation to show the formation of a solid (insoluble ionic compound) when the following solutions are mixed. Write *none* if no solid forms. (9.3)
a. $AgNO_3(aq)$ and $LiCl(aq)$
b. $NaCl(aq)$ and $KNO_3(aq)$
c. $Na_2SO_4(aq)$ and $BaCl_2(aq)$

9.106 Write the net ionic equation to show the formation of a solid (insoluble ionic compound) when the following solutions are mixed. Write *none* if no solid forms. (9.3)
a. $Ca(NO_3)_2(aq)$ and $Na_2S(aq)$
b. $Na_3PO_4(aq)$ and $Pb(NO_3)_2(aq)$
c. $FeCl_3(aq)$ and $NH_4NO_3(aq)$

9.107 Calculate the mass percent (m/m) of a solution containing 15.5 g of Na_2SO_4 and 75.5 g of H_2O. (9.4)

9.108 Calculate the mass percent (m/m) of a solution containing 26 g of K_2CO_3 and 724 g of H_2O. (9.4)

9.109 How many milliliters of a 12% (v/v) propyl alcohol solution would you need to obtain 4.5 mL of propyl alcohol? (9.4)

9.110 An 80-proof brandy is a 40.% (v/v) ethanol solution. The "proof" is twice the percent concentration of alcohol in the beverage. How many milliliters of alcohol are present in 750 mL of brandy? (9.4)

9.111 How many liters of a 12% (m/v) KOH solution would you need to obtain 86.0 g of KOH? (9.4)

9.112 How many liters of a 5.0% (m/v) glucose solution would you need to obtain 75 g of glucose? (9.4)

9.113 What is the molarity of a solution containing 8.0 g of NaOH in 400. mL of NaOH solution? (9.4)

9.114 What is the molarity of a solution containing 15.6 g of KCl in 274 mL of KCl solution? (9.4)

9.115 How many grams of solute are in each of the following solutions? (9.4)
a. 2.5 L of a 3.0 M $Al(NO_3)_3$ solution
b. 75 mL of a 0.50 M $C_6H_{12}O_6$ solution
c. 235 mL of a 1.80 M LiCl solution

9.116 How many grams of solute are in each of the following solutions? (9.4)
a. 0.428 L of a 0.450 M K_2CO_3 solution
b. 10.5 mL of a 2.50 M $AgNO_3$ solution
c. 28.4 mL of a 6.00 M H_3PO_4 solution

9.117 Calculate the final concentration of the solution when water is added to prepare each of the following: (9.5)
a. 25.0 mL of a 0.200 M NaBr solution is diluted to 50.0 mL
b. 15.0 mL of a 12.0% (m/v) K_2SO_4 solution is diluted to 40.0 mL
c. 75.0 mL of a 6.00 M NaOH solution is diluted to 255 mL

9.118 Calculate the final concentration of the solution when water is added to prepare each of the following: (9.5)
   a. 25.0 mL of a 18.0 M HCl solution is diluted to 500. mL
   b. 50.0 mL of a 15.0% (m/v) NH_4Cl solution is diluted to 125 mL
   c. 4.50 mL of a 8.50 M KOH solution is diluted to 75.0 mL

9.119 What is the initial volume, in milliliters, needed to prepare each of the following diluted solutions? (9.5)
   a. 250 mL of 3.0% (m/v) HCl from 10.0% (m/v) HCl
   b. 500. mL of 0.90% (m/v) NaCl from 5.0% (m/v) NaCl
   c. 350. mL of 2.00 M NaOH from 6.00 M NaOH

9.120 What is the initial volume, in milliliters, needed to prepare each of the following diluted solutions? (9.5)
   a. 250 mL of 5.0% (m/v) glucose from 20.% (m/v) glucose
   b. 45.0 mL of 1.0% (m/v) $CaCl_2$ from 5.0% (m/v) $CaCl_2$
   c. 100. mL of 6.00 M H_2SO_4 from 18.0 M H_2SO_4

9.121 Calculate the freezing point of each of the following solutions: (9.6)
   a. 0.580 mole of lactose, a nonelectrolyte, added to 1.00 kg of water
   b. 45.0 g of KCl, a strong electrolyte, dissolved in 1.00 kg of water
   c. 1.5 moles of K_3PO_4, a strong electrolyte, dissolved in 1.00 kg of water

9.122 Calculate the boiling point of each of the following solutions: (9.6)
   a. 175 g of glucose, $C_6H_{12}O_6$, a nonelectrolyte, added to 1.00 kg of water
   b. 1.8 moles of $CaCl_2$, a strong electrolyte, dissolved in 1.00 kg of water

   c. 50.0 g of $LiNO_3$, a strong electrolyte, dissolved in 1.00 kg of water

℞ Clinical Applications

9.123 An antacid tablet, such as Amphojel, may be taken to reduce excess stomach acid, which is 0.20 M HCl. If one dose of Amphojel contains 450 mg of $Al(OH)_3$, what volume, in milliliters, of stomach acid will be neutralized? (9.4)
$$Al(OH)_3(s) + 3HCl(aq) \longrightarrow 3H_2O(l) + AlCl_3 (aq)$$

9.124 Calcium carbonate, $CaCO_3$, reacts with stomach acid, (HCl, hydrochloric acid) according to the following equation: (9.4)
$$CaCO_3(s) + 2HCl(aq) \longrightarrow CO_2(g) + H_2O(l) + CaCl_2(aq)$$
Tums, an antacid, contains $CaCO_3$. If Tums is added to 20.0 mL of a 0.400 M HCl solution, how many grams of CO_2 gas are produced?

9.125 What is the osmolarity (Osm) of a half-normal 0.45% (m/v) NaCl solution? (9.6)

9.126 A Ringer's Injection solution contains Na^+ 147 mEq/L, K^+ 4 mEq/L, Ca^{2+} 4 mEq/L, and Cl^- 155 mEq/L. What is the osmolarity (Osm) of the solution? (9.6)

9.127 A patient on dialysis has a high level of urea, a high level of sodium, and a low level of potassium in the blood. Why is the dialyzing solution prepared with a high level of potassium but no sodium or urea? (9.6)

9.128 Why would a dialysis unit (artificial kidney) use isotonic concentrations of NaCl, KCl, $NaHCO_3$, and glucose in the dialysate? (9.6)

CHALLENGE QUESTIONS

The following groups of questions are related to the topics in this chapter. However, they do not all follow the chapter order, and they require you to combine concepts and skills from several sections. These questions will help you increase your critical thinking skills and prepare for your next exam.

9.129 In a laboratory experiment, a 10.0-mL sample of NaCl solution is poured into an evaporating dish with a mass of 24.10 g. The combined mass of the evaporating dish and NaCl solution is 36.15 g. After heating, the evaporating dish and dry NaCl have a combined mass of 25.50 g. (9.4)
   a. What is the mass percent (m/m) of the NaCl solution?
   b. What is the molarity (M) of the NaCl solution?
   c. If water is added to 10.0 mL of the initial NaCl solution to give a final volume of 60.0 mL, what is the molarity of the diluted NaCl solution?

9.130 In a laboratory experiment, a 15.0-mL sample of KCl solution is poured into an evaporating dish with a mass of 24.10 g. The combined mass of the evaporating dish and KCl solution is 41.50 g. After heating, the evaporating dish and dry KCl have a combined mass of 28.28 g. (9.4)
   a. What is the mass percent (m/m) of the KCl solution?
   b. What is the molarity (M) of the KCl solution?
   c. If water is added to 10.0 mL of the initial KCl solution to give a final volume of 60.0 mL, what is the molarity of the diluted KCl solution?

9.131 Potassium fluoride has a solubility of 92 g of KF in 100 g of H_2O at 18 °C. Determine if each of the following mixtures forms an unsaturated or saturated solution at 18 °C: (9.3)
   a. adding 35 g of KF to 25 g of H_2O
   b. adding 42 g of KF to 50. g of H_2O
   c. adding 145 g of KF to 150. g of H_2O

9.132 Lithium chloride has a solubility of 55 g of LiCl in 100 g of H_2O at 25 °C. Determine if each of the following mixtures forms an unsaturated or saturated solution at 25 °C: (9.3)
   a. adding 10 g of LiCl to 15 g of H_2O
   b. adding 25 g of LiCl to 50. g of H_2O
   c. adding 75 g of LiCl to 150. g of H_2O

9.133 A solution is prepared with 70.0 g of HNO_3 and 130.0 g of H_2O. The HNO_3 solution has a density of 1.21 g/mL. (9.4)
   a. What is the mass percent (m/m) of the HNO_3 solution?
   b. What is the total volume, in milliliters, of the solution?
   c. What is the mass/volume percent (m/v) of the solution?
   d. What is the molarity (M) of the solution?

9.134 A solution is prepared by dissolving 22.0 g of NaOH in 118.0 g of water. The NaOH solution has a density of 1.15 g/mL. (9.4)
   a. What is the mass percent (m/m) of the NaOH solution?
   b. What is the total volume, in milliliters, of the solution?
   c. What is the mass/volume percent (m/v) of the solution?
   d. What is the molarity (M) of the solution?

℞ **Clinical Applications**

9.135 A Pedialyte solution contains Na^+ 45 mEq/L, K^+ 20. mEq/L, Cl^- 35 mEq/L, citrate^{3-} 30. mEq/L, and glucose ($C_6H_{12}O_6$) 25 g/L. (9.6)
    a. What is the total positive charge of the electrolytes?
    b. What is the total negative charge of the electrolytes?
    c. What is the osmolarity (Osm) of the solution?

9.136 A lactated Ringer's solution with 5% glucose contains Na^+ 130. mEq/L, K^+ 4 mEq/L, Ca^{2+} 3 mEq/L, Cl^- 109 mEq/L, lactate$^-$ 28 mEq/L, and glucose ($C_6H_{12}O_6$) 50. g/L. (9.6)
    a. What is the total positive charge of the electrolytes?
    b. What is the total negative charge of the electrolytes?
    c. What is the osmolarity (Osm) of the solution?

ANSWERS

Answers to Selected Questions and Problems

9.1 a. NaCl, solute; water, solvent
    b. water, solute; ethanol, solvent
    c. oxygen, solute; nitrogen, solvent

9.3 The polar water molecules pull the K^+ and I^- ions away from the solid and into solution, where they are hydrated.

9.5 a. water   **b.** CCl_4
    c. water   **d.** CCl_4

9.7 In a solution of KF, only the ions of K^+ and F^- are present in the solvent. In an HF solution, there are a few ions of H^+ and F^- present but mostly dissolved HF molecules.

9.9 a. $KCl(s) \xrightarrow{H_2O} K^+(aq) + Cl^-(aq)$

    b. $CaCl_2(s) \xrightarrow{H_2O} Ca^{2+}(aq) + 2Cl^-(aq)$

    c. $K_3PO_4(s) \xrightarrow{H_2O} 3K^+(aq) + PO_4^{3-}(aq)$

    d. $Fe(NO_3)_3(s) \xrightarrow{H_2O} Fe^{3+}(aq) + 3NO_3^-(aq)$

9.11 a. mostly molecules and a few ions
    b. ions only
    c. molecules only

9.13 a. strong electrolyte
    b. weak electrolyte
    c. nonelectrolyte

9.15 a. 1 Eq   **b.** 2 Eq
    c. 2 Eq   **d.** 6 Eq

9.17 0.154 mole of Na^+, 0.154 mole of Cl^-

9.19 55 mEq/L

9.21 a. 130 mEq/L   **b.** above the normal range

9.23 a. unsaturated   **b.** unsaturated
    c. saturated

9.25 a. 68 g of KCl   **b.** 12 g of KCl

9.27 a. The solubility of solid solutes typically increases as temperature increases.
    b. The solubility of a gas is less at a higher temperature.
    c. Gas solubility is less at a higher temperature and the CO_2 pressure in the can is increased.

9.29 a. soluble   **b.** insoluble   **c.** insoluble
    d. soluble   **e.** soluble

9.31 a. No solid forms.
    b. $2Ag^+(aq) + 2NO_3^-(aq) + 2K^+(aq) + S^{2-}(aq) \longrightarrow$
             $Ag_2S(s) + 2K^+(aq) + 2NO_3^-(aq)$
      $2Ag^+(aq) + S^{2-}(aq) \longrightarrow Ag_2S(s)$
    c. $Ca^{2+}(aq) + 2Cl^-(aq) + 2Na^+(aq) + SO_4^{2-}(aq) \longrightarrow$
             $CaSO_4(s) + 2Na^+(aq) + 2Cl^-(aq)$
      $Ca^{2+}(aq) + SO_4^{2-}(aq) \longrightarrow CaSO_4(s)$

d. $3Cu^{2+}(aq) + 6Cl^-(aq) + 6Li^+(aq) + 2PO_4^{3-}(aq) \longrightarrow$
             $Cu_3(PO_4)_2(s) + 6Li^+(aq) + 6Cl^-(aq)$
    $3Cu^{2+}(aq) + 2PO_4^{3-}(aq) \longrightarrow Cu_3(PO_4)_2(s)$

9.33 a. 17% (m/m) KCl solution
    b. 5.3% (m/m) sucrose solution
    c. 10.% (m/m) $CaCl_2$ solution

9.35 a. 30.% (m/v) Na_2SO_4 solution
    b. 11% (m/v) sucrose solution

9.37 a. 2.5 g of KCl   **b.** 50. g of NH_4Cl
    c. 25.0 mL of acetic acid

9.39 79.9 mL of alcohol

9.41 a. 20. g of $LiNO_3$ solution
    b. 400. mL of KOH solution
    c. 20. mL of formic acid solution

9.43 a. 0.500 M glucose solution
    b. 0.0356 M KOH solution
    c. 0.250 M NaCl solution

9.45 a. 120. g of NaOH   **b.** 59.6 g of KCl
    c. 5.47 g of HCl

9.47 a. 1.50 L of KBr solution
    b. 10.0 L of NaCl solution
    c. 62.5 mL of $Ca(NO_3)_2$ solution

9.49 a. 10.4 g of $PbCl_2$
    b. 18.8 mL of $Pb(NO_3)_2$ solution
    c. 1.20 M KCl solution

9.51 a. 206 mL of HCl solution
    b. 11.2 L of H_2 gas
    c. 9.09 M HCl solution

9.53 a. 20. g of mannitol   **b.** 240 g of mannitol

9.55 2 L of glucose solution

9.57 3.0 mL of chlorpromazine solution

9.59 0.50 g of $CaCl_2$

9.61 Adding water (solvent) to the soup increases the volume and dilutes the tomato soup concentration.

9.63 a. 2.0 M HCl solution
    b. 2.0 M NaOH solution
    c. 2.5% (m/v) KOH solution
    d. 3.0% (m/v) H_2SO_4 solution

9.65 a. 80. mL of HCl solution
    b. 250 mL of LiCl solution
    c. 600. mL of H_3PO_4 solution
    d. 180 mL of glucose solution

9.67 a. 12.8 mL of the HNO_3 solution
    b. 11.9 mL of the $MgCl_2$ solution
    c. 1.88 mL of the KCl solution

9.69 1.0×10^2 mL

9.71 a. solution **b.** suspension

9.73 a. 2.0 moles of ethylene glycol in 1.0 kg of water will have a lower freezing point because it has more particles in solution.
b. 0.50 mole of $MgCl_2$ in 1.0 kg of water has a lower freezing point because each $MgCl_2$ dissociates in water to give three particles, whereas each KCl dissociates to give only two particles.

9.75 a. $-2.53\,°C$ **b.** $-15.6\,°C$ **c.** $-5.54\,°C$

9.77 a. 10% (m/v) starch solution
b. from the 1% (m/v) starch solution into the 10% (m/v) starch solution
c. 10% (m/v) starch solution

9.79 a. B 10% (m/v) sucrose solution
b. A 8% (m/v) albumin solution
c. B 10% (m/v) starch solution

9.81 a. 1.0 Osm **b.** 2.8 Osm

9.83 a. hypotonic **b.** hypotonic
c. isotonic **d.** hypertonic

9.85 a. NaCl **b.** alanine
c. NaCl **d.** urea

9.87 a. K^+, Na^+, Cl^- **b.** Ca^{2+}, Mg^{2+}
c. Ca^{2+}, Mg^{2+} **d.** K^+, Na^+, Cl^-

9.89 a. 1 **b.** 2 **c.** 1

9.91 a. 3 **b.** 1 **c.** 2

9.93 a. beaker 3
b. $Na^+(aq) + Cl^-(aq) + Ag^+(aq) + NO_3^-(aq) \longrightarrow$
$AgCl(s) + Na^+(aq) + NO_3^-(aq)$
c. $Ag^+(aq) + Cl^-(aq) \longrightarrow AgCl(s)$

9.95 The skin of the cucumber acts like a semipermeable membrane, and the more dilute solution inside flows into the brine solution.

9.97 a. 2 **b.** 1 **c.** 3 **d.** 2

9.99 Because iodine is a nonpolar molecule, it will dissolve in hexane, a nonpolar solvent. Iodine does not dissolve in water because water is a polar solvent.

9.101 a. unsaturated solution **b.** saturated solution
c. saturated solution

9.103 a. soluble **b.** soluble
c. insoluble **d.** soluble
e. insoluble

9.105 a. $Ag^+(aq) + Cl^-(aq) \longrightarrow AgCl(s)$
b. none
c. $Ba^{2+}(aq) + SO_4^{2-}(aq) \longrightarrow BaSO_4(s)$

9.107 17.0% (m/m) Na_2SO_4 solution

9.109 38 mL of propyl alcohol solution

9.111 0.72 L of KOH solution

9.113 0.500 M NaOH solution

9.115 a. 1600 g of $Al(NO_3)_3$ **b.** 6.8 g of $C_6H_{12}O_6$
c. 17.9 g of LiCl

9.117 a. 0.100 M NaBr solution
b. 4.50% (m/v) K_2SO_4 solution
c. 1.76 M NaOH solution

9.119 a. 75 mL of 10.0% (m/v) HCl solution
b. 90. mL of 5.0% (m/v) NaCl solution
c. 117 mL of 6.00 M NaOH solution

9.121 a. $-1.08\,°C$ **b.** $-2.25\,°C$ **c.** $-11\,°C$

9.123 87 mL of HCl solution

9.125 0.15 Osm

9.127 A dialysis solution contains no sodium or urea so that these substances will flow out of the blood into the solution. High levels of potassium are maintained in the dialyzing solution so that the potassium will dialyze into the blood.

9.129 a. 11.6% (m/m) NaCl solution
b. 2.40 M NaCl solution
c. 0.400 M NaCl solution

9.131 a. saturated **b.** unsaturated
c. saturated

9.133 a. 35.0% (m/m) HNO_3 solution
b. 165 mL
c. 42.4% (m/v) HNO_3 solution
d. 6.73 M HNO_3 solution

9.135 a. 65 mEq/L
b. 65 mEq/L
c. 0.25 Osm

10

Reaction Rates and Chemical Equilibrium

ANDREW WAS BORN 12 WEEKS EARLY WITH A

breathing problem called *infant respiratory distress syndrome* (IRDS). He was limp, purple, and not breathing. IRDS is caused by a lack of surfactant in underdeveloped lungs. Normally produced in the pulmonary alveoli, surfactants help the lungs inflate, and prevent the air sacs from collapsing. Without surfactants, a premature infant has difficulty breathing, which leads to decreased ventilation and hypoxia. Lack of oxygen can lead to the injury or death of cells and ultimately to irreversible brain damage. To prevent this, Andrew's metabolism needed to be slowed down.

At the hospital, Judy, a neonatal nurse, wrapped Andrew in a cooling blanket that lowered his body temperature to 33.5 °C. She attached electrodes to his head to monitor his brain activity. With a decrease in body temperature, Andrew's demand for oxygen was reduced. Artificial surfactants were administered to help him breathe more easily. When Andrew's oxygen levels in his bloodstream fell too low to maintain healthy tissues, Judy inserted a baby cannula in his nose that provided an air–oxygen mixture. Then more O_2 was picked up by Andrew's hemoglobin (Hb) at the lungs and released from the hemoglobin in the tissues.

$$Hb(aq) + O_2(g) \rightleftharpoons HbO_2(aq)$$

After Andrew successfully managed the three-day danger period, his body temperature was slowly restored to normal. Two weeks later, he was discharged from the hospital.

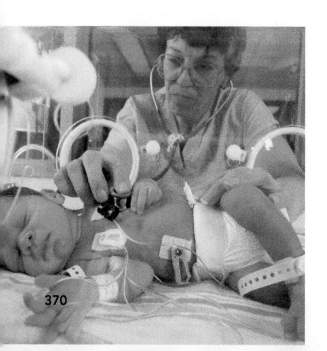

CAREER Neonatal Nurse

A neonatal nurse works with newborns that are premature, have birth defects, cardiac malformations, and surgical problems. Most neonatal nurses care for infants from the time of birth until they are discharged from the hospital.

A neonatal nurse monitors life support machines, medications, operates ventilators, and resuscitates a premature infant who stops breathing. Sufficient oxygen is provided for the tissues without injuring the organs. Many neonatal nurses take a national test to become part of a neonatal team or participate on an oxygenation team that provides heart–lung bypass for critically ill infants.

Earlier we looked at chemical reactions and determined the amounts of substances that react and the products that form. Now we are interested in how fast a reaction goes. If we know how fast a medication acts on the body, we can adjust the time over which the medication is taken. In construction, substances are added to cement to make it dry faster so that work can continue. Some reactions such as explosions or the formation of precipitates in a solution are very fast. When we roast a turkey or bake a cake, the reaction is slower. Some reactions such as the tarnishing of silver and the aging of the body are much slower (see Figure 10.1). We will see that some reactions need energy while other reactions produce energy. We burn gasoline in our automobile engines to produce energy to make our cars move. In this chapter, we will also look at the effect of changing the concentrations of reactants or products on the rate of reaction.

Up to now, we have considered a reaction as proceeding in a forward direction from reactants to products. However, in many reactions a reverse reaction also takes place as products collide to re-form reactants. When the forward and reverse reactions occur at the same rate, the amounts of reactants and products stay the same. When this balance in the rates of the forward and reverse reactions is reached, we say that the reaction has reached *equilibrium*. At equilibrium, both reactants and products are present. Some reaction mixtures contain mostly reactants and form only a few products, whereas others contain mostly products and a few reactants.

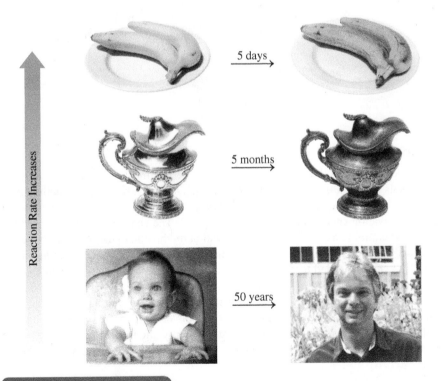

Reaction Rate Increases

5 days

5 months

50 years

FIGURE 10.1 ▶ Reaction rates vary greatly for everyday processes. A banana ripens in a few days, silver tarnishes in a few months, while the aging process of humans takes many years.

Ⓠ How would you compare the rates of the reaction that forms sugars in plants by photosynthesis with the reactions that digest sugars in the body?

CHAPTER READINESS*

🖩 KEY MATH SKILLS
- Solving Equations (1.4D)
- Writing Numbers in Scientific Notation (1.4F)

⚛ CORE CHEMISTRY SKILLS
- Using Significant Figures in Calculations (2.3)
- Balancing a Chemical Equation (7.1)
- Calculating Concentration (9.4)

*These Key Math Skills and Core Chemistry Skills from previous chapters are listed here for your review as you proceed to the new material in this chapter.

LEARNING GOAL

Describe how temperature, concentration, and catalysts affect the rate of a reaction.

10.1 Rates of Reactions

For a chemical reaction to take place, the molecules of the reactants must come in contact with each other. The **collision theory** indicates that a reaction takes place only when molecules collide with the proper orientation and sufficient energy. Many collisions can occur, but only a few actually lead to the formation of product. For example, consider the reaction of nitrogen and oxygen molecules (see Figure 10.2). To form nitrogen oxide (NO) product, the collisions between N_2 and O_2 molecules must place the atoms in the proper alignment. If the molecules are not aligned properly, no reaction takes place.

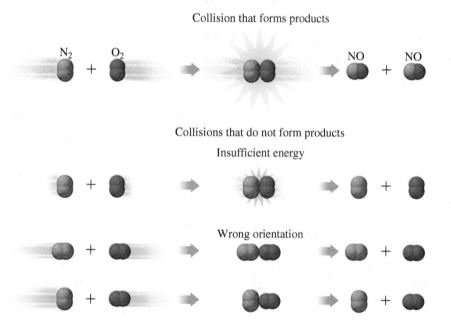

FIGURE 10.2 ▶ Reacting molecules must collide, have a minimum amount of energy, and have the proper orientation to form products.

Q What happens when reacting molecules collide with the minimum energy but don't have the proper orientation?

Activation Energy

Even when a collision has the proper orientation, there still must be sufficient energy to break the bonds between the atoms of the reactants. The **activation energy** is the minimum amount of energy required to break the bonds between atoms of the reactants. In Figure 10.3, activation energy appears as an energy hill. The concept of activation energy is analogous to climbing a hill. To reach a destination on the other side, we must have the energy needed to climb to the top of the hill. Once we are at the top, we can run down the other side. The energy needed to get us from our starting point to the top of the hill would be our activation energy.

In the same way, a collision must provide enough energy to push the reactants to the top of the energy hill. Then the reactants may be converted to products. If the energy provided by the collision is less than the activation energy, the molecules simply bounce apart and no reaction occurs. The features that lead to a successful reaction are summarized next.

Three Conditions Required for a Reaction to Occur

1. **Collision**   The reactants must collide.
2. **Orientation**   The reactants must align properly to break and form bonds.
3. **Energy**   The collision must provide the energy of activation.

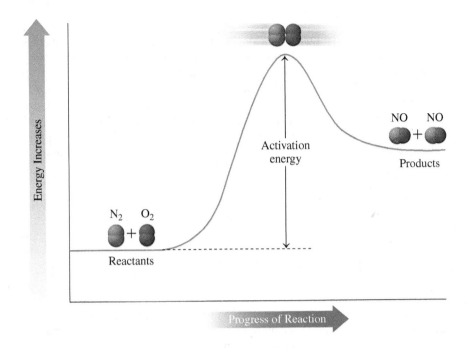

FIGURE 10.3 ▶ The activation energy is the minimum energy needed to convert the colliding molecules into product.

Q What happens in a collision of reacting molecules that have the proper orientation, but not the energy of activation?

Rate of Reaction

The **rate** (or speed) **of reaction** is determined by measuring the amount of a reactant used up, or the amount of a product formed, in a certain period of time.

$$\text{Rate of reaction} = \frac{\text{change in concentration of reactant or product}}{\text{change in time}}$$

We can describe the rate of reaction with the analogy of eating a pizza. When we start to eat, we have a whole pizza. As time goes by, there are fewer slices of pizza left. If we know how long it took to eat the pizza, we could determine the rate at which the pizza was consumed. Let's assume 4 slices are eaten every 8 minutes. That gives a rate of $\frac{1}{2}$ slice per minute. After 16 min, all 8 slices are gone.

Rate at Which Pizza Slices Are Eaten

Slices Eaten	0	4 slices	6 slices	8 slices
Time (min)	0	8 min	12 min	16 min

$$\text{Rate} = \frac{4 \text{ slices}}{8 \text{ min}} = \frac{1 \text{ slice}}{2 \text{ min}} = \frac{\frac{1}{2} \text{ slice}}{1 \text{ min}}$$

Reactions with low activation energies go faster than reactions with high activation energies. Some reactions go very fast, while others are very slow. For any reaction, the rate is affected by changes in temperature, changes in the concentration of the reactants, and the addition of catalysts.

Temperature

At higher temperatures, the increase in kinetic energy of the reactants makes them move faster and collide more often, and it provides more collisions with the required energy of activation. Reactions almost always go faster at higher temperatures. For every 10 °C increase in temperature, most reaction rates approximately double. If we want food to cook faster, we increase the temperature. When body temperature rises, there is an increase in the pulse rate, rate of breathing, and metabolic rate. If we are exposed to extreme heat, we may experience *heat stroke*, which is a condition that occurs when body temperature goes above 40.5 °C (105 °F). If the body loses its ability to regulate temperature, body temperature continues to rise, and may cause damage to the brain and internal organs. On the other hand, we slow down a reaction by decreasing the temperature. For example, we refrigerate perishable foods to make them last longer. In some cardiac surgeries, body temperature is decreased to 28 °C so the heart can be stopped and less oxygen is required by the brain. This is also the reason why some people have survived submersion in icy lakes for long periods of time. Cool water or an ice blanket may also be used to decrease the body temperature of a person with hyperthermia or heat stroke.

Reaction:

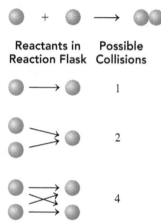

Reactants in Reaction Flask   Possible Collisions

Reactants	Collisions
	1
	2
	4

FIGURE 10.4 ▶ Increasing the concentration of a reactant increases the number of collisions that are possible.

Q Why does doubling the reactants increase the rate of reaction?

Concentrations of Reactants

For virtually all reactions, the rate of a reaction increases when the concentration of the reactants increases. When there are more reacting molecules, more collisions that form products can occur, and the reaction goes faster (see Figure 10.4). For example, a patient having difficulty breathing may be given a breathing mixture with a higher oxygen content than the atmosphere. The increase in the number of oxygen molecules in the lungs increases the rate at which oxygen combines with hemoglobin. The increased rate of oxygenation of the blood means that the patient can breathe more easily.

$$\underset{\text{Hemoglobin}}{Hb(aq)} \ + \ \underset{\text{Oxygen}}{O_2(g)} \longrightarrow \underset{\text{Oxyhemoglobin}}{HbO_2(aq)}$$

Catalysts

Another way to speed up a reaction is to lower the *energy of activation*. The energy of activation is the minimum energy needed to break apart the bonds of the reacting molecules. If a collision provides less than the activation energy, the bonds do not break and the reactant molecules bounce apart. A **catalyst** speeds up a reaction by providing an alternative pathway that has a lower energy of activation. When activation energy is lowered, more collisions provide sufficient energy for reactants to form product. During a reaction, a catalyst is not changed or consumed.

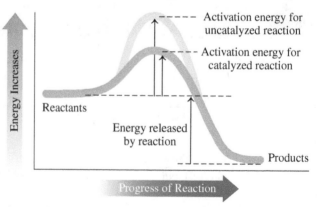

When a catalyst lowers the activation energy, the reaction occurs at a faster rate.

Catalysts have many uses in industry. In the manufacturing of margarine, hydrogen (H_2) is added to vegetable oils. Normally, the reaction is very slow because it has a high activation energy. However, when platinum (Pt) is used as a catalyst, the reaction occurs rapidly. In the body, biocatalysts called enzymes make most metabolic reactions proceed at rates necessary for proper cellular activity. Enzymes are added to laundry detergents to break down proteins (proteases), starches (amylases), or greases (lipases) that have stained clothes. Such enzymes function at the low temperatures that are used in home washing machines, and they are biodegradable as well.

The factors affecting reaction rates are summarized in Table 10.1.

Enzymes in laundry detergent catalyze the removal of stains at low temperatures.

▶ **SAMPLE PROBLEM 10.1 Factors That Affect the Rate of Reaction**

Indicate whether the following changes will increase, decrease, or have no effect on the rate of reaction:

a. increasing the temperature
b. increasing the number of reacting molecules
c. adding a catalyst

SOLUTION

a. A higher temperature increases the kinetic energy of the particles, which increases the number of collisions and makes more collisions effective, causing an increase in the rate of reaction.
b. Increasing the number of reacting molecules increases the number of collisions and the rate of the reaction.
c. Adding a catalyst increases the rate of reaction by lowering the activation energy, which increases the number of collisions that form product.

STUDY CHECK 10.1

How does using an ice blanket on a patient affect the rate of metabolism in the body?

ANSWER

Lowering the temperature will decrease the rate of metabolism.

TABLE 10.1 Factors That Increase Reaction Rate

Factor	Reason
Increase temperature	More collisions, more collisions with energy of activation
Increase reactant concentration	More collisions
Add a catalyst	Lowers energy of activation

Chemistry Link to the Environment
Catalytic Converters

For over 30 years, manufacturers have been required to include catalytic converters in the exhaust systems of gasoline automobile engines. When gasoline burns, the products found in the exhaust of a car contain high levels of pollutants. These include carbon monoxide (CO) from incomplete combustion, hydrocarbons such as C_8H_{18} (octane) from unburned fuel, and nitrogen oxide (NO) from the reaction of N_2 and O_2 at the high temperatures reached within the engine. Carbon monoxide is toxic, and unburned hydrocarbons and nitrogen oxide are involved in the formation of smog and acid rain.

A catalytic converter consists of solid-particle catalysts, such as platinum (Pt) and palladium (Pd), on a ceramic honeycomb that provides a large surface area and facilitates contact with pollutants. As the pollutants pass through the converter, they react with the catalysts. Today, we all use unleaded gasoline because lead interferes with the ability of the Pt and Pd catalysts in the converter to react with the pollutants. The purpose of a catalytic converter is to lower the activation energy for reactions that convert each of these pollutants into substances such as CO_2, N_2, O_2, and H_2O, which are already present in the atmosphere.

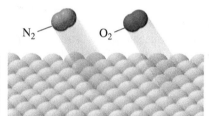

Exhaust Gases
Hydrocarbons, C_8H_{18}
Carbon monoxide, CO
Nitrogen oxide, NO

Catalytic
converter

Catalyst

Tail Pipe Emissions
Water, H_2O
Carbon dioxide, CO_2
Nitrogen, N_2
Oxygen, O_2

$$2NO(g) \longrightarrow N_2(g) + O_2(g)$$

NO absorbed on catalyst NO dissociates

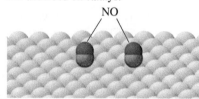

NO

N_2 O_2

Surface of metal (Pt, Pd) catalyst

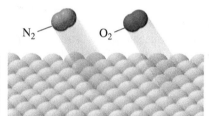

$$2CO(g) + O_2(g) \longrightarrow 2CO_2(g)$$

CO and O_2 absorbed on catalyst O_2 dissociates

CO

CO_2

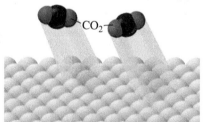

Surface of metal (Pt, Pd) catalyst

QUESTIONS AND PROBLEMS

10.1 Rates of Reactions

LEARNING GOAL Describe how temperature, concentration, and catalysts affect the rate of a reaction.

10.1 **a.** What is meant by the rate of a reaction?
 b. Why does bread grow mold more quickly at room temperature than in the refrigerator?

10.2 **a.** How does a catalyst affect the activation energy?
 b. Why is pure oxygen used in respiratory distress?

10.3 In the following reaction, what happens to the number of collisions when more $Br_2(g)$ molecules are added?

$$H_2(g) + Br_2(g) \longrightarrow 2HBr(g)$$

10.4 In the following reaction, what happens to the number of collisions when the temperature of the reaction is decreased?

$$2H_2(g) + CO(g) \longrightarrow CH_3OH(g)$$

10.5 How would each of the following change the rate of the reaction shown here?

$$2SO_2(g) + O_2(g) \longrightarrow 2SO_3(g)$$

a. adding some $SO_2(g)$
b. increasing the temperature
c. adding a catalyst
d. removing some $O_2(g)$

10.6 How would each of the following change the rate of the reaction shown here?

$$2NO(g) + 2H_2(g) \longrightarrow N_2(g) + 2H_2O(g)$$

a. adding some $NO(g)$
b. decreasing the temperature
c. removing some $H_2(g)$
d. adding a catalyst

10.2 Chemical Equilibrium

In earlier chapters, we considered the *forward reaction* in an equation and assumed that all of the reactants were converted to products. However, most of the time reactants are not completely converted to products because a *reverse reaction* takes place in which products collide to form the reactants. When a reaction proceeds in both a forward and reverse direction, it is said to be reversible. We have looked at other reversible processes. For example, the melting of solids to form liquids and the freezing of liquids to solids is a reversible physical change. Even in our daily life we have reversible events. We go from home to school and we return from school to home. We go up an escalator and we come back down. We put money in our bank account and we take money out.

An analogy for a forward and reverse reaction can be found in the phrase "We are going to the grocery store." Although we mention our trip in one direction, we know that we will also return home from the store. Because our trip has both a forward and reverse direction, we can say the trip is reversible. It is not very likely that we would stay at the store forever.

A trip to the grocery store can be used to illustrate another aspect of reversible reactions. Perhaps the grocery store is nearby and we usually walk. However, we can change our rate. Suppose that one day we drive to the store, which increases our rate and gets us to the store faster. Correspondingly, a car also increases the rate at which we return home.

Use the concept of reversible reactions to explain chemical equilibrium.

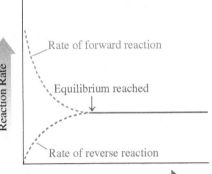

As a reaction progresses, the rate of the forward reaction decreases and that of the reverse reaction increases. At equilibrium, the rates of the forward and reverse reactions are equal.

Reversible Chemical Reactions

A **reversible reaction** proceeds in both the forward and reverse direction. That means there are two reaction rates: one is the rate of the forward reaction, and the other is the rate of the reverse reaction. When molecules begin to react, the rate of the forward reaction is faster than the rate of the reverse reaction. As reactants are consumed and products accumulate, the rate of the forward reaction decreases and the rate of the reverse reaction increases.

Equilibrium

Eventually, the rates of the forward and reverse reactions become equal; the reactants form products at the same rate that the products form reactants. A reaction reaches **chemical equilibrium** when no further change takes place in the concentrations of the reactants and products, even though the two reactions continue at equal but opposite rates.

At Equilibrium:
The rate of the forward reaction is equal to the rate of the reverse reaction.

No further changes occur in the concentrations of reactants and products, even though the two reactions continue at equal but opposite rates.

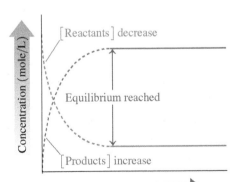

Equilibrium is reached when there are no further changes in the concentrations of reactants and products.

Let us look at the process as the reaction of H_2 and I_2 proceeds to equilibrium. Initially, only the reactants H_2 and I_2 are present. Soon, a few molecules of HI are produced by the forward reaction. With more time, additional HI molecules are produced. As the concentration of HI increases, more HI molecules collide and react in the reverse

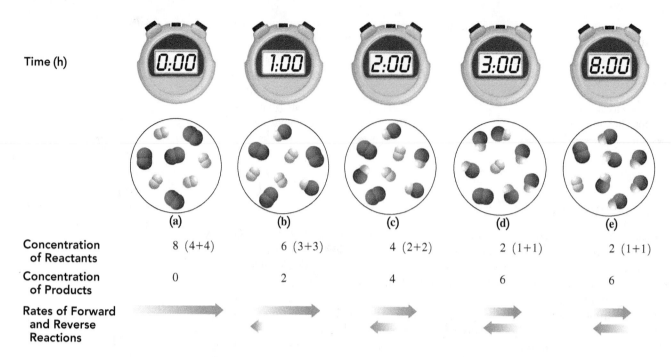

Time (h)					
	(a)	(b)	(c)	(d)	(e)
Concentration of Reactants	8 (4+4)	6 (3+3)	4 (2+2)	2 (1+1)	2 (1+1)
Concentration of Products	0	2	4	6	6
Rates of Forward and Reverse Reactions					

FIGURE 10.5 ▶ **(a)** Initially, the reaction flask contains only the reactants H_2 (white) and I_2 (purple). **(b)** The forward reaction between H_2 and I_2 begins to produce HI. **(c)** As the reaction proceeds, there are fewer molecules of H_2 and I_2 and more molecules of HI, which increases the rate of the reverse reaction. **(d)** At equilibrium, the concentrations of reactants H_2 and I_2 and product HI are constant. **(e)** The reaction continues with the rate of the forward reaction equal to the rate of the reverse reaction.

How do the rates of the forward and reverse reactions compare once a chemical reaction reaches equilibrium?

direction. As HI product builds up, the rate of the reverse reaction increases, while the rate of the forward reaction decreases. Eventually, the rates become equal, which means the reaction has reached equilibrium. Even though the concentrations remain constant at equilibrium, the forward and reverse reactions continue to occur. The forward and reverse reactions are usually shown together in a single equation by using a double arrow. A reversible reaction is two opposing reactions that occur at the same time (see Figure 10.5).

$$H_2(g) + I_2(g) \xrightleftharpoons[\text{Reverse reaction}]{\text{Forward reaction}} 2HI(g)$$

SAMPLE PROBLEM 10.2 Reaction Rates and Equilibrium

Complete each of the following with *equal* or *not equal*, *faster* or *slower*, *change* or *do not change*:

a. Before equilibrium is reached, the concentrations of the reactants and products _____.
b. Initially, reactants placed in a container have a _____ rate of reaction than the rate of reaction of the products.
c. At equilibrium, the rate of the forward reaction is _____ to the rate of the reverse reaction.

SOLUTION

a. Before equilibrium is reached, the concentrations of the reactants and products *change*.
b. Initially, reactants placed in a container have a *faster* rate of reaction than the rate of reaction of the products.
c. At equilibrium, the rate of the forward reaction is *equal* to the rate of the reverse reaction.

STUDY CHECK 10.2

Complete the following statement with *change* or *do not change*:
At equilibrium, the concentrations of the reactants and products _____.

ANSWER

At equilibrium, the concentrations of the reactants and products *do not change*.

We can also set up a reaction starting with only reactants or with only products. Let's look at the initial reactions in each, the forward and reverse reactions, and the equilibrium mixture that forms (see Figure 10.6).

$$2SO_2(g) + O_2(g) \rightleftharpoons 2SO_3(g)$$

If we start with only the reactants SO_2 and O_2 in the container, the reaction to form SO_3 takes place until equilibrium is reached. However, if we start with only the product SO_3 in the container, the reaction to form SO_2 and O_2 takes place until equilibrium is reached. In both containers, the equilibrium mixture contains the same concentrations of SO_2, O_2, and SO_3.

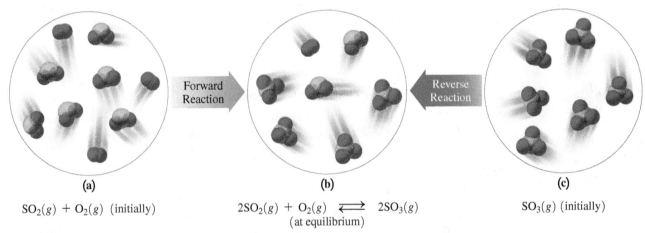

(a)   (b)   (c)

$SO_2(g) + O_2(g)$ (initially) $2SO_2(g) + O_2(g) \rightleftharpoons 2SO_3(g)$ $SO_3(g)$ (initially)

(at equilibrium)

FIGURE 10.6 ▶ Sample (a) initially contains $SO_2(g)$ and $O_2(g)$. At equilibrium, sample (b) contains mostly $SO_3(g)$ and only small amounts of $SO_2(g)$ and $O_2(g)$, whereas sample (c) contains only $SO_3(g)$.

Q Why is the same equilibrium mixture obtained from $SO_2(g)$ and $O_2(g)$ as from $SO_3(g)$?

QUESTIONS AND PROBLEMS

10.2 Chemical Equilibrium

LEARNING GOAL Use the concept of reversible reactions to explain chemical equilibrium.

10.7 What is meant by the term *reversible reaction*?

10.8 When does a reversible reaction reach equilibrium?

10.9 Which of the following are at equilibrium?
   a. The rate of the forward reaction is twice as fast as the rate of the reverse reaction.
   b. The concentrations of the reactants and the products do not change.
   c. The rate of the reverse reaction does not change.

10.10 Which of the following are not at equilibrium?
   a. The rates of the forward and reverse reactions are equal.
   b. The rate of the forward reaction does not change.
   c. The concentrations of reactants and the products are not constant.

10.11 The following diagrams show the chemical reaction with time:

$$A \rightleftharpoons B$$

If A is blue and B is orange, state whether or not the reaction has reached equilibrium in this time period and explain why.

| 1 h | 2 h | 3 h | 4 h |

10.12 The following diagrams show the chemical reaction with time:

$$C \rightleftharpoons D$$

If C is blue and D is yellow, state whether or not the reaction has reached equilibrium in this time period and explain why.

| 1 h | 2 h | 3 h | 4 h |

Calculate the equilibrium constant for a reversible reaction given the concentrations of reactants and products at equilibrium.

At equilibrium, the number of people riding up the lift and the number of people skiing down the slope are constant.

⚙ CORE CHEMISTRY SKILL

Writing the Equilibrium Constant Expression

10.3 Equilibrium Constants

At equilibrium, the concentrations of the reactants and products are constant. We can use a ski lift as an analogy. Early in the morning, skiers at the bottom of the mountain begin to ride the ski lift up to the slopes. After the skiers reach the top of the mountain, they ski down. Eventually, the number of people riding up the ski lift becomes equal to the number of people skiing down the mountain. There is no further change in the number of skiers on the slopes; the system is at equilibrium.

Equilibrium Constant Expression

At equilibrium, the concentrations can be used to set up a relationship between the products and the reactants. Suppose we write a general equation for reactants A and B that form products C and D. The small italic letters are the coefficients in the balanced equation.

$$aA + bB \rightleftharpoons cC + dD$$

An **equilibrium constant expression** for a reversible chemical reaction multiplies the concentrations of the products together and divides by the concentrations of the reactants. Each concentration is raised to a power that is equal to its coefficient in the balanced chemical equation. The square bracket around each substance indicates that the concentration is expressed in moles per liter (M). For our general reaction, this is written as:

$$K_c = \frac{[\text{Products}]}{[\text{Reactants}]} = \frac{[C]^c [D]^d}{[A]^a [B]^b}$$

Coefficients

Equilibrium constant expression

We can now describe how to write the equilibrium constant expression for the reaction of H_2 and I_2 that forms HI. The balanced chemical equation is written with a double arrow between the reactants and the products.

$$H_2(g) + I_2(g) \rightleftharpoons 2HI(g)$$

We show the concentration of the products using brackets in the numerator and the concentrations of the reactants in brackets in the denominator and write any coefficient as an exponent of its concentration (a coefficient 1 is understood).

$$K_c = \frac{[HI]^2}{[H_2][I_2]}$$

Coefficient of HI

▶**SAMPLE PROBLEM 10.3** **Writing Equilibrium Constant Expressions**

Write the equilibrium constant expression for the following reaction:

$$2SO_2(g) + O_2(g) \rightleftharpoons 2SO_3(g)$$

SOLUTION

STEP **1** Write the balanced chemical equation.

$$2SO_2(g) + O_2(g) \rightleftharpoons 2SO_3(g)$$

STEP **2** Write the concentrations of the products as the numerator and the reactants as the denominator.

$$\frac{[\text{Products}]}{[\text{Reactants}]} \longrightarrow \frac{[SO_3]}{[SO_2][O_2]}$$

STEP **3** Write any coefficient in the equation as an exponent.

$$K_c = \frac{[SO_3]^2}{[SO_2]^2[O_2]}$$

STUDY CHECK 10.3

Write the equilibrium constant expression for the following reaction:

$$2NO(g) + O_2(g) \rightleftharpoons 2NO_2(g)$$

ANSWER

$$K_c = \frac{[NO_2]^2}{[NO]^2[O_2]}$$

Guide to Writing the Equilibrium Constant Expression

STEP **1**
Write the balanced chemical equation.

STEP **2**
Write the concentrations of the products as the numerator and the reactants as the denominator.

STEP **3**
Write any coefficient in the equation as an exponent.

Calculating Equilibrium Constants

The **equilibrium constant, K_c,** is the numerical value obtained by substituting experimentally measured molar concentrations at equilibrium into the equilibrium constant expression. For example, the equilibrium constant expression for the reaction of H_2 and I_2 is written

$$H_2(g) + I_2(g) \rightleftharpoons 2HI(g) \qquad K_c = \frac{[HI]^2}{[H_2][I_2]}$$

In the first experiment, the molar concentrations for the reactants and products at equilibrium are found to be $[H_2] = 0.10\,M$, $[I_2] = 0.20\,M$, and $[HI] = 1.04\,M$. When we substitute these values into the equilibrium constant expression, we obtain its numerical value.

In additional experiments 2 and 3, the mixtures have different equilibrium concentrations for the system at equilibrium at the same temperature. However, when these concentrations are used to calculate the equilibrium constant, we obtain the same value of K_c for each (see Table 10.2). *Thus, a reaction at a specific temperature can have only one value for the equilibrium constant.*

The units of K_c depend on the specific equation. In this example, the units of $[M]^2/[M]^2$ cancel out to give a value of 54. In other equations, the concentration units do not cancel. However, in this text, the numerical value will be given without any units as shown in Sample Problem 10.4.

⚛ **CORE CHEMISTRY SKILL**

Calculating an Equilibrium Constant

TABLE 10.2 Equilibrium Constant for $H_2(g) + I_2(g) \rightleftharpoons 2HI(g)$ at 427 °C

Experiment	Concentrations at Equilibrium			Equilibrium Constant
	$[H_2]$	$[I_2]$	$[HI]$	$K_c = \dfrac{[HI]^2}{[H_2][I_2]}$
1	0.10 M	0.20 M	1.04 M	$K_c = \dfrac{[1.04]^2}{[0.10][0.20]} = 54$
2	0.20 M	0.20 M	1.47 M	$K_c = \dfrac{[1.47]^2}{[0.20][0.20]} = 54$
3	0.30 M	0.17 M	1.66 M	$K_c = \dfrac{[1.66]^2}{[0.30][0.17]} = 54$

▶ **SAMPLE PROBLEM 10.4** **Calculating an Equilibrium Constant**

The decomposition of dinitrogen tetroxide forms nitrogen dioxide.

$$N_2O_4(g) \rightleftharpoons 2NO_2(g)$$

What is the numerical value of K_c at 100 °C if a reaction mixture at equilibrium contains 0.45 M N_2O_4 and 0.31 M NO_2?

SOLUTION

STEP 1 State the given and needed quantities.

ANALYZE THE PROBLEM	Given	Need
	0.45 M N_2O_4, 0.31 M NO_2	K_c
	Equation	
	$N_2O_4(g) \rightleftharpoons 2NO_2(g)$	

STEP 2 Write the K_c expression for the equilibrium.

$$K_c = \frac{[NO_2]^2}{[N_2O_4]}$$

STEP 3 Substitute equilibrium (molar) concentrations and calculate K_c.

$$K_c = \frac{[0.31]^2}{[0.45]} = 0.21$$

STUDY CHECK 10.4

Calculate the numerical value of K_c if an equilibrium mixture contains 0.040 M NH_3, 0.60 M H_2, and 0.20 M N_2.

$$2NH_3(g) \rightleftharpoons 3H_2(g) + N_2(g)$$

ANSWER

$K_c = 27$

Guide to Calculating the K_c Value

STEP 1
State the given and needed quantities.

STEP 2
Write the K_c expression for the equilibrium.

STEP 3
Substitute equilibrium (molar) concentrations and calculate K_c.

QUESTIONS AND PROBLEMS

10.3 Equilibrium Constants

LEARNING GOAL Calculate the equilibrium constant for a reversible reaction given the concentrations of reactants and products at equilibrium.

10.13 Write the equilibrium constant expression for each of the following reactions:
a. $CH_4(g) + 2H_2S(g) \rightleftharpoons CS_2(g) + 4H_2(g)$
b. $2NO(g) \rightleftharpoons N_2(g) + O_2(g)$
c. $2SO_3(g) + CO_2(g) \rightleftharpoons CS_2(g) + 4O_2(g)$
d. $CH_4(g) + H_2O(g) \rightleftharpoons 3H_2(g) + CO(g)$

10.14 Write the equilibrium constant expression for each of the following reactions:
a. $2HBr(g) \rightleftharpoons H_2(g) + Br_2(g)$
b. $2BrNO(g) \rightleftharpoons Br_2(g) + 2NO(g)$
c. $CH_4(g) + Cl_2(g) \rightleftharpoons CH_3Cl(g) + HCl(g)$
d. $Br_2(g) + Cl_2(g) \rightleftharpoons 2BrCl(g)$

10.15 Write the equilibrium constant expression for the reaction in the diagram and calculate the numerical value of K_c. In the diagram, X atoms are orange and Y atoms are blue.

$$X_2(g) + Y_2(g) \rightleftharpoons 2XY(g)$$

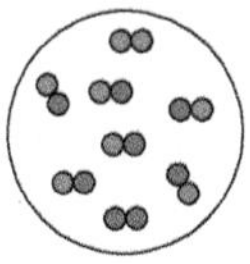

Equilibrium
mixture

10.16 Write the equilibrium constant expression for the reaction in the diagram and calculate the numerical value of K_c. In the diagram, A atoms are red and B atoms are green.

$$2AB(g) \rightleftharpoons A_2(g) + B_2(g)$$

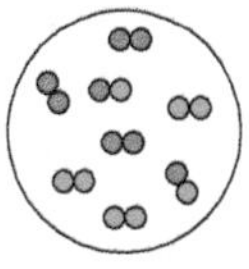

Equilibrium
mixture

10.17 What is the numerical value of K_c for the following reaction if the equilibrium mixture contains 0.030 M N_2O_4 and 0.21 M NO_2?

$$N_2O_4(g) \rightleftharpoons 2NO_2(g)$$

10.18 What is the numerical value of K_c for the following reaction if the equilibrium mixture contains 0.30 M CO_2, 0.033 M H_2, 0.20 M CO, and 0.30 M H_2O?

$$CO_2(g) + H_2(g) \rightleftharpoons CO(g) + H_2O(g)$$

10.19 What is the numerical value of K_c for the following reaction if the equilibrium mixture contains 0.51 M CO, 0.30 M H_2, 1.8 M CH_4, and 2.0 M H_2O?

$$CO(g) + 3H_2(g) \rightleftharpoons CH_4(g) + H_2O(g)$$

10.20 What is the numerical value of K_c for the following reaction if the equilibrium mixture contains 0.44 M N_2, 0.40 M H_2, and 2.2 M NH_3?

$$N_2(g) + 3H_2(g) \rightleftharpoons 2NH_3(g)$$

10.4 Using Equilibrium Constants

LEARNING GOAL

Use an equilibrium constant to predict the extent of reaction and to calculate equilibrium concentrations.

The values of K_c can be large or small. The size of the equilibrium constant depends on whether equilibrium is reached with more products than reactants, or more reactants than products. However, the size of an equilibrium constant does not affect how fast equilibrium is reached.

Equilibrium with a Large K_c

When a reaction has a large equilibrium constant, it means that the forward reaction produced a large amount of products when equilibrium was reached. Then the equilibrium mixture contains mostly products, which makes the concentrations of the products in the numerator higher than the concentrations of the reactants in the denominator. Thus at equilibrium, this reaction has a large K_c. Consider the reaction of SO_2 and O_2, which has a large K_c. At equilibrium, the reaction mixture contains mostly product and few reactants (see Figure 10.7).

$$2SO_2(g) + O_2(g) \rightleftharpoons 2SO_3(g)$$

$$K_c = \frac{[SO_3]^2}{[SO_2]^2[O_2]} \quad \frac{\text{Mostly product}}{\text{Few reactants}} = 3.4 \times 10^2$$

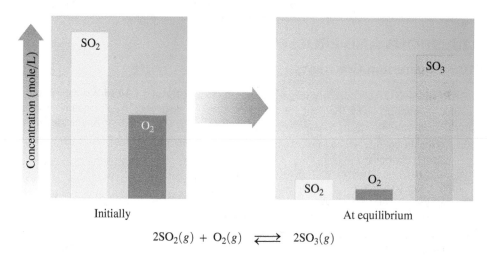

FIGURE 10.7 ▶ In the reaction of $SO_2(g)$ and $O_2(g)$, the equilibrium mixture contains mostly product $SO_3(g)$, which results in a large K_c.

🅠 Why does an equilibrium mixture containing mostly product have a large K_c?

$$2SO_2(g) + O_2(g) \rightleftharpoons 2SO_3(g)$$

Equilibrium with a Small K_c

When a reaction has a small equilibrium constant, the equilibrium mixture contains a high concentration of reactants and a low concentration of products. Then the equilibrium expression has a small number in the numerator and a large number in the denominator. Thus at equilibrium, this reaction has a small K_c. Consider the reaction for the formation of $NO(g)$ from $N_2(g)$ and $O_2(g)$, which has a small K_c (see Figure 10.8).

$$N_2(g) + O_2(g) \rightleftharpoons 2NO(g)$$

$$K_c = \frac{[NO]^2}{[N_2][O_2]} \quad \frac{\text{Few products}}{\text{Mostly reactants}} = 2 \times 10^{-9}$$

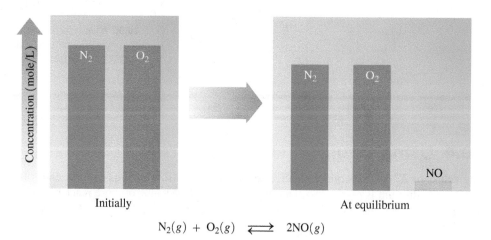

FIGURE 10.8 ▶ The equilibrium mixture contains a very small amount of the product NO and a large amount of the reactants N_2 and O_2, which results in a small K_c.

🅠 Does a reaction with a $K_c = 3.2 \times 10^{-5}$ contain mostly reactants or products at equilibrium?

$$N_2(g) + O_2(g) \rightleftharpoons 2NO(g)$$

A few reactions have equilibrium constants close to 1, which means they have about equal concentrations of reactants and products. Moderate amounts of reactants have been converted to products upon reaching equilibrium (see Figure 10.9).

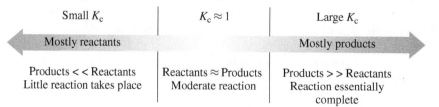

FIGURE 10.9 ▶ At equilibrium, a reaction with a large K_c contains mostly products, whereas a reaction with a small K_c contains mostly reactants.

🅠 Does a reaction with a $K_c = 1.2$ contain mostly reactants, mostly products, or about equal amounts of both reactants and products at equilibrium?

Table 10.3 lists some equilibrium constants and the extent of their reaction.

TABLE 10.3 Examples of Reactions with Large and Small K_c Values

Reactants		Products	K_c	Equilibrium Mixture Contains
$2CO(g) + O_2(g)$	$\rightleftharpoons$	$2CO_2(g)$	2×10^{11}	Mostly products
$2H_2(g) + S_2(g)$	$\rightleftharpoons$	$2H_2S(g)$	1.1×10^7	Mostly products
$N_2(g) + 3H_2(g)$	$\rightleftharpoons$	$2NH_3(g)$	1.6×10^2	Mostly products
$PCl_5(g)$	$\rightleftharpoons$	$PCl_3(g) + Cl_2(g)$	1.2×10^{-2}	Mostly reactants
$N_2(g) + O_2(g)$	$\rightleftharpoons$	$2NO(g)$	2×10^{-9}	Mostly reactants

Calculating Concentrations at Equilibrium

When we know the numerical value of the equilibrium constant and all the equilibrium concentrations except one, we can calculate the unknown concentration as shown in Sample Problem 10.5.

⚛ CORE CHEMISTRY SKILL

Calculating Equilibrium Concentrations

▶ **SAMPLE PROBLEM 10.5** Calculating Concentration Using an Equilibrium Constant

For the reaction of carbon dioxide and hydrogen, the equilibrium concentrations are 0.25 M CO_2, 0.80 M H_2, and 0.50 M H_2O. What is the equilibrium concentration of $CO(g)$?

$$CO_2(g) + H_2(g) \rightleftharpoons CO(g) + H_2O(g) \qquad K_c = 0.11$$

SOLUTION

STEP **1** State the given and needed quantities.

	Given	Need
ANALYZE THE PROBLEM	0.25 M CO_2, 0.80 M H_2, 0.50 M H_2O	[CO]
	Equation	
	$CO_2(g) + H_2(g) \rightleftharpoons CO(g) + H_2O(g)$ $\quad K_c = 0.11$	

Guide to Using the Equilibrium Constant

STEP **1**
State the given and needed quantities.

STEP **2**
Write the K_c expression for the equilibrium and solve for the needed concentration.

STEP **3**
Substitute the equilibrium (molar) concentrations and calculate the needed concentration.

STEP **2** Write the K_c expression for the equilibrium and solve for the needed concentration.

$$K_c = \frac{[CO][H_2O]}{[CO_2][H_2]}$$

We rearrange K_c to solve for the unknown [CO] as follows:

Multiply both sides by $[CO_2][H_2]$.

$$K_c \times [CO_2][H_2] = \frac{[CO][H_2O]}{[\cancel{CO_2}][\cancel{H_2}]} \times [\cancel{CO_2}][\cancel{H_2}]$$

$$K_c[CO_2][H_2] = [CO][H_2O]$$

Divide both sides by $[H_2O]$.

$$K_c \frac{[CO_2][H_2]}{[H_2O]} = \frac{[CO][\cancel{H_2O}]}{[\cancel{H_2O}]}$$

$$[CO] = K_c \frac{[CO_2][H_2]}{[H_2O]}$$

STEP **3** Substitute the equilibrium (molar) concentrations and calculate the needed concentration.

$$[CO] = K_c \frac{[CO_2][H_2]}{[H_2O]} = 0.11 \frac{[0.25][0.80]}{[0.50]} = 0.044 \text{ M}$$

STUDY CHECK 10.5

When the alkene ethene (C_2H_4) reacts with water vapor, the alcohol ethanol (C_2H_5OH) is produced. If an equilibrium mixture contains 0.020 M C_2H_4 and 0.015 M H_2O, what is the equilibrium concentration of C_2H_5OH? At 327 °C, the K_c is 9.0×10^3.

$$C_2H_4(g) + H_2O(g) \rightleftharpoons C_2H_5OH(g)$$

ANSWER

$$[C_2H_5OH] = 2.7 \text{ M}$$

QUESTIONS AND PROBLEMS

10.4 Using Equilibrium Constants

LEARNING GOAL Use an equilibrium constant to predict the extent of reaction and to calculate equilibrium concentrations.

10.21 If the K_c for this reaction is 4, which of the following diagrams represents the molecules in an equilibrium mixture? In the diagrams, X atoms are orange and Y atoms are blue.

$$X_2(g) + Y_2(g) \rightleftharpoons 2XY(g)$$

    A   B   C

10.22 If the K_c for this reaction is 2, which of the following diagrams represents the molecules in an equilibrium mixture? In the diagrams, A atoms are orange and B atoms are green.

$$2AB(g) \rightleftharpoons A_2(g) + B_2(g)$$

    A   B   C

10.23 Indicate whether each of the following equilibrium mixtures contains mostly products or mostly reactants:
    a. $Cl_2(g) + NO(g) \rightleftharpoons 2NOCl(g)$ $K_c = 3.7 \times 10^8$

    b. $2H_2(g) + S_2(g) \rightleftharpoons 2H_2S(g)$ $K_c = 1.1 \times 10^7$
    c. $3O_2(g) \rightleftharpoons 2O_3(g)$ $K_c = 1.7 \times 10^{-56}$

10.24 Indicate whether each of the following equilibrium mixtures contains mostly products or mostly reactants:
    a. $CO(g) + Cl_2(g) \rightleftharpoons COCl_2(g)$ $K_c = 5.0 \times 10^{-9}$
    b. $2HF(g) \rightleftharpoons H_2(g) + F_2(g)$ $K_c = 1.0 \times 10^{-95}$
    c. $2NO(g) + O_2(g) \rightleftharpoons 2NO_2(g)$ $K_c = 6.0 \times 10^{13}$

10.25 The equilibrium constant, K_c, for this reaction is 54.

$$H_2(g) + I_2(g) \rightleftharpoons 2HI(g)$$

If the equilibrium mixture contains 0.015 M I_2 and 0.030 M HI, what is the molar concentration of H_2?

10.26 The equilibrium constant, K_c, for the following reaction is 4.6×10^{-3}. If the equilibrium mixture contains 0.050 M NO_2, what is the molar concentration of N_2O_4?

$$N_2O_4(g) \rightleftharpoons 2NO_2(g)$$

10.27 The K_c for the following reaction at 100 °C is 2.0. If the equilibrium mixture contains 2.0 M NO and 1.0 M Br_2, what is the molar concentration of NOBr?

$$2NOBr(g) \rightleftharpoons 2NO(g) + Br_2(g)$$

10.28 The K_c for the following reaction at 225 °C is 1.7×10^2. If the equilibrium mixture contains 0.18 M H_2 and 0.020 M N_2, what is the molar concentration of NH_3?

$$3H_2(g) + N_2(g) \rightleftharpoons 2NH_3(g)$$

10.5 Changing Equilibrium Conditions: Le Châtelier's Principle

LEARNING GOAL

Use Le Châtelier's principle to describe the changes made in equilibrium concentrations when reaction conditions change.

We have seen that when a reaction reaches equilibrium, the rates of the forward and reverse reactions are equal and the concentrations remain constant. Now we will look at what happens to a system at equilibrium when changes occur in reaction conditions, such as changes in concentration, volume, and temperature.

Le Châtelier's Principle

When we alter any of the conditions of a system at equilibrium, the rates of the forward and reverse reactions will no longer be equal. We say that a *stress* is placed on the equilibrium. Then the system responds by changing the rate of the forward or reverse reaction in the direction that relieves that stress to reestablish equilibrium. We can use **Le Châtelier's principle**, which states that when a system at equilibrium is disturbed, the system will shift in the direction that will reduce that stress.

> ### Le Châtelier's Principle
> When a stress (change in conditions) is placed on a reaction at equilibrium, the equilibrium will shift in the direction that relieves the stress.

Suppose we have two water tanks connected by a pipe. When the water levels in the tanks are equal, water flows in the forward direction from Tank A to Tank B at the same rate as it flows in the reverse direction from Tank B to Tank A. Suppose we add more water to Tank A. With a higher level of water in Tank A, more water flows in the forward direction from Tank A to Tank B than in the reverse direction from Tank B to Tank A, which is shown with a longer arrow. Eventually, equilibrium is reached as the levels in both tanks become equal, but higher than before. Then the rate of water flows equally between Tank A and Tank B.

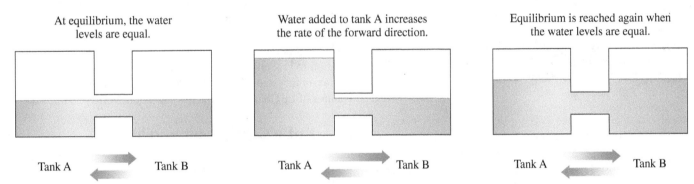

At equilibrium, the water levels are equal.	Water added to tank A increases the rate of the forward direction.	Equilibrium is reached again when the water levels are equal.
Tank A → ← Tank B	Tank A → ← Tank B	Tank A → ← Tank B

The stress of adding water to tank A increases the rate of the forward direction to reestablish equal water levels and equilibrium.

Effect of Concentration Changes on Equilibrium

⚛ **CORE CHEMISTRY SKILL**

Using Le Châtelier's Principle

We will now use the reaction of H_2 and I_2 to illustrate how a change in concentration disturbs the equilibrium and how the system responds to that stress.

$$H_2(g) + I_2(g) \rightleftharpoons 2HI(g)$$

Suppose that more of the reactant H_2 is added to the equilibrium mixture, which increases the concentration of H_2. Because a K_c cannot change for a reaction at a given temperature, adding more H_2 places a stress on the system (see Figure 10.10). Then the system relieves this stress by increasing the rate of the forward reaction. Thus, more products are formed until the system is again at equilibrium. According to Le Châtelier's principle, adding more reactant causes the system to *shift* in the direction of the products until equilibrium is reestablished.

$$\overset{\text{Add } H_2}{H_2(g) + I_2(g) \rightleftharpoons 2HI(g)}$$

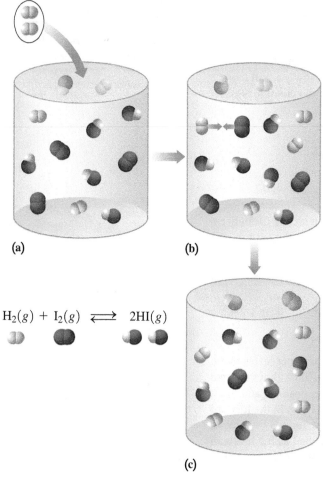

(a)   (b)

$$H_2(g) + I_2(g) \rightleftharpoons 2HI(g)$$

(c)

FIGURE 10.10 ▶ **(a)** The addition of H_2 places stress on the equilibrium system of $H_2(g) + I_2(g) \rightleftharpoons 2HI(g)$. **(b)** To relieve the stress, the forward reaction converts some reactants H_2 and I_2 to product HI. **(c)** A new equilibrium is established when the rates of the forward reaction and the reverse reaction become equal.

Q If more product HI is added, will the equilibrium shift in the direction of the products or reactants? Why?

TABLE 10.4 Effect of Concentration Changes on Equilibrium
$H_2(g) + I_2(g) \rightleftharpoons 2HI(g)$

Stress	Shift in the Direction of
Increase $[H_2]$	Products
Decrease $[H_2]$	Reactants
Increase $[I_2]$	Products
Decrease $[I_2]$	Reactants
Increase $[HI]$	Reactants
Decrease $[HI]$	Products

Suppose now that some H_2 is removed from the reaction mixture at equilibrium, which lowers the concentration of H_2 and slows the rate of the forward reaction. Using Le Châtelier's principle, we know that when some of the reactants are removed, the system will *shift* in the direction of the reactants until equilibrium is reestablished.

Remove H_2

$$H_2(g) + I_2(g) \rightleftharpoons 2HI(g)$$

The concentrations of the products of an equilibrium mixture can also increase or decrease. For example, if more HI is added, there is an increase in the rate of the reaction in the reverse direction, which converts some of the products to reactants. The concentration of the products decreases and the concentration of the reactants increases until equilibrium is reestablished. Using Le Châtelier's principle, we see that the addition of a product causes the system to *shift* in the direction of the reactants.

Add HI

$$H_2(g) + I_2(g) \rightleftharpoons 2HI(g)$$

In another example, some HI is removed from an equilibrium mixture, which decreases the concentration of the products. Then there is a *shift* in the direction of the products to reestablish equilibrium.

Remove HI

$$H_2(g) + I_2(g) \rightleftharpoons 2HI(g)$$

In summary, Le Châtelier's principle indicates that a stress caused by adding a substance at equilibrium is relieved when the equilibrium system shifts the reaction away from that substance. Adding more reactant causes an increase in the forward reaction to products. Adding more products causes an increase in the reverse reaction to reactants. When some of a substance is removed, the equilibrium system shifts in the direction of that substance. These features of Le Châtelier's principle are summarized in Table 10.4.

Effect of a Catalyst on Equilibrium

Sometimes a catalyst is added to a reaction to speed up a reaction by lowering the activation energy. As a result, the rates of both the forward and reverse reactions increase. The time required to reach equilibrium is shorter, but the same ratios of products and reactants are attained. Therefore, a catalyst speeds up the forward and reverse reactions, but it has no effect on the equilibrium mixture.

Effect of Volume Change on Equilibrium

If there is a change in the volume of a gas mixture at equilibrium, there will also be a change in the concentrations of those gases. Decreasing the volume will increase the concentration of gases, whereas increasing the volume will decrease their concentration. Then the system responds to reestablish equilibrium.

Let's look at the effect of decreasing the volume of the equilibrium mixture of the following reaction:

$$2CO(g) + O_2(g) \rightleftharpoons 2CO_2(g)$$

If we decrease the volume, all the concentrations increase. According to Le Châtelier's principle, the increase in concentration is relieved when the system shifts in the direction of the smaller number of moles.

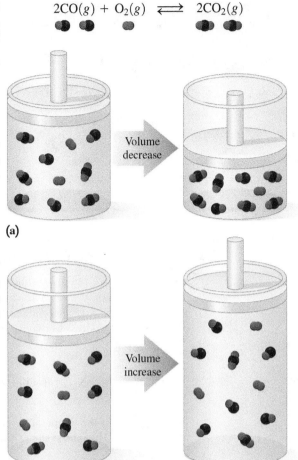

(a)

Decrease V

$$2CO(g) + O_2(g) \rightleftharpoons 2CO_2(g)$$
3 moles of gas $\qquad$ 2 moles of gas

On the other hand, when the volume of the equilibrium gas mixture increases, the concentrations of all the gases decrease. Then the system shifts in the direction of the greater number of moles to reestablish equilibrium (see Figure 10.11).

Increase V

$$2CO(g) + O_2(g) \rightleftharpoons 2CO_2(g)$$
3 moles of gas $\qquad$ 2 moles of gas

When a reaction has the same number of moles of reactants as products, a volume change does not affect the equilibrium mixture because the concentrations of the reactants and products change in the same way.

$$H_2(g) + I_2(g) \rightleftharpoons 2HI(g)$$
2 moles of gas $\qquad$ 2 moles of gas

FIGURE 10.11 ▶ **(a)** A decrease in the volume of the container causes the system to shift in the direction of fewer moles of gas. **(b)** An increase in the volume of the container causes the system to shift in the direction of more moles of gas.

Q If you want to increase the products, should you increase or decrease the volume of the container?

(b)

Chemistry Link to Health
Oxygen–Hemoglobin Equilibrium and Hypoxia

The transport of oxygen involves an equilibrium between hemoglobin (Hb), oxygen, and oxyhemoglobin (HbO_2).

$$Hb(aq) + O_2(g) \rightleftharpoons HbO_2(aq)$$

When the O_2 level is high in the alveoli of the lung, the reaction shifts in the direction of the product HbO_2. In the tissues where O_2 concentration is low, the reverse reaction releases the oxygen from the hemoglobin. The equilibrium expression is written

$$K_c = \frac{[HbO_2]}{[Hb][O_2]}$$

At normal atmospheric pressure, oxygen diffuses into the blood because the partial pressure of oxygen in the alveoli is higher than that in the blood. At an altitude above 8000 ft, a decrease in the atmospheric pressure results in a significant reduction in the partial pressure of oxygen, which means that less oxygen is available for the blood and body tissues. The fall in atmospheric pressure at higher altitudes decreases the partial pressure of inhaled oxygen, and there is less driving pressure for gas exchange in the lungs. At an altitude of

18 000 ft, a person will obtain 29% less oxygen. When oxygen levels are lowered, a person may experience *hypoxia*, characterized by increased respiratory rate, headache, decreased mental acuteness, fatigue, decreased physical coordination, nausea, vomiting, and cyanosis. A similar problem occurs in persons with a history of lung disease that impairs gas diffusion in the alveoli or in persons with a reduced number of red blood cells, such as smokers.

According to Le Châtelier's principle, we see that a decrease in oxygen will shift the equilibrium in the direction of the reactants. Such a shift depletes the concentration of HbO_2 and causes the hypoxia.

$$Hb(aq) + O_2(g) \longleftarrow HbO_2(aq)$$

Immediate treatment of altitude sickness includes hydration, rest, and if necessary, descending to a lower altitude. The adaptation to lowered oxygen levels requires about 10 days. During this time the bone marrow increases red blood cell production, providing more red blood cells and more hemoglobin. A person living at a high altitude can have 50% more red blood cells than someone at sea level. This increase in hemoglobin causes a shift in the equilibrium back in the

Hypoxia may occur at high altitudes where the oxygen concentration is lower.

direction of HbO_2 product. Eventually, the higher concentration of HbO_2 will provide more oxygen to the tissues and the symptoms of hypoxia will lessen.

$$Hb(aq) + O_2(g) \longrightarrow HbO_2(aq)$$

For some who climb high mountains, it is important to stop and acclimatize for several days at increasing altitudes. At very high altitudes, it may be necessary to use an oxygen tank.

Effect of a Change in Temperature on Equilibrium

We can think of heat as a reactant or a product in a reaction. For example, in the equation for an endothermic reaction, heat is written on the reactant side. When the temperature of an endothermic reaction increases, the system responds by shifting in the direction of the products to remove heat.

$$N_2(g) + O_2(g) + \text{heat} \quad \overset{\text{Increase } T}{\rightleftharpoons} \quad 2NO(g)$$

If the temperature is decreased for an endothermic reaction, there is a decrease in heat. Then the system shifts in the direction of the reactants to add heat.

$$N_2(g) + O_2(g) + \text{heat} \quad \overset{\text{Decrease } T}{\rightleftharpoons} \quad 2NO(g)$$

In the equation for an exothermic reaction, heat is written on the product side. When the temperature of an exothermic reaction increases, the system responds by shifting in the direction of the reactants to remove heat.

$$2SO_2(g) + O_2(g) \quad \overset{\text{Increase } T}{\rightleftharpoons} \quad 2SO_3(g) + \text{heat}$$

If the temperature is decreased for an exothermic reaction, there is a decrease in heat. Then the system shifts in the direction of the products to add heat.

$$2SO_2(g) + O_2(g) \quad \overset{\text{Decrease } T}{\rightleftharpoons} \quad 2SO_3(g) + \text{heat}$$

Table 10.5 summarizes the ways we can use Le Châtelier's principle to determine the shift in equilibrium that relieves a stress caused by the change in a condition.

TABLE 10.5 Effects of Condition Changes on Equilibrium

Condition	Change (Stress)	Shift in the Direction of
Concentration	Add a reactant	Products (forward reaction)
	Remove a reactant	Reactants (reverse reaction)
	Add a product	Reactants (reverse reaction)
	Remove a product	Products (forward reaction)
Volume (container)	Decrease volume	Fewer moles of gas
	Increase volume	More moles of gas
Temperature	**Endothermic reaction**	
	Increase T	Products (forward reaction to remove heat)
	Decrease T	Reactants (reverse reaction to add heat)
	Exothermic reaction	
	Increase T	Reactants (reverse reaction to remove heat)
	Decrease T	Products (forward reaction to add heat)
Catalyst	Increases rates equally	No effect

▶ **SAMPLE PROBLEM 10.6 Using Le Châtelier's Principle**

Methanol, CH_3OH, is finding use as a fuel additive. Describe the effect of each of the following changes on the equilibrium mixture for the following reaction:

$$2CH_3OH(g) + 3O_2(g) \rightleftharpoons 2CO_2(g) + 4H_2O(g) + 1450\ kJ$$

a. adding more CO_2
b. adding more O_2
c. increasing the volume of the container
d. increasing the temperature
e. adding a catalyst

SOLUTION

a. When the concentration of the product CO_2 increases, the equilibrium shifts in the direction of the reactants.
b. When the concentration of the reactant O_2 increases, the equilibrium shifts in the direction of the products.
c. When the volume increases, the equilibrium shifts in the direction of the greater number of moles of gas, which is the products.
d. When the temperature is increased for an exothermic reaction, the equilibrium shifts in the direction of the reactants to remove heat.
e. When a catalyst is added, there is no change in the equilibrium mixture.

STUDY CHECK 10.6

Describe the effect of each of the following changes on the equilibrium mixture for the following reaction:

$$2HF(g) + Cl_2(g) + 357\ kJ \rightleftharpoons 2HCl(g) + F_2(g)$$

a. adding more Cl_2
b. decreasing the volume of the container
c. increasing the temperature

ANSWER

a. When the concentration of the reactant Cl_2 increases, the equilibrium shifts in the direction of the products.

b. There is no change in equilibrium mixture because the moles of reactant are equal to the moles of product.

c. When the temperature for an endothermic reaction increases, the equilibrium shifts to remove heat, which is in the direction of the products.

Chemistry Link to Health

Homeostasis: Regulation of Body Temperature

In a physiological system of equilibrium called *homeostasis*, changes in our environment are balanced by changes in our bodies. It is crucial to our survival that we balance heat gain with heat loss. If we do not lose enough heat, our body temperature rises. At high temperatures, the body can no longer regulate our metabolic reactions. If we lose too much heat, body temperature drops. At low temperatures, essential functions proceed too slowly.

The skin plays an important role in the maintenance of body temperature. When the outside temperature rises, receptors in the skin send signals to the brain. The temperature-regulating part of the brain stimulates the sweat glands to produce perspiration. As perspiration evaporates from the skin, heat is removed and the body temperature is decreased.

In cold temperatures, epinephrine is released, causing an increase in metabolic rate, which increases the production of heat. Receptors on the skin signal the brain to constrict the blood vessels. Less blood flows through the skin, and heat is conserved. The production of perspiration stops, thereby lessening the heat lost by evaporation.

Blood vessels dilate
• sweat production increases
• sweat evaporates
• skin cools

Blood vessels constrict and epinephrine is released
• metabolic activity increases
• muscular activity increases
• shivering occurs
• sweat production stops

QUESTIONS AND PROBLEMS

10.5 Changing Equilibrium Conditions: Le Châtelier's Principle

LEARNING GOAL Use Le Châtelier's principle to describe the changes made in equilibrium concentrations when reaction conditions change.

10.29 In the lower atmosphere, oxygen is converted to ozone (O_3) by the energy provided from lightning.

$$3O_2(g) + \text{heat} \rightleftharpoons 2O_3(g)$$

For each of the following changes at equilibrium, indicate whether the equilibrium shifts in the direction of products, reactants, or does not change:

a. adding more $O_2(g)$
b. adding more $O_3(g)$
c. increasing the temperature
d. increasing the volume of the container
e. adding a catalyst

10.30 Ammonia is produced by reacting nitrogen gas and hydrogen gas.

$$N_2(g) + 3H_2(g) \rightleftharpoons 2NH_3(g) + 92 \text{ kJ}$$

For each of the following changes at equilibrium, indicate whether the equilibrium shifts in the direction of products, reactants, or does not change:

a. removing some $N_2(g)$
b. decreasing the temperature
c. adding more $NH_3(g)$
d. adding more $H_2(g)$
e. increasing the volume of the container

10.31 Hydrogen chloride can be made by reacting hydrogen gas and chlorine gas.

$$H_2(g) + Cl_2(g) + \text{heat} \rightleftharpoons 2HCl(g)$$

For each of the following changes at equilibrium, indicate whether the equilibrium shifts in the direction of products, reactants, or does not change:

a. adding more $H_2(g)$
b. increasing the temperature
c. removing some $HCl(g)$
d. adding a catalyst
e. removing some $Cl_2(g)$

10.32 When heated, carbon monoxide reacts with water to produce carbon dioxide and hydrogen.

$$CO(g) + H_2O(g) \rightleftharpoons CO_2(g) + H_2(g) + heat$$

For each of the following changes at equilibrium, indicate whether the equilibrium shifts in the direction of products, reactants, or does not change:
a. decreasing the temperature
b. adding more $H_2(g)$
c. removing $CO_2(g)$ as its forms
d. adding more $H_2O(g)$
e. decreasing the volume of the container

 Clinical Applications

Use the following equation for the equilibrium of hemoglobin in the blood to answer problems 10.33 and 10.34:

$$Hb(aq) + O_2(g) \rightleftharpoons HbO_2(aq)$$

10.33 Athletes who train at high altitudes initially experience hypoxia, which causes their body to produce more hemoglobin. When an athlete first arrives at high altitude,
a. What is the stress on the hemoglobin equilibrium?
b. In what direction does the hemoglobin equilibrium shift?

10.34 A person who has been a smoker and has a low oxygen blood saturation uses an oxygen tank for supplemental oxygen. When oxygen is first supplied,
a. What is the stress on the hemoglobin equilibrium?
b. In what direction does the hemoglobin equilibrium shift?

Clinical Update
An Iron-Rich Diet for Children's Anemia

Today, Andrew is a thriving two-year old toddler. However, his mother is concerned that Andrew looks pale, seems to have some trouble breathing, has a lot of headaches, and generally seems tired. At the clinic, Andrew and his mother see Judy, his neonatal nurse when he was an infant. Judy notes his symptoms and takes a blood sample, which shows that Andrew has *iron-deficiency anemia*. Judy explains to his mother that Andrew's red-blood cell count is below normal, which means that he has a low concentration of hemoglobin in his blood.

Hemoglobin, present in our red blood cells, is an iron-containing protein that carries oxygen from our lungs to the muscles and tissues of our body. Each hemoglobin molecule contains four heme or iron-containing groups. Because each heme group can attach to one O_2 in the lungs, one hemoglobin can carry as many as four O_2 molecules. The transport of oxygen involves an equilibrium reaction between the reactants Hb and O_2 and the product HbO_2.

$$Hb(aq) + O_2(g) \rightleftharpoons HbO_2(aq)$$

The equilibrium expression can be written

$$K_c = \frac{[HbO_2]}{[Hb][O_2]}$$

In the alveoli of the lungs where the O_2 concentration is high, the forward reaction is faster, which shifts the equilibrium in the direction of the product HbO_2. As a result, O_2 binds to hemoglobin in the lungs.

$$Hb(aq) + O_2(g) \longrightarrow HbO_2(aq)$$

In the tissues and the muscles where the O_2 concentration is low, the reverse reaction is faster, which shifts the equilibrium in the direction of the reactant Hb and releases the oxygen from the hemoglobin.

$$Hb(aq) + O_2(g) \longleftarrow HbO_2(aq)$$

Judy recommends to Andrew's mother that his diet include more high iron-containing foods such as chicken, fish, spinach, iron-fortified cereal, eggs, peas, beans, peanut butter, and whole-grain bread. After three months of an iron-rich diet, Andrew's hemoglobin was within normal range.

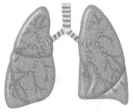  

| In the lungs, Hb binds O_2. | O_2 is carried as HbO_2 by red cells from the lungs to the tissues and muscles. | In the tissues and muscles, HbO_2 releases O_2. |

 Clinical Applications

10.35 For the hemoglobin equilibrium, indicate if each of the following changes shifts the equilibrium in the direction of the products, the reactants, or does not change:
a. increasing $[O_2]$
b. increasing $[HbO_2]$
c. decreasing $[Hb]$

10.36 For the hemoglobin equilibrium, indicate if each of the following changes shifts the equilibrium in the direction of the products, the reactants, or does not change:

a. decreasing $[O_2]$
b. increasing $[Hb]$
c. decreasing $[HbO_2]$

10.37 Andrew is diagnosed as being anemic. Why does Andrew not obtain sufficient oxygen in his tissues?

10.38 Andrew's diet is changed to include more iron-rich foods. How would an increase in iron affect his hemoglobin equilibrium?

REACTION RATES AND CHEMICAL EQUILIBRIUM

involves

Reaction Rates	Reversible Reactions	Le Châtelier's Principle
are affected by	when equal in rate give	indicates that equilibrium adjusts for changes in
Concentrations of Reactants	**Equilibrium Constant Expression**	**Concentration, Temperature, and Volume**
Temperature	is written as	
Catalyst	$K_c = \dfrac{\text{Products}}{\text{Reactants}}$	

Small K_c Has Mostly Reactants   **Large K_c Has Mostly Products**

CHAPTER REVIEW

10.1 Rates of Reactions
LEARNING GOAL
Describe how temperature, concentration, and catalysts affect the rate of a reaction.

- The rate of a reaction is the speed at which the reactants are converted to products.
- Increasing the concentrations of reactants, increasing the temperature, or adding a catalyst can increase the rate of a reaction.

10.2 Chemical Equilibrium
LEARNING GOAL Use the concept of reversible reactions to explain chemical equilibrium.

- Chemical equilibrium occurs in a reversible reaction when the rate of the forward reaction becomes equal to the rate of the reverse reaction.
- At equilibrium, no further change occurs in the concentrations of the reactants and products as the forward and reverse reactions continue.

10.3 Equilibrium Constants
LEARNING GOAL Calculate the equilibrium constant for a reversible reaction given the concentrations of reactants and products at equilibrium.

- An equilibrium constant, K_c, is the ratio of the concentrations of the products to the concentrations of the reactants, with each concentration raised to a power equal to its coefficient in the balanced chemical equation.

10.4 Using Equilibrium Constants
LEARNING GOAL Use an equilibrium constant to predict the extent of reaction and to calculate equilibrium concentrations.

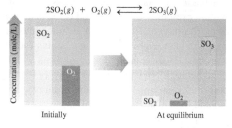

$$2SO_2(g) + O_2(g) \rightleftharpoons 2SO_3(g)$$

- A large value of K_c indicates that an equilibrium mixture contains mostly products and few reactants, whereas a small value of K_c indicates that the equilibrium mixture contains mostly reactants.
- Equilibrium constants can be used to calculate the concentration of a component in the equilibrium mixture.

10.5 Changing Equilibrium Conditions: Le Châtelier's Principle
LEARNING GOAL Use Le Châtelier's principle to describe the changes made in equilibrium concentrations when reaction conditions change.

- When reactants are removed or products are added to an equilibrium mixture, the system shifts in the direction of the reactants.
- When reactants are added or products are removed from an equilibrium mixture, the system shifts in the direction of the products.

- A decrease in the volume of a reaction container causes a shift in the direction of the smaller number of moles of gas.
- An increase in the volume of a reaction container causes a shift in the direction of the greater number of moles of gas.

- Increasing the temperature of an endothermic reaction or decreasing the temperature of an exothermic reaction will cause the system to shift in the direction of products.
- Decreasing the temperature of an endothermic reaction or increasing the temperature of an exothermic reaction will cause the system to shift in the direction of reactants.

KEY TERMS

activation energy The energy that must be provided by a collision to break apart the bonds of the reacting molecules.

catalyst A substance that increases the rate of reaction by lowering the activation energy.

chemical equilibrium The point at which the rate of forward and reverse reactions are equal so that no further change in concentrations of reactants and products takes place.

collision theory A model for a chemical reaction stating that molecules must collide with sufficient energy and proper orientation to form products.

equilibrium constant, K_c The numerical value obtained by substituting the equilibrium concentrations of the components into the equilibrium constant expression.

equilibrium constant expression The ratio of the concentrations of products to the concentrations of reactants, with each component raised to an exponent equal to the coefficient of that compound in the balanced chemical equation.

Le Châtelier's principle When a stress is placed on a system at equilibrium, the equilibrium shifts to relieve that stress.

rate of reaction The speed at which reactants are used to form product(s).

reversible reaction A reaction in which a forward reaction occurs from reactants to products, and a reverse reaction occurs from products back to reactants.

⚛ CORE CHEMISTRY SKILLS

The chapter section containing each Core Chemistry Skill is shown in parentheses at the end of each heading.

Writing the Equilibrium Constant Expression (10.3)

- An equilibrium constant expression for a reversible reaction is written by multiplying the concentrations of the products in the numerator and dividing by the product of the concentrations of the reactants in the denominator.
- Each concentration is raised to a power equal to its coefficient in the balanced chemical equation:

$$K_c = \frac{[\text{Products}]}{[\text{Reactants}]} = \frac{[\text{C}]^c [\text{D}]^d}{[\text{A}]^a [\text{B}]^b} \longrightarrow \text{Coefficients}$$

Example: Write the equilibrium constant expression for the following chemical reaction:

$$2NO_2(g) \rightleftharpoons N_2O_4(g)$$

Answer: $K_c = \dfrac{[N_2O_4]}{[NO_2]^2}$

Calculating an Equilibrium Constant (10.3)

- The equilibrium constant, K_c, is the numerical value obtained by substituting experimentally measured molar concentrations at equilibrium into the equilibrium constant expression.

Example: Calculate the numerical value of K_c for the following reaction when the equilibrium mixture contains 0.025 M NO_2 and 0.087 M N_2O_4:

$$2NO_2(g) \rightleftharpoons N_2O_4(g)$$

Answer: Write the equilibrium constant expression, substitute the molar concentrations, and calculate.

$$K_c = \frac{[N_2O_4]}{[NO_2]^2} = \frac{[0.087]}{[0.025]^2} = 140$$

Calculating Equilibrium Concentrations (10.4)

- To determine the concentration of a product or a reactant at equilibrium, we use the equilibrium constant expression to solve for the unknown concentration.

Example: Calculate the equilibrium concentration for CF_4 if $K_c = 2.0$, and the equilibrium mixture contains 0.10 M COF_2 and 0.050 M CO_2.

$$2COF_2(g) \rightleftharpoons CO_2(g) + CF_4(g)$$

Answer: Write the equilibrium constant expression.

$$K_c = \frac{[CO_2][CF_4]}{[COF_2]^2}$$

Rearrange the equation, substitute the molar concentrations, and calculate $[CF_4]$.

$$[CF_4] = \frac{K_c [COF_2]^2}{[CO_2]} = \frac{2.0 [0.10]^2}{[0.050]} = 0.40 \text{ M}$$

Using Le Châtelier's Principle (10.5)

- Le Châtelier's principle states that when a system at equilibrium is disturbed by changes in concentration, volume, or temperature, the system will shift in the direction that will reduce that stress.

Example: Nitrogen and oxygen form dinitrogen pentoxide in an exothermic, combination reaction.

$$2N_2(g) + 5O_2(g) \rightleftharpoons 2N_2O_5(g) + \text{heat}$$

For each of the following changes at equilibrium, indicate whether the equilibrium shifts in the direction of products, reactants, or does not change:

a. removing some $N_2(g)$
b. decreasing the temperature
c. increasing the volume of the container

Answer: **a.** Removing a reactant shifts the equilibrium in the direction of the reactants.

b. Decreasing the temperature shifts the equilibrium of an exothermic reaction in the direction of the products, which produces heat.

c. Increasing the volume of the container shifts the equilibrium in the direction of the greater number of moles of gas, which is in the direction of the reactants.

UNDERSTANDING THE CONCEPTS

The chapter sections to review are shown in parentheses at the end of each question.

10.39 Write the equilibrium constant expression for each of the following reactions: (10.3)

a. $CH_4(g) + 2O_2(g) \rightleftharpoons CO_2(g) + 2H_2O(g)$
b. $4NH_3(g) + 3O_2(g) \rightleftharpoons 2N_2(g) + 6H_2O(g)$
c. $C(s) + 2H_2(g) \rightleftharpoons CH_4(g)$

10.40 Write the equilibrium constant expression for each of the following reactions: (10.3)

a. $2C_2H_6(g) + 7O_2(g) \rightleftharpoons 4CO_2(g) + 6H_2O(g)$
b. $2KHCO_3(s) \rightleftharpoons K_2CO_3(s) + CO_2(g) + H_2O(g)$
c. $4NH_3(g) + 5O_2(g) \rightleftharpoons 4NO(g) + 6H_2O(g)$

10.41 Would the equilibrium constant, K_c, for the reaction in the diagrams have a large or small value? (10.4)

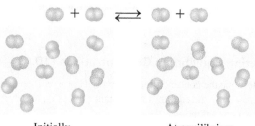

Initially   At equilibrium

10.42 Would the equilibrium constant, K_c, for the reaction in the diagrams have a large or small value? (10.4)

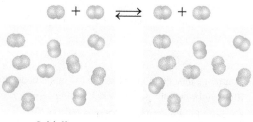

Initially   At equilibrium

10.43 Would T_2 be higher or lower than T_1 for the reaction shown in the diagrams? (10.5)

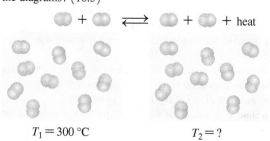

$T_1 = 300\ °C$ $T_2 = ?$

10.44 Would the reaction shown in the diagrams be exothermic or endothermic? (10.5)

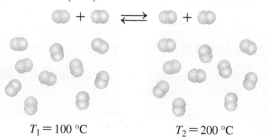

$T_1 = 100\ °C$ $T_2 = 200\ °C$

ADDITIONAL QUESTIONS AND PROBLEMS

10.45 For each of the following changes at equilibrium, indicate whether the equilibrium shifts in the direction of products, reactants, or does not change: (10.5)

$$C_2H_4(g) + Cl_2(g) \rightleftharpoons C_2H_4Cl_2(g) + heat$$

a. increasing the temperature of the reaction
b. decreasing the volume of the reaction container
c. adding a catalyst
d. adding more $Cl_2(g)$

10.46 For each of the following changes at equilibrium, indicate whether the equilibrium shifts in the direction of products, reactants, or does not change: (10.5)

$$N_2(g) + O_2(g) + heat \rightleftharpoons 2NO(g)$$

a. increasing the temperature of the reaction
b. decreasing the volume of the reaction container
c. adding a catalyst
d. adding more $N_2(g)$

10.47 For each of the following reactions, indicate if the equilibrium mixture contains mostly products, mostly reactants, or both reactants and products: (10.4)

a. $H_2(g) + Cl_2(g) \rightleftharpoons 2HCl(g)$ $K_c = 1.3 \times 10^{34}$
b. $2NOBr(g) \rightleftharpoons 2NO(g) + Br_2(g)$ $K_c = 2.0$
c. $2NOCl(g) \rightleftharpoons Cl_2(g) + 2NO(g)$ $K_c = 2.7 \times 10^{-9}$
d. $C(s) + H_2O(g) \rightleftharpoons CO(g) + H_2(g)$ $K_c = 6.3 \times 10^{-1}$

10.48 For each of the following reactions, indicate if the equilibrium mixture contains mostly products, mostly reactants, or both reactants and products: (10.4)

 a. $2H_2O(g) \rightleftharpoons 2H_2(g) + O_2(g)$ $K_c = 4 \times 10^{-48}$
 b. $N_2(g) + 3H_2(g) \rightleftharpoons 2NH_3(g)$ $K_c = 0.30$
 c. $2SO_2(g) + O_2(g) \rightleftharpoons 2SO_3(g)$ $K_c = 1.2 \times 10^9$
 d. $H_2(g) + S(s) \rightleftharpoons 2H_2S(g)$ $K_c = 7.8 \times 10^5$

10.49 Consider the reaction: (10.3)

$$2NH_3(g) \rightleftharpoons N_2(g) + 3H_2(g)$$

 a. Write the equilibrium constant expression.
 b. What is the numerical value of K_c for the reaction if the concentrations at equilibrium are 0.20 M NH_3, 3.0 M N_2, and 0.50 M H_2?

10.50 Consider the reaction: (10.3)

$$2SO_2(g) + O_2(g) \rightleftharpoons 2SO_3(g)$$

 a. Write the equilibrium constant expression.
 b. What is the numerical value of K_c for the reaction if the concentrations at equilibrium are 0.10 M SO_2, 0.12 M O_2, and 0.60 M SO_3?

10.51 The K_c for the following reaction is 5.0 at 100 °C. If an equilibrium mixture contains 0.50 M NO_2, what is the molar concentration of N_2O_4? (10.3, 10.4)

$$2NO_2(g) \rightleftharpoons N_2O_4(g)$$

10.52 The K_c for the following reaction is 15 at 220 °C. If an equilibrium mixture contains 0.40 M CO and 0.20 M H_2, what is the molar concentration of CH_3OH? (10.3, 10.4)

$$CO(g) + 2H_2(g) \rightleftharpoons CH_3OH(g)$$

10.53 According to Le Châtelier's principle, does the equilibrium shift in the direction of products or reactants when O_2 is added to the equilibrium mixture of each of the following reactions? (10.5)

 a. $3O_2(g) \rightleftharpoons 2O_3(g)$
 b. $2CO_2(g) \rightleftharpoons 2CO(g) + O_2(g)$
 c. $2SO_2(g) + O_2(g) \rightleftharpoons 2SO_3(g)$
 d. $2SO_2(g) + 2H_2O(g) \rightleftharpoons H_2S(g) + 3O_2(g)$

10.54 According to Le Châtelier's principle, does the equilibrium shift in the direction of products or reactants when N_2 is added to the equilibrium mixture of each of the following reactions? (10.5)

 a. $2NH_3(g) \rightleftharpoons 3H_2(g) + N_2(g)$
 b. $N_2(g) + O_2(g) \rightleftharpoons 2NO(g)$
 c. $2NO_2(g) \rightleftharpoons N_2(g) + 2O_2(g)$
 d. $4NH_3(g) + 3O_2(g) \rightleftharpoons 2N_2(g) + 6H_2O(g)$

10.55 Would decreasing the volume of the container for each of the following reactions cause the equilibrium to shift in the direction of products, reactants, or not change? (10.5)

 a. $3O_2(g) \rightleftharpoons 2O_3(g)$
 b. $2CO_2(g) \rightleftharpoons 2CO(g) + O_2(g)$
 c. $P_4(g) + 5O_2(g) \rightleftharpoons P_4O_{10}(s)$
 d. $2SO_2(g) + 2H_2O(g) \rightleftharpoons 2H_2S(g) + 3O_2(g)$

10.56 Would increasing the volume of the container for each of the following reactions cause the equilibrium to shift in the direction of products, reactants, or not change? (10.5)

 a. $2NH_3(g) \rightleftharpoons 3H_2(g) + N_2(g)$
 b. $N_2(g) + O_2(g) \rightleftharpoons 2NO(g)$
 c. $N_2(g) + 2O_2(g) \rightleftharpoons 2NO_2(g)$
 d. $4NH_3(g) + 3O_2(g) \rightleftharpoons 2N_2(g) + 6H_2O(g)$

CHALLENGE QUESTIONS

The following groups of questions are related to the topics in this chapter. However, they do not all follow the chapter order, and they require you to combine concepts and skills from several sections. These questions will help you increase your critical thinking skills and prepare for your next exam.

10.57 For each of the following K_c values, indicate whether the equilibrium mixture contains mostly reactants, mostly products, or similar amounts of reactants and products: (10.4)

 a. $N_2(g) + O_2(g) \rightleftharpoons 2NO(g)$ $K_c = 1 \times 10^{-30}$
 b. $H_2(g) + Br_2(g) \rightleftharpoons 2HBr(g)$ $K_c = 2.0 \times 10^{19}$

10.58 For each of the following K_c values, indicate whether the equilibrium mixture contains mostly reactants, mostly products, or similar amounts of reactants and products: (10.4)

 a. $Cl_2(g) + 2NO(g) \rightleftharpoons 2NOCl(g)$ $K_c = 3.7 \times 10^8$
 b. $N_2(g) + 2H_2(g) \rightleftharpoons 2N_2H_4(g)$ $K_c = 7.4 \times 10^{-26}$

10.59 The K_c at 100 °C is 2.0 for the decomposition reaction of NOBr. (10.3, 10.4, 10.5)

$$2NOBr(g) \rightleftharpoons 2NO(g) + Br_2(g)$$

In an experiment, 1.0 mole of NOBr, 1.0 mole of NO, and 1.0 mole of Br_2 were placed in a 1.0 L container.

 a. Write the equilibrium constant expression for the reaction.
 b. Is the system at equilibrium?
 c. If not, will the rate of the forward or reverse reaction initially speed up?
 d. At equilibrium, which concentration(s) will be greater than 1.0 mole/L, and which will be less than 1.0 mole/L?

10.60 Consider the following reaction: (10.3, 10.4, 10.5)

$$PCl_5(g) \rightleftharpoons PCl_3(g) + Cl_2(g)$$

 a. Write the equilibrium constant expression for the reaction.
 b. Initially, 0.60 mole of PCl_5 is placed in a 1.0 L flask. At equilibrium, there is 0.16 mole of PCl_3 in the flask. What are the equilibrium concentrations of PCl_5 and Cl_2?
 c. What is the numerical value of the equilibrium constant, K_c, for the reaction?
 d. If 0.20 mole of Cl_2 is added to the equilibrium mixture, will the concentration of PCl_5 increase or decrease?

10.61 Indicate how each of the following will affect the equilibrium concentration of NH_3 in the following reaction: (10.3, 10.5)

$$2NH_3(g) + 46\,kJ \rightleftharpoons N_2(g) + 3H_2(g)$$

 a. adding more $H_2(g)$
 b. increasing the temperature of the reaction
 c. increasing the volume of the container
 d. decreasing the volume of the container
 e. adding a catalyst

10.62 Indicate how each of the following will affect the equilibrium concentration of NH_3 in the following reaction: (10.3, 10.5)

$$4NH_3(g) + 5O_2(g) \rightleftharpoons 4NO(g) + 6H_2O(g) + 906\,kJ$$

 a. adding more $O_2(g)$
 b. increasing the temperature of the reaction
 c. increasing the volume of the container
 d. adding more $NO(g)$
 e. removing some $H_2O(g)$

10.63 Indicate if you would increase or decrease the volume of the container to *increase* the yield of the products in each of the following: (10.5)

a. $2SO_2(g) + O_2(g) \rightleftharpoons 2SO_3(g)$

b. $2CH_4(g) \rightleftharpoons C_2H_2(g) + 3H_2(g)$

c. $2H_2(g) + O_2(g) \rightleftharpoons 2H_2O(g)$

10.64 Indicate if you would increase or decrease the volume of the container to *increase* the yield of the products in each of the following: (10.5)

a. $Cl_2(g) + 2NO(g) \rightleftharpoons 2NOCl(g)$

b. $N_2(g) + 2H_2(g) \rightleftharpoons N_2H_4(g)$

c. $N_2O_4(g) \rightleftharpoons 2NO_2(g)$

ANSWERS

Answers to Selected Questions and Problems

10.1 a. The rate of the reaction indicates how fast the products form or how fast the reactants are used up.

b. At room temperature, the reactions involved in the growth of bread mold will proceed at a faster rate than at the lower temperature of the refrigerator.

10.3 The number of collisions will increase when the number of Br_2 molecules is increased.

10.5 a. increase   b. increase

c. increase   d. decrease

10.7 A reversible reaction is one in which a forward reaction converts reactants to products, whereas a reverse reaction converts products to reactants.

10.9 a. not at equilibrium   b. at equilibrium

c. at equilibrium

10.11 The reaction has reached equilibrium because the number of reactants and products does not change.

10.13 a. $K_c = \dfrac{[CS_2][H_2]^4}{[CH_4][H_2S]^2}$ b. $K_c = \dfrac{[N_2][O_2]}{[NO]^2}$

c. $K_c = \dfrac{[CS_2][O_2]^4}{[SO_3]^2[CO_2]}$ d. $K_c = \dfrac{[H_2]^3[CO]}{[CH_4][H_2O]}$

10.15 $K_c = \dfrac{[XY]^2}{[X_2][Y_2]} = 36$

10.17 $K_c = 1.5$

10.19 $K_c = 260$

10.21 Diagram **B** represents the equilibrium mixture.

10.23 a. mostly products   b. mostly products

c. mostly reactants

10.25 $[H_2] = 1.1 \times 10^{-3}\,M$

10.27 $[NOBr] = 1.4\,M$

10.29 a. Equilibrium shifts in the direction of the product.

b. Equilibrium shifts in the direction of the reactants.

c. Equilibrium shifts in the direction of the product.

d. Equilibrium shifts in the direction of the reactants.

e. No shift in equilibrium occurs.

10.31 a. Equilibrium shifts in the direction of the product.

b. Equilibrium shifts in the direction of the product.

c. Equilibrium shifts in the direction of the product.

d. No shift in equilibrium occurs.

e. Equilibrium shifts in the direction of the reactants.

10.33 a. The oxygen concentration is lowered.

b. Equilibrium shifts in the direction of the reactants.

10.35 a. Equilibrium shifts in the direction of products.

b. Equilibrium shifts in the direction of reactants.

c. Equilibrium shifts in the direction of reactants.

10.37 Without enough iron, Andrew will not have sufficient hemoglobin. When Hb is decreased, the equilibrium shifts in the direction of the reactants, Hb and O_2.

10.39 a. $K_c = \dfrac{[CO_2][H_2O]^2}{[CH_4][O_2]^2}$ b. $K_c = \dfrac{[N_2]^2[H_2O]^6}{[NH_3]^4[O_2]^3}$

c. $K_c = \dfrac{[CH_4]}{[H_2]^2}$

10.41 The equilibrium constant for the reaction would have a large value.

10.43 T_2 is lower than T_1.

10.45 a. Equilibrium shifts in the direction of the reactants.

b. Equilibrium shifts in the direction of the products.

c. There is no change in equilibrium.

d. Equilibrium shifts in the direction of the products.

10.47 a. mostly products

b. both reactants and products

c. mostly reactants

d. both reactants and products

10.49 a. $K_c = \dfrac{[N_2][H_2]^3}{[NH_3]^2}$ b. $K_c = 9.4$

10.51 $[N_2O_4] = 1.3\,M$

10.53 a. Equilibrium shifts in the direction of the products.

b. Equilibrium shifts in the direction of the reactants.

c. Equilibrium shifts in the direction of the products.

d. Equilibrium shifts in the direction of the reactants.

10.55 a. Equilibrium shifts in the direction of the products.

b. Equilibrium shifts in the direction of the reactants.

c. Equilibrium shifts in the direction of the products.

d. Equilibrium shifts in the direction of the reactants.

10.57 a. A small K_c value indicates that the equilibrium mixture contains mostly reactants.

b. A large K_c value indicates that the equilibrium mixture contains mostly products.

10.59 a. $K_c = \dfrac{[NO]^2[Br_2]}{[NOBr]^2}$

b. When the concentrations are placed in the expression, the result is 1.0, which is not equal to K_c. The system is not at equilibrium.

c. The rate of the forward reaction will increase.

d. The $[Br_2]$ and $[NO]$ will increase and $[NOBr]$ will decrease.

10.61 a. increase   b. decrease

c. decrease   d. increase

e. no change

10.63 a. decrease   b. increase

c. decrease

11

Acids and Bases

A 30-YEAR-OLD MAN HAS BEEN BROUGHT TO THE

emergency room after an automobile accident. The emergency room nurses are tending to the patient, Larry, who is unresponsive. A blood sample is taken then sent to Brianna, a clinical laboratory technician, who begins the process of analyzing the pH, the partial pressures of O_2 and CO_2, and the concentrations of glucose and electrolytes.

Within minutes, Brianna determines that Larry's blood pH is 7.30 and the partial pressure of CO_2 gas is above the desired level. Blood pH is typically in the range of 7.35 to 7.45, and a value less than 7.35 indicates a state of acidosis. Respiratory acidosis occurs because an increase in the partial pressure of CO_2 gas in the bloodstream prevents the biochemical buffers in blood from making a change in the pH.

Brianna recognizes these signs and immediately contacts the emergency room to inform them that Larry's airway may be blocked. In the emergency room, they provide Larry with an IV containing bicarbonate to increase the blood pH and begin the process of unblocking his airway. Shortly afterward, Larry's airway is cleared, and his blood pH and partial pressure of CO_2 gas return to normal.

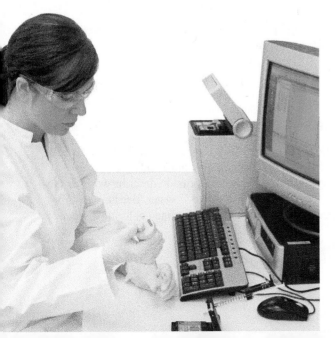

CAREER Clinical Laboratory Technician

Clinical laboratory technicians, also known as medical laboratory technicians, perform a wide variety of tests on body fluids and cells that help in the diagnosis and treatment of patients. These tests range from determining blood concentrations of glucose and cholesterol to determining drug levels in the blood for transplant patients or a patient undergoing treatment. Clinical laboratory technicians also prepare specimens in the detection of cancerous tumors, and type blood samples for transfusions. Clinical laboratory technicians must also interpret and analyze the test results, which are then passed on to the physician.

A cids and bases are important substances in health, industry, and the environment. One of the most common characteristics of acids is their sour taste. Lemons and grapefruits taste sour because they contain acids such as citric and ascorbic acid (vitamin C). Vinegar tastes sour because it contains acetic acid. We produce lactic acid in our muscles when we exercise. Acid from bacteria turns milk sour in the production of yogurt and cottage cheese. We have hydrochloric acid in our stomachs that helps us digest food. Sometimes we take antacids, which are bases such as sodium bicarbonate or milk of magnesia, to neutralize the effects of too much stomach acid.

In the environment, the acidity, or pH, of rain, water, and soil can have significant effects. When rain becomes too acidic, it can dissolve marble statues and accelerate the corrosion of metals. In lakes and ponds, the acidity of water can affect the ability of plants and fish to survive. The acidity of soil around plants affects their

Citrus fruits are sour because of the presence of acids.

growth. If the soil pH is too acidic or too basic, the roots of the plant cannot take up some nutrients. Most plants thrive in soil with a nearly neutral pH, although certain plants, such as orchids, camellias, and blueberries, require a more acidic soil.

The pH of a solution describes its acidity. The lungs and the kidneys are the primary organs that regulate the pH of body fluids, including blood and urine. Major changes in the pH of the body fluids can severely affect biological activities within the cells. Buffers are present to prevent large fluctuations in pH.

CHAPTER READINESS*

🖩 KEY MATH SKILLS
- Solving Equations (1.4D)
- Writing Numbers in Scientific Notation (1.4F)

⚛ CORE CHEMISTRY SKILLS
- Writing Ionic Formulas (6.2)
- Balancing a Chemical Equation (7.1)

- Using Concentration as a Conversion Factor (9.4)
- Writing the Equilibrium Constant Expression (10.3)
- Calculating Equilibrium Concentrations (10.4)
- Using Le Châtelier's Principle (10.5)

*These Key Math Skills and Core Chemistry Skills from previous chapters are listed here for your review as you proceed to the new material in this chapter.

LEARNING GOAL

Describe and name acids and bases.

11.1 Acids and Bases

The term *acid* comes from the Latin word *acidus*, which means "sour." We are familiar with the sour tastes of vinegar and lemons and other common acids in foods.

In 1887, the Swedish chemist Svante Arrhenius was the first to describe **acids** as substances that produce hydrogen ions (H^+) when they dissolve in water. Because acids produce ions in water, they are also electrolytes. For example, hydrogen chloride dissociates in water to give hydrogen ions, H^+, and chloride ions, Cl^-. It is the hydrogen ions that give acids a sour taste, change the blue litmus indicator to red, and corrode some metals.

$$HCl(g) \xrightarrow{\ H_2O\ } H^+(aq) + Cl^-(aq)$$

Polar molecular   Dissociation   Hydrogen
compound   ion

Naming Acids

Acids dissolve in water to produce hydrogen ions, along with a negative ion that may be a simple nonmetal anion or a polyatomic ion. When an acid dissolves in water to produce a hydrogen ion and a simple nonmetal anion, the prefix *hydro* is used before the name of the nonmetal, and its *ide* ending is changed to *ic acid*. For example, hydrogen chloride (HCl) dissolves in water to form $HCl(aq)$, which is named hydrochloric acid. An exception is hydrogen cyanide (HCN), which as an acid is named hydrocyanic acid, $HCN(aq)$.

When an acid contains oxygen, it dissolves in water to produce a hydrogen ion and an oxygen-containing polyatomic anion. The most common form of an oxygen-containing acid has a name that ends with *ic acid*. The name of its polyatomic anion ends in *ate*. If the acid contains a polyatomic ion with an *ite* ending, its name ends in *ous acid*.

The halogens in Group 7A (17) can form more than two oxygen-containing acids. For chlorine, the common form is chloric acid, $HClO_3$, which contains the chlorate polyatomic ion (ClO_3^-). For the acid that contains one more oxygen atom than the common form, the prefix *per* is used; $HClO_4$ is named *perchloric acid*. When the polyatomic ion in the acid has one oxygen atom less than the common form, the suffix *ous* is used. Thus, $HClO_2$ is named *chlorous acid*; it contains the chlorite ion, ClO_2^-. The prefix *hypo* is used for the acid that has two oxygen atoms less than the common form; HClO is named *hypochlorous acid*. The names of some common acids and their anions are listed in Table 11.1.

TABLE 11.1 Names of Common Acids and Their Anions

Acid	Name of Acid	Anion	Name of Anion
HCl	**Hydro**chloric acid	Cl^-	Chloride
HBr	**Hydro**bromic acid	Br^-	Bromide
HI	**Hydro**iodic acid	I^-	Iodide
HCN	**Hydro**cyanic acid	CN^-	Cyanide
HNO_3	Nitr**ic acid**	NO_3^-	Nitrate
HNO_2	Nitr**ous acid**	NO_2^-	Nitrite
H_2SO_4	Sulfur**ic acid**	SO_4^{2-}	Sulfate
H_2SO_3	Sulfur**ous acid**	SO_3^{2-}	Sulfite
H_2CO_3	Carbon**ic acid**	CO_3^{2-}	Carbonate
$HC_2H_3O_2$	Acetic acid	$C_2H_3O_2^-$	Acetate
H_3PO_4	Phosphor**ic acid**	PO_4^{3-}	Phosphate
H_3PO_3	Phosphor**ous acid**	PO_3^{3-}	Phosphite
$HClO_3$	Chlor**ic acid**	ClO_3^-	Chlorate
$HClO_2$	Chlor**ous acid**	ClO_2^-	Chlorite

Sulfuric acid dissolves in water to produce one or two H^+ and an anion.

Bases

You may be familiar with some household bases such as antacids, drain openers, and oven cleaners. According to the Arrhenius theory, **bases** are ionic compounds that dissociate into cations and hydroxide ions (OH^-) when they dissolve in water. They are another example of strong electrolytes. For example, sodium hydroxide is an Arrhenius base that dissociates completely in water to give sodium ions, Na^+, and hydroxide ions, OH^-.

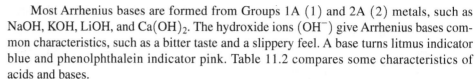

Most Arrhenius bases are formed from Groups 1A (1) and 2A (2) metals, such as NaOH, KOH, LiOH, and Ca(OH)$_2$. The hydroxide ions (OH$^-$) give Arrhenius bases common characteristics, such as a bitter taste and a slippery feel. A base turns litmus indicator blue and phenolphthalein indicator pink. Table 11.2 compares some characteristics of acids and bases.

$$NaOH(s) \xrightarrow{H_2O} Na^+(aq) + OH^-(aq)$$

Ionic   Dissociation   Hydroxide
compound   ion

An Arrhenius base produces cations and OH$^-$ anions in an aqueous solution.

TABLE 11.2 Some Characteristics of Acids and Bases

Characteristic	Acids	Bases
Arrhenius	Produce H$^+$	Produce OH$^-$
Electrolytes	Yes	Yes
Taste	Sour	Bitter, chalky
Feel	May sting	Soapy, slippery
Litmus	Red	Blue
Phenolphthalein	Colorless	Pink
Neutralization	Neutralize bases	Neutralize acids

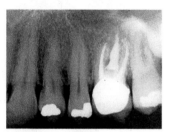

Calcium hydroxide, Ca(OH)$_2$, is used in the food industry to produce beverages, and in dentistry as a filler for root canals.

Naming Bases

Typical Arrhenius bases are named as *hydroxides*.

Base	Name
LiOH	Lithium **hydroxide**
NaOH	Sodium **hydroxide**
KOH	Potassium **hydroxide**
Ca(OH)$_2$	Calcium **hydroxide**
Al(OH)$_3$	Aluminum **hydroxide**

A soft drink contains H$_3$PO$_4$ and H$_2$CO$_3$.

▶ SAMPLE PROBLEM 11.1 **Names and Formulas of Acids and Bases**

a. Identify each of the following as an acid or a base and give its name:
  1. H$_3$PO$_4$, ingredient in soft drinks
  2. NaOH, ingredient in oven cleaner
b. Write the formula for each of the following:
  1. magnesium hydroxide, ingredient in antacids
  2. hydrobromic acid, used industrially to prepare bromide compounds

SOLUTION

a. 1. acid, phosphoric acid   **2.** base, sodium hydroxide
b. 1. Mg(OH)$_2$ **2.** HBr

STUDY CHECK 11.1

a. Identify as an acid or a base and give the name for H$_2$CO$_3$.
b. Write the formula for iron(III) hydroxide.

ANSWER

a. acid, carbonic acid   **b.** Fe(OH)$_3$

QUESTIONS AND PROBLEMS

11.1 Acids and Bases

LEARNING GOAL Describe and name acids and bases.

11.1 Indicate whether each of the following statements is characteristic of an acid, a base, or both:
    a. has a sour taste
    b. neutralizes bases
    c. produces H^+ ions in water
    d. is named barium hydroxide
    e. is an electrolyte

11.2 Indicate whether each of the following statements is characteristic of an acid, a base, or both:
    a. neutralizes acids
    b. produces OH^- ions in water
    c. has a slippery feel
    d. conducts an electrical current in solution
    e. turns litmus red

11.3 Name each of the following acids or bases:
    a. HCl   **b.** $Ca(OH)_2$ **c.** $HClO_4$
    d. HNO_3 **e.** H_2SO_3 **f.** $HBrO_2$

11.4 Name each of the following acids or bases:
    a. $Al(OH)_3$ **b.** HBr   **c.** H_2SO_4
    d. KOH   **e.** HNO_2 **f.** $HClO_2$

11.5 Write formulas for each of the following acids and bases:
    a. rubidium hydroxide   **b.** hydrofluoric acid
    c. phosphoric acid   **d.** lithium hydroxide
    e. ammonium hydroxide   **f.** periodic acid

11.6 Write formulas for each of the following acids and bases:
    a. barium hydroxide   **b.** hydroiodic acid
    c. nitric acid   **d.** strontium hydroxide
    e. acetic acid   **f.** hypochlorous acid

11.2 Brønsted–Lowry Acids and Bases

LEARNING GOAL

Identify conjugate acid–base pairs for Brønsted–Lowry acids and bases.

In 1923, J. N. Brønsted in Denmark and T. M. Lowry in Great Britain expanded the definition of acids and bases to include bases that do not contain OH^- ions. A **Brønsted–Lowry acid** can donate a hydrogen ion, H^+, and a **Brønsted–Lowry base** can accept a hydrogen ion.

A Brønsted–Lowry acid is a substance that donates H^+.

A Brønsted–Lowry base is a substance that accepts H^+.

A free hydrogen ion, H^+, does not actually exist in water. Its attraction to polar water molecules is so strong that the H^+ bonds to a water molecule and forms a **hydronium ion, H_3O^+**.

$$H - \ddot{O}: + H^+ \longrightarrow \left[H - \ddot{O} - H \right]^+$$
$$\quad | \qquad\qquad\qquad\qquad\qquad |$$
$$\quad H \qquad\qquad\qquad\qquad\qquad H$$

Water   Hydrogen   Hydronium ion
          ion

We can write the formation of a hydrochloric acid solution as a transfer of H^+ from hydrogen chloride to water. By accepting an H^+ in the reaction, water is acting as a base according to the Brønsted–Lowry concept.

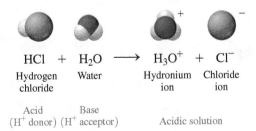

$$HCl \; + \; H_2O \longrightarrow H_3O^+ \; + \; Cl^-$$

Hydrogen   Water   Hydronium   Chloride
chloride   ion   ion

Acid   Base
$(H^+$ donor) $(H^+$ acceptor)   Acidic solution

In another reaction, ammonia, NH_3, acts as a base by accepting H^+ when it reacts with water. Because the nitrogen atom of NH_3 has a stronger attraction for H^+ than oxygen, water acts as an acid by donating H^+.

$$NH_3 \; + \; H_2O \; \rightleftharpoons \; NH_4^+ \; + \; OH^-$$

Ammonia	Water	Ammonium ion	Hydroxide ion
Base (H^+ acceptor)	Acid (H^+ donor)	Basic solution	

SAMPLE PROBLEM 11.2 Acids and Bases

In each of the following equations, identify the reactant that is a Brønsted–Lowry acid and the reactant that is a Brønsted–Lowry base:

a. $HBr(aq) + H_2O(l) \longrightarrow H_3O^+(aq) + Br^-(aq)$
b. $CN^-(aq) + H_2O(l) \rightleftharpoons HCN(aq) + OH^-(aq)$

SOLUTION

a. HBr, Brønsted–Lowry acid; H_2O, Brønsted–Lowry base
b. H_2O, Brønsted–Lowry acid; CN^-, Brønsted–Lowry base

STUDY CHECK 11.2

When HNO_3 reacts with water, water acts as a Brønsted–Lowry base. Write the equation for the reaction.

ANSWER

$$HNO_3(aq) + H_2O(l) \longrightarrow H_3O^+(aq) + NO_3^-(aq)$$

⚛ **CORE CHEMISTRY SKILL**

Identifying Conjugate Acid–Base Pairs

Conjugate acid–base pair

Donates H^+

HF F^-

Conjugate acid–base pair

Accepts H^+

H_2O H_3O^+

HF, an acid, loses one H^+ to form its conjugate base F^-. Water acts as a base by gaining one H^+ to form its conjugate acid H_3O^+.

Conjugate Acid–Base Pairs

According to the Brønsted–Lowry theory, a **conjugate acid–base pair** consists of molecules or ions related by the loss of one H^+ by an acid, and the gain of one H^+ by a base. Every acid–base reaction contains two conjugate acid–base pairs because an H^+ is transferred in both the forward and reverse directions. When an acid such as HF loses one H^+, the conjugate base F^- is formed. When the base H_2O gains an H^+, its conjugate acid, H_3O^+, is formed.

Because the overall reaction of HF is reversible, the conjugate acid H_3O^+ can donate H^+ to the conjugate base F^- and re-form the acid HF and the base H_2O. Using the relationship of loss and gain of one H^+, we can now identify the conjugate acid–base pairs as HF/F^- along with H_3O^+/H_2O.

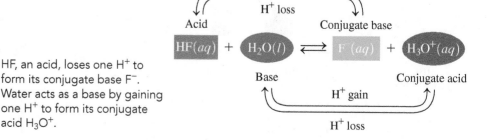

In another reaction, ammonia, NH_3, accepts H^+ from H_2O to form the conjugate acid NH_4^+ and conjugate base OH^-. Each of these conjugate acid–base pairs, NH_4^+/NH_3 and H_2O/OH^-, is related by the loss and gain of one H^+.

Ammonia, NH_3, acts as a base when it gains one H^+ to form its conjugate acid NH_4^+. Water acts as an acid by losing one H^+ to form its conjugate base OH^-.

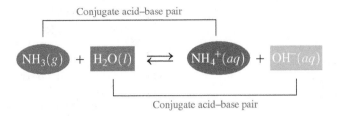

In these two examples, we see that water can act as an acid when it donates H^+ or as a base when it accepts H^+. Substances that can act as both acids and bases are **amphoteric** or *amphiprotic*. For water, the most common amphoteric substance, the acidic or basic behavior depends on the other reactant. Water donates H^+ when it reacts with a stronger base, and it accepts H^+ when it reacts with a stronger acid. Another example of an amphoteric substance is bicarbonate, HCO_3^-. With a base, HCO_3^- acts as an acid and donates one H^+ to give CO_3^{2-}. However, when HCO_3^- reacts with an acid, it acts as a base and accepts one H^+ to form H_2CO_3.

Amphoteric substances act as both acids and bases.

H_3O^+
H_2CO_3 ◄━━ Acts as a base ━━ H_2O / HCO_3^- ━━ Acts as an acid ━━► OH^- / CO_3^{2-}

▶**SAMPLE PROBLEM 11.3 Identifying Conjugate Acid–Base Pairs**

Identify the conjugate acid–base pairs in the following reaction:

$$HBr(aq) + NH_3(aq) \rightleftharpoons Br^-(aq) + NH_4^+(aq)$$

SOLUTION

ANALYZE THE PROBLEM	Given		Need
	HBr	Br^-	conjugate acid–base pairs
	NH_3	NH_4^+	

STEP 1 Identify the reactant that loses H^+ as the acid.
In the reaction, HBr donates H^+ to form the product Br^-. Thus HBr is the acid and Br^- is its conjugate base.

STEP 2 Identify the reactant that gains H^+ as the base.
In the reaction, NH_3 gains H^+ to form the product NH_4^+. Thus, NH_3 is the base and NH_4^+ is its conjugate acid.

STEP 3 Write the conjugate acid–base pairs.
HBr/Br^- and NH_4^+/NH_3

STUDY CHECK 11.3

Identify the conjugate acid–base pairs in the following reaction:

$$HCN(aq) + SO_4^{2-}(aq) \rightleftharpoons CN^-(aq) + HSO_4^-(aq)$$

ANSWER

The conjugate acid–base pairs are HCN/CN^- and HSO_4^-/SO_4^{2-}.

Guide to Writing Conjugate Acid–Base Pairs

STEP 1
Identify the reactant that loses H^+ as the acid.

STEP 2
Identify the reactant that gains H^+ as the base.

STEP 3
Write the conjugate acid–base pairs.

QUESTIONS AND PROBLEMS

11.2 Brønsted–Lowry Acids and Bases

LEARNING GOAL Identify conjugate acid–base pairs for Brønsted–Lowry acids and bases.

11.7 Identify the reactant that is a Brønsted–Lowry acid and the reactant that is a Brønsted–Lowry base in each of the following:
a. $HI(aq) + H_2O(l) \longrightarrow I^-(aq) + H_3O^+(aq)$
b. $F^-(aq) + H_2O(l) \rightleftharpoons HF(aq) + OH^-(aq)$
c. $H_2S(aq) + CH_3-CH_2-NH_2(aq) \rightleftharpoons$
$$HS^-(aq) + CH_3-CH_2-NH_3^+(aq)$$

11.8 Identify the reactant that is a Brønsted–Lowry acid and the reactant that is a Brønsted–Lowry base in each of the following:
a. $CO_3^{2-}(aq) + H_2O(l) \rightleftharpoons HCO_3^-(aq) + OH^-(aq)$
b. $H_2SO_4(aq) + H_2O(l) \longrightarrow HSO_4^-(aq) + H_3O^+(aq)$
c. $C_2H_3O_2^-(aq) + H_3O^+(aq) \rightleftharpoons HC_2H_3O_2(aq) + H_2O(l)$

11.9 Write the formula for the conjugate base for each of the following acids:
a. HF
b. H_2O
c. $H_2PO_3^-$
d. HSO_4^-
e. $HClO_2$

11.10 Write the formula for the conjugate base for each of the following acids:
a. HCO_3^-
b. $CH_3-NH_3^+$
c. HPO_4^{2-}
d. HNO_2
e. HBrO

11.11 Write the formula for the conjugate acid for each of the following bases:
a. CO_3^{2-}
b. H_2O
c. $H_2PO_4^-$
d. Br^-
e. ClO_4^-

11.12 Write the formula for the conjugate acid for each of the following bases:
a. SO_4^{2-}
b. CN^-
c. NH_3
d. ClO_2^-
e. HS^-

11.13 Identify the Brønsted–Lowry acid–base pairs in each of the following equations:
a. $H_2CO_3(aq) + H_2O(l) \rightleftharpoons HCO_3^-(aq) + H_3O^+(aq)$
b. $NH_4^+(aq) + H_2O(l) \rightleftharpoons NH_3(aq) + H_3O^+(aq)$
c. $HCN(aq) + NO_2^-(aq) \rightleftharpoons CN^-(aq) + HNO_2(aq)$
d. $CHO_2^-(aq) + HF(aq) \rightleftharpoons HCHO_2(aq) + F^-(aq)$

11.14 Identify the Brønsted–Lowry acid–base pairs in each of the following equations:
a. $H_3PO_4(aq) + H_2O(l) \rightleftharpoons H_2PO_4^-(aq) + H_3O^+(aq)$
b. $CO_3^{2-}(aq) + H_2O(l) \rightleftharpoons HCO_3^-(aq) + OH^-(aq)$
c. $H_3PO_4(aq) + NH_3(aq) \rightleftharpoons H_2PO_4^-(aq) + NH_4^+(aq)$
d. $HNO_2(aq) + CH_3-CH_2-NH_2(aq) \rightleftharpoons$
$$CH_3-CH_2-NH_3^+(aq) + NO_2^-(aq)$$

11.15 When ammonium chloride dissolves in water, the ammonium ion NH_4^+ donates an H^+ to water. Write a balanced equation for the reaction of the ammonium ion with water.

11.16 When sodium carbonate dissolves in water, the carbonate ion CO_3^{2-} acts as a base. Write a balanced equation for the reaction of the carbonate ion with water.

LEARNING GOAL

Write equations for the dissociation of strong and weak acids; identify the direction of reaction.

11.3 Strengths of Acids and Bases

In the process called **dissociation**, an acid or a base separates into ions in water. The *strength* of an acid is determined by the moles of H_3O^+ that are produced for each mole of acid that dissociates. The *strength* of a base is determined by the moles of OH^- that are produced for each mole of base that dissolves. Strong acids and strong bases dissociate completely in water, whereas weak acids and weak bases dissociate only slightly, leaving most of the initial acid or base undissociated.

Strong and Weak Acids

Strong acids are examples of strong electrolytes because they donate H^+ so easily that their dissociation in water is essentially complete. For example, when HCl, a strong acid, dissociates in water, H^+ is transferred to H_2O; the resulting solution contains essentially only the ions H_3O^+ and Cl^-. We consider the reaction of HCl in H_2O as going 100% to products. Thus, one mole of a strong acid dissociates in water to yield one mole of H_3O^+ and one mole of its conjugate base. We write the equation for a strong acid such as HCl with a single arrow.

$$HCl(g) + H_2O(l) \longrightarrow H_3O^+(aq) + Cl^-(aq)$$

There are only six common strong acids, which are stronger acids than H_3O^+. All other acids are weak. Table 11.3 lists the relative strengths of acids and bases. **Weak acids** are weak electrolytes because they dissociate slightly in water, forming only a small amount of H_3O^+ ions. A weak acid has a strong conjugate base, which is why the reverse reaction is more prevalent. Even at high concentrations, weak acids produce low concentrations of H_3O^+ ions (see Figure 11.1).

Many of the products you use at home contain weak acids. Citric acid is a weak acid found in fruits and fruit juices such as lemons, oranges, and grapefruit. The vinegar used in salad dressings is typically a 5% (m/v) acetic acid, $HC_2H_3O_2$, solution. In water, a few $HC_2H_3O_2$ molecules donate H^+ to H_2O to form H_3O^+ ions and acetate ions $C_2H_3O_2^-$. The reverse reaction also takes place, which converts the H_3O^+ ions and acetate ions $C_2H_3O_2^-$ back to reactants. The formation of hydronium ions from vinegar is the reason we notice the sour taste of vinegar. We write the equation for a weak acid in an aqueous solution with a double arrow to indicate that the forward and reverse reactions are at equilibrium.

Weak acids are found in foods and household products.

$$\underset{\text{Acetic acid}}{HC_2H_3O_2(aq)} + H_2O(l) \rightleftharpoons \underset{\text{Acetate ion}}{C_2H_3O_2^-(aq)} + H_3O^+(aq)$$

TABLE 11.3 Relative Strengths of Acids and Bases

Acid		Conjugate Base	
Strong Acids			
Hydroiodic acid	HI	I^-	Iodide ion
Hydrobromic acid	HBr	Br^-	Bromide ion
Perchloric acid	$HClO_4$	ClO_4^-	Perchlorate ion
Hydrochloric acid	HCl	Cl^-	Chloride ion
Sulfuric acid	H_2SO_4	HSO_4^-	Hydrogen sulfate ion
Nitric acid	HNO_3	NO_3^-	Nitrate ion
Hydronium ion	H_3O^+	H_2O	Water
Weak Acids			
Hydrogen sulfate ion	HSO_4^-	SO_4^{2-}	Sulfate ion
Phosphoric acid	H_3PO_4	$H_2PO_4^-$	Dihydrogen phosphate ion
Nitrous acid	HNO_2	NO_2^-	Nitrite ion
Hydrofluoric acid	HF	F^-	Fluoride ion
Acetic acid	$HC_2H_3O_2$	$C_2H_3O_2^-$	Acetate ion
Carbonic acid	H_2CO_3	HCO_3^-	Bicarbonate ion
Hydrosulfuric acid	H_2S	HS^-	Hydrogen sulfide ion
Dihydrogen phosphate ion	$H_2PO_4^-$	HPO_4^{2-}	Hydrogen phosphate ion
Ammonium ion	NH_4^+	NH_3	Ammonia
Hydrocyanic acid	HCN	CN^-	Cyanide ion
Bicarbonate ion	HCO_3^-	CO_3^{2-}	Carbonate ion
Methylammonium ion	$CH_3-NH_3^+$	CH_3-NH_2	Methylamine
Hydrogen phosphate ion	HPO_4^{2-}	PO_4^{3-}	Phosphate ion
Water	H_2O	OH^-	Hydroxide ion

Acid Strength Increases (vertical arrow, left)

Base Strength Increases (vertical arrow, right)

FIGURE 11.1 ▶ A strong acid such as HCl is completely dissociated ($\approx 100\%$), whereas a weak acid such as $HC_2H_3O_2$ contains mostly molecules and a few ions.

ⓠ What is the difference between a strong acid and a weak acid?

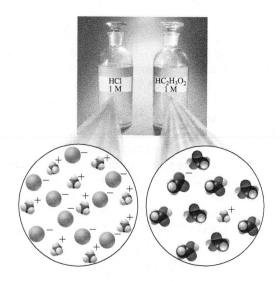

Diprotic Acids

Some weak acids, such as carbonic acid, are *diprotic acids* that have two H^+, which dissociate one at a time. For example, carbonated soft drinks are prepared by dissolving CO_2 in water to form carbonic acid, H_2CO_3. A weak acid such as H_2CO_3 reaches equilibrium between the mostly undissociated H_2CO_3 molecules and the ions H_3O^+ and HCO_3^-.

$$H_2CO_3(aq) + H_2O(l) \rightleftharpoons H_3O^+(aq) + HCO_3^-(aq)$$
Carbonic acid   Bicarbonate ion
                                              (hydrogen carbonate)

Because HCO_3^- is also a weak acid, a second dissociation can take place to produce another hydronium ion and the carbonate ion, CO_3^{2-}.

$$HCO_3^-(aq) + H_2O(l) \rightleftharpoons H_3O^+(aq) + CO_3^{2-}(aq)$$
Bicarbonate ion   Carbonate ion
(hydrogen carbonate)

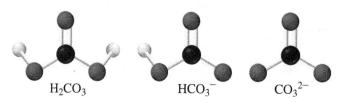

H_2CO_3 HCO_3^- CO_3^{2-}

Carbonic acid, a weak acid, loses one H^+ to form hydrogen carbonate ion, which loses a second H^+ to form carbonate ion.

Sulfuric acid, H_2SO_4, is also a diprotic acid. However, its first dissociation is complete (100%), which means H_2SO_4 is a strong acid. The product, hydrogen sulfate HSO_4^-, can dissociate again but only slightly, which means that the hydrogen sulfate ion is a weak acid.

$$H_2SO_4(aq) + H_2O(l) \longrightarrow H_3O^+(aq) + HSO_4^-(aq)$$
Sulfuric acid   Bisulfate ion
                                              (hydrogen sulfate)

$$HSO_4^-(aq) + H_2O(l) \rightleftharpoons H_3O^+(aq) + SO_4^{2-}(aq)$$
Bisulfate ion   Sulfate ion
(hydrogen sulfate)

In summary, a strong acid such as HI in water dissociates completely to form an aqueous solution of the ions H_3O^+ and I^-. A weak acid such as HF dissociates only slightly in water to form an aqueous solution that consists mostly of HF molecules and a few H_3O^+ and F^- ions (see Figure 11.2).

Strong acid: $HI(aq) + H_2O(l) \longrightarrow H_3O^+(aq) + I^-(aq)$ Completely dissociated
Weak acid: $HF(aq) + H_2O(l) \rightleftharpoons H_3O^+(aq) + F^-(aq)$ Slightly dissociated

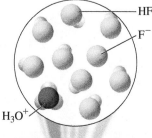

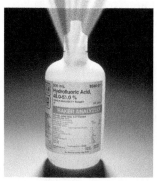

Hydrofluoric acid is the only halogen acid that is a weak acid.

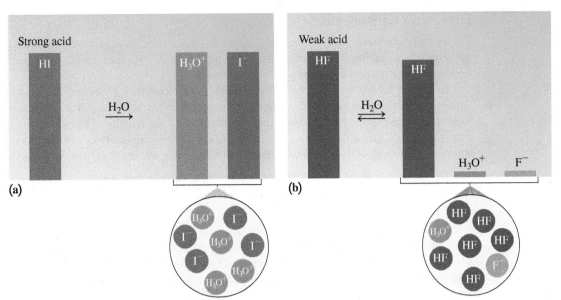

FIGURE 11.2 ▶ After dissociation in water, **(a)** the strong acid HI has high concentrations of H_3O^+ and I^-, and **(b)** the weak acid HF has a high concentration of HF and low concentrations of H_3O^+ and F^-.

🎯 How do the heights of H_3O^+ and F^- compare to the height of the weak acid HF in the bar diagram for HF?

Strong and Weak Bases

As strong electrolytes, **strong bases** dissociate completely in water. Because these strong bases are ionic compounds, they dissociate in water to give an aqueous solution of metal ions and hydroxide ions. The Group 1A (1) hydroxides are very soluble in water, which can give high concentrations of OH^- ions. A few strong bases are less soluble in water, but what does dissolve dissociates completely as ions. For example, when KOH forms a KOH solution, it contains only the ions K^+ and OH^-.

$$KOH(s) \xrightarrow{\text{H}_2\text{O}} K^+(aq) + OH^-(aq)$$

Strong Bases

Lithium hydroxide LiOH
Sodium hydroxide NaOH
Potassium hydroxide KOH
Rubidium hydroxide RbOH
Cesium hydroxide CsOH
Calcium hydroxide $Ca(OH)_2$*
Strontium hydroxide $Sr(OH)_2$*
Barium hydroxide $Ba(OH)_2$*

*Low solubility, but they dissociate completely

Weak bases are weak electrolytes that are poor acceptors of hydrogen ions and produce very few ions in solution. A typical weak base, ammonia, NH_3, is found in window cleaners. In an aqueous solution, only a few ammonia molecules accept hydrogen ions to form NH_4^+ and OH^-.

$$NH_3(g) + H_2O(l) \rightleftharpoons NH_4^+(aq) + OH^-(aq)$$
Ammonia   Ammonium hydroxide

Bases in household products are used to remove grease and to open drains.

Bases in Household Products

Weak Bases
Window cleaner, ammonia, NH_3
Bleach, NaOCl
Laundry detergent, Na_2CO_3, Na_3PO_4
Toothpaste and baking soda, $NaHCO_3$
Baking powder, scouring powder, Na_2CO_3
Lime for lawns and agriculture, $CaCO_3$
Laxatives, antacids, $Mg(OH)_2$, $Al(OH)_3$

Strong Bases
Drain cleaner, oven cleaner, NaOH

Direction of Reaction

There is a relationship between the components in each conjugate acid–base pair. Strong acids have weak conjugate bases that do not readily accept H^+. As the strength of the acid decreases, the strength of its conjugate base increases.

In any acid–base reaction, there are two acids and two bases. However, one acid is stronger than the other acid, and one base is stronger than the other base. By comparing their relative strengths, we can determine the direction of the reaction. For example, the strong acid H_2SO_4 readily gives up H^+ to water. The hydronium ion H_3O^+ produced is a weaker acid than H_2SO_4, and the conjugate base HSO_4^- is a weaker base than water.

$$H_2SO_4(aq) + H_2O(l) \longrightarrow H_3O^+(aq) + HSO_4^-(aq) \quad \text{Mostly products}$$

Stronger acid   Stronger base   Weaker acid   Weaker base

Let's look at another reaction in which water donates one H^+ to carbonate, CO_3^{2-}, to form HCO_3^- and OH^-. From Table 11.3, we see that HCO_3^- is a stronger acid than H_2O. We also see that OH^- is a stronger base than CO_3^{2-}. To reach equilibrium, the stronger acid and stronger base react in the direction of the weaker acid and weaker base.

$$CO_3^{2-}(aq) + H_2O(l) \rightleftharpoons HCO_3^-(aq) + OH^-(aq) \quad \text{Mostly reactants}$$

Weaker base   Weaker acid   Stronger acid   Stronger base

SAMPLE PROBLEM 11.4 Direction of Reaction

Does the equilibrium mixture of the following reaction contain mostly reactants or products?

$$HF(aq) + H_2O(l) \rightleftharpoons H_3O^+(aq) + F^-(aq)$$

SOLUTION

From Table 11.3, we see that HF is a weaker acid than H_3O^+ and that H_2O is a weaker base than F^-. Thus, the equilibrium mixture contains mostly reactants.

$$HF(aq) + H_2O(l) \rightleftharpoons H_3O^+(aq) + F^-(aq)$$

Weaker acid   Weaker base   Stronger acid   Stronger base

STUDY CHECK 11.4

Does the equilibrium mixture for reaction of nitric acid and water contain mostly reactants or products?

ANSWER

$$HNO_3(aq) + H_2O(l) \longrightarrow H_3O^+(aq) + NO_3^-(aq)$$

The equilibrium mixture contains mostly products because HNO_3 is a stronger acid than H_3O^+, and H_2O is a stronger base than NO_3^-.

QUESTIONS AND PROBLEMS

11.3 Strengths of Acids and Bases

LEARNING GOAL Write equations for the dissociation of strong and weak acids; identify the direction of reaction.

11.17 What is meant by the phrase "A strong acid has a weak conjugate base"?

11.18 What is meant by the phrase "A weak acid has a strong conjugate base"?

11.19 Identify the stronger acid in each of the following pairs:
   a. HBr or HNO_2
   b. H_3PO_4 or HSO_4^-
   c. HCN or H_2CO_3

11.20 Identify the stronger acid in each of the following pairs:
   a. NH_4^+ or H_3O^+
   b. H_2SO_4 or HCl
   c. H_2O or H_2CO_3

11.21 Identify the weaker acid in each of the following pairs:
   a. HCl or HSO_4^-
   b. HNO_2 or HF
   c. HCO_3^- or NH_4^+

11.22 Identify the weaker acid in each of the following pairs:
   a. HNO_3 or HCO_3^- **b.** HSO_4^- or H_2O **c.** H_2SO_4 or H_2CO_3

11.23 Predict whether each of the following reactions contains mostly reactants or products at equilibrium:
   a. $H_2CO_3(aq) + H_2O(l) \rightleftharpoons HCO_3^-(aq) + H_3O^+(aq)$
   b. $NH_4^+(aq) + H_2O(l) \rightleftharpoons NH_3(aq) + H_3O^+(aq)$
   c. $HNO_2(aq) + NH_3(aq) \rightleftharpoons NO_2^-(aq) + NH_4^+(aq)$

11.24 Predict whether each of the following reactions contains mostly reactants or products at equilibrium:
   a. $H_3PO_4(aq) + H_2O(l) \rightleftharpoons H_3O^+(aq) + H_2PO_4^-(aq)$
   b. $CO_3^{2-}(aq) + H_2O(l) \rightleftharpoons OH^-(aq) + HCO_3^-(aq)$
   c. $HS^-(aq) + F^-(aq) \rightleftharpoons HF(aq) + S^{2-}(aq)$

11.25 Write an equation for the acid–base reaction between ammonium ion and sulfate ion. Why does the equilibrium mixture contain mostly reactants?

11.26 Write an equation for the acid–base reaction between nitrous acid and hydroxide ion. Why does the equilibrium mixture contain mostly products?

11.4 Dissociation Constants for Acids and Bases

LEARNING GOAL

Write the expression for the dissociation constant of a weak acid or weak base.

As we have seen, acids have different strengths depending on how much they dissociate in water. Because the dissociation of strong acids in water is essentially complete, the reaction is not considered to be an equilibrium situation. However, because weak acids in water dissociate only slightly, the ion products reach equilibrium with the undissociated weak acid molecules. For example, formic acid $HCHO_2$, the acid found in bee and ant stings, is a weak acid. Formic acid is a weak acid that dissociates in water to form hydronium ion, H_3O^+, and formate ion, CHO_2^-.

$$HCHO_2(aq) + H_2O(l) \rightleftharpoons H_3O^+(aq) + CHO_2^-(aq)$$

HCHO₂

CHO₂⁻

Formic acid, a weak acid, loses one H^+ to form formate ion.

Writing Dissociation Constants

An acid dissociation constant expression can be written for weak acids that gives the ratio of the concentrations of products to the weak acid reactants. As with other dissociation expressions, the molar concentration of the products is divided by the molar concentration of the reactants. Because water is a pure liquid with a constant concentration, it is omitted. The numerical value of the acid dissociation constant expression is the **acid dissociation constant, K_a**. For example, the acid dissociation constant expression for the equilibrium equation of formic acid shown above is written

$$K_a = \frac{[H_3O^+][CHO_2^-]}{[HCHO_2]}$$

The value of the K_a for formic acid at 25 °C is determined by experiment to be 1.8×10^{-4}. Thus, for the weak acid $HCHO_2$, the K_a is written

$$K_a = \frac{[H_3O^+][CHO_2^-]}{[HCHO_2]} = 1.8 \times 10^{-4} \quad \text{Acid dissociation constant}$$

The K_a for formic acid is small, which confirms that the equilibrium mixture of formic acid in water contains mostly reactants and only small amounts of the products. (Recall that the brackets in the K_a represent the molar concentrations of the reactants and products). Weak acids have small K_a values. However, strong acids, which are essentially 100% dissociated, have very large K_a values, but these values are not usually given. Table 11.4 gives K_a and K_b values for selected weak acids and bases.

TABLE 11.4 K_a and K_b Values for Selected Weak Acids and Bases

Acids		K_a
Phosphoric acid	H_3PO_4	7.5×10^{-3}
Nitrous acid	HNO_2	4.5×10^{-4}
Hydrofluoric acid	HF	3.5×10^{-4}
Formic acid	$HCHO_2$	1.8×10^{-4}
Acetic acid	$HC_2H_3O_2$	1.8×10^{-5}
Carbonic acid	H_2CO_3	4.3×10^{-7}
Hydrosulfuric acid	H_2S	9.1×10^{-8}
Dihydrogen phosphate	$H_2PO_4^-$	6.2×10^{-8}
Hydrocyanic acid	HCN	4.9×10^{-10}
Hydrogen carbonate	HCO_3^-	5.6×10^{-11}
Hydrogen phosphate	HPO_4^{2-}	2.2×10^{-13}
Bases		K_b
Methylamine	CH_3-NH_2	4.4×10^{-4}
Carbonate	CO_3^{2-}	2.2×10^{-4}
Ammonia	NH_3	1.8×10^{-5}

Let us now consider the dissociation of the weak base methylamine:

$$CH_3-NH_2(aq) + H_2O(l) \rightleftarrows CH_3-NH_3^+(aq) + OH^-(aq)$$

As we did with the acid dissociation expression, the concentration of water is omitted from the base dissociation constant expression. The **base dissociation constant, K_b,** for methylamine is written

$$K_b = \frac{[CH_3-NH_3^+][OH^-]}{[CH_3-NH_2]} = 4.4 \times 10^{-4}$$

Table 11.5 summarizes the characteristics of acids and bases in terms of strength and equilibrium position.

TABLE 11.5 Characteristics of Acids and Bases

Characteristic	Strong Acids	Weak Acids
Equilibrium Position	Toward products	Toward reactants
K_a	Large	Small
$[H_3O^+]$ and $[A^-]$	100% of $[HA]$ dissociates	Small percent of $[HA]$ dissociates
Conjugate Base	Weak	Strong

Characteristic	Strong Bases	Weak Bases
Equilibrium Position	Toward products	Toward reactants
K_b	Large	Small
$[BH^+]$ and $[OH^-]$	100% of $[B]$ reacts	Small percent of $[B]$ reacts
Conjugate Acid	Weak	Strong

▶ **SAMPLE PROBLEM 11.5 Writing an Acid Dissociation Constant Expression**

Write the acid dissociation constant expression for the weak acid, nitrous acid.

SOLUTION

The equation for the dissociation of nitrous acid is written

$$HNO_2(aq) + H_2O(l) \rightleftarrows H_3O^+(aq) + NO_2^-(aq)$$

The acid dissociation constant expression is written as the concentration of the products divided by the concentration of the undissociated weak acid.

$$K_a = \frac{[H_3O^+][NO_2^-]}{[HNO_2]}$$

STUDY CHECK 11.5

Write the acid dissociation constant expression for hydrogen phosphate.

ANSWER

$$K_a = \frac{[H_3O^+][PO_4^{3-}]}{[HPO_4^{2-}]}$$

QUESTIONS AND PROBLEMS

11.4 Dissociation Constants for Acids and Bases

LEARNING GOAL Write the expression for the dissociation constant of a weak acid or weak base.

11.27 Answer *true* or *false* for each of the following: A strong acid
   a. is completely dissociated in aqueous solution
   b. has a small value of K_a
   c. has a strong conjugate base
   d. has a weak conjugate base
   e. is slightly dissociated in aqueous solution

11.28 Answer *true* or *false* for each of the following: A weak acid
   a. is completely dissociated in aqueous solution
   b. has a small value of K_a
   c. has a strong conjugate base
   d. has a weak conjugate base
   e. is slightly dissociated in aqueous solution

11.29 Consider the following acids and their dissociation constants:

$$H_2SO_3(aq) + H_2O(l) \rightleftharpoons H_3O^+(aq) + HSO_3^-(aq)$$
$$K_a = 1.2 \times 10^{-2}$$

$$HS^-(aq) + H_2O(l) \rightleftharpoons H_3O^+(aq) + S^{2-}(aq)$$
$$K_a = 1.3 \times 10^{-19}$$

   a. Which is the stronger acid, H_2SO_3 or HS^-?
   b. What is the conjugate base of H_2SO_3?

   c. Which acid has the weaker conjugate base?
   d. Which acid has the stronger conjugate base?
   e. Which acid produces more ions?

11.30 Consider the following acids and their dissociation constants:

$$HPO_4^{2-}(aq) + H_2O(l) \rightleftharpoons H_3O^+(aq) + PO_4^{3-}(aq)$$
$$K_a = 2.2 \times 10^{-13}$$

$$HCHO_2(aq) + H_2O(l) \rightleftharpoons H_3O^+(aq) + CHO_2^-(aq)$$
$$K_a = 1.8 \times 10^{-4}$$

   a. Which is the weaker acid, HPO_4^{2-} or $HCHO_2$?
   b. What is the conjugate base of HPO_4^{2-}?
   c. Which acid has the weaker conjugate base?
   d. Which acid has the stronger conjugate base?
   e. Which acid produces more ions?

11.31 Phosphoric acid dissociates to form hydronium ion and dihydrogen phosphate. Phosphoric acid has a K_a of 7.5×10^{-3}. Write the equation for the reaction and the acid dissociation constant expression for phosphoric acid.

11.32 Aniline, C_6H_5—NH_2, a weak base with a K_b of 4.0×10^{-10}, reacts with water to form C_6H_5—NH_3^+ and hydroxide ion. Write the equation for the reaction and the base dissociation constant expression for aniline.

11.5 Dissociation of Water

LEARNING GOAL

In many acid–base reactions, water is *amphoteric*, which means that it can act either as an acid or as a base. In pure water, there is a forward reaction between two water molecules that transfers H^+ from one water molecule to the other. One molecule acts as an acid by losing H^+, and the water molecule that gains H^+ acts as a base. Every time H^+ is transferred between two water molecules, the products are one H_3O^+ and one OH^-, which react in the reverse direction to re-form two water molecules. Thus, equilibrium is reached between the conjugate acid–base pairs of water.

Use the water dissociation constant expression to calculate the $[H_3O^+]$ and $[OH^-]$ in an aqueous solution.

Conjugate acid–base pair

:Ö—H + :Ö—H ⇌ H—Ö—H⁺ + ⁻:Ö—H

Conjugate acid–base pair

| Acid | Base | Acid | Base |
| (H^+ donor) | (H^+ acceptor) | (H^+ donor) | (H^+ acceptor) |

Writing the Water Dissociation Constant Expression, K_w

Using the equation for water at equilibrium, we can write its equilibrium constant expression that shows the concentrations of the products divided by the concentrations of the reactants. Recall that square brackets around the symbols indicate their concentrations in moles per liter (M).

$$H_2O(l) + H_2O(l) \rightleftharpoons H_3O^+(aq) + OH^-(aq)$$

$$K = \frac{[H_3O^+][OH^-]}{[H_2O][H_2O]}$$

By omitting the constant concentration of pure water, we can write the **water dissociation constant expression, K_w.**

$$K_w = [H_3O^+][OH^-]$$

Experiments have determined, that in pure water, the concentration of H_3O^+ and OH^- at 25 °C are each 1.0×10^{-7} M.

Pure water $[H_3O^+] = [OH^-] = 1.0 \times 10^{-7} M$

When we place the $[H_3O^+]$ and $[OH^-]$ into the water dissociation constant expression, we obtain the numerical value of K_w, which is 1.0×10^{-14} at 25 °C. As before, the concentration units are omitted in the K_w value.

$$K_w = [H_3O^+][OH^-]$$
$$= [1.0 \times 10^{-7}][1.0 \times 10^{-7}] = 1.0 \times 10^{-14}$$

Neutral, Acidic, and Basic Solutions

The K_w value (1.0×10^{-14}) applies to any aqueous solution at 25 °C because all aqueous solutions contain both H_3O^+ and OH^- (see Figure 11.3). When the $[H_3O^+]$ and $[OH^-]$ in a solution are equal, the solution is **neutral**. However, most solutions are not neutral; they have different concentrations of $[H_3O^+]$ and $[OH^-]$. If acid is added to water, there is an increase in $[H_3O^+]$ and a decrease in $[OH^-]$, which makes an acidic solution. If base is added, $[OH^-]$ increases and $[H_3O^+]$ decreases, which gives a basic solution. However, for any aqueous solution, whether it is neutral, acidic, or basic, the product $[H_3O^+][OH^-]$ is equal to K_w (1.0×10^{-14}) at 25 °C (see Table 11.6).

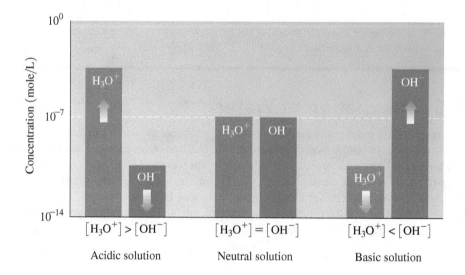

FIGURE 11.3 ▶ In a neutral solution, $[H_3O^+]$ and $[OH^-]$ are equal. In acidic solutions, the $[H_3O^+]$ is greater than the $[OH^-]$. In basic solutions, the $[OH^-]$ is greater than the $[H_3O^+]$.

Ⓠ Is a solution that has a $[H_3O^+]$ of 1.0×10^{-3} M acidic, basic, or neutral?

TABLE 11.6 Examples of $[H_3O^+]$ and $[OH^-]$ in Neutral, Acidic, and Basic Solutions

Type of Solution	$[H_3O^+]$	$[OH^-]$	K_w
Neutral	1.0×10^{-7} M	1.0×10^{-7} M	1.0×10^{-14}
Acidic	1.0×10^{-2} M	1.0×10^{-12} M	1.0×10^{-14}
Acidic	2.5×10^{-5} M	4.0×10^{-10} M	1.0×10^{-14}
Basic	1.0×10^{-8} M	1.0×10^{-6} M	1.0×10^{-14}
Basic	5.0×10^{-11} M	2.0×10^{-4} M	1.0×10^{-14}

Using the K_w to Calculate $[H_3O^+]$ and $[OH^-]$ in a Solution

If we know the $[H_3O^+]$ of a solution, we can use the K_w to calculate the $[OH^-]$. If we know the $[OH^-]$ of a solution, we can calculate $[H_3O^+]$ from their relationship in the K_w, as shown in Sample Problem 11.6.

$$K_w = [H_3O^+][OH^-]$$

$$[OH^-] = \frac{K_w}{[H_3O^+]} \qquad [H_3O^+] = \frac{K_w}{[OH^-]}$$

⊗ **CORE CHEMISTRY SKILL**

Calculating $[H_3O^+]$ and $[OH^-]$ in Solutions

▶ **SAMPLE PROBLEM 11.6** Calculating the $[H_3O^+]$ of a Solution

A vinegar solution has a $[OH^-] = 5.0 \times 10^{-12}$ M at 25 °C. What is the $[H_3O^+]$ of the vinegar solution? Is the solution acidic, basic, or neutral?

SOLUTION

STEP 1 State the given and needed quantities.

ANALYZE THE PROBLEM	Given	Need
	$[OH^-] = 5.0 \times 10^{-12}$ M	$[H_3O^+]$

STEP 2 Write the K_w for water and solve for the unknown $[H_3O^+]$.

$$K_w = [H_3O^+][OH^-] = 1.0 \times 10^{-14}$$

Solve for $[H_3O^+]$ by dividing both sides by $[OH^-]$.

$$\frac{K_w}{[OH^-]} = \frac{[H_3O^+][OH^-]}{[OH^-]} = \frac{1.0 \times 10^{-14}}{[OH^-]}$$

$$[H_3O^+] = \frac{1.0 \times 10^{-14}}{[OH^-]}$$

STEP 3 Substitute the known $[OH^-]$ into the equation and calculate.

$$[H_3O^+] = \frac{1.0 \times 10^{-14}}{[5.0 \times 10^{-12}]} = 2.0 \times 10^{-3} \text{ M}$$

Because the $[H_3O^+]$ of 2.0×10^{-3} M is larger than the $[OH^-]$ of 5.0×10^{-12} M, the solution is acidic.

STUDY CHECK 11.6

What is the $[H_3O^+]$ of an ammonia cleaning solution with $[OH^-] = 4.0 \times 10^{-4}$ M? Is the solution acidic, basic, or neutral?

ANSWER

$[H_3O^+] = 2.5 \times 10^{-11}$ M, basic

Guide to Calculating $[H_3O^+]$ and $[OH^-]$ in Aqueous Solutions

STEP 1
State the given and needed quantities.

STEP 2
Write the K_w for water and solve for the unknown $[H_3O^+]$ or $[OH^-]$.

STEP 3
Substitute the known $[H_3O^+]$ or $[OH^-]$ into the equation and calculate.

QUESTIONS AND PROBLEMS

11.5 Dissociation of Water

LEARNING GOAL Use the water dissociation constant expression to calculate the $[H_3O^+]$ and $[OH^-]$ in an aqueous solution.

11.33 Why are the concentrations of H_3O^+ and OH^- equal in pure water?

11.34 What is the meaning and value of K_w at 25 °C?

11.35 In an acidic solution, how does the concentration of H_3O^+ compare to the concentration of OH^-?

11.36 If a base is added to pure water, why does the $[H_3O^+]$ decrease?

11.37 Indicate whether each of the following solutions is acidic, basic, or neutral:
a. $[H_3O^+] = 2.0 \times 10^{-5}$ M
b. $[H_3O^+] = 1.4 \times 10^{-9}$ M
c. $[OH^-] = 8.0 \times 10^{-3}$ M
d. $[OH^-] = 3.5 \times 10^{-10}$ M

11.38 Indicate whether each of the following solutions is acidic, basic, or neutral:
a. $[H_3O^+] = 6.0 \times 10^{-12}$ M
b. $[H_3O^+] = 1.4 \times 10^{-4}$ M
c. $[OH^-] = 5.0 \times 10^{-12}$ M
d. $[OH^-] = 4.5 \times 10^{-2}$ M

11.39 Calculate the $[H_3O^+]$ of each aqueous solution with the following $[OH^-]$:
a. coffee, 1.0×10^{-9} M
b. soap, 1.0×10^{-6} M
c. cleanser, 2.0×10^{-5} M
d. lemon juice, 4.0×10^{-13} M

11.40 Calculate the $[H_3O^+]$ of each aqueous solution with the following $[OH^-]$:
a. NaOH, 1.0×10^{-2} M
b. milk of magnesia, 1.0×10^{-5} M
c. aspirin, 1.8×10^{-11} M
d. seawater, 2.5×10^{-6} M

Clinical Applications

11.41 Calculate the $[OH^-]$ of each aqueous solution with the following $[H_3O^+]$:
a. stomach acid, 4.0×10^{-2} M
b. urine, 5.0×10^{-6} M
c. orange juice, 2.0×10^{-4} M
d. bile, 7.9×10^{-9} M

11.42 Calculate the $[OH^-]$ of each aqueous solution with the following $[H_3O^+]$:
a. baking soda, 1.0×10^{-8} M
b. blood, 4.2×10^{-8} M
c. milk, 5.0×10^{-7} M
d. pancreatic juice, 4.0×10^{-9} M

LEARNING GOAL

Calculate pH from $[H_3O^+]$; given the pH, calculate the $[H_3O^+]$ and $[OH^-]$ of a solution.

11.6 The pH Scale

Personnel working in food processing, medicine, agriculture, spa and pool maintenance, soap manufacturing, and wine making measure the $[H_3O^+]$ and $[OH^-]$ of solutions. Although we have expressed H_3O^+ and OH^- as molar concentrations, it is more convenient to describe the acidity of solutions using the *pH scale*. On this scale, a number between 0 and 14 represents the H_3O^+ concentration for common solutions. A neutral solution has a pH of 7.0 at 25 °C. An acidic solution has a pH less than 7.0; a basic solution has a pH greater than 7.0 (see Figure 11.4).

Acidic solution	pH < 7.0	$[H_3O^+] > 1.0 \times 10^{-7}$ M
Neutral solution	pH = 7.0	$[H_3O^+] = 1.0 \times 10^{-7}$ M
Basic solution	pH > 7.0	$[H_3O^+] < 1.0 \times 10^{-7}$ M

When we relate acidity and pH, we are using an inverse relationship, which is when one component increases while the other component decreases. When an acid is added to pure water, the $[H_3O^+]$ (acidity) of the solution increases but its pH decreases. When a base is added to pure water, it becomes more basic, which means its acidity decreases and the pH increases.

In the laboratory, a pH meter is commonly used to determine the pH of a solution. There are also various indicators and pH papers that turn specific colors when placed in solutions of different pH values. The pH is found by comparing the color on the test paper or the color of the solution to a color chart (see Figure 11.5).

pH Value

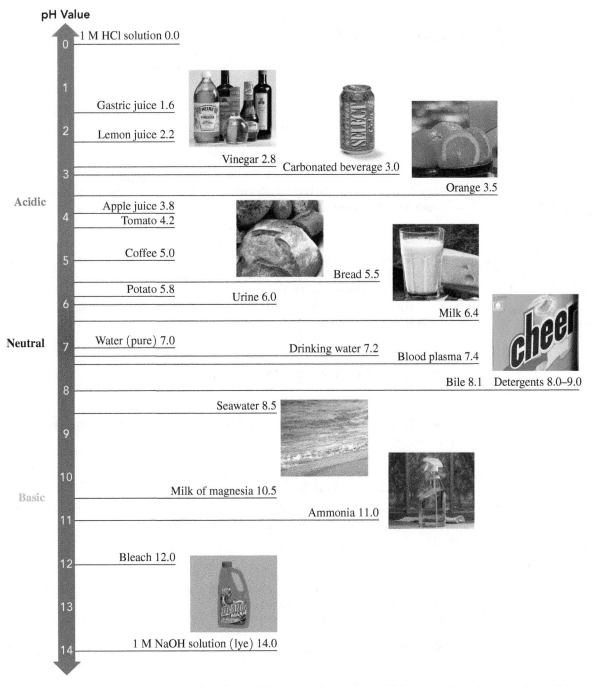

1 M HCl solution 0.0

Gastric juice 1.6

Lemon juice 2.2

Vinegar 2.8   Carbonated beverage 3.0

Orange 3.5

Acidic

Apple juice 3.8
Tomato 4.2

Coffee 5.0

Bread 5.5

Potato 5.8
Urine 6.0

Milk 6.4

Neutral   Water (pure) 7.0

Drinking water 7.2

Blood plasma 7.4

Bile 8.1   Detergents 8.0–9.0

Seawater 8.5

Basic

Milk of magnesia 10.5

Ammonia 11.0

Bleach 12.0

1 M NaOH solution (lye) 14.0

FIGURE 11.4 ▶ On the pH scale, values below 7.0 are acidic, a value of 7.0 is neutral, and values above 7.0 are basic.

Is apple juice an acidic, a basic, or a neutral solution?

(a)

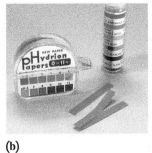
(b)

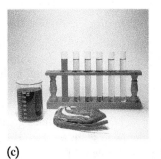
(c)

FIGURE 11.5 ▶ The pH of a solution can be determined using **(a)** a pH meter, **(b)** pH paper, and **(c)** indicators that turn different colors corresponding to different pH values.

If a pH meter reads 4.00, is the solution acidic, basic, or neutral?

A dipstick is used to measure the pH of a urine sample.

▶ **SAMPLE PROBLEM 11.7 pH of Solutions**

Consider the pH of the following body fluids:

Body Fluid	pH
Stomach acid	1.4
Pancreatic juice	8.4
Sweat	4.8
Urine	5.3
Cerebrospinal fluid	7.3

a. Place the pH values of the body fluids on the list in order of most acidic to most basic.
b. Which body fluid has the highest $[H_3O^+]$?

SOLUTION

a. The most acidic body fluid is the one with the lowest pH, and the most basic is the body fluid with the highest pH: stomach acid (1.4), sweat (4.8), urine (5.3), cerebrospinal fluid (7.3), pancreatic juice (8.4).
b. The body fluid with the highest $[H_3O^+]$ would have the lowest pH value, which is stomach acid.

STUDY CHECK 11.7

Which body fluid has the highest $[OH^-]$?

ANSWER

The body fluid with the highest $[OH^-]$ would have the highest pH value, which is pancreatic juice.

⊞ KEY MATH SKILL

Calculating pH from $[H_3O^+]$

Calculating the pH of Solutions

The pH scale is a logarithmic scale that corresponds to the $[H_3O^+]$ of aqueous solutions. Mathematically, **pH** is the negative logarithm (base 10) of the $[H_3O^+]$.

$$pH = -\log[H_3O^+]$$

Essentially, the negative powers of 10 in the molar concentrations are converted to positive numbers. For example, a lemon juice solution with $[H_3O^+] = 1.0 \times 10^{-2}$ M has a pH of 2.00. This can be calculated using the pH equation:

$$pH = -\log[1.0 \times 10^{-2}]$$
$$pH = -(-2.00)$$
$$= 2.00$$

The number of *decimal places* in the pH value is the same as the number of significant figures in the $[H_3O^+]$. The number to the left of the decimal point in the pH value is the power of 10.

$$[H_3O^+] = 1.0 \times 10^{-2} \qquad pH = 2.00$$

Two SFs   Two SFs

If soil is too acidic, nutrients are not absorbed by crops. Then lime ($CaCO_3$), which acts as a base, may be added to increase the soil pH.

Because pH is a log scale, a change of one pH unit corresponds to a tenfold change in $[H_3O^+]$. It is important to note that the pH decreases as the $[H_3O^+]$ increases. For example, a solution with a pH of 2.00 has a $[H_3O^+]$ that is ten times greater than a solution with a pH of 3.00 and 100 times greater than a solution with a pH of 4.00. The pH of a solution is calculated from the $[H_3O^+]$ by using the *log* key and changing the sign as shown in Sample Problem 11.8.

▶ **SAMPLE PROBLEM 11.8** Calculating pH from $[H_3O^+]$

Aspirin, which is acetylsalicylic acid, was the first nonsteroidal anti-inflammatory drug (NSAID) used to alleviate pain and fever. If a solution of aspirin has a $[H_3O^+] = 1.7 \times 10^{-3}$ M, what is the pH of the solution?

Acidic H
that dissociates in
aqueous solution

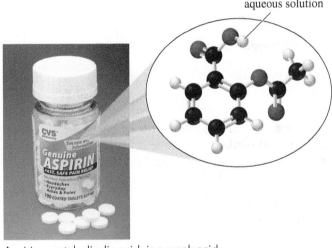

Aspirin, acetylsalicylic acid, is a weak acid.

> **Guide to Calculating pH of an Aqueous Solution**
>
> **STEP 1**
> State the given and needed quantities.
>
> **STEP 2**
> Enter the $[H_3O^+]$ into the pH equation and calculate.
>
> **STEP 3**
> Adjust the number of SFs on the *right* of the decimal point.

SOLUTION

STEP 1 State the given and needed quantities.

ANALYZE THE PROBLEM	Given	Need
	$[H_3O^+] = 1.7 \times 10^{-3}$ M	pH

STEP 2 Enter the $[H_3O^+]$ into the pH equation and calculate.

$$pH = -\log[H_3O^+] = -\log[1.7 \times 10^{-3}]$$

Calculator Procedure

$\boxed{+/-}$ $\boxed{\log}$ 1.7 $\boxed{\text{EE or EXP}}$ 3 $\boxed{+/-}$ $\boxed{=}$

Calculator Display

2.769551079

Be sure to check the instructions for your calculator.

STEP 3 Adjust the number of SFs on the *right* of the decimal point. In a pH value, the number to the *left* of the decimal point is an *exact* number derived from the power of 10. Thus, the two SFs in the coefficient determine that there are two SFs after the decimal point in the pH value.

Coefficient   **Power of ten**

1.7   × 10^{-3} M $pH = -\log[1.7 \times 10^{-3}] = 2.77$

Two SFs   Exact   Exact   Two SFs

STUDY CHECK 11.8

What is the pH of bleach with $[H_3O^+] = 4.2 \times 10^{-12}$ M?

ANSWER

pH = 11.38

When we need to calculate the pH from $[OH^-]$, we use the K_w to calculate $[H_3O^+]$, place it in the pH equation, and calculate the pH of the solution as shown in Sample Problem 11.9.

▶ **SAMPLE PROBLEM 11.9** Calculating pH from $[OH^-]$

What is the pH of an ammonia solution with $[OH^-] = 3.7 \times 10^{-3}$ M?

SOLUTION

STEP 1 State the given and needed quantities.

ANALYZE THE PROBLEM	Given	Need
	$[OH^-] = 3.7 \times 10^{-3}$ M	$[H_3O^+]$, pH

STEP 2 Enter the $[H_3O^+]$ into the pH equation and calculate. Because $[OH^-]$ is given for the ammonia solution, we have to calculate $[H_3O^+]$. Using the water dissociation constant expression, K_w, we divide both sides by $[OH^-]$ to obtain $[H_3O^+]$.

$$K_w = [H_3O^+][OH^-] = 1.0 \times 10^{-14}$$

$$\frac{K_w}{[OH^-]} = \frac{[H_3O^+]\cancel{[OH^-]}}{\cancel{[OH^-]}}$$

$$[H_3O^+] = \frac{1.0 \times 10^{-14}}{[3.7 \times 10^{-3}]} = 2.7 \times 10^{-12}\ \text{M}$$

Now, we enter the $[H_3O^+]$ into the pH equation.

$$pH = -\log[H_3O^+] = -\log[2.7 \times 10^{-12}]$$

Calculator Procedure

(+/−) (log) 2.7 (EE or EXP) 12 (+/−) (=)

Calculator Display

11.56863624

STEP 3 Adjust the number of SFs on the *right* of the decimal point.

2.7×10^{-12} M   pH = 11.**57**

Two SFs   Two SFs to the *right* of the decimal point

STUDY CHECK 11.9

Calculate the pH of a sample of bile that has $[OH^-] = 1.3 \times 10^{-6}$ M.

ANSWER

pH = 8.11

A comparison of $[H_3O^+]$, $[OH^-]$, and their corresponding pH values is given in Table 11.7.

Calculating $[H_3O^+]$ from pH

If we are given the pH of the solution and asked to determine the $[H_3O^+]$, we need to reverse the calculation of pH.

$$[H_3O^+] = 10^{-pH}$$

■ **KEY MATH SKILL**

Calculating $[H_3O^+]$ from pH

For example, if the pH of a solution is 3.0, we can substitute it into this equation. The number of significant figures in $[H_3O^+]$ is equal to the number of decimal places in the pH value.

$$[H_3O^+] = 10^{-pH} = 10^{-3.0} = 1 \times 10^{-3}\ \text{M}$$

TABLE 11.7 A Comparison of pH Values at 25 °C, $[H_3O^+]$, and $[OH^-]$

pH	$[H_3O^+]$	$[OH^-]$
0	10^0	10^{-14}
1	10^{-1}	10^{-13}
2	10^{-2}	10^{-12}
3	10^{-3}	10^{-11}
4	10^{-4}	10^{-10}
5	10^{-5}	10^{-9}
6	10^{-6}	10^{-8}
7	10^{-7}	10^{-7}
8	10^{-8}	10^{-6}
9	10^{-9}	10^{-5}
10	10^{-10}	10^{-4}
11	10^{-11}	10^{-3}
12	10^{-12}	10^{-2}
13	10^{-13}	10^{-1}
14	10^{-14}	10^0

Acidic

Neutral

Basic

Acids produce the sour taste of the fruits we eat.

For pH values that are not whole numbers, the calculation requires the use of the *10^x* key, which is usually a *2nd function* key. On some calculators, this operation is done using the inverse log equation as shown in Sample Problem 11.10.

▶ **SAMPLE PROBLEM 11.10 Calculating $[H_3O^+]$ from pH**

Calculate $[H_3O^+]$ for a urine sample, which has a pH of 7.5.

SOLUTION

STEP 1 State the given and needed quantities.

ANALYZE THE PROBLEM	Given	Need
	pH = 7.5	$[H_3O^+]$

STEP 2 Enter the pH value into the inverse log equation and calculate.

$$[H_3O^+] = 10^{-pH} = 10^{-7.5}$$

Calculator Procedure

[2nd] [log] [+/−] 7.5 [=]

Calculator Display

3.16227766 E −08

STEP 3 Adjust the SFs for the coefficient. Because the pH value 7.5 has one digit to the *right* of the decimal point, the coefficient for $[H_3O^+]$ is written with one SF.

$$[H_3O^+] = 3 \times 10^{-8}\,M$$
One SF

STUDY CHECK 11.10

What are the $[H_3O^+]$ and $[OH^-]$ of Diet Coke that has a pH of 3.17?

ANSWER

$[H_3O^+] = 6.8 \times 10^{-4}\,M$, $[OH^-] = 1.5 \times 10^{-11}\,M$

Guide to Calculating $[H_3O^+]$ from pH

STEP 1
State the given and needed quantities.

STEP 2
Enter the pH value into the inverse log equation and calculate.

STEP 3
Adjust the SFs for the coefficient.

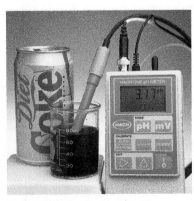

The pH of Diet Coke is 3.17.

Chemistry Link to Health

Stomach Acid, HCl

Gastric acid, which contains HCl, is produced by parietal cells that line the stomach. When the stomach expands with the intake of food, the gastric glands begin to secrete a strongly acidic solution of HCl. In a single day, a person may secrete 2000 mL of gastric juice, which contains hydrochloric acid, mucins, and the enzymes pepsin and lipase.

The HCl in the gastric juice activates a digestive enzyme from the chief cells called *pepsinogen* to form *pepsin*, which breaks down proteins in food entering the stomach. The secretion of HCl continues until the stomach has a pH of about 2, which is the optimum for activating the digestive enzymes without ulcerating the stomach lining. In addition, the low pH destroys bacteria that reach the stomach. Normally, large quantities of viscous mucus are secreted within the stomach to protect its lining from acid and enzyme damage. Gastric acid may also form under conditions of stress when the nervous system activates the production of HCl. As the contents of the stomach move into the small intestine, cells produce bicarbonate that neutralizes the gastric acid until the pH is about 5.

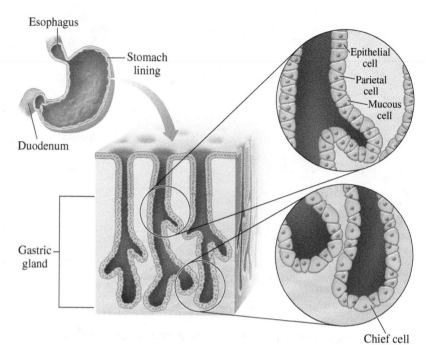

Parietal cells in the lining of the stomach secrete gastric acid HCl.

QUESTIONS AND PROBLEMS

11.6 The pH Scale

LEARNING GOAL Calculate pH from $[H_3O^+]$; given the pH, calculate the $[H_3O^+]$ and $[OH^-]$ of a solution.

11.43 Why does a neutral solution have a pH of 7.0?

11.44 If you know the $[OH^-]$, how can you determine the pH of a solution?

11.45 State whether each of the following solutions is acidic, basic, or neutral:
a. blood plasma, pH 7.38
b. vinegar, pH 2.8
c. coffee, pH 5.52
d. tomatoes, pH 4.2
e. chocolate cake, pH 7.6

11.46 State whether each of the following solutions is acidic, basic, or neutral:
a. soda, pH 3.22
b. shampoo, pH 5.7
c. rain, pH 5.8
d. honey, pH 3.9
e. cheese, pH 5.2

11.47 A solution with a pH of 3 is 10 times more acidic than a solution with pH 4. Explain.

11.48 A solution with a pH of 10 is 100 times more basic than a solution with pH 8. Explain.

11.49 Calculate the pH of each solution given the following:
a. $[H_3O^+] = 1 \times 10^{-4}$ M
b. $[H_3O^+] = 3 \times 10^{-9}$ M
c. $[OH^-] = 1 \times 10^{-5}$ M
d. $[OH^-] = 2.5 \times 10^{-11}$ M
e. $[H_3O^+] = 6.7 \times 10^{-8}$ M
f. $[OH^-] = 8.2 \times 10^{-4}$ M

11.50 Calculate the pH of each solution given the following:
a. $[H_3O^+] = 1 \times 10^{-8}$ M
b. $[H_3O^+] = 5 \times 10^{-6}$ M
c. $[OH^-] = 1 \times 10^{-2}$ M
d. $[OH^-] = 8.0 \times 10^{-3}$ M
e. $[H_3O^+] = 4.7 \times 10^{-2}$ M
f. $[OH^-] = 3.9 \times 10^{-6}$ M

℞ Clinical Applications

11.51 Complete the following table for a selection of foods:

Food	$[H_3O^+]$	$[OH^-]$	pH	Acidic, Basic, or Neutral?
Rye bread		6.3×10^{-6} M		
Tomatoes			4.64	
Peas	6.2×10^{-7} M			

11.52 Complete the following table for a selection of foods:

Food	$[H_3O^+]$	$[OH^-]$	pH	Acidic, Basic, or Neutral?
Strawberries			3.90	
Soy milk				Neutral
Tuna fish (canned)	6.3×10^{-7} M			

11.53 A patient with severe metabolic acidosis has a blood plasma pH of 6.92. What is the $[H_3O^+]$ of the blood plasma?

11.54 A patient with respiratory alkalosis has a blood plasma pH of 7.58. What is the $[H_3O^+]$ of the blood plasma?

11.7 Reactions of Acids and Bases

Typical reactions of acids and bases include the reactions of acids with metals, carbonates or bicarbonates, and bases. For example, when you drop an antacid tablet in water, the bicarbonate ion and citric acid in the tablet react to produce carbon dioxide bubbles, water, and salt. A **salt** is an ionic compound that does not have H^+ as the cation or OH^- as the anion.

LEARNING GOAL

Write balanced equations for reactions of acids with metals, carbonates or bicarbonates, and bases.

Magnesium reacts rapidly with acid and forms H_2 gas and a salt of magnesium.

Acids and Metals

Acids react with certain metals to produce hydrogen gas (H_2) and a salt. Active metals include potassium, sodium, calcium, magnesium, aluminum, zinc, iron, and tin. In these single replacement reactions, the metal ion replaces the hydrogen in the acid.

$$Mg(s) + 2HCl(aq) \longrightarrow H_2(g) + MgCl_2(aq)$$
Metal   Acid   Hydrogen   Salt

$$Zn(s) + 2HNO_3(aq) \longrightarrow H_2(g) + Zn(NO_3)_2(aq)$$
Metal   Acid   Hydrogen   Salt

⚛ CORE CHEMISTRY SKILL

Writing Equations for Reactions of Acids and Bases

Acids React with Carbonates or Bicarbonates

When an acid is added to a carbonate or bicarbonate, the products are carbon dioxide gas, water, and a salt. The acid reacts with CO_3^{2-} or HCO_3^- to produce carbonic acid, H_2CO_3, which breaks down rapidly to CO_2 and H_2O.

$$2HCl(aq) + Na_2CO_3(aq) \longrightarrow CO_2(g) + H_2O(l) + 2NaCl(aq)$$
Acid   Carbonate   Carbon   Water   Salt
                                dioxide

$$HBr(aq) + NaHCO_3(aq) \longrightarrow CO_2(g) + H_2O(l) + NaBr(aq)$$
Acid   Bicarbonate   Carbon   Water   Salt
                                dioxide

Acids and Hydroxides: Neutralization

Neutralization is a reaction between a strong or weak acid with a strong base to produce a water and a salt. The H^+ of the acid and the OH^- of the base combine to form water. The salt is the combination of the cation from the base and the anion from the acid. We can write the following equation for the neutralization reaction between HCl and NaOH:

$$HCl(aq) + NaOH(aq) \longrightarrow H_2O(l) + NaCl(aq)$$
Acid   Base   Water   Salt

If we write the strong acid HCl and the strong base NaOH as ions, we see that H^+ combines with OH^- to form water, leaving the ions Na^+ and Cl^- in solution.

$$H^+(aq) + Cl^-(aq) + Na^+(aq) + OH^-(aq) \longrightarrow H_2O(l) + Na^+(aq) + Cl^-(aq)$$

When we omit the ions that do not change during the reaction (*spectator ions*), we obtain the *net ionic equation*.

$$H^+(aq) + \cancel{Cl^-(aq)} + \cancel{Na^+(aq)} + OH^-(aq) \longrightarrow H_2O(l) + \cancel{Na^+(aq)} + \cancel{Cl^-(aq)}$$

The net ionic equation for the neutralization of H^+ and OH^- to form H_2O is

$$H^+(aq) + OH^-(aq) \longrightarrow H_2O(l) \quad \text{Net ionic equation}$$

When sodium bicarbonate (baking soda) reacts with an acid (vinegar), the products are carbon dioxide gas, water, and a salt.

Balancing Neutralization Equations

In a neutralization reaction, one H^+ always reacts with one OH^-. Therefore, a neutralization equation may need coefficients to balance the H^+ from the acid with the OH^- from the base as shown in Sample Problem 11.11.

> SAMPLE PROBLEM 11.11 Balancing Equations for Acids

Write the balanced equation for the neutralization of $HCl(aq)$ and $Ba(OH)_2(s)$.

SOLUTION

STEP 1 Write the reactants and products.

$$HCl(aq) + Ba(OH)_2(s) \longrightarrow H_2O(l) + salt$$

STEP 2 Balance the H^+ in the acid with the OH^- in the base. Placing a coefficient of 2 in front of the HCl provides $2H^+$ for the $2OH^-$ from $Ba(OH)_2$.

$$2HCl(aq) + Ba(OH)_2(s) \longrightarrow H_2O(l) + salt$$

STEP 3 Balance the H_2O with the H^+ and the OH^-. Use a coefficient of 2 in front of H_2O to balance $2H^+$ and $2OH^-$.

$$2HCl(aq) + Ba(OH)_2(s) \longrightarrow 2H_2O(l) + salt$$

STEP 4 Write the salt from the remaining ions. Use the ions Ba^{2+} and $2Cl^-$ and write the formula for the salt as $BaCl_2$.

$$2HCl(aq) + Ba(OH)_2(s) \longrightarrow 2H_2O(l) + BaCl_2(aq)$$

STUDY CHECK 11.11

Write the balanced equation for the reaction between $H_2SO_4(aq)$ and $K_2CO_3(s)$.

ANSWER

$$H_2SO_4(aq) + K_2CO_3(s) \longrightarrow CO_2(g) + H_2O(l) + K_2SO_4(aq)$$

Guide to Balancing an Equation for Neutralization

STEP 1
Write the reactants and products.

STEP 2
Balance the H^+ in the acid with the OH^- in the base.

STEP 3
Balance the H_2O with the H^+ and the OH^-.

STEP 4
Write the salt from the remaining ions.

Chemistry Link to Health

Antacids

Antacids are substances used to neutralize excess stomach acid (HCl). Some antacids are mixtures of aluminum hydroxide and magnesium hydroxide. These hydroxides are not very soluble in water, so the levels of available OH^- are not damaging to the intestinal tract. However, aluminum hydroxide has the side effects of producing constipation and binding phosphate in the intestinal tract, which may cause weakness and loss of appetite. Magnesium hydroxide has a laxative effect. These side effects are less likely when a combination of the antacids is used.

$$Al(OH)_3(s) + 3HCl(aq) \longrightarrow 3H_2O(l) + AlCl_3(aq)$$

$$Mg(OH)_2(s) + 2HCl(aq) \longrightarrow 2H_2O(l) + MgCl_2(aq)$$

Antacids neutralize excess stomach acid.

Some antacids use calcium carbonate to neutralize excess stomach acid. About 10% of the calcium is absorbed into the bloodstream, where it elevates the level of serum calcium. Calcium carbonate is not recommended for patients who have peptic ulcers or a tendency to form kidney stones, which typically consist of an insoluble calcium salt.

$$CaCO_3(s) + 2HCl(aq) \longrightarrow CO_2(g) + H_2O(l) + CaCl_2(aq)$$

Still other antacids contain sodium bicarbonate. This type of antacid neutralizes excess gastric acid, increases blood pH, but also elevates sodium levels in the body fluids. It also is not recommended in the treatment of peptic ulcers.

$$NaHCO_3(s) + HCl(aq) \longrightarrow CO_2(g) + H_2O(l) + NaCl(aq)$$

The neutralizing substances in some antacid preparations are given in Table 11.8.

TABLE 11.8 Basic Compounds in Some Antacids

Antacid	Base(s)
Amphojel	$Al(OH)_3$
Milk of magnesia	$Mg(OH)_2$
Mylanta, Maalox, Di-Gel, Gelusil, Riopan	$Mg(OH)_2$, $Al(OH)_3$
Bisodol, Rolaids	$CaCO_3$, $Mg(OH)_2$
Titralac, Tums, Pepto-Bismol	$CaCO_3$
Alka-Seltzer	$NaHCO_3$, $KHCO_3$

QUESTIONS AND PROBLEMS

11.7 Reactions of Acids and Bases

LEARNING GOAL Write balanced equations for reactions of acids with metals, carbonates or bicarbonates, and bases.

11.55 Complete and balance the equation for each of the following reactions:
  a. $ZnCO_3(s) + HBr(aq) \longrightarrow$
  b. $Zn(s) + HCl(aq) \longrightarrow$
  c. $HCl(aq) + NaHCO_3(s) \longrightarrow$
  d. $H_2SO_4(aq) + Mg(OH)_2(s) \longrightarrow$

11.56 Complete and balance the equation for each of the following reactions:
  a. $KHCO_3(s) + HBr(aq) \longrightarrow$
  b. $Ca(s) + H_2SO_4(aq) \longrightarrow$
  c. $H_2SO_4(aq) + Ca(OH)_2(s) \longrightarrow$
  d. $Na_2CO_3(s) + H_2SO_4(aq) \longrightarrow$

11.57 Balance each of the following neutralization reactions:
  a. $HCl(aq) + Mg(OH)_2(s) \longrightarrow H_2O(l) + MgCl_2(aq)$
  b. $H_3PO_4(aq) + LiOH(aq) \longrightarrow H_2O(l) + Li_3PO_4(aq)$

11.58 Balance each of the following neutralization reactions:
  a. $HNO_3(aq) + Ba(OH)_2(s) \longrightarrow H_2O(l) + Ba(NO_3)_2(aq)$
  b. $H_2SO_4(aq) + Al(OH)_3(s) \longrightarrow H_2O(l) + Al_2(SO_4)_3(aq)$

11.59 Write a balanced equation for the neutralization of each of the following:
  a. $H_2SO_4(aq)$ and $NaOH(aq)$
  b. $HCl(aq)$ and $Fe(OH)_3(s)$
  c. $H_2CO_3(aq)$ and $Mg(OH)_2(s)$

11.60 Write a balanced equation for the neutralization of each of the following:
  a. $H_3PO_4(aq)$ and $NaOH(aq)$
  b. $HI(aq)$ and $LiOH(aq)$
  c. $HNO_3(aq)$ and $Ca(OH)_2(s)$

11.8 Acid–Base Titration

LEARNING GOAL

Calculate the molarity or volume of an acid or base solution from titration information.

Suppose we need to find the molarity of a solution of HCl, which has an unknown concentration. We can do this by a laboratory procedure called **titration** in which we neutralize an acid sample with a known amount of base. In a titration, we place a measured volume of the acid in a flask and add a few drops of an **indicator**, such as phenolphthalein. An indicator is a compound that dramatically changes color when pH of the solution changes. In an acidic solution, phenolphthalein is colorless. Then we fill a buret with a NaOH solution of known molarity and carefully add NaOH solution to neutralize the acid in the flask (see Figure 11.6). We know that neutralization has taken place when the phenolphthalein in the solution changes from colorless to pink. This is called the neutralization **endpoint**. From the measured volume of the NaOH solution and its molarity, we calculate the number of moles of NaOH, the moles of acid, and use the measured volume of acid to calculate its concentration.

FIGURE 11.6 ▶ The titration of an acid. A known volume of an acid is placed in a flask with an indicator and titrated with a measured volume of a base solution, such as NaOH, to the neutralization endpoint.

Q What data is needed to determine the molarity of the acid in the flask?

⚛ **CORE CHEMISTRY SKILL**

Calculating Molarity or Volume of
an Acid or Base in a Titration

Guide to Calculations for an Acid–Base Titration

STEP 1
State the given and needed quantities and concentrations.

STEP 2
Write a plan to calculate the molarity or volume.

STEP 3
State equalities and conversion factors, including concentrations.

STEP 4
Set up the problem to calculate the needed quantity.

▶ **SAMPLE PROBLEM 11.12 Titration of an Acid**

If 16.3 mL of a 0.185 M $Sr(OH)_2$ solution is used to titrate the HCl in a 25.0-mL sample of gastric juice, what is the molarity of the HCl solution?

$$Sr(OH)_2(aq) + 2HCl(aq) \longrightarrow 2H_2O(l) + SrCl_2(aq)$$

SOLUTION

STEP 1 State the given and needed quantities and concentrations.

	Given	Need
ANALYZE THE PROBLEM	25.0 mL (0.0250 L) of HCl solution	molarity of the HCl solution
	16.3 mL of 0.185 M $Sr(OH)_2$ solution	
Neutralization Equation		
$Sr(OH)_2(aq) + 2HCl(aq) \longrightarrow 2H_2O(l) + SrCl_2(aq)$		

STEP 2 Write a plan to calculate the molarity.

| mL of $Sr(OH)_2$ solution | Metric factor | L of $Sr(OH)_2$ solution | Molarity | moles of $Sr(OH)_2$ | Mole–mole factor | moles of HCl | Divide by liters | molarity of HCl solution |

STEP 3 State equalities and conversion factors, including concentrations.

$$1 \text{ L of } Sr(OH)_2 \text{ solution} = 1000 \text{ mL of } Sr(OH)_2 \text{ solution}$$
$$\frac{1 \text{ L } Sr(OH)_2 \text{ solution}}{1000 \text{ mL } Sr(OH)_2 \text{ solution}} \text{ and } \frac{1000 \text{ mL } Sr(OH)_2 \text{ solution}}{1 \text{ L } Sr(OH)_2 \text{ solution}}$$

$$1 \text{ L of } Sr(OH)_2 \text{ solution} = 0.185 \text{ mole of } Sr(OH)_2$$
$$\frac{1 \text{ L } Sr(OH)_2 \text{ solution}}{0.185 \text{ mole } Sr(OH)_2} \text{ and } \frac{0.185 \text{ mole } Sr(OH)_2}{1 \text{ L } Sr(OH)_2 \text{ solution}}$$

$$2 \text{ moles of HCl} = 1 \text{ mole of } Sr(OH)_2$$
$$\frac{2 \text{ moles HCl}}{1 \text{ mole } Sr(OH)_2} \text{ and } \frac{1 \text{ mole } Sr(OH)_2}{2 \text{ moles HCl}}$$

STEP 4 Set up the problem to calculate the needed quantity.

$$16.3 \text{ mL } Sr(OH)_2 \text{ solution} \times \frac{1 \text{ L } Sr(OH)_2 \text{ solution}}{1000 \text{ mL } Sr(OH)_2 \text{ solution}} \times \frac{0.185 \text{ mole } Sr(OH)_2}{1 \text{ L } Sr(OH)_2 \text{ solution}} \times \frac{2 \text{ moles HCl}}{1 \text{ mole } Sr(OH)_2}$$

$$= 0.00603 \text{ mole of HCl}$$

$$\text{molarity of HCl solution} = \frac{0.00603 \text{ mole HCl}}{0.0250 \text{ L HCl solution}} = 0.241 \text{ M HCl solution}$$

Interactive Video

Acid-Base Titration

STUDY CHECK 11.12

What is the molarity of an HCl solution if 28.6 mL of a 0.175 M NaOH solution is needed to titrate a 25.0-mL sample of the HCl solution?

ANSWER

0.200 M HCl solution

QUESTIONS AND PROBLEMS

11.8 Acid–Base Titration

LEARNING GOAL Calculate the molarity or volume of an acid or base solution from titration information.

11.61 What is the molarity of a solution of HCl if 5.00 mL of the HCl solution is titrated with 28.6 mL of a 0.145 NaOH solution?

$$HCl(aq) + NaOH(aq) \longrightarrow H_2O(l) + NaCl(aq)$$

11.62 What is the molarity of the acetic acid solution if 29.7 mL of a 0.205 M KOH solution is required to titrate 25.0 mL of a solution of $HC_2H_3O_2$?

$$HC_2H_3O_2(aq) + KOH(aq) \longrightarrow H_2O(l) + KC_2H_3O_2(aq)$$

11.63 If 38.2 mL of a 0.163 M KOH solution is required to titrate 25.0 mL of a H_2SO_4 solution, what is the molarity of the H_2SO_4 solution?

$$H_2SO_4(aq) + 2KOH(aq) \longrightarrow 2H_2O(l) + K_2SO_4(aq)$$

11.64 If 32.8 mL of a 0.162 M NaOH solution is required to titrate 25.0 mL of a solution of H_2SO_4, what is the molarity of the H_2SO_4 solution?

$$H_2SO_4(aq) + 2NaOH(aq) \longrightarrow 2H_2O(l) + Na_2SO_4(aq)$$

11.65 A solution of 0.204 M NaOH is used to titrate 50.0 mL of a 0.0224 M H_3PO_4 solution. What volume, in milliliters, of the NaOH solution is required?

$$H_3PO_4(aq) + 3NaOH(aq) \longrightarrow 3H_2O(l) + Na_3PO_4(aq)$$

11.66 A solution of 0.312 M KOH is used to titrate 15.0 mL of a 0.186 M H_3PO_4 solution. What volume, in milliliters, of the KOH solution is required?

$$H_3PO_4(aq) + 3KOH(aq) \longrightarrow 3H_2O(l) + K_3PO_4(aq)$$

11.9 Buffers

The pH of water and most solutions changes drastically when a small amount of acid or base is added. However, when an acid or a base is added to a *buffer* solution, there is little change in pH. A **buffer solution** maintains the pH of a solution by neutralizing small amounts of added acid or base. In the human body, whole blood contains plasma, white blood cells and platelets, and red blood cells. Blood plasma contains buffers that maintain a consistent pH of about 7.4. If the pH of the blood plasma goes slightly above or below 7.4, changes in our oxygen levels and our metabolic processes can be drastic enough to cause death. Even though we obtain acids and bases from foods and cellular reactions, the buffers in the body absorb those compounds so effectively that the pH of our blood plasma remains essentially unchanged (see Figure 11.7).

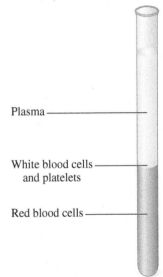

Whole blood consists of plasma, white blood cells and platelets, and red blood cells.

FIGURE 11.7 ▶ Adding an acid or a base to water changes the pH drastically, but a buffer resists pH change when small amounts of acid or base are added.

Q Why does the pH change several pH units when acid is added to water, but not when acid is added to a buffer?

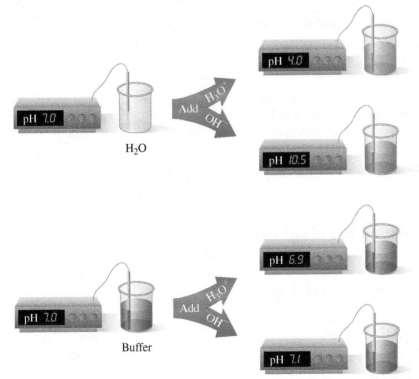

In a buffer, an acid must be present to react with any OH^- that is added, and a base must be available to react with any added H_3O^+. However, that acid and base must not neutralize each other. Therefore, a combination of an acid–base conjugate pair is used in buffers. Most buffer solutions consist of nearly equal concentrations of a weak acid and a salt containing its conjugate base. Buffers may also contain a weak base and the salt of the weak base, which contains its conjugate acid.

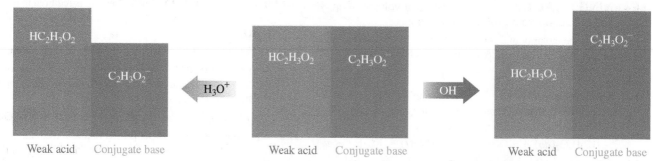

FIGURE 11.8 ▶ The buffer described here consists of about equal concentrations of acetic acid ($HC_2H_3O_2$) and its conjugate base acetate ion ($C_2H_3O_2^-$). Adding H_3O^+ to the buffer neutralizes some $C_2H_3O_2^-$, whereas adding OH^- neutralizes some $HC_2H_3O_2$. The pH of the solution is maintained as long as the added amount of acid or base is small compared to the concentrations of the buffer components.

Q How does this acetic acid–acetate ion buffer maintain pH?

For example, a typical buffer can be made from the weak acid acetic acid ($HC_2H_3O_2$) and its salt, sodium acetate ($NaC_2H_3O_2$). As a weak acid, acetic acid dissociates slightly in water to form H_3O^+ and a very small amount of $C_2H_3O_2^-$. The addition of its salt, sodium acetate, provides a much larger concentration of acetate ion ($C_2H_3O_2^-$), which is necessary for its buffering capability.

$$HC_2H_3O_2(aq) + H_2O(l) \rightleftharpoons H_3O^+(aq) + C_2H_3O_2^-(aq)$$
Large amount   Large amount

We can now describe how this buffer solution maintains the $[H_3O^+]$. When a small amount of acid is added, the additional H_3O^+ combines with the acetate ion, $C_2H_3O_2^-$, causing the equilibrium to shift in the direction of the reactants, acetic acid and water. There will be a slight decrease in the $[C_2H_3O_2^-]$ and a slight increase in the $[HC_2H_3O_2]$, but both the $[H_3O^+]$ and pH are maintained (see Figure 11.8).

$$HC_2H_3O_2(aq) + H_2O(l) \longleftarrow H_3O^+(aq) + C_2H_3O_2^-(aq)$$
Equilibrium shifts in the
direction of the reactants

If a small amount of base is added to this same buffer solution, it is neutralized by the acetic acid, $HC_2H_3O_2$, which shifts the equilibrium in the direction of the products acetate ion and water. The $[HC_2H_3O_2]$ decreases slightly and the $[C_2H_3O_2^-]$ increases slightly, but again the $[H_3O^+]$ and thus the pH of the solution are maintained.

$$HC_2H_3O_2(aq) + OH^-(aq) \longrightarrow H_2O(l) + C_2H_3O_2^-(aq)$$
Equilibrium shifts in the
direction of the products

CORE CHEMISTRY SKILL

Calculating the pH of a Buffer

Calculating the pH of a Buffer

By rearranging the K_a expression to give $[H_3O^+]$, we can obtain the ratio of the acetic acid/acetate buffer.

$$K_a = \frac{[H_3O^+][C_2H_3O_2^-]}{[HC_2H_3O_2]}$$

Solving for $[H_3O^+]$ gives:

$$[H_3O^+] = K_a \times \frac{[HC_2H_3O_2]}{[C_2H_3O_2^-]} \quad \begin{array}{l} \longleftarrow \text{ Weak acid} \\ \longleftarrow \text{ Conjugate base} \end{array}$$

In this rearrangement of K_a, the weak acid is in the numerator and the conjugate base in the denominator. We can now calculate the $[H_3O^+]$ and pH for an acetic acid buffer as shown in Sample Problem 11.13.

SAMPLE PROBLEM 11.13 Calculating the pH of a Buffer

The K_a for acetic acid, $HC_2H_3O_2$, is 1.8×10^{-5}. What is the pH of a buffer prepared with 1.0 M $HC_2H_3O_2$ and 1.0 M $C_2H_3O_2^-$?

$$HC_2H_3O_2(aq) + H_2O(l) \rightleftharpoons H_3O^+(aq) + C_2H_3O_2^-(aq)$$

SOLUTION

STEP 1 State the given and needed quantities.

ANALYZE THE PROBLEM	Given	Need
	1.0 M $HC_2H_3O_2$, 1.0 M $C_2H_3O_2^-$	pH
	Equation	
	$HC_2H_3O_2(aq) + H_2O(l) \rightleftharpoons H_3O^+(aq) + C_2H_3O_2^-(aq)$	

STEP 2 Write the K_a expression and rearrange for $[H_3O^+]$.

$$K_a = \frac{[H_3O^+][C_2H_3O_2^-]}{[HC_2H_3O_2]}$$

$$[H_3O^+] = K_a \times \frac{[HC_2H_3O_2]}{[C_2H_3O_2^-]}$$

STEP 3 Substitute [HA] and [A⁻] into the K_a expression.

$$[H_3O^+] = 1.8 \times 10^{-5} \times \frac{[1.0]}{[1.0]}$$

$$[H_3O^+] = 1.8 \times 10^{-5}\,M$$

STEP 4 Use $[H_3O^+]$ to calculate pH. Placing the $[H_3O^+]$ into the pH equation gives the pH of the buffer.

$$pH = -\log[1.8 \times 10^{-5}] = 4.74$$

> **Guide to Calculating pH of a Buffer**
>
> **STEP 1**
> State the given and needed quantities.
>
> **STEP 2**
> Write the K_a expression and rearrange for $[H_3O^+]$.
>
> **STEP 3**
> Substitute [HA] and [A⁻] into the K_a expression.
>
> **STEP 4**
> Use $[H_3O^+]$ to calculate pH.

STUDY CHECK 11.13

One of the conjugate acid–base pairs that buffers the blood plasma is $H_2PO_4^-/HPO_4^{2-}$, which has a K_a of 6.2×10^{-8}. What is the pH of a buffer that is prepared from 0.10 M $H_2PO_4^-$ and 0.50 M HPO_4^{2-}?

ANSWER

pH = 7.91

Because K_a is a constant at a given temperature, the $[H_3O^+]$ is determined by the $[HC_2H_3O_2]/[C_2H_3O_2^-]$ ratio. As long as the addition of small amounts of either acid or base changes the ratio of $[HC_2H_3O_2]/[C_2H_3O_2^-]$ only slightly, the changes in $[H_3O^+]$ will be small and the pH will be maintained. If a large amount of acid or base is added, the *buffering capacity* of the system may be exceeded. Buffers can be prepared from conjugate acid–base pairs such as $H_2PO_4^-/HPO_4^{2-}$, HPO_4^{2-}/PO_4^{3-}, HCO_3^-/CO_3^{2-}, or NH_4^+/NH_3. The pH of the buffer solution will depend on the conjugate acid–base pair chosen.

Using a common phosphate buffer for biological specimens, we can look at the effect of using different ratios of $[H_2PO_4^-]/[HPO_4^{2-}]$ on the $[H_3O^+]$ and pH. The K_a of $H_2PO_4^-$ is 6.2×10^{-8}. The equation and the $[H_3O^+]$ are written as follows:

$$H_2PO_4^-(aq) + H_2O(l) \rightleftharpoons H_3O^+(aq) + HPO_4^{2-}(aq)$$

$$[H_3O^+] = K_a \times \frac{[H_2PO_4^-]}{[HPO_4^{2-}]}$$

K_a	$\dfrac{[H_2PO_4^-]}{[HPO_4^{2-}]}$	Ratio	$[H_3O^+]$	pH
6.2×10^{-8}	$\dfrac{1.0\,M}{0.10\,M}$	$\dfrac{10}{1}$	6.2×10^{-7}	6.21
6.2×10^{-8}	$\dfrac{1.0\,M}{1.0\,M}$	$\dfrac{1}{1}$	6.2×10^{-8}	7.21
6.2×10^{-8}	$\dfrac{0.10\,M}{1.0\,M}$	$\dfrac{1}{10}$	6.2×10^{-9}	8.21

To prepare a phosphate buffer with a pH close to the pH of a biological sample, 7.4, we would choose concentrations that are about equal, such as $1.0\,M\ H_2PO_4^-$ and $1.0\,M\ HPO_4^{2-}$.

> **SAMPLE PROBLEM 11.14 Preparation of Buffers**
>
> What is the pH of a buffer made from 0.10 M formic acid ($HCHO_2$) and 0.10 M formate (CHO_2^-)? The K_a for formic acid is 1.8×10^{-4}.
>
> **SOLUTION**
>
> $$[H_3O^+] = K_a \times \frac{[HCHO_2]}{[CHO_2^-]}$$
>
> $$[H_3O^+] = 1.8 \times 10^{-4} \times \frac{[0.10]}{[0.10]} = 1.8 \times 10^{-4}\,M$$
>
> $$pH = -\log[1.8 \times 10^{-4}] = 3.74$$
>
> **STUDY CHECK 11.14**
>
> What is the pH of a buffer made from 0.10 M formic acid ($HCHO_2$) and 0.010 M formate (CHO_2^-)?
>
> **ANSWER**
>
> pH = 2.74

 # Chemistry Link to Health

Buffers in the Blood Plasma

The arterial blood plasma has a normal pH of 7.35 to 7.45. If changes in H_3O^+ lower the pH below 6.8 or raise it above 8.0, cells cannot function properly and death may result. In our cells, CO_2 is continually produced as an end product of cellular metabolism. Some CO_2 is carried to the lungs for elimination, and the rest dissolves in body fluids such as plasma and saliva, forming carbonic acid, H_2CO_3. As a weak acid, carbonic acid dissociates to give bicarbonate, HCO_3^-, and H_3O^+. More of the anion HCO_3^- is supplied by the kidneys to give an important buffer system in the body fluid—the H_2CO_3/HCO_3^- buffer.

$$CO_2(g) + H_2O(l) \rightleftharpoons H_2CO_3(aq) \rightleftharpoons$$
$$H_3O^+(aq) + HCO_3^-(aq)$$

Excess H_3O^+ entering the body fluids reacts with the HCO_3^-, and excess OH^- reacts with the carbonic acid.

$$H_2CO_3(aq) + H_2O(l) \longleftarrow H_3O^+(aq) + HCO_3^-(aq)$$
Equilibrium shifts in the direction of the reactants

$$H_2CO_3(aq) + OH^-(aq) \longrightarrow H_2O(l) + HCO_3^-(aq)$$
Equilibrium shifts in the direction of the products

For carbonic acid, we can write the equilibrium expression as

$$K_a = \frac{[H_3O^+][HCO_3^-]}{[H_2CO_3]}$$

To maintain the normal blood plasma pH (7.35 to 7.45), the ratio of $[H_2CO_3]/[HCO_3^-]$ needs to be about 1 to 10, which is obtained by the concentrations in the blood plasma of 0.0024 M H_2CO_3 and 0.024 M HCO_3^-.

$$[H_3O^+] = K_a \times \frac{[H_2CO_3]}{[HCO_3^-]}$$

$$[H_3O^+] = 4.3 \times 10^{-7} \times \frac{[0.0024]}{[0.024]}$$

$$= 4.3 \times 10^{-7} \times 0.10 = 4.3 \times 10^{-8} \text{ M}$$

$$\text{pH} = -\log[4.3 \times 10^{-8}] = 7.37$$

In the body, the concentration of carbonic acid is closely associated with the partial pressure of CO_2, P_{CO_2}. Table 11.9 lists the normal values for arterial blood. If the CO_2 level rises, increasing $[H_2CO_3]$, the equilibrium shifts to produce more H_3O^+, which lowers the pH. This condition is called *acidosis*. Difficulty with ventilation or gas diffusion can lead to respiratory acidosis, which can happen in emphysema or when an accident or depressive drugs affect the medulla of the brain.

A lowering of the CO_2 level leads to a high blood pH, a condition called *alkalosis*. Excitement, trauma, or a high temperature may cause a person to hyperventilate, which expels large amounts of CO_2. As the partial pressure of CO_2 in the blood falls below normal, the equilibrium shifts from H_2CO_3 to CO_2 and H_2O. This shift decreases the $[H_3O^+]$ and raises the pH. The kidneys also regulate H_3O^+ and HCO_3^-, but they do so more slowly than the adjustment made by the lungs during ventilation.

Table 11.10 lists some of the conditions that lead to changes in the blood pH and some possible treatments.

TABLE 11.9 Normal Values for Blood Buffer in Arterial Blood

P_{CO_2}	40 mmHg
H_2CO_3	2.4 mmoles/L of plasma
HCO_3^-	24 mmoles/L of plasma
pH	7.35 to 7.45

TABLE 11.10 Acidosis and Alkalosis: Symptoms, Causes, and Treatments

Respiratory Acidosis: $CO_2\uparrow$ pH$\downarrow$	
Symptoms:	Failure to ventilate, suppression of breathing, disorientation, weakness, coma
Causes:	Lung disease blocking gas diffusion (e.g., emphysema, pneumonia, bronchitis, asthma); depression of respiratory center by drugs, cardiopulmonary arrest, stroke, poliomyelitis, or nervous system disorders
Treatment:	Correction of disorder, infusion of bicarbonate
Metabolic Acidosis: $H^+\uparrow$ pH$\downarrow$	
Symptoms:	Increased ventilation, fatigue, confusion
Causes:	Renal disease, including hepatitis and cirrhosis; increased acid production in diabetes mellitus, hyperthyroidism, alcoholism, and starvation; loss of alkali in diarrhea; acid retention in renal failure
Treatment:	Sodium bicarbonate given orally, dialysis for renal failure, insulin treatment for diabetic ketosis
Respiratory Alkalosis: $CO_2\downarrow$ pH$\uparrow$	
Symptoms:	Increased rate and depth of breathing, numbness, light-headedness, tetany
Causes:	Hyperventilation because of anxiety, hysteria, fever, exercise; reaction to drugs such as salicylate, quinine, and antihistamines; conditions causing hypoxia (e.g., pneumonia, pulmonary edema, heart disease)
Treatment:	Elimination of anxiety-producing state, rebreathing into a paper bag
Metabolic Alkalosis: $H^+\downarrow$ pH$\uparrow$	
Symptoms:	Depressed breathing, apathy, confusion
Causes:	Vomiting, diseases of the adrenal glands, ingestion of excess alkali
Treatment:	Infusion of saline solution, treatment of underlying diseases

QUESTIONS AND PROBLEMS

11.9 Buffers

LEARNING GOAL Describe the role of buffers in maintaining the pH of a solution; calculate the pH of a buffer.

11.67 Which of the following represents a buffer system? Explain.
  a. NaOH and NaCl
  b. H_2CO_3 and $NaHCO_3$
  c. HF and KF
  d. KCl and NaCl

11.68 Which of the following represents a buffer system? Explain.
  a. $HClO_2$
  b. $NaNO_3$
  c. $HC_2H_3O_2$ and $NaC_2H_3O_2$
  d. HCl and NaOH

11.69 Consider the buffer system of hydrofluoric acid, HF, and its salt, NaF.

$$HF(aq) + H_2O(l) \rightleftharpoons H_3O^+(aq) + F^-(aq)$$

a. The purpose of this buffer system is to:
  1. maintain $[HF]$
  2. maintain $[F^-]$
  3. maintain pH

b. The salt of the weak acid is needed to:
  1. provide the conjugate base
  2. neutralize added H_3O^+
  3. provide the conjugate acid

c. If OH^- is added, it is neutralized by:
  1. the salt
  2. H_2O
  3. H_3O^+

d. When H_3O^+ is added, the equilibrium shifts in the direction of the:
  1. reactants
  2. products
  3. does not change

11.70 Consider the buffer system of nitrous acid, HNO_2, and its salt, $NaNO_2$.

$$HNO_2(aq) + H_2O(l) \rightleftharpoons H_3O^+(aq) + NO_2^-(aq)$$

a. The purpose of this buffer system is to:
   1. maintain $[HNO_2]$ 2. maintain $[NO_2^-]$
   3. maintain pH
b. The weak acid is needed to:
   1. provide the conjugate base   2. neutralize added OH^-
   3. provide the conjugate acid
c. If H_3O^+ is added, it is neutralized by:
   1. the salt   2. H_2O 3. OH^-
d. When OH^- is added, the equilibrium shifts in the direction of the:
   1. reactants   2. products   3. does not change

11.71 Nitrous acid has a K_a of 4.5×10^{-4}. What is the pH of a buffer solution containing 0.10 M HNO_2 and 0.10 M NO_2^-?

11.72 Acetic acid has a K_a of 1.8×10^{-5}. What is the pH of a buffer solution containing 0.15 M $HC_2H_3O_2$ and 0.15 M $C_2H_3O_2^-$?

11.73 Using Table 11.4 for K_a values, compare the pH of a HF buffer that contains 0.10 M HF and 0.10 M NaF with another HF buffer that contains 0.060 M HF and 0.120 M NaF.

11.74 Using Table 11.4 for K_a values, compare the pH of a H_2CO_3 buffer that contains 0.10 M H_2CO_3 and 0.10 M $NaHCO_3$ with another H_2CO_3 buffer that contains 0.15 M H_2CO_3 and 0.050 M $NaHCO_3$.

℞ Clinical Applications

11.75 Why would the pH of your blood plasma increase if you breathe fast?

11.76 Why would the pH of your blood plasma decrease if you hold your breath?

11.77 Someone with kidney failure excretes urine with large amounts of HCO_3^-. How would this loss of HCO_3^- affect the pH of the blood plasma?

11.78 Someone with severe diabetes obtains energy by the breakdown of fats, which produce large amounts of acidic substances. How would this affect the pH of the blood plasma?

Clinical Update

Acid Reflux Disease

Larry has not been feeling well lately. He tells his doctor that he has discomfort and a burning feeling in his chest, and a sour taste in his throat and mouth. At times, Larry says he feels bloated after a big meal, has a dry cough, is hoarse, and sometimes has a sore throat. He has tried antacids, but they do not bring any relief.

The doctor tells Larry that he thinks he has acid reflux. At the top of the stomach there is a valve, the lower esophageal sphincter, that normally closes after food passes through it. However, if the valve does not close completely, acid produced in the stomach to digest food can move up into the esophagus, a condition called *acid reflux*. The acid, which is hydrochloric acid, HCl, is produced in the stomach to kill bacteria, microorganisms, and to activate the enzymes we need to break down food.

If acid reflux occurs, the strong acid HCl comes in contact with the lining of the esophagus, where it causes irritation and produces a burning feeling in the chest. Sometimes the pain in the chest is called *heartburn*. If the HCl reflux goes high enough to reach the throat, a sour taste may be noticed in the mouth. If Larry's symptoms occur three or more times a week, he may have a chronic condition known as *acid reflux disease* or *gastroesophageal reflux disease* (GERD).

Larry's doctor orders an *esophageal pH test* in which the amount of acid entering the esophagus from the stomach is measured over 24 h. A probe that measures the pH is inserted into the lower esophagus above the esophageal sphincter. The pH measurements indicate a reflux episode each time the pH drops to 4 or less.

In the 24-h period, Larry has several reflux episodes and his doctor determines that he has chronic GERD. He and Larry discuss treatment for GERD, which includes eating smaller meals, not lying down for 3 h after eating, making dietary changes, and losing weight. Antacids may be used to neutralize the acid coming up from the stomach. Other medications known as *proton pump inhibitors* (PPIs), such as Prilosec and Nexium, may be used to suppress the production of HCl in the stomach (gastric parietal cells), which raises the pH in the stomach to between 4 and 5, and gives the esophagus time to heal. Nexium may be given in oral doses of 40 mg once a day for 4 weeks. In severe GERD cases, an artificial valve may be created at the top of the stomach to strength the lower esophageal sphincter.

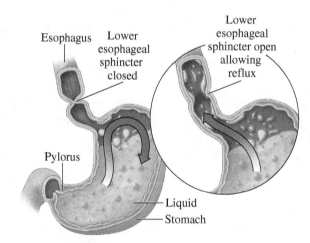

℞ Clinical Applications

11.79 At rest, the $[H_3O^+]$ of the stomach fluid is 2.0×10^{-4} M. What is the pH of the stomach fluid?

11.80 When food enters the stomach, HCl is released and the $[H_3O^+]$ of the stomach fluid rises to 4×10^{-2} M. What is the pH of the stomach fluid while eating?

11.81 In Larry's esophageal pH test, a pH value of 3.60 was recorded in the esophagus. What is the $[H_3O^+]$ in his esophagus?

11.82 After Larry had taken Nexium for 4 weeks, the pH in his stomach was raised to 4.52. What is the $[H_3O^+]$ in his stomach?

11.83 Write the balanced chemical equation for the neutralization reaction of stomach acid HCl with $CaCO_3$, an ingredient in some antacids.

11.84 Write the balanced chemical equation for the neutralization reaction of stomach acid HCl with $Al(OH)_3$, an ingredient in some antacids.

11.85 How many grams of $CaCO_3$ are required to neutralize 100. mL of stomach acid HCl, which is equivalent to 0.0400 M HCl?

11.86 How many grams of $Al(OH)_3$ are required to neutralize 150. mL of stomach acid HCl with a pH of 1.5?

CONCEPT MAP

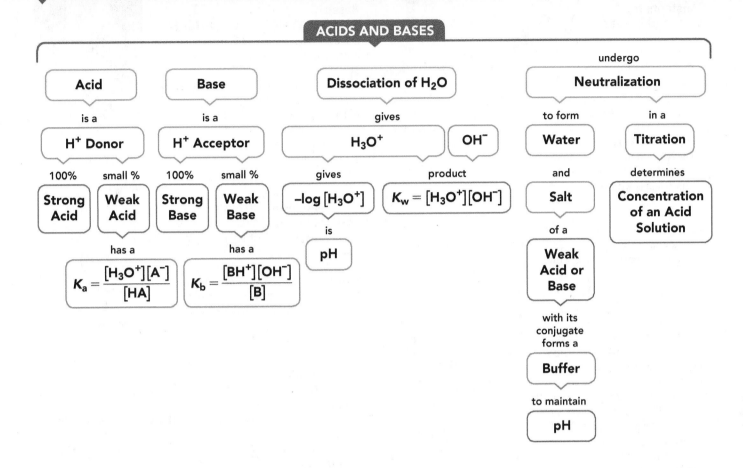

ACIDS AND BASES

Acid — is a — **H⁺ Donor**
- 100% → **Strong Acid**
- small % → **Weak Acid** — has a — $K_a = \dfrac{[H_3O^+][A^-]}{[HA]}$

Base — is a — **H⁺ Acceptor**
- 100% → **Strong Base**
- small % → **Weak Base** — has a — $K_b = \dfrac{[BH^+][OH^-]}{[B]}$

Dissociation of H₂O — gives — **H_3O^+** and **OH^-**
- gives → $-\log[H_3O^+]$ — is — **pH**
- product → $K_w = [H_3O^+][OH^-]$

Neutralization (undergo)
- to form → **Water** and **Salt** — of a — **Weak Acid or Base** — with its conjugate forms a — **Buffer** — to maintain — **pH**
- in a → **Titration** — determines — **Concentration of an Acid Solution**

CHAPTER REVIEW

11.1 Acids and Bases
LEARNING GOAL Describe and name acids and bases.

NaOH(s)

— OH⁻
— Na⁺
— Water

$$NaOH(s) \xrightarrow{H_2O} Na^+(aq) + OH^-(aq)$$
Ionic compound   Dissociation   Hydroxide ion

- An Arrhenius acid produces H⁺ and an Arrhenius base produces OH⁻ in aqueous solutions.
- Acids taste sour, may sting, and neutralize bases.
- Bases taste bitter, feel slippery, and neutralize acids.
- Acids containing a simple anion use a *hydro* prefix, whereas acids with oxygen-containing polyatomic anions are named as *ic* or *ous* acids.

11.2 Brønsted–Lowry Acids and Bases
LEARNING GOAL Identify conjugate acid–base pairs for Brønsted–Lowry acids and bases.

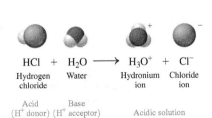

$$HCl + H_2O \longrightarrow H_3O^+ + Cl^-$$
Hydrogen chloride   Water   Hydronium ion   Chloride ion

Acid   Base
(H⁺ donor) (H⁺ acceptor)   Acidic solution

- According to the Brønsted–Lowry theory, acids are H⁺ donors and bases are H⁺ acceptors.
- A conjugate acid–base pair is related by the loss or gain of one H⁺.
- For example, when the acid HF donates H⁺, the F⁻ is its conjugate base. The other acid–base pair would be H_3O^+/H_2O.

$$HF(aq) + H_2O(l) \rightleftharpoons H_3O^+(aq) + F^-(aq)$$

11.3 Strengths of Acids and Bases
LEARNING GOAL Write equations for the dissociation of strong and weak acids; identify the direction of reaction.

HC₂H₃O₂ 1 M

- Strong acids dissociate completely in water, and the H⁺ is accepted by H₂O acting as a base.
- A weak acid dissociates slightly in water, producing only a small percentage of H_3O^+.
- Strong bases are hydroxides of Groups 1A (1) and 2A (2) that dissociate completely in water.
- An important weak base is ammonia, NH₃.

11.4 Dissociation Constants for Acids and Bases

HCHO₂   CHO₂⁻

LEARNING GOAL Write the expression for the dissociation constant of a weak acid or weak base.

- In water, weak acids and weak bases produce only a few ions when equilibrium is reached.
- Weak acids have small K_a values whereas strong acids, which are essentially 100% dissociated, have very large K_a values.
- The reaction for a weak acid can be written as
HA + H₂O ⇌ H₃O⁺ + A⁻. The acid dissociation constant expression is written as

$$K_a = \frac{[H_3O^+][A^-]}{[HA]}.$$

- For a weak base, B + H₂O ⇌ BH⁺ + OH⁻, the base dissociation constant expression is written as

$$K_b = \frac{[BH^+][OH^-]}{[B]}.$$

11.5 Dissociation of Water

LEARNING GOAL Use the water dissociation constant expression to calculate the $[H_3O^+]$ and $[OH^-]$ in an aqueous solution.

- In pure water, a few water molecules transfer H⁺ to other water molecules, producing small, but equal, amounts of $[H_3O^+]$ and $[OH^-]$.
- In pure water, the molar concentrations of H₃O⁺ and OH⁻ are each 1.0×10^{-7} mole/L.
- The *water dissociation constant expression*, K_w, $[H_3O^+][OH^-] = 1.0 \times 10^{-14}$ at 25 °C.
- In acidic solutions, the $[H_3O^+]$ is greater than the $[OH^-]$.
- In basic solutions, the $[OH^-]$ is greater than the $[H_3O^+]$.

H₃O⁺   OH⁻

$[H_3O^+] = [OH^-]$
Neutral solution

11.6 The pH Scale

LEARNING GOAL Calculate pH from $[H_3O^+]$; given the pH, calculate the $[H_3O^+]$ and $[OH^-]$ of a solution.

- The pH scale is a range of numbers typically from 0 to 14, which represents the $[H_3O^+]$ of the solution.
- A neutral solution has a pH of 7.0. In acidic solutions, the pH is below 7.0; in basic solutions, the pH is above 7.0.
- Mathematically, pH is the negative logarithm of the hydronium ion concentration,

$$pH = -\log[H_3O^+].$$

11.7 Reactions of Acids and Bases

LEARNING GOAL Write balanced equations for reactions of acids with metals, carbonates or bicarbonates, and bases.

- An acid reacts with a metal to produce hydrogen gas and a salt.
- The reaction of an acid with a carbonate or bicarbonate produces carbon dioxide, water, and a salt.
- In neutralization, an acid reacts with a base to produce water and a salt.

11.8 Acid–Base Titration

LEARNING GOAL Calculate the molarity or volume of an acid or base solution from titration information.

- In a titration, an acid sample is neutralized with a known amount of a base.
- From the volume and molarity of the base, the concentration of the acid is calculated.

11.9 Buffers

LEARNING GOAL Describe the role of buffers in maintaining the pH of a solution; calculate the pH of a buffer.

- A buffer solution resists changes in pH when small amounts of an acid or a base are added.
- A buffer contains either a weak acid and its salt or a weak base and its salt.
- In a buffer, the weak acid reacts with added OH⁻, and the anion of the salt reacts with added H₃O⁺.
- Most buffer solutions consist of nearly equal concentrations of a weak acid and a salt containing its conjugate base.
- The pH of a buffer is calculated by solving the K_a expression for $[H_3O^+]$.

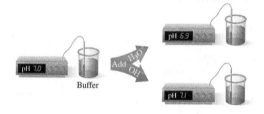
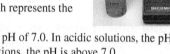
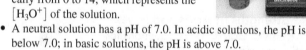

pH 7.0   Add H₂O / OH   pH 6.9

Buffer   pH 7.1

KEY TERMS

acid A substance that dissolves in water and produces hydrogen ions (H⁺), according to the Arrhenius theory. All acids are hydrogen ion donors, according to the Brønsted–Lowry theory.

acid dissociation constant, K_a The numerical value of the product of the ions from the dissociation of a weak acid divided by the concentration of the weak acid.

amphoteric Substances that can act as either an acid or a base in water.

base A substance that dissolves in water and produces hydroxide ions (OH⁻) according to the Arrhenius theory. All bases are hydrogen ion acceptors, according to the Brønsted–Lowry theory.

base dissociation constant, K_b The numerical value of the product of the ions from the dissociation of a weak base divided by the concentration of the weak base.

Brønsted–Lowry acids and bases An acid is a hydrogen ion donor; a base is a hydrogen ion acceptor.

buffer solution A solution of a weak acid and its conjugate base or a weak base and its conjugate acid that maintains the pH by neutralizing added acid or base.

conjugate acid–base pair An acid and a base that differ by one H^+. When an acid donates a hydrogen ion, the product is its conjugate base, which is capable of accepting a hydrogen ion in the reverse reaction.

dissociation The separation of an acid or a base into ions in water.

endpoint The point at which an indicator changes color. For the indicator phenolphthalein, the color change occurs when the number of moles of OH^- is equal to the number of moles of H_3O^+ in the sample.

hydronium ion, H_3O^+ The ion formed by the attraction of a hydrogen ion, H^+, to a water molecule.

indicator A substance added to a titration sample that changes color when the pH of the solution changes.

neutral The term that describes a solution with equal concentrations of $[H_3O^+]$ and $[OH^-]$.

neutralization A reaction between an acid and a base to form water and a salt.

pH A measure of the $[H_3O^+]$ in a solution; $pH = -\log[H_3O^+]$.

salt An ionic compound that contains a metal ion or NH_4^+ and a nonmetal or polyatomic ion other than OH^-.

strong acid An acid that completely dissociates in water.

strong base A base that completely dissociates in water.

titration The addition of base to an acid sample to determine the concentration of the acid.

water dissociation constant expression, K_w The product of $[H_3O^+]$ and $[OH^-]$ in solution; $K_w = [H_3O^+][OH^-]$.

weak acid An acid that is a poor donor of H^+ and dissociates only slightly in water.

weak base A base that is a poor acceptor of H^+ and produces only a small number of ions in water.

🖩 KEY MATH SKILLS

The chapter section containing each Key Math Skill is shown in parentheses at the end of each heading.

Calculating pH from $[H_3O^+]$ (11.6)

- The pH of a solution is calculated from the negative log of the $[H_3O^+]$.

$$pH = -\log[H_3O^+]$$

Example: What is the pH of a solution that has $[H_3O^+] = 2.4 \times 10^{-11}$ M?

Answer: We substitute the given $[H_3O^+]$ into the pH equation and calculate the pH.

$$pH = -\log[H_3O^+]$$
$$\boxed{+/-}\;\boxed{\log}\;2.4\;\boxed{\text{EE or EXP}}\;11\;\boxed{+/-}\;\boxed{=}$$
$$= 10.62 \quad \text{(Two decimal places equal the 2 SFs in the } [H_3O^+] \text{ coefficient.)}$$

Calculating $[H_3O^+]$ from pH (11.6)

- The calculation of $[H_3O^+]$ from the pH is done by reversing the pH calculation using the negative pH.

$$[H_3O^+] = 10^{-pH}$$

Example: What is the $[H_3O^+]$ of a solution with a pH of 4.80?

Answer:
$$[H_3O^+] = 10^{-pH}$$
$$= 10^{-4.80}$$
$$\boxed{2^{nd}}\;\boxed{\log}\;\boxed{+/-}\;4.80\;\boxed{=}$$
$$= 1.6 \times 10^{-5} \text{ M}$$
$$\text{(2 SFs in the } [H_3O^+] \text{ equal the two decimal places in the pH.)}$$

⚛ CORE CHEMISTRY SKILLS

The chapter section containing each Core Chemistry Skill is shown in parentheses at the end of each heading.

Identifying Conjugate Acid–Base Pairs (11.2)

- According to the Brønsted–Lowry theory, a conjugate acid–base pair consists of molecules or ions related by the loss of one H^+ by an acid, and the gain of one H^+ by a base.
- Every acid–base reaction contains two conjugate acid–base pairs because an H^+ is transferred in both the forward and reverse directions.
- When an acid such as HF loses one H^+, the conjugate base F^- is formed. When H_2O acts as a base, it gains one H^+, which forms its conjugate acid, H_3O^+.

Example: Identify the conjugate acid–base pairs in the following reaction:

$$H_2SO_4(aq) + H_2O(l) \rightleftharpoons HSO_4^-(aq) + H_3O^+(aq)$$

Answer: $H_2SO_4(aq) + H_2O(l) \rightleftharpoons HSO_4^-(aq) + H_3O^+(aq)$

     Acid   Base   Conjugate base   Conjugate acid

Conjugate acid–base pairs: H_2SO_4/HSO_4^- and H_3O^+/H_2O

Calculating $[H_3O^+]$ and $[OH^-]$ in Solutions (11.5)

- For all aqueous solutions, the product of $[H_3O^+]$ and $[OH^-]$ is equal to the water dissociation constant expression, K_w.

$$K_w = [H_3O^+][OH^-]$$

- Because pure water contains equal numbers of OH^- ions and H_3O^+ ions each with molar concentrations of 1.0×10^{-7} M, the numerical value of K_w is 1.0×10^{-14} at 25 °C.

$$K_w = [H_3O^+][OH^-] = [1.0 \times 10^{-7}][1.0 \times 10^{-7}]$$
$$= 1.0 \times 10^{-14}$$

- If we know the $[H_3O^+]$ of a solution, we can use the K_w expression to calculate the $[OH^-]$. If we know the $[OH^-]$ of a solution, we can calculate the $[H_3O^+]$ using the K_w expression.

$$[OH^-] = \frac{K_w}{[H_3O^+]} \quad [H_3O^+] = \frac{K_w}{[OH^-]}$$

Example: What is the $[OH^-]$ in a solution that has $[H_3O^+] = 2.4 \times 10^{-11}$ M? Is the solution acidic or basic?

Answer: We solve the K_w expression for $[OH^-]$ and substitute in the known values of K_w and $[H_3O^+]$.

$$[OH^-] = \frac{K_w}{[H_3O^+]} = \frac{1.0 \times 10^{-14}}{[2.4 \times 10^{-11}]} = 4.2 \times 10^{-4} \text{ M}$$

Because the $[OH^-]$ is greater than the $[H_3O^+]$, this is a basic solution.

Writing Equations for Reactions of Acids and Bases (11.7)

- Acids react with certain metals to produce hydrogen gas (H_2) and a salt.

$$\underset{\text{Metal}}{Mg(s)} + \underset{\text{Acid}}{2HCl(aq)} \longrightarrow \underset{\text{Hydrogen}}{H_2(g)} + \underset{\text{Salt}}{MgCl_2(aq)}$$

- When an acid is added to a carbonate or bicarbonate, the products are carbon dioxide gas, water, and a salt.

$$\underset{\text{Acid}}{2HCl(aq)} + \underset{\text{Carbonate}}{Na_2CO_3(aq)} \longrightarrow \underset{\substack{\text{Carbon} \\ \text{dioxide}}}{CO_2(g)} + \underset{\text{Water}}{H_2O(l)} + \underset{\text{Salt}}{2NaCl(aq)}$$

- Neutralization is a reaction between a strong or weak acid with a strong base to produce water and a salt.

$$\underset{\text{Acid}}{HCl(aq)} + \underset{\text{Base}}{NaOH(aq)} \longrightarrow \underset{\text{Water}}{H_2O(l)} + \underset{\text{Salt}}{NaCl(aq)}$$

Example: Write the balanced chemical equation for the reaction of $ZnCO_3(s)$ and hydrobromic acid $HBr(aq)$.

Answer:

$$ZnCO_3(s) + 2HBr(aq) \longrightarrow CO_2(g) + H_2O(l) + ZnBr_2(aq)$$

Calculating Molarity or Volume of an Acid or Base in a Titration (11.8)

- In a titration, a measured volume of acid is neutralized by an NaOH solution of known molarity.

- From the measured volume of the NaOH solution required for titration and its molarity, the number of moles of NaOH, the moles of acid, and the concentration of the acid are calculated.

Example: A 15.0-mL sample of a H_2SO_4 solution is titrated with 24.0 mL of a 0.245 M NaOH solution. What is the molarity of the H_2SO_4 solution?

$$H_2SO_4(aq) + 2NaOH(aq) \longrightarrow 2H_2O(l) + Na_2SO_4(aq)$$

Answer:

$$24.0 \text{ mL NaOH solution} \times \frac{1 \text{ L NaOH solution}}{1000 \text{ mL NaOH solution}}$$

$$\times \frac{0.245 \text{ mole NaOH}}{1 \text{ L NaOH solution}} \times \frac{1 \text{ mole } H_2SO_4}{2 \text{ moles NaOH}} = 0.00294 \text{ mole of } H_2SO_4$$

$$\text{Molarity (M)} = \frac{0.00294 \text{ mole } H_2SO_4}{0.0150 \text{ L } H_2SO_4 \text{ solution}} = 0.196 \text{ M } H_2SO_4 \text{ solution}$$

Calculating the pH of a Buffer (11.9)

- A buffer solution maintains pH by neutralizing small amounts of added acid or base.
- Most buffer solutions consist of nearly equal concentrations of a weak acid and a salt containing its conjugate base such as acetic acid, $HC_2H_3O_2$, and its salt $NaC_2H_3O_2$.
- The $[H_3O^+]$ is calculated by solving the K_a expression for $[H_3O^+]$, then substituting the values of $[H_3O^+]$, $[HA]$, and K_a into the equation.

$$K_a = \frac{[H_3O^+][C_2H_3O_2^-]}{[HC_2H_3O_2]}$$

Solving for $[H_3O^+]$ gives:

$$[H_3O^+] = K_a \times \frac{[HC_2H_3O_2]}{[C_2H_3O_2^-]} \quad \begin{matrix} \longleftarrow \text{ Weak acid} \\ \longleftarrow \text{ Conjugate base} \end{matrix}$$

- The pH of the buffer is calculated from the $[H_3O^+]$.

$$pH = -\log[H_3O^+]$$

Example: What is the pH of a buffer prepared with 0.40 M $HC_2H_3O_2$ and 0.20 M $C_2H_3O_2^-$, if the K_a of acetic acid is 1.8×10^{-5}?

Answer: $[H_3O^+] = K_a \times \frac{[HC_2H_3O_2]}{[C_2H_3O_2^-]} = 1.8 \times 10^{-5} \times \frac{[0.40]}{[0.20]}$

$$= 3.6 \times 10^{-5} \text{ M}$$

$$pH = -\log[3.6 \times 10^{-5}] = 4.44$$

UNDERSTANDING THE CONCEPTS

The chapter sections to review are shown in parentheses at the end of each question.

11.87 Determine if each of the following diagrams represents a strong acid or a weak acid. The acid has the formula HX. (11.3)

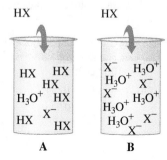

A   **B**

11.88 Adding a few drops of a strong acid to water will lower the pH appreciably. However, adding the same number of drops to a buffer does not appreciably alter the pH. Why? (11.9)

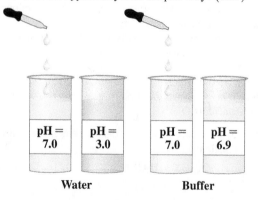

pH = 7.0   pH = 3.0   pH = 7.0   pH = 6.9

Water   **Buffer**

11.89 Identify each of the following as an acid or a base: (11.1)
    a. H_2SO_4 **b.** RbOH
    c. $Ca(OH)_2$ **d.** HI

11.90 Identify each of the following as an acid or a base: (11.1)
    a. $Sr(OH)_2$ **b.** H_2SO_3
    c. $HC_2H_3O_2$ **d.** CsOH

11.91 Complete the following table: (11.2)

Acid	Conjugate Base
H_2O	
	CN^-
HNO_2	
	$H_2PO_4^-$

11.92 Complete the following table: (11.2)

Base	Conjugate Acid
	HS^-
	H_3O^+
NH_3	
HCO_3^-	

℞ Clinical Applications

11.93 Sometimes, during stress or trauma, a person can start to hyperventilate. Then the person might breathe into a paper bag to avoid fainting. (11.9)
    a. What changes occur in the blood pH during hyperventilation?

b. How does breathing into a paper bag help return blood pH to normal?

Breathing into a paper bag can help a person who is hyperventilating.

11.94 In the blood plasma, pH is maintained by the carbonic acid–bicarbonate buffer system. (11.9)
    a. How is pH maintained when acid is added to the buffer system?
    b. How is pH maintained when base is added to the buffer system?

11.95 State whether each of the following solutions is acidic, basic, or neutral: (11.5)
    a. sweat, pH 5.2   **b.** tears, pH 7.5
    c. bile, pH 8.1   **d.** stomach acid, pH 2.5

11.96 State whether each of the following solutions is acidic, basic, or neutral: (11.5)
    a. saliva, pH 6.8   **b.** urine, pH 5.9
    c. pancreatic juice, pH 8.0   **d.** blood, pH 7.45

ADDITIONAL QUESTIONS AND PROBLEMS

11.97 Identify each of the following as an acid, base, or salt, and give its name: (11.1)
    a. $HBrO_2$ **b.** CsOH
    c. $Mg(NO_3)_2$ **d.** $HClO_4$

11.98 Identify each of the following as an acid, base, or salt, and give its name: (11.1)
    a. HNO_2 **b.** $MgBr_2$
    c. NH_3 **d.** Li_2SO_3

11.99 Complete the following table: (11.2)

Acid	Conjugate Base
HI	
	Cl^-
NH_4^+	
	HS^-

11.100 Complete the following table: (11.2)

Base	Conjugate Acid
F^-	
	$HC_2H_3O_2$
	HSO_3^-
ClO^-	

11.101 Using Table 11.3, identify the stronger acid in each of the following pairs: (11.3)
    a. HF or HCN   **b.** H_3O^+ or H_2S
    c. HNO_2 or $HC_2H_3O_2$ **d.** H_2O or HCO_3^-

11.102 Using Table 11.3, identify the stronger base in each of the following pairs: (11.3)
    a. H_2O or Cl^- **b.** OH^- or NH_3
    c. SO_4^{2-} or NO_2^- **d.** CO_3^{2-} or H_2O

11.103 Determine the pH for each of the following solutions: (11.6)
    a. $[H_3O^+] = 2.0 \times 10^{-8}$ M
    b. $[H_3O^+] = 5.0 \times 10^{-2}$ M
    c. $[OH^-] = 3.5 \times 10^{-4}$ M
    d. $[OH^-] = 0.0054$ M

11.104 Determine the pH for each of the following solutions: (11.6)
    a. $[OH^-] = 1.0 \times 10^{-7}$ M
    b. $[H_3O^+] = 4.2 \times 10^{-3}$ M
    c. $[H_3O^+] = 0.0001$ M
    d. $[OH^-] = 8.5 \times 10^{-9}$ M

11.105 Are the solutions in problem 11.103 acidic, basic, or neutral? (11.6)

11.106 Are the solutions in problem 11.104 acidic, basic, or neutral? (11.6)

11.107 Calculate the $[H_3O^+]$ and $[OH^-]$ for a solution with each of the following pH values: (11.6)
    a. 3.00   **b.** 6.2
    c. 8.85   **d.** 11.00

11.108 Calculate the $[H_3O^+]$ and $[OH^-]$ for a solution with each of the following pH values: (11.6)
    a. 10.00   **b.** 5.0
    c. 6.54   **d.** 1.82

11.109 Solution A has a pH of 4.5, and solution B has a pH of 6.7. (11.6)
   a. Which solution is more acidic?
   b. What is the $[H_3O^+]$ in each?
   c. What is the $[OH^-]$ in each?

11.110 Solution X has a pH of 9.5, and solution Y has a pH of 7.5. (11.6)
   a. Which solution is more acidic?
   b. What is the $[H_3O^+]$ in each?
   c. What is the $[OH^-]$ in each?

11.111 What is the $[OH^-]$ in a solution that contains 0.225 g of NaOH in 0.250 L of solution? (11.7)

11.112 What is the $[H_3O^+]$ in a solution that contains 1.54 g of HNO_3 in 0.500 L of solution? (11.7)

11.113 What is the pH of a solution prepared by dissolving 2.5 g of HCl in water to make 425 mL of solution? (11.6)

11.114 What is the pH of a solution prepared by dissolving 1.0 g of $Ca(OH)_2$ in water to make 875 mL of solution? (11.6)

CHALLENGE QUESTIONS

The following groups of questions are related to the topics in this chapter. However, they do not all follow the chapter order, and they require you to combine concepts and skills from several sections. These questions will help you increase your critical thinking skills and prepare for your next exam.

11.115 For each of the following: (11.2, 11.3)
   1. H_2S **2.** H_3PO_4
   a. Write the formula for the conjugate base.
   b. Write the K_a expression.
   c. Which is the weaker acid?

11.116 For each of the following: (11.2, 11.3)
   1. HCO_3^- **2.** $HC_2H_3O_2$
   a. Write the formula for the conjugate base.
   b. Write the K_a expression.
   c. Which is the stronger acid?

11.117 Using Table 11.3, identify the conjugate acid–base pairs in each of the following equations and whether the equilibrium mixture contains mostly products or mostly reactants: (11.2, 11.3)
   a. $NH_3(aq) + HNO_3(aq) \rightleftharpoons NH_4^+(aq) + NO_3^-(aq)$
   b. $H_2O(l) + HBr(aq) \rightleftharpoons H_3O^+(aq) + Br^-(aq)$

11.118 Using Table 11.3, identify the conjugate acid–base pairs in each of the following equations and whether the equilibrium mixture contains mostly products or mostly reactants: (11.2, 11.3)
   a. $HNO_2(aq) + HS^-(aq) \rightleftharpoons H_2S(g) + NO_2^-(aq)$
   b. $Cl^-(aq) + H_2O(l) \rightleftharpoons OH^-(aq) + HCl(aq)$

11.119 Complete and balance each of the following: (11.7)
   a. $ZnCO_3(s) + H_2SO_4(aq) \longrightarrow$
   b. $Al(s) + HNO_3(aq) \longrightarrow$

11.120 Complete and balance each of the following: (11.7)
   a. $H_3PO_4(aq) + Ca(OH)_2(s) \longrightarrow$
   b. $KHCO_3(s) + HNO_3(aq) \longrightarrow$

11.121 Determine each of the following for a 0.050 M KOH solution: (11.6, 11.7, 11.8)
   a. $[H_3O^+]$
   b. pH
   c. the balanced equation for the reaction with H_2SO_4
   d. milliliters of KOH solution required to neutralize 40.0 mL of a 0.035 M H_2SO_4 solution

11.122 Determine each of the following for a 0.10 M HBr solution: (11.6, 11.7, 11.8)
   a. $[H_3O^+]$
   b. pH
   c. the balanced equation for the reaction with LiOH
   d. milliliters of HBr solution required to neutralize 36.0 mL of a 0.25 M LiOH solution

11.123 One of the most acidic lakes in the United States is Little Echo Pond in the Adirondacks in New York. Recently, this lake had a pH of 4.2, well below the recommended pH of 6.5. (11.6, 11.8)
   a. What are the $[H_3O^+]$ and $[OH^-]$ of Little Echo Pond?
   b. What are the $[H_3O^+]$ and $[OH^-]$ of a lake that has a pH of 6.5?
   c. One way to raise the pH of an acidic lake (and restore aquatic life) is to add limestone ($CaCO_3$). How many grams of $CaCO_3$ are needed to neutralize 1.0 kL of the acidic water from the lake if the acid is sulfuric acid?

$$H_2SO_4(aq) + CaCO_3(s) \longrightarrow CO_2(g) + H_2O(l) + CaSO_4(aq)$$

A helicopter drops calcium carbonate on an acidic lake to increase its pH.

℞ Clinical Applications

11.124 The daily output of stomach acid (gastric juice) is 1000 mL to 2000 mL. Prior to a meal, stomach acid (HCl) typically has a pH of 1.42. (11.6, 11.7, 11.8)
   a. What is the $[H_3O^+]$ of the stomach acid?
   b. One chewable tablet of the antacid Maalox contains 600. mg of $CaCO_3$. Write the neutralization equation, and calculate the milliliters of stomach acid neutralized by two tablets of Maalox.
   c. The antacid milk of magnesia contains 400. mg of $Mg(OH)_2$ per teaspoon. Write the neutralization equation, and calculate the number of milliliters of stomach acid that are neutralized by 1 tablespoon of milk of magnesia (1 tablespoon = 3 teaspoons).

11.125 Calculate the volume, in milliliters, of a 0.150 M NaOH solution that will completely neutralize each of the following: (11.8)
   a. 25.0 mL of a 0.288 M HCl solution
   b. 10.0 mL of a 0.560 M H_2SO_4 solution

11.126 Calculate the volume, in milliliters, of a 0.215 M NaOH solution that will completely neutralize each of the following: (11.8)
  a. 3.80 mL of a 1.25 M HNO_3 solution
  b. 8.50 mL of a 0.825 M H_3PO_4 solution

11.127 A solution of 0.205 M NaOH is used to titrate 20.0 mL of a H_2SO_4 solution. If 45.6 mL of the NaOH solution is required to reach the endpoint, what is the molarity of the H_2SO_4 solution? (11.8)

$$H_2SO_4(aq) + 2NaOH(aq) \longrightarrow 2H_2O(l) + Na_2SO_4(aq)$$

11.128 A 10.0-mL sample of vinegar, which is an aqueous solution of acetic acid, $HC_2H_3O_2$, requires 16.5 mL of a 0.500 M NaOH solution to reach the endpoint in a titration. What is the molarity of the acetic acid solution? (11.8)

$$HC_2H_3O_2(aq) + NaOH(aq) \longrightarrow H_2O(l) + NaC_2H_3O_2(aq)$$

11.129 A buffer solution is made by dissolving H_3PO_4 and NaH_2PO_4 in water. (11.9)
  a. Write an equation that shows how this buffer neutralizes added acid.
  b. Write an equation that shows how this buffer neutralizes added base.
  c. Calculate the pH of this buffer if it contains 0.50 M H_3PO_4 and 0.20 M $H_2PO_4^-$. The K_a for H_3PO_4 is 7.5×10^{-3}.

11.130 A buffer solution is made by dissolving $HC_2H_3O_2$ and $NaC_2H_3O_2$ in water. (11.9)
  a. Write an equation that shows how this buffer neutralizes added acid.
  b. Write an equation that shows how this buffer neutralizes added base.
  c. Calculate the pH of this buffer if it contains 0.20 M $HC_2H_3O_2$ and 0.40 M $C_2H_3O_2^-$. The K_a for $HC_2H_3O_2$ is 1.8×10^{-5}.

ANSWERS

Answers to Selected Questions and Problems

11.1 a. acid **b.** acid
  c. acid **d.** base
  e. both

11.3 a. hydrochloric acid **b.** calcium hydroxide
  c. perchloric acid **d.** nitric acid
  e. sulfurous acid **f.** bromous acid

11.5 a. RbOH **b.** HF
  c. H_3PO_4 **d.** LiOH
  e. NH_4OH **f.** HIO_4

11.7 a. HI is the acid (hydrogen ion donor), and H_2O is the base (hydrogen ion acceptor).
  b. H_2O is the acid (hydrogen ion donor), and F^- is the base (hydrogen ion acceptor).
  c. H_2S is the acid (hydrogen ion donor), and $CH_3-CH_2-NH_2$ is the base (hydrogen ion acceptor).

11.9 a. F^- **b.** OH^-
  c. HPO_3^{2-} **d.** SO_4^{2-}
  e. ClO_2^-

11.11 a. HCO_3^- **b.** H_3O^+
  c. H_3PO_4 **d.** HBr
  e. $HClO_4$

11.13 a. The conjugate acid–base pairs are H_2CO_3/HCO_3^- and H_3O^+/H_2O.
  b. The conjugate acid–base pairs are NH_4^+/NH_3 and H_3O^+/H_2O.
  c. The conjugate acid–base pairs are HCN/CN^- and HNO_2/NO_2^-.
  d. The conjugate acid–base pairs are HF/F^- and $HCHO_2/CHO_2^-$.

11.15 $NH_4^+(aq) + H_2O(l) \rightleftharpoons NH_3(aq) + H_3O^+(aq)$

11.17 A strong acid is a good hydrogen ion donor, whereas its conjugate base is a poor hydrogen ion acceptor.

11.19 a. HBr **b.** HSO_4^- **c.** H_2CO_3
11.21 a. HSO_4^- **b.** HF **c.** HCO_3^-
11.23 a. reactants **b.** reactants **c.** products
11.25 $NH_4^+(aq) + SO_4^{2-}(aq) \rightleftharpoons NH_3(aq) + HSO_4^-(aq)$

  The equilibrium mixture contains mostly reactants because NH_4^+ is a weaker acid than HSO_4^-, and SO_4^{2-} is a weaker base than NH_3.

11.27 a. true **b.** false **c.** false
  d. true **e.** false

11.29 a. H_2SO_3 **b.** HSO_3^-
  c. H_2SO_3 **d.** HS^-
  e. H_2SO_3

11.31 $H_3PO_4(aq) + H_2O(l) \rightleftharpoons H_3O^+(aq) + H_2PO_4^-(aq)$

$$K_a = \frac{[H_3O^+][H_2PO_4^-]}{[H_3PO_4]}$$

11.33 In pure water, $[H_3O^+] = [OH^-]$ because one of each is produced every time a hydrogen ion is transferred from one water molecule to another.

11.35 In an acidic solution, the $[H_3O^+]$ is greater than the $[OH^-]$.

11.37 a. acidic **b.** basic
  c. basic **d.** acidic

11.39 a. 1.0×10^{-5} M **b.** 1.0×10^{-8} M
  c. 5.0×10^{-10} M **d.** 2.5×10^{-2} M

11.41 a. 2.5×10^{-13} M **b.** 2.0×10^{-9} M
  c. 5.0×10^{-11} M **d.** 1.3×10^{-6} M

11.43 In a neutral solution, the $[H_3O^+]$ is 1.0×10^{-7} M and the pH is 7.00, which is the negative value of the power of 10.

11.45 a. basic **b.** acidic
  c. acidic **d.** acidic
  e. basic

11.47 An increase or decrease of one pH unit changes the $[H_3O^+]$ by a factor of 10. Thus a pH of 3 is 10 times more acidic than a pH of 4.

11.49 a. 4.0 **b.** 8.5
  c. 9.0 **d.** 3.40
  e. 7.17 **f.** 10.92

11.51

Food	$[H_3O^+]$	$[OH^-]$	pH	Acidic, Basic, or Neutral?
Rye bread	1.6×10^{-9} M	6.3×10^{-6} M	8.80	Basic
Tomatoes	2.3×10^{-5} M	4.3×10^{-10} M	4.64	Acidic
Peas	6.2×10^{-7} M	1.6×10^{-8} M	6.21	Acidic

11.53 1.2×10^{-7} M

11.55 a. $ZnCO_3(s) + 2HBr(aq) \longrightarrow$
$$CO_2(g) + H_2O(l) + ZnBr_2(aq)$$
b. $Zn(s) + 2HCl(aq) \longrightarrow H_2(g) + ZnCl_2(aq)$
c. $HCl(aq) + NaHCO_3(s) \longrightarrow$
$$CO_2(g) + H_2O(l) + NaCl(aq)$$
d. $H_2SO_4(aq) + Mg(OH)_2(s) \longrightarrow 2H_2O(l) + MgSO_4(aq)$

11.57 a. $2HCl(aq) + Mg(OH)_2(s) \longrightarrow 2H_2O(l) + MgCl_2(aq)$
b. $H_3PO_4(aq) + 3LiOH(aq) \longrightarrow 3H_2O(l) + Li_3PO_4(aq)$

11.59 a. $H_2SO_4(aq) + 2NaOH(aq) \longrightarrow 2H_2O(l) + Na_2SO_4(aq)$
b. $3HCl(aq) + Fe(OH)_3(s) \longrightarrow 3H_2O(l) + FeCl_3(aq)$
c. $H_2CO_3(aq) + Mg(OH)_2(s) \longrightarrow 2H_2O(l) + MgCO_3(s)$

11.61 0.829 M HCl solution

11.63 0.124 M H_2SO_4 solution

11.65 16.5 mL

11.67 b and **c** are buffer systems. **b** contains the weak acid H_2CO_3 and its salt $NaHCO_3$. **c** contains HF, a weak acid, and its salt KF.

11.69 a. 3
b. 1 and 2
c. 3
d. 1

11.71 pH = 3.35

11.73 The pH of the 0.10 M HF/0.10 M NaF buffer is 3.46.
The pH of the 0.060 M HF/0.120 M NaF buffer is 3.76.

11.75 If you breathe fast, CO_2 is expelled and the equilibrium shifts to lower H_3O^+, which raises the pH.

11.77 If large amounts of HCO_3^- are lost, equilibrium shifts to higher H_3O^+, which lowers the pH.

11.79 pH = 3.70

11.81 2.5×10^{-4} M

11.83 $CaCO_3(s) + 2HCl(aq) \longrightarrow CO_2(g) + H_2O(l) + CaCl_2(aq)$

11.85 0.200 g of $CaCO_3$

11.87 a. This diagram represents a weak acid; only a few HX molecules separate into H_3O^+ and X^- ions.
b. This diagram represents a strong acid; all the HX molecules separate into H_3O^+ and X^- ions.

11.89 a. acid
b. base
c. base
d. acid

11.91

Acid	Conjugate Base
H_2O	OH^-
HCN	CN^-
HNO_2	NO_2^-
H_3PO_4	$H_2PO_4^-$

11.93 a. During hyperventilation, a person will lose CO_2 and the blood pH will rise.
b. Breathing into a paper bag will increase the CO_2 concentration and lower the blood pH.

11.95 a. acidic
b. basic
c. basic
d. acidic

11.97 a. acid, bromous acid
b. base, cesium hydroxide
c. salt, magnesium nitrate
d. acid, perchloric acid

11.99

Acid	Conjugate Base
HI	I^-
HCl	Cl^-
NH_4^+	NH_3
H_2S	HS^-

11.101 a. HF
b. H_3O^+
c. HNO_2
d. HCO_3^-

11.103 a. pH = 7.70
b. pH = 1.30
c. pH = 10.54
d. pH = 11.73

11.105 a. basic
b. acidic
c. basic
d. basic

11.107 a. $[H_3O^+] = 1.0 \times 10^{-3}$ M; $[OH^-] = 1.0 \times 10^{-11}$ M
b. $[H_3O^+] = 6 \times 10^{-7}$ M; $[OH^-] = 2 \times 10^{-8}$ M
c. $[H_3O^+] = 1.4 \times 10^{-9}$ M; $[OH^-] = 7.1 \times 10^{-6}$ M
d. $[H_3O^+] = 1.0 \times 10^{-11}$ M; $[OH^-] = 1.0 \times 10^{-3}$ M

11.109 a. Solution A
b. Solution A $[H_3O^+] = 3 \times 10^{-5}$ M;
Solution B $[H_3O^+] = 2 \times 10^{-7}$ M
c. Solution A $[OH^-] = 3 \times 10^{-10}$ M;
Solution B $[OH^-] = 5 \times 10^{-8}$ M

11.111 $[OH^-] = 0.0225$ M

11.113 pH = 0.80

11.115 a. 1. HS^-
2. $H_2PO_4^-$
b. 1. $\dfrac{[H_3O^+][HS^-]}{[H_2S]}$
2. $\dfrac{[H_3O^+][H_2PO_4^-]}{[H_3PO_4]}$
c. H_2S

11.117 a. HNO_3/NO_3^- and NH_4^+/NH_3; equilibrium mixture contains mostly products
b. HBr/Br^- and H_3O^+/H_2O; equilibrium mixture contains mostly products

11.119 a. $ZnCO_3(s) + H_2SO_4(aq) \longrightarrow$
$$CO_2(g) + H_2O(l) + ZnSO_4(aq)$$
b. $2Al(s) + 6HNO_3(aq) \longrightarrow 3H_2(g) + 2Al(NO_3)_3(aq)$

11.121 a. $[H_3O^+] = 2.0 \times 10^{-13}$ M
b. pH = 12.70
c. $2KOH(aq) + H_2SO_4(aq) \longrightarrow 2H_2O(l) + K_2SO_4(aq)$
d. 56 mL of the KOH solution

11.123 a. $[H_3O^+] = 6 \times 10^{-5}$ M; $[OH^-] = 2 \times 10^{-10}$ M
b. $[H_3O^+] = 3 \times 10^{-7}$ M; $[OH^-] = 3 \times 10^{-8}$ M
c. 3 g of $CaCO_3$

11.125 a. 48.0 mL of NaOH solution
b. 74.7 mL of NaOH solution

11.127 0.234 M H_2SO_4 solution

11.129 a. acid:
$H_2PO_4^-(aq) + H_3O^+(aq) \longrightarrow H_3PO_4(aq) + H_2O(l)$
b. base:
$H_3PO_4(aq) + OH^-(aq) \longrightarrow H_2PO_4^-(aq) + H_2O(l)$
c. pH = 1.72

CI.19 Consider the following reaction at equilibrium:

$$2H_2(g) + S_2(g) \rightleftharpoons 2H_2S(g) + heat$$

In a 10.0-L container, an equilibrium mixture contains 2.02 g of H_2, 10.3 g of S_2, and 68.2 g of H_2S. (7.5, 10.2, 10.3, 10.4, 10.5)

a. What is the numerical value of K_c for this equilibrium mixture?

b. If more H_2 is added to the equilibrium mixture, how will the equilibrium shift?

c. How will the equilibrium shift if the mixture is placed in a 5.00-L container with no change in temperature?

d. If a 5.00-L container has an equilibrium mixture of 0.300 mole of H_2 and 2.50 moles of H_2S, what is the $[S_2]$ if temperature remains constant?

CI.20 In wine-making, glucose ($C_6H_{12}O_6$) from grapes undergoes fermentation in the absence of oxygen to produce ethanol, C_2H_5OH, and carbon dioxide. A bottle of vintage port wine has a volume of 750 mL and contains 135 mL of ethanol which has a density of 0.789 g/mL. In 1.5 lb of grapes, there are 26 g of glucose. (2.7, 7.1, 7.5, 9.4)

When the glucose in grapes is fermented, ethanol is produced.

Port is a type of fortified wine that is produced in Portugal.

a. Calculate the volume percent (v/v) of ethanol in the port wine.

b. What is the molarity (M) of ethanol in the port wine?

c. Write the balanced chemical equation for the fermentation reaction of glucose in grapes.

d. How many grams of glucose from grapes are required to produce one bottle of port wine?

e. How many bottles of port wine can be produced from 1.0 ton of grapes (1 ton = 2000 lb)?

CI.21 A metal M with a mass of 0.420 g completely reacts with 34.8 mL of a 0.520 M HCl solution to form H_2 gas and aqueous MCl_3. (7.1, 7.5, 8.7, 11.7)

a. Write a balanced chemical equation for the reaction of the metal M(s) and HCl(aq).

b. What volume, in milliliters, of H_2 at 720. mmHg and 24 °C is produced?

c. How many moles of metal M reacted?

d. Using your results from part c, determine the molar mass and name of metal M.

e. Write the balanced chemical equation for the reaction.

When a metal reacts with a strong acid, bubbles of hydrogen gas form.

CI.22 A solution of HCl is prepared by diluting 15.0 mL of a 12.0 M HCl solution with enough water to make 750. mL of HCl solution. (9.4, 11.6, 11.7, 11.8)

a. What is the molarity of the HCl solution?

b. What is the $[H_3O^+]$ and pH of the HCl solution?

c. Write the balanced chemical equation for the reaction of HCl and $MgCO_3$.

d. How many milliliters of the diluted HCl solution is required to completely react with 350. mg of $MgCO_3$?

CI.23 A KOH solution is prepared by dissolving 8.57 g of KOH in enough water to make 850. mL of KOH solution. (9.4, 11.6, 11.7, 11.8)

a. What is the molarity of the KOH solution?

b. What is the $[H_3O^+]$ and pH of the KOH solution?

c. Write the balanced chemical equation for the neutralization of KOH by H_2SO_4.

d. How many milliliters of a 0.250 M H_2SO_4 solution is required to neutralize 10.0 mL of the KOH solution?

℞ Clinical Applications

CI.24 In a teaspoon (5.0 mL) of a liquid antacid, there are 400. mg of $Mg(OH)_2$ and 400. mg of $Al(OH)_3$. A 0.080 M HCl solution, which is similar to stomach acid, is used to neutralize 5.0 mL of the liquid antacid. (9.4, 11.6, 11.7, 11.8)

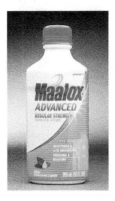

An antacid neutralizes stomach acid and raises the pH.

a. What is the pH of the HCl solution?

b. Write the balanced chemical equation for the neutralization of HCl and $Mg(OH)_2$.

c. Write the balanced chemical equation for the neutralization of HCl and $Al(OH)_3$.

d. How many milliliters of the HCl solution are needed to neutralize the $Mg(OH)_2$?

e. How many milliliters of the HCl solution are needed to neutralize the $Al(OH)_3$?

CI.25 A volume of 200.0 mL of a carbonic acid buffer for blood plasma is prepared that contains 0.403 g of $NaHCO_3$ and 0.0149 g of H_2CO_3. At body temperature (37 °C), the K_a of carbonic acid is 7.9×10^{-7}. (9.4, 11.6, 11.8, 11.9)

$$H_2CO_3(aq) + H_2O(l) \rightleftharpoons HCO_3^-(aq) + H_3O^+(aq)$$

a. What is the $[H_2CO_3]$?

b. What is the $[HCO_3^-]$?

c. What is the $[H_3O^+]$?

d. What is the pH of the buffer?

e. Write a balanced chemical equation that shows how this buffer neutralizes added acid.

f. Write a balanced chemical equation that shows how this buffer neutralizes added base.

CI.26 In the kidneys, the ammonia buffer system buffers high H_3O^+. Ammonia, which is produced in renal tubules from amino acids, combines with H^+ to be excreted as NH_4Cl. At body temperature (37 °C), the $K_a = 5.6 \times 10^{-10}$. A buffer solution with a volume of 125 mL contains 3.34 g of NH_4Cl and 0.0151 g of NH_3. (9.4, 11.6, 11.8, 11.9)

$$NH_4^+(aq) + H_2O(l) \rightleftharpoons NH_3(aq) + H_3O^+(aq)$$

a. What is the $[NH_4^+]$?
b. What is the $[NH_3]$?
c. What is the $[H_3O^+]$?
d. What is the pH of the buffer?
e. Write a balanced chemical equation that shows how this buffer neutralizes added acid.
f. Write a balanced chemical equation that shows how this buffer neutralizes added base.

ANSWERS

CI.19 a. $K_c = 248$
  b. If H_2 is added, the equilibrium will shift in the direction of the products.
  c. If the volume decreases, the equilibrium will shift in the direction of the products.
  d. $[S_2] = 0.280\ M$

CI.21 a. $2M(s) + 6HCl(aq) \longrightarrow 3H_2(g) + 2MCl_3(aq)$
  b. 233 mL of H_2
  c. 6.03×10^{-3} mole of M
  d. 69.7 g/mole; gallium
  e. $2Ga(s) + 6HCl(aq) \longrightarrow 3H_2(g) + 2GaCl_3(aq)$

CI.23 a. 0.180 M
  b. $[H_3O^+] = 5.56 \times 10^{-14}\ M$; pH = 13.255
  c. $2KOH(aq) + H_2SO_4(aq) \longrightarrow 2H_2O(l) + K_2SO_4(aq)$
  d. 3.60 mL

CI.25 a. 0.00120 M
  b. 0.0240 M
  c. $4.0 \times 10^{-8}\ M$
  d. 7.40
  e. $HCO_3^-(aq) + H_3O^+(aq) \longrightarrow H_2CO_3(aq) + H_2O(l)$
  f. $H_2CO_3(aq) + OH^-(aq) \longrightarrow HCO_3^-(aq) + H_2O(l)$

12

Introduction to Organic Chemistry: Hydrocarbons

AT 4:35 A.M., A RESCUE CREW RESPONDED TO A

call about a house fire. At the scene, Jack, a firefighter/emergency medical technician (EMT) found Diane, a 62-year old woman, lying in the front yard of her house. In his assessment, Jack, reported that Diane had second- and third-degree burns over 40% of her body as well as a broken leg. He placed an oxygen re-breather mask on Diane to provide a high concentration of oxygen. Another firefighter/EMT, Nancy, began dressing the burns with sterile water and cling film, a first aid material made of polyvinyl chloride, which does not stick to the skin and is protective. Jack and his crew transported Diane to the burn center for further treatment.

At the scene of the fire, arson investigators used trained dogs to find traces of accelerants and fuel. Gasoline, which is often found at arson scenes, is a mixture of organic molecules called alkanes. Alkanes or hydrocarbons are chains of carbon and hydrogen atoms. The alkanes present in gasoline consist of a mixture of 5 to 8 carbon atoms in a chain. Alkanes are extremely combustible; they react with oxygen to form carbon dioxide, water, and large amounts of heat. Because alkanes undergo combustion reactions, they can be used to start arson fires.

CAREER Firefighter/Emergency Medical Technician

Firefighters/emergency medical technicians are first responders to fires, accidents, and other emergency situations. They are required to have an emergency medical technician certification in order to be able to treat seriously injured people. By combining the skills of a firefighter and an emergency medical technician, they increase the survival rates of the injured. The physical demands of firefighters are extremely high as they fight, extinguish, and prevent fires while wearing heavy protective clothing and gear. They also train for and participate in firefighting drills, and maintain fire equipment so that it is always working and ready.

Firefighters must also be knowledgeable about fire codes, arson, and the handling and disposal of hazardous materials. Since firefighters also provide emergency care for sick and injured people, they need to be aware of emergency medical and rescue procedures, as well as the proper methods for controlling the spread of infectious disease.

443

At the beginning of the nineteenth century, scientists classified chemical compounds as inorganic and organic. An inorganic compound was a substance that was composed of minerals, and an organic compound was a substance that came from an organism, thus the use of the word *organic*. Early scientists thought that some type of "vital force," which could be found only in living cells, was required to synthesize an organic compound. This idea was shown to be incorrect in 1828 when the German chemist Friedrich Wöhler synthesized urea, a product of protein metabolism, by heating an inorganic compound, ammonium cyanate.

$$NH_4CNO \xrightarrow{\text{Heat}} H_2N-\overset{\overset{\textstyle O}{\|}}{C}-NH_2$$

Ammonium cyanate (inorganic)   Urea (organic)

The simplest organic compounds are the hydrocarbons that contain only the elements carbon and hydrogen. All the carbon-to-carbon bonds in a hydrocarbon known as an alkane are single C—C bonds. Some common alkanes include methane (CH_4), propane (C_3H_8), and butane (C_4H_{10}).

Alkenes are hydrocarbons that contain one or more carbon-to-carbon double bonds (C=C). Because double bonds are very reactive, they easily add hydrogen atoms (hydrogenation) or water (hydration) to the carbon atoms in the double bond. One important compound containing a double bond is ethene (ethylene), which is used to ripen fruit when ready for market. A common compound with a triple bond is ethyne (acetylene), which burns at high temperatures and is used in welding metals.

Learning about the structures and reactions of organic molecules will provide you with a foundation for understanding the more complex molecules of biochemistry.

CHAPTER READINESS*

⚛ CORE CHEMISTRY SKILLS
- Drawing Lewis Structures (6.6)
- Predicting Shape (6.8)

- Balancing a Chemical Equation (7.1)

---

*These Core Chemistry Skills from previous chapters are listed here for your review as you proceed to the new material in this chapter.

LEARNING GOAL

Identify properties characteristic of organic or inorganic compounds.

12.1 Organic Compounds

Organic chemistry is the study of carbon compounds. The element carbon has a special role because many carbon atoms can bond together to give a vast array of molecular compounds. **Organic compounds** always contain carbon and hydrogen, and sometimes other nonmetals such as oxygen, sulfur, nitrogen, phosphorus, or a halogen. We find organic compounds in many common products we use every day, such as gasoline, medicines, shampoos, plastics, and perfumes. The food we eat is composed of organic compounds such as carbohydrates, fats, and proteins that supply us with fuel for energy and the carbon atoms needed to build and repair the cells of our bodies.

We organize organic compounds by their *functional groups*, which are groups of atoms bonded in a specific way. Compounds that contain the same functional group have similar physical and chemical properties. The identification of functional groups allows us to classify organic compounds according to their structure, to name compounds within each family, and to predict their chemical reactions.

The formulas of organic compounds are written with carbon first, followed by hydrogen, and then any other elements. Organic compounds typically have low melting and boiling points, are not soluble in water, and are less dense than water. For example, vegetable oil, which is a mixture of organic compounds, does not dissolve in water but floats on top. Many organic compounds undergo combustion and burn vigorously in air. By contrast, many inorganic compounds have high melting and boiling points. Inorganic compounds that are ionic are usually soluble in water, and most do not burn in air. Table 12.1 contrasts some of the properties associated with organic and inorganic compounds, such as propane, C_3H_8, and sodium chloride, NaCl (see Figure 12.1).

Vegetable oil, a mixture of organic compounds, is not soluble in water.

TABLE 12.1 Some Properties of Organic and Inorganic Compounds

Property	Organic	Example: C_3H_8	Inorganic	Example: NaCl
Elements Present	C and H, sometimes O, S, N, P, or Cl (F, Br, I)	C and H	Most metals and nonmetals	Na and Cl
Particles	Molecules	C_3H_8	Mostly ions	Na^+ and Cl^-
Bonding	Mostly covalent	Covalent	Many are ionic, some covalent	Ionic
Polarity of Bonds	Nonpolar, unless a strongly electronegative atom is present	Nonpolar	Most are ionic or polar covalent, a few are nonpolar covalent	Ionic
Melting Point	Usually low	$-188\ ^\circ C$	Usually high	$801\ ^\circ C$
Boiling Point	Usually low	$-42\ ^\circ C$	Usually high	$1413\ ^\circ C$
Flammability	High	Burns in air	Low	Does not burn
Solubility in Water	Not soluble, unless a polar group is present	No	Most are soluble, unless nonpolar	Yes

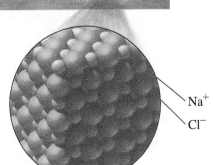

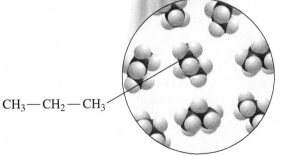

$CH_3 — CH_2 — CH_3$

Na^+

Cl^-

FIGURE 12.1 ▶ Propane, C_3H_8, is an organic compound, whereas sodium chloride, NaCl, is an inorganic compound.

Q Why is propane used as a fuel?

SAMPLE PROBLEM 12.1 **Properties of Organic Compounds**

Indicate whether the following properties are more typical of organic or inorganic compounds:

a. is not soluble in water
b. has a high melting point
c. burns in air

SOLUTION

a. Many organic compounds are not soluble in water.
b. Inorganic compounds are more likely to have high melting points.
c. Organic compounds are more likely to be flammable.

STUDY CHECK 12.1

What elements are always found in organic compounds?

ANSWER

C and H

Representations of Carbon Compounds

Hydrocarbons are organic compounds that consist of only carbon and hydrogen. In organic molecules, every carbon atom has four bonds. In the simplest hydrocarbon, methane (CH_4), the carbon atom forms an octet by sharing its four valence electrons with four hydrogen atoms.

The most accurate representation of methane is the three-dimensional *space-filling model* (**a**) in which spheres show the relative size and shape of all the atoms. Another type of three-dimensional representation is the *ball-and-stick model* (**b**), where the atoms are shown as balls and the bonds between them are shown as sticks. In the ball-and-stick model of methane, CH_4, the covalent bonds from the carbon atom to each hydrogen atom are directed to the corners of a tetrahedron with bond angles of 109°. In the *wedge–dash model* (**c**), the three-dimensional shape is represented by symbols of the atoms with lines for bonds in the plane of the page, wedges for bonds that project out from the page, and dashes for bonds that are behind the page.

However, the three-dimensional models are awkward to draw and view for more complex molecules. Therefore, it is more practical to use their corresponding two-dimensional formulas. The **expanded structural formula** (**d**) shows all of the atoms and the bonds connected to each atom. A **condensed structural formula** (**e**) shows the carbon atoms each grouped with the attached number of hydrogen atoms.

  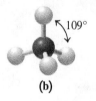

(a)	(b)	(c)	(d)	(e)

Three-dimensional and two-dimensional representations of methane: (**a**) space-filling model, (**b**) ball-and-stick model, (**c**) wedge–dash model, (**d**) expanded structural formula, and (**e**) condensed structural formula.

The hydrocarbon ethane with two carbon atoms and six hydrogen atoms can be represented by a similar set of three- and two-dimensional models and formulas in which each carbon atom is bonded to another carbon and three hydrogen atoms. As in methane, each carbon atom in ethane retains a tetrahedral shape. A hydrocarbon is referred to as a *saturated hydrocarbon* when all the bonds in the molecule are single bonds.

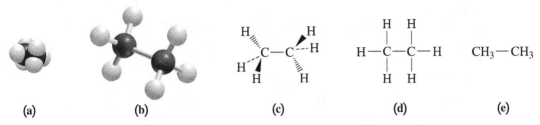

Three-dimensional and two-dimensional representations of ethane: **(a)** space-filling model, **(b)** ball-and-stick model, **(c)** wedge–dash model, **(d)** expanded structural formula, and **(e)** condensed structural formula.

QUESTIONS AND PROBLEMS

12.1 Organic Compounds

LEARNING GOAL Identify properties characteristic of organic or inorganic compounds.

12.1 Identify each of the following as a formula of an organic or inorganic compound:
   a. KCl   **b.** C_4H_{10}
   c. C_2H_6O **d.** H_2SO_4
   e. $CaCl_2$ **f.** C_3H_7Cl

12.2 Identify each of the following as a formula of an organic or inorganic compound:
   a. $C_6H_{12}O_6$ **b.** K_3PO_4
   c. I_2 **d.** C_2H_6S
   e. $C_{10}H_{22}$ **f.** C_4H_9Br

12.3 Identify each of the following properties as more typical of an organic or inorganic compound:
   a. is soluble in water
   b. has a low boiling point
   c. contains carbon and hydrogen
   d. contains ionic bonds

12.4 Identify each of the following properties as more typical of an organic or inorganic compound:
   a. contains Li and F   **b.** is a gas at room temperature
   c. contains covalent bonds **d.** produces ions in water

12.5 Match each of the following physical and chemical properties with ethane, C_2H_6, or sodium bromide, NaBr:
   a. boils at −89 °C   **b.** burns vigorously in air
   c. is a solid at 250 °C   **d.** dissolves in water

12.6 Match each of the following physical and chemical properties with cyclohexane, C_6H_{12}, or calcium nitrate, $Ca(NO_3)_2$:
   a. melts at 500 °C
   b. is insoluble in water
   c. does not burn in air
   d. is a liquid at room temperature

12.7 How are the hydrogen atoms of methane, CH_4, arranged in space?

12.8 In a propane molecule with three carbon atoms, what is the shape around each carbon atom?

Propane

12.2 Alkanes

More than 90% of the compounds in the world are organic compounds. The large number of carbon compounds is possible because the covalent bond between carbon atoms (C—C) is very strong, allowing carbon atoms to form long, stable chains.

The **alkanes** are a type of hydrocarbon in which the carbon atoms are connected only by single bonds. One of the most common uses of alkanes is as fuels. Methane, used in gas heaters and gas cooktops, is an alkane with one carbon atom. The alkanes ethane, propane, and butane contain two, three, and four carbon atoms, respectively, connected in a row or a *continuous chain*. As we can see, the names for alkanes end in *ane*. Such names are part of the **IUPAC** (International Union of Pure and Applied Chemistry) **system** used by chemists to name organic compounds. Alkanes with five or more carbon atoms in a chain are named using Greek prefixes: *pent* (5), *hex* (6), *hept* (7), *oct* (8), *non* (9), and *dec* (10) (see Table 12.2).

LEARNING GOAL

Write the IUPAC names and draw the condensed or line-angle structural formulas for alkanes and cycloalkanes.

TABLE 12.2 IUPAC Names of the First 10 Alkanes

Number of Carbon Atoms	Molecular Formula	Condensed Structural Formula	Line-Angle Structural Formula
1	CH_4	CH_4	
2	C_2H_6	$CH_3—CH_3$	—
3	C_3H_8	$CH_3—CH_2—CH_3$	
4	C_4H_{10}	$CH_3—CH_2—CH_2—CH_3$	
5	C_5H_{12}	$CH_3—CH_2—CH_2—CH_2—CH_3$	
6	C_6H_{14}	$CH_3—CH_2—CH_2—CH_2—CH_2—CH_3$	
7	C_7H_{16}	$CH_3—CH_2—CH_2—CH_2—CH_2—CH_2—CH_3$	
8	C_8H_{18}	$CH_3—CH_2—CH_2—CH_2—CH_2—CH_2—CH_2—CH_3$	
9	C_9H_{20}	$CH_3—CH_2—CH_2—CH_2—CH_2—CH_2—CH_2—CH_2—CH_3$	
10	$C_{10}H_{22}$	$CH_3—CH_2—CH_2—CH_2—CH_2—CH_2—CH_2—CH_2—CH_2—CH_3$	

CORE CHEMISTRY SKILL

Naming and Drawing Alkanes

Condensed and Line-Angle Structural Formulas

In a condensed structural formula, each carbon atom and its attached hydrogen atoms are written as a group. A subscript indicates the number of hydrogen atoms bonded to each carbon atom.

$$H—\underset{\underset{H}{|}}{\overset{\overset{H}{|}}{C}}— \ = \ CH_3— \qquad\qquad —\underset{\underset{H}{|}}{\overset{\overset{H}{|}}{C}}— \ = \ —CH_2—$$

Expanded   Condensed   Expanded   Condensed

When an organic molecule consists of a chain of three or more carbon atoms, the carbon atoms do not lie in a straight line. Rather, they are arranged in a zigzag pattern.

A simplified structure called the **line-angle structural formula** shows a zigzag line in which carbon atoms are represented as the ends of each line and as corners. For example, in the line-angle structural formula of pentane, each line in the zigzag drawing represents a single bond. The carbon atoms on the ends are bonded to three hydrogen atoms. However, the carbon atoms in the middle of the carbon chain are each bonded to two carbons and two hydrogen atoms as shown in Sample Problem 12.2.

Guide to Drawing Structural Formulas for Alkanes

STEP 1
Draw the carbon chain.

STEP 2
Draw the expanded structural formula by adding the hydrogen atoms using single bonds to each of the carbon atoms.

STEP 3
Draw the condensed structural formula by combining the H atoms with each C atom.

STEP 4
Draw the line-angle structural formula as a zigzag line in which the ends and corners represent C atoms.

▶ **SAMPLE PROBLEM 12.2** Drawing Expanded, Condensed, and Line-Angle Structural Formulas for an Alkane

Draw the expanded, condensed, and line-angle structural formulas for pentane.

SOLUTION

STEP 1 Draw the carbon chain. A molecule of pentane has five carbon atoms in a continuous chain.

$$C—C—C—C—C$$

STEP 2 Draw the expanded structural formula by adding the hydrogen atoms using single bonds to each of the carbon atoms.

$$H—\underset{\underset{H}{|}}{\overset{\overset{H}{|}}{C}}—\underset{\underset{H}{|}}{\overset{\overset{H}{|}}{C}}—\underset{\underset{H}{|}}{\overset{\overset{H}{|}}{C}}—\underset{\underset{H}{|}}{\overset{\overset{H}{|}}{C}}—\underset{\underset{H}{|}}{\overset{\overset{H}{|}}{C}}—H$$

STEP **3** Draw the condensed structural formula by combining the H atoms with each C atom.

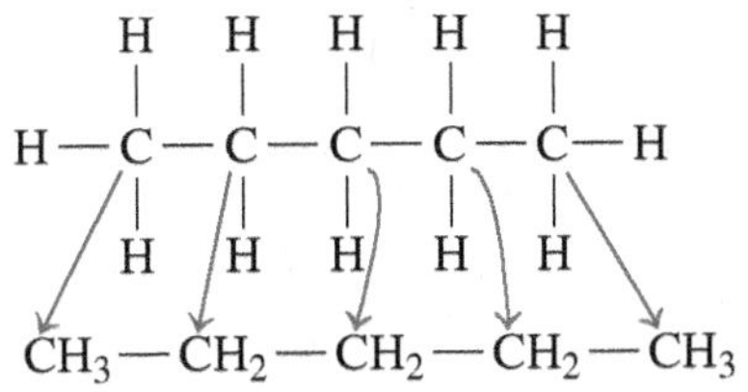

Expanded structural formula

Condensed structural formula

STEP **4** Draw the line-angle structural formula as a zigzag line in which the ends and corners represent C atoms.

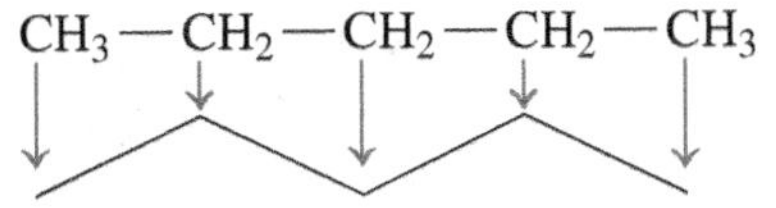

Condensed structural formula

Line-angle structural formula

STUDY CHECK 12.2

Draw the condensed structural formula and give the name for the following line-angle structural formula:

ANSWER

$CH_3-CH_2-CH_2-CH_2-CH_2-CH_2-CH_3$ heptane

Conformations of Alkanes

Because an alkane has only single carbon–carbon bonds, the groups attached to each C are not in fixed positions. They can rotate freely about the bond connecting the carbon atoms. This motion is analogous to the independent rotation of the wheels of a toy car. Thus, different arrangements, known as *conformations*, occur during the rotation about a single bond.

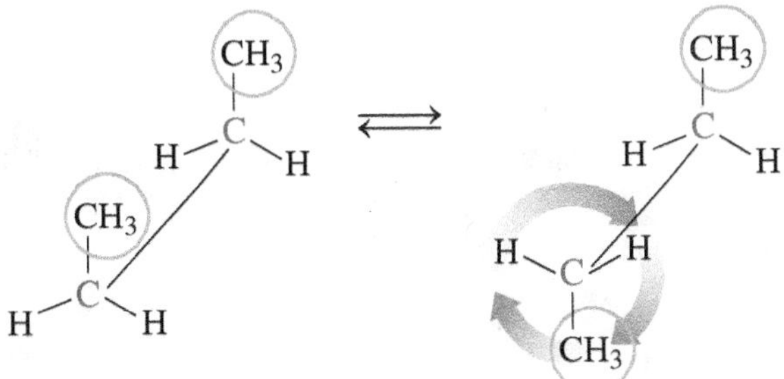

Suppose we could look at butane, C_4H_{10}, as it rotates. Sometimes the —CH_3 groups line up in front of each other, and at other times they are opposite each other. As the —CH_3 groups turn around the single bond, the carbon chain in the condensed structural formulas may appear at different angles. For example, butane can be drawn using a variety of two-dimensional condensed structural formulas as shown in Table 12.3. All these condensed structural formulas represent the same compound with four carbon atoms.

TABLE 12.3 Some Structural Formulas for Butane, C_4H_{10}

Expanded Structural Formula

Condensed Structural Formulas

Line-Angle Structural Formulas

Cycloalkanes

Hydrocarbons can also form cyclic or ring structures called **cycloalkanes**, which have two fewer hydrogen atoms than the corresponding alkanes. The simplest cycloalkane, cyclopropane (C_3H_6), has a ring of three carbon atoms bonded to six hydrogen atoms. Most often cycloalkanes are drawn using their line-angle structural formulas, which appear as simple geometric figures. As seen for alkanes, each corner of the line-angle structural formula for a cycloalkane represents a carbon atom.

The ball-and-stick models, condensed structural formulas, and line-angle structural formulas for several cycloalkanes are shown in Table 12.4. A cycloalkane is named by adding the prefix *cyclo* to the name of the alkane with the same number of carbon atoms.

TABLE 12.4 Formulas of Some Common Cycloalkanes

Name			
Cyclopropane	Cyclobutane	Cyclopentane	Cyclohexane

Ball-and-Stick Model

Condensed Structural Formula

Line-Angle Structural Formula

▶**SAMPLE PROBLEM 12.3** **Naming Alkanes and Cycloalkanes**

Give the IUPAC name for each of the following:

a.

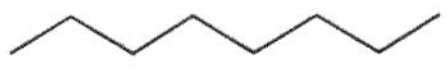

b.

SOLUTION

a. A chain with eight carbon atoms is octane.
b. The ring of six carbon atoms is named cyclohexane.

STUDY CHECK 12.3

What is the IUPAC name of the following compound?

ANSWER

cyclobutane

QUESTIONS AND PROBLEMS

12.2 Alkanes

LEARNING GOAL Write the IUPAC names and draw the condensed or line-angle structural formulas for alkanes and cycloalkanes.

12.9 Give the IUPAC name for each of the following alkanes and cycloalkanes:

a.

b. CH_3—CH_3

c.

d.

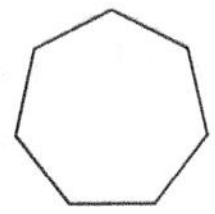

12.10 Give the IUPAC name for each of the following alkanes and cycloalkanes:

a. CH_4

b.

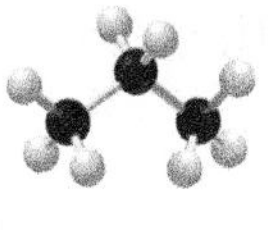

c.

d.

12.11 Draw the condensed structural formula for alkanes or the line-angle structural formula for cycloalkanes for each of the following:
  a. methane
  b. ethane
  c. pentane
  d. cyclopropane

12.12 Draw the condensed structural formula for alkanes or the line-angle structural formula for cycloalkanes for each of the following:
  a. propane
  b. hexane
  c. heptane
  d. cyclopentane

12.3 Alkanes with Substituents

When an alkane has four or more carbon atoms, the atoms can be arranged so that a side group called a *branch* or **substituent** is attached to a carbon chain. For example, there are different ball-and-stick models for two compounds that have the molecular formula C_4H_{10}. One model is shown as a chain of four carbon atoms. In the other model, a carbon atom is attached as a branch or substituent to a carbon in a chain of three atoms (see Figure 12.2). An alkane with at least one branch is called a *branched alkane*. When the two compounds have the same molecular formula but different arrangements of atoms, they are called **structural isomers**.

LEARNING GOAL

Write the IUPAC names for alkanes with substituents and draw their condensed and line-angle structural formulas.

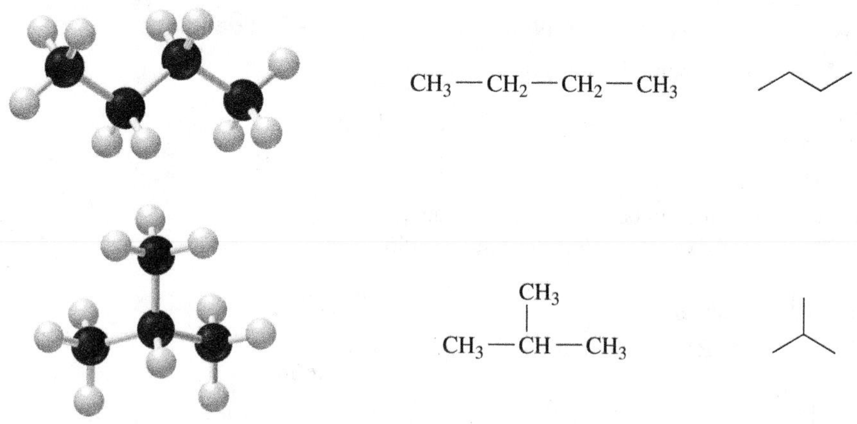

$$CH_3 - CH_2 - CH_2 - CH_3$$

$$\begin{array}{c} CH_3 \\ | \\ CH_3 - CH - CH_3 \end{array}$$

FIGURE 12.2 ▶ The structural isomers of C_4H_{10} have the same number and type of atoms but are bonded in a different order.

Ⓠ What makes these molecules structural isomers?

In another example, we can draw the condensed and line-angle structural formulas for three different structural isomers with the molecular formula C_5H_{12} as follows:

Structural Isomers of C_5H_{12}

Condensed	$CH_3 - CH_2 - CH_2 - CH_2 - CH_3$	$\begin{array}{c} CH_3 \\ | \\ CH_3 - CH - CH_2 - CH_3 \end{array}$	$\begin{array}{c} CH_3 \\ | \\ CH_3 - C - CH_3 \\ | \\ CH_3 \end{array}$
Line-Angle		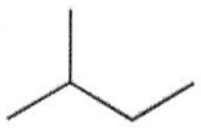	

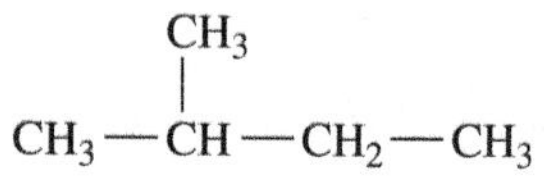

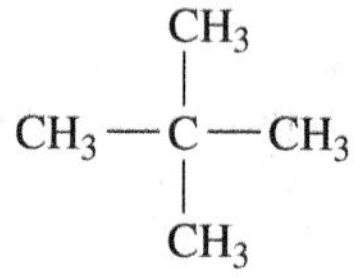

▶SAMPLE PROBLEM 12.4 Structural Isomers

Identify each pair of formulas as structural isomers or the same molecule.

a. 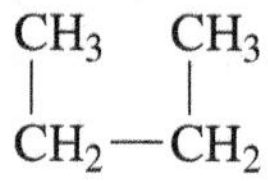 $\begin{array}{cc} CH_3 & CH_3 \\ | & | \\ CH_2 - CH_2 \end{array}$ and $\begin{array}{c} CH_2 - CH_2 - CH_3 \\ | \\ CH_3 \end{array}$

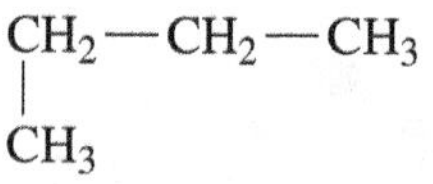

b. 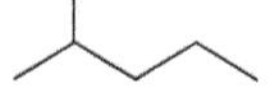 [line-angle structure] and [line-angle structure]

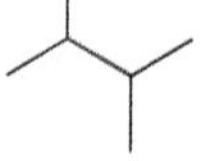

SOLUTION

a. When we add up the number of C atoms and H atoms, they give the same molecular formula C_4H_{10}. The condensed structural formula on the left has a chain of four C atoms. Even though the $-CH_3$ ends are drawn up, they are part of the four-carbon chain. The condensed structural formula on the right also has a four-carbon chain even though one $-CH_3$ end is drawn down. Thus both condensed structural formulas represent the same molecule and are not structural isomers.

b. When we add up the number of C atoms and H atoms, they give the same molecular formula C_6H_{14}. The line-angle structural formula on the left has a five-carbon chain with a $-CH_3$ substituent on the second carbon of the chain. The line-angle structural formula on the right has a four-carbon chain with two $-CH_3$ substituents, one bonded to the second carbon and one bonded to the third carbon. Thus there is a different order of bonding of atoms, which represents structural isomers.

STUDY CHECK 12.4

Why does the following formula represent a different structural isomer of the molecules in Sample Problem 12.4, part **b**?

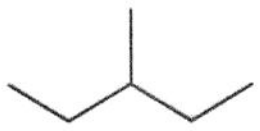

ANSWER

This formula represents a different structural isomer because the $—CH_3$ substituent is on the third carbon of the chain.

Substituents in Alkanes

In the IUPAC names for alkanes, a carbon branch is named as an **alkyl group**, which is an alkane that is missing one hydrogen atom. The alkyl group is named by replacing the *ane* ending of the corresponding alkane name with *yl*. Alkyl groups cannot exist on their own: They must be attached to a carbon chain. When a halogen atom is attached to a carbon chain, it is named as a *halo* group: *fluoro, chloro, bromo,* or *iodo.* Some of the common groups attached to carbon chains are illustrated in Table 12.5.

TABLE 12.5 Formulas and Names of Some Common Substituents

Formula	$CH_3—$			$CH_3—CH_2—$	
Name	methyl			ethyl	

Formula	$CH_3—CH_2—CH_2—$			$CH_3—CH—CH_3$	
Name	propyl			isopropyl	

Formula	$CH_3—CH_2—CH_2—CH_2—$	$CH_3—CH—CH_2—$ (with CH_3 branch)	$CH_3—CH—CH_2—CH_3$ (with branch)	$CH_3—C—CH_3$ (with CH_3 above and CH_3 below)
Name	butyl	isobutyl	sec-butyl	tert-butyl

Formula	$F—$	$Cl—$	$Br—$	$I—$
Name	fluoro	chloro	bromo	iodo

Naming Alkanes with Substituents

In the IUPAC system of naming, a carbon chain is numbered to give the location of the substituents. Let's take a look at how we use the IUPAC system to name the alkane shown in Sample Problem 12.5.

Interactive Video

Naming Alkanes

SAMPLE PROBLEM 12.5 Writing IUPAC Names for Alkanes with Substituents

Give the IUPAC name for the following alkane:

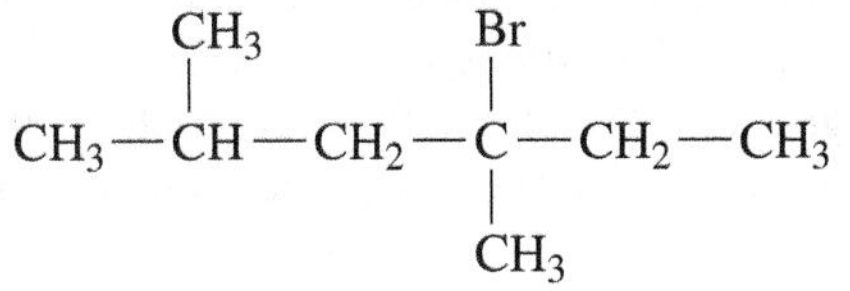

$$CH_3—CH—CH_2—C—CH_2—CH_3$$

(with CH_3 on second carbon, Br and CH_3 on fourth carbon)

SOLUTION

ANALYZE THE PROBLEM	Given	Need
	six carbon chain, two methyl groups, one bromo group	IUPAC name

<table>
<tr><td>

Guide to Naming Alkanes with Substituents

STEP 1
Write the alkane name for the longest chain of carbon atoms.

STEP 2
Number the carbon atoms starting from the end nearer a substituent.

STEP 3
Give the location and name for each substituent (alphabetical order) as a prefix to the name of the main chain.

</td></tr>
</table>

STEP 1 Write the alkane name for the longest chain of carbon atoms.

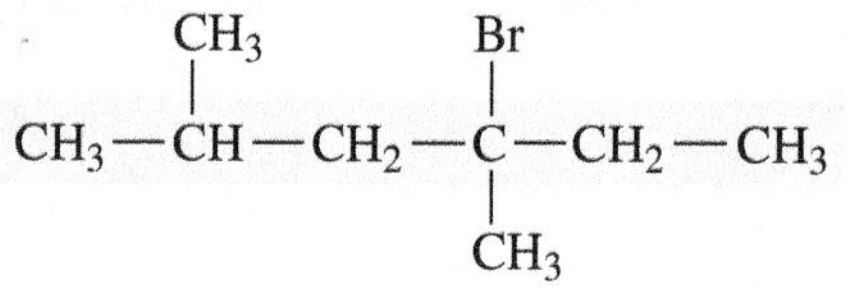

$$CH_3-CH-CH_2-C-CH_2-CH_3 \quad \text{hexane}$$
with CH₃ above the CH and Br above, CH₃ below the C

STEP 2 Number the carbon atoms starting from the end nearer a substituent. Carbon 1 is the carbon atom nearer a methyl group, —CH₃, on the left.

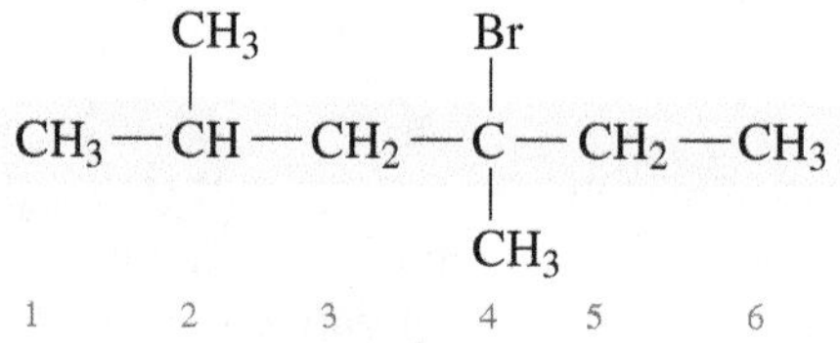

$$CH_3-CH-CH_2-C-CH_2-CH_3 \quad \text{hexane}$$

1   2   3   4   5   6

STEP 3 Give the location and name for each substituent (alphabetical order) as a prefix to the name of the main chain. The substituents, which are bromo and methyl groups, are listed in alphabetical order (bromo first, then methyl). A hyphen is placed between the number on the carbon chain and the substituent name. When there are two or more of the same substituent, a prefix (*di*, *tri*, *tetra*) is used in front of the name. However, these prefixes are not used to determine the alphabetical order of the substituents. Then commas are used to separate the numbers for the locations of the substituents.

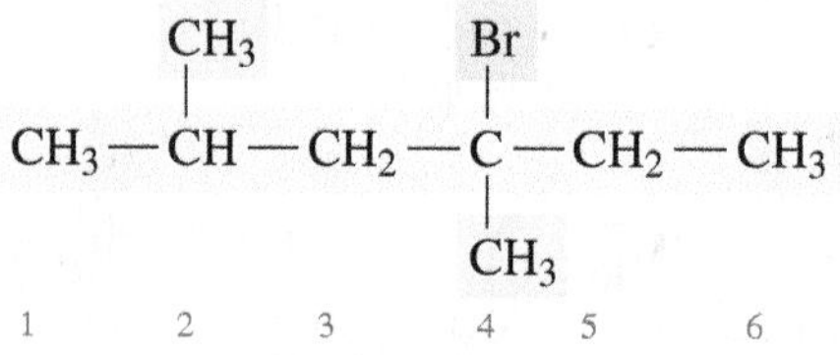

$$CH_3-CH-CH_2-C-CH_2-CH_3 \quad \text{4-bromo-2,4-dimethylhexane}$$

1   2   3   4   5   6

STUDY CHECK 12.5

Give the IUPAC name for the following compound:

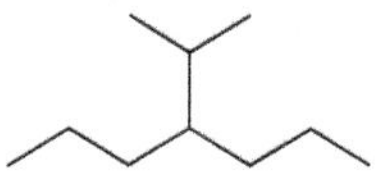

ANSWER
4-isopropylheptane

Naming Cycloalkanes with Substituents

When one substituent is attached to a carbon atom in a cycloalkane, the name of the substituent is placed in front of the cycloalkane name. No number is needed for a single alkyl group or halogen atom because the carbon atoms in the cycloalkane are equivalent. However, if two or more substituents are attached, the ring is numbered by assigning carbon 1 to the substituent that comes first alphabetically. Then we count the carbon atoms in the ring in the direction (clockwise or counterclockwise) that gives the lower numbers to the substituents.

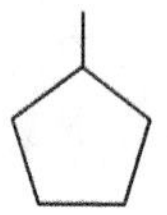

Methylcyclopentane 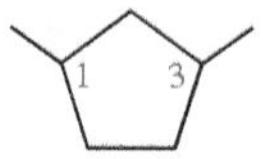   1,3-Dimethylcyclopentane 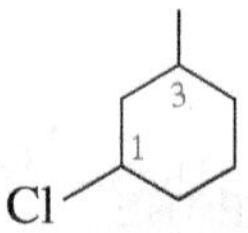   1-Chloro-3-methylcyclohexane

Haloalkanes

In a *haloalkane*, halogen atoms replace hydrogen atoms in an alkane. The halo substituents are numbered and arranged alphabetically, just as we did with the alkyl groups. Many times chemists use the common, traditional name for these compounds rather than the systematic IUPAC name. Simple haloalkanes are commonly named as alkyl halides; the carbon group is named as an alkyl group followed by the halide name.

Examples of Haloalkanes

Formula	CH_3-Cl	CH_3-CH_2-Br	$CH_3-\overset{\displaystyle F}{\underset{\displaystyle |}{CH}}-CH_3$	$CH_3-\overset{\displaystyle Cl}{\underset{\displaystyle \underset{\displaystyle CH_3}{|}}{\overset{\displaystyle |}{C}}}-CH_3$
IUPAC	Chloromethane	Bromoethane	2-Fluoropropane	2-Chloro-2-methylpropane
Common	Methyl chloride	Ethyl bromide	Isopropyl fluoride	*tert*-Butyl chloride

Drawing Condensed and Line-Angle Structural Formulas for Alkanes

The IUPAC name gives all the information needed to draw the condensed structural formula for an alkane. Suppose you are asked to draw the condensed structural formula for 2,3-dimethylbutane. The alkane name gives the number of carbon atoms in the longest chain. The names in the beginning indicate the substituents and where they are attached. We can break down the name in the following way:

2,3-Dimethylbutane

2,3-	Di	methyl	but	ane
Substituents on carbons 2 and 3	two identical groups	$-CH_3$ alkyl groups	four C atoms in the main chain	single (C—C) bonds

> **SAMPLE PROBLEM 12.6 Drawing Condensed Structures from IUPAC Names**

Draw the condensed and line-angle structural formulas for 2,3-dimethylbutane.

ANALYZE THE PROBLEM	**Given**	**Need**
	2,3-dimethylbutane	condensed and line-angle structural formulas

SOLUTION

STEP **1** Draw the main chain of carbon atoms. For butane, we draw a chain or a zigzag line of four carbon atoms.

$$C-C-C-C$$

STEP **2** Number the chain and place the substituents on the carbons indicated by the numbers. The first part of the name indicates two methyl groups —CH_3: one on carbon 2 and one on carbon 3.

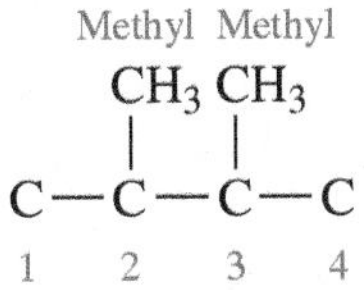

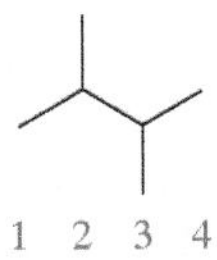

Guide to Drawing Structural Formulas for Alkanes with Substituents

STEP **1**
Draw the main chain of carbon atoms.

STEP **2**
Number the chain and place the substituents on the carbons indicated by the numbers.

STEP **3**
For the condensed structural formula, add the correct number of hydrogen atoms to give four bonds to each C atom.

STEP 3 For the condensed structural formula, add the correct number of hydrogen atoms to give four bonds to each C atom.

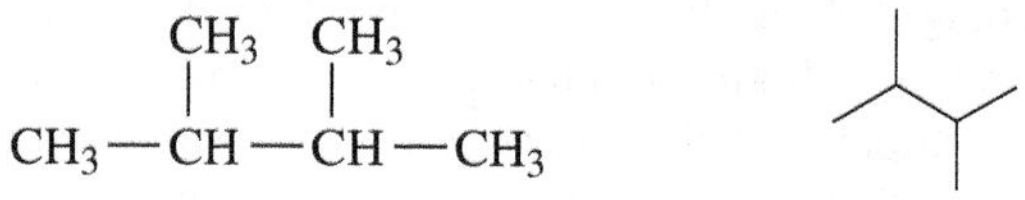

$$CH_3-\underset{\underset{CH_3}{|}}{CH}-\underset{\underset{CH_3}{|}}{CH}-CH_3$$

2,3-Dimethylbutane

STUDY CHECK 12.6

Draw the condensed and line-angle structural formulas for 2-bromo-3-ethyl-4-methylpentane.

ANSWER

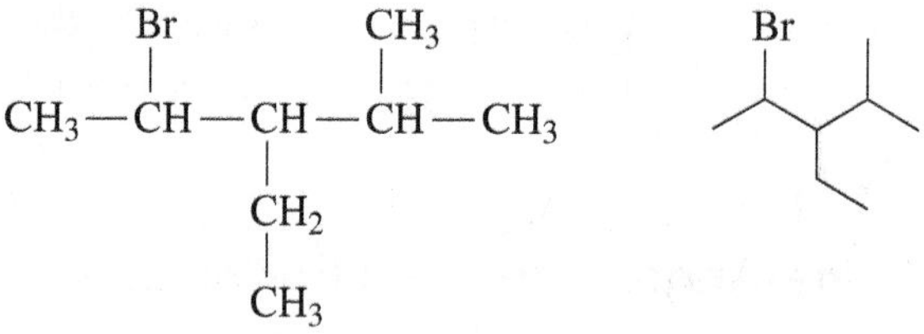

$$CH_3-\underset{\underset{}{\overset{\overset{Br}{|}}{}}}{CH}-\underset{\underset{\underset{CH_3}{|}}{\overset{\overset{}{|}}{CH_2}}}{CH}-\underset{\overset{\overset{CH_3}{|}}{}}{CH}-CH_3$$

QUESTIONS AND PROBLEMS

12.3 Alkanes with Substituents

LEARNING GOAL Write the IUPAC names for alkanes with substituents and draw their condensed and line-angle structural formulas.

12.13 Indicate whether each of the following pairs represent structural isomers or the same molecule:

a. 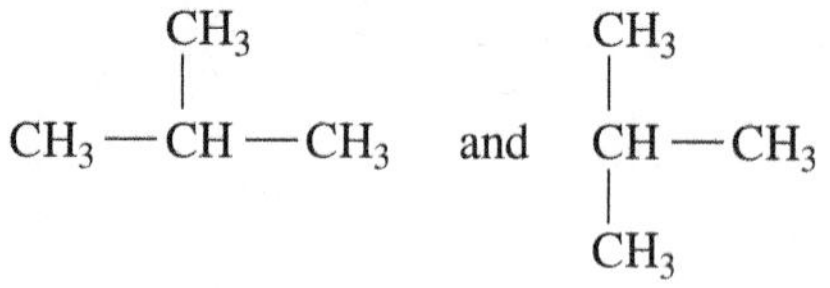 $CH_3-\underset{\underset{CH_3}{|}}{CH}-CH_3$ and $\underset{\underset{CH_3}{|}}{\overset{\overset{CH_3}{|}}{CH}}-CH_3$

b. 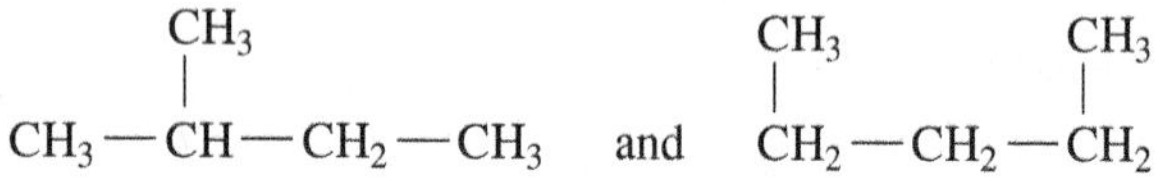 $CH_3-\underset{\underset{CH_3}{|}}{CH}-CH_2-CH_3$ and $\underset{\underset{}{\overset{\overset{CH_3}{|}}{}}}{CH_2}-CH_2-\underset{\overset{\overset{CH_3}{|}}{}}{CH_2}$

c. 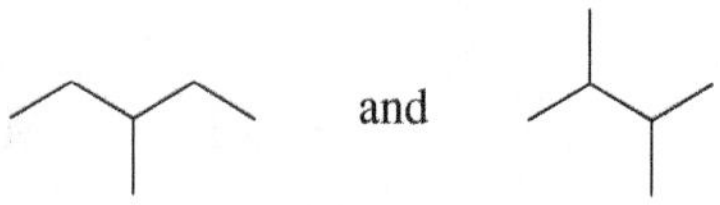 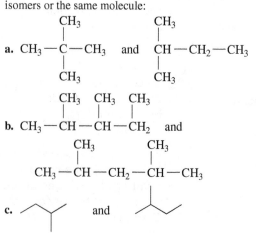   and

12.14 Indicate whether each of the following pairs represent structural isomers or the same molecule:

a. $CH_3-\underset{\underset{CH_3}{|}}{\overset{\overset{CH_3}{|}}{C}}-CH_3$ and $\underset{\underset{CH_3}{|}}{\overset{\overset{CH_3}{|}}{CH}}-CH_2-CH_3$

b. $CH_3-\underset{\underset{CH_3}{|}}{\overset{\overset{CH_3}{|}}{CH}}-\underset{\overset{\overset{CH_3}{|}}{}}{CH}-CH_2$ and
$CH_3-\underset{\underset{CH_3}{|}}{CH}-CH_2-\underset{\overset{\overset{CH_3}{|}}{}}{CH}-CH_3$

c.   and

12.15 Give the IUPAC name for each of the following:

a. 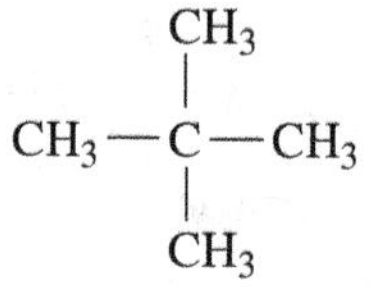 $CH_3-\underset{\underset{CH_3}{|}}{\overset{\overset{CH_3}{|}}{C}}-CH_3$ b.

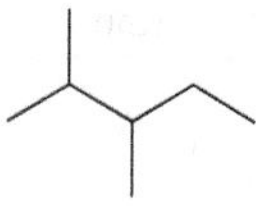

c. 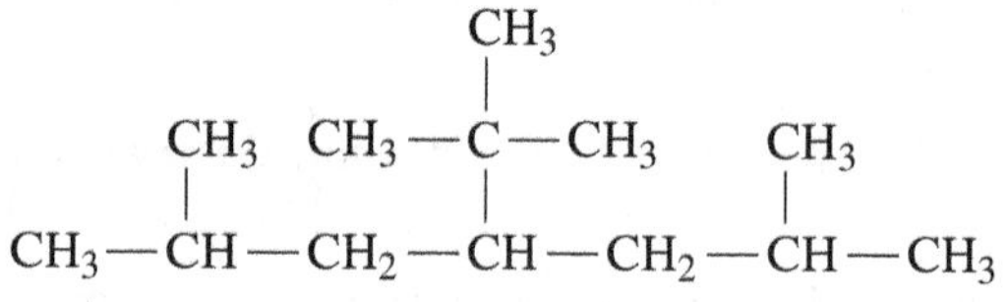 $CH_3-\underset{\underset{CH_3}{|}}{CH}-CH_2-\underset{\overset{\overset{CH_3}{|}}{\underset{}{\overset{}{C}}}}{\underset{CH_3}{|}}-CH_2-\underset{\overset{\overset{CH_3}{|}}{}}{CH}-CH_3$

d. 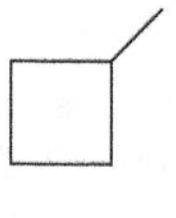   e.

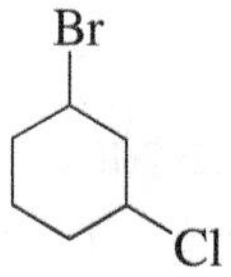

12.16 Give the IUPAC name for each of the following:

a. 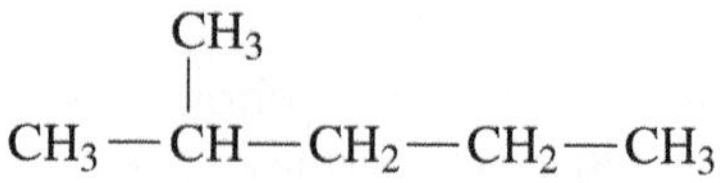 $CH_3-\underset{\underset{CH_3}{|}}{CH}-CH_2-CH_2-CH_3$

b.

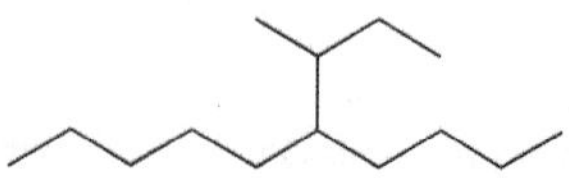

c. 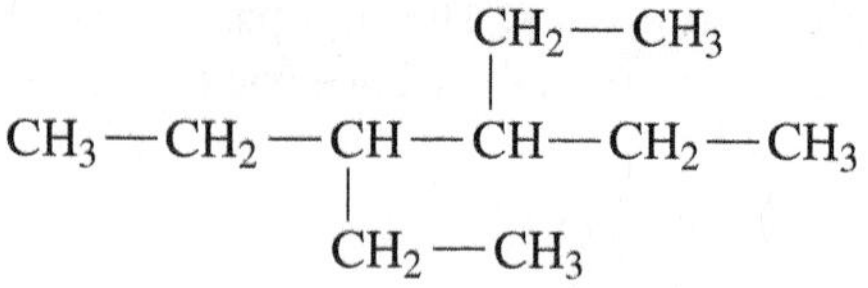 $CH_3-CH_2-\underset{\underset{CH_2-CH_3}{|}}{CH}-\underset{\overset{\overset{CH_2-CH_3}{|}}{}}{CH}-CH_2-CH_3$

d. 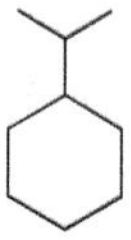   e.

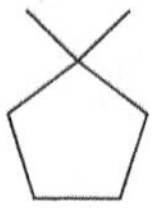

12.17 Draw the condensed structural formula for each of the following alkanes:
a. 3,3-dimethylpentane
b. 2,3,5-trimethylhexane
c. 3-ethyl-5-isopropyloctane
d. 1-bromo-2-chloroethane

12.18 Draw the condensed structural formula for each of the following alkanes:
a. 3-ethylpentane
b. 4-isopropyl-3-methylheptane
c. 4-ethyl-2,2-dimethyloctane
d. 2-bromopropane

12.19 Draw the line-angle structural formula for each of the following:
a. 3-methylheptane
b. 1-chloro-3-ethylcyclopentane
c. bromocyclobutane
d. 2,3-dichlorohexane

12.20 Draw the line-angle structural formula for each of the following:
a. 1-bromo-2-methylpentane
b. 1,2,3-trimethylcyclopropane
c. ethylcyclohexane
d. 4-chlorooctane

12.4 Properties of Alkanes

LEARNING GOAL

Identify the properties of alkanes and write a balanced chemical equation for combustion.

Many types of alkanes are the components of fuels that power our cars and oil that heats our homes. You may have used a mixture of hydrocarbons such as mineral oil as a laxative or petrolatum jelly to soften your skin. The differences in uses of many of the alkanes result from their physical properties, including solubility and density.

Some Uses of Alkanes

The first four alkanes—methane, ethane, propane, and butane—are gases at room temperature and are widely used as heating fuels.

Alkanes having five to eight carbon atoms (pentane, hexane, heptane, and octane) are liquids at room temperature. They are highly volatile, which makes them useful in fuels such as gasoline.

Liquid alkanes with 9 to 17 carbon atoms have higher boiling points and are found in kerosene, diesel, and jet fuels. Motor oil is a mixture of high-molecular-weight liquid hydrocarbons and is used to lubricate the internal components of engines. Mineral oil is a mixture of liquid hydrocarbons and is used as a laxative and a lubricant. Alkanes with 18 or more carbon atoms are waxy solids at room temperature. Known as paraffins, they are used in waxy coatings added to fruits and vegetables to retain moisture, inhibit mold, and enhance appearance. Petrolatum jelly, or Vaseline, is a semisolid mixture of hydrocarbons with more than 25 carbon atoms used in ointments and cosmetics and as a lubricant.

The solid alkanes that make up waxy coatings on fruits and vegetables help retain moisture, inhibit mold, and enhance appearance.

Melting and Boiling Points

Alkanes have the lowest melting and boiling points of all the organic compounds. This occurs because alkanes contain only the nonpolar bonds of C—C and C—H. Therefore, the attractions that occur between alkane molecules in the solid and liquid states are because of the relatively weak dispersion forces. As the number of carbon atoms increases, there is also an increase in the number of electrons, which increases the attraction because of the dispersion forces. Thus, alkanes with higher masses have higher melting and boiling points.

CH_4 $CH_3—CH_3$ $CH_3—CH_2—CH_3$ $CH_3—CH_2—CH_2—CH_3$ $CH_3—CH_2—CH_2—CH_2—CH_3$
Methane   Ethane   Propane   Butane   Pentane
bp = −164 °C   bp = −89 °C   bp = −42 °C   bp = 0.5 °C   bp = 36 °C

Number of Carbon Atoms Increases
Boiling Point Increases

The boiling points of branched alkanes are generally lower than the straight-chain isomers. The branched-chain alkanes tend to be more compact, which reduces the points of contact between the molecules. In an analogy, we can think of the carbon chains of straight-chain alkanes as pieces of licorice in a package. Because they have linear shapes, they can line up very close to each other, which gives many points of contact between the surface of the molecules. In our analogy, we can also think of branched alkanes as tennis balls in a can that, because of their spherical shapes, have only a small area of contact. One tennis ball represents an entire molecule. Because branched alkanes have fewer attractions, they have lower melting and boiling points.

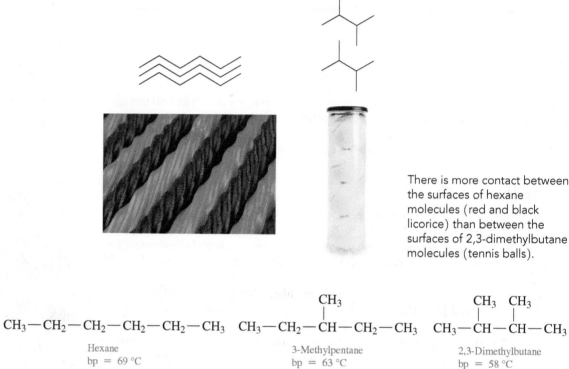

There is more contact between the surfaces of hexane molecules (red and black licorice) than between the surfaces of 2,3-dimethylbutane molecules (tennis balls).

$$CH_3-CH_2-CH_2-CH_2-CH_2-CH_3$$

Hexane
bp = 69 °C

$$CH_3-CH_2-\overset{\overset{\displaystyle CH_3}{|}}{CH}-CH_2-CH_3$$

3-Methylpentane
bp = 63 °C

$$CH_3-\overset{\overset{\displaystyle CH_3}{|}}{CH}-\overset{\overset{\displaystyle CH_3}{|}}{CH}-CH_3$$

2,3-Dimethylbutane
bp = 58 °C

Number of Branches Increases
Boiling Point Decreases

Cycloalkanes have higher boiling points than the straight-chain alkanes with the same number of carbon atoms. Because rotation of carbon bonds is restricted, cycloalkanes maintain a rigid structure. Cycloalkanes with their rigid structures can be stacked closely together, which gives them many points of contact and therefore many attractions to each other.

We can compare the boiling points of straight-chain alkanes, branched-chain alkanes, and cycloalkanes with five carbon atoms as shown in Table 12.6.

Combustion of Alkanes

The carbon–carbon single bonds in alkanes are difficult to break, which makes them the least reactive family of organic compounds. However, alkanes burn readily in oxygen to produce carbon dioxide, water, and energy.

$$\text{Alkane}(g) + O_2(g) \xrightarrow{\Delta} CO_2(g) + H_2O(g) + \text{energy}$$

For example, methane is the natural gas we use to cook our food and heat our homes. The equation for the combustion of methane (CH_4) is written:

$$CH_4(g) + 2O_2(g) \xrightarrow{\Delta} CO_2(g) + 2H_2O(g) + \text{energy}$$
Methane

TABLE 12.6 Comparison of Boiling Points of Alkanes and Cycloalkanes with Five Carbons

Formula	Name	Boiling Point (°C)
Straight-Chain Alkane		
$CH_3-CH_2-CH_2-CH_2-CH_3$	Pentane	36
Branched-Chain Alkanes		
$\begin{array}{c} CH_3 \\ \vert \\ CH_3-CH-CH_2-CH_3 \end{array}$	2-Methylbutane	28
$\begin{array}{c} CH_3 \\ \vert \\ CH_3-C-CH_3 \\ \vert \\ CH_3 \end{array}$	Dimethylpropane	10
Cycloalkane		
(pentagon)	Cyclopentane	49

In another example, propane is the gas used in portable heaters and gas barbecues (see Figure 12.3). The equation for the combustion of propane (C_3H_8) is written:

$$C_3H_8(g) + 5O_2(g) \xrightarrow{\Delta} 3CO_2(g) + 4H_2O(g) + \text{energy}$$
Propane

In the cells of our bodies, energy is produced by the combustion of glucose. Although a series of reactions is involved, we can write the overall combustion of glucose in our cells as follows:

$$C_6H_{12}O_6(aq) + 6O_2(g) \xrightarrow{\text{Enzymes}} 6CO_2(g) + 6H_2O(l) + \text{energy}$$
Glucose

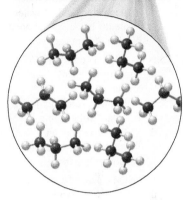

FIGURE 12.3 ▶ The propane fuel in the tank undergoes combustion, which provides energy.

Ⓠ What is the balanced equation for the combustion of propane?

Solubility and Density

Alkanes are nonpolar, which makes them insoluble in water. However, they are soluble in nonpolar solvents such as other alkanes. Alkanes have densities from 0.62 g/mL to about 0.79 g/mL, which is less than the density of water (1.0 g/mL).

If there is an oil spill in the ocean, the alkanes in the oil, which do not mix with water, form a thin layer on the surface that spreads over a large area. In April 2010, an explosion on an oil-drilling rig in the Gulf of Mexico caused the largest oil spill in U.S. history. At its maximum, an estimated 10 million liters of oil was leaked every day. Other major oil spills occurred in Queensland, Australia (2009), the coast of Wales (1996), the Shetland Islands (1993), and Alaska, from the *Exxon Valdez*, in 1989 (see Figure 12.4). If the crude oil reaches land, there can be considerable damage to beaches, shellfish, birds, and wildlife habitats. When animals such as birds are covered with oil, they must be cleaned quickly because ingestion of the hydrocarbons when they try to clean themselves is fatal.

Cleanup of oil spills includes mechanical, chemical, and microbiological methods. A boom may be placed around the leaking oil until it can be removed. Boats called skimmers then scoop up the oil and place it in tanks. In a chemical method, a substance that attracts oil is used to pick up oil, which is then scraped off into recovery tanks. Certain bacteria that ingest oil are also used to break oil down into less harmful products.

FIGURE 12.4 ▶ In oil spills, large quantities of oil spread out to form a thin layer on top of the ocean surface.

Ⓠ What physical properties cause oil to remain on the surface of water?

QUESTIONS AND PROBLEMS

12.4 Properties of Alkanes

LEARNING GOAL Identify the properties of alkanes and write a balanced chemical equation for combustion.

12.21 Heptane, used as a solvent for rubber cement, has a density of 0.68 g/mL and boils at 98 °C.
   a. Draw the condensed and line-angle structural formulas for heptane.
   b. Is heptane a solid, liquid, or gas at room temperature?
   c. Is heptane soluble in water?
   d. Will heptane float on water or sink?
   e. Write the balanced chemical equation for the complete combustion of heptane.

12.22 Nonane has a density of 0.79 g/mL and boils at 151 °C.
   a. Draw the condensed and line-angle structural formulas for nonane.
   b. Is nonane a solid, liquid, or gas at room temperature?
   c. Is nonane soluble in water?
   d. Will nonane float on water or sink?
   e. Write the balanced chemical equation for the complete combustion of nonane.

12.23 Write the balanced chemical equation for the complete combustion of each of the following compounds:
   a. ethane
   b. cyclopropane
   c. octane

12.24 Write the balanced chemical equation for the complete combustion of each of the following compounds:
   a. hexane   b. cyclopentane   c. butane

Butane in a portable burner undergoes combustion.

12.25 In each of the following pairs of hydrocarbons, which one would you expect to have the higher boiling point?
   a. pentane or heptane
   b. propane or cyclopropane
   c. hexane or 2-methylpentane

12.26 In each of the following pairs of hydrocarbons, which one would you expect to have the higher boiling point?
   a. propane or butane
   b. hexane or cyclohexane
   c. 2,2-dimethylpentane or heptane

LEARNING GOAL

Identify structural formulas as alkenes, cycloalkenes, and alkynes, and write their IUPAC names.

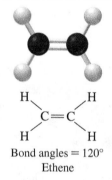

Bond angles = 120°
Ethene

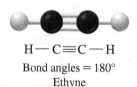

H—C≡C—H
Bond angles = 180°
Ethyne

FIGURE 12.5 ▶ Ball-and-stick models of ethene and ethyne show the double or triple bonds and the bond angles.

🔘 Why are these compounds called unsaturated hydrocarbons?

12.5 Alkenes and Alkynes

Alkenes and *alkynes* are families of hydrocarbons that contain double and triple bonds, respectively. They are called *unsaturated hydrocarbons* because they do not contain the maximum number of hydrogen atoms, as do alkanes. They react with hydrogen gas to increase the number of hydrogen atoms to become alkanes, which are *saturated hydrocarbons*.

Identifying Alkenes and Alkynes

Alkenes contain one or more carbon–carbon double bonds that form when adjacent carbon atoms share two pairs of valence electrons. Recall that *a carbon atom always forms four covalent bonds*. In the simplest alkene, ethene, C_2H_4, two carbon atoms are connected by a double bond and each is also attached to two H atoms. This gives each carbon atom in the double bond a trigonal planar arrangement with bond angles of 120°. As a result, the ethene molecule is flat because the carbon and hydrogen atoms all lie in the same plane (see Figure 12.5).

Ethene, more commonly called ethylene, is an important plant hormone involved in promoting the ripening of fruit. Commercially grown fruit, such as avocados, bananas, and tomatoes, are often picked before they are ripe. Before the fruit is brought to market, it is exposed to ethylene to accelerate the ripening process. Ethylene also accelerates the breakdown of cellulose in plants, which causes flowers to wilt and leaves to fall from trees.

In an **alkyne**, a triple bond forms when two carbon atoms share three pairs of valence electrons. In the simplest alkyne, ethyne (C_2H_2), the two carbon atoms of the triple bond are each attached to one hydrogen atom, which gives a triple bond a linear geometry. Ethyne, commonly called acetylene, is used in welding where it reacts with oxygen to produce flames with temperatures above 3300 °C.

Fruit is ripened with ethene, a plant hormone.

A mixture of acetylene and oxygen undergoes combustion during the welding of metals.

Naming Alkenes and Alkynes

The IUPAC names for alkenes and alkynes are similar to those of alkanes. Using the alkane name with the same number of carbon atoms, the *ane* ending is replaced with *ene* for an alkene and *yne* for an alkyne (see Table 12.7). Cyclic alkenes are named as *cycloalkenes*.

TABLE 12.7 Comparison of Names for Alkanes, Alkenes, and Alkynes

Alkane	Alkene	Alkyne
CH_3-CH_3	$H_2C=CH_2$	$HC\equiv CH$
Ethane	Ethene (ethylene)	Ethyne (acetylene)
$CH_3-CH_2-CH_3$	$CH_3-CH=CH_2$	$CH_3-C\equiv CH$
$\wedge$	$\wedge$	——— $\equiv$
Propane	Propene	Propyne

Examples of naming an alkene and an alkyne are seen in Sample Problem 12.7.

> **SAMPLE PROBLEM 12.7** Naming Alkenes and Alkynes
>
> Write the IUPAC name for each of the following:
>
> $$CH_3$$
> **a.** $CH_3-CH-CH=CH-CH_3$ **b.** $CH_3-CH_2-C\equiv C-CH_2-CH_3$
>
> **SOLUTION**
>
> **a.**
>
> | ANALYZE THE PROBLEM | Given | Need |
> |---|---|---|
> | | five-carbon chain, double bond, methyl group | IUPAC name |
>
> **STEP 1** Name the longest carbon chain that contains the double bond. There are five carbon atoms in the longest carbon chain containing the double bond. Replace the *ane* in the corresponding alkane name with *ene* to give pentene.
>
> $$CH_3$$
> $CH_3-CH-CH=CH-CH_3$ pentene

Guide to Naming Alkenes and Alkynes

STEP 1
Name the longest carbon chain that contains the double or triple bond.

STEP 2
Number the carbon chain starting from the end nearer the double or triple bond.

STEP 3
Give the location and name for each substituent (alphabetical order) as a prefix to the alkene or alkyne name.

STEP **2** Number the carbon chain starting from the end nearer the double bond. Place the number of the first carbon in the double bond in front of the alkene name.

$$CH_3-\underset{5}{C}H-\underset{4}{C}H=\underset{3}{C}H-\underset{2}{C}H_3 \qquad \text{2-pentene}$$
with CH_3 on carbon 4

Alkenes or alkynes with two or three carbons do not need numbers. For example, the double bond in ethene or propene must be between carbon 1 and carbon 2.

STEP **3** Give the location and name for each substituent (alphabetical order) as a prefix to the alkene name. The methyl group is located on carbon 4.

$$CH_3-\underset{5}{C}H-\underset{4}{C}H=\underset{3}{C}H-\underset{2}{C}H_3 \qquad \text{4-methyl-2-pentene}$$

b.

ANALYZE THE PROBLEM	Given	Need
	six carbon chain, triple bond	IUPAC name

STEP **1** Name the longest carbon chain that contains the triple bond. There are six carbon atoms in the longest chain containing the triple bond. Replace the *ane* in the corresponding alkane name with *yne* to give hexyne.

$$CH_3-CH_2-C\equiv C-CH_2-CH_3 \qquad \text{hexyne}$$

STEP **2** Number the carbon chain starting from the end nearer the triple bond. Place the number of the first carbon in the triple bond in front of the alkyne name.

$$\underset{1}{C}H_3-\underset{2}{C}H_2-\underset{3}{C}\equiv \underset{4}{C}-\underset{5}{C}H_2-\underset{6}{C}H_3 \qquad \text{3-hexyne}$$

STEP **3** Give the location and name for each substituent (alphabetical order) as a prefix to the alkyne name. There are no substituents in this formula.

STUDY CHECK 12.7

Name each of the following:

a.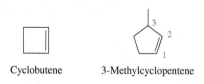

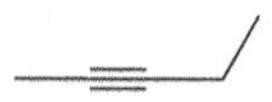

b. 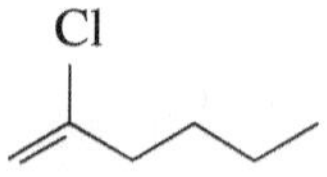 (structure with Cl)

ANSWER

a. 2-pentyne

b. 2-chloro-1-hexene

Naming Cycloalkenes

Some alkenes called *cycloalkenes* have a double bond within a ring structure. If there is no substituent, the double bond does not need a number. If there is a substituent, the carbons in the double bond are numbered as 1 and 2, and the ring is numbered in the direction that will give the lower number to the substituent.

Cyclobutene   3-Methylcyclopentene

Chemistry Link to the Environment
Fragrant Alkenes

The odors you associate with lemons, oranges, roses, and lavender are because of volatile compounds that are synthesized by the plants. The pleasant flavors and fragrances of many fruits and flowers are often because of unsaturated compounds. They were some of the first kinds of compounds to be extracted from natural plant material. In ancient times, they were highly valued in their pure forms. Limonene and myrcene give the characteristic odors and flavors to lemons and bay leaves, respectively. Geraniol and citronellal give roses and lemongrass their distinct aromas. In the food and perfume industries, these compounds are extracted or synthesized and used as perfumes and flavorings.

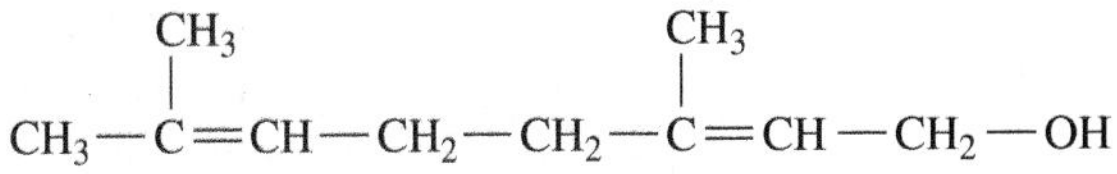

The characteristic odor of a rose is because of geraniol, a 10-carbon alcohol with two double bonds.

$$CH_3-\underset{\underset{CH_3}{|}}{C}=CH-CH_2-CH_2-\underset{\underset{CH_3}{|}}{C}=CH-CH_2-OH$$
Geraniol, roses

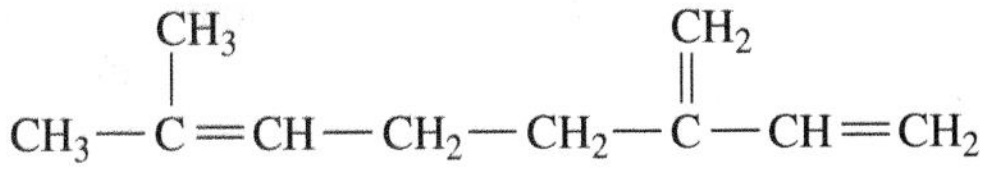

$$CH_3-\underset{\underset{CH_3}{|}}{C}=CH-CH_2-CH_2-\underset{\overset{CH_2}{||}}{C}-CH=CH_2$$
Myrcene, bay leaves

$$CH_3-\underset{\underset{CH_3}{|}}{C}=CH-CH_2-CH_2-\underset{\underset{CH_3}{|}}{CH}-CH_2-\overset{\overset{O}{||}}{C}-H$$
Citronellal, lemongrass

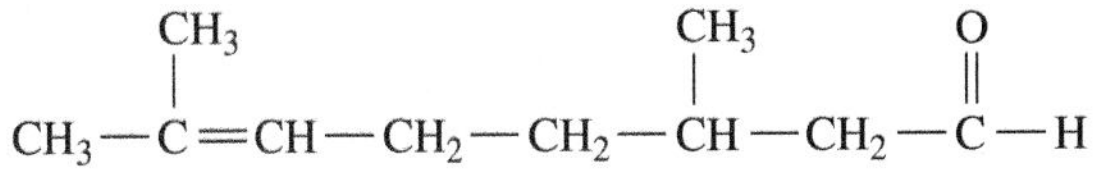

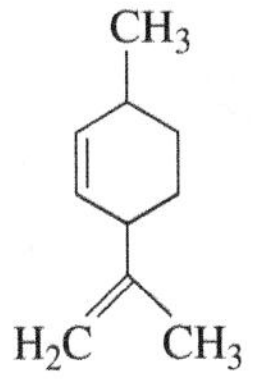

Limonene, lemons and oranges

QUESTIONS AND PROBLEMS

12.5 Alkenes and Alkynes

LEARNING GOAL Identify structural formulas as alkenes, cycloalkenes, and alkynes, and write their IUPAC names.

12.27 Identify the following as alkanes, alkenes, cycloalkenes, or alkynes:

a. 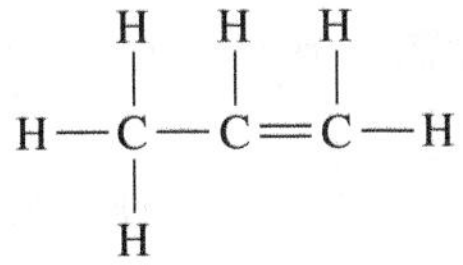 $H-\underset{\underset{H}{|}}{\overset{\overset{H}{|}}{C}}-\underset{\overset{H}{|}}{C}=\underset{\overset{H}{|}}{C}-H$ **b.** $CH_3-CH_2-C\equiv C-H$

c. 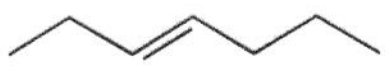 ∿∿ **d.** 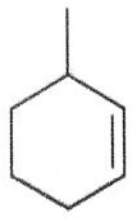 (cyclohexene with methyl)

12.28 Identify the following as alkanes, alkenes, cycloalkenes, or alkynes:

a.  (triangle) **b.**  (line-angle alkyne)

c. 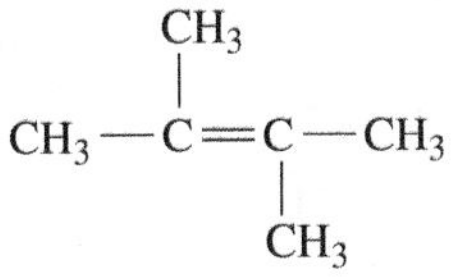 $CH_3-\underset{\underset{CH_3}{|}}{\overset{\overset{CH_3}{|}}{C}}=C-CH_3$ **d.** 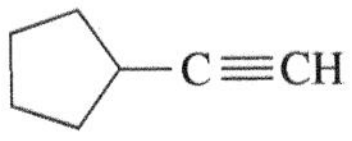 (cyclopentane)$-C\equiv CH$

12.29 Give the IUPAC name for each of the following:

a. 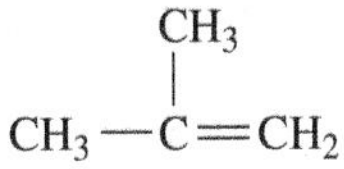 $CH_3-\underset{\overset{CH_3}{|}}{C}=CH_2$ **b.**

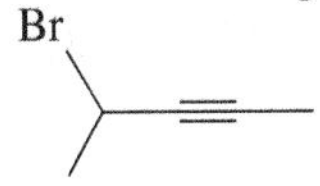

c. 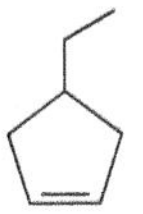 (cyclopentene with ethyl) **d.** 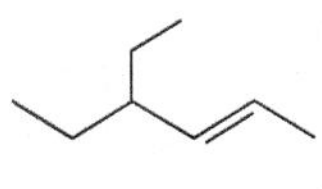 (branched alkene)

12.30 Give the IUPAC name for each of the following:

a. $H_2C=CH-CH_2-CH_2-CH_2-CH_3$

b. 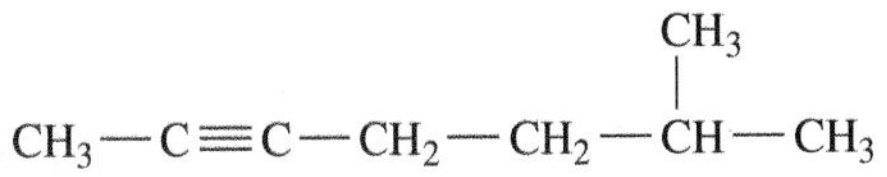 $CH_3-C\equiv C-CH_2-CH_2-\underset{\underset{CH_3}{|}}{CH}-CH_3$

c. (methylcyclohexene) **d.**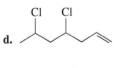

12.31 Draw the condensed structural formulas for **a** and **b** and line-angle structural formulas for **c** and **d**:
a. 1-pentene **b.** 2-methyl-1-butene
c. 3-methylcyclohexene **d.** 1-chloro-3-hexyne

12.32 Draw the condensed structural formulas for **a** and **b** and line-angle structural formulas for **c** and **d**:
a. 3-methyl-1-butyne **b.** 3,4-dimethyl-1-pentene
c. 1,2-dichlorocyclopentene **d.** 2-methyl-2-hexene

LEARNING GOAL

Draw the condensed and line-angle structural formulas and give the names for the cis–trans isomers of alkenes.

12.6 Cis–Trans Isomers

In any alkene, the double bond is rigid, which means there is no rotation around the double bond (see Explore Your World "Modeling Cis–Trans Isomers"). As a result, the atoms or groups are attached to the carbon atoms in the double bond on one side or the other, which gives two different structures called *geometric isomers* or *cis–trans isomers*.

For example, the formula for 1,2-dichloroethene can be drawn as two different molecules, which are cis–trans isomers. In the expanded structural formulas, the atoms bonded to the carbon atoms in the double bond have bond angles of 120°. When we draw 1,2-dichloroethene, we add the prefix *cis* or *trans* to denote whether the atoms bonded to the carbon atoms are on the same side or opposite sides of the molecule. In the **cis isomer**, the chlorine atoms are on the same side of the double bond. In the **trans isomer**, the chlorine atoms are on opposite sides of the double bond. *Trans* means "across," as in transcontinental; *cis* means "on this side."

$$Cl—CH=CH—Cl$$
1,2-Dichloroethene

Chlorine atoms are on the same side of the double bond.

Chlorine atoms are on opposite sides of the double bond.

cis-1,2-Dichloroethene   *trans*-1,2-Dichloroethene

Another example of a cis–trans isomer is 2-butene. If we look closely at 2-butene, we find that each carbon in the double bond is bonded to a —CH$_3$ group and a hydrogen atom. We can draw cis–trans isomers for 2-butene. In the *cis*-2-butene isomer, the —CH$_3$ groups are attached on the same side of the double bond. In the *trans*-2-butene isomer, the —CH$_3$ groups are attached to the double bond on opposite sides, as shown in their ball-and-stick models (see Figure 12.6).

FIGURE 12.6 ▶ Ball-and-stick models and line-angle structural formulas of the cis and trans isomers of 2-butene.

Q What feature in 2-butene accounts for the cis and trans isomers?

cis-2-Butene

trans-2-Butene

As with any pair of cis–trans isomers, *cis*-2-butene and *trans*-2-butene are different compounds with different physical properties and chemical properties. In general, trans isomers are more stable than their cis counterparts because the groups that are bigger than hydrogen atoms on the double bond are farther apart.

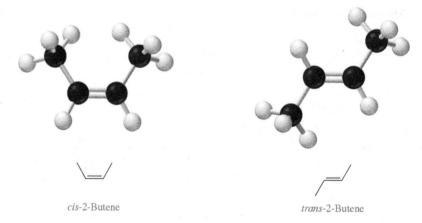

$$CH_3—CH=CH—CH_3$$
2-Butene

cis-2-Butene
(mp −139 °C; bp 3.7 °C)

trans-2-Butene
(mp −106 °C; bp 0.3 °C)

When the carbon atoms in the double bond are attached to two different atoms or groups of atoms, an alkene can have cis–trans isomers. For example, 3-hexene can be drawn with cis and trans isomers because there is one H atom and a CH_3—CH_2— group attached to each carbon atom in the double bond. When you are asked to draw the formula for an alkene, it is important to consider the possibility of cis and trans isomers.

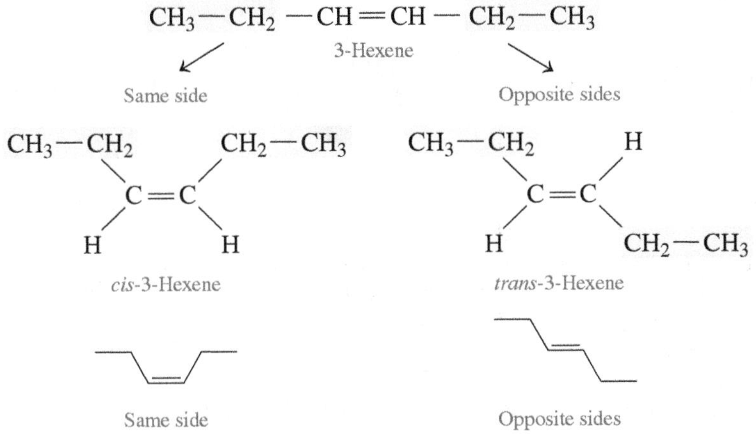

$$CH_3-CH_2-CH=CH-CH_2-CH_3$$

3-Hexene

Same side   Opposite sides

cis-3-Hexene

trans-3-Hexene

Same side   Opposite sides

When an alkene has identical groups on the same carbon atom of the double bond, cis and trans isomers cannot be drawn. For example, 1,1-dichloropropene has just one condensed structural formula and does not form cis–trans isomers.

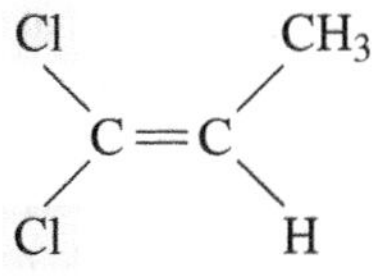

1,1-Dichloropropene

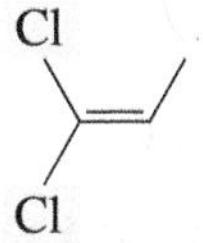

When identical groups are attached to carbon 1, there are no cis–trans isomers.

▶ **SAMPLE PROBLEM 12.8 Identifying Cis–Trans Isomers**

Identify each of the following as the cis or trans isomer and give its name:

a. 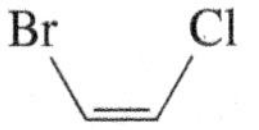 Br   Cl

b.

SOLUTION

a. This is a cis isomer because the two halogen atoms attached to the carbon atoms of the double bond are on the same side. The name of the two-carbon alkene, starting with the bromo group on carbon 1, is *cis*-1-bromo-2-chloroethene.

b. This is a trans isomer because the two alkyl groups attached to the carbon atoms of the double bond are on opposite sides of the double bond. This isomer of the five-carbon alkene, 2-pentene, is named *trans*-2-pentene.

STUDY CHECK 12.8

Give the name for the following compound, including cis or trans:

ANSWER

trans-3-hexene

Explore Your World

Modeling Cis–Trans Isomers

Because cis–trans isomerism is not easy to visualize, here are some things you can do to understand the difference in rotation around a single bond compared to a double bond and how it affects groups that are attached to the carbon atoms in the double bond.

Put the tips of your index fingers together. This is a model of a single bond. Consider the index fingers as a pair of carbon atoms, and think of your thumbs and other fingers as other parts of a carbon chain. While your index fingers are touching, twist your hands and change the position of your thumbs relative to each other. Notice how the relationship of your other fingers changes.

Now place the tips of your index fingers and middle fingers together in a model of a double bond. As you did before, twist your hands to move your thumbs away from each other. What happens? Can you change the location of your thumbs relative to each other without breaking the double bond? The difficulty of moving your hands with two fingers touching represents the lack of rotation about a double bond. You have made a model of a cis isomer when both thumbs point in the same direction. If you turn one hand over so one thumb points down and the other thumb points up, you have made a model of a trans isomer.

Cis-hands (cis-thumbs/fingers)

Trans-hands (trans-thumbs/fingers)

Using Gumdrops and Toothpicks to Model Cis–Trans Isomers

Obtain some toothpicks and yellow, green, and black gumdrops. The black gumdrops represent C atoms, the yellow gumdrops represent H atoms, and the green gumdrops represent Cl atoms. Place a toothpick between two black gumdrops. Use three more toothpicks to attach two yellow gumdrops and one green gumdrop to each black gumdrop carbon atom. Rotate one of the gumdrop carbon atoms to show the conformations of the attached H and Cl atoms.

Remove a toothpick and yellow gumdrop from each black gumdrop. Place a second toothpick between the carbon atoms, which makes a double bond. Try to twist the double bond of toothpicks. Can you do it? When you observe the location of the green gumdrops, does the model you made represent a cis or trans isomer? Why? If

your model is a cis isomer, how would you change it to a trans isomer? If your model is a trans isomer, how would you change it to a cis isomer?

Models from gumdrops represent cis and trans isomers.

Chemistry Link to the Environment
Pheromones in Insect Communication

Many insects emit minute quantities of chemicals called *pheromones* to send messages to individuals of the same species. Some pheromones warn of danger, others call for defense, mark a trail, or attract the opposite sex. In the past 40 yr, the structures of many pheromones have been chemically determined. One of the most studied is bom-

bykol, the sex pheromone produced by the female silkworm moth. The bombykol molecule contains one cis double bond and one trans double bond. Even a few nanograms of bombykol will attract male silkworm moths from distances of over 1 km. The effectiveness of many of these pheromones depends on the cis or trans configuration of the double bonds in the molecules. A certain species will respond to one isomer but not the other.

Scientists are interested in synthesizing pheromones to use as nontoxic alternatives to pesticides. When placed in a trap, bombykol can be used to capture male silkworm moths. When a synthetic pheromone is released in a field, the males cannot locate the females, which disrupts the reproductive cycle. This technique has been successful with controlling the oriental fruit moth, the grapevine moth, and the pink bollworm.

Pheromones allow insects to attract mates from a great distance.

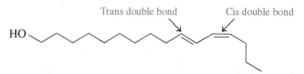

Bombykol, sex attractant for the silkworm moth

Chemistry Link to Health
Cis–Trans Isomers for Night Vision

The retinas of the eyes consist of two types of cells: rods and cones. The rods on the edge of the retina allow us to see in dim light, and the cones, in the center, produce our vision in bright light. In the rods, there is a substance called *rhodopsin* that absorbs light. Rhodopsin is composed of *cis*-11-retinal, an unsaturated compound, attached to a protein. When rhodopsin absorbs light, the *cis*-11-retinal isomer is converted to its trans isomer, which changes its shape. The trans form no longer fits the protein, and it separates from the protein. The change from the cis to trans isomer and its separation from the protein generate an electrical signal that the brain converts into an image.

An enzyme (isomerase) converts the trans isomer back to the *cis*-11-retinal isomer and the rhodopsin re-forms. If there is a deficiency of rhodopsin in the rods of the retina, *night blindness* may occur. One common cause is a lack of vitamin A in the diet. In our diet, we obtain vitamin A from plant pigments containing β-carotene, which is found in foods such as carrots, squash, and spinach. In the small intestine, the β-carotene is converted to vitamin A, which can be converted to *cis*-11-retinal or stored in the liver for future use. Without a sufficient quantity of retinal, not enough rhodopsin is produced to enable us to see adequately in dim light.

Cis–Trans Isomers of Retinal

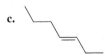

cis-11-Retinal   *trans*-11-Retinal

QUESTIONS AND PROBLEMS

12.6 Cis–Trans Isomers

LEARNING GOAL Draw the condensed and line-angle structural formulas and give the names for the cis–trans isomers of alkenes.

12.33 Give the IUPAC name for each of the following, using cis or trans prefixes:

a.

b.

c.

12.34 Give the IUPAC name for each of the following, using cis or trans prefixes:

a.

b.

c.

12.35 Draw the condensed structural formula for each of the following:
  a. *trans*-1-bromo-2-chloroethene
  b. *cis*-2-hexene
  c. *trans*-3-heptene

12.36 Draw the condensed structural formula for each of the following:
  a. *cis*-1,2-difluoroethene
  b. *trans*-2-pentene
  c. *cis*-4-octene

12.37 Which of the following cannot have cis–trans isomers? Explain.
  a. $H_2C{=}CH{-}CH_3$
  b. $CH_3{-}CH_2{-}CH{=}CH{-}CH_3$
  c.

12.38 Which of the following cannot have cis–trans isomers? Explain.
  a.
  b. $CH_3{-}CH_2{-}CH_2{-}CH{=}CH_2$
  c.

LEARNING GOAL

Draw the condensed or line-angle structural formulas and give the names for the organic products of addition reactions of alkenes. Draw a condensed structural formula for a section of a polymer.

12.7 Addition Reactions for Alkenes

The most characteristic reaction of alkenes is the **addition** of atoms or groups of atoms to the carbon atoms in a double bond. Addition occurs because double bonds are easily broken, providing electrons to form new single bonds.

The addition reactions have different names that depend on the type of reactant we add to the alkene, as Table 12.8 shows.

TABLE 12.8 Summary of Addition Reactions

Name of Addition Reaction	Reactants	Catalysts	Product
Hydrogenation	Alkene + H_2	Pt, Ni, or Pd	Alkane
Hydration	Alkene + H_2O	H^+ (strong acid)	Alcohol
Polymerization	Alkenes	High temperature, pressure	Polymer

⚛ CORE CHEMISTRY SKILL

Writing Equations for Hydrogenation, Hydration, and Polymerization

Hydrogenation

In a reaction called **hydrogenation**, H atoms add to each of the carbon atoms in a double bond of an alkene. During hydrogenation, the double bonds are converted to single bonds in alkanes. A catalyst such as finely divided platinum (Pt), nickel (Ni), or palladium (Pd) is used to speed up the reaction.

Some examples of the hydrogenation of alkenes follow:

$$CH_3-CH{=}CH-CH_3 + H_2 \xrightarrow{Pt} CH_3-CH_2-CH_2-CH_3$$

2-Butene   Butane

 + $H_2 \xrightarrow{Ni}$

Cyclohexene   Cyclohexane

▶ **SAMPLE PROBLEM 12.9** **Writing Equations for Hydrogenation**

Draw the structural formula for the product of each of the following hydrogenation reactions:

a. $CH_3-CH{=}CH_2 + H_2 \xrightarrow{Pt}$?
b. ⬠ + $H_2 \xrightarrow{Pt}$?

SOLUTION

In an addition reaction, hydrogen adds to the double bond to give an alkane.

ANALYZE THE PROBLEM	Given	Need
	alkene + H_2	structural formula of product

a. $CH_3-CH_2-CH_3$ **b.** ⬠

STUDY CHECK 12.9

Draw the condensed structural formula for the product of the hydrogenation of 2-methyl-1-butene, using a platinum catalyst.

ANSWER

$$CH_3-\overset{\overset{\textstyle CH_3}{|}}{CH}-CH_2-CH_3$$

Chemistry Link to Health
Hydrogenation of Unsaturated Fats

Vegetable oils such as corn oil or safflower oil are unsaturated fats composed of fatty acids that contain double bonds. The process of hydrogenation is used commercially to convert the double bonds in the unsaturated fats in vegetable oils to saturated fats such as margarine, which are more solid. Adjusting the amount of added hydrogen produces partially hydrogenated fats such as soft margarine, solid margarine in sticks, and shortenings, which are used in cooking. For example, oleic acid is a typical unsaturated fatty acid in olive oil and has a cis double bond at carbon 9. When oleic acid is hydrogenated, it is converted to stearic acid, a saturated fatty acid.

The unsaturated fats in vegetable oils are converted to saturated fats to make a more solid product.

Cis double bond

Oleic acid (found in olive oil and other unsaturated fats)

Single bond

Stearic acid (found in saturated fats)

Hydration

In **hydration**, an alkene reacts with water (H—OH). A hydrogen atom (H—) from water forms a bond with one carbon atom in the double bond, and the oxygen atom in —OH forms a bond with the other carbon. The reaction is catalyzed by a strong acid such as H_2SO_4, written as H^+. Hydration is used to prepare alcohols, which have the hydroxyl (—OH) functional group. When water (H—OH) adds to a symmetrical alkene, such as ethene, a single product is formed.

Interactive Video

Addition to an Asymmetric Bond

Ethene → Ethanol (ethyl alcohol)

← Functional group of alcohols

However, when H_2O adds to a double bond in an asymmetrical alkene, two products are possible. We can determine the prevalent product that forms using **Markovnikov's Rule**, named after the Russian chemist Vladimir Markovnikov. The rule states that when water adds to a double bond in which the carbon atoms are attached to different numbers of H atoms (an asymmetrical double bond), the H— from H—OH attaches to the carbon that has the *greater* number of H atoms and the —OH adds to the other carbon atom from the double bond. In the following example, the H— from H—OH attaches to the end carbon of the double bond, which has more hydrogen atoms, and the —OH adds to the middle carbon atom:

This C in the C=C has more H atoms.

Propene → 2-Propanol

▶ SAMPLE PROBLEM 12.10 Hydration

Draw the condensed structural formula for the product that forms in the following hydration reaction:

$$CH_3-CH_2-CH_2-CH=CH_2 + H_2O \xrightarrow{H^+}$$

SOLUTION

ANALYZE THE PROBLEM	Given	Need
	hydration, asymmetrical alkene	condensed structural formula for the product

For an asymmetrical alkene, the H— from water (H—OH) adds to the carbon with the *greater* number of hydrogen atoms, and the —OH bonds to the carbon with fewer H atoms.

$$CH_3-CH_2-CH_2-CH=CH_2 \xrightarrow{H^+} CH_3-CH_2-CH_2-\underset{OH}{CH}-CH_3$$

STUDY CHECK 12.10

Draw the condensed structural formula for the product obtained by the hydration of 2-methyl-2-butene.

ANSWER

$$CH_3-\underset{\underset{CH_3}{|}}{\overset{\overset{OH}{|}}{C}}-CH_2-CH_3$$

FIGURE 12.7 ▶ Synthetic polymers are used to replace diseased veins and arteries.

Ⓠ Why are the substances in these plastic devices called polymers?

Addition of Alkenes: Polymerization

A **polymer** is a large molecule that consists of small repeating units called **monomers**. In the past hundred years, the plastics industry has made synthetic polymers that are in many of the materials we use every day, such as carpeting, plastic wrap, nonstick pans, plastic cups, and rain gear. In medicine, synthetic polymers are used to replace diseased or damaged body parts such as hip joints, pacemakers, teeth, heart valves, and blood vessels (see Figure 12.7). There are about 100 billion kg of plastics produced every year, which is about 15 kg for every person on Earth.

Many of the synthetic polymers are made by addition reactions of small alkene monomers. Many polymerization reactions require high temperature, a catalyst, and high pressure (over 1000 atm). In an addition reaction, a polymer grows longer as each monomer is added at the end of the chain. A polymer may contain as many as 1000 monomers. Polyethylene, a polymer made from ethylene monomers, is used in plastic bottles, film, and plastic dinnerware. More polyethylene is produced worldwide than any other polymer. Low-density polyethylene (LDPE) is flexible, breakable, less dense, and more branched than high-density polyethylene (HDPE). High-density polyethylene is stronger, more dense, and melts at a higher temperature than LDPE.

Ethene (ethylene) monomers   Polyethylene section

Table 12.9 lists several alkene monomers that are used to produce common synthetic polymers, and Figure 12.8 shows examples of each. The alkane-like nature of these plastic synthetic polymers makes them unreactive. Thus, they do not decompose easily (they are not biodegradable). As a result, they have become significant contributors to pollution, on land and in the oceans. Efforts are being made to make them more degradable.

TABLE 12.9 Some Alkenes and Their Polymers

Recycling Code	Monomer	Polymer Section	Common Uses
2 HDPE 4 LDPE	$H_2C{=}CH_2$ Ethene (ethylene)	Polyethylene (PE)	Plastic bottles, film, insulation materials, shopping bags
3 V	$H_2C{=}CH$—Cl Chloroethene (vinyl chloride)	Polyvinyl chloride (PVC)	Plastic pipes and tubing, garden hoses, garbage bags, shower curtains, credit cards, medical containers
5 PP	$H_2C{=}CH$—CH_3 Propene (propylene)	Polypropylene (PP)	Ski and hiking clothing, carpets, artificial joints, plastic bottles, food containers, medical face masks, tubing
	$F{-}C{=}C{-}F$ Tetrafluoroethene	Polytetrafluoroethylene (PTFE)	Nonstick coatings, Teflon
	$H_2C{=}C$—Cl 1,1-Dichloroethene	Polydichloroethylene (Saran)	Plastic film and wrap, Gore-Tex rainwear, medical implants
6 PS	$H_2C{=}CH$ Phenylethene (styrene)	Polystyrene (PS)	Plastic coffee cups and cartons, insulation

You can identify the type of polymer used to manufacture a plastic item by looking for the recycling symbol (arrows in a triangle) found on the label or on the bottom of the plastic container. For example, the number 5 or the letters PP inside the triangle is the code for a polypropylene plastic. There are now many cities that maintain recycling programs that reduce the amount of plastic materials that are transported to landfills.

Today, products such as lumber, tables and benches, trash receptacles, and pipes used for irrigation systems are made from recycled plastics.

Tables, benches, and trash receptacles can be manufactured from recycled plastics.

Explore Your World

Polymers and Recycling Plastics

1. Make a list of the items you use or have in your room or home that are made of polymers.
2. Recycling information on the bottom or side of a plastic bottle includes a triangle with a code number that identifies the type of polymer used to make the plastic. Make a collection of several different kinds of plastic bottles. Try to find plastic items with each type of polymer.

Questions

1. What are the most common types of plastics among the plastic containers in your collection?
2. What are the monomers of some of the plastics you looked at?

Polyethylene

Polyvinyl chloride

Polypropylene

Polytetrafluoroethylene (Teflon)

Polydichloroethylene (Saran)

Polystyrene

FIGURE 12.8 ▶ Synthetic polymers provide a wide variety of items that we use every day.

Q What are some alkenes used to make the polymers in these plastic items?

▶ SAMPLE PROBLEM 12.11 Polymers

A firefighter/EMT arrives at a home where a premature baby has been delivered. To prevent hypothermia during transport to the neonatal facility, she wraps the baby in cling wrap. Draw and name the monomer unit and draw a portion of the polymer formed from three monomer units for cling wrap, which is polydichloroethylene (ethene).

SOLUTION

$$H_2C=C-Cl$$

1,1-Dichloroethene

$$-\overset{H}{\underset{H}{C}}-\overset{Cl}{\underset{Cl}{C}}-\overset{H}{\underset{H}{C}}-\overset{Cl}{\underset{Cl}{C}}-\overset{H}{\underset{H}{C}}-\overset{Cl}{\underset{Cl}{C}}-$$

STUDY CHECK 12.11

Draw the condensed structural formula for the monomer used in the manufacturing of PVC.

ANSWER

$$H_2C=CH-Cl$$

QUESTIONS AND PROBLEMS

12.7 Addition Reactions for Alkenes

LEARNING GOAL Draw the condensed or line-angle structural formulas and give the names for the organic products of addition reactions of alkenes. Draw a condensed structural formula for a section of a polymer.

12.39 Draw the structural formula for the product in each of the following reactions using Markovnikov's rule when necessary:

a. $CH_3-CH_2-CH_2-CH=CH_2 + H_2 \xrightarrow{Pt}$

b. $H_2C=\overset{\overset{\displaystyle CH_3}{|}}{C}-CH_2-CH_3 + H_2O \xrightarrow{H^+}$

c.  [line-angle structure] $+ H_2 \xrightarrow{Pt}$

d. 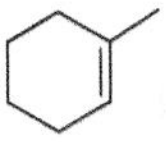 [cyclohexene with methyl] $+ H_2O \xrightarrow{H^+}$

12.40 Draw the structural formula for the product in each of the following reactions using Markovnikov's rule when necessary:

a. $CH_3-CH_2-CH=CH_2 + H_2O \xrightarrow{H^+}$

b. 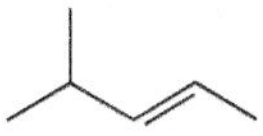 [line-angle structure] $+ H_2 \xrightarrow{Pt}$

c. 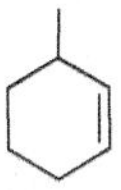 [methylcyclohexene] $+ H_2 \xrightarrow{Pt}$

d.  [line-angle structure] $+ H_2O \xrightarrow{H^+}$

12.41 What is a polymer?

12.42 What is a monomer?

12.43 Write an equation that represents the formation of a portion of polypropylene from three of its monomers.

12.44 Write an equation that represents the formation of a portion of polystyrene from three of its monomers.

12.45 The plastic polyvinylidene difluoride, PVDF, is made from monomers of 1,1-difluoroethene. Draw the expanded structural formula for a portion of the polymer formed from three monomers of 1,1-difluoroethene.

12.46 The polymer polyacrylonitrile, PAN, used in the fabric material Orlon is made from monomers of acrylonitrile. Draw the expanded structural formula for a portion of the polymer formed from three monomers of acrylonitrile.

$$H_2C=\overset{\overset{\displaystyle CN}{|}}{C}H$$

Acrylonitrile

12.8 Aromatic Compounds

In 1825, Michael Faraday isolated a hydrocarbon called **benzene**, which consists of a ring of six carbon atoms with one hydrogen atom attached to each carbon. Because many compounds containing benzene had fragrant odors, the family of benzene compounds became known as **aromatic compounds**. Some common examples of aromatic compounds that we use for flavor are anisole from anise, estragole from tarragon, and thymol from thyme.

LEARNING GOAL

Describe the bonding in benzene; name aromatic compounds, and draw their line-angle structural formulas.

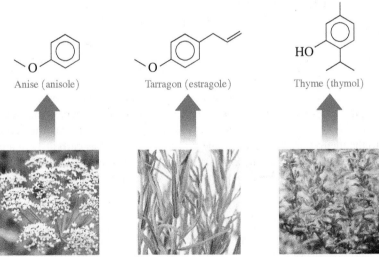

Anise (anisole)   Tarragon (estragole)   Thyme (thymol)

The aroma and flavor of the herbs anise, tarragon, and thyme are because of aromatic compounds.

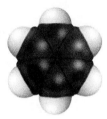

The space-filling model for benzene consists of a six-carbon ring with six hydrogen atoms.

In benzene, each carbon atom uses three valence electrons to bond to the hydrogen atom and two adjacent carbons. That leaves one valence electron, which scientists first thought was shared in a double bond with an adjacent carbon. In 1865, August Kekulé proposed that the carbon atoms in benzene were arranged in a flat ring with alternating single and double bonds between the adjacent carbon atoms. There are two possible structural representations of benzene in which the double bonds can form between two different carbon atoms. If there were double bonds as in alkenes, then benzene should be much more reactive than it is.

However, unlike the alkenes and alkynes, aromatic hydrocarbons do not easily undergo addition reactions. If their reaction behavior is quite different, they must also differ in how the atoms are bonded in their structures. Today, we know that the six electrons are shared equally among the six carbon atoms. This unique feature of benzene makes it especially stable. Benzene is most often represented as a line-angle structural formula, which shows a hexagon with a circle in the center. Some of the ways to represent benzene are shown as follows:

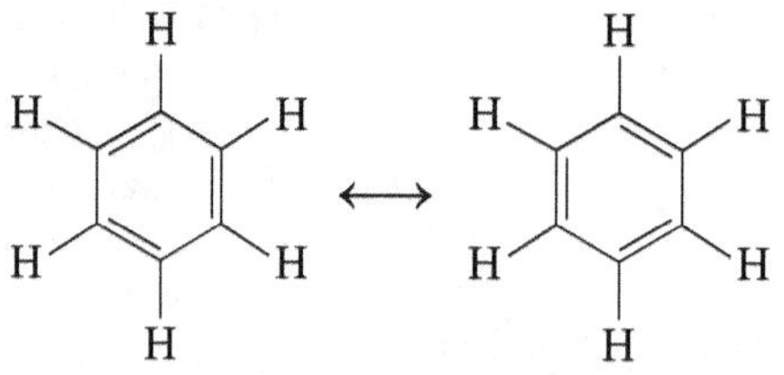

Equivalent structures for benzene

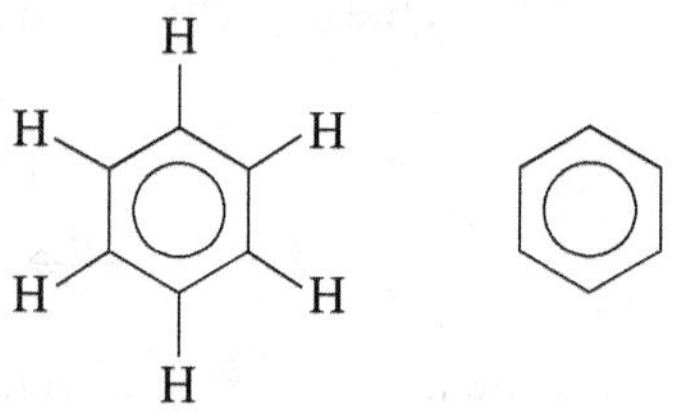

Structural formulas for benzene

Naming Aromatic Compounds

Many compounds containing benzene have been important in chemistry for many years and still use their common names. Names such as toluene, aniline, and phenol are allowed by IUPAC rules.

Toluene
(methylbenzene)

Aniline
(aminobenzene)

Phenol
(hydroxybenzene)

When a benzene ring is a substituent, —C_6H_5, it is named as a phenyl group.

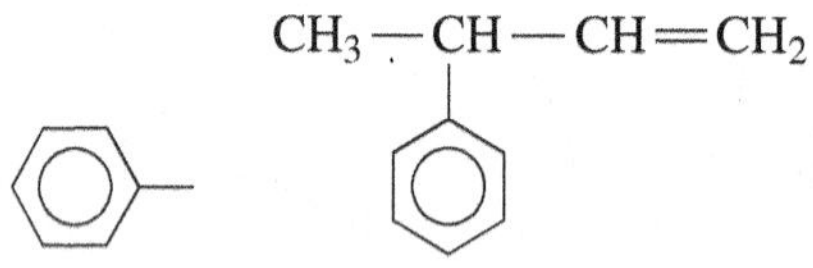

Phenyl group   3-Phenyl-1-butene

When benzene has only one substituent, the ring is not numbered. When there are two substituents, the benzene ring is numbered to give the lowest numbers to the substituents. When a common name can be used such as toluene, phenol, or aniline, the carbon atom attached to the methyl, hydroxyl, or amine group is numbered as carbon 1. In a common name, there are prefixes that are used to show the position of two substituents. The prefix **ortho** (*o*) indicates a 1,2-arrangement, **meta** (*m*) is a 1,3-arrangement, and **para** (*p*) is used for 1,4- arrangements.

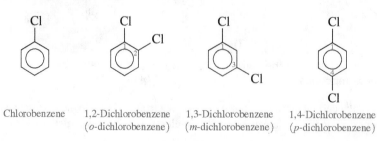

Chlorobenzene   1,2-Dichlorobenzene   1,3-Dichlorobenzene   1,4-Dichlorobenzene
                  (*o*-dichlorobenzene)   (*m*-dichlorobenzene)   (*p*-dichlorobenzene)

The common name xylene is used for the isomers of dimethylbenzene.

CH3
CH3
1
2
CH3
1
2
3
CH3
CH3
1
2
3
4
CH3

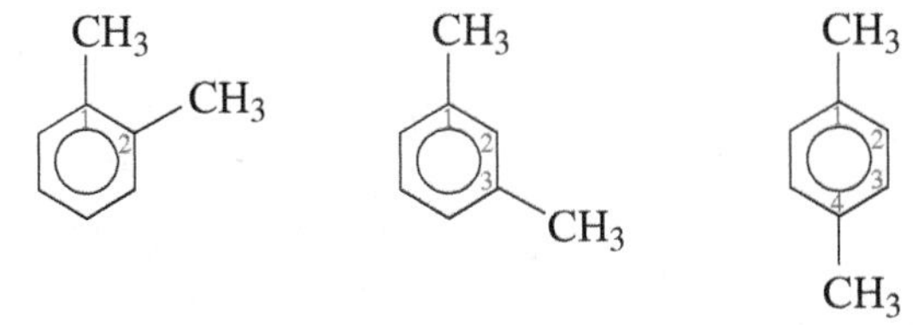

1,2-Dimethylbenzene (*o*-xylene) 1,3-Dimethylbenzene (*m*-xylene) 1,4-Dimethylbenzene (*p*-xylene)

When there are three or more substituents attached to the benzene ring, they are numbered in the direction to give the lowest set of numbers and then named alphabetically.

SAMPLE PROBLEM 12.12 Naming Aromatic Compounds

Give the IUPAC name for the following:

CH3
Cl
Br

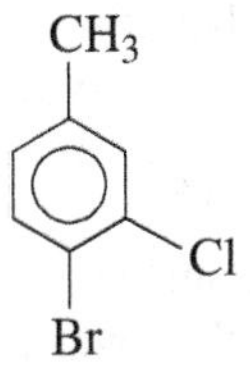

SOLUTION

4-bromo-3-chlorotoluene

STUDY CHECK 12.12

Give the IUPAC and common name for the following compound:

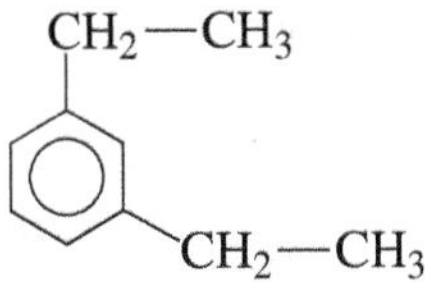

CH2—CH3
CH2—CH3

ANSWER

1,3-diethylbenzene (*m*-diethylbenzene)

Chemistry Link to **Health**

Some Common Aromatic Compounds in Nature and Medicine

Aromatic compounds are common in nature and in medicine. Toluene is used as a reactant to make drugs, dyes, and explosives such as TNT (trinitrotoluene). The benzene ring is found in some amino acids (the building blocks of proteins); in pain relievers such as aspirin, acetaminophen, and ibuprofen; and in flavorings such as vanillin.

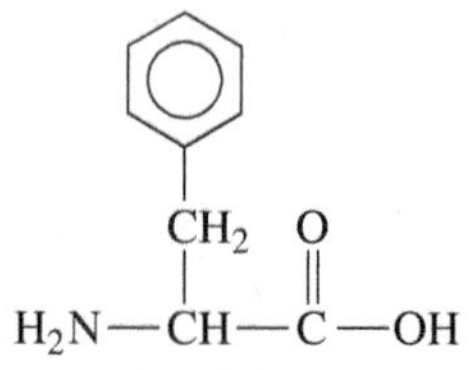

Phenylalanine
(amino acid)

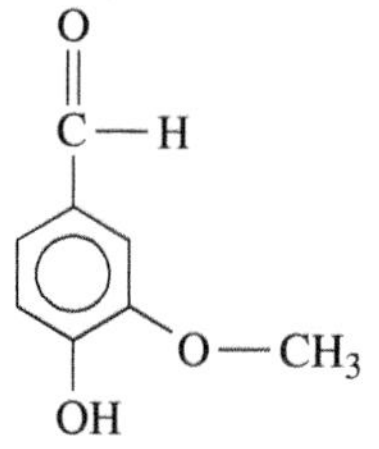

Vanillin

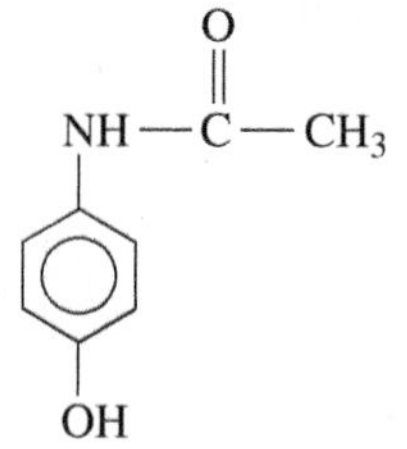

Acetaminophen

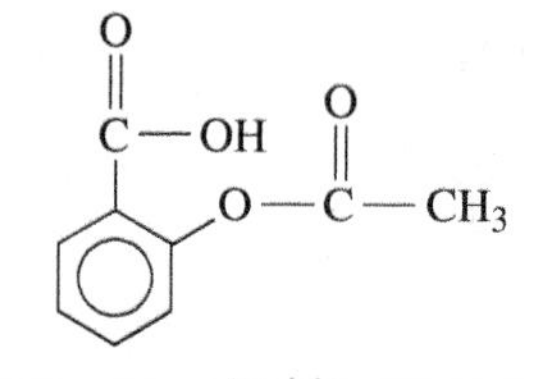

Aspirin

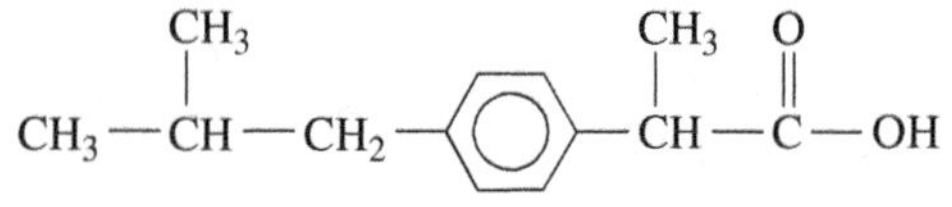

Ibuprofen

Properties of Aromatic Compounds

The flat symmetrical structure of benzene allows the individual cyclic structures to be very close together, which contributes to the higher melting points and boiling points of benzene and its derivatives. For example, hexane melts at −95 °C, whereas benzene melts at 6 °C. Among the disubstituted benzene compounds, the *para* isomers are more symmetric and have higher melting points than the *ortho* and *meta* isomers: *o*-xylene melts at −26 °C and *m*-xylene melts at −48 °C, whereas *p*-xylene melts at 13 °C.

Aromatic compounds are less dense than water, although they are somewhat denser than other hydrocarbons. Halogenated benzene compounds are denser than water. Aromatic hydrocarbons are insoluble in water and are used as solvents for other organic compounds. Only those aromatic compounds containing strongly polar functional groups such as —OH or —COOH will be somewhat soluble in water. Benzene and other aromatic compounds are resistant to reactions that break up the aromatic system, although they are flammable, as are other hydrocarbon compounds.

QUESTIONS AND PROBLEMS

12.8 Aromatic Compounds

LEARNING GOAL Describe the bonding in benzene; name aromatic compounds, and draw their line-angle structural formulas.

12.47 Give the IUPAC name and any common name for each of the following:

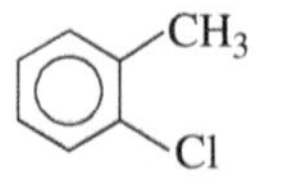

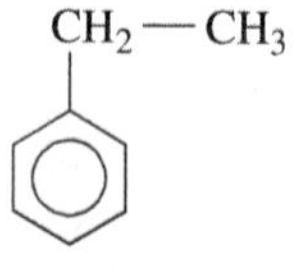

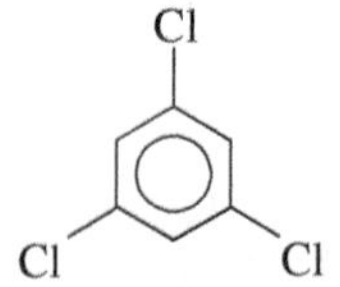

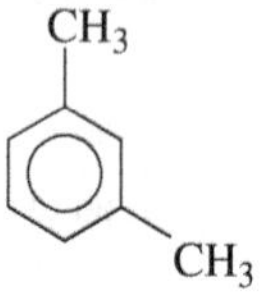

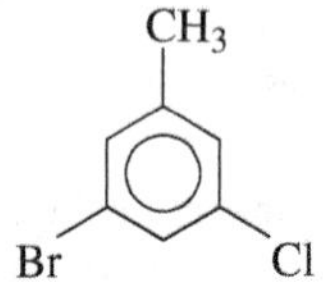

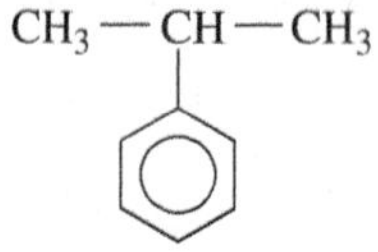

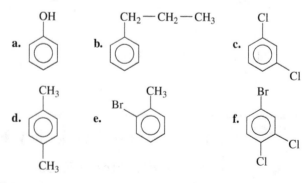

12.48 Give the IUPAC name and any common name for each of the following:

12.49 Draw the structural formula for each of the following:
   a. aniline
   b. 1-bromo-3-chlorobenzene
   c. 1-ethyl-4-methylbenzene
   d. *p*-chlorotoluene

12.50 Draw the structural formula for each of the following:
   a. *m*-dibromobenzene
   b. *o*-chloroethylbenzene
   c. propylbenzene
   d. 1,2,4-trichlorobenzene

Chemistry Link to Health

Polycyclic Aromatic Hydrocarbons (PAHs)

Large aromatic compounds known as *polycyclic aromatic hydrocarbons* (PAHs) are formed by fusing together two or more benzene rings edge to edge. In a fused-ring compound, neighboring benzene rings share two carbon atoms. Naphthalene, with two benzene rings, is well known for its use in mothballs; anthracene, with three rings, is used in the manufacture of dyes.

Naphthalene　　　Anthracene　　　Phenanthrene

When a polycyclic compound contains phenanthrene, it may act as a carcinogen, a substance known to cause cancer.

Compounds containing five or more fused benzene rings such as benzo[*a*]pyrene are potent carcinogens. The molecules interact with the DNA in the cells, causing abnormal cell growth and cancer. Increased exposure to carcinogens increases the chance of DNA alterations in the cells. Benzo[*a*]pyrene, a product of combustion, has been identified in coal tar, tobacco smoke, barbecued meats, and automobile exhaust.

Benzo[*a*]pyrene

Aromatic compounds such as benzo[*a*]pyrene are strongly associated with lung cancers.

Clinical Update

Diane's Treatment in the Burn Unit

When Diane arrived at the hospital, she was transferred to the ICU burn unit. She had second-degree burns that caused damage to the underlying layers of skin and third-degree burns that caused damage to all the layers of the skin. Because body fluids are lost when deep burns occur, a lactated Ringer's solution was administered. The most common complications of burns are related to infection. To prevent infection, her skin was covered with a topical antibiotic. The next day Diane was placed in a tank to remove dressings, lotions, and damaged tissue. Dressings and ointments were changed every eight hours. Over a period of 3 months, grafts of Diane's unburned skin were used to cover burned areas. She remained in the burn unit for 3 months and then was discharged. However, Diane returned to the hospital for more skin grafts and plastic surgery.

The arson investigators determined that gasoline was the primary accelerant used to start the fire at Diane's house. Because there was a lot of paper and dry wood in the area, the fire spread quickly. Some of the hydrocarbons found in gasoline include hexane, heptane, octane, nonane, decane, and cyclohexane. Some other hydrocarbons in gasoline are isooctane, butane, 3-ethyltoluene, isopentane, toluene, and 1,3-dimethylbenzene.

℞ Clinical Applications

12.51 The medications for Diane were contained in blister packs made of polychlorotrifluoroethylene (PCTFE). Draw the expanded structural formula for a portion of PCTFE polymer from three monomers of chlorotrifluoroethylene shown below:

Tablets are contained in blister packs made from polychlorotrifluoroethylene (PCTFE).

Chlorotrifluoroethylene

12.52 New polymers have been synthesized to replace PVC in IV bags and cling film. One of these is EVA, ethylene polyvinyl-acetate. Draw the expanded structural formula for a portion of EVA using an alternating sequence that has three of each monomer shown below:

Ethylene

Vinyl acetate

12.53 Write the balanced chemical equation for the complete combustion of each of the following hydrocarbons found in gasoline used to start a fire:
a. nonane
b. isopentane (2-methylbutane)
c. 3-ethyltoluene

12.54 Write the balanced chemical equation for the complete combustion of each of the following hydrocarbons found in gasoline used to start a fire:
a. isooctane (2,2,4-trimethylpentane)
b. cyclohexane
c. 1,3-dimethylbenzene

CONCEPT MAP

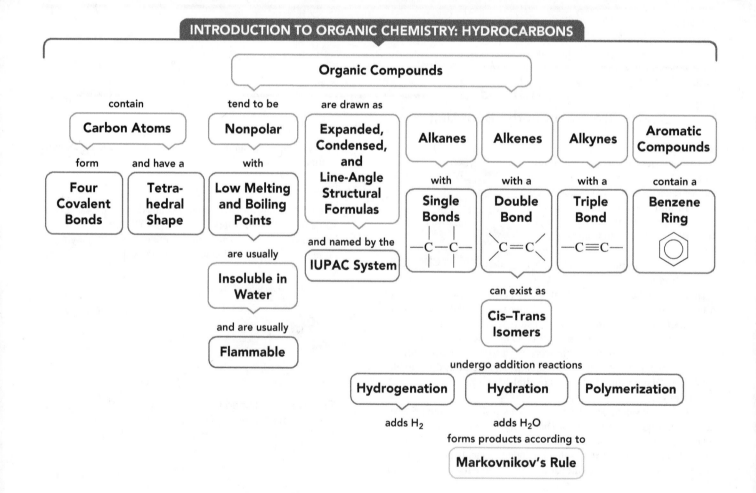

INTRODUCTION TO ORGANIC CHEMISTRY: HYDROCARBONS

CHAPTER REVIEW

12.1 Organic Compounds

LEARNING GOAL Identify properties characteristic of organic or inorganic compounds.

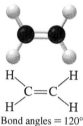

- Organic compounds have covalent bonds, most form nonpolar molecules, have low melting points and low boiling points, are not very soluble in water, dissolve as molecules in solutions, and burn vigorously in air.
- Inorganic compounds are often ionic or contain polar covalent bonds and form polar molecules, have high melting and boiling points, are usually soluble in water, produce ions in water, and do not burn in air.
- In the simplest organic molecule, methane, CH_4, the C—H bonds that attach four hydrogen atoms to the carbon atom are directed to the corners of a tetrahedron with bond angles of 109°.
- In the expanded structural formula, a separate line is drawn for every bond.

12.2 Alkanes

LEARNING GOAL Write the IUPAC names and draw the condensed or line-angle structural formulas for alkanes and cycloalkanes.

- Alkanes are hydrocarbons that have only C—C single bonds.
- A condensed structural formula depicts groups composed of each carbon atom and its attached hydrogen atoms.
- A line-angle structural formula represents the carbon skeleton as ends and corners of a zigzag line or geometric figure.
- The IUPAC system is used to name organic compounds by indicating the number of carbon atoms.
- The name of a cycloalkane is written by placing the prefix *cyclo* before the alkane name with the same number of carbon atoms.

12.3 Alkanes with Substituents

LEARNING GOAL Write the IUPAC names for alkanes with substituents and draw their condensed and line-angle structural formulas.

- Structural isomers are compounds with the same molecular formulas that differ in the order in which their atoms are bonded.
- Substituents, which are attached to an alkane chain, include alkyl groups and halogen atoms (F, Cl, Br, or I).
- In the IUPAC system, alkyl substituents have names such as methyl, propyl, and isopropyl; halogen atoms are named as fluoro, chloro, bromo, or iodo.

12.4 Properties of Alkanes

LEARNING GOAL Identify the properties of alkanes and write a balanced chemical equation for combustion.

- Alkanes, which are nonpolar molecules, are not soluble in water, and usually less dense than water.
- Alkanes undergo combustion in which they react with oxygen to produce carbon dioxide, water, and energy.

12.5 Alkenes and Alkynes

LEARNING GOAL Identify structural formulas as alkenes, cycloalkenes, and alkynes, and write their IUPAC names.

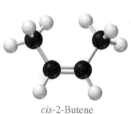

Bond angles = 120°
Ethene

- Alkenes are unsaturated hydrocarbons that contain carbon–carbon double bonds.
- Alkynes contain a carbon–carbon triple bond.
- The IUPAC names of alkenes end with *ene*, while alkyne names end with *yne*. The main chain is numbered from the end nearer the double or triple bond.

12.6 Cis–Trans Isomers

LEARNING GOAL Draw the condensed and line-angle structural formulas and give the names for the cis–trans isomers of alkenes.

cis-2-Butene

- Geometric or cis–trans isomers of alkenes occur when the carbon atoms in the double bond are connected to different atoms or groups.
- In the cis isomer, the similar groups are on the same side of the double bond, whereas in the trans isomer they are connected on opposite sides of the double bond.

12.7 Addition Reactions for Alkenes

LEARNING GOAL Draw the condensed or line-angle structural formulas and give the names for the organic products of addition reactions of alkenes. Draw a condensed structural formula for a section of a polymer.

- The addition of small molecules to the double bond is a characteristic reaction of alkenes.
- Hydrogenation adds hydrogen atoms to the double bond of an alkene to yield an alkane.
- Hydration adds water to a double bond of an alkene to form an alcohol.
- When a different number of hydrogen atoms are attached to the carbons in a double bond, the H— from water adds to the carbon with the greater number of H atoms (Markovnikov's rule).
- Polymers are long-chain molecules that consist of many repeating units of smaller carbon molecules called monomers.
- Many materials that we use every day are made from synthetic polymers, including carpeting, plastic wrap, nonstick pans, and nylon.
- Many synthetic materials are made using addition reactions in which a catalyst links the carbon atoms from various kinds of alkene molecules (monomers).
- Many materials used in medicine are made from synthetic polymers, including tubing, IV containers, and face masks.

12.8 Aromatic Compounds

LEARNING GOAL Describe the bonding in benzene; name aromatic compounds, and draw their line-angle structural formulas.

Ibuprofen

- Most aromatic compounds contain benzene, C_6H_6, a cyclic structure containing six carbon atoms and six hydrogen atoms.
- The structure of benzene is represented as a hexagon with a circle in the center.
- The IUPAC system uses the names of benzene, toluene, aniline, and phenol.
- In the IUPAC name, two or more substituents are numbered and listed in alphabetical order. In the common name, with two substituents, the positions are shown by the prefixes *ortho* (1,2-), *meta* (1,3-), and *para* (1,4-).

SUMMARY OF NAMING

Family	Structure	IUPAC Name	Common Name
Alkane	$CH_3-CH_2-CH_3$	Propane	
	$CH_3-CH(CH_3)-CH_2-CH_3$	2-Methylbutane	Isopentane
Haloalkane	$CH_3-CH_2-CH_2-Cl$	1-Chloropropane	Propyl chloride
Cycloalkane	(hexagon)	Cyclohexane	
Alkene	$CH_3-CH=CH_2$	Propene	Propylene
	(Br,H on C=C cis)	*cis*-1,2-Dibromoethene	
	(Br,H on C=C trans)	*trans*-1,2-Dibromoethene	
Cycloalkene	(triangle)	Cyclopropene	
Alkyne	$CH_3-C\equiv CH$	Propyne	
Aromatic	(toluene)	Methylbenzene; toluene	
	(1,3-dichlorobenzene)	1,3-Dichlorobenzene	*m*-Dichlorobenzene

SUMMARY OF REACTIONS

The chapter sections to review are shown after the name of the reaction.

Combustion (12.4)

$$CH_3-CH_2-CH_3(g) + 5O_2(g) \xrightarrow{\Delta} 3CO_2(g) + 4H_2O(g) + energy$$
Propane

Hydrogenation (12.7)

$$H_2C=CH-CH_3 + H_2 \xrightarrow{Pt} CH_3-CH_2-CH_3$$
Propene · Propane

Hydration (12.7)

Markovnikov's Rule

$$H_2C = CH - CH_3 + H_2O \xrightarrow{H^+} CH_3 - \overset{\displaystyle OH}{\underset{\displaystyle |}{CH}} - CH_3$$

Propene   2-Propanol

Polymerization (12.7)

$$H_2C = CH_2 + H_2C = CH_2 + H_2C = CH_2 \xrightarrow[\text{catalyst}]{\text{Heat, pressure,}} -CH_2 - CH_2 - CH_2 - CH_2 - CH_2 - CH_2 -$$

Ethene   Polyethylene

KEY TERMS

addition A reaction in which atoms or groups of atoms bond to a carbon–carbon double bond. Addition reactions include the addition of hydrogen (hydrogenation), and water (hydration).

alkane A hydrocarbon that contains only single bonds between carbon atoms.

alkene A hydrocarbon that contains one or more carbon–carbon double bonds ($C = C$).

alkyl group An alkane minus one hydrogen atom. Alkyl groups are named like the alkanes except a *yl* ending replaces *ane*.

alkyne A hydrocarbon that contains one or more carbon–carbon triple bonds ($C \equiv C$).

aromatic compound A compound that contains the ring structure of benzene.

benzene A ring of six carbon atoms, each of which is attached to a hydrogen atom, C_6H_6.

cis isomer An isomer of an alkene in which similar groups in the double bond are on the same side.

condensed structural formula A structural formula that shows the arrangement of the carbon atoms in a molecule but groups each carbon atom with its bonded hydrogen atoms

$$-CH_3, \ -CH_2-, \text{ or } -\overset{\displaystyle |}{CH}-.$$

cycloalkane An alkane that is a ring or cyclic structure.

expanded structural formula A type of structural formula that shows the arrangement of the atoms by drawing each bond in the hydrocarbon.

hydration An addition reaction in which the components of water, $H-$ and $-OH$, bond to the carbon–carbon double bond to form an alcohol.

hydrocarbon An organic compound that contains only carbon and hydrogen.

hydrogenation The addition of hydrogen (H_2) to the double bond of alkenes to yield alkanes.

IUPAC system A system for naming organic compounds devised by the International Union of Pure and Applied Chemistry.

line-angle structural formula A simplified structure that shows a zig-zag line in which carbon atoms are represented as the ends of each line and as corners.

Markovnikov's rule When adding water to alkenes with different numbers of groups attached to the double bonds, the $H-$ adds to the carbon that has the greater number of hydrogen atoms.

meta A method of naming that indicates substituents at carbons 1 and 3 of a benzene ring.

monomer The small organic molecule that is repeated many times in a polymer.

organic compound A compound made of carbon that typically has covalent bonds, is nonpolar, has low melting and boiling points, is insoluble in water, and is flammable.

ortho A method of naming that indicates substituents at carbons 1 and 2 of a benzene ring.

para A method of naming that indicates substituents at carbons 1 and 4 of a benzene ring.

polymer A very large molecule that is composed of many small, repeating monomer units.

structural isomers Organic compounds in which identical molecular formulas have different arrangements of atoms.

substituent Groups of atoms such as an alkyl group or a halogen bonded to the main carbon chain or ring of carbon atoms.

trans isomer An isomer of an alkene in which similar groups in the double bond are on opposite sides.

⚛ CORE CHEMISTRY SKILLS

The chapter section containing each Core Chemistry Skill is shown in parentheses at the end of each heading.

Naming and Drawing Alkanes (12.2)

- The alkanes ethane, propane, and butane contain two, three, and four carbon atoms, respectively, connected in a row or a *continuous* chain.
- Alkanes with five or more carbon atoms in a chain are named using the prefixes *pent* (5), *hex* (6), *hept* (7), *oct* (8), *non* (9), and *dec* (10).

- In the condensed structural formula, the carbon and hydrogen atoms on the ends are written as $-CH_3$ and the carbon and hydrogen atoms in the middle are written as $-CH_2-$.

Example: a. What is the name of $CH_3 - CH_2 - CH_2 - CH_3$?
b. Draw the condensed structural formula for pentane.

Answer: a. An alkane with a four-carbon chain is named with the prefix *but* followed by *ane*, which is butane.
b. Pentane is an alkane with a five-carbon chain. The carbon atoms on the ends are attached to three H atoms each, and the carbon atoms in the middle are attached to two H each. $CH_3 - CH_2 - CH_2 - CH_2 - CH_3$

Writing Equations for Hydrogenation, Hydration, and Polymerization (12.7)

- The addition of small molecules to the double bond is a characteristic reaction of alkenes.
- Hydrogenation adds hydrogen atoms to the double bond of an alkene to form an alkane.
- Hydration adds water to a double bond of an alkene to form an alcohol.
- When a different number of hydrogen atoms are attached to the carbons in a double bond, the H— from water adds to the carbon atom with the greater number of H atoms, and the —OH adds to the other carbon atom from the double bond.

Example: **a.** Draw the condensed structural formula for 2-methyl-2-butene.

b. Draw the condensed structural formula for the product of the hydrogenation of 2-methyl-2-butene.

c. Draw the condensed structural formula for the product of the hydration of 2-methyl-2-butene.

Answer: **a.** CH₃—C=CH—CH₃ with CH₃ group on the C

$$CH_3-\overset{\overset{\displaystyle CH_3}{|}}{C}=CH-CH_3$$

b. When H₂ adds to a double bond, the product is an alkane with the same number of carbon atoms.

$$CH_3-\overset{\overset{\displaystyle CH_3}{|}}{CH}-CH_2-CH_3$$

c. When water adds to a double bond, the product is an alcohol, which has an —OH group. The H— from water adds to the carbon atom in the double bond that has the greater number of H atoms.

$$CH_3-\overset{\overset{\displaystyle CH_3}{|}}{\underset{\underset{\displaystyle OH}{|}}{C}}-CH_2-CH_3$$

UNDERSTANDING THE CONCEPTS

The chapter sections to review are shown in parentheses at the end of each question.

12.55 Match the following physical and chemical properties with potassium chloride, KCl, used in salt substitutes, or butane, C₄H₁₀, used in lighters: (12.1)

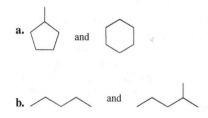

a. melts at −138 °C
b. burns vigorously in air
c. melts at 770 °C
d. contains ionic bonds
e. is a gas at room temperature

12.56 Match the following physical and chemical properties with octane, C₈H₁₈, found in gasoline, or magnesium sulfate, MgSO₄, also called Epsom salts: (12.1)
a. contains only covalent bonds
b. melts at 1124 °C
c. is insoluble in water
d. is a liquid at room temperature
e. is a strong electrolyte

12.57 Identify the compounds in each of the following pairs as structural isomers or not structural isomers: (12.3)

a. [cyclopentane with methyl] and [cyclohexane]

b. [line structure] and [line structure]

12.58 Identify the compounds in each of the following pairs as structural isomers or not structural isomers: (12.3)

a.

$$CH_2-CH_2-CH_2 \quad CH_2-CH_3$$
with CH₃ and CH₂—CH₃ groups   and   CH₃ ... CH₂—CH₂—CH₂—CH₃ with CH₃ group

b. [cyclohexane] and [methylcyclopentane]

12.59 Convert each of the following line-angle structural formulas to a condensed structural formula and give its IUPAC name: (12.3)

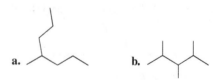

a. [line structure] **b.** [line structure with Cl and Br]

12.60 Convert each of the following line-angle structural formulas to a condensed structural formula and give its IUPAC name: (12.3)

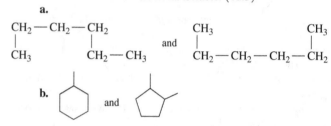

a. [line structure] **b.** [line structure]

12.61 Draw a portion of the polymer of Teflon, which is made from 1,1,2,2-tetrafluoroethene (use three monomers). (12.7)

Teflon is used as a nonstick coating on cooking pans.

12.62 A garden hose is made of polyvinyl chloride (PVC) from chloroethene (vinyl chloride). Draw a portion of the polymer (use three monomers) for PVC. (12.7)

A garden hose is made of polyvinyl chloride (PVC).

12.63 Give the number of carbon atoms and the types of carbon–carbon bonds for each of the following: (12.2, 12.3, 12.5)
a. propane
b. cyclopropane
c. propene
d. propyne

12.64 Give the number of carbon atoms and the types of carbon–carbon bonds for each of the following: (12.2, 12.3, 12.5)
a. butane
b. cyclobutane
c. cyclobutene
d. 2-butyne

ADDITIONAL QUESTIONS AND PROBLEMS

12.65 Give the IUPAC name for each of the following: (12.3)

a.
$$CH_3-CH_2-\underset{\underset{\displaystyle CH_3}{\overset{\displaystyle CH_3}{|}}}{\overset{|}{C}}-CH_3$$

b. CH_3-CH_2-Cl

c.
$$CH_3-CH_2-\underset{\displaystyle CH_3}{\overset{\displaystyle CH_3-CH_2}{|}}\;\;\underset{\displaystyle Br}{|}\\CH_3-CH_2-CH-CH_2-CH-CH_3$$

d.

12.66 Give the IUPAC name for each of the following: (12.3)

a.

b.
$$Cl-CH_2-\underset{\underset{\displaystyle Br}{|}}{CH}-CH_2-Br$$

c.
$$CH_3-\underset{\underset{\displaystyle CH_2}{\overset{\displaystyle CH_3}{|}}}{CH}-CH-CH_3\\ \qquad\qquad\underset{\underset{\displaystyle CH_2}{|}}{CH_2}\\ \qquad\qquad\underset{|}{CH_2}\\ \qquad\qquad CH_3$$

d.
$$CH_3-CH_2-\underset{\underset{\displaystyle CH_2}{\overset{\displaystyle Cl}{|}}}{C}-CH_2-CH_3\\ \qquad\qquad\underset{\underset{\displaystyle CH_2}{|}}{CH_2}\\ \qquad\qquad CH_3$$

12.67 Draw the condensed structural formula for alkanes or the line-angle structural formula for cycloalkanes for each of the following: (12.3, 12.5, 12.6)
a. 1,2-dibromocyclopentene
b. 2-hexyne
c. *cis*-2-heptene

12.68 Draw the condensed structural formula for alkanes or the line-angle structural formula for cycloalkanes for each of the following: (12.3, 12.5, 12.6)
a. *trans*-3-hexene
b. 2-bromo-3-chlorocyclohexene
c. 3-chloro-1-butyne

12.69 Give the IUPAC name for each of the following: (12.5, 12.6)

a.
$$\underset{\displaystyle H}{\overset{\displaystyle CH_3}{\diagdown}}C=C\underset{\displaystyle CH_2-CH_3}{\overset{\displaystyle H}{\diagup}}$$

b.

c.

12.70 Give the IUPAC name for each of the following: (12.5, 12.6)

a.
$$H_2C=\underset{\overset{\displaystyle |}{\displaystyle CH_3}}{C}-CH_2-CH_2-CH_3$$

b.

c.

12.71 Indicate if each of the following pairs represents structural isomers, cis–trans isomers, or identical compounds: (12.5, 12.6)

a. and

b.
$$\underset{\displaystyle H}{\overset{\displaystyle CH_3}{\diagdown}}C=C\underset{\displaystyle CH_3}{\overset{\displaystyle H}{\diagup}}\quad and\quad \underset{\displaystyle H}{\overset{\displaystyle CH_3}{\diagdown}}C=C\underset{\displaystyle H}{\overset{\displaystyle CH_3}{\diagup}}$$

12.72 Indicate if each of the following pairs represents structural isomers, cis–trans isomers, or identical compounds: (12.5, 12.6)

a.
$$H_2C=\underset{\underset{\displaystyle CH_3}{\overset{\displaystyle |}{CH_2}}}{\overset{\displaystyle CH}{\underset{\displaystyle |}{CH_2}}}\quad and\quad CH_3-CH_2-CH_2-CH=CH_2$$

b. and

12.73 Write the IUPAC name, including cis or trans, for each of the following: (12.5, 12.6)

a.
$$\underset{\displaystyle H}{\overset{\displaystyle CH_3-CH_2}{\diagdown}}C=C\underset{\displaystyle H}{\overset{\displaystyle CH_2-CH_2-CH_3}{\diagup}}$$

b. 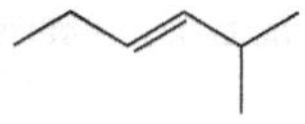

c. 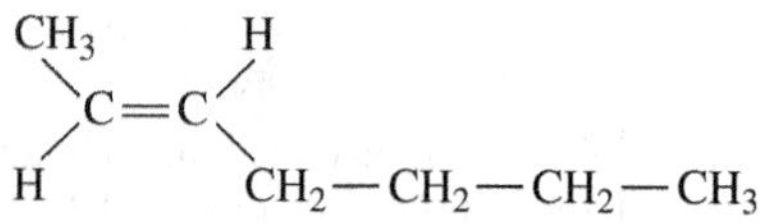

12.74 Write the IUPAC name, including cis or trans, for each of the following: (12.5, 12.6)

a. 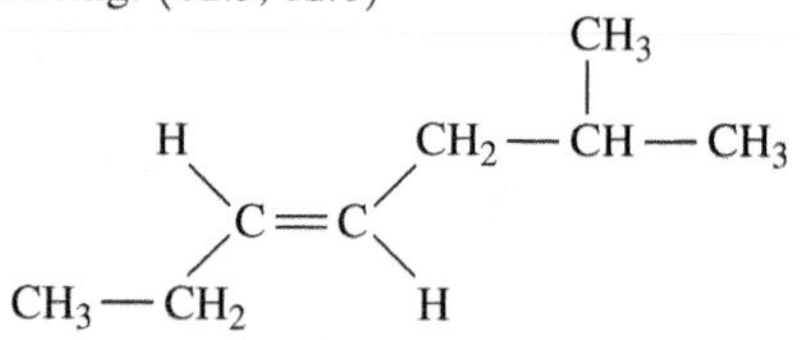

b. 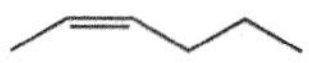

c. 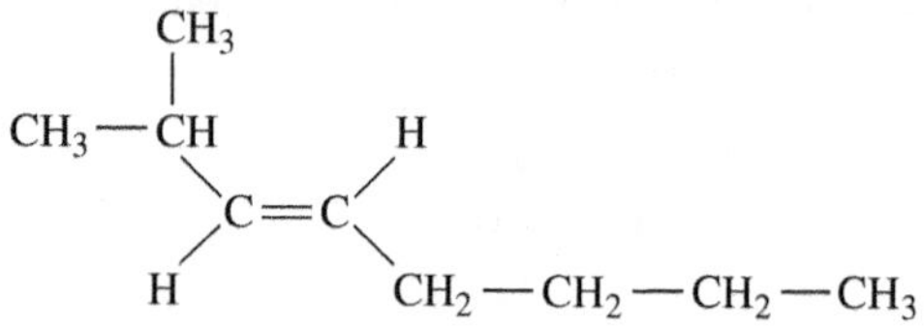

12.75 Draw the condensed structural formulas for the cis and trans isomers for each of the following: (12.5, 12.6)

a. 2-pentene **b.** 3-hexene

12.76 Draw the condensed structural formulas for the cis and trans isomers for each of the following: (12.5, 12.6)

a. 2-butene **b.** 2-hexene

12.77 Write a balanced chemical equation for the complete combustion of each of the following: (12.4, 12.5)

a. dimethylpropane
b. cyclobutane
c. 2-heptene

12.78 Write a balanced chemical equation for the complete combustion of each of the following: (12.4, 12.5)

a. cycloheptane
b. 2-methyl-1-pentene
c. 3,3-dimethylhexane

12.79 Give the name for the product from the hydrogenation of each of the following: (12.7)

a. 3-methyl-2-pentene
b. 3-methylcyclohexene
c. 2-butene

12.80 Give the name for the product from the hydrogenation of each of the following: (12.7)

a. 1-hexene
b. 2-methyl-2-butene
c. 1-ethylcyclopentene

12.81 Draw the structural formula for the product of each of the following: (12.7)

a. 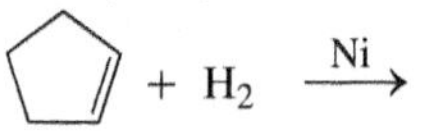

b. 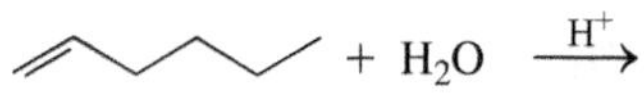

c. 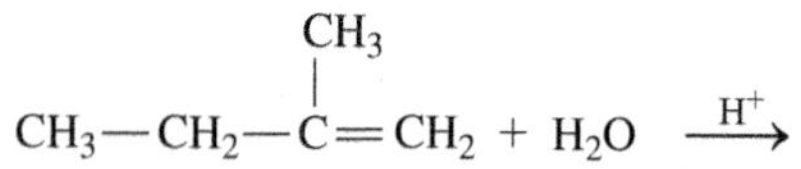

12.82 Draw the structural formula for the product of each of the following: (12.7)

a. 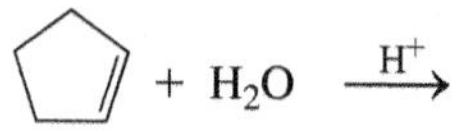

b. $CH_3—CH_2—CH_2—CH=CH_2 + H_2 \xrightarrow{Ni}$

c. 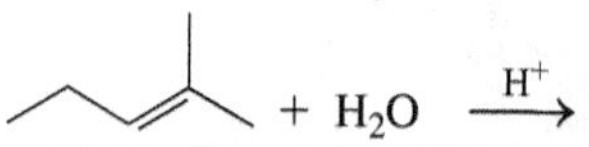

12.83 Copolymers contain more than one type of monomer. One copolymer used in medicine is made of alternating units of styrene and acrylonitrile. Draw the expanded structural formula for a section of the copolymer that would have three each of these alternating units. (12.7)

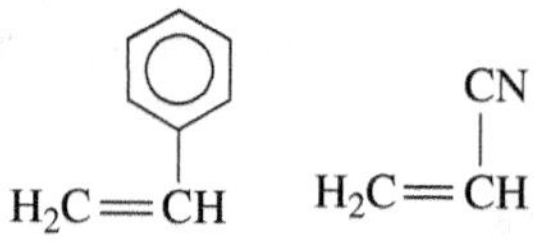

Styrene Acrylonitrile

12.84 Lucite, or Plexiglas, is a polymer of methyl methacrylate. Draw the expanded structural formula for a section of the polymer that is made from the addition of three of these monomers. (12.7)

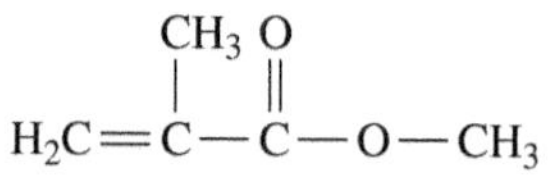

Methyl methacrylate

12.85 Name each of the following aromatic compounds: (12.8)

a. 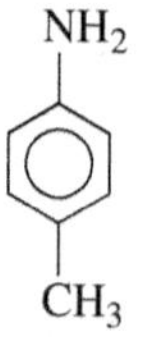

b. 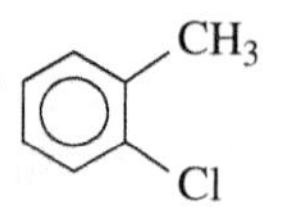

c. 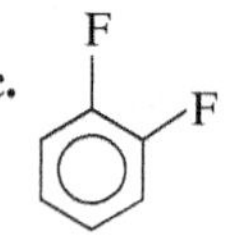

12.86 Name each of the following aromatic compounds: (12.8)

a. 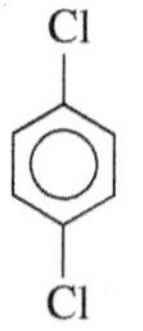

b. 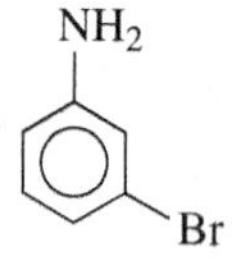

c. 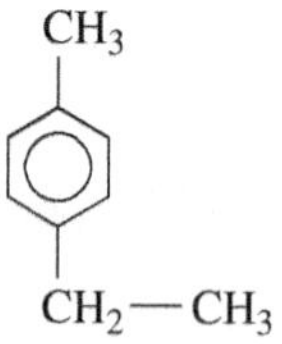

12.87 Draw the structural formula for each of the following: (12.8)

a. *p*-bromotoluene
b. 2,6-dimethylaniline
c. 1,4-dimethylbenzene

12.88 Draw the structural formula for each of the following: (12.8)

a. ethylbenzene
b. *m*-chloroaniline
c. 1,2,4-trimethylbenzene

CHALLENGE QUESTIONS

12.89 If a female silkworm moth secretes 50 ng of bombykol, a sex attractant, how many molecules did she secrete? (See Chemistry Link to the Environment "Pheromones in Insect Communication.") (7.2, 12.6)

12.90 How many grams of hydrogen are needed to hydrogenate 30.0 g of 2-butene? (12.7)

12.91 Draw the condensed structural formula for and give the name of all the possible alkenes with molecular formula C_5H_{10} that have a five-carbon chain, including those with cis and trans isomers. (12.5, 12.6)

12.92 Draw the condensed structural formula for and give the name of all the possible alkenes with molecular formula C_6H_{12} that have a six-carbon chain, including those with cis and trans isomers. (12.5, 12.6)

12.93 Explosives used in mining contain TNT or 2,4,6-trinitrotoluene. (12.8)

    a. The functional group *nitro* is —NO_2. Draw the structural formula for 2,4,6-trinitrotoluene.

    b. TNT is actually a mixture of structural isomers of trinitrotoluene. Draw the structural formula for two other possible structural isomers.

Explosives containing TNT are used in mining.

12.94 Margarine is produced from the hydrogenation of vegetable oils, which contain unsaturated fatty acids. How many grams of hydrogen are required to completely saturate 75.0 g of oleic acid, $C_{18}H_{34}O_2$, which has one double bond? (12.7)

Margarines are produced by the hydrogenation of unsaturated fats.

ANSWERS

Answers to Selected Questions and Problems

12.1 a. inorganic   **b.** organic   **c.** organic
    d. inorganic   **e.** inorganic   **f.** organic

12.3 a. inorganic   **b.** organic
    c. organic   **d.** inorganic

12.5 a. ethane   **b.** ethane
    c. NaBr   **d.** NaBr

12.7 In methane, the covalent bonds from the carbon atom to each hydrogen atom are directed to the corners of a tetrahedron with bond angles of 109°.

12.9 a. pentane   **b.** ethane
    c. hexane   **d.** cycloheptane

12.11 a. CH_4
    b. CH_3—CH_3
    c. CH_3—CH_2—CH_2—CH_2—CH_3
    d. △

12.13 a. same molecule
    b. structural isomers of C_5H_{12}
    c. structural isomers of C_6H_{14}

12.15 a. dimethylpropane
    b. 2,3-dimethylpentane
    c. 4-*tert*-butyl-2,6-dimethylheptane
    d. methylcyclobutane
    e. 1-bromo-3-chlorocyclohexane

12.17 a.
$$CH_3-CH_2-\overset{\overset{\displaystyle CH_3}{|}}{\underset{\underset{\displaystyle CH_3}{|}}{C}}-CH_2-CH_3$$

b.
$$CH_3-\overset{\overset{\displaystyle CH_3}{|}}{CH}-\overset{\overset{\displaystyle CH_3}{|}}{CH}-CH_2-\overset{\overset{\displaystyle CH_3}{|}}{CH}-CH_3$$

c.
$$CH_3-CH_2-\overset{\overset{\displaystyle CH_2-CH_3}{|}}{CH}-CH_2-\overset{\overset{\displaystyle CH}{|}}{\underset{}{CH}}\overset{\displaystyle CH_3\ CH_3}{}-CH_2-CH_2-CH_3$$

d. Br—CH_2—CH_2—Cl

12.19 a.

b.

c.

d.

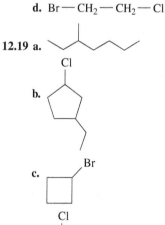

12.21 a. $CH_3-CH_2-CH_2-CH_2-CH_2-CH_2-CH_3$

b. liquid
c. no
d. float
e. $C_7H_{16}(g) + 11O_2(g) \xrightarrow{\Delta} 7CO_2(g) + 8H_2O(g) + energy$

12.23 a. $2C_2H_6(g) + 7O_2(g) \xrightarrow{\Delta} 4CO_2(g) + 6H_2O(g) + energy$

b. $2C_3H_6(g) + 9O_2(g) \xrightarrow{\Delta} 6CO_2(g) + 6H_2O(g) + energy$

c. $2C_8H_{18}(g) + 25O_2(g) \xrightarrow{\Delta}$
$16CO_2(g) + 18H_2O(g) + energy$

12.25 a. heptane   **b.** cyclopropane   **c.** hexane

12.27 a. alkene   **b.** alkyne
c. alkene   **d.** cycloalkene

12.29 a. 2-methylpropene   **b.** 4-bromo-2-pentyne
c. 4-ethylcyclopentene   **d.** 4-ethyl-2-hexene

12.31 a. $H_2C{=}CH-CH_2-CH_2-CH_3$

b. $H_2C{=}\overset{\overset{\displaystyle CH_3}{|}}{C}-CH_2-CH_3$

c.

d. Cl—

12.33 a. *cis*-2-butene
b. *trans*-3-octene
c. *cis*-3-heptene

12.35 a.

b.

c.

12.37 **a** and **c** cannot have cis–trans isomers because they each have two identical groups on at least one of the carbon atoms in the double bond.

12.39 a. $CH_3-CH_2-CH_2-CH_2-CH_3$

b. $CH_3-\overset{\overset{\displaystyle CH_3}{|}}{\underset{\underset{\displaystyle OH}{|}}{C}}-CH_2-CH_3$

c.

d.   OH

12.41 A polymer is a very large molecule composed of small units (monomers) that are repeated many times.

12.43 $3\ H_2C{=}CH \longrightarrow$

12.45

12.47 a. 2-chlorotoluene
b. ethylbenzene
c. 1,3,5-trichlorobenzene
d. 1,3-dimethylbenzene (*m*-xylene)
e. 3-bromo-5-chlorotoluene
f. isopropylbenzene

12.49 a.   **b.**

c.   **d.**

12.51

12.53

a. $C_9H_{20}(l) + 14O_2(g) \xrightarrow{\Delta} 9CO_2(g) + 10H_2O(g) + energy$

b. $C_5H_{12}(l) + 8O_2(g) \xrightarrow{\Delta} 5CO_2(g) + 6H_2O(g) + energy$

c. $C_9H_{12}(l) + 12O_2(g) \xrightarrow{\Delta} 9CO_2(g) + 6H_2O(g) + energy$

12.55 a. butane
b. butane
c. potassium chloride
d. potassium chloride
e. butane

12.57 a. structural isomers
b. not structural isomers

12.59 a. $CH_3-\overset{\overset{\displaystyle CH_3}{|}}{CH}-CH_2-\overset{\overset{\displaystyle CH_3}{|}}{CH}-CH_3$
   2,4-Dimethylpentane

b. $CH_3-\overset{\overset{\displaystyle Cl}{|}}{CH}-\overset{\overset{\displaystyle CH_3}{|}}{CH}-\overset{\overset{\displaystyle Br}{|}}{CH}-CH_2-CH_3$
   4-Bromo-2-chloro-3-methylhexane

12.61

12.63 a. three carbon atoms; two carbon–carbon single bonds
b. three carbon atoms; three carbon–carbon single bonds in a ring
c. three carbon atoms; one carbon–carbon single bond; one carbon–carbon double bond
d. three carbon atoms; one carbon–carbon single bond; one carbon–carbon triple bond

12.65 a. 2,2-dimethylbutane
   b. chloroethane
   c. 2-bromo-4-ethylhexane
   d. methylcyclopentane

12.67 a.

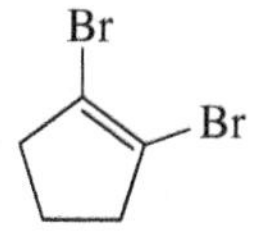

   b. $CH_3-C\equiv C-CH_2-CH_2-CH_3$

   c.

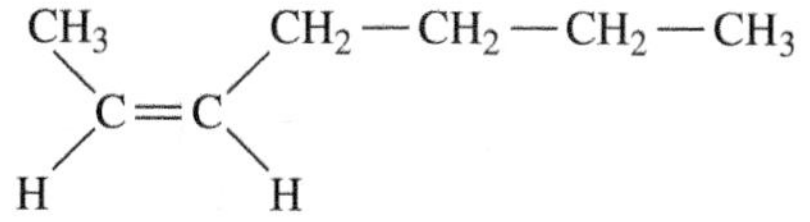

12.69 a. *trans*-2-pentene
   b. 4-bromo-5-methyl-1-hexene
   c. 1-methylcyclopentene

12.71 a. structural isomers
   b. cis–trans isomers

12.73 a. *cis*-3-heptene
   b. *trans*-2-methyl-3-hexene
   c. *trans*-2-heptene

12.75

   a.

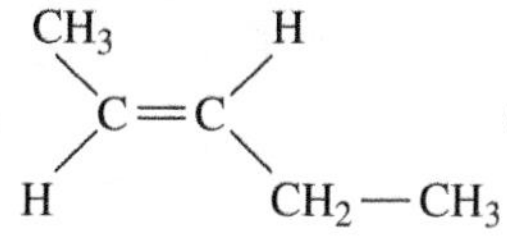

trans-2-Pentene

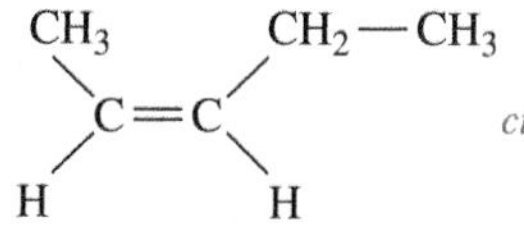

cis-2-Pentene

   b.

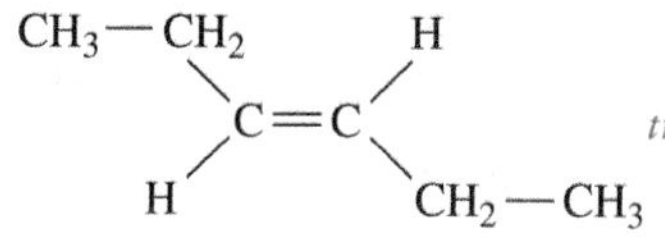

trans-3-Hexene

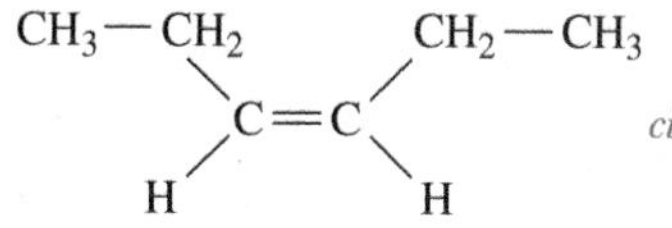

cis-3-Hexene

12.77 a. $C_5H_{12}(g) + 8O_2(g) \xrightarrow{\Delta} 5CO_2(g) + 6H_2O(g) + \text{energy}$

   b. $C_4H_8(g) + 6O_2(g) \xrightarrow{\Delta} 4CO_2(g) + 4H_2O(g) + \text{energy}$

   c. $2C_7H_{14}(l) + 21O_2(g) \xrightarrow{\Delta}$
   $14CO_2(g) + 14H_2O(g) + \text{energy}$

12.79 a. 3-methylpentane   **b.** methylcyclohexane
   c. butane

12.81 a.

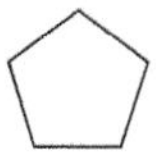

   b.

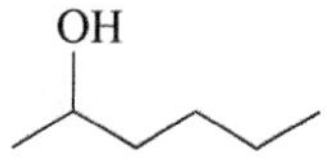

   c.

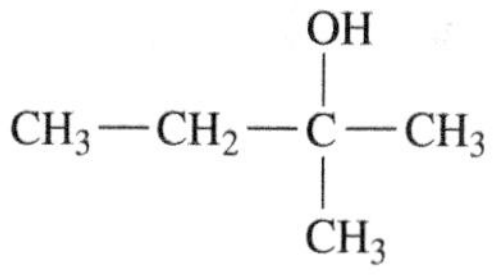

12.83

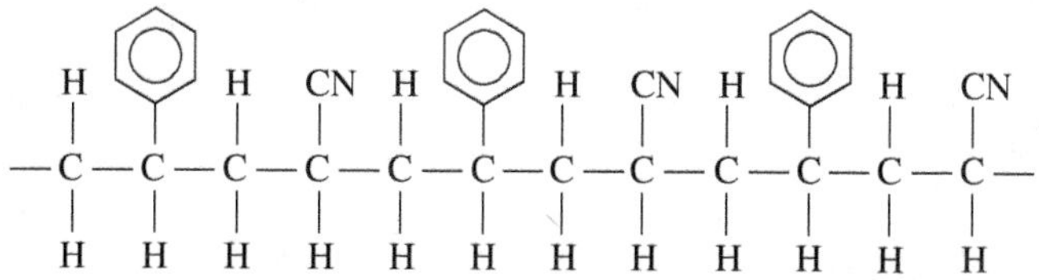

12.85 a. 3-methylaniline (*p*-methylaniline)
   b. 1-chloro-2-methylbenzene, 2-chlorotoluene
      (*o*-chlorotoluene)
   c. 1,2-difluorobenzene (*o*-difluorobenzene)

12.87 a.

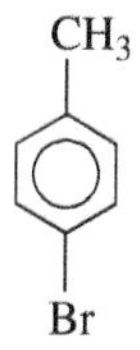

   b.

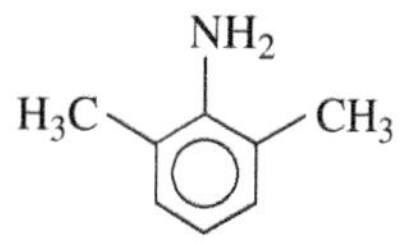

   c.

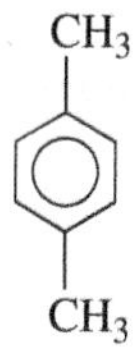

12.89 1×10^{14} molecules of bombykol

12.91 a. $H_2C=CH-CH_2-CH_2-CH_3$ 1-Pentene

   b.

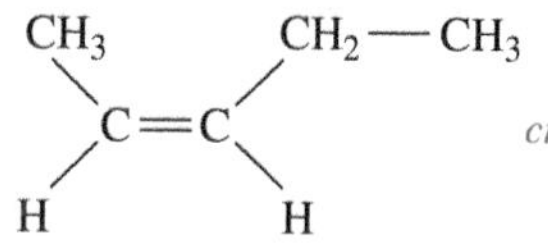

cis-2-Pentene

   c.

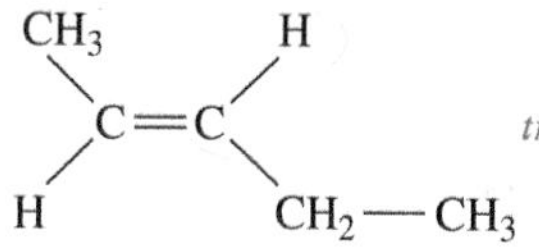

trans-2-Pentene

12.93 a.

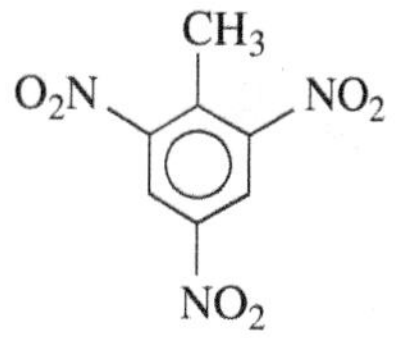

   b.

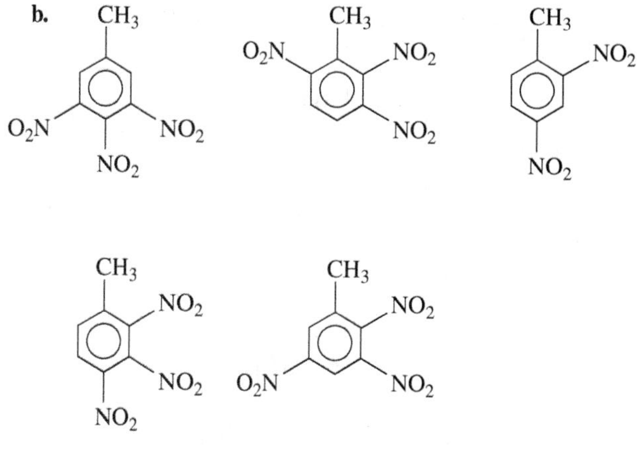

Credits

Photo Credits

p. 159   Pearson Science / Pearson Education
p. 160   HUMBERT / BSIP / Alamy
p. 163   Pearson Science / Pearson Education
p. 164   *bottom, center:* Don Farrall / Photodisc / Getty Images
p. 164   *bottom, left:* Kyodo / Newscom
p. 165   *bottom, left:* Food and Drug Administration
p. 165   *bottom, right:* Pearson Science / Pearson Education
p. 166   Jürgen Schulzki / Alamy
p. 169   Library of Congress Prints and Photographs Division[LC-DIG-matpc-22899]
p. 170   JIHAD SIQLAWI / AFP / Getty Images / Newscom
p. 171   Editorial Image, LLC / Alamy
p. 172   *center, left:* Burger / Phanie / SuperStock
p. 172   *bottom, center:* Lawrence Berkeley National Library / Photodisc / Getty Images
p. 172   *bottom, left:* Pasieka / Science Source
p. 173   GJLP / Science Source
p. 173   National Cancer Institute / Photodisc / Getty Images
p. 174   Cytyc Hologic Corporation
p. 177   Rolf Fischer / iStock / Getty Images
p. 178   Monkey Business Images / Shutterstock
p. 179   *center:* Don Farrall / Photodisc / Getty Images
p. 179   *bottom, center:* Lawrence Berkeley National Library / Photodisc / Getty Images
p. 181   Peter Buckley / Pearson Education

Chapter 6

p. 185   Don Hammond / Alamy
p. 186   buckarooh / Getty Images
p. 190   Pearson Education / Pearson Science
p. 192   *center:* Pearson Education / Pearson Science
p. 192   *top, left:* Richard Megna / Fundamental Photographs
p. 194   Eric Schrader / Pearson Education
p. 196   Gary Blakeley / Shutterstock
p. 197   mark huls / Fotolia
p. 198   *top, right:* Michael Neelon / Alamy
p. 198   *top, right:* Pearson Education / Pearson Science
p. 198   *right:* Pearson Education / Pearson Science
p. 199   Vladimir Smirnov / ITAR-TASS / Newscom
p. 200   Richard Megna / Fundamental Photographs, NYC
p. 201   theodore liasi / Alamy
p. 224   Don Hammond / Alamy
p. 226   Kameel4u / Shutterstock
p. 235   *bottom:* © Editorial Image, LLC / Alamy
p. 235   *center, right:* Augustin Ochsenreiter / AP Images
p. 235   *center, left:* Pearson Education / Pearson Science
p. 236   Family Safety Products Inc.

Chapter 7

p. 237   Craig Holmes Premium / Alamy
p. 239   *top, left:* Pearson Education / Pearson Science
p. 239   *top, right:* Pearson Education / Pearson Science
p. 240   Pearson Education / Pearson Science
p. 242   Pearson Education / Pearson Science
p. 243   Richard Megna / Fundamental Photographs
p. 246   Pearson Education / Pearson Science
p. 247   *bottom, left:* Pearson Education / Pearson Science
p. 247   *bottom, right:* Pearson Education / Pearson Science
p. 247   *top, center:* Tom Boschler
p. 248   *center, right:* Pearson Education / Pearson Science
p. 248   *bottom, left:* Sergiy Zavgorodny / Shutterstock
p. 250   Mitch Hrdlicka / Getty Images
p. 251   *bottom:* Pearson Education / Pearson Science
p. 251   *top, right:* Stephen Troell / iStock / Getty Images
p. 253   Pearson Education / Pearson Science
p. 254   *top, left:* Melissa Carroll / E+ / Getty Images
p. 254   *bottom, center:* Reika / Shutterstock
p. 255   Pearson Education / Pearson Science
p. 256   Michael Hill / E+ / Getty Images

p. 257   *top, right:* Helen Sessions / Alamy
p. 257   *bottom, left:* Pearson Education / Pearson Science
p. 258   Charles D. Winters / Science Source
p. 259   *top, left:* Pearson Education / Pearson Science
p. 259   *top, left:* Pearson Education / Pearson Science
p. 259   *top, right:* Pearson Education / Pearson Science
p. 259   *top, right:* Pearson Education / Pearson Science
p. 259   *center:* Pearson Education / Pearson Science
p. 259   *bottom, right:* ruzanna / Shutterstock
p. 260   Eric Schrader / Pearson Education
p. 262   *left:* Pearson Education / Pearson Science
p. 262   *right:* Pearson Education / Pearson Science
p. 262   *center:* Pearson Education / Pearson Science
p. 262   *top, center:* Tamara Kulikova / Getty Images
p. 263   *left:* Pearson Education / Pearson Science
p. 263   *right:* Pearson Education / Pearson Science
p. 263   *center:* Pearson Education / Pearson Science
p. 265   Thinkstock Images / Stockbyte / Getty Images
p. 267   Pearson Education
p. 269   Westend61 GmbH / Alamy
p. 271   NASA images
p. 276   *top:* Pearson Education / Pearson Science
p. 276   *bottom:* Richard Megna / Fundamental Photographs
p. 277   Craig Holmes Premium / Alamy
p. 278   Melissa Carroll / E+ / Getty Images
p. 279   *top, right:* NASA images
p. 279   *top, left:* Pearson Education / Pearson Science
p. 279   *center, left:* Pearson Education / Pearson Science
p. 279   *bottom:* Thinkstock Images / Stockbyte / Getty Images
p. 281   *top:* Gabriele Rohde / Fotolia
p. 281   *center:* Ljupco Smokovski / Fotolia
p. 283   *center:* Pearson Education / Pearson Science
p. 283   *bottom:* Pearson Education / Pearson Science
p. 287   *center:* MvH / E+ / Getty Images
p. 287   *bottom:* Pearson Education / Pearson Science

Chapter 8

p. 291   ADAM GAULT / Science Photo Library / Alamy
p. 294   Source: NASA
p. 296   *bottom, left:* Andersen Ross / Stockbyte / Getty Images
p. 296   *top, left:* Andrzej Gibasiewicz / Shutterstock
p. 296   *center, left:* Kenneth William Caleno / Shutterstock.com
p. 297   koszivu / Fotolia
p. 298   Levent Konuk / Shutterstock
p. 301   Mariusz Blach / Fotolia
p. 305   *top, left:* Pearson Education
p. 305   *top, right:* Pearson Education
p. 306   Andrey Nekrasov / Alamy
p. 309   Tomasz Wojnarowicz / Fotolia
p. 311   Yuri Bathan / Getty Images
p. 312   LoloStock / Shutterstock
p. 313   Mic Smith / Alamy
p. 314   Eric Schrader / Fundamental Photographs
p. 318   ADAM GAULT / Science Photo Library / Alamy
p. 319   *top, right:* Andrey Nekrasov / Alamy
p. 319   *bottom, right:* Eric Schrader / Fundamental Photographs
p. 322   Library of Congress, Prints & Photographs Division, Tissandier Collection, [LC-DIG-ppmsca-02284]

Chapter 9

p. 324   AJPhoto / Science Source
p. 326   *top, left:* Pearson Education / Pearson Science
p. 326   *top, right:* Pearson Education / Pearson Science
p. 327   *top, center:* Pearson Education / Pearson Science
p. 327   *bottom, left:* Thinkstock Images / Getty Images
p. 328   *top, left:* Pearson Education / Pearson Science
p. 328   *top, center:* Pearson Education / Pearson Science

p. 329   Pearson Education / Pearson Science
p. 330   *top, left:* Pearson Education / Pearson Science
p. 330   *center, left:* Pearson Education / Pearson Science
p. 332   Comstock Images / Stockbyte / Getty Images
p. 333   *bottom, left:* Pearson Education / Pearson Science
p. 333   *bottom, right:* Pearson Education / Pearson Science
p. 334   *bottom, right:* Remik44992 / Shutterstock
p. 334   *bottom, left:* Wellcome Image Library / Custom Medical Stock Photo
p. 335   Tom Biegalski / Shutterstock
p. 336   Pearson Education / Pearson Science
p. 337   *bottom, right:* CNRI / Science Source
p. 337   *top, left:* Pearson Education / Pearson Science
p. 337   *top, left:* Pearson Education / Pearson Science
p. 337   *top, right:* Pearson Education / Pearson Science
p. 337   *top, right:* Pearson Education / Pearson Science
p. 340   *top, left:* Pearson Education / Pearson Science
p. 340   *center, left:* Pearson Education / Pearson Science
p. 342   Pearson Education / Pearson Science
p. 343   *top, right:* Eric Schrader / Pearson Education
p. 343   *center, right:* Eric Schrader / Pearson
p. 346   *top, left:* Pearson Education
p. 346   *center, left:* Pearson Education
p. 349   *top, left:* Pearson Education / Pearson Science
p. 349   *top, right:* Pearson Education / Pearson Science
p. 349   *top, center:* Pearson Education / Pearson Science
p. 349   *bottom, left:* Pearson Education / Pearson Science
p. 349   *bottom, center:* Pearson Education / Pearson Science
p. 354   *top, left:* Jane norton / E+ / Getty Images
p. 354   *bottom, left:* photowind / Shutterstock
p. 356   Florida Images / Alamy
p. 358   *bottom, center:* Sam Singer / Pearson Education
p. 358   *bottom, center:* Sam Singer / Pearson Education
p. 358   *bottom, right:* Sam Singer / Pearson Education
p. 358   *bottom, right:* Sam Singer / Pearson Education
p. 358   *top, left:* Thinkstock Images / Stockbyte / Getty Images
p. 360   Picsfive / Shutterstock
p. 362   *top, left:* Pearson Education / Pearson Science
p. 362   *top, right:* Pearson Education / Pearson Science
p. 362   *bottom, right:* Pearson Education / Pearson Science
p. 363   Pearson Education / Pearson Science
p. 365   Stepan Popov / iStock / Getty Images
p. 366   Brand X Pictures / Getty Images

Chapter 10

p. 377   Fuse / Getty Images
p. 378   *top, left:* Pearson Education
p. 378   *top, right:* Pearson Education
p. 378   *center, left:* Pearson Education
p. 378   *center, right:* Pearson Education
p. 378   *bottom, left:* Pearson Education
p. 378   *bottom, right:* Pearson Education
p. 380   Pearson Education
p. 382   Pearson Education
p. 387   Gudellaphoto / Fotolia
p. 397   incamerastock / Alamy
p. 399   *center, right:* bikeriderlondon / Shutterstock
p. 399   *center, right:* Photobac / Shutterstock
p. 400   Fuse / Getty Images
p. 401   *bottom, right:* incamerastock / Alamy
p. 401   *bottom, center:* Gudellaphoto / Fotolia

Chapter 11

p. 399   Lisa S. / Shutterstock
p. 400   Kristina Afanasyeva / Getty Images
p. 402   *bottom, left:* Kesu / Shutterstock
p. 402   *top, left:* Kul Bhatia / Science Source
p. 407   Pearson Education / Pearson Science

p. 408 *top, right:* Pearson Education / Pearson Science
p. 408 *top, center:* Pearson Education / Pearson Science
p. 408 *bottom, left:* Richard Megna / Fundamental Photographs
p. 409 Eric Schrader / Pearson Education
p. 417 *top, left:* Pearson Education / Pearson Science
p. 417 *top, center:* Pearson Education / Pearson Science
p. 417 *top, right:* Pearson Education / Pearson Science
p. 417 *top, left:* Pearson Education / Pearson Science
p. 417 *center, right:* Pearson Education / Pearson Science
p. 417 *center, right:* Pearson Education / Pearson Science
p. 417 *center:* Pearson Education / Pearson Science
p. 417 *center:* Pearson Education / Pearson Science
p. 417 *bottom, left:* Pearson Education / Pearson Science
p. 417 *bottom, left:* Pearson Education / Pearson Science
p. 417 *bottom, center:* Pearson Education / Pearson Science
p. 417 *bottom, right:* Pearson Education / Pearson Science
p. 418 *top, left:* Alexander Gospodinov / Fotolia
p. 418 *bottom, left:* Wayne Hutchinson / Alamy
p. 419 Eric Schrader / Pearson Education
p. 421 *top, right:* Ana Bokan / Shutterstock
p. 421 *bottom, right:* Charles D. Winters / Science Source
p. 423 *bottom, right:* Eric Schrader / Pearson Education
p. 423 *top, right:* Richard Megna / Fundamental Photographs
p. 424 Renn Sminkey / Pearson Education
p. 425 *bottom, left:* Pearson Education / Pearson Science
p. 425 *bottom, center:* Pearson Education / Pearson Science
p. 425 *bottom, right:* Pearson Education / Pearson Science
p. 432 Lisa S. / Shutterstock

p. 433 Pearson Education / Pearson Science
p. 434 *bottom, center:* Pearson Education / Pearson Science
p. 434 *top, right:* Pearson Education / Pearson Science
p. 434 *top, right:* Richard Megna / Fundamental Photographs
p. 437 Geo Martinez / Getty Images
p. 438 Universal Images Group / SuperStock
p. 441 *bottom, left:* Charles D. Winters / Science Source
p. 441 *center, right:* Eric Schrader / Pearson Education
p. 441 *center:* isifa Image Service s.r.o. / Alamy
p. 441 *center, left:* Lynn Watson / Shutterstock

Chapter 12

p. 443 corepics / Fotolia
p. 445 *top, right:* Pearson Education / Pearson Science
p. 445 *bottom, left:* lillisphotography / E+ / Getty Images
p. 445 *bottom, right:* Pearson Education / Pearson Science
p. 457 Pearson Education / Pearson Science
p. 458 *center, left:* NatalieJean / Shutterstock
p. 458 *center, right:* Nyvlt-art / Shutterstock
p. 459 *top, right:* Pearson Education / Pearson Science
p. 459 *bottom, right:* roza / Fotolia
p. 460 LoloStock / Shutterstock
p. 461 *top, center:* Glen Jones / Shutterstock
p. 461 *top, left:* Tim Hall / Getty Images
p. 463 Petrenko Andriy / Shutterstock
p. 466 *center, right:* James Trice / Getty Images
p. 466 *bottom, left:* Nigel Cattlin / Alamy
p. 466 *top, right:* Pearson Education / Pearson Science
p. 466 *top, right:* Pearson Education / Pearson Science
p. 469 Pearson Education / Pearson Science
p. 471 Pearson Education / Pearson Science
p. 472 *bottom, left:* Eduardo Luzzatti Buy© / Getty Images

p. 472 *top, left:* Pearson Eduation / Pearson Science
p. 472 *top, right:* Pearson Education / Pearson Science
p. 472 *bottom, center:* Pearson Education / Pearson Science
p. 472 *bottom, right:* Pearson Education / Pearson Science
p. 472 *top, center:* Siede Preis / Photodisc / Getty Images
p. 473 *bottom, left:* Alexandr Kanõkin / Shutterstock
p. 473 *left:* Alexandr Kanõkin / Shutterstock
p. 473 *right:* dirkr / Getty Images
p. 473 *center:* vblinov / Shutterstock
p. 477 *center:* corepics / Fotolia
p. 477 *top, right:* Mediscan / Medical-on-Line / Alamy
p. 477 *bottom, right:* sumroeng / Fotolia
p. 479 *bottom, center:* Pearson Education / Pearson Science
p. 479 *bottom, right:* Pearson Education / Pearson Science
p. 479 *bottom, center:* roza / Fotolia
p. 482 *center, left:* Jason Nemeth / iStock / Thinkstock
p. 482 *bottom, right:* Eduardo Luzzatti Buy© / Getty Images
p. 482 *center, left:* Eric Schrader / Pearson Education
p. 483 Siede Preis / Photodisc / Getty Images
p. 485 *center, right:* igor kisselev / Shutterstock
p. 485 *top, right:* Ingram Publishing / Getty Images

Text Credits

Chapter 1

p. 4 John Horgan, 1993. Profile: Linus C. Pauling, Stubbornly Ahead of His Time, *Scientific American*, March 1993, 36–37

Chapter 11

p. 432 Based on 2004 MedicineNet, Inc.

Glossary/Index

Metric and SI Units and Some Useful Conversion Factors

Length SI Unit Meter (m)	Volume SI Unit Cubic Meter (m³)	Mass SI Unit Kilogram (kg)
1 meter (m) = 100 centimeters (cm)	1 liter (L) = 1000 milliliters (mL)	1 kilogram (kg) = 1000 grams (g)
1 meter (m) = 1000 millimeters (mm)	1 mL = 1 cm³	1 g = 1000 milligrams (mg)
1 cm = 10 mm	1 L = 1.06 quart (qt)	1 kg = 2.20 lb
1 kilometer (km) = 0.621 mile (mi)	1 qt = 946 mL	1 lb = 454 g
1 inch (in.) = 2.54 cm (exact)		1 mole = 6.02×10^{23} particles
		Water
		density = 1.00 g/mL (at 4 °C)

Temperature SI Unit Kelvin (K)	Pressure SI Unit Pascal (Pa)	Energy SI Unit Joule (J)
$T_F = 1.8(T_C) + 32$	1 atm = 760 mmHg	1 calorie (cal) = 4.184 J (exact)
$T_C = \dfrac{T_F - 32}{1.8}$	1 atm = 101.325 kPa	1 kcal = 1000 cal
$T_K = T_C + 273$	1 atm = 760 torr	**Water**
	1 mole of gas = 22.4 L (STP)	Heat of fusion = 334 J/g; 80. cal/g
	$R = 0.0821$ L·atm/mole·K	Heat of vaporization = 2260 J/g; 540 cal/g
	$R = 62.4$ mmHg·atm/mole·K	Specific heat (SH) = 4.184 J/g °C; 1.00 cal/g °C

Metric and SI Prefixes

Prefix	Symbol	Scientific Notation
Prefixes That Increase the Size of the Unit		
peta	P	10^{15}
tera	T	10^{12}
giga	G	10^{9}
mega	M	10^{6}
kilo	k	10^{3}
Prefixes That Decrease the Size of the Unit		
deci	d	10^{-1}
centi	c	10^{-2}
milli	m	10^{-3}
micro	μ (mc)	10^{-6}
nano	n	10^{-9}
pico	p	10^{-12}
femto	f	10^{-15}

Formulas and Molar Masses of Some Typical Compounds

Name	Formula	Molar Mass (g/mole)	Name	Formula	Molar Mass (g/mole)
Ammonia	NH_3	17.03	Hydrogen chloride	HCl	36.46
Ammonium chloride	NH_4Cl	53.49	Iron(III) oxide	Fe_2O_3	159.70
Ammonium sulfate	$(NH_4)_2SO_4$	132.15	Magnesium oxide	MgO	40.31
Bromine	Br_2	159.80	Methane	CH_4	16.04
Butane	C_4H_{10}	58.12	Nitrogen	N_2	28.02
Calcium carbonate	$CaCO_3$	100.09	Oxygen	O_2	32.00
Calcium chloride	$CaCl_2$	110.98	Potassium carbonate	K_2CO_3	138.21
Calcium hydroxide	$Ca(OH)_2$	74.10	Potassium nitrate	KNO_3	101.11
Calcium oxide	CaO	56.08	Propane	C_3H_8	44.09
Carbon dioxide	CO_2	44.01	Sodium chloride	NaCl	58.44
Chlorine	Cl_2	70.90	Sodium hydroxide	NaOH	40.00
Copper(II) sulfide	CuS	95.62	Sulfur trioxide	SO_3	80.07
Hydrogen	H_2	2.016	Water	H_2O	18.02